Modern Diesel Technology

Robert N. Brady
*Vancouver Community College
and HiTech Consulting Limited*

Prentice Hall
Englewood Cliffs, New Jersey   Columbus, Ohio

Library of Congress Cataloging-in-Publication Data
Brady, Robert N.
   Modern diesel technology / Robert N. Brady.
        p.   cm.
   Includes index.
   ISBN 0-13-288382-1 (hardcover)
   1. Diesel motor.   I. Title.
 TJ795.B66   1996
 621.43'6—dc20   95-17079
                                         CIP

Cover photo: Courtesy of Detroit Diesel Corporation, Detroit, Michigan
Editor: Ed Francis
Production Editor: Sheryl Glicker Langner
Design Coordinator: Julia Zonneveld Van Hook
Cover Designer: Brian Deep
Production Manager: Laura Messerly
Marketing Manager: Debbie Yarnell
Electronic Text Management: Karen L. Bretz

This book was set in Palatino and Eras by Carlisle Communication Ltd. and was printed and bound by Semline, Inc., a Quebecor America Book Group Company. The cover was printed by Phoenix Color Corp.

10 9 8 7 6 5 4 3 2 1

ISBN: 0-13-288382-1

Prentice-Hall Internation (UK) Limited, *London*
Prentice-Hall of Australia Pty. Limited, *Sydney*
Prentice-Hall of Canada, Inc., *Toronto*
Prentice-Hall Hispanoamericana, S.A., *Mexico*
Prentice-Hall of India Private Limited, *New Delhi*
Prentice-Hall of Japan, Inc., *Tokyo*
Simon & Schuster Asia Pte. Ltd., *Singapore*
Editora Prentice-Hall do Brasil, Ltda., *Rio de Janeiro*

Especially for Linda, Alanna, Alicia, Scott, Tracy and Adele!

To all of the creative individuals who have allowed me to gain knowledge and skills from their benchmark experiences, and to the many motivated students, friends and SAE colleagues within the diesel and automotive industry who have shared their standards of excellence. This book is a reflection of a diversity of backgrounds of truly remarkable people who provided me with their time and support. I trust that the finished product meets your high standards and expectations.

About the Author

Robert N. Brady has been involved in the automotive, heavy-duty truck and equipment field since 1959, having served a recognized five year apprenticeship as both an automotive and heavy-duty truck and equipment technician. He is a graduate of Stow College of Engineering in Glasgow, Scotland, with a degree in Mechanical Engineering Technology. He holds degrees both from the University of British Columbia, and the University of Alberta in Adult Education. He is a certified automotive, commercial transport and heavy-duty equipment technician.

His background experience includes positions as a shop foreman and service manager with Kenworth, fleet maintenance superintendent with North American Van Lines; factory service trainer for Canada, service representative, and sales application engineer with Detroit Diesel; Diesel Engineering and Diesel Mechanic/Technician college instructor, and college department head at Vancouver Community College. He is a director and Past President of the VCC Faculty Association. In 1987, he formed his own company, HiTech Consulting Ltd., specializing in technical training program design/implementation aimed specifically at heavy-duty, on- and off-highway equipment. He has designed and implemented training programs for a number of large truck fleets as well as for mining companies. He has set up fleet maintenance programs and been a speaker at a number of adult education seminars.

He is a prolific author of ten automotive, diesel, and heavy-duty truck books for Simon & Schuster's, Prentice Hall college division, where he has also been a book series editor. He has also written numerous technical articles for publication in local and national technical magazines. He is a member of SAE (Society of Automotive Engineers) International, in which he has held positions as the past chair of the local British Columbia Section. In 1989–1990, under his leadership, the section was presented an SAE Award of Merit for outstanding technical meetings. At the International level of SAE, he served three years on the Sections Board, and was both Vice-Chair and Chair. He co-chaired the 1992 Section Officers Leadership Seminar held in Warrendale, PA., for worldwide section officers, and returned in 1993 as Chair. Other activities within SAE at the Sections Board level include: Chair of the Executive Committee; Past-Chair of the Administrative Committee; member of the Section Evaluation and Awards Committee and the Section Activities; Chair of the Brazil Ad Hoc Committee and subsequently Chair of the International Sections and Affiliates Committee; member of the Regional Coordinators Committee where he was responsible for the provinces of British Columbia, Alberta and Manitoba, as well as an acting RC for the NW/Spokane-Intermountain and Oregon Sections; and member of the Total Quality Management Committee. He was appointed to the Board of Director's for SAE International for a three-year term covering 1994 to 1996, where he has been involved as a member of the DPCC (Development Project Coordinating Committee), the Appeals Board, and is currently a member of the Total Life Cycle Committee which is studying and implementing a Service Technician Society as part of SAE.

His military background includes service with the Army Emergency Reserve of the British Army in both the Paratroop Regiment and the R.E.M.E. (Royal Electrical Mechanical Engineers). He is a former Scottish amateur boxing champion, semi-professional soccer player, a very active long-distance cyclist and skier, and enjoys restoring older cars.

v

Preface

This text has been written by this author for Prentice Hall after detailed consultation with several hundred diesel industry personnel regarding their needs for a text that reflects the latest up-to-date information dealing with electronically controlled high-speed, heavy-duty diesel engines. The book is not meant to supplant the excellent service literature readily available from the major engine, truck, and equipment OEM's (Original Equipment Manufacturers), but is designed to supplement their outstanding training aids. A review of the chapter index will quickly highlight for you the major topics covered.

In conjunction with OEM service training courses and diversified technical literature, both college and vo-tech students, apprentices, and certified diesel engine, heavy-duty equipment, and commercial transport technicians have here a reference which includes the latest up-to-date technology related to current electronically controlled diesel engines. Although there is some basic information related to mechanically controlled diesel engines, the industry-wide adoption of electronic fuel injection systems has forced diesel technicians to become familiar and comfortable with the basic operation, diagnosis, and troubleshooting of these technologically advanced engines and systems. It has been ten years since the first electronically controlled diesel engine was released to the marketplace by Detroit Diesel Corporation in 1985. Today, all of the major engine OEM's manufacture and market high-speed, heavy-duty diesel engines equipped with electronic controls. Among the major engine OEM's, we can list Caterpillar, Cummins, Detroit Diesel, Mack, Volvo and Isuzu as major users of electronic controls. A thorough understanding of the design changes that have taken place in high-speed, heavy-duty diesel engines, and how each of the engine systems function and operate, is described in detail within this book.

Many U.S. states and Canadian provinces are now moving towards mandatory diesel technician certification. A recent study by the GAO (general accounting office) in the United States of over one-hundred highly skilled professions placed the needed skill levels of both automotive and diesel technicians on the same level as x-ray technicians and computer programmers. One of the areas most in need of skill development for automotive and diesel technicians is a solid understanding of electronics. In Chapter 5 of this book, you will find information describing how all of the various electronic diesel fuel injection systems operate. After studying this chapter, you will have a familiarization and solid background of just how similar most of these current fuel systems are.

No book of this type can truly reflect the wishes and needs of the diesel industry without the assistance and feedback of many of my colleagues. Within the acknowledgement list in this preface, you will find major OEM's who were kind enough to support me with information on their latest product offerings. I trust that the finished product is reflective of their commitment to excellence in all of their technological advancements.

I wish you well in your pursuit of new knowledge, since your study of this book, along with hands-on practical experience, will enhance your ability to understand, service, and diagnose the latest electronically controlled diesel engines and fuel systems. These skills will make you a very valuable addition to many employers, and will provide you with a rewarding, challenging, and fulfilling career for many years to come.

ACKNOWLEDGMENTS

1. Allied Signal Truck Brake Systems Company, Elyria, OH. 44036 U.S.A., Becky MacDonald, Manager, Communications.

2. Caterpillar Inc., 100 NE Adams Street, Peoria, IL. 61629 U.S.A., Mr. Randy R. Richards, Director, New Product Technology; Linda L. Schearer, Corporate Legal Asst., Patent Department.

3. Chevron Research and Technology Company, a division of Chevron U.S.A. Inc., San Francisco, CA. 94120, U.S.A. Mr. William P. Blum, Marketing Communications Manager; Mr. Steve Quan, Senior HRD Representative, Corporate Human Resources.

4. Corning Incorporated, Corporate Communications Div., Corning, N.Y. 14831.

5. Cummins Engine Company, Inc., Columbus, IN. 47202, U.S.A. Mr. John R. Keele, Director of Marketing, and Mr. Gary M. Gron, Corporate Patent Counsel.

6. DAF Trucks, DAF B.V., Eindhoven, Netherlands.

7. Davco Manufacturing Corporation, P.O. Box 487, Saline, MI. 48176, U.S.A., Mr. Paul B. Smith, VP Corporate Support & Engineering.

8. Detroit Diesel Corporation, 13400 Outer Drive West, Detroit, MI. 48239, U.S.A. Mr. Charles Yount, Manager, Advertising and Publishing.

9. Diesel & Gas Turbine Publications, 13555 Bishop's Court, Brookfield, WI. 53005, U.S.A., Mr. Robert A. Wilson, Publisher.

10. Donaldson Company, Inc., P.O. Box 1299, Minneapolis, MN. 55440. U.S.A., Mr. Jock Donaldson, Director of Marketing.

11. Engelhard Corporation, 101 Wood Avenue, Iselin, N.J. 08830, U.S.A. Mr. Richard A. Gay, Marketing Manager, Automotive Emissions Systems.

12. Farr Company, 2221 Park Place, El Segundo, CA. 90245, U.S.A. Mr. John W. Martin, Marketing Services Manager.

13. GMC Truck Division, General Motors Corporation, 31 Judson Street, Pontiac, MI. 48058. U.S.A.

14. Hastings Manufacturing Company, 325 N. Hanover Street, Hastings, MI. 49058, U.S.A. Mr. Norman W. Pugh, Manager Piston Ring Engineering.

15. Horton Industries, Inc., P.O. Box 9455, Minneapolis, MN. 55440. U.S.A., Mr. Nels C. Johnson, VP, Sales & Marketing.

16. Jacobs Manufacturing Company, Chicago Pneumatic Tool Co., 22 E. Dudley Town Road, Bloomfield, CT. 06002. U.S.A.

17. Kent Moore Division, SPX Corporation, 28635 Mound Road, Warren, MI. 48092, U.S.A. Andrea Kolton, Advertising Manager.

18. Kold Ban International, Ltd., 900 Pingree Road, Algonquin, IL. 60102, U.S.A. Mr. James O. Burke, VP Marketing.

19. Kwik-Way of Canada, 95 Norfinch Drive, Toronto, Ontario. M3N 1W8. Mr. Julio Giron, District Manager.

20. Mack Trucks, Inc., 2100 Mack Blvd. Allentown, PA. 18105, U.S.A. Mr. Bob Young, Coordinator Service Publications.

21. Neway Manufacturing, Inc., P.O. Box 188, Corunna, MI. 48817, U.S.A.

22. Parker Hannifin Corporation, Racor Division, 3400 Finch Road, Modesto, CA. 95353, U.S.A. Kathleen Edge, Marketing Services Manager.

23. Phillips & Temro Industries, Inc., Eden Prairie, MN. 55344, U.S.A., and Winnipeg Manitoba, Canada. Mr. Lance Toepper, General Manager, Industrial Division; Marion E. Lambrecht, Marketing Communications Manager.

24. Robert Bosch Inc., Mississauga, Ontario, L5N 1R1, Canada. Mr. Hans Ruschka and Mr. Krishna Pan, Technical Information.

25. SAE (Society of Automotive Engineers) International, Inc., 400 Commonwealth Drive, Warrendale, PA. 15096. U.S.A., Mr. Antenor R. Willems, Publications Group Director.

26. Stanadyne Automotive Products, Diesel Systems Division, 92 Deerfield Rd., Windsor, CT. 06095, U.S.A.

27. Sunnen Products Company, 7910 Manchester Avenue, St. Louis, MO. 63143. U.S.A., Mr. Bob Davis, Marketing Communications Manager.

28. Superflow Corporation, 3512 N. Tejon, Colorado Springs, CO. 80907, U.S.A. Mr. G. Neal Williams, President.

29. The Penray Companies Inc., 1801 Estes Ave., Elk Grove, IL. 60007, U.S.A., Mr. Ed Eaton, Director Technical Services.

30. Williams Controls Inc., 14100 SW 72nd Avenue, Portland, OR. 97224. Kathy Brown, Sales & Marketing Manager.

31. ZEXEL USA, Technology and Information Division, 37735 Enterprise Ct., Farmington Hills, MI. 48331. U.S.A. Mr. Shin Takeshita.

Contents

■ **4**

Fuel Filters, Fuel/Water Separators, and Fuel Heaters   98

■ **5**

Types of Fuel Systems   108

INTRODUCTION

The diesel engine business is an active industry in which the production of engines is based on the existing economy. In North America, production of both gasoline and diesel engines accounts for close to 30 million engines per year. Table A shows that North America production of gasoline and diesel engines ranged from 5 to 2000+ horsepower (hp), or 3.73 to 1492 kilowatts (kW), from 1991 through 1994.

In 1993, actual diesel engine industry sales to OEMs (Original Equipment Manufacturers) in North America consisted of 622,763 units, with Cummins Engine Company, Inc., Caterpillar Inc., Detroit Diesel Corporation, Navistar International Transportation Corporation, and Deere & Co. accounting for the majority of this total. At the time of this writing, final results were not in for total engine sales for 1994.

The AAMA (American Automobile Manufacturers Association) estimates that total diesel engine sales for *trucks* will be approximately 502,000, up 16% from the 1993 total of 431,164 units. Approximately 200,000 of these engines will have been sold for the Class 8 category of heavy-duty truck/tractors—a 15% increase from 1993's totals. Truck classifications are determined by weight; Table B lists the various classifications.

Cummins engine sales for 1994 will be close to 160,000 units, followed by Navistar, whose sales fell by around 8% due to a 20% decline in sales to Ford Motor Company, which accounts for more than 60% of Navistar's truck sales. Although Navistar has no sales to the heavy-duty portion of the truck market, it is the leader in the truck engine market segments with a total of around 115,000 units. Cummins accounted for approximately 34% of the engines sold for Class 8 trucks, and in the midrange truck market Cummins' sales grew by more than 50% over 1993's figures. Caterpillar sold approximately 73,700 engines in 1994; 56,500 of these went into heavy-duty truck applications. Detroit Diesel shifted more than 54,600 Series 60's of its 74,000 estimated sales in the heavy-duty market. These sales accounted for about 25% of the heavy truck market. Mack Trucks, Inc., placed all of its 24,900 diesel engines into its own heavy-duty vehicles—a 28% increase over 1993 levels. Volvo GM Heavy Truck delivered 2000 of its VE D12 engine models into its own Class 8 trucks, of a total of approximately 25,000 Class 8 trucks sold by Volvo in 1994 in North America. The other engines in these vehicles were from Cat, Cummins, or Detroit Diesel. In the lighter-duty truck field, Volvo delivered 1500 of its own 7 L diesels. In 1994, Volvo produced 60,000 heavy diesels at the Skovde engine factory in Sweden.

In the Class 8 (heavy-duty trucks) market, approximately 86% of the diesel engine share is accounted for by Caterpillar, Cummins, and Detroit Diesel. In off-highway applications, Deere is the leading supplier of engines, with approximately 43% of the market. Dollar sales of diesel engines in 1994 amounted to $4.7 billion for Cummins, $3.735 billion for Caterpillar, $1.7 billion for Detroit Diesel, and $570 million for Deere.

FUTURE ENGINE DEVELOPMENTS

Many heavy-duty, high-speed diesel engines now in use in long-haul trucking, as well as in industrial, marine pleasure craft, and off-highway applications, tend to have engine displacements in the range of 10 to 15 liters (L), or 610 to 915 cubic inches (cu in.). Current and ongoing development work at major engine manufacturers

TABLE A   North American engine production

Horsepower	1991	1992	1993	1994*
Gasoline				
<5	13,992,313	13,622,959	14,129,623	14,836,000
6–20	2,607,825	2,786,700	2,922,472	3,354,000
21–50	203,111	212,505	234,334	242,000
51–100	2,205,735	2,028,441	2,134,210	2,465,900
101–300	7,596,212	8,712,119	9,319,945	10,320,000
301–700	2,983	3,331	3,942	4,116
701–2000	592	630	690	745
2000+	69	88	96	133
Subtotal	26,608,840	27,366,773	28,745,312	31,222,894
Diesel				
<5	0	0	0	0
6–20	4,090	4,032	4,011	3,617
21–50	3,146	2,607	2,654	2,531
51–100	131,888	130,330	136,101	142,366
101–300	383,024	424,247	463,263	468,321
301–700	118,281	145,413	171,584	176,221
701–2000	7,679	7,539	7,544	7,589
2000+	843	785	925	1,044
Subtotal	648,951	714,953	786,082	801,689
Total	27,257,791	28,081,726	29,531,394	32,024,583

*Estimated
Source: Power Systems Research.

TABLE B   Truck weight classifications

Class 1 GVW*	6000 lb	2721.6 kg
Class 2 "	6001–10,000 lb	2722–4536 kg
Class 3 "	10,001–14,000 lb	4536.45–6350.4 kg
Class 4 "	14,001–16,000 lb	6350.85–7257.6 kg
Class 5 "	16,001–19,500 lb	7258–8845.2 kg
Class 6 "	19,501–26,000 lb	8845.65–11793.6 kg
Class 7 "	26,001–33,000 lb	11794–14968.8 kg
Class 8 "	33,001 lb and over	14969.25 kg

*Gross vehicle weight.
Notes: Class 1 and 2 are known as light-duty, 3 to 6 as medium-duty, and 7 and 8 as heavy-duty. Tractors are used from 50,000 lb GCW (gross combination weight) and above.
To convert pounds to kilograms, multiply the pounds by 0.4536.
Source: From Brady, R. N. (1989). *Heavy-Duty Truck Power Trains: Transmissions, Drive Lines, and Axles.* Englewood Cliffs, NJ: Prentice Hall.

indicates that engines of the future, 10 years hence and targeted at line-haul power units, will likely be in the 7 to 10 L (427 to 610 cu in.) displacement-size range. Through the use of newer, lighter weight materials, ceramics, hydraulically actuated electronic unit injectors (no camshaft actuation required), and two-stage turbocharging and turbo-compounding (waste heat from the turbocharger system passing into a large housing enclosing a turbine wheel that is geared back to the crankshaft), engine weight will be reduced substantially.

More importantly, however, the BSFC (brake specific fuel comsumption) will have been lowered to approximately 0.250 lb/bhp/hr, or 152.1 grams (g) per kilowatt hour (kWh), with outputs as high as 700 hp (522 kW). Compare this to the present-day electronically controlled engines, with the lowest BSFC rating being 0.297 lb/bhp/hr (180.7 g/kWh) on Detroit Diesel's Series 60. Consider also that the weight of these 700 hp (522 kW) engines will have dropped from approximately 9500 lb (4400 kg) in the 1950s to approximately 2300 lb (1043 kg) in an engine configuration the same basic size as a Cummins L10/M11, a Caterpillar 3176, or a Detroit Diesel Series 50.

To achieve these major improvements, engine designers are concentrating on how to minimize heat losses that currently exist from the cooling, exhaust, friction, and radiation areas as well as the oil pan. These heat losses will have to be reduced by up to 40% to meet the targeted BSFC goals. The wide use of ceramics will be one way in which these improvements can be achieved. Ceramics have been used sparingly to this point within IC (internal combustion) engines; in future models, ceramics will be used on valves, piston crowns, and a liner for the cylinder head fire deck to reduce heat loss from the current 18% level or so to approximately the 5% level. Existing two-piece crosshead and articulated pistons employing an air-gap thermal (heat) barrier are currently being developed by several major engine and piston manufacturers.

These changes should allow diesel engines to recover approximately 55% of the released fuel energy within the combustion chamber, compared to the 43% in today's electronically controlled engines. Engines using this turbo-compounding system have already been tested in research and development studies throughout the late 1980s and early 1990s. The options for this system are either an engine designed for a 6% better fuel economy, or an engine with an 11% improvement in horsepower. The turbo-compounding system also exhibits a 50% faster transient engine response when the operator depresses the throttle and a 13% lower exhaust-particulate emissions reading.

Two-stage series turbocharging using high-energy turbochargers, most probably with ceramic turbine wheels, and air-to-air aftercooling on trucks will also improve the engine response and its fuel economy. The adoption of a no-camshaft, heavy-duty, high-speed diesel engine is expected soon (and by the copyright date of this book, may very well be available from Caterpillar). At this time, the 93/94 Navistar T 444E and the 3126 Caterpillar engine employs a HEUI (hydraulically actuated electronic unit injector) system, which was designed by Caterpillar and closely coordinated with Navistar engineers. The Caterpillar no-cam engine technology uses computer-driven electrical solenoids and hydraulic amplifiers that between them generate the timing and force required to open the conventional in-head inlet and exhaust valves. This provides the ability to completely tailor valve timing, duration, and opening and closing speed to meet the changing demands placed on the engine during operation. In addition to the EUI (electronic unit injectors) now in wide use by major engine and fuel system design manufacturers such as Cummins, Caterpillar, Detroit Diesel, and Robert Bosch Inc., future engines will not have a conventional valve train, thereby allowing a less complex system. More importantly, the inertia and power losses associated with the conventional valve operating system will be reduced.

Existing heavy-duty, high-speed diesel engines are designed to produce their best fuel performance close to the power curve *torque or lug line,* although a number of them do show little difference in BSFC even through the range of 1500 to 1600 revolutions per minute (rpm). A cam-less engine will provide designers the opportunity to tailor the fuel map to match the operating point of the engine at any desired horsepower and throttle position.

In addition, all major engine manufacturers currently offer some form of alternate-fueled diesel engine. Methanol, CNG (compressed natural gas), and LNG (liquified natural gas) are but three of the most promising alternate fuels being studied and offered. A number of natural-gas-fueled engines that have been in use for some time employ pilot diesel fuel injected into the gas to create ignition. Some of these alternate fuels may be ignited by means of spark plugs similar to a gasoline engine. Research and development has shown, however, that directly injected natural gas has promising results; in this case, the gas is directly injected at high pressure into the combustion chamber and does not require a spark plug to ignite it. Thermal efficiency results similar to those for a diesel fuel engine have been documented.

REPAIR MARKET

Canada has approximately 15 million cars and trucks that by the year 1997 will generate a repair business worth about $13.5 billion. The U.S. market estimate is approximately $200 billion a year. Aftermarket players include companies making replacement products, wholesalers and distributors, and retailers and installers from car and truck dealers to local mechanics and technicians. In Canada the repair business employs about 230,000 people and in the United States the figure is conservatively estimated to be 5 million people. Due to the increasing use of electronics, cars and trucks are now more complex; consequently, do-it-yourself repairs are declining. Also mandatory vehicle testing often requires approved service and repair providers. Therefore, the market share of repair and service facilities is expected to increase for recognized brand-name dealers, independents, and specialty shops throughout the 1990s. In addition, many states and provinces are working toward certification of service and repair technicians in one or more areas. For these reasons, the standards for a heavy-duty truck or heavy-equipment technician career will demand that individuals continually upgrade their knowledge and skills. Many colleges and vocational/technical schools now offer a series of courses that allow a service technician to obtain a two-year diploma in either automotive or heavy-truck technology.

1

Diesel Engine Operating Fundamentals

OVERVIEW

In this chapter we discuss the operating fundamentals of two-stroke- and four-stroke-cycle diesel engines. This discussion will provide you with a solid foundation on which to pursue the other engineering characteristics relative to the diesel engine. Direct- and indirect-injection designs are described along with major terms and formulas such as horsepower, torque, piston speed, brake mean effective pressure, thermal efficiency, volumetric efficiency, mechanical efficiency, work, power, and energy.

TOPICS

- General engine designs and classifications
- Four-stroke-cycle operation
- Two-stroke-cycle operation
- Comparison of two- and four-stroke-cycle designs
- Engine firing orders
- Diesel engineering fundamentals
- Prefixes
- Heating value equivalents
- ISO standards
- Self-test questions

GENERAL ENGINE DESIGNS AND CLASSIFICATIONS

For many years the inline six-cylinder configuration diesel engine has been a standard design. Nevertheless, vee-type engine configurations have also been solid performers in many well-known engines. Vee-engine designs reduce both the length and the overall dimensions of a comparable six-cylinder inline engine that would produce the same horsepower characteristics. Vee engines are commonly available in all types of applications from V6 through V20. Some manufacturers of vee-type engines have adopted a range of engines with a standardized bore and stroke range to allow many common parts to be used in both their vee-type and inline engine configurations. Several examples are Detroit Diesel with its line of 71, 92, and 149 series two-stroke-cycle engines; Caterpillar's 3400, 3500, and 3600 series; Cummins' K series; and Mercedes-Benz with its 400 engine series.

Some of the major features of a typical six-cylinder inline engine for a heavy-duty, high-speed, electronically controlled unit injector Detroit Diesel Series 60 truck engine are illustrated in Figure 1–1. This engine, along with its four-cylinder Series 50 model, has an overhead camshaft design, two-piece crosshead pistons, a pulse recovery exhaust manifold, and high-efficiency turbocharger with a ceramic turbine wheel, injector rocker arms with ceramic rollers, and a silicon nitride rocker arm that produces fuel injector spray-in pressures of 28,000 pounds per square inch (psi), or 193,060 kilopascals (kPa). Air-to-air-charge cooling is a standard feature on these engines in on-highway truck applications. Figure 1–2 is a line drawing of a cross-sectional view of the 3406E Caterpillar engine, which also employs an overhead camshaft and electronic unit injectors. These engines, along with the Volvo VE D12 and the Isuzu Motors Ltd. 12L 6WA1TC, are the only four inline six-cylinder engines with the overhead camshaft design and electronic injector controls—features that make them leaders in their field.

Viewed from Any Angle...
the Series 60 is a World Class Engine

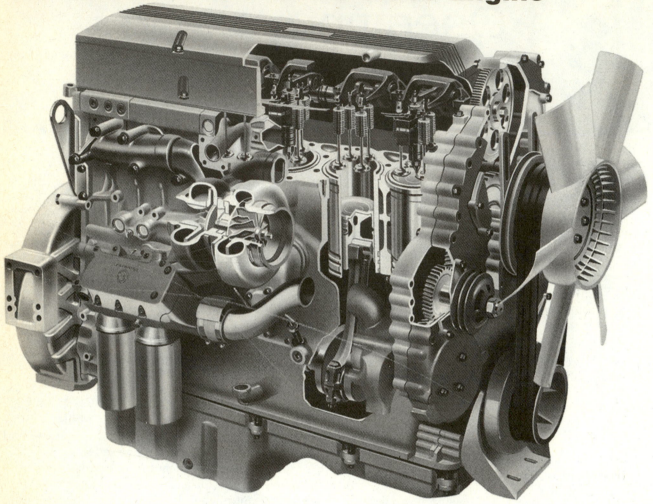

High Efficiency Turbocharger—*uses a pulse-recovery exhaust manifold that provides increased heat flow energy to the state-of-the-art turbocharger.*

Short Ports—*This unique configuration allows for very short intake and exhaust ports for efficient air flow, low pumping losses and reduced heat transfer.*

Iron Crosshead Pistons—*They allow the top ring to be placed much closer to the top of the piston. This reduces the dead volume above the top ring and improves fuel economy.*

Gasket Eliminator—*reduces engine service time since it is not necessary to get a separate gasket to complete a repair.*

Cylinder Liner, Flanges and Bores—*Plateau honing minimizes piston ring break-in and allows quicker ring seal. Flanges at the liner upper end seat in counterbores in the block deck and project slightly above it to compress the head gasket for a good seal. Cylinder bores feature replaceable, wet-type cylinder liners.*

Isolators—*reduce engine noise.*

Crankshaft, Main and Rod Bearings—*Crankshaft is forged, induction hardened steel for high strength, and features computer positioned oil passages to promote a thick oil film in the highest loaded sections. Large main and rod bearings increase bearing life and tolerance to wear.*

FIGURE 1–1 Major design features of a DDEC II (Detroit Diesel Electronic Controls, second generation) Series 60 four-stroke-cycle heavy-duty truck engine employing electronic fuel injection and governing, an overhead camshaft, and AAAC (air-to-air aftercooling). (Courtesy of Detroit Diesel Corporation.)

Fluid Weep Hole—*is provided in the unlikely occurrence of an upper seal water leak. It will leak externally instead of internally to the crankcase. This also allows easy identification of a problem before damage can occur.*

Overhead Camshaft—*design eliminates parts, is easy to inspect and service and optimizes intake and exhaust air passages in the cylinder head for easier engine breathing, and minimizes valve train losses.*

Eight Head Bolts per Cylinder—*provide a uniform load on the gasket and liner to reduce stress on the liner flange and block counterbore.*

Strong Cylinder Block—*block is extensively ribbed and contoured for maximum rigidity and sound reduction, without excessive weight.*

Redundant Internal Seals—*provide an extra seal in the event of primary seal malfunction.*

Grade Eight Metric Fasteners—*are stronger than are commonly used on heavy-duty engines, thus improving gasket loads and decreasing likelihood of breaking. Flanged fasteners eliminate washers.*

Generally speaking, the inline-type engine configuration is cheaper to produce for a given horsepower output. In no way can the inline six-cylinder engine be categorically characterized as better than a vee configuration, or vice versa. In North America, however, the trend seems to be away from V8-style engines in heavy-duty trucks to the long-used inline six-cylinder four-stroke-cycle direct injection engine design. Mack Trucks with its E7 series; Caterpillar with its 3406 and 3176 models; Cummins with its L10, M11, and 14L series; Detroit Diesel with its Series 60; and Volvo with its VE D12 have all chosen to use the inline six-cylinder engine configuration.

All midheavy and heavy-duty high-speed engines employ the direct-injection open-combustion-chamber design, where the injector sprays fuel directly into the cylinder, and the combustion chamber is formed basically by the shape of the piston crown. The injectors used with all of these engines are of the multihole variety.

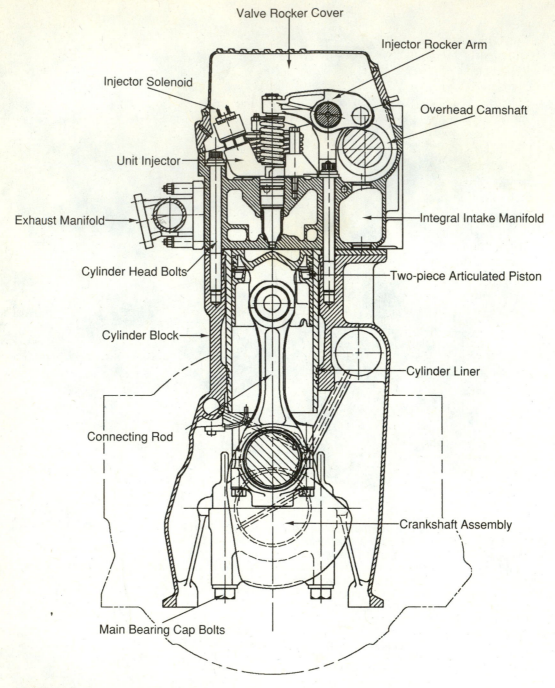

FIGURE 1–2   *Design features of a 3406E Caterpillar heavy-duty truck engine that employs an overhead camshaft, electronically controlled unit injectors and governing, and AACC (air-to-air-charge cooling). (Courtesy of Caterpillar Inc.)*

The following list summarizes the general advantages and design features of an inline engine in comparison to a vee.

- Many years of successful design experience and manufacture
- Ease of servicing and repair as well as usually being less expensive to overhaul than a vee of the same horsepower
- Generally ease of accessibility to auxiliary drive items, which can be mounted on the side of the engine block easier than on a vee
- Ease of installation due to a narrower width than a vee

- Engine that can be mounted horizontally or vertically in a bus application, for example
- Fewer moving parts in a six-cylinder than in a comparable V8 engine of the same power output
- Manufacturing costs that may be lower than those of a vee
- Ease of crankshaft balancing due to the firing order of the engine
- Easy to turbocharge, due to the cylinder arrangement and large crankshaft bearing area
- Good main and camshaft bearing life because of the accessible bearing surface area and space availability
- Fuel and oil consumption as well as exhaust emissions that are normally lower than those of a comparable V8 engine, due to fewer cylinders in the inline engine
- Noise level that, although not necessarily lower, does tend to be so compared with a V8 engine configuration

Diesel engines can be classified by two major characteristics: their operating cycle design and the type of combustion chamber they employ. By this we simply mean that the engine can operate on either the two-stroke- or four-stroke-cycle design. In addition, either one of these types of engine can be designed to operate on what is commonly referred to as the DI (direct-injection) open-combustion-chamber concept, or alternatively, on the IDI (indirect-injection) closed-combustion-chamber design. All heavy-duty high-speed diesel engines now in use operate on the direct injection principle. Figure 1–3 briefly illustrates the difference between DI and IDI combustion chamber design; combustion chambers are discussed in more detail in Chapter 2.

An understanding of the operation of two-stroke- and four-stroke-cycle diesel engines will facilitate your efforts when troubleshooting engines and fuel systems. The operating characteristics of each type of design will exhibit problems common only to that style of engine. The majority of high-speed diesel engines manufactured today are of the four-stroke-cycle design, so we begin with a study of its basic operating cycle. The fundamental operation of both four-stroke-cycle gasoline and diesel engines is the same: they require two complete revolutions of the engine crankshaft, or 720°, to complete the four piston strokes involved in one complete cycle of events.

FOUR-STROKE-CYCLE OPERATION

There are two major differences between a gasoline and a diesel engine:

1. A diesel engine requires a much higher compression ratio, because with no spark plug to initiate combustion, the heat generated by compressing the air in the cylinder is what causes the high-pressure injected diesel fuel to ignite.
2. On the intake stroke of a diesel engine, only air is supplied to the cylinder, whether the engine is naturally aspirated or turbocharged. In a gasoline engine a mixture of air and gasoline is taken into the cylinder on the intake stroke and then compressed. A spark plug then initiates combustion of this premixed fuel charge.

The four piston strokes in a four-stroke-cycle diesel engine are commonly known as (1) The intake stroke, (2) the compression stroke, (3) the power or expansion stroke, and (4) the exhaust stroke.

Figure 1–4 illustrates the four piston strokes in schematic form in a direct injection engine. Next, we consider the sequence of events involved in one complete cycle of operation of the four-stroke-cycle engine.
Intake Stroke.   During the intake stroke, the exhaust valves are closed but the inlet valves are open; therefore, the downward-moving piston induces a flow of air into the cylinder. This air pressure will be less than atmospheric on a naturally aspirated engine, whereas on a turbocharged or blower-equipped engine, this air pressure will be higher than atmospheric. Basically, the intake stroke accounts for 180° of piston movement, which is one-half of a crankshaft revolution. During this time the piston has completed one complete stroke down the length of the cylinder. The weight or percentage of air that is retained in the cylinder during this time is known as VE (volumetric efficiency). In most naturally aspirated engines that rely only on piston movement to inhale air, this VE is between 85% and 90% of atmospheric pressure. In turbocharged or gear-driven blower-type engines, the VE is always greater than atmospheric or 100%; therefore, VE values between 120% and 200% are common on these engines. The power output of any engine depends on the cylinder air charge at the end of the intake stroke. The engine crankshaft and flywheel have rotated through approximately 180°.
Compression Stroke.   During the compression stroke, both the intake and exhaust valves are closed as the piston moves up the cylinder. The upward-moving piston causes the trapped air to be placed under compression to approximately 450 to 550 psi (3103 to 3792 kPa) and 1000° to 1200° F (538° to 649° C) as a mean average. Both pressures and temperatures vary based on the actual engine design and compression ratio. Cylinder compression pressures and temperatures are affected by the ambient air tem-

Direct injection (a) defines the category where the fuel is injected directly into the combustion chamber volume formed between the cylinder head and the top of the piston. Mixing is achieved by using a multi-hole fuel injection nozzle and/or causing the intake air to swirl. High injection pressures are required (18,000–30,000 psi) (124110–206850 kPa) for fine atomization which promotes good con - tact between air and fuel.

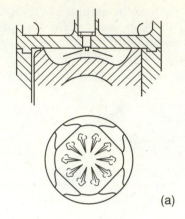

(a)

Indirect Injection (b) occurs where fuel is injected into a pre-chamber which communicates with the cylinder through a narrow passage. During the compression stroke, air enters the pre-chamber, which is usually about one half of the total compression volume. Mixing is achieved by spraying fuel into the turbulent air in the pre-chamber (generally with a single-hole pintle nozzle) where ignition occurs. The burning air-fuel mixture then enters the cylinder where it mixes with the remaining air to complete the combustion. This chamber has a small throat area so that inflow and exit velocities are high. Low injection pressures (5000–14,000 psi) (34475–96530 kPa) are used and the chamber is not as sensitive to the degree of fuel atomization.

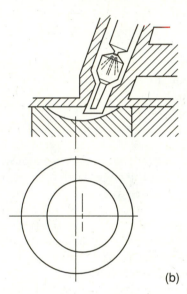

(b)

FIGURE 1–3 *Principles of DI (direct-injection) and IDI (indirect-injection) combustion chamber designs. (Reprinted with permission by Chevron Research and Technology Company, a division of Chevron U.S.A. Inc.; copyright Chevron Research Company [1995].)*

perature, the turbocharger boost pressure, engine compression ratio, valve timing, and engine speed and load. Consequently, some engines may exhibit compression pressures into the 600s, with their air temperature being at the high end of the figures quoted above. Just before the piston reaches the top of the cylinder, high-pressure diesel fuel is injected into this hot air mass and fuel is ignited, causing a substantial pressure and temperature rise within the combustion chamber. Fuel is injected continually to maintain this high pressure, with the number of degrees of injection being related to engine load and speed as well as to the specific model and type of engine being used. Once again the piston has completed approximately 180° of crankshaft rotation. Added to the crankshaft rotation from the intake stroke, the engine crankshaft and the flywheel have now rotated through approximately 360° or one full turn of rotation within the cycle of events.

Power or Expansion Stroke.   The combustion chamber of the cylinder is formed between the space that exists between the top of the piston (crown) and the cylinder head. The pressure released by the burning fuel in the combustion chamber forces the piston down the cylinder. The peak cylinder firing pressures on today's high-speed heavy-duty truck engines can range between 1800 and 2300 psi (12,411 to 15,856 kPa), with temperatures between 3000° and 4000°F (1649° to 2204°C) for very short time periods. This motion is transferred through the piston, the piston

4 CYCLE

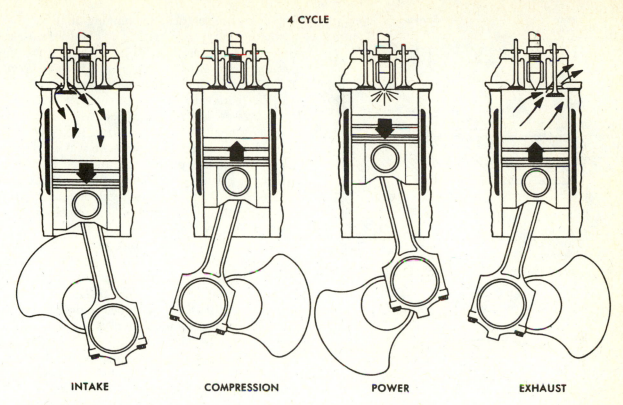

INTAKE   COMPRESSION   POWER   EXHAUST

FIGURE 1–4 *Sequence of individual piston and valve events for a four-stroke-cycle diesel engine. (Courtesy of Detroit Diesel Corporation).*

pin, and the connecting rod to the engine crankshaft and flywheel. Therefore, the straight-line motion of the piston is converted to rotary motion at the crankshaft and flywheel from the connecting rod. The length of the power stroke is controlled by how long the exhaust valves remain closed. Basically, the piston has moved down the cylinder from the top to the bottom and in so doing traveled through approximately 180°. Therefore, added to the already completed intake and the compression strokes, the crankshaft and flywheel have rotated through approximately 540° of the cycle of events.

Exhaust Stroke. The engine camshaft has now opened the cylinder exhaust valves; therefore, the exhaust gases, which are at a higher pressure than atmospheric, will start to flow out of the open exhaust valves. The upward-moving piston will positively displace these burned gases out of the cylinder as it moves from the bottom of its stroke to the top. This involves another 180° of crankshaft and flywheel rotation, which will complete the cycle of events within 720°, or two complete revolutions. Four piston strokes were involved to achieve one power stroke from this individual cylinder. The sequence of events will be repeated once again.

Valve Timing

During the four-stroke cycle of events just described, the opening and closing of the intake and exhaust valves are accomplished by the action of the gear-driven and rotating engine camshaft. Each engine manufacturer determines during the design phase just how long each valve should remain open to obtain the desired operating characteristics from that specific engine model. One simplified example of the sequence of events that occurs during a four-stroke-cycle engine's operation for one cylinder of a turbocharged engine is shown in a basic schematic in Figure 1–5. The following terms appear in the schematic:

- *TDC:* top dead center
- *BDC:* bottom dead center
- *EVC:* exhaust valve closes
- *EVO:* exhaust valve opens
- *IVO:* intake valve opens
- IVC: intake valve closes

NOTE: The valve timing diagram shown in Figure 1–5 represents 720° of crankshaft rotation. For simplicity, two complete circles have been superimposed on top of one another.

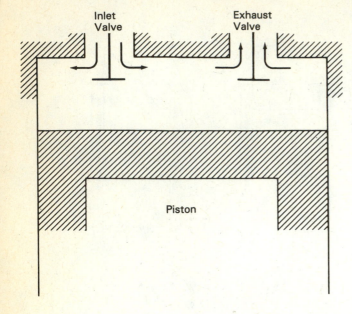

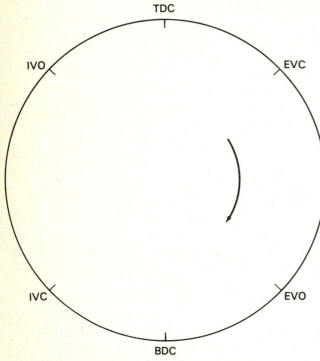

Four–Stroke Engine (Turbocharged)

FIGURE 1–5 *Simplified four-stroke-cycle diesel engine valve timing diagram showing the piston TDC (top dead center) and BDC (bottom dead center) positions, as well as the IVO (intake valve opens), IVC (intake valve closes), EVO (exhaust valve opens), and EVC (exhaust valve closes) positions.*

To ensure complete scavenging of all the exhaust gases from the cylinder at the end of the exhaust stroke and prior to the start of the intake stroke, the engine manufacturer actually has the camshaft open the intake valve before the upward-moving piston has completed its exhaust movement. The action of the burned gases flowing out of the exhaust valve ports allows a ram-air effect to occur once the intake valve is opened. This ensures complete removal of the exhaust gases. When the piston has reached TDC on its exhaust stroke and the piston starts to move down on its intake stroke, the exhaust valves remain open to ensure complete scavenging of any remaining exhaust gases caused by the inrushing air through the intake valve ports. The exhaust valves are closed a number of degrees ATDC (after top dead center) by the camshaft lobe action. The fact that the intake valves are opened before the piston reaches TDC on its exhaust stroke and the exhaust valves do not close until the piston is moving down on its intake stroke creates a condition known as *positive valve overlap*, which simply means that both the intake and exhaust valves are open at the same time for a specified number of crankshaft rotation degrees. For example, if the intake valves open 15° BTDC (before top dead center) and the exhaust valves do not close until 15° ATDC, the valve overlap condition is said to be 30°.

The downward-moving piston would reach BDC and start its upward stroke for the compression cycle. However, note in Figure 1–5 that the intake valves do not close until a number of degrees ABDC (after bottom dead center). This ensures that a full charge of air will be retained in the cylinder. Remember that the greater the air retained at the start of the compression stroke, the greater the engine's volumetric efficiency and power output capability. Simply put, VE is the difference in the weight of air contained in the cylinder with the piston at BDC with the engine stopped versus what it would be with the piston at BDC with the engine running.

The compression stroke begins only when the intake valves close (exhaust valves are already closed). Fuel is injected BTDC by the fuel injector or nozzle, depending on the type of fuel injection system used. Again, the start of fuel injection is determined by the engine manufacturer, based on the load and speed requirements of the engine. Fuel injection will begin earlier (farther away from TDC) with an increase in speed and load, whereas it will begin later (closer to TDC) under low speed and load conditions.

When the piston is forced down the cylinder by the pressure of the expanding and burning gases (air and fuel), the power stroke will continue until such times as the engine camshaft opens the exhaust

FIGURE 1–6 *Typical four-stroke-cycle diesel engine polar valve timing diagram showing the relative piston strokes, intake, compression, power, and exhaust. Specific degrees are also shown for the duration of each stroke as well as the actual start of fuel injection BTDC (before top dead center). (Courtesy of Mack Trucks, Inc.)*

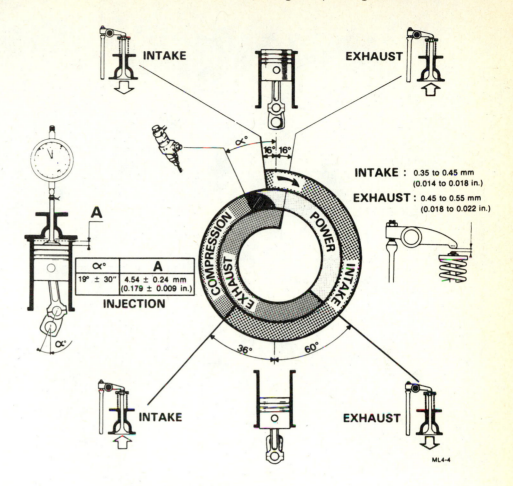

∝°	A
19° ± 30"	4.54 ± 0.24 mm (0.179 ± 0.009 in.)

INJECTION

INTAKE : 0.35 to 0.45 mm (0.014 to 0.018 in.)
EXHAUST : 0.45 to 0.55 mm (0.018 to 0.022 in.)

valves. In the simplified diagrams shown in Figures 1–4 and 1–5, the exhaust valves open BBDC (before bottom dead center) to allow the burned gases to start moving out and through the exhaust ports, exhaust manifold, exhaust piping, and muffler. When the piston turns at BDC and starts to come back up the cylinder, it will positively expel all of the burned exhaust gases from the cylinder. As the piston approaches TDC, the camshaft once again opens the intake valves for the cylinder, and the sequence of events is repeated over again.

Figure 1–6 illustrates one example of the duration of degrees involved in each piston stroke of a typical four-stroke-cycle Mack MIDS06.20.30 Midliner truck diesel engine. Such a diagram is commonly referred to as a *polar valve timing* diagram, since both TDC and BDC are always shown. The positions of both TDC and BDC are similar to that of the north and south poles on a globe of the earth, hence the technical term *polar valve timing*. Keep in mind that the actual number of degrees varies between engine makes and models. Typical stroke degrees for a high-speed diesel engine may include the following four conditions:

1. *Intake stroke.* Valves open at 16° BTDC and close at 36° ABDC; total duration is 232° of crankshaft rotation.
2. *Exhaust stroke.* Valves open at 60° BBDC and close at 16° ATDC; total duration is 256° of crankshaft rotation.
3. *Compression stroke.* Occurs when the intake valves close at 36° ABDC until TDC; total duration is 144°.
4. *Power stroke.* Starts at TDC and continues until the exhaust valves open at 60° BBDC; total duration is 120°.

NOTE: *BBDC,* before bottom dead center; *ABDC,* after bottom dead center; *BTDC,* before top dead center; *ATDC,* after top dead center.

Relative Piston Positions

The sequence of events just described represented the cycle of events in one cylinder of a multicylinder engine. In a six-cylinder four-stroke-cycle engine application, for example, six cylinders are in various stages

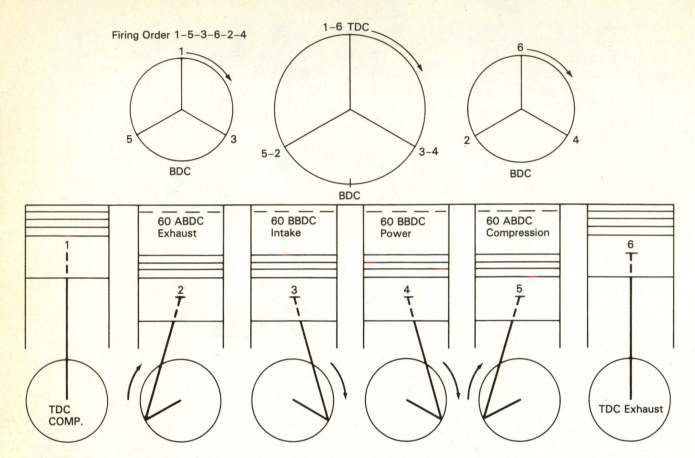

FIGURE 1–7   Relative piston firing positions for a six-cylinder inline four-stroke-cycle engine throughout 720° of crankshaft rotation; firing order is 1–5–3–6–2–4.

of events while the engine is running. The technician must understand what one cylinder is doing in relation to another at any given position of the crankshaft, because often when timing an injection pump to the engine or when adjusting exhaust valves or timing unit injectors, a specific sequence of adjustment must be followed. Knowing the firing order of the engine and what piston/cylinder is on what stroke can save you a lot of time when performing timing and valve adjustments. We mentioned earlier that the sequence of one cycle occurs within two complete revolutions of the crankshaft, or 720° of rotation of the engine. Therefore, in a six-cylinder four-stroke cycle engine each piston would be 120° apart in the firing stroke. Simply put, we would have six power strokes occurring within two crankshaft revolutions on a six-cylinder engine.

To demonstrate such an example, refer to Figure 1–7, which simplifies the complete cycle of events and where each piston would be and on what stroke when piston number 1 is at TDC starting its power stroke. For simplicity we have shown the 720° of crankshaft rotation in two individual circles as well as in one sketch that shows both circles superimposed on top of

one another, which is the commonly accepted method in the industry. The example shows a firing order of 1–5–3–6–2–4 for an engine that rotates CW (clockwise) when viewed from the front.

TWO-STROKE-CYCLE OPERATION

The largest manufacturer of two-stroke-cycle high-speed heavy-duty diesel engines in the world is Detroit Diesel, owned by Roger Penske. Although there are two-stroke-cycle engines that do not employ valves but operate on ports only, Detroit Diesel two-stroke-cycle engines employ a set of intake ports located around the center of the cylinder liner, with conventionally operated pushrod-type exhaust valves at the top of each cylinder. The operation of the two-stroke-cycle engine is illustrated in Figure 1–8, which depicts the layout of a vee-configuration engine. The only difference between the vee and inline two-stroke Detroit Diesel engines is in the basic cylinder arrangement.

In a four-stroke-cycle engine, 720 crankshaft degrees or two complete revolutions, plus four piston movements, are required to complete the intake,

FIGURE 1–8 *Two-stroke-cycle diesel engine principle of operation. (Courtesy of Detroit Diesel Corporation.)*

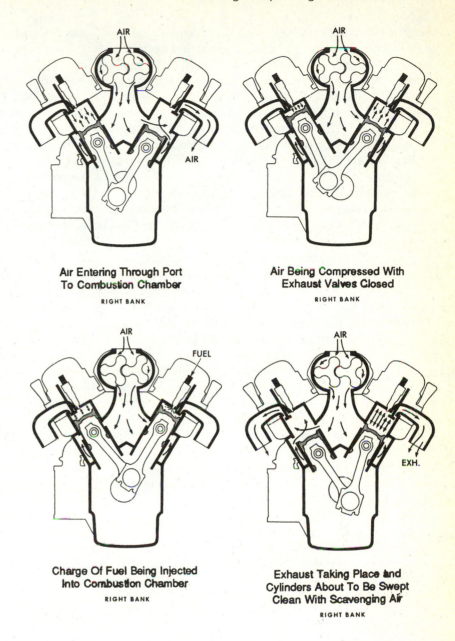

Air Entering Through Port
To Combustion Chamber
RIGHT BANK

Air Being Compressed With
Exhaust Valves Closed
RIGHT BANK

Charge Of Fuel Being Injected
Into Combustion Chamber
RIGHT BANK

Exhaust Taking Place and
Cylinders About To Be Swept
Clean With Scavenging Air
RIGHT BANK

compression, power, and exhaust strokes. On a two-stroke-cycle engine, this sequence of events is completed in only one complete turn of the crankshaft, or 360° of rotation involving only two piston movements. This is accomplished basically by eliminating the separate intake and exhaust strokes, which are a necessary part of four-stroke-cycle operation. During the intake and exhaust piston movements of the four-stroke cycle, the engine basically acts as an air pump by drawing air in and pumping burned exhaust gases out.

To achieve the elimination of these two specific strokes in the two-cycle engine requires the use of a gear-driven positive-displacement blower assembly, commonly known as a Roots-type blower. This blower supplies the airflow necessary for several actions:

- Scavenging of exhaust gases from the cylinder
- Cooling of internal engine components, such as the cylinder liner, the piston, and exhaust valves. Approximately 30% of the engine cooling is achieved by airflow from the blower and turbocharger.
- Combustion purposes
- Crankcase ventilation by controlled leakage of air past the oil control rings when the piston is at TDC

Most models of Detroit Diesel two-stroke-cycle engines are equipped with both a gear-driven blower and an exhaust-gas-driven turbocharger. The blower supplies a positive displacement of air, which is required at idle and light-load operation since the turbocharger does not receive a high enough exhaust gas pressure/flow to cause it to supply sufficient air to the engine. The blower is capable of producing approximately 4 to 7 psi (27 to 48 kPa) throughout the engine speed range. Under heavy loads the turbocharger boost will increase and supply between approximately 40 and 50 in. of mercury (in. Hg) or between 20 and 25 psi (140 to 172 kPa) to the intake ports in the cylinder liners. When the engine is operating under load, a bypass valve built into the gear-driven blower end plate opens and allows the air pressure on both sides of the blower (inlet and outlet) to equalize. In this way the horsepower required to drive the blower is reduced, and basically the airflow is being supplied by the exhaust-gas-driven turbocharger.

Two-stroke-cycle Detroit Diesel engines are equipped with exhaust valves only, with four per cylinder being used for better scavenging purposes. The cylinder liner is arranged so that it has a series of ports cast and machined around the liner circumference approximately halfway down its length. These ports act basically as intake valves.

The engine block is designed so that all liners are surrounded by an *air box* that runs the length of the block. The air box is somewhat like a plenum chamber, where the blower air is pumped into to ensure that there will always be an adequate volume for the four functions listed. Any time that a piston in a cylinder has uncovered the liner ports, the air box pressure is free to flow into and through a cylinder. The operational events are described next.

Scavenging.   During scavenging the liner ports are uncovered by the piston and the exhaust valves are open. The angled ports in the liner provides a unidirectional flow of pressurized air into and through the cylinder to scavenge the exhaust gases through the open exhaust valves. This action also cools the internal components, such as the piston, liner, and valves, with approximately 30% of engine cooling is provided by this airflow. This leaves the cylinder full of clean, cool fresh air for combustion purposes when the piston covers the liner ports.

Compression.   Compression begins when the piston moves up from BDC and covers the previously open liner intake ports. The exhaust valves are timed to close a few degrees after this occurs, to ensure positive scavenging along with a positive charge of fresh air for combustion purposes.

Power.   The initial start of fuel injection varies between series of engines and the year of manufacture; however, generally speaking, this is between 12° and 15° BTDC, with the engine running at an idle speed between 500 and 600 rpm. Advancement of injection occurs automatically through throttle movement via a helical cut plunger in non-DDEC-equipped engines, or

electronically in DDEC (Detroit Diesel Electronic Control) systems as the engine speed is increased.

When the unit injector sprays fuel into the combustion chamber, there is a small delay before ignition occurs; then the intense heat generated by combustion of the fuel increases both the temperature and pressure of the air/fuel charge. Injection continues for a number of degrees and the resultant force of the high-pressure gases drives the piston down the cylinder on its power stroke. The length of the power stroke in Detroit Diesel two-stroke-cycle engines will vary slightly, but at 90° to 95° ATDC, the exhaust valves will start to open. Compare this to a power stroke of between 120° and 140° on a four-stroke-cycle engine. But, although the power stroke is shorter on the two-cycle engine, there are twice as many of them. When the piston is at TDC, a regulated amount of air box pressure is designed to leak past the oil control ring drain holes of the piston to ensure positive crankcase ventilation.

Exhaust.   Exhaust occurs when the exhaust valves start to open by camshaft and rocker arm action. The power stroke, therefore, effectively ends at this point, as the burned gases escape into the exhaust manifold to either drive a turbocharger or to flow freely to a muffler. The exhaust valves have to open before the piston uncovers the liner ports; otherwise, the higher pressure of the exhaust gases would blow back into the air box against the much lower blower pressure.

Once the piston crown uncovers the liner ports, usually about 60° BBDC, the air box pressure is higher than the exhaust pressure and scavenging begins again. This continues until the piston has reached BDC and starts back up in the cylinder and ends when the piston has again recovered the liner ports to start the compression stroke once more.

Therefore, every upstroke of the piston in a two-stroke-cycle engine is basically a compression stroke, and every downstroke is a power stroke. The intake and exhaust events occur only during the time that the exhaust valves and liner ports are open. Scavenge blowthrough (liner ports open) takes place through approximately 120° of crankshaft rotation, although keep in mind that the exhaust valves open at about 90° to 95° ATDC and close several degrees after the piston has recovered the liner ports as it moves upward. The exhaust valves are therefore open for approximately 155° to 160° of crankshaft rotation.

Valve Timing

The polar valve timing diagram shown in Figure 1–9 illustrates one example of the various degrees of port opening, valves opening, and closure for a two-stroke-cycle non-DDEC–equipped Detroit Diesel V92 engine. The specific year of manufacture of the engine, the par-

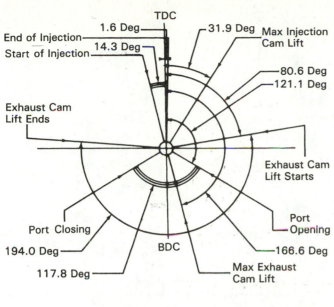

8V–92TA With Standard Cam
9A90 Injector with 1.480 Timing

TDC

End of Injection — 1.6 Deg
Start of Injection — 14.3 Deg

31.9 Deg — Max Injection Cam Lift

80.6 Deg
121.1 Deg

Exhaust Cam Lift Ends

Exhaust Cam Lift Starts

Port Opening

Port Closing
194.0 Deg
117.8 Deg

BDC

166.6 Deg

Max Exhaust Cam Lift

	.014 Hot Lash	.016 Cold Lash
Exhaust Valve Lift Starts—	98.2 Deg ATDC	98.9 Deg ATDC
Exhaust Valve Lift Ends—	246.0 Deg ATDC	243.0 Deg ATDC

Max. Injection Cam Lift– .2755
Max. Exhaust Cam Lift – .3270

FIGURE 1–9 *Example of a typical two-stroke-cycle diesel engine polar valve timing diagram. (Courtesy of Detroit Diesel Corporation.)*

ticular engine series, specific model, and application as well as the fuel delivery rate can result in different degrees of valve timing as well as injection duration.

If you compare this valve timing diagram with that shown in Figure 1–6 for the four-stroke-cycle engine, you will see that there are substantial differences in the duration of the various strokes and the number of crankshaft degrees involved. A thorough understanding of the differences between the two- and four-stroke operating cycles will serve you well when considering their operation and when attempting to troubleshoot the engine in some cases.

Piston Positions

In Figure 1–7 we considered an example of the relative piston positions for a six-cylinder four-stroke-cycle engine. This diagram allowed us to visually interpret where each piston is in relation to the others as well as what stroke each piston is on. Now assume that in the two-stroke-cycle Detroit Diesel engines we are to consider where each piston is at a given time and what

stroke it is on. Most of us would simply assume that since the sequence of events occurs in 360 crankshaft degrees, we can divide the degrees by the number of cylinders and we would know where each piston was. If we were to consider an 8V–71 or 92 series model, logic would tell us to divide 360° by 8 = 45°. This conclusion would be reasonable if the engine were a 90° vee configuration; in fact, however, these engines have a 63.5° angle between the banks. Therefore, the firing impulses between two cylinders has to add up to 90°. Figure 1–10 illustrates how Detroit Diesel does this on these series of engines for a right-hand rotation model with a firing order of 1L–3R–3L–4R–4L–2R–2L–1R. Keep in mind that the manufacturer determines the engine rotation from the front and identifies the left and right cylinder banks from the flywheel end, although it numbers the cylinders on each bank from the front of the engine. If we assume that cylinder 1 on, the left bank is at TDC compression, the other cylinders would be spaced 26.5°, 63.5°, 26.5°, and so on, throughout the firing order. By referring to Figure 1–9, which illustrates a typical example of a two-stroke 8V–92TA (turbocharged and aftercooled) engine polar valve timing diagram, you can determine exactly what stroke each piston is on in Figure 1–10.

COMPARISON OF TWO- AND FOUR-STROKE-CYCLE DESIGNS

Although the two-stroke-cycle engine has twice as many power strokes as that of its four-cycle counterpart, it does not produce twice the power output at the engine crankshaft or flywheel. This is due, in part, to the fact that the length of the power stroke is much shorter in the two-stroke engine than it is in the four-stroke. Average power stroke length in the two-cycle engine can be between 90 and 95 crankshaft degrees, while the four-cycle engine tends to have a power stroke of between 120° and 140°.

The two-stroke-cycle engine, however, generally delivers more power for the same weight and cylinder displacement, or the same basic horsepower, from a smaller-displacement engine size. We can compare the power differences as follows:

1. In a four-stroke-cycle engine, there is a longer period available for the scavenging of exhaust gases and the separation of the exhaust and inlet strokes. In addition, with a shorter valve overlap period versus the port/valve concept in the two-stroke engine, there tends to be a purer air charge at the start of the compression stroke in a four-cycle engine than in a conventional blower-air-supplied two-stroke engine. However, once a turbocharger is added to the two-stroke engine, the airflow delivery rate is increased substantially;

FIGURE 1–10 Example of the firing order and piston placement in degrees for a DDC two-stroke-cycle 63.5° V8 diesel engine with a right-hand firing order of 1L–3R–3L–4R–4L–2R–2L–1R, determined from the front of the engine.

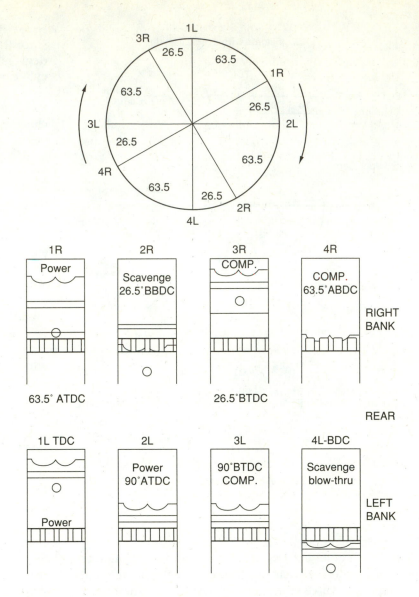

therefore, two-stroke-cycle engines such as Detroit Diesel's 71 and 92 series highway truck engines equipped with both a blower and a turbocharger match the characteristics of the four-stroke engine.

2. Both four-stroke- and two-stroke-cycle engines have pumping losses. The four-stroke-cycle losses occur during the intake and the exhaust strokes, whereas in the two-stroke-cycle engine the power losses required to drive the gear-driven blower reduces the net engine power output. In addition, two-stroke engines require a much larger airflow capacity to operate since the purpose of the airflow is to (a) scavenge the burned exhaust gases from the cylinder in a short interval (usually between 100° and 150°); (b) cool the internal engine components, such as the cylinder liner, the piston crown, and the exhaust valves; approximately 30% of the cooling of a two-stroke-cycle engine is done by airflow; (c) supply fresh air for combustion purposes; and (d) provide air leakage for positive crankcase ventilation.

3. Pumping losses occur in a four-stroke-cycle engine during the intake and exhaust strokes. Equivalent losses to drive the gear-driven blower exist in the two-stroke engine, plus as much as 40% of the engine friction. However, this has been reduced substantially in current Detroit Diesel two-cycle engines by the use of a bypass blower to reduce pumping losses once the turbocharger boost increases to a predetermined level. Generally, on a nonturbocharged two-cycle engine the blower power loss is less than the four-cycle pumping losses when the engines are operating at less than 50% of their rated speed. From 50% up to rated speed, however, the four-cycle engines' pumping losses tend to be about two-thirds that for the two-cycle engine. Two-cycle engines that employ both a turbocharger and a bypass blower, such as

Detroit Diesel 71, 92 and 149 series engines, have changed this ratio substantially.

4. The thermal (heat) loading on the piston, valves, cylinder head, and cylinder liner tend to be lower on a four-stroke-cycle engine because the power stroke occurs only once every two crankshaft revolutions versus once per revolution on a two-stroke engine.

5. It is easier to lubricate the pistons, rings, and liners in a four-cycle engine due to the absence of ports that are required in the two-cycle liner.

6. The two-cycle engine tends to have a slightly higher fuel consumption curve due to its double-power-stroke principle throughout the same 720° for a four-cycle engine.

7. Generally, the two-stroke-cycle engine can produce more power per cubic inch (cubic centimeter) of displacement than that for a four-cycle engine when high power applications are required, such as in high-output marine and off-highway mining trucks. In heavy-duty on-highway truck applications, one example is the Detroit Diesel 8V-92TA-DDEC model rated at 500 bhp (373 kW) at 2100 rpm from 736 cu in. (12.1 L). This same engine can pump out up to 765 bhp (571 kW) in high-output marine applications, which is more than 1 hp/cu in. of displacement. The Cat 3406E at 500 bhp has a displacement of 893 cu in. or 14.6 L, while the Cummins N14 at 500 bhp has a displacement of 855 cu in. (14 L). Mack's six-cylinder E7 model at 454 bhp (339 kW) from 728 cu in. (12 L), however, is a good example of high power from small displacement in a four-stroke-cycle engine.

8. The CR (compression ratio) on four-stroke engines tends to be lower than that on an equivalent rated two-cycle engine. Consider that the Caterpillar 3406E engine has a CR of 16.25:1; the Cummins N14 has a CR of 16.2:1; Detroit Diesel's Series 60 12.7L and Series 50 each have a CR of 15:1 while its two-cycle 92 has a CR of 17:1. (Refer to Figure 1–25 later in this chapter for a description of compression ratio.) However, Volvo's VE D12 electronically controlled six-cylinder four-stroke model has a CR of 17.5 to 1.

9. The BMEP (brake mean effective pressure), which is the average pressure exerted on the piston crown during the power stroke, is generally lower on a two-cycle engine. Consider that a Detroit Diesel 92 series engine rated at 450 bhp (336 kW) at 2100 would have a BMEP of 115 psi (793 kPa); the same engine at 500 bhp (373 kW) would have a BMEP of 128 psi (883 kPa). Compare this to the four-stroke-cycle engine models in the same general power rating category. The Caterpillar 3406E rated at 475 bhp (354 kW) at 1800 rpm would have a BMEP of 234 psi (1613 kPa), and at the peak torque point of 1200 rpm, its BMEP climbs to 295 psi (2037 kPa). A Cummins N14 at 500 bhp at 2100 rpm would develop a BMEP of 221 psi (1524 kPa). A Detroit Diesel Series 60 12.7L rated at 370 bhp (276 kPa) at 1800 rpm would develop a BMEP of 210 psi (1460 kPa); the same engine at 470 bhp (351 kW) would have a BMEP of 229 psi (1579 kPa). Mack's E7-454 bhp (339 kW) model has a BMEP of 274 psi (1890 kPa), while its E9 V8 rated at 500 bhp (373 kW) develops a BMEP of 209 psi (1440 kPa). Volvo's latest six-cylinder electronically controlled VE D12 rated at 415 bhp (310 kW) at 1900 rpm develops a BMEP of 234 psi (1612 kPa). As you can see, four-cycle engines tend to have BMEPs almost twice that for the two-cycle engines rated at the same horsepower. You may have noticed that the smaller the four-cycle engine displacement, the higher the BMEP value will be. Later in this chapter we discuss in more detail and describe how to determine the BMEP of any engine.

10. The BSFC (brake specific fuel consumption) of a two-stroke-cycle engine tends to be higher than that for a comparably rated four-cycle engine. BSFC is simply the ratio of fuel burned to the actual horsepower produced. Engine manufacturers always show their projected BSFC for an engine at different loads and speeds in their sales literature. Later in this chapter we discuss BSFC in more detail; examples of BSFC for several well-known engine makes and models are illustrated and discussed. Electronically controlled heavy-duty diesel engines are capable of returning fuel economy superior to mechanical models, which confirms that these engines have a higher *thermal efficiency* (heat efficiency) as well as the ability to meet the stringent exhaust emissions regulations of the U.S. EPA (Environmental Protection Agency).

We can summarize the two cycles by considering that the piston operation is divided into what is commonly referred to as a *closed* or *open* period. The closed period occurs during the power stroke, and the open period during the time the inlet and exhaust strokes are occurring. Consider the following sequence:

Two-Stroke Cycle

- *Closed period*
  a–b: compression of trapped air
  b–c: heat created by the combustion process
  c–d: expansion or power stroke
- *Open period*
  d–e: blow-down or escape of pressurized exhaust gases
  e–f: scavenging of exhaust gases by the blower and/or blower-turbocharger combination
  f–g: air supply for the next compression stroke

All of the above events occur within 360°, or one complete turn of the engine crankshaft/flywheel.

Four-Stroke Cycle

- *Closed period*
  a–b: compression of trapped air
  b–c: heat created by the combustion process
  c–d: expansion or power stroke
- *Open period*
  d–e: blow-down or escape of pressurized exhaust gases
  e–f: exhaust stroke
  f–g: inlet and exhaust valve overlap
  g–h: induction stroke
  h–i: compression

All of these events require 720° of crankshaft/flywheel rotation, in contrast to the 360° in the two-cycle engine.

ENGINE FIRING ORDERS

The number of cylinders and the engine configuration (inline versus vee) and the directional rotation of the engine determine the actual firing order. Chapter 11 and Chapter 13 discuss in detail the purpose and function of crankshaft counterweights, engine balance shafts, and vibration dampers in the overall balance of a running engine. Every cylinder in an engine produces what are commonly referred to as *disturbing forces* that act along the axis of each cylinder as a result of the acceleration and deceleration of the rotating connecting rod and piston assembly as the individual cranks rotate through 360°.

The actual firing order of an engine, and therefore the position of the individual cranks on the shaft, can be established today by computerized analysis. The following parameters must be considered:

- Main bearing loads when adjacent cylinders fire in sequence
- Engine balance
- Torsional vibrations of the crankshaft
- In some special cases, the airflow interference in the intake manifold

Figure 1–11 illustrates typical firing orders used for various engines with differing numbers of cylinders for both two-stroke- and four-stroke-cycle engines. Two-stroke crankshaft arrangements tend to be more complicated than those in a four-cycle engine, because the two-stroke engine must fire all cylinders in one crankshaft rotation (360° versus 720°). It is common in four-cycle engines to actually repeat, or "mirror," the two halves of the crankshaft to eliminate coupling forces (equal masses positioned opposite one another). This also often allows a number of firing orders to be obtained from a single crankshaft arrangement. The discussion of crankshaft balance and the forces involved is a specialized area in its own right, so we will not delve into details here. In many current high-speed vee-configuration engines the desired firing order is often achieved by employing off-set conrod (connecting rod) journals on the same throw of the crankshaft.

The most widely used six-cylinder firing order for a CW-rotation (from the front) two- or four-stroke cycle engine is 1–5–3–6–2–4. If the engine rotation is reversed, such as for some twin-engine marine applications, a typical firing order might be 1–4–2–6–3–5. When vee engine configurations are employed, the firing order is determined based on the engine rotation and whether it is a two- or four-stroke-cycle type. Most engine OEMs identify cylinder numbering from the front of the engine; however, in some cases the cylinder number is determined from the rear. In addition, on vee-type engines most manufacturers identify the left and right cylinder banks from the flywheel end.

Standard rotation on many engines is based on the SAE (Society of Automotive Engineers) technical standard in which rotation is determined from the flywheel end. Normally, this is CCW (counterclockwise), which results in a CW rotation when viewing the engine from the front. Opposite rotation according to the SAE is still viewed from the flywheel end; however, the engine crankshaft would rotate CCW when viewed from the front. Note that Caterpillar numbers its engine cylinders from the front to the rear, with No. 1 cylinder being on the right side and No. 2 cylinder on the left side when viewed from the rear. This means that the left and right engine banks on a vee model are determined from the flywheel end. For example, a four-cycle V12 Caterpillar 3512 engine model with a standard SAE rotation would have a firing order of 1–12–9–4–5–8–11–2–3–10–7–6; the cylinder numbering system would appear as illustrated in Figure 1–12. This same engine running in SAE opposite rotation would have a firing order of 1–4–9–8–5–2–11–10–3–6–7–12.

A two-stroke-cycle vee configuration, such as those manufactured by Detroit Diesel in V6, V8, V12, V16, and V20, determines left and right cylinder banks from the flywheel end, with the cylinders being numbered from the front to rear on each bank, as illustrated in Figure 1–13 for a series of vee models. In addition, Detroit Diesel engines determine the crankshaft rotation from the front of the engine, and *not* from the flywheel end. Anytime the engine rotation is changed from CW (right hand), to CCW (left hand), the engine firing order is always different, as indicated in Figure 1–13.

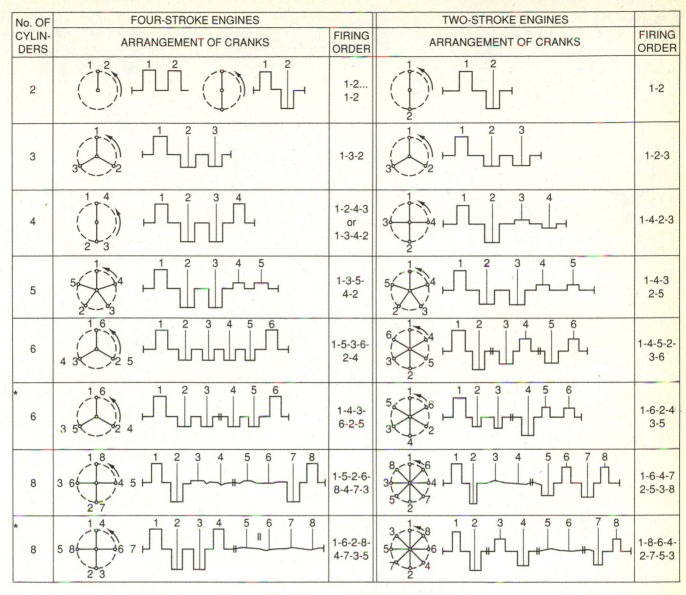

No. OF CYLIN-DERS	FOUR-STROKE ENGINES		TWO-STROKE ENGINES	
	ARRANGEMENT OF CRANKS	FIRING ORDER	ARRANGEMENT OF CRANKS	FIRING ORDER
2		1-2... 1-2		1-2
3		1-3-2		1-2-3
4		1-2-4-3 or 1-3-4-2		1-4-2-3
5		1-3-5-4-2		1-4-3-2-5
6		1-5-3-6-2-4		1-4-5-2-3-6
6		1-4-3-6-2-5		1-6-2-4-3-5
8		1-5-2-6-8-4-7-3		1-6-4-7-2-5-3-8
8		1-6-2-8-4-7-3-5		1-8-6-4-2-7-5-3

FIGURE 1–11 Typical crankshaft throw arrangements for both four- and two-cycle models for engines with between two and eight cylinder designs.

DIESEL ENGINEERING FUNDAMENTALS

This section deals with many of the more commonly used terms and operating conditions related to engine performance. No attempt is made to discuss the more advanced formulas that are required when designing an internal combustion engine, since these are not normally needed in a diesel technician's day-to-day duties. As either a diesel technician or engineering student studying heat engines or thermodynamics, your knowledge of these widely used terms will help you to understand and appreciate the operating philosophies

of how a diesel engine operates. A thorough understanding of these terms, along with a solid knowledge of the various operating principles discussed herein, will provide you with a clear and comfortable approach when you discuss these terms and concepts with your colleagues. Also, when you are analyzing and troubleshooting current mechanical or electronic engines, a mental picture of what actually occurs within the engine cylinders will allow you to recognize and trace possible problem areas.

In this section, English and metric equivalents have been used as much as possible. Use the English/metric conversion chart at the end of this chapter to review or

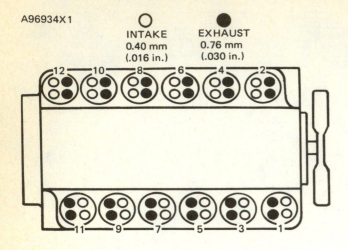

A96934X1

INTAKE
0.40 mm
(.016 in.)

EXHAUST
0.76 mm
(.030 in.)

CYLINDER AND VALVE LOCATION

FIGURE 1–12 Cylinder and valve location for a model 3512 (V12) four-stroke-cycle engine. (Courtesy of Caterpillar Inc.)

convert from either system. After using the chart for a short period of time, you will find that you will remember many of the more common conversion factors.

Energy

The first law of thermodynamics states that energy can neither be created nor destroyed. Only the form in which energy exists can be changed; for example, heat can be transformed into mechanical energy. All internal combustion engines apply the same principle by burning a fuel within the cylinder to produce heat. The high-pressure gases created due to combustion force the piston down the cylinder on its expansion or power stroke. The heat energy is converted into mechanical energy through the piston and connecting rod, which in turn rotates the engine crankshaft and flywheel to supply the power needed.

The second law of thermodynamics states that heat cannot be completely converted to another form of energy. For example, in an engine mechanical energy can be produced from a fuel, because heat passes only from a warmer to a colder body. The reverse of this process is only possible if energy is supplied.

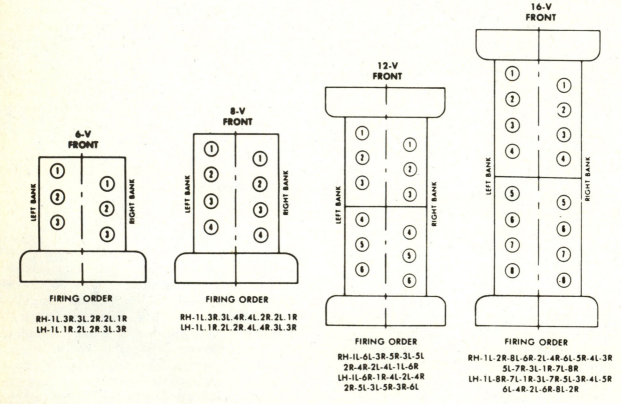

FIGURE 1–13 Engine cylinder designation and firing orders for two-stroke-cycle 6V, 8V, 12V, and 16V models. (Courtesy of Detroit Diesel Corporation.)

Work

Internal combustion engines are used extensively worldwide in 4500 plus applications to do *work*! What is work? If you exert a force to move an object through a given distance, the result of your efforts has produced energy, which we commonly refer to as work. For example, if you apply a force of 100 lb, or 45.36 kilograms (kg), that causes an object to move either vertically or horizontally through a distance of 10 ft or 3 meters (m), the work done would be expressed in foot-pounds (ft-lb) or newton-meters (N • m) in the metric system. Work, therefore, involves a force × a distance. If we consider the example of energy just described, we can show this as follows:

$$\text{work (W)} = \text{force (F)} \times \text{distance (d)}$$
$$\text{W (ft-lb)} = \text{F (lb)} \times \text{d (ft)}$$
$$\text{W} = 100 \times 10 = 1000 \text{ ft-lb (1356 N • m)}$$

Power

The term *power* is used to describe how much work has been done in a given period of time. The rate at which work can be done is measured in terms of power, or how many units of work (ft-lb) have been done in a unit of time. We can show this simply as

$$\text{power} = \frac{\text{work}}{\text{time}}$$

Normally, power is expressed as how many foot-pounds of work are done per minute. If enough work is performed in a given period of time, we can start to compare it to the word *horsepower*, which is used to describe the power output of all internal combustion engines. (A detailed description of horsepower occurs later in the chapter.)

Let us consider the example we used for the work that was produced by moving a weight of 100 lb (45.36 kg) through a distance of 10 ft (3 m); this was performed in a time of 4 seconds (sec or s). The power expended would be

$$\text{power} = \frac{\text{work}}{\text{time}} = \frac{1000 \text{ ft-lb}}{4 \text{ sec}} = 250 \text{ ft-lb per sec}$$

How much horsepower have we expended in doing this work? One horsepower is considered as being 550 ft-lb/sec, 33,000 ft-lb/min, or 1,980,000 ft-lb/hr. Therefore, we can compute horsepower as follows:

$$\text{horsepower} = \frac{250 \text{ ft-lb/sec}}{550 \text{ ft-lb/sec}} = 0.45 \text{ hp (0.33 kW)}$$

If this work were expended continually for a period of 1 min, the energy produced would be

$$\text{power} = \frac{\text{work}}{\text{time}} = \frac{1000 \text{ ft-lb}}{1 \text{ min}} = 1000 \text{ ft-lb/min}$$

and the horsepower produced would be

$$\text{horsepower} = \frac{1000 \text{ ft-lb/min}}{33,000 \text{ ft-lb/min}} = 0.030 \text{ hp}$$

From this simple example, you can see that if work is performed at a slower rate, less horsepower is produced; therefore, we can safely say that the word *horsepower* is an expression of how fast work can be done. In an internal combustion engine this work is produced within the cylinder due to the expanding gases. The faster the engine speed, the quicker the work is produced.

Metric Horsepower

In the metric system, power is expressed by the word *kilowatt* (kW) and was initially used to express the power of electrical machinery, where 1 hp was considered equal to 746 watts (W) in the English equivalent. (A watt is an ampere × a volt; amp is a measure of volume/quantity and V is a measure of electrical pressure.) Since 1 kW equals 1000 W, we can show 1 electrical hp as being equivalent to 0.746 kW. Conversely, 1 kW equals 1.341 hp. This 746 W of measurement is an American equivalent; in the metric system 1 hp is considered as being 735.5 W, or 75 kg-m/s. The German abbreviation for this unit of measurement is PS (*Pferdestärke*),where 1 PS (European horsepower) = 0.986 hp. The French equivalent is CV (*cheval vapeur*), where 1 ch = 1 PS = 0.07355 kW. This means that metric horsepower is approximately 1.5% less than the American unit of measurement! Other measures that you will encounter have been established by the ISO (International Standardization Organization), DIN (Deutsches Institut für Normung—German Institute for Standardization), and SAE (Society of Automotive Engineers [International] headquartered in Warrendale, (Pittsburgh) PA.

Horsepower Formulas

Work is done when a force is exerted over a distance. This can be defined mathematically as work equals distance (D) multiplied by a force (F). As we mentioned previously, horsepower is a measure of the rate (speed) at which the work is done. Therefore we can show this mathematically as:

330/350 HP

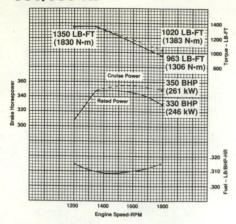

370/430 HP

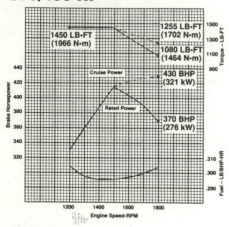

430/470 HP

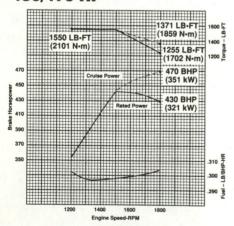

FIGURE 1–14 *Horsepower, torque, and brake specific fuel consumption curves for various electronically controlled Series 60 four-stroke-cycle engine models. (Courtesy of Detroit Diesel Corporation.)*

$$HP = \frac{D \times F}{33,000}$$

where the 33,000 is a constant figure determined by analysis and observation by James Watt when he studied the average rate of work for a horse with respect to the work his steam engine could do. He determined that the average horse could produce a work rate equal to 33,000 ft-lb/min (0.7457 kW/min), which he equated to 1 hp/min, or 550 ft-lb/sec (0.0124 kW/s).

Horsepower is generally considered as being one of two types:

1. bhp (brake horsepower) is actual useful horsepower developed at the crankshaft/flywheel. It can be determined by a known formula, but certain data must be readily available, such as the dynamometer information (weight on a brake arm × distance). Without the dynamometer information, this type of horsepower cannot be readily determined, unless the engine is run on a dynamometer with suitable horsepower, torque, and speed gauges. Many dynamometers also have a formula and data included on a riveted plate to allow you to mathematically compute the engine power being produced.

2. ihp (indicated horsepower) is the power developed within the cylinder based on the amount of heat released, but it does not take into account any frictional losses. The cylinder's mean indicated pressure can be monitored by installing a special test gauge to record the maximum firing pressure. If a maximum pressure indicator gauge is available and the cylinder pressure is known, you can factor out indicated horsepower using a formula.

Horsepower Performance Curves
The simplest way to view horsepower is to refer to Figure 1–14, which illustrates three performance curves for a Detroit Diesel Series 60 12.7 L (774 cu in.) displacement six-cylinder four-stroke-cycle engine. All of these heavy-duty truck engine models are equipped with electronically controlled unit fuel injectors. Note that at the 370 hp (276 kW) rating that this model produces 370 hp at 1800 rpm. This same engine, however, is programmed to increase the power output to approximately 430 hp (321 kW) at 1500 rpm, since this places the fuel consumption curve at close to its best point. In addition, on a gear-fast–run-slow truck application (actual numeric rear axle ratio) engaging the cruise control option to run at a preselected road speed will provide the additional horsepower necessary to

maintain a steady cruise speed even with changing road conditions.

NOTE: Horsepower is a value related to BMEP, but it is also influenced by both the speed of the engine and the cylinder/engine displacement.

The horsepower performance curve for the 430 bhp (321 kW) and the 470 bhp (351 kW) models shows that the rate of "cruise" horsepower increase is greater on the 370/430 hp (276 to 321 kW) model. The 470 hp (351 kW) model is programmed to maintain a "flatter" horsepower output from 1800 rpm down to approximately 1500 rpm.

Figure 1–15 illustrates the performance curve and relative information for the Caterpillar 3406E electronically controlled unit injector truck engine. This horsepower curve is similar to that shown in Figure 1–14 for the Detroit Diesel 370 bhp (276 kW) model. Figure 1–16 illustrates an engine performance curve for a Cummins N14-460E electronically controlled heavy-duty truck engine. Note in this example and others that the engine brake horsepower performance curve is tailored so that the maximum power and best fuel economy are achieved at a speed within the operating range where most of the actual driving is done on a heavy-duty truck application. Cummins refers to the point on the engine performance curve where this occurs as the *command point*. In Figure 1–17 note how the engine horsepower begins to drop as the operator revs the engine beyond 1700 rpm. Note also in Figure 1–16 that the engine torque starts to decrease fairly quickly beyond 1500 rpm and the fuel consumption starts to increase. This design feature "forces" the truck driver to use what is known as a *progressive shift pattern*. This means that the engine is accelerated only high enough to get the vehicle rolling; then a shift is made to the next higher gear. By using this shifting technique, not only does the higher engine *torque* move the vehicle gradually up to road speed, but it also keeps the engine within the most fuel efficient curve, as you can see from the BSFC line in Figures 1–14, 1–15, and 1–16. Most heavy-duty electronically controlled diesel-engine–mounted ECMs (electronic control modules) are programmed to provide this type of operational response. Both the fuel consumption and torque curves are discussed in detail later in this chapter.

The performance curves of brake horsepower we have been discussing are typical of most of the newer electronically controlled, unit injector, heavy-duty-truck-type engines manufactured by Caterpillar, Cummins, Detroit Diesel, Mack, Isuzu, and Volvo. On mechanically governed and injected engines, however, the horsepower generally tends to decrease with a reduction in engine speed (rpm) from its full-load rated setting as the engine rpm is reduced due to an increasing load, since the rate/speed of doing the work is slower. Electronic controls provide tremendous flexibility for tailoring engine performance that is not possible with mechanical controls. Proper selection of turbocharging and air-to-air-charge cooling, high top piston rings, piston bowl geometry, and the use of low-sulfur diesel fuel all help to provide this improvement in engine performance and reduce the exhaust emissions so that they can comply with the EPA-mandated limits.

Regardless of the type of horsepower calculated, most diesel technicians in the field choose to use the following simplified formula to determine horsepower, particularly when the engine torque and speed are known:

$$hp = \frac{torque \times rpm}{5252}$$

Brake Horsepower
The formula for brake horsepower can be stated as

$$bhp = \frac{2 \times \pi \times r \times rpm \times w}{33,000}$$

where, π (pi) = 3.1416
    r   = distance between the centerline of the engine crankshaft and the application of a weight on a brake arm in feet or meters
    rpm = speed of the engine in revolutions per minute
    w   = effective weight on a brake arm in pounds (kg).

Indicated Horsepower
The commonly accepted formula to determine indicated horsepower is

$$ihp = \frac{P \times L \times A \times N}{33,000}$$

where P = indicated brake mean effective pressure
    L = length of the piston stroke in feet
    A = area of the piston crown in square inches
    N = number of power strokes per cylinder per minute.

In two-stroke-cycle engines, N = the number of cylinders $\times$ rpm, while for four-stroke-cycle engines, N = the number of cylinders $\times$ rpm/2, since there are only half as many power strokes in the four-cycle engine versus the two-cycle. Using the known formula, let's determine the ihp developed from a four-cycle

3406E

Truck Engine Performance

475 (354) @ 1800 rpm

DM0479-00

1750 Peak Torque
50 State

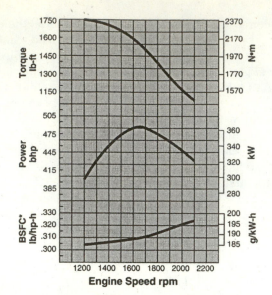

Rated		English		Maximum		Rated		Metric		Maximum	
475 hp				**485 hp**		**354 kW**				**362 kW**	
Engine Speed rpm	Engine Power w/o fan hp	Engine Torque lb ft	Engine BMEP psi	S Fuel Consum lb/hp-h	Fuel Rate gph	Engine Speed rpm	Engine Power w/o fan kW	Engine Torque N•m	Engine BMEP kPa	S Fuel Consum g/kW-h	Fuel Rate l/hr
2100	431	1078	182	.324	20.0	2100	322	1462	1254	197	75.6
2000	447	1173	198	.322	20.5	2000	333	1590	1364	196	77.7
1900	461	1275	215	.319	21.0	1900	344	1729	1483	194	79.5
1800	475	1387	234	.316	21.3	1800	354	1880	1613	192	80.8
1700	485	1499	253	.311	21.5	1700	362	2033	1745	189	81.3
1600	485	1593	269	.309	21.3	1600	362	2160	1854	188	80.8
1500	472	1653	279	.309	20.8	1500	352	2241	1923	188	78.9
1400	455	1705	288	.307	20.0	1400	339	2312	1984	187	75.7
1300	430	1738	293	.306	18.7	1300	321	2356	2022	186	70.9
1200	400	1751	295	.304	16.9	1200	298	2374	2037	185	64.0

Engine Speed rpm	Intake Manif Temp °F	Intake Manif Pres in-Hg	Intake Air Flow cfm	Exh Manif Temp °F	Exh Stk Temp °F	Exh Gas Flow cfm	Engine Speed rpm	Intake Manif Temp °C	Intake Manif Pres kPa	Intake Air Flow m³/min	Exh Manif Temp °C	Exh Stk Temp °C	Exh Gas Flow m³/min
2100	110	45.4	1164	911	671	2441	2100	43	153	33.0	488	355	69.2
2000	114	47.2	1168	938	695	2498	2000	45	159	33.1	503	368	70.8
1900	114	49.2	1161	965	717	2537	1900	45	166	32.9	518	381	71.9
1800	113	51.3	1143	993	741	2547	1800	45	173	32.4	533	393	72.2
1700	113	53.1	1108	1018	765	2519	1700	45	179	31.4	548	407	71.4
1600	112	54.1	1055	1041	790	2452	1600	44	182	29.9	561	421	69.5
1500	110	53.6	988	1061	815	2343	1500	43	181	28.0	571	435	66.4
1400	107	51.7	906	1080	840	2198	1400	41	174	25.7	582	449	62.3
1300	103	48.1	811	1099	871	2011	1300	39	162	23.0	593	466	57.0
1200	98	41.7	688	1121	914	1767	1200	36	140	19.5	605	490	50.1

Conditions

This engine performance data is typical of the engines approved by the Environmental Protection Agency (EPA) and the California Air Resources Board (CARB) for the calendar year 1994. This engine is approved for use in Canada. This data may change, subject to EPA and CARB approved engineering changes

* Brake Specific Fuel Consumption

Tolerance

Curves represent typical values obtained under lug conditions. Ambient air conditions and fuel used will affect these values. Each of the values may vary in accordance with the following tolerances.

Exhaust Stack Temperature	± 75°F ± 42°C	Power BSFC*	±3% ± 010 lb/hp-h
Intake Manifold Pressure-Gage	± 3 in. Hg ± 10 kPa	Fuel Rate	± 6 g/kW-h ± 5%
Torque	± 3%		

FIGURE 1–15 Model performance operating conditions for electronically controlled 3406E truck engine rated 475 hp (354 kW) (Courtesy of Caterpillar Inc.)

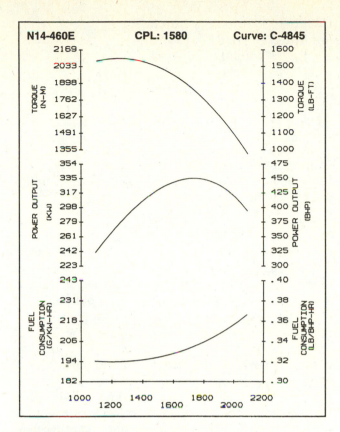

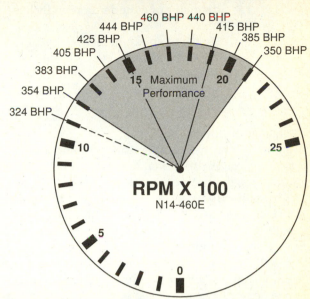

FIGURE 1–16 *Performance curves for N14-460E (855 cu in. displacement) electronically controlled Celect engine. (Courtesy of Cummins Engine Company, Inc.)*

FIGURE 1–17 *Performance graph of typical horsepower output versus engine speed for an electronically controlled heavy duty N14 engine. (Courtesy of Cummins Engine Company, Inc.)*

six-cylinder engine, with a bore of 5.4 in. (137 mm) and a stroke of 6.5 in. (165 mm), that develops an IMEP (indicated mean effective pressure) of 234 psi (1613 kPa) when operating at 1800 rpm.

$$\text{ihp} = \frac{\text{PLAN}}{33{,}000} = \frac{234 \times 6.5 \times 22.9 \times 1800 \times 6}{12 \times 33{,}000 \times 2}$$
$$= 474.96 \text{ ihp } (354 \text{ kW})$$

The number 12 on the bottom line of the formula is needed to convert the piston stroke into feet; however, if the stroke were 6 in. (152.4 mm) we could simply enter it on the upper line as 0.5 and remove the number 12 from the lower line. The answer of 474.96 ihp is actually the horsepower listed for the Cat 3406E electronically controlled unit injector engine shown in Figure 1–15.

If we were to use the same formula but apply it to a two-stroke-cycle engine such as a Detroit Diesel 6V-92 series engine with a bore of 4.84 in. (123 mm), a stroke of 5 in (127 mm), and a BMEP of 137 psi (944.6 kPa) and running at 2100 rpm, what would be the ihp?

$$\text{ihp} = \frac{\text{PLAN}}{33{,}000} = \frac{137 \times 5 \times 18.39 \times 2100 \times 6}{12 \times 33{,}000}$$
$$= 400.81 \text{ ihp } (299 \text{ kW})$$

Some people prefer to use these optional formulas for determining indicated horsepower:

- Two-stroke cycle
$$\text{ihp} = \frac{\text{plank}}{23{,}000 \times 12} \quad \text{or} \quad \frac{\text{PLANK}}{396{,}000}$$
- Four-stroke cycle
$$\text{ihp} = \frac{\text{plank}}{33{,}000 \times 12 \times 2} \quad \text{or} \quad \frac{\text{PLANK}}{792{,}000}$$

where n = rpm
k = number of cylinders.

Calculated Horsepower

If you wish to determine the calculated horsepower of an engine when the bhp and ihp data are incomplete, use the following formula:

$$\text{hp} = \frac{P \times D^2 \times L \times \text{rpm}}{C}$$

where P   =   mean effective pressure in psi (kPa),

D =   either bhp or ihp
diameter of cylinder bore in inches
(mm)

L =   length of stroke in inches

C =   1,010,000 for four-cycle engines or
505,000 for two-cycle engines

rpm = revolutions per minute of the output
shaft

Frictional Horsepower

No engine is capable of operating without frictional and heat losses! The frictional losses occur between all moving parts; the heat losses are assumed by the cooling, lube, and exhaust systems as well as the radiated engine heat. Because of these frictional losses, the ihp (indicated or apparent) and bhp (useful or true power) can never be the same. If we calculated from the ihp formula that an engine should develop 400 hp, but it only indicated 340 bhp on a dynamometer, then the frictional losses have accounted for a loss of 60 hp. One of the easiest ways to appreciate frictional hp losses (a method that is often used by a diesel technician) is when you short out a fuel nozzle or unit injector to determine both the cylinder and nozzle/injector condition during a low-power engine complaint.

Injectors can be shorted out on a running mechanical engine by loosening the high-pressure fuel line or by depressing and holding down the unit injector follower on two-stroke-cycle Detroit Diesel 53, 71, and 92 series engines. On electronically controlled engines that use unit injectors, such as those of DDC, Cat, Cummins, and Volvo, the injectors can be shorted out individually by use of the diagnostic equipment available.

What we are actually doing when shorting out individual cylinders one at a time is reducing the power from the engine. Assume that a six-cylinder engine develops 450 hp at 2100 rpm and that the engine is tested with each cylinder cut out in succession. Each time that a cylinder is cut out, the engine loses indicated horsepower from that cylinder, or the ihp developed by that cylinder when operating is equal to the total bhp of the engine minus the bhp when the cylinder is not firing. Therefore, the total sum of the losses in bhp when each cylinder is cut out is equal to the total ihp of the engine. Frictional horsepower losses can then be determined by this formula:

$$\text{frictional hp (fhp)} = \text{ihp} - \text{bhp}$$

Consider the following example for a 450 bhp engine running at 2100 rpm, with each cylinder cut out in succession one at a time.

Cylinder not firing	bhp at 2100 rpm	hp loss
1	366	84
2	356	94
3	364	86
4	358	92
5	362	88
6	362	88

Total hp loss = engine ihp = Frictional horsepower = 532 − 450 = 82. Therefore, the frictional losses in this sample engine are equal to 82.

Horsepower Ratings

Now that we are familiar with how to determine horsepower, let's discuss the different types of horsepower ratings applied to engines when installed in various applications. If you consider, for example, the same model engine in a different equipment application, the actual horsepower rating may not be the same. The reason for this is based on the loads and speed variation that the engine is subjected to throughout a typical working day. An engine in a heavy-duty on-highway truck tends to be exposed to what is known as an intermittent-continuous duty cycle as the operator revs the engine up and down during upshifting and downshifting of the transmission as a result of the geography and terrain in which the vehicle is operating. On the other hand, a diesel generator set is designed to start and run at a fixed speed, possibly with a fixed load or an alternating load based on the demands for electrical power. Consequently the horsepower (kW) rating for the gen-set (generator set) would be lower than that for the truck, because it is possible that the gen-set engine might run 24 hours a day, 7 days a week for a month or longer. To ensure optimum engine life and fuel economy, as well as factoring in some possible temporary overload capability into the gen-set application, most OEMs will derate this engine to 70% of maximum rated horsepower.

NOTE: All current heavy-duty diesel engines are equipped with either an engine identification plate or a series of stick-on decals attached to the rocker cover(s) that list the horsepower output at rated speed. In addition, an EPA compliance sticker confirms that the engine meets the mandated exhaust emissions limits for the year in which the engine was manufactured. Other information on these decals indicates the engine model, family and displacement, fuel injector delivery rate, initial injection timing, and intake and exhaust valve clearances. All specifications—even on U.S.–built engines—are now adopting the metric standard of measurement!

Basically there are seven general classifications of horsepower ratings with which you should be familiar: rated brake horsepower, intermittent rated, intermittent maximum, continuous horsepower, intermittent continuous, shaft horsepower, and road horsepower.

1. *Rated horsepower* is the net horsepower available from the engine with a specified injector fuel rate and engine speed, which is guaranteed within plus or minus 5% of that shown in an OEM's sales literature according to the SAE standard ambient conditions, elevation and air density. This is usually stated on the OEM sales literature, such as 77°F (25°C) and 29.31 in. Hg (99 kPa) barometer (dry).

2. *Intermittent rated* is used for variable speed and load applications where full output is required for short intervals of time. To obtain optimum life expectancy, the average load should not exceed 60% (turbo) and 70% (nonturbo) of full load at the average operating speed. Typical examples for this rating are a crew boat, a crane, a shovel, a railcar, a rail-yard switcher, front-end loader, earthmoving scraper, and off-highway rear-dump truck.

3. *Intermittent maximum* is a rating used for applications in which maximum output is desirable and long engine life between overhauls is of secondary importance, or in which the average load does not exceed 35% of the full load at the average operating speed. Typical examples for this rating include a bow thruster used for docking purposes on marine vessels, a standby gen-set, or a standby fire pump.

4. *Continuous horsepower* is a rating given to an engine running under a constant load for long periods of time without a reduction in speed or load. This rating gives the range of optimum fuel economy and longest engine life. The maximum speed for this rating is generally shown on a performance curve chart. The pump or injectors may or may not have reserve capacity for momentary overload demands. The average load should not exceed the continuous rating of the engine. Typical examples include a stationary air compressor, a quarry-rock crusher, a marine dredge, a gen-set, or a mud-pump in oil-well drilling applications.

5. *Intermittent continuous* is a rating used for applications that are primarily continuous but have some variations in load and/or speed. Average fuel consumption at this rating should not exceed that of the continuous rating. The injectors or pump may or may not have reserve capacity for momentary overload demands. Typical applications include a steering bow thruster on marine vessels, a workboat, a portable air compressor, a dredge, a gen-set, a railroad locomotive, and a bottom-dump earthmoving truck.

6. *Shaft horsepower* is the net horsepower available at the output shaft of an application, for example, the horsepower measured at the output flange of a marine gearbox.

7. *Road horsepower* is a rating of the power available at the drive wheels, for example, on a truck after losses due to the transmission, driveline, and so forth.

Engine Torque

Torque is a twisting and turning force that is developed at the engine crankshaft, and it is a measure of the engine's capacity to do work. The units of torque are expressed in pound-feet (lb-ft), or newton-meters (N • m) in the metric system. Smaller quantities of torque can be expressed in pound-inches (lb-in.) or N • m. An easy way to understand torque is to consider that as a heavy-duty truck is forced to move up a hill and the road speed and engine speed are decreased by the grade, the horsepower (rate of doing work) is slower but the engine torque increases with a reduction in speed. Therefore, it is the torque that keeps the crankshaft turning and actually pulls the truck up the hill. Similarly, when a tandem-axle dump truck is up to its axles in mud, it isn't horsepower that pulls it out of this mess (high hp occurs at an elevated speed, so revving the engine simply results in wheel slippage with no appreciable movement); once again it is the torque.

An attempt to move a heavily loaded truck from a parked position on a hill involves *gradeability* (percentage of hill steepness). What the vehicle needs is the ability to produce enough torque or *work power* to get moving and stay moving at a slow-vehicle speed. Therefore, the engine torque multiplied through the transmission and rear-axle ratios determines the truck's ability to overcome resistance to soft terrain or an uphill (gradeability) working position.

Figure 1–18 illustrates the conditions related to the development of torque, which is produced by a force (expanding high-pressure gases) pushing down on top of the piston crown. This force is measured in pounds per square inch (or in the metric system of measurement, kilopascals). The force on the piston is transferred through a lever (length and throw of the connecting rod), which in turn is connected to the crankshaft journal. The force exerted on the top (crown) of the piston decreases as the piston moves down the cylinder; this energy is used up in rotating the crankshaft. Torque depends on BMEP as well as engine cylinder displacement; therefore, the BMEP is the average pressure exerted on each square inch (square millimeter) of the piston crown throughout the actual "power stroke" within the cylinder multiplied by the area of the piston crown. This force (F) = area × BMEP.

The length of the connecting rod (lever) is shown in Figure 1–18. Torque can be described, therefore, as

FIGURE 1-18
Characteristics involved in
determining engine torque.

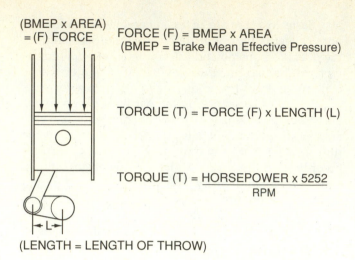

FORCE (F) = BMEP x AREA
(BMEP = Brake Mean Effective Pressure)

TORQUE (T) = FORCE (F) x LENGTH (L)

TORQUE (T) = $\dfrac{\text{HORSEPOWER} \times 5252}{\text{RPM}}$

(LENGTH = LENGTH OF THROW)

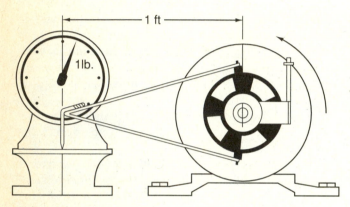

FIGURE 1-19 *Simplified concept of a load of 1 lb
(0.453 kg) applied through a lever 1 ft (.3M or 304.8
mm) long to an engine flywheel to produce* torque. *A
lb-ft is the moment created by a force applied to the
end of a lever. The term lb-ft indicates torque!*

the force (F) multiplied by the length of the lever (L)
and is best defined as

$$\text{torque (T)} = \frac{\text{hp} \times 5252}{\text{rpm}}$$

The number 5252 is a mathematical constant derived
from the basic horsepower (kilowatt) formula:

$$\text{hp} = \frac{DF}{33,000T}$$

Figure 1–19 illustrates the concept of a prony
brake, an early dynamometer that used an adjustable
weight on a lever to apply a large brake band to the
rotating engine flywheel. The diagram shows that a
weight of 1 lb (0.45 kg) placed at the end of a lever of
1 ft (0.3 m) results in an opposing torque (twisting and

turning force) at the flywheel of "one pound foot."
When applied to a prony brake, the formula therefore
becomes

$$\text{hp} = \frac{F \times 6.28 \, RN}{33,000} = \frac{FRN}{5252}$$

where F = force measured on the scale
      R = effective length of lever in feet or meters
      N = engine speed rpm
      6.28 = 2 pi (π)

We can determine the torque produced in a given
engine if we know some of the other specifications of
the engine. The formula for torque

$$T = \frac{5252 \times \text{hp}}{\text{rpm}}$$

is the simplest method to use if and when you want to
determine the given torque from an engine at a certain
operational speed. From our earlier discussion of
horsepower, we know that heavy-duty electronically
controlled engines are designed to produce their best
power and fuel consumption at a midrange rpm.
Figure 1–16 is one example, a Cummins N14 Celect
engine rated at 460 hp at 1700 rpm. What is important
here is that the torque drops off fairly quickly as the
engine speed is increased beyond this range. On the
other hand, as the rpm is reduced, the torque increases until at 1200 rpm it reaches its *peak torque point*,
which in this example is 1550 lb-ft (2101 N • m). The
1995-N14-460E+ was recalibrated to produce 1650 lb-ft
(2237 N • m) at 1200 rpm.

Refer now to Figure 1–15, which lists all of the
operational data for the 3406E Caterpillar engine
rated at 475 bhp at 1800 rpm. By using our torque for-

mula, we can confirm if the horsepower and torque are as stated in the figure. Let's see if the torque at full-load rated speed and the peak torque point checkout by using the formula:

$$T = \frac{5252 \times hp}{rpm} = \frac{5252 \times 475}{1800}$$
$$= 1386 \text{ lb-ft. } (1879 \text{ N} \cdot \text{m})$$

Another method is commonly used and can be applied to determine the torque from two-stroke-cycle and four-stroke-cycle engines if the engine displacement and its BMEP are known.

- Two-stroke cycle
$$torque = \frac{BMEP \times displacement}{75.4}$$

- Four-stroke cycle
$$torque = \frac{BMEP \times displacement}{150.8}$$

In both of these formulas the numbers 75.4 and 150.8 are constants derived from a mathematical procedure.

Once again refer to Figure 1–15 dealing with the 3406E and determine the torque at rated and peak torque speeds using the four-stroke-cycle engine formula.

$$torque \text{ at rated speed } (T) = \frac{BMEP \times displacement}{150.8}$$

$$= \frac{234 \times 893}{150.8} = 1385.68 \text{ lb-ft } (1879 \text{ N} \cdot \text{m})$$

$$peak \text{ torque at } 1200 \text{ rpm } (T) = \frac{BMEP \times displacement}{150.8}$$

$$= \frac{295 \times 893}{150.8} = 1747 \text{ lb-ft } (2369 \text{ N} \cdot \text{m})$$

As you can see from these calculations, there are minor variations in the final answer, but we have determined that these formulas do work!

Torque Rise

The term *torque rise* is another description that you will encounter often in reference to most of today's electronically controlled diesel engines, particularly with respect to heavy-duty on-highway truck applications. This term simply expresses in a percentage figure the increase in engine torque as the engine speed is reduced from its maximum no-load rpm or rated speed. For example, an engine develops 1000 lb-ft (1356 N • m) of torque at its rated speed of 2100 rpm and this torque increases to 1500 lb-ft (2034 N • m). When the rpm is reduced to 1200 rpm (known as the

peak torque point), the rate of torque rise is equal to 50%. If this 50% torque increase is divided by the 900 rpm drop from rated to peak torque rpm, this engine develops 5.55% torque rise for every 100 rpm decrease. Such a situation might occur when a heavy-duty truck is forced to climb a hill without the operator downshifting the transmission or changing the throttle position. Before the introduction of electronically controlled unit injector and pump-line-nozzle systems, OEMs employed various mechanical devices such as *torque springs* or two belleville washers within the governor, which could be adjusted to tailor the actual rate of torque rise of the engine. This function can now be programmed into the ECM on the engine to allow fine control of both the horsepower and torque curves. If the engine has been tailored for a high rate of torque rise with a decrease in engine speed, the operator downshifts the transmission less often. The engine, in truck driver jargon, "is able to hang onto the load a lot longer," such as when moving up a hill.

We can use the followng formula to determine the torque rise:

$$torque \text{ rise} = \frac{peak \text{ torque} - torque \text{ at rated speed}}{torque \text{ at rated speed}}$$

In Figure 1–15 note that the 3406E Caterpillar electronically controlled engine rated at 475 hp (354 kW) at 1800 rpm produces a torque of 1387 lb-ft (1880 N • m). The torque increases to 1751 lb-ft (2374 N • m) at 1200 rpm. Therefore, we can determine the torque rise of this engine from our formula:

$$torque \text{ rise} = \frac{1751 - 1387}{1387} = \frac{364}{1387} = 26.24\%$$

Some earlier models of mechanically governed engines exhibited torque rise figures as high as 60%; however, they had lower overall torque at rated speed than many of the current electronic model engines, which also offer numerous horsepower and torque ratings. Many of the electronic engines can have horsepower and torque altered simply by the technician connecting a diagnostic data reader to the ECM, entering the security password, and making the desired changes within the OEM's limits for that particular model of engine. In addition, the electronic engines have superior fuel economy and can develop both higher horsepower and torque ratings at lower engine speeds than their mechanical forerunners as well as being able to offer longer service life between overhauls. And most importantly, the electronic models can meet the severe EPA exhaust-smoke emissions standards more easily than the mechanical models could.

BMEP Formula

BMEP, or brake mean effective pressure, is the average pressure exerted on the piston crown during the working or power stroke. This factor is often described in terms of the performance capability of an engine model, because the BMEP is a measurement of how efficiently an engine is using its piston displacement to do work. Torque depends on BMEP as well as engine cylinder displacement. Horsepower is a value related to BMEP but it is also influenced by engine speed as well as displacement. Therefore, for a constant BMEP condition, torque increases in direct relation to the piston displacement of the engine. BMEP is actually difficult to define accurately since it is a parameter that doesn't specifically exist. It is the *theoretical* mean effective pressure developed during each power stroke which would in turn develop a power equal to a given horsepower or kilowatt figure.

BMEP is also equal to the IMEP (indicated mean effective pressure) times the mechanical efficiency of the engine. The BMEP must be calculated after the bhp or torque of the engine is known, and it can be determined using the conventional ihp formula stated earlier in this chapter. In the following formula, the BMEP (Pb) and bhp are used in place of IMEP (Pi) and ihp.

$$bhp = \frac{PbLAn}{33,000} \quad or \quad Pb = \frac{33,000\ bhp}{LAn}$$

where Pb = BMEP = brake mean effective pressure (psi or kPa)
    L = piston stroke in feet or meters
    A = piston crown area in square inches or square millimeters
    n = number of power strokes per minute

The total piston displacement (D) in cubic inches (or cubic centimeters or liters) of an engine is equal to the area of one piston times the stroke, times the number of cylinders. So the formula can be simplified somewhat for both two-stroke-cycle and four-stroke-cycle engines as follows:

- Four-stroke cycle
$$Pb = \frac{792,000\ bhp}{DN}$$

- Two-stroke cycle
$$Pb = \frac{396,000\ bhp}{DN}$$

where D = total piston displacement of the engine in either cu in. or cc
    N = engine speed in rpm

For example, using the above formula for a four-stroke-cycle Cummins engine with a displacement of 855 cu in. (14,011 cc, 14.011 L) developing 460 bhp at 1800 rpm, the BMEP would be

$$Pb = \frac{792,000\ bhp}{DN} = \frac{792,000 \times 460}{855 \times 1800}$$
$$= 236.72\ psi\ (1632\ kPa)$$

Using the same dimensions for a two-stroke-cycle engine, the BMEP would be

$$Pb = \frac{396,000\ bhp}{DN} = \frac{396,000 \times 460}{855 \times 1800}$$
$$= 118.36\ psi\ (816.1\ kPa)$$

Note that the two-stroke-cycle engine has a BMEP close to half that of a four-cycle model, even when running at the same horsepower setting. This is due to the fact that approximately only half as much fuel is injected for each power stroke on the two-stroke model versus the four-stroke model. Keep in mind, however, that the two-cycle model has "twice" as many power strokes as the four-cycle engine. For example, a 400 hp Detroit Diesel 92 series engine running at full load would have approximately 90 cu mm of fuel injected for each stroke of the injector plunger. The four-cycle engine set at the same horsepower rating would have approximately 180 cu mm plus of fuel injected on every stroke of the injector plunger. This does not mean that the two-cycle model is more fuel efficient than the four-cycle model. Generally, the two-cycle engine tends to be a little more thirsty than its four-stroke counterpart.

More simplified formulas can be used to determine BMEP if the engine torque and the engine displacement are known, for example:

- Two-stroke cycle
$$BMEP = \frac{75.4 \times torque}{displacement}$$

- Four-stroke cycle
$$BMEP = \frac{150.8 \times torque}{displacement}$$

Refer again to Figure 1–15. You will see that the BMEP at the rating and speed of 475 hp (354 kW) at 1800 rpm is 234 psi (1613 kPa). Take careful note that in any engine as the engine rpm is reduced under full-load operation toward the peak torque point, the BMEP increases accordingly. In the 475 hp (354 kW) 3406E engine, notice that the BMEP climbs to 295 psi (2037 kPa) at 1200 rpm. Using our formulas, let's determine if the BMEP is as listed for both the rated and 1200 rpm peak torque speeds.

- Rated speed (1800 rpm)

$$BMEP = \frac{150.8 \times torque}{displacement}$$

$$= \frac{150.8 \times 1387}{893} = 234.22 \text{ psi (1614.96 kPa)}$$

- Peak torque speed (1200 rpm)

$$BMEP = \frac{150.8 \times 1751}{893} = 295.6 \text{ psi (2039 kPa)}$$

Compare these answers to the values listed in Figure 1–15—they agree.

Piston Speed Formula

The speed of the piston within the cylinder is to some degree a measure of the wear rate within the cylinder and the wear rate of the piston ring. Piston speed can be determined by the following formula:

$$\text{piston speed} = \frac{L \times rpm \times 2}{12} \text{ or } \frac{\text{stroke (in.)} \times rpm}{6}$$

The number 2 appears in the first formula because the piston moves up and down for each crankshaft revolution. The number 12 on the bottom line of the formula is to convert the speed to feet per minute. In the second formula, we have simply substituted the number 6 and removed the 2 from the upper line. In either case the formula produces the same result. If an engine had a stroke of 6.5 in. (165 mm), what would its piston speed be in feet per minute (meters per minute) with the engine running at 1800 rpm?

$$\frac{L \times rpm \times 2}{12} = \frac{6.5 \text{ in. (165 mm)} \times 1800 \times 2}{12}$$
$$= 1950 \text{ ft/min (594 m/min)}$$

BSFC Formula

BSFC, or brake specific fuel consumption, is always listed on engine manufacturers' sales data literature and is usually shown in either lb/bhp/hr or g/kW-h (grams/kilowatt-hour). One lb/hp-hr is equal to 608.277 g/kW-h. Figure 1–15 illustrates an example of the BSFC for a Caterpillar 3406E model heavy-duty truck engine rated at 475 hp (354 kW) at 1800 rpm and a peak torque at 1200 rpm of 1750 lb-ft (2373 N • m). As you can readily see on the graph for BSFC, fuel consumption is approximately 0.316 lb/hp-hr (192 g/kW-h) for a fuel rate of 21.3 U.S. gallons (80.8 L/h) when running at 1800 rpm. At the peak torque rating of 1200 rpm, the fuel rate is 0.304 lb/hp/hr (185 g/kW-h) for a fuel consumption rate of 16.9 U.S. gallons (64 L/h). This same chart lists the various other important spec-

ifications and operating conditions for this engine rating, which can actually produce a maximum horsepower of 485 bhp (362 kW) at approximately 1650 rpm, for example, during a cruise control mode.

In the OEM's sales data for BSFC in Figure 1–15, the U.S. gallons per hour, or the fuel rate in liters per hour, is determined as follows. Let's consider the example listed with an engine speed of 1800 rpm and 475 hp (354 kW) where the BSFC is shown as 0.316 lb/hp-hr (192 g/kW-h). If we multiply 475 × 0.316 we get 150.1 lb/hr of fuel consumed, which is listed in the chart as being equivalent to 21.3 U.S. gallons/hr (80.8 L/h). If we divide 150.1 lb by 21.3, the weight of the fuel per U.S. gallon is 7.046 lb (3.196 kg). In Chapter 3, Table 3–1 indicates that this fuel has an API (American Petroleum Institute) gravity rating of approximately 36. The API rating of the fuel determines its heat value and therefore the Btu (British thermal unit) of heat content available from a pound or a gallon.

Based on the foregoing information, we can use the following formula to determine BSFC:

$$BSFC = \frac{\text{pounds of fuel per hour}}{bhp}$$
$$= \frac{150.1}{475} = 0.316 \text{ lb/hp-hr (192 g/kW-h)}$$

SPECIAL NOTE: All on-highway diesel engines sold in the United States must comply with the EPA exhaust emissions standards for the year in which they were manufactured. Information relative to the EPA standards for engine power output, fuel delivery rate, rpm, valve lash, and so on, can be found on a stick-on decal attached to the engine or its rocker cover area.

If manufacturers' information is not readily available, the BSFC could be determined by noting the fuel injection rate listed on the engine decal. If we were to assume that this was 249.36 cu mm per stroke of the injector, we could multiply this times the number of engine power strokes over a 1 hour time period. In the 3406E Cat engine described in Figure 1–15, we can calculate the total power strokes as follows:

$$\frac{1800 \times 6 \times 60}{2} = 324,000 \text{ power strokes per hour}$$

A cubic millimeter is 1/1000 of a cubic centimeter (cc); therefore, each injector will deliver 0.24936 cc per stroke (249.36 cu mm). To determine the fuel used, multiply 324,000 × 0.24936 cc, which equals 80,792 cc or 80.792 L/h, or 21.34 U.S. gallons/hr. The data for this engine listed in Figure 1–15 has been rounded off to show 80.8 L/h (21.3 U.S. gallons/hr).

Refer again to the information for the 3406E engine in Figure 1–15. Notice that the BSFC actually decreases, or improves, as the engine speed is reduced by load down to its peak torque of 1200 rpm (fewer injection cycles) where it is shown to be 0.304 lb/hp-hr (185 g/kW-h). Usually this occurs because the volumetric efficiency of the engine tends to increase with a reduction in engine speed due to the fact that the intake valves are open for a longer time at this lower speed and the intake manifold temperature is also usually lower.

Two-stroke-cycle engines tend to be a little more thirsty than their four-stroke-cycle counterparts. The two-stroke engine, however, is generally a faster accelerating and decelerating engine because of its power stroke every 360° (versus 720° in the four-stroke cycle). In addition, most two-stroke engines produce equal or greater horsepower from a smaller-displacement engine. Often they tend to be more compact and lighter, but there are exceptions when we factor in the latest design of four-cycle models that use new light-weight materials and electronic controls. We already know what a typical electronic four-cycle engine (Caterpillar 3406E) will consume in fuel through reference to Figure 1–15. Similarly, Figure 1–14 indicates

that the Detroit Diesel Series 60 engine has outstanding BSFC. Now let us consider the BSFC for an equivalent two-stroke engine such as the DDC 92 series with electronic controls and in the same basic horsepower rating category as the four-stroke Series 60 and the 3406E from the BSFC charts in Figure 1–14 and Figure 1–15. We can see that the Series 60, 470 bhp (351 kW) has a BSFC of 0.297 lb/hp-hr (181 g/kW-h) at a 1400–1450 rpm rate, which is better than that listed for the 3406E at the same speed and 475 bhp (354 kW), where the BSFC is 0.307 lb/hp-hr (187 g/kW-h). We must be careful, though, when reading such BSFC ratings, because they cannot be considered as completely accurate during normal day-to-day operation due to the many variables encountered. The 1994 Series 60 Detroit Diesel with a BSFC of 0.297 lb/hp-hr (181 g/kW-h) was the world's first high-speed heavy-duty engine to break the 0.300 lb/hp-hr (182.9 g/kW-h) BSFC barrier, followed closely by the Volvo VE D12 model with a BSFC of 0.300 lb/hp-hr at the 370 bhp (276 kW) variable torque rating.

Information for the two-stroke 8V-92TA DDEC engine rated at 500 bhp at 2100 rpm illustrated in Figure 1–20 indicates a BSFC of approximately 0.378

Performance Curves

450 BHP

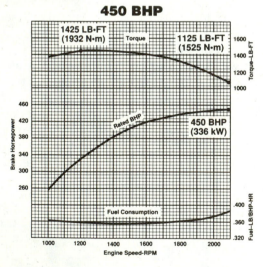

500 BHP

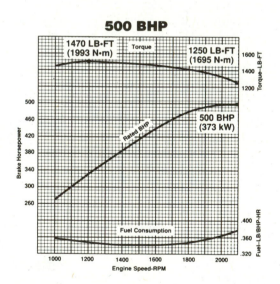

Rating Explanation

RATED BHP is the power rating for variable speed and load applications where full power is required intermittently.
FUEL CONSUMPTION CURVE shows fuel used in pounds per brake horsepower hour.

POWER OUTPUT guaranteed within 5% at rated ambient conditions.
THIS RATING does not include power requirements for accessory and standard equipment.

FIGURE 1–20 Sample horsepower (kW), torque, and BSFC (brake specific fuel consumption) performance curves for a two-stroke-cycle model 8V-92TA DDEC-equipped diesel engine rated at 450 hp (336 kW) and 500 hp (373 kW) at 2100 rpm. (Courtesy of Detroit Diesel Corporation.)

lb/hp-hr (0.230 g/kW-h). To be fair, this engine produces 475 bhp at a speed of approximately 1740 rpm, with a BSFC of approximately 0.344 lb/hp-hr (209 g/kW-h). At the peak torque speed of 1200 rpm, the 92 engine has a BSFC of 0.348 lb/hp-hr (212 g/kW-h) versus 0.304 (185) for the 3406E and 0.303 (184) for the Series 60. What this means is that if all engines were run at the speeds that produced this 470 to 475 bhp (351 to 354 kW) for 1 hour on a dynamometer under carefully controlled and equal conditions, we might expect each engine to consume the following amounts of fuel:

- Detroit Diesel 475 bhp 8V-92TA-DDEC at 1740 rpm = 475 × 0.344 = 163.4 lb/hr (74.11 kg) divided by its API 36 gravity rating of approximately 7.046 lb/U.S. gallon; this engine will burn 23.19 U.S. gallons/hr (87.78 L).
- DDC Series 60 at 470 bhp at 1800 rpm = 470 × 0.304 = 142.88 lb/hr (64.81 kg) divided by an API rating of 36 at 7.046 lb/U.S. gallon; this engine will burn 20.27 U.S. gallons/hr (76.76 L).
- Caterpillar 3406E at 475 bhp at 1800 rpm = 475 × 0.316 = 150.1 lb/hr (68.08 kg) divided by an API 36 fuel rating of 7.046 lb/U.S. gallon; the fuel consumption rate is 21.3 U.S. gallons/hr (80.63 L).

As you can see, the two-stroke-cycle engine would burn 2.92 U.S. gallons/hr (11.05 L) more than its Detroit Diesel Series 60 counterpart, and 1.89 U.S. gallons/hr (7.15 L) more than the 3406E Caterpillar engine.

SPECIAL NOTE: The BSFC curves shown at full-load conditions in OEMs' sales literature are *not* true indicators of fuel-tank mileage or fuel consumption over a 1 hour period, because the engine spends only a portion of time operating on the full-load curve. A significant amount of time is spent at various part-load conditions; therefore, full-load BSFC curves cannot be used to accurately reflect fuel-tank mileage or economy. Nevertheless, published figures can be used to approximate what the fuel economy might be under varying operating conditions—if the operator has a record of a typical daily operating cycle!

If an engine is being operated on a gaseous fuel such as LNG (liquid natural gas) or CNG (compressed natural gas), the BSFC is determined by the following formula:

$$BSFC = \frac{cu\ ft\ of\ gas\ burned \times heating\ value \times 60}{length\ of\ test\ (min) \times bhp}$$

For example, if an engine rated at 300 bhp (224 kW) used a gaseous fuel with a heating value of 1100 cu ft (31 cu m), and consumed 400 cu ft (11.3 cu m) of gas in 15 min, what would its BSFC be?

$$BSFC = \frac{400 \times 1100 \times 60}{15 \times 300} = \frac{26,400,000}{4500}$$
$$= 5867\ Btu/bhp/hr$$

Thermal Efficiency

TE (thermal efficiency) describes the *heat efficiency* of an internal combustion engine. Diesel and gasoline engines can consume either a liquid or gaseous fuel that is normally injected into the combustion chamber. The heat that is released as the fuel burns creates the high-pressure gases required to force the piston down the cylinder and rotate the engine crankshaft. The API fuel rating determines the Btu heat content contained within a given volume of fuel (see Chapter 3 and Table 3–1).

Let's determine the TE of the 3406E Caterpillar engine rated at 475 hp (354 kW) listed in Figure 1–15. We know from the information in the chart that at 1800 rpm this engine consumes 0.316 lb/hp-hr (192 g/kW-h); therefore, if we multiply the horsepower × the fuel we have 475 × 0.316 = 150.1 lb/hr (68 kg-h) of fuel consumed. We need to know the heat value of the fuel used, and we can determine this from the chart in Chapter 3 (Table 3–1); earlier we determined under the BSFC for this engine that it was in fact using an API fuel rated at 36. Each pound of this fuel contains a LHV (low heat value—see Chapter 3 for a description) of approximately 18,410 Btu; therefore, if we multiply the total fuel consumed in 1 hour, which was 150.1 lb, the total heat released into the engine combustion chambers was 150.1 × 18,410 = 2,763,341 Btu/hr. Divide this total heat released by the available horsepower of 475 and we can determine that to produce each horsepower in this engine required 5817.56 Btu (2,763,341 divided by 475 hp). Mathematical information indicates that a perfect engine requires 2545 Btu/hp-hr, so if we divide 2545 by 5817.56, which is what our engine used, we find that we have a thermal efficiency of 43.74%. If we were to use the HHV (high heat value) figure for this fuel, we would have a TE of 40.99%. In other words, for every dollar of fuel that we poured through this engine, we received approximately a LHV TE of 43.74 cents of a return at the flywheel.

All of the step-by-step procedures just described can be pulled into a simplified BTE (brake thermal efficiency) formula:

$$BTE = \frac{2545}{BSFC \times Btu\ per\ lb}$$

Using this formula, we can calculate the 3406E engine TE as follows using the LHV for this 36 API fuel of 18,414 Btu/lb.

$$\text{BTE} = \frac{2545}{0.316 \times 18{,}414} = \frac{2545}{5817.56} = 43.74\%$$

Keep in mind that these TE percentages have been determined under controlled test lab conditions as shown in Figure 1–15. In actual field operating conditions where changing speeds and loads are experienced along with ambient air temperatures and so forth, the TE may be lower. Notice in Figure 1–15 that for the 3406E engine the BSFC is quoted as being accurate within plus or minus 010 lb/hp-hr (± 6 g/kW-h), and the fuel rate is listed as being acceptable within ±5% of that shown. This means that the TE for the LHV could be as low as 40.99% less 5% (2.04%) = 38.95%, or for the HHV rating, 43.74% less 5% (2.187%) = 41.55%. These are impressive figures for TE. All of the latest electronically controlled DI (direct-injection) unit injector diesel engines from Caterpillar, Cummins, Detroit Diesel, Mack, and Volvo have thermal efficiencies in the same basic range. See the next section on heat losses for more versus information about thermal efficiency.

Heat Losses

Let us continue to use the TE example for the 3406E Caterpillar engine rated at 475 hp (354 kW). If we assume that our TE was in fact 43.74%, it means that we lost $100 - 43.74 = 56.26\%$ of the heat that was released into the cylinders. Where did this heat loss go? This heat loss can be related to four factors:

1. Cooling system (approximately 23% to 27%)
2. Exhaust system (approximately 23% to 27%)
3. Friction losses (approximately 7% to 9%)
4. Heat radiation (approximately 3%)

If we assume that we lost 23% to the cooling system, 23% to the exhaust (turbocharger driven), 7.26% to friction, and 3% to radiation, the total accounts for our heat losses of 56.26%. We calculated that this engine needed 5817.56 Btu to produce 1 hp-hr and that 2545 Btu of this was needed to produce that 1 hp-hr. Therefore, by multiplying each of the system's heat loss percentages times 5817.56, we expended the heat injected into the engine as follows:

Cooling   = 5817.56 × 0.23   = 1338 Btu
Exhaust   = 5817.56 × 0.23   = 1338 Btu
Friction   = 5817.56 × 0.0726 = 422.35 Btu
Radiation = 5817.56 × 0.03   = 174.52 Btu
1 horsepower/hr   = 2545 Btu
Total Btu of heat   = 5817.85 Btu

The heat losses chosen for the 3406E Cat engine are examples only and are not specific to this engine.

Nevertheless, they can be considered as fairly typical for high-speed heavy-duty electronically controlled unit injector diesel engines in use today.

Engine Speed Droop

All diesel engines use mechanical (weights versus a spring) or electronic (magnetic pickup) governors to control the idle and maximum speeds, or all speed ranges when desired. Unless the engine is equipped with an *isochronous* or *zero-droop* governor, the engine speed is always lower when operating under load than when it is running with no load on it. This speed difference is described in Chapter 6. The difference between these two operating speed conditions is commonly referred to as governor droop and can be determined as follows:

$$\text{speed droop} = \frac{\text{rpm at MNL speed} - \text{rpm at MFL speed}}{\text{RPM at MFL speed}}$$

NOTE: MNL = maximum no-load speed, often referred to as *high idle*; MFL = maximum full-load speed, often referred to as *rated*.

Engine rpm Formula

Invariably, the recommended engine speed is easily obtainable directly from the EPA and engine certification labels or decals that appear on either the engine or valve rocker cover(s). Alternatively, it is easily obtainable from the OEM's sales and service literature for a specific model and application of engine. From information that is readily available by using some of the formulas shown herein, we can determine the engine speed (rpm) as follows:

$$\text{rpm} = \frac{\text{hp} \times 5252}{\text{torque}}$$

Again, refer to the 3406E Caterpillar engine (Figure 1–15): 475 hp (354 kW) at 1800 rpm and producing 1387 lb-ft of torque. According to the rpm formula:

$$\text{rpm} = \frac{475 \times 5252}{1387} = \frac{2{,}494{,}700}{1387}$$
$$= 1798.63 \text{ rpm (or 1800 rpm)}$$

Joule's Equivalent

A common measure for determining the amount of work available from an engine based on its fuel heat value in Btu is Joule's equivalent, which states that 1 Btu is capable of releasing the equivalent of 778 ft-lb of work, or 1 ft-lb = 0.001285 Btu. Therefore, the horsepower-hour (kW-h) is the measure of 1 hp for a 1 hr period. Since we know that the amount of work required to produce a horsepower is equal to 550 lb-ft/sec, 33,000 ft-lb/min, or 1,980,000 ft-lb/hr, we can determine that a perfect engine with no heat losses would require 2545 Btu/hr to produce 1 hp by using the following formula:

$$1 \text{ hp/hr} = \frac{1,980,000}{778} = 2545 \text{ Btu}$$

Recall that in the metric system of measurement, horsepower is referred to as a kilowatt (kW), which is 1000 W (amp $\times$ V). Since 1 electrical hp is equal to 746 W or 0.746 kW, the kW is is referred to as to 1.341 hp-hr, and 1 kW-h = 2545 $\times$ 1.341 = 3413 Btu.

The foregoing information can be used to determine how much work can be extracted from a given quantity of fuel that is injected into a combustion chamber and burned. For example, consider again the 3406E Caterpillar engine (Figure 1–15) that we used as an example when calculating BSFC, thermal efficiency, and so on. We determined that this engine rated at 475 hp (354 kW) at 1800 rpm consumed 21.3 U.S. gallons/hr (80.8 L). We further determined that using an API fuel with a rating of approximately 36 provided us with about 18,410 Btu LHV. Using Joule's equivalent, we find that 18,410 $\times$ 778 = 14,322,980 ft-lb of work that can theoretically be extracted from each pound of fuel used. Since we know that fuel consumption and horsepower are equated over a 1 hr time period, this 150.1 lb of fuel consumed in 1 hr would release 150.1 $\times$ 18,410 = 2,763,341 Btu. The amount of work that can be extracted from this many Btu is 2,763,341 $\times$ 778 = 2,149,879,298 ft-lb/hr. We know that each horsepower developed needed 33,000 ft-lb of work per minute, or $\times$ 60 = 1,980,000 ft-lb/hr.

If we divided 2,149,879,298 by 1,980,000 we can determine that this much work effort would in fact compute to 1085.79 hp/hr or 809.99 kW. Of course, this does not mean that the engine will produce this horsepower rating at the flywheel, because we have to take into account the various heat losses to cooling, exhaust, friction, and radiation that we discussed earlier. We do know that the 3406E engine in our example produced 475 hp (354 kW) at 1800 rpm; therefore, we lost 1085.79 − 475 = 610.79 hp (455.64 kW).

Air Standard Cycles

Throughout our discussions of the operation of two- and four-stroke-cycle engines we have assumed that the engine operated with no heat losses. Factoring out an engine's performance using no assumed heat losses due to friction, radiation, cooling, and exhaust systems is known as *adiabatic compression and expansion*. This means that the calculated thermal efficiency is much higher than what would actually be found in a running engine when these losses are taken into account. Basically, there are three types of air-standard cycles that are applied to internal combustion gasoline and diesel engines: constant-pressure diesel cycle, constant-volume cycle, and dual combustion cycle.

Constant-Pressure Diesel Cycle

In the early history of the diesel engine, combustion was considered to produce a fairly constant pressure condition throughout the power stroke. Now we know that this does not actually occur. Instead, in current electronically controlled high-speed heavy-duty diesel engines, as the piston moves down the cylinder from TDC (top dead center), fuel continues to be injected for some number of crankshaft degrees. The duration varies between different makes and models of engines. However, as the piston moves down the cylinder on the power stroke, the pressure will remain somewhat constant for some given time period.

Constant-Volume Cycle

In the gasoline engine, the constant-volume (CV) cycle occurs where combustion is completed after the spark plug fires and during the instant the piston is at TDC (pressure increases, volume remains constant). This same combustion condition can be used as a reference cycle for diesel engines, particularly during light-load diesel operation when a small amount of fuel is injected and operating conditions are lean (high air volume, low fuel volume). During these idle or light-load conditions in the diesel engine, the heat-release period is so short that the assumption of zero heat release during this time can be compared to the gasoline or Otto cycle constant-volume condition.

Dual Combustion Cycle

This cycle is a combination of both the diesel and gasoline constant-pressure and constant-volume conditions. It is considered more appropriate when comparisons are made with "actual" diesel cycles based on the maximum cylinder pressure obtained during the heat-release period. Current high-speed heavy-duty diesel engines experience peak pressures of between 1800 and 2300 psi (12,411 to 15,858 kPa) when operating at full-load and peak torque conditions.

Pressure-Volume Curves

The information in this chapter about operating principles of two-stroke- and four-stroke-cycle engines allows us to understand what actually occurs during the intake, compression, power, and exhaust strokes. The energy required to compress the air to a very high pressure within the engine cylinder must be returned on the power stroke to ensure that the engine can overcome this energy loss as well as the frictional losses incurred during the additional intake and exhaust strokes. We can show how this work energy is created and expended by reference to a PV (pressure-volume) diagram, which is illustrated in Figure 1–21 for a four-stroke-cycle gasoline engine and in Figure 1–22 for a four-stroke-cycle diesel engine. The main advantage of the diesel engine over its gasoline counterpart is in the area of fuel economy, so studying the diagrams of both types of engines is important.

SPECIAL NOTE: A graph illustrating the PV curve for a four-stroke-cycle diesel engine during the actual injection of fuel, ignition delay period, combustion period, and afterburning period is illustrated in Figure 2–1 in Chapter 2.

The key information that can be interpreted from a PV diagram as far as we are concerned is the energy required to compress the cylinder charge versus the energy returned on the power stroke of both engines. Herein lies the basic clue to the difference in the fuel economy between the gasoline and diesel engines.

Gasoline Pressure-Volume Curves

In Figure 1–21 (gasoline engine), we start our study with the actual compression stroke at position A, which is the piston position at BDC (bottom dead center). Position B represents the piston at TDC (top dead center), having moved up the cylinder while compressing the air/fuel charge. The actual degrees BTDC

(before top dead center) at which the spark plug fires varies between engines and also with the speed of the engine. However, in this diagram the spark plug fires and ignites the air/fuel charge at position e to increase the pressure and temperature within the combustion chamber. This ignition, or flame front, is completed at point f, and the energy of the expanding gases (power stroke) starts at point B (peak cylinder pressure), which pushes the piston down the cylinder, rotating the crankshaft until it reaches BDC at point C.

If we now subtract the energy expended (negative work) in pushing or forcing the piston up the cylinder to compress the air/fuel mixture from the energy returned to drive the piston down the cylinder, we are left with what is commonly referred to as the *indicated work of the cycle*. This is shown in the PV diagram as that area under the curve AeB (negative work) versus the positive work under the curve at positions BfC in a clockwise direction on the diagram: AeBfC.

Keep in mind that the power stroke does not last from TDC all the way to BDC, because the exhaust valve(s) will be opened by the camshaft before the piston reaches BDC. On the PV diagram shown, the exhaust valve actually opens at position eo and a loss of pressure occurs since part of the gas pressure is moving out through the exhaust manifold. From BDC at position C, the piston is now moving up on its exhaust stroke, expelling or pushing the remaining gases out through the exhaust manifold at a pressure greater than atmospheric from position C to position D. All

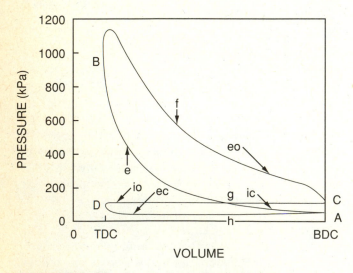

FIGURE 1–21 *Pressure-volume diagram for a four-stroke-cycle spark ignition gasoline engine at part-load throttle. (Reprinted with permission from SAE Paper PT-24, copyright 1982–84, Society of Automotive Engineers, Inc.)*

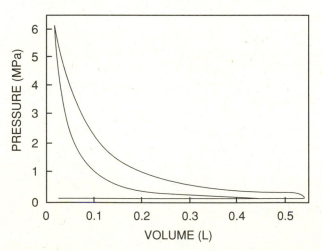

FIGURE 1–22 *Pressure-volume curve for an indirect injected four-stroke-cycle diesel engine at part load. (Reprinted with permission from SAE Paper PT-24, copyright 1982–84, Society of Automotive Engineers, Inc.)*

high-speed automotive gasoline engines in use today have a camshaft timed to open the cylinder intake valve BTDC and close the exhaust valve after TDC.

This condition allows the flow of exhaust gases, which are at a higher pressure than the intake (non-turbocharged engine), to cause a partial suction to the incoming fresh air, providing a better scavenging of the burnt gases and more complete filling of the cylinder.

On the PV diagram, the intake valve is opened by the engine camshaft at position io, while the exhaust valve closes at position ec.

The intake stroke that occurs from position D to A is caused by the fact that the air pressure in a non-turbocharged engine is less than atmospheric pressure (14.7 psi); therefore, intake manifold pressure is considered to be at a vacuum. The fact that atmospheric pressure exists above the throttle control valve is the reason that air is forced into the cylinder through the open intake valve. Generally, the pressure of air in the intake manifold varies, being dependent on throttle position and engine load. Most engines have pressures ranging from 85% to 90% at atmospheric, which is between 12.49 and 13.23 psi. This condition is known as *volumetric efficiency* and is the difference between the weight of air contained in the cylinder with the engine stopped and the piston at BDC, and the weight of air contained within the cylinder with the engine running and the piston at BDC. This weight of air will always be less with the engine running on an NA (naturally aspirated) engine.

The throttling of the air into the engine is one of the major reasons that the gasoline engine does not provide as good a fuel economy as the diesel engine, which does not restrict the airflow into the engine by use of a throttle. The air density or weight that is controlled by the throttle position also controls the amount of fuel that will be drawn or injected into the engine.

A further study of the PV diagram shown in Figure 1–21 illustrates the negative pumping work expended in the gas exchange process from positions CgDhA in a counterclockwise direction. The difference between the actual energy expended to cover the pumping losses incurred through the intake, compression, and exhaust strokes, and that returned to the engine on the power stroke, is the net work done by the expanding gases on the piston during one engine cycle (four strokes—intake, compression, power, and exhaust) and is represented by the points indicated on the PV diagram as positions AgBCgDhA.

We now have to take into account the energy or work lost in overcoming the frictional resistance in the piston and rings and the bearings and valve train components to arrive at the actual brake horsepower (usable power at the flywheel) delivered by the engine. These pumping losses are greatest at part-load conditions on the gasoline engine thereby affecting its fuel economy.

Diesel Pressure-Volume Curves

The diesel engine does not use a throttle to control the speed of the engine as the gasoline engine does. The throttle on the diesel engine is connected to a fuel control mechanism to vary the amount of fuel that is injected into the cylinder. No throttling of air takes place, which means that the diesel operates with a stratified charge or air/fuel in the cylinder under all operating conditions.

The net result of the unthrottled air in the diesel engine is that at idle rpm and light loads, the air/fuel ratio in the cylinder is very lean. Because of the excess amount of air (oxygen) contained in the cylinder of a diesel engine during idle and light-load situations, the average specific heat of the cylinder gases is lowered, which increases the indicated work obtained from a given amount of fuel. This condition, along with that of an unthrottled airflow, means that the diesel engine's efficiency increases as load is reduced in contrast to its gasoline counterpart, a condition that occurs much of the time in city-type driving modes.

Another condition that favors the diesel engine is that it is not limited by octane requirements as is the gasoline engine. The gasoline engine's compression ratio is limited by the availability of sufficiently high octane fuel, which at present in North America is about 93 octane unleaded. This limits the gasoline engine's CR (compression ratio) to about a maximum of 9.5:1, whereas the diesel engine, which does not depend on a fuel with a high octane rating, can have a CR of 23:1. If you compare the PV diagram of the diesel engine with that of the gasoline engine, you will notice that the negative pumping area is much less than that of the gasoline engine (see Figure 1–22).

Figure 1–23 is a PV diagram for a turbocharged and direct injected high-speed heavy-duty four-stroke-cycle diesel engine. Notice that from position 1 to 2 the piston moves down the cylinder on the intake stroke as it is charged with turbo boost air higher than atmospheric pressure, as indicated in line P1. Depending on the valve timing, actual inlet valve closure will control the degree of trapped cylinder air pressure. In this example, compression starts at position 2 as the piston moves up the cylinder. Fuel is injected at a number of degrees BTDC, and there is both a pressure and temperature rise as the fuel starts to burn from positions 3 to 4 (similar to what is illustrated in Figures 1–21 and 1–22). As the piston moves away from TDC on its power stroke, positions 4 to 5, the continuous injection of fuel provides a condition of somewhat "constant

FIGURE 1–23 Pressure-volume curve for a turbocharged and direct injected high-speed heavy-duty four-stroke-cycle diesel engine.

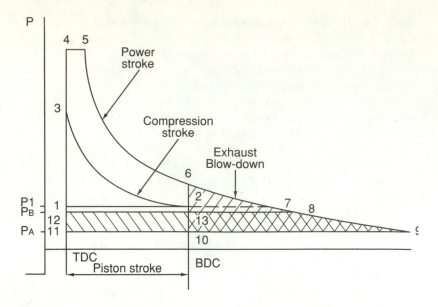

pressure" for a number of crankshaft degrees. From position 5 to 6, the piston is driven downward by the pressure of the expanding gases. The point at which the exhaust valves open BBDC depends on the make and model of engine used. The work represented by area 6–7–2 is available to the hot end of the turbocharger (turbine wheel) from the hot pressurized exhaust gases. Line P_A indicates atmospheric pressure along points 9–10–11. The exhaust manifold pressure is shown as line P_B and the exhaust gas blow-down energy is represented by points 6–9–10. The exhaust process from the engine cylinder is shown between points 6, 13, and 12, where 6 through 13 is the blow-down period when the exhaust valves open and the high-pressure gases expand into and through the exhaust manifold. From point 13 to 12 the piston moves from BDC to TDC, displacing most of the exhaust gas out of the cylinder.

Therefore, the potential work of the exhaust gases in this turbocharged engine is represented by the cross-hatched areas identified as points 10–11–12–13. The maximum energy to drive the turbine of the turbocharger is that shown in the area identified as points 6–9–10 and 10–11–12 and 13. Ideally, during points 6–9–10, if both the cylinder pressure and turbocharger inlet pressure could both be maintained at equal levels before the piston moves upward from BDC on its exhaust stroke, a system close to ideal would be created when using a *pulse turbocharger* system (see Chapter 20.) For ease of instruction, we have not shown the point at which the inlet valves open and the exhaust valves close, which would provide the valve overlap condition.

Gasoline Versus Diesel Engines

The thermal efficiency, or heat efficiency, of a diesel engine is superior to that of the spark-ignited gasoline (Otto cycle) engine. As we know from information discussed earlier in this chapter, the diesel engine employs compression ratios much higher than those of a gasoline engine. This is necessary to create a high enough cylinder air temperature for the injected diesel fuel to vaporize and start to burn. The much higher combustion pressures and temperatures allow a greater expansion rate and more energy to be extracted from the fuel. Tremendous improvements have occurred in gasoline spark-ignited engines, particularly in the 1990s when fuel consumption improvements due to changes in engine component design, combustion improvements, and electronic control of distributor-less ignition and fuel injection systems have resulted in thermal efficiencies in the area of 35% to 39%. Gasoline engines tend to return better fuel economy when held at a steady speed, such as during highway driving, but they suffer in city-driving cycles because of the intake manifold air-throttling effect and pumping losses that occur at lower speeds.

Diesel engines, on the other hand, do not suffer from a throttled air supply and operate with a stratified air charge in the cylinder under all operating conditions. The net result of the unthrottled air in the diesel engine is that at idle rpm and light loads, the air/fuel ratio in the cylinder is very lean (90 to 120:1). This excess air supply lowers the average specific heat of the cylinder gases, which in turn increases the indicated work obtained from a given amount of fuel.

To comply with EPA exhaust emissions standards, automotive gasoline engines have to operate close to a *stoichiometric* air/fuel ratio, which is approximately 14:1. In other words, about 14 kg of air is required to completely combust 1 kg of fuel. Another way to look at this is that approximately 10,000 L of air is required to burn 1 L of gasoline. Even under full-load operating conditions the diesel engine operates with an excess air factor of at least 10% to 20%, which usually results in air/fuel ratios in the region of 20:1 to 25:1. To meet exhaust emissions standards the gasoline engine relies on an exhaust-gas oxygen sensor to constantly monitor the "richness" or "leanness" of the exhaust gases after combustion. This oxygen sensor signal sends update information continuously to the on-board ECM (electronic control module) to allow operation in what is commonly known as a *closed-loop* operating mode. Failure of the oxygen sensor results in the engine falling back into an *open-loop* mode (no signal to the ECM), and the ECM automatically resorts to a "limp-home" condition that allows the engine to run but at a reduced performance. Because of their excess air factor of operation, most diesel engines at this time do not need an exhaust-gas oxygen sensor, or a catalytic converter, although some light- and midrange mechanically controlled truck engines are equipped with converters (see section titled "Exhaust Emissions Limits" in Chapter 2).

Another advantage that the diesel engine enjoys over its gasoline counterpart is that the diesel fuel contains about 11% more Btu per unit volume than does gasoline. Therefore, the diesel engine would have a better return per dollar spent on fuel.

Burn Rate

Information within this chapter has already indicated the sequence of events that occurs from the point the diesel fuel is first injected until it reaches the end of its burn. Figure 1–24 presents in graphic form one example of what this burn period may look like as the fuel is first introduced BTDC (before top dead center). Note the very high peak pressures that occur as a result of uncontrolled burning, followed by the decrease as the high-pressure fuel continues to be fed into an existing flame front. This creates a slight pressure rise during the controlled burning period to produce a fairly steady-state pressure condition as the piston arrives at TDC. As the piston changes direction and moves back down the cylinder on its "power" stroke, the rate of pressure drop depends on the speed of piston movement (engine rpm); in addition, the period of time that fuel is injected after TDC influences this condition. In this hypothetical example, assume that the start of injection occurs at 20° BTDC and the start of the burn occurs at 15° BTDC. Next comes an uncontrolled burning period that produces the high peak pressures (beyond the normal at TDC) of approximately 3° of crankshaft rotation. The fuel injection is cut off at approximately 1.5° ATDC (after top dead center) and the burn ends at approximately 18° ATDC, for a total burn rate time of about

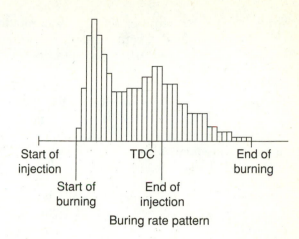

Start of injection   TDC   End of burning

Start of burning   End of injection

Buring rate pattern

FIGURE 1–24   *Graphic representation of a typical burning rate pattern for an engine cylinder both before and after top dead center.*

33 crankshaft degrees. The time required for all of this to happen is *extremely short* and one that few technicians consider when they think about what is going on within an engine during a full-load rpm condition of, say, 1800 rpm.

In this example of *burn rate* we can determine the times involved by considering the following data. First assume that the piston stroke is that for the 3406E Cat engine listed in Figure 1–15, that is 6.5 in., and the engine produces its rated horsepower at 1800 rpm. According to the piston speed formula, the piston travels at 1950 ft/min (594.3 m/min) or 32.5 ft/sec (9.9 m/s). In one complete turn of the engine crankshaft we rotate through 360°, which is equivalent to the piston stroke times two—6.5 × 2 = 13 in. (330.2 mm)—divided by 360; therefore, 1° = 0.0361 in. (0.917 mm). The time required to cover each degree is 0.0361 in. divided by 390 in., which is 0.0000925 sec. From the start of the injection period at 20° BTDC to the start of the burn at 15° BTDC, there is a 5° delay period equivalent to 0.0004625 sec. The uncontrolled burning period that creates the very high peak pressures and temperatures beyond those that normally occur later at TDC lasts for about 3°, or 0.000277 sec. Fuel is injected to about 1.5° ATDC, or 0.000143 sec, with the burn rate ending at approximately 18° ATDC, or for 0.000166 sec ATDC. Therefore, the total burn time lasts for approximately 33° (15 BTDC to 18 ATDC), or for about 0.003 sec. The expanding gases continue to push the piston down the cylinder until the exhaust valves start to open. If we assume that this engine has a power stroke that is 135° long, the time involved for this is about 0.0124 sec. It would take 0.0166 sec for the piston to cover its stroke and 0.033 sec for one complete turn of the crankshaft (360°). A four-cycle engine that requires 720° of crank rotation to run through the intake, compression, power, and exhaust cycle would need 0.0688 sec with the engine running at 1800 rpm.

At 1800 rpm, the crankshaft rotates through 360 × 1800 = 648,000°. If we multiply this number by 0.00009256 sec, we find that it adds up to 59.94 sec or 1 min—confirming all of the times and degrees that we factored out! Just think that in approximately 30,000 hours or 900,000 miles (1,448,370 km) of engine operation with a mean average speed of possibly 1400 rpm, the pistons would travel a total of 51,702.27 miles (83,204 km) and the crankshaft would rotate through 2,520,000,000 revolutions.

Mechanical Efficiency

The ME (mechanical efficiency) of an internal combustion engine is determined by comparing the actual usable hp (bhp) to the cylinder hp (ihp). The higher the mechanical efficiency of the engine, the lower the fuel consumption. The ME of an engine can be determined from the following formula:

$$ ME = \frac{bhp}{ihp} $$

If an engine produced 280 bhp with an ihp of 350, its ME would be

$$ \frac{bhp}{ihp} = \frac{280}{350} = 80\% $$

Volumetric Efficiency

The power that can be extracted from an internal combustion piston engine is related to the amount of air that can be consumed or fed into the engine cylinders and retained. The higher the percentage of air retained, the larger the quantity of fuel that can be injected and burned to completion.

The term *VE* (volumetric efficiency) refers to the weight of air retained in the engine cylinder at the start of the compression stroke. In NA (naturally aspirated) non-turbocharged or blower-equipped engines that rely on atmospheric air pressure to force its way into the cylinder, the resistance to airflow caused by the intake ducting (such as the diameter, number of bends, length, and air-cleaner restriction) and intake manifold design lower the VE. Because of these facts, the VE of an NA engine is always less than atmospheric pressure (14.7 psi or 101.35 kPa) at sea level. Most NA engines have a VE in the region of 85% to 90% of atmospheric pressure, or between 12.49 and 13.23 psi (86.1 to 91.2 kPa).

When a turbocharger or gear-driven blower is added to an engine, two- or four-stroke cycle, the VE can be greater than atmospheric pressure (that is, 100%). The critical factor in determining the cylinder air pressure before the start of the compression stroke is the timing of the intake valve closing on a four-stroke-cycle engine or the liner port and exhaust valve closing on a two-stroke-cycle Detroit Diesel type of engine. As an example refer to Figure 1–15, which lists operating conditions for Caterpillar's 3406E engine. Note that at 1800 rpm under full load this engine has an intake manifold pressure of 51.3 in. Hg. This 51.3 in. Hg is equivalent to 25.2 psi (173.7 kPa) and is supplied by the exhaust-gas–driven turbocharger on this four-cycle engine. As the engine speed is reduced under load, note that the turbocharger boost pressure at the peak torque point of 1200 rpm reduces to 41.7 in. Hg (20.5 psi or 141.2 kPa). The reason behind this is that with a slower running engine, the exhaust gas flow rate has decreased to 1767 cubic feet per minute (cfm), or 50 cubic meter per minute (cmm), from 2547 cfm (or 72 cmm) at 1800 rpm. Therefore, although the engine cylinder receives air at a pressure well above atmospheric, the valve timing is the final determining factor of what the trapped cylinder air pressure will be. On turbocharged engines, this can range anywhere between 130% and 200% higher than atmospheric.

People often talk about an engine as being "supercharged" and believe that as soon as an engine is fitted with a turbocharger or gear-driven blower that it automatically becomes so. Keep in mind that in technical classifications the intake valve timing on a four-cycle engine and the port and exhaust valve timing on a two-cycle model determine if the engine is actually supercharged. If the cylinder air pressure at the start of the compression stroke is higher than atmospheric, then basically the engine is supercharged. The degree of supercharging, however, is directly related to the actual cylinder air pressure charge!

Engine Displacement and Compression Ratio

Although there are many electronically controlled unit injector diesel engines on the market today with similar horsepower (kW) ratings, the torque developed by some of these engines is higher or lower than that of others in some instances. The displacement of the engine cylinders and the compression ratio are factors that can affect the developed torque at a given engine speed.

Displacement

The displacement of an engine can be determined from an OEM's sales or service literature. In the absence of this information, a cylinder's displacement can be determined by the following formulas. To determine the cubic inch or cubic centimeter displacement of a cylinder, we need to know the bore and stroke dimensions. For example, let's assume that an engine has a bore and stroke of 5.12 × 6.30 in. (130 × 160 mm). The first thing we need to do is compute the area of the piston crown from the known bore size of 5.12 in. (130 mm). Use this formula: area = $\pi R2$, where π = 3.1416; R = the radius of the bore squared (2). In our example, area = 3.1416 × 2.56 × 2.56 = 20.58 sq in. (132.83 sq cm). Now if we multiply the area of the piston by the stroke, we can determine the cylinder volume or displacement: 20.58 × 6.30 in. = 129.7 cu in. (2125.39 cc, or 2.125 L).

If the engine were a six-cylinder model, we would have an engine displacement of 6 × 129.7 = 778 cu in. (12,752 cc, or 12.7 L). Using the same formula for the 3406E engine in Figure 1–15, we would find a piston crown area of 22.9 sq in. (148 sq cm) multiplied by a stroke of 6.5 in. (165 mm) for a cylinder displacement of 148.85 cu in. (2349.2 cc). Since it is a six-cylinder engine, the total engine displacement is 893.1 cu in. (14.6 L).

To determine the *airflow requirements* of an engine, we need to be able to calculate the approximate volume of air required per minute in either cubic feet per minute (cfm), or cubic meters per minute (cmm) in the metric system of measurement. This can be determined by knowing the volume swept by all of the pistons during one stroke for each cycle, which can be determined simply by knowing the number of cylinders times the area of the piston crown in square feet (square meters) times the stroke in feet (meters) times the number of cycles per cylinder per minute.

$$\text{engine displacement per minute} =$$
$$N \times A \times S \times n \text{ (cfm)}$$

where N = number of cylinders
A = piston area in sq ft (sq m)
S = stroke in ft (m)
n = cycles per min for one cylinder
= rpm for two-cycle engines
= rpm/2 for four-cycle engines

Let's assume that we want to calculate the airflow requirements for the 3406E engine discussed in Figure 1–15—a six-cylinder, four-stroke-cycle engine with a bore of 5.4 in. (137 mm), a stroke of 6.5 in. (165 mm), and a rated horsepower (kW) at 1800 rpm.

$$\text{engine displacement per minute} = 6 \times \pi/4 \times 0.45^2$$
$$\times 0.541 \times 1800/2 = 6 \times 0.7854 \times 0.202 \times 0.541$$
$$\times 900 = 464 \text{ cfm}$$

This airflow requirement is for a non-turbocharged engine model. Once we turbocharge the engine and add an air-to-air-aftercooler system and electronic fuel injection controls to meet the mandated limits for exhaust emissions, the engine airflow requirement demands generally increase by turbocharger boost pressure ratios on the order of 2:1 and 3:1 in high-speed high-output models. In the case of the 3406E engine, note in Figure 1–15 that the specification for intake airflow calls for 1143 cfm (32.4 cmm) at 1800 rpm. Note also that the exhaust gas flow rate at 1800 rpm with the engine producing 475 bhp (354 kW) is quoted as 2547 cfm (72 cmm). Therefore, the 3406E engine actually requires an airflow rate that is 1143 cfm divided by 464 cfm (from the simplified formula calculation), which yields a ratio difference for this turbocharged and aftercooled engine that is 2.463 times greater than that for a naturally aspirated engine of the same displacement.

An alternate method to determine the airflow requirements is to use this formula:

$$\frac{\text{cubic inch displacement} \times \text{rpm}}{3456}$$
$$\times \text{volumetric efficiency} = \text{cfm}$$

Inserting the same data for the 3406E engine results in the following:

$$\frac{893 \times 1800}{3456} = 465 \text{ cfm} \times \text{VE} = \text{demand flow air}$$

We know from the specification sheet that this engine requires 2.46 times the air that a naturally aspirated model would require. Chapter 20 dealing with air inlet and exhaust systems discusses the airflow requirements for two- and four-stroke-cycle engines in more detail.

Compression Ratio

The term *CR* (compression ratio) is used to compare the difference in cylinder volume when the piston is at BDC (bottom dead center) versus when the piston is at TDC. Figure 1–25 is a CR comparison of a low-compression gas engine and a diesel engine. Most gasoline engines operate with CR values between 8:1 and 10.5:1, whereas diesel engines operate with much higher CR values, averaging between 14:1 and 17.5:1 on most current high-speed heavy-duty electronically controlled models of the DI (direct-injection) design. However, a number of IDI (indirect-injection) models run CRs as high as 23:1. Figure 1–25 indicates that the volume of air in the cylinder for the gasoline engine has been compressed to ⅛ its volume with the piston at TDC; in the diesel example, the volume has been reduced to 1/16 its volume with the piston at TDC.

FIGURE 1–25 This example of how the compression ratio is estimated shows that a gasoline engine operates with a much lower CR than does a diesel engine.

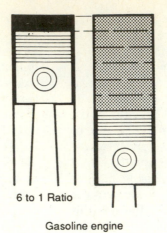
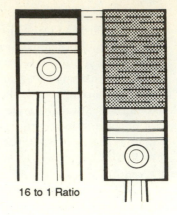

6 to 1 Ratio

Gasoline engine

16 to 1 Ratio

Diesel engine

The higher CR in diesel engines is one of the reasons that diesel engines are more thermally efficient than their gasoline counterparts. Higher CR results in greater expansion of the gases in the cylinder after combustion; therefore, a higher percentage of fuel energy is converted into useful work. Since a diesel engine does not use a spark plug for ignition of the fuel charge, the high CR raises the trapped cylinder air to a temperature that is above the self-ignition point of the injected diesel fuel. Typical CRs are 15.0:1 for the Detroit Diesel Series 50 8.5L and Series 60 12.7L (16:1 for the Series 60 11.1L model); 16.2:1 for the Cummins N14, and 16.25:1 for the 3406E Caterpillar model. Since we know that the engine displacement for the 12.7L Series 60 is 774 cu in./6 = 129 cu in. (2114 cc) divided by the CR of 15.0:1, the clearance volume (CV) between the piston crown and the underside of the cylinder head at TDC would be 129 divided by 15 = 8.6 cu in. (141 cc). The Series 60 11.1L model CV is 7 cu in. (115.5 cc). For the N14, with a displacement of 855 cu in. (14 L), the CV is 8.79 cu in. (144 cc). The 3406E, with a displacement of 893 cu in. (14.6 L) would have a CV of 9.16 cu in. (150.2 cc).

Keep in mind that both the engine torque and the horsepower of an engine are related to engine displacement, BMEP, and speed. Thus, the different torque figures that are listed on OEMs' sales sheets for engines of the same speed and horsepower settings are controlled by the variables of engine displacement, BMEP, valve timing, injector timing, turbocharger boost, air inlet temperature, air swirl, fuel injection spray-in pressure, distribution, and so on.

Compression Temperature. Engine compression ratio has a bearing on the final temperature of the cylinder air charge before injection of fuel. The temperature of the compressed air (boost) flowing from the turbocharger on high-speed heavy-duty engines at full-load operating conditions is usually in the region of 300°F (149°C). This air temperature drastically lowers the denseness of the air charge and affects the power output of the engine as well as its ability to meet mandated exhaust emissions standards. Therefore, an ATAAC (air-to-air aftercooler) is widely used on heavy-duty highway trucks, and industrial, off-highway, and marine engines employ JWAC (jacket water aftercooling) systems. These systems are described in Chapters 19 and 20. The ATAAC system lowers the turbo boost air to between 100° and 110°F (38° and 43°C). Typical high-speed heavy-duty diesel engines generate compression pressures in the range of 450 to 500 psi (3103 to 3792 kPa), which create cylinder air temperatures in the region of 900° to 1000°F (482° to 538°C). The relationship of temperature and pressure during the compression cycle can be considered to be in the region of about 2:1 and 3:1; the figure can be higher or lower depending on the engine compression ratio, air turbulence created during the upward movement of the piston, and of course the turbocharger boost ratio and the temperature of the air entering and being trapped within the cylinder. Final pressures and temperatures created during the power stroke are relative to the compression pressures and the quantity of fuel injected based on load/speed of the engine. Engines operating with boost pressure ratios in the region of 3:1 and ATAAC experience BMEPs between 180 and 295 psi (1241 to 2034 kPa) on most four-stroke-cycle engines for rated speed and peak torque rpm outputs, respectively. Because of their double power stroke, two-cycle engines have BMEPs that are normally about 100 psi (690 kPa) lower than an equivalent four-stroke model. Keep in mind, however, from the information shown in Figure 1–15, that peak cylinder pressures experienced in current high-speed heavy-duty engines can be between 1800 and 2300 psi (12,411 to 15,856 kPa).

Metric Measures

Most engines being manufactured today are built to metric standards. For example, what size is a 12.7 liter engine? There are 1000 cc in a liter, therefore a 12,700 cc engine has a displacement of 12.7 liters. To convert liters to cu in. refer to Figure 1–26.

The English standards of measurement are familiar to us, for example, the terms *thousandths* related to a micrometer and *inches* and *feet* related to a ruler or tape measure; the term *yards* is also employed for long distances. There are 12 inches in a foot, 3 feet in a yard, 5280 feet or 1760 yards in a mile. When we use a micrometer or vernier caliper scaled in the English standard of measurement, we are reading it to the closest one one-thousandth of an inch.

The metric system of length consists of terms such as *millimeters* (mm), *centimeters* (cm), *decimeters* (dm), *meters* (m), and *kilometers* (km). All of these measurements are constructed in multiples of 10 to a given power unit. In larger-length values, the meter has supplanted the yard as the standard length of measurement. A yard is 36 inches, but the meter is equal to 39.37 inches. Multiples of the meter are listed next:

1 micron (millionth of a meter)	μm = 0.00003937 in.
1 millimeter (thousandths of a meter)	mm = 0.03937 in.
1 centimeter (hundredths of a meter)	cm = 0.3937 in.
1 decimeter (tenths of a meter)	dm = 3.937 in.
1 meter (one one-thousandth of a kilometer)	m = 39.37 in.
1 decameter (tens)	dm = 393.7 in.
1 kilometer (thousand meters)	km = 39,370 in.

In the United States, drivers are used to driving miles per hour (mph). Road signs in kilometers are often confusing for U.S. citizens driving in Canada or Europe or other countries such as Japan that use metric measurements. A road sign indicating 50 km/h is equivalent to 31 mph, and a sign reading 100 km/h = 62 mph.

Let's consider some smaller measurement scales. There are 25.4 mm in 1 in., or 2.54 cm in 1 in. We can show 1 in. as 1″ or 1.000″. When using an English micrometer, the barrel is divided into graduations of 0 to 25, the stock is divided into segments of 25, 50, 75, 100 (1) 125, 150, 175, 200 (2), and so on, up to an inch. This requires us to rotate the movable barrel a total of 40 times to move it through 1″ (40 × 0.025 = 1.000″). The term *millimeter* (mm) is widely used with respect to inches, and we know that there are 25.4 mm in 1.000″; therefore, if we divide 1.000″ by 25.4 mm, we get 0.03937″, which is almost 39.5 thousandths. If we round off this figure to 40 (0.040″), each millimeter is equivalent to approximately 0.040″.

Engine specifications and measurements are shown in metric standards, including the intake and exhaust valve clearances for diesel engines. These clearances are found on a decal attached to either an engine rocker cover or a plate attached to the engine. The service technician simply has to select the correct metric feeler gauges to check or set the valve lash. If instead of metric feeler gauges, you had a set calibrated in English measurements, how would you convert from English to metric?

Let's try this example. An engine is quoted as having an intake valve clearance of 0.30 mm and an exhaust valve clearance of 0.36 mm. What are the equivalent English dimensions? We know that 1 mm = 0.03937″; if we multiply 0.30 mm by 0.03937″ we get 0.0118″ or approximately 12 thousandths (thou), 0.012″. Rather than using the cumbersome figure of 0.03937 every time, if we simply round off to 40 thou and multiply by 0.30 mm or 0.3, we can quickly arrive at an answer of 12 thou (0.012″). For the exhaust valve with a clearance of 0.36 mm, we multiply by the rounded-off figure of 40 thou (0.040″) and get 0.0144″, or for feeler gauge purposes, 14 thou (0.014″).

Other metric equivalents are used widely. Kilopascals (kPa) is used in place of pounds per square inch (psi): 1 psi = 6.895 kPa. Torque in the metric system is expressed as newton-meters (N • m); 1 lb-ft = 1.3558 N • m. When dealing with liquid volume such as diesel fuel or engine oil, we use the term *liters* (L) rather than quarts or gallons. One quart is equal to 0.94635 L, and one U.S. gallon = 3.7851 L. The Imperial gallon is equivalent to 4.546 L. When determining the cubic inch (cu in.) displacement of an engine, the equivalent metric measurement is cubic centimeters (cc): 1 cu in. is equal to 16.387 cc. Since there are 1000 cc in 1 L, when engine specification sheets indicate a displacement of 12.7 L, 14 L, or 14.6 L, the total cc displacement is 12,700, 14,000, or 14,600 cc, respectively. In the English system, the engine displacements rounded off would be 774, 855, and 893 cu in. These displacements are those for the larger Detroit Diesel Series 60, the Cummins N14, and the Caterpillar 3406.

The metric conversion chart shown in Figure 1–26 lists all of the commonly used conversion factors and allows you to quickly convert from English to metric and metric to English.

Velocity Rate

The term *velocity* basically means the speed and direction of an object. Often the term is used in engineering and mechanics to indicate the rate of motion or distance traveled per unit of time when an object is moving at a constant rate of speed and is equal to distance/time. For example, if a truck is moving at a steady highway speed of 1 mile (1.6 km) per minute, its velocity is the same as its speed. This means that in

Common Metric Prefixes

kilo (k) = 1000   milli (m) = 0.001
centi (c) = 0.01   micro (μ) = 0.000001

Multiply	By	To get	Multiply	By	To get
Length					
inches (in)	25.4	millimeters (mm)		0.03937	inches (in)
inches (in)	2.54	centimeters (cm)		0.3937	inches (in)
feet (ft)	0.3048	meters (m)		3.281	feet (ft)
yards (yd)	0.9144	meters (m)		1.094	yard (yd)
mile (mi)	1.609	kilometers (km)		0.6214	mile (mi)
microinch (μin)	0.0254	micron (μm)		39.37	microinch (μin)
micron (μm)	0.000001	meters (m)		1,000,000	micron (μm)
microinch (μin)	0.000001	inches (in)		1,000,000	microinch (μin)
Area					
square inches (in^2)	645.16	square millimeters (mm^2)		0.00:55	square inches (in^2)
square inches (in^2)	6.452	square centimeters (cm^2)		0.155	square inches (in^2)
square feet (ft^2)	0.0929	square meters (m^2)		10.764	square feet (ft^2)
Volume					
cubic inches (in^3)	16387.0	cubic millimeters (mm^3)		0.000061	cubic inches (in^3)
cubic inches (in^3)	16.387	cubic centimeters (cm^3)		0.06102	cubic inches (in^3)
cubic inches (in^3)	0.01639	liters (L)		61.024	cubic inches (in^3)
quarts (qt)	0.94635	liters (L)		1.0567	quarts (qt)
gallons (gal)	3.7851	liters (L)		0.2642	gallons (gal)
cubic feet (ft^3)	28.317	liters (L)		0.03531	cubic feet (ft^3)
cubic feet (ft^3)	0.02832	cubic meters (m^3)		35.315	cubic feet (ft^3)
Weight/Force					
ounces (av) (oz)	28.35	grams (g)		0.03527	ounces (av) (oz)
pounds (av) (lb)	0.454	kilograms (kg)		2.205	pounds (av) (lb)
U.S. tons (t)	907.18	kilograms (kg)		0.001102	U.S. tons (t)
U.S. tons (t)	0.90718	metric tons (t)		1.1023	U.S. tons (t)
Power					
horsepower (hp)	0.7457	kilowatts (kW)		1.341	horsepower (hp)
Torque/Work Force					
inch-pounds (lb-in)	0.11298	Newton-meters (N•m)		8.851	inch-pound (lb-in)
foot-pounds (lb-ft)	1.3558	Newton-meters (N•m)		0.7376	foot-pound (lb-ft)
Speed					
miles/hour (mph)	1.609	kilometers/hour (km/h)		0.6214	miles/hour (mph)
kilometers/hr (km/h)	0.27778	meters/sec (m/s)		3.600	kilometers/hr (km/h)
miles/hour (mph)	0.4470	meters/sec (m/s)		2.237	miles/hour (mph)
Pressure					
pounds per square inch (psi)	0.069	bar		14.50	pounds per square inch (psi)
pounds per square inch (psi)	6.895	kilopascals (kPa)		0.14503	pounds per square inch (psi)

Subtract	From	To get	Multiply	By	To get
Temperature					
32	Fahrenheit (°F) and divide by 1.8	Centigrade (°C)		1.8 and add 32	Fahrenheit (°F)

Fuel Consumption

$$\frac{235}{\text{miles per gallon (mpg) U.S.}} = \text{liters/100 kilometers (L/100 km)}$$

$$\frac{235}{\text{liters/100 kilometers (L/100 km)}} = \text{miles per gallon (mpg) U.S.}$$

$$\frac{282}{\text{miles per gallon (mpg) Imp.}} = \text{liters/100 kilometers (L/100 km)}$$

$$\frac{282}{\text{liters/100 kilometers (L/100 km)}} = \text{miles per gallon (mpg) Imp.}$$

FIGURE 1–26 Metric conversion chart

1 hr (60 min) the truck would be traveling at 60 mph (96.5 km). Since there is 5280 ft (1609.3 m) in a distance of 1 mile, we can show this velocity as follows:

$$\frac{1 \text{ mile}}{1/60 \text{ hr}} = 60 \text{ mph or } \frac{1 \text{ mile (5280 ft)}}{60 \text{ sec}} = 88 \text{ ft/sec}$$

Therefore, 60 mph (96.5 km) is the same velocity as 88 ft/sec or 26.8 m/s.

Acceleration Rate

Velocity (v) and acceleration (A) differ. When a body is not moving at a constant rate (velocity) but is accelerating, the velocity is said to be increasing; or during a deceleration condition, the velocity is becoming slower. If the rate of acceleration is constant, there is no increase or decrease from one second to the next.

$$A = \text{(ft/sec in each sec)}$$
$$= \frac{\text{final velocity (ft/sec)} - \text{initial velocity (ft/sec)}}{\text{time (sec)}}$$

Therefore, if a body is accelerating at a uniform velocity and its speed increases from, say, 40 ft/sec to 50 ft/sec in 3 sec, its rate of constant acceleration is

$$A = \frac{50 - 40}{3} = \frac{10}{3}$$

$$= 3.33 \text{ ft/sec change in velocity in 1 sec}$$

It is generally written as ft/sec/sec or ft/sec^2.

Another example of acceleration is related to the earth's force of gravity, which provides a constant rate of acceleration when a body is falling freely toward the earth. If we neglect the resistance of the air and drop a body, it will free-fall at a velocity of 32.2 ft/sec (9.81 m/s) at the end of the first second and 64.4 ft/sec (19.62 m/s) at the end of the next second. The rate of acceleration (g) is, therefore, 32.2 ft/sec^2 (9.81 m/s^2).

PREFIXES

Often the literature of engine and/or equipment manufacturers contains a variety of different prefixes and symbols whose meanings are questionable. The following table lists some of the more widely used prefixes and symbols.

Quantity	Multiplying Factor	Prefix	Symbol
Ten	$10 = 10^1$	deca	da
Tenth	$0.1 = 10^{-1}$	deci	d
Hundredth	$0.01 = 10^{-2}$	centi	c
Hundred	$100 = 10^2$	hecto	h
Thousand	$1,000 = 10^3$	kilo	k
Thousandth	$0.001 = 10^{-3}$	milli	m
Million	$1,000,000 = 10^6$	mega	M
Millionth	$0.000001 = 10^{-6}$	micro	μ
Billion	$1,000,000,000 = 10^9$	giga	G
Billionth	$0.000000001 = 10^{-9}$	nano	n
Trillion	$1,000,000,000,000 = 10^{12}$	tera	T
Trillionth	$0.000000000001 = 10^{-12}$	pico	p
Quadrillion	$1,000,000,000,000,000 = 10^{15}$	peta	p
Quadrillionth	$0.000000000000001 = 10^{-15}$	femto	f
Quintillion	$1,000,000,000,000,000,000 = 10^{18}$	exa	E
Quintillionth	$0.000000000000000001 = 10^{-18}$	atto	a

HEATING VALUE EQUIVALENTS

Typical heat value equivalents and their metric units for some of the more commonly used fuels are listed next.

Fuel	Imperial units	Metric units
Diesel	162,000 Btu/gallon	0.0377 GJ/L
Gasoline	146,000 Btu/gallon	0.0340 GJ/L
Propane	110,000 Btu/gallon	0.0255 GJ/L
	21,570 Btu/lb	0.0515 GJ/kg
Natural gas	1,000 Btu/cu ft	0.0372 GJ/m^3
Coal	8,500 to 15,000 Btu/lb	20 to 35 GJ/tonne
Electricity	3,412 Btu/kW-h	0.0036 GJ/kW-h

GJ = gigajoules, which is used to describe the metric quantity in billions (giga).

These heat values in Btu are average readings only and will vary in actual heat content of the gas or crude oil used. In the case of diesel fuel, refer to Chapter 3 which has a chart dealing with API (American Petroleum Institute) Btu heat values based on the fuels' API rating.

ISO STANDARDS

Not long ago the North American automotive, truck, and manufacturing industry regarded the European quality standards ISO 9000 with disdain; now it has embraced the standards as the core of a new global scheme to measure the performance of suppliers. Many manufactured products now contain a decal indicating that the component or item has been manufactured to ISO 9000 standards. This rating system is the core quality gauge for frontline parts makers to meet a set of industry-specific sets of standards.

ISO 9000 means global quality standards. Although *ISO* stands for International Standardization Organization, the term is used as a variant of the Greek word *isos*, meaning equal, and is pronounced *ice-oh*. The choice of the number 9000 was arbitrary. The North American manufacturing industry does not want variations in supplier standards within a country or between countries; rather the industry demands consistency of an agreed on standard at all levels. Since most of the ISO standards will be common, suppliers and OEMs will save time and money.

We have discussed the ISO 9000 standards, but there are others. The ISO standards can be grouped into the following categories:

- ISO 9000: An overview and introduction to the other standards, including definitions of terms and concepts related to quality that are used in the other standards
- ISO 9001: Comprehensive general standard for quality assurance in product design, development, manufacturing, installation, and servicing
- ISO 9002: Standards that focus on manufacturing and installation of products
- ISO 9003: Standards that cover final inspection and testing
- ISO 9004: Guidelines for managing a quality control system. More details on managing the quality systems that are called for in the other standards; intended for use in auditing quality systems

SELF-TEST QUESTIONS

1. List the strokes involved in one complete cycle of operation for a four-stroke diesel engine.
2. The four strokes in Question 1 involve
   a. 270° of crankshaft rotation
   b. 360° of crankshaft rotation
   c. 600° of crankshaft rotation
   d. 720° of crankshaft rotation
3. What are the two strokes that are effectively eliminated from a two-stroke-cycle diesel engine?
4. The working strokes of a two-stroke-cycle diesel engine are completed in the following number of crankshaft degrees:
   a. 180
   b. 360
   c. 540
   d. 720
5. Typical compression ratios used in heavy-duty high-speed diesel engines range between
   a. 8 and 10 to 1
   b. 10 and 13 to 1
   c. 14 and 17 to 1
   d. 19 and 22 to 1
6. Typical compression pressures produced in heavy-duty high-speed diesel truck engines run between
   a. 250 and 300 psi (1724 to 2068 kPa)
   b. 350 and 425 psi (2413 to 2930 kPa)
   c. 450 and 550 psi (3103 to 3792 kPa)
   d. 600 and 800 psi (4137 to 5516 kPa)
7. Technician A says that the term *thermal efficiency* is an expression of the mechanical efficiency of the engine, whereas technician B says that it is an indicator of the heat efficiency of the engine. Who is correct?
8. Thermal efficiency of a diesel truck engine generally runs between
   a. 24% and 28%
   b. 30% and 34%
   c. 34% and 38%
   d. 38% and 42%
9. Typical fuel performance figures for current high-speed heavy-duty diesel engines average between
   a. 0.380 and 0.395 lb/bhp/hr (231 to 240 g/kW/h)
   b. 0.350 and 0.370 lb/bhp/hr (213 to 225 g/kW/h)
   c. 0.315 and 0.340 lb/bhp/hr (192 to 207 g/kW/h)
   d. 0.300 and 0.315 lb/bhp/hr (183 to 192 g/kW/h)
10. One gallon of U.S. fuel is equal to
    a. 4.256 L
    b. 3.900 L
    c. 3.785 L
    d. 3.600 L
11. True or False: Btu means British thermal unit.
12. How may Btu are required to produce 1 hp in a perfect engine over a 1 hr period?
    a. 2040
    b. 2250
    c. 2415
    d. 2545
13. Technician A says that the term *work* is computed by multiplying the force times the distance. Technician B disagrees. Who is correct?
14. Technician A says that horsepower keeps the piston moving and is a measure of how fast work can be done by the engine. Technician B says that torque is the ability to move a load or do work. Who is correct?
15. Horsepower is accepted as being a given amount of work developed in a given time period. In English-speaking countries this is generally accepted as being equal to
    a. 28,000 ft-lb/min
    b. 33,000 ft-lb/min
    c. 35,550 ft-lb/min
    d. 37,300 ft-lb/min
16. Torque is a twisting and turning force that is developed at
    a. the piston
    b. the con-rod
    c. the crankshaft
    d. the flywheel
17. True or False: A constant-horsepower engine maintains a steady horsepower over a widerspeed band than does a conventional diesel engine.
18. Technician A says that all diesel truck engines develop their greatest torque value at about 65% of their rated speed under full loads, for example, 1200 rpm versus 1950 rpm. Technician B says that the greatest torque is developed at the rated speed and horsepower setting, for example, 1950 rpm and 400 hp. Which technician knows what he or she is talking about here?

19. Technician A says that torque is what pulls a truck up a hill with a decrease in speed. Technician B says that horsepower is what pulls the truck up the hill as the engine and road speed drop off. Who is right here?

20. Technician A says that a high-torque-rise diesel engine will allow fewer transmission shifts to have to be made over a conventional diesel-engine–equipped truck. Technician B says that there is no difference as long as the engine speed is kept at the rated value. Who is correct?

21. Technician A says that torque in the metric system is expressed in newton-meters (N • m), whereas technician B says that it is expressed in kilopascals (kPa). Who is correct?

22. Horsepower is expressed in kilowatts in the metric system of measurement, with 1 kilowatt equal to 1000 watts. Technician A says that 1 hp is higher in value than 1 kW. Technician B says that 1 hp is less than 1 kW. Is technician A or technician B correct?

23. A horsepower is equivalent to
    a. 0.674 kW
    b. 0.746 kW
    c. 0.940 kW
    d. 1.341 kW

24. Technician A says that brake mean effective pressure (BMEP) is the average pressure developed on the piston crown during the power stroke, whereas technician B says that it is the maximum pressure developed when the injected diesel fuel ignites. Who is correct?

25. Many heavy-duty highway-truck diesel engines use aftercooling to increase the horsepower of the engine. Technician A says that aftercooling reduces the exhaust heat loss of the engine and allows more heat for power. Technician B says that aftercooling lowers the temperature of the pressurized air from the turbocharger so that a denser charge is supplied to the engine cylinders, thereby producing more power. Is technician A or technician B correct?

26. Technician A says that the exhaust temperatures developed at the full-load rated rpm speed of an engine will be lower than that produced at the peak torque engine speed. Technician B disagrees. Who is correct?

27. Technician A says that the exhaust temperatures on a two-stroke-cycle engine tend to be slightly higher than those produced on an equivalent-horsepower four-stroke-cycle engine at rated rpm. Technician B says that he has this reversed; exhaust temperatures are cooler on the two-stroke-cycle engine. Who is correct?

28. True or False: The duration of the power stroke in crankshaft degrees is longer on a two-cycle diesel engine than it is on a four-cycle engine.

29. What is the principle on which the gasoline or Otto cycle engine is said to operate?

30. On what principle does the compression ignition or diesel engine operate?

31. True or False: Caterpillar manufactures both two- and four-stroke cycle engines.

32. To convert cubic inches to cubic centimeters, multiply by
    a. 6.895
    b. 12.7
    c. 16.387
    d. 22.32

33. A Caterpillar 3176 model engine has a displacement per cylinder of 1.7L. How many cu in. is this? Give the engine's total displacement in cu in. and L.

34. How many cubic centimeters make 1 L?

35. How many millimeters make 1 in.?

36. How many cubic inches make 1 L?

37. Determine the total cu in. displacement of a six-cylinder engine with a bore of 5.5 in. (139.7 mm), and a stroke of 6 in. (152 mm); then convert this answer to cc and L.

38. One micron is equal to one millionth of a meter. This can be expressed in decimal form as
    a. 0.03937"
    b. 0.003937"
    c. 0.0003937"
    d. 0.00003937"

39. To convert engine torque from lb-ft to its metric equivalent, by what should you multiply?

40. Describe briefly the definition of a "supercharged" engine?

41. Draw a circle and sketch in the duration of each individual stroke for a four-stroke-cycle diesel engine. Show the start and end of injection at an idle speed as well as the positive valve overlap condition that exists.

42. Repeat the same process described in Question 41 for a two-stroke-cycle diesel engine.

43. Sketch and show the relative piston firing positions for a six-cylinder CW rotation four-stroke-cycle engine with a firing order of 1–5–3–6–2–4 using the degrees created in Question 41, and describe where each piston is and what stroke it is on.

44. Repeat the same process that was described in Question 43 for a two-stroke-cycle engine.

45. Typical full-load rated horsepower air temperature leaving the outlet side of the turbocharger on high-speed diesel engines is approximately
    a. 65.5°C (150°F)
    b. 93°C (200°F)
    c. 149°C (300°F)
    d. 204°C (400°F)

46. True or False: VE (volumetric efficiency) refers to the weight of air contained in the cylinder with the piston at BDC stopped versus what it would be at BDC running.

47. True or False: Ihp (indicated horsepower) refers to usable power at either the engine crankshaft or flywheel.

48. Technician A states that 1 hp is considered equal to 33,000 lb-ft. (44,741 N • m) of work per minute. Technician B states that it is equivalent to 550 lb-ft (746 N • m) of work per second. Is only one technician correct or are both correct?

49. One Btu (kJ/kg) of released heat within a combustion chamber is capable of producing the following amount of mechanical work:
    a. 710 ft-lb (963 N • m)
    b. 758 ft-lb (1028 N • m)
    c. 778 ft-lb (1055 N • m)
    d. 876 ft-lb (1188 N • m)

50. Technician A states that current high-speed DI diesel engines develop peak firing pressures between 1200 and 1400 psi (6895 to 8274 kPa). Technician B says that this is too low and that peak pressures run between 1800 and 2300 psi (12,411 to 15,858 kPa). Who is correct?

51. List the advantages and disadvantages of a two-stroke-cycle engine in comparison to an equivalent four-cycle model.

52. Determine the following information for a six-cylinder four-stroke-cycle engine running at 1800 rpm:
    a. ihp; then convert it into kW; bore of 5.5 in. (140 mm) and a stroke of 6 in. (152 mm); a BMEP of 237 psi (1634 kPa)
    b. piston speed in feet/minute (m/min); then convert it to mph and km/h.
    c. torque in lb-ft; then into N • m
    d. convert BMEP to its metric equivalent of kPa
    e. thermal efficiency using a fuel consumption rate of 0.316 lb/bhp/hr (g/kW/h) with a calorific value of 19,100 Btu/lb (kJ/kW)

53. Determine the BMEP of a 365 bhp (272 kW) four-stroke-cycle engine using this formula

$$BMEP = \frac{792,000 \times bhp}{D \times N}$$

where D = total piston displacement of the engine in cu in. and/or cc employing the displacement from your answer in Question 52; N = rpm of 2100 rpm.

54. If an engine develops a torque of 1650 lb-ft (2237 N • m) at 1200 rpm, what horsepower (kW) would it produce?

55. If an engine develops 470 bhp (351 kW) at 1800 rpm, what torque would it produce in lb-ft and N • m?

56. Fuel injector spray-in pressures on several current high-speed electronically controlled diesel engines can range as high as
    a. 15,000 psi (103,425 kPa)
    b. 20,000 psi (137,900 kPa)
    c. 24,000 psi (165,480 kPa)
    d. 28,000 psi (193,060 kPa)

57. Technician A says that current heavy-duty high-speed DI diesel engines employ single-hole pintle-type injection nozzles. Technician B says that they employ multihole nozzles/injectors for better fuel distribution and penetration. Who is correct?

2

Combustion Systems

OVERVIEW

This chapter introduces and describes the fundamentals of internal combustion. As a result of contemporary environmental concerns, combustion has undergone major changes to ensure that diesel engines can comply with the stringent exhaust emissions regulations of the United States. We discuss the characteristics of air and fuel and the engine combustion chamber and piston designs that have been introduced to improve both the exhaust emissions and fuel economy of the engine.

TOPICS

- Combustion chamber designs
- Air turbulence
- Combustion dynamics
- Chemical theory of combustion
- Fuel injection timing
- Retarded versus advanced timing
- Fuel quantity requirements
- Thermal efficiency
- Exhaust emissions limits
- Self-test questions

The combustion phase of engine operation is the period during which the high-pressure diesel fuel is first injected into the compressed air mass within the cylinder, then ignited to produce both a high temperature and a high pressure rise within the combustion chamber. The resultant pressure created by the expanding gases forces the piston down the cylinder. The chemical energy released from the burning diesel fuel and air mixture is then converted to mechanical energy through the piston, connecting rod, and crankshaft to power the flywheel.

The design of combustion chambers used in automotive/truck diesel engines can take the form of either an IDI (indirect-injection) system or a DI (direct-injection) system. In Figure 1–3 we illustrated the basic differences between these two types of systems. Although the IDI design was used for many years in some diesel engines, as far as today's heavy-duty high-speed diesel engines are concerned, the DI system is dominant. In the DI system the fuel is injected directly into an open combustion chamber formed by the shape of the piston crown or bowl and the underside of the cylinder head fire deck. In the typical DI system shown in Figure 1–3, the injection nozzle is located in the cylinder head and extends directly into the engine cylinder. Note that the piston crown is shaped in such a manner that, in effect, it will form the combustion chamber when the piston approaches top dead center and fuel is injected.

Although the IDI design combustion chamber shown in Figure 1–3 has been used for many years, few engines being manufactured currently still use this design. The reason for this change is that the IDI engine has a 10% to 15% greater fuel consumption curve than a DI engine. Although the IDI engine gained some prominence during the late 1970s and early 1980s in automotive passenger cars and light pickup trucks, particularly in North America, it was chosen solely for its quieter operating characteristics and its ability to employ a glow plug for cold weather startability. In addition, at that time little technological research had been done on small-bore DI high-speed engines. Due to higher fuel consumption and exhaust emissions problems with the IDI engine, most engine manufacturers have now committed themselves to the DI concept. Although many of the older engines in lighter-duty truck applications use IDI, midheavy-duty and heavy-duty trucks are all using the DI principle of operation.

COMBUSTION CHAMBER DESIGNS

Although the term *combustion* is related to the actual burning of fuel within the combustion chamber, considerably more is involved in the actual combustion phase. One of the most important aspects of creating proper combustion is related to the engine's ability to inhale and trap a suitable air charge. In addition, the design of the actual piston crown, the intake and exhaust valves, and ports can do much to improve the engine's combustion cycle.

In Chapter 1 we discussed the basic design characteristics of heavy-duty truck diesel engines (Figure 1–3) and illustrated a typical piston design used with DI combustion chambers. Most heavy-duty high-speed diesel truck engines now employ not only exhaust-gas-driven turbochargers, but also air-to-air aftercooling, to reduce the temperature of the air charge leaving the compressor outlet of the turbo. By cooling the air charge, a denser mass of air under pressure can be supplied to the engine cylinders, thereby improving the horsepower and fuel economy characteristics. More importantly in these days of stringent exhaust emissions regulations, the cooler air improves the combustion cycle so that the by-products of combustion are reduced.

Two main piston crown designs are used today in DI diesel engines:

1. The Mexican hat–shaped piston shown in Figure 1–3 is the basic shape used by Detroit Diesel, Caterpillar, Cummins, and Mack, with minor variations among them.

2. The in-bowl type of piston shape (illustrated in Figure 15–4) is often referred to as the MAN type of system, since much research was undertaken by this German engine company in perfecting this shape. Others who use this type of piston crown shape include Perkins, Caterpillar, Cummins, and Detroit Diesel in their 8.2 L four-stroke-cycle engines.

The trends in piston design during the late 1990s seem to be following the DI design now in use by Detroit Diesel, Caterpillar, and Cummins and shown in Chapter 15. High top rings are necessary to sustain low oil consumption and to reduce transient particulate exhaust emissions. These emissions are reduced by minimizing the crevice volume between the top ring, the top of the piston, and the cylinder wall. Consider that in the Detroit Diesel Series 60 four-stroke-cycle engine piston design, the top ring is located only 0.150 in. (3.8 mm) from the top of the two-piece piston. The iron crown provides the support for the top ring and the strength required for future higher firing pressures. Higher firing pressures are designed to reduce exhaust soot because they provide a more homogeneous and thoroughly mixed charge. Cylinder pressures as high as 2300 psi (15,858 kPa) are common in high-speed heavy-duty engines.

Despite these higher pressures, the operating temperature of the top groove of the piston is not substantially greater because of the following three factors:

1. Heat transfer from the combustion bowl has been improved. High top rings tend to assist in the removal of heat transfer from the piston bowl to the cylinder liner. In addition, the use of pressurized oil flow to the underside of the piston crown through either oil cooling jets, or the "cocktail shaker" principle employed by Detroit Diesel, has tended to stabilize top groove temperatures.

2. As a result of engine design and combustion improvements, particularly as a consequence of electronic controls, engine speeds have tended to come down from the previous norm of 2100 rpm to 1800 or 1900 rpm in heavy-duty on-highway diesel engines. This speed reduction reduces piston temperature while still operating at the same BMEP (brake mean effective pressure) in the cylinder. Another benefit of lowering the engine speed is a reduction in engine noise.

3. With the adoption of air-to-air aftercooling systems in most turbocharged high-output truck engines, the air temperature entering the cylinder is lowered, which in turn lowers piston temperatures, improves fuel economy, and reduces nitric oxide emissions. The most popular method now in use to increase an engine's power output is through an increase in the BMEP, which is the average pressure exerted on the piston crown throughout the power stroke.

Refer to Chapter 1 for a discussion of typical examples of current electronically controlled engine BMEPs and the formula required to determine an engine's BMEP.

AIR TURBULENCE

The addition of turbulence to the incoming cylinder air charge does much to assist the combustion phase within an engine. In recent years this addition has been accomplished not only through turbocharging and aftercooling, but also by careful design of the intake and exhaust manifold systems. Tuned intake and exhaust manifolds are now commonplace in midrange and heavy-duty high-speed truck engines.

The intake air passage in the cylinder head is specially shaped to act as both a forcing cone and an air-twisting chamber. It accelerates the speed of the incoming air, then imparts a twisting turbulence or swirl so that when the air enters the cylinder/combustion chamber, this air motion is further enhanced by the toroidal shape of the piston bowl. As the piston compresses this turbulent air mass, it creates hundreds of miniature tornadoes circling in one violent vortex. When the piston moves up the cylinder on its normal compression stroke, the swirling air charge is compressed to $\frac{1}{17}$, for example, on an engine with a 17:1 compression ratio. This action raises the air temperature to about 1100°F (593°C) so that when the high-pressure diesel fuel is injected into the combustion chamber, the finely atomized fuel is immediately engulfed by the superhot, violently swirling air and ignition occurs shortly thereafter. The diesel fuel burns at a controlled rate and the tornadic air continues to mix and remix with each atom of fuel; the result is complete burning of the fuel for the highest possible extraction of its energy potential.

COMBUSTION DYNAMICS

Pressure–Volume Curve

Figure 2–1 will help you understand the processes that occur within the engine cylinder and combustion chamber. The figure illustrates what actually transpires during the two most important strokes within a four-stroke-cycle diesel engine. The PV (pressure–volume) diagram represents the piston from a position corresponding to 90° BTDC (before top dead center) as it moves up the cylinder on its compression stroke to 90° ATDC (after TDC) on its power stroke. The vertical lines in the diagram represent cylinder pressure, which can vary substantially between different makes and models of engines.

Typical cylinder pressures within the cylinder and combustion chamber at the start of injection would be approximately 550 to 600 psi (3793 to 4137 kPa) and the compressed air would be anywhere between 900° and 1100°F (482° to 593°C). Both the pressures and temperatures can, of course, vary with different compression ratios and engine design characteristics. Once the diesel fuel has been injected and starts to burn, peak cylinder pressures can run between 1800 and 2300 psi (12,411 to 15,859 kPa), with temperatures peaking to between 3500° to 4000°F (1927° to 2204°C) on high-speed heavy-duty truck direct-injected diesel engines.

FIGURE 2–1 *Graph illustrating the pressure–volume curve diesel engine combustion operating principle. (Courtesy of Zexel USA, Technology and Information Division.)*

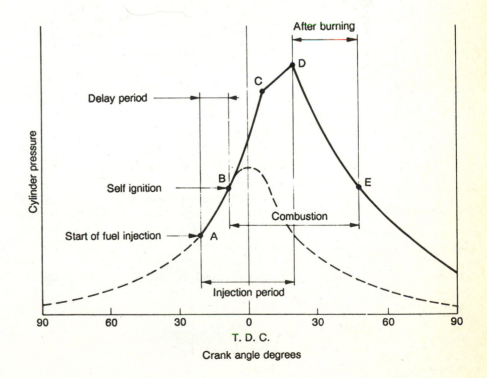

In Figure 2–1 the dashed line represents the increase in cylinder pressure BTDC and prior to fuel being injected when the engine is cranked over on the starter motor. For our close study of the actual four phases of combustion, we are concerned with the solid black line shown on the PV diagram. When the fuel is first injected at point A, the liquid-atomized fuel leaving the injector spray tip must vaporize and mix first in order to initiate combustion, due to the heat contained within the compressed air charge. The higher the cylinder pressure and temperature, the faster the fuel will vaporize and the quicker ignition will begin.

The ignition delay period extends from point A to point B; normal ignition delay periods range from 0.001 to 0.003 sec. When the injected fuel ignites at point B, a rapid rise in both pressure and temperature occurs within the cylinder. This phase is known as the uncontrolled burning or flame propagation period. The uncontrolled burning period ends at point C, which is followed by a controlled combustion period from point C to point D as the remaining fuel is injected. This action creates a gradual increase in cylinder pressure. The engine manufacturer determines through engineering analysis the actual rate of injection for this period. The actual rate of injection is simply the quantity or volume of diesel fuel injected in terms of either the injection pump camshaft angle degrees (multiple-plunger inline pump), or the engine camshaft angle degrees in a unit injector fuel system.

Note that between points B and C the piston has actually attained its TDC position and is being pushed down the cylinder by the pressure of the expanding gases. In this example the fuel injection duration ends at point D, with the piston being approximately 18° to 20° ATDC. The last droplets of fuel that were cut off at point D and any remaining unburned fuel particles will continue to burn between points D and E, thereby creating an afterburning period that produces the pressures to keep the piston moving on its power stroke. Note, however, that if the afterburning period takes too long due to poor mixing of the fuel and air, combustion temperatures will increase, with a subsequent decrease in the engine's thermal efficiency (heat efficiency). Thermal efficiency is discussed in more detail later in the chapter. One other problem of a long afterburn period is the generation of soot in the exhaust, as a result of incomplete combustion.

In the diesel engine, air only is drawn into the cylinder and subsequently compressed during the upward moving piston compression stroke. The diesel engine always operates with an excess air/fuel ratio due to the unthrottled entry of air. A diesel engine mechanically or electronically regulates the fuel flow and is therefore a leaner burning engine than its gasoline counterpart. At an idle rpm, the diesel engine tends to operate at an extremely lean air/fuel ratio with the excess air running between 600% and 1000%; at the high-speed end of the operating range, the diesel still has an excess air/fuel ratio of about 10% to 15% over its gasoline counterpart when producing its maximum horsepower. This excess air percentage can be shown as: excess air = lambda (λ) + 1.1−1.15, for the combustion to remain within acceptable exhaust smoke limits. The point at which fuel is injected directly into the compressed air varies between engines and also with the load and speed on the engine, similar to the way the spark plug firing point varies in a gasoline engine through the advance mechanism.

Compression ratios in the automotive precombustion chamber diesel engine average between 20 and 23 to 1, with resultant compression pressures from as low as 275 to 490 psi (1896 to 3378 kPa). Heavy duty, high-speed DI diesel engines used in highway trucks with compression ratios between 14 and 17:1, which are turbocharged and air-to-air aftercooled, obtain average compression pressures between 435 and 600 psi (30 to 41 bar) and compression temperatures before fuel is injected of between 700° and 900°C (1292° to 1652°F). Peak cylinder pressures and temperatures after the fuel is injected range anywhere between 1200 psi (8274 kPa) to as high as 2300 psi (15,858 kPa) on direct-injected high-speed heavy-duty diesel engines. Temperatures can peak as high as 2204°C (4000°F). The fuel injection pressures will depend on the type of system used, with pump-line-nozzle systems being incapable of delivering as high an injection pressure as the compact unit injector system. The fuel pressure required to open the nozzle needle valve in a pump line system generally ranges between 1800 and 3950 psi (12,411 to 27,235 kPa), although there are some that are capable of slightly higher pressure peaks. When this high-pressure fuel, or what is known as nozzle lift or release pressure, is forced through the very small holes in the tip, there is a fuel pressure increase similar to placing your thumb over a garden hose without a nozzle. The result is an increase in spray pressure and a reduction in volume so that spray-in pressure ranges between 18,000 and 19,600 psi (124,110 to 135,142 kPa). The number of holes in the spray tip and their diameter determine the fuel droplet size. Both have an impact on fuel vaporization times, combustion rate, and exhaust emissions levels. Generally, the fuel droplets range in size from 10 to 100 microns (μm) for a typical light distillate diesel fuel. Recall that 1 micron is 1 millionth of a meter; it can be written as a decimal: 0.00003937 in. Consequently, the fuel droplet size in inches would be 0.0003937 in. for a 10 μm droplet and 0.003937 in. for a 100 μm fuel droplet size. The final pressure at which the nozzle or unit injector needle valve opens depends on the compressive force of the needle valve spring and the area on which the increasing fuel pressure operates. However, many holes or orifices in the tip are usually between 0.005 and 0.010 in. (0.127 to 0.254 mm) in diameter on multiple-hole nozzles used in high-speed heavy-duty diesel engines.

The unit injector system is capable of producing spray-in pressures between 26,000 and 28,000 psi (179,270 to 193,060 kPa). The speed of penetration of the fuel leaving the injector tip can approach velocities as high as 780 mph (1255 km/h), which is faster than the speed of sound. The fact that the pump-line-nozzle systems cannot obtain as high a pressure for injection and control of exhaust emissions has forced fuel injection manufacturers to move toward adoption of the superior unit injector system. Detroit Diesel Corporation, which has always used unit injectors, has now been joined by Caterpillar, Cummins, Volvo, and Robert Bosch in using this type of injection system.

The injected fuel (atomized) is basically in a liquid state; therefore, for ignition to take place, the fuel must *vaporize* (known as distillation temperature; see the section on distillation range in Chapter 3). This means that the fuel must penetrate the air mass (high-pressure air/high temperature) to allow the fuel molecules to mix with the oxygen molecules within the combustion chamber. Unlike a gasoline engine, where the air/fuel mix has already taken place during the intake and compression strokes, the diesel fuel must achieve this after injection. For the fuel actually to reach a state of ignition, there is a time delay from the point of injection to the point of ignition. This time delay is approximately 0.001 sec and results in a slower-igniting fuel. The longer this time delay before the initial fuel that was injected takes to ignite, the greater the volume of injected fuel that will be collected within the combustion chamber. When this volume of fuel does ignite, there is a pressure increase within the combustion chamber. A time delay of longer than approximately 0.003 sec would be an excessively long ignition delay period and would therefore result in a rough-running engine (knocking). This knocking occurs at the start of combustion in a diesel engine instead of at the end of combustion in a gasoline engine.

Ignition delay and diesel knock can be reduced by consideration of the following methods, assuming that the compression ratio is suitably high for the fuel grade being used.

- Use the correct grade of fuel oil according to the engine manufacturer's recommendations. If the distillation range (vaporization point) of the diesel fuel is low enough and the cetane number (ignition quality) is high enough, diesel knock will be minimal.
- Ensure that the air intake temperature is high enough to promote fuel vaporization immediately after injection. This factor becomes very important when operating in low ambient (winter) conditions. The correct air intake temperature will create an increase in the cylinder temperature and the compression pressure. In summer operation, the correct air intake temperature can be ensured by use of an air-to-air aftercooler (see Figure 20–20).
- Retard (delay) ignition timing if necessary.

In a DI diesel engine, fuel that is injected and mixed during the ignition delay period will have a direct effect on the shape of the cylinder/combustion chamber pressure rise pulse. Fuel that is burned before the cylinder pressure reaches its peak value controls the peak height value developed within the cylinder. In other words, the peak rate of heat release determines the rapid rise in cylinder pressure that occurs immediately after ignition of the fuel. The peak in the heat release results from the rapid combustion of the diesel fuel, which was injected and premixed with the high-temperature cylinder air during the delay period. This rapid pressure rise after ignition contributes to the noise from the diesel combustion process that is characteristic of all diesel engines. A reduction in the cetane number of the diesel fuel being used increases the ignition delay period and contributes to a noisier combustion sound.

Fuel that is premixed during the ignition delay period, and therefore the peak rate of heat release and the peak rate of cylinder pressure increase in the combustion chamber, depends on the ignition delay and the quantity of fuel injected and mixed with the air. Ignition delay is affected by five factors:

1. The duration in crankshaft degrees of the actual delay period from the start of fuel injection until the fuel vaporizes and ignites, more commonly known as *ignition delay*
2. The temperature and pressure of the intake air
3. Engine compression ratio
4. The heat absorbed by the open cylinder air charge during the intake stroke and during the closed compression stroke from various surrounding engine surfaces

5. The cetane number of the fuel; the higher the rating, the shorter the ignition delay period

The amount or volume of diesel fuel injected and mixed with the cylinder air charge depends on five factors:

1. The rate of fuel injection. Different types of fuel injection systems have different rates or speeds at which they can actually deliver the fuel charge to the combustion chamber. Unit injector fuel systems, which create their fuel pressure rise within the body of the injector, tend to be able to accelerate the fuel charge quicker than do those produced in an inline pump system, which has to build up the long column of fluid contained within the steel delivery line from the pump to the nozzle. This action can vary the length of the ignition delay period.

2. The velocity (speed and direction) of the injected fuel leaving the spray nozzle or injector tip. With a higher injection pressure, more of the fuel penetrates the air mass rather than tending to have some fuel deposited on the combustion chamber wall and/or distributed in areas of the combustion chamber that are too lean to sustain burning of the fuel.

3. The actual fuel droplet size, which is dependent on the injection pressure and the number and size of holes for distribution purposes.

4. Combustion chamber/cylinder-induced air motion or swirl, which tends to affect the rate of diesel air/fuel mixing characteristics.

5. Cylinder air charge temperature and pressure. Turbocharging and aftercooling assist this part of the combustion phase.

Ignition lag will increase if the injection timing is either very late or very early, because the fuel will be injected into an air mass that has lost a lot of its compression heat (late timing) or not yet attained it through early injection timing. Since the injector will continue to inject fuel into this already burning mass, the pressure will rise to a peak pressure as the piston attains the TDC position. As the piston starts down into its power stroke, this additional injected fuel maintains a steady pressure as it starts to burn, thereby providing the diesel engine with the term *constant-pressure cycle*. In some engines, the fuel is cut off just BTDC, others may cut off fuel at TDC, while still others may not cut fuel off until after TDC. Because of the fact that diesel fuel continues to be injected into the already burning fuel of the combustion chamber as the piston moves down the cylinder on its power

stroke, the cylinder pressure is said to remain constant during the combustion process.

With the gasoline engine, the instantaneous ignition concept produces a very rapid rise in cylinder pressure with a very fast burn rate, resulting in a hammer-like blow on the piston crown. In the diesel cycle, the pressure rise is sustained for a longer period, resulting in a more gradual and longer push on the piston crown than that in the gasoline engine. Rudolf Diesel's original concept more than 100 years ago was that his engine would continue to have fuel injected during the power stroke and that no heat losses would occur in his uncooled engine. This concept was known as an *adiabatic diesel engine,* which in the true sense of the term meant that there would be no loss of heat to the cylinder walls while the piston moved up on its compression stroke. In addition, no cooling system would be used, resulting in the transfer of waste heat to the exhaust for a gain in thermal efficiency. Since no cooling system would be required, no frictional losses would occur through having to use a gear-driven water pump, and so on. We know this was impossible to achieve; however, Diesel's original idea of producing a true constant-pressure cycle, although never achieved, did attain some measure of success in the engines that now bear his name.

There is no internal combustion engine today that operates on either a true constant-pressure or constant-volume cycle under varying operating conditions, because they all require a few degrees of crankshaft rotation to complete combustion with a subsequent rise in cylinder pressure.

CHEMICAL THEORY OF COMBUSTION

Since both gasoline and diesel engines employ internal combustion to produce power, the ongoing legislation by the EPA in the United States, the ECE (Economic Commission for Europe) in Europe, and the Australian design Rule 30 to reduce exhaust emissions makes it important for the automotive heavy-duty truck technician to understand the actual theory of combustion in both these types of engines. Successful performance of any internal combustion engine is related to a quick change from chemical energy (fluid: that is, gas or diesel) of the fuel into heat energy in the combustion chamber, so that the piston will receive maximum effort from the expanding gases as it reaches TDC.

In a gasoline engine, the vaporization of the fuel can be done either in a carburetor or by fuel injection. This fuel injection can be done through TBI (throttle body injection) or by intake manifold port injection toward each cylinder's intake valve. In a diesel engine, air only is taken in on the intake stroke; therefore, vaporization of the diesel fuel occurs after the point of actual injection into the compressed air mass in the cylinder during the compression stroke as it mixes with the hot air in the cylinder. Combustion can take place only when the carbon and hydrogen in the fuel mixes with the oxygen (air) to provide combustion. This is why fuel vaporization is so important.

The actual horsepower (kilowatts) that any engine is capable of producing depends on a number of factors, but in the final analysis, the amount of air that the engine is capable of inhaling or swallowing on each intake stroke determines the final output from each cylinder. Once the air is trapped in the engine cylinder, the remaining power factor depends on just how much of the trapped air (oxygen) can be consumed (burned).

Let's look briefly at the chemistry of combustion within an engine cylinder to establish specifically what requirements constitute a successful combustion chamber burn. In our discussion of internal combustion engines we are concerned with liquid fuels that are made up of two main elements, hydrogen and carbon. Let's look at the atomic and molecular weights of these elements in relation to oxygen.

Atomic weights are generally compared to that of oxygen, which has an atomic weight of 16. The lightest atomic unit is that of hydrogen, which is approximately 1. Carbon's atomic weight is 12. The molecular weight of any element is simply its atomic weight times the number of atoms in a molecule of the element. Therefore, the molecular weight of hydrogen (H_2) is 1.008 times 2 = 2.016, oxygen (O_2) is 16 times 2 or 32, and carbon (C) is 12 times 1 = 12.

When considering the molecular weight of hydrogen for combustion calculations, we round it off from 2.016 to 2.000. The term *mole* is often used to express in simple terms the actual weight of a substance in relation to its molecular weight. Therefore, hydrogen with a molecular weight of 2 would indicate that a mole of hydrogen weighs 2 lb.

Makeup of Air

Air consists mainly of oxygen and nitrogen, along with very small amounts of argon, carbon dioxide (CO_2), hydrogen, and other gases. What we are concerned with in relation to air's combustion properties is the amount of oxygen and nitrogen it contains. The average molecular weight of dry air is about 29. Figure 2–2 lists the ratios of the component gases. When a fuel is burned, the ratio of nitrogen to oxygen is 3.76 moles of nitrogen to 1 mole of oxygen. Also, if we assume that a diesel fuel oil consists of some 15% hydrogen and 85% carbon by weight, this means that there will be 15 lb of hydrogen and 85 lb of carbon in every 100 lb of fuel oil.

	By volume		By weight	
	Percent	Ratio	Percent	Ratio
Nitrogen	79	3.76	76.8	3.32
Oxygen	21	1.00	23.2	1.00
Total	100		100	

FIGURE 2–2 *Nitrogen and oxygen content of air*

Combustion in the Cylinder

Internal combustion of gasoline or diesel fuel takes place within the engine cylinder. Both of these fuels are made up mainly of carbon and hydrogen. As a consequence of this combustion, by-products consisting of water vapor (H_2O), carbon dioxide (CO_2), and carbon monoxide (CO) are formed. Undesirable exhaust emissions emanating from this same combustion phase include NO_x (nitric oxides), HC (hydrocarbons), CO (carbon monoxide), CO_2 (carbon dioxide), soot, and particulates.

All diesel engines operate throughout their speed range with an excess of air in the combustion chamber. Depending on the load and speed range of the engine, the ratio of air to fuel can vary from as low as 18 or 20 to 1 under full load, to as high as 90 or 100 to 1 at an idle rpm. Another way to look at this excess air is to consider that the required weight of air for each pound of fuel burned would be 120% of 14.86 = 17.83 lb. One mole of a gas generally occupies 379 ft^3 at 60°F at 14.7 psi (atmospheric pressure), with the molecular weight of air being 29. Therefore, the volume of air required for the combustion of 1 lb of diesel fuel would be 379 $\times$ (17.83/29) = 233 ft^3.

From the foregoing information, a simplified chemistry of combustion can be calculated. The general ratio by weight of carbon to hydrogen in diesel fuel varies between 6 and 8. If we were to assume that the fuel burns with no excess air, the reactions for complete combustion could be equated as follows:

Chemical equations:

$$C + O_2 = CO_2 \quad \text{and} \quad 2H_2 + O_2 = 2H_2O$$

By molecular weight:

$$12 + 32 = 44 \quad \text{and} \quad 4 + 32 = 36$$

Therefore, 1 lb of hydrogen requires 32 + 4 or 8 lb of oxygen, and 1 lb of carbon requires 32 + 12 or 2.667 lb of oxygen for complete combustion. Since 1 lb of air contains 0.2315 lb of oxygen, 1 lb of hydrogen requires 8 ÷ 0.2315 or 34.56 lb of air, while 1 lb of carbon requires 2.667 ÷ 0.2315 or 11.52 lb of air for complete combustion. For complete combustion of an average fuel containing 1 part hydrogen and 7 parts carbon, the weight of air required is

$$\frac{34.56 + (7 \times 11.52)}{8} = 14.4 \text{ lb}$$

From these equations, under normal temperature and pressure conditions, 1 lb of air occupies 12.4 ft^3 and 1 lb of fuel with a specific gravity of 0.85 would occupy a volume of 0.01888 ft^3. Therefore, to completely burn 1 ft^3 of diesel fuel would require (14.4 × 12.4) ÷ 0.01888, or 9450 ft^3 of air. Generally speaking, then, it requires approximately 10,000 times the volume of air than fuel oil to burn the oil to completion.

Processes of Combustion: Diesel Engines
The full sequence of events in the engine cylinder consists of the following steps:

- The creation of air swirl during the open part of the cycle. (This was discussed in detail in the section "Air Turbulence" in this chapter.)
- The injection of the diesel fuel with control of timing and duration as well as possible modulation of the rate of injection as the piston nears TDC.
- The mixing of the diesel fuel and air under the conditions established by the air swirl in the cylinder/combustion chamber. The fuel must vaporize to cause ignition; therefore, there is a delay period.
- Initiation of combustion following the delay period.
- Subsequent combustion first under premixed and later under diffusion conditions.
- Separation of products and reactants under the combined action of density changes in a rapidly changing toroidal/swirling burning mass.
- Further air/fuel mixing and combustion occurring simultaeously.

The process just described generally occurs within three to four distinct periods. Briefly these are classified as follows:

1. The delay period. This is the time delay from the actual beginning of delivery of fuel, which enters the cylinder from the injector in a finely atomized state, until actual ignition. Unit injector needle valve popping pressures range between 2300 to 5300 psi (15,858 to 36,544 kPa); however, since fuel at this pressure must be forced through very small holes/orifices in the injector spray tip, the resultant injection pressures can average between 22,000 and 28,000 psi (151,690 to 193,060 kPa). The easiest way in which to conceive how this fuel pressure increases is to consider a garden hose

with no nozzle on the end of it: lots of volume but little pressure. If you install a spray nozzle or place your thumb over the end of the hose, there is a reduction in fluid flow but a substantial increase in pressure.

One of the most important factors that establishes the time delay period is the cetane number of the fuel, because a fuel with a higher cetane number vaporizes more readily and therefore propagates combustion quicker. Most high-speed diesel engines require a fuel with a cetane number of at least 40. This physical delay period exists because the injected fuel has to be atomized; it has to mix adequately with the air (oxygen) as well as vaporize so that combustion can be started.

2. Preflame reaction (chemical delay), which is parallel with or immediately behind the physical delay. The fuel is injected at speeds approaching 780 mph (1255 km/h), which is faster than the speed of sound. This fuel is ignited by contact with hot metal surfaces and/or the air temperature; burning usually starts with ignition of the vaporized fuel droplets in the first portion of the injected fuel. This premixed burning phase (chemically controlled) is the period during which the fuel that was injected during the ignition delay period starts to burn to create flame propagation and uncontrolled burning. This delay period is considerably longer for low-engine-load conditions, resulting in a higher proportion of the injected fuel remaining unburned. When the premixed burning starts, the chemically controlled rate of combustion is very high in all cases. In addition, during the low-load burning conditions, the large accumulation of unburned fuel during this longer delay period leads to a sharp pressure peak. In contrast, operation of the engine during a high-load condition, where the premixed phase merges and burns almost immediately, causes a lower pressure peak, due to the much smaller accumulation of fuel.

3. The diffusion period or burning phase, which is controlled by the mixing rate. The continually injected additional fuel burns in a controlled state as rapidly as it enters the combustion chamber, since a flame front was already established after the initial delay period. Peak flame temperatures will occur only when the combustion pressures are at their maximum and while the diesel fuel is still being injected. Combustion is generally considered to be smooth if the rate of cylinder pressure rise on small high-speed automotive engines is less than 30 psi (207 kPa) per degree of crankshaft rotation. However, on current high-speed heavy-duty truck diesel engines, the average maximum rate of cylinder pressure rise during injection varies between 50 psi/degree (3.45 bar/degree) and 90 psi per crankshaft degree (6.2 bar/degree). The maximum developed peak pressure in the combustion

chamber on small high-speed automotive engines generally averages between 900 and 1200 psi (6205 to 8274 kPa), whereas on high-speed heavy-duty diesel truck engines this pressure can run between 1800 and 2300 psi (12,411 to 13,790 kPa). These high pressures developed in high-speed heavy-duty diesel engines result in peak combustion chamber temperatures as high as 3500° to 4000°F (1926° to 2482°C).

4. An afterburning period during which late combustion of previously unburned fuel or intermediary products of combustion is completed. Because of ignition lag and combustion time, high-speed engines cannot attain constant-pressure combustion. It is therefore necessary to start injection earlier, with the result that much of the combustion occurs at a constant-volume condition similar to a gasoline engine, while the remainder of combustion occurs at constant pressure or nearly constant pressure. Studies indicate that a more efficient burn would occur at a constant-volume condition than at a constant-pressure condition. However, if all of the injected fuel were to burn at a constant-volume condition, the peak cylinder pressures would become excessively high (small volume and large fuel mass).

Because of incomplete mixing of the injected fuel with the air in the combustion chamber, some fuel droplets do not burn until late in the cycle. This means that the combustion chamber temperature is lower and there is also less oxygen to sustain the remaining burn; as a result, incomplete combustion occurs. This situation is reflected as smoke in the exhaust stack or pipe. White smoke results from incomplete combustion in overlean combustion chamber areas, by fuel spray impingement on metal surfaces, and also with low temperatures in the cylinder, such as when starting an engine (more so on cold days). Fuel with too high a cetane rating can also cause white smoke when used in high-ambient-temperature conditions. Gray or black smoke is the result of incomplete combustion in rich combustion chamber areas, caused by such conditions as engine overload, insufficient fuel injector spray penetration, or late ignition due to retarded injection timing. Air starvation can also cause black smoke.

FUEL INJECTION TIMING

Ignition lag in a diesel engine, as you now know, is related to such individual factors as the fuel's distillation range (vaporization temperature), the pressure and temperature of the compressed air within the combustion chamber, air turbulence, and engine load and speed. Engine manufacturers determine the best fuel injection timing point by experimentation in a test cell with the engine on a dynamometer. Actual fuel injection timing is then determined after consideration of the following factors:

- Horsepower output
- Fuel consumption
- Engine noise
- Exhaust gas denseness due to incomplete combustion (black soot)
- Exhaust gas temperatures
- Exhaust gas emissions with respect to NO_x (nitric oxides), HC (hydrocarbons), CO (carbon monoxide), CO_2 (carbon dioxide), and PM (particulate matter)

The actual start of fuel injection varies among makes and models of engines due to design differences; at an idle speed the variance can be anywhere between 5° and 15° BTDC. As the engine speed is increased and a greater volume of fuel is injected, timing must be advanced to allow the fuel to burn to completion because of the now-faster-moving piston, since there will be less time available. Consider that in an engine having a piston stroke of 6 in. (152.4 mm), at an idle speed of 600 rpm the speed of the piston will be 2 × 6 in., since the piston will move up the cylinder once and down the cylinder once for every 360° or each complete turn of the crankshaft. Therefore, piston speed can be determined by the following formula:

$$\text{piston speed} = \frac{2 \times \text{stroke length} \times \text{rpm}}{12}$$

So at a 600 rpm idle speed, the piston will travel 600 ft/min, or 60 × 600 in 1 hr. In 1 hr the piston travels 36,000 ft; if we divide by 5280 ft we can determine its speed in miles per hour, which in this case is 6.81 mph (11 km/h). At a maximum engine speed of 2100 rpm, the piston will travel at 2100 ft/min, or 23.86 mph (38.39 km/h). If the start of fuel pressurization within the fuel injection pump barrel was to occur at the same number of degrees BTDC at the high-speed as at the low-speed setting, then, as you can see in Figure 2–3, the piston would be closer to the top of its stroke before fuel injection actually began, while running at the higher speed. The start of fuel injection has therefore been retarded (begins later in the compression stroke of the upward-moving piston) at the higher speed. It becomes necessary to advance the start of fuel injection (inject fuel earlier) in the cylinder with an increase in engine speed. Figure 2–3 shows the actual beginning of fuel pressurization (beginning of compression) within the pumping plunger and barrel bore. In an inline multiple-plunger injection pump that uses long fuel lines to transfer the fuel from the pump to the injector and nozzle, there is

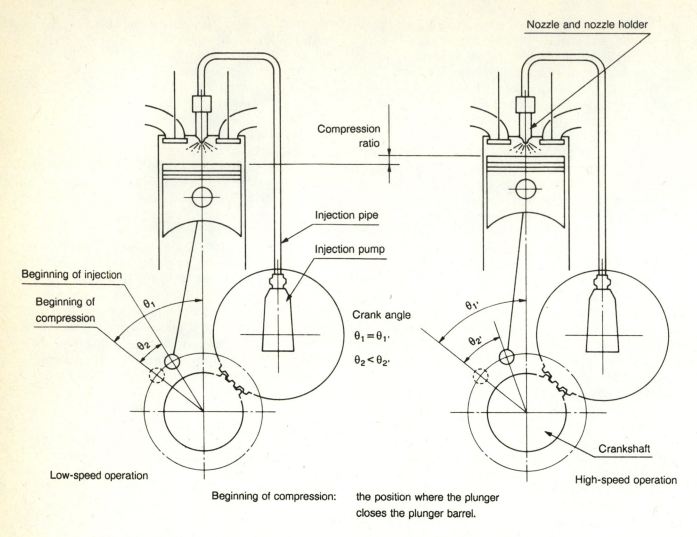

FIGURE 2-3 *Illustration of how the start of fuel injection into the combustion chamber must be advanced as the engine speed is increased. (Courtesy of Zexel USA, Technology and Information Division.)*

also a time delay required to create a high enough pressure in this long column of fuel before the nozzle will open and allow fuel injection to begin. This is important to understand since the speed of the engine/pump affects the actual start of injection.

Figure 2–4 illustrates a typical inline injection pump plunger and barrel assembly with the spring-loaded delivery valve assembled above the barrel. The connecting high-pressure fuel line and fuel nozzle are shown on the right-hand side. Once the upward-moving plunger has closed the fuel supply and discharge ports in the barrel, trapped fuel is placed under pressure or compression. The fuel must be at a high

enough pressure to overcome the fuel line residual pressure and the spring-loaded delivery valve above the barrel. T_1 is the time from the start of fuel pressurization/compression until the delivery valve actually opens. T_2 in the diagram is the time required for transmission of the high-pressure fuel inside the fuel pipe to the nozzle. T_2 is determined by the speed of the pressure wave transmission and the pipe length. In most high-speed diesel engines using inline pumps, this pressure wave transmission speed is approximately 1350 to 1400 m/s (4429 to 4593 ft/sec), which is a fuel speed of between 3020 and 3132 mph (4860 to 5040 km/h). Note that T_2 remains constant regardless

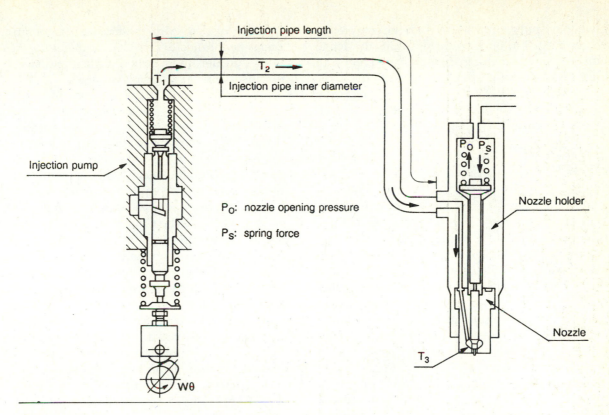

FIGURE 2–4 Three major areas that create injection lag in a multiple-plunger inline injection pump. (Courtesy of Zexel USA, Technology and Information Division.)

of injection pump speed. The time required for the residual pressure in the injection pipe to reach a high enough level that it can open the nozzle delivery valve is pressure T_3. Keep in mind that nozzle release pressures are adjustable by either an internal screw adjustment or by the use of shims. In both cases you effectively change the compressive force of the nozzle valve spring. This allows the same nozzle to be used in more than one particular model of engine. Pressure T_3 decreases as the injection pump speed increases, and increases (longer lag time) when the residual pressure in the fuel line decreases.

The injection lag time in a unit injector fuel system is shorter than that in an inline pump system because there is no long fuel line as a result of the fuel pressure being developed within the body of the unit injector. To give you an appreciation of just how short a time is involved in the fuel injection period, refer to Figure 2–5, which illustrates the time in milliseconds (thousandths of a second) required to complete the injection period in a typical high-speed diesel engine running at different rpm's.

If an engine idling at 500 rpm requires 15° of engine crankshaft rotation to inject its desired quantity of fuel, the actual time to complete this process will

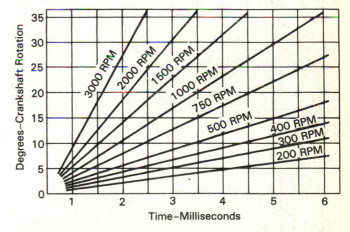

FIGURE 2–5 Graph illustrating the very short time period, in milliseconds (thousandths of a second), available for fuel injection purposes related to engine speed and the point at which injection begins BTDC (before top dead center).

be 5 milliseconds. If injection started at 15° BTDC at 2000 rpm, the time available for injection drops to approximately 1.75 milliseconds. The same engine running at a speed of 2000 rpm starting injection at 30°

BTDC will have only 3 milliseconds for the completion of the injected fuel to burn, which includes the actual injection time and the mixing of the atomized fuel with the compressed air charge, plus the vaporization of the fuel followed by burning. Advancement of the start of fuel injection can be obtained through either mechanical or electronic means.

RETARDED VERSUS ADVANCED TIMING

The reason that a variable injection/engine timing system is required on today's heavy-duty diesel engines, particularly in on-highway vehicles, is that the stringent exhaust emissions legislation mandated through the EPA in the United States was designed to reduce pollutants in the air that we breathe. In addition to limiting the exhaust emissions from the engine exhaust stack, however, the engine manufacturers want to improve the fuel economy and performance of their products. The two main culprits that EPA wants controlled are hydrocarbons and nitrogen oxides.

Just what are hydrocarbons? Unburned or partially burned fuel in the combustion chamber results in hydrocarbons—basically soot produced from the carbon in the diesel fuel. Nitrogen oxides, on the other hand, are what create the yellowish-brown smog that is so noticeable in cities such as Los Angeles. Nitrogen oxides are created when combustion chamber temperatures exceed 3000°F (1649°C), due to oxygen and nitrogen combining during this high-temperature phase. Since both oxygen and nitrogen are constituent parts of the air that we breathe, it is pretty hard to avoid these conditions completely.

To extract as much fuel economy and engine horsepower as possible from a particular model of diesel engine, injection timing must be advanced as the engine speed/load is increased. This is necessary to allow sufficient time for the additional fuel charge to burn at this higher speed, since diesel fuel burns at a fixed rate and the cycle time is shorter. This means that the fuel does not burn faster when the engine speed increases. Its burn rate is more or less constant. When an engine is running at normal injection timing (nonadvanced), the injection of fuel will be later than it would be in an advanced timing mode. In other words, fuel is injected later during normal timing (when the piston is closer to TDC). This results in a shorter ignition delay because of the higher pressure and temperature within the combustion chamber. Unfortunately, because of this later injection of fuel, the fuel will not mix as readily with the air; therefore, when ignition occurs, the combustion chamber temperatures are lower, but more important, so are the

nitrogen oxides. With these lower temperatures, the fuel is not burned to completion; therefore, we end up with a greater hydrocarbon content and smoke at the exhaust stack.

During normal (nonadvanced) injection timing, more of the fuel charge will burn at TDC. This is because of the shorter ignition delay (fuel is starting to burn before TDC), which means that the space above the piston is smaller than it would be at an advanced timing mode (longer ignition delay); the results are lower cylinder pressures, more complete combustion, and therefore more horsepower, without sacrificing engine durability or life. When injection timing is advanced, the fuel is injected earlier (piston is farther away from TDC). This means that the air pressure and temperature in the cylinder will be lower, resulting in an increased ignition delay period. However, this longer delay period allows the fuel more time to mix with the air charge, and when ignition does occur, because of the greater volume of fuel that has collected during this delay period, we end up with higher combustion chamber temperatures and pressures. These higher temperatures give us a higher nitrogen oxide content but fewer hydrocarbons, due to more complete burning of the fuel.

In summary, during *normal* injection timing, we have a lower nitrogen oxide content but a higher percentage of hydrocarbons. During *advanced* timing, we have a higher nitrogen oxide content but a lower hydrocarbon content.

FUEL QUANTITY REQUIREMENTS

The amount of fuel that the injection pump or unit injector must deliver to the engine to produce its rated horsepower can be determined by using the following formula:

$$Q \text{ (quantity)} = \frac{454,000 \times \text{bhp} \times \text{BSFC}}{60 \times N \times \text{sp. gr.}}$$
$$= \frac{7567 \times \text{bhp} \times \text{BSFC}}{N \times \text{sp. gr.}}$$

where Q = quantity of fuel per stroke of the pump or unit injector, measured in cubic millimeters (mm^3)

bhp = brake horsepower of one cylinder

BSFC = brake specific fuel consumption, in lb/bhp/hr

N = pump speed or unit injector speed (rpm) or injections per minute

sp. gr. = specific gravity of the diesel fuel being used

454,000 = volume of 1 lb of water, in mm^3

If a four-stroke-cycle six-cylinder heavy-duty truck diesel engine develops 425 bhp at a speed of 2100 rpm, it would develop 70.83 bhp per cylinder. If its BSFC is 0.310 lb/bhp/hr and it uses a diesel fuel with a specific gravity of 0.85, the quantity of fuel required per injection can be determined from the formula as

$$Q = \frac{7567 \times 70.83 \times 0.310}{(2100/2) \times 0.85} = 186.16 \text{ mm}^3$$

The fuel requirements for an engine can also be computed on the basis of cylinder/piston displacement. An average diesel fuel contains about 7 lb of carbon for each 1 lb of hydrogen, so complete combustion of 1 lb of fuel requires approximately 14.4 to 14.5 lb of air. Therefore, 1 ft^3 of diesel fuel with a specific gravity of 0.85 would require 9450 ft^3 of air for complete combustion. However, since most diesel engines operate with 1.5 times theoretical air supply, 1 ft^3 of fuel requires 14,170 ft^3 of air.

SPECIAL NOTE: The term *stoichiometric* is often used with respect to both gasoline and diesel engine combustion theory. What this means is that a specific amount of oxygen is required to provide complete combustion of the fuel charge. In both a gasoline and a diesel engine this requires an air/fuel ratio of approximately 14:1 (14 to 1), meaning that we need 14 times as much air as fuel to ensure complete combustion. However, since heavy-duty high-speed diesel engines are operated with no throttling of the air such as you find in a gasoline engine, the air/fuel ratio on a diesel at an idle speed can be as high as 100:1, dropping to somewhere in the region of 20 to 25:1 at a full-load speed setting.

If the volumetric efficiency (ability to inhale and retain percentage of atmospheric air) of a naturally aspirated engine is 90%, the fuel required for each injection in a 125 in.^{3} piston displacement per cylinder engine can be calculated from the following formula:

$$Q = \frac{\begin{array}{c}\text{piston displacement (in.}^3\text{)} \\ \times \text{ volumetric efficiency}\end{array}}{\text{ft}^3 \text{ of air required per ft}^3 \text{ of fuel}}$$

$$= \frac{125 \times 0.90}{14,170} = 0.008 \text{ in.}^3 \text{ per injection}$$

$$= 0.008 \times 16,387 = 131 \text{ mm}^3 \text{ per injection}$$

NOTE: We use the figure 16,387 in this calculation to get cubic millimeters from cubic inches.

From this formula, we can see that we more or less need 1 mm^3 of fuel for each cubic inch of piston displacement on a normally aspirated engine, which is an engine that relies on piston and valve opening alone to get atmospheric air into the cylinder. If the engine is turbocharged or supercharged, which is much more common on today's high-speed heavy-duty truck diesel engines, we have to use the following formula to determine the quantity of fuel required per injection:

$$Q \text{ (mm}^3\text{)} = \frac{P_a + P_g}{14.7} \times \text{piston displacement (in.}^3\text{)}$$

where P_a is the atmospheric pressure, in psia (psi absolute), and P_g is the turbo or supercharger pressure in psig (psi gauge). Atmospheric pressure at sea level is considered to be equivalent to 14.7 psi (101.35 kPa). If the atmospheric pressure is 14.2 psia and the engine intake manifold air pressure (turbo boost) is 15 psig, then

$$Q = \frac{14.2 + 15.0}{14.7}$$

$$= \frac{29.2}{14.7} = 1.986 \text{ mm}^3 \text{ of diesel fuel per cubic inch of piston displacement}$$

Therefore, the same 125 in.^{3} engine used in the normally aspirated engine would require $125 \times 1.986 = 248.25$ mm^3 of fuel per injection.

THERMAL EFFICIENCY

During the combustion cycle, the heat released from the burning fuel converts this *heat energy* into *mechanical energy* at the flywheel. How efficiently this is done is known as *thermal efficiency*, or how much energy an engine can extract from a given volume of fuel and turn it into power. Refer to Chapter 1 for the details of how to determine an engine's thermal efficiency.

EXHAUST EMISSIONS LIMITS

Both gasoline and diesel engines in North America are manufactured so that they *must* comply with the U.S. EPA exhaust emissions standards for the year in which they are produced. For heavy-duty on-highway diesel engines, these exhaust emissions fall into various categories that deal with hydrocarbons, carbon monoxide, nitrogen oxides, and particulate matter.

Exhaust gases have several major constituents.

- Carbon dioxide (CO_2), although nonpoisonous, does contribute to *global warming*. Complete combustion produces CO_2 and water.
- Carbon monoxide (CO) is a colorless, oderless, and tasteless gas. Inhalation of as little as 0.3% by

volume can cause death within 30 min. The exhaust gas from spark ignition engines at an idle speed has a high CO content. For this reason, *never* allow the engine to run in enclosed spaces such as a closed garage.

- Oxides of nitrogen (NO_x) have two classes. Nitrogen monoxide (NO) is a colorless, oderless, and tasteless gas that is rapidly converted into nitrogen dioxide (NO_2) in the presence of oxygen. NO_2 is a yellowish- to reddish-brown poisonous gas with a penetrating odor that can destroy lung tissue. NO and NO_2 are customarily treated together and referred to as oxides of nitrogen (NO_x).

- Hydrocarbons (HC) of many different types are present in exhaust gas. In the presence of nitrogen oxide and sunlight, they form oxidants that irritate the mucous membranes. Some hydrocarbons are considered to be carcinogenic. Incomplete combustion produces unburned hydrocarbons.

- Particulate matter (PM), in accordance with US legislation, includes all substances (with the exception of unbound water) that under normal conditions are present as solids (ash, carbon) or liquids in exhaust gases.

Future EPA regulations also extend into off-highway diesel equipment as well as marine applications. California, which has the strictest internal combustion engine exhaust emissions in the world, usually sets standards that are then followed by the EPA. California has enacted emission levels that extend to utility engines such as lawn mowers and garden equipment (gas or diesel). Separate standards are in place for handheld engines. Non-handheld engines have to meet two standards (three for diesels): total hydrocarbon plus nitrogen oxide level; carbon monoxide level; and, for diesels, a particulate matter limit.

The CARB (California Air Resources Board) now has laws in place covering all types of internal combustion engines in almost all types of applications; these laws cover retrofitted engines as well. The CARB requires certification test procedures and emission standards for heavy-duty (40 hp, 30kW, and over) construction and farm equipment for the 1995 model year and beyond. Also beginning in 1995, all new and heavy-duty off-highway engines must certify to emission standards of 1.3 g/bhp/hr for HC; 5.0 g/bhp/hr for NO_x, and 0.25 g/bhp/hr for PM. For the year 1999, all new heavy-duty off-highway engines must certify to 0.60 g/bhp/hr HC, 2.0 g/bhp/hr NO_x, and 0.1 g/bhp/hr for PM. All 1995 and later model year engines must comply with durability and warranty requirements similar to those imposed for on-highway engines in the state. All 1991

heavy-duty diesel engines rebuilt after 1995 must comply with a capping standard of 10 g/bhp/hr for HC and NO_x.

To reduce exhaust emissions from diesel engines, particularly heavy-duty on-highway models, engine advancements and after-treatment technologies have been adopted to ensure that all engines are in compliance with EPA standards. Exhaust emissions standards have become more stringent over the years; the latest major limits came into affect in 1994. By 1998 NO_x must drop by 20% from the 1994 limits to 4.0 g/bhp/hr. Most of the 1994 heavy-duty on-highway engines were able to meet the regulations through higher injection pressures, high top ring pistons, tailored intake and exhaust systems, and closely designed turbochargers using air-to-air-charge cooling systems. In addition, in October 1993 in the United States, legislation reduced the allowable sulfur content in diesel fuel to 0.05%, which has also helped in reducing emissions because 98% of the sulfur is combusted to sulfur dioxide and the rest is combusted to sulfates. This low-sulfur fuel still leaves about 0.01 g/bhp/hr sulfate in the raw exhaust. Diesel fuel contains molecules with between 8 and 15 carbon atoms, and engine lube oils tend to have molecules with more than 15 carbon atoms; diesel fuel and engine lube oil differ in molecular size.

Standards for particulate generation have been one of the tougher areas for engine designers. Many factors, such as a NO_x trade-off, are involved. By reducing particulate emissions through prolonged combustion and higher temperatures, researchers found that NO_x emissions tended to increase, and the reverse process also held true. Higher fuel injection pressures and electronic unit injector controls have helped tremendously in reducing exhaust emissions levels. Some manufacturers of midheavy diesel engines for trucks have had to resort to catalytic-type converters to meet 1994 EPA emissions standards. These included, but were not limited to, General Motors Corporation on its 6.5 L engine, Navistar on its T 444E (7.3 L), Cummins on its midrange B and C series engines, and Caterpillar on its 3116 truck engines.

For 1998, NO_x standards will be the primary target for heavy-duty engine designers. At that time the maximum limit drops to 4 g/bhp/hr. California however, has instituted a joint NO_x and HC limit of 3.9 g/bhp/hr for 1995 for medium-duty trucks. Further reductions in NO_x and particulates will probably be legislated after 1998.

Potential changes in engine design to meet NO_x in 1998 may include recycling of exhaust gas and retardation of fuel injection timing. Further use of DOCs (diesel oxidation catalysts), which can eliminate gases

FIGURE 2–6 Projected EPA off-highway exhaust emissions standards. (Courtesy of Diesel & Gas Turbine Publications.)

Net power kW (Hp)	HC g/kW-hr (g/bHp-hr)	CO g/kW-hr (g/bHp-hr)	NO$_x$ g/kW-hr (g/bHp-hr)	PM g/kW-hr (g/bHp-hr)	Smoke A/L/P* (%)
130 (175)	1.3 (1.0)	11.4 (8.5)	9.2 (6.9)	0.54 (0.4)	20/15/50
≥75 to <130 (100 to <175)	—	—	9.2 (6.9)	—	20/15/50
≥37 to <75 (50 to <100)	—	—	9.2 (6.9)	—	20/15/50

*Smoke opacity standards are reported in terms of percent opacity during an acceleration mode, a lug mode, and the peak opacity on either the acceleration or lug modes.

and SOFs (soluble oil fractions) in the exhaust, seem to have little effect on dry soot (carbon). However, the latest catalytic converters in use for diesel engines have shown that they can convert noxious carbon monoxide and hydrocarbon gases in the exhaust stream into carbon dioxide and water. Diesel exhaust filters are also capable of trapping particulates produced by buses and trucks; the soot is oxidized when the filter reaches its load limit, thus regenerating the filter. Examples of some of these exhaust aftertreatment devices are described in Chapter 20.

Federal emissions standards for diesel truck and bus exhaust in g/bhp/hr are shown here for 1994 and 1998:

Year	HC	CO	NO$_x$	PM	Fuel sulfur weight (%)
1994	1.3	15.5	5.0	0.1	0.05
1998	1.3	15.5	4.0	0.1	0.05

The only difference for urban buses is that the PM is 0.05 g/bhp/hr (for 1994 and 1998). Figure 2–6 lists the EPA off-highway emissions standards for CI (compression ignition) diesel engines, 37 kW (50 hp) or higher. The standards for HC, CO, and PM emissions for engines 130 kW (175 hp) and larger are consistent with standards adopted by the CARB. Figure 2–7 shows the EPA's implementation timetable for these emissions regulations based on engine size.

Alternative fuels will grow in importance throughout the 1990s and into the year 2000 and beyond as we struggle to limit the exhaust emissions released into our atmosphere. Some fuel options are discussed in Chapter 3.

SELF-TEST QUESTIONS

1. Technician A says that the most popular type of combustion chamber design for heavy-duty high-speed diesel truck engines is the IDI (indirect-injection) or PC (precombustion chamber) design. Technician B dis-

FIGURE 2–7 EPA's implementation timetable for off-highway engine exhaust emissions. (Courtesy of Diesel & Gas Turbine Publications.)

Engine size kW (Hp)	Implementation date
≥130 to <560 (≥175 to <750)	January 1, 1996
≥75 to <130 (≥100 to <175	January 1, 1997
≥37 to <75 (≥50 to <100)	January 1, 1998
>560 (>750)	January 1, 2000

agrees and says that the DI (direct injection) design is the most widely used type of combustion system. Which technician is correct?

2. Which of the following combustion chamber designs offers the best fuel economy when used in midheavy and heavy-duty diesel truck engines?
   a. Swirl chamber design
   b. Precombustion chamber design
   c. Direct injection design

3. Technician A says that a glow plug is not required for initial start-up of a precombustion chamber design engine. Technician B disagrees, stating that it is the direct injection engine type that does not require the use of a glow plug system for initial start-up. Who is right?

4. The MAN M-type combustion chamber design is one whereby
   a. the combustion chamber bowl is contained within the crown of the piston
   b. the combustion chamber is in fact a small antechamber contained within the cylinder head
   c. the combustion chamber is located off to the side of the main chamber

5. Technician A says that current cylinder firing pressures in high-speed heavy-duty engines average 1000 to 1200 psi (6895 to 8274 kPa). Technician B says this is

too low and that pressures of between 1800 and 2300 psi (12,411 to 15,858 kPa) are more common. Who is correct?

6. Technician A says that fuel injection pressures now in use in heavy-duty highway truck engines range between 19,000 and 28,000 psi (131,005 to 193,060 kPa). Technician B says this is impossible because such pressures would blow the engine apart. Is technician A or B correct?

7. Technician A says that the diesel engine operates on the constant-volume principle. Technician B disagrees, saying that the diesel engine operates on the constant-pressure cycle. Who is correct?

8. When the diesel fuel is injected into the combustion chamber, it is broken down into very fine particles. The term to describe this process is
   a. vaporization
   b. injection
   c. cetane explosion
   d. atomization

9. Ignition delay in a diesel engine is
   a. the time lag from initial injection to actual ignition
   b. the time required to raise the fuel pressure high enough to overcome the compression pressure in the cylinder
   c. the time delay required for the glow plug to reach its red-hot state
   d. the time lag for the injected vaporized fuel actually to atomize

10. Technician A says that a long ignition delay period would result in a rough-running engine. Technician B says that a long ignition delay period would result in an engine knocking sound, due to the high pressures created within the combustion chamber. Who is correct?

11. Technician A says that combustion in a diesel engine can take place only when the carbon and hydrogen molecules are atomized, whereas technician B says that the carbon and hydrogen must mix with the oxygen in the combustion chamber in a vaporized state to initiate successful combustion. Who is correct here?

12. Air used in a diesel engine for combustion is made up of oxygen and nitrogen. Technician A says that by volume, there is more nitrogen than oxygen in a given amount of air. Technician B says that there has to be more oxygen to sustain combustion. Which technician knows his or her basic chemistry?

13. Technician A says that a by-product of combustion is carbon dioxide, whereas technician B says that carbon monoxide is formed as a by-product of combustion. Who is right?

14. Technician A says that a diesel engine operates with an air/fuel ratio of approximately 25:1 under full load, whereas technician B states that it is closer to 100:1 under all conditions of operation. Who is correct?

15. List and describe briefly the four stages of combustion that occur in a diesel engine in order to achieve complete burning of the injected fuel.

16. List the main factors that affect the ignition delay period in the combustion chamber.

17. Technician A says that the letters EPA mean "European Protection Association," whereas technician B says that they mean "Environmental Protection Agency" Who is correct?

18. List the four main culprits that EPA wants controlled as a by-product of the combustion process in the exhaust of heavy-duty diesel engines.

19. Technician A says that when an engine is running at normal injection timing (nonadvanced), the injection of fuel will be later than it would be when running in an advanced timing mode. Technician B says that under normal timing, the fuel is injected earlier in the injection cycle. Who is correct?

20. True or False: During advanced injection timing, the fuel is injected earlier (piston is farther away from TDC). This means that the air pressure and temperature in the cylinder are lower, resulting in an increased ignition delay period.

21. Technician A says that during normal injection timing a lower nitrogen oxide content is produced at the exhaust but a higher percentage of hydrocarbons is produced. Technician B says that this is incorrect; instead, at normal injection timing there is a higher nitrogen oxide content but a lower hydrocarbon content. Who is correct?

22. True or False: Sulfur dioxide, which is a by-product of combustion, is caused by the sulfur content of the diesel fuel.

3 Diesel and Alternative Fuels

OVERVIEW

Diesel fuel is the liquid that powers most diesel engines; however, environmental concerns regarding exhaust emissions of internal combustion engines have spurred a drive toward alternative fuels. In this chapter we discuss in detail the characteristics of the federally legislated low-sulfur diesel fuels, the way various hydrocarbons in the fuels affect engine operation, and alternative fuels that are now being widely adopted for use in diesel engines.

TOPICS

- Crude oil and its refining process
- Diesel fuel oil grades
- Specific gravity of a fuel
- Heat value of a fuel
- Fuel recommendations
- Major characteristics of diesel fuels
- Diesel fuel operating problems
- Introduction to alternative fuels
- Methanol
- Dimethyl ether
- Ethanol
- Compressed natural gas
- Natural gas engine operation
- Liquified natural gas
- Propane
- Hydrogen
- Self-test questions

CRUDE OIL AND ITS REFINING PROCESS

Crude petroleum oil and natural gas are found in many areas of the world under pressures of up to several hundred psi, and both crude oil and natural gas are often obtained from the same well. The crude oil must be subjected to a refining process to remove the impurities; special additives are then blended with the fuel to make it commercially acceptable for use in both gasoline and diesel engines. Crude oils vary widely in composition and processing requirements. For example, Alaskan North Slope crude produces less gasoline than Arabian light crude. From a quality standpoint, however, Arabian light crude contains more sulfur than Indonesian Minas crude.

Products suitable for automotive engine fuels are blended using straight distilled fractions and processed components. Petroleum distillates normally used as fuel for diesel engines are composed of heavy hydrocarbons. The more volatile portions of the crude oil are used for gasoline, whereas the heavier distillates are used as diesel fuel and home heating oil.

The refining process for diesel fuel is not as complex as that for gasoline; therefore, it is less expensive to produce. Because of its heavier hydrocarbon content, diesel fuel contains more energy, or Btu per gallon, than gasoline or any other fuel now used in internal combustion engines, including liquid petroleum gas (LPG) and compressed natural gas (CNG). This greater heat value is one of the reasons that the diesel engine is more efficient than the gasoline engine.

The heat value of both diesel and gasoline varies slightly depending on the actual crude used, the refining process, and the grade of fuel desired. Distribution of products from an average barrel of crude oil is shown in Figure 3–1.

Diesel fuel is refined from crude petroleum oil, which is basically a mixture of many types of molecules containing only carbon (C) and hydrogen (H) atoms and referred to as a mixture of hydrocarbons. These are mixed with some sulfur and nitrogen compounds, small amounts of soluble organic compounds, and a few impurities, such as water and sediment.

Hydrocarbon molecules found in petroleum consist of a practically unlimited number of combinations of carbon and hydrogen atoms. These molecules are classified into three general groups: paraffin, naphthene, and aromatic. Varying proportions of these hydrocarbon molecules are found in all petroleum crude oils. These variations have caused a designation to be given to the type of crude oil in terms of the predominating hydrocarbon group: namely, paraffinic, mixed, naphthenic, or aromatic.

If there are too many heavy hydrocarbons in the fuel, incomplete combustion generally results. In contrast, if there are not enough of these hydrocarbons, the engine can lack power—a complaint received by heavy-duty truck mechanics/technicians on an ongoing basis. Good-quality diesel fuels are refined to ensure the correct blending of hydrocarbons to provide a smooth and continuous burn with the correct distillation range (temperature at which the fuel vaporizes).

Basically, 1 barrel of crude oil, which contains 191 L (42 Imperial gallons) or 189 L (50 U.S. gallons) when distilled and refined by local oil suppliers, produces only about 8 Imperial gallons (9.6 U.S. gallons), or 36 L, of diesel fuel. You can see how much crude oil is

actually required to produce a good grade of diesel fuel. The crude oil is heated to about 800°F (427°C) to basically distill the oil; then the lighter products contained within the crude oil, such as butane, gasoline, and LPG are removed. A further increase in the crude oil temperature allows such lighter distillate products as jet fuel (JP), kerosene, and the more highly refined No. 1 diesel fuel to be produced. From the remaining crude stock, the less volatile No. 2 diesel fuel as well as heavy turbine fuels are produced, followed by petrochemical feedstocks, lubricants, and other desirable products.

Refining residue from the paraffinic crudes is mostly *paraffin wax*, which is the cause of fuel filter plugging when ambient temperatures drop to the cloud point of the fuel oil. Naphthenic and aromatic crudes produce a residue that is composed mostly of asphalt. When crude oil is refined, it is heated and most of it is vaporized, so that the gases pass to a fractionating cooling tower where the various portions, such as gasoline, kerosene, gas oil (fuel oil), and other distillates, are separated from each other as they condense at different temperatures in the tower.

All crude oils contain varying amounts of soluble organic compounds of vanadium, nickel, iron, sodium, and other elements. Fuels with high concentrations of these elements can create rapid wear of internal engine components, although diesel fuels containing small amounts of vanadium, in the region of about 70 parts per million (ppm), generally give satisfactory results.

All diesel engine manufacturers issue fuel oil specification sheets that indicate the particular type of fuel that should be used in their engines for best performance and longest engine life. Conventional diesel fuels are distillates with a boiling range between approximately 149° and 371°C (300° to 700°F).

Figure 3–2 illustrates a typical refining procedure to produce diesel fuel from the crude oil supply. The crude oil enters a distillation unit where the crude is basically heated or distilled to boil off the hydrocarbons desired to produce the diesel fuel. The cracker actually splits or cracks the hydrocarbons into smaller, lighter components; the hydrocracking takes place in a hydrogen atmosphere. The coker is a variation of a thermal cracking unit that is applied to the heaviest crude streams not suitable for catalytic cracking. Other units take the process a step further by separating and condensing the newly formed hydrocarbon molecules into finished petroleum products, thereby allowing maximum production of quality fuel from each barrel of crude oil. The hydrotreater is designed to produce both home heating oils and diesel fuels through interaction of the middle distillates from the crude oil with

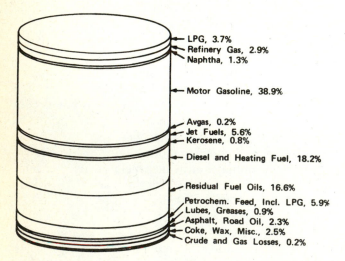

FIGURE 3–1   *Typical end products from a barrel of crude oil.*

LPG, 3.7%
Refinery Gas, 2.9%
Naphtha, 1.3%

Motor Gasoline, 38.9%

Avgas, 0.2%
Jet Fuels, 5.6%
Kerosene, 0.8%

Diesel and Heating Fuel, 18.2%

Residual Fuel Oils, 16.6%

Petrochem. Feed, Incl. LPG, 5.9%
Lubes, Greases, 0.9%
Asphalt, Road Oil, 2.3%
Coke, Wax, Misc., 2.5%
Crude and Gas Losses, 0.2%

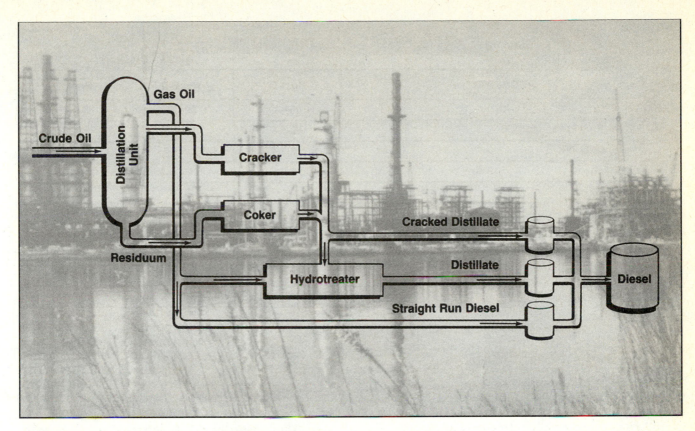

FIGURE 3–2 Crude oil refining and blending sequence to produce diesel fuel. (Reprinted with permission by Chevron Research and Technology Company, a division of Chevron U.S.A. Inc.; copyright Chevron Research Company [1995].)

hydrogen and a catalyst. Hydrotreating results in products with lower sulfur levels, which are required today to meet the U.S. EPA diesel fuel standards.

DIESEL FUEL OIL GRADES

Diesel fuel oil is graded and designated by the American Society for Testing and Materials (ASTM); its specific gravity and high and low heat values are also listed by the API (American Petroleum Institute). Each individual oil refiner and supplier attempts to produce diesel fuels that comply as closely as possible with the ASTM and API specifications. Because of different crude oil supplies, the diesel fuel end product may be on either the high or low end of the prescribed heat energy scale in Btu per pound or per gallon. Therefore, diesel fuel oils available from one supplier may vary slightly from those provided by another. At this time, only two recommended grades of fuel are considered acceptable for use in high-speed heavy-duty trucks and buses in North America. These are the No. 1D and No. 2D fuel oil classifications. The No. 1D fuel is a lighter distillate than a No. 2D. However, No. 1D fuel has less heat energy per gallon than does a No. 2D grade. The No. 1D fuel also costs more per gallon to produce than a No. 2D grade.For this reason, No. 1D tends to be used more widely in city bus applications, while the heavier No. 2D fuel grade with its greater energy (Btu per gallon) content is widely used in heavy-duty high-speed truck diesel engine applications.

Grade No. 1D

The No. 1D fuel rating comprises the class of volatile fuel oils from kerosene to the intermediate distillates. Fuels within this classification are suitable for use in high-speed engines in service that involves frequent and relatively wide variations in loads and speeds, and also in cases where abnormally low fuel temperatures are encountered, because the No. 1D fuel provides easier starting qualities in cold-weather operation. Therefore, for heavy-duty high-speed diesel truck operation in continued cold-weather environments, No. 1D fuel may allow better operation than the heavier distillate No. 2D.

Grade No. 2D

The No. 2D fuel rating includes the class of distillate gas oils of lower volatility. They are suitable for use in high-speed engines in service that involves relatively high loads and uniform speeds, or in engines that do not require fuels having the higher volatility or other properties specified for grade No. 1D. No. 2D fuel is more widely used by truck fleets, due to its greater heat value per gallon, particularly in warm to moderate climates. Although the No. 1D fuel has better properties for cold-weather operation, many fleets still prefer to use the No. 2D grade in the winter. They employ fuel heater/water separators to provide suitable starting as well as fuel additive conditioners, which are added directly to the fuel tank.

Classifications of diesel fuels below grades No. 1D and 2D are not considered acceptable for use in high-speed automotive or truck engines; therefore, they will not be discussed here.

On a volume basis, typical No. 2D fuel has about 13% more heating value in Btu per gallon than does gasoline; No. 1D fuel, which is a lighter distillate and therefore less dense than No. 2D, has approximately 10% more Btu content per gallon than gasoline.

Fuel Grade and Engine Performance

Selection of the correct diesel fuel is a must if the engine is to perform to its rated specifications. Generally, seven factors must be considered in the selection of a fuel oil:

1. Starting characteristics
2. Fuel handling
3. Wear on injection equipment
4. Wear on pistons
5. Wear on rings, valves, and cylinder liners
6. Engine maintenance
7. Fuel cost and availability

Several other considerations are also relevant to the selection of a fuel oil:

1. Engine size and design
2. Speed and load range
3. Frequency of load and speed changes
4. Atmospheric conditions

SPECIFIC GRAVITY OF A FUEL

The lighter a fuel's SG (specific gravity), the less heat value per gallon it will have. Conversely, the heavier the SG of a diesel fuel oil, the greater will be its energy content in Btu per gallon. SG is the ratio of the diesel fuel's weight to the weight of an equivalent volume of water; usually this is designated as "sp. gr. 60/60°F," which indicates that both the diesel fuel and water are weighed and measured at 60°F (15.5°C). API measures diesel fuel with a special hydrometer and assigns a gravity degrees API rating to it. An example of the type of chart used to show various API-rated fuels is shown in the left-hand column of Table 3–1. The specific gravity shown in the second column from the left indicates the weight of an Imperial gallon of fuel compared with an Imperial gallon of water, which weighs 10 lb. The third column shows the weight in pounds of a U.S. gallon of fuel.

HEAT VALUE OF A FUEL

The fourth and fifth columns from the left-hand side of Table 3–1 illustrate the *high* heat values in Btu per pound and also in Btu per gallon. The sixth and seventh columns list the Btu/lb and the Btu/gallon for the *low* heat values of the fuel. In North America, the thermal efficiency or heat efficiency of an internal combustion engine that uses liquid fuel is determined on the basis of the HHV (high heat value) of the fuel used. This means that the products of combustion are cooled to their original temperature, water vapor is condensed, and the total heat released is known as the gross or HHV of the fuel. High heat value is termed in Btu/lb for liquid fuel and in Btu/cubic foot for gaseous fuels such as propane and compressed natural gas. However, if the water vapor from combustion is not condensed, the latent heat of vaporization (an indication of the cooling effect when liquids are vaporized) of the water is subtracted to give the fuel's net or LHV (low heat value). The heat value of any given diesel fuel fluctuates based on its specification as a No. 1D or a No. 2D grade. In addition, the heat energy value of the fuel varies slightly between a summer and a winter blend, even from the same refining supplier. Since the diesel fuel grade recommended by TMC/ATA (The Maintenance Council, American Trucking Associations) for heavy-duty high-speed diesel engines in highway truck/tractors is grade No. 2D, we will use this as a generally accepted fuel energy equivalent. A No. 2D grade diesel fuel with an API (American Petroleum Institute) gravity rating number of 36 at 60°F (15.5°C) would be as shown in Table 3–1.

The greater the Btu content per gallon of fuel, the greater the energy that can be released in the combustion chamber when that fuel is ignited. Consider that each Btu of fuel energy is capable of releasing the equivalent of 778 ft-lb of mechanical work. Therefore,

TABLE 3–1   High and low heat values for API-rated diesel fuels[a]

Gravity (°API)	Specific gravity at 60°F	Weight fuel (lb/gal)	High heat value		Low heat value	
			Btu/lb	Btu/gal	Btu/lb	Btu/gal
44	0.8063	6.713	19,860	133,500	18,600	125,000
42	0.8155	6.790	19,810	134,700	18,560	126,200
40	0.8251	6.870	19,750	135,800	18,510	127,300
38	0.8348	6.951	19,680	137,000	18,460	128,500
36	0.8448	7.034	19,620	138,200	18,410	129,700
34	0.8550	7.119	19,560	139,400	18,360	130,900
32	0.8654	7.206	19,490	140,600	18,310	132,100
30	0.8762	7.296	19,420	141,800	18,250	133,300
28	0.8871	7.387	19,350	143,100	18,190	134,600
26	0.8984	7.481	19,270	144,300	18,130	135,800
24	0.9100	7.578	19,190	145,600	18,070	137,100
22	0.9218	7.676	19,110	146,800	18,000	138,300
20	0.9340	7.778	19,020	148,100	17,930	139,600
18	0.9465	7.882	18,930	149,400	17,860	140,900
16	0.9593	7.989	18,840	150,700	17,790	142,300
14	0.9725	8.099	18,740	152,000	17,710	143,600
12	0.9861	8.212	18,640	153,300	17,620	144,900
10	1.000	8.328	18,540	154,600	17,540	146,200

[a]It should be understood that heating values for a given gravity of fuel oil may vary somewhat from those shown.
Source: Bureau of Standards, Miscellaneous Publication No. 97, *Thermal Properties of Petroleum Products,* April 28, 1933.

if we multiply the total Btu/gal by this figure, we can determine the available work output that can be produced by the release of this heat energy. The total number of lb-ft of energy can then be divided by 33,000 ft-lb, which represents 1 hp/min. From this calculation we can equate just how much horsepower can be extracted from each gallon of diesel fuel.

Let us compare an API 34 fuel designation shown in Table 3–1, which has approximately 139,400 Btu/U.S. gallon with an API 36 with 138,200 Btu/U.S. gallon. The API 34 fuel can release 108,453,200 lb-ft of work output, while the API 36 fuel can release 107,519,600 lb-ft of work output. If we divide both totals by 33,000 lb-ft, which represents the work required to produce 1 hp/min, the API 34 fuel can produce an equivalent of 3286 hp divided by 60 to convert the total to horsepower developed in an hour, since all engines are computed on their ability to produce horsepower over a 1 hr period, we obtain 55 hp/hr. The API 36 fuel with its lower Btu heat content per gallon would produce slightly less at 54.3 hp/hr. However, on a 400 bhp engine, for example, that might consume 0.325 lb/hp/hr of diesel fuel, the engine would burn 130 lb of fuel in 1 hr. This figure is obtained by multiplying 0.325 × 400. If we divide the total fuel consumed in an hour by the weight of fuel per gallon, the API 36 fueled engine would consume 18.48 U.S. gal/hr, while the API 34 fueled engine would consume 18.26 U.S. gal/hr. Therefore, the engine running on the API 34 fuel would save 0.22 U.S. gal/hr. Projected over a 10 hr day, this is a savings of 2.2 U.S. gal. If the truck operates 7 days a week, we would save 15.4 U.S. gal/week. In a year, we would save 52 × 15.4 = 800.8 U.S. gal. Keep in mind, however, that we have to allow for heat, friction, and radiation losses from the engine, as well as the driving habits of the operator and the terrain and ambient temperatures in which the truck operates. However, taking two trucks with identical specifications, all things being equal, the truck engine using the API 34 fuel should return slightly better fuel economy than the one using API 36. For more details on thermal efficiency of an engine, refer to the section on thermal efficiency in Chapter 1.

FUEL RECOMMENDATIONS

Diesel fuel is a complex mixture of hydrocarbons that can include paraffins, olefins, naphthenes, and aromatics. For many years the paraffins plus naphthenes formed as much as 85% of the total fuel composition. As a direct result of the phasedown and eventual elimination of lead from gasoline and the greater octane requirement of unleaded gasoline, refiners have adopted new technologies to extend the division of products available from each barrel of crude oil that they refine. Consequently, this has led the refiners to increase severely the catalytic cracking process used to refine their crude oil supplies. In addition, the expanded use of octane-enhancing oxygenates (methyl *t*-butyl ether and alcohols such as ethanol) in gasoline has led to a gradual deterioration of diesel fuel quality and heating oil, since they are distilled off from what is left after extracting the lighter distillate gasoline.

This more severe catalytic cracking has raised the aromatic, olefinic, and sulfur contents, and the end result is that diesel cetane numbers have been lowered and exhaust particulates and smoke from diesel engines have tended to increase. However, several single-purpose additives have been used in diesel fuel to raise the cetane number, reduce the cloud and pour points, prevent oxidative and bacterial deterioration in storage, and reduce exhaust smoke. The introduction of electronically controlled diesel unit injectors with their higher spray-in pressures along with a series of ECM (electronic control module) engine/vehicle sensors has also resulted in some improvement in high-speed truck diesel operation.

The preferred grade of No. 2D diesel fuel that is recommended by TMC/ATA falls between an API 34 and 36 gravity rating at 60°F (15.5°C); refer to Table 3–1 to obtain the values for these two fuel numbers. Note that the HHV of the API 36 fuel is 19,620 Btu/lb, while the heat value for the API 34 fuel is 19,560 Btu/lb. Of special note, however, is the fact that the API 34 fuel contains more Btu/gal than does the API 36 fuel. The Btu/lb is obtained simply by dividing the Btu/gal by the weight of the fuel per gallon. The API 34 fuel grade is heavier than the 36, so we have less heat per pound but more heat per gallon.

For each API gravity number above 36, engine dynamometer tests have indicated that the engine will produce approximately 1% lower power; actual vehicle road tests indicate that the fuel mileage per gallon tends to be about 2% lower. Therefore, the difference between 32 and 40 API gravity can make a difference of as much as 15% in vehicle fuel costs. Consequently, the TMC/ATA recommendation lists a minimum diesel fuel of between 34 and 36 API and a minimum cetane index rating of 45. Generally within the range of 32° and 40° API gravity, a lower number, which indicates a heavier fuel, tends to provide more power and increased miles per gallon (km/L); in contrast, a higher number, which indicates a lighter distillate fuel blend, generally results in lower power and fewer miles per gallon. Although a minimum of 45 cetane is desirable, because of the deterioration in refined diesel fuel quality, the minimum should never be below 40.

Cetane is basically a measure of diesel fuel volatility. Unlike gasoline, where the higher octane number signifies greater resistance to self-ignition of the fuel, the higher the cetane number, the more readily the fuel will ignite when injected into the combustion chamber. This is a desirable feature when starting diesel engines in cold weather.

Table 3–2 lists the desirable and recommended diesel fuel characteristics that Detroit Diesel suggests for use in its line of two-stroke- and four-stroke-cycle engines. This fuel oil specification sheet is typical of the types readily available from all major fuel oil suppliers.

MAJOR CHARACTERISTICS OF DIESEL FUELS

Diesel fuels listed in the specification sheets in this chapter indicate a number of technical terms that are briefly listed and explained in the "Glossary of Fuel Terms" located at the end of this chapter. Table 3–3 lists diesel fuel properties and why each is important to the overall performance of the diesel engine and vehicle performance. The major characteristics of diesel fuel oil can best be explained by describing the individual properties.

Volatility (ASTM) Designation

Fuel volatility requirements depend on the same factors as cetane number. The more volatile fuels are best for engines in cars, buses, and trucks, where rapidly changing loads and speeds are encountered. Low-endpoint fuels tend to give better fuel economy, where their characteristics are needed for complete combustion, and they definitely produce less exhaust smoke, odor, deposits, crankcase dilution, and engine wear.

The importance of fuel endpoint increases with an increase in engine rpm. The endpoint of a fuel is established by a distillation test whereby a given volume of fuel is placed into a container that is then heated gradually. As the fuel boils, vapors pass through a tube located in an ice bath, where the vapors are condensed and collected in a graduated container. Because of the many types of hydrocarbons in fuel oils, different boil-

TABLE 3–2   Specifications chart for high-speed heavy-duty diesel engine diesel fuel oil.

General fuel classification	ASTM test	No. 1 ASTM 1-D	No. 2* ASTM 2-D
Gravity, °API#	D 287	40–44	33–37
Flash point, min. °F (°C)	D 93	100 (38)	125 (52)
Viscosity, kinematic, cST @ 100°F (40°C)	D 445	1.3–2.4	1.9–4.1
Cloud point °F#	D 2500	[See Note 1]	[See Note 1]
Sulfur content wt%, max.	D 1266	0.5 (0.05)$	0.5 (0.05)$
Carbon residue on 10%, wt%, max.	D 524	0.15	0.35
Accelerated stability total insolubles, mg/100 ml, max.#	D 2274	1.5	1.5
Ash, wt%, max.	D 482	0.01	0.01
Cetane number, min.+	D 613	45	45
Cetane index, min.+	D 4737	40	40
Distillation temperature, °F (°C)	D86		
IBP, typical#		350 (177)	375 (191)
10% typical#		385 (196)	430 (221)
50% typical#		425 (218)	510 (256)
90%+		500 (260) max.	625 (329) max.
End point#		500 (288) max.	675 (357) max.
Water and sediment %, max.	D 1796	0.05	0.05

*No. 2 diesel fuel may be used in city coach engine models that have been certified to pass federal and California emission standards.
#Not specified in ASTM D 975.
$By 1994 diesel fuel for U.S. highway vehicles will be limited to 0.05% sulfur content max.
+Differs from ASTM D 975.
Note 1: The cloud point should be 10°F (6°C) below the lowest expected fuel temperature to prevent clogging of fuel filters by wax crystals.
Note 2: When prolonged idling periods or cold weather conditions below 32°F (0°C) are encountered, the use of 1-D fuel is recommended.
Source: Courtesy of Detroit Diesel Corporation.

ing temperatures occur; therefore, during the test, boiling temperatures keep rising.

The temperature at which the first 10% of the fuel is recovered in the container is known as the 10% point; similarly, the temperature corresponding to 90% recovered is called the 90% point, and the highest boiling temperature reached at the end of the test is called the *endpoint*. The temperature at which the fuel vaporizes is more commonly called the *distillation temperature*.

Distillation Range

All diesel fuels are extracted from crude oil by a refining process that involves heating the crude to predetermined temperatures. The point at which various fuels are tapped off is known as the *distillation endpoint*. For example, if you look at Table 3–2, you can see that the endpoint of the preferred No. 2D grade fuel is listed as 675°F (357°C). This is the highest boiling temperature for this fuel. In other words, this diesel fuel will be completely evaporated or vaporized at this temperature.

The evaporation point of a diesel fuel becomes important to the operation of the engine combustion phase, since once the fuel is injected, the time that it takes to mix with the compressed air (oxygen) and change into a vapor from a liquid is known generally as the *ignition delay period*. Consider that if an engine developed a temperature at the end of the compression stroke of 550°F (288°C) while using a fuel with a

TABLE 3–3 *Properties of diesel fuels affecting performance.*

Property	Effect on Performance
Cetane number	Ignition quality measure—affects cold starting, smoke, and combustion
Sulfur content	Affects wear, deposits, and particulate emissions
Heating value	Affects power output and fuel economy
Volatility	Affects ease of starting and engine produces smoke
Flash point	Related to volatility and fire hazard in handling
API gravity	Related to heat content, affecting power and economy
Viscosity	Affects injector lubrication and atomization
Cloud and pour point	Affect low-temperature operation
Water and sediment	Affect life of fuel filters and injectors
Carbon residue	Measures residue in fuel—can influence combustion
Ash	Measures inorganic residues
Corrosion	Measures possible corrosive attack on metal parts

Source: Reprinted with permission by Chevron Research and Technology Company, a division of Chevron U.S.A. Inc.; copyright Chevron Research Company (1995).

distillation endpoint of 675°F (357°C), there would be a long ignition delay period caused by too low a combustion chamber temperature to readily vaporize the injected fuel. Poor engine performance would result. In most cases, however, if the cylinder temperature can reach 90% of the distillation temperature, successful and satisfactory ignition can occur. The 90% distillation temperature is shown in Table 3–2 along with the 50% and 10% specs. If possible, however, the full-range boiling point of the fuel should be used for proper fuel selection. The combustion chamber temperature depends on ambient or outside air temperature, engine speed, and load; therefore, poorer fuel vaporization tends to occur as ambient temperatures decrease and the engine is subjected to long periods of idling and/or light-load operation. Under such operating conditions, engines should use diesel fuels with lower distillation endpoint temperatures.

Cetane Number

Cetane number is a measure of the ignition quality of the fuel. It influences both the ease of starting and combustion roughness of an engine, because the ignition delay period is lengthened with a decrease in cetane number. A low cetane fuel permits a lot of the injected fuel to evaporate before the flame front actually begins. When the flame front begins, this previously injected fuel burns very rapidly, causing cylinder pressure to rise to very high peaks with resultant diesel knock.

Ignition delay was discussed in detail in Chapter 2. The duration of this delay is expressed in terms of cetane number (rating). Rapidly ignited fuels have

high cetane numbers (50 or above), whereas slowly ignited fuels have low cetane numbers (40 or below). The lower the ambient temperature, the greater the need for a fuel of a higher cetane rating so that it will ignite rapidly.

Difficult starting can be experienced if the cetane number of the fuel is too low. This can be accompanied by engine knock and puffs of white smoke during engine warm-up in cold weather.

High altitudes and low ambient temperatures require the use of a diesel fuel with an increased (higher) cetane number. Low-temperature starting is enhanced by the use of high-cetane fuel oil in the proportion of 1.5°F lower starting temperature for each cetane number increase in the fuel.

Current 1D and 2D diesel fuels have a cetane rating between 40 and 45. The cetane rating is actually a measure of the fuel oil's volatility; the higher the rating, the easier the engine will start and the smoother will be the combustion process within the ratings specified by the engine manufacturer.

Cetane rating differs from the octane rating that is used for gasoline. The higher the number of gasoline on the octane scale, the greater that fuel's resistance to self-ignition, which is a desirable property in gasoline engines with a high compression ratio. Using a low-octane fuel will cause preignition in a high compression engine.

The higher the cetane rating, the easier the fuel will ignite once injected into the diesel combustion chamber. In engines that are more sensitive to cetane number, however, the tendency toward black smoke is greater as the cetane number increases. This is due to

FIGURE 3–3 *Diesel fuel cetane number versus ignition delay. (Reprinted with permission by Chevron Research and Technology Company, a division of Chevron U.S.A. Inc.; copyright Chevron Research Company [1995].)*

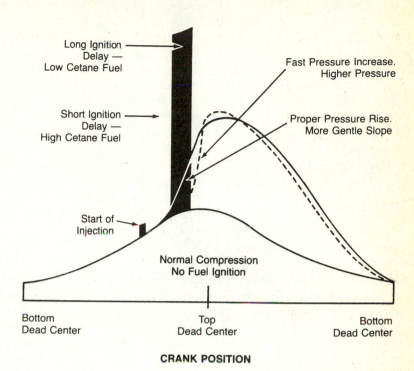

PRESSURE (and temperature) CYCLE IN A DIESEL ENGINE

Long Ignition Delay — Low Cetane Fuel

Short Ignition Delay — High Cetane Fuel

Fast Pressure Increase. Higher Pressure

Proper Pressure Rise. More Gentle Slope

Start of Injection

Normal Compression No Fuel Ignition

Bottom Dead Center

Top Dead Center

Bottom Dead Center

CRANK POSITION

the short ignition delay, which ensures that some raw fuel is sprayed into an established flame—which is why soot is produced. On the other hand, the use of a low cetane number fuel causes a longer ignition delay to occur once the fuel is injected into the combustion chamber, as well as harder starting in cold weather. Often, hexyl nitrate or amyl nitrate is added to the fuel at the refinery stage to increase the cetane number of the fuel, especially in areas that are subjected to cold-weather conditions.

Figure 3–3 illustrates conditions in the engine combustion chamber that result as a direct reflection of the cetane value or rating of the diesel fuel. When the delay is short, combustion is even and the engine runs smoothly.

Viscosity

Viscosity is a measure of the fuel's resistance to flow, and it will decrease as the fuel oil temperature increases. A high-viscosity (thick) fuel oil may cause extreme pressures in the injection system and will cause reduced atomization and vaporization of the fuel spray. See Figure 3–4.

Recommended fuel oil viscosity for high-speed diesel engines is generally in the region of 39 SSU

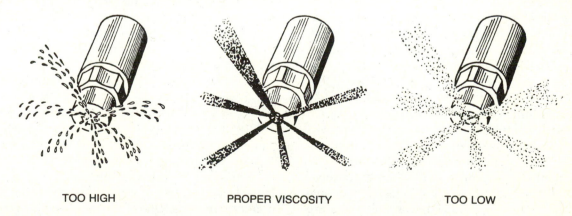

TOO HIGH

PROPER VISCOSITY

TOO LOW

FIGURE 3–4 Graphical representation of how diesel fuel viscosity can affect injection atomization and distribution. (Reprinted with permission by Chevron Research and Technology Company, a division of Chevron U.S.A. Inc.; copyright Chevron Research Company [1995].)

(seconds Saybolt universal) derived from a test that measures the time taken for a given quantity of fuel to flow through an orifice (restricted hole) in a tube. This viscosity rating of 39 SSU maximum provides good penetration into the combustion chamber and atomization of the fuel. The viscosity of diesel fuel also acts to lubricate the internal components of the injection system. The viscosity of diesel fuel is normally specified at 40°C (104°F). The Canadian average standard is between 1.2 and 4.1 centistokes (cSt), while the limits are 1.3 to 2.4 cSt for ASTM grade 1D and 1.9 to 4.1 cSt for grade 2D.

Gasoline has an API gravity rating of about 65; kerosene comes in at about 42; and average diesel fuel is about 35 to 36. Another interesting comparison between these three fuels is that gasoline has an almost nonexistent lubricating equality of 0.45 kinematic viscosity cSt at 40°C, while kerosene is 1.2 and diesel fuel runs between 1.9 and 3.4 kinematic viscosity cSt at 40°C. From this information, you can appreciate that use of other than a diesel fuel can cause serious problems as a result of lack of lubrication to injection system components. Many injection system components operate with clearances as small as 0.0025 mm (0.0000984 in.); therefore, it is imperative that the fuel used have an adequate viscosity to provide suitable lubrication for these finely lapped components. A high-viscosity (thick) oil may cause extreme pressures in the injection system and reduce atomization and vaporization of the fuel spray.

Carbon Residue

The amount of carbon residue left within the combustion chamber has a direct bearing on the engine deposits and cleanliness of combustion; therefore, the smaller the amount of carbon residue at the end of the combustion process, the longer the engine life will be and the cleaner the exhaust smoke. The amount of carbon in a fuel is determined by burning a given quantity in a sealed container until all that remains is carbon residue. Carbon residue is expressed as a percentage by weight of the original sample of the fuel oil.

Sulfur Content

Sulfur has a definite effect on the wear of the internal components of the engine, such as piston rings, pistons, valves, and cylinder liners as well as the crankshaft and connecting rod bearings. In addition, a fuel with high sulfur content requires more frequent changes of engine oil and filters due to the corrosive effects of the hydrogen sulfide in the fuel. There are two sulfur oxides in diesel fuel: sulfur dioxide (SO_2) and sulfur trioxide (SO_3). Sulfur formed during the combustion process reacts very rapidly with water

vapor in the exhaust and also forms sulfuric acid. In addition, in cold engines, condensation on the cylinder walls (dew point) causes the sulfur oxides to go into solution, thereby forming corrosive acids that can break down the engine lube oil, attack metal parts, and contribute to engine deposits. Always refer to the lube oil recommendations of the engine manufacturers to prevent these conditions from happening.

Low-Sulfur Fuels

For many years the ASTM D975-92 specification included five grades of diesel fuel: low-sulfur No. 1D, low-sulfur No. 2D, No. 1D, No. 2D, and No. 4D. Into the early 1990s, fuel sulfur in the No. 2D fuel from U.S. refineries was running about 0.25% to 0.30%. On October 1, 1993, however, regulations established by the EPA as a result of the U.S. Clean Air Act went into effect. Now operators of on-highway diesel equipment are required to use fuel that contains no more than 0.05% by weight sulfur fuel. Prior to this date, up to 0.5% sulfur by weight was allowable. Since off-highway diesel equipment is currently exempt from using this low-sulfur fuel, diesel fuel not intended for on-highway use (1D, 2D, and 4D) *must* be dyed with 1.4-dialkyl amino anthraquinone—a blue dye—to allow easy recognition of regulated and nonregulated fuels. For nonregulated diesel fuel, which is often characterized by a yellow-like color, the addition of the blue dye results in a blue-green or green appearance to the fuel. In addition, as illustrated in Table 3–2, the new low-sulfur diesel fuel must have a cetane index of at least 40, or a maximum aromatic content of 35 volume percent. The new U.S. EPA regulations also stipulate that when diesel fuel is blended with any other fuels such as jet fuels or kerosene, the resulting blend is considered diesel fuel and must meet the low-sulfur content levels if used in on-highway vehicles. The EPA will enforce these strict regulations for any on-highway fuels with sulfur in excess of 0.55%. Under the guidelines of the U.S. Clean Air Act, penalties for misfueling can range up to $25,000 per day, per violation, for on-highway vehicles.

On October 1, 1994, the Canadian oil industry voluntarily agreed to make available the same low-sulfur diesel fuel in Canada. Now that Mexico is part of NAFTA (North American Free Trade Agreement), we can expect to see it act similarly. The 0.05% sulfur fuel is mandated in Japan for October 1997.

This new clean diesel fuel is part of the technological changes being driven by ever-increasing air quality standards. One of the diesel exhaust emissions measured by the U.S. EPA is *particulates*, which compose a large portion of the black smoke emitted from a diesel exhaust stack. Lowering the sulfur content in the diesel fuel lowers the particulate exhaust emissions and helps to protect exhaust after-treatment devices in engines that require these devices to comply with mandated EPA exhaust emissions limits. The energy content of the low-sulfur fuel will not change from that of the higher-sulfur fuel used previously. This low-sulfur diesel fuel differs from off-highway fuel in that the off-highway higher sulfur fuel has a greenish appearance (due to the addition of the blue dye). All truck OEMs are required to label "Low-Sulfur Diesel Fuel Only" on the vehicle instrument panel as well as next to the filler inlet of the fuel tank(s).

Before the introduction of low-sulfur diesel fuel, the actual percentage of sulfur contained in a diesel fuel varied between suppliers and in different regions of North America. The percentage could range from a low of 0.08% for a No. 1 grade fuel to between an average of 0.1% and 0.28% for most No. 2 grade fuels. However, the sulfur content for off-highway and industrial diesel engines often exceeds even these averages.

Problems with High Sulfur Fuels

The sulfur content of the diesel fuel has a direct bearing on the life expectancy of a number of engine components. Active sulfur in a diesel fuel also attacks and corrodes injection system components in addition to contributing to combustion chamber and injection system deposits. When the continuous use of high-sulfur fuels greater than 0.5% is unavoidable, engine lubricant selection and oil drain intervals must be modified. The lube oil breaks down quicker due to the additional sulfur diluting the oil and causing sulfuric acid to form when it mixes with water vapor. Consequently, engine manufacturers will specify that a correct oil drain interval must be determined by lube oil analysis. Generally, the factor used to determine the condition of the engine oil is known as the TBN (total base number). A lubricant with a TBN above 10 is usually recommended. A reduction of the TBN to one-third of the initial new lube oil value can be used to determine a general guideline for a drain interval. TBN is a measure of a lube oil's ability to neutralize acids. TBN is important to control deposits in four-cycle engines and to neutralize the effects of high-sulfur fuels in all makes of diesel engines. As TBN increases, sulfated metallic ash residue deposits also increase. This ash residue is related to the oil's additive composition and is significant in predicting lubricants that may cause valve distress under certain operating conditions.

Initially, some fleet users complained that low-sulfur diesel fuel was causing reduced lubricity and increased wear in certain types of fuel injection pumps, as well as fuel pump O-ring and seal leakage problems. The seals in question were throttle shaft O-rings and gaskets made with a compound called Buna N, or nitrile rubber; some seals failed after as little as 3 week's exposure to the low-sulfur fuel. Some fleets paid from $200 to $600 per unit for repairs, with a consequent loss in vehicle productivity. Follow-up studies have indicated that these seal failures seemed to occur in older engines whose O-rings exhibited a compression set and were no longer elastic when exposed to lower aromatic fuels.

Another problem with the low-sulfur fuels is that their aromatic content was changed as a result of the hydrotreating process at the refinery. The severity of the hydrotreating process may contribute to the removal of *trace polar compounds* that compete for metal surfaces. When attached to metal surfaces, these compounds provide the boundary lubrication that is affected by trace amounts of nitrogen and oxygen compounds in the fuel. The fuel's viscosity is an indicator of the level of hydrodynamic lubrication! Therefore, diesel fuels of equal sulfur levels may exhibit different properties of lubricity. Aftermarket additive companies offer products that have lubricity additives and corrosion inhibitors to restore some lubricity to the fuel.

Major oil companies are aware of some of these problems and have reformulated, or are in the process of reformulating, their low-sulfur diesel fuel to prevent failure of injection components due to low lubricity problems. Customers will be using a cleaner burning diesel fuel that allows their engines to live longer and to emit fewer exhaust particulates.

Flash Point

Flash point has nothing to do with the combustion phase or performance of the fuel in the engine. Rather, it is a measure of the temperature at which the fuel oil vapors flash when in the presence of an open flame. Safety in handling and storage are the only points warranting consideration for flash point.

Cloud Point

Cloud point is the temperature at which the wax crystals in the fuel (paraffin base) begin to settle out, resulting in plugging of the fuel filter. This condition exists when cold ambient temperatures are encountered and is the reason that a thermostatically controlled fuel heater is required on vehicles that are to operate in cold-weather environments. Failure to use a fuel heater will prevent fuel from flowing through the filter, and the engine will not run. Cloud point generally occurs 5° to 8°C (9° to 14°F) above the pour point.

Pour Point

The pour point of the fuel determines the lowest temperature at which the fuel can be pumped through the system. Pour point is expressed as the temperature 5°F above the level at which the oil becomes solid or refuses to flow. Pour point averages about 10°F lower than the cloud point, although flow improvers can result in satisfactory fuel flow at about 9°C colder temperatures than is possible with untreated fuel.

Ash Content

Contained within the fuel oil are ash-forming materials in the form of abrasive solids or soluble metallic soaps. The solids cause wear of injection equipment, pistons, rings, and liners and also increase engine deposits. Ash from soluble soaps contributes to engine deposits and wear. Determination of ash content is established by burning a given weight of fuel oil in an open container until all the carbon deposits are consumed. Weight of the remaining ash is then expressed as a percentage of the weight of the original test sample of fuel oil.

Corrosion

Corrosion is the tendency of the fuel oil to react with copper, brass, or bronze parts of the fuel system. This specification does not indicate the corrosion of steel parts of the engine, which may occur from the use of high-sulfur fuels with low engine temperatures. Corrosion is determined by immersing a strip of polished copper in the fuel for a period of 3 hours at 212°F; the results are interpreted as (1) slight tarnish, (2) moderate tarnish, (3) dark tarnish, or (4) corrosion.

DIESEL FUEL OPERATING PROBLEMS

Fuel selection can cause operating problems in an engine such as unacceptable concentrations of exhaust smoke. White smoke in a diesel engine is caused by minute particles of unburned fuel—generally in cold-weather operation, especially on initial engine start-up—and is caused by low air temperatures in the engine. This condition disappears when the engine warms up unless there is water entering the cylinder.

Black smoke is generally caused by air starvation, some mechanical defect such as a faulty injector, use of a fuel with too high a boiling point, engine overload, or overfueling the engine through maladjustment. Blue/gray smoke results from oil being burned in the combustion chamber and usually is more noticeable on cold starts than when the engine warms up. The engine needs mechanical repair.

To prevent fuel-line freeze-up due to minute water particles in the fuel, a fuel-line water filter can

be used. Also, methyl or isopropyl alcohol can be added in the ratio of 0.0125%, or 1 part in 8000, which equals about 1 pint of isopropyl alcohol (isopropanol) to every 125 gallons of diesel fuel.

Fuel Temperatures

The temperature of diesel fuel can greatly affect the power output of the engine. Recall that when the ambient temperature drops to the cloud point of the fuel, wax crystals start to settle out. This action can reduce the fuel flow through the filter and lead to starvation, and in some cases the engine will not start. Temperature-controlled fuel heaters are now available from a variety of sources for protection against wax formation in cold-weather operation.

All engines in use today utilize a large percentage of the fuel circulated through the pump or injectors for cooling and lubrication purposes. Heat picked up by this fuel is returned to the fuel tank(s) where it circulates and cools. In certain applications, however, a lack of a constant flow of air around the tank(s) can result in an increase in fuel temperature. The lower the fuel level within the tank(s) system, the faster the temperature will increase.

In the summer when high ambient temperatures can be encountered, the temperature of the diesel fuel can also affect the engine's performance. Fuel temperature should run between 90° and 95°F (32° to 35°C). For every 10°F increase over this temperature, the engine loses about 1% of its gross horsepower due to expansion of the fuel (less dense); this is 1.5% on a turbocharged engine. Maximum fuel temperatures should never be allowed to exceed 150°F (65.5°C), because damage to the fuel injection components can result (lack of lubrication) as well as possible flash point danger.

Fuel temperature can be maintained at an acceptable level by attempting to keep the fuel tank reasonably full. Nevertheless, in applications where space limits the size of the fuel tank, or in cases where the tank is exposed to high ambient temperatures such as in a day tank in a marine application, a fuel cooler may be necessary.

Fuel Consumption

The temperature of a diesel fuel adversely affects the fuel mileage of a truck. This occurs because warmer fuel expands; therefore, a less dense charge of fuel is metered for injection purposes. Fuel mileage on heavy-duty trucks can vary significantly depending on factors such as driver expertise, operating terrain, weather changes, and mechanical problems on the vehicle. Ambient air temperature also can have a major effect on fuel mileage. Studies have shown that, on average, tank mileage decreases by several tenths of a mile per gallon in winter, and in very low ambient air conditions, a power loss is noticeable. The use of AAAC (air-to-air aftercoolers) is now fairly common on turbocharged heavy-duty diesel engines; the aftercooler is designed to reduce the charge air temperature of the turbo boost pressure. Most AAACs are capable of reducing the air charge under full-load operating conditions from approximately 300°F (149°C) to 100° to 110°F (38° to 43°C) at the intake manifold. The combination of cooler fuel and denser air tends to make the engine perform better, and truck drivers confirm that the engine does seem to have more flywheel horsepower, particularly in cool or colder weather.

The increased flywheel horsepower is usually offset by the fact that an increase in horsepower is needed to move the vehicle down the road against the denser ambient air through which the vehicle is moving. Other negatives are the higher rolling resistance of the tires and the increased friction in the drive train and wheel bearings. Detailed tests conducted by various engine-truck manufacturers indicate that the overall temperature effect on tank mileage is about a 2% reduction for every 10°F drop in ambient temperature, with a variation of approximately ½ mile per gallon (mpg), or 0.8 km, due to wind velocity and direction. On a test run, when the ambient temperature was 80°F (27°C) on a given day, the truck averaged 6.5 mpg (10.46 km); on a 30°F (−1°C) day, the same truck averaged only 5.85 mpg (9.41 km).

Injector Cleaners

Some commerical corporations offer a chemical injector cleaner that can be added to the diesel fuel. The cleaner is designed to remove carbon deposits from injectors and has the same properties as diesel fuel (flash point, specific gravity, cetane number, initial and final boiling point, and so forth). It has the same energy content as diesel fuel and thus does not adversely affect engine performance. For example, Cummins offers an injector cleaner known as Premium Plus which is claimed to improve emissions, clean the fuel system, reduce wear on the fuel pump and injector system, improve diesel fuel lubricity, have no effect on seals and gasket materials, have no effect on paint materials, and provide corrosion protection. Resin binders within the fuel tend to hold the carbon deposits together and to the injector parts; therefore, this cleaner allows its chemicals to attack the binders and cut the deposits into molecular particles that are soluble in the mixture of cleaner diesel fuel. The particles are injected into the cylinder along with the fuel and burned; they leave through the exhaust as normal combustion by-products. Cummins recommends that

1 quart (0.94 L) of the cleaner be added to the fuel every 10,000 miles (16,093 km) after filling the fuel tanks to minimize foaming of the cleaner.

There are a number of commercially available injector cleaning machines that can be connected to the engine fuel system without removing the injectors. Such systems are designed to flush the fuel system and injectors. A chemical cleaner is mixed with the diesel fuel while the engine is run for about 30 to 60 minutes to remove any varnish or carbon from the fuel system.

Fuel Additives

Generally, no additional aftermarket fuel additives are required when a suitable fuel is used. Certain characteristics of lower-quality fuel can be improved however, by treatment with aftermarket additives, which can be classified into the following six general types: cetane improvers, emission control additives, detergents, combustion improvers, smoke suppressants, and cold-weather flow improvers.

Table 3–4 illustrates the typical additives used by fuel refiners in automotive truck diesel fuels. Although the table shows barium being used as an antismoke additive, this is no longer true because of environmental concerns. A number of commercially available fuel additives are manufactured by several companies for both gasoline and diesel fuels. These additives are not normally required, because the fuel refiner ensures that its specific fuel meets, and in many cases exceeds, federal specifications.

Geographical location and operating conditions, along with type of fuel storage and handling and maintenance, play a part in determining whether some of these commercially available fuel additives might help a base fuel.

Three of the more commonly used aftermarket additives are described next:

1. *Cold-weather diesel additive.* This contains a pour-point depressant as well as a fuel conditioner and allows the fuel to flow down to 40°C below zero. This will assist in preventing waxing of the fuel in cold ambients so that the fuel filters do not become clogged.

2. *Diesel fuel treatment.* This additive eases starting and prevents corrosion; thereby it is claimed to keep the fuel lines, pumps, and injectors clean with an engine performance improvement.

3. *Biocide and conditioner.* This additive prevents fungi and bacteria from growing in the diesel fuel, either in bulk storage or inside the tank or fuel lines. Fuel kept in storage longer than 12 months can start to break

TABLE 3–4   Automotive diesel fuel additives (type and function)[a]

Additive	Type	Function
Detergents	Polyglycols, basic nitrogen-containing surfactants	Prevent injector deposits, increase injector life
Dispersants	Nitrogen-containing surfactants	Peptize soot and products of fuel oxidation, increase filter life
Metal deactivators	Cholating agents	Inhibit gum formation
Rust and corrosion inhibitors	Amines, amine carboxylates and carboxylic acids	Prevent rust and corrosion in pipelines and fuel systems
Cetane improvers	Nitrate esters	Increase cetane number
Flow improvers	Polymers, wax crystal modifiers	Reduce pour point
Antismoke additives or smoke suppressants	Organic barium compounds	Reduce exhaust smoke
Oxidation inhibitors	Low-molecular-weight amines	Minimize deposits in filters and injectors
Biocides	Boron compounds	Inhibit growth of bacteria and microorganisms

[a]No commercial additives reduce cloud point.
Source: Reprinted with permission (copyright 1989), Society of Automotive Engineers, Inc.

down. Microorganisms actually metabolize fuel, creating stringy, gooey masses that can plug filters and corrode metal components. Rubber and tank coatings also can be damaged. Evidence of fungi growth is usually noticed on filters as slimy, unfilterable blobs that may appear black, brown, or greenish.

Fuel additives specifically *not* recommended by most high-speed heavy-duty truck diesel engine manufacturers include lube oil mixed with diesel fuel and addition of gasoline to blend the fuel for better winter-operation characteristics. Several singe-purpose additives are available, however, that raise the cetane number by up to three to four numbers, depending on the base stock; reduce the cloud and pour points; prevent oxidative and bacterial deterioration in fuel storage; and tend to reduce exhaust smoke. Some additives on the market can have a positive effect on diesel fuel of lower quality. Typical advantages of these additives are that they allow No. 2D fuel to flow more easily in cold weather, eliminate the need to blend in No. 1D or kerosene during cold-weather winter operation, prevent fuel line and filter plugging, boost cetane, keep nozzles and injectors clean, improve fuel stability, and reduce exhaust smoke and pollution.

Before selecting an aftermarket fuel additive for diesel fuel, the equipment owner should determine from published information whether the product will cause these changes:

- Alter the cetane number of the fuel
- Increase the ash content of the fuel, which can cause increased engine wear rates, particularly from ash deposits in the piston ring groove area
- Destabilize fuel in storage, form particularly abrasive ash, or produce toxic exhaust emissions, if the additive contains any metallic compounds. If an additive contains halogenated compounds such as chlorine, fluorine, bromine, and sulfur, the lube oil can suffer through corrosive action as well as form sludge.
- Increase the fuel vapor pressure and possibly reduce the flash point of the fuel, which could create a safety hazard
- Change or alter the viscosity of the diesel fuel. Remember that one of the functions of a diesel fuel is to act as a lubricant for all of the injection system components.
- Form sludge in the fuel tank as a result of chemical reaction with sediment or water
- Change the cloud point or the pour point of the fuel

Some fuel additives can provide temporary benefits; however, they should not exclude proper fuel-handling practices. Although a fuel filter/water separator can help in trapping water before it reaches the filters and injection equipment, when water contamination is suspected, the use of a biocide treatment such as Biobor protects against microbe growth or black slime buildup in the fuel tank and filters.

Diesel Fuel Quality Tester

Often the cause of a lack-of-power complaint can be attributed directly to the quality of the fuel being used in the engine. Many hours can be spent in analyzing and troubleshooting performance complaints, only to find that nothing is out of adjustment and the engine is mechanically sound. Remember, the wrong grade of fuel can affect the horsepower developed by the engine. To determine if diesel fuel quality should be considered as a possible problem area when diagnosing a lack-of-power complaint, use a simple *diesel fuel quality tester*, which is basically a hydrometer. Figure 3–5 illustrates such a tester.

INTRODUCTION TO ALTERNATIVE FUELS

Diesel fuel is a complex mixture of hydrocarbons, which can include paraffins, olefins, naphthenes, and aromatics. Nationwide trends have led fuel oil distillers to reduce significantly the percentage of sulfur products in diesel fuels as one method of improving the combustion phase within the engine, and more importantly, to reduce exhaust emissions so that the existing 1994 and even more stringent 1998 EPA exhaust emission standards can be achieved.

There are strong governmental moves, from the state, province, and federal standpoint, to quickly and progressively reduce the exhaust emissions from passenger cars, light trucks, and heavy-duty trucks and buses. Legislation enacted in states such as Colorado, California, and Texas has severely curtailed the use of polluting internal combustion engines after the 1995 model year. Consequently, there has been and continues to be a tremendous amount of research and development taking place regarding the use of alternative types of fuels that can be applied to both gasoline and diesel internal combustion engines.

Although much has been written about alternative types of power plants, the basic design concept of the internal combustion engine as we know it today remains the most feasible option for the foreseeable future, albeit with dramatic improvements to the types of material used in its construction,

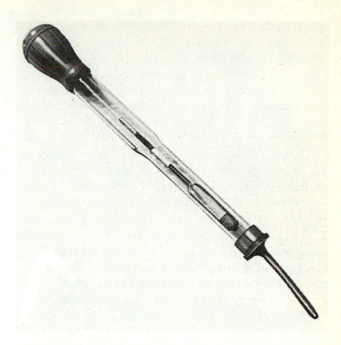

FIGURE 3–5 Diesel fuel quality tester. (Courtesy of Kent-Moore Division, SPX Corporation.)

combustion system changes, and alternative fuels available.

All available fuels can be placed in one of the following nine categories for use in either gasoline or diesel engines:

1. Diesel fuel
2. Gasoline
3. Methanol
4. Dimethyl ether
5. Ethanol
6. Reformulated gasoline or diesel fuel
7. Propane (gaseous fuel)
8. Compressed natural gas (gaseous fuel)
9. Hydrogen

Before we discuss alternative fuels in more detail, let us reconsider diesel fuel and gasoline.

Diesel Fuel Advantages

In this chapter we have already discussed the characteristics of diesel fuel. The main advantage of the diesel engine, of course, is its ability to extract more energy from a given amount of diesel fuel than any other type of engine now in use. The high thermal efficiency factor of the diesel engine certainly makes it the most feasible option at this time for heavy-duty truck operation, as well as a potential candidate for expansion into passenger cars, where it is very strong in

Great Britain and Europe. Improvements made to diesel fuel as well as improvements to the engine combustion phase now allow the diesel engine to meet the stringent EPA exhaust emissions standards.

To its benefit, the diesel has undergone dramatic design changes with regard to the types of material used in its construction; the use of high-efficiency air-to-air aftercoolers; a positive swing to the use of unit fuel injectors, with injection pressures higher than an inline pump system; the use of electronically controlled fuel injection; redesigned turbochargers; matched intake and exhaust flow systems; four-valve-head design improvements; low-flow cooling systems; and reductions in frictional losses to drive accessory components. Major high-speed diesel engine manufacturers, such as Detroit Diesel, Caterpillar, Cummins, Mack, and Volvo, are all committed to using on-board computers to control the fuel management aspects of their engines, and major manufacturers of fuel injection equipment such as Robert Bosch, Zexel USA, Nippondenso Company Ltd., and Lucas Automotive, Inc. all offer electronically controlled diesel fuel injection systems. Information presented in Chapter 2 dealing with combustion systems indicated that the diesel engine exhaust soot and particulate emissions as well as the NO_x (nitric oxide) content must be improved if the diesel engine is to remain the leading power plant for heavy-duty trucks and buses. It is possible that along with alternative fuels that can be burned within the diesel engine, we may see some merging of the technologies applicable to both gasoline and diesel engines.

Gasoline

Gasoline is a more volatile liquid than diesel fuel, and it is the fuel of choice for spark-ignited engines. However, gasoline has an energy content about 10% lower than that for an equivalent volume of diesel fuel. Gasoline weighs approximately 6 lb (2.7 kg) per U.S. gallon or 7.2 lb (3.2 kg) per Imperial gallon; therefore, it is lighter than diesel fuel. Depending on the grade of gasoline selected and whether we are dealing with U.S. or Imperial gallons, gasoline has a content of from 113,000 to 147,000 Btu, or 119,000 to 155,000 kilojoules (kJ), which is about 10% to 15% less than that for diesel fuel. Gasoline engines are thus less thermally efficient than diesel engines; in other words, the gasoline engine extracts less energy from each gallon because it has fewer Btu of heat energy release than does the diesel engine. In addition, since the diesel has a higher compression ratio, it extracts a greater heat release from each Btu of heat. Nevertheless, their lighter weight, faster acceleration, lower noise, lower exhaust soot emissions, lower degree of odor, and easier starta-

bility in cold weather have made gasoline engines a more socially acceptable choice for passenger cars. Exhaust emissions from gasoline engines are basically the same as those from diesel engines, with the exception of soot (carbon). These exhaust emissions include poisonous carbon monoxide (CO), nitrogen oxides (NO_x), some hydrocarbons (HC), and some carbon dioxide (CO_2). The NO_x and HCs tend to react photochemically with sunlight to form smog, while carbon dioxide tends to produce global-warming effects.

Major advancements in the design of gasoline engines have included the adoption of throttle body injection or multiport fuel injection along with distributor-less ignition systems, all of which are controlled electronically by an on-board computer. The adoption of exhaust-gas-driven turbochargers, gear- or belt-driven superchargers, or a "comprex" type of compressor, along with aftercoolers, four-valve cylinder heads, and combustion chamber improvements, has dramatically increased the miles per gallon (km/L) or thermal efficiency of the gasoline engine. The use of catalytic converters and exhaust gas oxygen sensors working in conjunction with the on-board computer has drastically reduced the exhaust emissions levels from gasoline engines. The fact remains, however, that these exhaust emissions have to be lowered to an acceptable level; therefore, extensive research and testing is under way to try to meet the stringent EPA emissions standards while using gasoline or an alternative fuel in the spark ignition engine.

METHANOL

Methanol can be produced from resources that are readily available worldwide from natural gas or flare gas. More importantly, methanol can be extracted from coal, of which both Canada and the United States have large, confirmed, and easily mineable deposits. Obtaining methanol from coal costs about 50% more than obtaining it from natural gas. Although methanol can also be extracted from wood, demands for wood products in other areas limit this supply. Biomass garbage can also be used to extract methanol; however, until such times as government legislation or improved technology extraction is available, garbage is not a major source for methanol. Methanol is formed by the synthesis of carbon monoxide and nitrogen from either one of the feedstocks just mentioned above. Since methanol is a liquid, it lends itself to easy adaptability for the internal combustion engine, which already operates on liquid-type fuels; therefore, there is a strong drive toward using this alternative fuel in internal combustion engines. Because of its excellent antiknock qualities, methanol is well suited for use in spark ignition (Otto cycle) engines that currently use gasoline.

Methanol is available in "neat" or "near neat" forms. *Neat* methanol is defined as M100, which is 100% methanol; *near neat* is defined as a methanol blend, with the most popular being M85, which contains 85% methanol and 15% unleaded gasoline. Methanol contains about 57,000 Btu/gallon of heat energy. Methanol, an alcohol fuel, has a chemical formula of CH_3OH, meaning that it is composed of carbon and hydrogen plus up to 50% oxygen by weight. It is similar in many respects to a hydrocarbon fuel such as gasoline and diesel. Methanol is also known as an oxygenated fuel, since it tends to carry this high oxygen-by-weight content into the combustion cycle. Hydroxy radical (OH) is also present in methanol.

Methanol is now being used for research and development purposes in a number of diesel-powered city bus fleets in the United States and Canada, with the major engines in use being two-stroke-cycle 92 series engines manufactured by Detroit Diesel. Using the DDEC (Detroit Diesel electronic controls), these bus engines have returned excellent results in regard to their ability to meet the tougher exhaust emissions standards for the 1990s.

The use of M85 methanol for a spark-ignited engine does not require major design modifications. The engine does require, however, adjustment to the air/fuel ratio, and an increase in the piston compression ratio to take advantage of the higher-octane rating of methanol, which is about 102 for M85 and closer to 110 for M100. Compare this to regular gasoline, which has an average octane rating of between 87 and 89; premium gasoline has an octane value of around 91 to 94 maximum. Adjustment of spark timing is also required to ensure that the difference in energy content in methanol, which is approximately 49% of that of gasoline and only 44% of diesel fuel, can be utilized to its maximum potential since the combustion characteristics associated with it, which differ from those of a gasoline or diesel engine, can be used advantageously.

Typical approximate heat values of gasoline, diesel, methanol, and ethanol are shown in Table 3–5.

SPECIAL NOTE: Alcohol fuels such as methanol and ethanol have a much greater cooling effect than does gasoline or diesel fuel when they are changed from a liquid to a vapor state. The common term used to describe this transition is *latent heat of vaporization*, which is an indication of the actual cooling effect on the cylinder/combustion chamber when liquids are vaporized for combustion purposes. This theory is a major consideration in the successful operation of internal combustion engines. If you consider that gasoline has a latent heat of vaporization of 800 Btu/gallon compared with 3300 Btu/gallon for methanol, this means that methanol has more than four times the cooling effect when it changes from a liquid to a vapor. This increased cooling effect, although providing a denser air/fuel mixture and subsequent higher engine power, mainly makes up for the reduced Btu content of the methanol fuel. Consequently, in warm-weather operation, this cooling effect has definite advantages and is one of the reasons that high-performance cars and racing vehicles choose to use methanol as a fuel source.

Methanol in Diesel Engines

The preceding information about methanol provides you with a good overview of the potential benefits for this liquid as an alternative fuel. We concentrate now on how methanol would react when used in a heavy-duty high-speed diesel engine.

The major benefit of using methanol as a fuel source in diesel engines is that it produces lower exhaust emission of particulates and nitrogen oxide. Methanol has a very low cetane value compared to conventional diesel fuel, approximately 3 versus 40 to 45 for diesel, so methanol is not suitable for use in an unmodified diesel engine because of its poor ignition quality. To use methanol successfully in a diesel engine, we have to employ either a glow plug (hot surface ignition) or a spark plug, and once the engine is

TABLE 3–5   *Heat values in Btu per gallon of various liquid fuels*

Fuel type	Btu/U.S. gal	Energy content compared to diesel fuel (%)	Energy content compared to gasoline (%)
No. 2 diesel	130,000 (LHV—36 API)	100	113
Gasoline	115,400 (LHV)	89	100
Methanol	56,600	44	49
Ethanol	75,700	58	66

running, high recirculation of hot exhaust gases is necessary to provide an auto-ignition capability for the methanol. The other option is to use fuel additives that contain ignition improvers. In a diesel engine the methanol is introduced into the combustion chamber; therefore, engine wear rates tend to be comparable to or less than that for an engine running on diesel fuel. More importantly, combustion with methanol produces reduced hydrocarbon emissions. Tests have indicated however, that the use of methanol reduces the engine lube oil's alkalinity reserve. Consequently, the oil's TBN (total base number) decreases. TBN is simply a measure of the lube oil's reserve alkalinity, or its ability to neutralize corrosive acids formed during combustion. Therefore, research and development are under way to counteract this situation by developing crankcase oils that will not react unfavorably to the use of methanol. The high heat of vaporization, or the fact that methanol does not vaporize quite as readily as does gasoline or diesel fuel, has a detrimental effect on engine startability in cold conditions. In fact, with the use of M100 (100% methanol), starting problems can occur at temperatures below 60°F (15.5°C).

Methanol-Fueled Engines

The first major OEM to receive U.S. and California emission certification in 1991 was Detroit Diesel for its 6V-92TA transit bus engine. After 8 years of development, this engine model was certified as a heavy-duty bus engine to run on M100 (100% methanol). In converting its engine to operate on methanol, which has a very low compression ignition quality, Detroit Diesel adapted its DDEC system to the methanol bus program. In addition, with the gear-driven blower being used for scavenging of exhaust gases, the DDEC system was programmed to recycle a percentage of these hot exhaust gases. A bypass air system meters and mixes the correct amounts of fresh air and retained exhaust gases to maintain the right temperature for compression ignition of the low-cetane-value methanol.

To start the engine on methanol, it is necessary to employ glow plugs located in a modified cylinder head, which is shown in Figure 3–6. The glow plugs are turned off when the engine reaches a predetermined operating temperature, which will allow the recirculated exhaust gases and fresh air to sustain compression ignition of the injected methanol. Methanol tends to swell O-ring seals, particularly in the unit injector, so a number of material changes were necessary to avoid this.

A substantial number of these methanol engines are in field service operation. Bus fleets that use the engines report that although methanol appears to match diesel fuel in performance, it is more expensive to operate: it takes about 2.5 times the amount of methanol to do what one U.S. gallon (3.785 L) of diesel fuel would do. In addition, some of the bus fleets

FIGURE 3–6 Unit fuel injector and glow plug arrangement for use in a two-stroke-cycle methanol-fueled engine. (Courtesy of Detroit Diesel Corporation.)

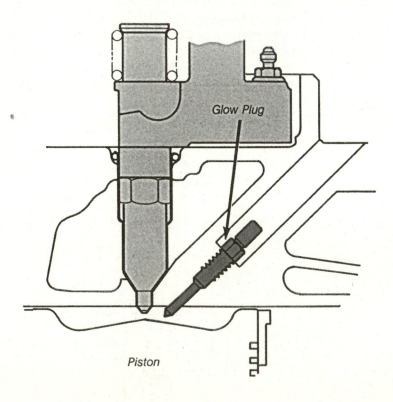

Glow Plug

Piston

report that the maintenance schedule for the methanol engines is almost doubled. Fuel filter changeouts are more frequent and injector life is shorter, although this can be extended by the use of a fuel additive made by Lubrizol, which adds about 1 cent a gallon to the cost of the fuel. Safety is another factor because of the toxicity of methanol.

Detroit Diesel, with both its 6V-92TA and Series 50G four-stroke-cycle natural gas engines, seems to be heading more toward the use of gaseous fuels than liquid methanol. Given the abundance of natural gas in both Canada and the United States, either CNG or LNG (liquified natural gas) is appearing as a more viable alternative.

DIMETHYL ETHER

Recent tests by Haldor Topsoe Inc., a Danish chemical company, in collaboration with Amoco and Navistar in the United States and the Austrian diesel engine research institute AVL, have shown that DME (dimethyl ether) is a clean-burning liquid fuel. When DME is used in diesel engines, exhaust emissions contain almost no soot particles, zero sulfur, a reduction in unburned hydrocarbons, and only approximately 20% of the normal level of NO_x; only CO_2 (carbon dioxide) emissions remain. This fuel could be a major candidate to meet the tough emissions standards that California plans to enact in 1998, particularly for diesel-powered equipment, since in testing DME exceeds the projected exhaust emissions limitations for both soot particles and oxides of nitrogen in g/hp/hr (grams per horsepower per hour).

In addition to its remarkable cleanliness, DME has a heat efficiency equal to diesel fuel, that is, returning close to 43% thermal efficiency. DME can be derived from methanol or natural gas and is prominent on the list of potential alternative fuels.

ETHANOL

Ethanol is an alcohol fuel that is now widely used in the United States as a gasoline extender, due to its ability to increase the octane level of gasoline. Approximately 10% of ethanol is used per gallon of gasoline, and the mixture is marketed under the name of *gasohol* in some areas. The ethanol, with an octane rating of 102, serves as an antiknock agent in spark-ignited engines. Since the early 1970s when the first energy crisis surfaced, ethanol has been used extensively in Brazil. The Brazilian government adopted a national energy policy to promote the extensive use of 100% ethanol fuel based on the country's ability to replenish its base feedstock continually from the large amounts of sugarcane and corn grown in Brazil.

Ethanol can also be manufactured from other agricultural products, such as barley, wheat, potatoes, and sugar beets. Most raw feedstocks are converted to starch first and then changed into sugar, where the ethanol is extracted by a distillation process. If sugar beets or sugarcane is used, the starch does not have to be converted to sugar in the actual manufacturing process. Little research has been gathered about cold-weather operation and emission controls that would be necessary in the colder ambient operating environments found in North America. We do know that ethanol use in cold-start and cold-driveability situations is worse than that for its other alcohol partner, methanol.

In Brazil, spark-ignited engines are generally of a dual-fuel nature: that is, they require initial start-up on gasoline, then a switch over to pure ethanol. This is due to the factor of high latent heat of vaporization, which we discussed earlier (see the special note for methanol). Ethanol has a latent heat of vaporization of 2600 Btu/gallon; for gasoline, it is only 800 Btu/gallon. Thus, ethanol has more than three times the cooling effect of gasoline, which affects its ability to vaporize in cold weather, even in temperatures as high as 40°F (4.5°C). In addition, ethanol has a heat energy value of only about 66% that of gasoline, and its emissions output parallels that for methanol described earlier. The chemical symbol for ethanol is C_2H_5OH. Ethanol differs from conventional hydrocarbon fuels in that it contains hydroxy radical (OH) in addition to both carbon and hydrogen. Therefore, ethanol contains about 35% oxygen by weight, giving it an approximate Btu content of about 76,000 Btu/gallon.

One of the major drawbacks of using ethanol, clean burning as it is, is that it emits larger quantities of CO_2 (carbon dioxide), which the U.S. EPA has directed to be reduced substantially. Current cost to produce ethanol is approximately four times that of gasoline. In the United States the federal government would have to subsidize the production of this alternative fuel to the amount of about 60 cents per gallon to keep the price at the pump competitive with gasoline. A suggested E85 fuel mix consisting of 85% ethanol and 15% conventional gasoline is one option that is being studied in the United States for use in spark-ignited engines; however, much research is still required before it could be considered as a direct replacement for gasoline.

COMPRESSED NATURAL GAS

Compressed natural gas (CNG) has been used for approximately 60 years to power internal combustion engines. World resources of natural gas are vast.

Sources of synthetic natural gas, such as coal gasification, sea kelp, and biomass, are other options. Natural gas is composed mainly of methane (CH_4), but hydrocarbons having a higher carbon-to-hydrogen ratio, such as ethane, propane, and butane, can also be present in natural gas. Natural gas can contain as much as 20% hydrocarbon. During the processing stage of natural gas, hydrocarbon content includes the removal of impurities, higher hydrocarbons, and water vapor. Today, many gasoline-powered vehicles have been converted to run on cheaper natural gas, specifically taxis and light delivery vehicles, particularly in North America. Much research is now under way to convert heavy-duty high-speed diesel truck and bus engines to run on natural gas. A number of companies in the United States and Canada have proved the feasibility of such a conversion.

At today's prices, CNG costs from one-third to one-half the price of gasoline based on 1 gallon of gasoline being equivalent to 100 ft^3 of natural gas. On an energy comparison, CNG has a lower energy content than either gasoline or diesel, with the heat value of CNG varying between 1000 and 1100 Btu (1055 to 1160 kJ) per cubic foot. This means that CNG contains roughly 32,154 Btu (33,332 kJ) per U.S. gallon at a stored pressure of 3000 psi (210 atmospheres). However, CNG has an octane equivalent of approximately 130, compared to 87 to 88 for regular gasoline; this higher octane rating would allow much higher compression ratios to be used in gasoline-type engines. When CNG is used in existing gasoline engines, the driver normally does not notice any great loss of power; however, under heavy-load situations and when climbing long, steep hills, a power loss of from 10% to 20% can be expected.

CNG is a clean-burning fuel and offers great potential as an alternative fuel source, since there is an existing infrastructure (house gas lines, for example) that could be utilized for refueling vehicles at home once acceptable air compressors have been developed and certified. CNG is stored at pressures of 3000 to 3200 psi (210 to 224 atm), so the fuel tanks are very expensive, and the range of the vehicle is reduced substantially. For example, taxicabs using CNG employ two or three tanks located in the trunk for a range of about 120 to 160 miles (193 to 257 km), with a CNG capacity of 322 ft^3 (9 m^3). However, heavy-duty diesel trucks using CNG would require too many fuel storage tanks to make it a feasible concept at this time. CNG conversions on city buses, however, have shown greater potential, because fuel tank storage is not as great a problem. In most cases there is adequate clearance underneath the bus to allow a number of CNG tanks to be installed. In addition, city buses do not accumulate as many miles in a day as do long-haul tractors/trailers. Buses can also be fueled locally at their depot by a fast-charge facility, which takes about the same amount of time as it would to fuel a diesel-powered bus.

It seems that the ideal CNG air/fuel ratio is approximately 16.5:1, which emits carbon monoxide levels that tend to be lower than that for a gasoline engine. In addition, hydrocarbons and oxides of nitrogen are reduced significantly in a CNG-fueled engine. On average, tests have indicated that both exhaust carbon monoxide and hydrocarbon emissions have been reduced by up to 90% when using CNG, while NO$_x$ (nitric oxide) emissions are lowered by about 70%.

The major advantages, in addition to lower exhaust emissions with CNG, are lower fuel costs and less engine wear, particularly to valves. Oil-change intervals are also doubled or tripled when using CNG in comparison to change intervals for gasoline. The safety factors of using CNG are well documented from users of long experience, such as Italy. Many large urban transit and city vehicle fleets are seriously considering the adoption of CNG. It is one alternative fuel that is bound to receive widespread attention throughout the 1990s for both gasoline- and diesel-powered internal combustion engines.

NATURAL GAS ENGINE OPERATION

With the move toward ever more stringent EPA exhaust emissions standards, a number of alternative fuels are being used in both gasoline and diesel engines. One that shows tremendous promise is natural gas in either its liquid form—LNG—or in its compressed form—CNG.

Natural gas, spark-ignited engines have been in operation for many years. Caterpillar and other major OEMs of large slow-speed engines have offered natural gas engines for many years in stationary engine applications. Caterpillar continues to develop some of its later model diesel engines to run on LNG or CNG. A number of major engine manufacturers around the world have adapted and converted diesel bus engines to operate on natural gas. These include MAN and Mercedes-Benz in Germany and Cummins and Detroit Diesel, particularly in the North American market. One of the first major manufacturers to adopt natural gas and receive certification to EPA standards was Detroit Diesel for its 6V-92 series two-stroke-cycle engine models used in transit bus applications, where Detroit Diesel has enjoyed the major share of the market for many years in North America. More recently, Detroit Diesel has offered its Series 50 four-stroke-cycle engine fueled by natural gas for transit bus applications.

Figure 3–7 illustrates the basic operating concept of natural gas engines in Detroit Diesel's two-cycle engines. The engine is controlled by the DDEC system, which is also used on diesel models. This engine, which was first offered in 1991, follows a pilot ignition natural gas operating principle; accordingly, an electronically controlled unit injector provides a pilot charge of diesel fuel into the combustion chamber. This high-pressure injected diesel fuel is used to initiate normal diesel combustion and is followed by ignition of the charge of natural gas, which would not self-ignite otherwise. The charge of natural gas is introduced into the cylinder through a high-speed gas valve shown in the diagram. Note that the gas valve is located just above the cylinder liner intake ports. At idle, the engine operates on 100% diesel fuel; however, at speeds above idle and depending on the speed/load cycle, the engine switches to burn primarily natural gas but using a small amount of pilot diesel fuel for continued combustion. A second DDEC ECM (electronic control module) performs the overall control function and determines whether the engine is in a diesel fuel only mode or in an operating mode that is a combination of pilot diesel fuel and natural gas. Figure 3–8 illustrates

the major modified components in the 6V-92 natural gas engine model.

If the engine runs out of natural gas, the vehicle can still "limp home" on its secondary diesel fuel supply. Continued operation of natural gas engines in city transit buses has shown that gas-fueled engines have lower particulate matter (brake specific particulate) exhaust emissions and lower peak and acceleration smoke than diesel engines. When the gas engine is equipped with a catalytic converter, it can meet the existing strict EPA exhaust emissions standards. The natural gas engine was a shared development of Detroit Diesel, DAI Technologies, the U.S. Gas Research Institute, Ortech International, and Stewart and Stevenson Power, Inc.

The latest addition to Detroit Diesel's natural gas lineup (certified in April 1994) involves the four-stroke-cycle Series 50 8.5L (519 cu in.) four-cylinder engine rated at either 250 or 275 bhp (186.5 to 205 kW) at 2100 rpm. This overhead camshaft engine utilizes a spark-ignited lean-burn natural gas combustion process with a distributor-less, high-energy ignition system and a wastegate turbocharger to direct exhaust gas flow around the turbo under certain operating conditions, thereby controlling the turbo boost airflow. These two features can be seen in Figure 3–9. Other

FIGURE 3–7 Basic layout for a Detroit Diesel 6V-92 two-stroke-cycle, pilot ignition, natural gas engine. (Courtesy of Detroit Diesel Corporation.)

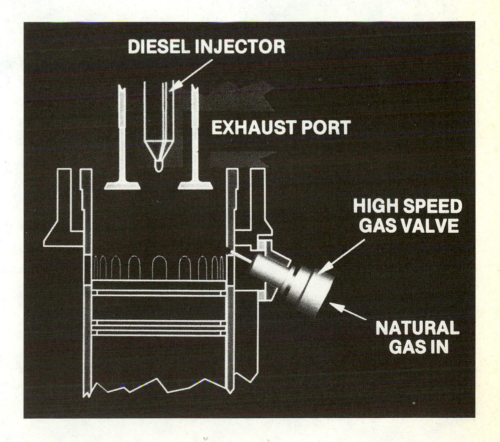

FIGURE 3–8 Modified engine components required to operate a 6V-92 two-stroke-cycle bus/coach engine on compressed natural gas. (Courtesy of Detroit Diesel Corporation.)

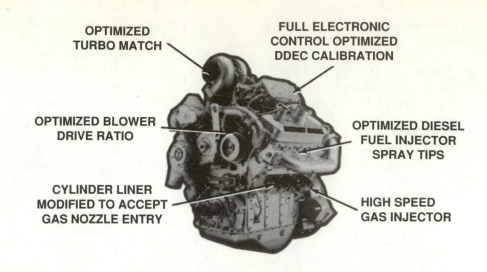

OPTIMIZED TURBO MATCH

FULL ELECTRONIC CONTROL OPTIMIZED DDEC CALIBRATION

OPTIMIZED BLOWER DRIVE RATIO

OPTIMIZED DIESEL FUEL INJECTOR SPRAY TIPS

CYLINDER LINER MODIFIED TO ACCEPT GAS NOZZLE ENTRY

HIGH SPEED GAS INJECTOR

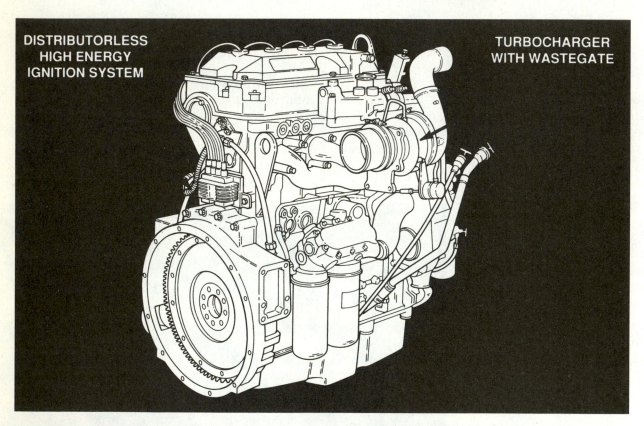

DISTRIBUTORLESS HIGH ENERGY IGNITION SYSTEM

TURBOCHARGER WITH WASTEGATE

FIGURE 3–9 Latest generation Series 50G four-stroke-cycle engine model illustrating the ignition and wastegate turbocharger for a natural gas engine for use in city buses/coaches. (Courtesy of Detroit Diesel Corporation.)

major features of the engine are illustrated in Figure 3–10. A low-pressure natural gas fuel supply regulator reduces the pressure to 70 psi (483 kPa) at the metering valve. The engine uses a 10:1 compression ratio piston and air-to-air-charge cooling of the turbo boost air prior to entering the engine. Natural gas fuel injection occurs downstream of the air-charge cooler, and the use of Detroit Diesel's electronic controls handles the air fuel ratio, spark timing, speed governing, and fuel flow. The engine meets all U.S. EPA emissions requirements, and the latest technology utilized in the Series 50G engine will enable it to surpass the emissions

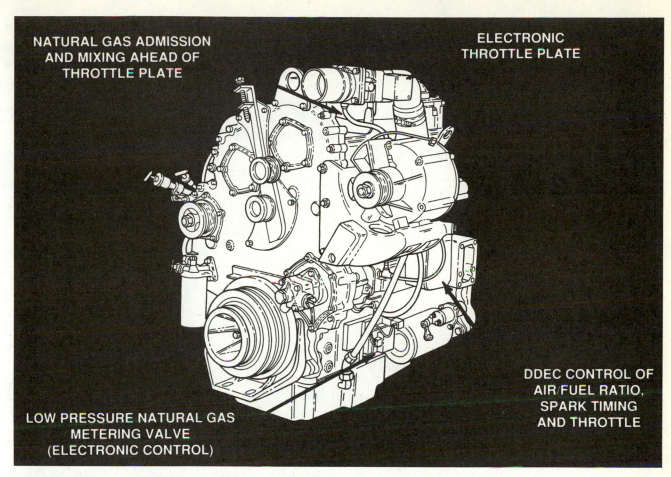

FIGURE 3–10 Natural gas components and DDEC controls for use in the Series 50G natural gas engine model. (Courtesy of Detroit Diesel Corporation.)

characteristics of other currently available lean-burn natural gas engines.

The 50G will also meet the CARB (California Air Resources Board) emissions standards because it has superior fuel economy and knock-free engine operation in contrast to aftermarket conversions that use carbureted controls. The natural gas metering valve is solenoid actuated and DDEC controlled, which allows the valve to meter and control the admission of low-pressure gas into the air intake stream, after the air-to-air-charge cooler and ahead of the throttle body. A catalytic converter is required, however, to meet the emissions standards; the converter is similar to that used on Detroit Diesel's alcohol-fueled methanol engines. The 50G engine carries a 2-year unlimited miles warranty, the same as that for the Series 50 diesel fuel model.

Safety Record of CNG Vehicles

Natural gas vehicles have proven safety records in Australia, New Zealand, Italy, Holland, Canada, and the United States. Being lighter than air, natural gas quickly dissipates in the event of a spill. It has a higher flash point than either gasoline or propane, and it burns within a narrower range of gas-to-air mixtures.

Figure 3–11 illustrates the typical constituents of natural gas. If natural gas is to be widely adopted for use in internal combustion engines, it must consist mainly of methane, and the impurities must be kept to low levels.

For natural gas vehicles to increase their penetration of the marketplace, an adequate refueling infrastructure must be in place. Electronically controlled engines are essential for fuel controls to allow stoichiometric-burn engines and extremely desirable lean-burn engines. One problem with natural gas is its slow flame speed, which is further reduced as the mixture becomes leaner. To speed up this process, highly turbulent conditions within the combustion chamber can be created by designing the intake manifold system to impart a swirling air charge. In addition, a specially designed piston crown with a high-squish region can

FIGURE 3–11 *Graphical representation of the typical components of natural gas. (Courtesy of TMC/ATA [The Maintenance Council, American Trucking Associations].)*

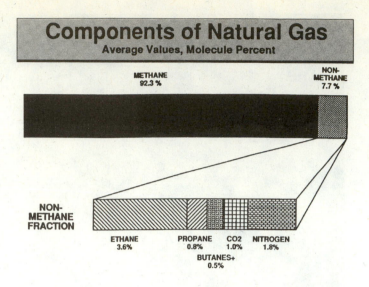

be used to accelerate the combustion rate. Tests indicate that lean-burn systems provide higher efficiency than a stoichiometric combustion system, and lean burn tends to reduce NO_x and carbon monoxide emissions. Also, lean-burn engines tend to operate cooler, thereby increasing engine durability. Combustion with a lean-burn engine can be troublesome, however, if the air/fuel mixture is too lean. This produces a condition in which the flame may fail to initiate or to travel across the combustion chamber.

Many major companies are involved in the research and development of CNG and LNG systems. Most likely, both systems will be used in more applications in the future.

LIQUIFIED NATURAL GAS

LNG (liquified natural gas) has one major advantage over CNG: in the liquid state, 625 cu ft. (17.7 cu m) takes up only 1 cu ft (0.028 cu m) of space. In addition, 1.5 gallons of LNG equals the mileage range of 1 gallon of gasoline, while 1.66 gallons of LNG equals the mileage range of 1 gallon of diesel fuel. LNG requires only twice the volume of diesel fuel compared to nine times for CNG. The major drawback of LNG is that it must be stored at $-260°F$ to remain in its liquid state. Other than in city buses where there is adequate below-floor space to install CNG cylinders, CNG is not a viable alternative. In line-haul trucks, for example, the time between necessary CNG fill-ups would be too short. LNG, on the other hand, is a possibility because of its lower space requirements, and it weighs only 1.2 times that of diesel fuel compared to five times for CNG. In addition, LNG can be delivered to areas not served at this time by natural gas pipelines.

To ensure that LNG remains in its liquid form, it must be delivered in insulated tank trucks similar to those used to transport liquid oxygen, nitrogen, and other industrial gases. When used in a vehicle as fuel, the LNG must be stored in a special *cryogenic tank*, which is somewhat similar to the concept of a thermos bottle. LNG is safe, and should a spill occur, it vaporizes quickly and does not puddle as do gasoline and diesel fuel. LNG can only burn when raised to ignition temperatures and mixed with air. Unlike methanol, natural gas is not toxic or corrosive. Almost all components required for use in LNG systems have been fully developed and field tested during the past 30 years plus. Experience gained in the U.S. space programs produced a body of knowledge on the production, storage, and handling of cryogenic liquids.

For LNG to meet the needs of a fleet operation, a small liquifier must be used. This unit can be designed so that when quantities of 1000 cu ft or 28 m³ per day of natural gas are available at pressures less than 100 psi (690 kPa), a compression-expansion cycle is utilized. A gas treatment system removes water and carbon dioxide; then the gas undergoes a compression-expansion cycle of varying complexity. An alternative liquifier approach is to take advantage of the local high-pressure gas pipeline where natural gas is piped to the end user at pressures in the typical range of 500 to 1200 psi (3447 to 8274 kPa). At the end user's facility, this gas pressure is reduced to between 60 and 100 psi (414 to 690 kPa). The refrigeration effect from this pressure drop can be harnessed to liquify a proportion of the gas required. It is cheaper to use this type of liquifier than the first model described. Figure 3–12 illustrates one example of an LNG-fueled vehicle. The LNG from the tank passes through a vaporizer to con-

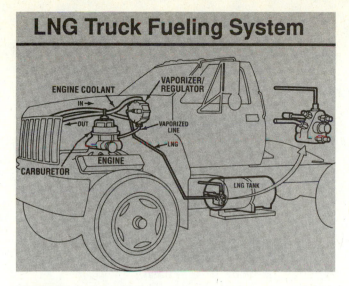

FIGURE 3–12 Basic component arrangement for a truck engine operating on LNG (liquified natural gas). (Courtesy of TMC/ATA [The Maintenance Council, American Trucking Associations].)

TABLE 3–6 Propane vapor pressure at a given ambient temperature

Ambient temperature	Vapor pressure
−45°F (−43°C)	0 psi (0 kPa)
−40°F (−40°C)	2 psi (14 kPa)
−20°F (−30°C)	13 psi (91 kPa)
0°F (−18°C)	28 psi (196 kPa)
70°F (21°C)	120 psi (840 kPa)
100°F (38°C)	190 psi (1330 kPa)

vert the liquid into a gaseous state for introduction into the engine through a device similar to a carburetor or throttle body injection unit.

PROPANE

Propane is extracted from natural gas along with butane, both in liquified form. A plus for propane is its relatively clean burn, which shows fairly low carbon monoxide content and hydrocarbon residues that are also fairly unreactive in the atmosphere. In addition, propane has an octane rating of about a 98 pump value, which is higher than that of available gasoline. In regard to energy propane has only about 74% the heat value equivalency of that for gasoline per liquefied gallon, and it must be stored in bulky fuel tanks that are capable of withstanding several hundred

pounds of pressure. This means that the initial installation for propane is much more costly than that for gasoline, and the available mileage on a tank of propane is less than that for gasoline.

Approximately 65% of the propane in the United States is extracted from natural gas wells and natural gas processing plants; the remaining 35% is obtained as a by-product of the gasoline refining process. Propane is a hydrocarbon fuel that differs from gasoline in its molecular structure. The chemical symbol for propane is C_3H_8, meaning that it contains three carbon atoms and eight hydrogen atoms. Compare this with gasoline, which has a chemical symbol of C_8H_{15}. Fuels with a lower carbon content usually exhibit a higher octane rating, which translates into less tendency for detonation, particularly in a spark-ignited engine. Propane has a specific gravity that is lighter than that of both gasoline and diesel fuel: 1 gallon of propane weighs about 4.25 lb (1.9 kg) per U.S. gallon or 5.08 lb (2.2 kg) per Imperial gallon.

At temperatures of lower than −45°F (−43°C), propane pressure in the tank will be at zero; therefore, since tank pressure is what is used to force the propane to the engine vaporizer valve, the fuel system will not operate at ambient temperatures below this level. Operation of a propane fuel system in warm ambient temperatures is ideal because fuel tank pressure can rise to 190 psi (1330 kPa). Consequently, the propane fuel tank must be capable of withstanding pressures between 250 and 325 psi (1724 to 2241 kPa), although tanks are tested at much higher pressures during the manufacturing process. Propane fuel is converted from a liquid to a vapor inside a vaporizer and is then delivered to the engine intake manifold in gaseous form. Consequently, engines using propane tend to operate more efficiently in cooler weather when a more dense air charge enters the cylinders. The vapor pressure of propane varies depending on the ambient temperature; Table 3–6 shows typical pressures at a variety of temperatures. Propane will boil or vaporize at a temperature of −44°F (−42°C), whereas CNG boils at −260°F (−162°C). Compare this to diesel fuel, which vaporizes between 500° and 675°F (260 to 357°C), depending on the grade being used, and gasoline, which vaporizes more slowly at temperatures just above freezing and much more quickly at elevated temperatures up to 400°F (204°C).

The major problem concerning propane use is that it is a by-product of crude oil. So if large numbers of vehicles were suddenly converted to run on propane, the infrastructure now in place would be unable to handle the demands.

Glossary of Fuel Terms

Fuel terms	Description	Effects
API gravity	Scale used to measure fuel weight	Heavy fuel is hard to burn and has a low API rating. Light fuel has less heat and less mpg performances, and has a high API value.
Viscosity	Measure of fuel thickness	Low viscosity can cause injector leaks and more wear. High viscosity means the fuel is hard to burn and gives poor injector spray.
Cetane	Ignition quality (startability)	Low cetane means poor starting. High cetane means good starting.
Distillation	Boiling range/lab test (vapor temperatures)	
IBP	Initial boiling point	Low BP means lighter fuel. High BP means hard to burn.
10%	10% vaporized	(Same as above.)
50%	50% vaporized	(Same as above.)
90%	90% vaporized	(Same as above.)
EP	End point	Low EP means less horsepower. High EP means more smoking, more deposits, more wear.
BS & W	Bottom sediment and water content	Nonusable material in fuel.
Conradson carbon residue on 10% bottoms	Measure of fuel's tendency to form injector deposits	High percent means injectors stick, increase wear, tip deposits.
Pour point	Jell temperature (solid fuel)	Fuel at pour-point temperature will not flow through lines or filters. Solid in tanks.
Cloud point	Wax formation temperature (crystals form)	Fuel at cloud point will flow but will have paraffin wax crystals suspended in fuel. This may plug filters and lines.
Flash point	Lab test of fuel vapor flame point	Low flash point means probable blending with lighter products (handling danger).
Sulfur content	Fuel contaminant, which is a major element in system corrosion and fuel acidity	High sulfur means increased wear, more deposits, oil contamination, more smoke.
Ash content	Noncombustible material	High ash content means increased wear, more smoke, lost fuel.
Recovery and residue	Lab test to determine maximum usable fuel content	Recovery is a lab measurement of usable fuel. Residue is a lab measurement of unusable fuel.
Lubricity	Measure of fuel's lubricating properties	Lack of proper lubrication will increase fuel pump and system wear.
Particulate content (inorganic)	Solid contaminants present in fuel	Higher amounts result in fuel system deposits, filter fouling, increased smoke, and loss of usable fuel. *Examples:* dirt, rust, and other foreign materials.
Microbial activity (organic)	Fungus or bacteria spores or growth in fuel	Microbial activity causes fuel filter plugging, injector fouling, system deposits, tank and line corrosion, loss of usable fuel, lower mpg, more smoke, low power, poor idling.

Glossary of Fuel Terms, *continued*

Fuel terms	Description	Effects
Oxidation stability	Free carbon formation in fuel due to fuel incompatibility	High test number means unstable fuel, engine deposits, system deposits, increased smoke, low power.
Trace metals	Contamination of fuel by small amounts of metal particles present in crude oil	Higher amounts mean more deposits, increased wear, decreased fuel stability, increased ash.
Hydrogen/ carbon ratio	Measure of fuel's major components; hydrogen and carbon content is used to determine the fuel's Btu content (fuel economy/ mpg)	Will tell the ultimate mpg the fuel will deliver when used.
Btu	The quantity of heat required to raise the temperature of 1 pound of water by 1°F	Measurement of fuel's energy output.

HYDROGEN

Research has been ongoing with hydrogen as a fuel source. Scientists anticipate that the greatest potential for clean air from the exhaust of internal combustion engines may be obtained with this fuel source. When hydrogen is burned in a combustion chamber with air, the result is water vapor plus traces of nitric oxides derived from the nitrogen content in the air. Hydrogen is one of the most natural and abundant elements in the world, and it combines with other elements, such as oxygen to form water. Hydrogen weighs only 0.6 lb (0.270 kg) per U.S. gallon and contains approximately 30,000 Btu/gallon. Therefore, each pound of hydrogen produces 51,600 Btu, which is substantially higher than that available from either gasoline or diesel fuel. Diesel fuel contains between 18,500 and 19,000 Btu per pound on average, with gasoline being about 10% lower per pound than diesel fuel.

The chemical symbol for hydrogen is H^2; liquid hydrogen is shown as LH^2 and gaseous hydrogen as GH^2. To use liquid hydrogen, it must be cooled below its boiling point of −423F (−252°C). Consequently, hydrogen is difficult to transport and to store; current technology uses heavy-duty tanks to hold the hydrogen in highly compressed form, or by liquid in heavier tanks. A third alternative for storing hydrogen is to employ hydride storage, which involves filling two-thirds of a tank with crushed iron titanium, then pumping hydrogen gas into the tank. The iron titanium absorbs the hydrogen similar to that of a sponge soaking up water. Applying heat to the storage tank from either the engine cooling or exhaust system results in the release of hydrogen from the iron titanium. Unfortunately, current technology does not allow a light enough fuel storage tank to make hydrogen from this process a feasible option. To obtain a 200 mile (322 km) range, the hydride tank would weigh about 600 lb (270 kg).

Hydrogen can be produced from natural gas, which in itself can be used as an alternative fuel as described in this chapter. Hydrogen can also be produced from coal gasification; however, this would create unacceptable pollution. Third, hydrogen can be produced from electrolysis of water by using an electric current to separate the hydrogen and oxygen. Although not an immediate answer to the problem of a clean-burning fuel, hydrogen does offer excellent potential. Ongoing research and development work is proceeding in several countries by major automotive manufacturers. It may be the early part of the twenty-first century before hydrogen is an optional alternative.

SELF-TEST QUESTIONS

1. Technician A says that crude oil petroleum distillates normally used as fuel for diesel engines are composed of heavy hydrocarbons, whereas technician B states that the more volatile portions of the crude oil are used to produce diesel fuel. Who is correct?

2. Technician A says that the refining process for diesel fuel is more complex than that for producing gasoline. Technician B disagrees. Who is correct?

3. Technician A says that diesel fuel contains more Btu per gallon than any other fuel now used in internal combustion engines, including gasoline, LPG, or CNG. Technician B believes that gasoline contains more heat

energy per gallon than does diesel fuel. Who is correct?

4. True or false: The average weight of diesel fuel per U.S. gallon is greater than that for a gallon of water.

5. The average weight of a U.S. gallon of diesel fuel is
   a. 5.8 lb
   b. 7.1 lb
   c. 8.6 lb
   d. 9.9 lb

6. Crude petroleum is a mixture of molecules that contain
   a. carbon and hydrogen atoms
   b. oxygen and carbon atoms
   c. hydrogen and oxygen atoms
   d. sulfur and nitrogen atoms

7. Technician A says that hydrocarbon molecules found in all liquid fuels are classified into three general groups: paraffin, naphthene, and aromatic. Technician B says that the three groups are gasoline, diesel, and aromatic. Who is correct?

8. Technician A says that the temperature at which the diesel fuel vaporizes is known as the distillation range. Technician B says that this is known as the temperature at which the fuel is atomized. Who knows what he or she is talking about here?

9. Technician A says that a barrel of crude oil contains only 42 Imperial gallons (191 L), whereas technician B says that the barrel contains 50 U.S. gallons. Who is correct?

10. Technician A says that to produce approximately 10 U.S. gallons of good-grade diesel fuel, we require 25 gallons of crude oil. Technician B disagrees and says that we need a barrel of crude oil to produce about 10 U.S. gallons of diesel fuel. Who is correct?

11. Technician A says that to distill crude oil, it has to be heated to temperatures of approximately 800°F (427°C), where the lighter products, such as butane, gasoline, and LPG, are removed. Technician B disagrees and says that 1500°F is necessary. Who is correct?

12. Technician A says that the cloud point of a diesel fuel is the temperature at which the refining residue from the paraffinic crudes known as paraffin wax will cause fuel filter plugging. Technician B says that the cloud point is where the fuel stops flowing due to solidifying. Who is correct?

13. Technician A says that fuel oils with high concentrations of soluble organic compounds such as vanadium, nickel, iron, and sodium will provide greater heat value per pound than fuels without these, and will also tend to reduce valve face wear. Technician B says that this is untrue since such fuels will create rapid wear of internal engine components. Who is correct?

14. True or false: Conventional diesel fuels are generally distillates with a boiling range of between approximately 300° and 700°F (149° to 371°C).

15. Diesel fuels in North America are graded and classified by ASTM. The letters ASTM stand for

   a. American Standards Test Median
   b. American Society for Testing Materials
   c. American Society of Test Manufacturers
   d. American Society of Truck Manufacturers

16. True or false: Diesel fuel oils are classified as being either a grade 1, 2, 3, or 4.

17. Technician A says that, depending on their grade classification, diesel fuel oils generally contain between 10% and 14% more Btu per gallon than gasoline does. Technician B says that gasoline contains more heat value per gallon than diesel. Who is correct?

18. Technician A says that the heating value of an API diesel fuel with an API number of 40 contains more Btu per gallon than does one rated at an API number of 34. Technician B says that it is the other way around—the lower the API number, the greater the heat value per gallon. Who is correct?

19. Technician A says that the term *cetane number* is a measure of the ignition quality of the fuel. Technician B says that the higher the cetane number, the more rapidly the fuel will ignite. Who is correct?

20. Technician A says that the lower the ambient temperature, the greater the need for a fuel of a lower cetane number or rating, so that it will ignite rapidly. Technician B says that a higher cetane number is desirable in cold-weather operations. Who is correct?

21. Technician A says that the diesel fuel cetane number differs from the octane number used for gasoline in that the higher the number of gasoline on the octane scale, the greater will be the gasoline fuel's resistance to self-ignition. Technician B says that the higher the cetane number of diesel fuel, the easier the fuel will ignite once injected. Who is correct?

22. Technician A says that the distillation range of a diesel fuel refers to the temperature at which the fuel will vaporize inside the combustion chamber, whereas technician B says that it is the maximum temperature at which the fuel can be circulated through the fuel system without damage to the operating components. Who is correct?

23. Technician A says that the term *viscosity* is a measure of the fuel's resistance to flow and that it will decrease as the fuel temperature increases. Technician B says that it is the term used to describe the temperature at which the wax crystals form in the fuel and cause fuel filter plugging. Who is correct?

24. Technician A says that the flash point of the fuel is the temperature at which the fuel oil will ignite inside the combustion chamber, whereas technician B says that it is the temperature at which the fuel oil vapors will flash when in the presence of an open flame. Who is correct?

25. Technician A says that a common by-product of combustion when hydrogen is burned in a diesel or gasoline engine is water vapor at the exhaust. Technician B says that water vapor is caused simply

by water in the fuel due to improper filtration. Who is correct?

26. Technician A says that in North America, the thermal efficiency of an internal combustion engine using liquid fuel is calculated on the low heat value of the fuel. Technician B insists that it is the high heat value of the fuel that is used to determine this. Who is right?

27. Technician A says that in the absence of suitable fuel/water filtration equipment, you should wait 5 to 10 minutes before drawing fuel from a newly filled storage diesel tank or drum. Technician B says that you should wait for 24 hours. Who is correct?

28. Technician A says that a No. 1 diesel fuel will offer easier starting in cold weather and is cleaner burning. Technician B says that a No. 2 fuel contains more Btu and would therefore be a better fuel for ease of starting in cold weather. Who is correct?

29. Technician A says that all things being equal, the use of a No. 2 diesel fuel will provide better fuel economy in a heavy-duty diesel truck than will the use of a No. 1 fuel. Technician B disagrees. Who is correct?

30. Technician A says that white smoke in an engine after initial start-up is indicative of a leaking cylinder head gasket. Technician B says that white smoke under such a condition is generally caused by minute particles of unburned fuel, particularly in cold-weather operation. Who is correct?

31. Technician A says that black smoke is usually caused by air starvation or using a fuel with too high a boiling point. Technician B says that this is incorrect. Who is right here?

32. Technician A says that the optimum temperature for fuel system operation is to maintain the fuel between 90° and 100°F (32° to 38°C); otherwise, there will be a loss in engine power. Not so, says technician B, who feels that the cooler the fuel, the greater the fuel charge and therefore the greater the engine power produced. Who is correct?

33. Three of the most important properties of any diesel fuel are
    a. cloud point, sulfur content, and pour point
    b. distillation range, pour point, and cetane rating
    c. cloud point, distillation range, and pour point
    d. sulfur content, cetane rating, and distillation range

34. The term *distillation* range refers to
    a. lubricity of the fuel oil
    b. ability of the fuel to flow at low ambient temperatures
    c. temperature at which the fuel is completely vaporized
    d. flammability of the fuel

35. High sulfur in a fuel oil will result in
    a. greater engine power
    b. longer fuel filter change intervals
    c. more frequent oil change periods

    d. premature wear, excessive deposit formation, and increased amounts of sulfur dioxide exhausted into the atmosphere

36. U.S. EPA maximum allowable standard for clean, reformulated diesel fuel sulfur content is now set at
    a. 0.5%
    b. 0.3%
    c. 0.15%
    d. 0.05%

37. True or false: The higher the octane number assigned to a gasoline, the greater the fuel's resistance to self- or auto-ignition.

38. A fuel with the designation M85, used in gasoline engines, refers to a mixture of
    a. 85% gasoline and 15% kerosene
    b. 85% gasoline and 15% diesel fuel
    c. 85% kerosene and 15% gasoline
    d. 85% methanol and 15% gasoline

39. An alternate fuel designated as M100 refers to
    a. 100% methanol
    b. 100% reformulated gasoline
    c. 100% kerosene
    d. 100% very-low-sulfur diesel

40. The term *SUS* related to fluid viscosity refers to
    a. specified user safe
    b. society universal sample
    c. summer universal specification
    d. seconds Saybolt universal

41. To start unaided, most diesel engines require that the diesel fuel obtain a 90% distillation point. For a No. 2 diesel fuel, this requires a temperature of approximately
    a. 246°C (475°F)
    b. 282°C (540°F)
    c. 310°C (590°F)
    d. 329°C (625°F)

42. What words do the following letters represent?
    a. API
    b. ASTM
    c. SAE

43. A No. 2 diesel fuel would have an ASTM gravity rating of between
    a. 40 and 44
    b. 36 and 40
    c. 33 and 37
    d. 28 and 30

44. Selection of a diesel fuel for use in cold-weather operation should preferably have its cloud point at least how many degrees below the lowest expected ambient air temperature?
    a. 6°C (10°F)
    b. 12°C (20°F)
    c. 18°C (32°F)
    d. 30°C (86°F)

45. Pour point refers to
    a. ambient temperature at which diesel fuel will no longer flow through fuel lines

b. rate at which the fuel will flow through a beaker
c. freezing temperature of the fuel
d. ability of the fuel to resist wax crystal formation

46. True or false: A No. 1 diesel fuel is a more volatile fuel than a No. 2.

47. True or fasle: A No. 1 diesel fuel has greater heat value per pound but less heat per gallon than a No. 2 diesel fuel.

48. True or false: A diesel engine will run on aviation jet fuel.

49. True or false: The addition of kerosene to diesel fuel can assist in lowering the cloud point in cold-weather operation.

50. True or false: In North America, thermal efficiency of an internal combustion engine using liquid fuel is calculated on the basis of LHV (low heat value).

51. True or false: In North America, thermal efficiency of an internal combustion engine using gaseous fuels (propane or natural gas) is calculated on the basis of HHV (high heat value).

52. The LHV of liquid fuels is about
a. 4% below the HHV
b. 6% below the HHV
c. 10% below the HHV
d. 20% below the HHV

53. The LHV of gaseous fuels is about
a. 8% below the HHV
b. 10% below the HHV
c. 14% below the HHV
d. 18% below the HHV

54. Fuel with an API gravity designation of 44 would have an HHV of approximately
a. 19,500 Btu/lb
b. 19,600 Btu/lb
c. 19,700 Btu/lb
d. 19,800 Btu/lb

55. The approximate Btu HHV per gallon for a No. 2, 36 API gravity rated diesel fuel is about
a. 133,500 Btu
b. 135,800 Btu
c. 138,200 Btu
d. 140,600 Btu

56. A No. 2, 36 API diesel fuel would have an approximate specific gravity at 15°C (60°F) of
a. 0.8448
b. 0.9120
c. 0.9872
d. 1.000

57. In one Imperial gallon, there are
a. 4.251 liters
b. 4.325 liters
c. 4.546 liters
d. 4.835 liters

58. One U.S. gallon contains
a. 3.625 liters
b. 3.785 liters
c. 3.835 liters
d. 3.920 liters

59. Diesel fuel with a high sulfur content causes
a. high exhaust emissions and associated engine wear caused by the corrosive effect of sulfuric acid formed from the combustion gases
b. engine wear through the need to use a multiviscosity oil
c. extended oil change intervals
d. hard starting and low power

60. Fuel sulfur wear in an engine can generally be recognized by
a. rapid piston ring wear
b. high crankcase pressure
c. badly worn crankshaft bearings
d. severe ring, liner, and exhaust valve guide wear

61. The BTU heat value per gallon of methanol fuel is approximately
a. 20% of diesel fuel
b. 33% of diesel fuel
c. 44% of diesel fuel
d. 58% of diesel fuel

62. Diesel fuel contains more heat value per gallon than does gasoline. It is approximately
a. 9% to 10%
b. 12% to 13%
c. 15% to 16%
d. 18% to 19%

63. Methanol can be extracted from
a. natural gas
b. flare gas
c. coal or wood
d. all of the above

64. Methanol fuel has a cetane value of approximately
a. 3 to 5
b. 8 to 10
c. 20 to 25
d. 35 to 40

65. True or false: CNG (compressed natural gas) has a higher heat content than does both gasoline and diesel fuel in an energy comparison.

66. CNG has an equivalent octane value to that of gasoline of approximately
a. 100
b. 110
c. 120
d. 130

67. Propane has an equivalent octane value to that of gasoline of approximately
a. 96
b. 98
c. 100
d. 102

68. CNG in its gaseous form is stored in tanks at approximately
a. 1000 psi (6895 kPa)
b. 2000 psi (13,790 kPa)
c. 3000 psi (20,685 kPa)
d. 4000 psi (27,580 kPa)

69. Propane storage pressure, when used in vehicles, varies with the surrounding ambient air temperature, but it is generally stored at approximate pressures of between
    a. 150 and 170 psi (1034 to 1172 kPa)
    b. 200 and 225 psi (1379 to 1551 kPa)
    c. 250 and 325 psi (1724 to 2241 kPa)
    d. 500 and 550 psi (3448 to 3792 kPa)

70. Propane pressure in a tank will drop as the ambient temperatures decrease. This tank pressure will drop to zero psi at
    a. approximately −45°F or −43°C
    b. approximately −50°F or −45.5°C
    c. approximately −55°F or −48°C
    d. approximately −60°F or −50°C

71. The heat value per cubic foot of natural gas at 15°C (60°F) falls between how many Btu for high heat value and how many Btu for low heat value?

72. True or false: Fuel economy or miles per gallon (L/100 km) is affected by the weight or API gravity of the diesel fuel being used.

73. The difference between high and low heat values in a diesel fuel depends on the proportion of what two of the following elements in the fuel?
    a. Oxygen and hydrogen
    b. Carbon and hydrogen
    c. Sulfur and oxygen

    d. Carbon and sulfur

74. Evidence of fungi, or bacterial growth, in a diesel fuel can be detected by
    a. the smell of carbon in the fuel (similar to burnt toast)
    b. very dark fuel oil color
    c. grayish/white fuel color
    d. slimy, unfilterable blobs (brown, black, or green) on the fuel filters

75. True or false: Diesel fuel tends to absorb and hold more water than does gasoline.

76. To preclude freeze-up of the fuel line in very cold ambients, use
    a. coolant antifreeze
    b. liquid ether (starting fluid)
    c. isopropyl alcohol
    d. solvent and diesel fuel mix

77. When using the liquid in your answer to Question 76, how much would you add to the fuel tank(s)?
    a. 1 U.S. pint (0.473 L) for each 125 U.S. gal/473 L
    b. 1 U.S. pint for each 150 U.S. gal/568 L
    c. 1 U.S. pint for each 175 U.S. gal/662 L
    d. 1 U.S. pint for each 200 U.S. gal/757 L

78. True or false: The process of mixing (blending) used engine lube oil and burning it in a high-speed diesel engine is a recommended practice by most engine manufacturers.

4

Fuel Filters, Fuel/Water Separators, and Fuel Heaters

OVERVIEW

Clean diesel fuel has always been paramount to obtaining long life from injection equipment. This is true even more with the introduction of electronically controlled diesel engines that operate with very high injection pressures. In this chapter we discuss the construction, operation, maintenance, and service of fuel filters; fuel filter/water separators; and thermostatically controlled heaters, which are used in cold-weather operation.

TOPICS

- Fuel filtration
- Fuel filters
- Fuel filter/water separators
- Fuel heaters
- Self-test questions

FUEL FILTRATION

Most diesel engines are equipped with at least a basic fuel filtration device. Yet, in the face of a general worldwide decline in the quality of diesel fuel itself, basic forms of filtration may not adequately protect precision components.

No matter how carefully fuel is handled, contaminants find their way into fuel during transfer, storage, or even inside vehicle tanks. Indeed, water, an engine's primary enemy, condenses directly from the air during normal daily heating and cooling cycles. In addition to water, solid and semisolid (microbiological) particulate contamination is prevalent. Rust, sand, and other small particles routinely find their way into diesel fuel. Sometimes larger identifiable objects such as pebbles, leaves, and paint chips are present. The most common culprits of plugged fuel filter elements, however, are oxidized organic semisolid contaminants such as gums, varnishes, and carbon. To be effective, fuel filtration devices must provide adequate solid-particle retention efficiencies while maintaining large capacities for the natural organic contaminants found in diesel fuel.

In addition to contaminant challenges, there is the potential for paraffin wax crystal formation in the fuel during cold-weather operations. These crystals form (at the cloud point of a fuel) and cause filters to plug just as if they were fouled by contamination.

Water—An Engine's Worst Enemy

Water is commonly found in diesel fuel due mainly to condensation, handling, and environmental conditions. Water contamination, although ever present, is more pronounced in humid areas and marine applications. The presence of water in diesel fuel systems may cause the following problems:

- Water causes iron components to rust and form loose aggregated particles of iron oxide that contribute to injector wear.
- At the interface of water and diesel fuel, microbiological growth occurs rapidly under proper conditions. These microbes form a sludge that can actually hinder filter effectiveness and injection performance.

- Water contamination combines with various forms of sulfur contamination to form sulfuric acid. This strong acid can damage injection systems and engine components.
- Water inhaled by the injection system can displace lubrication provided by the fuel oil itself, causing galling and premature wear.

Typical primary filtration devices do not have the capability to remove water, so they leave the engine prey to pump and injector damage and reduced efficiency. It is essential, therefore, to effectively separate water from the fuel prior to the final stages of solid-particulate filtration. In the absence of a water separator, standard primary elements become waterlogged and ineffective. When waterlogged, they are especially susceptible to waxing in cold temperatures.

An *upstream* water separator can significantly enhance the performance and life of primary filter elements. Frequent replacement of primary filters is required when the volume of contaminants is significant. In such cases, engine damage may result because filters are not immediately available for replacement, or operators are not aware of the need to replace. Therefore, upstream filtration capacity, water separation capability, and a 30 micron rating can, when properly applied, as much as triple the service life of the filtration system.

In addition to keeping dirt particles out of the diesel fuel, water in the fuel must be avoided. Water will cause severe lack of lubrication, leading to possible seizure of injection system components. In some cases water can cause the injector tip to be blown off, due to the high engine temperatures encountered in the combustion chamber, which leads to the water exploding as it passes through the injector tip orifices, causing serious engine damage. This condition is more pronounced in direct-injection diesel engines with multiple-hole nozzles. Because of the noncompressibility factor of water and the extremely high injection pressures created, water must not be allowed to enter the diesel fuel system. Even when the engine is not running, water in the fuel system can rust precision-fitted parts, thereby causing serious problems. Clean fuel should contain no more than 0.1% of sediment and water. Auxiliary filtering equipment must be used when sediment and water exceeds 0.1%; therefore, it is advisable to use a fuel/water separator. Another problem of water in the fuel is, of course, that it can lead to fuel-line freeze-up in cold-weather operation.

Most diesel fuel systems today employ a fuel return line that runs back to the fuel tank; this line carries warm fuel that has been used to cool and lubricate the injection pump and nozzles. When this warm fuel settles in the tank, condensation can form, leading to water vapor. To minimize water vapor, many fleets fill their fuel tanks up at night to displace any warm air in the tank. To prevent fuel-line freeze-up due to minute water particles in the fuel, a fuel/water filter and optional heater can be used, as well as the addition of methyl or isopropyl alcohol in the ratio of 0.0125% or 1 part in 8000, which equates to about 1 pint of isopropyl alcohol (isopropanol) to every 125 gallons of diesel fuel.

Water is found in diesel fuel in three forms: absorbed, emulsified, and in a free state. Of the three, water in a free state is by far the easiest to remove from diesel fuel. This free water is generally removed from the diesel fuel by using a mechanical filter employing the process of centrifugal force. Pleated paper separator systems provide filtration and water separation, and although they perform much better than a mechanical separator, they are not as good as the true *coalescing filter*. Fuel/water filters operate on the principle of *coalescence* to remove emulsified and coarsely dispersed water from the fuel oil. The dictionary defines *coalesce* as "to cause to grow together, to unite so as to form one body or association."

Emulsified droplets of water are very small and thus take considerable time to separate from the fuel by gravitational means. On the other hand, coarsely dispersed water droplets are large enough to separate by gravitational means in a short period of time. In the process of coalescing, droplets of water enter the filter assembly where they form into large droplets or globules and become large enough to settle in the fuel/water separator sump by gravitational means. Smaller droplets are trapped in the filtering element. Factors affecting the design and performance of a coalescing element are viscosity, specific gravity, solubility, surfactants (surface-active agents) and additives, concentration of contaminants, the degree of emulsification, solids content, and filter pressure drop.

FUEL FILTERS

The use of a suitable filtration system on diesel engines is a must to avoid damage to the closely fitted injection pump and injector components. These components are manufactured to tolerances of as little as 0.0025 mm (0.0000984 in.); therefore, insufficient fuel filtration can cause serious problems. Six principal filter element media have been used for many years:

1. Pleated paper
2. Packed cotton thread
3. Wood fibers

4. Mixtures of packed cotton thread and wood fibers
5. Wound cotton or synthetic yarn
6. Fiberglass

Filtering ability varies among type of engines and manufacturers. On high-speed diesel engines, a primary filter and a secondary filter are generally employed. The primary filter is capable of removing dirt particles down to about 30 microns (μm) and the secondary down to 10 to 12 μm, although final filters with a 3 to 5 μm rating are now more prevalent on truck diesel applications operating in severe-duty service. A micron is 1/1,000,000 of a meter, or 0.00003937 in.; therefore, 25.4 μm = 0.001 in. Fuel filters that employ wound cotton thread, pleated paper, or fiberglass media are typically rated only as low as 10 μm; therefore, current truck diesel engines often employ additional filtration in the form of either a fuel/water separator or injector filter. Some engines use only one fuel filter, but with a screen in the fuel tank to remove any larger dirt particles.

Pleated paper elements are made of resin-treated paper with controlled porosity. These fine pores hold solid contaminants but not water. Other factors related to the type of filtering media are the pressure drop across the filter and price of the replacement unit. Pleated paper elements are generally the lowest priced, and wound cotton yarn elements are more expensive. Fiberglass and cotton thread and wood fiber elements are usually the most expensive, but they offer the best protection and longest service life.

The degree of filtration is obviously related to the type and grade of fuel that has to pass through the filter; therefore, fuel filters are available with filter ratings of from as high as 60 to 70 μm down to an ultrafine 0.5 to 3 μm. The makeup of typical filters used in midrange and heavy-duty diesel fuel filters is as follows:

- Nominal 15 to 20 μm rating, consisting of 60% superfine wood fiber and 40% white cotton thread
- Nominal 10 to 15 μm rating, consisting of 40% wood fiber and 60% white cotton thread
- Nominal 5 to 10 μm rating, consisting of 85% white cotton thread and 15% synthetic thread
- Nominal 3 to 5 μm rating, consisting of 50% cotton thread and 50% cotton linters
- Nominal 0.5 to 3 μm rating, consisting of ultrafine 60% ground paper and 40% fine wood chips

The fuel system can be equipped with either a primary or a secondary fuel filter, depending on whether a fuel filter/water separator is employed. When a primary filter is used, it is usually manufactured from a cotton-wound-sock type of material and is designed to handle dirt removal down to 25 to 30 μm in size. On the other hand, the secondary filter is made from specially formulated and treated paper and is usually designed to remove dirt particles down to between 10 and 12 μm in size. For severe heavy-duty operating conditions, however, the secondary fuel filter will remove particles down to between 3 and 5 μm in size.

Filter Change Intervals

The engine application and environmental conditions determine the best change interval for both primary and secondary fuel filters. Often filters are changed at a specific accumulated mileage, number of hours, time period, or amount of fuel consumed by the engine. Each engine or equipment manufacturer specifies this in its operator and service manuals. For example, the specification may be to change filters every 16,000 km (10,000 miles), 250 hours, or 6 months—whichever comes first.

In cases where low engine power is noticed, with no unusual color exhaust smoke, a fuel pressure gauge can be installed in the inlet and outlet sides of the secondary filter head to determine if the filter is plugged. On the primary filter, a restriction check can be made of the fuel system on the suction side. This can be done by connecting a Hg (mercury) manometer or vacuum gauge to the outlet side of the primary filter head. Refer to Figures 20–53 through 20–56, which illustrate the use of manometers. Normally there is a small pipe plug that can be removed from the filter head so the vacuum gauge or manometer brass fitting can be installed. A small-bore rubber hose is then connected to the fitting, with the opposite end attached to the manometer. Start and run the engine at the recommended rpm, which is usually toward the high end of the speed range, and compare the reading on the manometer or vacuum gauge to the specs. For example, on both Caterpillar and Cummins engines, typical maximum allowable restriction is usually limited to 4 in. Hg on a clean system and 8 in. Hg with a dirty fuel filter. Detroit Diesel engines allow 6 in. Hg maximum on a clean system and 12 in. Hg on a dirty system. Values higher than this are indicative of fuel starvation due to plugged or collapsed hoses, hoses too small or kinked, plugging at the fuel tank inlet/suction pickup line, or a plugged filter. Also check for loose connections or fittings to determine if air is being drawn into the system.

When changing fuel filters, keep in mind that two types are commonly used: the S & E (shell and element) model or the SO (spin-on) type. The S & E model employs a steel canister that is retained in place by a bolt; the SO type is hand tightened. Fuel and lube oil filters are similar in external appearance and in liquid flow. Figures 18–25 and 18–26 illustrate an SO and an S & E lube oil filter. With the S & E type, the filter must

FIGURE 4–1 Applying a coat of clean engine lube oil to fuel filter gasket; priming fuel filter with clean filtered fuel. (Courtesy of Cummins Engine Company,

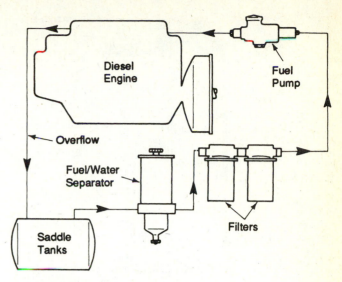

FIGURE 4–2 Typical installation arrangement for using a fuel filter/water separator.

be disassembled, washed in clean solvent, and reassembled with a new filter element and necessary gaskets. In the SO type, once the filter has been removed, it is discarded or recycled and a new unit is used. Figure 4–1 illustrates what to do before installing a new SO filter:

1. Clean the filter head of any dirt.
2. Apply a light coating of clean engine oil to the captive filter seal.
3. Pour clean filtered diesel fuel into the element to prime it.
4. Install the filter by hand and tighten it according to the directions on the attached label, which usually indicate that the filter should be rotated an additional one-half, two-thirds, or one full turn after the gasket makes contact.
5. With S & E type filters, use a torque wrench to correctly tighten the retaining bolt.
6. Inspect the filter for fuel leaks after starting the engine.

NOTE: If the engine runs rough after changing a fuel filter, it is likely that air has been trapped in the fuel system. Bleed all air from the filter by loosening off the bleed screw. In the absence of a bleed screw, individually loosen all external injector fuel lines (see Figure 22–7) until all air has been vented from the system and a steady flow of fuel is visible.

FUEL FILTER/WATER SEPARATORS

Due to the very fine tolerances of the injection components in today's diesel engines, not only is it necessary to ensure that a supply of clean fuel is maintained but also that no trace of water is allowed to enter the fuel injection system. For this reason, most diesel automotive,

heavy-duty truck, stationary, and marine engine applications employ fuel filters with built-in water separators. Figure 4–2 is a typical schematic for a heavy-duty diesel fuel system with a fuel filter/water separator that functions as a *primary* filtration system. Additional fuel filters serve as secondary filters with a finer dirt removal capability. Depending on the engine size and the application, filters can be of the SO or bolted-canister type.

Although there are many manufacturers of fuel filter/water separators, the concept of operation in all cases is to separate the heavier water from the lighter diesel fuel, usually by centrifugal action of the incoming fuel within the specially shaped housing. Figure 4–3 illustrates the flow of diesel fuel into, through, and out of the heavy-duty filter/water separator for a Racor Turbine Series model:

1. In the primary stage, liquid and solid contaminants down to 30 μm are separated out by centrifugal action created by the turbine centrifuge. Dirt and water, both being heavier than the fuel, tend to fall to the bottom of the clear bowl.
2. In the secondary stage, any minute particles of liquid contamination (lighter than the fuel) remain in suspension and flow up with the fuel into the lower part of the filter/separator shell where the minute particles tend to bead on the inner wall of the shell and the bottom of the specially treated filter element. Any accumulation of the water beads (heavier) will allow them to fall to the bottom of the filter/separator bowl.

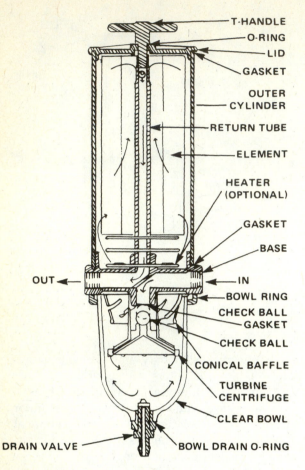

FIGURE 4–3 Fuel flow through a Racor Turbine Series fuel filter/water separator assembly. (Courtesy of Parker Hannifin Corporation, Racor Division.)

3. In the final filtration stage, the fuel flows through the replaceable filter element where the minute solids down to a 2 μm particle size are removed to a 96% rating.

Filter replacement in this model is achieved by loosening off the large T-handle on top of the assembly and opening the drain valve to remove accumulated water and fuel contaminants from the clear bowl. The filter can then be replaced.

In some models of fuel filter/water separators, the first stage of the filter assembly directs the diesel fuel through a tube of fine nylon fibers that are designed to *coalesce* any water. The fuel containing emulsified water passes through the coalescer element. The element retards the flow of water droplets, allowing them to combine to form larger drops of water. The larger drops of water emerging from the coalescer then gravitate to the filter reservoir at the bottom of the filter. The fuel then passes through the second stage of the filter assembly paper element, which is specially treated to restrict passage of small water droplets.

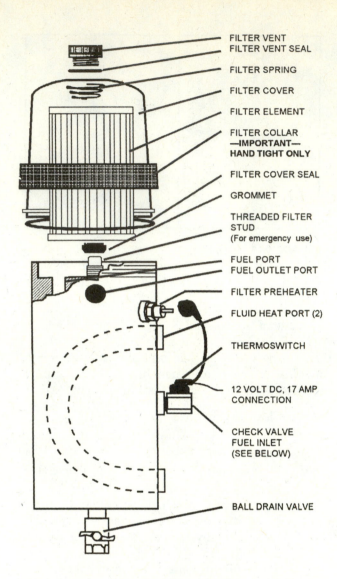

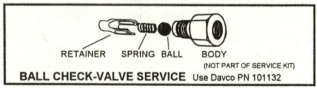

USE A BACK-UP WRENCH ON THE CHECK-VALVE WHEN INSTALLING OR REMOVING THE FUEL FITTING.

FIGURE 4–4 Component parts and features for a Fuel Pro 380 fuel filter/water separator assembly. (Courtesy of Davco Manufacturing Corporation.)

Another widely used filter assembly is the Davco Fuel Pro 380 illustrated in Figure 4–4. In this unique heavy-duty filter model, a clear cover on the upper half of the assembly allows the operator or maintenance technician to see the filter condition, and to check for signs of air in the incoming fuel, as shown in Figure 4–5. In addition, as filter restriction increases through dirt entrapment in the filter pores, dirt collects

FIGURE 4–5 Features of the Davco See-Chek clear filter bowl used with the Fuel Pro 380. (Courtesy of Davco Manufacturing Corporation)

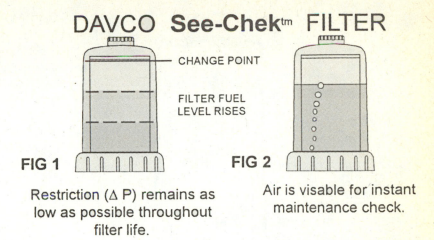

DAVCO See-Chek™ FILTER

FIG 1 — CHANGE POINT — FILTER FUEL LEVEL RISES

Restriction (Δ P) remains as low as possible throughout filter life.

FIG 2

Air is visable for instant maintenance check.

on the filter from the bottom up and the fuel level rises on the clear filter cover, indicating the remaining life to the next service interval. Any water in the fuel falls to the bottom of the filter assembly where it can be drained away using the rugged no-leak quick-drain valve at the base. Within the filter housing, a thermostatically controlled electric preheater warms the fuel to prevent waxing and gelling in cold ambient operating conditions. The standard fuel preheater is rated at 250 watts, 17 amps. An optional 150 watt, 10 amp model is also available. Many electric fuel heaters employ a PTC (positive temperature coefficient) ceramic heating element. A snap-disc thermostat in the heater assembly controls the operating temperature of the diesel fuel.

An optional engine coolant heater tube installed within the filter housing can also be used. The flow of engine coolant through this type of system is illustrated in Figure 4–6. A thermostat shuts off either the electric or engine coolant heater once the engine reaches a predetermined operating temperature. A check valve within the inlet port prevents fuel drain-back when the engine is shut down. This feature prevents loss of fuel prime and hard starting conditions after shutdown. The check valve also prevents fuel losses when the filter assembly is changed.

In the aluminum housing used with the Davco filter assembly, heat radiation from the filter is greater in warm weather than it is in some other filter housings. This reduces the temperature of the fuel and results in cooler fuel entering the system and in engines that run better with more power.

Another diesel fuel preheater system used on many heavy-duty truck applications is the *hot joint system*. This system is used with dual saddle-type fuel tanks that employ a balance line between the tanks on either side of the vehicle (Figure 4–7). The system prevents freeze-up at the fuel tank fitting in cold ambient

operating temperatures, which would create serious engine starting problems. The hot joints can be wired to operate with an ON/OFF toggle switch (used with a 4 minute timer) or a thermoswitch. Each of the hot joints is typically protected by use of individual 15 amp fuses or circuit breakers. If the ACC/IGN circuit will not handle 15 amps, a 20 amp relay can be used. An optional top-tank-mounted hot joint is also available. The hot joint heat probe shown in Figure 4–7 is thermostatically controlled for automatic operation from 40° to 60°F (4.5° to 15.5°C).

Figure 4–8 shows the *Fuel Manager* diesel filtration system. It includes an electronic water-in-fuel detection system to warn the operator or technician of excess water accumulation in the filter system. On diesel cars, pickup trucks, and light-duty trucks, this water sensor causes a light to illuminate on the vehicle dashboard. In many applications the operator can then simply activate a push-button drain valve located in the filter cover assembly or employ a mechanical lever system to automatically drain the accumulated water from the base of the filter assembly. The lamp extinguishes once the water has been drained, since the water acts as a ground system whereas the diesel fuel is more of an insulator.

FUEL HEATERS

Hot Line Fuel Heater
Some heavy-duty Class 8 trucks and truck/tractors employ an advanced solid-state electric fuel heater that is actually constructed within the fuel line from the fuel tank to the filter assembly. Figure 4–9 illustrates this type of fuel heater system which is commonly called a *hot line system* (or a Thermoline, manufactured by the Racor Division of the Parker Hannifin Corporation). Figure 4–10 illustrates the wiring system used with a hot line system on a vehicle with a single

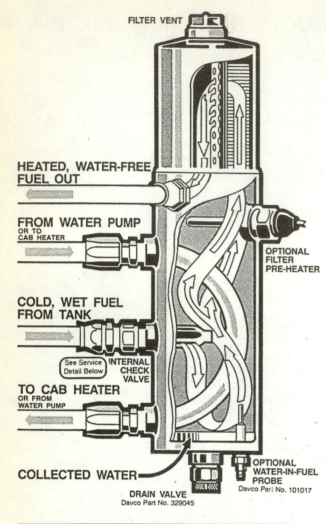

FILTER VENT

HEATED, WATER-FREE FUEL OUT

FROM WATER PUMP
OR TO CAB HEATER

OPTIONAL FILTER PRE-HEATER

COLD, WET FUEL FROM TANK

See Service Detail Below   INTERNAL CHECK VALVE

TO CAB HEATER
OR FROM WATER PUMP

COLLECTED WATER

OPTIONAL WATER-IN-FUEL PROBE
Davco Part No. 101017

DRAIN VALVE
Davco Part No. 329045

BODY
NOT A KIT PART

BALL   SPRING   RETAINER

BALL CHECK-VALVE SERVICE
USE DAVCO KIT 101132

FIGURE 4–6 *Features and plumbing arrangement for a Davco Fuel Pro Model 321 which employs engine-heated coolant running through the filter body. (Courtesy of Davco Manufacturing Corporation)*

fuel tank; a dual saddle-tank system is also available. In a dual-tank arrangement, two hot line heaters are used (one for each tank) and a three-way dash-mounted selector switch is activated by the truck driver. The driver can activate either fuel tank's heater for a closed, single draw/single-return system; however both tanks cannot be heated at the same time. Placing the dash switch in the center, or OFF position, turns off all power to both hot line heaters.

Cold-Weather Operation

The properties of diesel fuel and its contaminants, especially water, may be altered drastically in cold weather. Depending on the quality of the diesel fuel, its cloud point (the point at which paraffin crystals precipitate) may be −17° to 7.2°C (0° to 45°F). Paraffin crystals (which are found in most diesel fuels) quickly coat filter elements and prevent fuel flow and vehicle operation. In addition, water contamination in the form of icy slush compounds the problem by slowing fuel flow even more quickly. It is desirable, therefore, to heat diesel fuel as close to the filter element as possible to reliquify wax and ice crystals.

Several methods are available to heat diesel fuel to maintain operation in cold weather. The two most common are these:

1. Electric heaters
   a. Built into the diesel fuel filter/water separator
   b. An inline unit
2. Coolant heaters
   a. Built into the diesel fuel filter/water separator
   b. An inline unit

For most low-flow applications (under 1.89 lpm [liters per minute], .5 gpm [gallons per minute]), an efficient 150 to 200 watt electrical heater that is thermostatically controlled will economically provide immediate heat and maintain equipment operation. For higher-flow applications, the problem is more challenging. To ensure operation in cold conditions, a large amount of energy is required (for example, 1.5 gpm flow for a Cummins 350 to maintain operation). Several options are available: an efficient 350 to 500 watt electrical heater; a 150 to 300 watt start-up heater in conjunction with a coolant heater; and a combination coolant heater with an electrical heater. These options will prevent paraffin crystals from coating the filter medium and will assist in providing diesel fuel flow to the injection system in most cold-weather conditions. In extreme cold conditions (−76°C, −60°F) additional measures are required.

In a diesel engine, only a small percentage of the fuel that is delivered to the unit injectors is actually used for combustion purposes. As much as 80% is used for cooling and lubricating the injection pump and injector component parts. The high rate of return fuel has been filtered of its wax precipitants and has been warmed by the heat from the engine. On high-pressure in-line injection pumps, most of the fuel is returned from the pump, not from the nozzles.

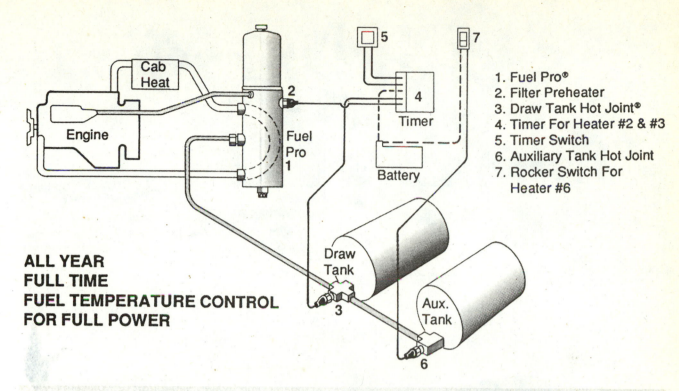

1. Fuel Pro®
2. Filter Preheater
3. Draw Tank Hot Joint®
4. Timer For Heater #2 & #3
5. Timer Switch
6. Auxiliary Tank Hot Joint
7. Rocker Switch For Heater #6

**ALL YEAR
FULL TIME
FUEL TEMPERATURE CONTROL
FOR FULL POWER**

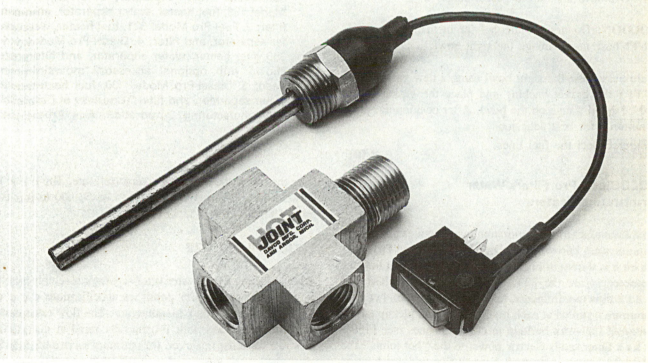

FIGURE 4–7 (a) Typical system schematic showing the Fuel Pro and hot joints located on a heavy-duty truck with saddle tanks; (b) components of the Davco hot joint assembly. (Courtesy of Davco Manufacturing Corporation.)

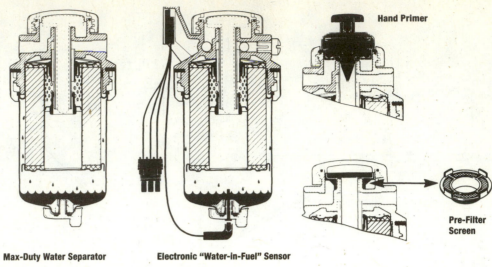

Hand Primer

Max-Duty Water Separator   **Electronic "Water-in-Fuel" Sensor**   **Pre-Filter Screen**

FIGURE 4–8   Marine engine Fuel Manager diesel fuel filtration system. (Courtesy of Stanadyne Diesel Systems.)

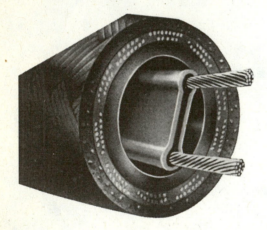

FIGURE 4–9   Close-up view of Thermoline diesel fuel heater. (Courtesy of Parker Hannifin Corporation, Racor Division.)

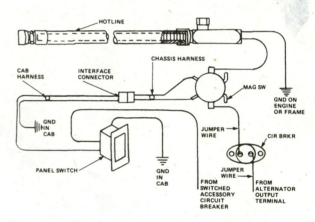

FIGURE 4–10   Electrical installation schematic of a single hot line heater. (Courtesy of Peterbilt Motors Company, Division of PACCAR.)

SELF-TEST QUESTIONS

1. Technician A says that material used in primary fuel filters generally consists of resin pleated paper, whereas technician B says that the primary filter is usually composed of cotton material. Who is correct?

2. Technician A says that a micron is one ten thousandth of a meter. Technician B says that a micron is equivalent to one millionth of a meter. Who is right?

3. After the discussion in Question 2, technician A says that a micron can be written as 0.003937 in., whereas technician B disagrees, saying that a micron is shown as 0.00003937 in. With whom do you agree?

4. Technician A says that the filtering capability of most primary filters used in regular service is rated as 30 μm. Technician B says that it is closer to 12 μm. Who is right?

5. Technician A says that secondary fuel filters used in what is classified as severe-duty service are generally rated at between 3 and 5 μm. Technician B disagrees, saying that this would cause too great a fuel flow restriction. Who is correct?

6. Technician A says that it is not necessary to use a separate primary filter when a good fuel filter/water separator assembly is used in the fuel system. Technician B disagrees, saying that you should

always use a primary fuel filter, regardless of what-ever else is used in the system. Who is correct?

7. Technician A says that water in the fuel will simply cause rusting of injection components. Technician B says that a slug of water can blow the tip off an injector. Who is correct?

8. Technician A says that water in a fuel tank can be caused by allowing the warm return fuel from the engine to cool in the tank. Technician B says that the only way that water can get into the tank is through improper handling of bulk fuel during fill-up. Who is right?

9. To minimize condensation in a fuel tank, you should
   a. always park the truck inside at night in a warm shop
   b. plug in a cylinder block coolant heater at night
   c. use a fuel tank heater
   d. instruct drivers to fill up the fuel tank at the end of each shift or at the end of the day if no shift work is performed

10. A truck fleet supervisor instructs a mechanic that if a fuel filter/water separator is not used on an engine fuel system, to prevent fuel line freeze-up add
    a. methyl or isopropyl alcohol
    b. liquid starting fluid as required
    c. kerosene to cut the fuel's specific gravity
    d. antifreeze in the ratio of 1 pint to every 125 gallons of diesel fuel

11. Fuel filter water separators generally operate on the principle of coalescence. This simply means
    a. droplets of water entering the fuel/water filter form into large globules or droplets, where they settle in the reservoir.
    b. water is broken down into tiny droplets to make it easier to spin them loose by gravitational forces.
    c. preheating the water to make it easier to trap in the filter.

12. Technician A says that the word *primary* and the word *secondary* are usually cast onto the fuel filter housing cover to prevent improper installation in the system. Technician B says that it doesn't matter, since the two fuel filters are the same physical size anyway. Who is correct?

13. Technician A says that fuel filters must be changed every 300 hours or 9000 miles. Technician B says that the filter change period can be determined by the truck fleet operating conditions. Who is correct?

14. Technician A says that fuel filters should be replaced when they become plugged. This can be determined when the engine loses horsepower. Technician B disagrees, saying that they should be changed at regular intervals to suit the operating conditions of the equipment. Who is correct?

15. Technician A says that to determine if the primary fuel filter is plugged you can make a fuel system restriction (vacuum) check. Technician B says that you should insert a fuel pressure gauge and determine the pressure drop through the filter assembly. What procedure would be acceptable?

16. True or false: A shell-and-element filter assembly is a throwaway type of unit.

17. A truck fleet mechanic says that after replacing diesel fuel filters you should always
    a. ensure that the filters have been filled up with clean filtered fuel
    b. fill the filters with unfiltered fuel since any dirt will be filtered out as it passes through the filter
    c. bleed (prime) the fuel system of all entrapped air
    d. fill up the fuel tank and crank the engine over until it starts

18. Technician A says that spin-on types of fuel filters should be tightened between one-half and two-thirds of a turn after the gasket contacts the base. Technician B says that the spin-on filter should be tightened securely with a strap wrench. Who is right?

19. Technician A says that if the engine runs rough or fails to run after changing the fuel filter assemblies, the most probable cause is a lack of fuel in the tank. Technician B says that it is more likely to be due to air trapped in the system. Who is correct?

20. True or false: Fuel filter/water separators contain internal heater units that must be switched ON/OFF in cold weather to prevent fuel line freeze-up.

21. Technician A says that water accumulation in a fuel filter/water separator must be drained off every day to prevent fuel filter damage. Technician B says that water accumulation has to be drained off only when the reservoir bowl is full or when the warning light on the vehicle instrument panel comes on. Who is correct?

22. Technician A says that all fuel filter/water separators contain a filter assembly that must be changed each time the regular fuel filters are changed. Technician B says that some models of fuel filter/water separators do not use a filter element at all and that the regular primary and secondary fuel filters are sufficient. Who is right?

23. Technician A says that a Thermoline unit is a heated fuel line that takes the place of the regular fuel line. Technician B says that a Thermoline unit is a fuel filter/water separator with a thermostatically controlled heating element. Who is correct?

24. The reason for using a fuel heater in winter is to
    a. increase the engine horsepower
    b. prevent waxing of the fuel filters, which would cause plugging
    c. stop any water in the fuel from freezing
    d. allow the engine to idle overnight without damage

25. Technician A says that fuel heaters are operated by warm coolant from the engine, whereas technician B says that only electrically operated fuel heaters are used. Who is correct?

Types of Fuel Systems

OVERVIEW

A number of different types of diesel fuel injection systems are in use today. Because of the move to strictly control engine exhaust emissions, most OEMs now produce electronically controlled fuel injection systems. Although these new fuel systems will dominate the rest of the 1990s and beyond, there are still millions of diesel engines in use with mechanically operated and controlled fuel injection systems that will continue to operate for years. In this chapter we discuss these mechanical systems briefly, but mainly we consider the latest electronically controlled fuel injection systems from major OEMs such as Cummins, Caterpillar, Detroit Diesel, Volvo, and Mack.

TOPICS

- Mechanical fuel systems
- High- and low-pressure fuel systems
- Pump-line-nozzle system operation
- Electronic PLN system
- Unit pump system
- Distributor pump system
- Electronic distributor pump
- Mechanical unit injectors
- Overview of electronic unit injectors
- System elements
- Sensors
- Operation of electronic unit injectors
- Electronic control modules
- Detroit Diesel electronic systems
- Caterpillar electronic fuel systems
- Cummins electronics
- HEUI fuel system
- Self-test questions

MECHANICAL FUEL SYSTEMS

It is not the intent within this chapter to discuss in detail the many models of mechanical fuel injection systems. Nevertheless, since there are literally millions of these systems still in use worldwide, we need to review briefly their basic way of operating. This knowledge will prepare us to understand and appreciate the differences between mechanical and electronically controlled systems.

Although all major OEMs now produce diesel engines with fuel systems that are electronically controlled, the procedure used to raise the trapped diesel fuel within the injection pump, or in a unit injector system, is still mechanical. In a multiple-plunger inline pump system similar to that shown in Figure 5–1, a rotating camshaft within the injection pump housing raises the individual cylinder pumping plungers as illustrated in Figure 5–2. In the unit injector system, a camshaft-actuated rocker arm assembly, or camshaft/pushrod-rocker arm assembly, forces a pumping plunger down to raise the fuel pressure. In the HEUI (hydraulically actuated electronic unit injector) system, which is employed by Caterpillar and Navistar, the pumping plunger is forced down by the use of hydraulic pressure. This action causes a high enough diesel fuel injection pressure to open the needle valve within the spray tip against spring force, so fuel can enter the combustion chamber.

HIGH- AND LOW-PRESSURE FUEL SYSTEMS

The terms *high pressure* and *low pressure* in relation to a fuel injection system refer to the type of injection pump

The eight major components are:

1. Fuel Tank
2. Primary Fuel Filter
3. Fuel Supply Pump
4. Secondary Filter
5. Injection Pump
6. High Pressure Fuel Lines
7. Injection Nozzles
8. Governor

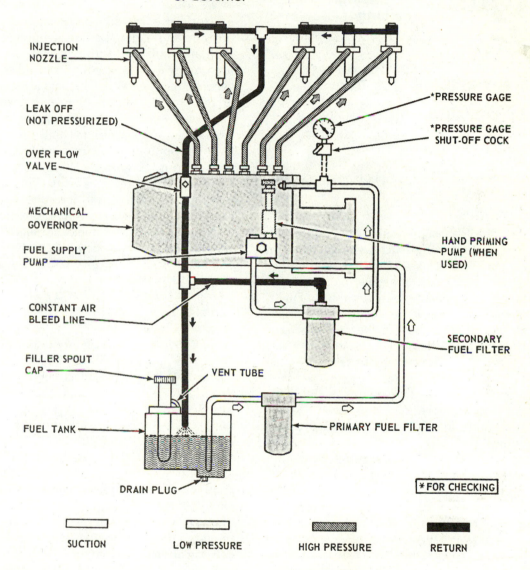

INJECTION NOZZLE

LEAK OFF (NOT PRESSURIZED)

OVER FLOW VALVE

MECHANICAL GOVERNOR

FUEL SUPPLY PUMP

CONSTANT AIR BLEED LINE

FILLER SPOUT CAP

FUEL TANK

VENT TUBE

DRAIN PLUG

*PRESSURE GAGE

*PRESSURE GAGE SHUT-OFF COCK

HAND PRIMING PUMP (WHEN USED)

SECONDARY FUEL FILTER

PRIMARY FUEL FILTER

*FOR CHECKING

SUCTION | LOW PRESSURE | HIGH PRESSURE | RETURN

FIGURE 5–1 Typical layout of a high-pressure multiple-plunger mechanical inline fuel injection pump system. (Courtesy of Mack Trucks, Inc.)

**Pressure Fuel
To Nozzle**

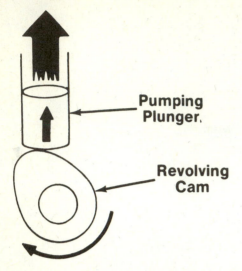

Pumping
Plunger

Revolving
Cam

FIGURE 5–2 *Basic concept of operation of a single-cylinder jerk pump system.*

used on the engine. If an engine employs an inline multiple-plunger injection pump such as that found on many six-cylinder four-stroke-cycle diesel engines, or uses a distributor-type pump, the metering and timing of the fuel are done within the injection pump. Fuel is then delivered to each cylinder nozzle in engine firing-order sequence through a steel fuel line since the delivery pressure will range between 1800 and 4000 psi (12,411 to 27,580 kPa). This is where the term *high-pressure fuel system* originates.

High-pressure fuel injection pumps of the inline variety are capable of delivering higher fuel pressures than those available from a smaller distributor-type pump assembly. The high fuel pressure delivered to the cylinder nozzle is then forced through a series of very small orifices (holes) in the nozzle tip, which causes an increase in the injected fuel pressure. This action can be compared to a garden hose that is turned on with no spray nozzle on its end. The result is substantial volume flow but little pressure other than that supplied by the city water mains. If you now place your finger, thumb, or a nozzle connection over the end of the hose, there is an immediate increase in velocity (speed and direction of the water) but a subsequent decrease in volume flow. At the nozzle, the same situation occurs, resulting in fuel spray-in pressures on the latest models of Robert Bosch and Caterpillar inline pump systems approaching 19,000 psi (1292 atm). Distributor pumps have spray-in pressures that are usually limited to between 11,000 and 14,000 psi (748 to 952 atm).

A low-pressure fuel system is one that delivers fuel to the unit injectors at pressures between 50 and 200 psi (345 to 1379 kPa). Typical fuel systems that use this type of system are all existing electronically controlled unit injector systems. Although the fuel delivery pressure is moderately low in comparison to the inline or distributor-type injection pump systems, a rocker-arm-activated injector plunger raises this supply pressure to between 4000 and 5000 psi (27,580 to 34,475 kPa) average. The fuel pressure then lifts the injector's needle valve from its seat against spring pressure and allows fuel to be injected into the combustion chamber. In a unit injector system, there is no need to create a long column of pressurized fuel oil between the pump and the nozzle as you must do on a high-pressure fuel system; therefore, the resultant injection pressures on a unit injector system are higher than those for an inline high-pressure pump system. The spray-in pressures on electronic unit injectors can run between 26,000 and 28,000 psi (1769 to 1905 atm). This produces a finer fuel spray (atomization), greater penetration into the compressed cylinder air mass, and usually a shorter ignition delay period. Consequently, mechanical or electronic unit injector systems are now being used by Detroit Diesel, Caterpillar, Cummins, and Volvo on diesel engines.

PUMP-LINE-NOZZLE SYSTEM OPERATION

One of the most widely used injection systems is known as the PLN (pump-line-nozzle) system (see Figure 5–1). Major manufacturers of the PLN system include Robert Bosch and their licensees which include Zexel (Diesel Kiki) and Nippondenso in Japan. In the United Kingdom, Lucas is a major producer of these types of fuel systems and at one time was closely allied with Robert Bosch. In the United States, Caterpillar, which manufactures its own system, employs a PLN fuel system similar in design and operation to that produced by Robert Bosch.

The basic function of the PLN fuel system is to provide a reservoir of diesel fuel, provide adequate circulation of clean, filtered fuel free of entrapped air, provide lubrication of the injection pump components, cool these components, and provide high-pressure fuel for injection purposes into the combustion chamber. Warm fuel is then recirculated back to the fuel tank(s) where it is allowed to cool. In the fuel system illustrated in Figure 5–1, fuel is pushed from the tank by atmospheric air and the suction created at the fuel supply pump after passing through a primary fuel filter. Any loose fittings between the tank and supply pump will cause air to be pulled into the fuel system and cause operating conditions such as a misfiring engine, rough running, and a possible no-start condition.

Fuel under low pressure from the supply pump is then forced through a secondary fuel filter before entering the injection pump. Within the injection pump housing, fuel at each individual jerk pump (see Figure 5–2) is metered, timed, and pressurized. Then it is delivered through a spring-loaded delivery valve, illustrated in Figure 5–3, where it passes through a steel line to the injector nozzle assembly. Each cylinder receives fuel in the engines firing order sequence. For example, on a six-cylinder engine this may be 1–5–3–6–2–4. The high-pressure fuel from the pumping plunger must be high enough to lift the nozzle needle valve from its seat against spring pressure to allow fuel to enter the combustion chamber. At the end of injection, the nozzle spring closes the needle valve, and the delivery valve within the injection pump starts to close. As the delivery valve closes, its design allows a percentage of the high-pressure fuel to flow back into the injection pump housing. This action lowers the PLN pressure below the opening level of the nozzle but maintains a residual pressure within the line in the region of 500 to 700 psi (3447 to 4826 kPa). A leak-off line from each nozzle permits fuel that is used for cooling and lubrication to return to a tee fitting at the injection pump, where warm fuel from the housing also returns to the fuel tank.

PLN Plunger Operation

Within the injection pump housing of the system shown in Figure 5–1, are six individual jerk pumps similar to the one shown in Figure 5–2. In Figure 5–4, with the plunger at the bottom of its stroke, both ports are uncovered by the top of the plunger, and the pump reservoir is full of fuel that will enter through both ports. The fuel delivery valve is closed at this time.

As the plunger is starting its upward travel (by rotation of the injection pump camshaft), some fuel will spill back out both ports into the reservoir until they are covered by the top land area of the plunger. This is termed *port closing* and is the basic start to injection. Note that the delivery valve is still on its seat.

The fuel pressure will continue to rise until it is high enough to lift or force the discharge valve off its seat, thereby allowing the displaced fuel to pass through the fuel line to the nozzle and on into the cylinder, with the delivery valve open. Injection will continue until the lower helical land uncovers the control port. This port is uncovered slightly ahead of the actual ending of the upward-moving plunger, which will displace the remaining fuel back to the reservoir.

The displaced fuel is allowed to escape down the relief area of the plunger and out the control port to the reservoir. The discharge valve closes, and the

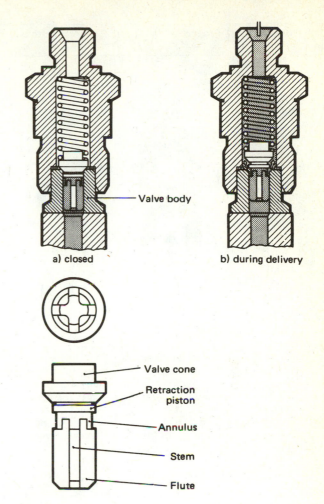

FIGURE 5–3 Nomenclature and concept of operation for a pump plunger spring-loaded delivery valve. (Courtesy of Robert Bosch Inc.)

plunger completes its stroke and is positively returned to the next intake stroke by the plunger return spring.

At the end of injection when the control port is uncovered, the high-pressure fuel in the pump chamber flashes back into the reservoir; therefore, to prevent eventual erosion of the pump housing, this pressure is deflected by the hardened end of the barrel locating screw. Two ports cut deflection pressures in half, while the conical port disperses the spill deflection.

Metering Principle

The amount or volume of the fuel charge is regulated by rotating the plunger in the barrel as shown in Figure 5–5 to effectively alter the relationship of the control port and the control helix on the plunger. This is done by means of a rack and a control collar or control sleeve. The *rack* is basically a rod with teeth on one side, which is supported and operates in bores in the housing. The rack is in turn connected to a governor.

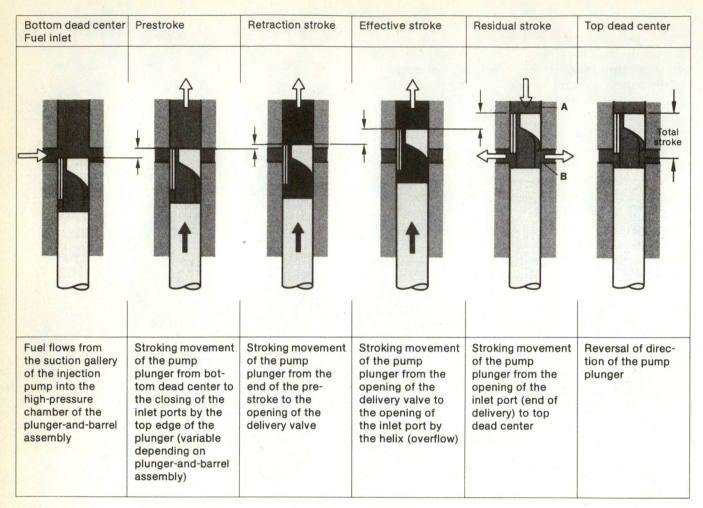

Bottom dead center Fuel inlet	Prestroke	Retraction stroke	Effective stroke	Residual stroke	Top dead center
Fuel flows from the suction gallery of the injection pump into the high-pressure chamber of the plunger-and-barrel assembly	Stroking movement of the pump plunger from bottom dead center to the closing of the inlet ports by the top edge of the plunger (variable depending on plunger-and-barrel assembly)	Stroking movement of the pump plunger from the end of the prestroke to the opening of the delivery valve	Stroking movement of the pump plunger from the opening of the delivery valve to the opening of the inlet port by the helix (overflow)	Stroking movement of the pump plunger from the opening of the inlet port (end of delivery) to top dead center	Reversal of direction of the pump plunger

FIGURE 5–4 *Phases of operation of the plunger stroke in a jerk pump injection system required to deliver fuel under pressure to the injection nozzles. (Courtesy of Robert Bosch Inc.)*

The geared segment or control collar is clamped to the top of the control sleeve with teeth that engage the rack. The control sleeve is a loose fit over the barrel and is slotted at the bottom to engage the wings on the plunger so that as the rack is moved it causes rotation of the collar, sleeve, and plunger.

The operation of Robert Bosch inline pumps is basically the same as that for other similarly designed pumps; however, let us quickly review the pumping plunger's operation and excess fuel device so that we thoroughly understand the principle.

The plunger within the barrel is moved up and down by the action of the rotating camshaft within the injection pump housing; it can also be rotated by the movement of the fuel control rack connected to the throttle and governor linkage. Any time that the stop control is moved to the engine shutdown position, the plunger is rotated as shown in Figure 5–5, whereby the vertical slot machined in the plunger will always be in alignment with the supply or control port. Therefore, regardless of the plunger's vertical position within the barrel, fuel pressure can never exceed that delivered by the fuel-transfer pump. This pressure will never be able to overcome the force of the delivery valve spring, so no fuel can be sent to the injector nozzles.

During any partial fuel delivery situation, the amount of fuel supplied to the injector will be in proportion to the *effective stroke* of the plunger, which simply means that the instant the supply port is covered by the upward-moving plunger, fuel will start to flow to the injector. This will continue as long as the control port is covered; however, as soon as the upward-moving plunger helix uncovers this port, fuel pressure to the injector is lost and injection ceases. Therefore, fuel is only effectively delivered to the injector as long as the control port is covered; this is shown in Figure 5–5

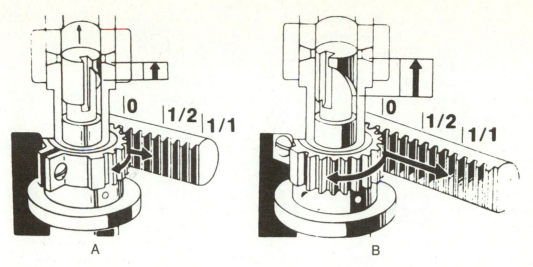

FIGURE 5–5 (a) Partial fuel delivery position; (b) maximum fuel delivery position of a gear/rack-controlled injection pump. (Courtesy of Robert Bosch Inc.)

for any partial throttle position. The effective stroke will vary in proportion to the throttle and rack position from idle to maximum fuel.

When the operator or driver moves the throttle to its maximum limit of travel, the effective stroke of the plunger, due to the rotation of the plunger helix, will allow greater fuel delivery because of the longer period that the control port is closed during the upward movement of the plunger by the pump camshaft.

Figure 5–5 shows the actual adjusting mechanism that alters the pumping element fuel delivery through the control rod (rack), which is connected to the throttle pedal through the governor assembly.

Injection Pump Delivery Valves

In single- or multiple-cylinder plunger injection pumps, a spring-loaded delivery valve is required. This valve has two main functions:

1. The pumping plunger within the barrel is sealed from the pump-to-nozzle delivery line until approximately 150 to 200 psi (1034 to 1379 kPa) is created by the upward-moving plunger.

2. At the end of the injection period, the fuel pressure in the pump-to-nozzle line needs to be lowered to prevent any fuel dribble into the cylinder. However, this fuel pressure should not be lowered back to zero; otherwise, it would require greater plunger lift at the start of each injection stroke to raise the fuel pressure high enough to reopen the spring-loaded nozzle needle. The delivery valve prevents a reversal of fuel flow from the injection line.

Figure 5–3 illustrates the delivery valve in open and closed positions. At the end of the injection period, once the injector nozzle closes, the high-pressure fuel tends to want to flow back into the injection pump. As this occurs, the delivery valve cone enters the bore of its holder, thereby removing a given volume of fuel from the injection line. This reduction in line volume decreases the existing fuel pressure and retains a residual fuel pressure, which is generally in the region of 700 to 900 psi (4826 to 6205 kPa). If, for example, a nozzle is adjusted to open at 3200 psi (22,064 kPa), the remaining residual pressure in the line allows a quick increase to occur as the pumping plunger rises and opens the delivery valve for the next injection period.

Inline Pump-to-Engine Timing

The purpose of this book is not to provide detailed information on the removal, installation, timing, repair, and troubleshooting of inline pumps for every model of engine. Due to similarity of design and application, the methods required to service and time these fuel injection pumps to typical midrange, midheavy, and heavy-duty on-highway trucks can be considered as being fairly similar to each other. Your guide when preparing to time an injection pump to the engine should always be the EPA exhaust emissions plate/label and tune-up specs decal. This decal is generally attached to the engine valve rocker cover and contains all the information you need.

Installation of an inline multiple-plunger fuel injection pump to an engine is a fairly straightforward procedure as far as actually mounting and bolting the pump into position is concerned. Prior to actual installation, however, it is necessary on some pumps to align a gear timing mark on the engine gear-train with a matching mark on the fuel injection pump-driven gear. On other models of engine an external reference timing mark, provided by the engine manufacturer, may be located on either the flywheel itself or on the crankshaft vibration damper or pulley located at the front of the engine. On some engines timing marks can be found on both the flywheel and vibration damper pulley, as illustrated in Figure 5–6a; Figure 5–6b shows the pump to drive coupling alignment marks.

Generally, the No. 1 piston is used as the reference cylinder on the compression stroke to align the marks with the stationary pointer, which is attached to either the engine gear timing cover at the front or at an accessory inspection plate cover on the flywheel. This is the procedure recommended by the majority of diesel engine manufacturers, with the No. 1 cylinder being determined from the vibration damper/pulley end of the engine. Note, however, that the specific make of engine determines what cylinder to use while on its compression stroke. On some engines the No. 1 cylinder is determined from the flywheel end (rear) of the engine; others may use cylinder 6 on its compression stroke as the reference point to align the injection pump-to-engine timing marks. Similarly, when timing an engine to an injection pump, the No. 1 pump within the housing is always located at the end closest to the drive coupling.

The timing marks on the flywheel or vibration damper pulley may indicate TDC for both cylinders 1 and 6, or possibly for all engine cylinders. Remember the TDC mark on a four-stroke-cycle engine can occur once every 360°. Since the timing mark must be aligned only on the compression stroke, always remove the valve rocker cover to determine if free play exists at the

FIGURE 5–6 (a) Example of engine-to-pump timing marks, which can be referenced when spill timing the pump to the engine; (b) example of the actual timing marks for injection pump to drive coupling. (Courtesy of Robert Bosch Inc.)

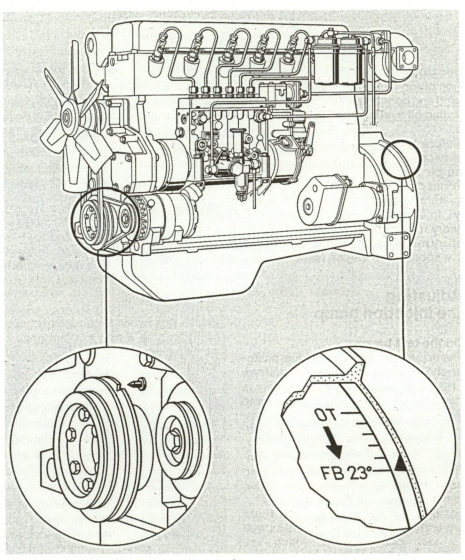

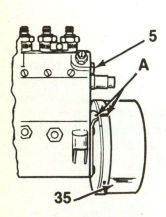

A. Alignment Marks
5. Injection Pump
35. Automatic Timer

B

A

valve operating mechanism on the cylinder being used as the reference point. Failure to do this can result in the piston being at TDC; however, it may be at TDC on the end of its exhaust stroke, which means that in fact the timing mark between the engine and injection pump would be 360° out of phase. This can be confirmed by checking for valve lash on the reference cylinder. If there is no valve lash, it is not on its compression stroke. Rotate the crankshaft manually another 360° to place the piston on its compression stroke.

Although we have discussed TDC for a particular cylinder, the static (engine stopped) pump-to-engine timing mark is always found on the engine exhaust emissions regulation plate or decal, which is usually attached to the valve rocker cover although on some engines it may be located elsewhere. Most engines have the static pump timing set for a number of degrees BTDC on the reference cylinder (No. 1); however, some engines use TDC as the actual pump-to-engine timing mark. On engines that have a BTDC timing mark, say 26° BTDC, then while rotating the engine over manually in its normal direction of rotation from the front, the pump-to-engine timing mark of 26° BTDC would appear before the TDC mark. If the TDC mark appears before the 26° marking, you are turning the engine over backwards. On some engines this timing mark may also have the letters BT or BTC, meaning before top or before top dead center, to assist you in aligning the correct marks. The letters OT, meaning over top, also indicate that it is after TDC as shown in Figure 5–6.

Static Spill Timing

When an injection pump is suspected of being out of time, or after the pump has been reinstalled onto an engine, a pump-to-engine timing procedure must be followed. A commonly employed procedure is known as *spill timing*. During this procedure the engine is stopped (static) and the pump-to-engine timing is performed by determining when the fuel is just starting to be delivered to the No. 1 cylinder. A small gooseneck-shaped line is attached to the top of the delivery valve holder so that the fuel flow can be monitored visually. An example of a gooseneck line or drip spout can be seen in Figure 5–7a.

Engine-to-pump timing can be determined by either a low- or high-pressure spill timing procedure. The low-pressure timing procedure involves using the hand priming pump attached to the transfer/lift pump shown in Figure 5–1, which supplies fuel to the No. 1 pumping plunger of the injection pump. Another low-pressure method uses regulated shop air to force the fuel through the injection pump. Both of these low-pressure spill timing procedures are commonly used

and are reasonably accurate. The drawback of the low-pressure procedure is that the technician must first remove the pumping plunger spring-loaded delivery valve. The delivery valve components can be seen in Figure 5–7b. Removal is necessary because the low fuel pressure created is insufficient to lift the delivery valve against the spring force. For more precise pump-to-engine timing, a high-pressure spill timing procedure is recommended. The high-pressure procedure uses an electric-motor-driven fuel pump system that creates fuel pressure high enough to open the spring-loaded delivery valve in the top of each pumping plunger assembly.

Regardless of what spill timing method is used, when the engine-to-pump timing marks are not in alignment, and the piston in the No. 1 cylinder is just starting its compression stroke, fuel will flow freely from the small gooseneck-shaped line attached to the No. 1 pumping plunger delivery valve holder shown in Figure 5–7a. This fuel flow occurs because the plunger is at the BDC (bottom dead center) position, which can be seen on the left-hand side of Figure 5–7c. This allows fuel under pressure from the injection pump gallery to flow in over the top of the plunger and exit out of the delivery valve holder at the top. As the engine is manually rotated in its normal direction of rotation, the injection pump camshaft will raise the pumping plunger (prestroke) until it closes off the fuel ports within the barrel. When this point is reached, fuel stops flowing out of the delivery valve holder, or the gooseneck-shaped fuel line if attached to the delivery valve holder. When the fuel from this line is reduced to 1 to 2 drops a minute (Figure 5–7d), this is the start of the static pump injection for that cylinder. The next step is to check the position of the engine flywheel or pulley timing marks to determine if the pump is correctly timed to the engine. If not, the pump or its drive coupling must be rotated to bring the engine and pump timing marks into proper alignment.

Once spill timing is complete and the fuel lines have been reinstalled, bleed the fuel system. Basically, bleeding of the system involves removing all entrapped air, which can be done by opening up the various bleeder screws on the fuel filter housing and the injection pump housing, then using the hand priming pump (Figure 5–1) to push fuel through the system.

Once the injection pump is free of air, confirmed by the fact that no air bubbles are evident in the spilling fuel, each one of the fuel injector high-pressure lines can be left loose about one-half to one-full turn. The engine priming pump can be used again to push fuel through the lines; however, it is usually better to crank the engine over until fuel free of air flows from

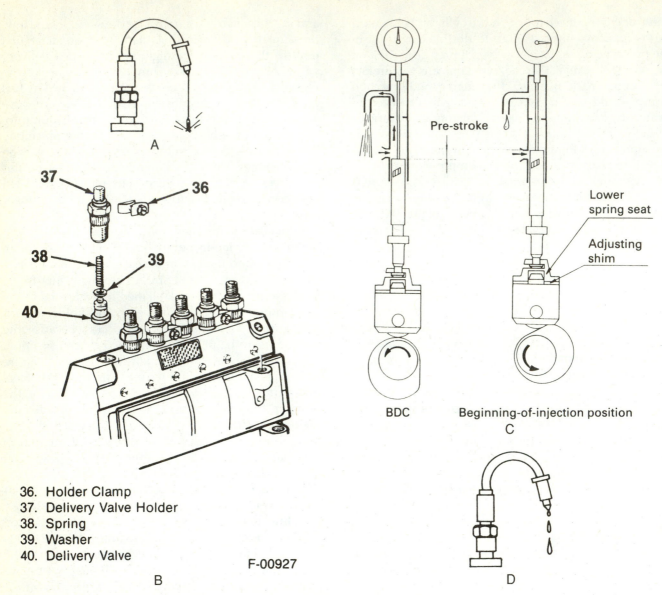

36. Holder Clamp
37. Delivery Valve Holder
38. Spring
39. Washer
40. Delivery Valve

F-00927

FIGURE 5–7   (a) Gooseneck fuel line attached to the top of the No.1 cylinder injection pump delivery valve holder (internal delivery valve/spring removed) showing a steady stream of fuel flowing from pumping chamber (barrel); (b) delivery valve components; (c) sequence to determine injection pump prestroke, or lift-to-port closure dimension using a dial indicator gauge and gooseneck fuel line to determine where and when the fuel flow stops; (d) stop crankshaft rotation when fuel flow changes from a solid stream to the formation of drops. (Courtesy of Zexel USA).

each line at the injector, after which time each line can be tightened up. Start the engine and check for any fuel leaks. If the engine still runs rough, rebleed the system. You can, however, loosen each fuel injector line one at a time to see if any air escapes as you hold a rag around the line nut; then retighten it when you are sure that there is no air left in the system.

ELECTRONIC PLN SYSTEM

For diesel engines to comply with mandated exhaust emissions standards in Europe, Japan, and the United States, it has been necessary to modify existing fuel injection systems so that a series of electrical sensors can continually monitor the changing operating conditions

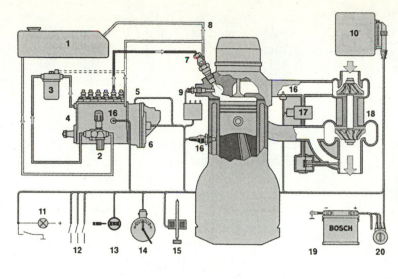

1 Fuel tank, 2 Supply pump, 3 Fuel filter,
4 In-line fuel-injection pump, 5 Timing
device, 6 Governor, 7 Nozzle-and-holder
assembly, 8 Fuel return line, 9 Sheathed-
element glow plug with glow control unit,
10 Electronic control unit, 11 Diagnosis indicator, 12 Switches for clutch, brake, exhaust
brake, 13 Speed selector lever, 14 Pedal
position sensor, 15 Engine-speed sensor,
16 Temperature sensor (water, air, fuel),
17 Charge-pressure sensor, 18 Turbocharger, 19 Battery, 20 Glow-plug and
starter switch.

FIGURE 5–8   Major components of a fuel injection system with an electronically
controlled inline fuel injection pump. (Courtesy of Robert Bosch Inc.)

of the engine and equipment. Figure 5–8 illustrates an electronically controlled PLN system for a high-speed heavy-duty diesel engine. Modifications to the mechanical injection pump assembly are best viewed by reference to Figure 5–9. Note that although the pumping plunger (8) still operates within a barrel (2), it also moves through a control sleeve (3). The sleeve can be moved to allow an adjustable prestroke to change the port closing, or to start injection. Compare this lift-to-port closure shown as h in Figure 5–9 with that for the mechanical pump illustrated in Figure 5–4. By moving the control sleeve upward in the direction of fuel delivery—closer toward TDC as per Figure 5–9—the plunger has to lift through a greater distance (longer prestroke) before it is able to close the control bore (6); therefore, injection starts later. If the sleeve is closer to BDC, injection starts earlier, since the control bore enters the sleeve earlier. The actual fuel delivery rate can be altered by the design of the injection pump camshaft lobe.

The cutaway view of a six-cylinder engine injection pump in Figure 5–10 highlights the control sleeve design on the pumping plunger. Both the injected fuel quantity and the start of injection are electronically controlled by means of linear solenoid actuators. The injection sequence is controlled from an ECU (electronic control unit) which receives electrical inputs from a number of engine sensors (see Figure 5–8). Each sensor is fed a voltage input from the ECU in the region of 5 volts, although this may be higher depending on the OEM using the system. Each sensor completes the electrical loop back to the ECU by sending

an output signal based on its existing operating condition. Each temperature sensor, for example, is designed to have a fixed resistance value when cold; as it warms up, the resistance value decreases. An oil, fuel, or coolant temperature sensor may be designed to have 115,000 ohms when cold and drop to 70 ohms when it is at normal operating temperature. What this means is that if the ECU outputs a 5 volt reference value to the sensor, the high resistance value will restrict the return signal to the ECU and the voltage value will be lower, usually in the region of 0.5 volts. For any operating temperature, therefore, the return voltage signal value to the ECU will vary between 0.5 and 5 volts. A pressure sensor, such as an oil or turbocharger boost, operates similarly to that described for the temperature sensors.

An inductive position sensor tells the ECU the position of the injection pump control rod/rack. An engine speed sensor (Figure 5–8; item 15) scans a pulse ring located to monitor the camshaft speed. A fuel temperature sensor monitors the fuel in the supply line to the injection pump. The accelerator pedal incorporates a variable resistor (potentiometer) so that the percentage of pedal opening can be relayed to the ECU. The throttle pedal is designed to show a high resistance value with a closed throttle at idle speed; consequently, the input voltage value of 5 volts is reduced to approximately 0.5 volts back to the ECU. At a WOT (wide open throttle) position, the return voltage back to the ECU is close to 5 volts, or the same as the input value. In addition, an intake manifold air-temperature sensor

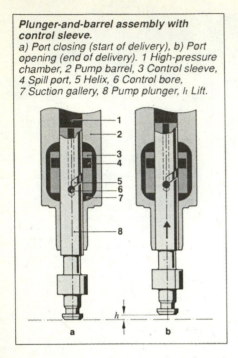

Plunger-and-barrel assembly with control sleeve.
a) Port closing (start of delivery), b) Port opening (end of delivery). 1 High-pressure chamber, 2 Pump barrel, 3 Control sleeve, 4 Spill port, 5 Helix, 6 Control bore, 7 Suction gallery, 8 Pump plunger, *h* Lift.

FIGURE 5–9 Components of an electronically controlled inline fuel injection pump plunger and barrel assembly. (Courtesy of Robert Bosch Inc.)

indicates to the ECU the denseness of the air flowing into the engine cylinders based on temperature. If a turbocharger is used, a turbo boost sensor functions to tell the ECU basically the load under which the engine is operating. A high boost pressure means greater load, while low boost pressure indicates a lower load level. An alternator speed signal can also be employed to drive an electronic tachograph. This signal, in turn, can be used to indicate to the ECU the vehicle's road speed. The clutch pedal position is indicated by a switch, and the stop-lamp switch provides information relative to the brake pedal position.

From all of the various sensor inputs, the ECU calculates and adjusts the electrical current to the rack actuator system of the fuel injection pump. Figure 5–11 illustrates the sequence of events involved in the EDC (electronic diesel control) system. The ECU compares the actual plunger/barrel port closing signal for the start of injection from a needle-motion sensor installed in one of the injector nozzle holders with an operating value that has been programmed into the computer map. The port closing actuator system is then adjusted by varying the control current so that the actual requested throttle/fuel demands are met. The travel of the injection pump rack electromagnet is

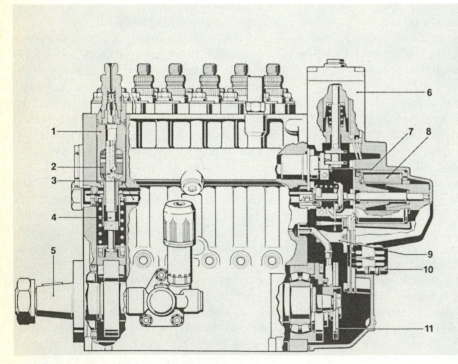

1 Pump cylinder, 2 Control sleeve, 3 Control rod, 4 Pump plunger, 5 Camshaft, 6 Port-closing actuator solenoid, 7 Control-sleeve setting shaft, 8 Rod-travel actuator solenoid, 9 Inductive rod-travel sensor, 10 Connector, 11 Inductive speed sensor.

FIGURE 5–10 Cutaway view of an electronically controlled inline injection pump illustrating main components. (Courtesy of Robert Bosch Inc.)

FIGURE 5–11 *Electronic open-loop and-closed loop control of the inline fuel injection pump with a control sleeve. (Courtesy of Robert Bosch Inc.)*

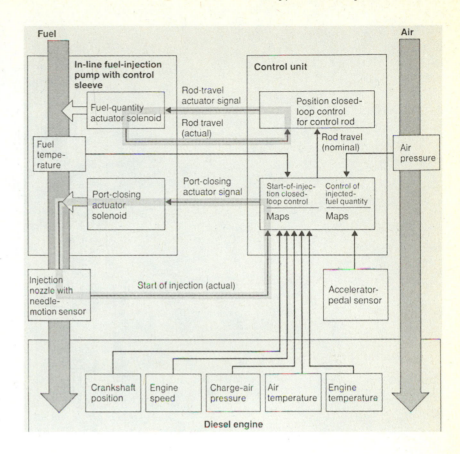

directly proportional to the current demands of injection. The end of injection caused by port opening is varied on the electronically controlled pump in the same way it is for the mechanical system; that is, the pump plunger is rotated through rack movement.

UNIT PUMP SYSTEM

A derivative of the basic jerk-pump system shown in Figure 5–2 is the camshaft-driven and electronically controlled unit pump system illustrated in Figure 5–12. This system is being used by Mercedes-Benz on its new 12L six-cylinder 1995 truck engine—a joint venture with Detroit Diesel. The engine is actually being manufactured in the United States by Detroit Diesel; it will be known as the OM457LA when marketed by Mercedes-Benz but as the Series 55 when distributed by Detroit Diesel. The individual unit pumps for each cylinder are connected by a short steel pipe to an eight-hole injector mounted in the four-valve per cylinder head. This new engine model will be the exclusive property of Mercedes-Benz (who controls Freightliner Trucks) for the first 12 months of its existence, after which time Detroit Diesel will have the right to market it as its own product for any OEM truck chassis.

DISTRIBUTOR PUMP SYSTEM

The mechanical distributor pump system shown in Figure 5–13a is found on small to medium-sized diesel engines and is often referred to as a rotary pump because its concept of operation is similar to an ignition distributor found on gasoline engines. A rotating member called a *rotor* within the pump distributes fuel at high pressure to the individual injectors in engine firing-order sequence. This system is classified as a high-pressure system and is limited to engine sizes up to about 2.0 L per cylinder. Distributor pumps do not have the capability to deliver sufficient fuel volume or to create high enough fuel injection pressures and delivery rates for heavy-duty large-displacement high-speed diesel engines used in trucks.

Distributor pumps are manufactured by Stanadyne Diesel Systems; Robert Bosch, whose VE model is widely used; and Lucas in England, with its legendary DPA (distributor pump assembly). Both Robert Bosch and Lucas have a number of licensees worldwide (for example, Zexel [Diesel Kiki] in Japan) who manufacture these distributor pumps for use in small lightweight and medium-duty diesel engines.

FIGURE 5–12 *Camshaft-driven electronically controlled unit pump illustrating a short pipe connected to the in-head injector. This design results in a "stiff" injection system for low exhaust emissions. (Courtesy of Detroit Diesel Corporation.)*

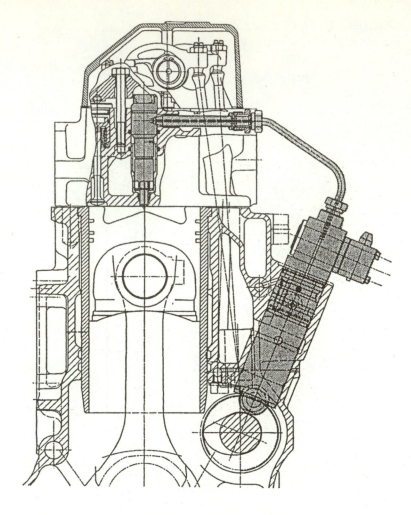

Fuel Flow

Figure 5–13a illustrates the model DB2 injection pump and its major component parts. Flow through the injection pump is as follows: Fuel at lift pump pressure from the secondary fuel filter enters the injection pump at the hydraulic head end (injection line end). This fuel passes into the vane-type transfer pump (2) through a filter screen (1). To control maximum delivery pressure of the shaft-driven transfer pump, a spring-loaded pressure regulating valve bypasses fuel back to the inlet side of the transfer pump. This fuel pressure is set with the injection pump mounted on a fuel pump test stand and is usually limited to a maximum of 130 psi (896 kPa).

Transfer pump fuel flows through the center of the rotor and past the retainers (4) and into the hydraulic head of the injection pump. Fuel then flows up to the fuel metering valve (8), which is controlled by throttle position and governor action through connecting passage (5) in the hydraulic head to the automatic timing advance (6) and continues on through the radial passage (9) to this valve.

The pump rotor, which is turning at injection pump speed (one-half engine speed), allows the rotor fuel inlet passages (10) to align with the hydraulic head fuel charging ports. Fuel flows into the pumping chamber, where two rotor plungers are moved toward each other by their rollers (11) contacting a cam ring lobe. The rollers force the plungers inward to increase the pressure of the trapped fuel, which is directed out of the rotor discharge passage to the single spring-loaded delivery valve and then to the injection nozzle fuel delivery line. This occurs in firing-order sequence as the rotor revolves.

The purpose of the air vent passage (12) in the hydraulic head is to allow a percentage of fuel from the transfer pump to flow into the injection pump housing. This fuel is used to vent air from the system and also to cool and lubricate the internal pump components. This fuel flows back to the fuel tank via a return line.

Charging and Discharging Cycle

Charging Cycle. Rotation of the rotor allows both inlet passages drilled within it to register with the cir-

FIGURE 5–13 (a) Features of a Stanadyne model DB2 mechanical distributor injection pump; (b) fuel flow during the pump charging cycle; (c) fuel flow during the pump discharge cycle. (Courtesy of Stanadyne Diesel Systems.)

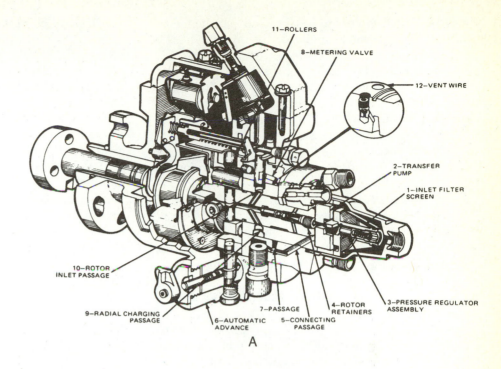

11—ROLLERS
8—METERING VALVE
12—VENT WIRE
2—TRANSFER PUMP
1—INLET FILTER SCREEN
3—PRESSURE REGULATOR ASSEMBLY
4—ROTOR RETAINERS
5—CONNECTING PASSAGE
7—PASSAGE
6—AUTOMATIC ADVANCE
9—RADIAL CHARGING PASSAGE
10—ROTOR INLET PASSAGE

A

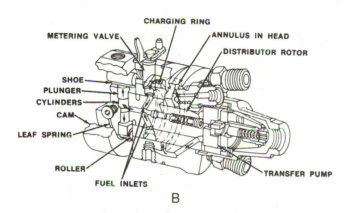

METERING VALVE
CHARGING RING
ANNULUS IN HEAD
DISTRIBUTOR ROTOR
SHOE
PLUNGER
CYLINDERS
CAM
LEAF SPRING
ROLLER
FUEL INLETS
TRANSFER PUMP

B

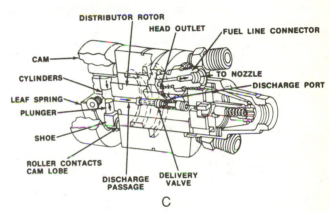

DISTRIBUTOR ROTOR
HEAD OUTLET
FUEL LINE CONNECTOR
CAM
CYLINDERS
LEAF SPRING
PLUNGER
SHOE
ROLLER CONTACTS CAM LOBE
DISCHARGE PASSAGE
DELIVERY VALVE
TO NOZZLE
DISCHARGE PORT

C

cular charging passage ports. The position of the fuel metering valve connected to the governor linkage controls the flow of transfer pump fuel into the pumping chamber and therefore how far apart the two plungers will be. The maximum plunger travel is controlled by the single leaf spring, which contacts the edge of the roller shoes. Maximum outward movement of the plungers will therefore occur only under full-load conditions. Figure 5–13b shows the fuel flow during the charging cycle. Any time that the angled inlet fuel passages of the rotor are in alignment with the ports in the circular passage, the rotor discharge port is not in registry with a hydraulic head outlet and the rollers are also off the cam lobes.

Discharging Cycle. The actual start of injection varies with engine speed since the cam ring is auto-

matically advanced by fuel pressure acting through linkage against it. Therefore, as the rotor turns, the angled inlet passages of the rotor move away from the charging ports. As this happens, the discharge port of the rotor opens to one of the hydraulic head outlets (see Figure 5–13c).

Also at this time, the rollers make contact with the lobes of the cam ring, forcing the shoes and plungers inward, thus creating high fuel pressure in the rotor discharge passage. The fuel flows through the axial discharge passage of the rotor and opens the spring-loaded delivery valve. Fuel then flows through the discharge port to the injection line and injector. This fuel delivery continues until the rollers pass the innermost point of the cam lobe, after which they start to move outward, thereby rapidly reducing the fuel pressure in the rotor's axial discharge passage and simultaneously allowing spring pressure inside the injection nozzle to close the valve.

Immediately after, the rotor discharge port closes totally; a residual injection line pressure of 500 to 600 psi (3447 to 4137 kPa) is maintained. In summation, the delivery valve will seal only while the discharge port is open, because the instant the port closes, residual line pressures are maintained by the seal existing between the close-fitting hydraulic head and rotor.

Fuel Return Circuit

The vent wire passage allows any air and a small amount of fuel to return to the fuel tank. Governor housing fuel pressure is maintained by a spring-loaded ballcheck return fitting in the governor cover of the pump.

ELECTRONIC DISTRIBUTOR PUMP

Major manufacturers of distributor pump systems such as Lucas with its DPA, Robert Bosch with its automotive VE model, and Stanadyne with its well-known DB and DS distributor pumps are three of the major OEMs that have switched to electronic control for various models. One example of such an arrangement is illustrated in Figure 5–14 for the Stanadyne DS model, which is widely used on the General Motors 6.5L V8 pickup truck application.

This DS pump model features a single high-speed solenoid to control both fuel and injection timing. A solenoid spill valve mounted in the hydraulic head area of the pump rotor, to minimize high-pressure volume, is a key to the higher injection pressures available from this pump model over its mechanical counterpart (the DB shown in Figure 5–13a). The geometry of the internal pump cam ring has been designed to ensure higher injection pressures as well as the desired control characteristics relative to the start, duration, and end of injection. The higher injection pressure has been enhanced through a new drive design that features a larger diameter zero-backlash drive shaft containing the cam rollers and four plunger tappets. In this way, the driving loads are isolated from the spinning distributor rotor. A higher gear-drive torque, as well as a belt-drive capability if desired, are accommodated with the larger-diameter drive shaft.

This DS pump model was the first to be offered in the U.S. light-truck consumer market; it was first introduced in 1994 Chevrolet and General Motors light trucks. The pump provides electronic control of both the fuel quantity and start of injection timing. The governor mechanism and fuel metering commonly used on the DB2-type mechanical pump models shown in Figure 5–13a have been replaced with a high-speed electrical actuator. Sensors provide information to an ECM (electronic control module), which

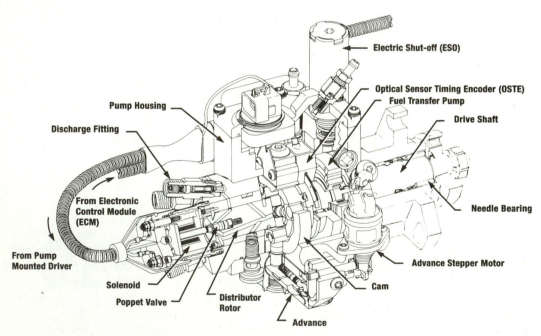

FIGURE 5–14 *Major features of the Stanadyne electronic model DS distributor pump used on General Motors 6.5L V8 pickup truck application. (Courtesy of Stanadyne Diesel Systems.)*

then computes the actual time in milliseconds that the fuel delivery and timing should be for any given condition of engine operation. Signals from the ECM instruct the pump-mounted driver electronics to supply the correct fuel injection PWM (pulse width modulated) signals.

Features of this electronic system can be seen in Figure 5–15; note the DS pump, the ECM, and the system sensors. These engine-mounted sensors send up-to-date operational data to the ECM. The pump speed and the angular pulse train data from the pump are also sent to the ECM. The programmed algorithms within the ECM process this information and send an appropriate inject command PWM signal to the PMD (pump-mounted driver). Some of the features of the DS pump are listed next:

- Shot-to-shot modification of fuel delivery and timing
- Complete governing flexibility with enhanced idle speed control
- Flexible controls for cold-engine operation
- Transient adaptation of fuel delivery and timing
- Complete flexibility of fuel metering and injection timing control
- Electronic spill control with a single 12 volt solenoid actuator for timing and fuel control
- Pump-mounted solenoid driver with poppet valve closure detection
- High-resolution pump-mounted angular encoder
- Four pumping plungers driven by the lobes on the internal pump cam ring
- Headless rotor drive to isolate torque loads from the rotor
- Fuel oil lubricated
- Fuel inlet at the top of the pump housing for vee-engine configuration and accessibility

Servicing of this DS model pump requires approximately 20 new service tools. Figure 5–16 is an example of a DS pump mounted on a fuel injection pump test stand; the pump is connected to a power supply/ECU. A conventional-type handheld scan tool can also be used with the correct software data cartridge to monitor fault codes, and so forth. Such a tool would be similar to that used on automotive gasoline engines and heavy-duty diesel engines with electronic unit injector systems.

MECHANICAL UNIT INJECTORS

The unit injector fuel system illustrated in Figure 5–17 is so named because all of the timing, atomization, metering, and pressurization is done as a *unit* within the injector body, rather than having a separate injection pump and nozzle connected with high-pressure fuel lines. Not only is this system much more compact and lighter than a PLN (pump-line-nozzle) system, but it also is capable of delivering much higher fuel injection pressures, a condition needed to meet stringent EPA exhaust emissions limits.

Detroit Diesel has used the unit injector system since 1937 in both its two-stroke-cycle and four-stroke-cycle engines. Later model two- and four-cycle DDC models now use an electronically controlled unit injector system that is discussed later in this chapter. Caterpillar uses the mechanical unit injector in both its 3114 and 3116 engine models and in early models of the 3500 and 3600 engines. In a typical fuel system arrangement used with the 6V–53/71/92 two-cycle DDC engine models employing a mechanical unit injector, fuel flows from the tank to and through either a fuel strainer (primary fuel filter) or a fuel/water separator assembly. The check valve is

FIGURE 5–15 *Illustration showing the basic operation of the model DS distributor pump, ECM, and system sensors which send up-to-date engine information to the ECM. Pump speed and the angular pulse train data from the DS pump are also sent to the ECM where customized algorithms process this information and send appropriate injection command signals to the PMD. (Courtesy of Stanadyne Diesel Systems).*

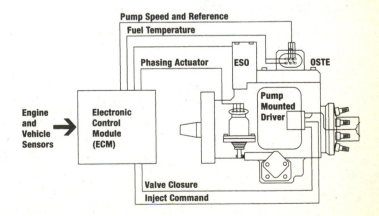

FIGURE 5–16 Model DS distributor injection pump mounted on a fuel pump test stand and connected to a special diagnostic test equipment package, which also includes a handheld DDR (diagnostic data reader—scan tool). (Courtesy of Stanadyne Diesel Systems.)

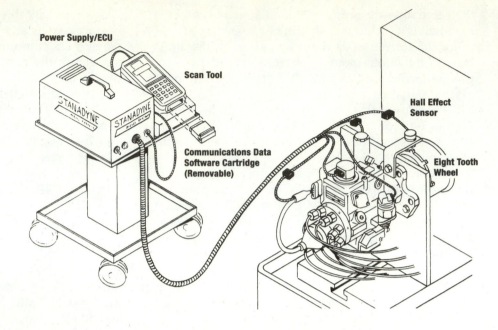

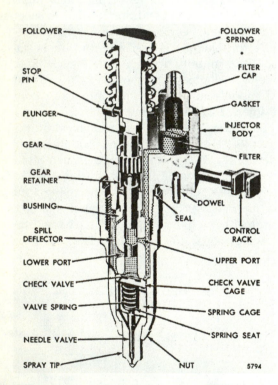

FIGURE 5–17 Cutaway view of a two-stroke-cycle engine mechanical unit injector assembly. (Courtesy of Detroit Diesel Corporation.)

used to prevent a loss of fuel system prime when the engine is stopped. The suction side of the system is between the inlet side of the pump and the tank; therefore, any loose fittings or connections will allow air to be drawn into the fuel system, resulting in rough running and a lack of power. Fuel leaving the outlet side of the fuel pump is under pressure of 50 to 70 psi (345 to 483 kPa) at rated engine speed. Fuel will show up as a fuel leak if any fittings are loose; this is the pressure side of the system. Fuel flows to the inlet manifold cast within each cylinder head and enters the injectors through a jumper line where fuel passes through an internal filter located under the injector fuel stud. Fuel that is not used for injection purposes is used to cool and lubricate the internal injector parts and exits the injector through a return fuel stud where it flows to the return fuel manifold cast internally within each cylinder head. Before leaving the head, the fuel must pass through a restricted fitting which is used to maintain a minimum fuel pressure within the return manifold of approximately 30 to 35 psi (207 to 241 kPa). The size of this restricted fitting is stamped on its body. For example, an R08 or R80 indicates that the fitting size is 0.080 in. (2.03 mm). The warm fuel then returns to the fuel tank where it can cool prior to recirculation.

Since there are still hundreds of thousands of mechanically equipped unit injector engines in operation, let's discuss how they operate before we look at the EUI models. Refer to Figure 5–17 which is a cross-sectional view of a typical MUI (mechanical unit injector). Basically, a needle valve contained in the injector spray tip is held on its seat (closed) by the action of a very strong spring. The engine-driven gear-type fuel pump creates flow and system pressure to deliver fuel

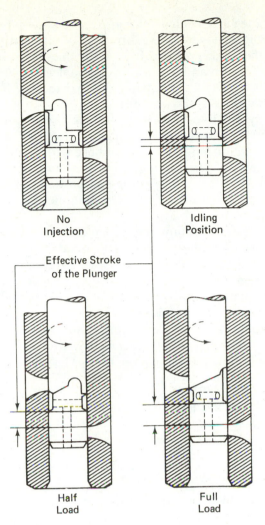

No Injection

Idling Position

Effective Stroke of the Plunger

Half Load

Full Load

FIGURE 5–18 *Sequence of events involved when the unit injector plunger is rotated by the movement of the fuel rack and internal gear to change the plungers effective stroke, and, therefore, the quantity of fuel injected. (Courtesy of Detroit Diesel Corporation.)*

to the injector inlet fuel stud that is located directly above the fuel rack. A small nylon mesh cone-type filter on newer injector models filters the fuel before it enters the MUI. When the rocker arm forces the plunger downward, the trapped fuel pressure is raised to a level high enough that it lifts the needle valve against its return spring. Normally the pressure is in the region of 3200 to 3900 psi (22,064 to 26,890 kPa) on later models. This is known as the injector *popping pressure.* Fuel is then forced through a series of small holes known as orifices into the combustion chamber. The fuel spray-in pressure is approximately 22,000 to 23,000 psi (151,690 to 158,585 kPa).

The fuel injector control tube and mechanical rack control lever are connected to the governor by a

fuel rod so that the speed of the engine can be changed by either manual operation of the throttle or by governor action. When the rack is moved in toward the injector body, fuel is increased; when the rack is pulled out all the way, this is the fuel shutoff position on Detroit Diesel engines. (Caterpillar models are opposite to this!)

Once the fuel from the pump reaches the injector, it performs the following four functions:

1. *Times injection.* Timing of the injector is accomplished by movement of the injector control rack, which causes rotation of the plunger within the injector bushing. Since the plunger is manufactured with a helical chamber area, this rotation either advances or retards the closing of the ports in the injector bushing, and therefore the start and end of the actual injection period. Pushrod adjustment establishes the height of the injector follower above the body. This in turn establishes the point or "time" that the descending plunger closes the bushing ports and therefore the start of the injection.

2. *Meters the fuel.* The rotation of the plunger by movement of the injector control rack advances or retards the start and end of the injection. If the length of time that the fuel can be injected is then varied, so will the amount of fuel be varied.

3. *Pressurizes the fuel.* Fuel that is trapped underneath the plunger on its downward stroke develops enough pressure to force its way past the check valve or needle valve, as the case may be, and therefore enter the combustion chamber.

4. *Atomizes the fuel.* Fuel under pressure that forces its way past the check or needle valve must then pass through small holes or orifices in the injector spray tip. This breaks down the fuel into a finely atomized spray as it enters the combustion chamber.

Phases of Injector Operation

The amount, rate, and timing of fuel injection is controlled by the injector plunger. Figure 5–17 shows that the top or neck of the plunger slides into a land area at the base of the injector follower. The follower is forced down by the action of the rocker arm; therefore, the plunger moves the same distance on each stroke. A circumferential groove cut in the plunger determines the timing and the quantity of fuel injected. The upper edge of this groove is cut in the shape of a helix; the lower edge is either straight or also cut in a helix shape. A flat on the upper portion of the plunger meshes with a flat on the inside diameter of the fuel control rack gear; therefore, when the fuel control rack is moved in or out it causes the plunger to rotate, thereby changing the position of the helix and thus the output of the injector.

The bushing actually has two ports, one on each side, and one is higher than the other. Anytime that both ports are uncovered by the plunger, fuel at pump pressure (45 to 70 psi; 310.27 to 482.65 kPa) is free to flow into and out of the bushing; therefore, no pressure beyond that being delivered by the pump is possible under this condition.

Figure 5–18 depicts the phases of injector operation through the vertical or downward movement of the plunger. With the plunger at the top of its stroke, fuel at pump pressure is free to flow into and out of the upper and lower ports of the bushing.

To change the amount of fuel delivered to the combustion chamber, we have to be able to lengthen or shorten the plunger's effective stroke. *Effective stroke* simply means that fuel is being injected. This is achieved by rotating the plunger within the bushing. When the fuel rack is moved, it causes the small gear shown in Figure 5–17 to rotate the plunger. The small flat area shown on the upper half of the plunger meshes with a flat within the bore of the gear. There is sufficient clearance, however, between the flats to allow the plunger to move/stroke through the bore of the gear as it is moved up and down by the rocker arm acting on the follower. The helix on the plunger will close the upper port earlier in its downward stroke when the rack is moved in toward the injector body. The upper port is covered later in the plunger's downward stroke when the rack is pulled away from the injector body. Consequently, the longer the effective stroke, the greater the amount of metered fuel that will be injected. Figure 5–18 illustrates the sequence of events as the plunger is rotated.

Fuel from the pump and cylinder head inlet manifold flows through the inlet fuel stud filter and drilled passages in the injector body, filling the cavity around the bushing. If the injector is not in an injection position, the fuel will flow through the upper and lower ports in the bushing and out of the injector return fuel stud.

When the injector rocker arm acting on the injector follower pushes it down, the plunger also moves down, causing the upper and lower ports in the bushing to be covered, thereby trapping fuel under the descending plunger. As the trapped fuel builds up pressure, it acts on the tapered land of the needle valve. Between 2300 and 3900 psi (15,858 and 26,890 kPa) on mechanically governed engines, the needle valve begins to lift against the pressure of the spring, exposing the seat portion of the needle valve to this high-pressure fuel. With this pressure now working on an increased area, the needle valve will lift very rapidly, allowing the fuel to flow into the spray tip sac and on through the tiny holes in the spray tip into the combustion chamber. The fuel must force its way through these small holes. Think again of turning on a garden hose with no nozzle on it; you get lots of volume but little pressure. If you place your thumb over the end of the hose, however, you restrict the flow (less volume) but increase the pressure.

The size and number of the holes in the spray tip varies on different unit injector models. Fuel can be injected at a pressure as high as 23,000 psi (158,585 kPa) on mechanical engines, causing the fuel to enter the combustion chamber in a finely atomized state. When the downward travel of the plunger ceases, fuel pressure drops off very rapidly, allowing the needle valve spring to seat the needle valve sharply and crisply, thus preventing any further injection.

Injector Sizes

To change the horsepower setting of any engine, either a two-stroke-cycle or a four-stroke-cycle design, two methods are common:

1. Increase the maximum governed speed of the engine.
2. Increase the fuel delivery rate at the same engine speed.

For example, if we were to look at a Detroit Diesel mechanical injector with the tag N65 on it, this would mean that this injector would be a needle valve design and would flow 65 mm^3 of fuel out if its spray tip every time the rocker arm pushed the injector follower down while the injector rack was in the full-fuel position. Changing an injector from one size, say, an N60 to an N65, would result in an increase in horsepower, depending on the size and model of engine that it is in at the same governed rpm. Each successive move up the scale in multiples of 5 mm^3 will continue to increase the horsepower setting in a similar fashion.

The maximum no-load governed rpm for any engine is always stamped on either the engine rocker cover option plate and/or paper-laminate label.

Care and Testing of Unit Injectors

Unit injectors provide many hours and/or miles (kilometers) of successful operation if the fuel system filters are changed regularly and the system is kept free of water. Other than when the cylinder head is being removed for service, the engine is being repaired/overhauled, or the injectors are being changed at a predetermined service interval, perform the following checks before condemning the unit injector as faulty.

1. On two-stroke-cycle 53, 71, and 92 Detroit Diesel engines, with the engine running at an idle speed, push and hold the injector follower down with a large screwdriver or special tool. This action effectively prevents the lower port from closing and, therefore, shorts the injector out, similar to a spark plug in a gasoline engine. When this is done, there should be a positive change to the operational sound of the engine along with a reduction in rpm; otherwise, it is an indication that the injector was not operating correctly. A contact pyrometer placed on each individual exhaust manifold outlet will allow you to check the temperature of each cylinder on 149 series engines. Generally, if the temperature differs by more than 50°F (10°C) between cylinders, it can indicate a faulty injector, but it may be low compression in that particular cylinder. The air box inspection covers can be removed on all Detroit Diesel two-cycle engines for a visual check of the piston rings, and a compression check may be required to confirm low compression if the rings appear to be free and do not show signs of excessive wear.

2. On 8.2 L four-stroke-cycle Detroit Diesel engines, the shorting out of the injector cannot be done, because the injector rocker arm pushrod is not threaded into the rocker arm assembly as it is on the two-stroke-cycle 53, 71, and 92 engines. If you attempt to hold the injector follower down, the pushrod will either fly out of the engine or will fall out of its socket and bend itself. To check the injector on this engine, start and run the engine at an idle speed, and using injector flooding bar Kent-Moore J 29522 or a modified slotted screwdriver, individually push one injector rack at a time to the full-fuel position (inward). This is known as flooding the cylinder, since full fuel is being delivered to the combustion chamber. If the engine does not pick up speed when you do this, the injector is faulty.

3. On DDEC-equipped engines (two- or four-stroke-cycle) the injector follower is still mechanically operated by the rocker arm, although there is no injector rack. A small electrically operated solenoid controls the duration of fuel injection. Shorting out of these injectors can be done by selecting individual cylinders with the use of the DDR (diagnostic data reader) illustrated in Figure 5–40.

Mechanical Injector Tests

Unit injectors can be checked and tested on a pop tester stand for spray pattern and atomization. However, because of the design of the injector, the actual popping pressure or pressure at which the internal needle valve lifts from its seat against spring force can be done only by installing the internal parts on a special adapter. This means you must loosen the injector body nut, remove the component parts below the injector bushing, and assemble these onto the special adapter along with the injector nut and seal. Only then can the actual injector popping pressure be determined on a special test stand.

In addition, the injector's delivery rate can be checked on a calibration test stand to determine if in fact the injector assembly is delivering the correct amount of fuel. There are several test stands and pop testers on the market that can be used to test Detroit Diesel unit injectors.

OVERVIEW OF ELECTRONIC UNIT INJECTORS

This overview provides a simplified picture of how an electronically controlled fuel injection system operates without the specifics of a particular system. Details on particular systems are provided in subsequent sections of the chapter.

Environmental concerns about exhaust emissions from the internal combustion engine were the force that motivated diesel engine manufacturers to adopt *electronic engine control systems*. You may recollect from other discussions in this book that the adoption of electronics for diesels followed closely the process that was initiated for gasoline passenger car engines in the late 1970s and early 1980s. In the gasoline engine, the carburetor and contact breaker point ignition system was superceded by breaker-less ignition systems and by either TBI (throttle body injection) or MPFI (multi-port fuel injection).

Mechanically governed and mechanically controlled fuel injection systems on diesel engines had reached their limit of efficiency. The next logical technological move was to adopt a series of electrical engine sensors, an EFPA (electronic foot pedal assembly), and an on-board ECM (electronic control module) programmed to extract the optimum fuel economy and engine performance.

Initially, heavy-duty high-speed diesel engine electronic fuel injection systems were add-on items attached to existing PLN (pump-line-nozzle) systems such as those manufactured by Robert Bosch, Zexel, Nippondenso, Lucas, and Caterpillar. The first major OEM to release full-authority electronic controls was the Detroit Diesel Division of General Motors Corporation, now owned by Roger Penske and called Detroit Diesel Corporation. Detroit Diesel introduced the DDEC I (Detroit Diesel electronic controls) system in September 1985; DDEC II in September 1987, and DDEC III in September 1993. This EUI (electronic unit injector) system is employed on the company's two-stroke-cycle and four-stroke-cycle engine models.

Caterpillar introduced its PEEC (programmable electronic engine control) system on its PLN fuel system for its 3406B truck engine in 1987. This was followed in 1988 by the release of its EUI system on the 3176 truck engine. The PEEC system on the 3406B and C engine models was superceded by the EUI system beginning in late 1993 and early 1994 with the introduction of the 3406E engine model. Both the 3500 and 3600 Caterpillar engines also employ EUI systems. Cummins introduced its first-generation ECI (electronically controlled injection) system in 1988. This was followed in 1990 by its Celect (Cummins Electronics) fuel system. The Celect system is available on Cummins' 14L, M11, L10, and K series engine models. In 1994 Volvo introduced its VE D12 overhead camshaft 12L truck engine equipped with VE, for Vectro (Volvo electronics) controlled unit injectors, which are similar to the DDEC system.

Mack has used a system known by the acronym VMAC (vehicle management and controls) on its PLN Bosch fuel injection pumps for several years now. Robert Bosch, who is a major PLN OEM, recently purchased 49% of the Diesel Technology Equipment Division Inc., of Detroit Diesel; therefore, we can expect Bosch to offer electronic unit injectors to many engine OEMs in place of its long-used PLN fuel systems. Mercedes-Benz, the majority owner of Freightliner, has signed a cooperative venture with Detroit Diesel to manufacture a 12L diesel engine using Detroit Diesel electronics; technology.

From this information, it is apparent that the majority of engine OEMs are now committed to using electronically controlled diesel fuel injection systems. The trend at this time is to replace PLN systems with electronic unit injectors. Electronic diesel control means an advanced technology electronic fuel injection and control system that offers significant operating advantages over traditional mechanically governed engines. Electronic systems optimize control of critical engine functions that affect fuel economy, exhaust smoke, and emissions. These electronic systems provide the capability to protect the engine from serious damage resulting from conditions such as high engine coolant temperatures, high oil temperature, and low engine oil pressure conditions.

SYSTEM ELEMENTS

Although there are unique differences in the electronic fuel systems employed by each OEM, overall there are more similarities than differences. Since Cummins, Caterpillar, Detroit Diesel and Volvo all use electronically controlled unit fuel injectors, which are mechanically actuated, each system employs a series of engine and vehicle sensors that are continually fed an electrical *input* signal from the ECM. Most sensors are designed to accept a 5.0 volt DC (direct current) input signal from the ECM. Depending on the operating condition at the sensor, it will *output* a signal back to the ECM ranging between 0.5 to 5.0 VDC (volts direct current), although some systems can range as high as 5.25 to 5.5 VDC. The ECM then determines and computes a digital PWM (pulse width modulated) electrical signal based on predetermined calibration tables in its memory to control the time that each injector actually delivers fuel to the combustion chamber. This type of system allows tailoring of the start, duration, and end of fuel injection to ensure optimum engine performance at any load and speed. Fuel is delivered to the cylinders by the EUIs, which are driven by an overhead camshaft on Detroit Diesel Series 50 and 60 engines, the Caterpillar 3406E, the Volve VE D12, and the Isuzu 12L 6WA1TC, or by an in-block camshaft and pushrod on Caterpillar's 3176B and Cummins' N14, M11, and L10 models, to provide the mechanical input for sufficient pressurization of the fuel, resulting in injector spray-in pressures as high as 28,000 psi (193060 kPa).

Figure 5–19 is a simplified schematic of an electronically controlled unit injector fuel system common to Caterpillar, Cummins, Detroit Diesel, and Volvo high-speed diesel engines. Figure 5–20 is a simplified line diagram of an electronic unit injector fuel system arrangement that shows the engine crankshaft TRS (timing reference sensor), the gear train SRS (synchronous reference sensor), the basic layout of the ECM components, the electronically controlled unit injector solenoid, most of the sensors used, and the operator interfaces, which indicate to the ECM when a function is desired. The number of engine/vehicle sensors and their location varies in makes and models of engines; in all, however, the ECM continually monitors each sensor for an *out-of-range condition*. When this occurs, a dash-mounted warning light system is activated and a trouble code is stored in ECM memory. This code can be extracted by the technician by means of a DDR. The sensors and engine protective features employed by each engine OEM normally have the following elements.

1. *TRS* (timing reference sensor): tells the ECM where the rotation of the engine is or when each cylinder is firing. Some OEMs (for example, Cummins) refer to this sensor as an EPS (engine position sensor). Caterpillar employs an engine speed timing sensor

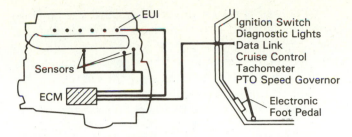

ECM–Electronic Control Module
EUI–Electronic Unit Injectors

FIGURE 5–19 Simplified schematic of the engine-mounted ECM, sensors, and EUI (electronic unit injectors), plus the inputs and connections from the electronic foot pedal assembly and various switches for a DDEC system. (Courtesy of Detroit Diesel Corporation.)

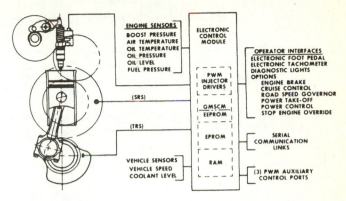

FIGURE 5–20 Various inputs and outputs between the engine, sensors, and ECM of the DDEC system. (Courtesy of Detroit Diesel Corporation.)

that provides a PWM signal to the ECM, which the ECM interprets as a crankshaft position and engine speed reference.

2. *SRS* (synchronous reference sensor): advises the ECM when the No. 1 cylinder is at TDC on the compression stroke.

3. *TBS* (turbo boost sensor): provides information on intake manifold air pressure to the ECM and is used for control of white smoke and emissions.

4. *OPS* (oil pressure sensor): advises the ECM of the engine main oil gallery pressure. Engine protective features programmed into the ECM are calibrated to trigger an engine speed and power reduction feature when the oil pressure drops to a point lower than desired. If a dangerous oil pressure is sensed, the ECM warns the operator by flashing a dash-mounted red light; on some engine/vehicles it may be accompanied by an audible buzzer. If the ECM is so programmed, automatic engine shutdown will occur after 30 seconds of low oil pressure. In some cases, the system may be equipped with a manual override button to provide an extra 30 seconds of running time to allow the operator to pull a vehicle over to the side of the road safely.

5. *OTS* (oil temperature sensor): indicates the engine oil temperature at all times to the ECM. Normally, the ECM and engine protective features can be programmed to provide the same safety features as those described for a low oil pressure condition. However, a yellow dash-mounted warning light is triggered first when the oil temperature exceeds a safe, normal limit. Continued oil temperature increase to a preset maximum limit results in an engine power-down feature, followed by engine shutdown similar to that for the OPS. Many electronic engines

employ this sensor at engine start-up to advise the ECM to provide a fast idle speed, particularly during cold ambient conditions. In some engines the coolant temperature sensor provides the input signal to the ECM for this operating condition. This signal causes the ECM to vary the fuel injection PWM time to control white smoke on a cold engine. Normal idle speed is automatically resumed when the oil or coolant temperature reaches a predetermined limit or after a programmed engine running time.

6. *CTS* (coolant temperature sensor): used to advise the ECM of the engine coolant temperature. This sensor can be used to trigger an engine protection response; it has an automatic power-down feature and shutdown similar to that for the OPS and OTS. In addition, many heavy-duty trucks now employ this sensor to activate thermatic fan controls.

7. *CLS* (coolant level sensor): monitors the level of coolant in the radiator top tank or in a remote surge tank. Normally, this sensor is tied into the ECM engine protection system and initiates an automatic engine shutdown sequence at a low coolant level. In addition, the engine will fail to start when this sensor senses a low coolant level, and it will trigger a dash-mounted warning light.

8. *ACLS* (auxiliary coolant level sensor): indicates when the coolant level requires topping up. Positioned within the top rad tank or remote surge tank, this sensor is located above the CLS.

9. *CPS* (coolant pressure sensor): normally employed on larger-displacement engines to closely monitor water pump/engine block pressure.

10. *CPS* (crankcase pressure sensor): usually found on larger-displacement engines in mining, stationary, and marine engine applications. This sensor

can be profiled to monitor crankcase pressure direct; on two-stroke-cycle engines, it monitors air pressure inside the air box of the two-stroke-cycle engine block. Caterpillar refers to this sensor as an *atmospheric pressure sensor,* which measures the atmospheric air pressure in the crankcase and sends a signal to the ECM.

11.   *FPS* (fuel pressure sensor): usually monitors the fuel pressure on the outlet side of the secondary fuel filter. This sensor is used for diagnostics purposes.

12.   *FTS* (fuel temperature sensor): provides fuel temperature information to the ECM and is normally located on the secondary fuel filter head. Changes in fuel temperature allow the ECM to adjust the PWM signal to the unit injectors, since warmer fuel expands, resulting in less horsepower.

13.   *ATS* (air temperature sensor): indicates intake manifold temperature to the ECM to allow the ECM to alter the injector PWM signal for emissions control.

14.   *EFPA* (electronic foot pedal assembly): indicates to the ECM the percentage of throttle pedal depression, and therefore how much fuel is being requested by the operator. Current EFPAs are equipped with an IVS (idle validation switch) that indicates a closed throttle pedal condition and therefore that an idle speed is being requested.

15.   *ITS* (idle timer shutdown): a programmable engine idle shutdown feature ranging from as low as 3 minutes to 99 minutes depending on the make of engine. For example, on a Caterpillar 3176B/3406E engine, 90 seconds before the programmed idle time is reached, the dash-mounted diagnostic lamp starts to flash rapidly. For the idle shutdown timer to function, the following operating conditions must be met:

- Idle shutdown timer feature has been programmed into the ECM.
- Vehicle parking brake must be activated/set.
- Engine must be at normal operating temperature.
- Vehicle speed must be at zero mph (km/h).
- Engine is running under a no-load condition.
- Parking brake switch has been installed to alert the ECM and the idle timer when to start the idle time-down feature.

16.   *IAS* (idle adjust switch): located on the instrument panel and can be toggled to alter the hot idle rpm to eliminate shaky mirrors. Usually provides a plus 100 rpm and minus 25 rpm.

17.   *EBC* (engine compression brake controls): compatible with cruise control features on trucks. While in the cruise mode, the engine brakes can be programmed to come on and off automatically to maintain a preset cruise speed. The engine brakes can be programmed to a set road speed above the cruise speed to improve the driveability of the vehicle.

18.   *PGS* (pressure governor system): used on fire trucks to maintain a set water pressure by varying the engine rpm.

19.   *SLS* (starter lockout sensor): indicates the engine condition to the ECM once the engine is running. This sensor prevents starter engagement to prevent grinding of the flywheel and starter pinion gears.

20.   *VSS* (vehicle speed sensor): used to monitor the transmission or drive wheel speed to advise the ECM how fast the vehicle is moving. This magnetic pickup sensor is provided by the truck OEM and is necessary when cruise control, vehicle speed limiting, maximum overspeed with/without fuel (throttle pedal position), and engine brake usage are involved.

21.   *VSG* (variable speed governor): supplied in the form of a hand throttle to maintain engine speed at a fixed rpm regardless of engine load; usually programmed within the ECM to provide a zero-droop condition (no speed change regardless of load).

22.   *CEL* (check engine light): an amber or yellow light on the dash used to indicate to the operator that a system fault has been detected by the ECM. When activated, a trouble code is stored in the ECM memory. Depending on the severity of the condition, the engine may lose speed and power, but it will provide limp-home capability.

23.   *SEL* (stop engine light): a red light on the dash that illuminates when a serious engine operating condition is detected. If the ECM has been programmed for automatic engine shutdown, the engine will shut down usually within a 30 second time period. An optional feature such as an STEO (stop engine override) button can be provided to allow a temporary override condition so the operator can safely pull a truck or bus over to the side of the road.

24.   *EPS* (engine protection system): a programmable feature within the ECM that provides a method to sense an out-of-range operating condition in the engine. When a sensor indicates to the ECM that the sensed condition is outside of the normal parameter (condition), the ECM systematically illuminates either the yellow or red warning lamp on the dash, and typically ramps down the engine speed and power setting. The degree of power reduction varies in different makes of engines, but it is usually from 100% to 70%; a further reduction down to about 40% occurs after the SEL (red) illuminates. Trigger sensors for this protection system usually include coolant temperature, oil temperature, oil pressure, and coolant level.

25.   *VDL* (vehicle deceleration light): located on the rear of a truck or bus and illuminates when the driver takes his or her foot off the accelerator pedal, indicating that the vehicle is slowing down.

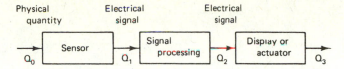

FIGURE 5–21 Simplified sensor measurement operational system.

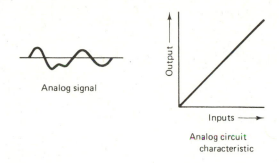

FIGURE 5–22 Analog-wave signal shape.

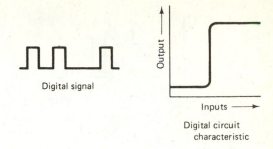

FIGURE 5–23 Digital-wave signal shape.

FIGURE 5–24 Digital voltage signal in an ON/OFF mode (5 V reference or trigger signal).

26. *PWM* (pulse width modulation): the term used to describe the duration of time that the injector solenoid is energized and fuel is being delivered to the engine. Timed in milliseconds, or thousandths of a second, but measured in degrees of rotation of the engine crankshaft.

SENSORS

Basic Sensor Arrangement

Figure 5–21 is a simplified diagram of the basic sensor measurement system, where the sensor itself absorbs either a heat or pressure signal from a monitored engine condition. The sensor converts this signal into an electrical output and relays it to the signal processor. Within the signal processor, the sensor signal is amplified so that it can be sent to an analog or digital display; or alternatively, it may be used to activate a specific actuator on the engine or vehicle.

Signal processing can be accomplished with either analog devices or digital devices. Analog signals resemble the human voice and have a continuous waveform signal, whereas a digital signal forms a series of boxes to indicate an ON or OFF voltage condition. Analog signal processing involves amplifiers, filters, adders, multipliers, and other components; digital signal processing uses logic gates. In addition, digital processing requires the use of counters, binary adders, and microcomputers.

The IC (integrated circuit) can be analog or digital. The analog-type IC is one that handles or processes a wave-like analog electrical signal, such as that produced by the human voice; it is also similar to that shown on an ignition oscilloscope. An analog signal

changes continuously and smoothly with time as shown in Figure 5–22. Its output signal is proportionate to its input signal.

Digital signals, on the other hand, show a more rectangular wavelength, as shown in Figure 5–23. These signals change intermittently with time, which means that, simply put, they are either on or off. This, of course, is quite different from the analog operating mode. The general characteristic of operation of the digital circuit can best be explained as follows: When the input voltage signal rises to a predetermined level, the output signal is then triggered into action. For example, assume that a sensor is feeding a varying 5 volt (V) maximum reference signal to a source such as a diode. In this condition, the output signal remains at zero until the actual input signal has climbed to its maximum of 5 V.

This is why digital signals are classified as being either on or off. ON means that a signal is being sent, and OFF means that a signal is not being sent. For convenience sake, in electronics terminology, when a voltage signal is being sent (ON), the numeral 1 is used. When no voltage signal is being sent (OFF), this is indicated by the numeral 0. These numerals are used so that the computer can distinguish between an ON and OFF voltage signal.

Figures 5–24 and 5–25 show how this numeric system operates. Most sensors in use today in automotive applications are designed to operate on a 5 V reference signal. Anything above this level is considered as being in an ON, or numeral 1, condition, and any voltage below this value is considered as OFF, or 0 numeral, since the voltage signal is too low to trigger a diode response. Digital systems consist of many

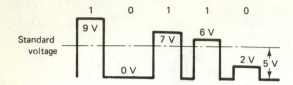

FIGURE 5–25 Digital wave signal when the voltage values are either above or below the standard voltage references.

numbers of identical *logic gates* and *flip-flops* to perform the necessary computations.

A simplified example of an analog signal is that generated from a speedometer sensor that changes continuously as the vehicle speed increases or decreases. An example of an applied digital signal that is either on or off can be related to the opening and closing of a car door. When open, the interior light comes on; therefore, the signal is at its maximum of 12 V. If, on the other hand, the door is closed, the signal is at 0 V.

Types of Sensors

Various engine/vehicle sensors are described in this chapter. The physical operating characteristics of each unit depend on the following design types: two-wire design, three-wire design, and pulse-counter design. Each of these operating types is illustrated and explained next to show how various sensors operate.

1. *Two-wire design.* Figure 5–26 illustrates the two-wire design type of sensor, which is basically a variable resistor in series with a known-fixed resistor contained within the ECM. Sensors that use the two-wire type of design are the CTS, OTS, FTS, MAT (manifold air temperature), and OAT (outside air temperature) units. All of these sensors operate on a varying resistance; their resistance varies inversely with temperature (thermistor principle).

Since most sensors in use in automotive applications use a base voltage input of 5 V (some use 8 V), the value of the variable resistor can be determined from the base voltage along with the known voltage drop across the fixed resistor.

The coolant and oil temperature sensors are mounted on the engine, while the fuel sensor is mounted on the fuel filter. Each sensor relays temperature information to the ECM. The ECM monitors a 5 V reference signal, which it applied to the sensor signal circuit through a resistor in the ECM. Note that these sensors are in reality a thermistor, which means that they change their internal resistance as the temperature changes. Specifically, when the sensor is cold, such as when starting up an engine that has been sitting for some time, the sensor resistance is high, and the ECM monitors a high signal voltage. As the engine warms

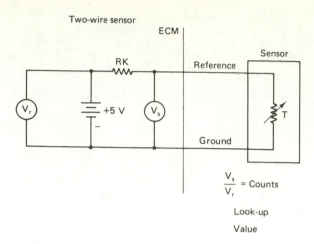

FIGURE 5–26 Basic arrangement of a two-wire design sensor unit.

up, however, the internal resistance of the sensor decreases and causes a similar decrease in the reference voltage signal. Therefore, the ECM interprets this reduced voltage signal as signifying a warm engine. The range of the coolant and oil temperature sensors varies with various engine/vehicle manufacturers, but normally it is between –10° and 300°F. At the low-temperature end of the scale, the resistance of the sensor tends to be about 100,000 ohm (Ω), while at the high range its internal resistance would have dropped to only 70 Ω. Figure 5–27 illustrates how a temperature of 150°F (65.5°C), which is an analog signal, is converted from analog to digital within the A/D (analog/digital) converter. In Fig. 5–27 we see a typical upward-moving sine wave which is representative of the changing voltage output signal from the oil or coolant sensor as the engine temperature increases because of the decreasing resistance value of the sensor. At a temperature of 150°F, the sensor analog output voltage is sampled by the A/D converter, which converts values into a *binary number value* or code.

2. *Three-wire design.* Figure 5–28 illustrates the three-wire design type of sensor arrangement, which is commonly in use in TPS (throttle position sensors), MAP (manifold absolute pressure), and BARO (barometric pressure sensors). These types of sensors have a reference voltage, a ground, and a variable wiper, with the lead coming off the wiper being the actual signal feed to the ECM. A change in the wiper's position automatically changes the signal voltage being sent back to the ECM.

3. *Pulse counters.* Figure 5–29 illustrates the basic operation of a pulse counter. Sensors relying on this type of counting system are typically the VSS, the rpm or engine speed sensor, which could be a crankshaft-

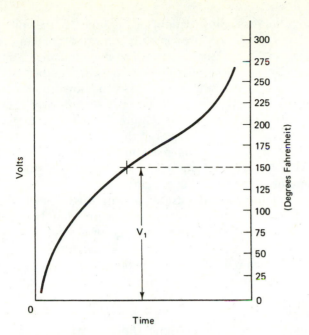

FIGURE 5–27 *Coolant temperature versus analog output voltage signal.*

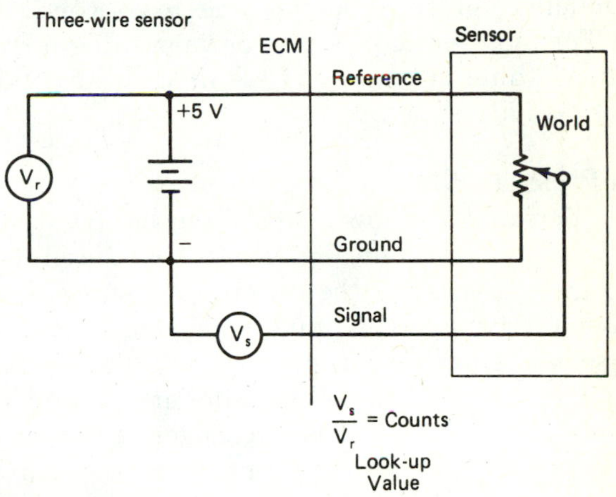

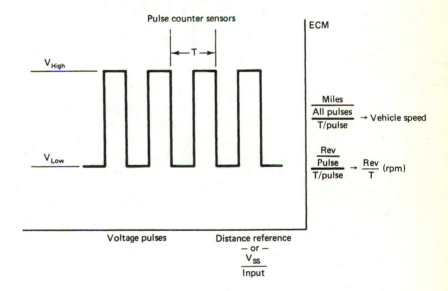

FIGURE 5–28 *Basic arrangement of a three-wire design sensor unit.*

FIGURE 5–29 *Pulse counter mode of operation.*

or camshaft-sensed Hall-effect type on various makes of vehicles, and also the distributor reference sensor on vehicles employing this style of ignition system.

Consider, for example, that many gasoline-powered cars and light-duty trucks today have a distributor-less ignition system. These systems rely on a crankshaft- or camshaft-mounted sensor, or both, to pick up a gear position, usually through the use of a raised tooth on the gear wheel. The resultant voltage signal produced is relayed by the sensor to the ECM, which then determines when to trigger the ignition pulse signal to the respective spark plug. On heavy-

duty truck engines such as those employing the Detroit Diesel Series 60 four-stroke-cycle DDEC engines, an electronic TRS (timing reference sensor) extends through an opening in the engine gear case and is positioned to provide a small air gap between it and the teeth of the crankshaft timing gear. The TRS sends a voltage signal to the ECM, which uses it to determine fuel injector solenoid operation/timing. This same engine employs an SRS (synchronous reference sensor) that is mounted to the rear of the engine gear case, where it is positioned to provide a small air gap between it and the rear of a bull gear driven from the crankshaft gear. The SRS sends a voltage signal to the ECM, which uses this information to determine engine speed.

The speed at which sensor signals are transmitted and monitored by the ECM microprocessor are usually updated a given amount of times in a second.

For those on request sensor values, the nominal response time in current ECMs used in heavy-duty trucks is 100 milliseconds.

Oil Pressure Sensor Operation

To understand just how a typical sensor operates in a heavy-duty electronically controlled diesel truck engine, let's consider the oil pressure sensor as one example. The sensor outputs an analog signal, with the sensor resistance changing as a result of engine oil pressure changes. This oil pressure and sensor resistance change, in turn, creates changes in the sensor–resistor–battery circuit current flow. Any current increase will similarly create an increase in the voltage value across the resistor. Consequently, during engine operation, any oil pressure change is reflected by a sensor voltage output that the analog-to-digital subsystem will process accordingly.

Consider that the oil pressure sensor used on the DDEC system has a sensor range between 0 and 65 psi (0 to 448 kPa) with a sensor output update rate of once per second and a resolution of 0.5 psi per bit. During engine operation, if the sensor failed, the check engine light would illuminate on the dash; if low oil pressure at the current engine speed is sensed, the check engine light will illuminate and the ECM would power down the engine. Unsafe oil pressure would result in the SEL (stop engine light) illuminating, followed 30 seconds later by an ECM-actuated engine shutdown procedure. If the engine is equipped with an SEO (stop engine override), the shutdown sequence can be delayed by holding the SEO button in for a couple more times only, after which the ECM shuts the engine off.

For ease of instruction, let's assume that the voltage across the oil pressure sensor is converted from an analog to a digital signal by an A/D converter in the form of a VCO (voltage-controlled oscillator), where the sensor voltage varies from 0 to 10 V. As you know from earlier information, the digital system is a square-wave signal typical of that shown in Figure 5–29. The amplitude (voltage strength) changes of the digital signals would have very fast ON/OFF reactions, varying from 0 to 5 V, with 0 V representing a logic number 0 and the 5 V amplitude representing a logic number 1.

Figure 5–30 illustrates a simplified system that represents this oil pressure sensor function. If a scale is selected to represent a change of engine oil pressure of from 0 to 65 psi (0 to 448 kPa), a change in voltage from 0 to 10 V can be used to duplicate/scale this change in oil pressure. If we assume that the VCO's output oscillates back and forth between 0 and 10 V based on changing engine oil pressure, the frequency of the voltage signal (how often it happens) in our scaled example would vary between 400 and 1000 hertz (Hz), or 400 to 1000 times a second, based on the 0 to 10 V input signal to the VCO. A change in voltage from 0 to 10 V would cause a change in frequency of 600 (= 1000 − 400) Hz in our example. The voltage output of the VCO is connected to one input of an AND logic gate. (For a description of an AND gate and its truth table combination refer to *Mid-Heavy Duty Truck Electrical and Electronic Systems* by Robert N. Brady published in 1991 by Prentice Hall Englewood Cliffs, N.J.)

Due to the operation of the AND logic gate shown to the immediate right of the VCO in Figure 5–30, the output of the VCO is connected to one input of the AND gate, while the other input is held to a logic level 1. This results in the output of the AND gate being a reproduction of the VCO's output. But when the second input from the VCO is at logic 0, the output of the AND gate would be a steady logic 0. Therefore, by

FIGURE 5–30 *Simplified electronic oil pressure sensor system. (Reprinted with permission, copyright 1995, Society of Automotive Engineers, Inc.)*

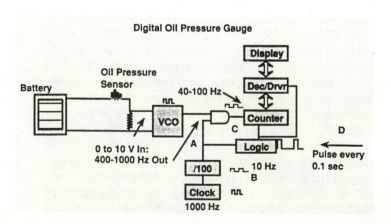

actively controlling the logic levels on the second input, the VCO's output pulse can be gated through for a given amount of time, then blocked, then gated through again, with the process being repeated over and over.

For scaling purposes, let's consider that when a zero engine oil pressure exists, we will also have zero volts across the oil pressure sensor resistor. At 0 lb oil pressure, we will equate this to a frequency of 400 Hz. With the engine running and the oil pump creating 65 psi (448 kPa) of pressure, the voltage value is 10 V and the frequency is equivalent to a VCO output of 1000 Hz. If we also assume that the engine oil pressure rises linearly (gradual straight-line increase), there is a direct relationship created between the oil pressure, the voltage, and the frequency. Since our scale runs between 400 and 1000 Hz to represent 0 to 65 psi (0 to 448 kPa), this means that over the 600 Hz range between these two numbers, we can scale the VCO's output frequency to represent any given oil pressure. For example, based on our graduated scale, a 32.5 psi (224 kPa) oil pressure would correspond to a signal of 5 V and a frequency halfway between 400 and 1000, which would be 700 Hz. Therefore, as you can see, it is quite easy to convert a given oil pressure at the sensor into a voltage input at the VCO, along with a frequency output from the VCO. The engine oil pressure sensor used on the DDEC system on Detroit Diesel's 71, 92, and Series 60 heavy-duty truck diesel engines have an update rate of once per second; therefore, when the oil pressure is 65 psi (448 kPa), the VCO will be outputting a signal every second that is representative of this pressure. In our descriptive example, this would be equivalent to the VCO outputting 1000 square-wave pulses (digitally shaped) per second. For better resolution or monitoring of the changing oil pressure system, we could choose to set the logic gate up so that it is open for 0.1 second. This can be achieved by directing a signal to the second AND gate input, which has a logic 1 period equal to 0.1 second.

We can ensure this operating condition by employing a square-wave oscillating clock with a fixed frequency of 1000 Hz. The output can then be directed through a series of logic ICs (integrated circuits) that effectively divide the input count by 10, then by a further 10. Reference to Figure 5–30 indicates this clock system is identified as /100 above the 1000 Hz clock. This means that the 1000 Hz signal is divided by 100 to produce a square output wave with a 10 Hz frequency. Consequently, the signal would have a time period of 1/10 or 0.1 second.

If the logic gate pulses open for 0.1 second, it is closed, then opened once again on a continuing basis;

then every time the logic gate is opened, 100 square waves will pass through as long as the oil pressure remains at 65 psi (448 kPa). If the engine speed is reduced, or the oil pressure were to drop to 32.5 psi (224 kPa), the VCO frequency would be reduced from 1000 to 700 Hz. This means that in a 0.1 second period, only 70 square-wave pulses will pass through the logic gate. When the 10 Hz signal is a logic 1 input, the VCO's output will pass through the AND gate. When the 10 Hz signal is logic 0, the AND gate's output is logic 0. Therefore, when the oil pressure is 65 psi (448 kPa), the internal digital clock counter will count 100 pulses in 0.1 second. At a pressure of 32.5 psi (224 kPa), it will count 70 pulses every 0.1 second. With zero oil pressure, the counter will register 40 pulses every 0.1 second. The clock counter's output is then input to a decoder/driver IC to drive a digital display that allows the truck driver to visually determine the engine oil pressure condition at a glance. Generally, the output of the decoder/driver is a latched output. This means that the output value changes only when a latch pulse, shown as item D in Fig. 5–30, is input to a latch input.

Electronic Foot Pedal Assembly

A unique feature of the electronic fuel system is that the foot throttle pedal assembly consists of a small potentiometer (variable resistor) rather than a direct mechanical linkage as is found on mechanical engines. This throttle arrangement is often referred to as a *drive by wire system*, since no mechanical linkage is used; only electrical wires transmit the position of the throttle to the ECM. The potentiometer is electrically connected to the ECM.

The throttle position sensor shown in Figure 5–31 contains a potentiometer (variable resistor) that is designed to output a voltage in direct response to the depression of the pedal. This sensor is designed to receive a 5 V input reference signal from the ECM. However, the output voltage is totally dependent on how far down the pedal is pushed for any given condition. When the throttle pedal is at its normal idle position, its voltage output is low; therefore, the signal sent to the ECM advises the system of its relative position, and the solenoid on each fuel injector is activated for a short pulse-width time. This results in a small delivery of fuel to each cylinder and therefore a low idle speed.

As the operator pushes the throttle pedal down, the voltage signal from the sensor increases, and when the ECM recognizes this voltage change, it sends out a signal to activate the solenoid on each fuel injector for a longer pulse width period. This results in a greater amount of fuel being delivered to the cylinders and therefore a higher speed. The actual quantity of fuel delivered and therefore the horsepower produced by

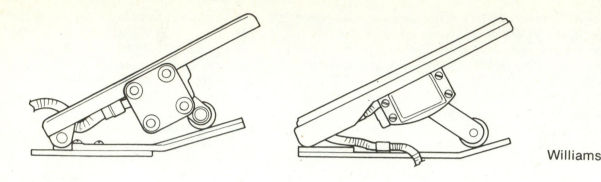

Bendix   Williams

Electronic Foot Pedal Assemblies

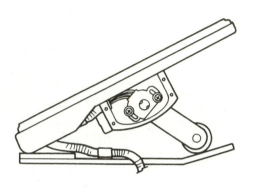

Throttle Position Sensor

FIGURE 5–31 EFPA (electronic foot pedal assembly) designs also showing the TPS (throttle position sensor). (Courtesy of Detroit Diesel Corporation.)

the engine also depend on the engine coolant temperature, the turbocharger boost pressure, and both the oil pressure and temperature sensor readings. Each one of these sensors is continually relaying a voltage signal back to the ECM, which then computes the injector pulse width signal.

Newer models of the EFPA (electronic foot pedal assembly) feature an integrated idle validation switch/sensor that combines two electrical signal generators: the accelerator position sensor (APS) and the idle validation switch (IVS) in a single housing. The two components are isolated electrically but are actuated by a common mechanical link to the accelerator pedal. The calibration between the two signals is set at the factory and will maintain uninterrupted adjustment throughout the life of the unit.

Detroit Diesel, Caterpillar, and Cummins employ the same basic EFPA assembly, although the installation angle of the EFPA on its mounting plate varies to suit different truck floor pan installations. The pedal moves through approximately 20° from idle to WOT (wide open throttle), thereby varying the voltage signal back to the ECM. The EFPA receives a 5 V input

reference voltage signal from the ECM, and the return voltage signal is based on the percentage of throttle depression. Another feature of this EFPA with IVS and APS is that the automatic transmission shift point-control can be regulated by the integrated sensor. At a specified voltage, the transmission can be downshifted to a lower gear range. An engine retarder signal may be utilized to invoke an exhaust brake or other engine transmission retarder device through the idle validation setting within the EFPA.

OPERATION OF ELECTRONIC UNIT INJECTORS

This section describes briefly the operation of an electronically controlled unit injector. At this time, the high-speed heavy-duty electronic unit injectors employed by Detroit Diesel, Caterpillar, Cummins, Volvo, and Robert Bosch depend on an engine camshaft rocker arm activation system. The exception is the HEUI (hydraulically actuated electronic unit injector) codesigned by Caterpillar and Navistar for use on Navistar's T 444E (7.3 L) medium-duty truck engine.

FIGURE 5–32 (a) EUI (electronic unit injector) cam-in-block actuation mechanism for a 3176 model engine; (b) EUI overhead cam actuation mechanism for a 3406E model engine: 1, electronically controlled unit injector; 2, adjusting nut; 3, rocker arm assembly; 4, camshaft. (Courtesy of Caterpillar Inc.)

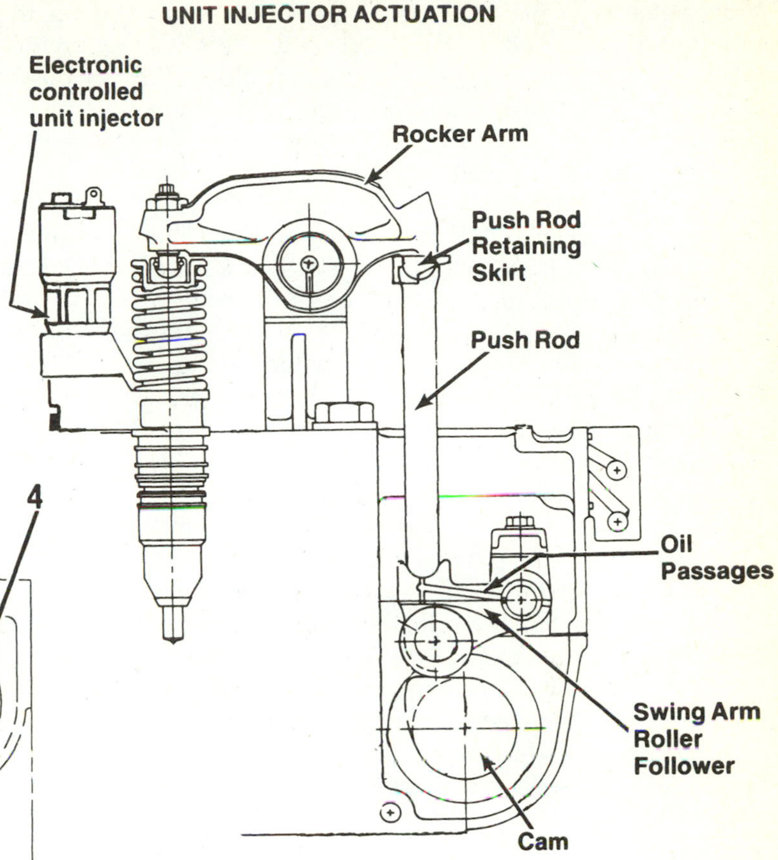

UNIT INJECTOR ACTUATION

Electronic controlled unit injector

Rocker Arm

Push Rod Retaining Skirt

Push Rod

Oil Passages

Swing Arm Roller Follower

Cam

A

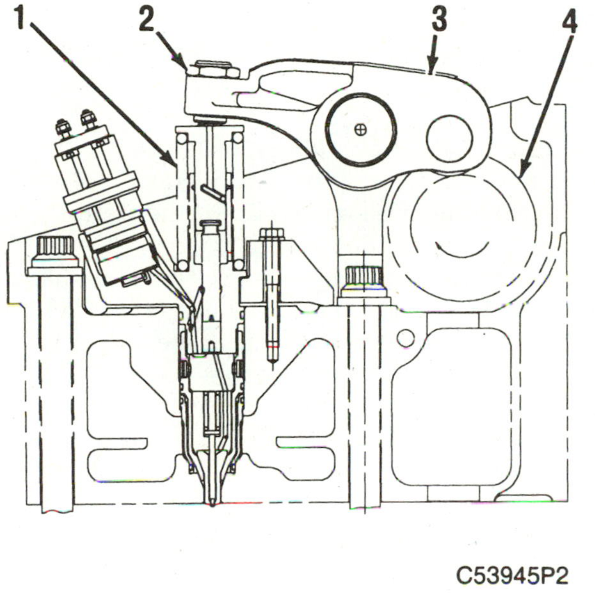

1   2   3   4

C53945P2

Unit Injector Mechanism
(1) Electronically controlled unit injector. (2) Adjusting nut.
(3) Rocker arm assembly. (4) Camshaft.

B

The electronic unit injector has an electric solenoid that receives a command signal from an ECM, which determines the start of injection as well as the amount of fuel metered. As we discussed earlier, a series of electronic engine and vehicle sensors are used to advise the ECM of the various operating conditions, much the same as those now in wide use on passenger cars.

System Operation
Figure 5–20 illustrates the basic arrangement of an EUI (electronic unit injector) system on a heavy-duty truck engine. This diagram shows a simplified layout of the system. Each system employs a throttle position sensor which contains a potentiometer (variable resistor) assembled into the pedal assembly. There is no direct

connection between the throttle pedal and the injectors, since the position of the pedal sends out a signal to the ECM to let it know the percentage of throttle opening. In addition to the pedal position, the ECM receives input signals from a number of sensors, such as the engine turbo boost, intake manifold air temperature, fuel temperature, oil pressure, oil temperature, coolant level or coolant temperature, engine speed, and vehicle road speed. Prior to start-up, the engine receives signals from both a timing reference sensor and a synchronous reference sensor, so that the ECM knows the relative piston positions and can then initiate fuel delivery to the injectors. Some unit injectors, such as the Detroit Diesel two-stroke-cycle 71 and 92 models, the Caterpillar 3176 engine model, and the Cummins Celect system are operated through an engine-camshaft-actuated pushrod and rocker arm assembly (see Figure 5–32a). On Detroit Diesel's Series 60, the Caterpillar 3406E, and the Volvo VE D12, an overhead camshaft operates the unit injector rocker arm (see Figure 5–32b). Each injector is controlled by an injector-mounted electric solenoid.

There is no mechanically operated fuel rack on any electronically controlled unit injector; therefore, the amount of fuel metered and the timing are controlled by the signal generated at the ECM, based on the various sensor outputs and the throttle position. This ECM signal to the injector, known as a PWM (pulse width modulated) signal, lasts for a given amount of crankshaft degrees. For a given speed, the longer the solenoid is energized, the greater the amount of fuel injected. Conversely, the shorter the PWM signal, the lower the volume of fuel injected into the combustion chamber. Generation of high-enough fuel pressure for injection purposes requires the action of the rocker arm assembly, as shown in Figure 5–32. Figure 5–33 illustrates the internal injector plunger, which is forced down by the rocker arm inside its barrel/bushing. Note that a small spill valve is shown to the right-hand side of the diagram; this spill valve is held open by a spring that will prevent any fuel pressure increase beyond that created by the fuel system's fuel supply pump. As the injector plunger moves down, fuel will simply flow or spill from this valve and return to the fuel tank. For injection to begin, this spill valve must be closed by a signal from the ECM energizing the small electric solenoid, which sits on top of the injector. Once the solenoid is energized by the PWM signal from the ECM, the downward-moving injector plunger will create a rapid increase in the trapped fuel pressure below it. Once this pressure is high enough, the needle valve

in the injector spray tip will be opened against its return spring, allowing fuel to be injected into the combustion chamber. Any time that the injector solenoid is de-energized, the small spill valve is opened by its spring, and fuel injection comes to an immediate end.

The basic difference between a mechanically operated and rack-controlled unit injector plunger, and the injector used on electronic-equipped engines, is that there is no helix on the electronic injector plunger; it is simply a solid plunger (see Figure 5–34). Each one of the electronic unit injector systems is equipped with an electronic speed control system, which is a part of the solid-state circuitry contained within the ECM housing. On some systems, the ECM is cooled by routing diesel fuel through a cooling plate attached to the ECM mounting bracket to maintain the electronic components at an acceptable operating temperature.

Series 50 and 60 Fuel System

Before we study how the EUI operates, let's briefly look at the fuel system layout for the Detroit Diesel Series 50 and 60 EUI engine models. Figure 5–35 illustrates that the fuel system is similar to that used with the MUI engines in that a gear-type fuel transfer pump driven from the rear of the air compressor assembly on truck applications creates the flow requirements for the system. Fuel leaves the fuel tank and passes through either a primary fuel filter or fuel/water separator assembly to the inlet side of the fuel pump. This is the suction side of the fuel system; therefore, any loose fittings or connections will allow air to be drawn into the system, resulting in a rough running engine and a lack of power. From the outlet side of the pump, fuel under pressure flows through a cooling plate EDU (electronic distributor unit) bolted to the ECM (electronic control module) on certain applications to maintain the internal operating temperature of the electronics components within the ECM at an acceptable level. This fuel cooler is not normally required on heavy-duty highway truck Series 60 engines unless fuel temperatures are consistently above 140°F (60°C), although it is used on Series 50 models in transit bus applications. Fuel now enters the secondary fuel filter and exits to the rear of the cylinder head where it flows through an internally cast manifold to feed each EUI. Fuel that isn't required for injection purposes is used to cool and lubricate the internal components of the injector. Return fuel leaves the injector where it flows through an internal fuel return manifold cast within the cylinder head. Fuel leaves the head at the rear through a restricted fitting as shown in Figure 5–36 and returns to the fuel tank.

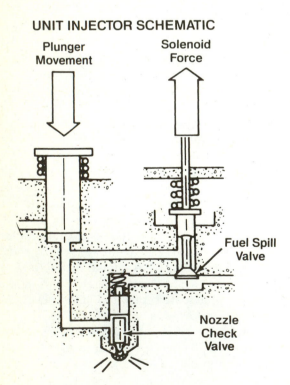

UNIT INJECTOR SCHEMATIC

Plunger Movement

Solenoid Force

Fuel Spill Valve

Nozzle Check Valve

FIGURE 5–33 Basic concept of operation for an electronically controlled unit fuel injector. (Courtesy of Caterpillar Inc.)

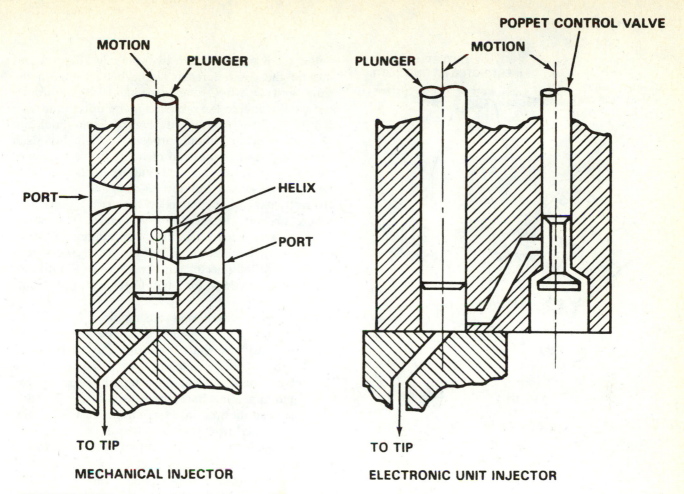

MECHANICAL INJECTOR

ELECTRONIC UNIT INJECTOR

FIGURE 5–34 Comparison of the unit injector plunger design differences between a mechanical and electronically controlled model. (Courtesy of Detroit Diesel Corporation.)

FIGURE 5–35 Schematic layout of the fuel system for a Series 60 four-stroke-cycle EUI engine model. (Courtesy of Detroit Diesel Corporation.)

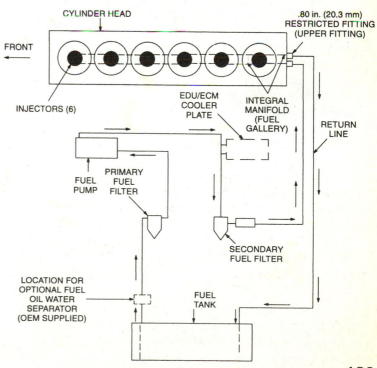

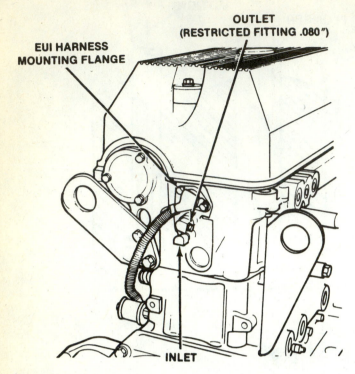

FIGURE 5–36 *Series 60 engine model fuel gallery inlet and outlet fittings at the rear of the cylinder head. (Courtesy of Detroit Diesel Corporation.)*

UPDATE: The Series 60 engine uses an R80 (0.080 in. 2.05 mm) fuel restricted fitting. DDC recommends that where power output and engine response complaints are received, the R80 fitting can be drilled out to as much as 0.093 in. (2.36 mm). This resulting increase in fuel flow supplies the injectors with fuel that is slightly lower in temperature. This denser, lower-temperature fuel has a higher energy content, so it provides slightly more horsepower to each cylinder. The restricted fitting modification should be attempted only after the fuel system has been checked for filter plugging, supply line restriction to flow, leaks, or contamination. In addition, after modifying the restricted fitting, check the fuel system pressure, which should not be allowed to drop below 83 kPa (12 psi) at an engine idle speed of 600 rpm; otherwise, an unstable hunting or rolling condition will lead to performance concerns.

Fuel Injector Operation

In the DDEC injector used with Detroit Diesel's Series 50 and 60 engines, the fuel feed to the injector is similar to that found on other electronic engines. The fuel

enters the injector through two fuel inlet filter screens around the circumference of the body between the third and fourth O-rings (seals). All the injectors receive this fuel in the same manner, through the inlet manifold fitting shown in Figure 5–36. Fuel not required for combustion purposes, but which is used for cooling and lubrication of internal injector parts, exits the injector at the small fuel return hole located between the second and third O-rings and flows out of the restricted fitting connection shown in Figure 5–36, where it returns directly to the fuel tank.

The actual identification of component parts is clearly shown in Figure 5–37 for the Series 60 electronically controlled injector. The functions of the injector are the same as those for a non-DDEC-equipped unit:

- Creates the high pressure required for efficient injection. This is achieved by the action of the overhead camshaft pivoting the rocker arm through its roller follower to force the injector follower down against its external return spring. Therefore, a mechanical means is still required to force the internal injector plunger down to raise the trapped fuel to a high enough pressure to lift the needle valve at the bottom of the injector off its seat.

- Meters and injects the precise amount of fuel required to handle the load. This quantity of fuel is determined by the ECM, which in turn continually receives input signals from the various engine sensors. The ECM sends out a pulse width signal to close the small internal poppet valve. This action allows the downward-moving plunger to increase the pressure of the fuel to lift the needle valve from its seat and injection begins. Injection lasts as long as the ECM is sending out a signal to energize the EUI (electronic unit injector) solenoid. As soon as the ECM deenergizes the solenoid, a spring opens the small poppet valve and the high fuel pressure that was holding the needle valve open is lost to the return line; therefore, injection ends. The longer the pulse width time, the greater the volume of fuel that will be injected.

- Atomizes the fuel so that it will penetrate the air mass within the cylinder and initiate combustion. This atomization is achieved by the downward-moving plunger, which has to increase the fuel pressure to approximately 5000 psi (34,475 kPa) to lift the needle valve from its seat. The fuel is then forced through the multiple small holes (orifices) in the spray tip, which causes the fuel droplets to break down into a finely atomized state as they approach injection pressures of 28,000 psi (193,060 kPa).

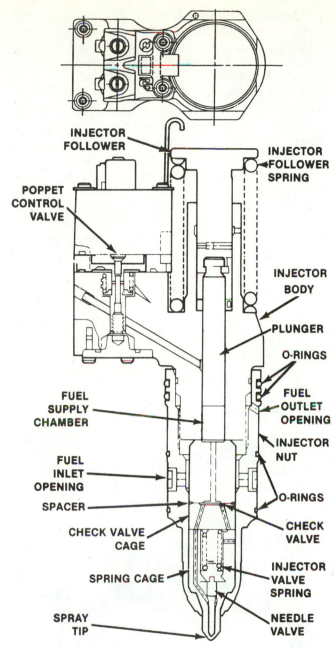

**INJECTOR
FOLLOWER**

**POPPET
CONTROL
VALVE**

**INJECTOR
FOLLOWER
SPRING**

**INJECTOR
BODY**

PLUNGER

O-RINGS

**FUEL
SUPPLY
CHAMBER**

**FUEL
OUTLET
OPENING**

**INJECTOR
NUT**

**FUEL
INLET
OPENING**

SPACER

O-RINGS

**CHECK VALVE
CAGE**

**CHECK
VALVE**

SPRING CAGE

**INJECTOR
VALVE
SPRING**

**SPRAY
TIP**

**NEEDLE
VALVE**

FIGURE 5–37 *Cross-sectional view and identification of major parts of a Series 60 engine electronically controlled unit injector assembly. (Courtesy of Detroit Diesel Corporation.)*

- Permits continuous fuel flow in excess of that required for combustion purposes to ensure cooling and lubrication of all injector components.

The injection timing (start of injection) and metering (quantity) are controlled by the pulse width signal from the ECM through to the EUI. The longer the EUI solenoid is energized, the longer the small poppet

valve will remain closed and the greater the amount of fuel that will be injected. In effect, by holding the poppet valve closed longer, we are lengthening the effective stroke of the downward-moving plunger, since it will always move down the same distance regardless of the pulse width time. This is so because the lift of the camshaft lobe will always be the same.

When the poppet valve is closed by the EUI solenoid activation, which is called *response time feedback,* the ECM uses the information to monitor and adjust fuel injection timing. This action ensures that there will be no injector-to-injector variation in the start of injection timing. The EEPROM (electrically erasable programmable read-only memory) chip set within the ECM is programmed with a pulse width program for each particular engine and application; therefore, the maximum amount of fuel injected depends on this EEPROM information.

ELECTRONIC CONTROL MODULES

All electronically controlled engines incorporate an engine-mounted ECM or ECU (electronic control module or unit). Illustrations in this chapter indicate the location of various ECMs in different engine makes. The wiring harness connections to and from the ECM differ slightly in engine makes; however, all systems generally incorporate several types of wire harness:

- The engine harness connector to connect all of the sensors and switches to the ECM. This harness is supplied by the engine manufacturer to allow the engine to run.
- The injector harness to allow unit injector operation
- The power harness to carry battery power to the ECM
- An OEM harness to interface with all of the cab controls and ECM-controlled instrumentation.

Each engine manufacturer uses a generic ECM across its line of engines. Thus when the engine reaches the end of the assembly line, it is a simple matter to program it according to the end user's requirements and desired options as indicated on the sales order data sheet. Figure 5–38 illustrates how this is accomplished by connecting a PC (personal computer) to the engine ECM. Information stored in the factory mainframe computer downloads specific engine operating, parameters through the PC and into the engine ECMs double-EE prom chip, more commonly identified by the letters EEPROM (electrically erasable programmable read-only memory). This information contains the engine calibration configurations such as maximum engine governed speed, governor droop characteristics,

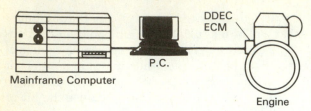

EEPROM CALIBRATION

Basic Rating
- BHP/RPM
- Governor Features
  - Low & High Idle
  - Droop

Customer Options
- Engine Protection
  (Warning or Shutdown)
- Road Speed/Cruise Control
  - Max Speed
  - Axle Ratio
  - Tires Rev./Mile
  - Transmission Data
  - Vehicle Speed Sensor
- Power Control
- Special Application Features

FIGURE 5–38 Example of EEPROM (electrically erasable programmable read only memory) end-of-line ECM program calibration for an electronically controlled heavy-duty diesel engine. (Courtesy of Detroit Diesel Corporation.)

cruise control features, maximum vehicle road speed, transmission gear-down protection, PTO (power take-off) operating features, idle shutdown timer, fuel injector information, horsepower rating, engine data list, diagnostic trouble codes, and engine/trip data. Once the vehicle or equipment is placed into service, a number of ECM operating parameters can be changed by an authorized OEM through use of a *programming station* similar to the one featured in Figure 5–39. This suitcase-mounted system includes a laptop computer and special telephone modem and engine hookup harnesses to allow connection to the factory mainframe computer when it is necessary to change engine horsepower settings, and so on. If an engine horsepower setting is altered, or if major alterations to the engine parameters are required while the engine is still under warranty, the OEM needs to know what changes are being made. This reprogramming feature can cost the engine user from several hundred to several thousand dollars, particularly if a higher horsepower setting is desired, because experience proves that higher horsepower engines tend to cost more because of service failures

Programming Station

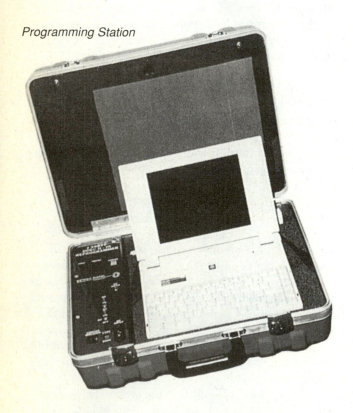

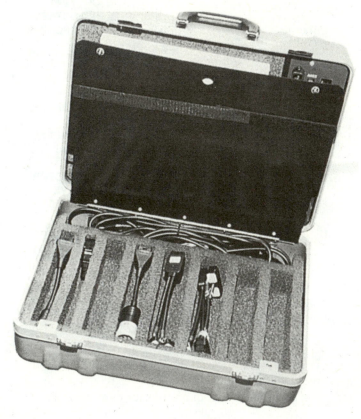

FIGURE 5–39 Portable technician briefcase with a laptop computer, special adapters, and electronic controls to allow ease of ECM reprogramming. (Courtesy of Detroit Diesel Corporation.)

than do lower power-rated engines. The user pays extra dollars to cover the anticipated possible failure costs charged back to the OEM while the engine is under an extended warranty period.

A field service technician can access ECM information with the use of handheld DDR (diagnostic data reader) similar to the MPSI (Microprocessor Systems, Inc.) Pro-Link 9000 model shown in Figure 5–40. Access is controlled by the adoption of an electronic password, which is usually selected by the end user at the time of ordering the engine. Thousands of passwords are available and can be chosen by the owner or fleet management personnel. Without knowledge of the specific password (name or numbers), no changes can be made to the system operating parameters; therefore, system security is maintained. System security is usually offered to users in three forms:

1. No password. This option allows anyone to change selected options within a given range using a handheld DDR connected to the DDL (diagnostic data link) of the engine ECM.

2. Changeable password. Only individuals with access to the password can make selected changes utilizing the DDR.

3. System lockout. A specific password is provided that allows only an authorized representative of the engine dealer to make changes to various options such as the horsepower or major engine settings.

ECM Operational Description

The ECM is the brains of the system. It continually receives input voltage signals from the various engine and vehicle sensors and computes these signals to determine the length of the EUI pulse width modulated signal. The longer the injector solenoid is energized, the greater will be the fuel delivered to the combustion chamber. Because of the high current switching requirements necessary for operation of the individual electronic unit injectors, the voltage signal from the ECM is sent to a built-in EDU (electronic distributor unit) contained within the single ECM housing.

The various sensors used with each system were discussed earlier in this chapter. Sensors continually input voltage signals to the ECM when the engine is first cranked and is running. The idle rpm, fuel input, and therefore the horsepower developed at a given load/speed are determined by the injector solenoid pulse width signal, based on the various inputs from all the sensors used with the system.

The timers used are the basis for the fuel delivery system and have the following major functions:

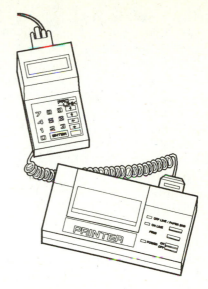

FIGURE 5–40   Handheld Pro-Link 9000 model DDR (diagnostic data reader) connected to a miniprinter to capture a hard copy of engine operational data and logged trouble codes. (Courtesy of Detroit Diesel Corporation.)

- Time between cylinders (measured as crank degrees)
- Time from reference signal to injector solenoid turn on
- Solenoid response time
- Solenoid ON time
- Real-time program events

For each cylinder, a timer requests the beginning of injection (BOI), and the pulse width (PW) time (effective injector plunger stroke) is converted from degrees of crankshaft angle to a time reference.

Initiation of a cylinder injection sequence is started with the time delay between the beginning of the timing reference signal to actually turn the solenoid on. This time delay is estimated from the time between the last two sets of timing signals and subsequently reduced by the previously measured solenoid response time. Pulse width or injector solenoid ON time (fuel being injected) is determined by converting the requested crank angle degrees sensor signal to an equivalent time period plus the solenoid response time.

ECM Control Functions

The ECM receives the various sensor voltage signals and sends out a command pulse to the unit injector based on throttle position and engine speed. The peak torque rpm and actual torque shaping are determined by scheduling fuel pulse width (injector plunger effective stroke) based on engine speed at full throttle. The speed governor is designed to maintain a precise speed setting for all engine loads from the information stored in the calibration EEPROM. From this information, the governor has the ability to calibrate droop, which is the difference between maximum full-load and maximum no-load speeds. The system is designed for closed-loop control, whereby all sensors are providing input signals to the ECM so that the desired idle speed can be set for accessory performance and fuel economy; therefore, PTO (power takeoff) functions can be handled by establishing a new set speed when a load is applied to the engine.

On each system there is a built-in flexibility feature for calibrating droop from 0 to 150 rpm, to provide the best performance from engine speed/vehicle gearing. Zero droop can be programmed into the system to limit vehicle speed by setting the maximum full-load engine speed to match the maximum vehicle road speed. In addition, the system can be programmed for two-speed logic, whereby the maximum full-load rpm of the engine can be reduced any time that the transmission is in top gear. One or more switches can be used to indicate what gear the transmission is in, to limit vehicle speed or allow an extended rpm operating range in one or more gears for better fuel economy or performance improvement. The rated speed is determined by a switch input to the ECM. Improved cold starting of the engine is established by using a voltage signal from the engine oil temperature sensor to provide a 15% improvement over a nonelectronic engine.

Another feature of the electronic system is reducing white smoke on initial start-up of a cold engine by increasing the idle speed setting, along with advanced injection timing to allow faster engine warm-up. The idle speed is reduced and the injection timing is retarded as the engine warms up to ensure lower fuel consumption, reduced exhaust emissions, and lower combustion noise. If the ECM has been programmed to do so, a 3- to 100-minute idle shutdown can be incorporated into the electronic system. This shutdown timer starts its count once the engine is idling and the vehicle spring parking brakes are activated. An engine airflow turbocharged discharge pressure transducer sensor set for approximately 2 atmospheres (29.4 psi) absolute, along with an engine speed sensor, provides improved engine acceleration as well as an improvement in engine torque because of the faster response of the electronic system. An air temperature sensor is also used to provide optimum timing for best fuel consumption based on changing air temperatures.

The electronic distributor unit (EDU) contained within the ECM functions as the high-current switching unit for actuation of the unit injector solenoids as well as monitoring the solenoid voltage waveform to sense valve closure. The EDU sources its current through a linearly controlled pass transistor circuit from the vehicle battery. Because of the high current generated by the current regulators, a cold plate using the engine fuel flow as the cooling medium provides a heat sink for the ECM on some electronic engine applications. The average current draw for various truck engine models is between 1 and 3 amps at idle speed to between 3 and 8 amps at full-load engine rpm based on the number of cylinders and governed engine speed.

The cruise control interface system can use either the vehicle or the engine speed as the control input, while vehicle brake, set/coast, and resume/acceleration switch inputs provide drive commands. The engine brake operates when the ECM senses that the engine is in an unfueled state so that the engine brake can be applied. Output from the ECM is provided to interface with the engine braking system.

Each ECM contains two types of memory.

1. The EEPROM (electronically erasable programmable read-only memory) unit, which has been designed for use with a particular engine speed and horsepower setting, and coded for use in a particular truck based on its transmission and axle ratios as well as tire size, and so on. The EEPROM chip allows any engine to have its speed and horsepower settings changed without completely replacing the ECM.
2. The RAM (random-access memory) unit, which continually receives updated information from all of the various engine/vehicle sensors to allow the ECM to be advised of any changes to the operating parameters for the engine vehicle during operation. In effect, the RAM unit becomes the working scratch pad of the ECM during engine operation.

ECM Safety Precautions

When working around electronic engines, major safety precautions must be observed.

1. *Welding.* Disconnect the vehicle batteries and the plug-in harnesses to the ECM to prevent any possibility of ECM damage during welding.
2. *Electrical shock:* Never disconnect or connect any wires or harness connectors, particularly at the ECM, when the engine is running or when the ignition key switch is turned on. Also, remember that electronic unit injectors receive a PWM signal from the ECM that can range as high as 90 V when the engine is running. *Do not* come in contact with the injector terminals while the engine is running!

When handling an electronic part that has an electrostatic discharge sensitive sticker (Figure 5–41), follow

FIGURE 5–41   Typical industry standard warning label/decal to indicate electrostatic discharge. (Courtesy of Detroit Diesel Corporation.)

these guidelines to reduce any possible electrostatic charge build-up on your body and the electronic part:

- Do not open the package until it is time to install the part.
- Avoid touching electrical terminals of the part.
- Before removing the part from its package, ground the package to a known good ground on the vehicle.
- Always touch a known good ground before handling the part. This should be repeated while handling the part and more frequently after sliding across the seat, sitting down from a standing position, or walking a distance.

3. *Turbocharger shield.* It is sometimes necessary to operate an engine with the ducting to the intake side of the turbocharger disconnected. Never operate any engine without first installing a turbo "guard" similar to the one illustrated in Chapter 20 (Figure 20–33).

ECM Diagnostic Access

All electronically controlled engines are designed to store or log a trouble code in ECM memory when a sensor is operating in an out-of-range condition. When a problem is sensed and relayed back to the ECM, the severity of the problem will cause either the yellow or red diagnostic instrument panel light to illuminate. When the yellow light is illuminated, there may be a rampdown (power reduction) of both engine power and speed. If the red light is illuminated, the sensed operating problem is serious enough to trigger an engine shutdown condition if the ECM has been programmed to do so. Some electronic systems are equipped with a *diagnostic toggle switch* that can be activated to cause the dash-mounted CEL to illumi-

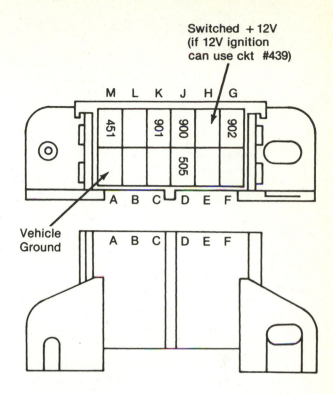

12 Pin DDL Connector P/N 12020043

FIGURE 5–42   Diagram of a DDEC I and DDEC II engine 12-pin DDL (diagnostic data link) connector normally located in the cab area of a heavy-duty truck to allow plug-in of the interface cable from the DDR shown in Figure 5–40. Trouble codes can be withdrawn by using the DDR or by using a jumper wire connected between terminals A and M of the DDL connector, then turning the ignition key on to monitor the flash codes. (Courtesy of Detroit Diesel Corporation.)

nate and to flash rapidly, thereby allowing the driver or technician to determine the *flash code number.*

In some electronic systems, the technician can use a *jumper wire* across two diagnostic connector terminals to cause any stored ECM trouble codes to "flash" the dash-mounted vehicle diagnostic light. Figure 5–42 illustrates one such example of a 12-pin DDL (diagnostic data link) connector, which is generally located within the truck cab area (placement varies by OEM). This particular example is for a DDEC I or DDEC II Detroit Diesel system. To extract a flash trouble code, with the ignition key switch off, insert a jumper wire between terminals A and M, which are clearly marked on the connector. When the ignition switch is turned back on, closely watch the dash-mounted yellow diagnostic light. An example of how to interpret stored flash trouble codes is illustrated in Figure 5–43. A flash code 13, for example, on a DDEC system (I or II) indicates that a

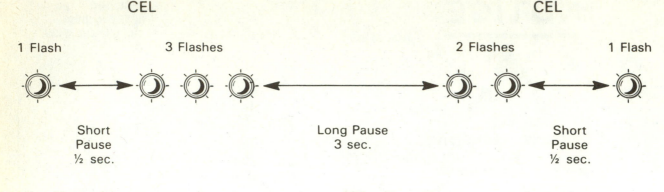

FIGURE 5–43 *Example of how a stored DDEC I or DDEC II model ECM trouble code would cause the yellow warning light—CEL (check engine lamp)—on the vehicle dash to flash a code 13 and a code 21 when a jumper wire is installed across terminals A to M of the DDL shown in Figure 5–42. (Courtesy of Detroit Diesel Corporation).*

coolant level sensor has detected low coolant. A code 21 on this system indicates that the TPS (throttle position sensor) has detected a high circuit voltage reading.

Some vehicles with electronic dashboards can provide a direct readout of engine diagnostic codes similar to the example illustrated in Figure 5–44. This system, known as a ProDriver unit, can continually update the driver on engine and vehicle operating conditions, for example, an instant mpg/km/L fuel consumption reading.

Although flash codes are helpful, a more thorough analysis of system trouble codes and problem areas can be performed by the service technician using a handheld diagnostic reader, which is more commonly referred to as a DDR (diagnostic data reader). The type of diagnostic reader used to withdraw stored trouble codes varies in design among engine manufacturers; however, some major OEMs of diagnostic tools now offer a generic tool that can handle any make of engine, in addition to transmission and antiskid brake electronic controls, simply by removing and inserting an electronic cartridge assembly into the handheld DDR. One such diagnostic tool (Figure 5–40) is manufactured by MPSI (Microprocessor Systems, Inc., Sterling Heights, MI). This tool is distributed through Kent-Moore Division, SPX Corporation. Refer to the sections in this chapter dealing with Caterpillar and Cummins for specifics on their special diagnostic tooling.

The DDR, which is connected to a DDL (diagnostic data link) connector located on the vehicle, can be used for troubleshooting and diagnostic purposes. It also can be used to provide unique capabilities such as

these: running engine cylinder cutout, injector solenoid response times, injector calibration update, engine trip data, engine/vehicle speed calibration changes, cruise control speed setting changes, idle shutdown and transmission progressive shift changes, engine and engine protection configuration changes, parameter versus engine speed (or time), engine snapshot data, and limited ECM reprogramming when customer changes are desired and/or required within the operating conditions/parameters of the engine OEM.

By using any of the readily available DDRs from one of the major suppliers, the technician can access the ECM memory storage bank and monitor the sensor outputs and the diagnostic trouble codes. The technician can also confirm what ECM options have been programmed into the system, such as cruise control, automatic engine shutdown in the event of a major engine system problem, idle control time limit, and so forth.

The DDR can be operated from the vehicle battery power supply, as can the printer (plug into the cigarette lighter). A 110 V power supply is also available to run the printer and is preferable when the DDR and printer are to be used for any length of time.

Technicians can extract and/or download ECM data into either a PC, laptop computer, or a small printer to produce a hard copy of the stored information within the ECM. A small printer is shown connected to a handheld DDR in Figure 5–40.

ECM SAE Trouble Codes

The trouble code numbering system and interpretation stored in ECM memory are not the same in engines

FIGURE 5–44 *Example of how an instrument-panel-mounted ProDriver diagnostic readout screen might appear to a truck driver or service technician. (Courtesy of Detroit Diesel Corporation.)*

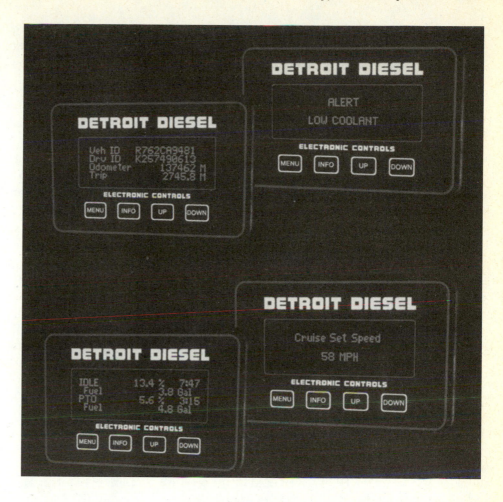

from different OEMs. For example, flash code 35 does not have the same meaning on Caterpillar, Cummins, Detroit Diesel, Mack, and Volvo engines. The SAE (Society of Automotive Engineers, International), through its technical standards committees, has been working with engine OEMs to arrive at a standard system of electronic coding and meaning. To encourage industry-wide acceptance of electronic serial data communication links between engines, SAE has created SAE-J reference standards, which are now in use.

- *SAE J1587.* This standard enables the ECM to "talk" with diagnostic service tools, trip recorder and vehicle management information systems, electronic dash displays, and satellite communication systems. In other words, the J1587/J1708 data link provides sensor(s) and engine data to other vehicle modules.
- *SAE J1922 and J1939.* These two standards give the ECM the capability to communicate with and provide control data to other vehicle systems such as antilock braking systems, electronic transmissions, and antislip ASR systems (traction control devices). The on-vehicle communications harness assembly connects the ECM's J1922 and J1939 control data ports to other vehicle systems. The J1939 data link uses the CAN (controller area network) protocol.
- *SAE J1924.* This is a PC-software-compatible standard to allow the PC to interface with and translate the data link signal from the ECM. The software is installed as a TSR (terminate and stay resident) program.

When a technician uses a handheld DDR similar to the one shown in Figure 5–40 to interpret stored ECM trouble codes, these codes are now displayed in the SAE International technical standard format. Previously, stored trouble codes appeared on the DDR screen as a two- or three-digit number. The technician then referred to a flash code listing in the engine service manual or on a small plastic card provided by the OEM that allowed him or her to interpret the specific trouble code. The technician then referred to the trouble code number in the engine service manual and followed a step-by-step procedure to locate and correct the source of the problem. Although the technician can still follow this procedure, flash codes no longer appear on the screen of the DDR in newer electronic engine systems.

The flash codes have been replaced by parameter and system identification descriptions known as PID (parameter identification) and SID (system identification) numbers. After the PID and SID numbers is an FMI (failure mode identifier), which defines the area where the fault has occurred. The following are summary descriptions of these numbers:

- PID: This appears on the screen of the DDR as a single- or double-byte character to identify data of varying length, for example, the ECM data list of engine operating parameters, which would include items related to oil pressure, oil and coolant temperature, TPS (throttle position sensor) and so on.
- SID: This appears only as a single-byte character to identify field-repairable or field-replaceable subsystems for which failures can be detected or isolated. Such a code would identify an injector problem.
- FMI: This describes the type of failure detected in a subsystem and identified by the PID or SID. The FMI and either the PID or SID combine to form a given diagnostic code as defined by the SAE J1587 technical standard.

Currently, SAE FMIs list 15 numbers that are used in conjunction with either PIDs or SIDs. All of these numbers appear on the DDR screen used by the service technician to recall stored trouble codes from the ECM. Most of the FMIs that accompany either a PID or SID tend to be either a 3 or a 4, and they are included in the following list of the SAE numbers currently in use:

Failure Mode Identifiers (FMIs)

0   Data valid but above normal operational range (that is, engine overheating)
1   Data valid but below normal operational range (that is, engine oil pressure too low)
2   Data erratic, intermittent, or incorrect
3   Voltage above normal or shorted high
4   Voltage below normal or shorted low
5   Current below normal or open circuit
6   Current above normal or grounded circuit
7   Mechanical system not responding properly
8   Abnormal frequency, pulse width, or period
9   Abnormal update rate
10 Abnormal rate of change
11 Failure mode not identifiable
12 Bad intelligent device or component
13 Out of calibration
14 Special instructions
15 Reserved for future assignment by the SAE data format subcommittee

For example, the DDR illustrated in Figure 5–40, when connected to a DDEC III system, may display on its screen the following sequence:

Code p 91 3 = EFPA circuit failed high
3 = High Voltage
4 = Low Voltage

When using the DDR, the screen will display (when prompted) whether there are *active* and *inactive* trouble codes stored in the ECM memory. Such a diagnostic request might display the following sequence for a DDEC III system:

[The engine serial number]
Diagnostic Code List
NO ACTIVE CODES
INACTIVE CODES
Engine Throttle Sensor Input Voltage Low
    PID:91   FMI:4 (Flash Code 22)
Engine Oil Pressure Sensor Input Voltage Low
    PID:100   FMI:4 (Flash Code 36)
Engine Turbo Boost Sensor Input Voltage Low
    PID:102   FMI:4 (Flash Code 34)
Coolant Level Sensor Input Voltage High
    PID:111   FMI:3 (Flash Code 16)

The foregoing information indicates to the technician that there are no active codes and 4 inactive codes. Note, however, that the flash codes would show on a DDEC II system DDR screen, but not on a DDEC III system DDR screen! A dash-mounted flash code diagnostic request toggle switch can be activated on the DDEC III system to extract these types of codes.

Even though all engine manufacturers conform to the SAE technical standards, the flash codes are still different. Assume we are using a DDR and we uncover a PDI/FMI number 100/01 on a Cummins, Caterpillar, or Detroit Diesel engine. This SAE code means that the engine ECMs have detected from the sensor input that a low oil pressure condition has been logged. The flash code on the Caterpillar would be a No. 46; on the Detroit Diesel, it would be No. 45; and on the Cummins, it would be No. 143. A PDI/FMI number 110/00 means a high coolant temperature warning; it would exhibit a flash code No. 61 on the Caterpillar, a No. 44 on Detroit Diesel, and a No. 151 on the Cummins. The adoption of the standardized SAE fault codes ensures that all engine manufacturers using electronic fuel injection systems will display the same PIDs and FMIs regardless of individual flash code numbering systems.

Active/Inactive Codes
When an engine or vehicle speed sensor detects an out-of-range operating condition, the ECM receives a high or low signal based on the failure mode detected.

The ECM then logs a trouble code into its memory bank for extraction by the technician at a later date. For example, say the ECM was programmed to record a high engine oil temperature condition beginning at 250°F (121°C). When this condition is noted by the OTS (oil temperature sensor), the signal to the ECM will cause the yellow dash-mounted warning light to illuminate. This condition is known as an *active code* situation. If the ECM has been programmed for engine protection, the engine will usually start to lose speed and power to a level that was the average power occurring prior to the fault condition. If, however, the oil temperature continues to increase, at a preprogrammed point, the red SEL (stop engine light) on the dash will illuminate. Then a 30 second automatic ramp down (power reduction) will begin, followed by engine shutdown if the system has been programmed to do so. In some situations, if the fleet management or owners/operators have previously selected a temporary override option, the driver may push an STEO (stop-engine override) button on the dash to provide another 30 seconds of engine operation, so the vehicle can be pulled safely to the side of the highway.

In this same condition of high engine oil temperature, let's assume that the ECM is programmed to illuminate the dash-mounted yellow warning light at 251°F (122°C) and to shut the engine down at 261°F (127°C). The yellow light illuminates when the low-end temperature of the lube oil is reached, and a trouble code is stored in ECM memory. If the vehicle operating condition triggered this light when moving up a long hill and while heavily loaded, it is possible that once the hill is covered, the engine oil temperature condition would drop back into a normal operating range. This would cause the yellow light to go out; nevertheless, the trouble code would remain stored in ECM memory. This type of a condition is referred to as an *inactive code* (sometimes called a "historic" code). An active code indicates to the vehicle driver that an out-of-range condition has been detected, and an inactive code indicates to the service technician that a problem was detected by a sensor/ECM at some time during engine/vehicle operation. Most current ECMs are programmed not only to log and retain trouble codes, but also to record how many times they occurred and at what hours or miles.

Examples of the various trouble codes—PIDs, SIDs, and FMIs—are listed for Detroit Diesel, Caterpillar, and Cummins engines in subsequent sections of this chapter.

Clearing Codes
After trouble codes have been stored in ECM memory and you want to remove them, you must select the menu option from the DDR that indicates to the technician whether you wish to erase all stored codes. All current electronic systems require this method. In some first-generation systems the stored trouble codes could be erased either by using the DDR or simply by removing the power supply fuses to the ECM for 10 seconds, then reinserting them. The disadvantage of these systems is that after an operator removes the codes, any record of troubles that may have occurred on a trip would be lost, and the service technician or fleet maintenance manager would have no knowledge of any engine or vehicle problems.

SPECIAL NOTE: The information contained within this section dealing with the DDEC (Detroit Diesel Electronic Controls) systems is designed to provide an overview of the system operation and the special diagnostic tools that can be used to troubleshoot the system. It is *not* intended to supplant the excellent printed literature and audiovisual materials readily available from Detroit Diesel. If you intend to perform service diagnostics on DDEC systems, you should acquire the following service publications from your local Detroit Diesel service dealer: Publication No. 7SA708, *DDEC III Application and Installation Manual*; Publication No. 6SE492, *DDEC III Troubleshooting Guide*, which contains all of the system trouble codes, wiring diagrams, and step-by-step diagnostic troubleshooting procedures to quickly and effectively analyze system problems; and an engine service manual related to the particular Detroit Diesel engine that you will be working on; for example, the Series 60 service manual is available under Publication No. 6SE483.

DETROIT DIESEL ELECTRONIC SYSTEMS

In September 1985 Detroit Diesel Corporation was the first major engine OEM in the world to release electronic unit fuel injection controls in a high-speed diesel engine. This system was known as DDEC I (Detroit Diesel Electronic Controls), and was followed in September 1987 by the more advanced DDEC II system. In September 1993, DDC released its third-generation system known as DDEC III.

DDEC III: Evolution and Advantages
DDEC III evolved as a result of a unique set of events: requests from customers for additional electronic engine features and more information; the need to meet increasingly stringent air quality standards; improvements in microprocessor capabilities; and significant strides in the electronics industry.

The DDEC III development team included engineers working together from Detroit Diesel, Motorola Inc., and Pi Research, Ltd. Motorola, one of the world's leading providers of electronic equipment, systems, components, and services, designed the hardware and manufactures the electronic control module. Pi Research, headquartered in Cambridge, England, is known for its dashboard display and on-board sensors designed for cars such as those that race in the Indianapolis 500. This experience, combined with development of DDEC II allowed Pi Research to write the DDEC III software and assist in numerous hardware designs.

The DDEC III computing capability is eight times faster and memory capacity is seven times larger than that of DDEC II; the result is faster engine information response, expanded features, and more precision from the engine control systems. DDEC III represents a major step in providing management information to the fleet operator.

One of the benefits of the extra memory capacity provided by DDEC III is the ability to have multiple ratings in one engine. Multiple ratings enable customers to order one engine with up to four ratings. When the customer orders an engine, the truck manufacturer selects the rating that meets the customer's specification. The additional DDEC III also allows several control functions to be incorporated into one ECM, thereby reducing cost and complexity while improving system reliability. The ECM can control the engine brakes, so a separate brake controller is not necessary. The fan can be engaged by the ECM based on a variety of input signals that could call for fan operation. The low coolant system no longer needs its own control module because it is managed by the DDEC III ECM.

Reprogramming of DDEC software is now much easier than it was in the DDEC I or DDEC II systems. All software can now be reprogrammed using the in-cab six-pin connector, illustrated in Figure 5–45, through advances to DDEC memory chips. Connecting either the DDR shown in Figure 5–40 or the reprogramming unit shown in Figure 5–39 reduces reprogramming time and improves reliability, because removal of the ECM or wire harness connector is no longer required.

Field tests and in-house vehicle tests have shown that the DDEC III system, combined with the stronger engine-rated torque curves, is preferred by drivers of heavy-duty highway trucks for responsiveness and extra pulling power. In addition, the DDEC III system has shown an approximately 3% fuel economy improvement over an equivalent rated DDEC II engine model. Detroit Diesel is the first high-speed heavy-duty engine manufacturer to

break the 300 brake specific fuel consumption barrier, coming in at 0.297 lb/bhp/hr (0.180 g/kW/h), a truly outstanding achievement!

Engine Sensors and Location

All of the existing heavy-duty electronically controlled diesel engines employ similar sensors to monitor operating conditions using fairly common technology. Figure 5–46 illustrates the location of various DDEC III engine sensors, and they are described here:

- Air temperature sensor located in the intake manifold allows the ECM to adjust engine timing to reduce white smoke on startup, improve cold starts, and provide engine protection should the intake manifold air become too hot.
- Turbo boost sensor monitors turbocharger compressor discharge pressure and provides data to the ECM for smoke control during engine acceleration.
- Oil pressure sensor activates the engine protection system when the oil pressure falls below a normal oil pressure at a given engine rpm. A dash-mounted warning light can be used to warn the driver of a low oil pressure condition.
- Oil temperature sensor tells the ECM the engine operating temperature; oil temperature is a closer reflection of engine operation than is coolant. This information optimizes idle speed (fast idle at cold startup) and injection timing to improve cold startability and reduce white smoke. In addition, this sensor activates the engine protection system if the oil temperature is higher than normal. A dash-mounted warning light can be used to warn the driver of a high oil temperature condition.
- Fuel temperature sensor, usually located at the secondary fuel filter, provides a signal to the ECM to calculate fuel consumption for instant readout at the push of a button on a truck instrument panel such as the Detroit Diesel ProDriver option. The ECM also utilizes the fuel temperature signal to adjust the unit injector PWM time for changes in the fuel density with a change in temperature.
- Coolant level sensor, mounted on the radiator top tank, triggers the engine protection feature when a low coolant condition is sensed. An additional coolant level sensor located higher in the radiator top tank indicates, through either a dash-mounted warning lamp or the ProDriver readout module, that the engine coolant is low, but not enough to activate the DDEC engine protection feature.
- Coolant temperature sensor, located on the right side of the engine, also triggers the engine protection system if the coolant temperature exceeds

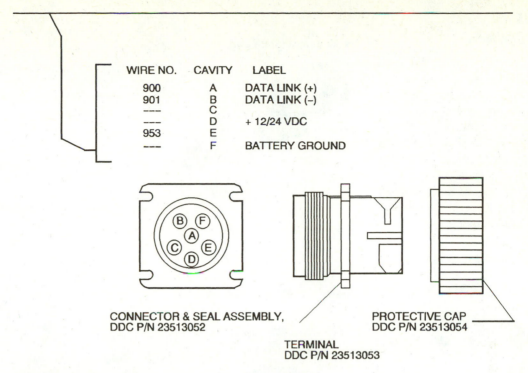

WIRE NO.	CAVITY	LABEL
900	A	DATA LINK (+)
901	B	DATA LINK (−)
---	C	
---	D	+ 12/24 VDC
953	E	
---	F	BATTERY GROUND

CONNECTOR & SEAL ASSEMBLY,
DDC P/N 23513052

TERMINAL
DDC P/N 23513053

PROTECTIVE CAP
DDC P/N 23513054

FIGURE 5–45 DDEC III ECM six-pin diagnostic connector used to connect the DDR shown in Figure 5–40 to enable the technician to access engine data, stored SAE standard trouble codes, conduct various engine tests, and to reprogram the ECM when desired by the customer. (Courtesy of Detroit Diesel Corporation.)

specified limits. A warning light can be provided on the dash to inform the driver when this situation occurs.

- SRS (synchronous reference sensor) provides a once per cylinder signal to the ECM.
- TRS (timing reference sensor) provides a 36 per crankshaft revolution signal from a toothed wheel bolted behind the crankshaft gear. Working in conjunction, the SRS and TRS tell the ECM which cylinder is at TDC for firing purposes. Precise monitoring of piston position allows for optimum injection timing, resulting in excellent fuel economy and performance with low emissions.
- Vehicle speed sensor is usually mounted over the vehicle transmission output shaft to provide the ECM with the speed of the vehicle. This signal is used for cruise control, vehicle speed limiting, and automatic progressive application of the engine Jake brakes to maintain a preprogrammed maximum vehicle speed. In addition, engine fan braking engages the cooling fan clutch automatically when the engine brakes are on *high*. This feature adds 20 to 45 bhp (15 to 33.5 kW) to the engine retardation for slowing down the vehicle.

- On fire truck applications, a fire pump water pressure sensor is used to monitor the pressure governor system. The signal back to the ECM changes engine rpm to allow the fire water pump to maintain a water pressure during pumping operation.
- Throttle position sensor is located within the body of the electronic foot pedal assembly (which was featured in Figure 5–31). An idle validation switch within the throttle sensor assembly tells the ECM when the throttle is at an idle position. In addition, as the operator depresses the pedal or hand throttle on a marine application, the percentage of throttle opening is relayed to the ECM. Throttle response is fast and accurate. Later model throttle sensors are self-calibrating (idle validation) and require no maintenance.

On larger model Detroit Diesel two-stroke-cycle 149 series engine models, a crankcase pressure sensor and a coolant pressure sensor are two additional sensors unique to these models. On the smaller model 71 and 92 two-cycle engines, the sensor locations vary from those on the Series 50 and 60 engines but function in the same manner. In addition, the 71 and 92 engines

DDEC III
How It Works. . .

The major components of the system consist of the electronic control module (ECM), the electronic unit injectors (EUI) and the various system sensors. The purpose of the sensors is to provide information to the ECM regarding various engine performance characteristics. The information sent to the ECM is used to instantaneously regulate engine and vehicle performance.

■ **Electronic Unit Injector (EUI)**

■ **Electrical Connectors**

■ **Air Temperature Sensor**

■ **Coolant Temperature Sensor**

■ **Fire Truck Pump Pressure Sensor**

■ **The SRS and TRS Sensors**

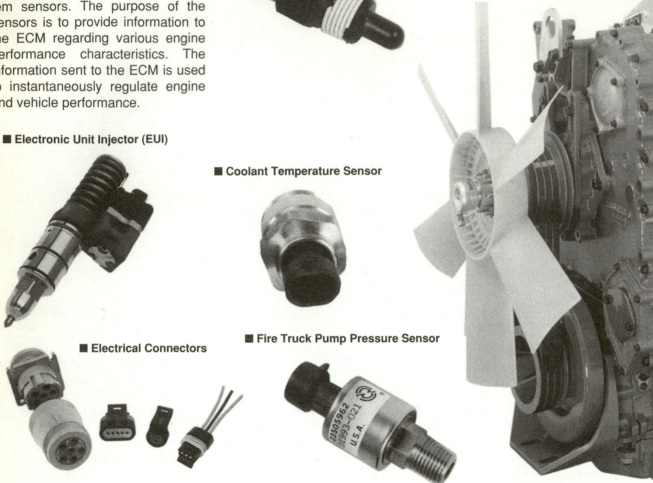

FIGURE 5–46 The DDEC III system—how it works and the various sensors needed for the electronic control system to function and operate properly. (Courtesy of Detroit Diesel Corporation.)

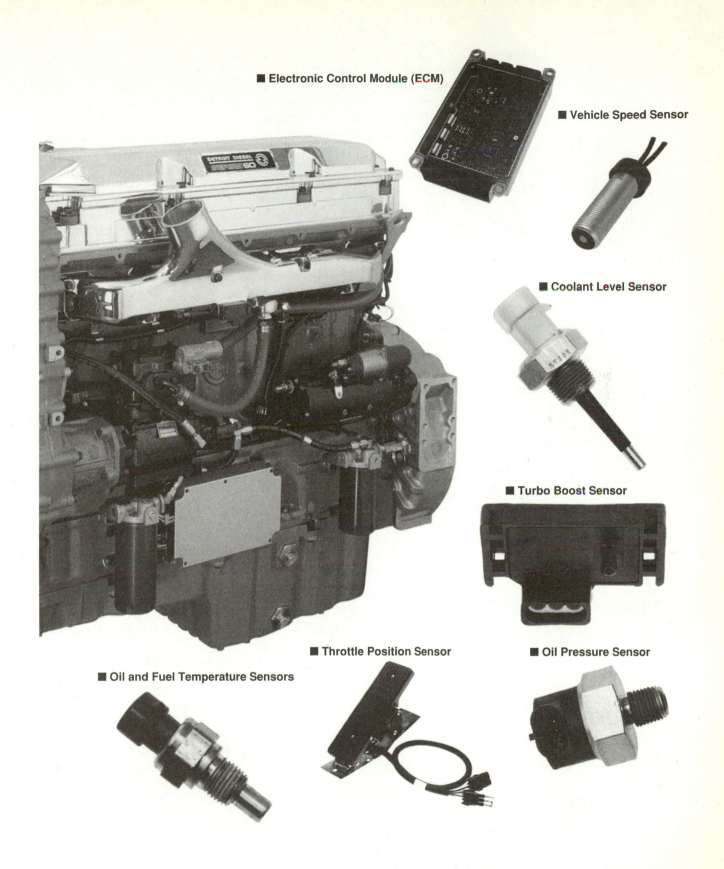

■ Electronic Control Module (ECM)

■ Vehicle Speed Sensor

■ Coolant Level Sensor

■ Turbo Boost Sensor

■ Throttle Position Sensor

■ Oil Pressure Sensor

■ Oil and Fuel Temperature Sensors

usually mount the ECM above and in front of the engine blower assembly; the SRS and TRS sensors pick up their signals from the left front camshaft accessory drive pulley. On 149 engines two ECMs are used, a "master" and "slave" to handle the additional electrical loads on these larger displacement engine models.

The DDEC system has several additional features:

1. Throttle inhibit system can disable the accelerator pedal on a passenger bus application when the doors are open or on a fire truck when the pressure governor fire pump is active.

2. A deceleration light typically used on buses can be mounted on the dash and at the rear of the vehicle to indicate that the vehicle is slowing down when the operator takes his or her foot off of the throttle pedal.

3. A starter motor lockout is commonly used on buses to prevent starter activation after the engine is already running.

4. A green cruise control light illuminates when "cruise" is selected to alert the driver of this condition.

5. A fan clutch override switch can engage the cooling fan at any time when either the engine oil, coolant, or intake manifold temperatures exceed their preset values.

6. A low DDEC voltage light illuminates on the dash when the ECM records a voltage less than 10 V on either a 12 or 24 V vehicle system. This light is typically used on fire truck applications.

Engine Protection System

An engine protection system is programmed into the ECM and operates based on out-of-range operating conditions from the individual engine and vehicle-mounted sensors. On the DDEC III system, the ECM initiates the protection procedure when it receives an out-of-range signal from the oil pressure, oil temperature, coolant temperature, coolant level, and intake manifold air temperature sensors. The system can be programmed for one of three protection features: shutdown, rampdown, or warning.

A warning feature alerts the driver by illuminating a yellow dash-mounted warning light with 100% engine power still available. For example, the oil temperature sensor may be programmed to illuminate the light at 250°F (121°C). If the oil temperature continues to increase, a gradual loss of engine power will occur down to approximately the 70% level, at which time the red dash light will illuminate, for example, at 260°F (127°C). The operator must then choose to pull the vehicle over and shut it down. If the vehicle or marine unit is equipped with a ProDriver feature such as the one illustrated in Figure 5–44, oil temperature can be monitored by the push of a button.

A rampdown condition alerts the driver also by illuminating the yellow dash warning light and reducing the engine power from 100% to 70%, at which time the red dash light will illuminate and the engine power will quickly be reduced to a 40% level.

A shutdown condition occurs similarly to the rampdown mode, except that 30 seconds after illumination of the red light, the ECM has been programmed to automatically shut the engine down.

When toggled or pushed, an STEO (stop engine override) switch located on the instrument panel will allow the engine to return to a 70% power level every 30 seconds while the engine is running. In other words, the operator must activate this switch manually after the red light is illuminated and before the 30 second time interval expires, otherwise the engine will shut down and will not restart.

Engine Diagnostics

The DDEC III system provides an indication of engine and vehicle malfunctions by illuminating the yellow CEL (check engine light) or red SEL (stop engine light) at any time that a sensor or system fault is detected. When the yellow CEL is illuminated, it signifies that a fault has been detected; however, the fault is not serious enough to activate the automatic engine shutdown feature if it has been programmed within the ECM. The condition should be diagnosed as soon as possible; if the vehicle is equipped with a ProDriver diagnostic system similar to the one shown in Figure 5–44, the operator can determine what the fault condition is. This allows the operator to contact a service facility or the home service base and report the problem to the service/maintenance personnel.

Any faults that are stored in ECM memory can be accessed in one of three ways:

1. Connect a DDR (diagnostic data reader) such as the model shown in Figure 5–40 to the DDL connector of the vehicle. See Figure 5–42 for DDEC II systems. For DDEC III systems, depending on the vehicle or equipment in which the engine is installed, the diagnostic connector shown in Figure 5–45 may be located in several areas; therefore refer to the vehicle/equipment service manual for the exact location. On heavy-duty trucks, this connector is usually within the cab area and located under the dash, behind a side kick panel.

2. Use a jumper wire on DDEC II systems similar to that described earlier and shown in Figure 5–42 across terminals A to M on the 12-pin connector to activate the yellow CEL flash codes. On DDEC III systems, flash codes *cannot* be activated in this manner; instead, a diagnostic request switch mounted on the dash must be toggled.

3. Connect a PC or a laptop to the ECM vehicle diagnostic connector on either a DDEC II or a DDEC III system as illustrated in Figure 5–39 and 5–47. The use of a DDEC translator device converts the SAE J1708 standard to an RS232 serial output protocol. Refer to Figure 5–40 where the small printer shown is connected to the RS232 serial port on the side of the DDR. This same PC hookup can be employed with Detroit Diesel software called TRAC (Trip Record Access) release 3.00, which is a programmed package that extracts operational data stored in the ECM. These data can be used to automate fleet record keeping or analyzed to evaluate fleet performance in key areas such as miles (kilometers) driven, engine hours, fuel consumed, total idle/PTO time, total idle fuel used. Fault codes and ECM setup parameters can also be reviewed to aid in troubleshooting when necessary.

Remember that there are two types of trouble codes that can be stored and extracted from the ECM memory system. When an inactive code is logged in ECM memory, it is "time stamped" with the following information: (1) the first occurrence of each diagnostic code in engine hours on all engine applications; (2) the last time that each diagnostic code occurred in engine hours; (3) the number of STEO actions recorded during a trouble code condition; and (4) the total time in seconds that the diagnostic code was active.

SPECIAL NOTE: When disconnecting or connecting ECM or sensor wire harnesses, the ignition switch power *must* always be in the OFF position to prevent serious damage to the various circuits. The ignition system is fuse protected; nevertheless, make certain that no power is on when connecting or disconnecting diagnostic equipment or special tester tools.

ECM and Special Tools

Figure 5–48 illustrates the DDEC II ECM with all of the wiring harness connectors at one end. Figure 5–49 shows the DDEC III ECM which has wiring harness connectors on both ends of the electronic control module.

If it becomes necessary to trace a wiring circuit fault in a DDEC system, open up the alligator-style wiring harness protective cover by prying it apart with your hands. Each wire is identified by an ink-stamped number that corresponds to the system wiring diagram. In addition, each ECM connector pin is identified in the DDEC system wiring diagram as to the wire number to which it connects. Thus it is a reasonably easy task for the service technician to trace all wires for possible faults. However, *never* attempt to pierce the insulation on any wire to probe for a reading with a multimeter. Breaking the insulation causes serious

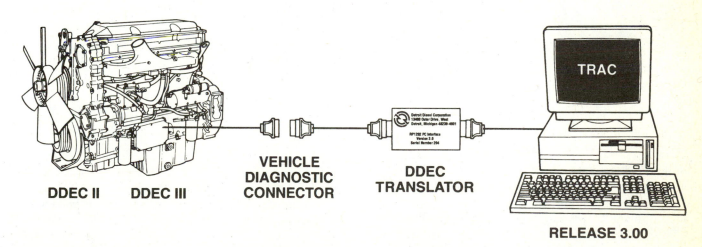

DDEC II   DDEC III   VEHICLE DIAGNOSTIC CONNECTOR   DDEC TRANSLATOR   TRAC   RELEASE 3.00

FIGURE 5–47   Hookup required to the engine ECM for downloading or data extraction system of stored ECM and data hub information. Hookup allows translation to a PC software file for electronic engine and vehicle management control. (Courtesy of Detroit Diesel Corporation.)

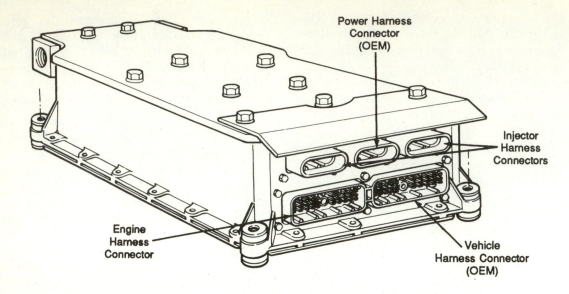

Electronic Control Module (ECM)

FIGURE 5–48 *DDEC II ECM and engine/vehicle interface electrical connectors. (Courtesy of Detroit Diesel Corporation.)*

FIGURE 5–49 *DDEC III ECM and engine/vehicle interface electrical connectors. (Courtesy of Detroit Diesel Corporation.)*

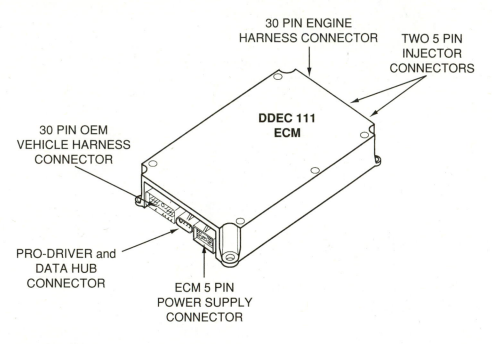

problems from corrosion and/or short circuits. When it becomes necessary to trace the wiring circuits and/or possible faults in wire harness connectors, or within the ECM, refer to Figure 5–50, which illustrates a BB (breakout box) designed specifically for this purpose. When connected into the system, the probes of a multimeter can be inserted into the lettered and numbered BB sockets that correspond to the engine wiring diagram connections. Readings can then be safely taken according to the BB directions or diagnostic step-by-step procedure for tracing a specific trouble code in the engine service manual.

Figure 5–51 illustrates a Kent-Moore special DDEC jumper wire set with its various probe connectors that are designed for insertion into either the ECM female or male connection points and harness connectors. Multimeter leads can then be inserted into the opposite ends of these special probe connectors to safely determine a voltage or resistance value. This reading can then be compared to the service manual specs.

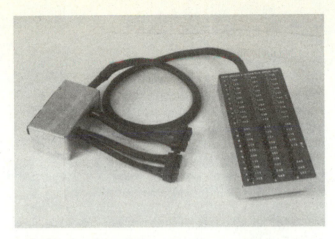

FIGURE 5–50 ECM breakout box (J35634) for use in testing and troubleshooting possible DDEC system problems. (Courtesy of Kent-Moore Division, SPX Corporation.)

FIGURE 5–51 Model J35751 DDEC jumper wire kit for effective electrical troubleshooting and problem diagnosis. (Courtesy of Kent-Moore Division, SPX Corporation.)

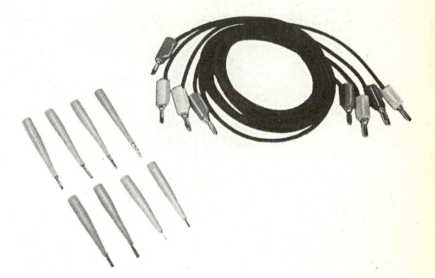

What's A Break-Out Box?
It's a hand held device which allows the technician to "Break-Out" or access electronic circuits so they can be checked for proper voltage, resistance, and continuity.

Why Use The Break-Out Box?
• The Break-Out Box allows complete interrogation of any DDEC circuit (engine or vehicle) from one convenient device at a comfortable position away from the engine compartment.
• No need to probe the back of the harness connectors or pierce wire insulation to pick-readings.
• All testing is done after "one" initial hook-up of the Break-Out Box. No Individual jumper wires to install in male and female connectors. No chance of error in locating the proper circuit.

How Is The Break-Out Box Used?
• Simply disconnect the vehicle and engine harness at the Electronic Control Module (ECM) and connect to the Break-Out Junction Box. The vehicle and engine connectors from the junction box are then connected to the ECM.
• The probes from a Volt/Ohm Meter (such as Kent-Moore J 34039-A) are then inserted into the proper sockets to take readings with ignition on and with or without engine running.

Specifications
• Uses same connectors as found in DDEC.
• Six foot cable between junction box and probe panel.
• Sixty socket probe panel with connector cavities marked to correspond with vehicle and engine connectors (DDEC II) and J1A and J1B (DDEC I).
• Includes handy reference card to identify connector cavities.

Should it become desirable to individually check the various DDEC system sensors, refer to Figure 5–52 which illustrates a special Kent-Moore sensor tester. Simply disconnect the snap wire harness connector from one or more sensors and attach the correct mating sensor tester harness. Rotate the sensor tester dial knob to the sensor that you want to check; then insert the multimeter test leads into the two probe holes on the tester to read the sensor value and compare it to service manual specs.

Diagnostic Codes
In accordance with SAE industry-wide technical standardization trouble codes, all engine OEMs now employ the same PIDs, SIDs, and FMIs to indicate the same problem area with their systems. Refer back to the section in this chapter titled, "ECM SAE Trouble Codes" for a description of these.

ECM flash codes, which were described and shown in Figure 5–43, are shown in Figure 5–53 for DDEC systems. Keep in mind that these flash codes appear on the DDR screen in DDEC I and DDEC II systems but not on DDEC III systems, which reveal only the PIDs, SIDs, and FMIs. Flash codes can be extracted from DDEC III systems only if a diagnostic request switch has been wired into the ECM system. Figure 5–53 lists SID-PID-FMI trouble code to flash code cross-references used on DDEC III systems for SAE standard J1587.

Using the MPSI DDR
The MPSI Pro-Link 9000 DDR illustrated in Figure 5–40 is designed to provide the service technician with a

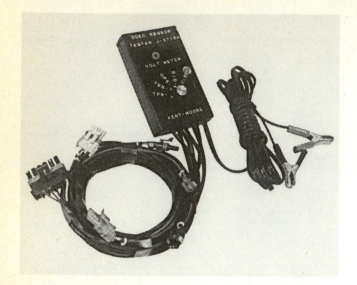

FIGURE 5–52 DDEC engine sensor tester tool used to isolate possible faulty sensors or wire harness faults. Sensors can be checked on or off the engine. Tester requires a 12 V battery power source and the use of a digital multimeter. (Courtesy of Kent-Moore Division, SPX Corporation.)

number of functions. It contains an operational soft-touch *keypad* (with 16 keys) similar to that illustrated in Figure 5–54. The MPSI reader can be used with all current heavy-duty diesel electronic systems. However, since each engine and vehicle manufacturer has chosen its own computer operating system, the Pro-Link 9000 DDR can have its software cartridge changed to suit the engine or transmission type. The slip-in cartridge can be easily removed or installed from the rear of the DDR with light pressure.

Figure 5–54 lists the MPSI DDR reader functions that can be used to access the engine ECM. The DDR shown in Figure 5–40 contains 10 numeric keys and 4 arrow keys. The up and down arrow keys can be used to scroll through the digital screen readout displays, while the right and left arrow keys can be used to toggle back and forth between choices on the display. The Function key is used to choose one of the functions listed in Figure 5–54. The Enter key must be pressed once you have selected a function from the readout window screen to confirm your choice or instruct the DDR to continue to the next step.

NOTE: Within the DDR Pro-Link is a 2 amp fuse; failure of the unit to power up and display information on the window screen may indicate a blown fuse.

DDR operation requires connection of a special cable with a 15-pin terminal to the top of the housing, as shown in Figure 5–40. Once installed, lightly tight-en the two captive plastic thumbscrews to secure the cable connection. If a printer is being used, connect it as shown in Figure 5–40.

Troubleshooting with the DDR

Always make sure that the ignition switch/key is OFF before connecting or disconnecting the DDR connectors. When the DDR is connected to the ECM diagnostic data link connector, the technician can select any of the items listed in Figure 5–54. Scroll through the selections illuminated on the DDR screen with the up and down arrows. When you see the function you want, you may have to use the left and right arrow keys to place the brackets [ ] around your selection when prompted to do so on the screen. Then you have to press the Enter key. As you select a given function, the DDR screen prompts you about what to do next. If you want to extract stored trouble codes, or short out engine cylinders automatically or by cylinder selection, you can do so using the Function and Enter keys. After a short practice period with the DDR, you will become relatively comfortable using it.

Injector Calibration with the DDR

Injectors in the 1994 later-production DDEC III engines have performance *bar codes* and are individually programmed into the ECM after installation. This feature is shown in Figure 5–55 where the injector load plate has a bar code label on it plus a calibration code number that can range from 00 to 99. This number must be entered into the ECM using the DDR when injectors are replaced. By doing so, we can ensure a cylinder balancing feature to help control engine horsepower variability in each cylinder. This variability occurs due to mass production tolerances that result in variations in cylinder compression pressures, fuel injector delivery volume, and so forth. Use of the calibration number results in improved engine response and fuel efficiency because the ECM is able to accurately compute many factors, including each injector's performance, and meter an exact fuel quantity into each cylinder.

Figure 5–56 illustrates the procedure required when the DDR is used to recalibrate injectors; the following description explains the procedure in more detail. When using the DDR to calibrate injectors, select ENGINE from the screen and hit the Enter key. Using the arrow keys, scroll to FUEL INJECTOR INFO on the screen and press the Enter key. Scroll with the arrow keys again until CAL-UPDATE appears on the DDR screen and press the Enter key. From DO YOU WANT TO UPDATE THE CALIBRATION select [VIEW] and hit the Enter key. The DDR screen will display the various injector calibration codes. Compare the two-digit calibration numbers shown on the injectors (see Figure

DDEC III — Flash Codes — SAE Faults

TO READ CODES: Use the diagnostic data reader or depress and hold the diagnostic request switch with the ignition on, engine at idle or not running. Press and hold the switch. Active codes will be flashed on the stop engine light, followed by the inactive codes being flashed on the check engine light. The cycle will repeat until the operator releases the diagnostic request switch.

Flash Code	DDEC III Description
11	VSG input low
12	VSG input high
13	Coolant level circuit low
14	Intercooler, coolant or oil temp. circuit high
15	Intercooler, coolant or oil temp. circuit low
16	Coolant level circuit high
17	Bypass position circuit high
18	Bypass position circuit low
21	TPS circuit high
22	TPS circuit low
23	Fuel temp. circuit high
24	Fuel temp. circuit low
25	No codes
26	Aux. shutdown #1or #2 active
27	Air temp. circuit high
28	Air temp. circuit low
31	Aux. output short or open circuit (high side)
32	SEL short or open circuit
33	Boost pressure circuit high
34	Boost pressure circuit low
35	Oil pressure circuit high
36	Oil pressure circuit low
37	Fuel pressure circuit high
38	Fuel pressure circuit low
41	Too many SRS (missing TRS)
42	Too few SRS (missing SRS)
43	Coolant level low
44	Intercooler, coolant or oil temp. high
45	Oil pressure low
46	Battery voltage low
47	Fuel pressure high
48	Fuel pressure low
52	A/D conversion fail
53	EEPROM write or nonvolatile checksum fail
54	Vehicle speed sensor fault
55	J1939 data link fault
56	J1587 data link fault
57	J1922 data link fault
58	Torque overload
61	Injector response time long
62	Aux. output open or short to battery
63	PWM open or short to battery
64	Turbo speed circuit failed
67	Coolant pressure circuit high or low
68	IVS switch fault, open or grounded circuit
71	Injector response time short
72	Vehicle overspeed
75	Battery voltage high
76	Engine overspeed with engine brake
81	Oil level or crankcase pressure circuit high
82	Oil level or crankcase pressure circuit low
83	Oil level or crankcase pressure high
84	Oil level or crankcase pressure low
85	Engine overspeed
86	Water pump or baro. pressure circuit high
87	Water pump or baro. pressure circuit low
88	Coolant pressure low

SAE Fault	Flash Code	DDEC III Description
p 052 0	44	Intercooler temp. high
p 052 3	14	Intercooler temp. circuit high
p 052 4	15	Intercooler temp. circuit low
p 072 3	17	Bypass position circuit high
p 072 4	18	Bypass position circuit low
p 073 3	86	Pump pressure circuit high
p 073 4	87	Pump pressure circuit low
p 084 0	72	Vehicle overspeed (fueled)
p 084 11	72	Vehicle overspeed (absolute)
p 084 12	54	Vehicle speed sensor fault
p 091 3	21	TPS circuit high
p 091 4	22	TPS circuit low
p 092 0	58	Torque overload
p 094 0	47	Fuel pressure high
p 094 1	48	Fuel pressure low
p 094 3	37	Fuel pressure circuit high
p 094 4	38	Fuel pressure circuit low
p 098 0	83	Oil level high
p 098 1	84	Oil level low
p 098 3	81	Oil level circuit high
p 098 4	82	Oil level circuit low
p 100 1	45	Oil pressure low
p 100 3	35	Oil pressure circuit high
p 100 4	36	Oil pressure circuit low
p 101 0	83	Crankcase pressure high
p 101 1	84	Crankcase pressure low
p 101 3	81	Crankcase pressure circuit high
p 101 4	82	Crankcase pressure circuit low
p 102 3	33	Boost pressure circuit high
p 102 4	34	Boost pressure circuit low
p 103 8	64	Turbo speed circuit failed
p 108 3	86	Baro. pressure circuit high
p 108 4	87	Baro. pressure circuit low
p 109 1	88	Coolant pressure low
p 109 3	67	Coolant pressure circuit high
p 109 4	67	Coolant pressure circuit low
p 110 0	44	Coolant temp. high
p 110 3	14	Coolant temp. circuit high
p 110 4	15	Coolant temp. circuit low
p 111 1	43	Coolant level low
p 111 3	16	Coolant level circuit high
p 111 4	13	Coolant level circuit low
p 121 0	76	Eng. overspeed with eng. brake
p 168 0	75	Battery voltage high
p 168 1	46	Battery voltage low
p 172 3	27	Air temp. circuit high
p 172 4	28	Air temp. circuit low
p 174 3	23	Fuel temp. circuit high
p 174 4	24	Fuel temp. circuit low
p 175 0	44	Oil temp. high
p 175 3	14	Oil temp. circuit high
p 175 4	15	Oil temp. circuit low
p 187 3	12	VSG input high
p 187 4	11	VSG input low
p 187 7	11	VSG interface not responding
p 190 0	85	Engine overspeed
p 251 10	--	Clock module abnormal rate
p 251 13	--	Clock module failure
s 001 0	61	Injector #1 response time long
s 001 1	71	Injector #1 response time short
s 002 0	61	Injector #2 response time long
s 002 1	71	Injector #2 response time short
s 003 0	61	Injector #3 response time long
s 003 1	71	Injector #3 response time short
s 004 0	61	Injector #4 response time long
s 004 1	71	Injector #4 response time short
s 005 0	61	Injector #5 response time long
s 005 1	71	Injector #5 response time short
s 006 0	61	Injector #6 response time long
s 006 1	71	Injector #6 response time short
s 007 0	61	Injector #7 response time long
s 007 1	71	Injector #7 response time short
s 008 0	61	Injector #8 response time long
s 008 1	71	Injector #8 response time short
s 009 0	61	Injector #9 response time long
s 009 1	71	Injector #9 response time short
s 010 0	61	Injector #10 response time long
s 010 1	71	Injector #10 response time short
s 011 0	61	Injector #11 response time long
s 011 1	71	Injector #11 response time short
s 012 0	61	Injector #12 response time long
s 012 1	71	Injector #12 response time short
s 013 0	61	Injector #13 response time long
s 013 1	71	Injector #13 response time short
s 014 0	61	Injector #14 response time long
s 014 1	71	Injector #14 response time short
s 015 0	61	Injector #15 response time long
s 015 1	71	Injector #15 response time short
s 016 0	61	Injector #16 response time long
s 016 1	71	Injector #16 response time short
s 020 3	81	Dual fuel BOI input failed high
s 020 4	82	Dual fuel BOI input failed low
s 021 0	41	Too many SRS (missing TRS)
s 021 1	42	Too few SRS (missing SRS)
s 025 11	26	Aux. shutdown #1 active
s 026 3	62	Aux. Output #1 short to battery
s 026 4	62	Aux. Output #1 open circuit
s 040 3	62	Aux. Output #2 short to battery
s 040 4	62	Aux. Output #2 open circuit
s 047 0	61	Injector #17 response time long
s 047 1	71	Injector #17 response time short
s 048 0	61	Injector #18 response time long
s 048 1	71	Injector #18 response time short
s 049 0	61	Injector #19 response time long
s 049 1	71	Injector #19 response time short
s 050 0	61	Injector #20 response time long
s 050 1	71	Injector #20 response time short
s 051 3	31	Aux. Output #3 open circuit
s 051 4	31	Aux. Output #3 short to ground
s 052 3	31	Aux. Output #4 open circuit
s 052 4	31	Aux. Output #4 short to ground
s 053 3	62	Aux. Output #5 short to battery
s 053 4	62	Aux. Output #5 open circuit
s 054 3	62	Aux. Output #6 short to battery
s 054 4	62	Aux. Output #6 open circuit
s 055 3	62	Aux. Output #7 short to battery
s 055 4	62	Aux. Output #7 open circuit
s 056 3	62	Aux. Output #8 short to battery
s 056 4	62	Aux. Output #8 open circuit
s 057 3	63	PWM #1 short to battery
s 057 4	63	PWM #1 open circuit
s 058 3	63	PWM #2 short to battery
s 058 4	63	PWM #2 open circuit
s 059 3	63	PWM #3 short to battery
s 059 4	63	PWM #3 open circuit
s 060 3	63	PWM #4 short to battery
s 060 4	63	PWM #4 open circuit
s 061 11	26	Aux. shutdown #2 active
s 230 5	68	IVS switch fault, open circuit
s 230 6	68	IVS switch fault, grounded circuit
s 231 12	55	J1939 data link fault
s 238 3	32	SEL short to battery
s 238 4	32	SEL open circuit
s 239 3	32	CEL short to battery
s 239 4	32	CEL open circuit
s 240 2	--	FRAM checksum incorrect
s 248 8	55	Proprietary link fault (master)
s 248 9	55	Proprietary link fault (slave)
s 249 12	57	J1922 data link fault
s 250 12	56	J1587 data link fault
s 253 2	53	Nonvolatile checksum incorrect
s 253 12	53	EEPROM write fail
s 253 13	--	Incompatible cal version
s 254 0	--	Failed external RAM
s 254 1	--	Failed internal RAM
s 254 6	--	Entered boot via switches
s 254 12	52	A/D Conversion fail

FIGURE 5–53 Listing of DDEC III system flash codes and SAE standard fault codes. (Courtesy of Detroit Diesel Corporation.)

5–55) with the numbers shown on the DDR screen. If no changes are required, press the Function key and turn off the ignition; then disconnect the DDR.

If some of the injector codes differ from those shown on the DDR screen, press the Function key to return to the FUEL INJECTOR INFO menu. Select UPDATE and press the Enter key. Type in the four-digit update injector calibration password for the DDR and press Enter. If this feature is not password protected, type 0000 and press the Enter key. A message will appear telling you to use the up and down arrow keys to SELECT FUNCTION (in this case the cylinder number), and TYPE # (the injector calibration code). An asterisk (*) will highlight the first cylinder number in the list. Using the arrow keys, scroll to the cylinder requiring the code change and type in the new two-digit injector calibration code number; then press the Enter key. Repeat the same procedure for each cylinder that requires a change to the injector code number. Note, however, that the Enter key must be pressed before the DDR will allow selection of another cylinder number!

DDEC III   MPSI Reader Functions

Engine Selections

ENGINE DATA LIST

Active Codes	Intercooler Temp	Cruise Set Speed
Inactive Codes	Oil Pressure	SRS Received
Engine RPM	Fuel Pressure	Idle Speed RPM
Pulsewidth	Baro Pressure	Engine Governor
Turbo Boost	Crankcase Pressure	% Torque Limit
TPS Counts	Coolant Pressure	Half Engine
TPS Percent	External Pump	Engine Brake
VSG Counts	Oil Level	Fuel Rate
VSG SETRPM	Coolant Level	Fuel Economy
BOI	Bypass Valve	ISD Option
Oil Temp	Engine Load	PWM #1
Coolant Temp	Torque	PWM #2
Fuel Temp	ECM Volts	PWM #3
Air Inlet Temp	Vehicle Speed	PWM #4

DIAGNOSTIC CODES
Active Codes
Inactive Codes
Clear Codes

CALIBRATION CONFIGURATION
Engine & Engine Protection Configurations
VSG & Cruise Control Configurations
Idle Shutdown & Progressive Shift Configurations
ECM Input & Output Configurations

FUEL INJECTOR INFORMATION
Cylinder Cutout
Response Times
Calibration Update
Change Injector Password

ENGINE/TRIP DATA

Fuel	Idle Hours	VSG Hours
Engine Hours	Idle Fuel	Cruise Hours
Miles	Engine Brake Hours	Fuel Economy,
		(MPG - km/L)

CALIBRATION CHANGES
Reprogram Options
Change Password

SWITCH/LIGHT STATUS

ACTIVATE OUTPUTS

MID MESSAGES BEING RECEIVED

Pro-link Selections

RS-232 SERIAL PORT   **CUSTOM DATA LIST**
 PRINTER OUTPUT   Display Standard
  Engine Data   Display Custom
  Diagnostic Codes   Edit Custom
  Calibration Configuration   Reset Custom
  CCO Test Results
  Snapshot Data   **CONTRAST ADJUST**
  Injector Response Times
  Trip Data   **ENGLISH/METRIC**
  Total Engine Data
 TERMINAL OUTPUT   **SNAPSHOT**
 P.C. INTERFACE
 PORT SETUP   **RESTART**

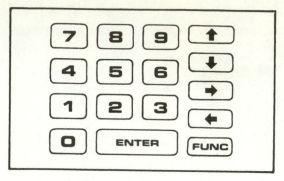

FIGURE 5–54   DDEC III system MPSI DDR (see Figure 5–40) Pro-Link 9000 selections available by using the various function keys on the handheld tool. (Courtesy of Detroit Diesel Corporation.)

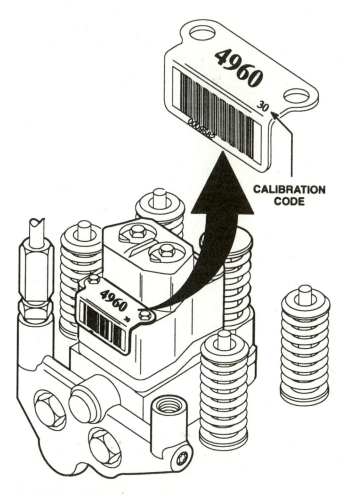

FIGURE 5–55   Electronic unit injector calibration code location on the load plate for all DDEC III systems. (Courtesy of Detroit Diesel Corporation.)

When all cylinders have been updated with the required new injector calibration code numbers, press the Function key. Select YES from the display and press Enter to reprogram the ECM with the revised injector calibration codes. Turn the ignition key to the OFF position and wait a minimum of 5 seconds before starting the engine.

NOTE: Always replace removed injectors back into the same cylinder after a service operation; otherwise, correct cylinder balance will not occur. If you have placed injectors back into a different cylinder from which they were removed, they will have to be rechecked with the DDR as just described and updated.

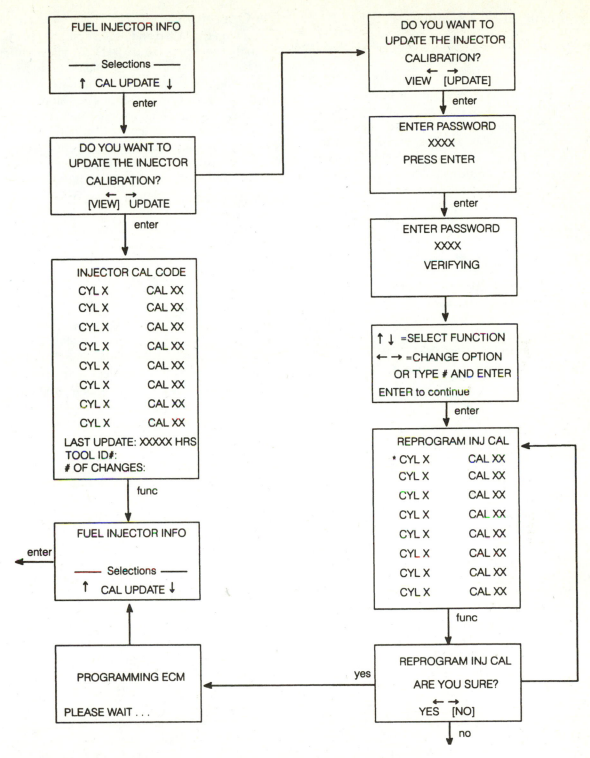

FIGURE 5–56 Step-by-step sequence that would be followed on the handheld Pro-Link 9000 diagnostic data reader when recalibrating new or rebuilt DDEC III electronic unit injectors. (Courtesy of Detroit Diesel Corporation.)

CATERPILLAR ELECTRONIC FUEL SYSTEMS

SPECIAL NOTE: The information contained within this section dealing with the Caterpillar EUI (electronic unit injector) fuel system is designed to provide an overview of the system operation and the special diagnostic tools that can be used to troubleshoot the system. It is *not* intended to supplant the excellent printed literature and audiovisual materials readily available from Caterpillar. If you intend to perform service diagnostics on Caterpillar 3176B and 3406E engine products, you should acquire the following service publications from your local Caterpillar service dealer: Publication No. SENR5561–01, *3176B Diesel Truck Engine; Systems Operation, Testing and Adjusting*; Publication No. SENR5574, *3176B and 3406E Diesel Truck Engine Schematic (Wiring System NS Sensor Locations)*; Publication No. SENR5582–01, *3176B and 3406E Diesel Truck Engine; Electronic Troubleshooting*; and Publication No. SENR5578, *3406E Diesel Truck Engine; Systems Operation, Testing and Adjusting*.

Caterpillar Inc. introduced its first electronic control system in early 1987 on its 3406B model heavy-duty highway truck engine series, which was known by the acronym PEEC (programmable electronic engine control). This system retained the conventional PLN (pump-line-nozzle) system that had been in use by Caterpillar for many years. This first system was retained through the 3406C model until the introduction in late 1993 of the 3406E model, which uses an overhead cam design and EUIs (electronic unit injectors) similar to those used by Detroit Diesel. Caterpillar however first released its EUI system in 1988 on its on-highway truck 3176 model engine, which is now in its second generation and is known as the 3176B. Additional Caterpillar engines that employ PEEC electronic controls are the 3408/3412 engines using PLN fuel systems, particularly on marine applications. Larger Caterpillar products that now use EUI systems are the 3500 and 3600 series engines.

The EUI system illustrated in Figures 5–57 and 5–58 is now in use on the 3176B and 3406E on-highway truck engines, and on both the 3500 and 3600 series large-displacement industrial and marine engines. We will concentrate on the EUI system as it pertains to the 3176B and 3406E, since there are substantially more of these engines in field service use. The 3176B was also released into high-power-output marine applications for the first time in the 1994 model year.

EUI Operation

The EUI on the 3176B and 3406E operates in a way similar to that shown in Figure 5–33; the visual difference is that the 3406E unit has its solenoid mounted at an angle. The 1994 EUIs were manufactured with pre-radius nozzle orifices to eliminate erosion, reduce emissions, and decrease engine performance variability.

The operation of the EUI on both the 3176B and the 3406E engines is the same, except that the activation of the injector follower is different. On the 3176B engine, the camshaft is block mounted and employs a short pushrod as shown in Figure 5–32a. On the 3406E engine which uses an overhead camshaft located in the cylinder head, a roller follower attached to the rocker arm is actuated by the camshaft directly, as shown in Figure 5–32b. Keep in mind that all of the sensor inputs, as well as the position of the EFPA (electronic foot pedal assembly) sending signals to the ECM, are what determines the start, duration, and end of injection. The length of the PWM signal from the ECM to the injector solenoid controls the fuel delivery rate and the power developed by the engine. The EUI on the 3406E engine produces a fuel spray-in pressure similar to that of the Series 50 and 60 Detroit Diesel models, which is approximately 28,000 psi (193,060 kPa); for the 3176B engine, the spray-in pressure is approximately 25,500 psi (175,822 kPa).

EUI Electronics

For the 1994 model year both engines used new electronic controls referred to by the acronym ADEM (advanced diesel engine management), which provide fleet managers with the power of information such as tracking trip and lifetime data through stored data from the ECM. Figure 5–59 illustrates the ECM layout for the 3176B and 3406E with its dual microprocessors which have reduced calculation times for critical engine control parameters and improved engine efficiency and performance response. This same ECM is installed in the 3176B–3406E–3500 and 3600 series engines. The ECM continues to be diesel-fuel cooled to greatly reduce damaging thermal (heat) cycles and increase reliability/durability under the most extreme operating temperatures.

Information from the ECM can be displayed on an optional dash display or downloaded to a PC (see Figure 5–47). A generic ECM is used across all applicable engine lines so that the ECM can be programmed for the specific application of the engine. This new ECM has eight times the memory capacity, processes data from twice as many sensor inputs, and makes calculations four times faster. Engine/vehicle parameters that can be monitored are total miles, average fuel consumption, and speed

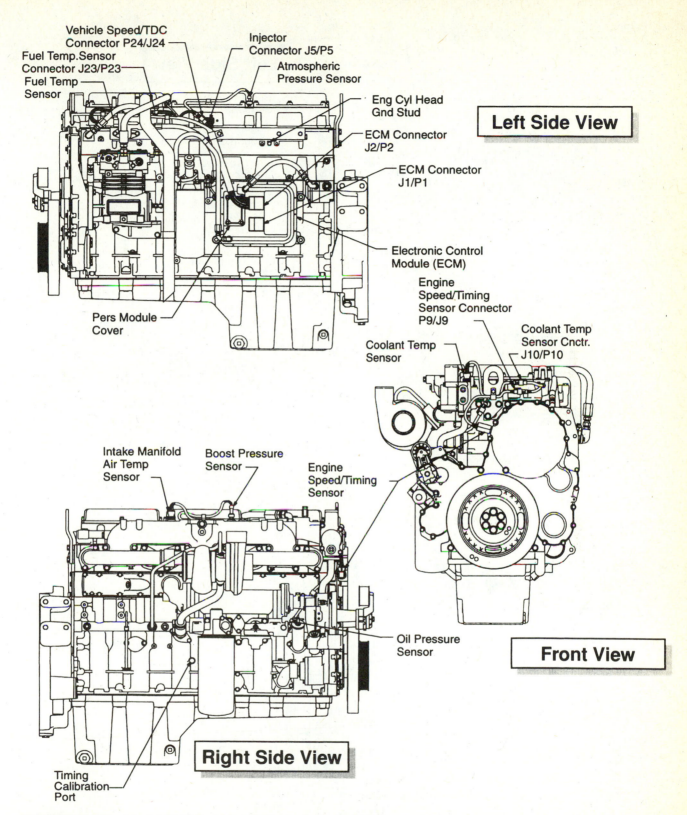

FIGURE 5–57 Model 3176B electronically controlled unit injector engine component locations. (Courtesy of Caterpillar Inc.)

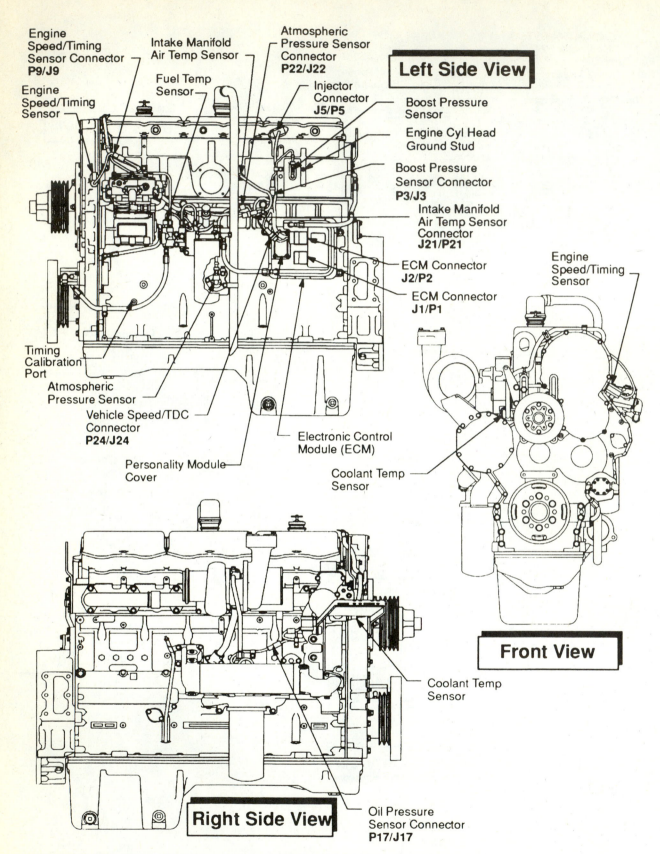

Engine
Speed/Timing
Sensor Connector
P9/J9

Engine
Speed/Timing
Sensor

Intake Manifold
Air Temp Sensor

Fuel Temp
Sensor

Atmospheric
Pressure Sensor
Connector
P22/J22

Injector
Connector
J5/P5

Left Side View

Boost Pressure
Sensor

Engine Cyl Head
Ground Stud

Boost Pressure
Sensor Connector
P3/J3

Intake Manifold
Air Temp Sensor
Connector
J21/P21

ECM Connector
J2/P2

ECM Connector
J1/P1

Timing
Calibration
Port

Atmospheric
Pressure Sensor

Vehicle Speed/TDC
Connector
P24/J24

Personality Module
Cover

Electronic Control
Module (ECM)

Engine
Speed/Timing
Sensor

Coolant Temp
Sensor

Front View

Coolant Temp
Sensor

Right Side View

Oil Pressure
Sensor Connector
P17/J17

FIGURE 5–58 Model 3406E electronically controlled unit injector engine component locations. (Courtesy of Caterpillar Inc.)

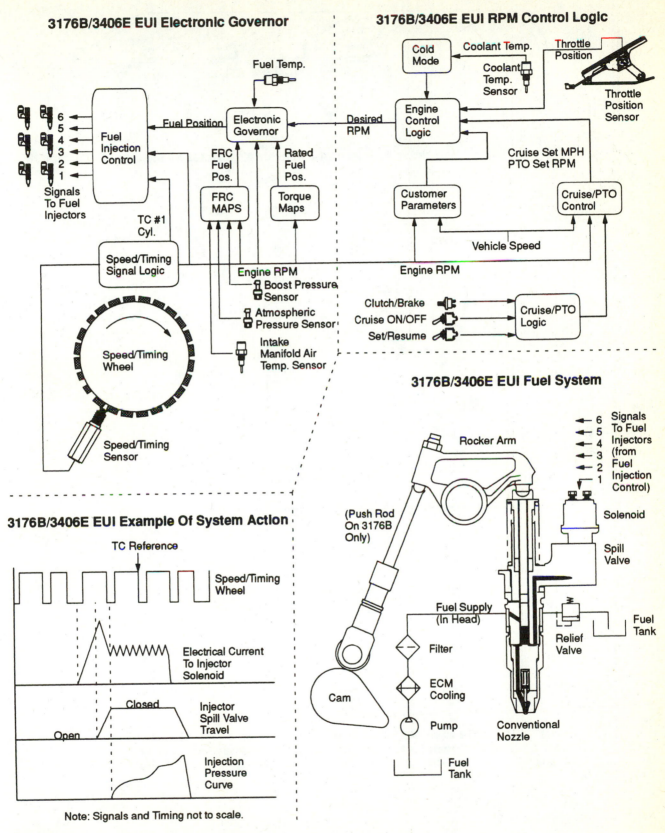

FIGURE 5–59 Model 3176B and 3406E EUI electronic governor, engine rpm control logic, and EUI fuel system operational paths. (Courtesy of Caterpillar Inc.)

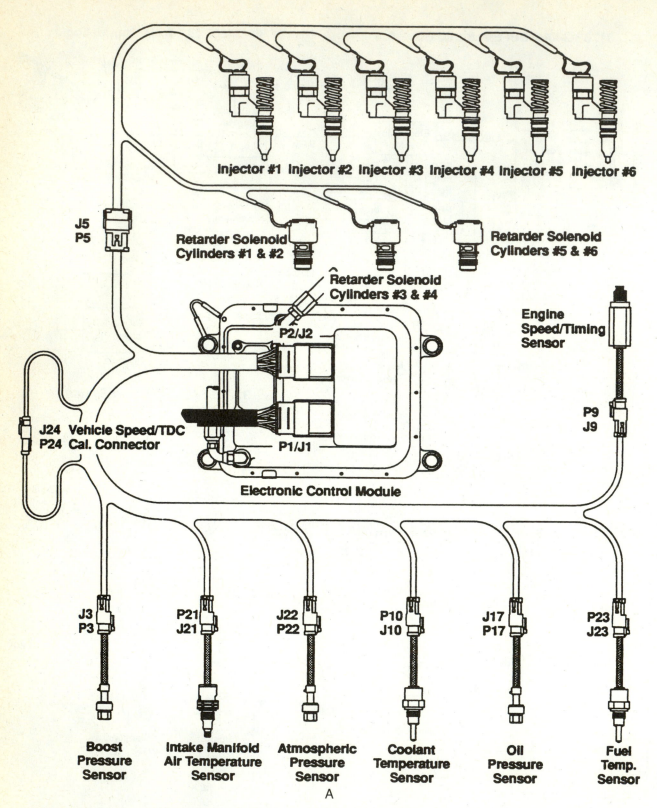

Injector #1　Injector #2　Injector #3　Injector #4　Injector #5　Injector #6

J5
P5

Retarder Solenoid
Cylinders #1 & #2

Retarder Solenoid
Cylinders #5 & #6

Retarder Solenoid
Cylinders #3 & #4

P2/J2

Engine
Speed/Timing
Sensor

J24　Vehicle Speed/TDC
P24　Cal. Connector

P1/J1

P9
J9

Electronic Control Module

J3
P3

P21
J21

J22
P22

P10
J10

J17
P17

P23
J23

Boost
Pressure
Sensor

Intake Manifold
Air Temperature
Sensor

Atmospheric
Pressure
Sensor

Coolant
Temperature
Sensor

Oil
Pressure
Sensor

Fuel
Temp.
Sensor

A

FIGURE 5–60 (a) 3176B/3406E engine electronic control system EUI, engine sensor, ECM, and engine retarder solenoid schematic; (b) electronic foot pedal assembly, switches, and warning lights schematic for 3176B/3406E engine models. (Courtesy of Caterpillar Inc.)

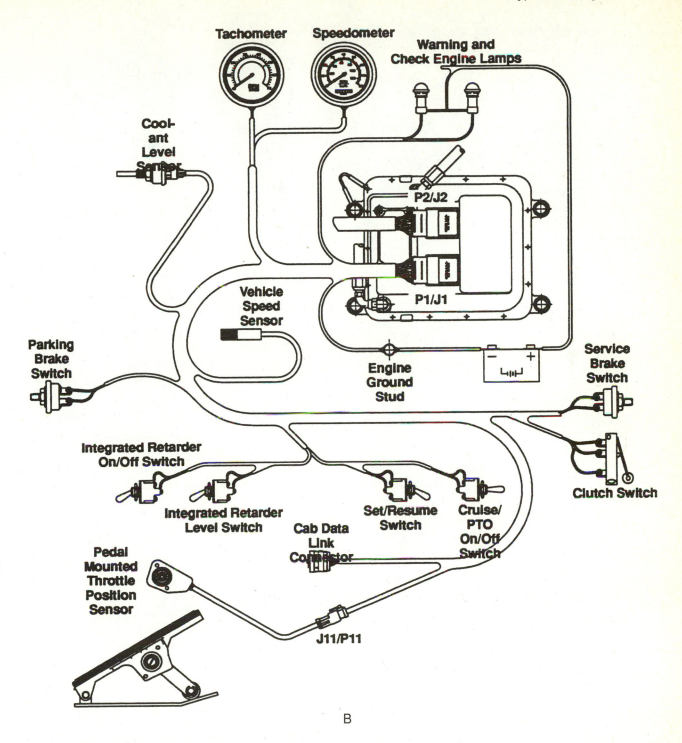

B

and load factors. This information can be used for management software to help determine precise maintenance intervals. With dual microprocessors, engine performance, response, and fuel economy are improved. Fault codes are logged in memory, and the ECU also records engine parameters immediately before a fault and shortly after it has occurred. The ECM processes information supplied by a fuel temperature sensor locat-

ed in the fuel manifold and makes adjustments to compensate for fuel warming, thereby avoiding the possibility of a power loss. If fuel temperature exceeds 150°F (65.5°C), the ECM logs a fault code.

For vehicle PTO operation, the rate of speed increase can be controlled. As an option, the Caterpillar "softcruise" speed control system modulates fuel delivery above and below the set speed, particularly when a truck is running over rolling terrain, to eliminate abrupt fuel cutoffs, and it helps to keep turbo boost spooled up for the next hill. The ECM is soft mounted to the engine and cooled by diesel fuel piped through a cooler plate to ensure that radiated engine heat does not affect the operation of the electronics components. Mounted within the ECM is the engine's *flash memory chip,* which contains the engine's control software. The flash memory technology enables software to be downloaded directly to the ECM and eliminates the need for the replaceable "personality module" for individual engine ratings as was the case with the earlier 3406B and C PEEC and 3176A engines. New software previously stored in 3176A personality modules can be downloaded directly to the ECM via a PC. All sensors are connected to the ECM by two Deutsch 40 pin connectors. One of the 40 pin connectors provides the electrical interface between the engine and vehicle.

Figure 5–60 is a 3406E/3176B electronic system block diagram that allows you to visually trace the system components and wiring arrangement. The sensors shown along the bottom row of Figure 5–60a receive a 5 V input signal from the ECM. Their output voltage value varies between 0.5 and 4.5 V based on the changing resistance value at the sensor, and whether it is a pressure or temperature type. The PMTPS (pedal-mounted throttle position sensor) shown in Figure 5–60b receives an 8 V input signal from the ECM. Other switches operate on a 12 V battery supply. Injector solenoids are pulsed on and off by ECM voltage signals. A good injector solenoid exhibits a resistance value between 0.5 and 2.0 ohms, while the resistance value from either injector solenoid terminal to the injector case should always be greater than 20,000 ohms (K ohms). Other 1994 changes in the ECM include SAE J1922 power-train data link to allow the engine to communicate with ABS (antibrake skid), new automatic transmissions, and traction control ASR systems. A pedal-mounted TPS (throttle position sensor) similar to that shown in Figure 5–31, which is basically the standard EFPA now used by all heavy-truck OEMs, replaces Caterpillar's own earlier and bulkier TPS system. The newer ECM system also provides either 12 or 24 V Jake brake control and speedometer and tachometer inputs to eliminate OEM sensors. The system also includes both an SAE J1708/J1587 satellite communications interface and improved diagnostics. As with other competitive systems, the Caterpillar system provides a programmable droop feature up to 150 rpm above the truck engine limit to provide fewer transmission shifts in rolling terrain, driver comfort, and improved fuel economy. Another improvement is the incorporation of the previously external truck speed buffer into the ECM to minimize the need for cleaning

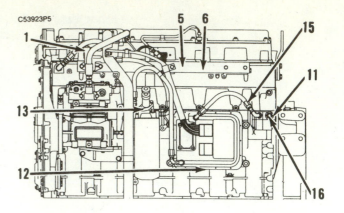

Fuel System Components
(1) Adapter (siphon break). (5) Fuel return manifold. (6) Fuel supply manifold. (11) Fuel transfer pump. (12) Electronic control module (ECM). (13) Fuel priming pump. (14) Fuel filter. (15) Fuel outlet (to ECM). (16) Fuel inlet (from tank).

A

FIGURE 5–61 (a) Component location for model 3176B electronic engine external fuel system; (b) fuel system schematic and flow. (Courtesy of Caterpillar Inc.)

up the signal from the OEM-provided truck speed sensor. The ECM continuously monitors battery voltage and logs a diagnostic code if battery voltage decreases below an acceptable limit. This provides a continuous health check of the wiring and pinpoints system problems that may affect engine operation.

The previous transducer module used on the 3406B and 3406C engine PEEC system has been eliminated, because new technology sensors allow remote mounting of these units, thereby doing away with needed hose connections. The radiator engage/disengage fan system is automatically turned on when the engine retarder *high mode* is applied to provide increased engine braking. The ECM continuously monitors coolant temperatures, intake manifold air temperature, the engine compression brake position and the air-conditioning system pressure to determine if and when the radiator fan should be activated.

An electronic full-range governor features a programmable low idle rpm (600 to 750 rpm), with a factory setting of 600 rpm and 20 rpm overrun. There is no need for a mechanical air/fuel ratio control system, since the intake manifold air temperature sensor, turbo boost pressure sensor, and atmospheric pressure sensor allow electronic control of engine fuel delivery.

Fuel System Layout
The fuel systems used on the 3176B and 3406E EUI-equipped engines, although similar in function and operation, differ slightly in layout. Figure 5–61a and

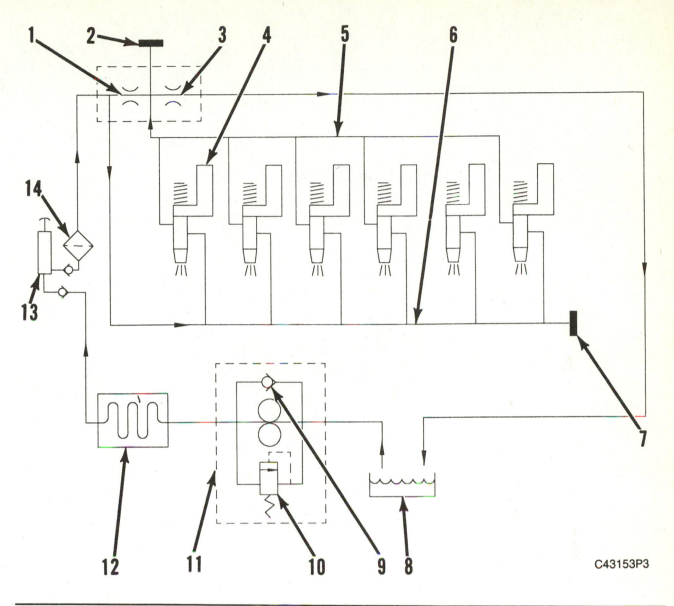

Fuel System Schematic
(1) Siphon break passage. (2) Vent plug. (3) Pressure regulating orifice. (4) Electronically controlled unit injectors. (5) Fuel manifold (return path). (6) Fuel manifold (supply path). (7) Drain plug. (8) Fuel tank. (9) Check valve. (10) Pressure regulating valve. (11) Fuel transfer pump. (12) Electronic control module (ECM). (13) Fuel priming pump. (14) Fuel filter (secondary).

B

5–61b illustrate the location of the major fuel system external components and the actual fuel flow through the system for the 3176B model, while Figures 5–62a and 5–62b represent the fuel system arrangement and flow for the 3406E.

In Figure 5–62b you can see that the fuel supply to the system's electronically controlled unit injectors (3) is provided by a gear-type fuel pump (9) which pulls fuel from the tank (12). Within the pump body, a check valve (11) allows fuel flow around the gears when the fuel priming pump (item 2 in Figure 5–62a) located on top of

the filter housing is used, for example, when priming the fuel system after the filters have been changed or service work has been performed on the system.

Also within the fuel pump body is a pressure regulating valve (item 10 in Figure 5–62b) to limit and protect the system from extreme pressure. Fuel under pressure from the pump (91 psi, 630 kPa, at rated speed) is directed through cored passages in the distribution block (8), around the hand-priming pump (7), and into the fuel filter (6), which is rated at 5 microns (0.00020 in.). Fuel enters a cooler plate bolted to the ECM (5) to

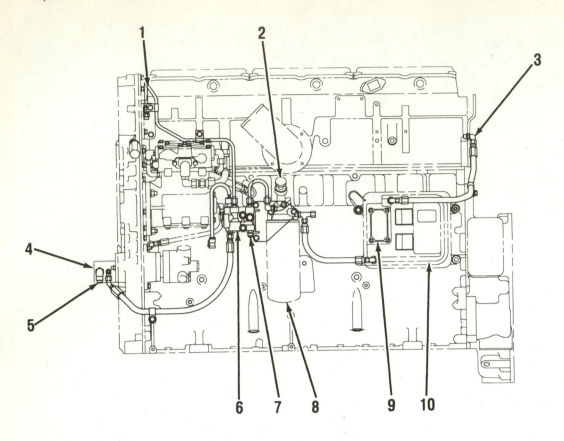

Component Locations
(1) Fuel return line. (2) Fuel priming pump. (3) Fuel inlet line. (4) Fuel transfer pump. (5) Fuel inlet from fuel tank. (6) Distribution block. (7) Fuel return to tank. (8) Fuel filter. (9) Personality module. (10) Electronic control module (ECM).

A

FIGURE 5–62   (a) Component location for model 3406E electronic engine external fuel system; (b) fuel system schematic and flow. (Courtesy of Caterpillar Inc.)

maintain the operating temperature of the electronics components within the ECM at an acceptable level. Fuel leaves the ECM and enters the fuel manifold (2) at the rear of the cylinder head where it is distributed equally to all injectors from the common-rail design. An amount of fuel over and above that required for injection purposes is circulated through the EUIs. Fuel not required for injection purposes is used for cooling and lubrication of the EUIs (3) as well as purging any air from the system. Fuel then leaves the cylinder head through the fuel return manifold (4) and is directed back into the fuel distribution block (8) where a regulating valve is designed to maintain sufficient pressure within the fuel return manifold to ensure that the EUIs remain filled with fuel. This warm fuel then travels back to the fuel tank (12) where it cools before being recirculated through the system. Minimum fuel transfer pump flow for the 3176B engine is 3.5 L/min (0.93 U.S. gallons) at 1800 engine rpm. On the 3406E, the

minimum pump flow is quoted as being 3.2 L/min (0.83 U.S. gallons) at a speed of 840 rpm and with a delivery pressure of 310 kPa (45 psi).

The fuel pump for the 3176B engine is located as shown in Figure 5–61a at the left rear corner of the engine. It is mounted to a spacer block and is driven by the camshaft through a pair of helical gears. On the 3406E engine shown in Figure 5–62a, the fuel pump is located at the left front corner of the engine where it is mounted to the timing gear cover (plate) and is driven from the engine gear train.

The 3176B and 3406E fuel systems are very similar; the normal fuel pressure for both engines is 91 psi (630 kPa). A low fuel pressure condition would be 75 psi (517 kPa); check the fuel filters for plugging. A high system pressure would be 100 psi (690 kPa) or higher; remove the fuel regulating valve from the adaptor behind the return fuel line fitting and check for debris plugging the orifice holes. The injector pop-

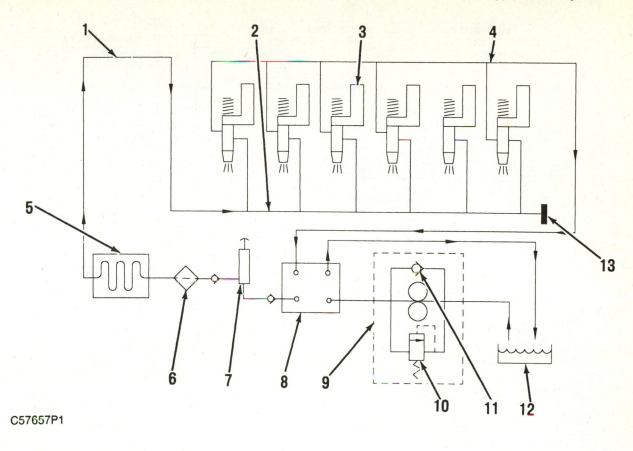

C57657P1

Fuel System Schematic
(1) Fuel supply line. (2) Fuel gallery (supply path). (3) Electronically controlled unit injectors. (4) Fuel gallery (return path). (5) Electronically controlled module (ECM). (6) Fuel filter. (7) Fuel priming pump. (8) Distribution block. (9) Fuel transfer pump. (10) Pressurized regulating valve. (11) Check valve. (12) Fuel tank. (13) Drain plug.

B

ping pressure on the 3406E is 5003 ± 275 psi (34,474 ± 1896 kPa), while it is 5500 psi (37,931 kPa) for the 3176B. Both injector solenoids receive a 90 V signal from the ECM to determine the start of injection.

System Troubleshooting

When an operational complaint is lodged by an operator on any electronic engine, always keep in mind that the engine fuel system or a mechanical problem may be the cause for the complaint. Always consider that simple items such as a plugged air filter, plugged fuel filters, or high exhaust back pressure can be the reason for a low power complaint. To help a truck driver determine the cause on a 3176B or a 3406E engine, refer to the engine performance chart shown in Figure 5–63.

This chart is also helpful for the service technician to use before performing a series of checks and tests to pinpoint the problem. By using the various special tools and diagnostic equipment illustrated in Figure 5–64, then referring to the various SAE standard codes

listed in Figure 5–65, the service technician can systematically determine the cause of the performance complaint. For more details on the SAE standardized trouble codes, refer to the section earlier in this chapter titled, "ECM SAE Trouble Codes."

Both the 3176B and 3406E engines are equipped with an ECM that is programmed to offer three levels of engine protection during operation. These three situations are triggered by sensor values that change based on engine operating conditions. The ECM programming feature will initiate the following type of engine protection actions: a dash-mounted *warning* light illumination condition; an engine *derate* or *shutdown* condition; and an engine *shutdown* condition. Figure 5–65b indicates the PID-FMI (parameter identifier-failure mode identifier) sensor-induced trouble code condition that will cause each one of these condtions to occur.

All electronic diesel engines today are password protected by factory inserted alpha/numeric (letter/number) codes. Factory passwords are calculated on a

DIAGNOSTIC FLASH CODE/ENGINE PERFORMANCE RELATIONSHIP–3176B/3406E							
	EFFECT ON ENGINE PERFORMANCE				SUGGESTED DRIVER ACTION		
Diagnostic Flash Code	Engine Misfire	Low Power	Engine Speed Reduced	Engine Shutdown	Shutdown Vehicle	Service ASAP	Schedule Service
01 - Idle Shutdown Override							
02 - Event Recorder Data Lost							✓
12 - Coolant Level Sensor Fault ²							✓
13 - Fuel Temp. Sensor Fault							✓
14 - Retarder Solenoid Fault							✓
19 - A/C High Pressure Switch Open Circuit							✓
21 - Sensor Supply Voltage Fault ¹,²		✓					✓
24 - Oil Pressure Sensor Fault ²							✓
25 - Boost Pressure Sensor Fault ¹		✓					✓
26 - Atmospheric Pressure Sensor Fault ¹							✓
27 - Coolant Temperature Sensor Fault ¹,²							✓
28 - Check Throttle Sensor Adjustment							✓
31 - Loss Of Vehicle Speed Signal			✓				
32 - Throttle Position Sensor Fault			✓			✓	
34 - Engine RPM Signal Fault	✓		✓	✓		✓	
35 - Engine Overspeed Warning							
36 - Vehicle Speed Signal Fault			✓				✓
38 - Intake Air Temperature Sensor Fault ¹,²							✓
41 - Vehicle Overspeed Warning							✓
42 - Check Sensor Calibrations		✓					
46 - Low Oil Pressure Warning		✓	✓	✓	✓	✓	
47 - Idle Shutdown Occurrence				✓			
51 - Intermittent Battery Power To ECM	✓	✓		✓		✓	
53 - ECM Fault	✓	✓	✓	✓		✓	
55 - No Detected Faults							
56 - Check Customer/System Parameters		✓	✓				✓
58 - Powertrain Data Link Fault							✓
59 - Incorrect Engine Software							✓
61 - High Coolant Temperature Warning		✓		✓		✓	
62 - Low Coolant Level Warning		✓		✓		✓	
64 - High Intake Air Temperature Warning							✓
65 - High Fuel Temperature Warning							✓
72 - Cylinder 1 or 2 Fault	✓	✓				✓	
73 - Cylinder 3 or 4 Fault	✓	✓				✓	
74 - Cylinder 5 or 6 Fault	✓	✓				✓	

¹ - These Diagnostic Flash Codes may affect the system only under specific environmental conditions, such as engine start-up at cold temperature, cold weather operation at high altitudes, etc.
² - These Diagnostic Flash Codes reduce the effectiveness of the Engine Monitoring feature when active.
Shutdown Vehicle: Drive the vehicle cautiously off the road and get immediate service. Severe engine damage may result.
Service ASAP (As Soon As Possible): The driver should go to the nearest qualified service location.
Schedule Service: The driver should have the problem investigated when convenient.

FIGURE 5–63 Form for determining diagnostic flash code and engine performance relationship on 3176B and 3406E electronic engines. (Courtesy of Caterpillar Inc.)

computer system available only to Caterpillar dealers to protect the customer-selected engine operating parameters. Passwords are selected by the end user or customer.

Both the 3176B and 3406E electronic systems have some ability to self-diagnose. When a problem is detected, a diagnostic code is generated and the diagnostic *check engine lamp* is turned on, and in most cases the code is stored in permanent memory within the ECM for extraction by a service technician. Codes that present current faults are known as *active* because they indicate an existing problem. *Logged* codes stored in ECM memory may have been temporary conditions and record "events" rather than actual failures. By using the ECAP (electronic control analyzer programmer) diagnostic tool shown in Figure 5–64, all stored trouble codes, engine operating parameters and conditions, shorting out of individual injectors, and fault tracing can be performed. When a diagnostic code occurs, the ECM records the time when this happened in engine hours as well as the engine operating parameters for 9.6 seconds before and 3.4 seconds after the code was detected.

When using the ECAP, which is powered by vehicle 12 V supply, always ensure that the ignition key switch is off during connector hookup or when test wires are being disconnected. The ECAP is connected to the system through the DDL (dash data link) connector by means of one of the adapters shown in Figure 5–64. The ignition key can be turned on to power up the ECAP, which will operate with the engine running or stopped as long as the key is on.

The ECAP window screen presents you with a choice of functions. Select one simply by pressing the desired control keys or scroll through the ECAP menu until you find the operating parameter or condition that you want to enter. You can reprogram the ECM personality module by connecting up a communication adapter and PC as illustrated in Figure 5–66. Figure 5–67 is an example of what a service technician may encounter on the information screen of the ECAP

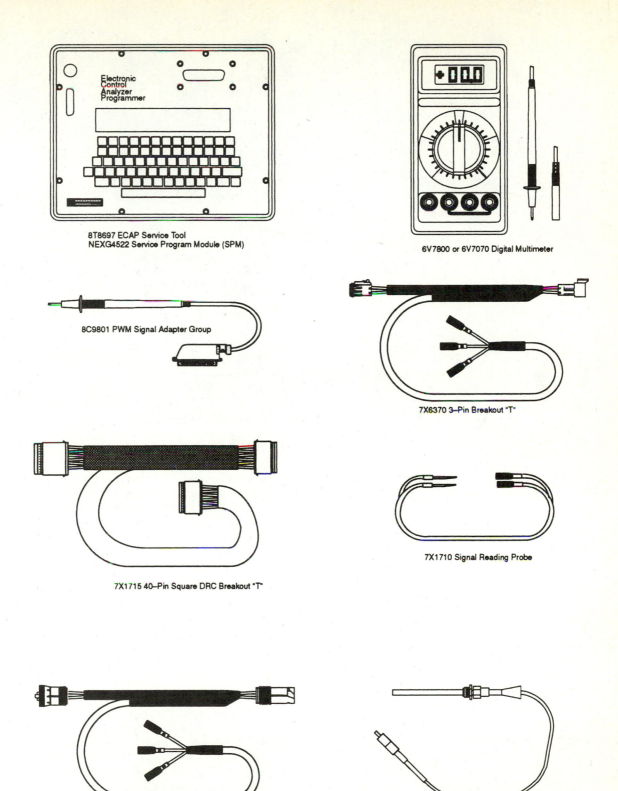

8T8697 ECAP Service Tool
NEXG4522 Service Program Module (SPM)

6V7800 or 6V7070 Digital Multimeter

8C9801 PWM Signal Adapter Group

7X6370 3–Pin Breakout "T"

7X1715 40–Pin Square DRC Breakout "T"

7X1710 Signal Reading Probe

8T8726 3–Pin Breakout "T"

Magnetic Pick–up Sensor
for Timing Calibration 6V2197

FIGURE 5–64 Electronic engine service diagnostic tools for use with the 3176B and 3406E engine models. (Courtesy of Caterpillar Inc.)

FIGURE 5–65 (a) 3176B and 3406E engine models SAE standard diagnostic troubleshooting code description as well as flash code numbers. (b) engine ECM warning and protection system PID-FMI trouble code features that will initiate various operating parameters on 3176B and 3406E engines. (Courtesy of Caterpillar Inc.)

PID-FMI	FC	Diagnostic Code Description
1-11	72	Cylinder 1 Fault
2-11	72	Cylinder 2 Fault
3-11	73	Cylinder 3 Fault
4-11	73	Cylinder 4 Fault
5-11	74	Cylinder 5 Fault
6-11	74	Cylinder 6 Fault
22-13	42	Check Timing Sensor Calibration
41-03	21	8 Volt Supply Above Normal
41-04	21	8 Volt Supply Below Normal
71-00	01	Idle Shutdown Override
71-01	47	Idle Shutdown Occurence
84-00	41	Vehicle Overspeed Warning
84-01	31	Loss of Vehicle Speed Signal
84-02	36	Invalid Vehicle Speed Signal
84-08	36	Vehicle Speed Out of Range
84-10	36	Vehicle Speed Rate of Change
91-08	32	Invalid Throttle Signal
91-13	33	Throttle Sensor Calibration
100-01	46	Low Oil Pressure Warning
100-03	24	Oil Pressure Sensor Open Circuit
100-04	24	Oil Pressure Sensor Short Circuit
100-11	46	Very Low Oil Pressure
102-00	25	Boost Pressure Reading Stuck High
102-03	25	Boost Pressure Sensor Open Circuit
102-04	25	Boost Pressure Sensor Short Circuit
102-13	42	Boost Pressure Sensor Calibration
105-00	64	High Intake Manifold Air Temperature Warning
105-03	38	Intake Manifold Air Temperature Sensor Open Circuit
105-04	38	Intake Manifold Air Temperature Sensor Short Circuit
105-11	64	Very High Intake Manifold Air Temperature
108-03	26	Atmospheric Pressure Sensor Open Circuit
108-04	26	Atmospheric Pressure Sensor Short Circuit
110-00	61	High Coolant Temperature Warning
110-03	27	Coolant Temperature Sensor Open Circuit
110-04	27	Coolant Temperature Sensor Short Circuit
110-11	61	Very High Coolant Temperature
111-01	62	Low Coolant Level Warning
111-02	12	Coolant Level Sensor Fault
111-11	62	Very Low Coolant Level
121-05	14	Retarder Solenoid Lo/Hi Open Circuit
121-06	14	Retarder Solenoid Lo/Hi Short Circuit
122-05	14	Retarder Solenoid Med/Hi Open Circuit
122-06	14	Retarder Solenoid Med/Hi Short Circuit
168-02	51	Low or Intermittent Battery Power to ECM
174-00	65	High Fuel Temperature Warning
174-03	13	Fuel Temperature Sensor Open Circuit
174-04	13	Fuel Temperature Sensor Short Circuit
190-00	35	Engine Overspeed Warning
190-02	34	Loss of Engine rpm Signal
228-03	19	A/C High Pressure Switch Open Circuit
232-03	21	5 Volt Supply Above Normal
232-04	21	5 Volt Supply Below Normal
244-02	02	Event Recorder Data Lost
249-11	58	Powertrain Data Link Fault
252-11	59	Incorrect Engine Software
253-02	56	Check Customer or System Parameters
254-12	53	ECM Fault

Programmed to WARNING

PID-FMI	Flash Code	Description of code:	Warning Lamp	45 MPH Max	160 HP Max	1350 RPM Max
100-01	46	Low Oil Pressure Warning	SOLID	NO	NO	NO
100-11	46	Very Low Oil Pressure	SOLID	NO	NO	NO
105-00	64	High Intake Manifold Air Temp. Warning	SOLID	NO	NO	NO
105-11	64	Very Hi Intake Manifold Air Temp.	SOLID	NO	NO	NO
110-00	61	High Coolant Temperature Warning	SOLID	NO	NO	NO
110-11	61	Very High Coolant Temperature	SOLID	NO	NO	NO
111-01	62	Low Coolant Level Warning	SOLID	NO	NO	NO
111-11	62	Very Low Coolant Level Warning	SOLID	NO	NO	NO

Programmed to DERATE or SHUTDOWN

PID-FMI	Flash Code	Description of code:	Warning Lamp	45 MPH Max	160 HP Max	1350 RPM Max
100-01	46	Low Oil Pressure Warning	SOLID	NO	NO	NO
100-11	46	Very Low Oil Pressure	FLASH	YES	YES	YES
105-00	64	High Intake Manifold Air Temp. Warning	SOLID	NO	NO	NO
105-11	64	Very High Intake Manifold Air Temp.	SOLID	NO	NO	NO
110-00	61	High Coolant Temperature Warning	FLASH	YES	YES	NO
110-11	61	Very High Coolant Temperature	FLASH	YES	YES	NO
111-01	62	Low Coolant Level Warning	SOLID	NO	NO	NO
111-11	62	Very Low Coolant Level Warning	FLASH	YES	YES	NO

Programmed to SHUTDOWN

PID-FMI	Flash Code	Description of code:	Warning Lamp	Time to Shutdown	Start Restart Time
100-01	46	Low Oil Pressure Warning	SOLID	NO	NO
100-11	46	Very Low Oil Pressure	FLASH	30 sec.	18 sec.
105-00	64	High Intake Manifold Air Temp. Warning	SOLID	NO	NO
105-11	64	Very High Intake Manifold Air Temp.	SOLID	NO	NO
110-00	61	High Coolant Temperature Warning	FLASH	NO	NO
110-11	61	Very High Coolant Temperature	FLASH	20 sec.	60 sec.
111-01	62	Low Coolant Level Warning	SOLID	NO	NO
111-11	62	Very Low Coolant Level	FLASH	30 sec.	80 sec.

when it is powered up and he or she has selected "system configuration parameters." By pressing the up and down arrows on the ECAP keyboard pad, the technician can scroll through the information for that selected menu. As with the DDR used on the DDEC system, with continued use you will master the use of the ECAP tool and be able to quickly diagnose performance complaints.

The built-in MI (maintenance indicator) calculates service intervals for PM 1 (preventive maintenance 1), PM 2 (preventive maintenance 2), and coolant flush/fill maintenance procedures. The customer has the option of programming a specific number of hours or miles (kilometers) or even, based on engine oil sump quantity, the optimal PM 1 time interval. Note, however, that the PM 2 and coolant flush intervals are

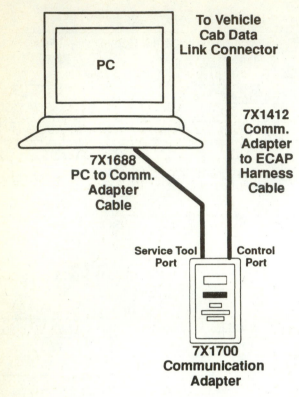

FIGURE 5–66 *Optional diagnostic tooling required to reprogram the engine ECM for both the 3176B and 3406E engine models. (Courtesy of Caterpillar Inc.)*

not programmable but are based on the recommended mileage or hours from the operation and maintenance manual. Within the ECM, the maintenance indicator sends a signal via the SAE J1587 data link to a hand-held service tool similar to that shown in Figure 5–40, to a dash display (see Figure 5–44), or to the fleet management program and indicates that maintenance is due 3,000 miles (4828 km) prior to the estimated service. Once the MI has been alerted, it can be reset using the handheld or ECAP service tool (see Figure 5–64) or the dash display controls.

A trip data system that includes two trip data registers is an optional item that allows the driver to view a dash-mounted display with a reset feature and permits the owner/fleet user to download stored data into a PC from the ECM. Typical items that can be monitored or recorded include these:

- Start engine hours, current engine hours, trip hours
- Start miles, current miles, trip miles (kilometers)
- Current/total trip time, idle time
- Fuel consumed at idle
- Average load factor
- Average speed
- Average mpg (L/100 km), average fuel rate

In addition, with a diagnostic tool connected to the data link, the technician can monitor or record engine rpm, mph (kph), fuel rate in gph (Lph), fuel rate with correction factor, average engine load factor, mph in increments of 5 mph (8 km); and engine rpm in increments of 100 rpm. Using programmable data screens, the technician can record additional engine and vehicle parameters such as coolant temperature, oil pressure, and cruise operation.

Breakout Cable Assemblies
Figure 5–50 showed a *breakout box* that can be used on the DDEC systems to check system wiring and harness connections with the aid of a multimeter. Wiring and harness connections on Caterpillar's 3176B and 3406E engine models can be checked using the various wire harness breakout tees shown in Figure 5–64 to speed up electrical troubleshooting. These cables allow the probe tips of a multimeter to be safely inserted into the tip jacks to obtain a signal from any harness wire. The 7X6370 three-pin breakout T-harness is inserted in series between a 3176B/3406E harness jack and plug to permit voltage measurement on an operating system. The 8T8726 T-harness is only required to check a remote-mounted throttle position sensor, which receives a battery signal between 11 and 13.5 V.

CUMMINS ELECTRONICS

SPECIAL NOTE: The information contained within this section dealing with the Cummins Celect (Cummins Electronics) system is designed to provide an overview of the system operation and the special diagnostic tools that can be used to troubleshoot the system. It is *not* intended to supplant the excellent printed literature and audiovisual materials readily available from Cummins. If you intend to perform service diagnostics on Cummins Celect equipped engines such as the L10, M11 and N14, you should acquire the following service publications from your local Cummins dealer: Bulletin No. 3810389, *Celect Fault Code Manual*; Bulletin No. 3810469, *Troubleshooting and Repair Manual, CELECT System, N14 Engines* (or order for an L10 or M11 engine); *Celect Wiring Diagram* (plasticized); and the engine service manual for your engine model.

Cummins Engine Company first ventured into engine electronics in the 1980s with its PACE and PT/PACER systems. Basically those had an add-on cruise control system, plus an engine monitoring system that could be used with Cummins mechanically controlled PT (pressure-time) fuel system on its 444 hp (331 kW), 855 cu in. (14L) six-cylinder heavy-duty truck engines.

In late 1988, Cummins released its first-generation electronically controlled injection system, known as

```
                Read System Configuration Parameters
Selected Engine Rating
      Rating #:                                      1        # 4
      Rating Type:                           Standard
      Rated Power:                               445  HP
      Rated RPM:                                1700  RPM
      Rated Peak Torque:                        1650  LB FT
 more... Press   ↑ or ↓ to move through the rest of the parameters.
```

```
      Rated Peak Torque RPM:                    1200  RPM
      Top Engine Limit–RPM Range:          1620–2120  RPM
      Test Spec:                               0T1234
              with BrakeSaver:                 0T5678
      Last Service tool to change system parameters:   TMCA1000
      Last Service tool to change customer parameters: TMCA1000
      Full Load Setting:                          10       # 0
      Full Torque Setting:                        10       # 0
      Personality Module Code:                     1       # 0
      Personality Module P/N:              12T4321–02
      Personality Module Release Date:          OCT91
      Electronic Control Module S/N:        XXX–000000
      Vehicle ID:                          1234509876      #2
      Engine Serial Number:                  XXX 01234
      Total  Tattletale:                          60
```

FIGURE 5–67 *Sample information screen called up on the ECAP (Electronic Control Analyzer Programmer) when "system configuration parameters" was selected. (Courtesy of Caterpillar Inc.)*

ECI (electronically controlled injection). This was followed in April 1990 by the current Celect (Cummins Electronics) system, which was released on the L10, and in mid-1990 on the N14 series of on-highway truck engines. This system is also now in use on the M11 which will supersede the L10, as well as on the larger industrial, marine, and off-highway K series engines. Figure 5–68 is a schematic of the Celect system as applied to a six-cylinder engine configuration.

Celect Fuel System Flow
The fuel pump shown in Figure 5–68 is driven from the rear of the air compressor on an N14 engine. Refer to Figure 5–69 to see more clearly the location of the fuel system components. The fuel pump is a gear type and operates similarly to the gear transfer pump that was used on earlier PT (pressure-time) fuel systems. Figure 5–70a is a cross-sectional view of the fuel pump and the flow through the housing, and Figure 5–70b illustrates the basic fuel flow into and through the electronically controlled injector. Fuel is drawn from the tank by the pump where it can pass through a primary fuel filter or fuel/water separator filter assembly before it flows into and through a cooler plate bolted to the rear of the ECM assembly. The purpose of direct-

ing fuel through the cooling plate is to ensure that the electronics package components are maintained at an acceptable operating temperature level during engine operation. Fuel then flows through a filter and on to the inlet side of the gear-type transfer pump. The system pressure and flow rate will vary proportionally to engine speed; therefore, the maximum system operating pressure is generally 140 psi (965 kPa) at rated engine speed. Within the fuel pump, a spring-loaded bypass valve opens to bypass fuel back to the suction side of the pump to regulate fuel pressure. Fuel under pressure is directed through the electric solenoid on top of the fuel pump, which is similar to that used in the earlier PT fuel systems. When the ignition key is switched on, this solenoid is energized. Turning the key switch off deenergizes the fuel pump solenoid to allow engine shutdown by blocking further fuel flow out of the pump assembly. Fuel from the gear pump flows into the rear of the cylinder head on N14 engines where a common rail allows all injectors to receive fuel through the cast manifold within the cylinder head.

The pump is designed to circulate an excess amount of fuel to and through the injectors, so that fuel not used for injection purposes is used to cool and lubricate the internal components, as well as to purge any air

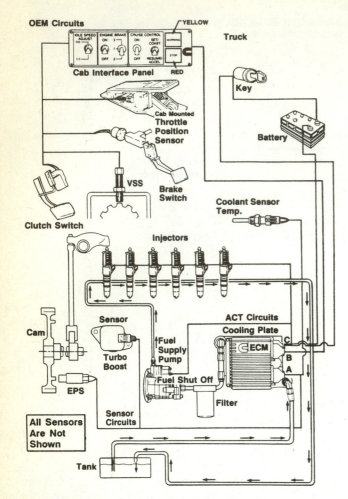

FIGURE 5–68 Celect (Cummins Electronics) system layout and basic fuel flow path for a six-cylinder heavy-duty diesel engine. (Courtesy of Cummins Engine Company, Inc.)

from the fuel system and injectors. Fuel from the inlet manifold enters the injector as shown in Figure 5–70b at the left center of the body through a small circular filter screen similar to that for the PT injector systems. Fuel is then directed up to and around a small poppet valve. This poppet valve is electrically controlled by a signal from the ECM. Injection can only occur when this PWM signal closes this small internal poppet valve as the injector pushrod is activating the injector rocker arm assembly. Rocker arm motion is required to raise the trapped fuel pressure within the injector body to a high enough level to lift the needle valve from its seat in the spray tip (cup). Therefore, the start of injection, the quantity of fuel metered, and the duration of injection are electronically controlled by the ECM. The operation of the Celect injector is similar to that of the unit injectors used by other engine manufacturers such as Detroit Diesel, Caterpillar, Volvo, and Mack.

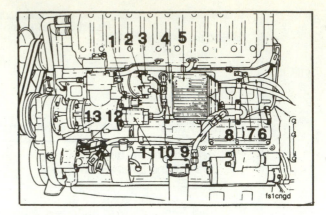

FIGURE 5–69 Location of various Celect engine components on a 14L six-cylinder Cummins heavy-duty truck model. 1, fuel shutoff valve; 2, oil pressure sensor; 3, turbocharger boost sensor; 4, ECM cooling plate; 5, ECM; 6, actuator wiring harness; 7, OEM wiring harness; 8, sensor wiring harness; 9, fuel inlet; 10, fuel outlet; 11, gear-type fuel transfer pump; 12, oil temperature sensor; 13, engine position speed sensor. (Courtesy of Cummins Engine Company, Inc.)

ECM Connectors

The ECM has three wire harnesses plugged into it to control the Celect system. Figure 5–71 illustrates these three individual wire harnesses:

1. The sensor harness identified as A receives electrical signals from all of the engine-mounted sensors, which are shown in Figure 5–69. The sensors tell the ECM the current state of the engine operation regarding throttle position, air intake manifold temperature, ambient pressure, turbocharger boost temperature, engine piston position from a sensor located to monitor a pin attached to the engine camshaft gear, engine coolant and oil temperature, and oil pressure. Some engines are equipped with a fuel pressure and fuel temperature sensor.

2. The OEM (original equipment manufacturer such as a truck builder) harness identified as item B is wired to all of the vehicle instrument panel control switches. These include the cruise control switch and the vehicle speed sensor which monitors the transmission output shaft rpm, an instant readout of fuel consumption, engine compression brake controls, and the cab interface panel. This harness is not supplied by Cummins but by the truck or equipment manufacturer.

ECI Injector

Fuel Supply Pump

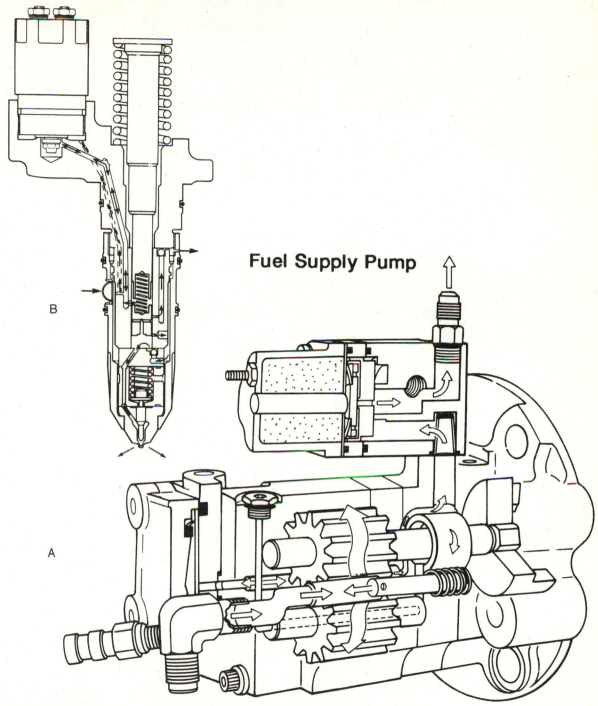

FIGURE 5–70 (a) Celect engine gear-type fuel supply pump; (b) ECI injector assembly and basic fuel flow into and out of the body. (Courtesy of Cummins Engine Company, Inc.)

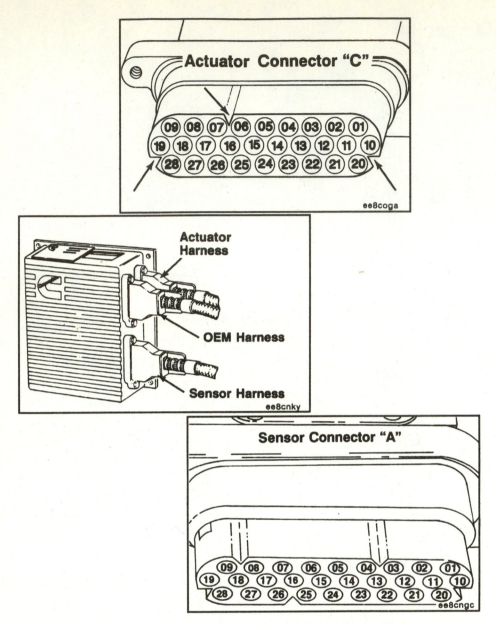

FIGURE 5–71 *Location and identification of the three main wire harness connections and pin numbers of the Celect system ECM. (Courtesy of Cummins Engine Company, Inc.)*

3. The actuator harness identified as item C controls the injector solenoids.

The three ECM harness connectors cannot be inadvertently installed into the wrong position. This is ensured by the fact that each connector has a different *key design feature* as illustrated in Figure 5–71 so that each connector is readily identifiable by the letter A, B, or C. Note also that each connector pin is identified by a number that can be traced back through the system wiring diagram. Figure 5–72a illustrates the wires that are connected to the oil temperature sensor ECM connector A. This example shows wires 3 and 6. If this sensor and wires were operating outside a designed limit, the ECM would log a fault code 215 (SAE-PID = parameter identifier 175, and FMI = failure mode identifier 1).

Figure 5–72b illustrates the OEM–ECM connector B. This example shows wires 17 and 26, which are the two wires connected to the engine tachometer. Figure 5–72c illustrates the ECM actuator harness C. This example shows how the battery is connected

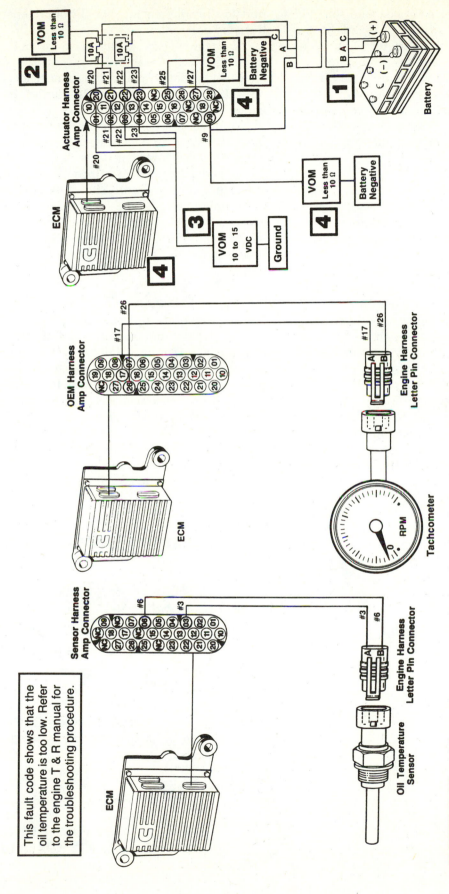

FIGURE 5–72 (a) Sensor harness example showing the oil temperature sensor wiring—Fault Code 215 (PID 175, FMI 1); (b) OEM wiring harness connection showing the wiring to the electronic engine tachometer—Fault Code 234 (PID 190, FMI 0); (c) actuator harness connector illustrating typical wire connections—Fault Code 434 (SID 251, FMI 4). (Courtesy of Cummins Engine Company, Inc.)

into the system, some of the fuses used, and some of the typical multimeter readings that might be obtained when checking the system. By using these wiring diagrams and a *breakout box* similar to that shown for the DDEC system in Figure 5–50, or by using special pin-out jumper wires inserted into specific numbered connector holes, a multimeter can be employed to check any wire system for a voltage or resistance value. Then compare the values to Cummins' specs.

Sensors

The sensors used on Celect engine models vary in physical shape based on the year of manufacture of the engine. The 1991 model L10 and N14 engines employed a square flange mount design sensor, which can be seen in Figure 5–69 (items 2 and 3). In June 1993, the L10 and M11 entered production with threaded pressure sensors for oil, turbo boost, and ambient air temperature. The N14 engines implemented the same sensor change in July 1993. These threaded pressure sensors have the same internal components as the flange mount design but in a different shell. This sensor shape change did not require a change to the sensor harness on the L10 engine models, but on the N14 engines the oil pressure sensor was relocated to the oil rifle (gallery), which created the need for a new sensor harness. In addition, the ambient air pressure sensor was relocated to the rear of the ECM. Note that it is not necessary to convert the remaining sensor(s) to the threaded design in these engine models. Cummins does offer, however, a threaded sensor kit to update an earlier engine model from the flange to the threaded design.

Both the M11 and N14 1994 engine models entered production with the threaded pressure sensor design. Note that the flange mount design must *not* be installed on a 1994 model M11 or N14 engine. In the 1994 engines, the threaded turbo boost sensor is a higher set unit, ranging from 0 to 50 psi (0 to 348 kPa), whereas the earlier flange model ranged from 0 to 32 psi (0 to 222 kPa). *Do not* interchange the 32 psi sensor with the 50 psi model. Figure 5–73, which illustrates differences in the turbo boost sensors, shows that the 1994 model has a unique round wire harness instead of the oval shape of the 1991 model. The function and operation of all the engine/vehicle sensors is similar to that already described for the Detroit Diesel and Caterpillar engine systems.

Electronic Protection System

The purpose of the Celect engine protection system is similar to that found on DDC and Cat engines, that is, to prevent and/or limit damage to the engine when it operates outside specific temperature and pressure parameters (conditions). The system is always active; however, one customer-selectable feature of the system is the option to shut down the engine if an *out-of-limit condition* is detected. Should the ECM not be programmed for this shutdown feature, the engine will simply derate in both speed and power. The shutdown protection feature can be activated at any time by connecting one of Cummins' electronic diagnostic tools

FIGURE 5–73 *Differences between 1991 and 1994 engine turbocharger boost sensors. (Courtesy of Cummins Engine Company, Inc.)*

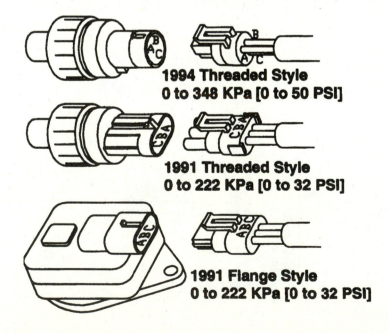

Boost Pressure Sensor Detail

1994 Threaded Style
0 to 348 KPa [0 to 50 PSI]

1991 Threaded Style
0 to 222 KPa [0 to 32 PSI]

1991 Flange Style
0 to 222 KPa [0 to 32 PSI]

(Compulink, Echek, or INSITE). Sensors that provide information to the ECM on the Celect system for engine protection include coolant temperature, coolant level, oil pressure, oil temperature, and intake manifold temperature.

When an out-of-limit condition is detected, several activities occur. A dash-mounted engine protection lamp illuminates to warn the driver that an out-of-parameter condition has been detected. As long as the problem exists, this warning lamp remains lit. In addition, within the ECM memory storage system, a *fault code* is logged into memory; it indicates the specific fault detected, the time of the occurrence, and the elapsed time and maximum value of the out-of-limit condition. Low coolant level and low oil pressure are two main faults that will immediately cause the ECM to derate the engine speed and power, and if so programmed, they will initiate the engine shutdown sequence. First a dash light begins to flash. When the operator sees this, he or she has 30 seconds to pull the vehicle over to the side of the road or come to a controlled stop. If the sensors detect that the coolant level or oil pressure is once again within a safe operating limit, the system will reset itself and the process will start again if operating conditions warrant.

It is possible during engine/vehicle operation for the engine protection system (coolant, oil, and intake manifold temperature) to cause the engine protection lamp to illuminate without shutting the engine down. For example, when climbing a long steep hill fully loaded in warm weather, the engine oil temperature condition may reach a level beyond 250°F (121°C). This would cause the warning light to illuminate and remain lit as long as the oil temperature remains above the low out-of-range condition of 250°F. However, if the oil temperature climbs to, say, a high-end safe operating limit of 260°F (137°C), the light will start flashing and the engine will automatically start a sequence of speed and power reduction, followed 30 seconds later by an automatic engine shutdown.

During an engine derate caused by a low out-of-range sensor condition, the power and speed reduction helps to protect the engine and provide "limp-home" capability by reducing the engine speed to not less than 1400 rpm. Information stored in the ECM can be extracted by the service technician to help reconstruct the sequence of events which led to the derate or engine shutdown action.

Troubleshooting the Celect System

To troubleshoot the Celect system, special diagnostic tooling can be used to access the information stored within the ECM memory. This can be done by using

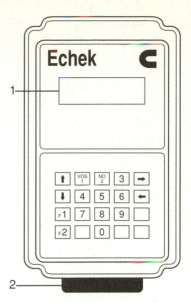

FIGURE 5-74 *Handheld diagnostic Echek reader for use with Cummins Celect engines. Note the digital display window (1) which shows data and messages to the user and the various available memory cartridges (2) which contain the necessary software to test Cummins and other electronic engines when connected to the diagnostic data link. (Courtesy of Cummins Engine Company, Inc.)*

Cummins Compulink, Echek, or INSITE electronic equipment. In addition, several major tool and equipment manufacturers offer generic diagnostic handheld tools that can be used on all of the various makes of electronic engines in use today. A specific test cartridge must be inserted into the DDR similar to the one shown in Figure 5–74 for the Echek system or the MPSI 9000 model shown in Figure 5–40.

SPECIAL INFORMATION: For more details on troubleshooting the Celect system, Cummins offers through its dealers a series of videotapes, slides, and information booklets. Obtain the three following Cummins publications: *Bulletin No. 3666018* is a plasticized wiring diagram foldout; *Bulletin No. 3810389* (*Celect Fault Code Manual*), a guide to a given procedure for any fault code called up from the ECM; and *Bulletin No. 3810469* (*Troubleshooting and Repair Manual CELECT System N14 Engines*)–a similar publication is available for both the L10 and M11 engines as well as the larger K engine models.

Approach electonic engine troubleshooting in a systematic manner just as you would for a mechanically equipped and governed engine. Plugged fuel filters or air filters will result in the same basic complaints on either engine type, namely, a lack of power and visible exhaust smoke. This book cannot provide the test sequences that should be followed to successfully troubleshoot all of the various trouble codes for a Cummins engine. Refer to the Cummins Celect troubleshooting manual and follow closely the *troubleshooting trees* in the performance of each repair; these will guide you through a sequence of possible causes and symptoms.

Vehicle Cab Interface Panel

The dash mounted cab interface panel illustrated in Figure 5–75 can be activated by the driver through a series of small toggle-type switches. This panel contains several elements:

1. An idle speed adjust switch can be used to adjust the engine idle speed between 550 and 800 rpm. Each time the switch is moved briefly to either the + or − position, the idle speed changes by approximately 25 rpm.

2. The engine compression brake control switch has an ON/OFF position to activate either a Jacobs or Cummins C brake system. The other toggle switch used with the engine brake control can be placed into position 1, 2, or 3. In position 1, on NT (14L) engines, only two cylinders are activated; position 2 activates the compression brake on four cylinders, and position 3 allows all six engine cylinders to provide compression braking.

3. The cruise control panel has two toggle switches; one of these is simply the ON/OFF switch. The second one is actually the cruise control position select switch that the truck driver actually uses to set and adjust the cruise control speed while driving. This toggle switch can be used to set and adjust the engine speed while the PTO is in operation. Take careful note that some truck manufacturers may choose to employ a labeling system with a cruise control system that reads SET/ACCEL and RESUME/COAST instead of what is shown in the example of Figure 5–75 which is SET/COAST and RESUME/ACCEL. The cruise control switch operates in the same manner as that found on most passenger cars equipped with a cruise control feature. The cruise control will not operate if the brake pedal has been depressed. In addition, the cruise control will not operate below 30 mph (48 km/h).

To adjust the cruise control set speed up, move the control select switch briefly to the ACCEL position once for 1 mph increments, or twice to this same position for 2 mph increments. To reduce the speed, use the COAST select switch in the same manner just described. The engine PTO is controlled from the cruise control switches while the vehicle is in a parked position, although there are certain Cummins-approved applications that allow the vehicle to move up to 6 mph (10 km/h) during PTO operation.

FIGURE 5–75   Procedure required to activate and use the step forward or step backward to a fault code number. When choosing to engage the instrument-panel-mounted idle speed, adjust + or − toggle switch. (Courtesy of Cummins Engine Company, Inc.)

4. On the right-hand side of this control panel are two warning lights. One of these is yellow in color and is labeled WARNING, while the lower one is red in color and is labeled STOP (see Figure 5–75). When the yellow warning light is illuminated during engine operation, this indicates that a Celect system problem has been detected and recorded in ECM memory. The vehicle can still be operated since the problem is not serious enough to warrant engine shutdown; however, the driver should have the system checked out at the earliest available opportunity. Should the red stop light illuminate during engine operation, the truck driver should bring the vehicle to the side of the road as soon as possible, shut off the engine, and make the necessary adjustments to have a service technician from the closest Cummins dealer determine the reason for the engine shutdown.

To withdraw stored trouble codes from ECM memory without using the Compulink or Echek system, a diagnostic switch that can be either an ON/OFF design or a jumper connection cap located in the cab instrument panel area similar to that illustrated in Figure 5–75 can be used. Activation of the diagnostic system will cause the yellow and red fault lights to illuminate and flash a specific code sequence that indicates a given trouble code number. As a means of confirming that both the yellow warning and red stop lights are operational, each time the ignition key is turned on while the diagnostic switch is off, both lights should illuminate and then go out after approximately 2 seconds. Both lights will remain off until a fault code is detected, at which time either the yellow warning light (can still operate the vehicle) or the red stop light (bring the vehicle to a halt and shut the engine off) will illuminate. To check the ECM memory for stored fault codes, the ignition key switch should be off; place the dash-mounted diagnostic toggle control switch into the ON position. Now turn the ignition key switch on.

SPECIAL NOTE: If no fault codes are stored in ECM memory, the yellow warning and red stop lights will simply illuminate. However, if active fault codes are in ECM memory, both the yellow and red lights will begin to flash the code of the recorded faults.

Figure 5–43 illustrates a similar example of the sequence that the yellow and red warning lights would go through to indicate a code. The system will continue to flash the same codes until the system is instructed to move to another function. To show any other fault codes in ECM memory, refer to Figure 5–75 and move the idle INC/DEC + or − toggle switch momentarily to the INC position. If you desire to back up to the previous fault code, move the idle toggle control switch to the DEC (−) position momentarily. Should there be only one active fault code stored in ECM memory, the system will continue to display the same fault code continually. When finished withdrawing fault codes, simply turn the diagnostic toggle switch off as well as the ignition key switch off.

ECI Cylinder Misfire Test

SPECIAL NOTE: When attempting to diagnose a Celect engine cylinder misfire condition, *do not* touch or remove the injector electric wire leads, since this can cause you to receive a serious electric shock!

To check the electronically controlled injectors individually for signs of a suspected misfire condition, two individual procedures can be used.

1. Use the same basic procedure as that for a mechanically controlled Cummins engine by inserting rocker lever actuator Cummins P/N 3823609 or a wrench on an injector rocker lever as illustrated in Figure 13–45. The engine must be running at a speed between 800 and 1000 rpm using the throttle pedal. Do *not* use the idle or PTO controls to raise the engine speed. Hold the injector plunger down while the engine is running, which will stop fuel flow to the injector. If the engine rpm decreases when an injector plunger is held down, the injector is good. This same procedure can be used to detect smoking cylinders. If the exhaust smoke disappears when a cylinder is cut out, this cylinder is the one causing the exhaust smoke problem.

2. Use the Cummins Compulink, Echek handheld diagnostic data reader illustrated in Figure 5–74, or the INSITE unit plugged into the engine OEM harness access connector, which is usually located inside the vehicle cab. Make sure that the ignition key switch

is off. The diagnostic connector location differs on different makes of trucks. Turn the ignition key switch back on. By selecting the desired menu command and depressing the correct keys on the face of the Echek tool, with the engine running, the ECM will cycle the engine through an automatic cylinder cut-out sequence to allow you to determine if a specific injector is misfiring. This is the preferred method. An Echek handheld diagnostic tool provides you with the ideal diagnostic capability to effectively troubleshoot the system. The keypad used with the Echek system feeds a command pulse into the Echek and then into the Celect ECM to extract stored trouble codes or to cause the engine to react to a specifically chosen test parameter condition.

Celect Fault Code Information

Figure 5–76 provides information dealing with Celect fault codes. A number of different SAE standard fault codes, which have been stored in ECM memory, can be extracted by the technician using either the Compulink, Echek, or INSITE diagnostic tools. In addition, if the vehicle is equipped with a cab interface panel (see Figure 5–75) it can be used to obtain flash codes from ECM memory. Details on SAE (SIDs, PIDs, and FMIs) were discussed in detail earlier in this chapter.

HEUI FUEL SYSTEM

The first high-speed diesel engine to adopt HEUI (hydraulically actuated electronic unit injection) was released in 1994 on the Navistar 7.3L (444 cu in.) direct-injected turbocharged V8 diesel engine for use in light- and mid-duty trucks. This system was a combined effort of Navistar and Caterpillar design engineers. This system is being used on Ford and Navistar truck applications. The system does not use a camshaft-operated rocker arm to activate the injector.

The 1995 edition of Cat's 3116 engine has been reconfigured from 1.1L per cylinder to 1.2L per cylinder and is now known as the 3126, which is a 7.2L displacement six-cylinder engine. This engine has switched from mechanical unit injectors to the HEUI fuel system. The engine is also turbocharged and aftercooled with a bore and stroke of 110×127 mm and employs a new deep skirted block with a *parent bore* design (no liners).

Figure 5–77 (p. 188) illustrates the five main components of this system, and Figure 5–78 (p. 188) is a schematic of the HEUI system where oil is supplied from a Rexroth high-pressure axial piston pump through oil manifolds on each bank of the vee engine. These oil manifolds serve as accumulators for the eight injectors. The high-pressure oil manifold and the

LAMPS: R = Red   Y = Yellow   EP = Engine Protection Lamp
ABBREV: SH = Sensor Harness   AH = Actuator Harness   OH = OEM Harness

FAULT CODE LAMP	PID(P) SID(S) FMI	EFFECT
115 R	P190 2	Current to injectors turned off. Engine dies.
121 Y	P190 10	None. Possible fueling or timing shift.
122 Y	P102 3	Derate to no-air setting.
123 Y	P102 4	Derate to no-air setting.
131 R	P091 3	Severe derate (power and speed). Power to get off road, or limp home if throttle pedal is held down.
132 R	P091 4	Severe derate (power and speed). Power to get off road or limp home if throttle pedal is held down.
135 Y	P100 3	No engine protection for oil pressure.
141 Y	P100 4	No engine protection for oil pressure.
143 EP	P100 1	Progressive power derate with increasing time after alert.
144 Y	P110 3	Possible white smoke. Fan on if ECM controlled. No engine protection for coolant temperature.
145 Y	P110 4	Possible white smoke. Fan on if ECM controlled. No engine protection for coolant temperature.
151 EP	P110 0	Progressive power and speed derate with increasing temperature.
153 Y	P105 3	Fan clutch engaged if ECM controlled. No engine protection for manifold air temperature.
154 Y	P105 4	Fan clutch engaged if ECM controlled. No engine protection for manifold air temperature.
155 EP	P105 0	Progressive power and speed derate with increasing temperature.
212 Y	P175 3	No engine protection for oil temperature.
213 Y	P175 4	No engine protection for oil temperature.
214 EP	P175 0	Progressive power derate with increasing temperature.
221 Y	P108 3	Power derate by 15%.
222 Y	P108 4	Power derate by 15%.
234 R	P190 0	Fuel shutoff valve closed. Opens when RPM falls to 2000.
235 EP	P111 1	Progressive power derate with increasing time after alert.
241 Y	P084 2	Engine speed limited to "Max. Engine Speed W/O VSS" Compulink value. Cruise control, progressive shift, gear down protection and road speed governor will not work.
243 Y	P121 4	ECM turns off engine brake supply voltage. Engine brakes can't be activated.
245 Y	S033 4	ECM turns off fan clutch supply voltage. Fan won't turn on. Possible engine overheat if ECM controlled fan in use.
254 R	S017 4	ECM turns off fuel shutoff valve supply voltages. Engine dies.
255 Y	S026 3	None on performance. Fuel shutoff valve or fan clutch or brake enable supply voltage stays on.

FIGURE 5–76 Celect fault code SAE information listing for use with Cummins engines. (Courtesy of Cummins Engine Company, Inc.)

fuel manifold are illustrated in Figure 5–79 (p. 189). The ECM is a variant of Ford's EEC-1V control module. The HEUI is illustrated in Figure 5–80 (p. 189) and consists of four main components. In the operational schematic of the system shown in Figure 5–81 (p. 190), the high-pressure oil pump is gear driven and draws oil through both an oil filter and an oil cooler from the engine oil sump. The oil circuit consists of both a low- and high-pressure section: the low side from the engine oil pump operates at pressures of approximately 300 kPa (43.5 psi), and the high side, which provides the oil to the injectors, operates at a range between 4 and 23 Mpa (580 to 3336 psi) depending on the speed of the engine. Although this high oil pressure is used to cause injector plunger operation, the start, duration, and ending of injection is controlled electronically by a PWM signal from the ECM.

The high-pressure oil flow is controlled by an RPCV (regulator pressure control valve) that opens and dumps oil directly back to the engine oil pan. The fuel transfer pump draws fuel from the tank and delivers it through a filter to the injectors through a passage within each cylinder head, which is visible in Figure 5–79. Fuel pressure is usually in the range of 200 kPa

FAULT CODE LAMP	PID(P) SID(S) FMI	EFFECT
311 Y	S001 6	Speed derate to 1400-1600 RPM. Current to injector is shut off.
312 Y	S005 6	Speed derate to 1400-1600 RPM. Current to injector is shut off.
313 Y	S003 6	Speed derate to 1400-1600 RPM. Current to injector is shut off.
314 Y	S006 6	Speed derate to 1400-1600 RPM. Current to injector is shut off.
315 Y	S002 6	Speed derate to 1400-1600 RPM. Current to injector is shut off.
321 Y	S004 6	Speed derate to 1400-1600 RPM. Current to injector is shut off.
322 Y	S001 5	Speed derate to 1400-1600 RPM. Current to injector is shut off.
323 Y	S005 5	Speed derate to 1400-1600 RPM. Current to injector is shut off.
324 Y	S003 5	Speed derate to 1400-1600 RPM. Current to injector is shut off.
325 Y	S006 5	Speed derate to 1400-1600 RPM. Current to injector is shut off.
331 Y	S002 5	Speed derate to 1400-1600 RPM. Current to injector is shut off.
332 Y	S004 5	Speed derate to 1400-1600 RPM. Current to injector is shut off.
333 Y	S254 12	Speed derate to 1400-1600 RPM.
335 R	S254 12	Unpredictable - possible no start (no power to either fuel solenoid or injectors).
341 R	S254 12	Unpredictable - possible no start (no power to either fuel solenoid or injectors).
342 R	S253 12	Engine won't start (no power to fuel solenoid).
343 Y	S254 12	None on performance.
351 Y	S254 12	Possible no noticeable effects. Possible reduced performance.
352 Y	S254 4	Cruise control/PTO, engine brakes don't work. 431 fault code - Compulink shows all switches open... OR... derate to no air and simultaneous logging of fault codes, 123, 141, 145, 154, 213, 222 and 422.
411 Y	S249 3	Control device may not work properly.
412 Y	S250 3	Compulink or Echek may not work properly.
413 Y	S249 9	Control device may not work properly.
414 Y	S250 9	Compulink or Echek may not work properly.
415 EP	P100 1	Progressive power and speed derate with increasing time after alert.
422 Y	P111 2	No engine protection for coolant level.
431 Y	P091 2	None on performance.
432 R	P091 11	Engine will only idle.
433 Y	P102 2	Derate to no-air setting.
434 Y	S251 4	Possible no noticeable performance effects. Possibility of engine dying or difficulty in starting engine.

(29 psi) and is controlled by a regulating valve, with very little fuel returning to the tank; therefore, a fuel cooler is not required with this system. The actual fuel injection pressures range from 19 to 120 MPa (2756 to 17,404 psi) based on the speed of the engine.

An example of the electronic control system is illustrated in Figure 5–82 (p. 191), with all of the sensors shown, along with the various switches and data links. A Caterpillar-type ECAP (electronic control analyzer and programmer) is shown. This data reader can of course be used to withdraw stored trouble codes from ECM memory as well as to troubleshoot the system. Refer to the Caterpillar electronic fuel system description for the 3176B and 3406E engines in this chapter for more information on using the ECAP or a similar hand-held diagnostic data reader that is discussed in the sec-

tions on the Detroit Diesel and Cummins fuel systems.

Eventually this HEUI system will be used in larger horsepower engines, more than likely Caterpillar's own models. When used in heavy trucks and buses (Classes 6 through 8), the electronic system will include an additional microprocessor-based module, known as the vehicle personality module, which was commonly used by Caterpillar in its 3406 PEEC systems as well as in the 3176A model. Given the advances in electronics, however, it is more than likely that the ECM will be designed similarly to those now in use on Caterpillar's 3176B and 3406E engines as well as the DDEC system used by Detroit Diesel on its engines. These ECMs will offer multipower ratings from one system that can be altered through use of the DDR similar to that shown in Figure 5–40.

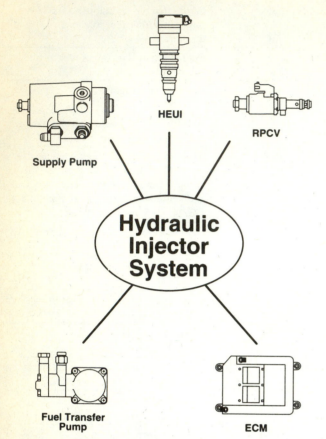

HEUI

RPCV

Supply Pump

Hydraulic Injector System

Fuel Transfer Pump

ECM

FIGURE 5–77 Major operating components of the HEUI (hydraulically actuated electronic unit injector) system used with the Caterpillar 3126 EUI engine model. This system is also employed by Navistar in its 7.3L/T 444 E cu in. direct-injected V8 engine in its own vehicles, as well as by Ford in a number of its truck models using the Navistar engine. (Reprinted with permission from SAE Paper 930271, copyright 1993, Society of Automotive Engineers, Inc.)

FIGURE 5–78 Schematic arrangement of the high-pressure lube oil side of the HEUI fuel injector mechanism. (Reprinted with permission from SAE Paper 930269, copyright 1993, Society of Automotive Engineers, Inc.)

SELF-TEST QUESTIONS

1. Detroit Diesel engines use a fuel system known as
   a. a high-pressure system
   b. a low-pressure recirculatory system
   c. a common-rail system
   d. a distributor pump system
2. Identify the basic functions of a unit injector fuel system.
   a. Supplies clean fuel and cools and lubricates the injectors
   b. Purges the system of air and maintains adequate pressure
   c. Self primes, lubricates, and supplies pressure
   d. Both (a) and (b) are correct
3. Technician A says that installing too small a fuel inlet/suction line from the fuel tank can result in a high fuel system restriction to the suction side of the fuel transfer pump. Technician B says that too small a line can cause lack of power under load. Who is right?
4. Technician A says that he would perform a fuel system restriction check by performing a fuel spill-back check. Technician B says that she would use a mercury manometer at the primary filter. Who knows the correct procedure?
5. Technician A says that if air is drawn into the fuel system, it can occur only between the fuel tank and inlet side of the fuel pump. Technician B says that you could also suck air at the secondary fuel filter if the gasket is not sealing properly. Who is right?
6. Technician A says that normal fuel system pressure on a Detroit Diesel engine is between 30 and 45 psi (207 to 310 kPa). Technician B says that this is too low and that it should be between 50 and 70 psi (345 to 483 kPa). Who is right?
7. Technician A says that the Detroit Diesel fuel system restricted fitting is installed at the fuel inlet manifold. Technician B disagrees, saying that it is located at the fuel outlet/return fuel manifold. Who is correct?

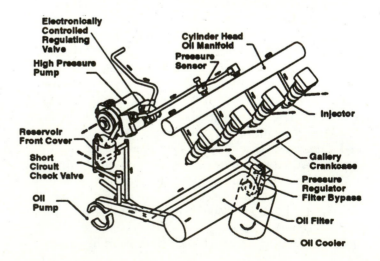

FIGURE 5–79 Cross-section of the cylinder head showing the location of the high-pressure lube oil manifold and the diesel fuel gallery in the 7.3L/T 444 E Navistar engine. (Reprinted with permission from SAE Paper 930269, copyright 1993, Society of Automotive Engineers, Inc.)

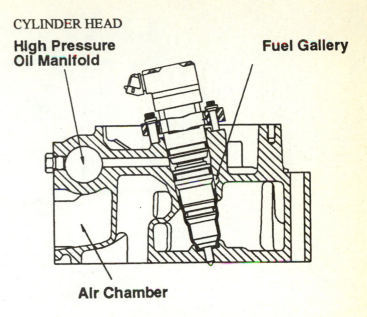

CYLINDER HEAD

High Pressure Oil Manifold

Fuel Gallery

Air Chamber

HEUI – Cross Section

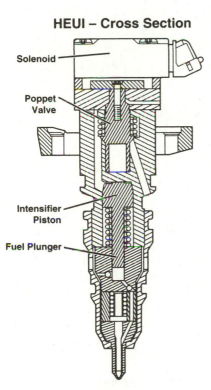

Solenoid

Poppet Valve

Intensifier Piston

Fuel Plunger

FIGURE 5–80 Cross-section of an HEUI electronically controlled unit injector mechanism. (Reprinted with permission from SAE Paper 930271, copyright 1993, Society of Automotive Engineers, Inc.)

8. Technician A says that the purpose of the fuel system restricted fitting in all Detroit Diesel engines is to maintain a minimum pressure of 35 psi (241 kPa) at the inlet fuel manifold. Technician B says that the

restricted fitting is to limit the fuel flow to the injectors to limit the engine horsepower. Who understands the purpose of this fitting?

9. Technician A says that the size of the restricted fitting orifice is stamped on the brass fitting. Technician B says that all restricted fittings on Detroit Diesel engines are the same. Who is correct here?

10. Technician A says that a fuel spill-back check is used to confirm that the fuel pump pressure is up to specs. Technician B says that this check can confirm whether there is air in the system and if the fuel filters are plugged. Who is right?

11. Technician A says that an R08 or R80 stamping on a fuel system restricted fitting indicates that the orifice size is 0.080 in. Technician B says that it means that the orifice size is 0.8 mm. Who is correct in this instance?

12. Technician A says that the four functions of the unit injector are to time, atomize, meter, and pressurize the fuel. Technician B says that the four functions are to time, meter, inject, and atomize the fuel. Who is correct?

13. Technician A says that you should not intermix unit injectors in the engine. Technician B says that you can since they will physically fit. Who is correct?

14. Technician A says that the basic horsepower on Detroit Diesel mechanical engines (non-DDEC) can be changed by installing a larger or smaller injector size. Technician B says that to change the horsepower setting, you have to increase the maximum full-load engine speed. Who is right?

15. Technician A says that to change the horsepower setting on a Detroit Diesel electronically controlled fuel injection system engine (DDEC), you would have to alter the EEPROM (electrically erasable programmable read-only memory) in the ECM. Technician B says that you would have to physically remove the existing

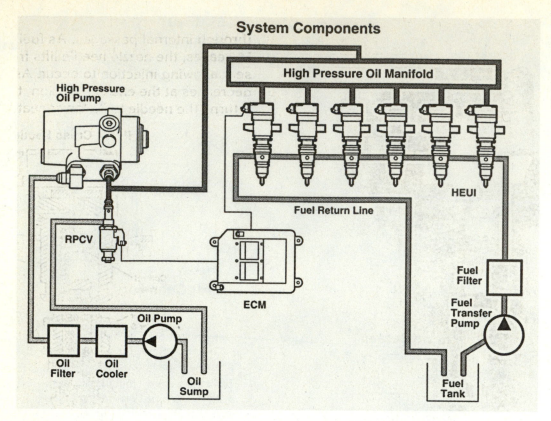

FIGURE 5–81 *Simplified layout and arrangement of the system components used with the HEUI fuel injection system. (Reprinted with permission from SAE Paper 930270, copyright 1993, Society of Automotive Engineers, Inc.)*

PROM chip and install a new one that has been recalibrated for a new setting. Who is correct?

16. Technician A says that metering of the fuel inside a mechanical unit injector is accomplished by the position of the rack, which alters the helix position and therefore the fuel delivery rate. Technician B says that the length of the plunger effective stroke does this function. Who is right?

17. Technician A says that the injector popping pressure is the pressure required to atomize the fuel. Technician B says that it is the pressure required to lift the internal needle valve. Who is right?

18. Technician A says that the fuel delivery rate in DDEC-equipped engines is controlled by rocker arm movement and the governor linkage connection. Technician B says that the ECM regulates the fuel delivery by a PWM electrical signal. Who is correct?

19. Technician A says that in a *matched* set of injectors, they all flow at the same fuel rate when tested on a calibration test stand. Technician B says that all the injectors are set to the same timing height. Who is correct?

20. Technician A says that spray tips are generally blown off an injector by high fuel delivery pressures.

Technician B says that this is usually a direct result of water in the fuel. Who is right?

21. Technician A says that excessive carbon buildup on the injector tip is usually an indication of low popping pressure and poor atomization, whereas technician B says that water in the fuel will cause this. Who is right?

22. Technician A says that engine tune-up must be performed every 50,000 miles (80,465 km) to ensure that the engine exhaust emissions comply with EPA regulations. Technician B says that tune-up is required only when a low-power complaint is received and the air and fuel systems are mechanically sound. Who is correct?

23. Technician A says that to clear the ECM trouble codes from DDEC memory, you simply have to pull the inline system fuses for 10 seconds. Technician B says that you have to employ an electronic DDR (diagnostic data reader). Who is correct?

24. Technician A says that stored ECM DDECII trouble codes can be determined by shorting out jumper pins A to M on the 12-pin DDL truck connector and watching the CEL illumination flashes. Technician B says

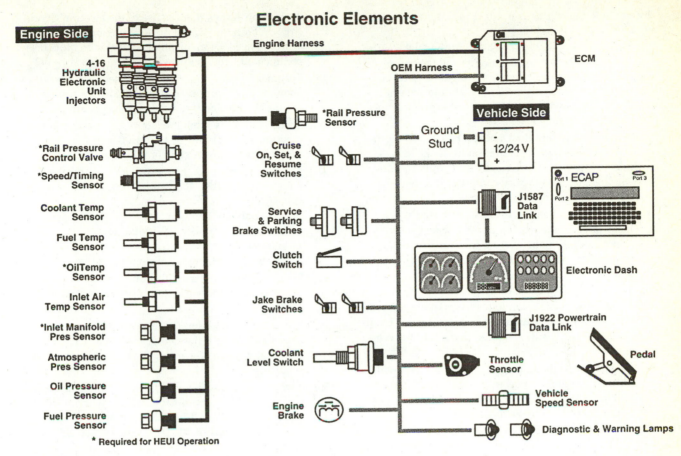

FIGURE 5–82 Electronic components arrangement of HEUI fuel injection system. (Reprinted with permission from SAE Paper 930270, copyright 1993, Society of Automotive Engineers, Inc.)

that you must use the DDR (diagnostic data reader). Who is right?

25. Technician A says that diesel fuel is used to cool the ECM in the DDEC system. Technician B says that engine coolant is routed through the ECM housing for this purpose. Who is correct?

26. Technician A says that if a DDEC-equipped engine shuts down repeatedly after idling for 5 minutes, this is a normal condition controlled by the ECM. Technician B says that this indicates a plugged primary fuel filter and the engine is simply using the fuel volume contained within the secondary filter assembly. Who is right?

27. A bus driver with a DDEC-equipped coach complains that the engine fails to rev up when the coach is parked and idling with the passenger door open. Technician A says that this is a normal condition. Technician B says that this is an abnormal condition. Who is correct?

28. Technician A says that the throttle pedal on a DDEC system uses a sensor, which is basically a variable potentiometer that changes the voltage output signal

proportional to throttle depression. Technician B says that the throttle pedal is connected to a mechanical linkage running to a TPS sensor and then to the electronic governor. Who is correct?

29. Technician A says that the throttle position sensor is nonadjustable. Technician B says that you can adjust the TPS. Who is right?

30. Technician A says that when the CEL (check engine light) on the dash illuminates, a trouble code has been logged into ECM memory and that the driver should have the DDEC system checked at the first available opportunity. Technician B says that when the CEL illuminates, within 30 seconds the engine/ECM will initiate an engine shutdown sequence. Who is correct here?

31. Technician A says that the SRS and TRS must be adjusted on all DDEC-equipped engines. Technician B says that this has to be done only on DDEC-equipped two-stroke-cycle 71 and 92 series engines. Who is right?

32. Technician A says that the EUI used on the DDEC systems can be effectively checked in the engine by using a special tester. Technician B says that you have to use a large screwdriver and hold the injector follower

down while the engine is running in order to check its operation. Who is right?

33. Technician A says that when checking the DDEC system wiring for either a resistance or voltage value, it is acceptable to puncture the wiring to gain a good connection. Technician B says that you should never do this because this will expose the weatherproof connections to the elements. Who is correct?

34. Technician A says that the DDR can be used to reprogram part of the engine calibration in the ECM. Technician B says that this can be done only by connecting the DDR to a factory computer interface hookup. Who is correct?

35. A fuel system problem is generally indicated when
    a. black smoke emanates from the exhaust stack.
    b. white smoke emanates from the exhaust stack.
    c. the engine loses power with no abnormal exhaust smoke
    d. high crankcase pressure is apparent.

36. Technician A says that high fuel system operating temperatures will result in high horsepower. Technician B says that this will result in a loss of horsepower. Who is correct?

37. Technician A says that a low fuel spill-back rate with normal fuel pressure would indicate air in the fuel system. Technician B says that this is probably due to too small a restricted fitting. Who is right?

38. Technician A says that too large a restricted fitting can cause a loss of fuel pressure at the injectors. Technician B says that this can cause a high fuel spill-back rate. Who is correct?

39. Technician A says that to check an injector for a misfiring condition in a non-DDEC 71 or 92 engine, you can run the engine at idle and simply depress the injector follower (hold it down). Technician B says that you should individually push each injector rack into the full-fuel position and see if the engine picks up speed. Who knows the correct procedure?

40. Since all direct-injection engine nozzles are of the multiple-hole design, technician A says that you can intermix nozzles between engines. Technician B says that you should never unilaterally switch nozzles between engines without first checking part numbers, and so on. Who is right?

41. True or False: Carbon should be removed from a nozzle tip with a brass-bristle brush, *not* with a wire brush.

42. Technician A says that the unit injectors used on the 3176 Caterpillar engine are capable of injection pressures of 25,000 psi + (17,237 bar). Technician B says that they are only capable of pressures as high as 15,000 psi (1033 bar). Who is right?

43. Technician A says that the 3176 Caterpillar engine injectors create their high pressures through electronic means. Technician B says that the high pressures necessary for injection are created mechanically by the pushrod acting on the injector follower. Who is right?

44. Technician A says that the use of the electronic controls on both the 3176 and 3406E engines does away with the need for an air/fuel control unit. Not so says technician B; you still need the unit. Who is right?

45. Technician A says that there is no need for a hydramechanical governor on an electronically controlled engine. Technician B disagrees. Who is correct?

46. Technician A says that the letters TPS mean throttle position sensor, while technician B says that they mean throttle power switch. Who is right?

47. The throttle pedal on an electronically controlled engine such as the 3406E and 3176 Caterpillar engine is basically
    a. a variable potentiometer
    b. a hydraulic/pneumatic cylinder
    c. an ON/OFF relay switch
    d. a mechanical/electrical circuit breaker

48. True or False: Both the 3406E and the 3176 engines rely on various engine sensors for operating condition feedback to the computer.

49. Technician A says that the term PROM means programmable read-only memory, whereas technician B says that it means power road override module. Who is correct?

50. Technician A says that an EEPROM unit is an electrically erasable programmable read-only memory, whereas technician B says that it is an electric engine power road override module. Who is correct?

51. Technician A says that to prevent unauthorized adjustment of the engine power setting on the 3406E and 3176 models, an electronic password is required. Technician B says that you can alter the engine horsepower setting by removing and installing another PROM assembly. Who is right?

52. Technician A says that when an electronic engine is started, the driver controls the start and duration of injection through the TPS. Technician B says that this is done through the ECM ratings personality module (PROM). Who is right?

53. Technician A says that to cool the ECM power control module on 3406E and 3176 engines, engine coolant is circulated around the housing. Technician B says that diesel fuel is used for this purpose. Who is correct?

54. Technician A says that the ECM determines injection timing, fuel delivery rate, and governor reaction/setting. Technician B says that this is done by manipulation of the TPS. Who is right?

55. Technician A says that to withdraw stored trouble codes from computer memory in the 3406E or 3176 engines you require special Caterpillar diagnostic equipment. Technician B says that you can also activate and use the flashing trouble lamp mounted on the vehicle dash. Who is correct?

56. Technician A says that the normal fuel delivery pressure to the unit injectors on 3176 and 3406E engines is

between 45 and 70 psi (310 to 483 kPa). Technician B says that it is higher and runs between 90 and 91 psi (620 to 627 kPa). Who is correct here?

57. Technician A says that in the 3176 engine, the fuel in the return manifold is returned to the tank from a relief valve that is set to open between 50 and 60 psi (345 to 414 kPa). Technician B disagrees, stating that it opens between 60 and 80 psi (414 to 552 kPa). Who is right?

58. Technician A says that a relief valve that sticks open in the return fuel manifold of a 3176 engine will cause the engine to run at a fast idle speed. Technician B says that this would cause the engine to run rough, misfire, and fail to pickup the load. Who is correct?

59. True or False: The time taken for the electronic unit injector fuel spill valve to close in a 3176 engine is approximately 1 millisecond.

60. Technician A says that a simple gear pump controls fuel system pressure in a Celect system. Technician B says that the Celect fuel system pressure is controlled by the size of the fuel pump button recess as in the PT system. Who is correct?

61. Technician A says that the Celect system operates at an approximate fuel pressure of 200 psi (1379 kPa). Technician B says that this is too high and that it is usually around 140 psi (965 kPa). Who is correct?

62. True or False: Current Celect-equipped engines do *not* have a separately housed PDM (power distribution module).

63. Technician A says that the purpose of the PDM on a Celect system is to receive electrical power from the vehicle batteries and relay it to the ECM. Technician B says that the purpose of the PDM is to protect the ECM from possible electrical charging system voltage surges and possible reversals of polarity during a battery boost condition. Are both mechanics correct in their statements, or is only one?

64. Technician A says that diesel fuel routed through the ECM cooling plate functions to keep the internal solid-state components at a safe operating temperature. Technician B says that the purpose of the cooling plate is to allow ECM warm-up in cold ambient temperatures. Who is correct here?

65. Technician A says that the purpose of the EPS (engine position sensor) on a Celect system is to monitor engine rpm. Technician B disagrees and says that its function is to provide both a piston position and engine speed condition to the ECM. Who is right?

66. Technician A says that on a Celect-equipped engine, only the engine coolant temperature sensor signal to the ECM will determine the engine idle speed at start-up. However, technician B states that it is the engine oil temperature sensor signal that determines the initial idle speed at start-up. Who is correct?

67. Technician A says that when an oil or coolant sensor signal on the Celect system is outside normal operat-

ing parameters, the ECM will lower the engine's maximum speed automatically. Technician B says that only a low coolant level sensor will do this. Who knows the Celect system best?

68. Technician A says that the TPS (throttle position sensor) on the Celect system is mounted on the PT fuel pump housing, whereas technician B says that it is located within the throttle pedal in the vehicle cab. Who is correct?

69. On a Celect-equipped engine, technician A says that any time the throttle pedal is in any position but idle, both the PTO and engine brakes will be deactivated. Technician B says that depressing the throttle pedal past idle will allow the cruise control feature to be overridden. Are both mechanics correct, or only one of them?

70. The term *PWM* refers to
   a. the duration in crankshaft degrees that the injector actually delivers fuel
   b. the length of signal duration from the engine position sensor
   c. the percentage of throttle depression
   d. the fuel pressure created in the fuel rail to the electronically controlled injectors

71. Technician A says that each time the idle speed adjust switch is toggled once on a Celect engine, the idle rpm will increase by approximately 50 rpm. Technician B says that the speed change is closer to 25 rpm. Who is right?

72. Technician A says that the maximum fuel system pressure in the Celect system is controlled by a spring-loaded bypass valve within the gear pump. Technician B says that a restricted fuel return fitting in the fuel rail to the injectors controls the fuel pressure. Who is right?

73. On a Celect-equipped engine, technician A says that the injector is manually operated by a rocker arm and pushrod similar to that used on a PT system to create the pressures necessary for injection. Technician B says not so, that the injector is operated by an electric solenoid to create the high fuel pressures necessary for injection purposes. After all, he asks, isn't that what electronic fuel injection is all about? Which technician understands how the Celect system operates?

74. Technician A says that for injection to occur within the ECI Celect injector, a metering spill port must be closed. Technician B says that there is no metering spill port and that injection begins and ends based on the PWM signal to the injector from the ECM. Who is correct?

75. Technician A says that metering ends in the ECI Celect injector when the small electric control valve is opened by a signal from the ECM. Technician B says that fuel metering is controlled by gear pump pressure. Who is right?

76. Technician A says that fuel system performance checks of the Celect system can be performed only by using a handheld electronic diagnostic data reader. Technician B says that a fuel supply restriction check, fuel drain line restriction check, and cooling plate restriction check can be performed in a similar manner to that for a PT-equipped engine. Which technician is correct?

77. Technician A says that the valve and injector adjustment on a Celect-equipped engine follows the same basic procedure as that for a PT-equipped engine. Technician B says that no injector adjustment is required since the injector is electronically controlled. Which technician is correct?

78. Technician A says that the ECI injector can be checked for a misfire condition in the same manner as for a PT injector. Technician B says that an electronic diagnostic data reader is required to effectively short out the ECM signal to the injector solenoid. Who is right?

6 Mechanical and Electronic Governors

OVERVIEW

The diesel technician today needs to understand fully the operation of both mechanical and electronic governor systems, because each controls fuel flow to the engine cylinders and consequently can affect the vehicle (or equipment or vessel) performance. In this chapter we discuss how both of these control systems function.

TOPICS

- General terms
- Types of governors
- Why a governor is required
- Basic mechanical governor operation
- Governor droop
- Maximum engine speed adjustment
- Zero-droop governors
- Electronic governors
- Self-test questions

GENERAL TERMS

All diesel engines must operate with a governor mechanism to control the speed and response of the engine under varying load and throttle opening conditions. As a foundation for our discussion of governor types and their operation, study the following governor terms; they are commonly used in reference to engine speed regulation.

Although most engine and fuel injection equipment manufacturers use the same general terms,

phraseology fluctuates between specific engine manufacturers. Common meanings, and the different terms, will be discussed where applicable.

1. *Maximum no-load speed* or *high idle* is a term used to describe the highest engine rpm obtainable when the throttle linkage is moved to its maximum position with no load applied to the engine. This rpm can be adjusted to suit changing conditions or applications according to the engine manufacturer's limits and recommendations.

2. *Maximum full-load speed* or *rated speed* indicates the engine rpm at which a particular engine will produce its maximum designed horsepower setting as stated by the manufacturer.

3. *Idle* or *low idle speed* is the term used to indicate the normal speed at which the engine will rotate with the throttle linkage in the released or closed position. Normally, truck idle speed settings range between 500 and 700 rpm and are adjustable.

4. *Work capacity* describes the amount of available work energy that can be produced at the governor's terminal or output shaft. Each specific mechanical or hydromechanical governor assembly is designed to have enough work output to ensure that it can move the associated linkage that is connected to it. The work capacity is generally expressed in inch-pounds or foot-pounds.

5. *Stability* refers to the condition of the governor linkage after a load or speed setting change. The governor must be able to return the engine to a new speed/load setting without any tendency for the engine speed to drift up or down (fluctuate) before settling down at the new setting. Stability of a governor is usually indicated by the number of corrective movements it makes and the time required to correct fuel flow for any given load change.

6.   *Speed droop* is the term used to express the difference between the no-load (high idle) speed setting and the full-load (rated) speed setting. In other words, it is the increase in rpm above the maximum rated horsepower setting as the full load is reduced to zero power output without adjustment to the governor. It is expressed as a percentage of rated speed and can be shown by this equation:

$$\text{speed droop} = \frac{\text{MNL} - \text{MFL}}{\text{MFL}} \times 100\%$$

where the MNL is the maximum no-load (high idle) rpm and the MFL is the maximum full-load (rated) rpm. For example, if the rated full-load speed setting of an engine was 2100 rpm, and the no-load speed is 2310 rpm, the speed droop is 10%. Speed droop is adjustable on some types of governors, namely, hydromechanical and electronic units.

7.   *Sensitivity* is an expression of how quickly the governor responds to a speed change. For example, a governor that responds to a speed change of 5% is more sensitive than a governor that responds with a 10% speed change. Once the governor has sensed a speed change, it must produce a corrective movement of the fuel control mechanism.

8.   *Response time* is tied closely to the governor's sensitivity and is normally the time taken in seconds for the fuel linkage to be moved from a no-load to a full-load position.

9.   *Isochronous* is the term used to indicate zero-droop capability. In other words, the full-load (rated) and no-load (high idle) speeds are the same.

10.   *Speed drift* is usually most noticeable at an idle speed and more commonly referred to as *hunting* or *surging,* where the set speed tends to rise above or below the initial governed setting. Speed drift is usually easily adjustable by means of a buffer screw or a bumper spring on the governor housing.

11.   *Overrun* is a term used to express the action of the governor when the engine tends to exceed its maximum governed speed. Generally, overrun occurs when the engine is driven by the vehicle road wheels, such as when descending a steep hill.

12.   *Underrun* is simply a term used to describe the governor's inability to prevent the engine speed from dropping below a set idle, particularly when the throttle has been moved rapidly to a decreased fuel setting from a high idle or maximum full-load position. This can generally result in the engine stalling.

13.   *Deadband* is the term used to describe a very narrow speed range during which no measurable correction is made by the governor.

14.   *State of balance* is the common term used to describe the speed at which the centrifugal force of the rotating governor flyweights matches and balances the governor speeder spring force. This can occur at any speed in an all-range governor as long as the speed of the engine can develop sufficient horsepower to carry the load applied.

TYPES OF GOVERNORS

There are a number of different types or styles of governors used on diesel engines. Some of these are common to industrial, marine, and power generator set applications. Basic types of governors can be classified in the following six categories:

1.   Mechanical centrifugal flyweight style, which relies on a set of rotating flyweights and a control spring; used since the inception of the diesel engine to control its speed. Millions of these are still used in one form or another on mechanically operated and controlled diesel fuel injection systems.

2.   Power-assisted servomechanical style, which operates similarly to that described in 1 but also employs engine oil under pressure to move the operating linkage. Used on many engines, such as Caterpillar products, in a variety of applications.

3.   Hydraulic governor, which relies on the movement of a pilot valve plunger to control pressurized oil flow to a power piston, which in turn moves the fuel control mechanism. Commonly used on industrial, marine, and power generator set engine applications.

4.   Pneumatic governor, which is responsive to the airflow (vacuum) in the intake manifold of the engine. A diaphragm within the governor housing is connected to the fuel control linkage, which changes its setting with increases or decreases in the vacuum.

5.   Electromechanical governor assembly, which uses a magnetic speed pickup sensor on an engine-driven component to monitor the rpm. The sensor sends a voltage signal to an electronic control unit, which in turn controls the current flow to a mechanical actuator connected to the fuel linkage. Commonly used on stationary power plants and generator sets.

6.   Electronic governor assembly, which uses a magnetic speed sensor to monitor the engine rpm. The sensor continuously feeds a signal back to an ECM (electronic control module).

The ECM then computes this signal along with information from other engine/vehicle sensors, such as the throttle position sensor, turbocharger boost sensor, engine oil pressure and temperature, engine coolant level or temperature, and fuel temperature to limit the engine speed. The ECM actually alters the PWM (pulse width modulated) electrical signal to the electronically controlled injectors to control how long fuel is injected over a given amount of crankshaft degrees. This type of governor is typical of that now in use on Detroit Diesel, Caterpillar, Cummins, Mack, and Volvo engines.

The governors used on highway truck applications fall into one of two basic categories:

1. *Limiting-speed governors,* sometimes referred to as *minimum/maximum* models since they are intended to control the idle and maximum speed settings of the engine. Generally, there is no governor control in the intermediate range, which is regulated by the position of the throttle linkage by the driver/operator.
2. *Variable-speed* or *all-range governors,* which are designed to control the speed of the engine regardless of the throttle setting.

NOTE: A constant-speed-range governor assembly is another type of governor that allows the engine to go immediately to a fixed-speed setting after startup and stays there minus the droop unless it is capable of isochronous control. This type is used for industrial applications only.

WHY A GOVERNOR IS REQUIRED

The speed and horsepower capability of any internal combustion engine is regulated by the volume of air that can be retained within the engine cylinders and the volume of fuel that can be delivered and consumed during the engine power stroke. More than likely you have a driver's license, so you are aware of the fact that when you drive a car or truck equipped with a gasoline engine, *you* determine the rate of fuel supplied to the engine by manipulation of the gas or throttle pedal. Regardless of whether the engine is carbureted or fuel injected, throttle movement controls the flow of air into the engine cylinders and thus the desired fuel flow.

Therefore, a mechanical or electronic governor assembly is not necessary on a gasoline engine. Nevertheless, some gasoline engines in industrial and truck applications are equipped with a governor to control the maximum speed and power of the engine/vehicle. In addition, some models of passenger cars are equipped with an electronic ignition cutoff system to control the maximum speed of the vehicle. Remember, a governor is not a "must" with a gasoline engine as it is with a diesel engine.

Why then does a diesel engine require a governor assembly? The main reason has to do with the fact that the throttle pedal controlled by the operator does not regulate the airflow into the diesel engine but controls the fuel flow. Current gasoline engines in passenger cars have electronic controls for both the ignition and fuel systems and are designed to operate at air/fuel ratios that allow the engine to comply with existing U.S. EPA exhaust emissions standards. Through the use of an exhaust gas oxygen sensor, the air/fuel ratio is in *closed loop* operation (oxygen sensor receives an input reference voltage signal from the ECM and returns a system operating condition signal back to the ECM to complete the circuit). The oxygen sensor monitors the percentage of oxygen in the exhaust gases leaving the engine. The ECM then either leans out or enriches the air/fuel mixture to try and maintain a *stoichiometric* air/fuel ratio, which is between 14.6 and 14.7 parts of air to one part of fuel (gasoline).

Due to the unthrottled air supply condition, a diesel engine at an idle speed runs very lean, with air/fuel ratios being between 90 and 120:1 depending on the specific model of engine in question. Under full-load conditions, this air/fuel ratio is approximately 25 to 30:1.

Let's assume for instructional purposes that a given four-stroke-cycle diesel engine is designed to produce 400 bhp (298 kW) at 2100 rpm full-load speed. If we also assume that, to produce this power, each fuel injector is designed to deliver 185 cu mm of fuel into each cylinder for each power stroke, then by manual operation of the throttle we might assume that at an idle speed of 600 rpm, the fuel delivery rate to each cylinder might be only 18.5 cu mm with the engine producing possibly 40 bhp (30 kW). A similarly rated two-stroke-cycle engine would inject approximately half as much fuel per power stroke, but since there are two power strokes for every one in the four-cycle engine, both engines will consume approximately the same amount of fuel.

If the engine/vehicle is stationary and the throttle is placed into a WOT (wide open throttle) position, the engine does not need to receive full fuel (185 cu mm) to accelerate to its maximum no-load speed. The engine can be accelerated with very little additional fuel being supplied to the cylinders, because with no load on the engine, we have to overcome only the resistance to motion from the engine components, as well as any accessory driven items that need more horsepower to drive them at this higher speed. In addition, if the engine has very little additional load from what it had at an idle rpm, the faster rotating fly-wheel will store enough inertia (centrifugal force generated at the higher speed) to keep the engine turning over smoothly at this higher no-load speed.

Once the engine obtains this higher no-load speed, in this example, say, 2250 rpm, the same amount of fuel (or slightly more) that was supplied at idle will basically maintain this higher speed. However, on a diesel engine, remember that manual operation of the throttle controls the fuel flow and *not* the airflow as happens on a gasoline engine. Therefore, by opening the throttle to a WOT position in this engine, we actually deliver 185 cu mm of fuel to the engine cylinders, or *10 times more* than we did at idle speed; but all we need to maintain this higher no-load rpm is basically the same volume of fuel that we used at idle (18.5 cu mm) at 600 rpm, or slightly more. If we generated 40 bhp (30 kW) at 600 rpm, at WOT we might develop an additional 10 to 15 hp (7.5 to 11 kW) to handle the increased power requirements of the various accessory items such as a fan, air compressor, or generator. We certainly do not require the 400 bhp (298 kW) rated power output of the engine under this operating condition.

Without a governor assembly, a WOT position grossly *overfuels* the engine in this high-idle no-load example by about 10 times its needs. Since we know from earlier discussions that the diesel engine always operates with an excess air supply, we have sufficient air to burn this full-fuel delivery rate. The result will be that with 10 times more fuel than necessary, the engine rpm will continue to climb in excess of a safe operating speed. Under such a nongoverned over-fueled condition most diesels will quickly self-destruct as a result of valves striking piston crowns and connecting rods punching through the engine block as well as possible crankshaft breakage.

When a load is applied to a diesel engine, more fuel delivery is obviously required to generate the extra heat energy to produce the higher horsepower required. In our simplified example, this engine can produce 400 bhp (298 kW) at 2100 rpm WOT full-load operating conditions. It is only under such a condition that this engine needs its 185 cu mm of fuel delivery to each cylinder. Refer to the engine performance curve charts illustrated in Chapter 1; you can see that the power produced by the engine increases with speed, since horsepower is considered as being the rate or speed at which work is done by the engine. To prevent the engine from over-revving and running

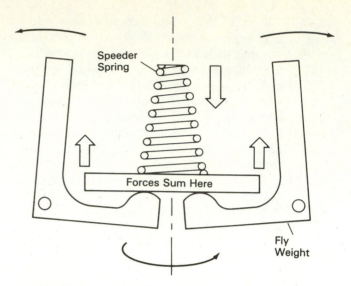

FIGURE 6–1 *Weight force versus spring force to achieve governor speed balance—often referred to as SOB (state of balance).*

away, we must have some type of control mechanism that will limit the amount of fuel injected to the engine cylinders under all operating conditions. In other words, we need either a mechanical or electronic governor assembly on the engine!

BASIC MECHANICAL GOVERNOR OPERATION

The mechanical governor assembly uses two main components: a set of engine-driven flyweights and a spring. Figure 6–1 illustrates a basic mechanical governor with its set of weights and spring. Each of these components serves a purpose in *all* mechanical governors. The force of the spring is designed to move the fuel control linkage to an *increased* setting under all operating conditions. The centrifugal force generated by the engine-driven flyweights is designed to *decrease* the fuel control linkage setting under all operating conditions.

When the engine is stopped, the force of the governor spring is therefore attempting to place the fuel control racks into a full-fuel position. On some engines, the governor is arranged so as to provide excess fuel for start-up purposes, whereas on some turbocharged engine models, a mechanical adjustment device limits start-up fuel to half-throttle to minimize exhaust smoke. In these simplified governor diagrams, we show the manual throttle control as being connected directly above the governor spring; in reality, seldom is this the case. Instead, additional linkage

FIGURE 6–2 *Concepts of basic governor reaction: (a) state of balance condition where the centrifugal force of the weights balances the spring force; (b) load decrease causes a speed increase, resulting in a decrease in the fuel setting; (c) load increase causes a speed decrease resulting in an increase in the fuel setting.*

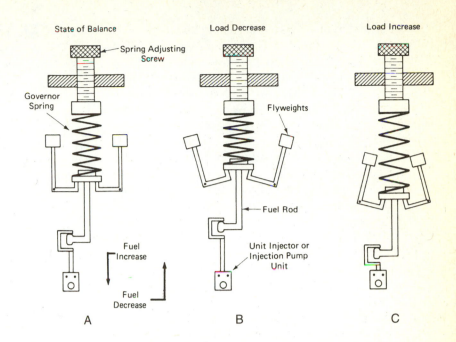

is used to transfer the manual operation of the throttle to the governor spring assembly.

Increasing the force of the governor spring through the throttle linkage when the engine is running manually increases the fuel rack setting, resulting in an increase in engine speed and power. As the engine accelerates, the centrifugal force generated by the rotating flyweights becomes stronger and the flyweights oppose the force of the spring. For a given throttle setting, the force applied to the spring will cause the weights to generate an equal and opposing force. When the spring force and weight forces become equal for a given engine load and speed, the governor is said to be in a *state of balance*, and the fuel racks will be held in a stationary position with the engine producing a specific horsepower at a given rpm.

Since the governor weights are engine driven, the governor assembly is said to be *speed sensitive*. An engine speed change due to a load increase or a load decrease will affect the rotational speed of the flyweights and, therefore, the state of balance condition that exists between the weights and the governor spring for any throttle setting position.

GOVERNOR DROOP

An engine operating at WOT with no load on it will run at a higher speed than it does at WOT under full load! Why will the engine not run at the same speed loaded or unloaded? The answer has to do with the term *governor droop*, or how "sensitive" the governor assembly is to an engine speed change. How much speed will be lost or gained depends on the govenor

reaction. The difference between the engine MNL (maximum no-load) speed (high idle) and the MFL (maximum full-load) speed (rated) is known as governor droop. This can be determined as follows:

$$\text{droop} = \frac{\text{MNL} - \text{MFL}}{\text{MFL}} \times 100\%$$

$$= \frac{2250 - 2100}{2100} \times 100\% = 7.14\%$$

In this example, the droop is actually 150 rpm, which is a full-load droop speed. Regardless of the speed at which the engine is running, this droop percentage will remain constant; however, the rpm will change. Seven percent of 2250 rpm versus 7% of 1200 rpm results in droop readings of 150 and 84 rpm, respectively. An engine idling at 600 rpm with no load would result in a speed loss of 42 rpm when fully loaded.

What causes droop? To describe this condition, let's refer to the three simplified diagrams illustrated in Figure 6–2. When the engine is stopped the weights are collapsed and the spring force pushes the fuel rack to the maximum position for startup purposes. When the engine is cranked and fires, the centrifugal force generated at the weights starts to compress the spring, while at the same time pulling the fuel rack to a decreased fuel setting. When the weight and spring forces are equal, the governor is said to be in a *SOB* (state of balance) condition. The position of the fuel rack is held at a position corresponding to this SOB. For example, with the throttle held at an idle position, the engine would run at this speed setting, which can be adjusted by a screw to change the spring force.

If in Figure 6–2a the weights and spring are at a SOB condition and the spring is compressed to 102 mm (4 in.), let's assume the spring has a stored energy (force) of 10 lb (4.5 kg). If we now apply a load to the engine at this fixed throttle position as shown in Figure 6–2c, the engine requires more power to maintain this SOB condition. The additional load will cause the engine speed to drop, which will upset the SOB condition between the weights and spring. This allows the spring to expand and give up some of its stored energy in moving the fuel racks to an increased position. Let's assume that the spring is now 108 mm (4.25 in.) long, with a stored energy of only 9 lb (4 kg); the centrifugal force generated by the rotating flyweights will be able to obtain a new SOB with this longer and weaker spring at a lower engine speed. The engine will now be running at a slower rpm, but with more fuel being delivered to the cylinders it will produce more horsepower to handle the additional load. The difference in engine speed due to this rebalancing between the weights and spring is what causes the "droop."

With the engine running at a fixed throttle position and a SOB condition similar to that shown in Figure 6–2a, we are now going to decrease the load as shown in Figure 6–2b. Once again we upset the SOB between the weights and spring in favor of the weights because the engine would now tend to pick up speed. As the weights fly outward due to the higher engine rpm, the spring is compressed as the fuel rack is pulled to a decreased fuel setting. Let's assume that the spring is now 95.25 mm (3.75 in.) long and has a stored energy of 11 lb (5 kg); with a shorter and stronger spring, the weights will have to rotate faster to maintain a new governor SOB condition. However, with the fuel rack at a decreased setting due to a lighter load, the engine now runs slightly faster but produces less horsepower. Once again "droop" has entered the speed change picture.

In a variable-speed (all-range) governor, the weights and spring can control any speed setting selected by the operator. In a limiting-speed (minimum/maximum) governor, however, the speed control is designed to operate only at the lower and higher ends of the speed zones. Between these speeds, the operator controls engine speed by manual operation of the throttle. Regardless of the type of governor employed on an engine and the speed at which it is running, a load increase or a load decrease situation results in governor reactions similar to those illustrated in Figure 6–2.

MAXIMUM ENGINE SPEED ADJUSTMENT

When as a diesel technician you have to adjust the maximum no-load speed of an engine, you must know how sensitive the governor is so that you can determine the difference between the MNL and MFL speeds due to droop. With a 10% sensitive governor, all this means is that the speed difference at MNL rpm will be 10% higher than what it will be at MFL rpm. Here is another way to look at this: for every 100 rpm at which the engine is running with no load, it will lose 10 rpm for each 100 the engine is running at when a full load is applied to it. Therefore, at an MNL speed of 2310 rpm, the MFL speed is approximately 2100 rpm. Failure to set the MNL speed high enough will result in a low MFL speed, and the engine will not produce its rated horsepower.

Let's consider the fairly narrow droop rpm zone of a particular engine with the governor adjusted to an MNL speed of 2250 rpm and its MFL speed at 2100 rpm. Within this 150 droop rpm area, as load is applied to the engine the centrifugal force of the flyweights is reduced as they slow down. This action upsets the SOB that existed between the weights and spring in favor of the spring, which will expand and push the fuel racks toward an increasing fuel delivery setting to create more cylinder horsepower. In this example the engine may have been producing 45 hp (33.5 kW) at 2250 rpm no load with an 18.5 cu mm fuel setting, but at 2100 rpm full load, it will be receiving 185 cu mm of fuel and producing 400 hp (298 kW). As you can see from this example, a large fuel increase occurs within a fairly narrow speed droop range.

ZERO-DROOP GOVERNORS

A *zero-droop governor*, or isochronous (single time) governor, is a governor that is capable of maintaining the engine speed the same, loaded or unloaded. This governor assembly is designed for adjustable droop through either an internal or external adjustment screw mechanism. The adjustable-droop feature may range from 0% to 10% depending on the model of governor used. A zero-droop condition is one in which the engine runs at the same rpm loaded or unloaded. The adjustable-droop feature allows the internal governor linkage fulcrum point to be adjusted, so that after a load change the spring force is returned to the same length and strength. This ensures that the engine will continue to rotate at the same rpm.

A governor with adjustable droop is commonly used on a diesel power generator set. It is needed to ensure that when one or more engines are electrically tied together in a parallel arrangement, each engine can handle its share of the load in proportion to its gen-set rating. Generally, one engine governor is adjusted for zero droop to monitor the system, and the other engine governors are set to allow equal load sharing. Even if we select two identical model engines set at the same horsepower and driving equal sized gen-sets, mass production of parts prevents every engine from being able to produce the exact same horsepower at the same rpm. Variations in cylinder pressures and fuel delivery rates account for characteristic changes in both horsepower and acceleration. Adjustable-droop governors allow us to set up each engine for equal-load sharing capabilities.

ELECTRONIC GOVERNORS

The introduction of electronically controlled diesel fuel injection systems on Detroit Diesel, Caterpillar, Cummins, Volvo, Mack, and Mercedes-Benz heavy-duty high-speed truck engines has allowed the speed of the diesel engine to be controlled electronically rather than mechanically. In an electronic governor, the same type of balanced condition to that shown in Figure 6–1 for a mechanical governor occurs. The major difference is that in the electronic governor, electric currents (amperes) and voltages (pressure) are summed together instead of mechanical weight and spring forces. This is possible through the use of an MPS (magnetic pickup sensor), which is in effect a permanent-magnet single-pole device. This magnetic pickup concept is being used on all existing electronic systems; therefore, its operation can be considered common to all of them. MPSs are a vital communicating link between the engine crankshaft speed and the on-board computer, known as the ECM. The MPS is installed next to a drive shaft gear made of material that reacts to a magnetic field. As each gear tooth passes the MPS, the gear interrupts the MPS's magnetic field. This, in turn, produces an alternating current signal that corresponds to engine rpm. This signal is then sent to the ECM.

Figure 6–3 illustrates a simplified wiring diagram for a TRS (timing reference sensor) which is located on the engine block. Refer to Chapter 5 to see where this sensor is mounted on specific engines; usually this sensor picks up cylinder positions from a raised pin attached to either the crankshaft or camshaft gear. The sensor is installed so that a small air gap exists between the end of the sensor and the gear teeth or pickup pin.

The TRS generally receives a 5 V timing reference signal from the ECM and then returns a signal based

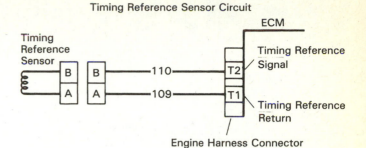

FIGURE 6–3 *Simplified example of a timing reference sensor circuit for an electronically governed engine. (Courtesy of Detroit Diesel Corporation.)*

on engine speed to the ECM, which then converts this signal to determine the speed of engine rotation. The rotation of the ferrous (metal) gear teeth past the end of the sensor causes the magnetic field or magnetic flux level to change every time a gear tooth passes through this electrically generated signal field since the air gap space is reduced. This action induces a voltage signal that is transmitted through the TRS return wire to the ECM. The shape and spacing of the gear teeth determine the electrical waveform of the sensor output voltage. The number of teeth on the gear determines the number of pulses per revolution of the gear. An 80 tooth gear, for example, rotating at 2100 rpm would produce 168,000 pulses per minute or 2800 pulses per second. This 2800 pulses per second in electronics terminology would be referred to as 2800 Hz (hertz), which is the frequency of the generated TRS signal. This TRS signal is used by the ECM to establish the amount of fuel that should be injected into combustion chambers of the engine.

The components described above compose a closed-loop system of measurement, which is illustrated in Figure 6–4 in a simple line diagram. The output of the magnetic speed pickup sensor is connected to a speed sensor circuit inside the ECM. This circuit converts the AC magnetic pickup signal to a DC voltage whose level is proportional to the speed of the engine. An analog-to-digital converter within the speed control circuit provides this DC signal since the ECM circuitry is designed to operate only on DC signals. The DC voltage signal is compared to the speed reference voltage; therefore, if a difference or an error exists, the ECM output signal from the built-in amplifier causes the injector PWM signal to lengthen or shorten. This change to the PWM signal causes the injector fuel delivery cycle to last for a greater or shorter duration of crankshaft degrees, thereby changing the engine speed and fuel setting.

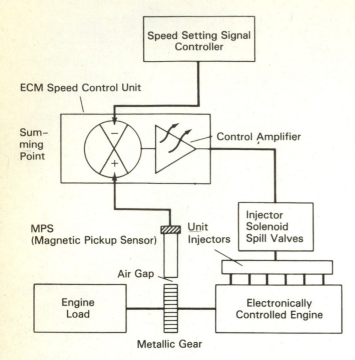

FIGURE 6–4 *Simplified schematic showing the concept of operation for a closed-loop control electronic governor assembly.*

For the electronic governor system within the ECM to control the speed and fueling of the engine, it must know the following conditions:

- Speed of the engine
- Percentage of throttle depression
- Turbo boost/load on the engine
- Intake manifold temperature

The degree of throttle pedal depression at the EFPA (electronic foot pedal assembly) inputs a desired engine speed request to the ECM. The feedback signal to the ECM from the engine speed sensor alerts the ECM to the actual engine speed. If the desired engine speed request from the EFPA is greater than the actual engine speed, the ECM lengthens the electronic injector solenoid PWM signal to produce more fuel to the combustion chambers. If, on the other hand, the desired engine speed from the EFPA is less than the actual engine speed, then less fuel is desired. The ECM shortens the PWM signal to reduce the quantity of fuel injected.

This basic scenario is best viewed in the illustration in Figure 6–5, which depicts in one diagram the timing and injection control system for a Caterpillar 3176B and 3406E heavy-duty truck electronically controlled unit injector system. As you can see, the *summing point* within the ECM governor control system continually receives a throttle percentage request to the positive side of the system, while the actual engine speed is fed to the negative side of the system. The ALU (arithmetic/logic unit) within the ECM computes the various sensor inputs and accesses a *lookup table* in its memory for the desired output to the fuel injectors. The turbo boost sensor signal is needed to tell the ECM the air pressure, and the intake manifold temperature sensor indicates to the ECM the denseness of the air flowing into the engine cylinders from the intake manifold. To control exhaust emissions and engine performance, the ECM must know the pressure and temperature of the intake air to control the air/fuel ratio circuit (or the PWM signal to the unit injectors). The net result is shown in Figure 6–3, where injector timing and duration are controlled by sensor signal inputs to the ECM from the engine speed and timing reference sensors, the EFPA, the turbo boost sensor, and intake manifold temperature sensor.

SELF-TEST QUESTIONS

1. Technician A says that a diesel engine requires the use of a governor because the air is not throttled into the engine. Technician B says that the governor is required to stop the diesel engine from stalling at an idle speed. Who is right?

2. Technician A says that mechanical and hydraulically assisted governors are speed-sensitive devices. Technician B says that they are load-sensitive devices. Who is correct?

3. Technician A says that at an idle speed, the air/fuel ratio in a diesel engine can be as high as 30:1, whereas technician B says that it is much higher, being as lean as 130:1. Who is correct?

4. Technician A says that the recommended idle speed of an engine can usually be found stamped on the exhaust emissions decal on the engine, whereas technician B says it will always be found on the governor ID tag itself. Who is right?

5. *High idle speed* is a term used by some manufacturers to indicate
   a. a higher-than-normal idle rpm used in cold-weather operation only
   b. the maximum no-load speed setting of the engine
   c. the maximum full-load speed setting of the engine
   d. the speed setting when the vehicle is stationary and a PTO (power takeoff) is being used.

6. Technician A says that the engine will use less fuel when running at a maximum no-load speed of, say, 2100 rpm than it will at a full-load speed of 1950 rpm. Technician B believes that it will use more fuel at the higher speed. Which mechanic knows the basic governor operation?

7. When the engine is running under full load (say, 1950 rpm) and its speed is slowly reduced to its peak torque speed of, say, 1200 rpm, why is the horsepower

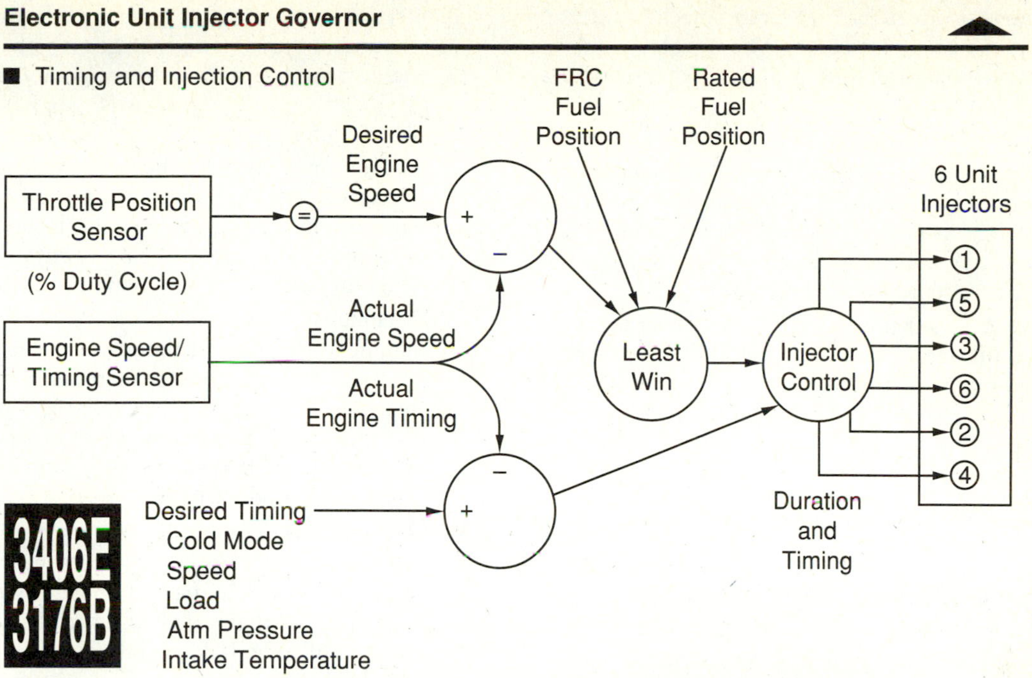

Electronic Unit Injector Governor

■ Timing and Injection Control

FIGURE 6–5 Electronic unit injector governor timing and injection control circuit arrangement schematic for the 3176B and 3406E engine models. FRC means "fuel ratio control." (Courtesy of Caterpillar Inc.)

not constant if the engine is still receiving full-load fuel from the governor?

8. Why does the engine produce more torque under load at a lower engine speed (for example, at 1200 rpm) than it does at its full-load speed of, say, 1950 rpm if the governor is still supplying maximum fuel to the fuel injectors?

9. Technician A says that as the engine speed increases from its maximum full-load rpm to its no-load rpm, the governor will decrease the fuel delivered to the injectors. Technician B disagrees, saying that the governor would have to increase the fuel delivery rate to allow an increase in speed. Who is correct?

10. Technician A says that a state of balance condition in a mechanical governor can exist only when the engine is running at an idle speed. Technician B says that a state of balance condition can exist at any speed throughout the governor control range as long as the weight and spring forces are equal. Who is correct?

11. In a limiting-speed mechanical governor, the governor controls
   a. the idle speed
   b. the maximum speed
   c. all speed ranges between idle and maximum
   d. both a and b

12. Technician A says that governor droop is the difference in speed between the maximum no-load and maximum full-load engine rpm. Technician B says that it is the difference between high idle and rated speed. Who is correct?

13. Technician A says that governor droop is generally expressed as a percentage figure. Technician B says that droop is expressed as an rpm. Who is correct?

14. Technician A says that the term *governor sensitivity* is generally expressed as an rpm value, whereas technician B says that it is expressed as a percentage value. Who is right?

15. Technician A says that in a mechanical governor assembly, the force of the governor spring is always trying to increase the fuel delivery rate to the injectors. Technician B says that this is incorrect, and that the centrifugal force of the rotating flyweights are always attempting to increase the fuel to the engine. Who is correct?

16. A minimum/maximum governor is designed to control
   a. the idle and maximum speed of the engine
   b. the idle, intermediate, and maximum speed settings of the engine
   c. the idle and intermediate speed settings only
   d. the idle speed setting only

17. A variable-speed governor is designed to control
   a. idle speed
   b. idle, intermediate, and maximum speeds
   c. idle and intermediate speeds
   d. idle and maximum speed settings

18. Technician A says that when an engine using a mechanical minimum/maximum or limiting-speed mechanical governor is stopped and the engine is ready to start, the fuel control mechanism will be held in the full-fuel position. Technician B says that when

the engine is stopped, the fuel control mechanism must be in the no-fuel position. Who is right?

19. True or False: The maximum engine speed settings are usually found stamped on the engine compliance/exhaust emissions label.

20. Technician A says that if an engine lacks power, the reason should be investigated. Technician B says that if an engine lacks power, the maximum speed setting of the engine should be increased until it performs according to specification. Who is correct?

21. Technician A says that if an engine was governed at a maximum full-load speed setting of 2100 rpm, then during operation, if the speed were allowed to increase to 2175 rpm, the engine would develop more horsepower. Technician B disagrees, saying that the horsepower would be less due to the action of the governor. Who is correct here?

22. Technician A says that if a truck running down a long steep incline is not slowed by use of an engine brake, retarder, or service brakes, engine overspeed can occur, causing damage to the engine. Technician B says that this cannot happen since the governor will automatically regulate the engine speed. Who is correct here?

23. Technician A says that to increase the truck road speed setting, the mechanical governor can be opened up and adjusted to raise the maximum no-load speed engine rpm setting. Technician B says that this should never be done. Who is correct here?

24. Supply the missing words in the following statement: When a load is applied to an engine, the speed will _____ and the governor will _____ the fuel setting.

25. Supply the missing words in the following statement: When a load is decreased on an engine, the speed will _____ and the governor will _____ the fuel setting.

26. Technician A says that the term *isochronous* means that the governor is capable of a zero-droop setting, which means that the no-load and full-load speeds are the same. Technician B says that no engine can operate at the same speed loaded and unloaded; since it has to work harder under load, it will run slower. Who is right?

27. The letters MPS mean
    a. magnetic pickup sensor
    b. mean position sensor
    c. motor point system
    d. motor position sensor

28. Technician A says that a rotating fiber gear tooth is used to interrupt the MPS field on a regular basis. Technician B disagrees, saying that the gear must be a metallic gear to operate. Who is correct?

29. Technician A says that the signal generated from the MPS is a DC signal, whereas technician B says that it is an AC signal. Who is correct?

30. Technician A says that the size of the air gap between the end of the MPS and the gear tooth determines the field strength and the proper operation. Technician B says that the width of the MPS gap has no bearing on its operation. Who is correct?

31. Technician A says that most sensors used on truck electronic governor systems receive a 5 V reference signal from the ECM to operate. Technician B says that they operate on the 12 V battery supply power source. Who understands the system best?

32. Technician A says that on the Detroit Diesel Series 60 engine, the ECM uses the sensor value from the throttle pedal to determine the start and amount of fuel injection. Technician B says that the TRS (timing reference sensor) is used by the ECM to establish the amount of fuel that should be injected into the combustion chamber. Who is correct?

33. Technician A says that the frequency of electrical sensor signals is determined by the engine speed and number of teeth on the pickup gear. Technician B says that the ECM determines the frequency of sensor signal output. Who is correct here?

34. Technician A says that the maximum no-load engine speed on a mechanical governor can be altered. Technician B says that the engine maximum no-load speed should never be tampered with. Who is right?

35. Technician A says that the amount of droop (rpm loss) on all engines equipped with mechanical governors can be offset by setting the maximum no-load rpm higher than the full-load speed desired. Technician B says that both the full-load and no-load speeds are one and the same since the governor will compensate for any speed loss as the engine load is applied. Who is right here?

36. A state of balance in a mechanical governor means that
    a. the force of the weights and springs is equal
    b. the operator is controlling the engine speed
    c. the correct gear in the transmission has been selected to keep the engine at a steady speed
    d. the turbocharger boost and fuel delivery pressures are equal

37. Technician A says that the term *high idle* means the same as *maximum no-load* engine speed. Technician B says that it means the same as *rated* engine speed. Who understands the meaning of this terminology?

38. Technician A says that on a mechanical or hydramechanical governor, the fuel rack will be pushed into an increased fuel delivery position with a drop in engine speed from high idle to rated rpm. Technician B says that there will be less fuel delivered under such an operating condition. Who knows governor theory here?

7 Safe Working Habits

OVERVIEW

This chapter deals with a critical topic: personal safety of yourself and others when working around diesel engines and machinery. Several considerations are discussed that should become second nature to every technician who performs repairs, service, or maintenance.

TOPICS

- Slinging an engine
- Chain-fall and web-type slings
- Do-not-operate warnings
- Self-test questions

SLINGING AN ENGINE

All diesel technicians and truck and heavy-duty equipment mechanics/technicians *must* be well versed in the safe and efficient methods required to safely lift and remove or install a variety of heavy-duty component parts from equipment. Failure to recognize and understand the severity of poorly slung or retained parts can result in serious personal injury and even death.

When it becomes necessary to remove an engine from a piece of equipment, whether it is in a truck, a bus, a marine craft—any industrial or stationary application—there are a number of common accessory items that must be disconnected and/or removed before attaching suitable lifting slings/shackles to the engine block. Under no circumstances should the engine mounts be loosened and removed prior to

ensuring that a sling(s) has been strategically and safely bolted into position. The type of lifting tackle that is used depends to some extent on the engine application and the access afforded to the service personnel. Many service facilities are equipped with an overhead crane that runs lengthwise up and down as well as across the shop. This is ideal in a large shop that services mobile equipment such as buses, trucks, and off-highway equipment (for example, logging trucks, mining trucks, front-end loaders, crawler tractors, bottom dumps, and road graders). Portable rock drills and air compressors can also have their diesel engines removed in this manner.

For marine pleasure craft, it is usually necessary to dock the vessel alongside a repair facility that employs a swing-out hoist to remove the engine. On much larger pleasure craft, workboats, tugboats, pusher tugs, and so forth, it is often necessary to unbolt or cut out the deck plates to gain access to the engine room, so that the engine can be removed if necessary. Removal is usually undertaken only if either the engine block or crankshaft is damaged. Normally, an in-frame type of engine overhaul can be performed where new cylinder kits and major accessory items are exchanged for rebuilt or new ones. If a large diesel marine engine must be removed, often the vessel is placed in dry dock. On very large deep-sea vessels, the engine room is generally designed with suitable overhead lifting facilities to allow removal of heavy engine components during a refit of the main engine.

When dealing with high-speed heavy-duty diesel engines, a variety of specialized jib cranes, load rotors, and heavy-duty self-locking positioning slings are available to facilitate the process of safely securing the engine before removal from its application. Many diesel

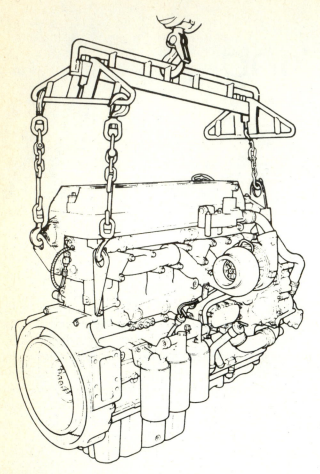

FIGURE 7–1 *Recommended sling arrangement for lifting a heavy-duty engine using chain falls and a spreader bar. (Courtesy of Detroit Diesel Corporation.)*

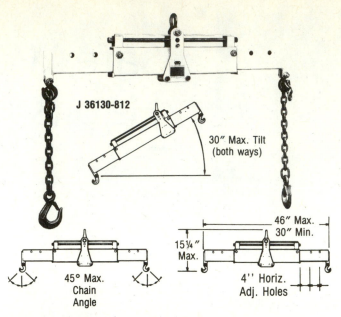

FIGURE 7–2 *Heavy-duty lifting tackle with adjustable spreader bar and tilting mechanism. (Courtesy of Kent-Moore Division, SPX Corporation.)*

engines leave the factory with a number of lifting eyes bolted in place on the engine to facilitate installation in and removal from its intended application. *Always* use these lifting points when they are readily available, since they ensure a safe and balanced lift. The diagrams in this chapter illustrate a number of the more commonly used portable lifting tackle.

Figure 7–1 illustrates how to safely lift a Detroit Diesel four-stroke-cycle Series 60 engine assembly from mobile equipment installations. Note that suitable spreader bars and strategically located slings are used to allow the engine to be removed in a balanced position. There is no danger of the engine dropping to one side or falling. The lifting tackle chosen must be rated for the intended load to be lifted. Generally WCB (Workers Compensation Board) inspectors visit shops regularly to ensure that all load rotors, chains, steel cables, lifting hooks, and soft slings are in safe working order and clearly marked as to their identified safe working limit.

Figure 7–2 illustrates an example of a commonly used load rotor. In this case, this load rotor is rated at 6000 lb (2722 kg) and it can be used with a floor jib crane or overhead hoist. This load rotor features a self-locking positioning screw with a 1 in. (25.4 mm) hex head. Angle adjustments up to 30° are possible. The lifting eye has a 1⅝ in. (41.3 mm) opening. The working length is adjustable in three positions from 30 in. (762 mm) to 46 in. (1168 mm). Two ⁵⁄₁₆ in. (8 mm) alloy chains, 2 ft (0.6 m) long with an eye hook, are included. Figure 7–3 illustrates a heavy-duty self-locking load rotor that is capable of handling either a 2000 or 4000 lb (907 or 1814 kg) load limit, with positioning slings that can be used with a crane or hoist. A self-locking worm-and-gear set in the sling's head permits rapid adjustment of the angle of the engine or component being handled. The engine can be tilted or leveled by merely turning the sling's ⅝ in. (16 mm) hex drive end with a common speed handle and socket. The gear ratio is generally about 34:1 for the lighter model and 82:1 for the heavier model; therefore, the technician can gently and easily alter the angle of the lift, which is often required when attempting to remove an engine from a heavy-duty truck application.

Figure 7–4 illustrates a typical heavy-duty shop jib crane that combines the capability of a 6000 lb (2722 kg) capacity floor crane, a 10,000 lb (4536 kg) capacity one-end lift, and a 4000 lb (1814 kg) capacity wheel dolly attachment all on the same frame. Shop cranes such as this have a low profile, yet they are able to lift

**Military Spec:
MIL-S-45944 (WE)**

TILTS LOAD
TO ANY ANGLE

FIGURE 7–3 *Heavy-duty self-locking load rotor positioning slings. (Courtesy of Kent-Moore Division, SPX Corporation.)*

as high as 130 in. (3302 mm). The telescoping legs allow the technician to adjust for stability with load changes. A wheel dolly attachment allows easy removal of the largest truck and tractor wheels with ease. Figure 7–5 illustrates a heavy-duty engine jib crane and engine stand that combined allow the technician to safely and easily remove or install this vee-configuration diesel engine from the COE (cab-over-engine) Class 8 truck in the background. In places where limited overhead space is a problem, a boom extension can be bolted onto the end of the jib crane as shown in Figure 7–6 to simpify the job (for example, servicing COE trucks). This 45° adjustment provides horizontal entrance of the boom into the work area.

Once an engine has been removed safely from its equipment, it should be mounted into an engine stand similar to the one shown in Figure 7–7. This type of engine stand allows rapid disassembly of any engine, because the engine can be easily rotated through 360° assisted by a 60:1 ratio self-braking worm gear system in the hand-operated rotation drive unit. In addition, a hand-operated hydraulic jack allows the technician to precisely tilt the engine to any suitable angle. This engine stand has a 36 in. (914 mm) centerline height and angled center-post design to permit fast and easy engine mounting with a low center of gravity for the utmost in safety and stability. Concealed casters and screw-down floor brakes allow the technician to safely and easily move around the shop floor yet quickly secure the unit in a stationary position. A wide variety of universal engine-to-stand adapter plates allows this model to be used with all of the popular OEM diesel engines.

As the technician removes diesel engine components, he or she can use a portable parts rack such as the one illustrated in Figure 7–8 (p. 210) to keep all parts with the engine and to ensure organization during the disassembly procedure. Use of the rack improves shop efficiency by decreasing engine overhaul time. Four shelves of expanded steel mesh with a total of approximately 60 sq ft (5.57 sq m) of storage space allow all engine components to be stacked safely and securely in one area. Another major advantage of this open-mesh type of parts rack is that dirty components can be steam cleaned or high-pressure washed without being removed from the racks. Large 6 in. (152 mm) diameter steel wheels permit the rack to be pushed easily around the shop facility.

CHAIN-FALL AND WEB-TYPE SLINGS

The two most common slings in use today for heavy equipment are the chain-fall type and web type. All chains and web slings are rated for a given safe working load, and these loads should never be exceeded! Figure 7–9 (p. 210) illustrates commonly used lifting chains and hooks, with safety catches on each hook. Cast into the hook is a safe working limit to guide usage.

The following three terms are generally applied to both chains and web-type slings:

1. *Ultimate tensile strength* (or ultimate strength, breaking strength) is the term used to indicate the minimum load at which brand-new chain (wire rope, web strapping, and so on) may fail. The ultimate tensile strength of a cable, webbing, or chain is equal to the load required to break the cable!

2. *Proof strength* (or proof test load, proof load) is the term used to ensure no defects in material or manufacture have occurred in a product. The manufacturer tests the sling to a predetermined load. In the case of a chain, the proof strength is typically 50% of the ultimate tensile strength.

3. *Safe working load* (or working load limit, safe working load limit) has two meanings:
   a. The maximum load (as warranted by the manufacturer or by a professional engineer), repeatedly applied, that the sling is capable of withstanding with complete safety throughout its normal service life; or
   b. When the manufacturer or professional engineer has not designated the safe working load, a value equal to 25% of the ultimate tensile strength of the sling as supplied by the manufacturer.

FIGURE 7–4 Repair shop portable jib crane. (Courtesy of Kent-Moore Division, SPX Corporation.)

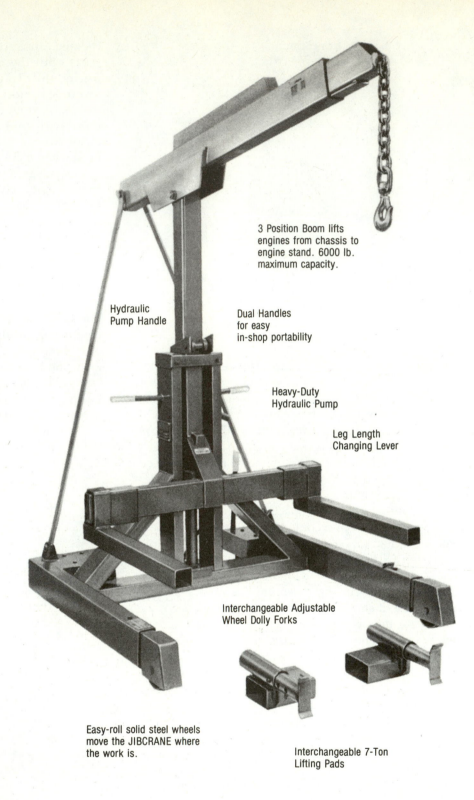

3 Position Boom lifts engines from chassis to engine stand. 6000 lb. maximum capacity.

Hydraulic Pump Handle

Dual Handles for easy in-shop portability

Heavy-Duty Hydraulic Pump

Leg Length Changing Lever

Interchangeable Adjustable Wheel Dolly Forks

Easy-roll solid steel wheels move the JIBCRANE where the work is.

Interchangeable 7-Ton Lifting Pads

FIGURE 7–5 Heavy-duty jib crane being securely connected to a Class 8 truck engine to remove the engine from its overhaul stand. (Courtesy of Kent-Moore Division, SPX Corporation.)

FIGURE 7–6 Heavy-duty jib crane equipped with a tilt mechanism to position a diesel engine into a truck application. (Courtesy of Kent-Moore Division, SPX Corporation.)

FIGURE 7–7 Commonly used mounting stand for overhaul or repair of heavy-duty diesel engines. (Courtesy of Kent-Moore Division, SPX Corporation.)

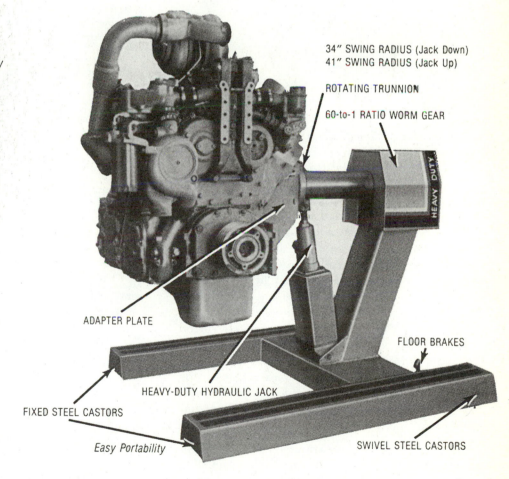

34" SWING RADIUS (Jack Down)
41" SWING RADIUS (Jack Up)

ROTATING TRUNNION

60-to-1 RATIO WORM GEAR

ADAPTER PLATE

FIXED STEEL CASTORS

Easy Portability

HEAVY-DUTY HYDRAULIC JACK

FLOOR BRAKES

SWIVEL STEEL CASTORS

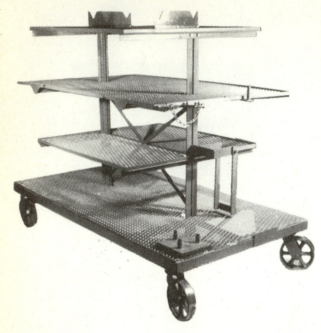

FIGURE 7–8 *Heavy-duty diesel engine parts dolly to securely and safely store removed engine components. (Courtesy of Kent-Moore Division, SPX Corporation.)*

Chain Grades and Connector Links

The information in Table 7–1 describes in detail the grade and suggested application of chain falls. Table 7–2 is a *guideline* for the safe working load for each grade of chain, which will vary depending on the chain-link size and the type of steel material used.

A variety of chain connector links are commonly used with chain falls (see Figure 7–10). In the absence of engine manufacturers' lifting brackets on the engine or on a component part or equipment, lifting brackets similar to those shown in Figure 7–1 can be used *only* after determining that they are safely rated for the intended load. When severe bending loads will be imposed on the lifting bracket, avoid using a 45° offset because this can overstress the bracket. It is better to use a straight pull on a straight bracket that can be retained by a suitably selected grade of bolt. The following information describes some of the more common chain links in use:

NOTE: In addition to the various chain links available, remember the heavy-duty adjustable chain sling (Figure 7–9). Each chain can be shortened or lengthened independently by inserting the link into the slot of the bracket assembly chain link by chain link (short hooking).

- Thimbles should be used when attaching hooks, chains, clevises, or similar devices to the cable.

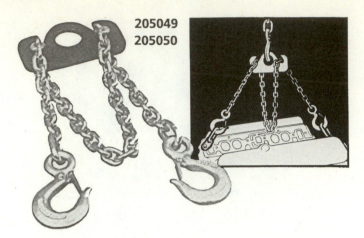

205049
205050

FIGURE 7–9 *Heavy-duty adjustable chain slings. (Courtesy of Kent-Moore Division, SPX Corporation.)*

TABLE 7–1 *Grades of Industrial Chain Sizes and Recommended Applications*

Grade	Application
Grade 80 or Alloy Chain Identified by A, 8, 80, or 800 on links	Overhead lifting, slinging, load binding Flail chains, choker chains, skidder chains *Use no other chain for overhead lifting.*
Grade 70 or Transport Chain Identified by 7, 70, or 700 on links	Trucking railways, logging, construction, farming, towing, load binding, deck lashing, heavy-duty tie-down applications, security chains
Grade 50 or High Test Chain Identified by 4 or 5 on links	Railway tie-down chains, load bindings, cargo lashings, logging and farm operations, towing and moving jobs, in oil fields, industry and for trucking
Grade 30—Short Link or BBB Identified by 3B or BBB	Tow chains, pocket wheels, railway brake chains, sugar cane slings, bundling chains
Grade 30—Regular Line or Proof Coil Identified by 3 or PC on links	Boom chains, barrier chains, decoration, pipeline hanging, tailgate guardrail, tow chains
Loading-Decking Chain Identified with DL or 3L on links	Light-duty tie-down applications.

TABLE 7–2 Chain Grade, Trade Size, and Safe Working Load Limits

Grade	Trade size		Working load limit	
	Millimeters	Inch	Kilograms	Pounds
80	7	¼	1 660	3,650
	10	⅜	2 980	6,550
	13	½	5 180	11,400
	16	⅝	8 590	18,900
	20	¾	11 890	26,150
	22	⅞	15 700	34,550
70	7	¼	1 410	3,100
	8	5⁄16	2 020	4,450
	10	⅜	2 820	6,200
	11	7⁄16	3 960	8,750
	13	½	4 890	10,750
50	7	¼	1 330	2,200
	8	5⁄16	1 930	3,200
	10	⅜	2 430	4,000
	11	7⁄16	2 858	6,300
	13	½	4 670	7,700
BBB	7	¼	601	1,325
	8	5⁄16	884	1,950
	10	⅜	1 247	2,750
	13	½	2 154	4,750
	16	⅝	3 288	7,250
DL	7	¼	612	1,350
	8	5⁄16	862	1,960
	10	⅜	1 202	2,650
	13	½	2 086	4,600
PC	7	¼	567	1,250
	8	5⁄16	850	1,875
	10	⅜	1 190	2,625
	13	½	2 041	4,500
	16	⅝	3 084	6,800
	20	¾	4 309	9,500

- If saddle and U-bolt *cable clamps* are utilized as shown in Figure 7–11, the U-bolt must bear against the dead or free end.
- At least two saddle and U-bolt clamps are to be used for cable sizes up to and including 11 mm (7⁄16 in.).
- At least three saddle and U-bolt clamps must be used on 13 mm (½ in.) cable.
- If a winch-type tightening device is used,
  a. the winch must be specifically designed for use with wire cable, as illustrated in Figure 7–12.
  b. the wire rope must be protected against cutting and be anchored securely to the drum.

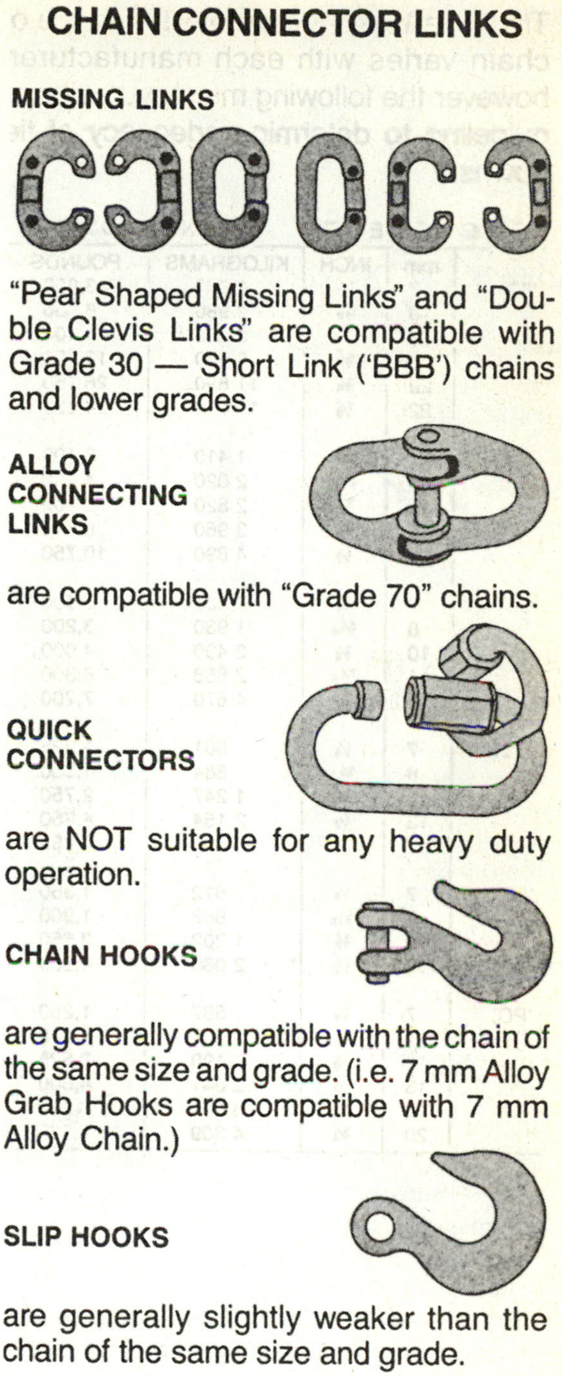

CHAIN CONNECTOR LINKS

MISSING LINKS

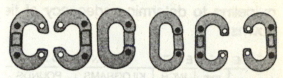

"Pear Shaped Missing Links" and "Double Clevis Links" are compatible with Grade 30 — Short Link ('BBB') chains and lower grades.

ALLOY CONNECTING LINKS

are compatible with "Grade 70" chains.

QUICK CONNECTORS

are NOT suitable for any heavy duty operation.

CHAIN HOOKS

are generally compatible with the chain of the same size and grade. (i.e. 7 mm Alloy Grab Hooks are compatible with 7 mm Alloy Chain.)

SLIP HOOKS

are generally slightly weaker than the chain of the same size and grade.

FIGURE 7–10 Chain connector links.

Nylon Webbing Slings

Nylon webbing straps/slings must be permanently marked by the manufacturer with the safe working load limit. Since the strength of the nylon webbing depends not only on its external dimensions but also on its internal construction, the manufacturer's rating is the only safe method of determining its capacity. As a general

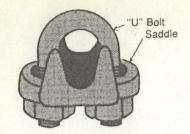

FIGURE 7–11   Lifting cable U-bolt saddle.

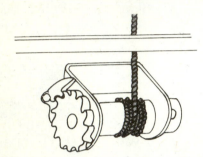

FIGURE 7–12   Rope and/or wire cable ratcheting and tightening mechanism.

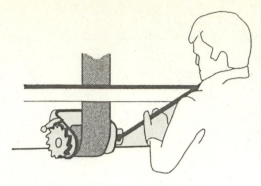

FIGURE 7–13   Ratcheting and tightening mechanism for nylon webbing sling.

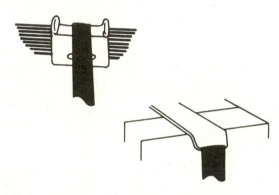

FIGURE 7–14   Nylon webbing sling protective devices to prevent chafing or tearing at sharp corners of the secured load.

guideline, you can assume a load rating of 530 kg (1168 lb) per 1 cm (0.400 in.) of width. Nylon webbing straps are acceptable for lifting and securing loads when winch-tightening devices mounted in a fixed position are utilized, or on an adjustable installation where the winches may be mounted on a slide bar or track. Of course, many nylon webbing slings are manufactured with a loop on both ends to facilitate hooking onto an engine or component part, or to allow threading one end through the opposite loop to tighten up on a lifting area. Figure 7–13 illustrates that a nylon webbing sling can be drawn tight through the use of a winch and bar arrangement. Care must be exercised to ensure that the webbing is protected from abrasive surfaces or sharp edges such as the two examples shown in Figure 7–14.

Inspection for Wear

Regardless of the type of lifting sling used, the diesel technician should always ensure prior to use that there is no physical damage that could lead to failure during use. Chains, load binders attachments, and anchor points *must* be maintained in good condition. The following conditions would render any lifting sling unfit for further use:

- Chain containing cracked welds or links
- Chain containing bent, twisted, stretched, or collapsed links
- Chain links weakened by gouges, nicks, or severe pitting (rust)

- Chains repaired incorrectly
- Links obviously worn or showing other visible evidence of loss of strength
- Knots in any portion of the chain, wire rope, or webbing
- spread or disturbed grab hooks
- Cuts, nicks, or splits in nylon webbing
- Wire cable with missing strands or wraps
- An anchor point that is weakened or shows loss of strength due to cracks, breaks, or distortion

DO-NOT-OPERATE WARNINGS

When working on or around diesel engines and/or heavy equipment, extreme care must *always* be exercised to prevent serious injury to yourself or others. Throughout this book, note the safety practices that *must* be followed.

One of the most common ways to prevent operators or service technicians from attempting to start an engine or move a piece of equipment is to clearly indicate that the engine, vehicle, or equipment is *out of service.* Figure 7–15 illustrates a typical *do-not-operate*

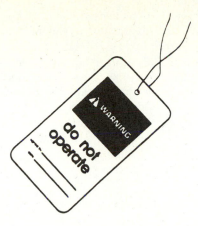

FIGURE 7–15 Typical do-not-operate safety tag that should be placed on engines and equipment during service and repair. (Courtesy of Caterpillar Inc.)

warning tag that can be placed on or wired to the ignition key switch (or starter button) or controls area. In addition, a larger tag with a white background and prominent red letters can be attached securely to the machine that is under repair or service.

NOTE: Do-not-operate tags are readily available from major tool suppliers as well as from equipment and engine OEMs.

An additional safety method is to disconnect the starter motor batteries. On compressed air starters, bleed off the air supply from the reservoir tanks. When servicing or repairing electric power generation (gen-set) equipment, make sure that the unit is *off-line* (disconnected from the utility and/or other generator power) and either locked out or tagged *do not operate*. Follow these safety procedures; failure to do so could result in injury or death.

- Make sure the generator engine is stopped.
- Make sure all batteries are disconnected.
- Make sure all capacitors are discharged.
- Make sure residual voltage in the gen-test rotor, stator, and generator is discharged.

When power generation equipment must be in operation to make tests and/or adjustments, remember that high voltage and current are present. Improper test equipment may fail and present the danger of a high-voltage shock. Make sure the testing equipment is designed for, and correctly operated for, high-voltage conditions and the tests being conducted.

SPECIAL NOTE: When operating turbocharged engines during service or repair when the air inlet ducting may be disconnected, *always* install a safety shield (see Figure 20–33).

SELF-TEST QUESTIONS

1. True or False: Engine or equipment retaining bolts or mounts should be loosened prior to supporting the engine on a secure sling.

2. True or False: Complete engine and marine gear replacement in a vessel may require that the deck plates be removed or be cut open to gain access to the engine room area.

3. True or False: Many manufacturers install lifting brackets/eyes on their engines or equipment to facilitate ease of removal.

4. True or False: When using lifting equipment to support or remove an engine from any installation, spreader bars should always be used to prevent shifting of the load.

5. True or False: All lifting tackle should be checked to determine that it is capable of supporting the intended load. This can usually be determined by looking for a load decal or painted safe load number on the equipment.

6. True or False: All chain- and web-type slings are rated for a specific load-carrying capability.

7. The term *ultimate tensile strength* rating for a sling means
   a. the safe working load for that sling assembly
   b. the minimum load at which a new sling may fail
   c. you should never exceed 50% of the stated load rating
   d. the load carrying capability is three times the rating

8. True or False: The term *proof strength* is used to indicate that the manufacturer has tested the sling to a predetermined load.

9. True or False: The proof strength of a chain is typically 50% of the ultimate tensile strength.

10. True or False: The term *safe working load* means the maximum load, as warranted by the manufacturer, that a sling will repeatedly withstand.

11. True or False: Grades of chain can be identified by an alphabetical letter or number on the links.

12. Refer to Table 7–2 and explain the safe working load limit for each of the following chain assemblies:
    a. Grade DL
    b. Grade BBB
    c. Grade 80
    d. Grade 50

13. Technician A says that when using a chain assembly for an overhead lifting or slinging situation, he would select an assembly rated Grade 30 or BBB. Technician B disagrees and says that she would choose a Grade 80 chain link assembly. Who is correct?

14. Refer to Table 7–2 and determine the working load limit for the following chain link assemblies:
    a. Grade 80, 13 mm (½ in.) link
    b. Grade 70, 13 mm (½ in.) link
    c. Grade DL, 13 mm (½ in.) link
    d. Grade PC, 13 mm (½ in.) link

15. Technician A says that "quick connectors" are acceptable to use when performing any heavy-duty lifting operation with a chain fall. Technician B disagrees and says that quick connectors are *not* suitable for any heavy-duty operation. Who has safe working habits?

16. An alloy connecting chain link is suitable for use with Grade 80 chain according to technician A. Technician B disagrees, saying that these links are compatible only with a Grade 70 chain link assembly. Which technician is correct?

17. Technician A says that chain hooks are generally compatible with the chain of the same size and grade. Technician B says that hooks should always be rated at least twice the strength of the chain fall assembly. Who is correct here?

18. Technician A says that slip hooks are generally slightly weaker than the chain of the same size and grade. Technician B says that the slip hook is normally stronger, not weaker. Which technician is correct?

19. True or False: The rated safe working load of webbing slings can be found stitched to a label on the sling.

20. True or False: If a web-type sling is frayed at the edges, it is still safe to use.

Engine Disassembly

OVERVIEW

In this chapter we discuss general engine overhaul procedures that can be applied to the many diesel engines used in thousands of applications worldwide. The purpose of the chapter is not to describe details relative to specific engine makes or models, but rather to consider the most appropriate and safest method to employ for any engine overhaul process. In this process, it is extremely important to avoid removing any damaging marks that may indicate one or more reasons for failure. Also, care must be exercised so that no additional damage to the components is introduced.

TOPICS

- Overhaul procedures
- Engine cleaning procedures
- Safe work habits when cleaning
- The in-frame overhaul
- Major engine overhaul
- Fundamentals of failure analysis
- Self-test questions

OVERHAUL PROCEDURES

The physical size and application/installation of a diesel engine will determine the best process to employ during repair. Often it is not possible to completely remove the engine from its application/installation because of its size, for example, the very large slow-speed engines used in large marine or industrial applications. These engines are overhauled in place by removal of component parts as necessary. In addition, in some pleasure craft, workboat marine applications, or mobile equipment such as heavy duty trucks, maintenance management personnel may choose to complete an *in-frame overhaul* rather than a major overhaul that requires complete removal of the engine from its application. If the engine assembly can be removed from its application, a more thorough cleaning, inspection, and repair can be performed.

In many large fleets, it is customary to stock one or more overhauled engines, so that when required, an engine can be removed from a piece of equipment and quickly replaced with a like model. In this way, equipment downtime is kept to a minimum, and the efficiency of the equipment is maintained. This practice is common in long-distance on-highway trucks and in mobile mining equipment applications. In these cases the engine is usually mounted on a subframe assembly that facilitates quick and easy removal. The removed engine can then be systematically disassembled and overhauled to an as-new condition.

ENGINE CLEANING PROCEDURES

All states and provinces currently have in place regulations about the disposal of hazardous chemicals. The concerned diesel technician today should be familiar with the local laws concerning the use and disposal of any cleaning agent that is commonly used in maintaining diesel-powered equipment, regardless of the application. Failure to follow the regulations can result in serious environmental damage as well as danger to the user. Substantial monetary fines are being levied on a daily basis against many companies and individuals who fail to follow responsible disposal practices.

Proper cleaning of assemblies and individual parts is essential when servicing and rebuilding engine and accessory drive components such as manual gearshift, automatic and powershift transmissions, marine gears, power pumps, generator sets, and so forth. Proper cleaning is especially critical for parts with operating components that cannot be completely disassembled. Also, partly disassembled components, such as tapered roller bearing cones and cups and planetary gear pinions that are often left mounted in a housing or on a shaft, require special procedures for thorough cleaning.

When it becomes necessary to perform an overhaul or repair of an engine or major drive component, the main objective in removing and disassembling any component is to replace or repair damaged and worn parts. Therefore, all parts must be cleaned thoroughly before they are inspected to determine their suitability for reuse. Any varnish, sludge, dirt, and other foreign material must be removed from usable parts before a component is reassembled.

The skilled diesel technician must be aware that to prevent damage to certain components, the correct cleaning method and chemicals must be used. Adopting the wrong cleaning method or agent can be as harmful as no cleaning at all. Bearing races and rollers, polished shafts, or gear teeth exposed to moisture, acids, or caustic solutions during the cleaning process can quickly water spot, stain, rust, or corrode. Returning such parts to the engine can cause rapid wear and premature failure. The methods discussed herein are general in nature and should not be considered an all encompassing guide for cleaning and degreasing components. Specific cleaning methods and cleaning agents required for a particular component or assembly are usually available from commercial chemical cleaning companies; information is also available in the service literature of engine manufacturers.

SAFE WORK HABITS WHEN CLEANING

Some alkalis, detergents, and solvents can irritate the skin or be harmful to the eyes. Adequate ventilation is a must when working around and with cleaning chemicals. When working with potentially harmful substances, carefully read and heed the cautions and warnings on the product labels. *Always* wear safety equipment such as safety glasses, a face shield, gloves, and apron. Exercise extreme care when spraying to prevent injury to other personnel and to avoid an accident! Components such as cylinder liners, oil cooler cores, and radiators usually require special treatment when cleaned.

Steam Cleaning

Steam cleaning should be done only to remove heavy deposits of dirt and grease from exterior surfaces of the engine block and major drive components. Heavy grease deposits should first be scraped and brushed away. Internal engine components should not be steam cleaned, because the process may remove the protective oil film and cause the parts to water spot and rust. During an in-frame overhaul, if no other cleaning agent is readily available, steam cleaning may be done but cautiously, and all parts should be thoroughly flushed, blown-dry with compressed air, and quickly relubricated to prevent rusting.

Pressurized Oil Sprays

Oil-based mineral solvents and fuel oils under pressure can be used to flush varnish, sludge, and dirt from cylinder block internal passages and surfaces of component part housings. Drain holes or other openings through which these solvents can be flushed must be adequate to carry away dirt and flushing oils. All flushing oils must be drained completely from the components to prevent contamination from lubricants added to the reassembled components.

Heated Solvents

Many smaller engine and drive assembly components can be thoroughly and safely cleaned by flushing, soaking, or mechanically agitating them in heated petroleum solvents. Oils and solvents used for this purpose, however, must be capable of being heated to the required temperature without producing safety or health hazards from volatile or harmful vapors. Naptha, white gas, varnish remover, and similar solvents obviously should not be heated under any circumstances.

Small parts such as bearings and gears can be suspended on metal wires, or placed in wire baskets, and submerged in the heated solvent tank to soak off grease, varnish, and sludge. Mechanical agitation of the solvent or parts will increase the effectiveness of the cleaning solvents. Extremely tough scale and varnish can be brushed loose. Exercise care to keep loose brush bristles out of assembled parts.

After cleaning all parts, machined and polished surfaces of components, bores, housings, and their internal parts should be protected from rust and corrosion with a coating of oil or light grease. Small parts can be kept in shallow pans and covered with oil until needed. Larger parts should be coated with grease or oil and wrapped in polyethelene film or oil-proof paper.

Hot Tank Cleaning

Hot tank cleaning is a method commonly used for all ordinary cast iron or steel engine parts, and it is usually required when heavy scale buildup is evident within the engine block coolant passages. However, many companies that rebuild engines now employ glass or walnut beads to clean off engine blocks. The engine block is placed in an enclosure with a rotating table. The doors of the enclosure are then securely closed and the table is rotated with the engine bolted securely in place. The engine block or parts are bombarded by the beading agent to effectively clean the part without having to use chemicals.

Generally, a hot tank can be filled with a variety of commercially available cleaning chemicals; selection and strength are determined by the type of metal to be cleaned. One of the most commonly used cleaning agents for both cast iron and steel parts consists of a commercial heavy-duty alkaline solvent with a tank big enough to accept the largest engine block or component part to be cleaned. To increase the effectiveness of the cleaning process, the engine block can be lowered onto a steel grade below the level of the alkaline; then the solvent is heated to approximately 160°F (71°C) and a mechanically driven device moves the grate backward and forward to create an agitating action. In some cases, air can also be injected into the solution.

The time required to clean a component part in the alkaline solvent hot tank is determined by the degree of scale and so forth that has to be removed and the type of chemical being used. It can be as short as 20 minutes or as long as an overnight soak. For example, cylinder blocks and cylinder heads that are heavily scaled may require extra cleaning by agitating the parts in a bath of inhibited commercial pickling acid and leaving them in the acid until the bubbling action stops, which is usually between 20 and 30 minutes.

CAUTION: When using commercial pickling acid, take care to prevent electrolysis between dissimilar metals such as aluminum, copper, and other nonferrous metals with the cast iron or steel engine block or head(s). These metals should be removed from the parts before they are treated with acid. Two examples are aluminum square head plugs and the injector copper tubes that are used within the cylinder head area.

After the bubbling action stops, lift the parts, allow them to drain, then reimmerse them for another 10 minutes. Repeat as necessary to completely remove all scale from the block or head coolant passages. Rinse all parts thoroughly in clean, hot water or with steam. Neutralize any remaining acid by immersing the parts in an alkali bath. Finally, rinse the parts in clean, hot water or with steam; dry the parts with compressed air; and oil all machined surfaces to prevent rusting.

Cold Tank Solvent Cleaning

Cold tank solvent cleaning can be used for most of the steel and aluminum parts of the engine. Make sure that the strength of the chemical solvent will not attack tin-coated parts such as those found on some pistons and/or liners. Cold tank cleaning is also good for removing the rustproofing compound from service replacement parts. In addition to solvents, diesel fuel oil can also be used for cleaning purposes, particularly when working with injector components. To clean a part using the cold tank method, follow these three steps:

1. Immerse and agitate the part in a suitable tank.
2. Use a soft-bristle brush to go over and through oil and water passages so that all deposits are removed.
3. When parts are thoroughly clean, rinse them in clean fuel oil and allow them to air dry, or carefully use compressed air for this purpose.

Cleaning Aluminum Parts

Aluminum parts can be cleaned safely in diesel fuel or in a detergent solution, but *never* one containing an *alkali!* Detergents can be used at room temperature, in a heated tank with mechanical agitation, or in a steam cleaner. To detergent-clean aluminum parts follow these five steps:

1. Prepare a solution of heavy-duty detergent in a hot tank, cold tank, or a steam cleaner.
2. Agitate the parts in the detergent or steam clean with the detergent–water solution until all grease and dirt are removed.
3. Rinse the parts thoroughly in a tank of hot water, with a high-pressure hot water rinse, or with steam.
4. Dry all parts with compressed air.
5. If further cleaning is required, perform each of the following steps:
   a. Brush on a commercial, chlorinated solvent suitable for aluminum and leave it on the part for several hours.
   b. Steam clean the part with a solution of detergent and water.
   c. Rinse the part in clean water and dry with compressed air.

THE IN-FRAME OVERHAUL

An in-frame overhaul does not involve removal of the engine block from the frame, but it does include removal of the cylinder head(s) and oil pan to access the cylinder components. Accessory components such as the turbocharger, gear-driven blower, and other items can also be removed and overhauled or replaced with new items. However, the crankshaft and all related parts remain in place, although the oil pump and oil cooler can be removed and serviced. The main disadvantage of performing an in-frame overhaul is that the engine block cannot be cleaned or descaled, since there is no way of using flushing or hot tanking that can compare with hot tank cleaning of a disassembled engine. Dirt and other foreign materials that are easily removed from the passages of the block by agitation in a hot tank must be removed more painstakingly with steam and compressed air, or high-pressure wash cleaning, when an in-frame overhaul is performed. Generally during an in-frame overhaul, the crankshaft main and thrust bearings can be replaced by rolling them out and in.

When performing an in-frame overhaul, make sure that the engine block is cleaned as thoroughly as possible. To minimize dirt and debris falling into internal areas of the engine block, tool suppliers offer various plastic plugs. For example, disposable block plugs can be inserted into the push-tube cavities of the block deck of a Cummins 14L engine to prevent debris from falling into the block. Plastic metal chip catchers can be placed in the lower packing area of the cylinder block liner to prevent metallic chips from being dispersed throughout the lower crankshaft area. A small hand-held super-vacuum unit that operates on shop air and comes with a large reusable bag can be employed to remove metal chips instead of blowing them around inside the engine. For best results with in-frame overhauls, most engine manufacturers suggest that you follow the steps outlined next. The procedures are described briefly since each one can be found in detail in other chapters of this book as well as in the service/shop manuals of engine manufacturers.

Dissassembly

1. Before removing any engine components, always use steam cleaning or high-pressure wash cleaning on the exterior of the engine. Wear suitable safety clothing and eye and face protection. Take care that any engine openings (intake, exhaust, breather, coolant) have been securely closed or taped off to prevent dirt from entering the engine. *Caution:* During cleaning, the engine should not be running. *Never* direct steam pressure or high-pressure hot water against an aluminum-type fuel injection pump housing, especially when the engine is running, because the heat can cause the housing to distort, resulting in scoring or seizure of the injection pump steel plunger within the barrel/bushing internally. Always dry the exterior of the engine with compressed air.

2. Remove the turbocharger and/or gear-driven blower as well as the one-piece or multiple cylinder heads. Remove the engine oil pan. Remove all cylinder components, and cover the exposed bearing surfaces of the crankshaft with masking tape or rags taped around each journal. Hone the block bores if necessary (refer to Chapter 16 for details).

3. Remove the oil cooler assembly and lube oil filters in preparation for steam cleaning the inside of the block. Note that on two-stroke-cycle Detroit Diesel engines you can remove the hand-hole inspection covers along the side of the block as well as the air box drain tubes.

4. Steam clean all exposed lube system passages in the block. On two-stroke DDC engines, clean the air box as well as the camshaft and balance shaft pockets (vee engines and inline models). Clean the cylinder bores and the various inlet and outlet openings in the block and crankcase.

5. Quickly follow up the steam cleaning procedure by drying all components of the engine with compressed air; then remove the masking tape from the crankshaft throws and clean with compressed air. You can also use stiff-bristle brushes to push through the crankshaft oil holes to ensure that all debris has been removed. If you can gain access to the crankshaft oil passage *Allen-head screws* in the crank throws, remove these and use the same brushes to clean all oil passages; then blow them dry with compressed air. Be *sure* to replace all oil passage screws back into position after the cleaning operation and torque them to specifications.

6. Wash and blow-dry the oil cooler housing and the lube oil filter spin-on adapter. Always replace the filter element(s) and clean the oil pan and oil lines by washing and blow-drying. A portable engine preluber can be used to thoroughly flush dirt and steam cleaning solution out of all oil passages.

Assembly

1. Lubricate all components thoroughly and reassemble the engine after inspecting all components as described in various chapters in this textbook. Torque all nuts and bolts as indicated in Figure 8–1.

2. After reassembly, follow the instructions contained in Chapter 21 for starting new or newly overhauled engines. Prelube the engine main oil gallery by attaching a hydraulic hose assembly from a shop air-driven or electric-motor-driven preluber

Standard Torque For Metric Fasteners

NOTE: Take care to avoid mixing metric and inch dimensioned fasteners. Mismatched or incorrect fasteners can result in vehicle damage or malfunction, or possible injury. Exceptions to these torques are given in the Service Manual where needed.

NOTE: Prior to Installation of any hardware, be sure components are in near new condition. Bolt and threads must not be worn or damaged. Hardware must be free of rust and corrosion. Clean hardware with a non-corrosive cleaner and apply engine oil to threads and bearing face. If thread lock or other compounds are to be applied, do not apply engine oil.

METRIC NUTS AND BOLTS		
Thread Size Metric	Standard Torque	
	N·m	lb ft
M6	12 ± 3	9 ± 2
M8	28 ± 7	20 ± 5
M10	55 ± 10	40 ± 7
M12	100 ± 20	75 ± 15
M14	160 ± 30	120 ± 22
M16	240 ± 40	175 ± 30
M20	460 ± 60	340 ± 45
M24	800 ± 100	600 ± 75
M30	1600 ± 200	1200 ± 150
M36	2700 ± 300	2000 ± 225

METRIC TAPERLOCK STUDS		
Thread Size Metric	Standard Torque	
	N·m	lb ft
M6	8 ± 3	6 ± 2
M8	17 ± 5	13 ± 4
M10	35 ± 5	26 ± 4
M12	65 ± 10	48 ± 7
M16	110 ± 20	80 ± 15
M20	170 ± 30	125 ± 22
M24	400 ± 60	300 ± 45
M30	650 ± 80	480 ± 60
M36	870 ± 100	640 ± 75

Standard Torque For Inch Fasteners

Exceptions to these torques are given in the Service Manual where needed.

INCH NUTS AND BOLTS		
Thread Size Inch	Standard Torque	
	N·m	lb ft
1/4	12 ± 3	9 ± 2
5/16	25 ± 6	18 ± 4.5
3/8	47 ± 9	35 ± 7
7/16	70 ± 15	50 ± 11
1/2	105 ± 20	75 ± 15
9/16	160 ± 30	120 ± 20
5/8	215 ± 40	160 ± 30
3/4	370 ± 50	275 ± 35
7/8	620 ± 80	460 ± 60
1	900 ± 100	660 ± 75
1 1/8	1300 ± 150	950 ± 100
1 1/4	1800 ± 200	1325 ± 150
1 3/8	2400 ± 300	1800 ± 225
1 1/2	3100 ± 350	2300 ± 250

INCH TAPERLOCK STUDS		
Thread Size Inch	Standard Torque	
	N·m	lb ft
1/4	8 ± 3	6 ± 2
5/16	17 ± 5	13 ± 4
3/8	35 ± 5	26 ± 4
7/16	45 ± 10	33 ± 7
1/2	65 ± 10	48 ± 7
5/8	110 ± 20	80 ± 15
3/4	170 ± 30	125 ± 22
7/8	260 ± 40	190 ± 30
1	400 ± 60	300 ± 45
1 1/8	500 ± 70	370 ± 50
1 1/4	650 ± 80	480 ± 60
1 3/8	750 ± 90	550 ± 65
1 1/2	870 ± 100	640 ± 75

FIGURE 8–1 *Standard nut-, bolt-, and stud-tightening torque values for various thread sizes in inch and metric units. (Courtesy of Caterpillar Inc.)*

(see Figure 18–42). This ensures that all components will not run dry on initial engine start-up and reduces the time required for the lube oil pump to fill the various filters and oil passages. Fill the crankcase to the proper level with the recommended grade of lube oil. It is advisable to leave the rocker cover(s) off so you can liberally pour fresh engine oil over the rocker arm assemblies and camshaft.

3. Upon initial engine start-up, don't race the engine (let it idle or run at a fast idle speed). Leave the turbocharger oil supply line loose to check for oil flow, and tighten it up as soon as you see signs of oil flow. Look for oil under pressure flowing from the rocker arm shaft assemblies, and check the oil pressure gauge for signs of sufficient oil pressure.

4. Check the manufacturer's recommendations in regard to when the oil and filters should be changed after overhaul.

MAJOR ENGINE OVERHAUL

Major engine overhaul involves a much more complete engine repair procedure than does an in-frame overhaul. The major overhaul involves the removal of the engine from its equipment, cleaning, complete engine and component disassembly, hot tank cleaning of the engine and some ferrous metal components, close inspection of all major parts leading to possible remachining of cylinder heads and the cylinder block flat surfaces, cylinder block boring (honing), alignment boring of the crankshaft main bearing bores, and regrinding of the crankshaft journals and thrust bearing surfaces.

Figure 7–7 in Chapter 7 illustrates a heavy-duty high-speed diesel engine mounted in an engine overhaul stand that allows the engine to be rotated through 360° to facilitate quick and easy removal of all engine components. The disassembly procedure varies slightly in specific makes and applications of engines based on design variations such as inline versus vee-model engines. Variations also occur based on the optional accessory items used with a given engine application, as well as the type of fuel injection system used and whether the engine is naturally aspirated, turbocharged, turbocharged/aftercooled, or gear-driven blower-equipped, such as on a two-stroke-cycle DDC model.

Regardless of the make and model of engine to be disassembled, always approach the teardown procedure carefully, keeping in mind that you may be reusing all or many of the removed parts. In a teardown procedure that involves an engine failure, particularly one that will be subject to a warranty claim, extreme care must be exercised during disassembly to avoid inflicting damage that was not a part of the original cause of failure. Before removing parts, match-mark all components to their respective location in the engine so that if they are reused, they can be reinstalled in the same position from which they were removed. Use a metal marker, or if the part is an external casting, carefully use a sharp center punch to identify mating surfaces.

All parts removed should be tagged and/or identified in some way, so that on closer analysis wear marks and failure causes can be logically traced. Typical parts to match-mark include cylinder liner flanges to the engine block counterbore and pistons that can be marked in reference to their respective cylinder and position, front or rear, if they do not have a cast or stamped number on the crown. Con-rods are generally marked with a cylinder number on the rod and cap halves to facilitate correct installation. However, con-rod and main bearings should be taped together with masking tape to keep them as a one-piece assembly formed into a circle. Use a felt-tip pen to write the journal number on the outside of the tape. Camshaft roller followers and intake and exhaust valves should also be match-marked (metal marker on the valve head) to their respective position in the cylinder head assembly.

The following step-by-step procedure is general enough for the disassembly of any high-speed diesel engine. Obviously, specific differences will exist between two-stroke-cycle and four-stroke-cycle engines; nevertheless, for purposes of general engine disassembly, the sequence presented is typical. With both engine oil and coolant drained, follow these steps to remove the engine components:

1. Remove the fan assembly on a radiator-type cooling system.
2. Remove accessory drive items such as the alternator, starter motor, air compressor, air-conditioning pump, power steering pump, and fuel injection pump if its drive gear does not require access through the removal of the engine front timing cover.
3. Remove the turbocharger(s).
4. Remove the exhaust manifold(s).
5. Remove the water pump.
6. Remove the oil pan.
7. Remove the lube oil pump.
8. Remove the flywheel.
9. DDC two-stroke-cycle engines: Remove the blower driveshaft cover and snap-ring; pull out the blower driveshaft.
10. DDC: Remove the blower drive gear assembly at the flywheel housing after removing the blower-to-drive-gear oil supply line.

11. DDC: Remove the governor cover and disconnect the fuel rod(s); loosen the hose clamp(s) for the fuel rod hose.

12. DDC: Remove the fuel pump hoses.

13. DDC: Remove the blower hold-down bolts. Place lifting eyes into the blower housing and lift it clear from the engine.

14. Remove the flywheel housing.

15. Remove the crankshaft pulley and vibration damper.

16. Remove the engine front cover or timing cover.

17. Remove the rocker covers.

18. Remove the intake manifold(s) and JWAC (jacket water aftercooler) if used.

19. Remove the rocker arms and push rods and the overhead camshaft if used.

20. Remove the unit injectors or nozzles from their bores.

21. Remove the cylinder head hold-down bolts and sling the head for safe removal.

22. Remove the con-rod bolts and cap one at a time.

23. Remove the piston oil spray nozzles by loosening the retaining bolts that are along the side of the engine block or accessible from the underside of the block.

24. Remove the piston and con-rod assemblies or the cylinder pack as a unit.

25. If an idler gear is used in the gear train, remove it.

26. If the engine camshaft is an in-block design, remove it along with its gear.

27. Loosen and remove the crankshaft main bearing cap bolts and/or stabilizers. Note that some engines also employ side bolts that are screwed into the main bearing caps. These bolts are accessible from the side of the engine block.

28. Remove the main bearing caps. If these are tight, you can either tap them with a rubber mallet or, in some cases, if tapped bolt holes are used, employ two slide hammers to pull the caps free.

29. Remove the crankshaft thrust washers if they are separate from the main bearing caps.

30. Carefully sling the crankshaft and lift it clear of the block.

31. On two- or three-piece blocks such as those used by Detroit Diesel on its two-stroke-cycle 12V-92, 16V-71, 16V-92, 12-16, and 20V-

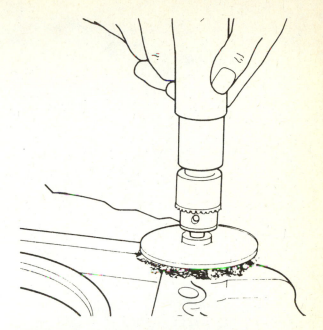

FIGURE 8–2 *Using a high-speed drill and Scotch-Brite disc to safely and effectively remove gasket eliminator material from a machined jointing surface. (Courtesy of Detroit Diesel Corporation.)*

149 series engines, place the assembled engine blocks on their ends and sling the blocks securely. Then remove all of the retaining bolts so that the individual blocks can be split apart for service if necessary by using a suitable overhead shop crane.

32. Remove all plugs from the various passages in the coolant, fuel, and lube oil systems so that the engine block(s) and cylinder heads can be cleaned successfully in a hot tank.

Removing Gasket Eliminator

Many new heavy-duty high-speed, high-horsepower diesel engines have numerous aluminum components. Some of these surfaces are considered *dimensionally critical*, which means that if they are to be cleaned, for example, of old gasket material, conventional scraping methods can seriously nick or score the mating surfaces. In cases where gasket eliminator or RTV (room temperature vulcanizing) was used to form a seal (gasket), remove this old material from both mating surfaces prior to reassembly, since it will form a very thin film. Avoid using gasket scrapers or emery cloth to do this.

The recommended procedure for removing gasket eliminator is to use an electric- or air-powered hand drill capable of a rotating speed of 15,000 to 18,000 rpm and equipped with a 4 in. (100 mm) diameter 3M Scotch-Brite Surface Conditioning Disc similar to that illustrated in Figure 8–2. In addition, a coarse pad

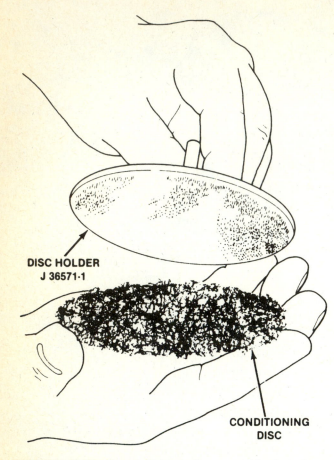

FIGURE 8–3 *Scotch-Brite surface conditioning disc and disc holder. (Courtesy of Detroit Diesel Corporation.)*

(Kent-Moore J36571-2 or 3M 07450, brown color) similar to that shown in Figure 8–2 is suitable to use on steel surfaces, while a medium pad (Kent-Moore J36571-3 or 3M 07451, maroon color) is recommended for aluminum surfaces. All of these pads are easily interchangeable using a disc holder (Kent-Moore J 36571-1 or 3M 07492) as shown in Figure 8–3.

Special Measuring Tools

Now that the engine has been disassembled and cleaned thoroughly, the following chapters in this book dealing with major engine components will indicate what dimensional checks are required to determine the wear limit characteristics of these parts. Because of space limitations we will not discuss every possible special gauge and tool required; however, Figures 8–4 through 8–7 illustrate five measuring tools that are widely used and applicable to dimensional check procedures when any engine is overhauled. In addition, the use of precision dial indicator gauges for measuring cylinder block bores, liner bores, block counterbores, crankshaft end

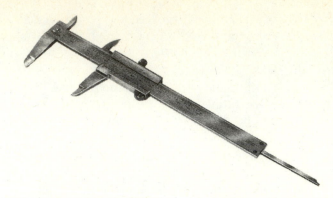

Tool No.	Size	Vernier Scale
J 26900-5	6" x 150MM	.001" x 0.02MM

The Dial Hand makes one complete revolution per every one hundred thousandths. One revolution of the Hand coincides with the smallest graduation on the main beam. The Dial Face is colored in non-reflective green.

"QUADRI" 4-Way Measuring Feature
1. Outside
2. Inside
3. Step
4. Depth

Tool No.	Range	Measuring Capacity	Graduation
J 26900-6	English 6"	6"	.001
J 26900-7	Metric 150MM	150MM	0.02MM

FIGURE 8–4 *Two types of vernier calipers that can be used to record an inside, outside, step, or depth dimension. The calipers are readily available in either English or metric measuring capacities. (Courtesy of Kent-Moore Division, SPX Corporation.)*

float, flywheel and housing concentricity, and so forth, are illustrated in respective chapters.

FUNDAMENTALS OF FAILURE ANALYSIS

When a component part fails in or on an engine or piece of equipment, do not automatically replace the part. Instead, attempt to determine the cause for failure; in this way you may avoid a repeat failure within

FIGURE 8-5 The outside micrometer ("mike") is a widely used precision measuring tool generally available in the increments shown in the accompanying chart (larger-dimension units are available). This particular model is a combination English/metric mike that indicates an inch value on the thimble, while its metric equivalent is registered on the digital counter. (Courtesy of Kent-Moore Division, SPX Corporation.)

Tool No.	Thimble	Range Counter	Graduation Thimble	Counter
J 26900-1	0-1"	00.00-25.40MM	.0001"	0.01MM
J 26900-2	1-2"	25.40-50.80MM	.0001"	0.01MM
J 26900-3	2-3"	50.80-76.20MM	.0001"	0.01MM
J 26900-4	3-4"	76.20-101.60MM	.0001"	0.01MM
J 26900-30	4-5"	101.60-127.00MM	.0001"	0.01MM
J 26900-32	5-6"	127.00-152.00MM	.0001"	0.01MM

Telescoping Gages

(3/4" to 2-1/8") Double Action (self-centering for quick checking of inside measurements).

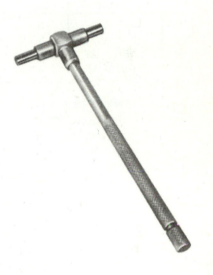

- Uniform contact pressure.
- Plunger or gage expands in hole to be measured, locked in place and gage is removed from hole. Final hole size is obtained by measuring over contacts with micrometer.
- Constant spring tension for uniform feel.
- Rigid handle with self-centering feature.
- Satin chrome finish.
- Contact points are of hardened tool steel and precision ground on the end measuring radius.

Tool No.	Range	Overall Length
J 26900-16	3/4" - 1 1/4" (19-32MM)	4.400"
J 26900-23	1 1/4 - 2 1/8" (32-54MM)	5.850"

FIGURE 8-6 The telescoping gauge is a spring-loaded two-plunger device that can be used to accurately measure the inside diameter of a machined bore or hole. The dimension is then checked by using an outside micrometer across both plungers. (Courtesy of Kent-Moore Division, SPX Corporation.)

a short time period. A second failure is often more disastrous than the first due to the cumulative effect on the other components that work together in harmony.

During the course of any maintenance, repair, or overhaul of engines and equipment, there will be times when you are faced with deciding the reason for failure of one or more component parts. Although the reasons for some failures may be fairly evident, often it is necessary to look for specific clues. In some cases you will need to systematically piece together unusual or abnormal signs to pinpoint the original cause of failure. When disassembling a failed engine or other equip-

ment components, it is extremely important that you do so in a manner that prevents obliteration of signs that lead to identification of the cause of a failure condition. Carefully lay all parts out on a bench, or on a wooden pallet on the floor, in a process that will allow you to view these components just as they would fit together in normal operation.

Failure analysis can be broken down into four major procedural steps:

1. Make a preliminary investigation.
2. Prepare parts for examination.

Small Hole Gages

Extra long for gaging deep and shallow holes, slots and similar work.

J 26900-14
Set of 4 Small Hole Gages

- Gaging surface is a full-round with a flat bottom; permits use in smallest of shallow holes, slots and grooves, etc.
- Knurled knob at end of handle is used for size adjustment. Hole size is obtained by measuring over the contact points with a micrometer.
- Gauging surface is fully hardened to insure long tool life.
- Supplied 4 gages in a fitted case.

Range		Overall	Probe
English	Metric	Length	Depth (L)
.125" - .200"	(3-5MM)	3 5/8"	.880:
.200" - .300"	(5-7.5MM)	3 7/8"	1.200"
.300" - .400"	(7.5-10MM)	4"	1.600"
.400" - .500"	(10-13MM)	4 1/4"	1.600

FIGURE 8–7 *Small-hole gauges have a split ball at one end that can be expanded by turning the upper knurled knob. Typically used to measure intake and exhaust valve guides for wear, the ball dimension is checked by means of an outside micrometer. (Courtesy of Kent-Moore Division, SPX Corporation.)*

3. Determine the type and cause of failure.
4. Correct the failure and its cause.

Although failure analysis is a skill that is developed through experience, the technician must have a complete working knowledge of the operation of the engine and/or equipment to mentally visualize how each part interacts with the other during normal operation. Your accumulated knowledge will also provide you with a frame of reference that will help you judge abnormal wear signs.

The preliminary investigation consists of these three tasks: observation, inquiry, and review of engine history. Any preliminary investigation includes a study of the past performance of the engine. This should include a review of the service records regarding the frequency of preventive maintenance, along with careful inspection of what failures have occurred. More particularly, determine if a major repair and parts replacement was undertaken fairly recently in the area of failure or in an area that might have contributed to the failure. Ask the engine or equipment operator about the conditions that were present during and immediately prior to the failure.

Were there any telltale signs of unusual operation (speed and/or sound changes)? Did instrumentation gauges register outside the normal operating limits? In regard to engine failure problems, what color was the exhaust smoke—white, gray, black, or blue? Did the operator smell any burning conditions? High operating temperatures are usually accompanied by a burning oil condition. Also, raw diesel fuel can be smelled in the exhaust; a fuel leak dripping onto a hot engine or exhaust manifold is quickly noticeable by fumes and smell, as is an engine oil leak or an antifreeze leak in the area of a hot exhaust manifold.

Sometimes you may be faced with determining the cause of failure from failed parts that have been shipped to you from another maintenance facility. It is very important that all parts be packed in a manner to prevent further damage during shipment. For example, crankshaft main and con-rod bearings should be taped together with masking tape so that the upper and lower bearings are matched. Similarly pistons, rings, and liners should be kept together, and injectors should be labeled with the cylinder number in which they were operating.

In subsequent chapters of this book dealing with crankshafts, shell bearings (mains and rods), and pistons and liners, several examples of failures are illustrated and information is presented that will assist you in determining the possible cause for failure. Refer to these specific chapters as a general guide when faced with determining a reason for failure.

At the conclusion of your inspection of a failure, you need to formulate an opinion based on factual information from the evidence at hand. Therefore, when reporting a failure indicate the equipment or engine serial number, what happened, where it happened, when it happened, and why it happened.

The equipment or engine *serial number* identifies and stores in records a history of operation, costs involved in operation, actual operating miles, kilometers, or hours, downtime, and so on. Describing *what happened* confirms what you saw when the failed components were analyzed. *Where* it happened indicates what type of terrain or conditions were evident and what was around the engine or equipment when the failure occurred. *When* it happened indicates what the actual operating conditions were at the time of failure. *Why* it happened is what you consider the cause of the failure. Keep in mind that when a failure occurs to a component, often the fault is not necessarily in that part; rather, the component failure is triggered by a primary failure in another mating component or operating condition.

SELF-TEST QUESTIONS

1. True or False: When degreasing or cleaning dirty engines and equipment, you can dump or drain oil and filters into a city drain.

2. Technician A says that heavy-duty ball or roller bearing assemblies can be cleaned safely by submerging them into a hot tank of caustic solution. Technician B disagrees strongly, saying that this can cause water spotting and acid etching of the components and should not be attempted; it is better to wash the components carefully in a clean solvent. Who is correct?

3. After a ball or roller bearing has been cleaned, technician A says that it is acceptable to spin the bearing with compressed air to ensure that all dirt particles have been removed. Technician B says that this action can severely damage the bearing and in some cases cause the bearing to disintegrate. Which technician knows safe work habits?

4. Technician A says that regardless of what type of cleaning agent is being used, you should always work in a well-ventilated area and wear safety glasses, an eye shield, gloves, and an apron. Technician B says that this is necessary only when using a caustic solution in a hot tank. Who is correct?

5. Technician A says that you should never heat naptha, white gas, varnish remover, and similar solvents under any cleaning condition. Technician B says that as long as you do not exceed 93°C (200°F) there is no danger. Who is correct?

6. Technician A says that after any cleaning procedure, all machined surfaces should be oiled lightly to prevent rust and corrosion from forming. Technician B says that this is a bad idea because the oil tends to attract dust. Who is correct?

7. True or False: A common hot tank cleaning solution for use with both cast iron and steel parts consists of a commercial heavy-duty alkaline solvent solution.

8. Technician A says that when using a commercial pickling acid in a hot tank it is not necessary to remove nonferrous metals such as copper and aluminum engine parts. Technician B says that if you do not remove these parts, an electrolytic action between dissimilar metals will cause them to be eaten away. Who is right?

9. True or False: The time required to clean a component part of scale accumulation depends on the strength of the cleaning solution.

10. True or False: After hot tank cleaning all parts should be thoroughly rinsed with clean hot water or steam and dried with compressed air, and machined surfaces should be lightly oiled.

11. True or False: Aluminum parts should never be cleaned in a solution containing alkali.

12. Technician A says that an in-frame engine overhaul is just as effective as a complete rebuild that involves removing the engine from its application. Technician B says that you cannot achieve as successful a job of internal cleaning of the engine block with an in-frame repair. Who is correct?

13. Technician A says that during an in-frame overhaul the crankshaft main bearings can be changed by rolling them in and out by use of a special pin inserted into the crankshaft journal oil hole. Technician B says that this is impossible and that the crankshaft *must* be removed to do this. Who is right?

14. If an engine block is to be steam cleaned externally for any reason, technician A says that the engine should always be running to allow equal distribution of the heat from the engine block. Technician B says that this is unsafe: Steam heat applied to an aluminum injection pump housing can result in severe distortion of the housing; internal plunger-to-barrel clearances can be affected, thereby causing scuffing or scoring. Which technician knows safe working procedures best?

15. Technician A says that when disassembling an engine, you should follow a systematic procedure that allows you to minimize damage to components and to get to other components as required. Technician B says that it doesn't matter how you pull the engine apart, because most components will be replaced anyway. Who is correct?

16. To facilitate and assist the technician in determining the possible cause for an engine failure, technician A says that all mating parts should be carefully labeled and identified. In addition, care should be taken not to scratch, score, or damage the parts during disassembly. Technician B says that this is not necessary—why waste time since new parts will be installed. Which technician has better standards of excellence?

17. After reassembly of an engine and prior to initial start-up, technician A says that you should place the throttle at full fuel to facilitate start-up and to allow a higher oil pump flow to quickly lubricate the internal parts. Technician B says that you should always pre-lube the main oil gallery and oil filter to ensure a minimum time delay for the oil to start flowing through the engine. Who is a better technician?

18. True or False: Once the engine has started after being rebuilt, you should leave the turbocharger oil supply line loose to ensure that it is receiving an adequate flow of oil. If no oil flow is visible after 20 to 30 sec, you should shut down the engine.

19. True or False: After initial engine start-up, the engine should be run at fast idle rather than wide open throttle.

20. During initial engine running after a rebuild, what signs should the technician be checking for? On a separate sheet of paper, list major checks that you would perform.

21. Technician A says that all engine parts that are not already marked by the manufacturer should be match-marked to allow reinstallation in the same position. Technician B says that this doesn't matter since all parts will be cleaned anyway and position does not make any difference. Which technician is correct?

22. Technician A says that intake and exhaust valves can be match-marked to their respective valve guide by using a sharp center punch to dot the head of the valve with its number. Technician B says that it is better to use a metal marker to do this and/or place the respective valves in a numbered wooden or cardboard valve holder. Which technician is correct?

23. On a separate sheet of paper, list the four major procedural steps required in a failure analysis.

24. Technician A says that it is extremely important that all nuts and bolts be correctly torqued and that the same-size diameter bolt have the same torque value as a taperlock stud. Technician B disagrees, saying that taperlock studs do not have as high a torque rating as a nut or bolt. Which technician is correct? Refer to the standard nut and bolt chart (Figure 8–1).

9 Cylinder Blocks

OVERVIEW

In this chapter we discuss the major structural part of any engine: the cylinder block, which serves as the foundation for all other components. The physical size of the engine dictates whether the block can be completely stripped of components for repairs or whether an in-frame type of repair must be done. The chapter describes the major checks, tests, and inspections that must be performed on an engine block, along with the necessary machining and repairs that may have to be performed to return the engine block to service.

TOPICS

- Sizes of engine block assemblies
- Engine block design flexibility
- Block cleaning procedures and safe work habits
- Pressure testing the block
- Inspection of the cylinder block
- Repair of cylinder block cracks
- Replacement cylinder blocks
- Self-test questions

SIZES OF ENGINE BLOCK ASSEMBLIES

Classification of engines is generally related to governed speed range; therefore, engines are generally classed as slow-speed, medium-speed, or high-speed design. Slow-speed engines are usually governed to run between 60 and 500 rpm; a medium-speed engine runs in the range of 500 to 1000 rpm; and anything beyond 1000 to 1200 rpm is considered a high-speed engine. Heavy-duty on-highway truck engines such as those manufactured by Caterpillar, Cummins, Detroit Diesel, Mack, Volvo, Scania, Mercedes-Benz, MAN, DAF Trucks, and so forth, are usually governed at speeds in the range of 1800 to 2500 rpm.

In this chapter you will see that large slow-speed engines and some medium-speed engines do not use a conventional cast cylinder block; instead they have fabricated and welded subsections. Some medium-speed engine models can employ a combination cast and prefabricated block arrangement. High-speed engines invariably employ a cast iron cylinder block; however, often several sections are bolted together to form a complete assembly. Regardless of the speed and physical size of the engine, the various engine checks and tests required are common in approach and outcome.

The cylinder block is the main structural part of the engine and acts as the foundation for all other components. It has to provide rigidity and strength to ensure proper alignment of the block bores for the cylinder liners as well as for the crankshaft and camshaft. In addition, the cylinder head(s) and other accessory drive components add additional stress—each in its own way—to the block structure during engine operation.

Although heavy-duty high-speed diesel engines are commonly designed to both vee-type and inline configuration, the most widely used model is the inline six-cylinder unit of the four-stroke-cycle type. Figure 9–1 illustrates an engine block of this type, minus the cylinder head(s), and the relative locations of the major components that form the complete engine assembly.

Ref No.	Part Name	Req	Remarks
	CYLINDER BLOCK **OPTION BB1004**		Engine block includes cylinder block, liners, crankshaft, bearings and associated block hardware, non-targeted piston cooling nozzles. Draincock supplied in kit.
1	Block, Cylinder	1	
2	Dowel, Rear Main	2	
3	Dowel, Pin	6	
	Pin, Roll	2	
4	Screw, Hexagon Head Cap	14	3/4 - 16 x 6 5/8 inch
5	Cap, Main Bearing	3	
6	Cap, Main Bearing	3	
7	Cap, Main Bearing	1	
8	Bushing	4	
9	Bushing	4	
10	Bushing	2	
11	Washer, Plain	14	3/4 inch
12	Washer, Plain	14	7/8 inch
13	Plug, Pipe	4	1/8 NPT
14	Plug, Threaded	1	7/8 - 18 UNS
15	Plug, Threaded		
16	Plug, Pipe	2	1/2 NPT
17	Plug, Expansion	1	
18	Plug, Pipe	3	3/8 NPT
19	Plug, Threaded	2	9/16 - 18 UNF
20	Seal, O-ring	2	
21	Plug, Threaded	1	1 3/16 - 12 UN
22	Seal, O-ring	1	
23	Plug, Threaded	2	3/4 - 16 UNF
24	Seal, O-ring	2	
25	Plug, Threaded	1	1 5/8 - 12 UN
26	Seal, O-ring	1	
27	Plug, Threaded	1	3/8 - 24 UNF
28	Seal, O-ring	1	
29	Nozzle, Piston Cooling	1	
30	Seal, O-ring	1	
31	Screw, Captive Washer Cap	6	3/8 - 16 x 3/4 inch
32	Ring, Liner Seal	6	0.0205 inch (white)
32	Ring, Liner Seal	A/R	0.0195 inch (black)
32	Ring, Liner Seal	A/R	0.0215 inch (orange)
32	Ring, Liner Seal	A/R	0.031 inch
32	Ring, Liner Seal	A/R	0.062 inch
33	Block, Cylinder	1	
34	Nipple, Coupling	1	
35	Seal, O-ring	1	
36	Pin, Roll	1	

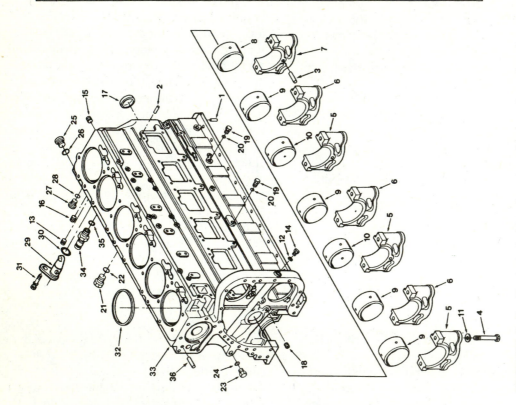

FIGURE 9–1 Exploded view showing the location of major component parts in a typical heavy-duty high-speed six-cylinder engine cylinder block. (Courtesy of Cummins Engine Company, Inc.)

The majority of high-speed heavy-duty diesel engine blocks in use today employ replaceable cylinder liners; the wet type is more dominant than the dry type. As illustrated in Figure 9–14, flanges at the upper ends of the liner are designed to seat in a machined counterbore of the block's upper deck with a slight protrusion of the liner flange to provide for compression of the cylinder head gasket, which acts as a compression seal. A wet liner has engine coolant in direct contact with its outside diameter. At the lower end of the liner, a series of seal rings are used to prevent coolant leakage between the block water jacket and the crankcase (oil). An integral coolant manifold is cast within the block, and it distributes the water pump flow along the complete length of the block. In addition, oil galleries are machined into the oil cooler side of the block. If we view an inline six-cylinder engine block from the underside as illustrated in Figure 9–2, we can see the integral crankshaft main bearing webs, cast to provide extreme rigidity and strength, plus front and rear bulkheads that support the engine crankshaft in seven main bearing saddles. The integral oil galleries direct the oil pump flow through the external oil cooler and filters to the main oil gallery and then to drilled passages in the crankcase webs, which supply oil under pressure to each crankshaft main bearing.

The vee-configuration engine block is a popular alternative to the widely used inline six model; V6, V8, V10, V12, V16, and V20 models are readily available for a wide variety of applications. The V6 and V8 models are commonly used in both on-highway and off-highway, marine, and some industrial and gen-set applications. Mercedes-Benz offers V10 on-highway truck power and Detroit Diesel offers V12-71/92 units in off-highway logging truck applications. In larger categories of horsepower, bigger displacement engines running between 700 and 1800 rpm are offered by Caterpillar in its 3500 and 3600 models in 6, 8, 12, and 16 cylinders, Cummins K series in both V12 and V16, and Detroit Diesel V8, V12, V16, and V20 149 series, where the V20 employs two V6 and one centrally located V8 engine block configuration to form the V20. Detroit Diesel also offers V16 configuration blocks in its Series 71 and Series 92 range. Of these various larger engine sizes, the Caterpillar 3600 engine is the largest; it has a bore and stroke of 11 × 11.8 in. (280 × 300 mm) for a displacement per cylinder of 1127.25 cu in. (18,472.24 cc or 18.472 L) and a V16 model displacement of 295.6 L (18,036 cu in.), with a dry engine weight of 60,700 lb (27,510 kg) in an approximate 6600 hp (4924 kW) rating. The engine idle speed is 350 rpm and it has a 13:1 compression ratio.

The 3616 lube oil system requires 322 U.S. gallons (1217 L) of 40 weight oil. Figure 9–3 illustrates a V16 engine block for a Caterpillar 3600 engine, and Figure 9–4 illustrates an engine block for a Detroit Diesel 16V-149 two-stroke-cycle model. You can see in Figure 9–4 that the V8's are bolted together to form a V16 model. In the larger type of 149 lineup, DDC offers up to a V20 model, which consists of a centrally mounted V8 block with two V6 blocks bolted to each end of the V8. The 149 engines are commonly referred to as *square engines* since both the bore and stroke are the

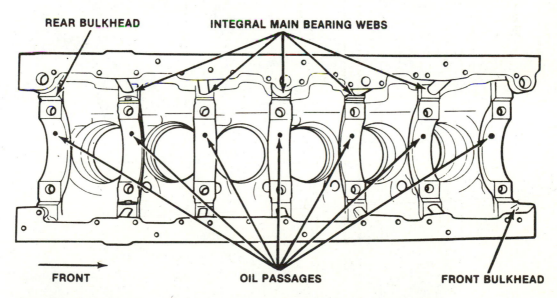

FIGURE 9–2 Bottom view of a six-cylinder heavy-duty high-speed diesel engine cylinder block highlighting the integral crankshaft main bearing webs and saddle, along with the upper main bearing pressurized lube oil passages. (Courtesy of Detroit Diesel Corporation.)

FIGURE 9–3 Construction arrangement of a heavy-duty 16-cylinder vee-configuration model 3616 Cat cylinder block, which is cast from alloy gray iron. The block features large main bearing inspection openings. It also has a cast-in air-intake manifold for increased block rigidity. (Courtesy of Caterpillar Inc.)

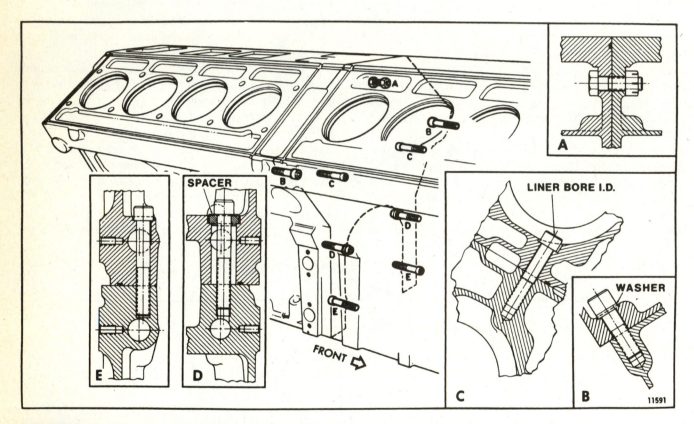

FIGURE 9–4 Example of a V16 cylinder block arrangement for a two-stroke-cycle DDC model 149 series engine. This block consists of two V8 blocks bolted together in the middle and incorporates a two-piece bolted crankshaft assembly. (Courtesy of Detroit Diesel Corporation.)

same (5.75 in., or 146 mm) for an individual cylinder displacement of 149 cu in. (2422 cc). Thus, the 20V-149 model has a total displacement of 2980 cu in. (48.83 L).

Other well-known two-stroke-cycle engines are the models manufactured by the General Motors Electro-Motive Division (GM-EMD), which are widely used in railroad locomotives, mining equipment, marine propulsion, and industrial generating unit applications. These engines are available in V8, V12, V16, and V20 configurations, with the largest model being the 710, which refers to its cubic inch displacement per cylinder (11.64 L). This engine has a bore of 9⅟₁₆ in. (230.19 mm) and a stroke of 11 in. (279.4 mm) with a 45° vee angle between the banks. The crankcase (block) and oil pan are of welded steel construction rather than the conventional heavy cast iron block design.

Cummins also manufactures a four-stroke-cycle V16 K model with a displacement of 50.25 L (3067 cu in.). All of these larger-size engines employ individual cylinder heads, plus the Caterpillar 3600 and DDC 149 models have segmented camshafts that allow removal of one part of a camshaft only during service and repair, or for replacement at overhaul.

Large Slow-Speed Engine Blocks

Many larger slow-speed diesel engines with very high horsepower do not use one-piece or multipiece blocks bolted together; instead they employ what is known as an *A-frame* design (not unlike some wood construction houses). Many of these engines are as high as a two-story house. Multi A-frame designs are welded and/or bolted together in sections to form the desired length of engine base. Consider, for example, that the K90MC/E engine model used in deep-sea ships and designed and built by a consortium consisting of Hyundai Engine & Machinery Company, MAN, and Burmeister & Wain (B&W) has a bore of 900 mm (35.43 in.) and a stroke of 2550 mm (100.39 in.) and can produce 47,307 kW (63,414 hp) from its two-stroke-cycle design concept at 90 rpm. There are several other engines with strokes as long as 3056 mm (120.31 in.), which is a little larger than 10 ft (3.048 m). Figure 9–5a illustrates the A-frame engine design used with these very-large-displacement slow-speed engines. To appreciate the actual dimensions of these engines, note the size of the man standing atop the upper area of the A-frame. The cast or fabricated and welded upper A-frame cylinder jacket assemblies (the number being related to the number of cylinders) in the example shown in Figure 9–5a are then bolted to a base or *bedplate*, which may be cast or fabricated and is designed to retain the massive crankshaft assembly. A very large engine bedplate is shown on the left-hand side of Figure 9–5b; note the crankshaft already mounted into the bedplate assembly. Note also on the right-hand side of this illustration a similar bedplate, but with the massive crankshaft lying alongside the bedplate. A technician wearing a hardhat is standing atop the bedplate with the crankshaft main shell bearings ready to be inserted.

Bedplates and crankcases are fabricated by welding low-carbon steels with small quantities of niobium added to improve their strength without affecting their other properties. Some larger engines now use nodular iron with low percentages of sulfur and phosphorous. Magnesium, cerium, or both are added,

which transforms the graphite flakes typical of cast gray irons into spheroids of graphite. These metals are then known as either spheroidal or nodular irons.

Large slow-speed engines of this massive size and displacement are generally used strictly as stationary industrial power units, or more commonly in marine applications in deep-sea ships. The rotative speed of many of the super-large diesel engines can be as low as 57 rpm, with speeds seldom exceeding 500 rpm on the medium-sized slow-speed units. These larger slow-speed engines are available in configurations ranging from 5, 6, 7, 8, 9, 10, 12, 14, 16, and 18 cylinders.

High-Speed Block Construction

High-speed diesel engine cylinder blocks are generally manufactured from gray flake graphite cast iron with a good percentage of silicon distributed throughout the casting. If the pistons are to operate directly in the block bore without the use of replaceable liners, a relatively high-phosphorous iron is employed to provide a network of hard iron phosphide that is fairly resistant to wear. In special applications, or in many lighter-duty diesel engines, aluminum alloys are common. A unique engine block design is illustrated in Figure 9–6 for the 3176, 629 cu in. (10.3 L) Caterpillar engine, one of the new generation of electronically controlled unit injector engines. The engine block is a two-piece design consisting of a cast gray iron crankcase and an aluminum permanent-mold spacer deck. The gray iron has a minimum strength of 207 kPa (30 ksi), or 30,000 psi. This configuration eliminates the requirement for a counterbore liner seat in the top of the machined upper deck of the block, which is common in engines with wet- and dry-type liners. The engine block uses a mid-supported cylinder liner supported by the top deck of the crankcase immediately below the aluminum spacer deck plate. For more information on a mid-supported liner, refer to Chapter 16. The aluminum spacer deck provides the liner water jacket, camshaft support, and an oil manifold that supplies oil to the camshaft bearings and valve mechanism. In addition, its structural rigidity provides an overall engine weight reduction as well as eliminating O-ring grooves on the liner and a water jacket in the crankcase area of the block.

ENGINE BLOCK DESIGN FLEXIBILITY

Many engine manufacturers today have standardized the bore and stroke of many of their engines. This feature offers a reduction in production and design costs and makes the interchangeability of parts a major benefit to the end user. For example, Cummins has standardized its four- and six-cylinder B series engines, as well as its K series larger-bore engines. Caterpillar has standardized its 3100, 3300, 3400, 3500, and 3600 models. Mercedes-Benz also uses a common bore and stroke arrangement with many of its engine models. In large-bore high-horsepower locomotive and marine engines, the GM-EMD has always had a common bore and stroke feature for its series of engines, with the 567, 645, and 710 cu in. (9292, 10,570, and 11,635 cc) per cylinder V8, V12, V16, and V20 two-stroke-cycle models. In the smaller high-speed engines, Detroit Diesel has always employed a common bore and stroke in its various two-cycle engines such as the 53, 71, 92, and 149 models. Detroit Diesel employs two V6 blocks to produce a 12V-92 or 12V-149 engine model, and two V8 blocks to produce a 16V-71, 92, or 149 engine model. Its latest V20-149 engine utilizes two V6 and one V8 engine block to produce this configuration. All of the engine models within a given series of DDC two-stroke-cycle engines use the same bore and stroke, while in the Series 60 engines (11.1L and 12.7L) models the engines have the same bore but the stroke is longer in the larger 12.7L model. The Series 50 engine is simply a four-cylinder Series 60 12.7L unit.

Consider that the engine blocks such as those manufactured and used by Detroit Diesel on its three-, four, and six-cylinder 71 series inline engines are symmetrical (identical in design and dimensions) except for length. Therefore, the two ends of the block are similar, which means that the flywheel housing and gear train can be assembled on either end of the block. This is important for reassembling the block at overhaul. Any one of eight different engine model designations can be obtained depending on the chosen engine rotation (CW or CCW from the front end) and the actual side of the engine on which the gear-driven blower and exhaust manifold are located. The blower will mount on only one side of the engine on a machined pad, but its location as to left-hand or right-hand side is determined by what end of the block has the flywheel housing bolted to it. This provides tremendous flexibility of application installation in on-highway and off-highway, marine, stationary, or industrial applications since an A, B, C, or D model engine designation is possible in either a left-hand or right-hand crankshaft rotation for the eight various models. Figure 9–7 illustrates a typical six-cylinder inline 71 series DDC engine block. Detroit Diesel's vee-type engine blocks are also similar in design to inline engines that allow eight different engine models. This commonality of engine design makes it much easier for the service technician to readily adapt to the maintenance, repair and overhaul, tuneup, and troubleshooting requirements of a given engine series whether there are 6, 8, 12, 16, or 20 cylinders!

A

FIGURE 9–5   (a) This engine block consists of a series of A-frame sections welded together and is commonly used on slow-speed, very-large-bore, high-output diesel engines in stationary and deep-sea marine applications. Note the size of the technician standing on top of the block assembly. (Courtesy of Hyundai Engine & Machinery Co., Ltd., Seoul, Korea.)(b) Illustration shows the production floor of a heavy-industries plant. The physical size of these very large slow-speed diesel engines for deep-sea marine vessels can be gauged by noting the size of the various technicians throughout. On the right-hand side of the illustration note the technician standing on top of the engine bedplate alongside the crankshaft shell bearings, with the crankshaft lying alongside the bedplate ready for installation. On the left-hand side note the crankshaft sitting in its bedplate. In the top center two technicians are working—one on the second story and the other on the third story catwalk of the assembled engine. (Courtesy of Hyundai Engine & Machinery Co., Ltd., Seoul, Korea.)

BLOCK CLEANING PROCEDURES AND SAFE WORK HABITS

Once an engine has been disassembled, the block assembly must be cleaned completely to determine if it needs any major repairs prior to determining whether it can be reused. Begin by carefully scraping all gasket material from the block using a gasket scraper so as not to create any deep nicks or scratches on machined sur-

B

faces. This task can be facilitated by spraying on a commercially available liquid such as Loctite Chisel, which penetrates and cleans complex gasket material shapes and reduces the need for excessive scraping. In addition, drill-motor-driven surface conditioning pad discs are excellent for cleaning gasket surfaces after they have been scraped off. These discs are a safe way to clean flange areas and mating surfaces of gasketing residue. Both coarse and medium discs are made from a three-dimensional nonwoven fiber material that allows controlled cleaning of metal surfaces. These discs can be used with ¼ in. (6.3 mm) air or electric power tools. In addition, a carbon-removing wire brush set of various sizes can be used with a ¼ in. (6.3

mm) drill for removing carbon buildup. Also remove all oil gallery and core hole plugs, as well as any non-ferrous metals (copper and aluminum), to allow any caustic or alkaline cleaning solution to contact the inside of all oil and water passages, so that any scale buildup can be removed. The engine service manual usually includes a foldout diagram identifying the location, size, and torque values for all removed plugs.

Before using any steam cleaner, high-pressure washer, or hot cleaning tank, make sure that you wear protective clothing, gloves, safety glasses, and a face shield. Securely attach the block to a suitable lifting tackle similar to that shown in Figure 7–1 for engine removal and disassembly. Usually two or more eyebolts

FIGURE 9–6 Six-cylinder 3176 engine model block that employs a thick aluminum spacer deck plate between the top of the block and the cylinder head. Wet-type replaceable cylinder liners are used. (Courtesy of Caterpillar Inc.)

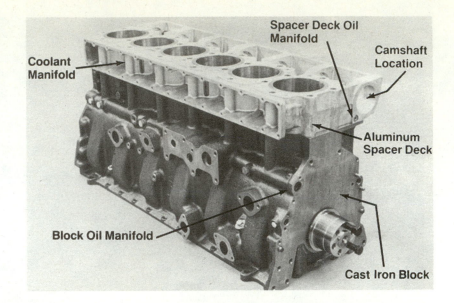

Coolant Manifold

Spacer Deck Oil Manifold

Camshaft Location

Aluminum Spacer Deck

Block Oil Manifold

Cast Iron Block

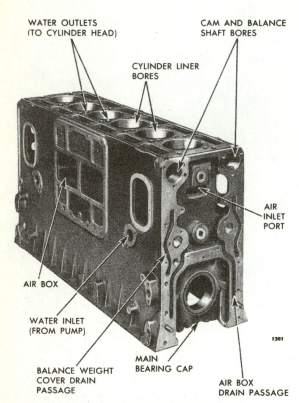

WATER OUTLETS (TO CYLINDER HEAD)

CAM AND BALANCE SHAFT BORES

CYLINDER LINER BORES

AIR INLET PORT

AIR BOX

WATER INLET (FROM PUMP)

BALANCE WEIGHT COVER DRAIN PASSAGE

MAIN BEARING CAP

AIR BOX DRAIN PASSAGE

FIGURE 9–7 Two-stroke-cycle 6-71 series DDC engine block, which is manufactured as a symmetrical block allowing the engine gear train, flywheel, and flywheel housing to be assembled onto either end of the block assembly. This concept provides for eight different engine models to be constructed from one engine block. Dry slip-fit cylinder liners are used. (Courtesy of Detroit Diesel Corporation.)

installed into the upper deck of the block (cylinder head bolt holes) at opposite ends of the block can be used. Use a spreader bar between both lifting points similar to that illustrated in Figure 7–1 and Figure 7–2 to prevent the engine block from sliding to one side. This type of a spreader bar allows three working lengths from 30 to 46 in. (762 to 1168 mm) plus angle adjustments of up to 30°. The bar is rated at 6000 lb (2722 kg); always ensure that the load-rotor spreader bar selected is capable of handling its intended load.

To clean the engine block, follow these eight steps:

1. Carefully steam clean or high-pressure wash the exterior of the engine block to minimize contamination of the cleaning solution.

NOTE: Either clean the block in a commercial heavy-duty alkaline solution, or if the coolant passages are heavily scaled, submerge the block in a bath of inhibited phosphoric acid.

2. Slowly lower the engine block into the hot or cold tank of a commercial heavy-duty alkaline cleaning solution or inhibited phosphoric acid as shown in Figure 9–8.

3. Once the block has been submerged into the solution, close the lid and activate the switch that will agitate the block support within the tank.

4. The time that the block should remain in the cleaning solution depends on how heavily scaled it is in the coolant passages and the strength of the solution. Rely on past experiences or refer to the cleaning manufacturer's suggested time period. When using inhibited phosphoric acid, as soon as the block is low-

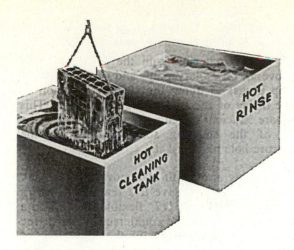

FIGURE 9–8 Process commonly used to clean and descale a cylinder block. (Courtesy of Detroit Diesel Corporation.)

ered into the bath, you will notice a bubbling action as the chemicals react with the scale buildup within the coolant passages. Leave the block in the bath until the bubbling action has stopped; this takes about 30 minutes. If coolant scale is still evident after you remove the block, lower the block back into the bath for another 10 minutes. Repeat this routine until you are satisfied that the block coolant passages are clean and free of scale.

5. After the block is removed from the cleaning solution, allow enough time for excess liquid to drain from it before swinging it clear from the tank. If a hot water rinsing tank is readily available, as shown in Figure 9–8, submerge the block into this bath since the cleaning solution can be neutralized in this way. If no rinsing tank is available, wash the block in hot water or steam clean it to remove the alkaline solution.

6. In addition to the hot water bath, you can neutralize the acid that may cling to the block casting by immersing it in an alkaline bath, then washing the block in hot water or by steam cleaning.

7. Dry off the block with compressed air adjusted to approximately 40 psi (276 kPa), and blow out all of the bolt holes and plug passages with compressed air.

8. Use an engine oil squirt gun and lightly coat all machined surfaces on the engine block to prevent these from rusting.

9. Refer to the block plugging instructions in the service manual. If new precoated plugs are not available, precoat the used plug threads with a recommended nonhardening sealant such as Loctite 620 and tighten them to the specified torque. Many of these plugs have square heads in them and are easily installed using a suitably sized square drive socket extension.

PRESSURE TESTING THE BLOCK

Pressure testing of the cylinder block is required to determine if any unseen internal oil or coolant passages are cracked. This can be done in two ways, but both methods include sealing off all coolant and oil passages with suitable gaskets and steel plates bolted into position. In addition, cylinder liners and O-seal rings must be installed and clamped into position to isolate the water jackets during the test procedure.

Method 1

This method is the more common of the two, since the block can be pressure tested while in place in the vehicle or equipment during an in-frame overhaul, or when removed and cleaned as a bare engine block. Which coolant and oil passages require plugging depends on the specific model and make of engine block to be tested.

To check an engine block that uses dry liners, no liners have to be installed to block off any coolant during the test. Cylinder head water seal rings can be used as gaskets between blank-off plates and the block; then bolts or nuts can be inserted and tightened securely. Any other water openings in the engine block can be blocked off using suitable gaskets and steel plates bolted into position. For example, on most engines it will be necessary to use water hole cover plates over the water pump inlet openings on the block. Select one of the sealing plates, and drill and tap it to take a compressed air fitting.

On the other hand, if the engine employs wet-type liners, the liners and their seal rings have to be installed, then clamped in place to perform the pressure check. Figure 9–9 illustrates a method used to seal off the top of the block on a four-stroke-cycle Series 60 DDC engine that uses wet-type cylinder liners. Special steel plate strips and test rings are required along with a series of bolts to clamp down a sealing gasket underneath the plates. In addition, a water pump inlet cover plate must be secured to the engine block at the front.

SERVICE TIP: Prior to installation of one of the top deck sealing plates, fill the engine coolant passages with a mixture of water and 1 gallon of permanent antifreeze. The antifreeze will penetrate a crack easier and its color will make it more readily visible to the naked eye.

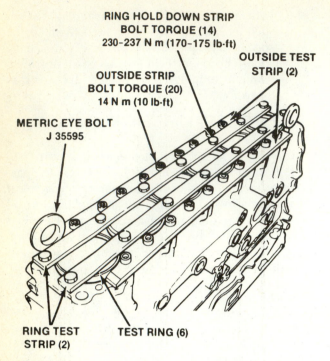

RING HOLD DOWN STRIP
BOLT TORQUE (14)
230-237 N·m (170-175 lb·ft)

OUTSIDE TEST
STRIP (2)

OUTSIDE STRIP
BOLT TORQUE (20)
14 N·m (10 lb·ft)

METRIC EYE BOLT
J 35595

RING TEST
STRIP (2)

TEST RING (6)

FIGURE 9–9   *Preparing a cylinder block for a pressure test to determine if any cracks are evident. Test strips are bolted as shown to seal off the coolant passages. (Courtesy of Detroit Diesel Corporation.)*

Dry liner engines should have a maximum air pressure applied to them of 40 psi (276 kPa), whereas wet liner engines should never have air pressure in excess of 20 psi (138 kPa) applied to them. Allow the air pressure to be maintained for at least 2 hours. At the end of the test period, carefully inspect the outside diameter of wet liner flanges and the underside of the block on Cummins or Caterpillar engines for any signs of liner O-seal ring leakage. Note, however, that on Detroit Diesel Series 50 and Series 60 engines (see Figure 16–5) coolant weep holes located alongside the engine block allow any coolant that leaks past the top liner seal ring to exit at the holes. Check the various oil passages, crankcase, and exterior of the block for any signs of water and antifreeze leakage, which would confirm that either the block is cracked or a liner seal ring is leaking. Most manufacturers recommend that a cracked block be replaced with a new one. There are, however, methods that are sometimes used to repair a small crack that is not located in an area close to either the cylinder liner or cylinder head sealing surfaces.

Method 2

This method can be used only if a large enough water tank is available to completely submerge the engine block. The same block sealing procedure as described for the first method is used. If the water in the tank can be heated to normal engine coolant operating temperature, the test will more truly resemble engine operating conditions. Submerge the block using a suitable lifting device; then allow the block to sit in the heated water for 10 to 15 minutes before applying 40 psi (276 kPa) on a dry liner engine or a maximum of 20 psi (138 kPa) on a wet liner engine. Any air bubbles appearing in the tank will indicate that a leak or crack exists in that area.

At the end of either method 1 or 2, release the air pressure gradually; then remove the sealing plates and gaskets. Blow out all of the passages in the block, particularly the oil passages, with compressed air, and lightly lubricate all of the machined surfaces to prevent rusting.

Nondestructive Block Testing

It is possible to check the engine block for cracks by using a number of nondestructive testing methods. These methods are described in detail in Chapter 11.

INSPECTION OF THE CYLINDER BLOCK

Once an engine block has been pressure tested and found to be free of cracks, a number of checks must be made to determine if remachining is required for the block to meet acceptable used standard wear limits as defined in the engine service manual. The following list indicates the various checks that should be performed:

- Check the cylinder block bore diameter for wear, ovality, and taper, particularly dry liner engines.
- Carefully inspect the block bore area on wet liner engines to check for the same conditions as described in the previous item. Also check the liner seal ring area and the dry area of the block bore when a partially wet liner is used.
- Check the cylinder liner counterbore area in the block for signs of fretting (liner movement), depth, and squareness.
- Use a straightedge and feeler gauges to check the machined top deck surface both longitudinally and transversely for signs of warpage.
- Check all other machined surfaces on the engine block as described in the previous item.
- Inspect all threaded holes and clean them with a suitable tap. If any bolt holes are stripped, they will have to be repaired using either a *helicoil* or a *Tap-lok* insert.
- Check the crankshaft bores throughout all of the main bearing caps for signs of distortion or misalignment (wear, taper, and ovality).

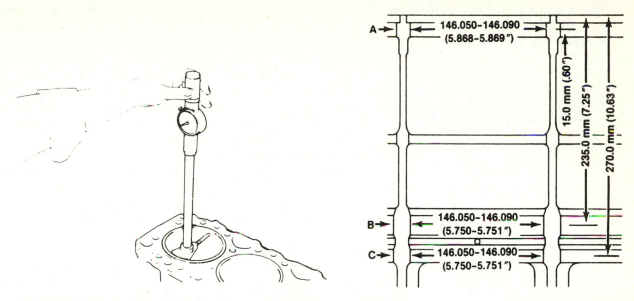

MAXIMUM ALLOWABLE CYLINDER BLOCK BORE DIAMETER

A → 146.050–146.090 (5.868–5.869″)

15.0 mm (.60″)

235.0 mm (7.25″)

270.0 mm (10.63″)

B → 146.050–146.090 (5.750–5.751″)

C → 146.050–146.090 (5.750–5.751″)

FIGURE 9–10 *Using a precision dial bore gauge to determine wear, ovality, and taper within a cylinder block bore. (Courtesy of Detroit Diesel Corporation.)*

- Check each main bearing cap for signs of fretting at their machined parting line, which would indicate cap movement.
- Check each main bearing cap for signs of bluing, which would indicate overheating has occurred.
- Check the camshaft bores on a non-overhead cam engine design for wear, ovality, and taper and any signs of damage.

Block Bore Diameter

The cylinder block must be checked with a dial bore gauge to determine if taper and out-of-round (ovality) readings are within worn limit specifications. The number of readings taken and their spacing throughout the block bore length depend on whether the block has been designed as a *parent bore* (no liner), a dry liner, or a wet liner. In dry liner engines, or engines with a parent bore, measure the bore diameter throughout its length at five or six places and at 90° to each other. An example of taper and ovality is discussed in Chapter 16 dealing with cylinder liners and can be equally applied to a cylinder bore. On a four-stroke-cycle wet liner engine, dial reading checks are taken at three positions, A, B, and C, as illustrated in Figure 9–10 for a Series 50 or Series 60 DDC model. On two-stroke-cycle DDC engines, only the upper half of the liner is directly in contact with the engine coolant (above the cylinder liner ports—port belt area); therefore, dial bore checks would be taken as shown in Figure 9–11.

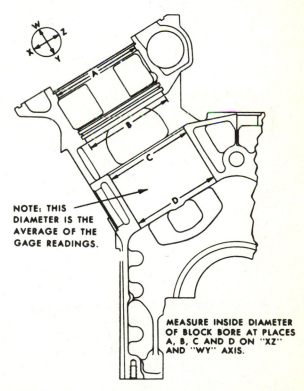

NOTE: THIS DIAMETER IS THE AVERAGE OF THE GAGE READINGS.

MEASURE INSIDE DIAMETER OF BLOCK BORE AT PLACES A, B, C AND D ON "XZ" AND "WY" AXIS.

FIGURE 9–11 *Recommended positions used to check a cylinder block bore in a two-stroke-cycle DDC 92 series engine with a precision dial bore gauge or inside micrometer. (Courtesy of Detroit Diesel Corporation.)*

In blocks using either dry or wet liners, any physical damage to the liner surface usually requires installation of a new cylinder liner. In DDC two-stroke-cycle 71 series engines, a dry slip-fit liner is used; so if the liner inside diameter is lightly scuffed or scored, or the liner outside diameter exhibits some discoloration (dark spots), contact is not occurring. The cylinder block can be lightly cleaned with a fixed hone to accept a 0.001 in. (0.0254 mm) oversize outside diameter liner. If boring is required, oversize outside diameter liners are readily available from DDC in 0.005, 0.010, 0.020, or 0.030 in. (0.125, 0.254, 0.508, or 0.762 mm) outside diameter *only*. No liners with larger size inside diameter are available; therefore, a standard diameter piston is always used.

In some light- and medium-duty diesel engines, no cylinder liners are used, and the piston operates directly within the engine block (parent bore). Visually inspect the block bore for any signs of scuffing or scoring; if there are signs, the block bore may have to be power honed or bored to take an oversize piston. If the block bore requires boring beyond the largest size of oversize piston available, a replacement press-fit sleeve could be obtained to salvage the block. The block must be bored to accept the outside diameter of the sleeve (allow a press fit of 0.002 to 0.003 in., or 0.0508 to 0.0762 mm). Then rebore the inside diameter of the sleeve after pressing it into the block to bring it back to the replacement piston size.

Honing Versus Reboring

Any service technician who is involved in major engine repairs must be well versed in the various techniques of honing the cylinder block bore and liner, including knowing when to hone and when to correct the block bore by remachining with a boring tool. In all cases, the initial use of a cylinder hone is simply to remove minor imperfections from the block or liner inside diameter before employing a dial gauge to determine bore or liner condition for reuse with respect to diameter, out-of-round condition, and taper. Cylinder liners that fall outside specifications should be replaced automatically with new liners. Honing can also be done to break any cylinder wall glaze, so that new piston rings can be seated on a nonpolished surface. Chapter 16 discusses the various types of hones available and how to use them to create the proper crosshatch pattern on the cylinder bore or liner wall as specified in the engine service manual.

A hone or ridge-reamer is also required to remove any minor ridge (see Figure 16–19) at the top of the block bore or cylinder liner formed by the old piston ring travel. Attempting to hand-hone a cylinder block to accept oversize liners in excess of 0.001 in. (0.0254

mm) or oversize pistons, which generally are available in 0.010, 0.020, and 0.030 in. (0.254, 0.508, and 0.762 mm) sizes, can be done correctly only by using a boring bar. A portable boring bar such as the one illustrated in Figure 9–12a can be used to perform an in-frame repair; or at major engine overhaul, the block assembly can be mounted and clamped into a floor-mounted model such as the one illustrated in Figure 9–12b. An optional method that is widely used to prepare a cylinder block to accept oversize outsize diameter liners, or oversize pistons in a parent bore block, is to use a *power hone* similar to the one illustrated in Figure 9–13.

Attempting to enlarge a cylinder bore with a hand hone powered by an air or electric drill motor would require considerable time; in addition, the hone would tend to follow the existing imperfections in the block bore. If reboring is necessary in any parent block bore, or to accept an oversize outside diameter liner, only remove enough material to clean up the bore and to accept the first oversize piston or liner available; in this way, future reboring at major overhaul is possible. If you are boring to accept an oversize piston, determine from service information just what piston-to-block clearance is specified. For example, if the piston-to-liner clearance for an aluminum piston is specified as being between 0.006 and 0.007 in. (0.152 to 0.177 mm), then you want to bore to within 0.002 to 0.003 in. (0.050 to 0.076 mm) or slightly less to allow you to finish by honing the block bore. This would allow you to obtain the proper crosshatch pattern and surface finish on the cylinder wall. For details on the crosshatch pattern and how to obtain it, refer to Chapter 16.

Some engine manufacturers do *not* offer oversize diameter pistons for some of their engines. One example is the Caterpillar 3116 truck engine. Caterpillar determined that it was not practical to rebore the blocks for oversize pistons. In this case the procedure to salvage a cylinder block with major cylinder bore damage is to bore the cylinder oversize and employ a press-in sleeve, which can then be rebored to produce the correct size bore while leaving enough material to allow for a properly honed crosshatch pattern.

Block Counterbore

The cylinder liner flange is supported in a machined counterbore at the top area of the block. This counterbore must be checked closely because many liners are press fit into this bore to ensure that no coolant or compression leakage occurs. Check the counterbore, outside diameter, depth, and slope, and signs of fretting that indicate liner movement.

To check the counterbore diameter, use a dial bore gauge similar to the one shown in Figure 9–10. If you use a telescoping gauge, check the dimension with an

FIGURE 9–12 (a) Cylinder block portable boring bar mounted on the top surface of the engine block in preparation for boring the cylinder bores to accept oversize outside diameter dry-type slip-fit liners. (Courtesy of Detroit Diesel Corporation.) (b) Example of an engine block bolted securely into a precision floor mounted boring machine.

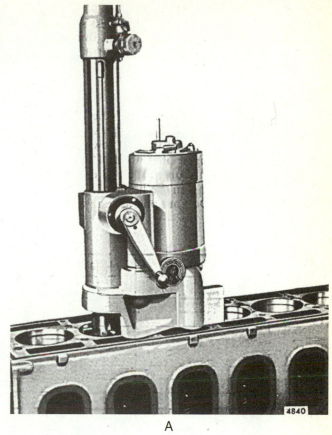

A

ACP 155-2/B
Cylinder blocks boring machine
Min. and max. boring range:
mm 73 ÷ 155 (2.875"–6.093")
Max. boring spindle travel, automatic:
mm 360 (14.125")

B

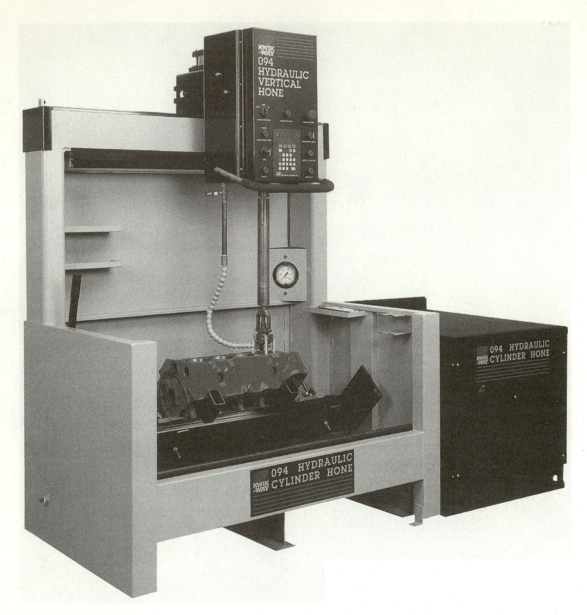

FIGURE 9–13 Power honing machine used to hone a cylinder block bore to accept either an oversize liner or piston assembly. (Courtesy of Kwik-Way Manufacturing Co.)

outside micrometer and compare to specs. For example, Figure 9–14 illustrates a counterbore check for a Cummins 14L (855 cu in.) engine. The liner is press fit in the counterbore, so first measure the counterbore in the area shown on the left-hand side of the diagram. The right-hand side of the diagram shows where the standard liner flange diameter is press fit in the block counterbore. Standard liner flange diameters can be used in this example if the diameter measured does not exceed 166.713 mm (6.5635 in.). If the reading exceeds this, the block counterbore will have to be remachined to accept an oversize outside diameter liner flange.

To check the depth and slope of the counterbore in the block, you can use either a depth micrometer or a dial indicator mounted on a sled gauge as shown in Figure 9–15 and compare the readings to spec. Figure 9–16 illustrates that the counterbore must be checked at four places and in positions 1 and 2 to determine if any slope exists. Readings should not vary more than 0.03 mm (0.001 in.) around the circumference of the counterbore. In addition, if the counterbore depth exceeds the specifications, it has to be remachined by installing a sleeve. After remachining, you can choose to use shims under the liner flange to obtain the correct protrusion

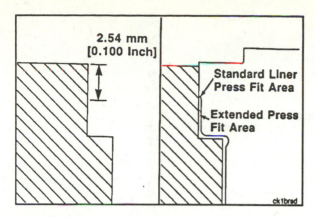

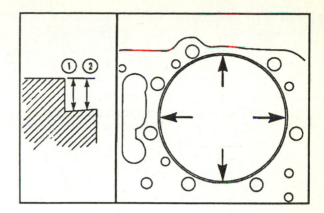

FIGURE 9–14 Close-up of how the top flange area of the cylinder liner is designed to press fit into the cylinder block counterbore area. (Courtesy of Cummins Engine Company, Inc.)

FIGURE 9–16 Recommended locations at which to check the cylinder block liner flange counterbore for signs of sloping or distortion. (Courtesy of Cummins Engine Company, Inc.)

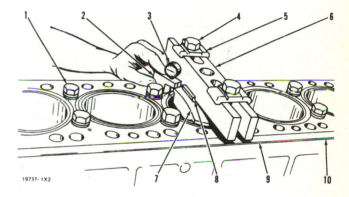

FIGURE 9–15 Checking the depth of the cylinder block liner flange counterbore with a dial indicator mounted on a sled gauge. (Courtesy of Detroit Diesel Corporation.)

FIGURE 9–17 Using a bolted cylinder liner hold-down clamp to effectively check the liner protrusion with a dial sled gauge similar to the one illustrated in Figure 9–15. (Courtesy of Caterpillar Inc.)

cleaned lightly with fine emery cloth. Severe marks would mean remachining. A downward sloping or concave counterbore can cause liners to crack at the flange area due to insufficient support. The measured reading between position 2 and 1 in Figure 9–16 must not vary more than 0.036 mm (0.0014 in.).

Block Spacer Plates

Some engine models employ cylinder block aluminum deck spacer plates similar to that shown earlier in Figure 9–6 for the 3176 Cat engine. The Caterpillar 3406B/C and E models employ a steel spacer plate located between the top of the engine block and the underside of the cylinder head; however, this spacer plate is much thinner than the one used on the 3176 engines. Figure 9–17 illustrates the location of the spacer plate (9) and gasket (10) clamped into position on top of the engine block in preparation for a check of

above the block deck (see Figure 16–1), or you can use oversize flange liners. Cummins offers either a standard liner with a regular outside diameter and flange thickness or an oversize outside diameter flange that is 0.51 mm (0.020 in.) over standard and has a 0.25 mm (0.010 in.) thicker flange.

Visually inspect the counterbore machined surface closely for any signs of counterbore slope and for any raised metal burrs or nicks. Minor imperfections can be cylinder liner flange projection. At engine rebuild, a 0.076 mm (0.003 in.) thinner spacer plate is available as an alternative to counterboring all six cylinder liner seats to increase average liner projection to within the specified range of 0.03 to 0.15 mm (0.001 to 0.006 in.). Earlier engines used an aluminum spacer plate, but that has been replaced by a steel spacer plate.

Note the other numbered components in Figure 9–17:

1   Spacer plate temporary retaining bolts
2   Dial gauge body
3   Dial indicator
4   Cylinder liner hold-down clamp bolt
5   Bolt spacer plate
6   Caterpillar 8B7548 Push-Puller plate
7   Cylinder liner adapter plate
8   3H465 plate installed upside down

On Caterpillar 3406B/C engine blocks, new cylinder liner seat inserts are available to salvage engine blocks that have been damaged from fretting, erosion, corrosion, wear steps, or cracks on top of the cylinder block under the cylinder liner flange. These inserts are 0.05 mm (0.002 in.) thinner or thicker than the standard liner inserts, and the nominal thickness is marked on each new insert. These inserts provide additional repair options within each counterbore depth range. They also help alleviate the need to counterbore to the next available depth range if the original counterbore measures out of the specification range. If machining of the block liner counterbore is required, deburr the edges with emery paper or No. 400 wet-dry sandpaper. Always install the inserts in the counterbore with the chamfered edge of the insert facing down and without a sealant applied to them. Different inserts may be required to ensure that they provide the correct cylinder liner projection limits. Liner inserts are available in standard, oversize, and undersize to suit the conditions encountered.

Repairing Damaged Counterbores

When a cylinder block counterbore is found to be outside wear limit specifications as presented in the service manual, or if there are signs of possible cracking in this area as illustrated in Figure 9–18, there are a variety of special tools available to repair the block while it is still in the vehicle or equipment. The Kent-Moore Division of SPX Corporation manufactures and offers portable repair equipment under the name of Porta-Tool. These special tools can be used to repair any area of the cylinder block.

Counterbore areas with cracks or excessively worn counterbore ledges, or blocks that have been counterbored to their maximum depth, can result in

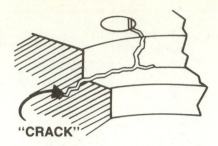

FIGURE 9–18 *Location of a typical crack that might appear in the highly stressed cylinder block liner counterbore area. (Courtesy of Kent-Moore Division, SPX Corporation.)*

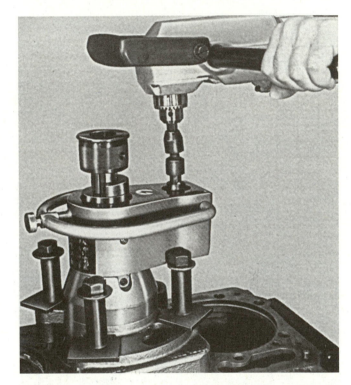

FIGURE 9–19 *Using a power driven Porta-Matic tool for an in-frame repair of a cracked or damaged counterbore area of the cylinder block liner. (Courtesy of Kent-Moore Division, SPX Corporation.)*

the scrapping of the engine block long before its useful life is over. Figure 9–19 illustrates a Porta-Matic upper-deck boring tool that can be used on Cummins, Caterpillar, Detroit Diesel, Mack, Navistar, and Komatsu Dresser Company engines. This tool is used to enlarge the damaged counterbore for installation of a repair bushing to form a watertight counterbore. It can also be used to bore the counterbore for installation of oversize liners. The tool cutter is powered by a drill motor once the feed mechanism, depth, and

A

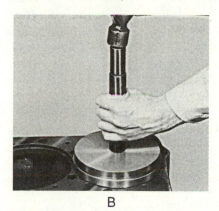

B

FIGURE 9–20 (a) Installing a new cylinder block liner counterbore repair sleeve onto the special tooling; (b) using a hammer to drive the sleeve into the block counterbore. (Courtesy of Kent-Moore Division, SPX Corporation.)

diameter have been set. The machine hydraulically controls the rate of feed in relation to the power source rpm and will "free wheel" once the preset dimension is reached. Figure 9–20 illustrates the Porta-Matic tool removed from the cylinder block after remachining and the technician preparing for the installation of the OEM-approved counterbore repair bushing. The repair bushing is centrifugally cast from high-tensile alloy and machined on all surfaces to exacting tolerances.

The bore and the outside surface of the repair bushing are cleaned using a Loctite primer. Then the outside surface of the bushing is coated with a special Loctite retaining compound prior to driving the repair bushing into the block counterbore as shown in Figure 9–20b with the special driver tool. This type of repair can be completed in less than 30 minutes (including setup time). A similar hand-powered tool is available from Porta-Tool. It has a T-handle and can be used for cleaning counterbores, recutting counterbores prior to shimming, and finishing the counterbore ledge in a newly installed repair sleeve.

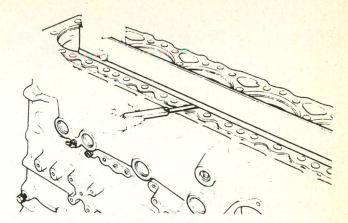

FIGURE 9–21 Using a precision steel straightedge and feeler gauge to carefully check the machined surface of the engine block for signs of distortion or flatness. (Courtesy of Detroit Diesel Corporation.)

Lower-Bore Repair

Close inspection of the lower area of the block/liner bore may disclose stress cracks and erosion on engines with wet-type liners in the lower packing bore region. In Cummins, Caterpillar, J. I. Case, Tenneco Inc., and Komatsu engines particularly, you may have to install a specially designed prefinished repair bushing to return the block to acceptable serviceability.

Block Flatness Check

All machined surfaces of the cylinder block must be checked for flatness using a nick-free straightedge and feeler gauge as shown in Figure 9–21. The service manual specs should be your guide as to allowable differences in measurement both longitudinally and transversely. If the machined surface of the block deck is not within tolerances, it will have to be resurfaced. The metal that can be removed from the top surface of the block is limited to a small amount.

Grinding Block Deck Surface

If the procedure in Figure 9–21 indicates that the block deck surface is outside the engine service manual tolerances, or if deep nicks or scratches and/or pitting exists around the water passage holes, the block will have to be resurfaced. This can be performed by installing the block into a grinding or milling machine such as the one illustrated in Figure 9–22. The machine operator can then lower a high-speed rotating grinding wheel (flat surfaces) downward by use of a micrometer feed control, or by an automatic feed control, to remove metal from the deck surface. The grinding machine is also placed into an automatic longitudinal feed so that its speed across the length of the block surface remains constant to provide an even and true finish.

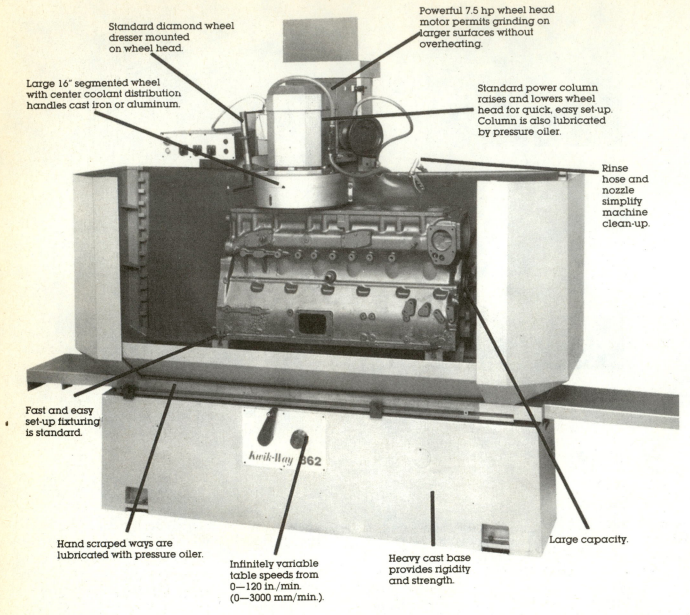

Standard diamond wheel dresser mounted on wheel head.

Large 16" segmented wheel with center coolant distribution handles cast iron or aluminum.

Powerful 7.5 hp wheel head motor permits grinding on larger surfaces without overheating.

Standard power column raises and lowers wheel head for quick, easy set-up. Column is also lubricated by pressure oiler.

Rinse hose and nozzle simplify machine clean-up.

Fast and easy set-up fixturing is standard.

Hand scraped ways are lubricated with pressure oiler.

Infinitely variable table speeds from 0—120 in./min. (0—3000 mm/min.).

Heavy cast base provides rigidity and strength.

Large capacity.

Kwik-Way 862

FIGURE 9–22 Illustration shows a diesel engine securely mounted and precision leveled to allow a grinding and milling machine to resurface the top deck of the engine block. This same type of a machine can be used to resurface the cylinder head. (Courtesy of Kwik-Way Manufacturing Co.)

NOTE: The amount of metal that can be removed from the top surface of the block is limited by the dimension from the centerline of the engine crankshaft to the top surface of the deck as shown in Figure 9–23a. Some engine manufacturers recommend checking this deck height as shown in Figure 9–23b.

Removing too much material from the top of the engine block deck can cause the piston crown to strike the underside of the cylinder head as well as change the liner counterbore depth. Consequently cylinder liner intrusion (two-cycle DDC engines) or liner protrusion (Cummins, Cat, and four-cycle Detroit Diesel models) can be too high or too low.

If the block has been resurfaced previously, the amount of stock removed will usually be stamped somewhere on the cylinder block on a machined pad area close to the top of the deck. A cylinder block deck height checker similar to the one illustrated in Figure 9–24 can be used to accurately measure the distance from the top deck to the main bearing bore. This tool,

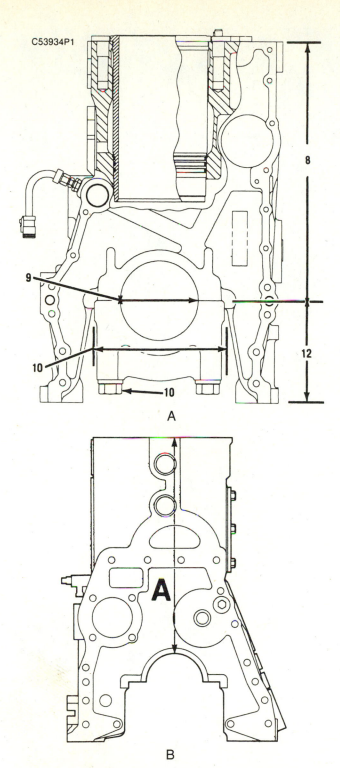

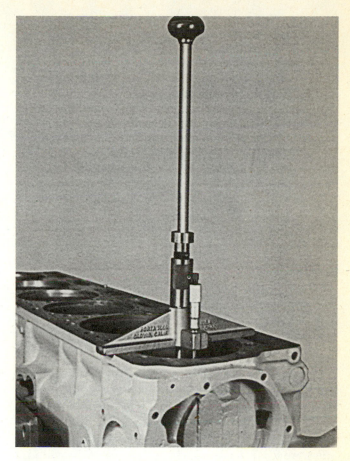

FIGURE 9–24 Universal block deck height checking tool used to accurately measure the distance from the top deck to the main bearing bore. This tool allows the service technician to measure exactly how much material can be surfaced from the block at overhaul. (Courtesy of Kent-Moore Division, SPX Corporation.)

FIGURE 9–23 (a) Example of where the technician would check the cylinder block deck height to crankshaft centerline on a 3406E heavy-duty high-speed engine. (Courtesy of Caterpillar Inc.) (b) Dimension A is one example of where the engine manufacturer requires the technician to closely check the cylinder block deck height to upper main bearing saddle area. (Courtesy of DAF Trucks, Eindhoven, Netherlands.)

with its attachments, allows the service technician to check block heights ranging between 8 and 24 in. (203 to 610 mm). A built-in micrometer comes with a setting standard to ensure complete accuracy. In this way, the technician knows how much material can be safely removed from the top deck surface. After the block has been resurfaced, you can measure both ends of the block with the machined pad resting on the block, as shown in Figure 9–24, to make certain that the block deck has been resurfaced straight and square.

SERVICE TIP: Some engine manufacturers offer thicker cylinder head gaskets for use with resurfaced cylinder blocks. On Caterpillar 3116 truck engines, a 0.25 mm (0.010 in.) thicker head gasket is intended for use *only* when the block height (distance from the centerline of the main bearing bore to the top deck of the block) is less than 321.75 mm (12.667 in.). If the height is less than 321.50 mm (12.657 in.), however, the block should be replaced!

FIGURE 9–25 *Engine block thread repair bushing, which is sealed at the bottom to eliminate coolant leakage. (Courtesy of Kent-Moore Division, SPX Corporation.)*

Threaded Holes

A very important task is to closely inspect and clean out all threaded holes in the block. Failure to do so can result in stripped and damaged bolts as well as incorrect torque readings. A set of readily available shop taps can be used. If, however, stripped or cracked bolt holes are found, particularly in the area of the cylinder head and main bearing capscrew holes, the insertion of either a *helicoil* or *Tap-lok* insert will be required. Although this can be done by hand, it is extremely important that the insert is installed squarely; otherwise, the stresses placed on the bolt or capscrew can result in bolt breakage and the consequences associated with this.

A small Porta-Tool thread repair kit that contains a sturdy base plate and drill jig to ensure perfect alignment is maintained during the reaming and tapping operations can be used. Two types of thread repair bushings are available, as shown in Figure 9–25. One of these is hollow and open at both ends. For cylinder head bolt repairs, the insert is sealed at the bottom end to eliminate coolant leakage. Once the damaged hole has been located and the base plate centered, the damaged hole can be reamed out as shown in Figure 9–26. The hole is then retapped using this same basic equipment to ensure perfect alignment. Remember to wear safety glasses when using compressed air to clean out the hole. Then with the new thread insert screwed onto a bolt and locked in place, tighten the threaded bushing into place as shown in Figure 9–27.

For repair of smaller cylinder block bolt holes in both English and metric sizes, a *Master thread repair kit*

FIGURE 9–26 *Using a power drill, base plate, and drill jig to maintain alignment during the reaming and tapping operation prior to installing a thread repair bushing into the engine block. (Courtesy of Kent-Moore Division, SPX Corporation.)*

FIGURE 9–27 *Installing a thread repair bushing into the engine block upper deck surface using a threaded bolt and lockout assembly. (Courtesy of Kent-Moore Division, SPX Corporation.)*

similar to the one shown in Figure 9–28 can be used without the need for the special tools illustrated in Figures 9–26 and 9–27. The kit shown provides a range of high-performance, carbon steel threaded inserts for quick positive repair of damaged threads in

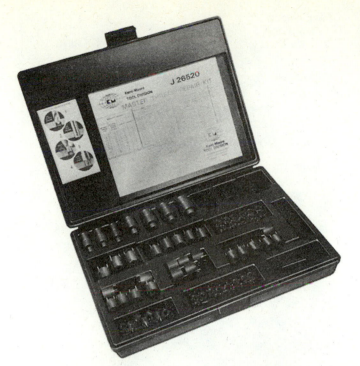

J 26520 Master Thread Repair Kit

High performance, carbon steel threaded inserts for quick positive repair of damaged threads in cold rolled steel, cast iron, aluminum, magnesium, and plastics.

Fast, permanent installation in 4 easy steps... with standard drills and taps!

DRILL OUT OLD THREADS

TAP NEW THREADS

SCREW IN INSERT

DRIVE TABS DOWN

EXCLUSIVE LOCKING "TABS" PREVENT INSERT ROTATION

FIGURE 9–28 Contents of a typical master thread repair kit for repairing stripped or damaged holes on an engine block or piece of equipment. (Courtesy of Kent-Moore Division, SPX Corporation.)

cold rolled steel, cast iron, aluminum, magnesium, and plastics. The inserts feature an exclusive TABS lock insert that, once installed, cannot rotate, particularly when the bolt is removed at a later date. Replacement threaded inserts can be purchased to restock the kit at any time.

Main Bearing Cap Alignment

When an engine has accumulated many miles (kilometers) or hours of operation, some slight misalignment may occur in the main bearing caps. In cases of engine failure, main bearing failure, or crankshaft damage, close visual inspection during engine disassembly will usually indicate where suspected mis-

alignment may exist. The main bearing bores can be checked for misalignment in three ways (the third method is the most accurate):

1. Use a dial bore gauge as shown in Figure 9–29 set to the specified setting and compare the various readings. Take careful note, however, that measuring the inside diameter of individual bores will *not* determine if the bores are on the same centerline.

2. Install the crankshaft and new main bearings lubricated liberally, and torque the main bearing caps in sequence. Manually rotate the crankshaft each time you tighten each cap. Any misalignment will cause the crankshaft to tighten up or fail to rotate, indicating at

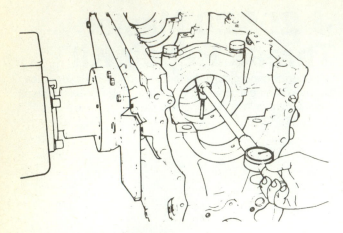

FIGURE 9–29 *Gauging the engine block crankshaft main bearing bores with a precision dial bore gauge. (Courtesy of Detroit Diesel Corporation.)*

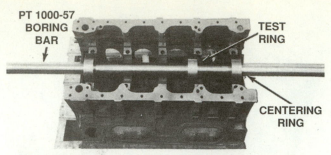

Installation of the Centering Rings

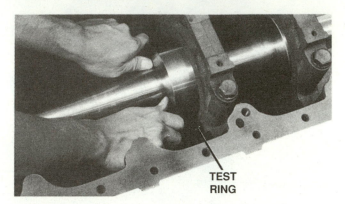

FIGURE 9–30 *Cylinder block crankshaft bore alignment checking tools. Once the centering rings are installed at each end of the block and the main bearing caps are installed, slide the correct test ring through the journal caps. If the test ring fails to pass through freely, mark this bore for repair. (Courtesy of Kent-Moore Division, SPX Corporation.)*

what main bearing cap the misalignment exists. If the crankshaft does not rotate freely by hand after installation and torquing of main bearing caps, the reason may be one of these: normal wear or use, improper installation of block stabilizers, improper bearing cap bolt torque, improper line boring techniques, improper block alignment, improper outboard bearing installation, or lack of crankshaft end-play.

There are several reasons why the bearing bore centers may be off centerline: foreign material between bearing shell and block bore, incorrect bearing shell size, bent crankshaft, two- or three-piece blocks misaligned, crankshaft bore damaged or misaligned, or incorrect installation of the bearing shell.

3. Use a dummy shaft (pilot mandrel) for the specific engine make and model. This mandrel is the same dimension as the inside diameter of the main bearing caps, less a small oil clearance. With the mandrel installed into the main bearing saddles of the block and the caps torqued into place individually, attempt to rotate the checking bar. Failure of the mandrel to rotate as each main bearing cap is tightened indicates misalignment at this cap. Other checking kits include a series of guide rings and a bar. The ring group contains two centering rings and one test ring. To use, simply install a centering ring at each end of the block and reinstall all bearing caps as shown in Figure 9–30. Install the bar and test ring; then slide the test ring through the journals to be checked. If the test ring does not pass through any bore, mark this area for repair (line boring).

When misalignment of the crankshaft main bearing bores exists, the crankshaft block saddles and caps have to be rebored or honed. The block can be sent to a machine shop or the technician can use a line boring tool that can be powered by a heavy-duty drill motor as

illustrated in Figure 9–31. Line-boring kits come with a wide variety of options and guide ring groups to suit various engine makes and models. The portable line boring kit contains a special micrometer base assembly. This micrometer is used to preset the selected size range cutter bit when mounted in its holder to the bore diameter, which can range between 3 and 7 in. (76 to 178 mm). The system comes equipped with a fully automatic hydraulic feed unit that totally controls the rate by directly relating it to cutter speed, which in turn is driven by a suitably rated drill motor. The Sunner CH-100 line bore unit can be used on Cummins, Caterpillar, Detroit Diesel, Mack, Navistar, and Komatsu diesel engines. In addition, it may also be necessary to remachine the main bearing thrust surfaces after completion of a line boring procedure. Designed for easy manual operation, the thrust cutter attaches to the end of a Porta-Tool line boring bar and cuts the thrust surface. An adjustable feed collar is graduated in increments of 0.001 in. (0.0254 mm) to precisely set the cutting depth. Both large and small cutter assemblies are included to provide universal application.

FIGURE 9–31 *Cylinder block crankshaft line honing repair tools and equipment installed into the engine to correct for misalignment. (Courtesy of Sunnen Products Company.)*

Main Bearing Saddle Repair

Although line boring can be used to realign the crankshaft bearing bore in the main bearing cap saddles, in some cases this distortion or severely worn or damaged saddles may require metal removal that exceeds the available oversize outside diameter bearings. If this occurs, a bushing will have to be inserted to salvage the block. This involves using the line boring tools shown in Figure 9–31 to bore the saddles to accept a prefinished bushing. Figure 9–32 illustrates that, once the block has been line bored, a semicircular bushing similar in shape to a main bearing shell is inserted into the saddle. A bushing hold-down clamp kit shown in this same diagram is then installed to securely hold the bushing in position. While the bushing is clamped, rivet holes are drilled and retaining rivets are installed. The bushing is then line bored to the engine manufacturer's specifications, which would be equal to the standard outside diameter of the replacement bearing shells. Once the bushings have been installed and line bored, remove any excess material as shown in Figure 9–33 with the use of a good, clean, smooth file.

Thermospray Coating

Repair or reworking of main bearing saddle areas in the block can also be done by applying a thermospray coating to the spun area of the saddle. The coating is a one-step, self-bonding machinable stainless steel type. It is a nickel-chromium, molybdenum, aluminum composite, and it is applied in powder form. The strongly bonded coating rebuilds the damaged saddle inside diameter half-sections, which are built up to slightly oversize, then machined to final specifications. The powdered metal composite is available from Metco Inc., Westbury, NY. This spray method is fast and easy and does not require removal of base metal, as does conventional line boring and insert-type repair. Coatings as thin as 0.001 in. (0.0254 mm) and as thick as 0.100 in. (2.54 mm) can be applied.

The application procedure for repairing the saddle area of the block begins with close examination to determine if the block is salvageable. If it is, the block is degreased, then blasted with a coarse G-25 chilled iron grit or angular steel to roughen the surface and improve subsequent bonding. Areas surrounding the section to be flame sprayed have to be masked off, and

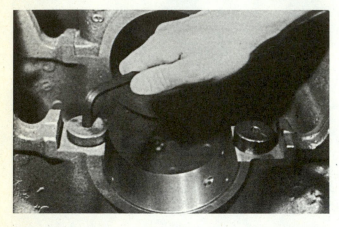

FIGURE 9–32 Engine block hardware kits designed to seat and clamp the crankshaft saddle repair bushing into the machined saddle bores. While the bushing is clamped, rivet holes are drilled and retaining rivets are installed. The repair bushing is then bored to OEM specifications. (Courtesy of Kent-Moore Division, SPX Corporation.)

FIGURE 9–33 Using a hand file to carefully remove excess material from the block crankshaft bore saddle area after an installed repair bushing has been line bored. (Courtesy of Kent-Moore Division, SPX Corporation.)

the area to be rebuilt is preheated to 200 to 300°F (93 to 149°C) maximum using a Type 6P-H thermospray gun. A Type 3MP positive-pressure powder feeding unit with a dial on the control unit sets the precise feed rate desired. Once the feeder is started, the self-bonding metal powder is applied to produce a strong bond as a result of the exothermic reaction that occurs.

A sealer material designed to make machining of the area easier is applied to the built-up area while it is still warm. The wax sealer melts, impregnating the pores of the heated surface, and also serves as a tooling lubricant for the tungsten carbide tool bit during final machining. This metal spraying process has gained in popularity and is much cheaper and less time consuming than regular machining.

Camshaft Bearing Bore

The camshaft bearing bores can be checked for taper and ovality by means of a spring-loaded telescoping gauge; then the dimension is checked with an outside micrometer and compared to service manual specs. A special *cam boring tool attachment kit* can be used with the line boring tool kit illustrated in Figure 9–30. These attachments can be used to repair damaged cam bores, and if no oversize outside diameter cam bearings are available, prefinished repair bushings can be installed to accept a standard outside diameter cam bushing assembly. If the cam bearing bores are acceptable, however, new standard bushings can be installed using a suitable cam bearing installer tool. Figures 13–27 through 13–30 in Chapter 13 illustrate one cam bearing service kit.

REPAIR OF CYLINDER BLOCK CRACKS

When an engine block has been cracked, the location, length, and depth of the crack are the determining factors in whether it is technically acceptable and financially suitable to attempt to repair the crack, or whether the engine block should be replaced. Earlier we described how cylinder block counterbores and damaged bolt holes could be repaired using special tools and equipment. Attempting to repair cracks other than these can be "touchy" at best, although many repair facilities offer these services. The technician or service maintenance management must decide whether they want to take a chance on such procedures, since there is usually no guarantee that the repairs will withstand indefinitely the rigors of heavy-duty, day-to-day diesel operations.

In some repair procedures for major cracks, the block can be welded after preheating to relieve stresses, then normalized after the welding procedure. This process involves uniquely designed metal locks and threaded pins to repair cracked and broken castings. This metal stitching system is a cold repair process that does not require preheating as in a welding repair. The metal stitching pins are manufactured from alloy steel and come in several lengths and sizes. The pin design incorporates the tight sealing of a tapered pin along with the controlled-stress feature of a straight pin. The pin is designed with a hex head that snaps off at a predetermined torque value just above the surface of the block.

REPLACEMENT CYLINDER BLOCKS

Should it become necessary to replace a cylinder block assembly, always check the latest OEM service bulletin information to ensure you can use some of the existing major components such as the crankshaft, camshaft, liners, and pistons. Engine manufacturers update products continually, so you may find that the block you require is no longer available. Usually the upper liner area of the block has been changed, the crankshaft diameter has been increased, and newer style pistons have been introduced with top rings that are located closer to the top of the crown to produce LCV (lower crevice volume) and meet the more stringent exhaust emissions regulations. Use of newer pistons in an older model block usually results in insufficient top ring cooling and ring breakage or seizure. In Caterpillar 3406C engines, the upper liner area of the newer block has been changed to allow a higher coolant path because of the new 8 mm (0.315 in.) top ring distance LCV pistons. The new block also uses a new liner with lower O-ring locations: the top liner O-ring now resides below the lower bore chamfer in the block. Always take special care to determine what used parts can be reused when the cylinder block is changed!

SELF-TEST QUESTIONS

1. Technician A says that most high-speed diesel engine cylinder blocks are made from aluminum alloy. Technician B disagrees, stating that gray cast iron alloys with a fairly high silicon content ensure superior durability. Who is correct?

2. Technician A states that all high-speed diesel engines employ one-piece cylinder blocks. Technician B says that a number of larger high-speed engines employ two- and even three-piece bolted blocks. Who knows the product information best?

3. True or False: The most widely used high-speed engine cylinder block is a six-cylinder inline configuration.

4. Technician A says that when cylinder block bores become worn, the block should be replaced. Technician B says that the block can be rebored or a new cylinder sleeve (liner) can be used. Who is correct?

5. True or False: A square engine block design means that the bore and stroke are the same dimension.

6. Technician A says that very large slow-speed engines such as those used in deep-sea marine tankers and freighters employ blocks of the A-frame design, which are welded sections. Technician B says that this is not so, because this type of construction would not allow a strong enough configuration; instead, large cast iron sections must be employed. Which technician is correct?

7. Technician A says that very large slow-speed diesel engines often run as slow as 57 rpm. Technician B says that the slowest speed an engine can operate at is about 400 rpm. Which technician is correct?

8. True or False: Many engine blocks in use today that employ the same bore and stroke simply keep adding cylinders to meet the desired horsepower rating.

9. Technician A says that when overhauling an engine, it is very important to remove any scale buildup from the internal coolant passages to prevent overheating during operation. Technician B says that as long as you thoroughly steam clean these passages, there should be no problem. Which technician has higher standards of excellence?

10. Technician A says that it isn't necessary to pressure test a cylinder block at major overhaul if no visible cracks are apparent during inspection when you are using nondestructive testing methods. Technician B says that you should always perform a pressure check to confirm that no cracks exist, since you cannot always detect hairline cracks using the nondestructive method. Which technician is correct?

11. True or False: All machined surfaces of an engine block should always be checked with a straightedge and a feeler gauge for any signs of distortion.

12. True or False: Cylinder block crankshaft bore alignment should be checked at major overhaul even if no bearing damage is evident.

13. True or False: If a cylinder block crankshaft bore is misaligned, the block should be replaced.

14. True or False: Signs of fretting at the main bearing cap parting line are indicative of movement of the main bearing cap.

15. True or False: A dry-type cylinder liner is always press fit in the block bore.

16. Technician A says that a dry press fit cylinder liner can normally be pressed in the block bore by hand. Not so says technician B; a hydraulic press is necessary to install it. Which technician is correct?

17. Technician A says that to recondition a cylinder block bore, either an adjustable/fixed power hone (see Figure 9-13) can be used, or a boring bar can be used. Technician B says that a boring bar should be used to enlarge the block bore and that a hone should be used only to finish the bore crosshatch. Which technician is correct?

18. List the conditions for which cylinder block counterbores should always be checked.

19. Damaged cylinder liner block counterbores can be remachined to repair them, according to technician A. Technician B says that the block would have to be replaced. Who is correct?

20. Technician A says that when remachining of the top deck of the cylinder block is necessary, you are limited to how much metal can be removed and should be guided by the dimension from the centerline of the crankshaft to the top of the deck. Technician B says that you can remove as much metal as necessary from the top deck surface; simply employ a thicker cylinder head gasket to offset the removed deck metal. Which one of these technicians would you follow?

21. Cylinder block camshaft bores can also be remachined at engine overhaul if necessary, according to technician A. Technician B says that the block would require replacement. Who is right?

22. To determine if the cylinder block bore is within the allowable limits regarding wear, ovality, and taper, use
    a. a precision dial indicator
    b. inside calipers
    c. an inside micrometer
    d. a tape measure

10 Flywheels and Housings

OVERVIEW

The flywheel and housing, which provide the power takeoff point from the engine, require special consideration. In this chapter we discuss the different types of flywheels—their identification, SAE size category, and bolt pattern. We also discuss dial indicator runout checks needed to ensure that the flywheel rotates concentrically within tolerance limits.

TOPICS

- Purposes of flywheels
- Flywheel forces
- Flywheel designs and SAE sizes
- Flywheel timing marks
- Removing and inspecting the flywheel
- Ring gear replacement
- Pilot bearing replacement
- Flywheel installation
- Flywheel runout
- Flywheel housing
- Self-test questions

PURPOSES OF FLYWHEELS

The engine flywheel illustrated in Figure 10–1 is generally manufactured from cast iron or cast steel. It is designed for multiple purposes such as those described next.

1.   The engine flywheel is fitted with a ring gear shrunk onto the circumference of the assembly. The

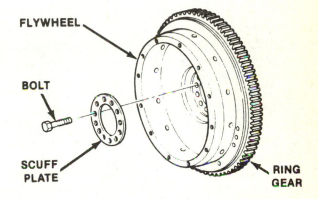

FIGURE 10–1 Heavy-duty high-speed engine pot-type flywheel showing the starter motor ring gear and self-locking retaining bolt scuff plate. (Courtesy of Detroit Diesel Corporation.)

starter motor drive gear engages this ring gear to rotate the engine crankshaft to start the engine.

2.   The flat machined surface or face of the flywheel serves as a power transfer mounting point for various elements:

- Heavy-duty friction clutch disc (standard transmission)
- Clutch pressure plate (standard transmission)
- Flex disc for an automatic or powershift transmission
- Bolted and toothed ring to accept a rubber drive flex plate for hydraulic marine gear
- Drive ring attachment for a power generator
- Mounting surface for a PTO (power takeoff)
- Mounting surface for a multiple-belt/chain drive pulley

253

- Direct bolting surface for a drive plate and universal joint

3. The mass of the rotating flywheel produces a high centrifugal force to provide energy for operating the engine between power impulses. The amount of energy absorbed and returned by the flywheel is relative to the work developed, which is based on the number of engine cylinders, whether the engine is a two- or four-stroke-cycle, the power of the engine, and the engine's speed of rotation. The flywheel reduces the variation in the rotative speed of the crankshaft during individual cylinder power impulses. On a two-stroke-cycle engine, the number of degrees between each cylinder power stroke will be closer together than on an equivalent four-stroke-cycle engine. During the exhaust, intake, and compression strokes of a four-stroke-cycle engine, and on the compression stroke of a two-cycle engine, the energy stored in the flywheel on the power stroke keeps the engine rotating. Obviously, the greater the number of cylinders, the less energy the flywheel has to store to keep the engine rotating at a steady speed. Therefore, the actual diameter and weight of the flywheel used on any engine depend on the number and the size of the cylinders, the engine rpm, and the allowable speed fluctuation desired. On engine applications that operate at varying speeds throughout the governed operating range, if quick acceleration or engine response is required, a light flywheel is desirable (for example, on a parallel diesel gen-set application where the frequency must be kept very close).

FLYWHEEL FORCES

The forces incurred in a rotating flywheel depend on flywheel mass (weight), diameter, and rotative speed. Consider that the rotative speed of the flywheel rim is at a very high velocity (speed and direction). Place a chalk or paint mark on the rim of the flywheel and watch it as the engine accelerates, to gain an appreciation for the velocity that occurs. On a high-speed heavy-duty diesel engine, if a 26 in. diameter (2.166 ft or 0.66 m) flywheel was used, and if the engine was governed at a maximum full-load speed of 2100 rpm, the velocity of the flywheel would be 14,296 ft/min (4357 m/min), or 163 mph (261 km/h). The larger the flywheel diameter, the higher the rotative speed of the flywheel rim. Allowable flywheel rim velocities depend on flywheel design, the grade of material used, and the diameter of the flywheel. On very large diesel engines a 10 ft (3 m) diameter flywheel on an engine running at 100 rpm would have a rim velocity of 3142 ft/min (958 m/min), or 36 mph (57 km/h).

The tensile stresses incurred in a rotating flywheel can be substantial. Consider that in a cast iron flywheel with a velocity of 6000 ft/min (1829 m/min), the tensile stresses at the flywheel rim would be approximately 970 psi (6688 kPa), but when rotating at a velocity of 21,000 ft/min (6400 m/min), the rim stresses increase to 13,000 psi (89,635 kPa, or 90 MPa). Because of the stresses incurred in a rotating flywheel, large slow-speed engine flywheels are usually aligned and supported on either one or more keyways, while many high-speed engines employ hardened dowel pins. The flywheel bolts used are never less than a Grade 8 classification.

FLYWHEEL DESIGNS AND SAE SIZE

Some flywheels are designed with a flat machined surface, whereas others employ what is commonly referred to as a *pot-type* design. Figure 10–1 illustrates a pot-type flywheel design along with the starter motor ring gear and a self-locking retaining bolt scuff plate. Various threaded bolt holes are located around the flywheel to allow bolting of drive assemblies. Closer inspection of the flywheel will reveal that there are a number of drilled holes spaced unevenly around the assembly. These holes are to provide for static and dynamic balance. Also in pot-type flywheels, a series of circumferential holes are drilled around the flywheel to allow any dirt or dust accumulations to be centrifuged out when the engine is running. These holes also allow airflow through the flywheel for cooling purposes, for example, when using a clutch drive.

Flywheel diameters and the spacing of the various bolt holes are not all the same. An acceptable industry standard for flywheels is that provided by the SAE. Figure 10–2 illustrates how the various flywheel dimensions for high-speed heavy-duty diesel engines are determined. Note that the larger diameter flywheel is assigned an SAE number of double zero (00), and the smallest flywheel dimension shown is a No. 6. This same numbering sequence is used for the flywheel housing assembly on the engine. For example, you cannot install a 00 flywheel into a No. 2 SAE housing, since the flywheel is physically too large to fit into the bore of the housing, as you can see from the chart.

Dual-Mass Flywheels

Flywheels used in some light- and medium-duty truck applications employ what is commonly called a *dual-mass flywheel* design. Figure 10–3 illustrates the component parts. The design has been used for a number of years by Ford and Navistar in their 6.9L and 7.3L diesel engine models and by GMC in its current 6.5L

FIGURE 10–2 *SAE flywheel and flywheel housing sizes and bolt pattern dimensions.*

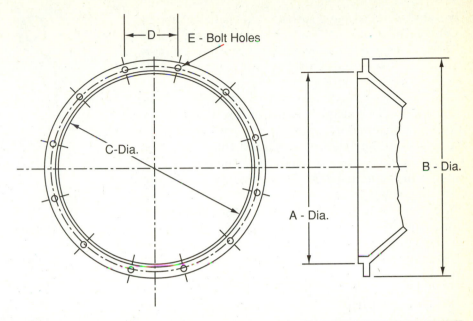

SAE No.	A	B	C	D	E	
					No.	Size
00	31	34 3/4	33 1/2	6 17/32	16	17/32
0	25 1/2	28	26 3/4	5 13/64	16	17/32
1/2	23	25 1/2	24 3/8	6 5/16	12	17/32
1	20 1/8	21 3/4	20 7/8	5 13/32	12	15/32
2	17 5/8	19 1/4	18 3/8	4 3/4	12	13/32
3	16 1/8	17 3/4	16 7/8	4 3/3	12	13/32
4	14 1/4	15 7/8	15	3 57/64	12	13/32
5	12 3/8	14	13 1/8	5 1/64	8	13/32
6	10 1/2	12 1/8	11 1/4	4 19/64	8	13/32

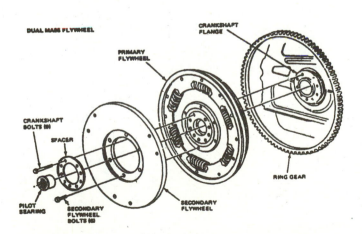

FIGURE 10–3   Concept of a dual-mass flywheel used by Ford and Navistar on their 6.9L and 7.3L V8 diesel engine models and by GMC on its 6.5L V8 diesel powered pickup truck. (Courtesy of Navistar International Corporation.)

turbocharged diesel pickup truck engine. The flywheel has a primary section with a spring-loaded insulator. Due to diesel engine torsional vibrations, the plastic spring retainers may crack or the spring may break; therefore, the flywheel should be taken apart each time a clutch repair job is to be performed. The secondary section, or clutch friction surface, must be checked with a straightedge for taper, cracks, and hard spots caused by heat. This surface may require regrinding to a maximum limit of 0.040 in. (1 mm). After flywheel installation onto the crankshaft flange, alignment with the flywheel housing should be within a maximum limit of 0.008 in. (0.2 mm).

FLYWHEEL TIMING MARKS

Flywheel rims are usually scribed on all four-stroke-cycle engines to assist the diesel technician with setting valves, starting cylinder positions on large slow-speed direct-air-start engines, respective cylinder TDC positions, and fuel injection pump timing degree marks BTDC. High-speed two-stroke-cycle engines such as those manufactured by Detroit Diesel do not have flywheel timing marks because technicians are not required to align any injection pump (because they use unit injectors) or to set the valves or injectors during a tuneup procedure.

Figure 10–4 illustrates flywheel rim timing marks. The TDC or the degree marks on the flywheel are aligned with a stationary pointer; in some engines slotted marks on the flywheel are aligned with a bolted-on degree marker plate. The flywheel timing marks are visible through an inspection cover hole on the flywheel housing. Some four-stroke-cycle engines also employ engine timing marks on the crankshaft pulley located at the front of the engine, plus injection pump timing marks that are visible after removing an inspection cover from the pump housing.

REMOVING AND INSPECTING THE FLYWHEEL

The engine flywheel is an extremely heavy component. When removing it, use a suitable safety sling or specially adaptable flywheel lifting tool that can be bolted into position, and attach a chain hoist or overhead crane as shown in Figure 10–5a to safely support its weight. Remove all of the flywheel retaining bolts except for one, as shown in Figure 10–5b. Install two flywheel guide studs with slotted heads; then remove the flywheel after removing the single retaining bolt. Many flywheels are supported on the rear crankshaft flange by two hardened dowel pins. You may have to lightly tap the flywheel to loosen it from these dowels, or use a heel bar to pry it loose without damaging the ring gear.

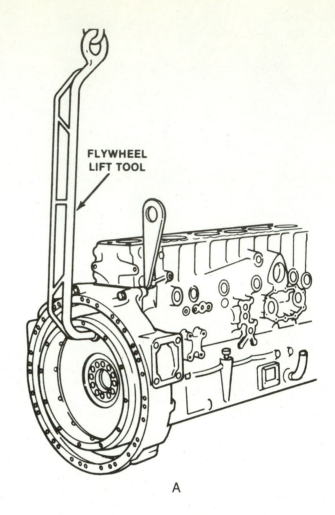

A

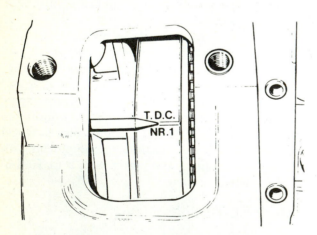

FIGURE 10–4   Example of flywheel timing marks that can be aligned with the stationary pointer when checking injection-pump-to-engine timing or when placing the No. 1 piston at TDC. (Courtesy of DAF Trucks, Eindhoven, Netherlands.)

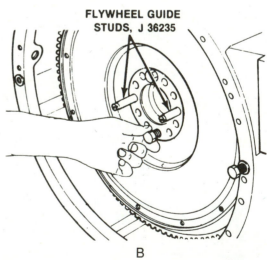

B

FIGURE 10–5   (a) Using a special lifting tool to either remove or install the flywheel safely; (b) using two guide studs threaded into the rear mounting flange of the crankshaft to facilitate removal or installation of the flywheel assembly. (Courtesy of Detroit Diesel Corporation.)

A flywheel is usually removed when the engine is given a major overhaul or when the machined flat face surface has been damaged, for example, due to a slipping clutch or drive member. Another reason to remove the flywheel is to replace a damaged starter motor ring gear (see Figure 10–1). Carefully inspect the contact surfaces of both the rear of the crankshaft and the flywheel for any signs of nicks, burrs, high spots, or scoring or signs of possible overheating, which will be visible as discoloration. The rear of the crankshaft is generally a hardened surface, so you may have to use a small finger grinder to remove any high spots, although a smooth file or rough-grade emery cloth will often do the job. Any radii on the flywheel surface or crankshaft flange should be maintained during any cleanup procedure.

Inspect the flat machined surface of the flywheel, particularly when a heavy-duty clutch is involved. Minor heat checks are acceptable, but use a straightedge and a feeler gauge or a dial indicator and sled gauge to determine what warpage exists on this surface. Severe discoloration is an indication of excessive heat buildup caused by a slipping clutch friction disc. The flat machined clutch surface may be reground providing that the following two conditions are met:

1. There should be no cracks within 5 mm (0.200 in.) from the inner or outer edge, unless they are minor heat checks.
2. No more than the recommended metal should be ground from the flywheel face. Check the service manual for the allowable minimum flywheel thickness.

If the flat machined surface is damaged, the flywheel face can be remachined on a flywheel grinder (Figure 10–6). The amount of metal removed should only be sufficient to provide a new, clean, flat surface. If too much material is removed, the induction hardened surface will be penetrated and short face life will result. Often the engine service manual specifies a minimum flywheel thickness dimension after any regrind procedure. If this dimension is exceeded, then a new flywheel will be required.

Refer to the following typical acceptable limits when grinding flywheels:

Flat Type

6, 7, 8 in. (152, 178, 203 mm)	Limit = 0.020 in. (0.5 mm)
9, 10 in. (229, 254 mm)	Limit = 0.030 in. (0.75 mm)
11, 12 in. (279, 305 mm)	Limit = 0.040 in. (1 mm)
13, 14 in. (330, 356 mm)	Limit = 0.060 in. (1.5 mm)
15, 15.5 in. (381, 394 mm)	Limit = 0.090 in. (2.29 mm)

Recess Type

13, 14, 15 in. (330, 356, 381 mm)	Limit = 0.090 in. (2.29 mm)

NOTE: Flywheel thickness is normally measured from the crankshaft bolt surface to the clutch or PTO disc friction surface. After any regrinding, to ensure that there is no clutch disc hangup, always place the clutch driven disc in or onto the flywheel and check the clearance between the disc hub damper springs, and the clearance between the heads of the crankshaft bolts.

RING GEAR REPLACEMENT

The steel flywheel ring gear that is driven by the starter motor drive pinion is press fit (shrunk) onto the rim of the flywheel. Figure 10–7 illustrates the ring gear and the machined lip on the flywheel over which it is pressed.

Ring Gear Removal
To remove the ring gear, lay the flywheel flat and support it on blocks as shown in Figure 10–8 so that the ring gear faces down. *Always* protect your eyes when attempting to remove or install a ring gear. The ring gear can be removed with a suitable brass punch and hammer by working around the circumference of the gear to avoid possible cocking and binding. Alternatively, you can use a sharp hand chisel to cut the ring gear between two of the teeth. A third method you can employ is an oxyacetylene torch to cut the ring gear between one-half to three-fourths of the way through, while exercising extreme care that the flame does not touch the flywheel. This action will expand and weaken the ring gear, which can then be easily tapped from its seat on the flywheel assembly.

Ring Gear Installation
Before installing a new ring gear, clean up the rim area using emery cloth; if nicks, burrs, or scores are evident, carefully use a small-mill smooth file. Closely inspect the new ring gear to ensure that it is the same as the removed unit. Many flywheel ring gears are manufactured with a chamfered tooth side, but some do not have a chamfer. If a chamfer is evident, the ring gear must be installed so that the chamfer on the teeth faces the starter motor drive gear pinion as it engages it.

Follow these steps to install a ring gear:

1. Support the flywheel upside down on a solid flat surface.

CAUTION: To install a new ring gear, you can use either an oxyacetylene torch or temperature-controlled oven to expand the ring gear enough to drop over the

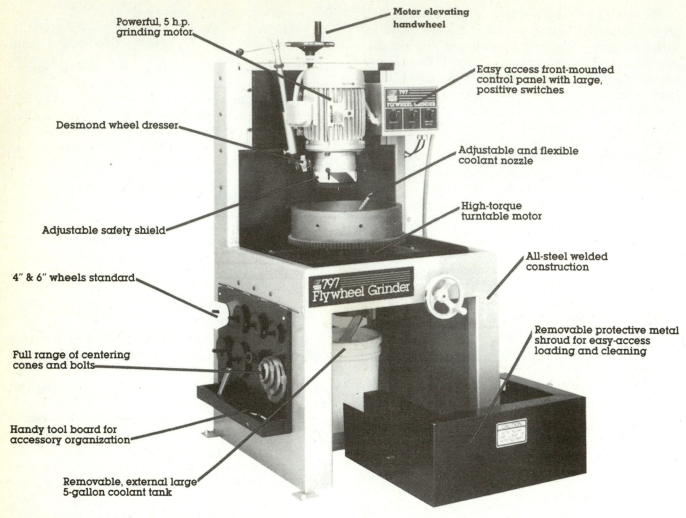

Powerful, 5 h.p. grinding motor.

Motor elevating handwheel

Desmond wheel dresser.

Easy access front-mounted control panel with large, positive switches

Adjustable and flexible coolant nozzle

Adjustable safety shield

High-torque turntable motor

4" & 6" wheels standard.

All-steel welded construction

Full range of centering cones and bolts.

Removable protective metal shroud for easy-access loading and cleaning

Handy tool board for accessory organization.

Removable, external large 5-gallon coolant tank

797 Flywheel Grinder

FIGURE 10–6 Grinding a heavy-duty engine flywheel clutch surface. (Courtesy of Kwik-Way Manufacturing Co.)

flywheel rim. Since the ring gear and teeth are hardened, excessive heat *can* withdraw the temper from the teeth causing them to wear rapidly. The engine service manual usually states the maximum temperature to use when heating the ring gear, for example, Cummins 14L—600°F (316°C) maximum; Cummins C engine—260°F (127°C); Detroit Diesel Series 92, 50 and 60 engines—400°F (204°C). Be sure to check the service manual.

2. To ensure that you do *not* exceed the temperature for expanding the ring gear, use a heat-indicating crayon (Thermomelt or Tempilstik), which is similar to a wax-type crayon. A label on the crayon indicates its melting temperature. Although you can lay a small piece of the crayon on the ring gear, it is acceptable to simply mark the ring gear in several places around its circumference. Use

the torch to move around the ring gear so that even heat distribution is ensured during the heating operation.

3. Place the ring gear on a flat metal surface. While wearing a pair of welding gloves, heat the ring gear uniformly with an oxyacetylene torch by moving the torch around the circumference. *Do not* allow the end of the flame to lick directly onto the ring gear.

4. Pay close attention to the crayon markings. When they start to become fluid, the ring gear has been heated sufficiently. Use a pair of large tongs to lift and place the ring gear into position over the flywheel rim, ensuring that the chamfered teeth are facing in the proper direction. Quickly tap the ring gear squarely into position until it bottoms gently against the flywheel shoulder. Should the

FIGURE 10–7 *Example of how the flywheel ring gear is attached to the flywheel assembly by a shrink-fit procedure onto a stepped flange area. 8 = bolt; 9 = flywheel; 10 = pin; 11 = ring gear; 12 = ball bearing. (Courtesy of DAF Trucks, Eindhoven, Netherlands.)*

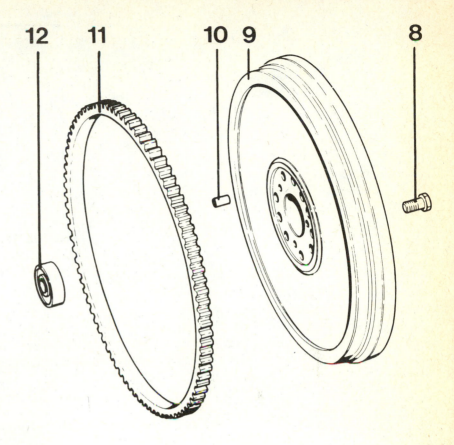

FIGURE 10–8 *Using a hammer and punch to remove the flywheel ring gear while supporting the flywheel on wooden blocks. (Courtesy of Cummins Engine Company, Inc.)*

ring gear not drop into position (become severely cocked), remove it, reheat it, and try again.

5. Allow the ring gear and flywheel to cool. *Do not* pour cold water over the ring gear to cool it, because this can cause a change to the structural properties of the metal.

PILOT BEARING REPLACEMENT

Many engine applications such as those bolted to a heavy-duty truck transmission require that a sealed (pilot) ball bearing shown in Figure 10–7 be pressed into the center bore of the flywheel assembly. In some engines, a split-tube-type retainer is driven into the end of the crankshaft to prevent the pilot bearing from entering the crankshaft cavity. The purpose of this bearing is to support and align the transmission input shaft. In other applications, a bushing may be used in place of a bearing. If it is necessary to remove this bearing, it can be replaced without removing the flywheel from the crankshaft. The bearing can be removed easily by using a special slide hammer puller similar to the one illustrated in Figure 10–9. By turning the slide hammer threaded rod in or out, the two small jaws can be expanded to suit the inside bore size of the pilot bearing. Then by using the slide hammer, the bearing is removed with little effort. The replacement bearing can be driven into place with a suitable installer.

FLYWHEEL INSTALLATION

During flywheel installation, use the same tooling that was described to remove it. Normally, the flywheel

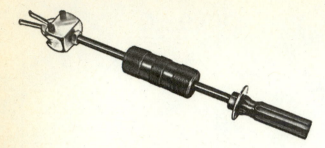

FIGURE 10–9 Slide-hammer-type flywheel bearing puller. (Courtesy of Kent-Moore Division, SPX Corporation.)

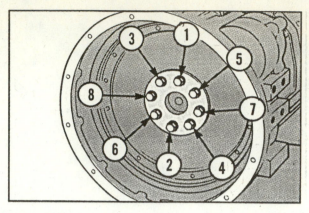

FIGURE 10–10 Flywheel torquing sequence for a C model diesel engine. (Courtesy of Cummins Engine Company, Inc.)

bolts onto the rear of the crankshaft in only one direction to ensure that the respective timing marks are aligned properly. If the flywheel bolt holes are not offset to guide you during installation, manually rotate the engine over to place the No. 1 cylinder on TDC on its compression stroke. Install the flywheel so that the No. 1 TDC scribe mark on the rim is aligned with the stationary pointer visible through the flywheel housing inspection cover hole, similar to that illustrated in Figure 10–4. If no dowel pins are used on the rear face of the engine crankshaft, to facilitate flywheel installation, refer to Figure 10–5 and install two guide studs threaded into the crankshaft at the 3 and 9 o'clock positions. Using the lifting arrangement shown in Figure 10–5, lift the flywheel into position and slide it over the guide studs or onto its dowel pins. If a scuff plate similar to the one illustrated in Figure 10–1 is used, install a new one. If a new one is not available, reverse the scuff plate and install two bolts 180° apart and tighten them to 50 lb-ft (68 N·m) to hold the flywheel in place while you remove the guide studs and the lifting tool. Replace bolt lock plates if used.

Most manufacturers specify that you should lightly lubricate the threads of the flywheel retaining bolts as well as the underside of the bolt head contact area with 15W-40 engine oil. If the bolt holes are "blind" (don't run right through), however, *do not* use excessive amounts of lubricant since this can create a hydrostatic lock in the hole. If you use a bolt lubricant such as International Compound No. 2 or equivalent, apply it to the bolt threads so that they are completely filled with compound and wipe off the excess. Also, apply this same compound to the underside of the bolt heads or hardened washers. Lubricating the bolts ensures that a minimum friction is created, thereby resulting in an accurate torque tightening value.

SERVICE TIP: Most high-speed engine manufacturers recommend what is known as a *torque-turn method* when tightening the flywheel bolts. This procedure provides a more consistent clamping load on the bolts.

In addition, many engine manufacturers now state that flywheel mounting bolts are considered *one use items* and cannot be reused. New mounting bolts must be installed when attaching the flywheel. Using old bolts can lead to either a loss of torque or bolt breakage during engine operation, resulting in serious engine damage.

Follow these five steps to install the flywheel:

1. After the flywheel is lifted into position over the two guide studs, install two bolts and torque them to 50 lb-ft (68 N·m).

2. Install all remaining bolts, lubricated as described, and snug them.

3. Remove the two bolts installed in step 1 and lubricate them with International Compound No. 2 or equivalent.

4. Using an accurately calibrated torque wrench, tighten each bolt to 50 lb-ft (68 N·m) using a star or diagonally opposite pattern sequence similar to that shown in Figure 10–10.

5. Mark the heads of the bolts to the flywheel with chalk; rotate each bolt the recommended number of additional degrees as specified in the service manual. Figure 10–11 illustrates one manufacturer's torque-turn method chart. It indicates that once the 50 lb-ft torque is achieved, the bolts would be rotated an additional 120°, or the equivalent of two flats on a six-point bolt head.

FLYWHEEL RUNOUT

Once the flywheel has been installed, it is important to carefully check its concentricity (running true) and face runout. This can be done by means of a dial indi-

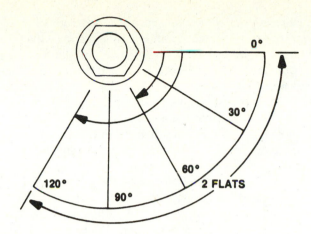

FIGURE 10–11 *Example of a torque-turn method used to accurately tighten the flywheel retaining bolts. (Courtesy of Detroit Diesel Corporation.)*

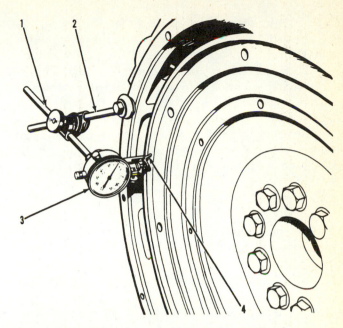

FIGURE 10–12 *Using a dial indicator gauge to check the flywheel bore runout. (Courtesy of Caterpillar Inc.)*

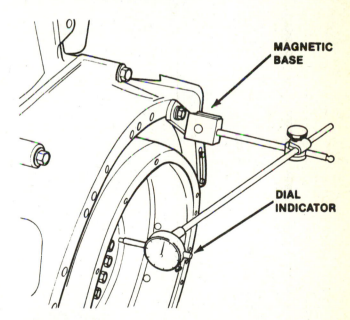

FIGURE 10–13 *Measuring flywheel clutch face surface runout. (Courtesy of Detroit Diesel Corporation.)*

cator attached to the flywheel housing. Attach the dial indicator by using a magnetic base type or by using a bolt to hold the indicator bracket to the flywheel housing. In Figure 10–12 the dial gauge is set up to check the bore runout of the flywheel to the flywheel housing. The contact tip of the indicator has been preloaded against the inside diameter of the flywheel bore, and the gauge has been set to zero. The service manual will specify the maximum allowable runout, which is usually stated as TIR (total indicator reading). This means that if the TIR is given as a maximum of 0.010 in. (0.25 mm), then the total of the plus and minus readings on the dial gauge must not exceed this specification. If the TIR does exceed the spec, loosen the flywheel bolts, remove the flywheel, and closely inspect the flywheel-to-crankshaft mounting surface for dirt, scores, nicks, or damage. Also, closely check the dowel pins (if used) in the rear of the crankshaft flange for signs of wear. Replace them if they are worn. Reinstall the flywheel and repeat the dial indicator reading procedure.

Also mount a dial indicator against the flat machined surface of the flywheel as illustrated in Figure 10–13. The gauge tip should be approximately 140 mm (5.5 in.) from the centerline of the crankshaft for a high-speed diesel engine, or approximately in the mid-travel area of the clutch surface. This check is used to determine the axial (end to end) runout of the flywheel. To accurately determine this axial runout, you must push the flywheel fully forward; otherwise, the normal crankshaft end float will create an erroneous reading. With the crankshaft in the fully forward position, zero the dial indicator tip against the machined surface of the flywheel. Manually rotate the flywheel and compare the reading obtained with that stated in the service manual for the engine. Once

again, if the reading exceeds specifications, remove the flywheel and determine the cause. In the absence of manufacturers' specifications use these: A 16 in. (406 mm) diameter flywheel would have an average acceptable TIR runout of approximately 0.008 in. (0.203 mm). Allowable runout would increase by approximately 0.002 in. (0.05 mm) for each additional

2 in. (51 mm) diameter of the flywheel. Therefore, a 32 in. (813 mm) diameter flywheel would have an allowable TIR runout of approximately 0.016 in. (0.406 mm).

Flywheels used in heavy-duty trucks that employ a mechanical clutch use a pilot bearing, which is shown as item 12 in Figure 10–7. After flywheel installation, mount a dial indicator gauge as illustrated in Figure 10–14 to check the bore runout of the clutch pilot bearing. Compare the obtained reading to the service manual specifications.

FLYWHEEL HOUSING

The flywheel housing is generally bolted to the rear of the engine and encloses the flywheel assembly. It is designed to provide the mounting surface for the bolted engine mounts, and it is machined to accept the installation of the press-fit rear crankshaft oil seal in its centerbore area. In addition, the housing provides the structural mounting surface to which is bolted a transmission, marine gear, pump, gen-set, torque converter, and so forth. Accessory drive items such as a vehicle alternator, air compressor, and hydraulic pump, may also be mounted to the flywheel housing and driven by a gear or belt drive from the rear gear train if used. The engine starter motor is bolted to the forward side of the flywheel housing, which is generally a one-piece casting manufactured from either cast iron or aluminum. Figure 10–15 illustrates an aluminum flywheel housing and identifies component parts.

Removal of Flywheel Housing
The flywheel housing can be removed with the engine in position in its application; however, the transmission or drive unit would have to be removed first. The engine

must be supported securely by a jack or stands or slung to an overhead crane. As an example, assume that the engine is mounted into an engine overhaul stand such as the one illustrated in Figure 7–7. First, the flywheel has to be removed to access the flywheel housing. The number of bolts that you have to loosen varies between different makes and models of engines. Before removing the housing, it is generally helpful to thread in several long guide studs to the rear of the engine block or mounting plate surface. This facilitates pulling the housing away from the block squarely, since some housings are positioned over several dowel pins. It is advisable to sling the housing during removal, unless it is small and light enough for you to handle manually. Many housings are equipped with tapped threaded holes to facilitate the installation of eyebolts, to which a chain-fall or bracket-and-web sling can be attached.

Inspection of Flywheel Housing
After cleaning any dirt, grime, and old gasket material from the flywheel housing, inspect the housing for signs of stress cracks, particularly at the engine mount bolt area as well as the area to which the transmission is bolted. At the time of a major overhaul, the crankshaft rear oil seal should be removed and replaced. Inspect the oil seal bore for any signs of damage that might lead to oil leakage. All flat surfaces of the flywheel housing should be checked for any signs of severe distortion or warpage. If any bolt holes show signs of thread damage, you may have to install a helicoil, a Tap-lok insert, or a Rexnord-type *Keensert* (which is similar to a Tap-lok unit).

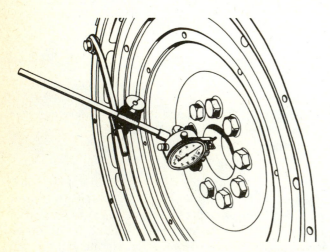

FIGURE 10–14 *Measuring bore runout of the flywheel clutch pilot bearing. (Courtesy of Caterpillar Inc.)*

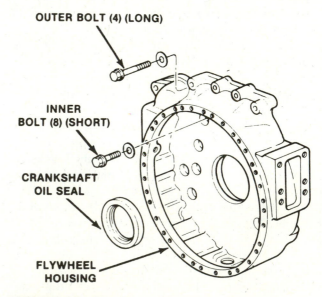

FIGURE 10–15 *Series 60 engine aluminum flywheel housing and related parts. (Courtesy of Detroit Diesel Corporation.)*

Installation of Flywheel Housing

Some flywheel housings are mounted directly to the rear face of the engine block. Others are bolted to an adaptor plate that has already been bolted to the engine block, such as those used on Detroit Diesel two-stroke-cycle engine models. Figure 10–16 illustrates that the flywheel housing on these engines forms the complete rear cover for the rear-mounted gear train. A gasket may be used between the housing and block. Alternatively, you can apply a continuous 1/16 in. (1.6 mm) bead of gasket eliminator (RTV-type sealant or equivalent) as illustrated in Figure 10–17 prior to housing installation. Some engines may require a wider bead than this, but seldom would you need more than a 1/8 in. (3.175 mm) bead. These types of sealants usually cure fairly quickly—within 5 to 10 minutes after application. Therefore, don't apply the sealant until you are ready to install the flywheel housing. If the flywheel housing has a new rear crankshaft oil seal installed in it, always use a seal protector during housing installation to prevent possible damage or rolling of the seal lip. Seal protectors are usually made from thin steel or plastic and offer a tapered surface for the seal to easily slide over during installation. It may be necessary to install an oversize seal along with a Speedi-Sleeve to the rear crankshaft flange area if a worn groove has formed. Refer to Chapter 11 on crankshafts for information on this procedure.

Use two long guide studs to ensure that the flywheel housing is installed squarely. Install all of the necessary bolts (lubricated) and torque them in sequence according to instructions in the service manual. Figure 10–18 illustrates one example of how to tighten the flywheel housing bolts. Once the flywheel housing has been securely bolted in place, install two dial indicators as illustrated in Figure 10–19, with the gauges supported on a base post threaded into the bolt holes of the flywheel. These gauges are required to check the bore concentricity and face runout of the flywheel housing to ensure that a square fit exists between the engine drive train and the drive option (for example, transmission, PTO, or marine gear). If the flywheel has not yet been installed, you can simply attach the dial gauge base to one of the holes in the rear crankshaft flange area and use dial gauge extension rods to allow the gauge tips to contact the reading areas. The top gauge in the diagram has its tip preloaded and zeroed against the flat bolted flange sur-

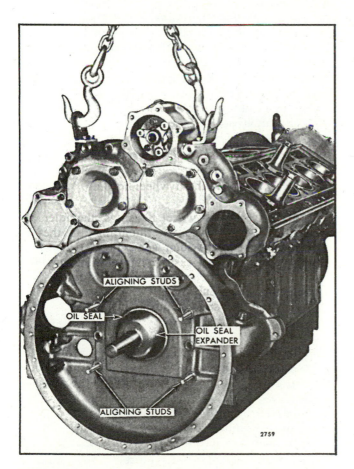

FIGURE 10–16 *Installing flywheel housing to the rear of a V71/92 two-stroke-cycle engine using lifting brackets, aligning studs, and an oil seal expander. (Courtesy of Detroit Diesel Corporation.)*

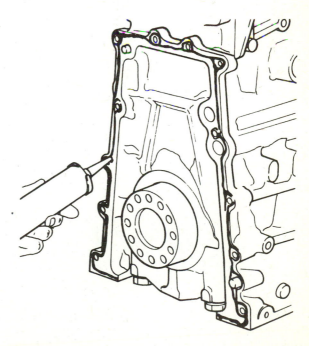

FIGURE 10–17 *Gasket eliminator installation to the rear of the Series 60 engine block. (Courtesy of Detroit Diesel Corporation.)*

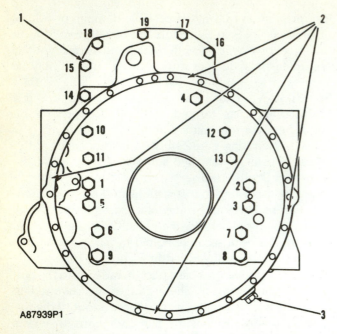

A87939P1

FIGURE 10-18 Torquing sequence for flywheel housing bolts for a 3406E Caterpillar engine. Item 2 indicates that the flywheel face runout should be checked at four main points with a dial indicator. (Courtesy of Caterpillar Inc.)

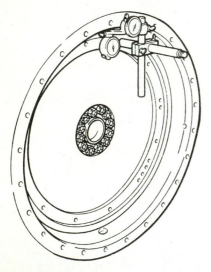

FIGURE 10-19 Measuring bore concentricity and bolting flange runout of flywheel housing. (Courtesy of Detroit Diesel Corporation.)

face of the housing to check for runout. The lower of the two gauges has its tip bearing against the inside bore of the flywheel bell housing.

Manually pry the crankshaft toward one end of the block to ensure that endplay does not affect any of

the readings. Take dial guage readings at four places 90° apart and compare them with the service manual specs. If the flywheel housing readings exceed the specs, remove the housing and check for dirt, metal particles, or anything that might prevent the housing from seating fully or squarely.

SELF-TEST QUESTIONS

1. Flywheels and housings are available in different diameters that are manufactured to meet standards set by which one of the following associations?
   a. ASTM
   b. API
   c. SAE
   d. ISO

2. True or False: No. 1 size flywheel is smaller than a No. 4.

3. Technician A says that the starter ring gear is usually pinned or bolted to the flywheel assembly. Technician B says that the ring gear is a shrink fit to the flywheel. Who is correct?

4. Technician A says that to replace the flywheel ring gear you have to remove the flywheel from the crankshaft. Technician B says that you simply have to unbolt it and replace it with a new ring gear. Who is correct?

5. Technician A says that a scuff plate used on a flywheel is designed to prevent scuffing of the machined surface by a clutch assembly. Technician B says that the scuff plate is used as a self-locking plate for the retaining bolts. Who is correct?

6. True or False: One of the functions of the mass contained in the flywheel is to store energy and return it to the crankshaft during engine operation. This maintains a steady engine speed between the firing impulses of the cylinders.

7. Technician A says that all engine flywheels contain engine timing marks to facilitate in-service checks. Technician B disagrees, saying that two-cycle Detroit Diesel engines do not use any flywheel timing marks, since they are not necessary when a unit injector fuel system is used. Who is correct?

8. True or False: All flywheels are mounted on the rear of the engine and supported on dowel pins as well as being bolted onto the rear of the engine crankshaft.

9. Technician A says that many engine flywheels can be installed in only one position to align the retaining bolt holes. Technician B says that flywheels can be installed in any position, because the bolt holes are always drilled the same center-to-center distance apart. Who is correct?

10. True or False: If a flywheel is capable of being installed in any of several positions, you should manually rotate the crankshaft over to place the No. 1 piston at TDC; then install the flywheel so that the No. 1 TDC mark is aligned with the stationary pointer.

11. True or False: Slight discoloration and a series of small cracks on the machined surface of a flywheel that employs a heavy-duty clutch or PTO requires that the flywheel be replaced.

12. Technician A says that a worn flywheel pilot bearing can be replaced without having to remove the flywheel from the engine crankshaft. Technician B says that this is not possible; you must remove the flywheel assembly. Who is correct?

13. True or False: Using excessive heat on a flywheel ring gear can destroy the surface hardness of the teeth.

14. Technician A says that to prevent overheating a flywheel ring gear, you can use a heat-indicating crayon or install the ring gear into a temperature-controlled oven. Technician B says that heat should never be applied to a flywheel ring gear. Who is correct?

15. Technician A says that it is advisable to thread two guide studs into the rear of the crankshaft mounting flange when installing the flywheel and to use a suitable lifting bracket and sling to facilitate installation. Technician A says that it is easier to manually lift the flywheel into position and rotate it to line up the bolt holes. Which technician knows safer work habits?

16. True or False: Many engine manufacturers recommend that flywheel bolts be changed at major overhaul regardless of the visible condition of the bolts.

17. Technician A says that flywheel retaining bolts that thread into "blind" holes should be heavily lubricated prior to installation. Technician B says that this can cause a hydrostatic lock in the hole; therefore, only a light coating of oil should be used on the threads, plus a small amount of oil under the bolt head. Who is correct?

18. Technician A says that when flywheel retaining bolts are to be tightened, they should be pulled up in increments using a diagonal tightening sequence until the correct torque is obtained. Technician B says that most high-speed engine manufacturers specify that the flywheel bolts be tightened using the torque-turn method, which is more accurate. Which technician is correct?

19. True or False: Flywheel housing concentricity or runout should always be checked with a dial indicator gauge after tightening the retaining bolts.

20. Technician A says that a flywheel housing bore that is not concentric after installation can cause oil leakage from the rear oil seal. Technician B disagrees, saying that this could not happen since the oil seal is press fit in the bore. Which technician is correct?

21. After flywheel installation, what runout checks would you perform using a dial indicator?

22. Technician A says that excessive flywheel runout can lead to complaints of engine vibration and heavy-duty clutch problems. Technician B says that this is not possible if the flywheel is torqued to the right spec. Who is correct?

23. True or False: Distortion of the machined flywheel face surface could cause clutch slippage.

24. Technician A says that if the rear crankshaft oil seal which is press fit in the flywheel housing bore leaks, the flywheel must be removed to replace the seal. Technician B says that the problem can be solved in place by drilling two small holes in the seal housing, inserting two self-tapping screws, and using a slide hammer to remove the seal. Which technician is correct?

Crankshafts, Bearings, Seals, and Dampers

OVERVIEW

The crankshaft is the largest and usually the most expensive rotating component within the engine block. In this chapter we discuss the various types of crankshaft designs, safe handling, removal, inspection, measurement, nondestructive testing, and reinstallation procedures. The chapter also describes the shell-type bearings used to support the crankshaft in the engine block, the types of oil seals used, and the importance of a properly maintained vibration damper assembly.

TOPICS

- Purpose of crankshafts
- Design and materials
- Crankshaft removal
- Polishing the journals
- Grinding the crankshaft
- Crack detection methods
- Failure analysis of the crankshaft
- Multiple piece crankshafts
- Crankshaft web deflection
- Crankshaft installation
- Main and con-rod bearings
- Crankshaft seals
- Crankshaft vibration dampers
- Crankshaft pulleys
- Self-test questions

PURPOSE OF CRANKSHAFTS

The main purpose of a crankshaft is to change the *reciprocating* (backward and forward) motion of the pistons into *rotary* motion at the crank via the con-rod and piston pin. Figure 11–1 illustrates a typical six-cylinder high-speed engine crankshaft that consists of seven main bearings; a four-cylinder or a V8 engine configuration would contain five main bearings. Since the main bearing journals support the weight of the rotating crank shaft and the mass of both the con-rod and piston, there is always one more main journal than con-rod journals. The number of individual cranks (for con-rods) on any shaft, and their placement, is dictated naturally by the number of cylinders and the firing order chosen for the engine. The cranks are usually equally spaced to provide a uniform angle between piston power impulses. In vee-type engines, the angle between the cylinder banks is also a determining factor for the locations of crank con-rod journals.

When an engine is running, the rotation of the crankshaft and the lower end of the con-rod creates a centrifugal force that acts on the crank main bearings. In multicylinder engines, these forces are often counteracted by other cranks to prevent vibration; however, the main bearings are still exposed to these additional loads. To effectively counteract these centrifugal forces, crankshaft counterweights strategically placed opposite the crankpins are designed to produce equal and opposite centrifugal forces. They also reduce bending stresses and minimize main bearing loads.

Complete static and dynamic balance of the crankshaft is achieved by the placement of counterweights (static); these weights are then drilled to remove material to provide a rotating (dynamic) balance. If you look closely at any crankshaft, you will notice that not all the weights are drilled to the same depth and location. Depending on engine size, most crankshaft counterweights are forged as part of the

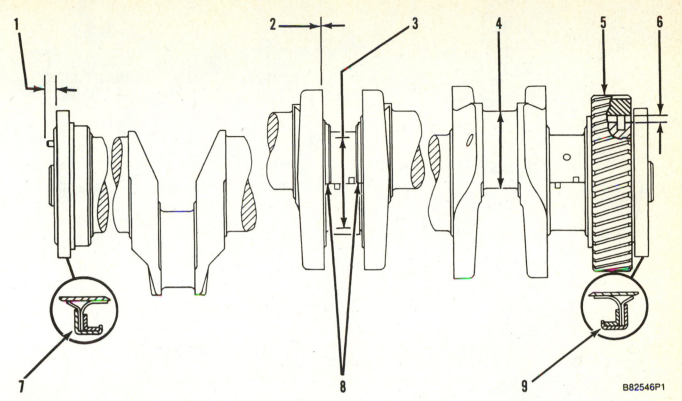

FIGURE 11–1   Identification of crankshaft components for a 3406E model inline six-cylinder high-speed, heavy-duty diesel engine. 1 = maximum length of pin out of crankshaft face; 2 = end play for crankshaft (new); 3 = main bearing journal; 4 = connecting rod bearing; 5 = maximum permissible temperature of the gear for installation on crankshaft; 6 = length of dowel out of crankshaft; 7 = 2W1734 seal group (rear); 8 = thrust plates for center main bearing only; 9 = 2W1733 seal group (front). (Courtesy of Caterpillar Inc.)

crank; however, on larger slow-speed engines, the weights are often bolted or welded into position.

DESIGN AND MATERIALS

The crankshaft is the longest, largest rotating component part of any engine; consequently, it is usually the most expensive component to replace. Smaller-displacement engine crankshafts can be manufactured from shell-molded nodular iron castings. Medium- and high-speed heavy-duty engine crankshafts with less than a 305 mm (12 in.) bore are generally manufactured from one-piece forged alloy steel containing carbon manganese, molybdenum, nickel, and chromium. The crankshaft is then heat-treated to relieve stresses, machined, induction hardened, and ground.

The main and con-rod bearing journal surfaces and fillets are induction hardened to provide high endurance limits at the most heavily stressed area of the crankshaft, which is at the rolled *fillet radius* as

shown in Figure 11–2. Surface hardening of the main and con-rod journal is usually obtained by flame hardening or induction hardening, whereby the surfaces to be hardened are rapidly heated and then water quenched. The degree of hardening obtained depends on the carbon content of the steel used, heating time, and so forth. In highly stressed crankshafts, the shaft is exposed to gas nitriding or carbon nitriding using ammonia and hydrocarbon gases at around 500° to 600°C (932° to 1112°F); the time factor is controlled by the actual steel used and the thickness of hardness penetration desired. Hardness layers up to 0.25 mm (0.010 in.) thick, measuring 700 to 800 DHN (designated hardness number, in this case, Rockwell C scale of 52), can be obtained with this process or by *tufftriding*, which uses a bath of liquid salts to achieve a similar result.

Figure 11–1 illustrates a typical six-cylinder heavy-duty high-speed engine one-piece crankshaft forged from chrome-alloy steel and heat-treated to ensure strength and durability. Cat's 3176 engine crankshaft

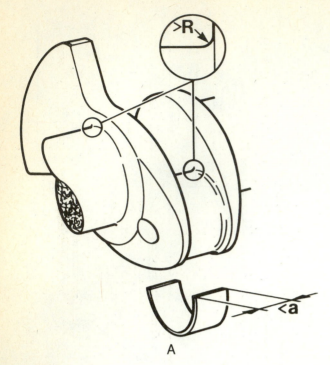

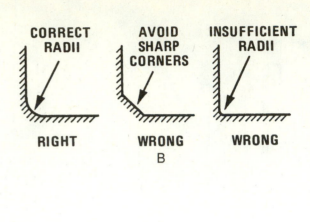

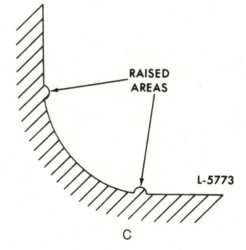

FIGURE 11–2 (a) Location of crankshaft main and con-rod journal fillet radius, which must meet the engine manufacturer's specifications after any regrind procedure to prevent the bearing from riding on the fillets; (b) examples of right and wrong journal fillet radius after crankshaft regrinding; (c) example of how some engine manufacturers employ a special rolling process in the fillet radius area for added strength. (Courtesy of Detroit Diesel Corporation.)

has seven main bearing journals and eight counterweights. It is forged from strand-cast high-carbon micro-alloy steel with each counterweight milled to specific dimensions for balance purposes, maximum internal load cancellation, and minimum crankshaft weight. Most manufacturers now employ a three-dimensional *boundary element analysis* system to evaluate the torsional stresses developed in the crankshaft, as well as to determine the ideal location for the placement of the oil hole drillings to optimize the oil film thickness and pressure and the bearing fillet geometries.

All high-speed crankshafts are drilled to provide oil passages running from the concentrically rotating main bearings to the individual con-rod bearing journals as shown in Figure 11–3. Three-dimensional analysis has shown that by drilling the main bearing journal oil holes offset from center, a 50% thicker oil film can be maintained on the main bearing journals during engine operation. A cross-sectional view of a crankshaft showing offset main bearing journal oil holes is illustrated in Figure 11–4. Note that when off-

set oil holes are used, they are usually designed to rotate in only one direction; this is referred to as a *uni-directional crankshaft*. Therefore, right-hand rotation cranks cannot be used in left-hand rotating engines and vice versa. On high-speed multicylinder engines, the crankshaft is often made in two or three sections and bolted together at the mating flanges. A common example of this principle can be found in Detroit Diesel two-stroke-cycle 16V-71, 16V-92, 12V-149, 16V-149, and 20V-149 engines.

For very large low-speed high-output engines, low-alloy forged steel is used. Very large engine crankshafts are generally built in precast sections (usually referred to as a semibuilt crankshaft) with the webs and journals often being made separately. Consider that many large deep-sea marine slow-speed diesel engines are capable of producing up to 55,000 to 60,000 hp (41,103 to 44,742 kW). Figure 11–5 illustrates one example of a very large slow-speed engine crankshaft. In engines this large we are dealing with a stroke size of 1,050 mm (41.33 in.) and a crankshaft that can be up

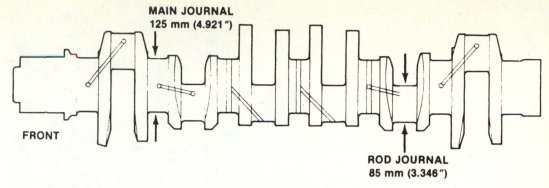

FIGURE 11-3 Location of drilled holes within the crankshaft assembly to carry pressurized engine lube oil from the main bearing to the con-rod bearing journal surface. (Courtesy of Detroit Diesel Corporation.)

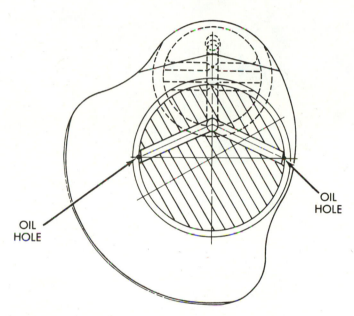

FIGURE 11-4 Cross-sectional view of a crankshaft showing an offset connecting-rod journal in addition to the relocated main bearing journal oil holes to provide increased oil flow under load. (Courtesy of Detroit Diesel Corporation.)

to 12,000 mm (472.4 in., or 39.37 ft) long and weighing approximately 21t300 (21 tons 300 kg) in the forward section and 21t100 (21 tons 100 kg) in the aft section. In semibuilt crankshafts this large, the webs can be bored to size and shrunk onto the journals. In some cases, locking dowels or pins are fitted to assist in retaining the web to the journal. If the crankshaft is made from a one-piece bar, a special-purpose partial heating furnace for throw-by-throw (crank journal by crank journal) heating is used. Then the red-hot bar section is placed over a throw-by-throw forge where tremendous hydraulic pressure applied to the upsetting dies

forms the crankshaft journal by journal. This same process is used on smaller high-speed crankshafts; however, the complete crankshaft can be drop forged in one process.

Methods commonly used to increase crankshaft wear resistance and fatigue life include these:

- Induction hardening of all journals usually to a Brinell hardness number between 400 and 650
- Case-hardening
- Gas nitriding (ammonia and hydrocarbon gases)
- Tufftriding (salt-bath nitriding)
- Pressure rolling of the journal fillet radii
- Induction hardening of the fillet radii

Located at the back of this chapter is a glossary of terms that lists and describes many of the technical terms associated with engine crankshafts and bearings.

CRANKSHAFT REMOVAL

During any major engine overhaul, the crankshaft must be removed to allow proper cleaning and hot tanking of the block coolant passages to remove scale buildup as well as any dirt or sludge from the oil passages. In addition, after the crankshaft is removed, we can conduct a series of inspection checks to determine the suitability of the crankshaft assembly for reuse. The crankshaft is checked and inspected for possible cracks, signs of overheating and distortion or bending, and whether the connecting rod journals or main bearing journals need regrinding due to severe scoring, taper, or ovality.

Removal of the crankshaft can be considered a common procedure for most high-speed engines. If, however, you are working on a slow- to medium-speed large displacement engine and the crankshaft has been damaged, the removal process is more complicated.

FIGURE 11–5 Example of a very large diesel engine crankshaft with a length of approximately 11.5 m (38 ft) and weighing 32 tons. (Courtesy of Maschinefabrik Alfing, Kessler, GmbH, Germany.)

Individual cylinder boxes or A-frames would have to be removed to allow removal of a sectionalized (semi-built) crankshaft. If the crankshaft was a one-piece unit, the complete engine would have to be disassembled in a way similar to that for a high-speed engine to allow removal of the large crankshaft from the lower part of the engine, which is commonly referred to as the *bed*.

At the time of major overhaul and prior to disassembly of components of a high-speed engine, common practice is to first steam clean or high-pressure wash the engine block and components. Next, mount the engine block securely into an engine overhaul stand similar to the one illustrated in Figure 7–7. Ensure that the engine block is securely bolted onto the engine stand before releasing the lifting sling(s) from the engine. To facilitate bolting of the engine to the overhaul stand, you may have to remove a number of accessory items so that the engine-to-stand block adaptor plate can be bolted into place. With both engine oil and coolant drained, remove all of the components in the sequential procedure described in Chapter 8.

Procedure

With the engine mounted in a revolver-type rotatable stand and the engine stripped to its essentials, follow these five steps to remove the crankshaft:

1. Remove the main bearing cap bolts.
2. Remove the caps. If the caps do not come off easily, and if they have tapped holes in them for stabilizer brackets or for securing oil pump pickup tubes, you can thread two slide hammers into these holes to facilitate removal. Alternatively, you can tap the caps with a rubber or plastic mallet to help free them.
3. Remove the crankshaft *end float thrust washers* from each side of the main bearing cap. The location of these thrust washers varies among engine manufacturers; some put them at the rear or center main bearing cap.
4. Refer to Figure 11–6 and securely sling the crankshaft with two web slings, as illustrated, or with two large hooks protected with heavy rubber hose that will accept the diameter of the journals. You can also use a rope sling at two crank throws. Similarly, if chain falls are used, they should be used with bolts and brackets threaded into each end of the crankshaft.
5. Using an overhead hoist, slowly and carefully raise the crankshaft from the engine block or bed and lay it securely on a flat surface.

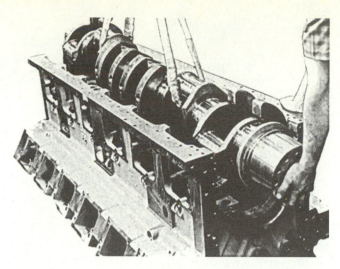

FIGURE 11–6 *Using nylon webbing slings to support the crankshaft during removal or installation. (Courtesy of Cummins Engine Company, Inc.)*

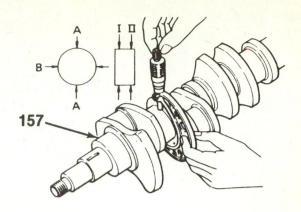

157. Crankshaft   W-00867

FIGURE 11–7 *Using an outside micrometer to accurately measure the crankshaft journals for taper, wear, and ovality. (Courtesy of GMC Trucks.)*

Initial Cleaning

If severe damage to the crankshaft is evident, don't waste energy cleaning it. If the crankshaft can be cleaned, remove the oil passage Allen-head plug screws from the individual crankshaft webs. Wear a pair of safety glasses. Clean the crankshaft using fuel oil and a parts cleaning brush. Pay particular attention to cleaning out all oil passages with a stiff-wire bristle brush. Blow all oil passages clear with compressed air regulated to about 40 psi (276 kPa). Dry the crankshaft using compressed air and lint-free rags.

Initial Inspection

Prior to detailed measurement of the crankshaft, make an initial careful inspection. Suggested checks are listed next:

- Check for signs of excessive overheating, which normally means crankshaft replacement is needed. Overheating of journals indicated by discoloration such as bluing or straw color can draw the hardness from the main and con rod journals.
- Check all crankshaft main and rod journals, as well as the thrust washer surfaces, for signs of scratches, nicks, and scores. Deep imperfections require that the crankshaft be reground and new undersize bearings be used.
- Closely inspect the front and rear crankshaft seal surface areas for signs of a rough or grooved condition. These imperfections cause oil leakage when the engine is operating. A replaceable sleeve can be pressed over these worn areas and an oversize oil seal can be used.

- Inspect the crankshaft thrust surfaces for signs of overheating, severe wear, or grooving. If damage is evident, these surfaces have to be reground.
- Check the crankshaft gearing (some have a front gear, others have a rear gear, some have both) for worn, chipped, or damaged teeth. Also check the condition of the gear woodruff key and keyway for signs of wear.
- Inspect the crankshaft for cracks.
- Carefully measure each crankshaft main and rod journal for wear, ovality, and taper.

Journal Measurement

To accurately measure the condition of the journals, use an outside micrometer as illustrated in Figure 11–7 or a dial indicator placed against the journal to determine how much taper and ovality exist. Wear is determined by comparing the various journal readings to the limits listed in the service manual. Either mount the crankshaft assembly into a lathe or support it on its front and rear journals in two V blocks. If neither of these methods is available to you, install the front and rear upper main bearing shells into the engine block saddle and lower the crankshaft into position.

The crankshaft main and rod journals should be measured and recorded on two planes (axes) 90° apart; use the letters X and Y as shown in Figure 11–8. These two planes may be described with an A and B axis designation by some engine manufacturers. In addition, it is customary to measure each journal in at least three places (A, B, C) along each axis as shown in Figure 11–8. These positional measurements are required so that both the taper and ovality of the journal can be gauged accurately.

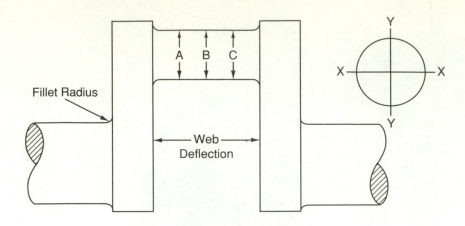

FIGURE 11–8 *Locations that should be checked on a crankshaft journal when measuring with an outside micrometer. Also check the web deflection dimension.*

Let's assume that a standard diameter for a new journal was listed in the service manual specifications as 5.000 in. (127.00 mm) and that the micrometer measurements for a worn journal along the X or Y axis shown in Figure 11–8 were as follows:

Axis X

Position A	4.9990 in.	(126.974 mm)
Position B	4.9985 in.	(126.961 mm)
Position C	4.9980 in.	(126.949 mm)

From these readings, we can determine that the journal is tapered 0.001 in. (0.0254 mm)—the difference between position A and C. If we take a second set of readings at right angles to the first set, we will be able to determine the ovality of the journal by comparing the two sets of readings.

Now we take micrometer readings at 90° to the set taken for taper, but in the same positions (namely, A–B–C), so we can determine the out-of-round condition, or ovality, of the journal.

Axis Y

Position A	4.9980 in.	(126.949 mm)
Position B	4.9980 in.	(126.949 mm)
Position C	4.9975 in.	(126.936 mm)

A comparison of the two sets of readings taken 90° apart indicates that the largest variation is between the A points on the X and Y axes. This indicates that the journal has in fact a worn ovality of 0.001 in. (0.0254 mm) in addition to its taper of 0.001 in. (0.0254 mm). To determine maximum wear, simply take the lowest reading and subtract it from the standard journal size. In this example, the lowest reading is at position C on the Y axis, so the wear is 0.0025 in. (0.0635 mm).

Figure 11–9 illustrates a working sheet that you can use when checking a crankshaft for taper, wear, and ovality. On the upper half of the diagram, enter the micrometer readings for all of the main journals (three measurements along each journal, A–B–O, and at 90° to each other on the A and B axes). Repeat the same procedure for the con-rod journals and enter the readings in the windows on the bottom half of the diagram. Also closely inspect the rear crankshaft oil seal area for a wear groove; if necessary, install a thin-wall Speedi-Sleeve and use an oversize oil seal.

If either the taper, ovality, or wear exceeds the engine manufacturer's specifications, the crankshaft journals have to be reground to accept *undersize* bearings. After regrinding, the crankshaft journals would be smaller in diameter than new journals. Oversize bearings refer to a bearing shell set that is larger on its outside diameter to compensate for block metal that has been removed by *line boring,* or lower boring, used to realign the main bearing cap and saddle bores. Where possible, it is desirable to maintain the use of standard-inside-bore diameter bearing shells. Refer to the section in this chapter dealing with crankshaft bearings as well as to Chapter 9 for more detailed information on both undersize and oversize bearings.

Thrust Surface Inspection

The crankshaft thrust washer bearing surfaces must also be checked for signs of overheating, scoring, and wear. On larger engines, this surface can be a separate flange that can be checked with an outside micrometer and compared to specifications. On many high-speed diesel engines this surface is formed on both ends of one main bearing journal. The distance between the two thrust surfaces can be measured by means of a telescoping gauge. In both cases, visual inspection can quickly indicate the condition of the thrust surfaces. If minimal scuffing is apparent on the crankshaft thrust surfaces, clean them using fine emery cloth soaked in fuel oil.

POLISHING THE JOURNALS

If micrometer measurements indicate that all readings are within the maximum allowable diameter specs, but minor scuffing or fine scratching on journals is

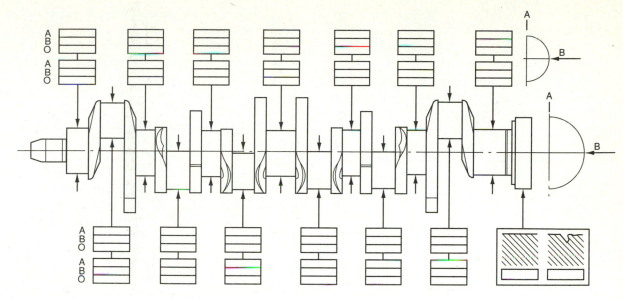

FIGURE 11–9 *Sample measurement chart that can be used to enter all of the various micrometer readings obtained from both the main and con-rod journals of the crankshaft.*

evident, the crankshaft journals can be polished. Secure the crankshaft in a machine lathe. Tighten the rear seal end in the chuck. You can wrap emery cloth (grit side inward) around the seal end once to protect the seal surface from the jaws. Support the front end of the crankshaft on a roller-bearing-supported "live" center at the tailstock end.

Polishing the crankshaft journals is not intended to reduce the journal diameters to accept an undersize bearing, as does grinding. Nevertheless, many engine manufacturers and bearing suppliers do offer 0.001 in. (0.0254 mm) or 0.002 in. (0.0508 mm) undersize bearings expressly to maintain correct bearing oil clearances after polishing. All journals polished *must* meet the engine manufacturer's dimensional specifications as stated in the service manual. To polish the individual journals, follow these steps:

1. Wear a pair of safety glasses. Ensure that no clothing is loose to prevent any possibility of becoming caught in the rotating lathe and crankshaft components.

2. Select a moderate chuck speed on the lathe gearbox.

3. Obtain several rolls of strip emery cloth. Select 220 and 320 grit; use the rougher grit (220) to remove any scratches or minor grooves. Use the 320 grit to give the journal its final polish. Rougher-grit emery cloth can be used to remove any ridges; however, the polished journals will be subject to excessive

wear unless they are polished smooth with nothing coarser than 240 grit! Ensure that the width of the emery cloth matches that of the journal if possible, because this will make it easier to polish the complete journal width in one operation.

4. Fill a container with clean diesel fuel, which you will use as a lubricant during the polishing process.

5. Rip the strip emery cloth into a long enough length to allow you to hold onto each end when it is wrapped around the journal to be cleaned. Usually 30 to 36 in. (762 to 915 mm) is sufficient. An alternative is to use a piece of rawhide or suitable rope wrapped around the emery cloth and drawn back and forth to ensure a round journal.

6. Soak the length of emery cloth in the container of fuel oil.

7. Drive the lathe in the direction of normal crankshaft rotation. Stand on the side with the crankshaft rotating away from you.

8. Start by placing the length of strip emery cloth around a main bearing journal that rotates concentrically, so that you can securely hold onto equal lengths of the cloth with both hands.

9. Before starting the lathe, be prepared to allow the length of emery cloth to slip back and forth by moving one hand ahead and back of the other.

10. Start the lathe and follow the backward and forward motion with your hands while applying light pressure to the emery cloth to allow it to cut/polish the journal.

11. Stop the lathe after 20 to 30 seconds—the usual time for this stroking action to remove minor journal imperfections. Remove the emery cloth. Carefully wipe the journal clean with a lint-free rag and visually inspect the journal finish. If necessary, continue polishing until the journal appears smooth.

12. Give the journal a final polish using the finer-grit emery cloth.

13. Repeat the same process for all of the other main bearings.

14. Follow the same procedure to polish the con-rod journals; however, since the rod journals rotate eccentrically (off center) to the lathe chuck, be prepared to roll with this action during the polishing process. This will take some practice before you feel comfortable with it, so select a very fine strip length of emery cloth when attempting to polish the first rod journal. Practice until you are confident that you have the emery cloth action in synchronization with the rotating crankshaft motion.

15. Use fine emery cloth to clean the main bearing thrust washer surfaces.

16. When complete, remove all of the crankshaft oil passage screw plugs. Use a stiff-bristle brush and fuel oil to thoroughly clean out all debris from the diagonal oil passages within the crankshaft assembly. Clean the complete crankshaft in fuel oil or solvent and blow it dry with compressed air at about 40 psi (276 kPa).

17. Recheck all main and con-rod journals for diameter using an outside micrometer. Be sure that you have not removed too much material and increased the bearing-to-journal clearance beyond service manual limits.

18. If journals require excess material removal during polishing, the crankshaft should be reground to accept new undersize bearings.

GRINDING THE CRANKSHAFT

A crankshaft that exhibits visual discoloration such as bluing or straw color has induction hardened surfaces that have been damaged. Such a crankshaft should *not* be ground but replaced with a new one.

Crankshafts are generally reground when excessive taper, ovality, or wear are evident at major overhaul, or after a bearing failure has occurred or ridging of the journal from dirt and foreign material has taken place. Material stock removed from crankshaft journals should only be enough to allow the first undersize bearings to be used according to the service manual normal specification. The first undersize bearing available from most engine manufacturers and bearing suppliers for high-speed diesel engines is usually 0.010 in. (0.254 mm); this is followed by one of 0.020 in. (0.508 mm) and then one of 0.030 in. (0.762 mm). Some engine manufacturers do allow up to 0.050 in. (1.27 mm) to be removed from the main and con-rod journals; they do specify, however, that if more than 0.010 in. (0.254 mm) is to be removed, the crankshaft has to be nitrided. (The nitriding process was discussed earlier in this chapter.)

Although larger undersize bearings are available in some cases from jobber parts suppliers, engine manufacturers limit their parts to a stated maximum in their service specifications. Removing more material than this from a crankshaft can weaken the induction hardening on the journal surfaces, as well as increase the stresses in the critical areas of the crankshaft. Crankshaft thrust washers are also available in thicker sizes to compensate for grinding of these surfaces; they are usually available in standard 0.005 in. (0.127 mm) or 0.010 in. (0.254 mm) oversizes.

A crankshaft requires regrinding even if only one or two journals are damaged (main or rods). Always grind every main journal to the same size. Similarly, all rod journals should be reground to the same diameter if one is worn. Once a crankshaft has been reground, the machinist usually indicates how much material has been removed from both the main and con-rod journals by stamping the crankshaft web. Some engine rebuilders or machinists simply stamp the stock amount removed, whereas others use a code that can be interpreted by looking at the crankshaft information area in the service manual. For example, the letter H would indicate the main journal, the letter D the crankpin or con-rod, and the letter N that the journals have been nitrided for hardness. These letters are followed by a figure, which indicates the number of times that the crankshaft has been ground. For example, a 1 indicates that the crankshaft has been reground to 0.010 in. (0.254 mm) undersize; each additional number (2, 3, 4, 5) indicates an additional 0.010 in. (0.254 mm) of stock removal. The highest number, 5, is equal to a 0.050 in. (1.27 mm) undersize. Consider the following example letters and numbers stamped on a crankshaft:

A

FIGURE 11–10 (a) Crankshaft journals being reground. (Courtesy of Berco S.p.A., Ferrara, Italy.) (b) Crankshaft grinding and polishing rotation. (Courtesy of Detroit Diesel Corporation.)

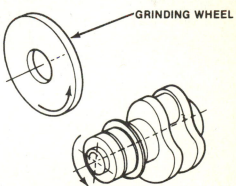

GRINDING WHEEL

FRONT OF CRANKSHAFT
GRIND AS SHOWN

CRANKPIN AND MAIN JOURNAL GRINDING
SHOULD BE PERFORMED WITH CRANKSHAFT
ROTATION OPPOSITE TO ACTUAL ENGINE ROTA-
TION, WHILE POLISHING SHOULD BE PERFORMED
WITH THE CRANKSHAFT ROTATION IN THE SAME
DIRECTION AS ENGINE ROTATION.

B

- H1 = main journal has been reground to the first undersize.
- D2N = con-rod journals have been reground to the second undersize.

Crankshaft grinding can be performed on a special machine as shown in Figure 11–10a, where a large grinding stone removes the desired amount of material. It is extremely important that during main or rod journal grinding the crankshaft be rotated *opposite* to normal engine rotation (Figure 11–10b). After grinding of any journal, the *fillet radius* of the journal must be maintained (see Figure 11–2). The radius can be checked with a fillet radius gauge. When the gauge is held against the radius, no space or light should be visible between the gauge and the fillet radius, otherwise the radius is incorrect. The fillet radius is extremely important because the most highly stressed areas of the crankshaft occur in this location. When too sharp a fillet radius exists, load stresses on the crankshaft between the crank cheek and journal will be increased, because these loads are distributed over a smaller cross-sectional area. Similarly, when sharp corners are left in the fillet area, the con-rod or main bearing will ride up on these and cause severe twisting to occur, which leads to serious crankshaft and engine damage. On the other hand, if too great a fillet radius was left after regrinding, the main and rod bearings would not fit into place over the journal.

At the completion of crankshaft grinding, the shaft should be checked for magnetic particles to determine if any cracks originated as a result of the grinding operation. Demagnetize the crankshaft after this check! Finally, remove all oil passage plugs; then use fuel oil or solvent along with a stiff-bristle nylon brush to carefully clean all traces of grinding dust from the crank. Dry the shaft with compressed air at approximately 40 psi (276 kPa); reinstall the plugs immediately.

CRACK DETECTION METHODS

Basically there are two major types of loads imposed on a crankshaft during operation, a bending force or a twisting force. Normally these load forces will not affect the life of the crankshaft in a well-maintained and properly operated engine. Figure 11–11a illustrates certain areas of the crankshaft that are exposed to these loads more than others and are commonly referred to as *critical load zones*.

Visually inspect the crankshaft for cracks, particularly around the journal oil holes; the cracks tend to follow the journal surface at a 45° angle. Other areas to check include the highly stressed areas shown in Figure 11–11a and highlighted in Figure 11–11b, along with fatigue cracks at the cheek and web. Cracks of this nature require that the crankshaft be discarded and replaced with a new one. Often cracks are not

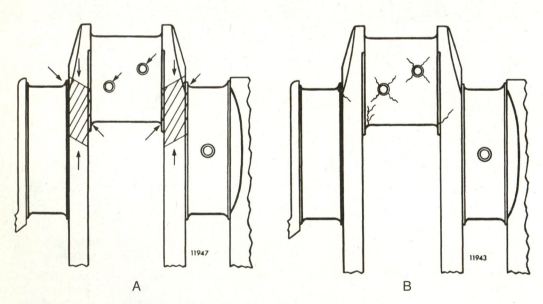

A   B

FIGURE 11–11   (a) Location of typical crankshaft loading zones for a heavy-duty high-speed diesel engine; (b) example of the location where crankshaft fatigue cracks would appear. (Courtesy of Detroit Diesel Corporation.)

readily visible to the naked eye; therefore, several methods are recommended for detecting cracks, and we discuss them next.

Magnetic Particle Method

The magnetic particle method usually involves mounting the crankshaft in a machine-lathe-type support structure (Figure 11–12). A circular magnet that surrounds the crankshaft is then activated and moved lengthwise along the crank to completely magnetize it. A small, rubber, hollow spray bulb is filled with a fine magnetic powder or solution. This is sprayed onto the magnetized crankshaft, where any cracks or flaws will cause the powder or solution to form a small local magnet in the damaged area, thereby effectively marking the crack. The crankshaft *must* be demagnetized after the test by use of the sliding collar.

Portable kits of this type are readily available from major tool suppliers. Figure 11–13a illustrates an electromagnet that can be used with 110 V AC or 6 to 12 V DC battery power. It contains solid-state construction with a built-in transformer and momentary ON/OFF switch. The kit contains the electromagnet, 1 lb (0.45 kg) of flux powder, spray bulb funnel, DC adapter, and storage box. A similar kit is available with two industrial-grade permanent magnets polyencapsulated and cable connected for flexibility. These are ideal for checking round-type components or an around-corner application. This kit contains the same materials as those illustrated in Figure 11–13a.

Fluorescent Magnetic Particle Method

The fluorescent magnetic particle method is similar to the magnetic particle method, but it employs magnetic

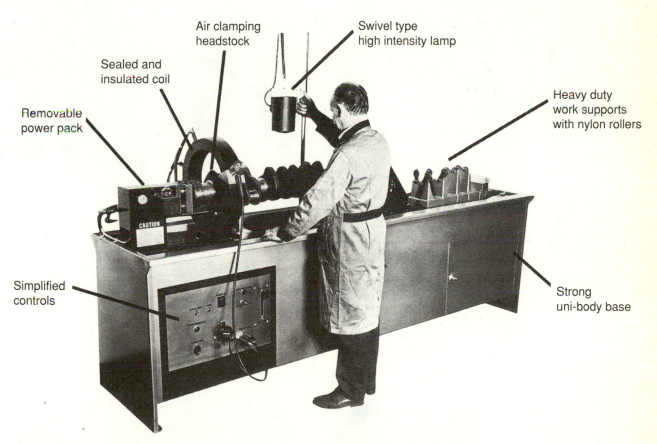

FIGURE 11–12 *Magnetic particle inspection of a crankshaft using a circular-shaped sealed and insulated coil, which can be moved along the length of the crankshaft to magnetize it. This model (MPI-259) offers 10,000 amps at the coil and 3000 amps between the headstock and tailstock of the work support table. Using the high-intensity light, the technician can detect exterior cracks or flaws in the crankshaft assembly. (Courtesy of Kwik-Way Manufacturing Co.)*

particles that are fluorescent and glow under a portable *black light*. This allows detection of very fine cracks that might be missed under the nonfluorescent method. Cracks on discolored or dark surfaces in particular can be detected with this fluorescent method.

Fluorescent Penetrant Method

The fluorescent penetrant method can be used on both ferrous and nonferrous (nonmagnetic) materials such as aluminum. The highly fluorescent liquid penetrant is sprayed on the surface of the part to be tested; then the excess penetrant is removed from the surface and the part is dried. A developing powder is sprayed on the part, which helps to draw the penetrant out of any cracks by a capillary action. Inspection can then be carried out under a black light.

Figure 11–13b illustrates the Flaw Finder crack detection kit, which can be used on cast iron, steel, and aluminum materials. There are four different spray cans in this kit: two cans labeled *cleaner* (only one is required at a time); a can labeled *dye penetrant*, which contains a dark-red liquid; and a can labeled *developer*. The cleaner is sprayed on the area to be checked and wiped dry. The cleaned area is then sprayed with the dye penetrant and allowed to air-dry for about 5 minutes. When dry, the developer powder is sprayed on and allowed to dry for 1 to 2 minutes. As the developer powder dries, flaws and cracks are outlined with red marks on a white background.

FAILURE ANALYSIS OF THE CRANKSHAFT

The engine crankshaft is designed to absorb the firing impulses that provide the rotary motion at the flywheel. All crankshafts are designed to withstand the high firing pressures and forces under which they constantly operate. They are designed to "give a little" when pressures are exerted on them. Any unusual forces placed on the crankshaft during oper-

FIGURE 11–13 (a) Component parts of a portable handheld electromagnetic crack detection kit which can be used with either an AC or DC power source; (b) optional Flaw Finder spray-on kit which includes a cleaner, dye penetrant, and powder developer. (Courtesy of Kent-Moore Division, SPX Corporation.)

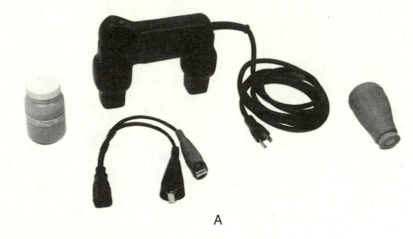

A

Ordering Information

Tool No.	Description
PT 7191	Flaw Finder Kit
PT 7191-1	Cleaner
PT 7191-2	Dye Penetrant
PT 7191-3	Developer

B

ation that cause it to twist or bend abnormally, or excessive thrust forces, can severely test crankshaft durability. Major crankshaft failures due to breakage are not regular occurrences; therefore, when a crankshaft fails or breaks, the cause can usually be traced back to an abnormal operating condition. The diesel technician must research the cause(s) that led to the failure to prevent a repeat situation. Cracks in any vital area require that the crankshaft be replaced. A crack cannot be repaired or removed; a crack will continue to spread and will soon result in a crankshaft failure.

Types of Breaks

Basically two types of breaks occur in any crankshaft. A bending break occurs at 90° to the centerline of the crankshaft. A torsional break occurs at 45° to the centerline of the crankshaft.

Categories of Failure

Crankshaft failures can be categorized as follows: longitudinal cracking, bearing seizure, torsional fatigue, and bending fatigue.

Longitudinal Cracking

Longitudinal cracking is the most common cause of crankshaft failure. In this case the oil film has been destroyed in a small area, causing metal-to-metal contact, which produces a hot spot. The localized heat from the hot spot destroys the journal surface hardness and causes tiny cracks to form on the surface. Often these cracks are located about 1 in. (25.4 mm) from the oil hole in the opposite direction from crankshaft rotation; the cracks are caused by the lower oil flow to this area. The problem is accentuated by severe, heavy loads being applied to the engine or by continual lugging of the engine at full load under low speeds. The tiny crack eventually grows larger until the journal is so weakened that it fails in torsion. The torsional break progresses from the crank in the opposite direction and at 45° from each end of the crack. In later-designed crankshafts, engine manufacturers have relocated the oil hole to an offcenter position to alleviate the oil flow problem. Crank journals that have become barrel shaped due to wear and that have not been corrected by grinding can create this condition of uneven load on the crank journal and bearing, as can an improperly ground grinding wheel stone.

Bearing Seizure

Seizures differ from longitudinal cracks in that the whole oil film breaks down, causing the bearing to invariably break down. Usually the crank fails in a jagged break starting at the fillet radius of the journal. The break is rough with a series of longitudinal cracks running out both sides. Bearing seizure can usually be traced to several causes:

- Lack of bearing-to-journal clearance caused by improper installation such as overtorquing, improper torquing sequence, distorted cap or saddle, crankshaft misalignment, or uneven seating of the bearing in the cap or saddle
- Excessive clearance in the main bearings that decrease oil pressure, leading to starvation of con-rod bearings
- Dirty or clogged oil passages
- Excessive oil temperatures or improper grade of oil

Torsional Fatigue

Torsional fatigue failures result from vibration that takes place at high frequency. A combination of abnormal speed and load conditions may cause the

FIGURE 11–14 *Example of a torsional fatigue failure that has occurred through the crank journal near the rear of the crankshaft at a 45° angle to the axis of the crankshaft. (Courtesy of Detroit Diesel Corporation.)*

twisting forces to set up a vibration commonly referred to as *torsional vibration* (twisting or turning force), which imposes high stresses at the locations highlighted in Figure 11–11a. Torsional stress may produce a fracture in either the con-rod journal or the crank cheek. Con-rod journal failures usually break at a 45° angle to the centerline of the shaft as illustrated in Figure 11–14.

The two main indications to look for during inspection are circumferential fillet cracks at critical areas and 45° cracks to the axis of the shaft starting from either the critical fillet locations or the con-rod journal holes. These may be accompanied by a jagged line break through the cheek parallel to the centerline of the crankshaft, or possibly through the web as short lines parallel to the centerline of the shaft. The break may also occur at one or two positions through the oil hole.

Torsional vibrations can be caused by several factors:

- A loose, damaged, or defective vibration damper
- Overspeeding the engine, for example, when a heavy truck is allowed to descend a hill and the rear wheels become the driving member because the operator does not check or control the road speed by applying the engine brake, hydraulic retarder, or service brakes
- Maximum engine speed set higher than recommended
- Running the engine at critical speeds. Critical speed is the engine speed at which the firing impulses of the engine coincide or synchronize with the natural vibrations of the crankshaft. Each engine generally has an identifiable operating speed at which a slight vibration is noticeable—usually somewhere in the midpoint speed range. When this occurs, the shaft is in danger of being fractured by the abnormal stresses. Never run an engine at its critical speed (either operate it beyond that speed, or slow it down below that speed). During normal operation most engines never suffer this critical speed condition under full load, because the engine application usually requires operation between the peak torque point rpm and rated full-load speed.
- An unbalanced cylinder load possibly caused by irregular fuel distribution to one cylinder or faulty injector or by low compression
- A loose flywheel (broken or stretched bolts caused by overtorquing), worn bolts, and undertorquing
- Overtightened belt drives.
- Homemade alterations to the engine setup that require a torsional vibration analysis to ensure that no problems are evident. Such additional items as heavy front pulleys or couplings, and large PTOs, generators, or pulleys on the drive end, require this type of analysis.
- Faulty engine foundation or engine mounts

Bending Failures
Bending failures result from bending the crankshaft, which takes place once per revolution. The crankshaft is supported between each of the cylinders by a main bearing, and the load imposed by the gas pressure on top of the piston is divided between the adjacent bearings. Stress is usually highest in the con-rod journals next to the point of the bend. Fatigue starts at the rod journal and advances through the crank cheek area, often extending into the main bearing fillet section. Bending breaks can usually be identified by the fact that they occur at 90° to the crankshaft centerline. This type of a crack or break usually occurs in the web and normally starts at the fillet radius. It is identified by a series of lines at right angles to the centerline of the crankshaft. An abnormal bending stress in the crankshaft, particularly in the crank fillet, can impose a bending load on the crankshaft. The areas of the crankshaft that are most susceptible to high stresses are the cheeks between the main and con-rod journals, as well as the rod fillets. These areas are highlighted in Figure 11–11a, and Figure 11–15 illustrates a bending break in a crankshaft that was not properly supported.

Typical operating conditions that impose abnormal bending stresses on the crankshaft may be a result of misalignment of the main bearing bores, improperly fitted bearings, bearing failures, a loose or broken bearing cap, unbalanced drive pulleys, multiple drive belts that are too tight, or excessive side loads applied to either the front or rear of the shaft. When the engine was last overhauled, if the main bearing caps were misaligned and were not line bored to correct this condition, crankshaft failure is imminent. Misalignment can also be caused by a flywheel or housing that is incorrectly installed and/or a drive member, such as a heavy-duty transmission, PTO, or marine gear, being bolted to the flywheel and housing.

We can summarize the causes of bending failures as follows:

- Too sharp a fillet radius caused by a poor grinding procedure. Make sure the fillet radius meets the manufacturer's specs after any regrind process by the use of a fillet radius gauge set. Fillet radius is specified in the engine manufacturer's service manual literature and is generally not less than 1/16 of the pin or journal diameter. Cold rolling the fillet to its

FIGURE 11–15 Example of a bending break where the crankshaft broke because it was not supported properly. (Courtesy of Detroit Diesel Corporation.)

final size provides a burnished finish and places the surface under initial compressive stress. Both of these conditions increase fatigue resistance.

- Notches, grinding burr marks, or deep scratches on the crank
- Misalignment of the main bearing cap bores. On large slow-speed heavy-duty engines, check the bed alignment.
- A bad bearing or loose bearing cap caused by improperly torqued bolts or an obstruction between the cap and block surface, which cannot support the crankshaft at this point so it subjects the shaft to abnormal bending stresses
- Excessive end thrust on the crankshaft, which removes the lube oil between the crankshaft and the main bearing thrust washers, thereby subjecting the washers to rapid wear. The debris and heat from disintegrating thrust washers can "wipe out" the main bearings, which will cause a loss of bearing support and subsequently impose a bending stress on the crankshaft.
- Misalignment between the front and rear blocks on two- or three-piece engine blocks such as those used by Detroit Diesel in its 16V-71, 12V-92, 16V-92, 12V-149, 16V-149, and 20V-149 models. This can impose a bending load on either side of the crankshaft where the blocks are bolted together at the flange coupling points as shown in Figure 11–16. Misalignment subjects two- or three-piece crankshafts to stress and fatigue.
- Misalignment of PTOs, transmissions, gen-sets, and so forth, to the engine, which can side load the crankshaft excessively and impose bending

stresses in the shaft at the rear main bearing and con-rod journal locations.

MULTIPLE-PIECE CRANKSHAFTS

Many larger high-speed engines, as well as some very large medium- and slow-speed diesel engines, use a design that incorporates a crankshaft with two, three, or more sections. Thus one or more damaged sections can be replaced at the time of major engine overhaul or at the time of a crankshaft failure.

In the high-speed diesel engine market, examples of two- and three-piece crankshafts are those used by Detroit Diesel in its 16V-71, 12V-92, 16V-92, 12V, and 16V-149 series engines; the more recent 20V-149 engine uses a three-piece crankshaft assembly. In all cases, the crankshafts are bolted together as illustrated in Figure 11–16. Follow these 10 steps to bolt crankshaft sections together when placing the crankshaft back into service at a major repair procedure:

1. Ensure that the two or three sections of the cylinder block as described in Chapter 9 have been properly aligned and that the retaining bolts have been torqued to specifications.
2. With the upper main bearing shells and thrust washers in position and liberally lubricated, lower the two or three individual pieces of the crankshaft into the bearing saddles.
3. Install all of the main bearing caps and bearings (lubricated) except for the two center caps (each side of the bolted crankshaft flange or flanges).

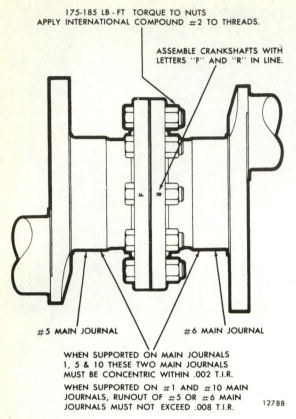

175-185 LB - FT TORQUE TO NUTS
APPLY INTERNATIONAL COMPOUND #2 TO THREADS.

ASSEMBLE CRANKSHAFTS WITH
LETTERS "F" AND "R" IN LINE.

#5 MAIN JOURNAL   #6 MAIN JOURNAL

WHEN SUPPORTED ON MAIN JOURNALS
1, 5 & 10 THESE TWO MAIN JOURNALS
MUST BE CONCENTRIC WITHIN .002 T.I.R.

WHEN SUPPORTED ON #1 AND #10 MAIN
JOURNALS, RUNOUT OF #5 OR #6 MAIN
JOURNALS MUST NOT EXCEED .008 T.I.R.

12788

FIGURE 11–16 *Assembly instructions used to bolt together a two-piece crankshaft for a 12V or 16V-92 two-stroke-cycle engine model. (Courtesy of Detroit Diesel Corporation.)*

4. Torque down all main bearing cap bolts in the proper sequence.

5. Check that the crankshaft sections rotate freely.

6. Refer to Figure 11–16 and rotate each section of the crankshaft until the timing marks are in alignment at the respective flanges. Coat the flange bolt threads with International Compound No. 2 or equivalent and wipe the excess compound from the bolt threads. Install three bolts through the flange holes so that they are 120° apart.

7. Snug up these bolts.

8. Place a dial indicator on the flange surface as well as on the two adjacent crankshaft journals. The allowable runout varies by manufacturer based on the physical size of the crankshaft assembly; however, always try to obtain a minimum runout. For example, in high-speed diesel engines, runout is specified as being within 0.001 in. (0.0254 mm). Tap the flanges while rotating the crankshaft to minimize the dial indicator runout.

9. Install the remaining flange retaining bolts and nuts and alternately torque each bolt/nut 180° apart until all bolts have been tightened.

10. Recheck the runout again after the bolts have been tightened.

CRANKSHAFT WEB DEFLECTION

In large-displacement high-horsepower diesel engines in the low-, medium-, and high-speed categories, a check of crankshaft deflection is common procedure. It is done when bearing failure has occurred and after a two- or three-piece crankshaft has been reinstalled into the engine block(s) or bedplate assembly. The amount of crankshaft deflection or bending that occurs during engine operation is relative to the overall length of the shaft and is usually quite small. However, since the various points on the crankshaft alternate between compressive and tension stress once every revolution, if any operating condition causes these stresses to be too high, the shaft may ultimately break in the same way that a metal wire that has been bent back and forth many times will do.

Figure 11–17a and b illustrates in exaggerated form a crankthrow flexing through one-half revolution on an out-of-line crankshaft assembly. The stresses produced due to bending are greatest in the crankshaft web along the plane (axis) A–A. The critical area occurs at point B where the fillet radius section stresses are magnified. The crankpin fillet at position B is continually placed in tension (Figure 11–17a) and then into compression, as shown in Figure 11–17b. If the centerline of the crankshaft could be maintained perfectly straight during engine operation, with no flex occurring, then the bending stresses at the fillets would be minimized. Because of the high loads transmitted to the crankshaft during operation, however, the stresses cannot be avoided entirely.

The acceptable method of checking crankshaft alignment in high-speed engines is by installing a mandrel (see Figure 9–30) into the pretorqued main bearing caps. Make sure the mandrel can be rotated freely. In addition, a dial indicator can be inserted into the main bearing bores to check for misalignment. On very large diesel engines, this is not easy; although a bridge gauge can be set up over each main bearing journal, and with the aid of a pull-down bar, the crank can be placed under a mock load. The dimension from a fixed point on the bridge gauge to the crank journal can then be taken and compared to other readings for the remaining journals to determine if a misalignment exists.

FIGURE 11–17 Out-of-line crankshaft problems: (a) exaggerated example of how a crankshaft journal and its webs flex or deflect (open) during one-half revolution; (b) resultant stress areas induced into the crankshaft journal and web area as the shaft rotates back through the other half cycle of rotation.

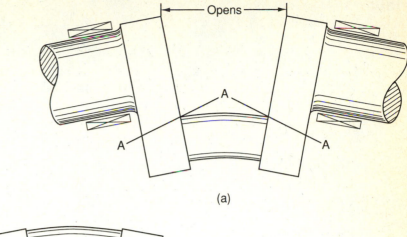

(a)

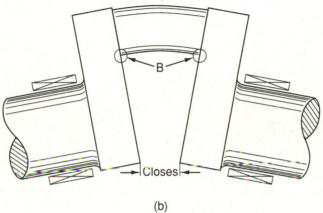

(b)

An acceptable practice on both high- and low- speed diesel engines is to employ a dial indicator placed between the crankwebs, as illustrated in Figure 11–18, to determine the amount of flexing motion that occurs between the webs as the crankshaft is rotated over very slowly. Many large engines have premarked center punch holes on the inside face of each counterweight cheek to facilitate supporting of the dial indicator points. The placement of the dial gauge between the cheeks causes the deflection to vary; therefore, if no prepunched center punch holes are provided, always check the engine manufacturer's service literature to determine just where you should place these.

SERVICE TIP: The center punch marks should be small and made with a very sharp punch. The accuracy of the dial readings may be affected if the marks are too large or are not made with a sharp punch. The center punch marks (dimension X) from the journal, as shown in Figure 11–18, are usually accepted as being equal to one-half of the engine stroke on very large slow-speed engines.

On high-speed engines, web deflection can be checked as the crankshaft is being reinstalled at a major overhaul. If a crankshaft problem is suspected during engine service, however, web deflection can be checked by removing one of the cylinder block inspection covers to gain access to the crankshaft. Similarly, on very large slow-speed diesel engines, web deflection can be checked by removing either a crankcase explosion door or the main engine cylinder access cover to get to the crankshaft assembly. A truer reading of web deflection is obtained when the engine is completely assembled, since the weight of all of the cylinder components is truly representative of the strain of these parts and the crankshaft tends to assume a more natural shape. On some large engines, when the crankshaft deflection gauge is in place, you will not be able to turn the engine over a complete revolution due to interference from some component parts. You may have to move the gauge further out on the webs to gain more crank rotation. Keep in mind, however, that this action will cause a higher deflection to occur.

Follow these steps to check crankshaft web deflection.

1. If the engine is warm, place the dial gauge assembly on or near the engine, so that the gauge will expand to the same basic temperature as the engine. In this way, there should

FIGURE 11–18 *Checking crankshaft web deflection with the use of a dial indicator installed between opposing webs.*

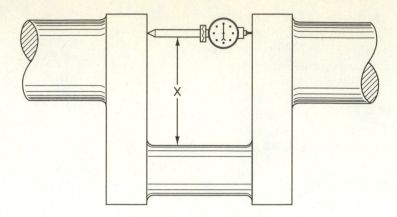

be a minimum amount of gauge expansion during the test to affect any readings. Where possible, web deflection gauge readings should be taken while rotating the engine crankshaft at least 90° in both directions. Note and record the dial readings at the 3, 6, and 9 o'clock positions. Some manufacturers of larger slow-speed engines suggest that you take at least five readings: 12:30, 3, 6, 9, and 11:30 positions.

SAFETY TIP: Disconnect any starting motor batteries and compressed air supply, or shut off all compressed air to direct-air-start engines and leave the cylinder cocks at each cylinder head fully open. Lock out all possibilities of anyone attempting to engage the engine starting system!

2. Carefully place the dial gauge between the webs and adjust it outward to provide sufficient tension to hold it snugly in place.

3. With the crank at or near BDC, twirl the gauge with your thumb and forefinger and note the pointer reading. Do this several times to ensure that the pointer does not change position.

4. When the gauge maintains a constant reading after several twirls between the center punch marks, set the needle to zero and retwirl the gauge to recheck a zero setting.

5. Slowly turn the crankshaft in the direction of normal engine rotation and record any gauge readings—plus or minus! If the gauge pointer moves toward the plus side of zero, it indicates that the webs are opening; any needle movement to the minus side of zero indicates that the webs are closing. If the crankshaft has all plus deflection readings, the webs are open and the crankshaft is convex upward. All minus deflections close the webs and the crank is convex downward.

6. Consider this rule of thumb: Web deflection is usually in the range of 0.001 in. (0.0254 mm) per 1 in. (25.4 mm) of engine stroke. Nevertheless, if available, use the specifications of the engine manufacturer, because shafts with large fillets can normally sustain larger deflections than a more rigid shaft with smaller fillets.

7. When crank web deflections exceed the manufacturer's specs, check for worn bearings, engine foundation deformation, and loose tie rods. Also check the PTO assembly, transmission, marine gear, or power generator for improper installation and realign as necessary.

CRANKSHAFT INSTALLATION

Although crankshaft installation can be considered simply as the reverse procedure of removal, there are a number of procedures that will ensure proper operation on completion of the installation.

Whether a used, reground, or new crankshaft is to be installed, the crankshaft and its oil holes *must* be spotlessly clean. On many new crankshafts, the assembly is coated with a rust-preventive substance that requires the service technician to steam clean or wash the assembly in clean solvent with a stiff-bristle brush to ensure that all oil passages are clear and clean. Always use compressed air to blow-dry the passages. Install all oil passage plugs and tighten to specs.

NOTE: Refer to the next section dealing with crankshaft main bearings and install the upper main bearing shells into the saddle area of the engine block. If used bearing shells are to be reused, after careful examination, install them in the same location from which they were removed. If the crankshaft has been reground, all new main and con-rod bearings and thrust washers must be installed.

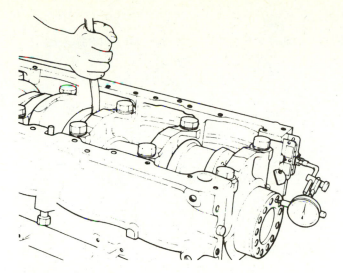

FIGURE 11–23 Using a pry bar to force the crankshaft toward a dial indicator to determine the crankshaft end play. (Courtesy of Detroit Diesel Corporation.)

ing engine operation due to heat expansion and due to the thrust loads experienced on the flywheel. The amount of end play varies between engines. On high-speed diesel engines, this normally is in the region of 0.004 to 0.018 in. (0.10 to 0.457 mm).

- If the end play is less than specs, loosen the cap screws slightly and shift the crankshaft toward the front and then the rear of the engine. Retorque the cap bolts in sequence once again; recheck the end clearance.

- If end clearance is insufficient, or too much, carefully check that the correct thickness of thrust washers is being used. If the crank thrust surfaces have been reground, thicker thrust washers are required.

SERVICE TIP: It is acceptable to use different thicknesses of thrust washers on each side of the main bearing cap to obtain the necessary end play. For example, you may use standard thickness thrust washers (upper and lower) on one side and 0.010 in. oversize washers (upper and lower) on the opposite side, or any combination that will provide the correct crankshaft end float.

- If main bearing cap side bolts are used, torque these to specifications now. Recheck the crankshaft end float again. If main bearing bolt flat metal locks are used, bend one end of the lock around the cap and the other end against one flat surface of the nut or bolt head.

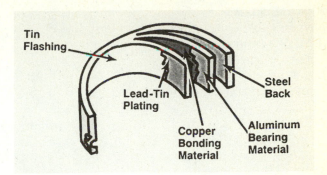

FIGURE 11–24 Construction concept of precision shell bearings. (Courtesy of Caterpillar Inc.)

MAIN AND CON-ROD BEARINGS

Designs

All low- and high-speed engines now employ thinwall *shell* bearings manufactured from a wide range of surface lining materials to suit a diversified cross-section of engine models and operating conditions. Although some shell bearings are manufactured from aluminum alloys, most are manufactured as illustrated in Figure 11–24 for typical high-speed diesel engine crankshaft main, con-rod, and camshaft bearing construction. The crankshaft and con-rod bearings are formed mainly of a series of layers that consist of the following arrangement:

- *Flashing.* A thin tin coating or flashing covers the bearing operating surface to protect the shaft and bearing from possible corrosion prior to installation. In addition, this tin coating acts as a metal lubricant to protect the crankshaft journal and the bearing during the initial start-up of a rebuilt engine during the critical run-in period.

- *Overlay.* The metal overlay generally is a trimetal (three metal) combination consisting of lead, tin, and copper to provide an almost friction-free operation with minimum bearing strength loss. This trimetal arrangement also provides good embedability for any minute dirt particles flowing in the oil system to minimize possible scoring of the crankshaft journal surface. These dirt particles work themselves into the bearing where they are then covered over by the bearing surface material, so that a smooth surface is again presented to the crankshaft journal. The overlay also provides good conformability to the shape of the bearing journal, plus protection against any condition of marginal lubrication during engine operation, particularly during start-up.

FIGURE 11–25
Nomenclature of the various areas of a flange-type and plain-type precision shell bearing assembly. (Courtesy of Cummins Engine Company, Inc.)

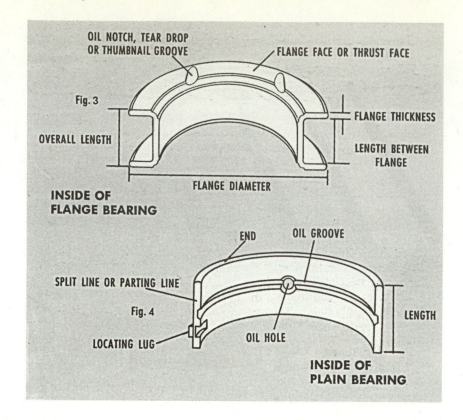

- *Barrier:* The barrier coating is usually designed to prevent any metallurgical interaction between the dissimilar materials used for the lining and overlay. Nickel or a copper bonding material is commonly used for this barrier or dam.
- *Lining:* The lining is usually a trimetal composition consisting of copper with lead and tin for maximum fatigue strength, although an aluminum bearing material can also be used.
- *Backing:* The backing, which is made from steel, acts as the foundation for other bearing metals; it provides both rigidity and mechanical strength.

The thickness of the shell bearing varies, based on the diameter of journal that it is to fit. Typical shell bearing thicknesses on heavy-duty high-speed diesel engines of up to 3000 hp (2237 kW) usually range between 0.155 and 0.170 in. (3.937 to 4.318 mm), but some are thicker for certain engine makes and models. All crankshaft main bearings are generally designed as a *plain bearing;* however, some engines employ a *flange bearing* that incorporates the crankshaft thrust washers (see Figure 11–25). To prevent rotation of the bearing shell in a running engine, the bearing is held in the cap or saddle by a locating tang, lug, or tab, which is also illustrated in Figure 11–25. In some larger engines, the bearing shell may be retained by a dowel in the cap or saddle that fits into a mating hole in the bearing.

Shell bearings are manufactured so that in their free state (not installed in place) they actually form an oval or off-center shape. Figure 11–26a illustrates the bearing in its *free state,* or free spread, where the shell OD (outside diameter) at the mating faces is slightly larger than the bearing bore diameter. This difference in diameter ensures that the bearing will not move during engine operation; it also ensures good contact between the bearing backing and the cap or saddle seating surface. Figure 11–26b illustrates that the bearing shells sit slightly higher than the main bearing split parting line. The purpose of this design concept, known as *bearing crush,* is that when the main bearing or con-rod bolts are torqued to specifications, the crush on the bearing ensures that the bearing shells are tightly seated in their bores formed by the cap and saddle.

Both the main and con-rod bearings have distinct *upper* and *lower* halves. Figure 11–27 illustrates one example of a set of main bearings in which the upper shell is constructed with an oil supply hole. Sometimes an elongated groove can be used to allow pressurized engine lube oil to lubricate both the upper and lower shells. The lower shell usually has no oil hole or groove; therefore, there is a greater cross-sectional area for bearing support. To assist you in identifying the upper from the lower bearing, Figure 11–27 illustrates the information on the backside of the bearing: manufacturing code/date, part number, location (whether

FIGURE 11–26 (a) Design concept of the off-center or shell bearing free spread when the bearing is out of its saddle; (b) installed bearing in its saddle highlighting the extension above the saddle known as bearing crush. (Courtesy of Detroit Diesel Corporation.)

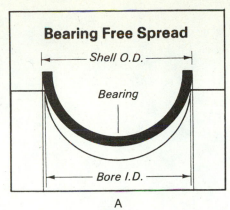

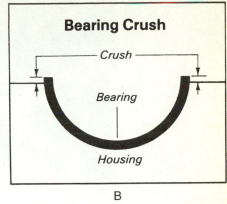

A

B

the bearing is the upper or lower shell), size classification (standard, 0.010 in., 0.020 in., 0.030 in., or 0.254, 0.508, 0.762 mm), and the bearing manufacturer's trademark, which in this example is DDC.

The locating tang on the bearing back usually prevents any possibility of switching the upper and lower shells during installation. No oil could flow to the main bearings or the con-rods if the bearings were reversed. To prevent an error, some bearing manufacturers place the locating tang on the bearing backs in different positions. Although the con-rod bearings are similar in appearance to the main bearings, they always have a smaller diameter. The lower con-rod bearing normally contains an annular oil groove. The groove permits pressurized oil from the crankshaft to lubricate the connecting rod bearing and to continue through two small notches at the side of the upper bearing shell to allow pressurized lube oil to enter the base of the rifle-drilled con-rod where the oil travels up to both the piston pin and bushings. The oil then leaves through a spray nozzle at the top of the rod to cool the underside of the piston dome. On engines that do not use rifle-drilled con-rods but employ strategically placed oil cooling pipes or nozzles, the upper bearing will not contain any notches.

Bearing Loads

Shell bearings must support the full impact of the high pressures applied to the pistons by engine combustion and transferred to the crankshaft by the con-rods. Bearing loads vary with the particular model of engine. In a two-stroke-cycle engine, for example, every upstroke is compression and every downstroke is power. This means that two-cycle bearing loads are in the upper half of the rod bearing and the lower half of the main bearing, with the exception of low compression pressures and very high-speed operation. An analysis of several popular high-speed turbocharged four-stroke-cycle diesel engines indicates that bearing loads can average between 4000 and 6000 psi (27,580 to

41,370 kPa); substantially higher loads than this are encountered in some of the newer electronically controlled diesel engines. Average con-rod bearing loads can range between 5300 and 7800 psi (36,544 to 53,781 kPa). Shell bearings are lubricated and cooled by pressurized oil flow from the crankshaft oil holes and by contact with the bearing cap or saddle.

In-Frame Bearing Removal

When engine bearings wear, particularly the main bearings, engine lube oil pressure decreases, because the oil that flows from the engine main oil gallery flows directly to the crankshaft and passes through the drillings in the crankshaft to the main bearings. Oil then flows through intersecting crank oil passages to feed the con-rod bearings. Worn main bearings allow a large volume of oil to exit between the sides of the main bearings and the crank journal, where the oil drops into the oil pan. Consequently, the overall oil pressure decreases and the con-rod and other lubricated components within the engine suffer due to oil starvation.

During normal engine life, between overhauls, it may become necessary to replace the crankshaft main bearings while the crankshaft and engine are still in the equipment. Reasons for replacement may be bearing failure from deterioration (acid formation) of the oil or loss of oil. Some engine manufacturers indicate that to achieve longer life between rebuilds, the main bearings should be replaced in-frame at specific mileage (kilometer) intervals. Upper shell bearing removal can be performed successfully by inserting a *roll-out pin* into the crankshaft main journal oil hole, and slowly rotating the crankshaft over in its normal direction of rotation to carefully remove the upper main bearing from its saddle. Figure 11–28 illustrates a roll pin being inserted, and Figure 11–29 illustrates a special Kent-Moore upper main bearing shell remover/installer tool set recommended for Detroit Diesel Series 50 and 60 engine models. The kit includes a dummy main bearing cap, a dummy main bearing

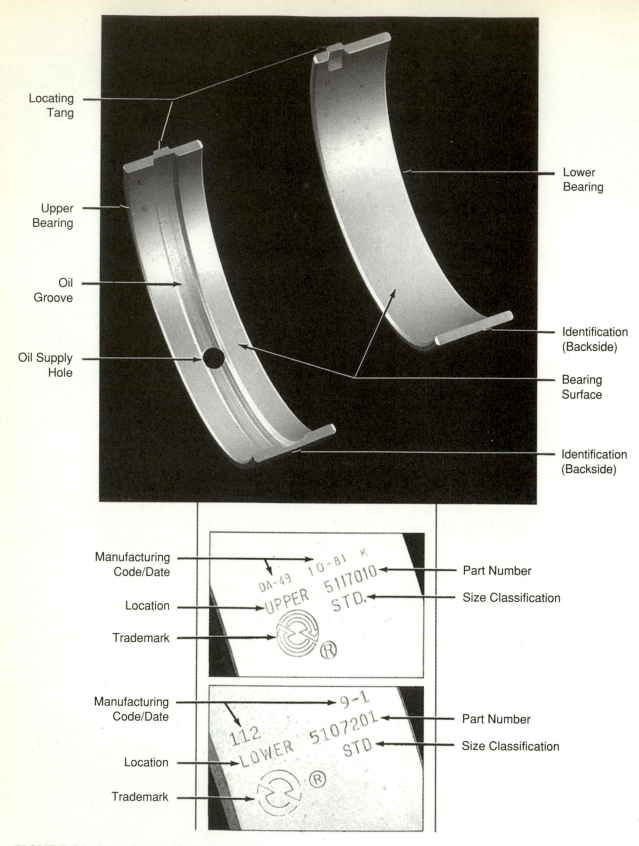

Locating Tang

Upper Bearing

Oil Groove

Oil Supply Hole

Lower Bearing

Identification (Backside)

Bearing Surface

Identification (Backside)

Manufacturing Code/Date

Location

Trademark

Part Number

Size Classification

DA-49 10-81 K

UPPER 5117010

STD.

Manufacturing Code/Date

Location

Trademark

Part Number

Size Classification

9-1

112

LOWER 5107201

STD

FIGURE 11–27 Identification of the upper and lower main bearing shells and the various information contained on the back side of the shell bearing assembly. (Courtesy of Detroit Diesel Corporation.)

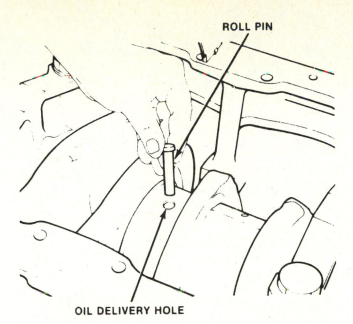

FIGURE 11–28 *Installing a special roll pin into the crankshaft main bearing journal oil hole to allow rolling in or out of the upper shell bearing while the crankshaft is in position in the engine block. (Courtesy of Detroit Diesel Corporation.)*

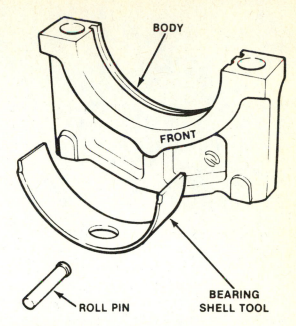

FIGURE 11–29 *A special main bearing shell remover/installer tool set (Kent-Moore J36187). (Courtesy of Detroit Diesel Corporation.)*

shell tool, and the roll pin. This same tool can be used to effectively remove the No. 6 main bearing thrust washers on the Series 60 engine.

The new upper main bearing shell can then be rolled into position using the special tooling just described. If special tooling is not available, select a capscrew/bolt that will fit into the oil hole of the crankshaft, but *grind* the bolt head so that it is thin enough to prevent jamming the bolt as you rotate the crankshaft, or to prevent grooving or scoring of the block bearing saddle area. You can also grind a circular contact area into the bolt head area to assist in proper bearing removal.

Bearing Inspection

When a main or con-rod bearing assembly is removed, either during an in-frame repair or at the time of major engine teardown for complete rebuild, the bearings should always be carefully inspected. If bearings are being considered for possible reuse, check them as follows:

1. Check for etching, flaking, pitting, scoring, minute bearing overlay material cracks, loss of material, or signs of overheating (discoloration).

2. Check the lower main bearing shells that carry the load; they normally show signs of distress before the upper shells.

3. Inspect the backs of the bearing shells for signs of bright or shiny spots, which indicate that the

bearing has been moving in its cap or saddle and therefore should be discarded. This would usually require line boring of the main bearing cap bores and resizing or replacement of the con-rods.

4. Using a ball micrometer (ball against the bearing surface), measure the thickness of the bearing shells as shown in Figure 11–30 across the center of the bearing. If a ball micrometer is not available, use a small ball bearing; subtract the diameter of the ball from the shell thickness and compare to the service manual specs.

5. If old or new bearings are to be used, particularly after grinding of a crankshaft or line boring of the main bearing caps, check the bearing oil clearance. This is best done by using a special extruded plastic thread that is referred to by its trade name of *Plastigage*. This product is readily available from major parts suppliers. Plastigage is available in four thicknesses; choose one based on the desired oil clearance that you are checking. Each box of Plastigage contains 12 envelopes of a given color and size. Bearing clearances for a given engine can be found in the service manual. Plastigage is widely used in four main sizes, which are identified by the color-coded packets green, red, blue, and yellow:

- Green = 0.001 to 0.003 in. (0.025 to 0.076 mm)
- Red = 0.002 to 0.006 in. (0.051 to 0.152 mm)
- Blue = 0.004 to 0.009 in. (0.102 to 0.229 mm)
- Yellow = 0.009 to 0.020 in. (0.23 to 0.51 mm)

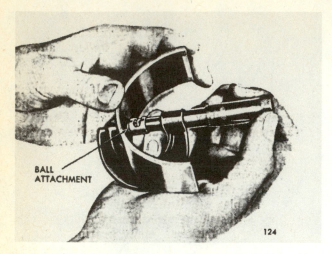

BALL ATTACHMENT

124

FIGURE 11–30 *Using a special outside micrometer with a captive ball-bearing attachment to allow measurement of the shell bearing thickness. (Courtesy of Detroit Diesel Corporation.)*

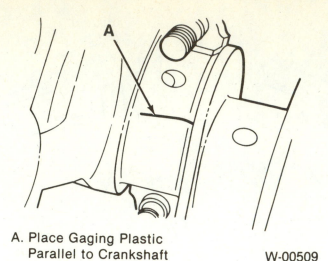

A

A. Place Gaging Plastic Parallel to Crankshaft   W-00509

FIGURE 11–31 *Placing a strip of Plastigage lengthwise across the crankshaft journal. (Courtesy of GMC Trucks.)*

Plastigage offers a fast and accurate method of checking the clearances of both main and con-rod bearings. To use Plastigage correctly, make sure it is at room temperature; then follow these steps:

1. If the engine is turned upside down, lay a strip of Plastigage equivalent to the width of the bearing journal across it and parallel to the crankshaft centerline.

2. If the main bearing clearances are being checked with the engine in position in its equipment, support the weight of the crankshaft and the flywheel by means of a jack under the counterweight adjoining the bearing being checked; otherwise, a false reading will be obtained.

3. Cut or tear off a length of the paper envelope that contains the Plastigage to the bearing width required. Avoid squeezing the envelope during this action, because if the Plastigage is compressed, a false reading may result or the Plastigage may become stuck to the envelope.

4. Carefully roll or remove the strip of Plastigage from the envelope by cutting with a pair of scissors or a knife.

5. Wipe any oil from the bearing shell or journal.

6. Place the Plastigage across the full width of the bearing journal or bearing shell as shown in Figure 11–31.

7. Reinstall the bearing cap and tighten the bolts to the recommended torque value.

8. Loosen the bolts and carefully remove the bearing cap.

9. Lay the Plastigage envelope, which is printed with a series of graduations, alongside the flattened Plastigage as shown in Figure 11–32 until one of the numbered graduations equals the Plastigage width. One side of the envelope is graduated in thousandths of an inch, while the opposite side is in metric dimensions.

10. If the bearing clearance is too small or too large, try to determine the cause(s). Too small a clearance can be caused by high spots behind the bearing shell in the cap or saddle; therefore, check for nicks, burrs, or dirt behind the bearing. Too large a clearance may be due to worn bearings, worn journals, or use of the wrong size of bearings on a reground crankshaft.

11. Remove Plastigage by flooding it with clean engine oil and scraping it from a journal with a fingernail. Do not scratch or etch a bearing surface (non-hardened). Plastigage will self-destruct during engine operation.

Bearing Failure Analysis

Bearing failure analysis is necessary to determine the cause(s) for failure if either bearing damage or crankshaft damage is evident. If the engine is still under *warranty,* it is critical that all bearings be taped together and identified in regard to the position in which they were located. Use masking tape to tape the individual bearing sets (upper and lower shells) together

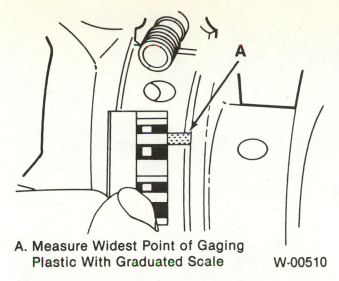

A. Measure Widest Point of Gaging
Plastic With Graduated Scale   W-00510

FIGURE 11–32 *Using the Plastigage paper packet measuring strip to determine the bearing to crankshaft journal clearance. (Courtesy of GMC Trucks.)*

in a circular shape, or tape them together in a semicircular fashion. The engine serial number and miles or hours should be clearly marked on the tape. In addition, a metal marker or a wide, black felt-tip pen can be used to write the number of the bearing location on the back of the shell.

Worn main and con-rod bearings can usually be detected by lower than normal oil pressure accompanied by a distinct knocking sound. Usually excessive oil consumption and a blue smoky exhaust are also evident. A properly fitted precision shell bearing generally appears dull gray in color after a reasonable period of service, which indicates that it has been running on a good, clean oil film. A con-rod knock is generally more noticeable when the engine is unloaded; therefore, alternately load and unload the engine to focus on the noise difference. On the other hand, a main bearing noise is usually more evident when the engine is loaded. Wiped-out or badly worn thrust washers can be detected by measuring the crankshaft end float.

Minor scuffing may be apparent on the top layer of the bearing material, but as long as the wear has not penetrated to the second or third layer of the bearing, the wear is normal. Severe scratches or scoring indicates, of course, dirt or foreign particles in the lube oil. This section will present some examples of bearing failures and their causes. In addition, most engine manufacturers publish excellent booklets dealing with inspection and analysis and causes of specific types of bearing failures; you can obtain these booklets from any local dealer.

Investigation of bearing failures should always procure facts related to these questions:

- When did it occur: at engine start-up, during engine operation, or at shutdown?
- Where did it happen: on a downgrade, on an upgrade, or on level ground?
- How was it identified: an operator complaint, unusual engine noises, a stopped engine, or an engine alarm or low oil pressure gauge?
- Were there any previous engine operating complaints such as history of excessive white, blue, or black exhaust smoke, particularly within the past day or two?
- Does a review of previous service maintenance records suggest any clues such as previous engine repairs, lube oil consumption problems, engine coolant use, or previous lube oil analysis tips?
- What is the condition of external oil lines? Condition of oil filter elements? Amount of lube oil in system? Amount of engine coolant? Condition of air filter elements?

Primary causes of shell bearing damage and their frequency of occurrences are listed next:

Dirt, foreign particles	45%
Misassembly	13%
Misalignment	13%
Insufficient lubrication	11%
Overloading	9.5%
Corrosion	4%
Other causes	4.5%

If a shell bearing is replaced without first determining the cause for failure, most likely the same problem will occur again, and in a much shorter time than the first failure. Basically, analyzing the types of failures involves consideration of bearing appearance, damaging action, possible causes, and corrective action.

Figure 11–33 illustrates the process of bearing fatigue. If the bearing lining exhibits small, irregular pieces of missing surface material, this is usually due to excessive, heavy pulsating-type loads, improper assembly, or incorrect reconditioning of main bearing block bores during line boring. These actions cause the bearing surface to crack from metal fatigue. With continued operation, these cracks widen and become deeper perpendicular to the bonding line. As these fatigue cracks approach the bond line, they tend to turn and run parallel to the bond line, eventually joining and causing pieces of surface material to flake out. All bearing shells should be replaced when this condition occurs and the engine condition that caused this to occur should be corrected. The equipment operator

FIGURE 11–33 *Sequential process of how bearing fatigue can eventually damage the surface layer. (Courtesy of Detroit Diesel Corporation.)*

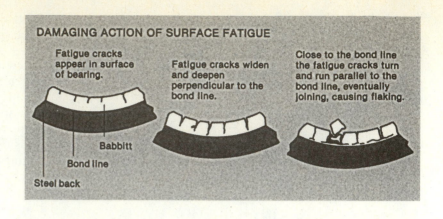

FIGURE 11–34 *How foreign particles trapped between the bearing shell and the crankshaft journal create a high spot leading to bearing and journal damage. (Courtesy of Detroit Diesel Corporation.)*

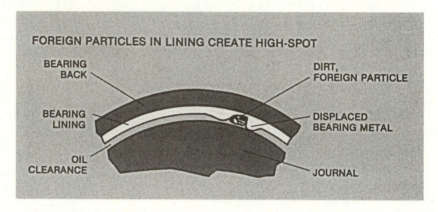

should be counseled to avoid *hot-rodding* and not to lug the engine down below the peak torque and rpm point. Corrosion does not affect all bearings in the same manner because of different bearing alloys. Blowby from combustion gases always creates deterioration of the lube oil. Deterioration is affected by the amount of sulfur in the fuel, the operating temperature of the engine, and any coolant or antifreeze additives that enter the lube system. A sulfuric acid formation results from this oil degradation, and this leads to pitting of the bearing overlay, which creates a porous and extremely weak copper matrix that is easily fatigued by the dynamic loads applied to the surface during engine operation.

Figure 11–34 illustrates foreign particles embedded in the lining material. Dust, dirt, abrasives, or metallic particles present in the oil tend to displace bearing surface metal and crowd the crankshaft journal, thereby creating a *high spot* as shown. This can lead to a rubbing action that eventually breaks down the bearing lining; alternatively, the protruding material can cause a grinding wheel action. Poor rebuild practices that allow dust, dirt, and foreign material to enter the engine, as well as road dirt and sand entering the air intake or breather system, add to the problem. Fitting of tight parts during a rebuild or lack of prelubrication before initial start-up after a rebuild can also cause metal fragments to enter

the lube system. Similarly, operating engines in subzero weather, using too heavy an engine oil, or not using a coolant block or oil heater can accelerate wear on internal engine component parts and lead to a high wear rate and introduction of metal particles in the lube system. Other practices can lead to foreign particles in the lining material: poor maintenance procedures; long intervals between draining and changing oil and filters; poor air cleaner maintenance, particularly on off-highway equipment where heavy dust concentrations are allowed to enter the secondary filter element; and loose air intake duct work clamps. One of the most detrimental lapping compounds for cylinder components is unfiltered air (dust or dirt) that mixes with the engine lube oil.

A bearing failure due to metal-to-metal contact causes a wiping action. This type of failure can be caused by improper installation practices such as too thick a replacement bearing shell. You can reinstall bearing shells that appear to be serviceable, but if the crankshaft is polished, always check the bearing clearance with Plastigage. Too much oil clearance results in excessive oil throw-off, loss of oil pressure, bearing knocking, and failure of other engine parts due to oil starvation.

Figure 11–35 illustrates foreign particles lodged behind the back of the bearing shell and the cap or saddle. The cause can be nicks, burrs, or scores that were

FIGURE 11–35 How foreign particles trapped between the back side of the bearing shell and saddle can distort the bearing. (Courtesy of Detroit Diesel Corporation.)

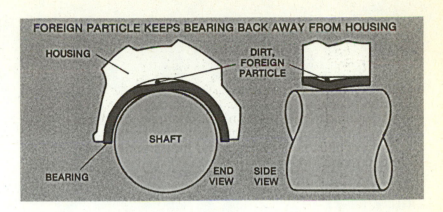

FOREIGN PARTICLE KEEPS BEARING BACK AWAY FROM HOUSING

HOUSING

DIRT, FOREIGN PARTICLE

SHAFT

BEARING

END VIEW   SIDE VIEW

not removed during the inspection and preparation process, as well as dirt, dust, abrasives, or other metallic particles that were not cleaned from the engine block area during the rebuild procedure. As you can see in the diagram, the bearing shell is unable to seat properly in its bore. This creates poor bearing contact and a hotter running bearing. In addition, this uneven distribution of the load creates a very high, concentrated pressure area in contact with the crankshaft hardened journal surface. The result is rapid wear of the bearing surface as well as scoring of the journal surface.

During line boring of the main bearing caps, or honing of the con-rod bores, excessive crush on the shell bearings can result if close tolerances are not maintained or if distortion and an out-of-round condition of the bores have not been corrected. Too much bearing crush results in high compressive forces that cause the bearing to actually bulge inward at the parting faces as shown in the example in Figure 11–36; this is usually referred to as *side pinch*. On the other hand, if insufficient bearing crush is evident, the bearing shells tend to move back and forth during engine operation as shown in Figure 11–37. Close inspection will reveal highly polished areas at the bearing backs as well as at the edge of the bearing parting line area. Poor contact between the back of the shell bearing and its bore will cause insufficient heat transfer, and the resultant overheating problem will cause deterioration of the bearing surface. Poor bearing contact can be the result of nicks or burrs at the cap parting line or distortion (stretch) of the bearing cap. Insufficient bolt/nut torque, or failure to replace the bolts at major overhaul, can cause the cap to be loose.

Figure 11–38 illustrates a problem caused by the technician using a socket with too thick a body, which crowded the cap and shifted it to one side during installation. So one side of each bearing shell half is forced against the crankshaft journal at the parting line. That metal-to-metal contact accompanied by excessive pressure will lead to severe bearing surface

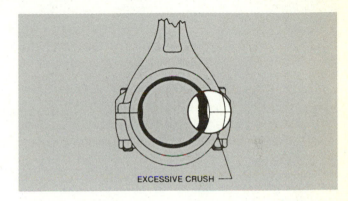

EXCESSIVE CRUSH

FIGURE 11–36 How excessive bearing shell crush can cause bearing distortion at the parting faces (side pinch). (Courtesy of Detroit Diesel Corporation.)

wear and eventual fatigue. This condition can also be caused by reversing the bearing cap, not match-marking numbers on con-rods or main bearings, or by switching caps with others. Poor installation procedures such as insufficient torque, incorrect torquing sequence, or enlarged cap bolt holes can be another factor in this type of a failure.

Other problems caused by technicians are improperly installing engine bearing shells, installing an offset con-rod in the wrong direction, reversing bearing halves, and failing to align the bearing retaining lug with its mating notch in the cap or saddle. Crankshaft journals that are tapered or oval and are not in accord with specifications always cause short bearing life. Figure 11–39 illustrates three typical examples that can be found in diesel engine crankshafts. A taper-shaped journal can usually be traced to uneven wear as a result of misalignment or improper machining of the journal during grinding. An hourglass or barrel-shaped journal is always traceable to improper machining. Out-of-round main or con-rod bearing bores always create excessive wear areas near the parting lines on both sides of the top and bottom shells. This is usually

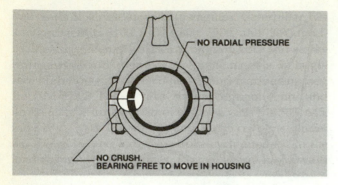

FIGURE 11–37   How a shell bearing with insufficient crush is free to move back and forth within the saddle area. (Courtesy of Detroit Diesel Corporation.)

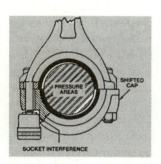

FIGURE 11–38   How a shifted or uncentered rod bearing cap can produce excessive bearing pressure areas. (Courtesy of Detroit Diesel Corporation.)

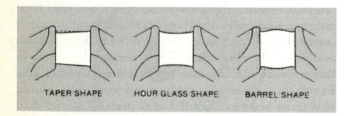

FIGURE 11–39   Three typical irregular shapes that indicate a worn crankshaft journal (Courtesy of Detroit Diesel Corporation.)

accompanied by reduced oil clearance near the parting line, and metal-to-metal contact takes place between the bearing and journal as illustrated in Figure 11–40.

Incorrect crankshaft journal fillet radius can result in the edge of the bearing riding up on the fillet, which manifests itself as excessive wear on the outer edges of the bearing shell surface. Figure 11–41 illustrates this type of a problem. Always check journal fillets after any regrinding with a set of fillet radius gauges to determine if the fillets have been ground correctly;

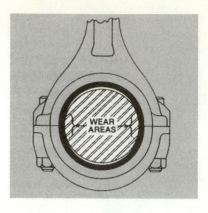

FIGURE 11–40   How insufficient or decreased bearing shell oil clearance causes excessive wear. (Courtesy of Detroit Diesel Corporation.)

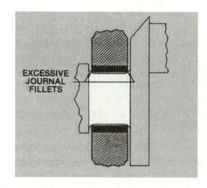

FIGURE 11–41   Problems created when a reground crankshaft journal fillet radius area is too great. (Courtesy of Detroit Diesel Corporation.)

otherwise, early bearing and possible crankshaft failure will result. Also, keep in mind that measuring the individual main bearing cap bores inside diameters *will not* determine if the bores are on the same centerline. Use a mandrel or make sure that the crank rotates freely after installing new lubricated bearings and torquing them to specifications.

Avoidance of Main Bearing Damage

Shell bearings are precision manufactured to offer long service life, but incorrect operation or engine starting conditions can result in premature damage and early replacement of main bearings. High-speed light-load operation of the engine before establishing proper bearing oil films often results in main bearing damage. On most engines, main bearings are loaded heavier than rod bearings when the engine is operating at light- or no-load conditions. Any residual oil in the crankshaft oil holes flows to the rod bearings due to centrifugal force from the rotating crankshaft. Main bearing damage usually originates with a plastic flow of the bearing overlay material (that is, the metal overlay starts to change from a solid to a liquid) and progresses based on the oil pressure time delay and associated engine speed. In addition, both rod bearings and the turbocharger bearings can be damaged by the improper operating conditions. To avoid early failure of main bearings, avoid the following conditions:

- Fast start: increasing engine speed immediately after initial start-up
- Fast/cold start: increasing engine speed immediately after starting combined with oil pressure delay due to cold oil temperatures
- Dry start: starting an engine, particularly after an overhaul, with dry or empty oil filters or after prolonged engine shutdown or storage. *Always prelube* the oil system as described and illustrated in Figure 18–42.
- Fast/dry start: starting the engine with dry or empty oil filters and immediately increasing engine speed before the oil film is established
- Starting an engine by using ethyl-ether starting fluid: This creates an uncontrolled engine speed, which depends on the amount of ether injected. In this case, the engine rpm can exceed the high idle (maximum no load) governed speed, as the fuel injection pump/unit injector governor has no control.
- Engine overspeed: This is a common occurrence with heavy-duty highway tractor trailers or dump trucks. The vehicle road wheels become the driving member in downhill loaded hauls, particularly with mechanical drive transmissions where the operator fails to check and slow the vehicle speed by use of an engine compression or exhaust brake or by application of a hydraulic or electric retarder assembly and/or the normal vehicle service brakes. Other causes of engine overspeed can be entry of an external fuel or gas flow through the intake air system.

CRANKSHAFT SEALS

All engines employ a crankshaft oil seal at both the front and rear to retain lube oil within the crankcase and gear train housing area. Seals are generally made from an oil-resistant synthetic silicone rubber for the carrier and a *Teflon* material for the sealing lips. These seals are circular lip-type seals and contain a garter spring behind the seal to allow firm pressure to be applied around the circumference of the crankshaft hardened and polished sealing surfaces. Figure 11–42 illustrates the general makeup of a crankshaft oil seal designed as a unidirectional single-lip type. In cases

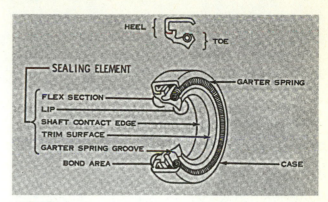

FIGURE 11–42 *General construction and nomenclature of a typical crankshaft seal. (Courtesy of Caterpillar Inc.)*

where fluids are present on both sides of the seal, a double-lip seal can be used to prevent mixing of the fluids. The side of the seal that contains the garter spring faces the oil to be sealed. As shown in the diagram, the main parts of a lip-type seal are the case, sealing element, and garter spring. Many crankshaft oil seal lips are now coated with Teflon, which is transferred to the crankshaft or wear sleeve for proper sealing; therefore, never use engine lube oil on the seal lip. Read the seal package directions carefully to determine the proper installation procedure.

The specific location of the front and rear seals differs slightly depending on engine make and model. Usually, the *front seal* is located in the engine front gear case cover, but in some cases the seal may be within the oil pump cover, which is bolted to the front end of the engine. The *rear seal* is normally pressed into the bore of the flywheel housing, although some engines such as the Cummins N14 models employ a small rear cover bolted to the rear of the engine block that can be removed without having to remove the flywheel housing. It is generally good practice to replace the front or rear oil seal any time that you have to remove and reinstall the flywheel housing or front cover. When replacing either the front or rear seal, the engine crank pulley-damper and/or flywheel must be removed first to gain access to the seal.

Rear Seal Replacement and Installation

If the rear crankshaft oil seal leaks, it can be replaced without removing the engine from its equipment. However, the engine's optional drive mechanism, such as a transmission, torque converter housing, PTO, or marine gear, has to be removed to gain access to the flywheel, which must be removed.

After removing the flywheel, drill two or three small holes in the seal casing 120° to 180° apart that

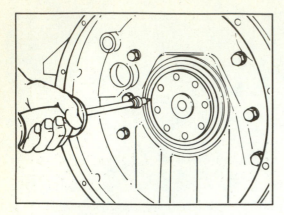

FIGURE 11–43 Using a slide hammer and dent puller attachment to carefully remove a rear crankshaft oil seal from the flywheel housing. (Courtesy of Cummins Engine Company, Inc.)

FIGURE 11–44 Installing a new crankshaft rear oil seal into the flywheel housing bore with a special installer set. (Courtesy of Detroit Diesel Corporation.)

will accept No. 10 self-tapping sheet metal screws. Then install the screws with flat washers on them. Remove the seal by prying against the flat washers with two pry bars. Alternatively, you can use a slide hammer(s) or dent puller attachment as illustrated in Figure 11–43 to remove the seal from its bore area.

To *install* the rear crankshaft oil seal, follow these six steps:

1. Thoroughly clean and dry the sealing surface area in the flywheel housing bore and the crankshaft area.
2. Use a seal kit, which generally provides a seal pilot made from plastic. If not, obtain a suitable plastic or steel seal protector.
3. Install the seal pilot onto the rear of the crankshaft.

SERVICE TIP: Many seal manufacturers indicate that new seals should go on dry (no lube oil) because the seal surface is coated with Teflon and requires no lubricant. In addition, the outside diameter of the seal is also often coated with plastic that acts as a sealant. *Do not* remove this coating or lubricate it. Non-Teflon-coated seals usually require liberal lubrication with clean engine oil to the inside lip of the seal as well as to the crankshaft or sleeve area and seal pilot. Failure to do so can result in seal lip damage on initial engine start-up (dry start). Always read the new seal package or box directions carefully to determine the installation procedure.

4. With the lip of the seal pointing toward the engine, carefully push the seal over the end of the pilot seal protector and onto the crankshaft. Remove the seal expander.

5. Using a seal alignment tool installer similar to that illustrated in Figure 11–44 along with two guide studs threaded into the crankshaft/flywheel bolt holes, use a hammer to drive the seal into the flywheel housing squarely. In some cases, the seal is designed to bottom in the bore of the housing. If not, take care that the seal is not driven in too far. Refer to the engine service manual for details.

6. Confirm that the seal is sitting squarely in its bore by mounting a dial indicator onto the rear of the crankshaft flange. Pry the crankshaft forward and set the gauge tip against the seal housing metal face. Note the readings at the 12, 3, 6, and 9 o'clock positions; generally, these should not vary more than 0.010 to 0.015 in. (0.254 to 0.381 mm).

Front Seal Replacement and Installation

The crankshaft front oil seal is pressed into the gear case cover housing bore. If the seal requires replacement, your first step on most engines will be to remove the crankshaft pulley and vibration damper assembly and the gear case housing. Once these items have been removed, you can drive the seal from the housing bore by using a brass drift and hammer. Alternatively, you can use a circular plate slightly smaller in diameter than the seal bore, and either hammer it out or use a hydraulic press to remove the seal. Always clean the crankshaft seal lip area with fine emery cloth, as well as the bore within the gear case cover. The seal can also be

FIGURE 11–45
Arrangement and design concept of a crankshaft wear sleeve and an oversize front or rear oil seal assembly. (Courtesy of Detroit Diesel Corporation.)

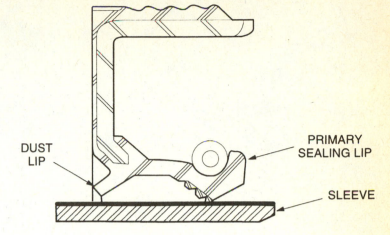

replaced without removing the gear case cover in the same manner as that described for rear seal removal.

If the seal lip surface on the crankshaft is worn or grooved, *installing* a new standard seal will not correct the oil leakage problem. To effectively repair this type of a condition, a thin-walled oil seal sleeve must be pressed over the worn surface of the crankshaft. This is the preferable method for correcting the worn condition. In certain engine models where space permits, a seal spacer can be used to relocate the seal lip to an unworn surface on the crankshaft. The thin-walled sleeves are often referred to as *Speedi-Sleeves*, since a repair to the leaking area can be done fairly quickly and easily. When a sleeve is used, the new seal selected must be oversize on its inside diameter to accommodate the sleeve. Figure 11–45 illustrates the arrangement of a new oversize seal and hardened sleeve assembly. It is designed to be installed as a unit (seal and sleeve), which simplifies seal and sleeve installation and reduces the possibility of seal lip damage that can occur when the sleeve and the seal are installed one at a time. The diagram shows a unidirectional hydrothread-type Teflon primary sealing lip and a secondary dust sealing lip. It also has an integral spring that helps to insure proper seal lip tension.

Special tooling is required to install this oversize front or rear seal and wear sleeve on an engine. Tooling varies for makes and models of engines and is readily available from major tool suppliers. Worn front or rear seals can be removed as described for rear crankshaft seal removal without removing the flywheel housing or the front gear case cover by using self-tapping screws and a slide hammer puller arrangement. Follow these steps to install the new seal:

1. With the worn seal removed, use crocus cloth or very fine emery cloth to remove any minor irregularities from the crankshaft seal contact surface.

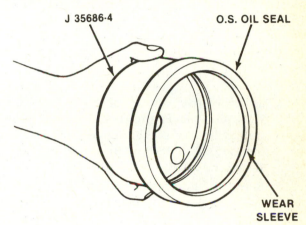

FIGURE 11–46 Tool setup for oil seal wear sleeve installation. O.S. = oversize. (Courtesy of Detroit Diesel Corporation.)

2. Coat the area of the crankshaft where the sleeve will be positioned with Permatex No. 3 sealant or equivalent.

3. Keep the seal and sleeve together! Figure 11–46 illustrates the new oversize seal and sleeve assembly on the special installer. The seal and sleeve supplier states that if the seal is separated from the sleeve, both parts must be scrapped. The reason is that the Teflon lip seal may be damaged when attempting to reinstall it over the wear sleeve. In addition, the seal will probably have lost its Teflon coating and will invariably leak if installed.

4. If special tooling is not available, press the sleeve onto the shaft using a suitable sleeve installer with an inside diameter that is a slip-fit over the crankshaft surface and with a wide enough outside diameter to fully contact the sleeve diameter. Special tooling has guide studs to allow centering of the sleeve and seal

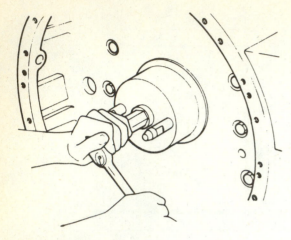

FIGURE 11–47 *Using special oil seal and sleeve installation tooling to successfully press the seal and sleeve into the flywheel housing and onto the rear flange of the crankshaft. (Courtesy of Detroit Diesel Corporation.)*

assembly over the crankshaft. Two guide studs shown in Figure 11–47 allow the technician to thread these through the base and into the crankshaft 180° apart to square up the sleeve and seal.

5. Refer to Figure 11–47 and with the tooling arranged as shown, install the thrust bearing tool with the case side toward the installer housing. Install the hex nut onto the center screw as illustrated.

6. Refer to Figure 11–47 and after tightening the hex nut by hand, use a ratchet and socket to tighten the hex nut. This will pull the seal and sleeve into position over the worn crankshaft surface until the seal and sleeve are correctly positioned.

7. If special tooling is not available, always check the seal for squareness; follow step 6 for installing a rear seal.

CRANKSHAFT VIBRATION DAMPERS

One of the most important components on any high-speed heavy-duty diesel engine is the crankshaft vibration damper, which is located at the front end of the engine and bolted to a flange on the crankshaft. The purpose of the damper is said briefly in its name—vibration damper. It is designed to reduce torsional flexing of the crankshaft caused by gas pressures in the engine cylinders as well as inertia forces resulting from the reciprocating and rotating parts of the engine. Rotating components within the engine assembly can create torsional vibration amplitudes and resonance at varying frequencies. If these destructive couples are

not dampened or detuned, crankshaft breakage and other engine component damage can result.

Although not all diesel engines require expensive dampers, normally some means of altering the frequency of the vibration forces to reduce the energy to a safe level is necessary. Therefore, a damper is designed to develop an antiphase and opposing torque to the vibratory torque within the engine.

Types of Dampers

The size, displacement, and rotating speed of the engine determines the size and type of vibration damper. Dampers basically fall into four basic categories:

1. A series of coil springs or rubber buffer blocks sandwiched between two coupling halves and fitted in curved axial slots machined around the outer circumference of the couplings to connect the two halves together. The components are retained against the developed centrifugal force by a cover assembly. This type of damper is often mounted behind the engine front cover rather than being exposed to view as are the other three more commonly used types. This spring system is usually found only in very large slow- and medium-speed engines and will not be described in detail here.

2. A single-rubber damper bolted to a hub and cone.

3. A double-rubber damper consisting of a light damper, a heavy damper, a hub, and an inner and outer cone.

4. A viscous damper consisting of a sealed outer shell, an internal flywheel, and a quantity of highly viscous fluid.

The most widely used vibration dampers described in categories 2 through 4 are attached to the front of the crankshaft by a hub mechanism and bolted into position. Figure 11–48 illustrates the component parts of a single-rubber damper assembly bolted to the front of the engine crankshaft. This damper is relatively inexpensive to manufacture and is widely used on production automotive gasoline engines as well as on a number of lighter and midrange model diesel engines. The smaller and lighter inner solid metal hub is connected to the heavier and larger-diameter outer hub by a chemically bonded rubber insert. This rubber ring is radially compressed so that during engine operation, the torques transmitted through the crankshaft-mounted damper inner hub tend to want to shear the rubber. A properly operating damper usually exhibits some heat during engine operation due to this twisting and shearing action. The inherent elastic-

66. Vibration Damper
67. Crankshaft Pulley
68. Washer
69. Bolt
70. Washer
71. Bolt

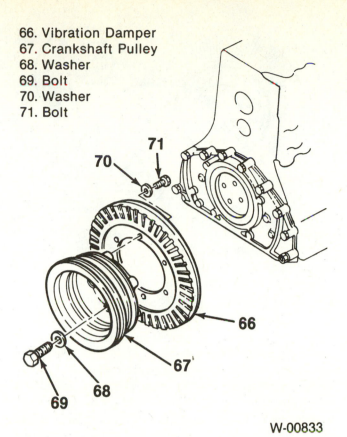

W-00833

FIGURE 11–48 Identification of component parts for a rubber-type engine crankshaft vibration damper and pulley assembly. (Courtesy of GMC Trucks.)

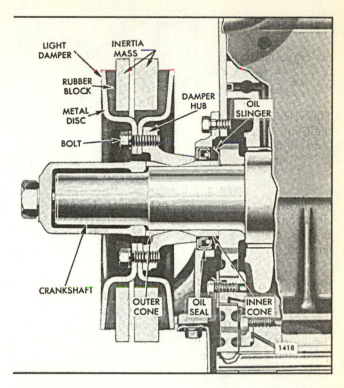

FIGURE 11–49 Side view of the component parts of a double-rubber crankshaft vibration damper assembly. (Courtesy of Detroit Diesel Corporation.)

ity of the rubber reduces the transmitted torques and vibrations to the larger outer hub to reduce the frequency to a safe level. The stiffness of the rubber ring and the inertial mass of the damper hubs can be engineered to suit either a low- or high-vibration frequency so that consistent damping or hysteresis properties are achieved.

The double-rubber damper assembly illustrated in sectional view in Figure 11–49 operates on principles similar to those described for the single-rubber model. The double model is used on heavier-duty engine models and consists of both a light and heavy damper assembly constructed of rubber blocks bonded to an inertia mass in the form of a metal ring on one side and a stamped metal disc on the opposite side. The metal components are separated and free to move within prescribed limits through their bonded rubber blocks. The light and heavy dampers are bolted and doweled together and supported on a hub. The driving hub is supported on an inner and outer cone, and the bolted crankshaft cap or pulley secures the assembly in position.

The most widely used type of damper on high-speed heavy-duty diesel engines where the equipment

requires frequent speed and load changes is the viscous type. This damper provides faster response to load and speed changes, and high temperatures have less adverse effect on it than on the rubber type. The viscous damper was originally designed by the Houdaille-Hershey Corporation in 1946 and is still the standard; it is the most widely used type of most OEMs of heavy-duty engines. Either a single or double configuration is appropriate, depending on the engine displacement, speeds, and loads generated. Similarly, the diameter of the damper(s) varies by engine size.

Figure 11–50 is a sectionalized view of a single viscous damper assembly attached to the front of the crankshaft. The viscous damper assembly consists of a sealed outer shell with an internal solid flywheel that is free floating in a quantity of highly viscous silicone fluid. Various silicones are chosen depending on damper design. Note in Figure 11–51 that very little clearance exists between the solid internal flywheel and the damper outer housing or shell. Due to the drag, or shearing, of the silicone fluid, when the engine is accelerated the flywheel is driven but at a much slower speed than the housing because of the friction created. When the engine is decelerated, the internal flywheel tends to freewheel. During operation the damper outer housing, which is bolted to the crankshaft, rotates at engine speed. Two distinct extreme

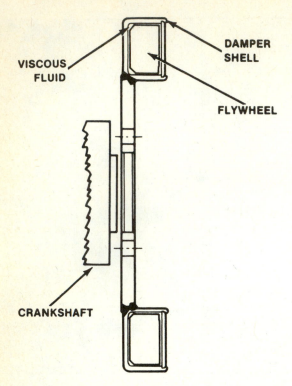

FIGURE 11–50 Simplified diagram illustrating the solid flywheel suspended in a viscous fluid within the vibration damper housing. (Courtesy of Detroit Diesel Corporation.)

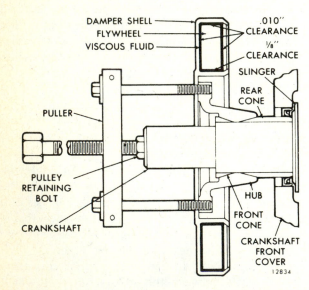

FIGURE 11–51 Using a special puller assembly to carefully and successfully remove the viscous-type crankshaft vibration damper. (Courtesy of Detroit Diesel Corporation.)

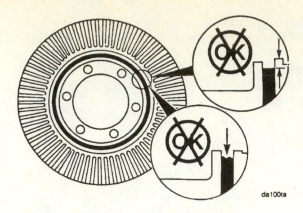

FIGURE 11–52 Inspection of a rubber type vibration damper to identify signs of missing rubber pieces or to determine if the rubber bonding is more than ⅛ in. (3.175 mm) below the metal surface. (Courtesy of Cummins Engine Company, Inc.)

vibratory conditions occur. At low speeds and vibration amplitudes, the inertia mass of the flywheel rotates at close to engine speed. At higher speeds and during engine acceleration, very large vibration amplitudes are transmitted to the slower turning flywheel mass due to the fluid-drive condition that exists through the silicone. This slippage allows the slower turning flywheel to absorb and dampen the amplitude of excessive torsional vibrations in the crankshaft, thereby reducing the value to a safe level.

A properly operating viscous damper always exhibits a warm to hot housing temperature when touched after stopping a running engine that has been cycled through various speeds and loads for at least 30 minutes. A typical surface temperature on a properly functioning damper is approximately 180°F (82°C). If safety shrouds are used around the damper, they must allow for adequate airflow to keep the damper operating at an acceptable temperature; otherwise, high operating temperatures could cause the fluid within the damper to break down. Make the damper safety shroud from meshed or expanded metal material.

Inspecting Rubber Vibration Dampers

Regardless of the type of damper used, an engine that continually throws accessory drive belts from the crankshaft pulley could indicate a failed damper assembly. Visual inspection of the damper on the engine should be done only after cleaning the assembly using a mild detergent and warm water. Look for signs of any cracks in the damper hub, and closely inspect the elastic member for deterioration or sponginess. If pieces of rubber are missing or the rubber bonding is more than ⅛ in. (3.175 mm) below the metal surface diameter as shown in Figure 11–52, or if the outer flywheel flat surface is more than 0.050 in. (1.25 mm) out of alignment with the hub, replace the assembly. Most rubber dampers have two index lines between the inner and outer hub areas as shown in Figure 11–53. If the lines are more than ¹⁄₁₆ in. (1.59 mm) out of alignment, replace the damper.

Run the engine and visually check the damper for any signs of wobble from the front and side. If you suspect some runout, clean the outer diameter of the damper and place a dial indicator against the circumferential outer surface. Manually rotate the engine over. If the runout exceeds more than approximately 0.004 in./1 in. (0.10 mm/25.4 mm) of damper diameter, replace the damper. Place the dial indicator against the front side of the damper and thrust the crankshaft toward the rear to remove crankshaft end float; otherwise, a false reading may be obtained. Set the gauge to zero and rotate the engine through 360°. If the wobble exceeds 0.007 in./1 in. (0.177 mm/25.4 mm) of radius, replace the damper.

Inspecting Viscous Dampers

An engine that continually throws accessory drive belts from the crankshaft pulley is a good indication of a failed vibration damper. A damper can become inoperative without showing signs of damage on the outside. For this reason, some engine manufacturers suggest that the viscous damper be replaced at 10,000 hours on marine applications or at engine overhaul, whichever comes first. On off-highway units, the dampers would be replaced at 20,000 hours or at overhaul. Industrial and power generator units need replacement at overhaul, as do on-highway truck applications. Since a viscous damper that shows no visible signs of damage cannot be checked thoroughly in the field, the damper manufacturer will conduct a *damper check* for a service fee when all other checks indicate no damage.

To check a viscous damper assembly with the engine stopped, clean the housing with a good solvent cleaner. Do not steam clean it, because this can alter the internal silicone fluid temperature. Replace the damper if any of the following conditions are found:

- Visually inspect the housing for any signs of dents, nicks, deep scratches, raised surfaces, or other physical damage.
- Look carefully around the mounting bolt area for signs of cracking.
- Check the rolled lip at the outer circumference of the damper where there is usually a raised lip. If the back is flush with the outer edge, the damper has internal damage.
- Check for signs of fluid leakage.
- Refer to Figure 11–54 and use emery cloth to remove paint at four positions on both sides of the damper 90° apart. Check the thickness of the damper about ⅛ in. (3.175 mm) from its outer diameter at these four places. Variations in thickness should not be greater than 0.010 in. (0.254 mm).
- Check the damper for runout using a dial indicator for eccentricity by placing the gauge against the outer circumference. Rotate the damper through 360°. Readings should not exceed 0.004 in./1 in. (0.1 mm/25.4 mm) of damper diameter.
- Check the damper for wobble by setting a dial indicator against the front face of the housing. Push the crankshaft rearward to avoid any false reading from crankshaft end float. The readings should not exceed 0.007 in./1 in. (0.177 mm/25.4 mm) of damper radius.

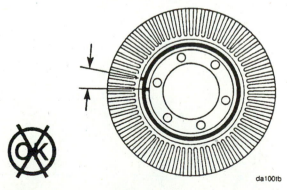

FIGURE 11–53 *Checking to see if the rubber bonding index lines between the inner and outer hub are misaligned. (Courtesy of Cummins Engine Company, Inc.)*

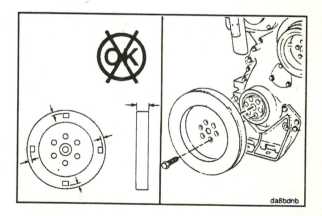

FIGURE 11–54 *Removing paint from the viscous damper at four points and checking the thickness with an outside micrometer. After reinstalling the damper, check it for wobble and runout using a precision dial indicator. (Courtesy of Cummins Engine Company, Inc.)*

- Remove the damper from the engine. *Never* strike a viscous damper with a hammer; many dampers have drilled and tapped holes to allow use of a suitable puller assembly similar to that illustrated in Figure 11–51.
- Shake the damper back and forth. If a metallic rattling sound is heard, a loss of fluid is indicated and the damper *must* be replaced.
- Refer to Figure 11–55 and spray the damper with spot-check developer (type SKD-NF or equivalent). Place the damper in a temperature-controlled oven with the rolled lip side down and heat the damper at 200°F (93°C) for at least 30 minutes. Remove the damper from the oven using protective gloves. Check for any signs of fluid sweating or leaks.
- Check for loose or deteriorated engine mounts.

CAUTION: Loose engine mounts allow the engine to move during operation, which can cause damage to the vibration damper by adding an extra couple to the damper action. If severe damage to the viscous damper is found, it is possible that crankshaft damage has occurred. Therefore, it is wise to remove the crankshaft for inspection. If the engine is being overhauled, this inspection would be performed routinely. When an in-frame overhaul is being done, the crankshaft should be checked *very carefully!*

CRANKSHAFT PULLEYS

Closely inspect the crankshaft and all other pulley assemblies for cracks and signs of severe belt wear in the pulley grooves. Most heavy-duty diesel engines employ multiple-groove pulley assemblies that use V-style belts or poly-V belts. A poly-V type crankshaft pulley assembly is shown in Figure 11–56.

High polish in the pulley grooves usually is indicative of belt slippage, misalignment, or damaged pulley assemblies. Short belt life (tearing and rolling) is usually an indication that the pulley grooves are worn or misaligned. If you do not have a pulley groove checking tool, lay new belt into the pulley groove and check how far it falls into the groove compared to how far it falls in a new pulley. Most belts in new pulleys normally sit fairly close to the surface. Figure 11–49 illustrates a vibration damper assembly along with the location of the front crankshaft oil seal within the engine front support. Worn oil surfaces can be repaired by installing a Speedi-Sleeve and oversize oil seal as described earlier in this chapter. When tightening the damper or pulley retaining bolts, prevent the engine crankshaft from rotating by jamming the flywheel ring gear. On some engines an accessory drive pulley retaining nut can be held by a socket and breaker bar to prevent engine rotation.

GLOSSARY OF TERMS*

Aluminum contamination   Failure of aluminum components in an engine, contributing aluminum debris into the lubrication system, that is,

*Courtesy of Detroit Diesel Corporation.

FIGURE 11–55 *Cleaning and spraying the viscous damper housing with spot-check developer. Then place the damper into a temperature-controlled oven for 30 minutes. After removal, check it for signs of fluid sweat or leaks. (Courtesy of Cummins Engine Company, Inc.)*

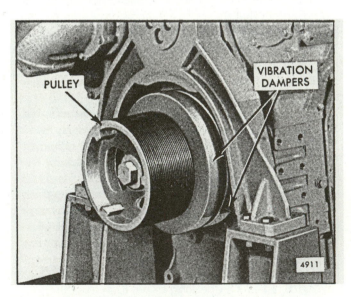

FIGURE 11–56 *Example of a poly-V, multiple-grooved front crankshaft pulley assembly. (Courtesy of Detroit Diesel Corporation.)*

blower(s), intermediate camshaft bearings, flywheel housings, turbochargers, oil pump housings, and governor housings.

Bearing alloy   Any alloy that is used as a bearing lining surface.

Bearing cap   The removable half of the housing that holds the bearing shells in place.

Bearing corrosion   Chemical attack evident on bearing surfaces by metal loss or discoloration.

Bearing housing bore   The housing into which the bearing shells are assembled.

Bearing lining material   Trimetal alloy mainly of copper with lead and tin for maximum fatigue strength.

Bearing lower (half shell)   The bearing half that is made for assembly in the bearing cap.

Bearing material fatigue   The cracking and eventual "chunking out" of bearing material associated with repeated loading in excess of the fatigue strength for the material.

Bearing upper (half shell)   The bearing half that is made for assembly in the engine block or connecting rod as opposed to the bearing cap.

Bearing wall thickness   The dimension of the bearing shell through the radial cross section as measured by a micrometer with ball attachment.

Bore (housing)   The inside diameter of the main bearing/connecting rod bore into which the bearing shells are assembled.

Bore geometry   Bore diameter, roundness, taper, and alignment (main bearing).

Cavitation erosion   Cavitation is the formation of bubbles in a fluid (lube oil) which may occur when the fluid is subjected to low pressures. The high energy dissipated when these bubbles collapse near the bearing surface causes gradual erosion and pitting of same. This condition is called cavitation erosion and is generally not harmful to bearing performance.

Clearance (diametral bearing)   The difference between the bearing housing bore ID and bearing journal OD.

Connecting rod   The structural member that transfers the force from the piston to the crankpin.

Connecting rod bearing   The bearing at the big end of the connecting rod in which the crankpin rotates.

Copper exposed   A condition where the bearing shell has been worn through the overlay and into the copper bearing lining as evidenced by a copper color.

Corrosion   *See* Bearing corrosion.

Crankcase   The enclosure for the crankshaft formed by the oil pan and the lower portion of the engine block.

Crankpin   The crankshaft journal around which the connecting rod bearing shells are installed.

Crankshaft   The main shaft of an engine; contains the main bearing journals and crankpins.

Crown   The center area of a bearing shell.

Crush   The circumferential interference fit necessary to hold two bearing halves securely in the housing bore. In a bearing half, the amount of circumference in excess of a half circle.

Crush relief   Metal removed on the bearing surface at the parting faces extending the full width of the bearing.

Debris   *See* Foreign material.

Dilution   Either fuel or coolant in the lubrication system mixing with the lubrication oil.

Dirt   *See* Foreign material.

Edge loading   Unequal loading of a bearing shell evidenced by taper wear across the length of the bearing.

Embedability   The ability of the bearing material to absorb foreign material without causing serious bearing damage.

Embedded   The enclosure of solid particles into the surface of a bearing shell, for example, dirt, shavings, metal grinding dust.

End clearance (end play)   The possible forward and backward movement of the crankshaft in the main bearing bore or connecting rods on the crankpin.

Engine block   The main casting of an internal combustion engine containing the cylinder bores and main bearing bores.

Fatigue   *See* Bearing material fatigue.

Fatigue strength   Ability of a bearing material to withstand the repeated loads incurred during engine operation.

Foreign material   Any extraneous material not intended to be present, for example, particles of steel, cast iron, dirt, sand.

Free spread diameter   *See* Spread.

"Hot short"   Term used to describe a condition where the bearing lining becomes unbonded from the steel bearing back because of an excessively high bearing temperature. The high bearing temperature is almost always a result of the heat generated during a scoring failure. This condition does not indicate an initial defective bearing lining to steel back bond. It merely indicates that a high enough bearing temperature was reached during a scoring failure to "hot shot" or "melt" the bond layer.

Hydraulic erosion   The eating away of the bearing overlay by the action of the oil flow past the surface.

Insufficient lubrication   Inadequate flow rate of lube oil for satisfactory bearing performance.

Journal   The part of a shaft that revolves in a bearing.

Limit   A size or dimension either plus or minus the tolerance (high and low limit.)

Line bore   To machine the crankshaft main bearing bores, creating bore centers that fall on a true centerline.

Lining   *See* Bearing lining material.

Lining fatigue   *See* Bearing material fatigue.

Locating tang   A projection on a bearing back that locates in a machined slot in the bearing seat; used to locate the bearing in the housing bore and keep it from moving laterally.

Lubricant   A substance capable of reducing friction between mating surfaces in relative motion through separation by an oil film.

Main bearing   A bearing that is used to support the crankshaft in the cylinder block.

Main bearing journal   A crankshaft journal that is supported by a main bearing.

Main bearing saddle   The area in the cylinder block machined to receive the upper main bearing.

Normal wear   The amount of bearing wear experienced during normal engine operation.

Oil   A viscous fluid; insoluble in water.

Oil clearance   *See* Clearance (diametral bearing).

Oil film   The thin layer of oil that protects the journal and bearing surfaces by separating them and preventing journal-to-bearing contact while the engine is in operation.

Oil gallery (main)   The main oil supply line in an engine block; often referred to as the header. Oil flows from this major supply route under pressure to the many parts that are to be lubricated.

Oil groove   A canal machined in the surface of a bearing to spread oil on a friction area or to permit the transfer of oil to another part.

Oil hole   A hole drilled through a bearing wall or crankshaft journal to allow for the passage of the oil.

Oil starvation   A condition of inadequate oil flow or supply.

Out-of-round   An inside or outside diameter, designed to be perfectly round, having varying diameters when measured at different points across its diameter.

Overlay checking   The bearing overlay cracking indicating the beginning stages of overlay fatigue.

Overlay fatigue   The cracking and eventual loss of overlay material associated with repeated loading in excess of the fatigue strength of the overlay material.

Overload   A bearing load in excess of the load the bearing was designed to carry.

Oversize   Either an inside or outside diameter that is greater than standard size.

Parting edge   The edge formed where the inside or outside surface of the bearing joins the parting face.

Parting face   The surface that is in contact with the other bearing half when the bearing is assembled.

Parting line   The theoretical line formed by the contacting parting faces.

Spread   The excess of diameter at the outside parting edges in the free state over the housing bore into which the bearing is to be installed.

Spun bearing   Bearing set that has adhered to the journal and turned in the bore for various reasons, for example, dirt, lack of lubrication, or improper lubrication.

Thrust bearing   A flat bearing used to control the crankshaft end play.

Tolerance   An acceptable range for dimensions to provide accuracy in finished parts.

Undersize   Either an inside or outside diameter that is less than standard size.

Wear   The gradual decrease in bearing thickness.

SELF-TEST QUESTIONS

1. Technician A says that there is generally one more main bearing journal than there are cylinder numbers. Technician B says that the crankshaft must have the same number of main bearing journals and cylinders. Who is correct?

2. True or False: Crankshaft counterweights are employed to produce greater torque when the engine is running.

3. True or False: Most high-speed engine crankshafts are manufactured from a one-piece forged alloy steel billet.

4. True or False: Built or semibuilt crankshafts are sectional crankshafts that are used on larger slow-speed engines.

5. True or False: The crankshaft fillet radius is used to relieve the stresses at each journal by spreading the load across a greater cross-sectional area.

6. Technician A says that crankshaft main and con-rod journals are always induction hardened to fairly shallow depths. Technician B says that all journals are hardened all the way through. Which technician is correct?

7. True or False: Offset crankshaft journal oil holes are designed to provide a 50% thicker oil film during engine operation.

8. What washers maintain crankshaft end float or end play?

9. Give three ways to minimize flexing of main bearing caps during engine operation.

10. Technician A says that crankshaft oil passages can be effectively cleaned by removing the Allen-head screws and using a stiff-bristle brush pushed and pulled through the oil hole drillings. Technician B says that it is better to submerge the crankshaft in a tank of hot caustic solution. Who is correct?

11. On a separate sheet of paper, list the various checks and tests that you would perform on a crankshaft at overhaul.

12. Technician A says that minor imperfections on crankshaft journals can be removed only by regrinding. Technician B says that this can be done by polishing the crankshaft in a metal lathe using fine emery cloth and diesel fuel as a lubricant. Which technician is correct?

13. When a crankshaft is reground, technician A says that you would want to use *oversize* bearings to account for the metal that has been removed. Technician B says that you would want to use *undersize* bearings in this case. Which technician understands the philosophy behind this procedure?

14. True or False: If the crankshaft thrust surfaces have been reground, you usually have to employ thicker thrust washers to maintain the correct end float.

15. Technician A says that to maintain crankshaft end float within specs, it is acceptable to use either thicker or thinner thrust washers on either side of the crankshaft. Technician B says that this cannot be done; instead, the same thickness thrust washers are required on both sides of the thrust surfaces. Which technician is correct?

16. True or False: If a crankshaft requires regrinding, both the main and con-rod journals must have the same amount of material removed from their surfaces.

17. Generally a high-speed crankshaft is reground to a diameter that is smaller by one of three sizes. List the three sizes.

18. Most high-speed engine manufacturers specify that the maximum amount of metal that can be removed from a crankshaft journal be limited to
    a. 0.762 mm (0.030 in.)
    b. 1.000 mm (0.03937 in.)
    c. 1.500 mm (0.060 in.)

19. When measuring a crankshaft journal with a micrometer, it should be checked at how many different positions and how many axes?

20. True or False: To determine taper on a crankshaft journal, you should compare the readings from one axis with those of another.

21. True or False: To determine ovality on a crankshaft journal, you should compare readings along one axis.

22. True or False: If either a front or rear crankshaft oil seal surface is badly worn, the crankshaft can be repaired using a Speedi-Sleeve and an oversize oil seal assembly.

23. True or False: To determine if the crankshaft webs are misaligned or overflexed, a dial indicator inserted between the webs can be used.

24. Crankshafts can be checked for signs of cracks using what three nondestructive methods?

25. If a crankshaft suffers a break, list the two types of breaks that can occur and the angle at which they usually occur.

26. Crankshaft failures can generally be categorized into four main areas. What are these?

27. When installing a crankshaft with new bearings that are properly lubricated and main bearing caps torqued to spec, technician A says that if the crankshaft rotates freely, you do not need to check each individual bearing for the proper clearance. Is this an acceptable service procedure? Explain why or why not.

28. Crankshaft bearing clearance can be accurately checked by using
    a. wire solder
    b. Plastigage
    c. layout ink
    d. Prussian blue

29. The majority of high-speed diesel engines employ main and con-rod bearings that are generally referred to as
    a. ball bearings
    b. roller bearings
    c. shell bearings
    d. needle bearings

30. True or False: Some high-speed diesel engines employ ball bearings to support the engine crankshaft.

31. Most shell bearings consist of five layers of material. List the layers and their materials.

32. True or False: Normally the size of a shell bearing is stamped on the back face of the bearing assembly.

33. Shell bearings are prevented from spinning during engine rotation by the use of a
    a. locating tang
    b. dowel pin
    c. retaining bolt

34. Shell bearings dissipate their heat by being compressed into the cap or saddle; this is known as
    a. free diameter
    b. bearing crush
    c. press fit
    d. slip fit

35. True or False: All shell bearings can be installed in either the upper or lower position without any problems occurring.

36. True or False: Upper main shell bearings can be removed and replaced during an in-frame overhaul by the use of a roll pin.

37. When inspecting shell bearings at overhaul, bright or shiny spots appearing on the back side of the bearing are usually indicative of
    a. overheating
    b. bearing shell movement
    c. insufficient bearing clearance
    d. too much bearing clearance

38. Excessive main bearing clearance will result in
    a. low oil pressure
    b. high oil pressure
    c. aeration of the oil
    d. engine vibration

39. Bearing shells can be checked for thickness using a
    a. dial indicator
    b. depth micrometer
    c. vernier caliper
    d. ball micrometer

40. True or False: A properly fitted and operating shell bearing usually appears dull gray in color after a reasonable period of service.

41. Technician A says that a main bearing noise is usually more evident when the engine is loaded. Technician B says that a con-rod bearing noise is generally more noticeable when the engine is unloaded. Do you agree with both of these statements? Explain why or why not.

42. True or False: Worn main and con-rod bearings are usually accompanied by lower than normal oil pressure, excessive oil consumption, and blue smoke in the exhaust.

43. Severe scratches or scoring on the surface of a shell bearing is usually indicative of
    a. lack of oil
    b. overheating
    c. metal-to-metal contact between the bearing and journal
    d. dirt or foreign particles in the oil

44. The most common cause of shell bearing damage can usually be attributed to
    a. overloading
    b. dirt and foreign particles
    c. corrosion
    d. lack of lubrication

45. True or False: Technician A says that a typical cause of main bearing failure can be traced to fast/dry starts after an engine oil filter change.

46. Technician A says that many new crankshaft oil seals are precoated with a special lubricant and should not, therefore, have the lip prelubricated with oil. Technician B says that you should always coat the oil seal lip with clean engine lube oil. Who is correct?

47. The most effective type of engine crankshaft vibration damper on high-speed diesel engines is the
    a. single-rubber type
    b. double-rubber type
    c. viscous type

12 Gear Trains

OVERVIEW

The gear train allows us to correctly time the engine as well as to drive the camshaft. It can also provide power take off points for accessory drive items. Either spur-cut or helical-cut gears can be used. In this chapter we discuss some of the common types of engine gear trains being used in electronically controlled diesel engines and how to check gear backlash and the condition of gear teeth.

TOPICS

- Purposes
- Examples
- Gear backlash
- Engine gear timing
- Gear lubrication
- Gear removal
- Gear bearing preload check
- Self-test questions

PURPOSES

All diesel engines employ a series of gears referred to as the *gear train* that are housed either behind the engine front cover or behind the flywheel housing. Some larger-displacement engines have a gear train at both the front and rear of the engine, for example, Detroit Diesel 16V-71, 12 and 16V-92, and 12, 16, and 20V-149 engine models. Regardless of the location of the gear train, these meshing gears are required for the following two purposes:

1. To time the crankshaft and camshaft together so that both valve and fuel injection pump (or unit injector) operation occur at the right time throughout the various piston strokes
2. To transfer power from the crankshaft to drive an accessory item such as a blower (two-stroke-cycle engine), air compressor, water pump, oil pump, fuel injection pump or fuel transfer pump, hydraulic pump(s) and power steering, and heavy-duty alternator (some buses—although most are belt driven from an accessory drive pulley, as is the air-conditioning pump)

The gears can be of two types: the spur (straight)-cut design, or the helical (angled teeth)-type design. The helical type is quieter in operation than the spur type, so many engine manufacturers use these. A number of electronically controlled engines now use a combination of helical and high-contact-ratio spur gears to achieve reduced gear tooth bending stresses and lower noise. Regardless of the type of gears used, the crankshaft gear is normally a carburized and hardened assembly that is a press fit to the crankshaft. All other gears are generally nitrided and hardened steel.

The important thing about the gear train is that various gears must be timed to one another during engine overhaul, or any time that they have been disturbed for a service repair procedure. On four-stroke-cycle engines, the engine camshaft must rotate at half the speed of the crankshaft (one power stroke every 720°, or two crankshaft revolutions). On two-stroke-cycle engines, the camshaft rotates at the same speed as the crankshaft (one power stroke every 360°). The number of gears in the gear train differs by engine

309

make and model; the smallest number of gears is usually two when a chain drive is used between them (this method is common only to light-duty diesel engines). This arrangement ensures that the camshaft gear rotates in the same direction as the crankshaft gear. In addition, the number of teeth on the camshaft gear is twice that on the crankshaft to allow the camshaft to rotate at half the speed on a four-stroke-cycle engine. A two-stroke-cycle engine camshaft can have the same number of teeth as the crankshaft. If no chain drive is used (smaller, lighter diesels) then a minimum of three gears must be employed: the crankshaft gear, an idler gear (to rotate the camshaft in the same direction as the crankshaft), and the camshaft gear.

The number of teeth used on the idler gear is chosen to allow the camshaft to rotate according to whether it is a two- or four-stroke-cycle engine. Take careful note, however, that a number of engines employ a gear ratio between the adjustable idler gear and the camshaft drive gear that results in what is commonly referred to as a *hunting tooth* condition. This occurs when the number of teeth on the idler gear does not match those on either the crankshaft or camshaft gear. For example, if the crankshaft gear had 78 teeth, the idler gear had 68, and the camshaft gear had 78, then the idler would be overdriven at a ratio of 1.147:1 for one complete rotation of the crankshaft. However, since the idler has to drive the larger camshaft gear with the same number of teeth as the crankshaft (78), the camshaft gear ends up rotating at the same speed as the crankshaft. This arrangement is often required because the engine height and design require that a different sized idler gear be used to link the crankshaft and camshaft.

SERVICE TIP: When a hunting tooth arrangement is used, once you have aligned the respective gear timing marks, if you rotate the engine over, don't be fooled into thinking that the engine is now mistimed because the gear timing marks are no longer in alignment. In the example quoted with the 78- and 68-tooth gear layout, the hunting gear arrangement requires you to turn the engine over approximately 33 times to realign all of the gear timing marks. This is a classic example of the hunting tooth concept.

EXAMPLES

Not all engines employ the same number of gears. The diagrams in this chapter highlight some of the gear trains now in use on the latest high-speed heavy-duty electronically controlled diesel engines. Figure 12–1 illustrates the gear train used by Detroit Diesel on its Series 50 and Series 60 four-stroke-cycle electronically

controlled engines; there are 10 gears in constant mesh. Note that the gear drive ratios for the Series 50 and 60 engines are shown in the figure. These engine models also employ an adjustable idler gear (Figure 12–2) to allow for changes in gear lash should the cylinder head or engine block require machining at overhaul. The gear train on the Series 50 and 60 engines has helical-cut teeth on the crankshaft, oil pump, bull gear, water pump, air compressor, fuel pump, and accessory drive pulley. Located behind the bull gear is a straight-cut spur gear which drives the spur-toothed adjustable idler and camshaft drive gear. The high-contact-ratio spur gears provide reduced gear tooth bending stresses as a result of the very high (28,000 psi, or 193,060 kPa) unit injection pressures encountered with an overhead camshaft design and electronic controls. This combination of both helical and spur-toothed gears, commonly referred to as a *split gear train*, provides both the strength and quietness of operation desired with an overhead camshaft design. It also reduces the thrust loads and provides better load capacity. Figure 12–2 also shows the correct gear train timing marks for the Series 60 engine.

Figure 12–3 illustrates a gear train for a Caterpillar 3176 engine with eight constant-mesh gears clearly identified in regard to their function. Figure 12–4 illustrates the timing gear layout for the 3406E Caterpillar engine. This gear train is somewhat similar in arrangement to the DDC Series 50 and 60 models in that it also employs a combination of helical and spur gears. The crankshaft, oil pump, water pump, and rear gear of the cluster idler are helical, while the front gear of the cluster gear is a high-contact-ratio spur gear, as are the remaining gears. This gear train employs an adjustable idler gear to accommodate about 0.45 mm (0.018 in.) of movement to allow for shaving (remachining) of the block or cylinder head at overhaul, yet to maintain the desired gear tooth backlash.

The Cat gear train is rather unique, however, in that it employs a *pendulum absorber* type of camshaft drive gear. The camshaft gear is unusual because it contains several unique features including the machined TDC and timing slots for the speed timing sensor for the ECM. The tuned pendulum absorber illustrated in Figure 12–5 reduces the high impact loads transferred to the overhead camshaft caused by the injector pressure pulses. This pendulum mass within the overhead camshaft gear employs eight trapped and hardened steel rollers that soften shock loads and reduce noise, vibration, and gear train loads. It accomplishes this damping feature in the same general way that a rotating engine flywheel does by storing inertia in its mass. The pendulum mass absorbs the energy created by each injector pulse and allows the

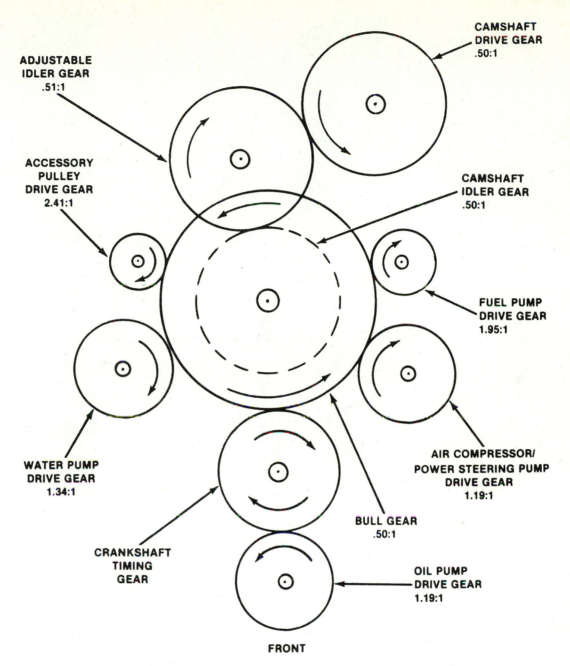

CAMSHAFT DRIVE GEAR .50:1

ADJUSTABLE IDLER GEAR .51:1

ACCESSORY PULLEY DRIVE GEAR 2.41:1

CAMSHAFT IDLER GEAR .50:1

FUEL PUMP DRIVE GEAR 1.95:1

WATER PUMP DRIVE GEAR 1.34:1

AIR COMPRESSOR/ POWER STEERING PUMP DRIVE GEAR 1.19:1

CRANKSHAFT TIMING GEAR

BULL GEAR .50:1

OIL PUMP DRIVE GEAR 1.19:1

FRONT

FIGURE 12–1 *Gear train components of Series 60 four-stroke-cycle electronically controlled unit injector model engine. Note location of overhead camshaft gear. (Courtesy of Detroit Diesel Corporation.)*

camshaft to maintain a more even speed of rotation, rather than trying to slow down between injections, and speeding up at the start of the next injection cycle. This design has reduced the transmitted loads by more than 50%, and Caterpillar has patented the idea.

All of the gear trains illustrated so far are for four-stroke-cycle engines. Now we consider the two-stroke-cycle engine. Figure 12–6 illustrates the gear train arrangement for a DDC 92 series engine, and

Figure 12–7 illustrates the gears used in both the front and rear gear train of a 12V, 16V, and 20V-149 series engine with the respective timing marks between the gears shown clearly. Several gears in the gear train must be *timed* to one another when assembling the engine or replacing the gears after a service repair procedure to ensure that the valves and the fuel injection pump or the unit fuel injectors will open/close and inject fuel during the correct piston

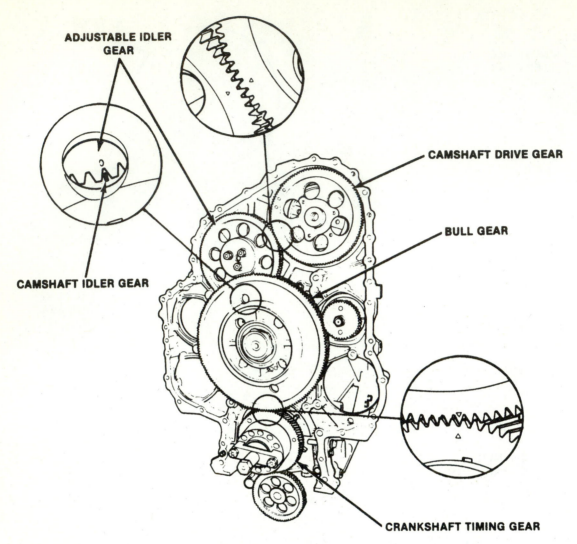

FIGURE 12–2 *Series 60 engine gear timing marks and adjustable idler gear. (Courtesy of Detroit Diesel Corporation.)*

stroke and at the proper time. In some engines, several other gears must be timed for balance purposes, such as the balance shaft gear on inline DDC two-stroke engines, the air compressor gear on some Cummins engines, and the oil pump to underslung balance shafts used on a number of high-speed diesel engines. Camshaft and crankshaft gears are generally pressed on and keyed to their respective shafts, with each being secured by a retaining nut and often a gear nut retainer to ensure that it will not loosen off during engine operation.

To time the various gears to one another involves starting at the crankshaft and aligning the timing marks that have been stamped or etched on the face of the gears to one another. Each manufacturer chooses its own markings, which may be numbers, letters, or triangular or diamond shapes. These can be seen in the earlier diagrams of the various engine manufacturers gear trains.

GEAR BACKLASH

All gears that are in mesh must have an allowable backlash to prevent binding as they heat up during engine rotation and the gear and engine damage that would result. Engine service manuals list the allowable maximum limit for gear backlash. Excessive gear lash will reflect itself as a noisy rattling sound, particularly at an idle speed and when the load is removed from the engine and the engine is accelerated again. This noise can also be caused by chipped, pitted, or burred gear teeth or excessive wear of the gear support shaft bearing. Insufficient gear backlash will show up as a high-pitched whine and excessive heat in the gear train cover area.

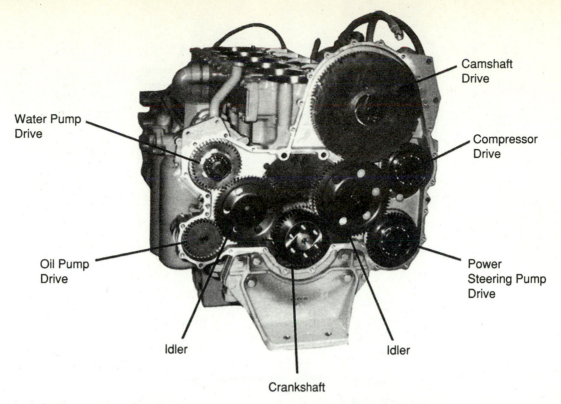

FIGURE 12–3 Front-mounted gear train for a 3176 Cat model electronic unit injector engine employing a high mounted camshaft design with short pushrods. (Courtesy of Caterpillar Inc.)

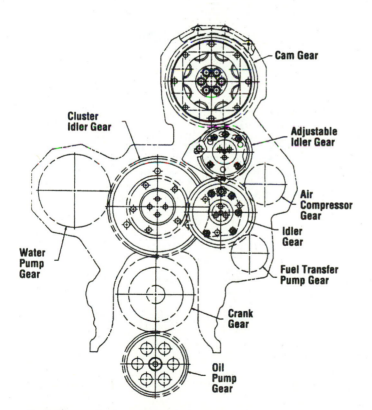

FIGURE 12–4 Caterpillar 3406E heavy-duty truck overhead camshaft engine gear train arrangement. (Courtesy of Caterpillar Inc.)

FIGURE 12–5 Unique 3406E engine camshaft gear pendulum absorber to dampen any shock and vibration cycles. (Courtesy of Caterpillar Inc.)

Although gear backlash can be determined by using finger-type feeler gauges between the meshing gear teeth, the use of a dial gauge is easier and generally more accurate. To use a dial gauge to accurately measure gear lash, refer to Figure 12–8. Preload the gauge tip against one of the gear teeth of the gear that you wish to check. Then rotate one of the gears in mesh as far as it will go in one direction; keep pressure

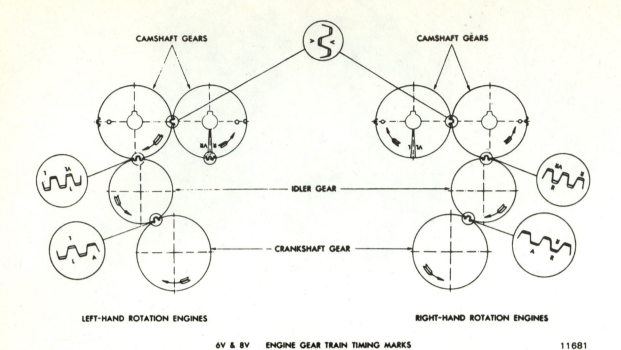

FIGURE 12–6 Gear trains forming either a correct figure 7 or a reverse figure 7 on two-stroke-cycle DDC V71 or V92 engine models. Note gear timing mark alignment required to properly time the engine. (Courtesy of Detroit Diesel Corporation.)

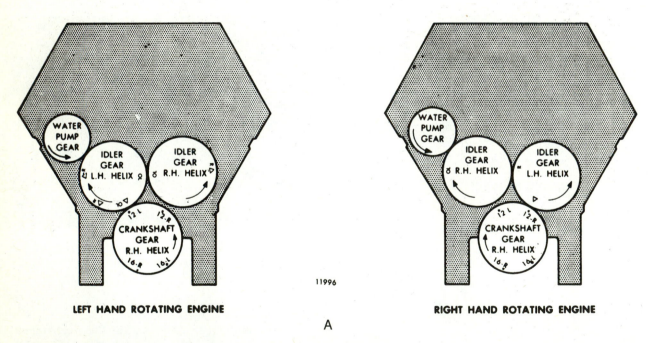

FIGURE 12–7 (a) DDC 149 series two-stroke-cycle engine models show front gear train timing marks and identification of helical cut of individual gears; LH = left hand; RH = right hand. (Courtesy of Detroit Diesel Corporation.) (b) DDC 149 series two-stroke-cycle engine models show rear gear train timing marks and identification of helical cut of individual gears. (Courtesy of Detroit Diesel Corporation.)

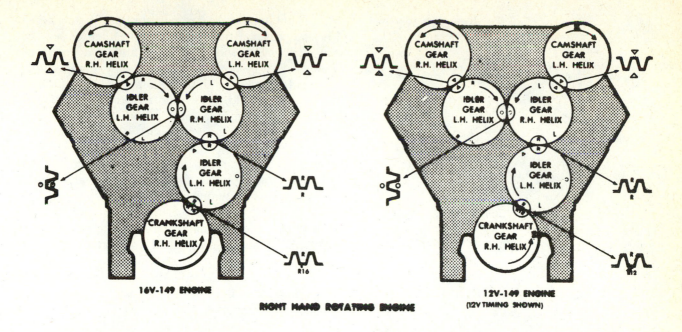

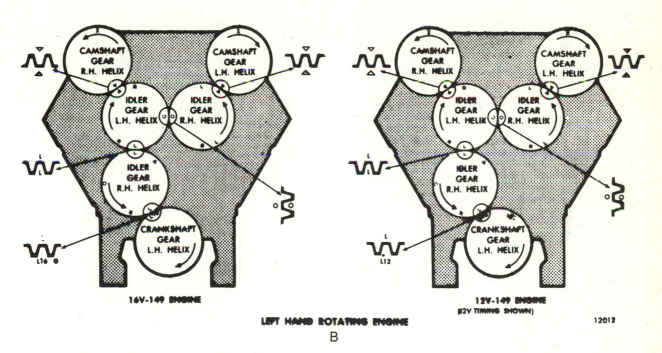

B

on it without actually causing the gear to rotate. Bring the dial gauge to zero; then pry the gear back against the dial gauge, record the backlash, and compare it to service manual specs. Repeat the same procedure for all of the meshing gears in the gear train. A number of diesel engines employ oil pumps that are mounted below the crankshaft centerline, and their housing is mounted on a machined pad. To alter the crankshaft gear to oil pump gear lash, shims can be added or taken away from the mounting pad area of the pump housing.

A number of newer electronically controlled engines such as the DDC Series 50 and 60 models, and the Caterpillar 3406E model employ adjustable idler gear hubs that allow the technician to dial-in the recommended gear backlash requirements.

GEAR TIMING

Most service manuals list the procedure to follow to determine if an engine is out of time. An engine that is out of time may result in preignition, uneven running,

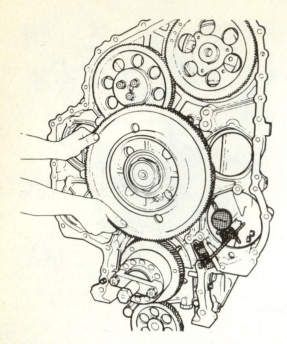

FIGURE 12–8 *Using a precision dial indicator to accurately check the gear backlash between the crankshaft gear and the bull gear of Series 50 and 60 engine models. (Courtesy of Detroit Diesel Corporation.)*

and a loss of power, as well as the possibility of the valves coming into contact with the piston crown or bending of the valve pushrods (when used). Although the gear cover or flywheel housing can be removed to confirm that all gears are in time, this can be time consuming when an engine is in a piece of equipment.

On engines that have timing marks on the flywheel similar to those illustrated in Figure 10–4, the engine can be manually rotated over to place the No. 1 cylinder at TDC compression. Then the intake and exhaust valves can be checked to determine if any valve-to-rocker arm clearance exists (valve lash). If the engine is timed correctly, both the intake and exhaust valves should have clearance. If the valve lash has been set properly and no valve lash exists, the engine is out of time. You can also check for correct gear train timing by rotating the engine flywheel over to place the injection pump (when used) timing marks in alignment; then spill time the No. 1 cylinder (see Figure 5–7, assuming that the pump has been correctly installed). On some engines, a timing bolt can be placed through a hole in the flywheel housing to engage a hole in the flywheel. This locks the No. 1 piston at TDC compression! The timing can then be confirmed by checking the valves as well as the fuel injection pump timing. The fuel injector on the No. 1 cylinder can be removed and a dial indicator extension used to confirm that the piston is actually at TDC compression when the timing pointer is aligned with either the flywheel or front pulley timing marks.

If information regarding camshaft lift and degrees is readily available to you, use a dial gauge on the valves in conjunction with a circular timing degree wheel attached to the front crankshaft pulley/damper or flywheel to check that all valves are opening and closing when they should, as per a polar valve timing diagram. Another problem with out-of-time engines can sometimes be traced to the wrong parts being installed. Now that the US EPA exhaust smoke emissions regulations are in force, a number of engine manufacturers have changed their camshaft profiles and valve timing. Installation of the wrong camshaft for the year-of-manufacture engine can create serious problems with timing and engine operation and may cause the valves to actually come into contact with the piston crown during engine operation. Piston crowns have also been redesigned (see Chapter 15) to allow them to meet these emissions levels. Careful checks of what parts have been installed at overhaul will ensure that engine timing will be correct for the engine's year of manufacture.

In two-stroke Detroit Diesel Corporation DDC engines (53, 71, 92, 149 series) there are no flywheel or front pulley timing marks to guide you in an engine timing check, since a unit injector is used with these engines. The exhaust valves are adjusted by rotating the engine over until the unit injector follower is at the bottom of its stroke (injection position); adjustment of the unit injectors is performed when the exhaust valves are wide open. You can check engine timing on all DDC two-stroke engines by removing the No. 1 injector and using a dial gauge to find true piston TDC compression. Follow these steps:

1. Place and lock the stop lever in the no-fuel position. (We are assuming that for this engine rotation is right-hand [CW] from the front end.)

2. Choose any cylinder for this check. Most service technicians usually prefer to use the No. 1 cylinder. On vee-type engine models, it doesn't matter which bank you choose.

3. Remove the No. 1 injector from the cylinder head.

4. Slide a rod about 12 in. (30 mm) long through the injector copper tube hole until it contacts the piston crown.

5. Slowly rotate the crankshaft over while holding onto the rod, and try to determine when the piston has reached TDC.

6. Manually turn the engine opposite its normal direction of rotation between 1/16 and 1/8 of a turn.

7. Mount a dial indicator with a long enough extension to contact the piston crown into

position over the cylinder and through the injector copper tube. The dial gauge should be capable of at least 1 in. (25.4 mm) of travel and be graduated in 0.001 in. (0.0254 mm) increments. Preload the dial gauge and set it to zero.

8. Fabricate a temporary timing pointer (piece of 1/16 in., 1.587 mm, oxyacetylene welding rod) that can be temporarily bolted over the front cover so that it hangs over the vibration damper assembly. Grind the end of the rod to a point if desired.

9. Place a piece of masking tape over the damper circumference that is several inches (50 mm) long underneath the timing pointer.

10. Manually rotate the crankshaft in its normal rotation until the dial indicator pointer stops moving. Slowly rock the crankshaft forward and then back until you find the exact point where the needle stops moving.

11. Draw a clean sharp pencil line across the tape directly opposite the timing pointer rod to establish a reference point. Although this step is not necessary, some technicians find it helpful.

12. With the dial set to zero, continue to rotate the crankshaft in its normal direction until the dial indicator registers 0.010 in. (0.254 mm).

13. Scribe another line on the masking tape opposite the pointer.

14. Slowly rotate the crankshaft opposite its normal rotation until the gauge needle stops moving. Continue this rotation until the needle just starts to move. Reset the dial gauge to zero.

15. Turn the crankshaft opposite normal rotation until the dial needle registers 0.010 in. (0.254 mm) and scribe another pencil line opposite the timing pointer.

16. Accurately measure between the two widest pencil lines and find the exact midpoint; scribe a line here because this represents *true TDC.*

17. Reinstall the fuel injector along with the rocker arm assemblies and torque it to specs. Adjust the exhaust valves and time the unit injector. When the injector is adjusted, the valves have to be wide open (this will place the TDC pencil mark on the damper masking tape toward BDC).

18. Install a dial gauge and set it to zero with its extension rod resting on the flat top of the No. 1 unit injector follower.

19. Slowly rotate the engine in its normal direction of rotation from the front until the damper TDC pencil mark is directly opposite the stationary timing pointer. Read the dial gauge and compare it to the service manual specifications; this will confirm if the gear train timing is correct, advanced, or retarded. Details of this procedure and the respective dial indicator readings for correct timing can be found in Section 1.7.1 of all Detroit Diesel service manuals for two-stroke-cycle engines.

GEAR LUBRICATION

Depending on the make and model of engine, some gears may be pressure lubricated. In most cases, the gear train is lubricated by oil splash or overflow oil from the engine camshaft or drain holes from the upper part of the cylinder block. Tapped oil supply holes from the main oil gallery usually align with the gear case cover to carry oil through spray nozzles to specific gears that require pressure lubrication. In some engines, gears requiring pressure-fed oil can have main oil pressure fed through their support hub, which aligns with the oil hole in the front or rear of the engine block depending on where the gear train is located. Pressure lubricated gears are usually the idler gear, the camshaft gear(s), and the bull gear (for example, in the DDC Series 50 and Series 60 engines). Oil then drains back to the crankcase.

GEAR REMOVAL

Always carefully check all gears for signs of overheating (discoloration), pitting, scoring, or chipped or broken teeth at overhaul, or when a problem has been discovered during engine operation. The procedure for removing a gear from a gear train depends on whether the gear is a press fit or is supported on a set of tapered roller bearings that ride on a hub bolted to the engine block by one or more bolts. In cases such as the latter, the retaining bolts are sometimes designed with a left-hand thread to prevent loosening off of the bolts during gear rotation when the engine is running. The location of the gear in the gear train and its rotation determine whether its retaining bolt is left- or right-hand thread.

Gears that are a press fit usually require a suitable mechanical or hydraulic puller to remove them without damage. For example, crankshaft gears which drive all other gears within the gear train are correctly located on the crankshaft by the use of a Woodruff key and keyway. Camshaft gears are also usually keyed into position to ensure that timing will not change as a result of a slipping gear/shaft condition. Figure 12–9

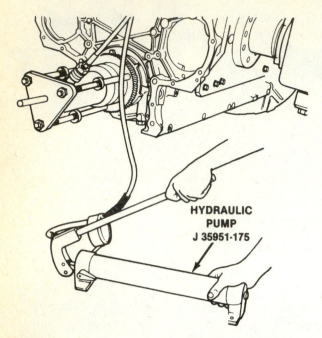

FIGURE 12–9 *Using a special hydraulic puller mounted as shown to safely and effectively remove the crankshaft timing gear from the front of the crankshaft on Series 50 and 60 DDC engine models. (Courtesy of Detroit Diesel Corporation.)*

illustrates one example of special tooling installed in place to remove the crankshaft gear with the aid of a portable hydraulic press. Hydraulic pressure of as much as 3.5 to 4 tons is often required for this purpose. To reinstall the crankshaft gear, additional adapters are used with this same tooling to hydraulically force the gear back into position. Camshaft gears can be removed or reinstalled by placing the camshaft and gear in a shop press to safely and hydraulically apply the needed force on the gear. Most engine manufacturers recommend special adapters for removal and installation of the various gears on their engines. Engine service manuals illustrate these and indicate the tool supplier part number.

GEAR BEARING PRELOAD CHECK

Gears that are supported on two opposed tapered roller bearings between the gear and support hub have to be assembled and lubricated, and the retaining nut or bolts torqued to specs, to apply normal force to the bearing assemblies. The engine service manual will illustrate and recommend how to check the gear bearing preload on either a used or new assembly. This is a very important check because if a used bearing is being considered for reuse, too little preload will result in noisy operation, and the bearing may collapse dur-

ing engine operation. If the preload is too tight, the bearing will run hot, which can lead to siezure. Before installing the bearings into the gear hub, always check for any burrs or contaminants and remove these as necessary so that there is no possibility of the bearing being damaged or being too hard to rotate.

Figure 12–10 illustrates one method used to check bearing preload on the bull gear that is used on DDC Series 50 and 60 electronically controlled engines. The process involves mounting the gear into a special holding fixture, wrapping a cord around the outside of the bull gear at least two complete revolutions, and attaching the end of the looped cord to a spring-loaded spring scale or to a digital readout scale or force gauge. To obtain an accurate reading of bearing preload, take at least four readings so that you can average out the force required to rotate the gear in its holding fixture. In this particular example, the recommended preload should be between 1 and 3 lb (0.453 to 1.360 kg). A selective spacer ring is available to adjust the bearing preload within specs. A thinner spacer ring is required when the bearing preload is too low; using a thicker spacer ring reduces the turning torque. Not all engine manufacturers offer a means to adjust the bearing preload. If the bearing preload cannot be adjusted to within specifications, or a bearing with no adjustment is outside of the specs, a new bearing will have to be installed and checked in the same manner.

SELF-TEST QUESTIONS

1. On a separate sheet of paper list the various functions of the engine gear train.

2. Technician A says that all gear trains employ spur-cut gear teeth. Technician B says that this is not so; helical-cut gears are used more often since they offer the advantage of quieter operation. Which technician is correct?

3. Why do some gear trains employ idler gears? Give your reasons on a seperate sheet of paper.

4. What does the term *hunting tooth* condition mean with respect to a gear train?

5. Technician A says that the term *split gear train* refers to the fact that both spur-cut and helical-cut gears are employed in the gear train arrangement. Technician B says that the term means that a gear train is used at both the front and rear of the engine block, similar to that found on DDC 149 series engine models. Which technician is correct?

6. What current high-speed engine employs what is known as a *pendulum absorber* in its gear train arrangement?

7. What is the purpose of using the pendulum absorber to drive the camshaft in this engine?

8. Why do various gears within a gear train have to be timed to one another?

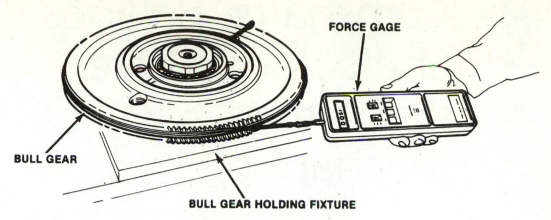

FORCE GAGE

BULL GEAR

BULL GEAR HOLDING FIXTURE

FIGURE 12–10 *Series 50 and 60 DDC engine model bull gear mounted to a special holding fixture. The digital readout force gauge and string wrapped around the body of the gear are used to pull (rotate) the gear around its support bearings to check the bearing preload or turning torque. (Courtesy of Detroit Diesel Corporation.)*

9. Technician A says that insufficient gear backlash between the gears in a gear train can result in noisy operation. Technician B says that the result would be a high-pitched sound during engine operation. Which technician is correct?

10. Gear backlash is usually best checked by using a
    a. feeler gauge
    b. dial indicator gauge
    c. spring-loaded pull-type gauge and recording the force required to rotate a given gear

11. True or False: A quick engine gear train timing check can usually be done by rotating the engine over manually and placing the No. 1 piston at TDC (check with a dial indicator), then checking to see if the flywheel or damper timing marks are in proper alignment.

12. True or False: Each engine manufacturer specifies in its respective service manual a detailed procedure that can be used to check for accurate gear train timing.

13. True or False: A polar valve timing diagram allows the technician to determine when both the intake and exhaust valves open and when the injector begins to inject fuel into the combustion chamber.

14. Technician A says that current EPA-regulated diesel engines indicate the initial engine timing setting on an engine decal. Technician B says that you need to consult the engine manufacturer's technical literature for this information. Who is correct?

15. True or False: All gears within an engine gear train are pressure lubricated.

16. Technician A says that gears that are supported on two opposed roller bearings should always have the bearing preload checked using a spring-loaded pull-type scale. Technician B says that this check is required only when using old parts. Who is correct?

13 Camshafts, Balance Shafts, and Valve Operating Mechanism

OVERVIEW

In this chapter we consider the importance of the engine camshaft and its relationship to the opening, duration, and closing of the intake and exhaust valves. The chapter describes how the camshaft activates the unit injector follower, even on electronically controlled engines. We also discuss engine balance shafts and the components of both an in-block and overhead camshaft arrangement as they relate to the valve operating mechanism. The chapter concludes with a description of engine compression brakes.

TOPICS

- Functions of the camshaft
- Cam lobe shape
- Camshaft types
- Camshaft timing
- Camshaft removal
- Camshaft inspection
- In-block camshaft bushing replacement
- Camshaft end float
- Balance shafts
- Valve and injector operating mechanism
- Valve bridge (crosshead, yoke)
- Valve and injector adjustment
- Rocker arm ratio
- Pushrod inspection
- Rocker arm inspection
- Cam follower inspection
- Engine compression brakes
- Self-test questions

FUNCTIONS OF THE CAMSHAFT

The engine camshaft illustrated in Figure 13–1 is designed to control the opening, closing, and duration in crankshaft degrees of the intake and exhaust valves. In engines that employ either mechanical or electronic unit injectors, or a system similar to the Cummins PT fuel system, the camshaft is the mechanism used to actuate the injector follower. The engine camshaft consists of a shaft with a series of bumps or projections on it throughout its length, which are commonly referred to as *cam lobes*. Figure 13–2a identifies the number of lobes used per cylinder.

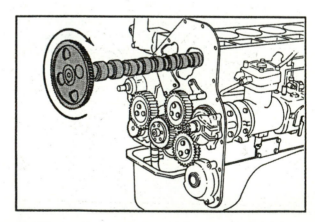

FIGURE 13–1 Typical location of an in-block camshaft design for an L10 model engine showing its drive gear in relation to the engine gear train. (Courtesy of Cummins Engine Company, Inc.)

CAM LOBE SHAPE

Figure 13–2b illustrates a typical camshaft and lobe; the camshaft is circular throughout one half and is designed with an oval-shaped lobe. The highest point on the cam lobe is known as the nose, and the sloped sides are known as the ramp or flank. Camshaft forces originate from the valve springs and the inertia forces that occur during the rapid opening and closing processes, as well as from the forces generated by the cylinder gas pressure when the valves open. These forces tend to increase with the square of the speed; therefore high-speed engine camshafts require very careful design. Today they are usually designed by computer simulation methods.

Although the shape of the cam lobe may appear similar on most engines, actually it is designed for a given amount of lift as well as for the rate and speed (acceleration and deceleration) at which it begins to activate the valves and injectors. The sloping sides (ramp) of the lobe are critical to the acceleration and deceleration characteristics of both the valves and injectors. Given today's emissions standards, engines require a much faster start and end to injection (fewer crankshaft degrees) than did earlier diesel engines. Similarly, the number of crankshaft degrees that the injector plunger is actually moving down is closely controlled by the shape of the camshaft lobes, as are intake and exhaust valve opening and closing. Each engine manufacturer determines these degrees during the initial stage of engine design. Examples of the degrees of duration for intake and exhaust valves on typical high-speed heavy-duty diesel engines, (both four-stroke and two-stroke-cycle engines) are given in Chapter 1. Unlike automotive gasoline engine applications where different camshaft profiles can be used as aftermarket devices to obtain longer intake and exhaust valve openings for increasing overall engine performance, diesel engine camshafts cannot be replaced for this purpose.

CAMSHAFT TYPES

There are two common types of camshaft systems used in diesel engines. The first type is referred to as an *in-block design*, which is illustrated in Figure 13–1. Later model high-speed heavy-duty electronically controlled unit injector engines such as the Series 50 and 60 Detroit Diesel models, the Caterpillar 3406E, the Volvo 12.1L D12A models, and the Isuzu 12L 6WA1TC, are designed with an *overhead* or high-mounted camshaft that is located within the cylinder head area rather than in the engine block. All of these engines employ similar camshaft mountings. Figure 13–3 (p. 324) illus-

trates an overhead camshaft used by Detroit Diesel in its Series 50 and 60 engines. The camshaft is located on top of the cylinder head and actuates the intake and exhaust valves as well as the mechanically operated but electronically controlled unit injector.

The accurately ground overhead camshaft ensures efficient and quieter operation than an in-block system. An overhead camshaft design eliminates pushrods and lifters while making the injector and valve operating mechanism much stiffer and less complex. This results in precise control of injection and valve events with much lower inertia forces. The overhead camshaft design requires no pushrod assemblies; the cam lobes act directly on a hardened roller follower located at the rear of the rocker arm unit as shown in Figure 13–4 (p. 325). Detroit Diesel uses a silicon nitride cam follower roller in its injector rocker arm on the Series 50 and 60 engines to provide low-wear properties, and to generate very high injection pressures of 28,000 psi (193 Mpa) while maintaining long roller life. An overhead camshaft assembly has relatively low contact stress, fewer parts, and up to 40 fewer wear surfaces in a six-cylinder engine than does an in-block camshaft. In addition, it is much easier to service an overhead camshaft. Advantages of overhead camshafts are summarized next:

- Easier removal and installation
- Less chance of valve float due to more positive drive
- Much lower inertia forces (tendency of a moving object to keep moving in the same direction)
- More positive opening and closing of the valves to provide a higher possible engine rpm if desired
- Stronger activation of valves and injectors, particularly unit injectors with very high injection pressures
- Especially advantageous for four-valve-cylinder heads

The DDC Series 60 camshaft shown in Figure 13–3 is supported by seven bearing assemblies, which are precision-type, replaceable bearing shell inserts that are split at their centerline. The lower bearing shell is positioned in a saddle that is integral with the cylinder head. Since the camshaft retaining caps are line bored after assembly to the head at the factory, the caps are not interchangeable. Therefore, do not interchange the numbered caps with other caps of the same part number from parts stock or from a different cylinder head! Although Caterpillar uses an overhead camshaft design in its recent 3406E model engine, the design differs from that used by Detroit Diesel in its Series 50 and 60 models. In the Caterpillar design, the camshaft is supported by seven bearings in an internal align-bored cavity running the length of the cylinder head. Therefore, removal and installation of the camshaft require that access covers on the front and rear of the cylinder head be removed to allow the camshaft to be withdrawn from either end of the head.

Camshafts are usually manufactured from induction-hardened carbon steel or cast iron, depending on the stresses encountered, with different forms of surface hardening and treatment. The lobes are heat-treated to provide a hard wear surface. The arrangement of the cam lobes on the shaft determines the engine firing order, and the actual shape or contour of the valve lobes controls the time and rate of opening and closing of the valves. The injector cam lobe on mechanical fuel systems is designed to control the start of fuel injection, its duration, and the end of injection. On electronically controlled engines using unit injectors, the cam lobe determines the start of the injector plunger lift required to create the high pressures required to open the needle valve and to begin atomization of the fuel droplets into the combustion chamber. On electronic engines, the ECM determines the actual start, duration, and end of fuel injection by varying the PWM electrical signal sent to the injector solenoid. This action controls the effective stroke of the solid injector plunger used with electronic engines.

Engines employing inline or distributor-type injection pump systems do not require an injector cam lobe. In addition, the camshaft is supported by a series of concentric journals usually located between each cylinder. These journals can run directly in the camshaft bore of the engine block or be supported by a number of thin- or thick-wall bearings or bushings. The support journals are usually larger in diameter than the cam lobes to allow ease of both removal and installation on in-block camshaft designs. The camshaft is timed to the engine crankshaft gear directly, or as is the case in most heavy-duty engines, it is gear driven from the engine crankshaft by one or more idler gears (similar to the examples illustrated for the gear train in Chapter 12). Some smaller diesel engines may have a chain drive or a cogged/toothed belt drive such as that used by Volkswagen in its small passenger car and industrial models. The camshaft drive gear is correctly located in position by the use of a key or keyway and is normally a press fit over the tapered end of the camshaft assembly, where it is then retained in position by the use of a large retaining nut or by several bolts.

On four-stroke cycle-engines, the camshaft is driven at half the speed of the crankshaft, because there is only one power stroke produced throughout the 720° (two full turns) of the intake, compression, power, and

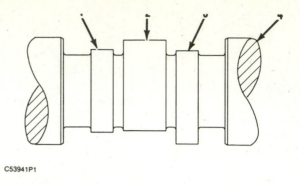

C53941P1

(1) Exhaust lobe.

(2) Injector lobe.

(3) Intake lobe.

(4) Camshaft journal. Diameter of camshaft journal

A

FIGURE 13–2   (a) General camshaft identification (Courtesy of Caterpillar Inc.). (b) Typical inlet and exhaust cam lobe contours. (Courtesy of Mack Trucks, Inc.)

exhaust strokes. In an engine running at 2000 rpm, the camshaft would rotate at 1000 rpm. On two-stroke-cycle engines, the camshaft rotates at the same speed as the crankshaft since a power stroke is produced once every 360°.

Two-Stroke Engine Camshafts

Camshafts on two-stroke-cycle engines differ from those on four-stroke-cycle engines mainly because they are driven at engine crankshaft speed rather than at half speed. In addition, their mounting arrangement and location differ slightly from those used on most four-stroke-cycle diesel models.

For example, the larger-displacement 149 series Detroit Diesel engine models employ a high-mounted camshaft on each engine bank that is supported in bearing saddles and retained by half-shell-type bearing caps similar to those used in the Series 60 overhead cam design shown in Figure 13–3. On V12, V16, and V20 engine models the camshafts are segmented: a V12 consists of two V6 engine blocks, the V16 has two V8 engine blocks, and the V20 consists of a V6–V8–V6 configuration bolted together. Therefore, the front, intermediate, and rear camshaft in each bank of the engine are bolted together through an intermediate flexible coupling attached to the flange end of each camshaft, an example of which is illustrated in Figure

INLET AND EXHAUST CAM CONTOURS

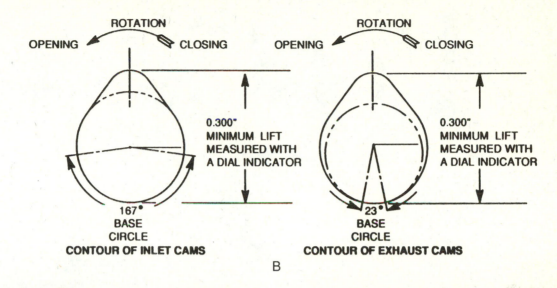

ROTATION
OPENING ← → CLOSING

0.300"
MINIMUM LIFT
MEASURED WITH
A DIAL INDICATOR

167°
BASE
CIRCLE
CONTOUR OF INLET CAMS

ROTATION
OPENING ← → CLOSING

0.300"
MINIMUM LIFT
MEASURED WITH
A DIAL INDICATOR

23°
BASE
CIRCLE
CONTOUR OF EXHAUST CAMS

B

13–5. The camshafts are driven by a rear gear train on engine models that employ both a front and rear gear train assembly. Camshafts are etched with letters, A, B, C, and so on at each flange end for proper installation at the time of assembly.

The camshaft(s) in the smaller-displacement Detroit Diesel two-stroke-cycle engine models are mounted high in the engine block and toward the inside of the vee (toward the blower assembly) on the vee models. Figure 13–6 illustrates the cam location in a six-cylinder inline Series 71 DDC engine model. The camshaft is supported front and rear by an end bearing bolted to the block, as well as by a series of intermediate aluminum alloy bearings throughout the length of the camshaft. These intermediate bearings are formed by two half shells held together by two circular snap rings. To prevent spinning of the camshaft intermediate bearings during engine operation, a setscrew located in a drilled hole in the block upper deck locks the bearings in position. Located at the right-front side of the camshaft of vee models is a water pump drive gear, while at the left-front side of the camshaft is an accessory drive pulley. Thrust washers are located on both sides of the rear end support bearing to maintain camshaft end float within specs. All gears and pulleys are keyed onto the ends of the camshaft for timing and balance purposes.

Camshafts in high-speed engines are generally one-piece designs; however, many larger-displacement engines employ sectional camshafts that are bolted together (flanges used) for ease of service and repair. In very-large-displacement slow-speed diesel engines, each cylinder can employ an individual camshaft segment connected to the others by a suitable drive connection. Figure 13–7 illustrates a segmented camshaft that is used in the Caterpillar 3600 engine series. The illustration shows a special service tool used to support the cam segment during removal or installation. Note also that the camshaft segment shown is machined with two flanges to allow bolting to the other camshaft segments once it has been correctly aligned with the proper timing marks for the cylinder.

The transfer of motion from the camshaft lobes to the valves or injector varies between the in-block and the overhead cam design. Figure 13–8 illustrates that in the in-block design, a flat or roller-type follower (sometimes called a tappet or lifter) is raised and lowered by the rotating cam lobe. Flat tappets are mushroom shaped, and the offset position of the tappet against the cam lobe causes the tappet to rotate as it lifts the pushrod. A pushrod seated within the follower activates the intake and exhaust or injector rocker arm assembly as illustrated in Figure 13–9.

CAMSHAFT TIMING

The camshaft drive gear is usually aligned with a timing mark on an idler gear placed between the cam and crankshaft. Some engines have the camshaft gear in direct mesh with the crankshaft gear. Some engines are

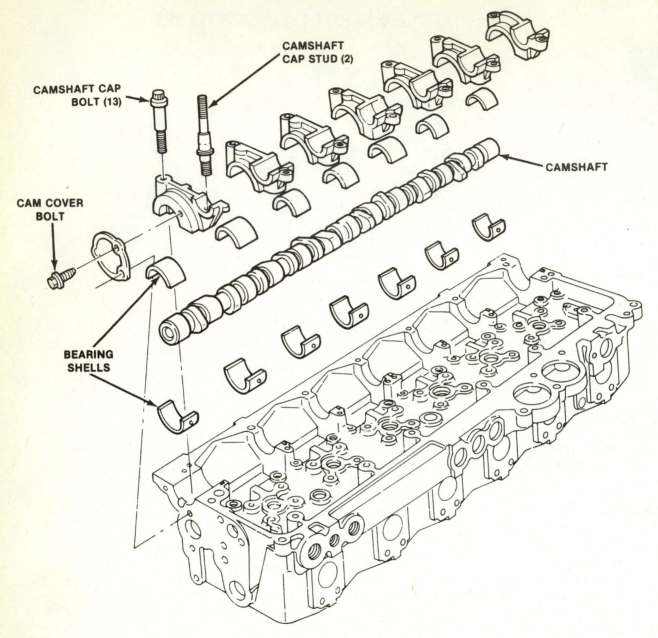

FIGURE 13–3 *Details of the overhead camshaft design used in the Series 50 and 60 DDC heavy-duty four-stroke-cycle engine models. (Courtesy of Detroit Diesel Corporation.)*

designed with an A (advanced) timing mark on the crankshaft gear; if this mark is aligned with the camshaft timing mark, the engine cam timing is advanced. (Refer to Chapter 12 for specific information on gear timing marks.)

A number of camshaft-actuated fuel injector engines vary cam gear timing (advanced or retarded) by installing various offset keys in the camshaft-to-gear keyway. Figure 13–10 illustrates one example of

this offset key arrangement. Engine manufacturers' service manuals detail the various keys by part number and degree of offset required to change the camshaft timing. Cummins uses these types of keys on its L10 and 14L engines employing mechanical fuel injectors. Detroit Diesel uses a similar arrangement on its 71 and 92 series mechanically governed engine models. On 14L Cummins engines, camshaft timing can be changed by adding (advances) or removing

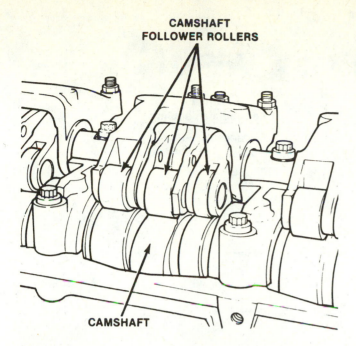

CAMSHAFT FOLLOWER ROLLERS

CAMSHAFT

FIGURE 13–4 *Close-up showing the Series 50 and 60 overhead camshaft design and the roller followers. The two outer ones operate the intake and exhaust valves, while the center roller follower operates the unit injector. (Courtesy of Detroit Diesel Corporation.)*

(retards) gaskets located between the cam follower housing and the engine block. Figure 13–11 illustrates the location of the three cam follower housings, which are bolted to the side of the engine block alongside the in-block camshaft. Each one of these cam follower housings contains the component parts shown in Figure 13–12, which support the pivoted cam follower levers and pushrods for the intake and exhaust valves as well as the injector pushrod. This six-cylinder engine employs three cylinder heads (one head per each two cylinders); therefore, a front, center, and rear cam follower box is used.

Figure 13–13 illustrates the sequence required to check the engine-to-injector timing on a Cummins L10, M11, N14, or K model engine series. Since this diagram represents various piston and crankshaft front damper positions, let's call the circular diagram in the center sub figure I, and the others subfigure a, b, c, and d. To perform the timing check accurately, two special dial gauges have to be installed as shown. One gauge measures the piston travel, while the other measures injector pushrod travel. On a six-cylinder N14 Cummins model engine, the injectors on cylinders 1, 3, and 5 must be removed to check the timing at each one of the three cylinder heads, since each rocker arm assembly

is connected to its own individual cam follower housing (identified as item 3 in Figure 13–12). On L10, M11, and K engine models only one injector has to be removed.

Now follow these steps to check camshaft timing:

1. With the injector removed from either cylinder 1, 3, or 5 and the dial gauges installed, manually rotate the engine crankshaft clockwise slowly from the front.

2. Confirm that you are on the compression stroke by checking to see that both dial indicator gauge needles are rotating in the same direction.

3. Adjust the height of each gauge, if necessary, to ensure that they do not bottom out before the piston reaches TDC. Allow approximately a 0.5 mm (0.020 in.) safety clearance.

4. When the piston gauge indicates TDC, slowly rock the crankshaft back and forward to confirm true TDC and set the dial gauge to zero.

5. Place a chalk mark on the damper as shown in Figure 13–13, subfigure II, to indicate TDC for that cylinder.

6. Refer to subfigure III and manually rotate the engine over until the chalk mark on the damper is at approximately 90° ATDC.

7. Loosen off and push down on the pushrod dial gauge and let it come back up until approximately 0.75 mm (0.030 in.) free travel exists. Rotate the dial gauge bezel to set the needle to zero.

8. Rotate the crankshaft damper opposite the direction of normal rotation, or CCW, until the damper chalk mark is again at TDC as shown in subfigure IV. Check that the piston dial gauge is still at TDC. If not, carefully reset it to zero.

9. Continue rotating the damper CCW to place the chalk mark at approximately 45° BTDC as shown in subfigure IV. At this position the piston dial gauge will register about 5.58 mm (0.220 in).

10. Refer to subfigure V and very slowly rotate the damper CW while watching the piston dial gauge. When this gauge registers 5.16 mm (0.2032 in.), the piston is at 19° BTDC on its compression stroke.

11. Read the injector pushrod dial gauge; note the dimension and compare this to the service manual or engine CPL (control parts list) data.

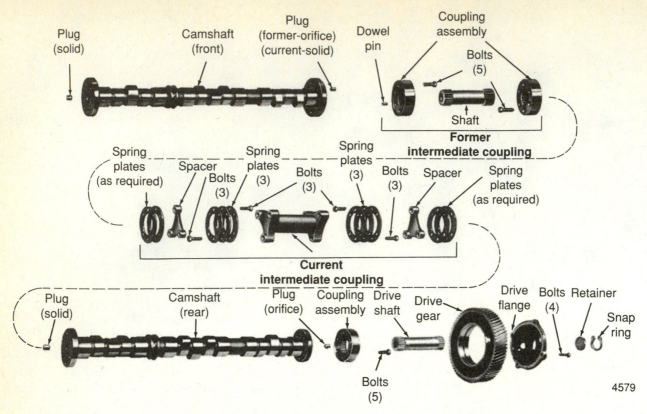

FIGURE 13–5 Design arrangement of the two- or three-piece camshaft used by DDC on various two-stroke-cycle V12, V16, and V20 engine models. The front, center, and rear camshaft sections are bolted together by the use of a flexible spring plate coupling and drive shaft. (Courtesy of Detroit Diesel Corporation.)

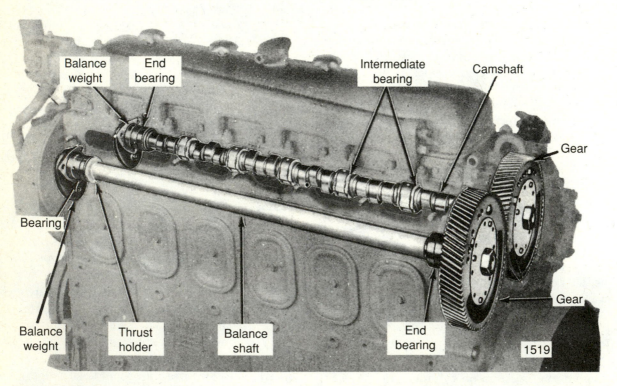

FIGURE 13–6 Location of the camshaft and the balance shaft assemblies in a Series 6-71 model two-stroke-cycle engine. (Courtesy of Detroit Diesel Corporation.)

FIGURE 13–7 Illustration of a segmented camshaft assembly used on the 3600 series Caterpillar engine model. A high overlap cam for heavy fuel or a standard overlap cam for distillate and marine diesel fuels is available. (Courtesy of Caterpillar Inc.)

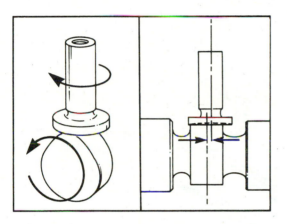

FIGURE 13–8 Design of a flat or mushroom-type camshaft follower (tappet) assembly, which tends to rotate for even wear during engine operation. (Courtesy of Cummins Engine Company, Inc.)

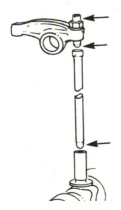

FIGURE 13–9 Flat follower, pushrod, and rocker arm assembly used with an in-block camshaft design. (Courtesy of Cummins Engine Company, Inc.)

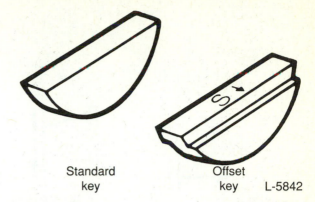

Standard   Offset
key   key   L-5842

FIGURE 13–10 Example of a standard camshaft key and an offset cam key used to alter the camshaft-to-gear-train timing. (Courtesy of Cummins Engine Company, Inc.)

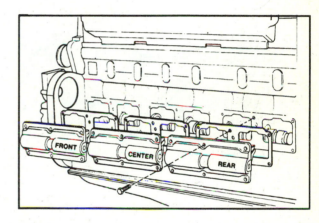

FIGURE 13–11 Identification of the cam follower boxes mounted along the side of an inline six-cylinder model N14 (855 cu in.) displacement engine. (Courtesy of Cummins Engine Company, Inc.)

On the engine CPL plate attached to the engine front timing cover, two letters are listed; for example, let's assume that the timing code was CH. Cummins data indicate that the injector pushrod reading should be 1.32 mm (0.052 in.). A value lower than this indicates that the injection timing is fast or too early, whereas a value greater than the spec indicates that the timing is slow or late. Early and late timing are best explained by referring to Figures 13–14 and 13–15. To alter the injection timing on a 14L engine model, refer to Figure 13–12, which indicates that the cam follower housing gasket(s), item 15, must be changed. Figure 13–16 illustrates that adding gaskets (1) *advances* the timing while removing gaskets (2) *retards* the timing. This reason is that the pivoting camshaft lever roller contacts the rotating camshaft either earlier or later

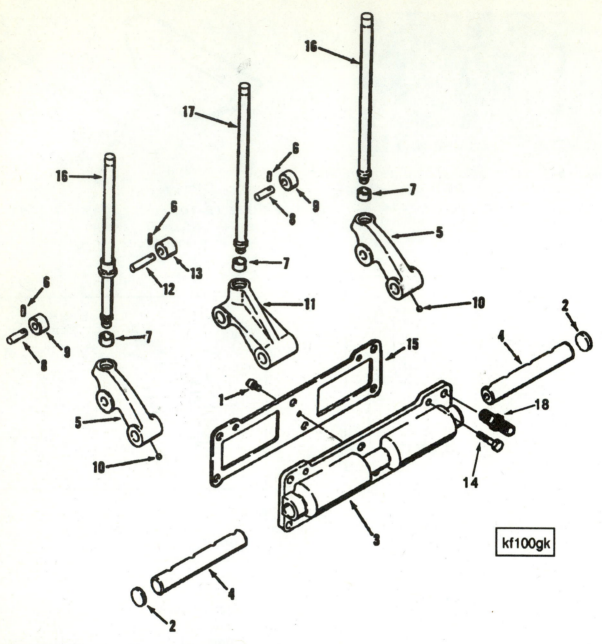

FIGURE 13–12 Details of the cam follower components used to transfer the in-block camshaft rotation/lift to the valve and injector rocker arm assemblies of an N14 (855 cu in.) Cummins engine model. 1 = screw, lock; 2 = plug, expansion; 3 = housing, cam follower; 4 = shaft, cam follower; 5 = lever, cam follower; 6 = pin, roll; 7 = socket, cam follower; 8 = pin, cam follower roller; 9 = roller, cam follower; 10 = plug, ball; 11 = lever, cam follower; 12 = pin, cam follower roller; 13 = roller, cam follower; 14 = capscrew, hexagon head; 15 = gasket, cam follower housing; 16 = rod, push; 17 = rod, push injector; 18 = capscrew, hexagon head. (Courtesy of Cummins Engine Company, Inc.)

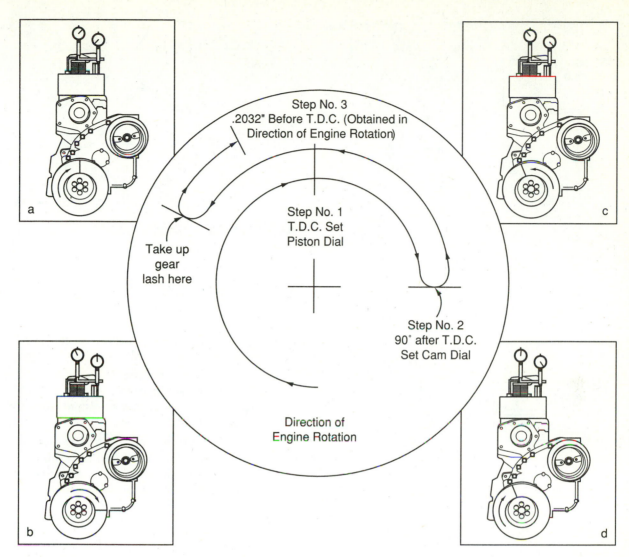

FIGURE 13-13 Four-step procedure required to accurately check the engine piston travel to injector pushrod lift on a Cummins N14 (855 cu in.) engine model. (Courtesy of Cummins Engine Company, Inc.)

during engine operation. On L10, M11, and K series engines, an offset camshaft gear key must be installed to correct any injection timing irregularities.

Another cam timing check recommended by Caterpillar for its 3406 mechanical engines suggests adjusting the No. 1 cylinder intake valve clearance to specs first. Then mark TDC for this cylinder on the vibration damper or pulley (this can also be confirmed by installing a timing bolt through the flywheel housing into the flywheel). Place a dial gauge on top of the No. 1 cylinder intake valve; rotate the crankshaft in the normal direction of rotation. On the 3406B, for example, stop when the dial gauge reads 0.075 in. (1.91 mm) and check the location of the previously marked TDC mark that was placed on the front pulley/damper. Depending on the engine serial number and camshaft

used, the TDC mark should be within a given number of degrees ATDC to confirm that camshaft timing is within specs. Refer to Caterpillar service information.

Refer to Chapter 12 for a detailed engine camshaft timing check for two-stroke DDC engines. On engines using mechanical inline fuel injection pumps such as those of Robert Bosch, Caterpillar, ZEXEL USA, Nippondenso, and Lucas a fuel spill-timing procedure described in Chapter 5 can be used to check fuel injection timing.

CAMSHAFT REMOVAL

Removal of Overhead Model
Removing an overhead camshaft is a fairly straightforward process: take off the rocker cover assembly first,

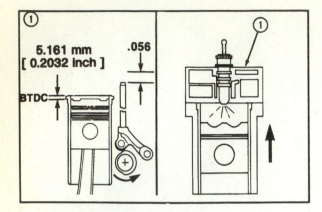

FIGURE 13–14 Early fuel injection as a result of too small an injector pushtube lift BTDC is registered on the face of the dial indicator mounted on top of the pushrod as shown in Figure 13–13. (Courtesy of Cummins Engine Company, Inc.)

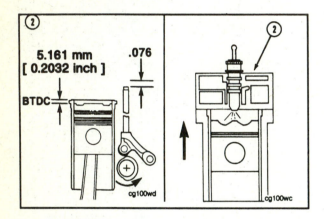

FIGURE 13–15 Late fuel injection as a result of too large an injector pushtube lift BTDC is registered on the pushtube dial indicator shown in Figure 13–13. (Courtesy of Cummins Engine Company, Inc.)

then proceed to remove the camshaft. You will find minor variations in makes of engines, but in engines such as the Caterpillar 3406E, the Isuzu 12L-6WA1TC, the Volvo D12A, and Detroit Diesel Series 50 and 60 engines, the general procedure can be considered common. Refer to Figure 13–3, which illustrates the DDC Series 60 engine camshaft, and follow these steps:

1. Remove the valve rocker cover.
2. Remove the five bolts that secure the camshaft drive gear access cover located on the front gear case as illustrated in Figure 13–17.
3. Refer to Figure 13–18 and loosen off all of the locknuts on the rocker arm adjusting screws. This removes excess spring pressure from the valves and injectors.

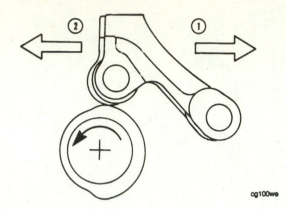

FIGURE 13–16 Cummins model N14 engine injector pushtube lift is adjusted by varying the thickness of the cam follower box gaskets. By removing gaskets we retard the injector timing. By adding gaskets we advance the timing. (Courtesy of Cummins Engine Company, Inc.)

4. Remove the rocker arm shaft bolts and nuts that retain the assemblies to the cylinder head.
5. Hook special tooling (Kent-Moore J-35996) into place as illustrated in Figure 13–19 and carefully lift the rocker arm shafts and rockers clear of the cylinder head.
6. Install a special holding tool (Kent-Moore J-35652), which is illustrated in Figure 13–20, to remove the camshaft drive gear-to-camshaft bolt. Install the tool by inserting the leg through one of the machined lightening holes of the camshaft gear as shown in the diagram. To retain the tool, thread two of the access cover bolts into the gear case and snug them up. If you cannot align these two bolts, you may have to gently rotate the engine crankshaft over by inserting a 3/4 in. (19 mm) square drive into the matching hole in the center of the crankshaft pulley.
7. Install a 27 mm impact socket and breaker bar over the camshaft drive gear-to-camshaft bolt to loosen and then remove it.
8. Remove the holding tool that you installed in step 6.
9. Refer to Figure 13–20 and locate the two camshaft thrust plate mounting bolts. You may have to rotate the crankshaft over to expose these bolts through the machined lightening holes in the gear. Remove both bolts.

SERVICE TIP: Prior to removing these two bolts, you may want to temporarily install a shop towel into the gear case opening to catch the bolts; otherwise, they may drop into the gear case.

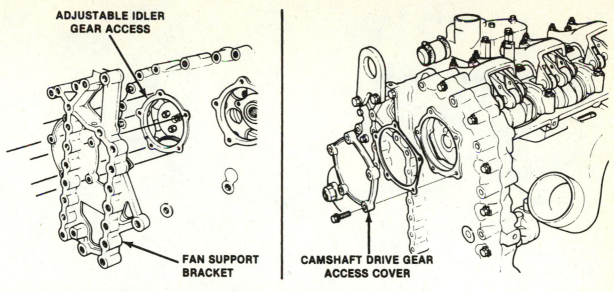

FIGURE 13–17   *Series 60 engine camshaft drive gear and adjustable idler gear access cover. (Courtesy of Detroit Diesel Corporation.)*

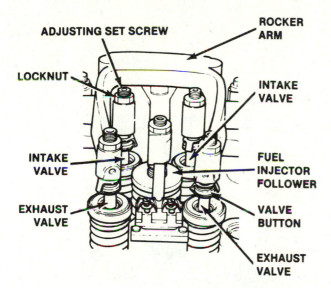

FIGURE 13–18   *Valve and unit injector mechanism and adjustment screws for the four-cycle Series 60 electronically controlled engine model. (Courtesy of Detroit Diesel Corporation.)*

10. To pull the gear from the front of the camshaft, use a puller similar to the one shown in Figure 13–21. Retain the puller onto the gear case by inserting three of the bolts that were removed earlier. Thread the large center puller screw bolt into the threads in the end of the camshaft drive gear hub until tight.

11. Rotate the gear puller bolt until the camshaft drive gear hub and thrust plate have moved forward about 1/4 in. (6 to 7 mm). This will

allow the thrust plate seal to clear the camshaft front bearing cap and cylinder head as illustrated in Figure 13–22.

SPECIAL NOTE: If only the camshaft is being removed, *do not* remove the special tool shown in Figure 13–21, but do remove the large center screw bolt from the tool at this time. This tool *must* be left in place, minus the center screw, to hold the camshaft gear in contact with the adjustable idler gear; otherwise, you will have to retime the cam gear to the idler gear. This would require removal of the crankshaft damper and pulley as well as the gear case cover!

12. Refer to Figure 13–23 and remove the rear camshaft cover by taking out the three retaining bolts.

13. Remove all of the camshaft bearing cap bolts. You will have to use a special Kent-Moore tool (J-36003 or equivalent) to remove the No. 1 and No. 7 studs.

14. Remove all of the camshaft bearing caps along with their upper shells. Ensure that all shells remain with their respective caps and that all caps are identified as to their correct position for reinstallation purposes.

15. Manually slide the camshaft toward the rear of the engine to disengage the dowel from the hub. Carefully lift the camshaft from the cylinder head.

16. Remove the lower cap bearing shells and match them to their respective upper bearing shell and cap assembly.

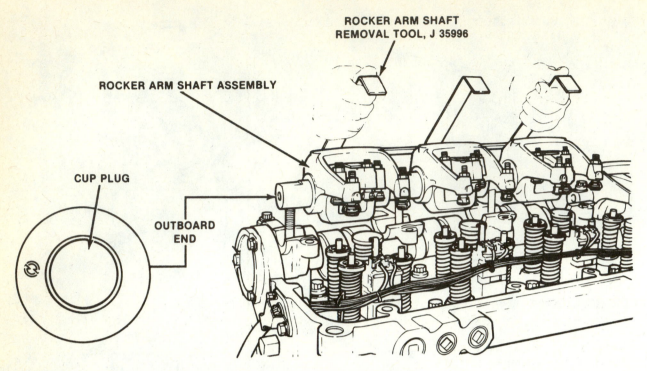

FIGURE 13–19 Removal or installation of Series 60 engine model overhead camshaft rocker arm using special Kent-Moore tooling (J-35996). (Courtesy of Detroit Diesel Corporation.)

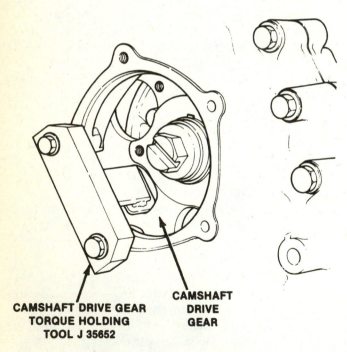

FIGURE 13–20 Installation of Kent-Moore torque holding tool in Series 60 overhead camshaft drive gear. (Courtesy of Detroit Diesel Corporation.)

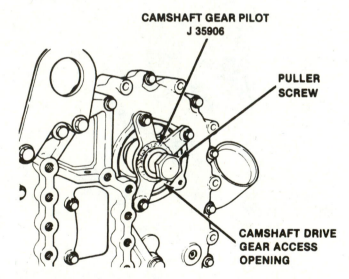

FIGURE 13–21 Series 60 overhead camshaft gear puller pilot tooling arrangement. (Courtesy of Detroit Diesel Corporation.)

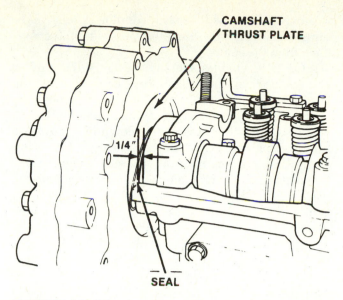

FIGURE 13–22 *Series 60 overhead camshaft thrust plate clearance (Courtesy of Detroit Diesel Corporation.)*

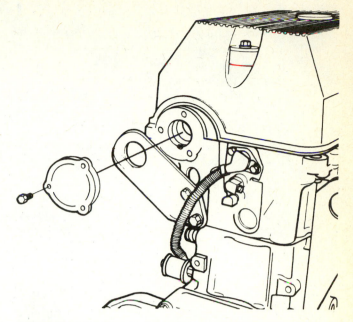

FIGURE 13–23 *Series 60 overhead camshaft rear access cover. (Courtesy of Detroit Diesel Corporation.)*

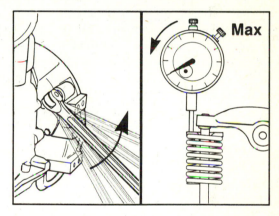

FIGURE 13–24 *Manually barring the engine crankshaft over at the flywheel end to determine the camshaft lift at the valve using a dial indicator. (Courtesy of Cummins Engine Company, Inc.)*

In-Block Camshaft Check

If the camshaft in an in-block design is suspected of being worn on one or more lobes—indicated by a rough running engine—the camshaft lobes can only be visually inspected by removing the camshaft. Alternatively, you can measure the valve lift to check for wear in the valve train. This is done by adjusting the valve lash on the suspected cylinder to a *zero lash* position by placing the rocker arms in the correct valve-set position. Follow these steps:

1. Refer to Figure 13–24 and mount a dial indicator on top of the valve spring retainer as illustrated.
2. Preload the dial slightly and set the gauge to zero. Bar the engine in the direction of rotation until the dial gauge reaches its maximum value in one direction and just starts to move back.
3. Refer to the engine service manual to determine what the camshaft lift should be for either the intake, exhaust, or injector lobe and compare the dial gauge reading to the spec.
4. If there is no wear on the rocker lever or pushrod and the camshaft lobe lift is less than the spec, check the camshaft and lifter (tappets) for wear.

Removal of In-Block Model
Procedure for a Four-Stroke Engine

The procedure for removing the camshaft on in-block engines varies by engine make and model. In most cases, you must steam clean the front timing cover area of the engine first. Then follow these steps:

1. Loosen off and remove any drive belts.
2. Use a suitable puller to remove the vibration damper and any pulleys from the front of the crankshaft.
3. On some engines remove accessory drive pulleys to gain access to the gear train timing cover.
4. Remove the front gear train timing cover after removing all bolts. Manually rotate the engine over until all timing gear marks are in alignment. Take careful note of these marks for reinstallation purposes.

5. Remove the valve rocker cover(s).

6. Loosen off all rocker arm adjusting screw nuts and back off the adjusting screws so you can remove the valve pushrods as well as the injector pushtubes on some engines. In addition, you may have to remove the flat lifters or followers that sit on top of the cam lobes on some engines.

7. On Cummins 14L engines, remove the cam follower cover assemblies from the side of the block. (See Figure 13–11.)

8. On some engines, loosen and remove the camshaft thrust washer flange retaining bolts. These can be accessed through holes in the cam gear, which you may have to rotate to expose the bolt heads.

9. Grasp the camshaft gear and using a twisting motion similar to that shown in Figure 13–1, slowly rotate the camshaft by turning the gear, which will allow you to carefully screw twist it from the bore. As the camshaft passes through each bushing in the block bore it will tend to drop under its own weight; therefore, exert up and down pressure on the gear to facilitate cam removal. If the engine has been removed from the equipment for major overhaul, the block can be mounted on its flywheel housing and the camshaft can be easily removed by using an overhead hoist to pull the cam straight out of the engine block.

SERVICE TIP: In some engines where you can access the camshaft through holes in the block, you can fabricate a heavy wire hook that will allow you to lift up on the end of the camshaft to help guide it through each bushing bore. *Do not*, however, try to lift it by sticking your fingers through the access holes in the block; serious injury can result. As more of the camshaft is exposed during the withdrawal process, grasp part of the camshaft with one hand to facilitate easier removal. Take care that you do not cut your hands on the sharp edges of the cam lobes or support journals. Wear a pair of thick gloves similar to those used for arc welding.

Procedure for a Two-Stroke Engine
On 149 series Detroit Diesel engines, the camshafts (see Figure 13–5) can be accessed by removing the valve rocker covers, the fuel lines to the unit injectors, rocker arm mechanisms, the flywheel housing camshaft gear covers, the camshaft drive shaft snap ring, and the retainer from the drive flange. Remove the drive shaft. If removal of the complete camshaft(s) assembly is desired, loosen the intermediate shaft coupling bolts prior to removing the rear camshaft drive shafts.

Remove the intermediate shaft couplings. Remove the camshaft bearing caps. Sling the camshafts and remove them from the engine.

On DDC engines such as the 53, 71 (both inline and vee models), and V-92 models, the cooling system has to be drained first, since you have to remove the cylinder head(s), flywheel, and flywheel housing to be able to remove the camshaft(s) shown in Figure 13–6 from the engine block. Remove the gear-driven water pump and the engine front balance weight cover. Remove the bolts and step-up gear, if used, from the rear right-bank camshaft gear. (The left and right banks on vee-model engines are determined from the flywheel end). Remove the four bolts that retain the large camshaft gear nut lock plates. Wedge a clean, folded rag between the rear camshaft meshing gears to jam them together, and remove the gear retaining nut from the front and rear ends of the camshaft. If you choose, you can simply remove the left-bank front camshaft nut and accessory drive pulley, or right-bank front camshaft gear; then pull either one from the camshaft with a suitable puller assembly. You will be able to pull the camshaft with the rear gear still in position; however, you should still loosen off the large rear retaining nut because it is easier to do at this time than after the camshaft has been removed.

Rotate the camshaft gears to reveal the end bearing retaining bolts; loosen and remove these. Loosen off and remove the intermediate camshaft bearing retaining setscrews (do not attempt to remove the bearing snap rings). Grasp the rear camshaft gear, and rotate and pull the camshaft from the engine block. The intermediate half-shell bearings can now be separated by removing the two snap rings. Inspect the intermediate and end support bearings after removal and replace them if they are worn beyond the limits or show signs of scoring or damage.

CAMSHAFT INSPECTION

The condition of the camshaft in an overhead cam engine can be determined with the cam in or out of the engine. Similarly, on in-block camshafts where access covers are used (such as on Cummins 14L engines), a visual inspection of the cam lobes can be made with the camshaft in the engine. If inspection reveals possible cam lobe damage, the camshaft should be removed.

Overhead camshafts can be checked while still in place in the engine as illustrated in Figure 13–25; the rocker arms and camshaft caps must be removed. Select a small straightedge, or square steel block, and lay it across each camshaft lobe as shown. Select a feeler gauge and install it between the leading side of the camshaft (injector rise side) or on the intake and

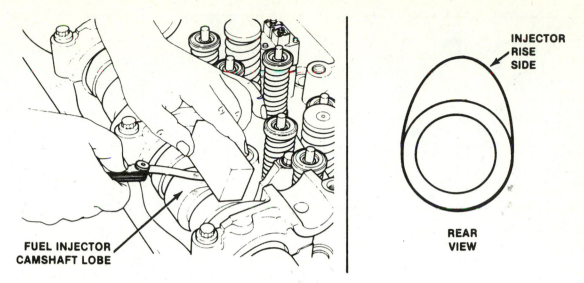

FUEL INJECTOR
CAMSHAFT LOBE

INJECTOR
RISE
SIDE

REAR
VIEW

FIGURE 13–25 Using a machined block and feeler gauge to check the overhead camshaft lobes for wear. (Courtesy of Detroit Diesel Corporation.)

exhaust valve lobe leading faces. Measure the flat on the camshaft lobes as illustrated. Refer to the manufacturer's service manual specs for the allowable tolerance. For example, the Series 50 and 60 DDC engines quote a maximum tolerance with a feeler gauge of 0.003 in. (0.076 mm). Minor imperfections on cam lobes can be stoned or smoothed over with fine emery cloth. Another method to determine if the camshaft is bent is to place a dial gauge as illustrated against the center support journal. If the camshaft runout exceeds the manufacturer's specs when rotated through 360°, it should be replaced. In many high-speed engines, this tolerance is usually as low as 0.002 in. (0.050 mm).

After a camshaft has been removed, clean it with fuel oil or solvent and dry it with compressed air and lint-free rags. Some camshafts are drilled throughout their length with an oil supply passage; in this case, run a wire brush through the oil gallery to remove any foreign material. Lightly lubricate the lobes and journals with engine oil to prevent rusting. Visually inspect the camshaft lobes for signs of scuffing, scoring, scratches, cracks, or other damage. After many miles or hours of operation, it is not unusual to see a light wear pattern on the lobes from the roller follower contact path. Closely inspect the lobes and use a straight piece of hard steel material and a feeler gauge to determine the extent of the cam lobe wear. Refer to the service manual specs for tolerances.

SERVICE TIP: Place the camshaft in a lathe or support it on two vee blocks and use either a dial gauge or outside micrometer as shown in Figure 13–26 to measure the camshaft support journals and each cam lobe. By manually rotating the camshaft with a dial gauge in place, you can quickly determine the lift of each lobe and check for variations. You can also check to see if the camshaft is bent.

IN-BLOCK CAMSHAFT BUSHING REPLACEMENT

Removal
At the time of engine overhaul, the camshaft bushings (bearings) should be closely inspected for wear. They should be checked with a telescoping gauge and outside micrometer to determine if the inside bores are worn beyond the specified limits. On overhead camshaft engines, the cam bearing shells can be accessed easily to determine their condition. Removal and installation is accomplished by removing the camshaft bearing caps as shown in Figure 13–3.

On in-block camshafts, the cam bearings are a little tougher to access, because they are located within the cam bore, which runs the length of the engine block. Figure 13–27 highlights one of seven cam bearings used with a six-cylinder heavy-duty high-speed diesel engine. The cam bushings can be replaced with the engine in place or with the engine block disassembled during major repair. Camshaft bushings can only be removed with the assistance of a special cam bearing puller. Various types of pullers are readily available from major tool suppliers or from engine dealers. The puller comes with a number of expandable adapters to suit different diameter bushings which are a press fit in the block bore.

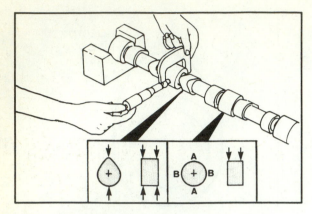

FIGURE 13–26 Using an outside micrometer to measure the camshaft lobes at two places 90° apart. (Courtesy of Cummins Engine Company, Inc.)

Figure 13–28 illustrates one example of a cam bearing puller set with a slide hammer located over the end of the shaft assembly. In this example, the No. 1 bushing is removed first by inserting the tool through the camshaft bore until the driver sits flush against the bushing. By moving the slide hammer against the shaft, the bushing can be driven from its bore. The remaining six bushings can be removed in order from the front to the rear. However, to remove the No.7 bushing, you have to insert the puller assembly as shown in Figure 13–29 so you can slide through the bushing length with the adaptor until the pins of the puller are engaged behind the bushing. The bushing adaptor can then be expanded from the front of the tool to ensure a tight fit behind the thin wall of the bushing. Hit the slide hammer against the T-handle until the bushing is removed from its bore. Take care when removing or installing these bushings to avoid damaging the bore within the block or the bushing. Also be aware of the sharp casting area that tends to exist around each cam bushing bore. Keep your fingers clear!

Cam Bore Inspection
Inspect the condition of all cam bushing bores within the block. Use fine emery cloth to remove burrs or minor irregularities. Check the bushing and block bore using either a dial bore gauge or a telescoping gauge and outside micrometer. Compare these readings with the service manual specifications. Remove and replace any worn or damaged bushings.

Bushing Installation
Bushing installation is basically the reverse of removal. Remember to carefully check the part numbers stamped on the backs of the bushings. Some will have

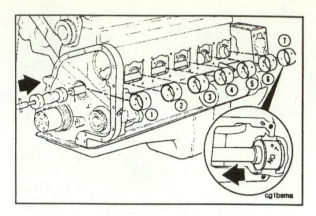

FIGURE 13–27 Using a special slide hammer tool set which extends throughout the camshaft bearing bores within the block to remove the cam bearings from an N14 engine model. (Courtesy of Cummins Engine Company, Inc.)

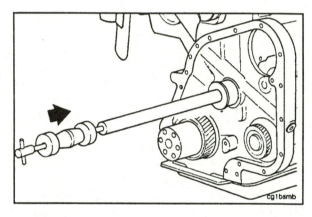

FIGURE 13–28 Removing the No. 1 cam bearing from the block bore of an N14 engine. (Courtesy of Cummins Engine Company, Inc.)

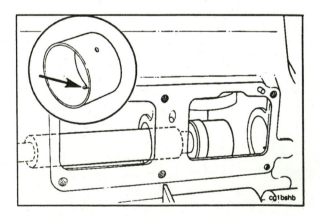

FIGURE 13–29 Identification of the cam bearing locating notch shown at approximately the 6 o'clock position; the oil locating hole is shown at 12 o'clock. (Courtesy of Cummins Engine Company, Inc.)

the numbers 1 through 7 clearly stamped in place. These numbers are important because in some engines the bushings are not all the same diameter. In our example of a six-cylinder 14L Cummins engine, install the cam bushings in this order: 7, 6, 5, 4, 3, 2, and 1. Cam bushings are generally drilled with one or more oil holes in them for lubrication purposes; therefore, be sure to align each bushing with its mating oil supply hole during installation. Some bushings may have a locating notch to guide you.

Figure 13–29 illustrates one example of a locating notch in the No. 7 bushing which should be toward the rear of the engine and at the 6 o'clock position. Using the correct bushing adaptors on the special tool, along with a guide bushing installed in the No. 5 and No. 6 bores, install the No. 7 bushing into its bore by hitting the slide hammer against the shaft assembly until the oil holes are aligned with the drillings in the block bore. To ensure that the bushing oil holes are aligned, insert a small wire rod as shown in Figure 13–30 to confirm proper installation of the bushing. The remaining bushings, No. 6 through No. 1, should have the locating notch facing the rear of the engine and be located at the 9 o'clock position. Use the same installation procedure described for the No. 7 bushing. Carefully inspect all installed bushings. Check them with a telescoping gauge and outside micrometer to ensure that they have not buckled or distorted during the installation process.

Squirt liberal amounts of clean engine oil into each bushing. Then reinstall the camshaft thrust washer with the oil grooves facing toward the camshaft gear; otherwise, thrust washer failure will occur. Lubricate both sides of the washer with Lubriplate 105 or equivalent. Carefully grasp the camshaft with one hand and the gear with the other for support (use gloves to protect your hands from sharp edges). Use a gentle twisting motion during installation as you carefully work the camshaft into position. Make sure before engaging the camshaft gear that the timing reference marks are correctly aligned with mating gears. Check camshaft gear backlash (see Chapter 12).

CAMSHAFT END FLOAT

All camshafts, both overhead and in-block, employ some form of thrust washer to maintain the end float within acceptable tolerances. To check the end float, or end play, you can mount a dial indicator gauge as shown in Figure 13–31 for an overhead cam arrangement. The gauge pin is sitting against the rear end of the camshaft with the inspection cover removed. Alternatively, on either overhead or in-block cam

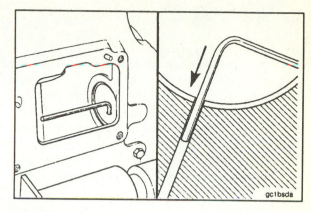

FIGURE 13–30   Using a rod or Allen key to determine if the installed cam bushing is correctly aligned with the engine block oil feed supply hole. (Courtesy of Cummins Engine Company, Inc.)

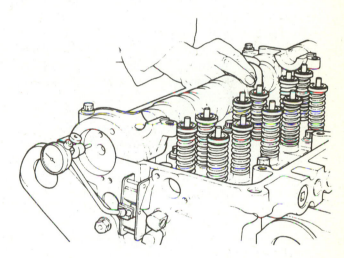

FIGURE 13–31   Measuring overhead camshaft end play with a dial indicator mounted as shown. (Courtesy of Detroit Diesel Corporation.)

engines, you can mount the dial gauge against the camshaft gear. Gently thrust the camshaft to one end; you can use a small heel bar behind the gear, but be careful! Preload and set the dial indicator to zero; then move the camshaft as far as possible in the opposite direction while reading the gauge. The amount of end play will be stated in the service manual; this tolerance usually falls within 0.003 to 0.015 in. (0.076 to 0.381 mm) on most high-speed heavy-duty engines. If the end play is outside of the tolerance, check to make sure that the new parts have been installed correctly. If necessary, you can replace the camshaft thrust plate or washer; on some models of engines, you can add or remove shims from the thrust plate stack-up. Recheck the camshaft end float.

BALANCE SHAFTS

Many inline four-cylinder four-stroke-cycle engines have an inherent vibration caused by the motion of the piston, pin, and small end of the con-rod. Detroit Diesel's Series 50 four-cylinder 8.5L engine (four-cylinder version of the Series 60, 12.7L model) employs counterrotating balance shafts which cancel out the vertical shaking force. Figure 13–32 illustrates these two shafts, which are gear driven and attached to the underside of the engine inside the oil pan. The gears must be phased and timed so that their designed-in weights cancel out the unwanted vertical forces. This system allows the four-cylinder engine to operate as smoothly as its larger six-cylinder sibling. A similar arrangement is used by Caterpillar in its four-cylinder model 3114 (4.4L) mechanically governed unit injector engine (see Figure 13–33). The balancer shaft gears must be phased and timed to the engine by marked teeth on the gears.

Two-stroke-cycle Detroit Diesel inline model engines (such as the 53 and 71 series) employ a balance shaft that sits in the block opposite the camshaft (see Figure 13–6). This balance shaft is needed to provide an extremely smooth running engine assembly, because the two-stroke-cycle engine with its uneven firing impulses (twice as many as a four-stroke-cycle model) causes an uneven couple, which tends to want to rock the engine. The balance shaft is the same length and weight as the camshaft. At one end of both the cam and balance shaft (front of engine) are two balance weights, which are installed and located in the same position by a key or keyway and large retaining nut. At the opposite end of both shafts are two gears (flywheel end), which are also installed and located by a key (keyway) and which weigh the same as the weights used at the front of both shafts. Notice in the diagram that each gear is designed so that half of the gear is solid while the other half is open. The solid (heavy) half of each gear is located 180° opposite the weights at the front, so that as the engine rotates, the centrifugal forces developed by these rotating weights produce a force that is equal and opposite to that developed by the uneven firing impulses of the engine. On Detroit Diesel vee-configuration two-stroke-cycle engines, each bank employs its own camshaft, so there is no need for a separate balance shaft assembly.

VALVE AND INJECTOR OPERATING MECHANISM

In-block camshaft designs require individual pushrods to transfer the cam action to the valves, or valves and injectors, through the rocker arm assemblies. Pushrods are manufactured in either solid or

FIGURE 13–32   Series 50 8.5L four-cylinder engine counter-rotating balance shafts, which are located below the engine crankshaft within the oil pan. (Courtesy of Detroit Diesel Corporation.)

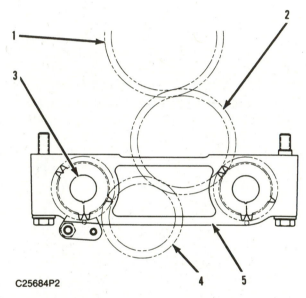

C25684P2

FIGURE 13–33   Example of counter-rotating balancer shafts (3) and gears (1, 2, 4) used with the Cat 3114 engine model. 5-oil pump housing. (Courtesy of Caterpillar Inc.)

tubular form and are provided with ball ends at the rocker arm and lifter end. One example of the components used to operate the valve and injector mechanism in the Caterpillar 3176 EUI-controlled engine is illustrated in Figure 13–34 and Figure 13–35. The camshaft is high mounted in the engine—located within the aluminum spacer deck that sits atop the gray cast iron cylinder block. The camshaft is located just below the cylinder head to minimize pushrod length and to provide a very stiff actuating mechanism. Note that this system has *swing arm* roller followers and that due to the skewed valve arrangement in the cylinder head, two different rocker arm lengths

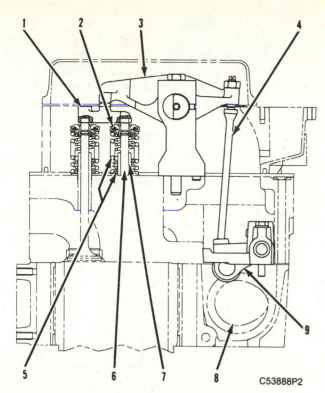

C53888P2

FIGURE 13-34 Cat model 3176 engine valve operating mechanism. 1 = intake bridge; 2 = rotocoil; 3 = intake rocker arm; 4 = pushrod; 5 = valve springs (inner and outer); 6 = intake valves; 7 = valve guide; 8 = camshaft; 9 = lifter. (Courtesy of Caterpillar Inc.)

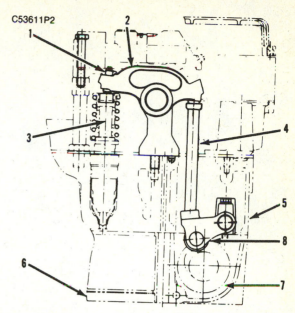

C53611P2

FIGURE 13-35 Cat model 3176 engine electronically controlled, but mechanically actuated, unit injector operating mechanism. 1 = adjusting nut; 2 = rocker arm assembly; 3 = electronically controlled unit injector; 4 = pushrod; 5 = cylinder head; 6 = spacer block; 7 = camshaft; 8 = lifter (Courtesy of Caterpillar Inc.)

are used. Detroit Diesel also uses roller followers (non-swing type) and short pushrods with its 53, 71, and 92 series two-stroke-cycle engines; all of these components are assembled into the cylinder head as illustrated in Figure 13–36, where the parts are held in position by a bolted guide plate attached to the cylinder head at the bottom and a snap ring at the top end of the follower body which fits into a machined groove in the cylinder head.

The heavy-duty 14L models of Cummins employ pivoted roller folllowers and pushrods (see Figure 13–12). Figure 13–4 illustrates the Detroit Diesel overhead cam design with a roller follower attached to the rear side of the rocker arms. This design is also used in the Volvo D12A engine with a four-valve head and electronically controlled, but mechanically actuated, unit injector. The forward side of the rocker arm (adjusting screw end) contacts the center of a valve bridge to open two valves at once. Another example of an overhead cam engine using a valve bridge mechanism is the Isuzu 6WA1TC 12L six-cylinder heavy-duty high-speed truck diesel, which has a self-centering wear button in the end of the rocker arm valve lash adjusting screw.

A rather unique rocker arm mechanism arrangement is that employed by Detroit Diesel in its Series 50 and 60 engines (Figure 13–37). The arrangement allows for two long and two short rocker arm assemblies without having to resort to a valve bridge mechanism to open the two intake and two exhaust valves per cylinder. Note the internal oil holes to lubricate the self-centering adjusting screw button, rocker shaft, and roller follower, as well as the various profiles of the camshaft lobes for the intake, exhaust, and unit injector. As you can see, the actual cam lobe profiles are quite different for each system.

VALVE BRIDGE (CROSSHEAD, YOKE)

The term *bridge* is used by Detroit Diesel and Caterpillar, Cummins prefers the term *crosshead*, and Mack refers to a *yoke*. In two-valve head engines, the rocker arm pallet acts directly on the end of the valve stem, while in four-valve heads the rocker arm acts on a valve bridge (crosshead, yoke) to open two valves at once (two intake and two exhaust valves on four-stroke-cycle engines, and four exhaust valves on two-stroke-cycle engines).

Figure 13–38 illustrates a typical valve yoke (bridge, crosshead) which is supported on a guide pin pressed into the upper deck of the cylinder head. The

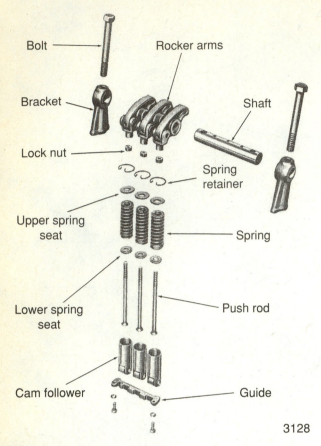

Bolt

Rocker arms

Bracket

Shaft

Lock nut

Spring retainer

Upper spring seat

Spring

Lower spring seat

Push rod

Cam follower

Guide

3128

FIGURE 13–36 *Valve and mechanical unit injector operating mechanism used on 53, 71 and 92 series DDC two-stroke-cycle engines. (Courtesy of Detroit Diesel Corporation.)*

yoke is pushed down by the rocker arm contacting its pallet surface, which allows two valves to open and close simultaneously. The yoke must be adjusted to ensure that it sits squarely on its guide stud and will open both valves equally. It can be adjusted in place or during cylinder head or rocker arm service or repair. If the engine or cylinder heads are being overhauled, the yoke will be accessible; therefore, place it into a soft-jaw vice and loosen off the locknut on the adjusting screw. Place the yoke over its guide stud so that it contacts both valve stems.

To adjust the bridge (yoke, crosshead), some designs allow a strip of thin shim stock or a feeler gauge to be placed between the end of each valve stem and the bridge. The thickness of feeler gauge used doesn't really matter, although thinner gauges provide a better feel. Some manufacturers specify 0.0015 in. (0.038 mm), while others specify up to 0.010 in. (0.0254 mm). Place light finger pressure onto the bridge rocker arm contact area, or if the rocker arms are in place, refer to Figure 13–39 and apply light pressure to the rocker

arm. Rotate the adjusting screw clockwise until a slight step-up in effort is felt as the bridge screw just makes contact with the valve stem or the feeler gauges. Hold the screw and tighten the locknut. Check to see if the drag on each feeler gauge is the same. If not, readjust. If the rockers are not in place, you can remove the bridge and replace it into a soft-jaw vice. Hold the lockscrew securely and torque the locknut to specifications.

VALVE AND INJECTOR ADJUSTMENT

Valve Adjustment

Valve lash adjustment can only be performed when the valves are in a fully closed position or on the base circle of the camshaft. By following the engine firing order, all valves and unit injectors can be adjusted on four-stroke engines in two complete crankshaft revolutions (720°); on two-stroke-cycle engines, all valves and injectors can be adjusted in one full turn (360°) of the crankshaft. All later model engines have several decals attached to the engine or rocker cover(s) that indicate U.S. EPA emissions certification as well as the intake and exhaust valve clearances and the injector setting information.

The procedure required to check or set both the valves and injectors on different makes of engines can be considered common; however, the position of the valves and injectors and *specific* setting processes do vary. First we will discuss a general procedure, then specific procedures for a number of well-known high-speed heavy-duty diesel engines, many of which are using electronically controlled unit fuel injectors. On engines that have nozzles rather than unit-type injectors, either a distributor-type or inline multiple-plunger injection pump is used. Therefore, no adjustment is required to the nozzle while it is in the engine, although the nozzle popping pressure can be adjusted by the use of shims or a setscrew during nozzle service.

General Procedure

Valves can be checked and adjusted by rotating the engine over in its normal direction of rotation and choosing one of the following methods for four-stroke-cycle engines.

1. Visually determine when the inlet valve starts to open and the exhaust valve has just closed. This procedure is commonly referred to as the *rocking motion* of valve adjustment. For example, consider an inline six-cylinder engine with a conventional firing order of 1–5–3–6–2–4. The valves to be adjusted on a given cylinder can be determined as follows:

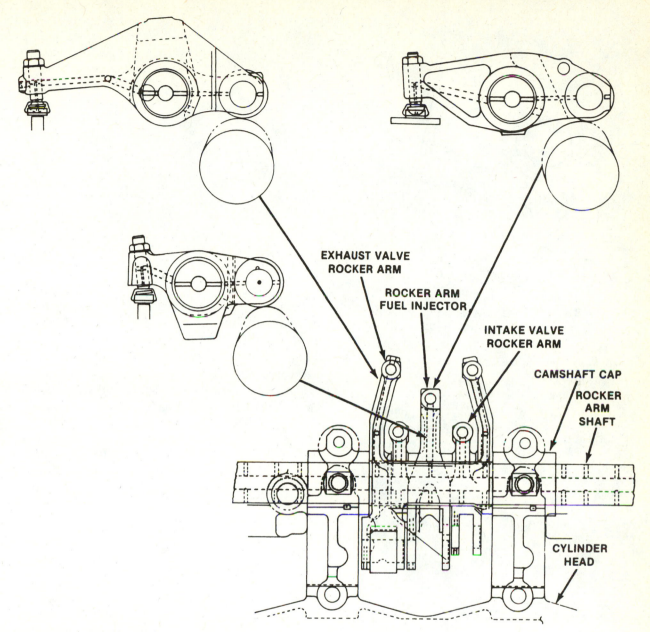

FIGURE 13–37 Unique overhead camshaft valve and injector operating mechanism components used on the Series 50 and 60 electronic engine models. Note that there is no need for valve bridges with this design. (Courtesy of Detroit Diesel Corporation.)

Rocking cylinder	Cylinder/valves to be adjusted
6	1
2	5
4	3
1	6
5	2
3	4

Figure 13–40 illustrates a feeler gauge installed between the end of the rocker arm and the valve stem on a two-valve head engine model. On four-valve head models, the clearance is checked between the rocker arm and the valve bridge pallet surface. To accomplish valve adjustment, loosen off the locknut on the pushrod located at the rear of the rocker arm; then rotate the slotted screw either CW or CCW until the desired lash is achieved. Tighten the nut to specs while securely holding the adjusting screw. The next cylinder intake and exhaust valves can then be adjusted by rotating the engine over manually

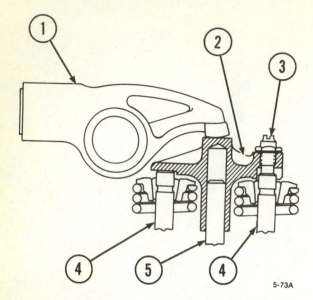

FIGURE 13–38 Close-up view of a four-valve-head rocker arm (1), yoke/bridge/crosshead (2), yoke adjusting screw (3), valve stem (4), and yoke guide pin (5). (Courtesy of Mack Trucks, Inc.)

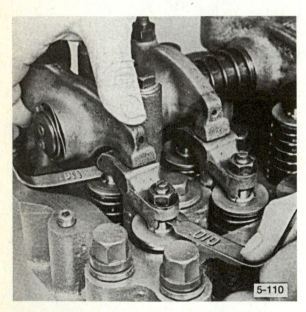

FIGURE 13–39 Using a feeler gauge between the end of the valve stem and the yoke (bridge) mechanism of a four-valve-head engine to check for accurate adjustment and squareness. (Courtesy of Mack Trucks, Inc.)

another 120°, or one-third of a turn. Continue this process until all valves have been adjusted.

2.   Once again let's consider an inline six-cylinder engine. On a two-valve head there are 12 valves (6

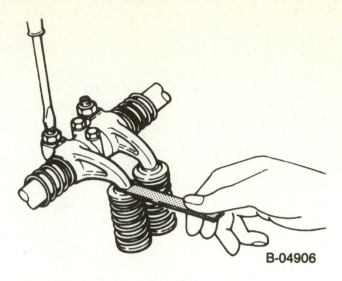

FIGURE 13–40 Location of feeler gauge to check clearance of the rocker arm pallet to valve stem on a two-valve-head engine. (Courtesy of GMC Trucks.)

intake and 6 exhaust). On a four-valve head there are 24 valves (12 intake and 12 exhaust); however, two valves (one set) are opened at once through the bridge mechanism. If we use what is commonly referred to as the *thirteen system* (front to rear of engine), we can easily set both the intake and exhaust valves as follows:

- Starting from the front of the engine, note that the valves or valve sets (2) are numbered consecutively 1 through 12 for either a two- or four-valve head.
- To set any valve clearance, visually determine when any valve(s) is fully open while rotating the engine manually.
- Assume that valve 5 is fully open. To obtain a count of 13, we check and adjust the valve clearance on valve 8. Similarly, if valve 9 is fully open, we check and adjust valve 4. By following this procedure, we can quickly check and adjust all valves.

On a four-cylinder four-stroke engine, a *nine system* is used to check and adjust the valve clearances.

Mack Engines

The vibration damper at the front of the crankshaft is marked in 120° increments on the six-cylinder models; the paired cylinders are 1–6, 5–2, and 3–4 for the firing order of 1–5–3–6–2–4. On the V8 models, the vibration damper is marked in 90° increments; the paired cylinders are 1–6, 5–3, 4–7, and 8–2 for a firing order of 1–5–4–8–6–3–7–2. On the six-cylinder engines when the cylinder markings are aligned with a stationary pointer marked "valve" above the damper, they provide the 30° ATDC damper relationship for valve lash adjustment. On the V8 models the cylinder markings, when aligned with the stationary pointer, indicate TDC for each cylinder piston! When a paired cylinder damper mark is aligned with the stationary pointer, check the rocker arms of both numbered cylinders to determine which one has free play. Adjust the valves on this cylinder only. Rotate the engine CW to bring up the next numbered pair of cylinders and repeat the process until all intake and exhaust valves have been adjusted to the correct clearance.

Cummins Engines

The valves on the B and C series four-stroke engine models can be adjusted in the same sequence as that described for general valve adjustments. Some Cummins engines, however, employ actual VS (valve set) marks (A,B,C) located on an accessory drive pulley (L10/M11, N14, and K series) that are aligned with a stationary gear train housing mark. Figure 13–41 illustrates these VS marks. When any VS mark is aligned with the stationary pointer located on the engine front gear train housing, the piston in one of the mating cylinders is 90° ATDC. Since this is a six-cylinder engine, there are three coupled cylinders with a firing order of 1–5–3–6–2–4. This means that there are always two pistons in the same cylinder position throughout the engine's rotation (refer to Chapter 1 if you need to review relative piston positions). Note the following markings around the circumference of the engine accessory drive pulley:

- TDC 1-6 (1-6 TC)
- Letter A—indicating that the valves can be set on either cylinder 1 or 6
- Letter B—indicating that the valves can be set on either cylinder 5 or 2
- Letter C—indicating that the valves can be set on either cylinder 3 or 4

To determine which valves can be checked or set, grasp the rocker arm assemblies on both of the matched cylinders. For example, if letter A was aligned, grasp the rocker arms on cylinders 1 and 6. Whatever one indicates free play or looseness is the cylinder that is 90° into its power stroke.

SERVICE TIP: Because the high pressures created within the injector place a greater load on the rocker arm and camshaft than does valve operation, some engine manufacturers suggest that you set or adjust the injector before the valve lash. Otherwise, due to the clearance that exists between the valve operating mechanism, the injector load setting may alter the valve lash. Cummins makes this recommendation, but Detroit Diesel does not.

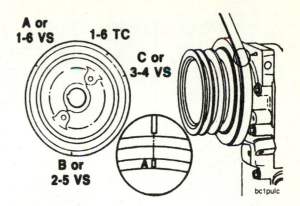

FIGURE 13–41 Location of engine accessory drive pulley valve set markings and stationary pointer on the engine front gear case of Cummins N14 (855 cu in.) engine model. (Courtesy of Cummins Engine Company, Inc.)

Injector and Valve Adjustment Sequence			
Bar Engine in Direction of Rotation	Pulley Position	Set Cylinder Injector	Valve
Start	A	3	5
Advance to	B	6	3
Advance to	C	2	6
Advance to	A	4	2
Advance to	B	1	4
Advance to	C	5	1
Firing Order: 1-5-3-6-2-4			

FIGURE 13–42 Injector and valve adjustment sequence chart for a Cummins six-cylinder mechanical engine PT fuel system engine. (Courtesy of Cummins Engine Company, Inc.)

Since Cummins L10/M11, 14L, and K series engines employ pushrod operated injectors (mechanical or Celect engines), valves and injectors can be set according to the procedure listed in Figure 13–42 for mechanical PT engine models. The electronic (Celect) models can have the valves and injectors set on the same cylinder in the procedure listed in Figure 13–43. Set the valve clearances by using a feeler gauge between the rocker arm pallet and the crosshead contact surface. Always torque the locknut to specifications after adjustment and recheck the valve lash. To adjust the Cummins injector, refer to either Figure 13–42 or Figure 13–43 to determine what injector to set at a given VS mark. In some engines, the injector can be set by backing off the adjusting nut and screw of the injector rocker arm and performing the recommended adjustment. Look at the engine CPL (control

Injector and Valve Adjustment Sequence			
Bar Engine In Direction of Rotation	**Pulley Position**	**Set Cylinder Injector and Valves**	
Start	A	1	
Advance to	B	5	
Advance to	C	3	
Advance to	A	6	
Advance to	B	2	
Advance to	C	4	
Firing Order: 1-5-3-6-2-4			

FIGURE 13–43 *Injector and valve adjustment sequence chart for N14 STC OBC engine model, or for use with a six-cylinder Celect-equipped engine. (Courtesy of Cummins Engine Company, Inc.)*

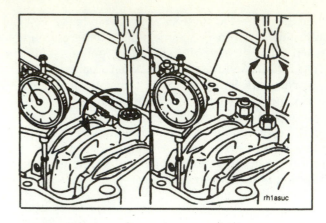

FIGURE 13–44 *Using a dial indicator mounted on top of the injector follower of a model N14 engine, then backing off the adjustment screw. (Courtesy of Cummins Engine Company, Inc.)*

parts list) data plate located on the side of the engine front timing cover. Under injector information, you will find a dimension (for example, 0.170 in., 4.318 mm, for a non-top-stop injector) or the letters T.S. (top-stop Injector) which is adjusted for zero lash.

On some models of engines, the injector adjusting screw is tightened to a recommended inch-pound torque value, which you may have to locate in the engine service manual. If the injector calls for a dimensional setting, mount a dial indicator over the injector as shown in Figure 13–44 with the dial extension contacting the top of the injector plunger. The injector must be forced down several times until the plunger bottoms to squeeze the fuel from the cup. This can be done by placing a wrench or socket and breaker bar over a special hooked adapter connected to the rocker arm assembly as illustrated in Figure 13–45. With the injector plunger bottomed in the cup, set the dial gauge to zero; then release the socket and bar slowly to allow the injector plunger to return to its full upward position while carefully reading the dial gauge measurement. If the dimension is incorrect, rotate the rocker arm adjusting screw until it is correct; then torque the locknut. Recheck the setting once more.

If top-stop injectors have been removed from the engine and their adjustment is disturbed for any reason, they have to be set on a special dial gauge fixture to provide a specific injector plunger travel similar to that described for the non-top-stop injector. If you are setting the injector on the engine, once the VS mark is in position to allow injector adjustment for that cylinder, loosen off the adjusting screw and use the special Cummins T-handle torque wrench (5 to 6 in. lb) or equivalent to tighten it to specs. Tighten the locknut as shown in Figure 13–46 to 54 to 61 N·m (40 to 45 lb-ft).

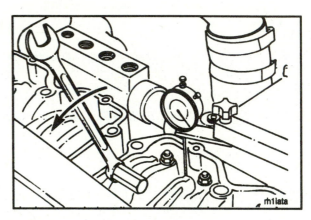

FIGURE 13–45 *Using a rocker lever actuator tool (ST-1193) to depress the injector plunger, then allowing it to return while carefully noting the reading on the dial indicator gauge. (Courtesy of Cummins Engine Company, Inc.)*

On Celect engine models (L10/M11 or N14), refer to the VS chart shown in Figure 13–43 and back out the adjusting screw. Bottom the injector three or four times to remove the fuel from the cup in a manner similar to that described for a non-top-stop injector. Rotate the injector rocker arm adjusting screw CW until it stops. Back out the screw equivalant to two flats on the locknut (120°). Hold the screw and torque the locknut (usually 40 to 45 lb-ft, 54 to 61 N·m). A dial indicator can be used on the injector plunger to obtain the lash recommended in the service manual.

Detroit Diesel Four-Stroke-Cycle Engines

Figure 13–18 illustrates the adjusting screws required to check and adjust the valves and electronic unit injectors

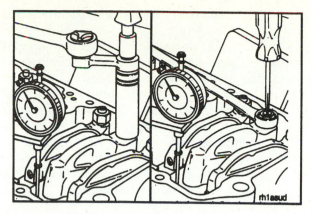

FIGURE 13–46 *Tightening the injector rocker arm adjusting screw using either an ST-669 torque wrench or a screwdriver and combination wrench. (Courtesy of Cummins Engine Company, Inc.)*

on Detroit Diesel Series 50 and 60 four-stroke-cycle models. Since the engine has a firing order of 1–5–3–6–2–4, refer to Figure 13–47. Bar the engine over manually until one of the injector followers has just started to move down. This procedure allows all of the valves and injectors to be set in two complete crank rotations (720°). Refer to Figure 13–48 and adjust all four valves (two intake and two exhaust) on this cylinder using the procedure illustrated. From the information provided in Figure 13–47, set the fuel injector height on the mating (companion) cylinder. For example, if we had just set the valve lash on cylinder No. 1, we would now set the injector on the No. 6 cylinder. The unit injector is adjusted for a listed dimensional height (indicated on the engine decal) from the top machined surface of the follower to the injector body by using a *timing pin* which fits into a drilled hole in the injector body as shown in Figure 13–49. Adjust the injector height as illustrated in Figure 13–50 until a slight drag is felt on the flag of the gauge as it passes over the top of the injector follower. Tighten the locknut when done and recheck the injector height.

SERVICE TIP: Some experienced technicians like to place a small amount of clean engine oil onto the injector follower. When the timing height gauge is rotated over the follower, a small half-circle shape, which is visible as the oil is wiped off, confirms that the injector is correctly set. Other technicians simply rely on feel as the gauge is moved backward and forward over the follower, which is machined with a small chamfer on its circumference.

NOTE: DDC recommends that after a new or overhauled engine has been in service for a given time period, both the valve lash and the injector heights on all Series 50/60 engines should be checked and reset if necessary. For truck engines, the time for checking is at 60,000 miles (96,000 km) or 24 months, whichever

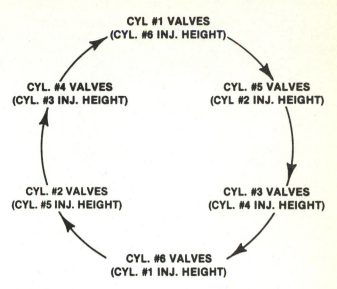

FIGURE 13–47 *Timing circle chart that can be used to check and adjust all of the valve and injector settings on a DDC Series 60 four-stroke-cycle engine. (Courtesy of Detroit Diesel Corporation.)*

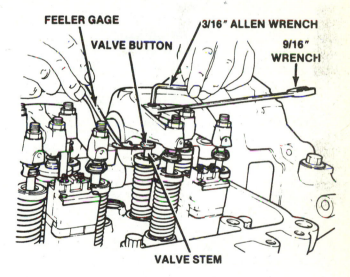

FIGURE 13–48 *Setting the valve clearance adjustment on a Series 50 or 60 overhead cam design engine model. The valve clearance specs can be found on the decal attached to the valve rocker cover. (Courtesy of Detroit Diesel Corporation.)*

occurs first. On stationary and industrial engine applications, check at 1,500 hours or 45,000 miles (72,000 km). Failure to check these clearances and settings may result in gradual loss of engine performance and reduced fuel efficiency.

Detroit Diesel Two-Stroke-Cycle Engines

On two-stroke-cycle Detroit Diesel engines all valves are exhaust. To check and set the valves, simply rotate

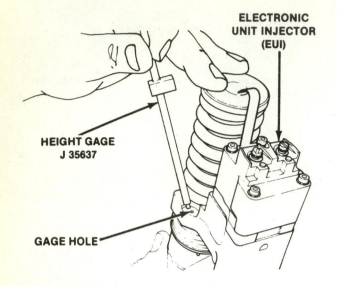

FIGURE 13–49 *Location of the injector timing height gauge pin hole to check and adjust the injector-body-to-follower dimension, which can be found on the engine decal attached to the valve rocker cover. (Courtesy of Detroit Diesel Corporation.)*

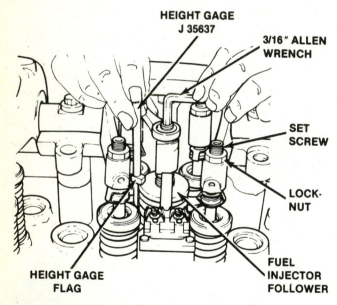

FIGURE 13–50 *Using an Allen key and wrench to adjust and lock the electronic unit injector screw after setting the fuel injector body to follower height dimension. (Courtesy of Detroit Diesel Corporation.)*

the engine over (normally CW from the front) until the unit injector follower is fully depressed or all the way down. Adjust the valve clearance on that particular cylinder. On Series 53, 71, and 92 models the pushrod is threaded into the back side of the rocker arm; therefore, to adjust the valve lash you will have

to rotate the pushrod by placing a wrench onto the square shoulder provided after loosening off the locknut. On 149 series engines the valve and injector adjustment require that you loosen off a locknut at the forward side of the rocker arm; then use an Allen (hex) key to perform the adjustment similar to that shown for the Series 60 engine. To adjust the injector timing height, rotate the engine over in its normal rotation until the exhaust valves are fully open on the cylinder. Refer to the engine decal to determine the correct injector setting. Use the correct timing height gauge similar to the one illustrated in Figure 13–49 for Series 50 and 60 engines. Use the same injector checking procedure described for these engines; then lock the nut.

Caterpillar Valve and Injector Set

The sequence used to check and set the valve lash and unit injectors on all six-cylinder Caterpillar engines follows the same basic procedure, except for the actual valve and injector clearance specs and the location of the engine flywheel turning mechanism. Check the engine data plate information to determine the valve lash clearance specification. The following procedure describes the adjustments for the 3176 EUI engine. The valve operating mechanism is illustrated in Figure 13–34 and the injector mechanism in Figure 13–35. All of the valves and injectors can be adjusted by placing the piston in the No. 1 cylinder at TDC compression for three cylinder adjustments and at TDC exhaust for the remaining cylinder valves and injectors. TDC is obtained by manually rotating the engine over in its normal direction of rotation, which is CW from the front, or CCW from the rear (flywheel end). The easiest method to use to rotate these engines is to refer to Figure 13–51a. Remove the two bolts and remove the cover from the flywheel housing. Use a 1/2 in. (12.7 mm) drive ratchet along with special Cat tool 9S9082, which engages the flywheel ring gear to turn the engine flywheel over in the normal direction of rotation—CCW when viewed from the flywheel end of the engine (see Figure 13–51b).

You will know when No. 1 piston is at TDC compression by the fact that approximately 5 to 6 in. (127 to 152 mm) above the ratchet turning hole in the flywheel housing there is a provision that allows one of the bolts (item 1 in Figure 13–51a) removed from the cover to be installed through this timing hole and thread into a mating hole in the flywheel. Slowly rotate the flywheel while watching the position of the valves on the No. 1 cylinder; both should be closed when No.1 piston is at TDC compression. Check that both rocker arms can be moved by hand. If not, you are 360° or one full turn off, and the piston is at TDC

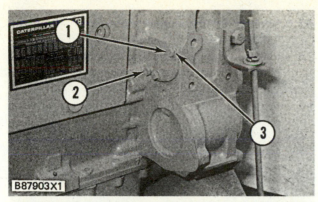

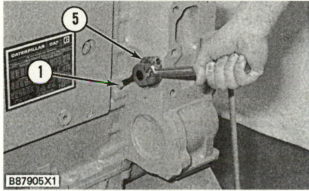

FIGURE 13–51 (a) Inspection plate cover location at the flywheel housing (left side of engine) on a 3406 model. Use timing bolt (1) to thread into the flywheel (2); bolt storage location is indicated (3). This will place the No. 1 piston at TDC compression. (b) 3406 engine flywheel ring gear special turning tool (5) 9S9082 attached to the end of a 1/2 in. (12.7 mm) ratchet. (Courtesy of Caterpillar Inc.)

but on its exhaust stroke. You can start the valve and injector adjustment procedure at either TDC compression or TDC exhaust as long as the timing bolt has been threaded into the flywheel hole.

SPECIAL NOTE: The valve clearance spec when checking lash is stated as 0.56 to 0.72 mm (0.022 to 0.028 in.) for the exhaust valves and 0.30 to 0.46 mm (0.012 to 0.018 in.) for the intake valves. When actually adjusting the valve lash, the spec is 0.38 mm (0.015 in.) for the intake valve and 0.64 mm (0.025 in.) for the exhaust valve.

If you are starting at TDC compression for the No. 1 piston, proceed as follows:

1. Check and adjust the intake valve clearance if required on cylinders 1, 2, and 4 using a feeler gauge between the end of the rocker arm and the valve bridge pallet surface.
2. Check and adjust the exhaust valve clearance if required on cylinders 1, 3, and 5. Refer to

Figure 13–34 which illustrates that the valve clearance can be set by loosening off the locknut and rotating the adjusting screw as necessary. Tighten the locknut to 25+ or −7 N·m (18+ or −5 lb-ft.) after adjustment and doublecheck the lash before moving onto the next valve check.

3. Make an adjustment to the unit injector, on cylinders 3, 5, and 6 by loosening off the adjusting nut and screw shown in Figure 13–35 and rotating the screw CW until contact is made with the unit injector. Turn the screw an additional 180°, or one-half turn CW. Hold the screw and torque the nut to 55+ or −10 N·m (41+ or −7 lb-ft.).

4. When all valves have been set with the No. 1 piston at TDC compression, remove the timing bolt from the flywheel. Rotate the flywheel another full turn (360°) in a CCW direction when using the turning ratchet from the rear of the engine. Reinstall the timing bolt back into the threaded hole in the flywheel. No. 1 piston is now at TDC exhaust.

5. Check and adjust the intake valve lash on cylinders 3, 5, and 6 and for the exhaust valves on cylinders 2, 4, and 6 using the same procedure described earlier.

6. Adjust the unit injectors on cylinders 1, 2, and 4.

7. Remove the timing bolt from the flywheel when all adjustments have been performed as well as the ratchet turning mechanism. Reinstall the flywheel housing cover and bolts.

NOTE: A similar procedure to that described for the 3176 engine can also be used on the 3116 and 3406E engines as well as on the 3406B and C models, except that the B and C do not use electronic unit fuel injectors. The injector follower height on the 3116 engine is set similar to that shown earlier for the Series 50 and 60 DDC engine models; however, a dial gauge is used for this purpose.

ROCKER ARM RATIO

The term *rocker arm ratio* refers to the distance between the centerline of the rocker arm and both ends of the rocker arm assembly. This is usually determined from the midpoint of the rocker arm support shaft, which acts as the pivot point for the transfer of the lever action from an upward motion at the camshaft, to the resultant downward force at the valve or injector end.

If we assume that a rocker arm is 4 in. (101.6 mm) long, and that this distance is split equally either side of the centerline, we have 2 in. (50.8 mm) on both sides of the rocker arm shaft center. This means that a 3/8 in. (9.52 mm) cam lobe lift would cause the valve or injector to move through this same distance, thereby providing a 1:1 rocker arm ratio. If, however, the length of the rocker arm was offset so that the dimension at the camshaft end was twice as long (2 in., or 50.8 mm) as that from the centerline to the valve or injector (1 in., or 25.4 mm) then a 3/8 in. (9.52 mm) cam lift would result in the valves or injector only opening half this distance, or 3/16 in. (4.76 mm). The rocker arm ratio would be 0.5:1, since the mechanical advantage at the valve is cut in half. If we were to reverse these dimensions so that the valve or injector opened twice as far as the cam lift, namely 3/4 in. (19 mm), then we would have a rocker arm ratio of 2:1. The mechanical advantage has been doubled at the valve or injector end from a 1 in. (25.4 mm) long rocker arm at the cam end to 2 in. (50.8 mm) at the opposite end.

Rocker arm ratio is not changed in diesel engines. In some high-performance gasoline engines, along with long duration camshafts, different rocker arm ratios are often used.

PUSHROD INSPECTION

When pushrods are removed from the engine, match-mark them using a metal marker pen so that they can be reinstalled in the same position. This is necessary because the ends of a pushrod take up the wear pattern of its own particular tappet (lifter) at the lower end and also of the ball end of the rocker arm at its top end. In engines that employ pushrods to operate the valves and injectors, the pushrods should be inspected carefully at overhaul for uneven wear or scratches, particularly at the rounded ends as well as at the cup. Figure 13–52 illustrates what to look for during inspection. The pushrods must also be checked for straightness visually or by rolling them on a surface table as shown in Figure 13–53. A bent pushrod will hop as you roll it. For hollow pushtubes such as those used by Cummins in its 14L engines, refer to Figure 13–54. Hold the pushrod horizontally and drop it from a height of about 6 in. (152.4 mm) onto a concrete floor or flat metal surface. If there is a ringing sound, the pushrod can be reused. If a dull thud or nonringing sound is heard, the pushrod contains engine oil and it should be replaced.

ROCKER ARM INSPECTION

Rocker arm assemblies should also be numbered or kept in a sequence that allows reinstallation into the same position because of the wear pattern that takes

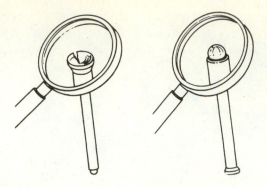

FIGURE 13–52   Close inspection of the ball and cup ends of the pushrod to determine if physical damage exists. (Courtesy of Cummins Engine Company, Inc.)

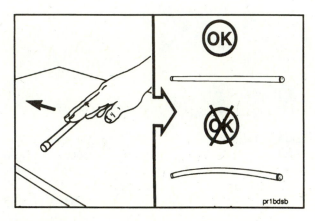

FIGURE 13–53   Rolling a pushrod across a flat surface to determine if it is bent (indicated by a hop). (Courtesy of Cummins Engine Company, Inc.)

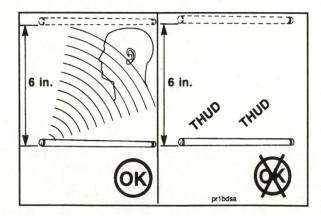

FIGURE 13–54   Dropping a hollow pushrod onto a flat surface to determine if it is reusable (ringing sound). A dull thud indicates that the hollow pushtube is filled with oil and should be replaced. (Courtesy of Cummins Engine Company, Inc.)

place between the pushrod and valve end. The rocker arm assemblies should be closely inspected at overhaul as shown in Figure 13–55 for signs of excessive wear at the pallet surface that contacts either the valve stem or valve bridge (crosshead) on four-valve head engines. The pallet surface can be reground on a special adapter used on a valve face grinding machine. Take careful note, however, that the pallet surface although smooth is *not* flat, but it is ground to form a radius. This is so because when the engine is operating the rocker arm moves through an arc of travel as it rocks back and forth to open the valves or activate the injector follower. If you fail to use a rocker arm adapter when grinding, and it ends up with a flat rather than a surface with a radius, severe stresses can occur, resulting in damage to the end of the valve stem, or the rocker arm can crack through the tip end. In addition, remove only as little material as is required to smooth off the end of the rocker arm. Generally, this is limited to approximately 0.010 in. (0.254 mm).

Check the rocker arm bore for signs of wear by using either a telescoping gauge or inside caliper fitted with a dial indicator as shown in Figure 13–56. Check the bore or the bushing at several positions and 90° apart. Measure the telescoping gauge dimension with an outside micrometer and if it is beyond wear limits, replace the bushing or the rocker arm assembly. Cracks found in a rocker arm indicate that complete replacement is necessary. Inspect the rocker arm shaft for signs of wear visually; also use an outside micrometer to determine its condition. Excessively worn shafts should be replaced. If rocker arm shaft pedestals are used, check them carefully for any signs of cracking, particularly at the hold-down bolt holes. Many hold-down bolts are T-drilled to allow pressurized engine oil to flow to the shaft and rocker assemblies. Carefully inspect the bolts for signs of stretch, damaged threads, or rounded flats on the head. Replace the bolts if any damage is found.

Check the rocker arm valve and injector adjusting screws and retaining nuts. The adjusting screws often have ball ends on them that can be damaged; use the inspection procedure followed for the pushrod ends. If the threads are damaged or the locknut is rounded on the flats, replace as required.

CAM FOLLOWER INSPECTION

Loose rocker levers and the need to frequently reset the valve and injector clearances can be an indication of cam lobe or tappet and/or roller follower wear. Flat tappets such as those illustrated in Figure 13–57 can be inspected for socket wear, stem and face wear, and signs of cracks or other visible damage. Part A in

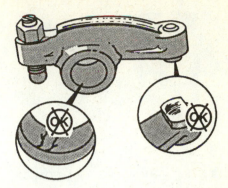

FIGURE 13–55 *Close inspection of the rocker arm assembly to check for possible cracks and severe wear at the pallet end. (Courtesy of Cummins Engine Company, Inc.)*

FIGURE 13–56 *Using an inside caliper attached to a dial gauge to determine the bore size of the rocker arm bushing. (Courtesy of Cummins Engine Company, Inc.)*

the diagram illustrates normal wear; B and C show conditions of abnormal wear, and the tappet should be replaced. Use an outside micrometer to measure the tappet stem diameter and a small telescoping gauge to check the tappet bore in the engine block. Always clean the tappet bore in the block with a good stiff-bristle brush on a drill motor prior to measuring it for wear.

Roller-type cam followers should be inspected for support pin wear, spalling, wear or damage to the roller surface, and the inside and outside diameter of the roller as well as the outside diameter of the cam follower body (similar to those used by Detroit Diesel in its 53, 71, and 92 series engines and illustrated in Figure 13–36) and the inside bore diameter for the follower body in the cylinder head or engine block on some makes of engines. Roller side-to-side clearance between the roller and its cam follower leg should also be checked and compared to specs. Check the free and

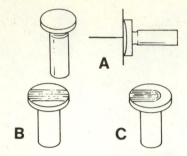

FIGURE 13–57 Checking a flat tappet for socket wear, stem and face wear, and signs of cracks or physical damage. (Courtesy of Cummins Engine Company, Inc.)

compressed length of the cam follower spring and compare to specs. Also check the spring for signs of an off-square condition, which is similar to that for a valve spring. Shiny spots on the spring coils indicate rubbing action with the bore area. Visually inspect all other component parts used with the follower assembly.

ENGINE COMPRESSION BRAKES

Many attempts were made over the years to design an engine brake on a diesel engine that would use high compression air as some form of braking device. Basically, the idea was to convert the engine into an air compressor when power was not required but braking was. The person who finally succeeded in doing this was Clessie M. Cummins, founder of the Cummins Engine Company in the United States. In his early youth, he experienced brake fade while driving a fully laden vehicle down a hill and vowed to invent some form of auxiliary engine braking for diesel engines.

In its simplest form, the Jacobs engine brake opens the cylinder exhaust valves just before top dead center; the result is a net loss of power. In other words, the energy required to compress the air charge in the cylinder is released through the exhaust manifold so that no energy is returned to the piston. In effect, the engine becomes an *air compressor*.

The first brake of this type was installed in the United States in 1959. Some minor problems were evident, however, and the brake was redesigned and reappeared in 1961. Since that time it has been tremendously successful and used extensively on diesel engines in North America, and it is becoming more popular in other areas of the world.

The brake's name comes from the fact that it is manufactured by the Jacobs Manufacturing Company, which is well known for its production of drill and lathe chucks and so on, and is now a part of the

Chicago Pneumatic Tool Company. The *Jake brake,* as it is commonly known, is widely used on the following diesel engines: Caterpillar, Cummins, Detroit Diesel, and Mack.

In addition to the well known Jake brake, Cummins also offers a compression brake commonly called the C brake. This brake is basically a Jake brake with minor design and operational changes. Mack offers an engine compression brake on its diesel engines known as a *Dynatard* model; although its design is somewhat different from that of the Jake, it operates in a similar fashion. Pacific Diesel Brake, another manufacturer, offers an engine compression brake known as the PACBRAKE for Cat, Cummins, Detroit Diesel, and Mack engines. Other diesel engine OEMs who offer compression brakes with operational characteristics similar to a Jake brake include Volvo, Scania, and Mercedes-Benz.

Brake Controls Schematic

The controls used with the Jake brake vary between a mechanically governed and an electronically controlled engine. Figure 13–58 is a schematic of a Jake brake system for a mechanical non-Celect-equipped N14 Cummins engine. Note these features:

- A dash-controlled switch. This is an ON/OFF switch manually activated by the truck driver.
- A clutch switch on a truck equipped with a standard transmission. When the clutch is engaged (foot of the pedal), the switch contacts are closed, thereby completing the circuit.
- A fuel pump switch that is located alongside the PT fuel pump throttle lever. Note that on different model OEM engines, this switch is generally located so that it can be opened and closed by throttle pedal linkage movement.
- A three-position dash-mounted switch to allow the driver to select either two-, four-, or six-cylinder braking on a six-cylinder engine.

For the Jake electrical circuit to function, all of these switches must be ON. Therefore, to complete the circuit to the engine brake solenoids located under the valve rocker covers, the following conditions must be met:

- Dash control switch ON.
- Throttle pedal in the idle position.
- Clutch pedal released (up) to engage the clutch.
- Three-position switch in any position—1, 2, or 3.

In an electronically controlled engine, the Jake brake signal is normally arranged to interface with and receive its control signals from the ECM. Figure

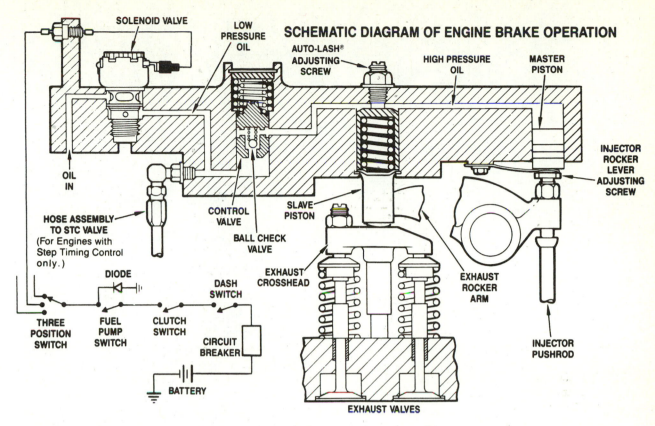

FIGURE 13–58 *Operational schematic of a Jake brake for use on a four-stroke-cycle mechanically governed diesel engine. (Courtesy of Jacobs Manufacturing, Chicago Pneumatic Tool Co.)*

13–59 illustrates the Jake brake schematic for a model 3406E Cat heavy-duty truck engine. Note that the main difference between this system and that shown in Figure 13–58 for the mechanical engine is that the *solenoid valve* is controlled from the lead wire (2), which is connected to the ECM brake logic controller.

Brake Operation

The brake consists of electrically operated solenoid valves mounted above each engine cylinder as illustrated for both the mechanical and electronically controlled engine models (see Figures 13–58 and 13–59). To achieve engine *compression braking,* the cylinder exhaust valves are opened by a *slave piston* located directly above the valve bridge or exhaust valve crosshead, or the rocker arm in the case of the 3406E engine model. Opening of the exhaust valves near the top of the normal engine compression stroke releases the high-pressure air to the exhaust manifold and into the atmosphere. At the same time, fuel to the injector is cut off. The result is no return of energy to the engine piston on the power stroke; therefore, a net energy loss

occurs, which is taken from the rear wheels of a truck to provide the braking action, since the power expended to compress the cylinder air is not returned to the engine crankshaft.

Let's describe the complete operation of the Jake brake for the system illustrated in Figure 13–59—the 3406E electronically controlled electronic unit injector engine. On this engine only the valves and valve mechanism for the exhaust side of the cylinders are used; only one of the two exhaust valves for each cylinder is used during engine braking. The Jake controls allows one, two, or three brake housings to be activated, resulting in two-, four-, or six-cylinder progressive braking.

Pressurized engine oil is fed from the rocker arm shaft supports to the solenoid valve (1) when it is activated by a signal from the ECM Jake logic. The solenoid valve movement closes the oil drain passage back to the crankcase and allows pressurized engine oil into the oil passage (15) where it flows to the control valve (4) and pushes it up in its chamber against the force of the return spring (3). A groove in the

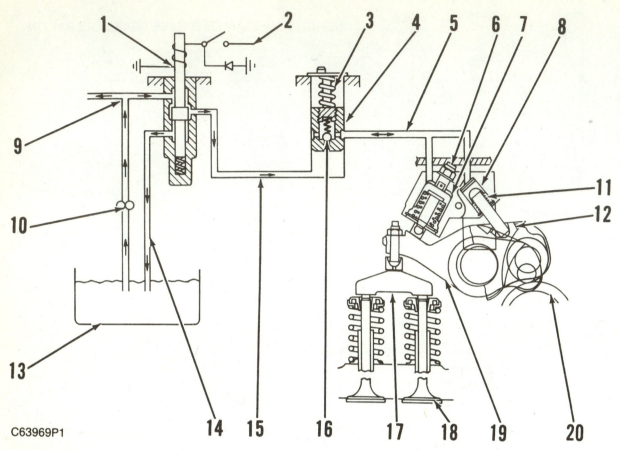

C63969P1

FIGURE 13–59 *Operational schematic of a Jake brake for use with a 3406E Cat electronically controlled EUI heavy-duty high-speed truck engine. 1 = solenoid valve; 2 = lead wire (from Jake brake to solenoid valve; 3 = spring; 4 = control valve; 5 = high-pressure oil passage; 6 = slave piston adjustment screw; 7 = slave piston; 8 = master piston; 9 = rocker arm shaft oil passage; 10 = engine oil pump; 11 = spring; 12 = injector rocker arm; 13 = engine oil pan; 14 = oil drain passage; 15 = low-pressure oil passage; 16 = ball check valve; 17 = exhaust valve bridge; 18 = exhaust valve; 19 = exhaust valve rocker arm; 20 = camshaft. (Courtesy of Caterpillar Inc.)*

valve (4) in alignment with the high-pressure oil passage (5) directs oil to the slave piston (7) and the master piston (8). The small ball check valve (16) is forced open, which allows the high-pressure oil passage (5) and the chambers behind both the slave and master piston assemblies to be filled. The resultant oil pressure forces the master piston downward until it comes into contact with the cylinder injector rocker arm (12). During the cylinder compression stroke, camshaft lift of the injector rocker arm pushes the master piston (8) upward to increase the pressure of the trapped oil and close the small ball check valve (16). Continued movement of the master piston by camshaft rotation results in the trapped engine oil in passage (5) forcing the slave piston (7) down against

the exhaust rocker arm (19) of the same cylinder with sufficient force to open the exhaust valve(s) on that specific cylinder just before the piston reaches TDC. This action requires approximately one-fifth of a second to operate.

The greatest degree of braking occurs when the vehicle is running down a hill on a closed throttle; the road wheels are the driving member allowing the engine to run at its rated speed (for example, 2100 rpm). The percentage of braking available depends on the make of engine and the model of engine compression brake. As an example, a Cat 3406E rated at 460 hp (343 kW) obtains approximately 400+ braking horsepower when running at its rated speed. Individual cylinder compression braking occurs in the firing order sequence of the engine. Some engine models feature a slave piston for each exhaust valve to improve response and decrease the load applied back to the camshaft during braking.

When the solenoid valve (1) is deenergized, the engine oil supply passage is closed by the internal spring pushing the valve upward to uncover the drain passage (14) to the sump. This permits the oil below the control valve (4) to vent to drain, and the spring (3) pushes the valve to the bottom of its bore. High-pressure oil in the passage (5) drains into the chamber above the control valve piston (4) where the oil vents to the atmosphere from the chamber outside of the Jake brake housing located under the valve rocker cover. The spring (11) pushes the master piston (3) to a released position away from the injector rocker arm (12). This release action takes approximately one-tenth of a second.

Jake Brake Adjustment

The clearance of the slave piston to the rocker arm, (or to the valve bridge, or crosshead, on some engines) must be adjusted to ensure that the Jake brake operates correctly. Figure 13–60 shows the Jake brake adjusting arrangement for the 3406E engine. To correctly adjust the slave piston clearance, follow these steps:

1. Manually rotate the engine over to place No. 1 piston at TDC on its compression stroke (intake and exhaust valves fully closed) by inserting the timing bolt into the flywheel. (Refer to Figure 13–51.)
2. Insert a 0.69 mm (0.027 in.) feeler gauge between the slave piston (2) and rocker arm (3).
3. Loosen the slave piston adjusting screw locknut and rotate the adjustment screw (1) clockwise until the feeler gauge drag is correct. Tighten the locknut to 26 lb-ft (35 N·m) and recheck the drag. Readjust if necessary.
4. Repeat steps 2 and 3 for cylinders 3 and 5.
5. Rotate the engine over manually to place No. 6 piston at TDC on its compression stroke (place timing bolt in the flywheel).
6. Adjust the clearance of the slave piston to the rocker arm for cylinders 2, 4, and 6. Remove the flywheel timing bolt.

Figure 13–61 illustrates the engine brake housing components for a Series 60 Detroit Diesel engine using a Model 760 Jake brake assembly. To adjust the slave piston clearance, refer to Figure 13–47 which shows the *timing circle chart* used to set the valves and injectors on the Series 60 engine. Follow these steps to set the slave piston clearance for the Jake brake:

FIGURE 13–60 *Jake brake adjustment screw location for a 3406E Cat engine model. (Courtesy of Caterpillar Inc.)*

1. Refer to Figure 13–61 and back out the leveling screw in the slave piston crosshead until the end of the screw is beneath the surface of the crosshead.
2. Refer to Figure 13–62 and insert a 0.020 in. (0.50 mm) feeler gauge between the solid side of the slave piston opposite the leveling screw and the exhaust valve rocker arm adjusting screw.
3. Loosen the slave piston adjusting screw locknut on the top of the brake housing as shown in Figure 13–63. Then slowly rotate this screw CW or CCW until a light drag is felt on the 0.020 in. (0.50 mm) feeler gauge.
4. Firmly hold the adjusting screw in this position and tighten the locknut to 25 lb-ft (35 N·m).
5. Now go back to the leveling screw in the Jake crosshead that was initially loosened off in step 1. Using a 0.020 in. (0.50 mm) feeler gauge between the leveling screw and the rocker arm adjusting screw, rotate the leveling screw clockwise until a light drag is apparent on the feeler gauge (see Figure 13–64.)
6. Firmly hold the leveling screw while torquing the locknut to a value of 25 lb-ft (35 N·m).
7. Repeat this procedure for all cylinders.

Jake Brake Options

On electronically controlled truck diesel engines, the engine brake can provide engine brake capability when the vehicle is in cruise control. For example, if a vehicle is in cruise control mode and running down a hill while the engine brake is ON, the ECM will control the amount of engine braking with respect to the cruise

EXPLODED VIEW
Model 760 Housing Assembly

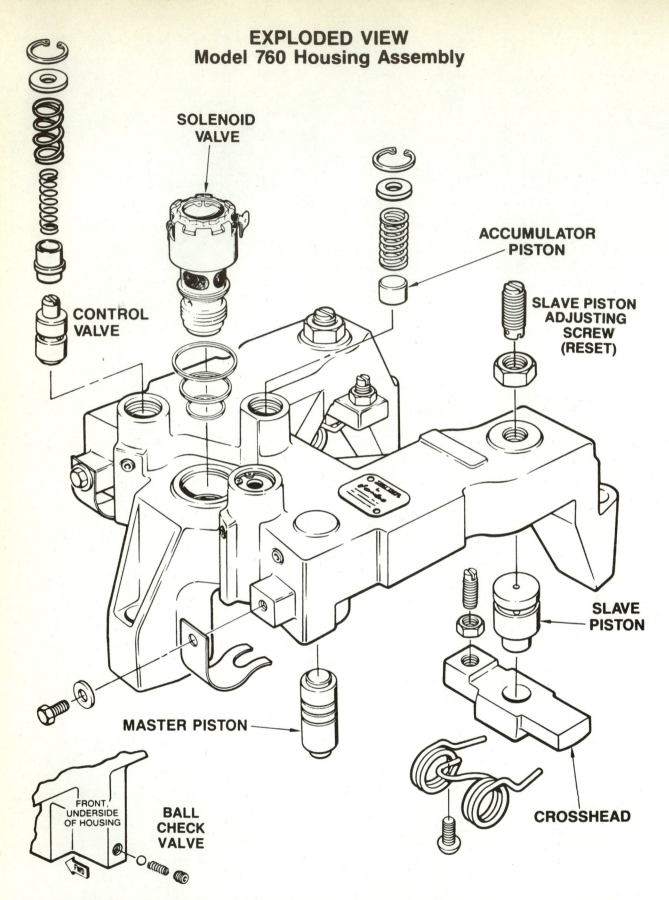

SOLENOID
VALVE

ACCUMULATOR
PISTON

SLAVE PISTON
ADJUSTING
SCREW
(RESET)

CONTROL
VALVE

SLAVE
PISTON

MASTER PISTON

CROSSHEAD

FRONT,
UNDERSIDE
OF HOUSING

BALL
CHECK
VALVE

FWD

FIGURE 13-61 Exploded view of the Jake brake components for a model 760 unit used on Detroit Diesel Series 60 electronically controlled engine. (Courtesy of Jacobs Manufacturing, Chicago Pneumatic Tool Co.)

FIGURE 13–62 Insertion location of a 0.020 in. (0.5 mm) feeler gauge between the solid side of the slave piston and exhaust rocker arm adjusting screw for a DDC Series 60 engine. (Courtesy of Jacobs Manufacturing, Chicago Pneumatic Tool Co.)

FIGURE 13–64 Adjustment procedure on a Series 60 engine model using a 0.020 in. (0.5 mm) feeler gauge between the slave piston leveling screw and the rocker arm adjusting screw. (Courtesy of Jacobs Manufacturing, Chicago Pneumatic Tool Co.)

0FIGURE 13–63 Rotation of Jake slave piston adjusting screw CW until a light drag is felt on the feeler gauge. (Courtesy of Jacobs Manufacturing, Chicago Pneumatic Tool Co.)

control set speed. The level of engine brake (low, medium, high) selected with the dash switches will be the maximum amount of engine braking that the ECM allows. If the driver activates the ON/OFF switch, or air brake pedal or depresses the clutch during this automatic engine brake control mode, cruise control is disabled. The Jake brake selection switch (position 1, 2, or 3) outputs are connected to the digital input ports of the engine ECM. On trucks equipped with automatic transmissions featuring a hydraulic transmission retarder, a digital output is switched to battery ground whenever the throttle is in the 0% position and cruise control is inactive. This signal in conjunction with a relay may be used to control the transmission hydraulic retarder.

In addition, electronically controlled diesel engines may be equipped with a *deceleration light* option to warn those behind that the vehicle is slowing down. A digital output is switched to ground whenever the throttle is closed (0%) and the cruise control is inactive. This digital output from the ECM can be used to drive a deceleration light or a small relay which drives the deceleration lights. Similarly, an engine brake *active* light can be wired into the system to illuminate on the dash whenever the engine brake is active. A special feature now used on many electronically controlled diesel engines is the *dynamic engine brake* option. It turns on the engine cooling fan when the engine brake level is in the high mode. This creates about 40 hp (30 kW) of additional engine braking power.

SELF-TEST QUESTIONS

1. Technician A says that camshafts on high-speed heavy-duty diesel engines are generally belt or chain driven. Technician B says that camshafts are gear driven on high-speed heavy-duty diesel engines. Who is correct?

2. Technician A says that the camshaft on electronically controlled unit injector diesel engines is only required to operate the intake and exhaust valves, since the injector is controlled from the ECM. Technician B disagrees, stating that the camshaft is needed to operate the injector plunger to create the high pressures required for injection. Which technician is correct?

3. Technician A says that the highest point on the camshaft is generally referred to as the *nose*; technician B says that it is called the *base circle*. Who is right?

4. True or False: A camshaft that is located within the engine block rather than in the cylinder head is known as an *overhead camshaft*.

5. List four high-speed heavy-duty diesel engines that employ an overhead camshaft design.

6. Which one of the four engines listed in question 5 employs a silicon nitride cam follower roller in its injector rocker arm assembly?

7. On a seperate sheet of paper, list six advantages of using an overhead camshaft versus an in-block type.

8. Technician A says that the camshaft on a four-stroke-cycle engine is driven at half the speed of the crankshaft, while on a two-cycle engine it is driven at the same speed. Technician B disagrees, stating that the camshaft on the two-cycle must turn twice crankshaft speed since there is a power stroke every crankshaft revolution. Who is correct?

9. True or False: Many larger diesel engines employ segmented, or bolted together, camshaft sections.

10. Technician A says that on two-stroke-cycle DDC 71 and 92 engine models, only one camshaft is used to operate the valves and injectors, similar to that commonly found on V8 gasoline engines. Technician B disagrees, saying that each cylinder bank has its own camshaft assembly. Who is right here?

11. Technician A says that in addition to aligning the timing marks between the camshaft and idler or crankshaft gear, several major engine manufacturers use offset camshaft gear keys to allow specific camshaft timing arrangements. Technician B says that all camshaft gear keys are straight and that any camshaft timing advancement must be made by the engagement of the cam and crank gear timing marks. Who is correct?

12. What make and model of high-speed heavy-duty diesel engine can have its camshaft timing altered by adding or removing cam follower box gaskets?

13. In Question 12, technician A says that adding gaskets retards the camshaft timing, whereas removing gaskets advances the timing. Technician B says that A has this backwards; instead, adding gaskets advances timing, and removing gaskets retards the timing. Which technician is correct?

14. True or False: To alter the camshaft timing on a Cummins L10 or M11, you can add or remove cam follower box gaskets.

15. Technician A states that to check the camshaft timing on a Cummins N14, L10, M11, or K series engine you need to remove an injector and set up two dial indicator gauges so that both the piston travel and the injector pushrod travel can be monitored. Not so says technician B; you only have to use one dial gauge to check the piston travel and compare its position with the marks on the accessory drive pulley at the front of the engine. Which technician knows the material best?

16. Technician A says there are no flywheel timing marks on two-cycle DDC engine models for timing reference purposes. Technician B says all engines need flywheel and/or pulley marks to allow for engine timing checks. Which technician knows the products better?

17. True or False: Most Caterpillar engines are equipped with a flywheel timing bolt that can be inserted to lock the engine at TDC for the No. 1 cylinder.

18. Technician A says that when an in-block camshaft lobe is suspected of being worn, you can check it by placing a dial indicator gauge on top of the valve spring retainer and setting the rocker arm for zero lash (or on the injector follower), rotating the engine over, and comparing the cam lift to specs. Technician B says that you need to remove the camshaft from the block to check its worn lobe condition. Who is correct?

19. Technician A says that to effectively clean a camshaft after removal, you should soak it in a hot tank of caustic solution. Technician B says that you should clean it with either diesel fuel or solvent and dry it with compressed air and lint-free rags. Who is correct?

20. Technician A says to quickly check a removed camshaft for individual lobe lift, place it between two vee blocks and employ a dial indicator. Technician B says place it into a metal lathe self-centering chuck and use a dial gauge. Are both technicians correct in their statements?

21. Technician A says that to replace the camshaft bushings on an in-block design, the engine needs to be completely disassembled. Technician B says that once the engine gear train or front cover has been removed, you can pull the camshaft and employ an expandable bearing (bushing) puller to replace them. Which technician is correct?

22. True or False: When replacing camshaft bushings, you can install them in any position without aligning locating notches.

23. Technician A says that camshaft end float must be checked in a manner similar to that used for a crankshaft. Technician B says that this isn't necessary, since the camshaft end play is controlled by the gear lash that exists between the various gears in mesh. Which technician is correct?

24. Technician A says that inline model two-stroke DDC engine models has a balance shaft driven from the oil pump drive gear. Technician B disagrees, saying that the balance shaft is located on the side of the block opposite the camshaft. Who is correct?

25. True or False: DDC two-cycle engines employ balance weights within the cam and balance shaft gears to produce a force that is equal and opposite to that developed by the uneven firing impulses of the pistons.

26. True or False: The valve bridge (crosshead, yoke) is designed to allow two valves to be opened at the same time.

27. Technician A says that valve bridges require occasional adjustment. Technician B disagrees, stating that no adjustment is provided or required. Which technician is correct?

28. Which make of engine uses VS (valve set) timing marks located on the accessory drive pulley at the front of the engine and the letters A, B, and C?

29. Technician A says that if the rocker arm pallet (comes in contact with the valve stem or bridge) is worn, you can regrind the surface on a valve grinding machine. Technician B says that this would weaken the rocker arm and should not be attempted. Which technician is correct?

30. True or False: Cracks in rocker arms require replacement of the assembly.

31. Technician A says that many rocker arm pedestal hold-down bolts are T-drilled to carry pressurized lube oil to the rocker arm shaft. Technician B says that this would weaken the bolt and that splash lubrication is more common. Which technician is correct?

32. Make a list of the items you would check on a flat or mushroom-type lifter (follower) at overhaul?

33. Make a list of the items you would inspect and check on a roller-type cam follower at overhaul?

34. List two methods for determining if a pushrod is bent.

35. Technician A says that when timing the injector on a two-stroke-cycle DDC engine, the exhaust valves should be fully closed. Technician B says that the exhaust valves should be fully open. Which technician is correct?

36. Technician A says that to time the injector on both non-DDEC- and DDEC-equipped engines, you have to set the height between the injector body and the top of the injector follower to a given dimension, which is listed on the engine decal attached to the rocker cover. Technician B says that you only have to do this setting on non-DDEC engine models, since the DDEC injectors are electronically controlled. Who knows what they are talking about?

37. Technician A says that when setting the injectors on a DDC Series 50 or 60 four-stroke-cycle engine, the valves and injectors cannot be set at the same time on the same cylinder. Technician B says that the injector can only be set when both the intake and exhaust valves are on the rock, that is, when the intake valve(s) is opening and the exhaust valve(s) is closing. Who is right?

38. Technician A says that a Jacobs engine brake is an exhaust-type brake device. Technician B says that it is an engine compression brake that converts a power producing engine into an air compressor. Who is correct here?

39. Technician A says that Clessie M. Cummins, founder of the Cummins Engine Company, perfected the Jacobs engine brake operation. Technician B says that Robert Bosch was the individual who did this. Who is correct?

40. True or False: The Jacobs Manufacturing Company is now a part of the Cummins Engine Company.

41. Technician A says that the Jacobs engine brake has been used in heavy-duty truck diesel engines since 1927. Technician B says the brake was fully perfected in the early 1960s. Who is right?

42. What are the three main switches that are used to control the operation of a Jake brake?

43. Technician A says that for the Jake brake to operate, the clutch and throttle pedals must both be in the upward position. Technician B disagrees, saying that only the throttle pedal has to be in the idle position. Who is correct?

44. Technician A says that on a six-cylinder engine equipped with a Jake brake, two, four, or six cylinders can be activated for a difference in braking action. Technician B says that all six cylinders are engaged any time that the Jake brake is applied. Who is correct?

45. Technician A says that once the Jake brake is activated, it will come on in about 2 seconds. Technician B says that it will act much faster, coming on in about one-fifth of a second. Who is correct?

46. Technician A says that the Jake brake relies on electricity for movement of both the slave and master pistons. Technician B disagrees saying that trapped oil pressure causes the master and slave pistons to function. Who is right?

47. Technician A says that the cylinder exhaust valves are opened just after TDC on the power stroke when the Jake brake is ON. Technician B says that the exhaust valves are opened just before TDC on the compression stroke. Who is right?

48. Technician A says that the individual Jake brake cylinder master piston assemblies are normally pushrod operated. Technician B says that they are electrically energized. Which technician understands the system operation best?

49. Technician A says that the slave piston operates an exhaust valve crosshead (bridge) or rocker arm. Technician B says that it is the master piston that actually performs this task. Which technician is correct?

50. Technician A says that the major Jake brake adjustment is the master piston clearance. Technician B says that it is the slave piston that must be adjusted for proper clearance between the valve crosshead (bridge) or rocker arm. Who is correct?

51. Technician A says that when using a test light to check the operation of the clutch or throttle pedal microswitches, the test light should not illuminate when the pedals are in their released position with the Jake control switch ON. Technician B says that the test light should illuminate under this condition. Which technician is correct?

52. Technician A says that the Jake brake electric solenoids can be removed and their O-ring seals replaced. Technician B says that these solenoids are sealed and cannot be repaired. Which technician is correct?

14 Cylinder Head and Valves

OVERVIEW

The cylinder head and valves enclose the combustion chambers of the engine and allow fresh air and exhaust gases to enter and leave the engine smoothly. In this chapter, we discuss various types of cylinder heads and designs—two-valve and four-valve types. The cylinder head also contains fuel inlet and outlet passages for the injector assemblies and is sealed to the cylinder block deck by a special gasket. Some cylinder heads cover all cylinders, whereas others enclose one, two, or three cylinders based on engine design and configuration.

TOPICS

- Purpose and functions
- Cylinder head materials
- Design and construction
- Intake and exhaust valves
- Valve construction
- Valve rotators
- Cylinder head removal
- Disassembly and descaling of the cylinder head
- Detection of cracks
- Fire deck flatness check
- Cylinder head machining
- Valve guide inspection
- Valve seat inserts
- Valve and seat inspection
- Valve grinding
- Valve seat insert grinding
- Valve springs
- Cylinder head gaskets
- Cylinder head installation
- Self-test questions

358

PURPOSE AND FUNCTIONS

The purpose of the cylinder head assembly illustrated in Figure 14–1 is to seal the top of the cylinders and to form the combustion chamber between the underside of the head and the bowl of the piston crown. Combustion gas pressures are effectively sealed between the cylinder head and block by the use of a suitably designed and constructed gasket. A number of bolts are employed to retain and clamp the head to the cylinder block upper deck. In addition, the cylinder head has a number of other major functions:

- Retain the intake and exhaust valves, springs, and porting
- Retain the valve seat inserts and guides
- Retain the fuel injectors and their sleeves (either copper or stainless steel)
- Provide the foundation for the overhead camshaft assembly
- Provide a foundation for the valve operating mechanism (rocker arms and followers) for both overhead and in-block camshaft arrangements
- Contain oil, air, fuel, exhaust and coolant passages

Although the cylinder head may seem to be a rather insignificant component in the overall performance of the engine, it plays a role in the five key elements in performance development of any heavy-duty diesel engine: fuel consumption, ratings, exhaust emissions, drivability, and white smoke. In recent years, engine manufacturers have made a number of design changes to pistons and fuel injectors to meet the stringent EPA exhaust emissions standards of the U.S. EPA. Other redesigned features include the cylinder head with the incorporation of an overhead camshaft, intake

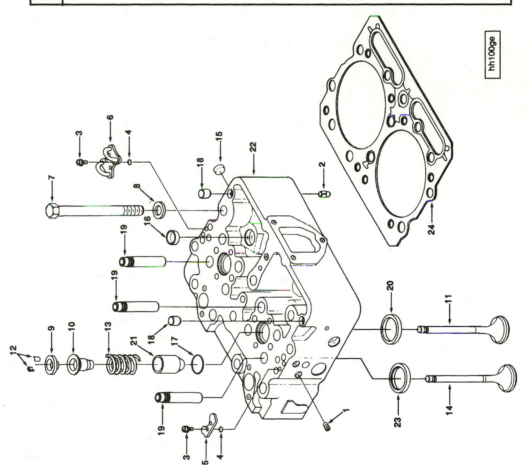

Ref No.	Part Name	Req
	CYLINDER HEAD OPTION HH1003	
1	Pipe, Plug	10
2	Pin, Groove	6
3	Screw, Filh Springtite	12
4	Seal, O-ring	12
5	Plate, Cover	2
6	Connection, Fuel Crossover	2
7	Screw, Hexagon Head Cap	36
8	Washer, Plain	36
8	Assb, Cylinder Head (TLA)	3
9	Retainer, Valve Spring	8
10	Seal, Valve Stem	8
10	Kit, Intake Valve	4
11	Valve, Intake	1
12	Collet, Half Valve	2
13	Spring, Valve	8
13	Kit, Exhaust Valve	4
14	Valve, Exhaust	1
12	Collet, Half Valve	2
15	Plug, Expansion	3
16	Plug, Expansion	8
17	Seal, O-ring	2
18	Dowel, Ring	2
19	Guide, Valve Stem Intake	8
20	Insert, Valve Exhaust	4
21	Sleeve, Injector	2
22	Head, Cylinder	1
23	Insert, Valve Intake	4
24	Gasket, Cylinder Head	3

FIGURE 14–1 Exploded view of the cylinder head and its components for a six-cylinder N14 Cummins engine model. One head covers two cylinders each. (Courtesy of Cummins Engine Company, Inc.)

and exhaust valve placement and materials, tuned intake and exhaust valve air and gas flow porting, placement of electronic unit injectors within the head, and use of stronger materials such as a silicon nitride injector rocker arm follower roller to allow operation at very high 28,000 psi (193,060 kPa) injection pressures. Four valve heads with crossflow air design concepts and closely designed and tuned intake and exhaust manifolds using stainless steel exhaust port inserts have come into vogue for engines of the 1990s.

One of the major functions of the cylinder head is to retain both the intake and exhaust valves and through the valve rocker arm mechanism, opens and closes both valves to allow airflow from the turbocharger to enter the cylinder and, at the end of the power stroke, to allow the exhaust gases to exit the cylinder, thereby giving up heat energy to drive the turbocharger. Tuned intake and exhaust manifolds, often with helical-shaped or semiquiescent intake ports and newly configured exhaust ports, are designed to improve efficiency by as much as 30%. The intake ports produce a swirl to the incoming air within the cylinder to achieve good mixing of air and fuel as well as to impart maximum energy from the exhaust gases being directed into the turbocharger. The result is a reduction in peak cylinder pressures and combustion face temperatures, both of which can help extend durability and valve and head life.

CYLINDER HEAD MATERIALS

Newer high-speed heavy-duty diesel engines are developing peak cylinder pressures in the range of 2350 psi (16,203 kPa), with peak temperatures often approaching 3500° to 4000°F (1927° to 2204°C). These operating conditions place tremendous stress on any cylinder head casting. As a rule, therefore, materials used for the head include chromium-molybdenum alloy gray cast iron, but for less highly stressed smaller engines, a chrome alloy is usually sufficient. Material strengths for head castings are generally in the range of 300 MPa. Some smaller light-duty diesel engines employ cast aluminum alloy heads.

DESIGN AND CONSTRUCTION

The cylinder head design used on diesel engines can vary considerably based on the bore, stroke, speed, and horsepower requirements of the engine. In addition, the engine design and application have a bearing on whether a single-, two-, three-, or one-piece multicylinder head concept is used. Figure 14–1 illustrates a Cummins N14 one-piece cylinder head assembly that covers two cylinders of a six-cylinder inline four-stroke-

cycle high-speed truck engine configuration. This particular cylinder head employs two intake and two exhaust valves for each cylinder, a design commonly referred to as a *four-valve head*. Figure 14–2 illustrates a single-cylinder round *pot-head* containing four exhaust valves that is used to seal one individual cylinder on a high-speed high-horsepower two-stroke-cycle Detroit Diesel 149 series engine. Current heavy-duty high-speed electronically controlled four-stroke-cycle truck diesel engines such as the overhead cam Volvo D12A, the Isuzu 12L-6WA1TC, the 3406E Caterpillar, and the Detroit Diesel Series 50 and 60 models all employ one-piece cylinder heads, as does the Caterpillar 3176 EUI model and the Cummins B, C, and L10/M11 models. Detroit Diesel has also retained one-piece heads on its DDEC-equipped two-stroke 71 and 92 series engines. Some smaller-bore engines such as auxiliary diesels used in sailboats and many air-cooled Deutz diesels employ one head for each cylinder. One head per cylinder is also common in large-displacement engines in the high-speed field; Cummins on its K models, Detroit Diesel on its 149 series engines, and Caterpillar on its 3500 and 3600 engines are good examples. You will also find the one-head-per-cylinder design concept used in very-large-bore medium- and slow-speed diesel engines from Grande Motori Trieste, Mitsubishi, Sulzer Bros., and so on, which are widely used in deep-sea marine applications such as oil tankers, freighters, and passenger cruise ships. Other engines such as those used by Cummins and Mack have used one cylinder head covering two cylinders for many years on some vee models.

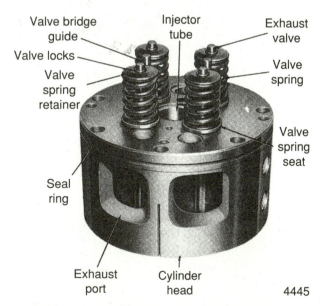

FIGURE 14–2 *Components of a single-cylinder round pot-type cylinder head for a DDC 149 series two-stroke-cycle engine. (Courtesy of Detroit Diesel Corporation.)*

Major engine manufacturers in North America such as Caterpillar, Cummins, Detroit Diesel, and Mack have employed four-valve heads for many years. In contrast, European and Japanese diesel engine manufacturers have only recently adopted this superior principle along with overhead camshafts in their designs. Most cylinder heads in use today (two- or four-valve design) employ what is known as a *crossflow* design concept, with the intake manifold on one side and the exhaust manifold on the other. Figure 14–3 illustrates a four-valve head design with the air entering the cylinder head from one side and the exhaust gases leaving on the opposite side. This design provides for a smoother and more efficient air and exhaust flow into and out of the cylinder head, and it also removes the high heat radiation to the intake manifold that can occur from the exhaust manifold when the manifolds are mounted on the same side. This heat radiation tends to reduce the denseness of the air charge, thereby affecting engine performance, fuel economy, exhaust emissions, and the service life of components such as the valves and pistons.

For many years, an in-block camshaft arrangement has been used in the majority of diesel engines. This design requires that a tappet, or lifter, be employed in conjunction with a pushrod to open the valves (similar to that shown in Figure 13–9). Because of the drive

toward cleaner burning engines with improved fuel economy and performance, a swing toward overhead camshaft engines contained within the cylinder head is now underway. Figure 14–4 illustrates the arrangement of the overhead camshaft, four-valve head design used by DDC on its Series 50 and 60 heavy-duty engines. This same concept is also used in the Volvo D12A, the Isuzu 12L-6WA1TC, and the Caterpillar 3406E engine models.

High-speed heavy-duty engine models today favor both an overhead camshaft and four-valve head design. Two intake and two exhaust valves are common on four-stroke-cycle models, and four exhaust valves per cylinder are common on two-stroke cycle engines. Use of four valves per cylinder has the advantage of reducing the inertia forces induced when the intake and exhaust valves open and close because two of the valves are smaller and lighter. For example, in a two-valve head with one intake and one exhaust valve per cylinder the single larger valve is heavier and does not create as effective a swirl or turbulence to the air entering or leaving the cylinder. In addition, if a single intake valve had a head diameter of 2.125 in. (53.97 mm), it would create an airflow area in square inches of 3.554 in. (90.27 mm). Using two smaller intake valves with a head diameter of 1.625 in. (41.27mm) would provide an airflow area equivalent to 4.146 in. (105.3 mm). As you can readily appreciate in this simple example, the two smaller intake valves provide a freer breathing engine. Similarly, two exhaust valves in place of one larger unit can also provide a larger flow area from which the exhaust gases can escape.

The use of four-valve heads with the crossflow design concept improves engine volumetric efficiency, or ability to breathe more easily. This results in a better charge of air to the cylinders as well as allowing smoother flow out of the exhaust system. The valve placement in a crossflow head design employing an overhead camshaft (Figure 14–3) used by DDC on its Series 50 and 60 four-stroke models is known as a *parallel port configuration* where the four valves are located 90° from their position on traditional engines. This design allows for very short, unobstructed intake and exhaust ports for more efficient airflow, lower pumping losses, and reduced heat transfer; thus the engine is able to breathe more freely and to run cooler under load. With all intake valves on one side of the head and all exhaust valves on the other side, the valve and port design results in a simpler head casting and lower fire deck thermal stresses between the valves. This one-piece overhead cam cylinder head design minimizes the number of parts, thereby enabling more uniform bolt loading. Eight cylinder head bolts around each cylinder are almost equally spaced to provide uniform loading on the head gasket and cylinder liner flange.

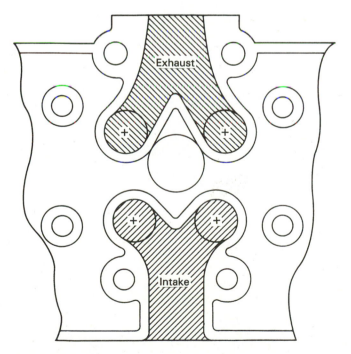

FIGURE 14–3 *Unique design of the crossflow intake and exhaust valve arrangement used on Detroit Diesel Series 50 and 60 engines. (Courtesy of Detroit Diesel Corporation.)*

FIGURE 14–4 Example of the arrangement of the valve operating mechanism used on the Series 60 DDC engine model with an overhead camshaft design. (Courtesy of Detroit Diesel Corporation.)

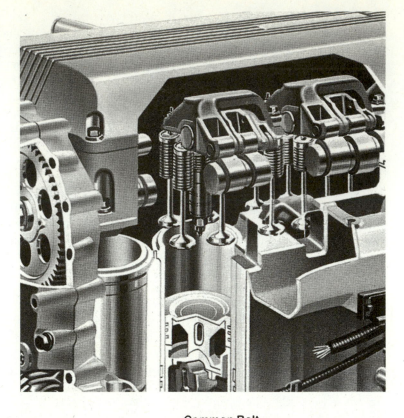

FIGURE 14–5 "Siamesed" (joined together) intake and exhaust valve airflow arrangement used on the 3176 model EUI Cat engine. (Courtesy of Caterpillar Inc.)

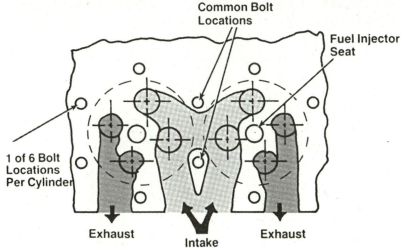

The retaining force, therefore, is approximately 1 million lb (453,600 kg) between the head and cylinder block. This design concept results in acceptable mechanical and thermal stresses.

A somewhat similar crossflow overhead camshaft design is used by Caterpillar in its 3406E engine. The intake and exhaust systems employ a series flow arrangement skewed 6° to provide space on the top deck for the electronic unit injector body and valve springs. The exhaust port within the head contains a stainless steel sleeve within the last 2.3 in. (60 mm) to form an air gap between the sleeve and port wall. This design reduces heat rejection to the coolant, and with

the exhaust ports terminating in a round shape equal to 100% of the exhaust valve opening area, more efficient exhaust flow heat energy to the turbocharger is promoted. This combination of steel sleeves and gas flow improves the overall thermal efficiency of the 3406E engine.

Figure 14–5 illustrates the valve arrangement used by Caterpillar on its 10.3L-3176 EUI model. The intake and exhaust valves were designed to be the same diameter as those used in the 40% larger-displacement 14.6L-3406 engine. These larger valves and the low-loss port (manifold) system were designed to minimize fuel consumption and improve engine response. In this design the intake and exhaust ports are located on one side of the cylinder head to form what is commonly referred to as a *uniflow design*. The quiescent intake ports of adjacent cylinders are "siamesed" (joined together) to one of three large plenums, and there are individual exhaust ports for each cylinder. The four-valve-per-cylinder arrangement is skewed to shorten the exhaust port length, which reduces heat rejection and minimizes the flow interference between the exhaust valves in each port. Later model 3176 truck engines have newer style cylinder heads, spacer blocks, and head gaskets. The new spacer block and cylinder head have increased top or bottom deck surface areas to allow for greater clamping surface at the joint of the head to spacer block.

Within all cylinder head castings, are coolant passages, oil passages, and fuel passages to deliver pressurized fuel to the electronically controlled unit injectors. Engine coolant from the engine block enters the cylinder head water jacket through various mating passages with the block. An increase in coolant velocity (speed and direction) is often acheived by using strategically positioned water directional nozzles pressed into the underside of the cylinder head. Small orifices in the nozzles direct increased coolant around the hotter exhaust valve casting area. This design concept is shown more clearly in Figure 14–6, which also illustrates the coolant flow around the unit injector copper tube. Most engines, particularly those employing unit injectors (mechanical and electronically controlled), are designed to contain a press-fit copper tube within the cylinder head such as the one illustrated in Figure 14–6 and used by DDC on its two-stroke-cycle engine designs, which is a full-length injector body tube. However, the injector tube used by DDC in its four-cycle Series 50 and 60 electronically controlled engines employs a half-tube length copper design, and the Caterpillar 3406E has a stainless steel injector sleeve. These tubes not only support the injector in the cylinder head, but since these tubes (sleeves) are surrounded by engine coolant within the cylinder head, they ensure that the injector and fuel temperature are maintained within acceptable operating limits. Sealing of this sleeve is achieved by employing a press fit at the bottom side, with most sleeves rolled by special tooling to ensure a water- and gas-tight seal. The top of the sleeve is sealed with one or two O-rings in grooves in the head or sleeve assembly. In some heads, such as the 3406E Cat engine, the cylinder head water jacked is divided into both an upper and lower compartment by a water shelf design. Coolant entering the head from the block is directed along the bottom deck by the shelf and flows between the ports and up around the unit injector stainless steel tube (sleeve). The upper part of the shelf then

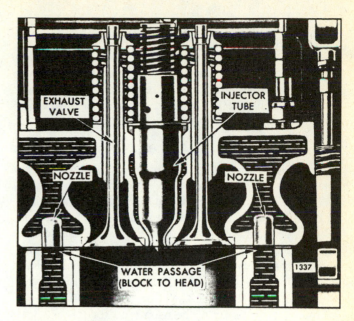

FIGURE 14–6 *Cross-sectional view of the coolant passages surrounding the exhaust valves and the unit fuel injector copper sleeve (tube) on a two-cycle DDC engine model. (Courtesy of Detroit Diesel Corporation.)*

allows the coolant to flow longitudinally throughout the length of the head to the thermostat area.

Cylinder head lube oil passages are designed to provide oil flow to the valve train through the rocker arms and rocker arm stands (pedestals), as well as to provide oil for the overhead camshaft support bearings when this design is employed. Some cylinder heads such as the 3406E Cat engine employ a single fuel passage to supply the electronic unit injectors; the warm fuel that has picked up heat from its cooling and lubrication purposes within the unit injector is returned back to the tank. Others such as the Detroit Diesel Series 50 and 60 and two-stroke models, as well as the Cummins N14 models, employ two fuel passages (an inlet and a return) to and from the electronic unit injectors.

INTAKE AND EXHAUST VALVES

Both the intake and exhaust valves are mechanically actuated, or opened, by a rocker arm assembly and closed by the action of the valve coil spring. The rocker arm can be activated by either a pushrod or an overhead camshaft through a roller assembly. Figure 14–1 illustrates a typical valve assembly items 11 and 14 commonly referred to as a *poppet-type valve*. The material used in the manufacture of the intake and exhaust valves varies in engine makes based on operating design features. The valves operate within a replaceable guide (see Figure 14–1, item 19, which is press fit in a bore within the cylinder head.

Common materials used for intake valves include iron for the valve head with chrome-nickel-alloy-hardened steel stems screwed or shrunk onto the head. The intake valve, which operates at cooler temperatures than the exhaust valve, is usually made in a cold-heading process; naturally aspirated engines use En 24, 52, or 59 alloyed steel. In turbocharged engines, however, inlet valve temperatures as high as 700°C (1292°F) can be encountered; therefore, 21-4N or 21-12N alloy steels are used. The exhaust valve, which runs hotter than the intake valve, can be exposed to temperatures averaging 800° C (1472°F); therefore, it can be made from a variety of materials such as special steel alloys using chrome, manganese, nickel, and tungsten—a chrome-cobalt-tungsten alloy is popular. Exhaust valve heads are frequently made of a highly heat-resistant material such as Nimonic 80 fraction welded to a less highly alloyed stem. For small engines, 21-4N or 21-12N with a lower manganese content may be used, and for larger high-speed highly rated engines, Nimonic 80A or 81 with a Brinell hardness range of 250 to 350 is fraction welded to a less highly alloyed stem. In the 7.3L Navistar 444 HEUI (hydraulically controlled electronic unit injector), the cylinder head features integrally cast induction-hardened valve seats for both the intake and exhaust valves. The exhaust valve is made from hot forged 21-2N steel material and requires no hard facing, while the intake valve is made in a cold-heading process.

To minimize corrosion and wear, some engine manufacturers protect the valve head seats by welding on a facing of Stellite or similar high nickel-cobalt-chromium material. Inconel (high nickel alloy) exhaust valves are often incorporated to better withstand high exhaust temperatures, and valve rotators are often used on both the intake and exhaust valves to reduce valve guide wear. Triballoy intake valves are also an option for long-hour-life, severe-duty applications.

To effectively seal the high pressures generated within the engine combustion chamber, the valve face rests against a valve seat insert, which is shrink fit into the cylinder head. The intake and exhaust valve seat inserts can be seen in Figure 14–1 as items 20 and 23. These inserts are often made from a Stellite material containing a highly alloyed steel containing nickel, chrome, and cobalt to provide excellent heat and wear characteristics. For the valve to dissipate its heat, it must have good surface contact between the valve face to seat insert in the cylinder head, as well as between the valve stem and the guide within the head. Poor valve contact can result in the valve running several hundred degrees hotter than normal, causing short valve life. Both the intake and the exhaust valves receive additional cooling from the airflow entering the cylinder during the intake stroke. On turbocharged and aftercooled engines, this cooler air is also used to

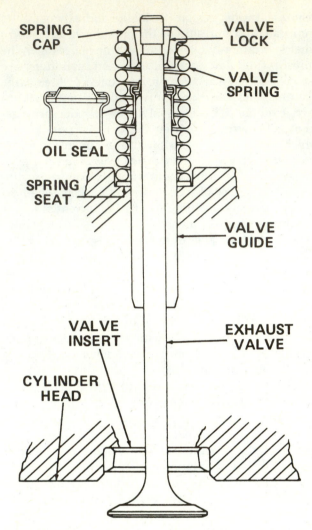

FIGURE 14–7 *Details of a typical valve, spring, and seat configuration. (Courtesy of Detroit Diesel Corporation.)*

cool the piston crown, cylinder liner, valves, and cylinder head fire deck area. The use of smaller valves, such as on a four-valve head versus a two-valve head design, also ensures a greater surface area; plus with the increased air turbulence from the greater number of valves, they tend to run cooler.

VALVE CONSTRUCTION

The most widely used valves in internal combustion engines are commonly referred to as *mushroom* or *poppet* design assemblies. Figure 14–7 illustrates the major components of the valve retaining mechanism for an exhaust valve assembly installed in position within the cylinder head. The valve is installed into a replacement guide within the cylinder head assembly where it moves up and down. A set of split valve locks (two), which are often referred to as keepers or collets, retain the valve in place. These keepers fit into machined grooves toward the top end of the valve stem. Sandwiched between the top of the valve and the top side of the cylinder head is the lower valve spring seat; often it is machined directly into the cylinder head surface.

Some engines employ a single valve spring, whereas others may have two valve springs (an inner and an outer). At the top of the spring is the valve spring cap. The spring cap is machined with a tapered bore to match the outside taper of the valve locks, thereby securing the valve in position in the head. In some engines, a *positive valve rotator* is used in place of the valve spring cap. Depending on the engine make and design, one or more valve stem seals may be used to control valve stem lubrication while limiting oil consumption. Faulty valve stem seals allow engine oil to flow down between the valve stem and guide. This seal is usually an O-ring type design made from nylon or neoprene (or a combination of both) or graphite and impregnated Teflon as shown in Figure 14–7. In cases where oil consumption is a problem, an umbrella-type valve stem seal may also be used.

VALVE ROTATORS

The heat absorbed by a valve in a running engine must be dissipated through contact between the valve stem and guide. Most of the heat is transferred through the contact that exists between the valve face and its seat insert in the cylinder head. It is not unusual for exhaust valves to experience temperatures of 800°C (1472°F) in today's heavy-duty high-speed electronically controlled diesel engines. During engine operation, the normal vibrations created within the engine tend to assist the intake and exhaust valves to rotate very slightly each time they open.

To provide a more even-wearing valve face-to-seat contact condition, and to minimize carbon buildup between the face and seat, many heavy-duty high-speed diesel engines employ what are commonly referred to as *positive valve rotators*. The positive valve rotator spring cap is used in place of the regular top valve spring seat at the tip end of the valve stem. This type of a rotator assists rotation of the valves during engine operation and produces a wiping action to remove any deposit buildup on the valve face, thereby allowing the valve head to run cooler. There are two basic types of rotators: one allows the valve to rotate as it opens, and the other is designed to rotate the valve as it starts to close.

Figure 14–8 illustrates in more detail a typical positive valve rotator, which is thicker than the conventional spring cap. The rotator is manufactured in two parts and consists of the seating collar (A) and the retainer cap (B) which are spun together and enclose a flexible washer and ball bearings in inclined races. As the valve is opened by camshaft rotation, the flexible washer (C) flexes and applies pressure to the balls (D), forcing them to roll down the inclined races (E) as shown in the diagram. This action produces relative motion between the two parts of the cap and thus rotates the valve usually in the range of 1° to 3° each time that the valve is opened. As the valve closes and pressure on the flexible washer is released, the small internal springs (F) return the balls to their original position.

Failure of the valve rotator to function correctly can lead to shortened valve life as a result of accelerated valve face and seat wear or eventual valve face-to-seat burning. Valve face guttering can occur with pieces of the valve breaking up and dropping into the cylinder, leading to either piston damage or a combination of piston and cylinder head damage. Check the rotator(s) for proper operation as follows:

1. Remove the valve rocker cover(s).
2. Ensure that all valve lash clearances are set correctly.
3. Wipe oil from the top of each rotator and place a visible mark (dot or line) on each rotator cap directly in front of the rocker arm. Use light-colored chalk or a metal marker.
4. Start and idle the engine.
5. Carefully watch the top of each valve rotator assembly and note if the mark applied in step 3 slowly rotates each time the valve opens or closes (1° to 3° is typical of a properly operating rotator).
6. If any rotator fails to operate, replace it. You do not have to remove the cylinder head. Manually rotate the engine to place the piston at TDC. Then compress the valve spring with a suitable tool to allow removal of the keepers and rotator asssembly.

CYLINDER HEAD REMOVAL

Removal of the cylinder head is required any time that service, repair, or maintenance of con-rods, pistons, liners, valves, or injector sleeves is necessary. Cylinder head removal may be necessary because of problems such as these:

- Leaking head gasket and low compression
- Water in the lube oil
- Compression leakage into the coolant system
- Cracked cylinder head
- Leaking injector sleeve
- Fuel oil contamination of the lube oil
- Dropped valve
- Worn valve guides
- Poor valve seating (low compression)

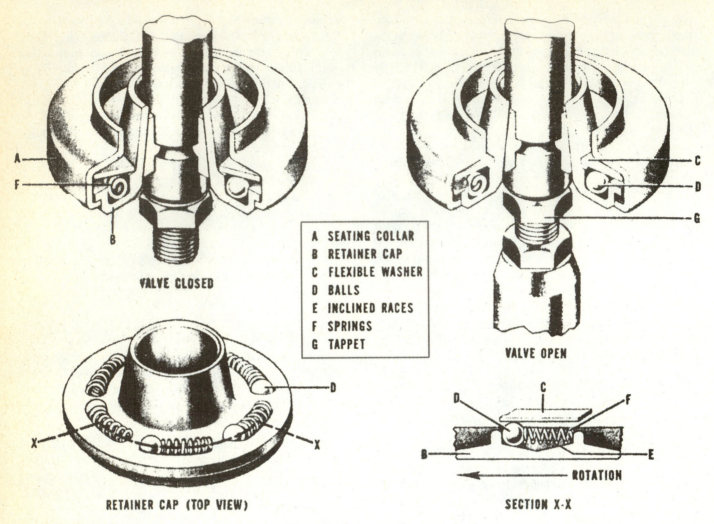

FIGURE 14–8 *Details of the parts of a positive valve rotator assembly.*
(Courtesy of Caterpillar Inc.)

Due to differences in makes and models of engines, the cylinder head removal procedure will vary. Nevertheless, for general descriptive purposes, the following sequence can be considered typical. Note that on engines using an in-block camshaft rather than an overhead arrangement, removal of the camshaft would not apply.

1. Drain the cooling system. Remove the thermostat housing hose to the radiator along with any deaeration lines.

2. Drain the engine oil. Although this is not specifically necessary, some technicians prefer to do so because engine coolant can often drain into the crankcase during the head removal procedure.

3. Disconnect the exhaust piping from the turbocharger. Seal the turbocharger intake and exhaust sides with plastic shipping protectors.

4. Disconnect the turbocharger oil supply and drain lines. Seal all lines with plastic shipping caps.

5. Remove the turbocharger assembly from the exhaust manifold.

6. Remove the air cleaner ducting (piping) and air crossover connection or tube if used.

7. If a jacket water aftercooler is used and is bolted to the cylinder head(s) (some Cat and Cummins models), remove it.

8. On Cummins N14 engines, remove the water manifold that is bolted to each one of the three cylinder heads.

SERVICE TIP Always identify (tag) all components related to the valve operating mechanism and injectors to ensure that these parts are reinstalled in the same position if they are to be reused, since all operating parts develop a wear pattern to their mating components. Also identify all of the intake and exhaust valves.

9. Remove the valve rocker cover(s).

10. Remove the valve operating mechanism, rocker levers, shafts, housings, valve bridges, and pushrods.

11. Disconnect any electrical connections from electronic unit injectors or engine compression brakes. You may have to disconnect the wiring harness clips and pull the harness clear of the cylinder head assembly.

12. On DDC two-stroke-cycle engines, disconnect the fuel rod(s) from between the mechanical governor and the injector control tube assembly on the cylinder head.

13. If the engine is using an overhead camshaft, remove the access plate at the front of the engine to gain access to the camshaft drive gear. The gear retaining bolts must be loosened off and removed to facilitate gear removal from the front end of the camshaft. To remove the camshaft on engines such as the Detroit Diesel Series 50 and 60, the Volvo 12.1L, and the Isuzu 12L models, the camshaft cap retaining bolts have to be removed. On the Caterpillar 3406E, the camshaft is contained within a bore of the head and can be withdrawn from either the front or rear of the head. On smaller-bore high-speed diesel engines, the overhead camshaft is often cog-belt driven. Loosen off the belt tensioner and remove the belt.

14. Disconnect the required supply and return fuel lines; seal all fuel line and fitting openings with plastic shipping caps to prevent the entrance of dirt.

15. Remove the fuel injectors. (Although not necessary, this step is usually recommended to prevent any possible damage to the injector tips, particularly when laying the head on the bench; it is always advisable to support removed heads on wooden blocks.) Number all injectors so that they can be replaced in the same cylinder. Wrap all injectors and place them in a safe location.

16. Remove the exhaust manifold. You may need to tap the manifold with a rubber mallet to break the seal between the gasket and the head. (If special lifting brackets are not readily available for the cylinder head, you may choose to leave this item on to facilitate lifting the head.) If an exhaust pyrometer is used, disconnect the wiring from the sensor.

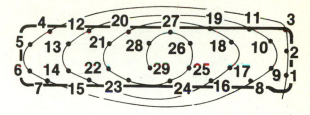

FIGURE 14–9 *Recommended cylinder head loosening sequence for studs, bolts, or nuts. (Courtesy of GMC Trucks.)*

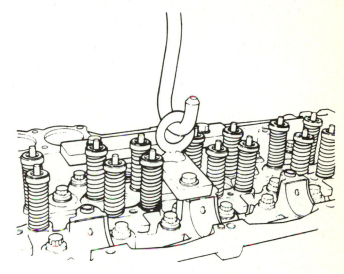

FIGURE 14–10 *One example of a special lifting bracket used to safely remove a cylinder head assembly from the engine block. (Courtesy of Detroit Diesel Corporation.)*

17. Remove the intake manifold. Use a rubber mallet to tap it loose if necessary. (Once again this is an option; if no special lifting brackets are available, you may choose to leave it in place). If a turbo boost sensor is used, disconnect the wire harness.

18. Loosen or remove the cylinder head bolts in the reverse tightening sequence as shown in Figure 14–9. On vee engines, leave at least one bolt loose, in place, to prevent the head from sliding off prior to slinging the head.

19. Use special cylinder head lifting brackets to facilitate easy and safe removal of the cylinder head(s). Each engine manufacturer offers one or more. Figure 14–10 illustrates a bracket used by Detroit Diesel on its four-cycle Series 50 and 60 engines. If no special brackets are available, you can usually screw in two eyebolts into the rocker head area, assemble shackles through the eyebolts, and

use either a chain- or web-type sling to support the head during the removal process.

20. Once the head(s) have been removed, support them on suitable wooden blocks. This will protect the machined surface of the head from scratching or scoring. In addition, some heads have roller-type cam followers extending from the underside of the head that need to be protected.

21. Remove and discard the cylinder head gasket.

SERVICE TIP: If only the cylinder head is to be serviced after removal and no major overhaul is to be performed on the engine block, install plastic cylinder blanking plugs and mating plugs into all other block openings. If these are not available, a cardboard or thin plywood cover can be used and retained in place by several bolts. Alternatively, use heavy plastic sheeting to cover the top of the engine block to avoid dust and dirt.

DISASSEMBLY AND DESCALING OF THE CYLINDER HEAD

Sometimes it is necessary to overhaul the cylinder head, for example, when remachining the fire deck surface or replacing or refacing the valves, the guides, the valve seat inserts, or the injector sleeve (tube). Remove the head from the engine as just described. Remove the valve springs using a conventional compressor shown in Figure 14–11 or the spring compressor in Figure 14–12 for an overhead cam engine, and carefully remove the valve locks. Air-operated spring compressor tools are also available. Carefully release the force on the compressed spring. Now remove the tool; then remove the spring retainer, spring, seals, and lower spring seat if used. In cases where the top of the valve stem may have been pounded or mushroomed, you will have to deburr or lightly grind this area to allow the valve to be pushed through the valve guide. Use a block of wood with numbered holes drilled through it to allow you to retain all valves, so that they can be identified and replaced in the same guide. Alternatively, mark the valve heads with a metal marker. If the cylinder head is to be cleaned in a hot tank to remove scale buildup in the coolant passages with a strong industrial chemical, you will have to remove all of the nonferrous metals first, such as the injector copper sleeves and copper coolant directional nozzles.

It is extremely important to inspect a cylinder head for signs of scale buildup within the coolant passages, because scale can seriously inhibit the heat transfer from the head to the coolant passages. The cleaning procedure is similar to that used for the engine block during major overhaul. Heavy scale buildup can result in cylinder head cracking. To determine the condition

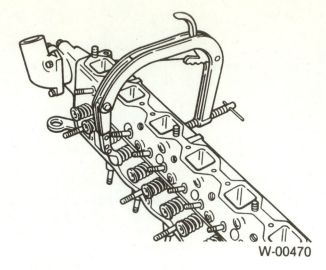

FIGURE 14–11   Using an adjustable C-clamp tool to compress the valve spring during either removal or installation. (Courtesy of GMC Trucks.)

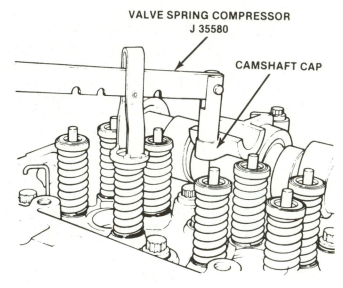

FIGURE 14–12   Using a spring compressor to remove the valve spring. (Courtesy of Detroit Diesel Corporation.)

of scale within the cylinder head, remove the various threaded access plugs or frost plugs to the coolant passages. In addition, remove the injector sleeve to quickly determine the degree of scale buildup within the coolant passages. Heavy scale should be removed by stripping the cylinder head of all threaded or frost plugs, along with all injector sleeves and nonferrous metals. Then submerge the head assembly in a descaling bath; various commercial chemical cleaners are available for this purpose. Some can be used cold, whereas others require heating in a sealed container. In both cases, the cylinder head is totally submerged in the liquid chemical.

FIGURE 14–13 (a) Using a sealing gasket (1) and thick steel plate (2) bolted to the underside of an L10 cylinder head in preparation for a pressure test. (Courtesy of Cummins Engine Company Inc.) (b) Test strips and suitable gaskets bolted to the underside of a Series 60 cylinder head in preparation for a pressure test. (Courtesy of Detroit Diesel Corporation.)

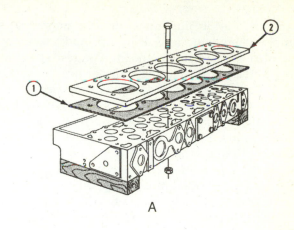

A

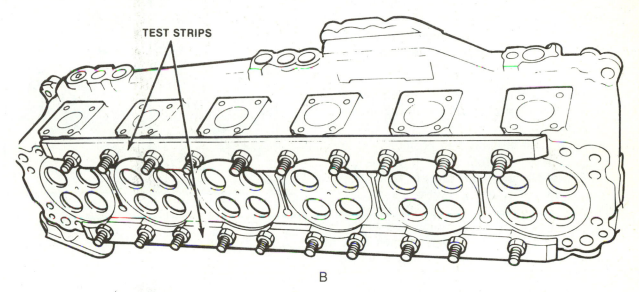

TEST STRIPS

B

SAFETY NOTE: Always use suitable eye protection, protective gloves, and an apron when dealing with cleaning chemicals.

When the head is removed from the cleaning solution, steam clean it or flush it liberally with warm water; then blow-dry it with compressed shop air. Prior to checking the valve guides, valve seat inserts, head flatness, and so forth, do a pressure check to determine if the head is reusable and to ensure that no cracks exist.

DETECTION OF CRACKS

Once the cylinder head has been removed, disassembled, and steam cleaned and the carbon has been scraped off, visually inspect the fire deck area for signs of cracks. Most cracks appear between the exhaust valves, or between the exhaust valves and the injector since this is the hottest and most highly stressed area of the head. Sometimes it is difficult to spot a hairline crack, particularly when the head is cold. It is also very difficult to determine by visual observation if a crack exists within the internal casting of the cylinder head.

Four basic methods can be used to determine if the cylinder head is cracked: magnetic particle method, fluorescent magnetic particle method, fluorescent penetrant method, and pressure check method. Refer to Chapter 11 for details on each of the first three methods. The following information describes the pressure check method.

This method is used when the other three methods are not available or when a suspected crack cannot be confirmed visually by these methods. The pressure checking method is widely used since it is fairly easy to perform and is very effective not only in determining if a crack(s) exists but also if there are coolant leaks at the injector sleeves. Different heads require special blank-off plates and gaskets, although many service technicians employ sheet rubber or neoprene gaskets and steel plates to seal off the various coolant passages (see Figure 14–13a). One of the blank-off plates must be drilled and tapped to accept a compressed air fitting such as at the sealing plate bolted in place over the thermostat housing cover opening with a quick-couple connector for an air hose attachment.

Figure 14–13b illustrates another pressure test example where two metal test strips and gaskets are assembled to the cylinder head. The test strips are bolted to the head using the cylinder head bolts and nuts. If the cylinder head has been descaled, install all of the removed plugs. If new plugs are used, they are usually precoated with a sealer. If the old plugs are being reused, coat the plugs with Loctite, pipe sealant, or Teflon tape and torque them to the spec listed in the service manual. If new cup plugs or frost plugs are used, coat them with a good grade of non-hardening sealant such as Loctite 620 or equivalent. Similarly, if injector sleeves (tubes) have been removed, new ones have to be installed prior to the pressure check.

Minor variations will exist between engines and models, follow these basic steps in the pressure check method:

1. Install the coolant passage blank-off plates along with a compressed air fitting into a coolant passage.

2. Install dummy injectors into position in each injector bore sleeve (tube). If dummy injectors are not readily available, use old scrap ones torqued into place. If an injector sleeve holding tool kit similar to the one illustrated in Figure 14–14a for a Cummins L10 engine model is available, install and tighten these components in place for each cylinder as shown.

3. Use one of these two methods to check the cylinder head.

    a. Submerge the head in a tank of preheated water usually at a temperature between 82° and 93°C (180° to 190°F). Apply the recommended air pressure to the coolant water jacket for at least a 20 minute period (see Figure 14–14b).

    b. If a tank is not available, fill the coolant jackets with a mixture of antifreeze and water; bolt the blank-off plates into position; apply the recommended regulated air pressure to the air fitting and leave it under pressure for 1 to 2 hours to allow the antifreeze mixture to penetrate any cracks.

NOTE: The air pressure applied to the cylinder head will vary depending on the type of injector and sleeve used. On replaceable sleeves (tubes) that are surrounded by coolant, the recommended air pressure is between 30 and 40 psi (207 to 276 kPa). However, some designs of cylinder heads suggest air test pressure of between 80 and 100 psi (552 to 690 kPa). *Always* closely check the engine manufacturer's service literature

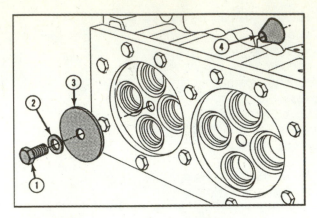

FIGURE 14–14   (a) Installing special injector retaining sleeve tooling to an L10 cylinder head prior to pressure checking. 1 = capscrew; 2 = flat washer; 3 = ST-1179-4 anvil; 4 = ST-1179-2 mandrel; (b) L10 cylinder head submerged in a tank of hot water with a fitting attached to a compressed air line supply; signs of air bubbles indicate a cracked head, assuming that no leaks are evident at the sealing plates and gaskets. (Courtesy of Cummins Engine Company Inc.)

to ensure that you do not exceed the recommended pressure!

4. Air bubbles appearing when the head is submerged in a tank of heated water are indicative of cracks (see Figure 14–14b). Closely inspect the area to ensure that any leak is not from one of the gaskets and blank-off plates. If so, the head may be distorted and require remachining. (Refer to the next section dealing with fire deck flatness check.)

5. Note any signs of leakage of antifreeze mixture which would indicate a crack in the cylinder head.

Although cylinder heads can be repaired by welding, and a number of specialty shops offer this service, most engine manufacturers suggest that all cracked heads be replaced.

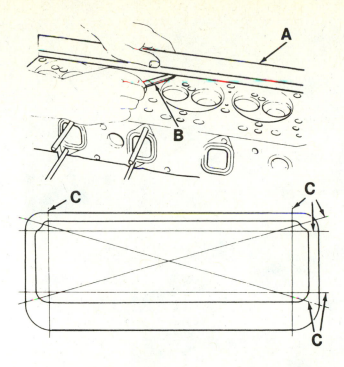

A. Straightedge
B. Feeler Gage
C. Check in Six Directions   W-00803

FIGURE 14–15 *Using a precision steel straightedge and a feeler gauge to check the machined surface of the cylinder head for warpage longitudinally and transversely, as well as diagonally. (Courtesy of GMC*

FIRE DECK FLATNESS CHECK

After descaling and cleaning the cylinder head, the machined surface of the fire deck can be polished lightly using 240 to 400 grit emery on a sanding block or an orbital sander. Check the surface with a true steel straightedge and a feeler gauge as illustrated in Figure 14–15. The length and width of the cylinder head determine how many positions should be checked; however all heads must be checked *longitudinally, transversely,* and *diagonally* as indicated in the diagram. Refer to the engine service manual for the allowable distortion limits. Typically, on high-speed electronically controlled heavy-duty six-cylinder engines using a one-piece head, this limit is approximately 0.005 in (0.127 mm) longitudinally and 0.003 in. (0.076 mm) transversely.

CYLINDER HEAD MACHINING

When a cylinder head is distorted and fails to pass the limits relative to flatness on the fire deck, it can be remachined as shown in Figure 14–16a and 14–16b on a surface grinder (see Figure 9–22) and reused if the finished head thickness falls within the engine manufacturer's limits for minimum head thickness. The reasons for this are related to the valve seat inserts and the valve head protrusion above the fire deck. On overhead camshaft models, resurfacing of the cylinder head or engine block affects the position of the camshaft in relation to the adjustable cam idler gear as well as the gear train backlash. The service manual lists the recommended minimum cylinder head thickness after regrinding. Figure 14–16c illustrates a typical example of where this measurement would be taken on an overhead camshaft cylinder head. It is customary for the technician to *stamp* or *etch* the amount of stock removed from the cylinder head on a machined pad somewhere on the head. This serves as a guide for another technician who has to determine if the head has been remachined previously.

VALVE GUIDE INSPECTION

The valve stem-to-guide clearance is very important. Insufficient clearance can result in the valve sticking or siezing in the guide, and excessive clearance results in a rocking action every time the valve opens and closes. Too much valve guide wear results in poor seating of the valve face-to-seat insert due to a rocking action as well as causes engine oil to be pulled down the stem-to-guide clearance, particularly the intake valve during the intake stroke. Not only will high oil consumption occur, but blue exhaust smoke will be evident, particularly when the engine is at idle, light loaded, or running down a hill with a closed throttle on a truck application.

A badly worn valve guide offers little support and guidance for the valve stem. Continued operation with worn valve guides also results in heavy carbon deposits at the neck of the valve (burning oil and usually low compression and incomplete combustion), which can create a restriction to both air and exhaust gas flows.

SPECIAL NOTE: If you suspect excessive valve guide wear, but want to confirm this before removing the cylinder head, follow these steps: Remove the rocker cover(s), rotate the engine to TDC on one cylinder at a time, depress the valve spring, and remove the valve locks (keepers) and spring. Refer to Figure 14–17 and place a dial indicator tip against the valve stem. Rotate and rock the valve to determine the stem-to-guide wear and compare it to the service manual specifications.

With the cylinder head removed and disassembled, use a small valve guide bore cleaning brush of nylon or wire construction attached to a drill motor to remove all gum, varnish, or carbon deposits. Then carefully inspect the guide for signs of cracks, chipping, scoring, or excessive wear. Use a small hole (ball)

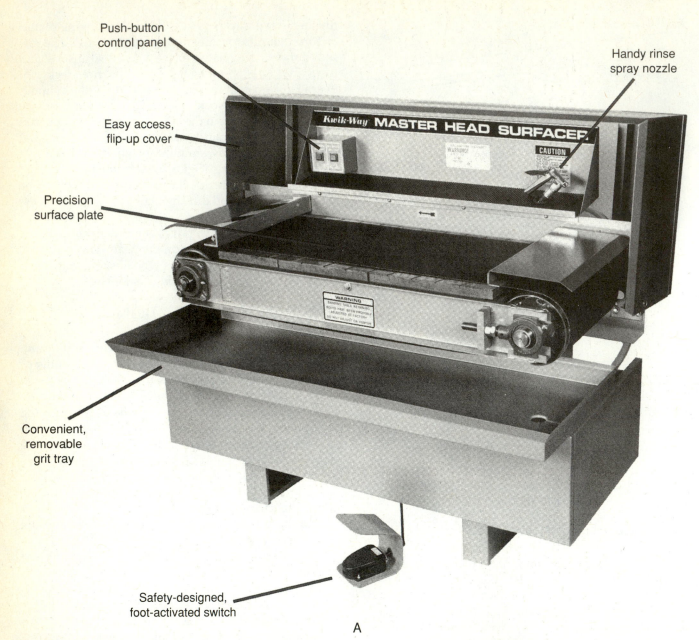

Push-button
control panel

Handy rinse
spray nozzle

Easy access,
flip-up cover

Kwik-Way **MASTER HEAD SURFACER**

Precision
surface plate

Convenient,
removable
grit tray

Safety-designed,
foot-activated switch

A

FIGURE 14-16 (a) Rotating belt sander model 870 cylinder head resurfacer; (b) placement of two 25 lb (11.3 kg) weight bags provide additional pressure when needed, saving time and labor. (Courtesy of Kwik-Way Corporation.) (c, at the top of p. 373) Example of the dimensional thickness tolerance for a Series 60 engine model cylinder head. The technician records the amount of material that has been removed from the head as shown in the example (0.010 in.). (Courtesy of Detroit Diesel Corporation.)

The two 25 lb. weight bags provide additional pressure when needed, saving time and labor.

B

FIGURE 14–16 *continued*

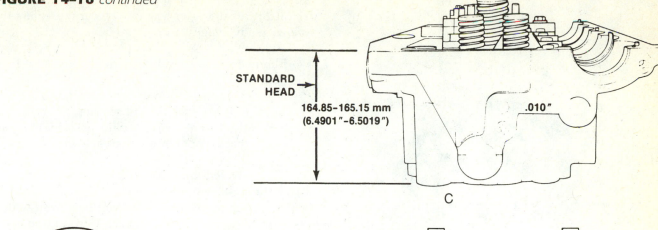

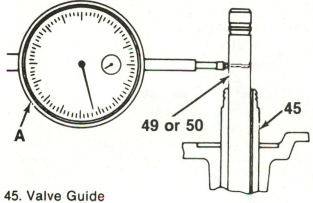

45. Valve Guide
49. Exhaust Valve
50. Intake Valve
A. Dial Indicator

W-00805

FIGURE 14–17 *One method of checking valve stem-to-guide clearance with the cylinder head still in position on the engine. Place a dial indicator as illustrated against the valve stem while rocking the valve back and forth. (Courtesy of GMC Trucks.)*

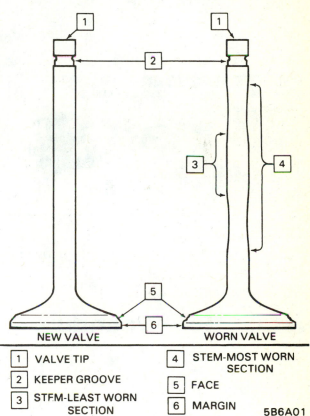

1	VALVE TIP		4	STEM-MOST WORN SECTION
2	KEEPER GROOVE		5	FACE
3	STFM-LEAST WORN SECTION		6	MARGIN

5B6A01

FIGURE 14–18 *Typical areas to inspect for valve wear at major overhaul. (Courtesy of GMC Trucks.)*

adjustable gauge (see Figure 8–7) within the guide bore and adjust the gauge to produce a slight drag; then remove the gauge, check it with an outside micrometer, and compare the dimension to the service manual specs. Check the guide diameter in three places (top, middle, and bottom) and the measurements at 90° to one another. Check the diameter of the valve stem with an outside micrometer to the published specs, and compare the valve stem diameter with that of its mating guide to determine the actual valve stem-to-guide wear. Figure 14–18 illustrates a comparison between a new valve stem and a worn valve stem for instructional purposes only. Clearances beyond worn limits require that the valve guide be replaced on most diesel engines. However, some engine manufacturers (mainly light-duty automotive) offer oversize outside diameter valve stems to bring the clearance within specs.

Another method that can be used to avoid replacement of chilled or hardened valve guides is to *knurl* the inside diameter of the guide with special equipment, or to bore the worn guide and install a bronze valve guide liner. In both cases, a reamer is used to resize the guide after this procedure. Figure 14–19 illustrates a *valve guide knurling kit* that comes with a variety of different sized guide knurling tools, from 0.236 in. (6.0 mm) up to 0.562 in. (14.27 mm). Knurling is a process that basically cuts a spiral screw-type thread within the bore of the guide without removing the guide from the cylinder

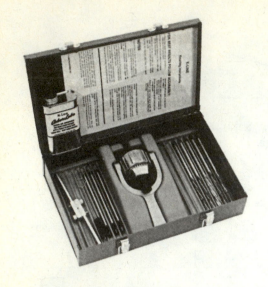

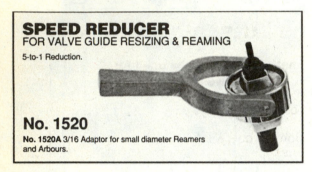

FIGURE 14–19 *Valve guide knurling and reamer set used to recondition worn valve guides. (Courtesy of Hastings Manufacturing Co.)*

head. Often, knurling is apparent on guides direct from the factory. Knurling of a worn valve guide offers the following advantages:

- Eliminates costly valve guide removal and replacement
- Stops oil consumption due to valve guide wear
- Reduces valve sticking and scoring
- Reconditions the valve guide area in cylinder heads that do not use a replaceable guide

The threaded-knurling-type spiral arbor can be driven through the worn valve guide by using a speed-reducer assembly in the kit that can be driven with a 1/4 in. (6.35 mm) drill motor and can recondition valve guides with up to 0.010 in. (0.254 mm) wear. Another method is to bore the worn guide and install a bronze valve guide sleeve. Figure 14–20 illustrates the procedure that can be used to bore and install a bronze guide liner as well as how to use the optional guide spiral (knurling) and finish ream the guide insert.

Replacement valve guides are press fit within their mating bore in the cylinder head. To remove the valve guides, you can use one of several methods: a hammer and properly sized shouldered punch, a mechanical threaded guide puller, or an air impact hammer and chisel arrangement similar to that illustrated in Figure 14–21. Removal or installation of the guide with the air chisel hammer requires that you employ special tools that must be held vertical to the cylinder head and forced tight against the guide to prevent pounding of the end of the guide. When a

Installation Procedure

I.D. FINISHING METHODS

BALL BROACH   **SPIRAL & FINISH REAM**

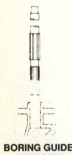 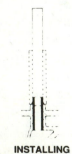    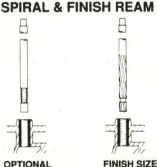

BORING GUIDE OVERSIZE
Select proper tooling and bore out old guide. Both H.S. and Carbide Boring Tools are available

INSTALLING "BRONZE LINER" IN GUIDE
Lube guide, push guide-liner into holder, select guide driver and hammer into place.

TRIMMING BRONZE LINER
Insert tool point into the seam, push down to guide top and turn once to remove excess material.

FINISH SIZE OPERATION
To finish I.D., select appropriate Ball Broach and drive through guide. Flex-hone with high RPM drill.

OPTIONAL GUIDE SPIRAL
For closer than normal stem to guide clearance, spiraling is suggested for added lubrication.

FINISH SIZE OPERATION
To finish ream, lubricate reamer with bronze-lube and run through guide. Both H.S. and Carbide Reamers are available.

FIGURE 14–20 *Installation and finishing procedures required to successfully and accurately recondition a worn valve guide by the insertion of a precision wear sleeve. (Courtesy of Hastings Manufacturing Co.)*

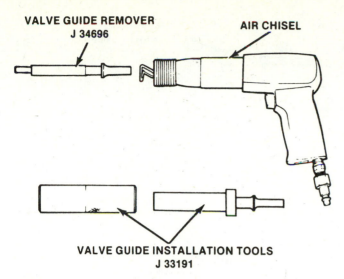

VALVE GUIDE REMOVER
J 34696

AIR CHISEL

VALVE GUIDE INSTALLATION TOOLS
J 33191

FIGURE 14–21   Special air chisel and adaptor tools required to remove or install a valve guide. (Courtesy of Detroit Diesel Corporation.)

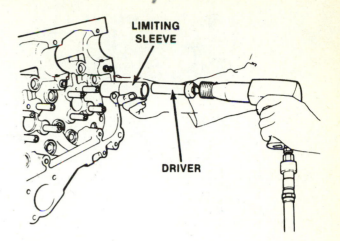

LIMITING SLEEVE

DRIVER

FIGURE 14–22   Using a special air chisel and tooling to install a new valve guide into the cylinder head. (Courtesy of Detroit Diesel Corporation.)

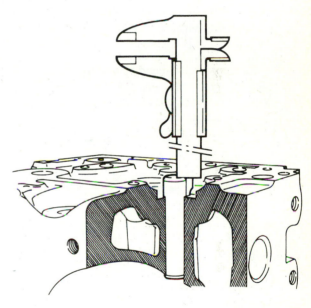

3-2-4

FIGURE 14–23   Using a vernier caliper to measure the installation height of a valve guide. (Courtesy of DAF Trucks, Eindhoven, Netherlands.)

guide has been removed, use a stiff-wire brush similar to that used to clean the inside of the guide; run the brush through the bore in the cylinder head to remove any minor imperfections. Insert the chamfered end of the new valve guide into its bore from the top side of the cylinder head. Then, make sure you have the correct guide installer, as shown in the example in Figure 14–22, and use the air impact chisel to drive the guide into place in the cylinder head from the top side.

NOTE: If you do not have the correct guide installation tools, take extreme care when installing a new guide. Do not drive the guide too far into the head bore. Either measure the height of a guide that is still in place or refer to the service manual to ensure that you install the new guide to its specified height above the cylinder head using a vernier caliper as shown in Figure 14–23.

In some engines employing aluminum alloy cylinder heads, a nonferrous valve guide is used. Often, this means that you must heat the head in boiling water or a temperature-controlled oven to safely remove the guide. To safely install the new guide, the head can be preheated and the guide chilled before installation.

VALVE SEAT INSERTS

The cylinder head contains replaceable hardened valve seat inserts, which can be seen in Figure 14–1 and 14–7. These inserts are shrink (press fit) within a machined bore of the cylinder head. If close inspection during servicing indicates that the inserts are worn or pitted, they can be reground or cut with special tooling (see the sections on valve and seat grinding later in

this chapter). If the inserts are severely worn or cracked, however, they have to be removed and replaced. If the inserts are loose in their bore or the bore is damaged, the cylinder head has to be remachined to accept an oversize outside diameter insert.

Insert Removal

To effectively remove and install a valve seat insert requires special tooling. A number of major tool manufacturers supply a variety of these tools. Figure 14–24 illustrates a cam-operated type of valve seat remover.

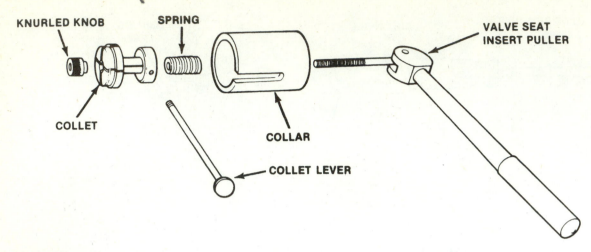

FIGURE 14-24 *An example of a valve seat insert removal tool. (Courtesy of Kent-Moore Division, SPX Corporation.)*

This tool is available with a number of different sized collets to fit a wide variety of diesel engines. To use this tool, follow these five steps:

1. Place the cylinder head assembly on a flat surface with the valve seat inserts facing up.

2. Assemble the seat remover tool, similar to that shown in Figure 14–24, using the proper collet for the insert to be removed.

3. Rotate the handle of the tool into the knurled knob so that the split collet has been expanded to slightly less than the bore size of a new valve seat insert.

4. Insert the assembled tooling squarely into the bore of the valve seat insert to be removed. With the collet lever in position, hold the handle and rotate the lever to expand the split collet until it is tight. This will expand the collet within the bore of the seat insert.

5. Pull down on the handle of the tooling to allow the cam to apply pressure on the collar, which will remove the valve seat insert from its bore in the cylinder head. Some seat removers are equipped with a slide hammer and expandable collet to allow valve seat insert removal.

Insert Installation

Always clean the insert counterbores with a suitable wire brush. If a brush is not available, scrape any foreign material from the bore and use fine emery cloth to carefully clean the seat area and the outside diameter. Clean any new valve seat insert with a suitable solvent and dry it off.

Refer to Figure 14–25 and obtain a shouldered valve seat insert installer tool with a machined step at

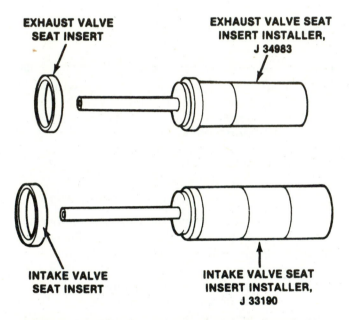

FIGURE 14-25 *Special valve seat insert installation tools. (Courtesy of Detroit Diesel Corporation.)*

its base to facilitate correct installation without damage. Refer to Figure 14–26 and squarely place the new insert into the bore of the cylinder head. Using the seat installer tool, slide the pilot into position in the bore of the valve guide. Now use a hammer to drive the insert carefully into position until you hear a dull thud. This sound indicates that the insert has reached bottom. Lightly tap the hammer against the installation tool to confirm that the insert is all the way home. Do not continue to pound on the insert, because you may bounce it away from the bore in the head.

Although new valve seat inserts are preground, you will have to select a dial gauge and valve guide adapter as shown in Figure 14–27 to check the valve seat

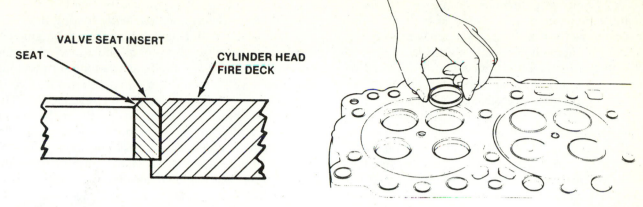

FIGURE 14–26 *Placement of valve seat insert into the cylinder head prior to final tooling insertion. (Courtesy of Detroit Diesel Corporation.)*

insert concentricity to the valve guide. Generally, this reading should not exceed 0.002 in. (0.05 mm). If it is within specs, the insert and valve guide are OK. If it is not, you will have to lightly grind the seat insert to "square it up". If new valve guides are to be installed, do this before you attempt to regrind a valve seat insert. In cases where the cylinder head fire deck surface has been resurfaced, the valves will have to be seated deeper to maintain the valve head recess when seated within specs. Since valve seat inserts are hardened, rather than attempting to grind them down, use new valve seat inserts that are 0.010, 0.020, or 0.030 in. (0.254, 0.508 and 0.762 mm) thinner in overall thickness. When a reduced-thickness valve seat insert is used, however, a correspondingly thicker valve spring seat is necessary to ensure that the valve stem protrusion and valve spring installed height and compression remain the same.

VALVE AND SEAT INSPECTION

Valves are made from heat-treated alloys with precision-ground head faces and stems, and stem ends that are hardened to minimize wear. Nevertheless, after many hundreds of thousands of miles (kilometers), the valve face that seats on the hardened alloy valve seat insert can exhibit signs of wear or pounding. Similarly, the valve stem-to-guide clearance can exceed the normal wear limits. When valve faces become distorted or burned, compression leakage can result. When the valve stem-to-guide wear becomes excessive, the rapid opening and closing action of the valve actually causes the valve assembly to rock back and forth within the guide. As a result, the valve face-to-seat contact changes all the time; the consequences are poor valve sealing and usually a ridge on the valve face. In addition, the guide wear allows engine oil to be pulled down the guide between the valve stem, resulting in burning of oil in the combustion chamber as well as carbon forma-

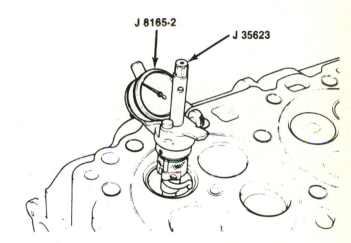

FIGURE 14–27 *Using a special dial gauge and adapter to check the concentricity (runout) of the valve guide to the valve seat insert. (Courtesy of Detroit Diesel Corporation.)*

tion around the neck of the valve. Excessive carbon restricts the airflow into and the exhaust gas flow out of the cylinder. Burning oil can lead to varnish buildup on the stem, and coupled with the carbon formation, the valve can actually fail to close properly.

This can cause the piston to actually strike the valve, thereby causing either a bent or broken valve. If a valve head breaks off and becomes jammed between the piston crown and the underside of the cylinder head fire deck, total destruction of the engine will occur.

Efficient combustion in the engine cylinders requires an airtight seal between the valve face and its seat as well as correct valve stem-to-guide clearance. In addition, the valve clearance must be maintained to allow opening and closing of the valves when necessary. Excessive idling and continuous light-load operation of an engine results in low operating temperatures and incomplete combustion (cold running).

These conditions lead to poor sealing of the piston rings and formation of carbon around the valves and related parts, as well as a greater tendency for contamination of the engine lube oil and sludge formation.

When you disassemble the cylinder head at major overhaul, or any time that you suspect that the valves are not seating properly, carefully inspect the valve face seating area for pitting and poor sealing and the valve stem-to-guide clearance. The valve face can be checked visually first to determine if signs of pitting or seat roughness and pounding are evident. Next determine the condition of the valve seat contact area, the seat width, and the seat's actual location across the valve face.

Although the valve dissipates most of its heat through contact at the valve face to seat, too wide a contact area can cause foreign material such as carbon to be trapped between the valve face and seat. This leads to pitting at the seat area and therefore poor sealing. On the other hand, if the seat contact is too narrow, the valve will run hotter and can end up overheating, distorting, and burning, again causing poor sealing and short valve life. Therefore, each engine manufacturer specifies in the service literature (1) the recommended valve face contact width and (2) the location of the seat contact on the face.

When checking a used valve, or a valve and seat that have both been reground, the seat width and location must be checked closely to determine if acceptable valve face-to-seat insert contact is visible. This can be done in two ways:

1. Place a series of light lead pencil marks around the valve face as shown in Figure 14–28. Then after placing the valve back into its respective guide, place light pressure against the valve head while manually rotating the stem. This action will cause the pencil marks to be erased, which indicates where the valve-to-seat contact exists and how wide it is.

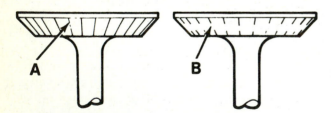

A. Pencil Marks Before Contact
B. Pencil Marks After Proper Contact

W-00482

FIGURE 14–28 *Placing lead pencil marks across the valve face (A) prior to face-to-seat checking. (B) Inspection of the valve face-to-seat contact area after proper contact. (Courtesy of GMC Trucks.)*

2. A more positive and easily visible valve seat pattern can be determined by *lightly* coating the valve face with machinist's Prussian Blue paste (contained in a tube similar to toothpaste) as illustrated in Figure 14–29. Place the valve into its guide without touching the coated valve face. Then either bounce it once or rotate the valve back and forth in the seat about 1/8 in. (3 mm) without any pressure on the valve head. Carefully withdraw the valve from its guide; again, be careful not to touch the face seating area. Now the location of the valve-to-seat contact area as well as the width of the seat can be determined visually: a clean surface area will appear on the valve face.

VALVE GRINDING

Before attempting to regrind any valve, the stem should be checked with a micrometer for wear, the stem tip should be checked for excessive pounding or cracking, and the valve head rim or margin thickness shown in Figure 14–18 must be thick enough so that after grinding it is still within the minimum allowable limits. The valve head margin thickness should generally not be less than 1/16 in. (1.58 mm). Valve heads with a thickness less than this will end up in a weak head and face area, resulting in pounding, valve head distortion, and burning of the valve. The minimum margin thickness is usually in the engine service manual specifications.

Valves can be cleaned of deposits and carbon on a powered bench grinder soft-wire wheel. Where extremely heavy carbon is evident, the valves can be submerged in a suitable commercial cleaner and allowed to soak until the carbon has been chemically removed. Rinse off and dry the valves when complete.

When valve faces are badly pitted or worn, the valve can be reground using the special grinding equipment illustrated in Figure 14–30. Although a variety of tool suppliers manufacture this type of equipment, there are basically two methods used for regrinding.

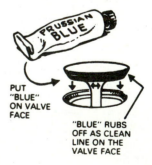

FIGURE 14–29 *Use of Prussian Blue paste spread lightly across the valve face. Bounce the valve once on its seat, then carefully remove it and check the seat contact area and width. (Courtesy of Neway Manufacturing, Inc.)*

1. Mount the valve stem into a self-centering chuck, adjust the machine for the correct angle of cut, lightly feed the valve face with the micrometer feed into the rotating grinding stone as illustrated in Figure 14–31. Special cutting oil is supplied to the valve face during the grinding process. A typical valve grinding machine is also capable of grinding valve stem tips and rocker arm pallets. A diamond tip grinding tool allows the technician to retrue the grinding stone face when worn. When finished grinding the valve face, use a vee-block attachment and spring holder to lightly hold the valve stem, so that a dial indicator can be used on the valve stem and valve head to determine if the valve is bent or if the head is concentric to the stem.

2. Use a *"hand-operated valve refacer"* tool that incorporates durable tungsten carbide cutter blades. The tool is simple to operate and actually allows the operator to feel the amount of material being removed while providing a near perfect concentric cut. Figure 14–32 illustrates a Neway handheld valve refacer kit.

Some engine manufacturers recommend that the valve and seat angle be ground or cut to between a 1/2 to 1 degree difference, a term and condition known as an *interference angle* where the valve face has been ground to a smaller angle than the seat insert. The purpose of using a different angle is to allow a fairly narrow seat width contact surface when the valve is cold. This produces high seat contact pressure and tends to minimize carbon created from incomplete combustion in a cold engine from being pounded between the face and seat. When the engine achieves normal operating temperature, the valve head expands and forms a full-seat contact area as desired from the initial grind process. Figure 14–33 illustrates an interference angle where the valve face has been ground to 29° 30', and the valve seat insert in the cylinder head has been ground to 30°. Item A in the diagram is the seat contact area, and B is the minimum width of the valve head margin. Another common interference angle is a 30° valve face and a 31° seat insert angle, which is currently used by a

Wheel head
Sealed, lubricated ball bearings, pre-loaded to eliminate end play. Features two wheels mounted back to back. One for grinding valve faces. One for valve butts and rocker arm pads. Special wheel for stellite valve faces is supplied standard. (Optional fixtures required for butt grinding and rocker arm pads.)

Wheel Drive
Two speeds for maximum versatility.

Diamond wheel dresser
Mounted on machine...in position for use without removing valve from chuck. Pops up and down for fast wheel dressing.

Self-contained circulating oil system
Features a long-life impeller pump in easy to clean drawer type reservoir. Capacity: 3 gallons (11.3 liters). Water-soluble grinding fluid assures stress-free cutting action. Captures grit and chips.

Workhead
"Ground in assembly" workhead with sealed, pre-lubricated ball bearings pre-loaded to eliminate end play. Air actuated, hardened and ground collets, with adjustable end stop, handle any stem diameter from .175" to .800" (4.5 mm to 20.3 mm). **Two-speed drive** provides correct rotation speeds for head diameters up to 4" (102 mm).

Valve face angle adjustment
Can be set and locked at any angle from 0 to 75.

Feed screw
Turns in ball bearing and oilite bushing. Feed nut and screw bearing are end loaded to eliminate backlash. Feed screw and nut are sealed off from dirt and chips. In-feed graduated in .001" increments.

FIGURE 14–30 Model VR-6500 precision valve refacer is used to grind metal from the valve face with a rotating grinding wheel (stone). (Courtesy of Sunnen Products Company.)

Air-actuated hardened and ground collets speed production, assure pinpoint chucking of valves.

Valve butt chamfering attachment (standard) removes sharp edges after grinding process.

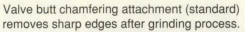

Valve butt grinding attachment (optional) has quick action cam lock and micrometer feed.

Rocker arm grinding attachment (optional) grinds pad parallel to the bore of shaft type rocker arms.

FIGURE 14–31   *Four of the common grinding jobs that can be performed to a valve and rocker arm using the model VR-6500 valve refacer machine. (Courtesy of Sunnen Products Company.)*

number of major high-speed heavy-duty diesel engine manufacturers (some recommend a 44° and 45° combination). These interference angles are easily obtained by setting the valve face grinder and seat grinder to the desired angles.

VALVE SEAT INSERT GRINDING

When valve seat inserts show signs of pitting or wear, they can be reground by one of three methods using either a grinding stone or a tungsten carbide cutter:

1. Use a *concentric grinder*, the grinding stone contacts the full-seat face width.
2. Use an *eccentric grinder* and stone, similar to Figure 14–34, which is designed so that the rotating grinding wheel contacts the seat at only one point at any time as it rotates around the seat. A micrometer feed on the handle of

the drive motor permits very fine adjustment of the amount of material to be removed.

3. Use an adjustable seat cutter employing tungsten carbide blades that can cut thousands of seats before showing wear and can produce a very fine surface finish. This system is superior to a grinding stone, which requires refacing and or replacing much more frequently.

Although the concentric and eccentric valve seat grinders have been used for many years, they do have some drawbacks. The concentric valve seat stone grinder that contacts the full-seat circumference at one time tends to retain the fine grinding dust during the grinding process and can actually pound these filings back into the seat. Consequently, it does not produce as fine a seat surface finish as the eccentric grinder shown in Figure 14–34, which only contacts one part of the seat at any given time as it rotates off-center

FIGURE 14–32 *Cutting (machining) a valve face with a hand-operated valve refacer kit. The valve is safely and securely held in a vise to protect the stem. (Courtesy of Neway Manufacturing, Inc.)*

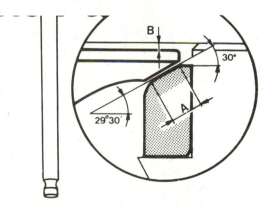

FIGURE 14–33 *Example of a valve face-to-seat insert interference angle. (Courtesy of DAF Trucks, Eindhoven Netherlands.)*

around the valve seat. The eccentric grinder does, however, take longer to grind the seat than does a concentric grinder. Both the concentric and the eccentric valve seat grinders employ grinding stones and holders that are threaded onto the end of the drive motor chuck. Stones are readily available in a wide variety of diameters and seat angles. Stones can be reground using a diamond point tool attachment when worn. Stones are available in different grits and colors; their makeup is relative to the type of material to be ground. Cast iron heads and regular steel inserts usually employ a gray-colored stone, whereas hardened Stellite-type inserts require a white stone.

The main advantage of a seat cutter with a tungsten carbide blade shown in Figure 14–35 is that it does not require regular resharpening as a grinding stone does. It retains seat-to-guide concentricity much better, and it can grind thousands of seats with one set of blades, which are replaceable when required. This

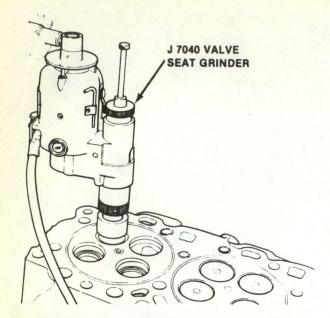

A

FIGURE 14–34 *Grinding a valve seat insert within the cylinder head using an eccentric valve seat grinder and stone. (Courtesy of Detroit Diesel Corporation.)*

type of seat cutter can cut a seat in the same time that it takes to dress a stone, plus it cuts in far fewer revolutions and produces a true flat seat at an exact angle with a superior finish.

The important part of the valve seat grinding process is to ensure that the insert, when finish ground, will produce the desired valve seat contact width along with the proper location on the valve face. The width required on the valve face-to-seat contact area is determined by the overall valve head diameter and is specified by the engine manufacturer in the service literature. For example a 2 in. (50.8 mm) diameter valve might call for a 0.060 to 0.090 in. (1.5 to 2.25 mm) face width. The seat face contact should start at about the midpoint of the valve face and move toward the head of the valve but stop short of the rim (margin). To accurately achieve this, often you must use a *three-angle cutting sequence* on the valve seat insert in the cylinder head by employing three stones (cutters) ground or adjusted to these three separate angles. This allows you to perform what is commonly referred to as *overcutting* or *undercutting* to position the seat on the desired location of the valve face. In addition, the cutting sequence allows you to obtain the recommended face seat width accurately.

To effectively produce a three-angle valve seat, the technician can employ a 15°, 30°, and 60° cutter set similar to that shown in Figure 14–35, or if available, can use the special Kwik-Way tooling illustrated in Figure 14–36. This tooling is designed to produce a

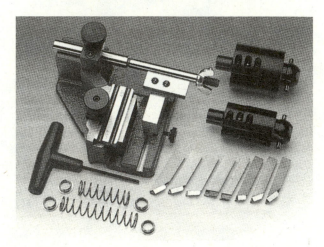

VGS-500 three-blade, three-angle seat cutting kit.

B

FIGURE 14–35 *(a) Using a model VGS-20 valve seat insert cutter machine; (b) VGS-500 three-blade, three-angle seat cutting kit attachments. (Courtesy of Sunnen Products Company.)*

three-angle cut using a carbide tip tool that cuts all three valve seat angles at once. The tooling allows manual operation by hand or an electric cutting motor drive assembly. It features a carbide pilot and articulated spindle holder with a ball-mounted spindle for self-aligning tooling.

When cutting a three-angle valve seat as shown in Figure 14–37, note that area 4 has been cut with a 60° cutter or stone, while area 3 has been cut with a 15° stone. Item 1 in the diagram is the *minimum* valve seat width, which in this example is 0.060 in (1.5 mm); item 2 is the *maximum* seat width of 0.090 in. (2.25 mm). Both item 1 and item 2 are a 30° angle. Once the seat has been initially cut or ground to 30°, it should not

FIGURE 14–36 Model
045 valve seat forming center.
(Courtesy of Kwik Way
Manufacturing Co.)

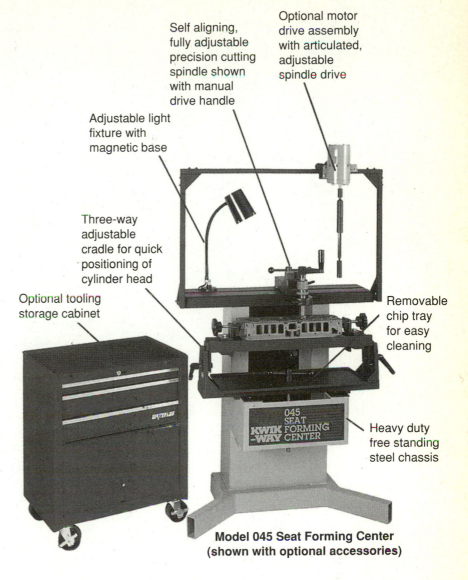

Self aligning,
fully adjustable
precision cutting
spindle shown
with manual
drive handle

Optional motor
drive assembly
with articulated,
adjustable
spindle drive

Adjustable light
fixture with
magnetic base

Three-way
adjustable
cradle for quick
positioning of
cylinder head

Optional tooling
storage cabinet

Removable
chip tray
for easy
cleaning

Heavy duty
free standing
steel chassis

**Model 045 Seat Forming Center
(shown with optional accessories)**

require recutting if the service technician applied the 15° and 60° cutters or stones very gently to obtain the desired seat width and location on the valve face when checked with Prussian Blue paste.

Seat Grinding Procedure

Ideally, the cylinder head should be mounted securely onto a suitable support stand at a comfortable working height similar to that shown in Figure 14–36 before attempting to remove or install valve guides or seats and during any attempt to regrind the seat inserts. The cylinder head can also be bolted to an adapter on an engine overhaul stand or any other suitable head-retaining fixture. To achieve concentricity between the valve seat and guide, the guide should be within acceptable worn limits. The more square the guide, the better the chance that the seat will be at right angles to the guide. Regardless of the type of grinding stone

(cutter) used, a valve guide pilot must be inserted to support the rotating stone (cutter) holder. Most pilots have a diameter stamped on the body to guide you. Similarly, the diameter and angle of grinding stones and cutters are labeled.

Now follow these steps in the seat grinding procedure:

1. Select a valve guide pilot. Use either a solid pilot, which is the same basic diameter as the valve stem, or an expandable pilot, which usually provides an adjustment of approximately 0.020 in (0.5 mm). When using a solid pilot, insert it into the valve guide using a slight twisting motion until it is tight (Figure 14–38). Note that the pilot shoulder should not touch the guide; if it does, use a smaller or larger pilot as appropriate. If you are using an expandable pilot as shown in Figure 14–39, select a pilot as close to the valve stem diameter as possible and insert the pilot into the guide. The valve

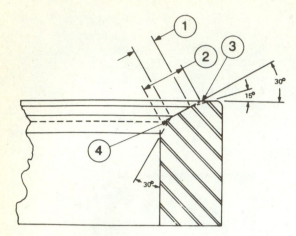

FIGURE 14–37   *Illustration of a 30° valve seat insert. The minimum seat width is shown as item 1; item 2 is the maximum recommended seat width. The seat width and its location to the valve face can be achieved by using a 15° stone to remove metal from the top side at position 3, a method known as undercutting. Position 4 at the throat area can be overcut by using a 60° stone. (Courtesy of Cummins Engine Company Inc.)*

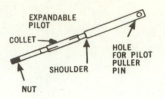

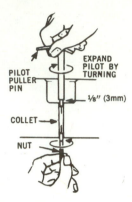

FIGURE 14–39   *Identification of an expandable valve guide pilot. (Courtesy of Neway Manufacturing, Inc.)*

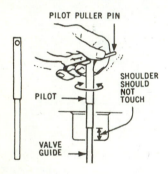

FIGURE 14–38   *Installing or removing the valve guide pilot, which is required to accept a valve seat grinding stone (cutter). (Courtesy of Neway Manufacturing, Inc.)*

guide should be longer than the expandable section of the pilot collet, as shown in Figure 14–39, which must remain inside the valve guide when tightened up. The pilot shoulder should be about 1/8 in. (3 mm) above the valve guide. Insert the pilot puller pin into the pilot hole at the top, and while holding onto the lower nut, rotate and expand the pilot until tight.

2. If you are using a grinding stone, refer to Figure 14–34, which illustrates an eccentric seat grinder supported on a valve guide pilot. By adjusting the drive motor micrometer handle, the stone will automatically be lowered onto the seat, and the internal drive mechanism will allow the stone to slowly rotate around the seat until it has finished the rotation.

If you are using a concentric grinding stone, you control how hard the stone contacts the seat (downward pressure) and for how long. Therefore, be very careful that you do not remove too much stock from the seat. Start the drive motor and lightly and quickly allow the stone to contact the seat; then inspect it to see how much material has been removed. Carefully continue to grind the seat until it is completely cleaned up.

3. If you are using a valve seat cutter with tungsten carbide blades, you can select a cutter of the same basic diameter as the valve head that has been set to the correct angle. Refer to Figure 14–40 and place the cutter over the valve guide pilot. Slowly lower the cutter to the valve seat face, since dropping it can damage the cutter blade and seat. Place a T-handle or motor-driven power unit over the hex drive of the cutter, and while maintaining a centered light downward pressure, rotate the cutter clockwise through several complete revolutions. Carefully remove the cutter and inspect the seat surface as shown in Figure 14–41 to determine the condition of the surface finish. This procedure will allow you to gauge just how much material needs to be removed to square up the seat.

4. Whether you are using a grinding stone or a cutter arrangement, once the seat has been cleaned to satisfaction, remove the tooling, apply Prussian Blue paste to the valve as shown earlier in Figure 14–29, and inspect the valve face for the seat width and location. Normally, if you have used only one stone (cut-

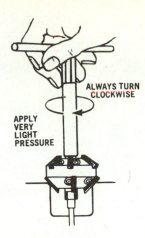

FIGURE 14–40 Using a valve seat insert cutter tool to restore a worn seat. (Courtesy of Neway Manufacturing, Inc.)

FIGURE 14–41 Close inspection of the valve seat insert to determine how much material needs to be removed to square up the seat. (Courtesy of Neway Manufacturing, Inc.)

ter) set to the recommended angle (30°, for example), the seat width will normally be too wide. You will have to *overcut* or *undercut* to raise or lower the seat location and to achieve the desired seat width.

5. Figure 14–42 illustrates that by using a stone (cutter) with a steeper angle (overcutting 60°, for example), you can successfully raise the bottom edge of the seat contact surface, since the removed material no longer contacts the valve face. This is known as a *bottom narrowing cut*.

6. Figure 14–43 illustrates that by using a narrower stone (cutter)—undercutting 15°, for example—you can remove valve seat insert material from the top edge of the seat contact surface area, thereby lowering the top edge of the valve face seat. This is known as a *top narrowing cut*.

7. If the top and bottom narrowing cuts have been performed very lightly and with adequate care, the seat will be centered between both cuts as illustrated in Figure 14–44. If the seat width is too narrow, you will have to use the 30° stone (cutter) again. If the

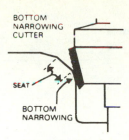

FIGURE 14–42 Overcutting a seat insert by using a 60° cutter to raise the bottom edge of the valve face seat contact surface. (Courtesy of Neway Manufacturing, Inc.)

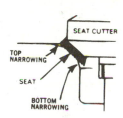

FIGURE 14–43 Undercutting a seat insert by using a 15° cutter to lower the valve face seat contact surface. (Courtesy of Neway Manufacturing, Inc.)

FIGURE 14–44 Centering of the valve seat insert to the valve face contact surface by narrowing both the top and bottom seat areas. (Courtesy of Neway Manufacturing, Inc.)

seat is too wide, or the seat location is too high or too low, you may have to overcut or undercut to achieve the correct seat location and width.

8. Always confirm the seat width and location by use of Prussian Blue paste on the valve face as described earlier. Refer to Figure 14–45 and gently tap the valve up and down slightly. Apply finger pressure to the top of the valve head and to the stem tip until you have achieved a clean valve face seat contact area. If an *intereference angle* is being used, the valve face seat contact area will appear as a *ring mark* or narrow line, rather than the wider seat that occurs when no interference angle is used. The ring mark should appear about one-third of the way down the valve face from the rim (margin). If the mark is too high, cut the top narrowing angle

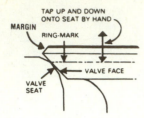

FIGURE 14–45 *Determining the contact location of the valve face to valve seat insert by tapping the valve onto the seat by hand. After removal, check the Prussian Blue paste as described in Figure 14–29 to determine seat width and actual location. (Courtesy of Neway Manufacturing, Inc.)*

FIGURE 14–46 *Using a lapping stick and suction cup on top of the valve head to lightly lap the valve seat to the insert while using a small amount of lapping paste on the valve face. (Courtesy of Cummins Engine Company Inc.)*

slightly to lower the mark. If the mark is too low, cut the seat angle at the bottom to raise the mark. If an open spot appears on the valve face seat contact area and it is greater than 12.7 mm (1/2 in.), reuse the seat stone (cutter) over the pilot and gently attempt to blend it in by turning the stone (cutter) by hand only. Small noncontact spots on the valve seat face tend to peen themselves into a full-face contact pattern within a very short time after initial engine start-up.

9.   After any valve seat cutting (grinding) procedure, install a small dial gauge on a pilot (as illustrated in Figure 14–27) with its extension point resting against the valve seat. Set the gauge to zero and gently rotate it at least one complete turn to determine the runout that exists between the valve guide and seat insert. This will indicate if the valve seat is concentric to the guide; although stated in the engine service manual specs, the maximum reading is usually 0.05 mm (0.002 in.), but check the engine service manual specs. Excessive runout readings can be traced to a worn valve guide or grinding equipment that has not been set up or used properly.

10.   While wearing protective eye gear and clothing, thoroughly clean the cylinder head in a solvent bath or by steam cleaning and high pressure washing. Then blow-dry the cylinder head with compressed shop air.

11.   After the valves, springs, seals, and keeper locks have been reassembled, check the seat sealing surface of the valves by using either a hand-operated or electric-motor-driven vacuum pump with the suction cup placed over the valve head. Failure of the vacuum pump gauge to rise and hold its value indicates that the seat-to-valve face is leaking. If no vacuum pump is available, lay the cylinder head on its side and pour diesel fuel into the intake and exhaust ports. Check for any signs of fuel pouring from the valve head area. A minor leak or sweat is usually acceptable. If a serious vacuum or fuel leak is evident, however,

remove the valve and carefully check that no foreign material has been wedged between the face and seat. If the valve seats have already been reground to satisfaction, or there is insufficient material left to regrind the seat, you can attempt one of these procedures:

- Apply a light coating of valve lapping compound to the valve face seat. In Figure 14–46 a small suction cup and valve stick are used to rotate the valve so that it can be lightly ground to the seat insert. Do not rotate the valve excessively; remove it after six to ten full rotations, clean it off, and inspect the seat contact, which will appear as a dull-gray surface finish. Relap as necessary without creating a step in the face of the valve.
- Replace the valve seat inserts; possibly use new valves.

SPECIAL NOTE: Any time that the valve seats or the valves have been reground, it is very important that you check the *valve head recess* which can be done by using a dial indicator mounted onto a sled-gauge as illustrated in Figure 14–47. Always check the engine service manual to determine the allowable dimension! If the valve head is too low in its seat, *valve guttering* will occur. In other words, the valve will fail to open wide enough and may result in a restriction to both the air inlet and exhaust gas flow to and from the combustion chamber and cylinder. Rough engine operation will result along with low power, poor fuel economy, smoke at the exhaust stack, incomplete combustion, and carbon buildup around the neck of the valves. In some cases where both a new valve and seat insert are being used, the seat insert *may* require grinding to lower the valve head sufficiently to avoid contact with the piston crown. This situation can occur when a cylinder head

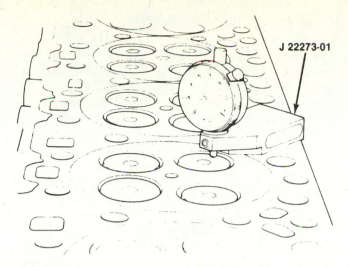

FIGURE 14–47 Using a dial indicator mounted on a sled to determine the valve head protrusion or intrusion. (Courtesy of Detroit Diesel Corporation.)

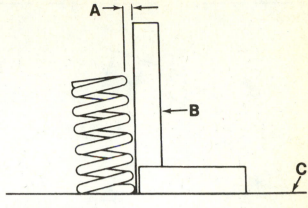

A. Inclination
B. Square
C. Surface Plate   W-00476

FIGURE 14–48 Using a small try square to check the valve spring for straightness and squareness. (Courtesy of GMC Trucks.)

fire deck has been resurfaced and new standard thickness inserts have been installed. Reduced thickness inserts of 0.010, 0.020, and 0.030 in. (0.254, 0.5, and 0.75 mm) should be installed to handle the same amount of material ground from the fire deck. Note that maximum values for valve *protrusion* and *intrusion* are specified. If the valve sits too high above the fire deck, regrind the seat insert. If it sits too far below the fire deck, replace the insert. If the valve head rim (margin) is too thin, replace the valve.

VALVE SPRINGS

Figure 14–7 illustrates the location of the valve spring, which is used to keep the valve securely closed during the compression and power stroke within the engine. Some engine manufacturers use a single spring, whereas others may use two or even three springs for this purpose. Obviously when more than one spring is used, the inner springs are smaller in outside diameter than the outer spring so that they can be stacked inside one another. Spring materials are made from high-strength alloy steels that contain a high modulus of elasticity, because the constant compression-to-tension cycle that they experience during engine operation places high stresses on them.

When checking valve springs, look for signs of polishing on the outer coils. Such signs may indicate that the spring has been rubbing on some component within the valve operating mechanism during engine operation. They may also indicate that a spring is off square as a result of weakness, distortion, or coil breakage. Also check the valve springs for overheating

(indicated by spring coil discoloration), squareness, and free and compressed length. Spring squareness can be checked as illustrated in Figure 14–48 by sitting the spring on a flat surface and placing a small try square alongside it. Any appreciable gap between inclination (A) and square (B) would require spring replacement. Using a vernier caliper as shown in Figure 14–49, check the free length of the spring and compare it to the dimension in the service manual. Replace the spring if it is too short. The compressed length of the spring can be checked on a special spring tester to determine if it agrees with the value in the service manual. The tester is equipped with a ruler and a spring pressure scale as shown in Figure 14–50. With the tester set to a specific spring height, place the spring between the top and bottom surface tables and read the gauge to determine if the compressed force of the spring is acceptable. If not, replace the spring.

If a valve spring breaks during engine operation, the valve may or may not come into contact with the piston crown. When you replace a broken spring, also replace the valve spring seat or rotator and use new valve lock keepers. Also carefully inspect the valve for signs of damage in the keeper area, and check to see if the valve has been bent. You can conduct this check without removing the cylinder head. Rotate the engine over manually to place the piston at TDC; then use an external spring compressor or suitable tooling to remove the valve spring retainer or rotator, the keepers, spring, and seal(s). Manually rotate the valve to determine any visible bending, or install a dial indicator against the valve stem and rotate the valve. A bent valve requires removal of the cylinder head.

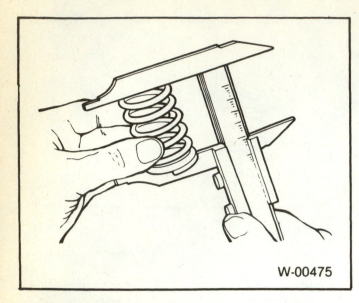

W-00475

FIGURE 14–49 *Measuring the free length of a valve spring with a vernier caliper. (Courtesy of GMC Trucks.)*

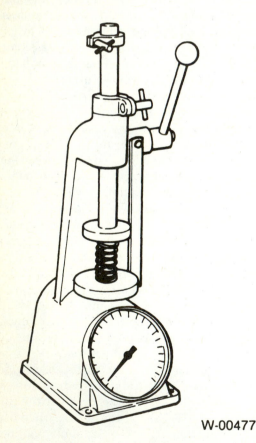

W-00477

FIGURE 14–50 *Measuring the compressed length of a valve spring. (Courtesy of GMC Trucks.)*

CYLINDER HEAD GASKETS

Heavy-duty high-speed diesel engines that are electronically controlled generally have cylinder head gaskets that are manufactured as a sandwich-type design. For example, the 3176 Cat cylinder head gasket is made with a stainless steel perforated core and graphite coating material, and it employs a stainless steel flange wrapping the fire rings and capturing a water hole to help prevent coolant leaks. These head gaskets are usually precoated, so they do not require the service technician to apply any type of sealer to the gasket or head surface prior to installation.

All necessary O-rings for coolant and lube oil passages from the engine block to the cylinder head are captured within the one-piece gasket assembly. A typical one-piece head gasket design is illustrated in Figure 14–1. On some engines such as the two-stroke-cycle DDC models, individual round cylinder liner compression gaskets such as those illustrated in Figure 16–32 are employed. In addition, there are individual O-rings for coolant and lube oil passages. These O-rings sit in machined counterbores on top of the cylinder block and are compressed to form an effective seal when the head is torqued down.

Because of their raised free-shape design, all cylinder head gaskets are compressed flat by the cylinder head when the bolts are torqued to specifications. This deformation characteristic provides an effective compression and coolant seal. The gaskets do not return to their original shape once the cylinder head has been removed; therefore, the head gasket is a "one-time item." Always replace the head gasket with a new one each time the cylinder head has been removed for any reason. In emergency situations, a used head gasket may be reinstalled, but there is no guarantee that it will seal indefinitely.

Current steel-type cylinder head gaskets *do not* require retorquing after initial engine run-in after overhaul or when a new gasket has been installed during service repair. However, some engine manufacturers state that when a steel cylinder head gasket has been removed for a head repair, a nonsteel gasket should be used as a replacement. In cases such as this, they often suggest that the cylinder head bolts or nuts be retightened after the accumulation of between 500 and 2500 km (311 to 1553 miles). Always check the engine manufacturer's service manual for information.

CYLINDER HEAD INSTALLATION

After a cylinder head has been overhauled, or if the head has been removed to replace a gasket, make sure that all cylinders are clean and free of any foreign material. All piston domes and the head and engine block machined surfaces must be smooth and free of any nicks or burrs. The cylinder head bolt holes in the engine block should be cleaned with a tap to minimize any false torque reading values. Similarly, the threads of the bolts or studs should be cleaned on a wire brush. Make sure that none of the head bolt holes are filled with water or oil, since when the bolt is tightened into a *blind hole* a cracked block hole can occur from the hydrostatic lock that results as the bolt is torqued.

Although many cylinder blocks are fitted with two dowel pins to guide the head into place upon installation, it is advisable to install at least two *guide studs* as shown in Figure 14–51. These can be manufactured from old head bolts or cold-rolled steel stock. On engines with cylinder head studs and nuts, the studs should be installed and tightened into position prior to lowering the head into position. Use either two nuts locked together or a stud remover and installer with a 1/2 in. (12.7 mm) square drive to facilitate tightening of the head studs to the specified torque or installed height. Carefully check the cylinder head gasket to ensure that it is installed in the correct direction. Usually the word *top, front,* or a part number indicates the top side of the head gasket and how it should be installed. Some gaskets fit onto the block in only one direction due to offset oil, water, or bolt hole placement. The head gasket usually employs raised and rolled lips around the cylinder bore areas and/or coolant and oil passages. These raised areas are on the top side of the gasket.

Follow these steps to install the cylinder head.

1. On four-stroke-cycle engines, carefully install the one-piece head gasket over the dowels and guide studs. Note that some DDC two-stroke-engine models employ a special strip/steel shim at each end of the cylinder block. These shims are required to prevent cylinder head bolt breakage. Prior to installing new shims, remove the adhesive paper and place the support shims in position at each end of the block. On these same engines, individual cylinder liner compression gaskets are used with a series of O-rings that are inserted into counterbores in the engine block top deck to seal both coolant and lube oil flowing from the block to the cylinder head.

2. Using the same cylinder head lifting brackets that were used for removal, lift the head into position using an overhead hoist and carefully direct the head over the guide studs.

3. On engines using individual coolant or oil O-seal rings, carefully see that all O-rings are in place just before lowering the head down.

4. Visually inspect the cylinder head capscrews for damaged threads, corroded surfaces, pitting, or a reduced diameter due to capscrew stretching. Signs of

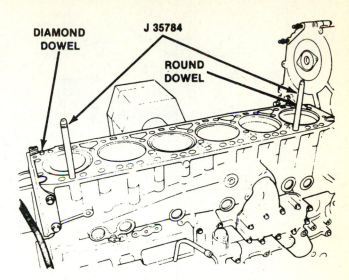

FIGURE 14–51 *Use of cylinder head guide studs to assist in the removal and installation alignment of the head. (Courtesy of Detroit Diesel Corporation.)*

rounding on the hex head area of the bolt would also be sufficient reason to replace the cylinder head capscrews.

5. Before installing the head bolts or nuts, refer to the engine manufacturer's service manual to determine what type of lubricant should be applied to the bolt threads. Some suggest that a small amount of clean engine oil be used (usually 15W-40); others specify that International Compound No. 2 or equivalent be used on the bolt threads as well as under the bolt head or nut contact area. Failure to use a lubricant can lead to insufficient bolt and nut torque, resulting in a leaking head gasket.

6. Note that each manufacturer specifies a head bolt torquing sequence, which generally starts at the center of the cylinder head and moves outward in a clockwise direction. Follow this process if you do not have a service manual to guide you. A specific example of the head bolt torquing sequence for a DDC Series 60 four-stroke-cycle electronically controlled DDEC engine using a one-piece cylinder head is shown in Figure 14–52. Figure 14–53 illustrates the head bolt torquing sequence for a Cummins N14 Celect engine model. In both cases tighten the bolts at the middle of the head first and move outward in a clockwise direction.

SPECIAL NOTE: On very large bore engines, such as those found in industrial, oil pipeline, gen-set, and deep-sea marine applications, torquing of the large cylinder head bolts cannot be performed using a conventional type torque wrench, since the physical size of the retaining nuts and bolts prevents a manual tightening routine. To effectively tighten cylinder head bolts and nuts on these types of engines, a *hydraulic tensioner* device unit

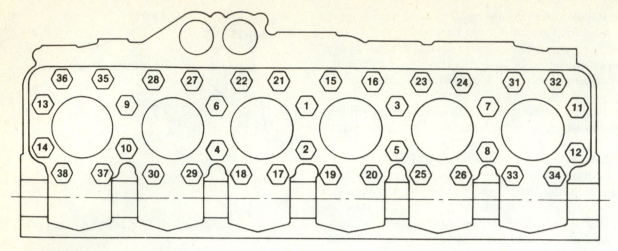

FIGURE 14–52 *Example of a cylinder head bolt tightening sequence for a Series 60 engine model. (Courtesy of Detroit Diesel Corporation.)*

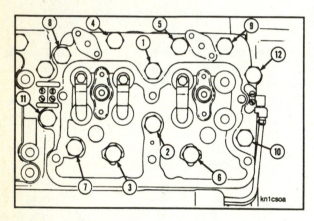

FIGURE 14–53 Cylinder head bolt tightening sequence for a model N14 (855 cu in.) engine. (Courtesy of Cummins Engine Company, Inc.)

FIGURE 14–54 *Using four hydraulic tensioner machines to tighten the cylinder head retaining studs on a Cat 3600 Series engine. Use these same tensioners to tighten the main bearing caps. (Courtesy of Caterpillar Inc.)*

similar to that shown in Figure 14–54 for a Caterpillar 3600 series engine is used. Four units are shown in position on the cylinder head at one time to allow equal and accurate torque to be applied to the head studs. This same type of hydraulic device is used to tension the main bearing caps on these engine models.

SERVICE TIP: Cylinder head bolts should never be tightened to their final torque in one step! From specs, determine the final torque value; then pull the bolts down in three steps. For example, if the final torque is listed as 220 lb-ft. (298 N·m), step 1 should be approximately 50 lb-ft. (68 N·m), step 2 might be to 125 lb-ft. (170 N·m), and step 3 is the final torque setting. Once the final torque value has been reached, go back over the tightening sequence to verify that all bolts are in fact torqued to spec. Many existing torque wrenches are equipped with a battery-operated digital readout to confirm final torque values.

·7.   Install the individual injectors into their respective bores. These should have been numbered when they were removed! If new injectors are being installed, it doesn't matter what cylinder they are placed into. Make certain that new copper washers of the correct thickness are used on nozzles employed with high-pressure inline injection pump fuel systems (Robert Bosch, Zexel USA, Nippondenso, Lucas, and so forth). On unit injectors, make sure that the injector crab hold-down washer has the hemispherical washer (beveled side) facing down toward the cylinder head, and tighten the hold down crab bolt or nuts to the specified torque value.

SERVICE TIP: Overtightening the hold-down crab on mechanical unit injectors can result in a sticking fuel rack.

8.   Remember that on overhead camshaft designs, the cam idler gear must be adjusted and locked to provide the correct gear backlash. This condition requires a special tool (see Chapter 13).

9. Install the rocker arm and shaft assemblies and tighten them to the correct torque value. Reset the intake and exhaust valve bridges (crossheads) as well as the valve clearance. Adjust the unit injector timing height or preload. If the engine is a two-stroke-cycle DDC mechanical model, adjust the governor gap, injector racks, idle and no-load speeds, the buffer screw, throttle delay mechanism, and the starting-aid screw.

10. Reconnect the electronic unit fuel injector wiring harness and the engine compression brake wiring.

11. If the engine coolant thermostats have not been installed, clean the gasket surface area and install new thermostats, seals, and gasket. Tighten the thermostat housing into place.

12. Install the intake and exhaust manifolds with new gaskets and torque in sequence and to specifications. Install the wiring harness from the turbo boost and intake manifold temperature and exhaust temperature sensors.

13. Install the aftercooler, if removed, using new gaskets.

14. Install the turbocharger with new gaskets; reconnect any intake and exhaust piping.

15. Install the top rad hose and deaeration lines from the thermostat housing.

16. Fill and vent the cooling system until all signs of air have been displaced by a steady stream of coolant from the vent line connection.

17. Double-check that all other accessory items and fittings such as lube and fuel lines have been reconnected.

18. Refill the engine with clean engine oil and a new lube filter. If the engine has been completely rebuilt, prime the lube oil system first using a suitable pressure primer until lube oil is visible at the rocker arm shaft assemblies.

19. Bleed the fuel system with a priming pump to displace all air.

20. Start and run the engine and check carefully for fuel, coolant, lube oil, and exhaust and intake manifold air leaks.

SELF-TEST QUESTIONS

1. List the five major functions of the cylinder head.
2. Cylinder heads are generally cast from what type of materials?
3. Material strengths for cylinder heads are generally about
   a. 100 MPa
   b. 175 MPa
   c. 250 MPa
   d. 300 MPa
4. Technician A says that the term *four-valve head* refers to an engine with a total of four valves within the cylinder head. Technician B says the term means that each cylinder covered by the head contains four valves. Who is correct?
5. Technician A says that the term *crossflow cylinder head* means that the intake manifold is on one side while the exhaust manifold is on the opposite side. Technician B says that the term means that the inlet air enters one side of the head, flows across the piston crown, and flows back out of the same side to induce swirl to the exhaust gases during the valve overlap cycle. Which technician is correct?
6. Technician A says that all DDC two-stroke-cycle engines only use exhaust valves. Technician B says that all engines need both intake and exhaust valves to operate. Which technician knows engine operating theory best?
7. Technician A says that Detroit Diesel, Caterpillar, and Cummins employ individual cylinder heads on their larger-displacement engines. Technician B says that the only engine manufacturers that employ these feature are those that build very-large-displacement slow-speed engines such as those for marine applications. Which technician is correct?
8. List the advantages of using four valves per cylinder over two valves.
9. True or False: A parallel port valve configuration in a cylinder head means that the valves are located 90° from the position used on traditional engines.
10. The Caterpillar 3406E engine has a stainless steel sleeve at the exhaust port within the cylinder head. What is the purpose of this feature?
11. True or False: Water or coolant directional nozzles within the cylinder head are designed to increase the velocity (speed and direction) of the block coolant entering the head to improve the coolant flow around the valve and injector areas.
12. Technician A says that most high-speed heavy-duty diesel engine injectors are screwed into the cylinder head. Not so says technician B; they are held in place by a hold-down clamp arrangement. Which technician is correct?
13. True or False: Most unit injectors are inserted into a copper or stainless steel injector tube within the cylinder head to allow for adequate cooling of the injector assembly.
14. The shape of the intake and exhaust valves in diesel engines is commonly referred to as a
   a. reed valve
   b. poppet valve
   c. gate valve
   d. rotating valve
15. Exhaust valves in diesel engines are exposed to average operating temperatures as hot as
   a. 600°C (1112°F)
   b. 700°C (1292°F)
   c. 800°C (1472°F)
   d. 900°C (1652°F)

16. List some of the common metal alloys from which exhaust valves are manufactured.

17. List some of the more common materials from which intake valves are made.

18. How do intake and exhaust valves manage to dissipate their absorbed heat?

19. What does a Stellite valve seat insert material consist of, and why would it be used?

20. Technician A says that both the intake and exhaust valves are retained in place in the cylinder head by the use of split locks (keepers). Technician B says that the spring retainer performs this function. Who is correct?

21. What is the purpose of a positive valve rotator assembly?

22. Describe the method you would use to determine if a positive valve rotator assembly was operating correctly in an engine.

23. Technician A says that faulty valve stem seals will result in combustion blowby, low compression, and hard starting. Technician B says that oil will be pulled down the valve guide, resulting in burning of oil and blue smoke in the exhaust gas. Which technician is correct?

24. Technician A says that worn valve guides can cause a rocking action as the valve opens and closes, resulting in poor valve face-to-seat contact and early valve failure from burning. Technician B says that oil pulled down the guides will cause blue smoke in the exhaust gas. Are both statements correct?

25. Technician A says that worn valve guides can sometimes be repaired by a knurling procedure. Technician B says that when worn, all valve guides must be replaced. Who is correct?

26. Technician A says that if a cylinder head does not contain replaceable valve guides, when the head is worn it must be replaced. Technician B says that the head can be machined to accept press-fit valve guide assemblies. Which technician is correct?

27. True or False? Valve seat inserts are shrink fit in the cylinder head.

28. Technician A says that all valves should be marked at removal to ensure that they will be replaced into the same guide position upon reassembly. Technician B says that it doesn't matter where they are placed after repair. Which technician is correct?

29. Technician A says that if injectors are being reused at an engine rebuild, they can be serviced and then replaced into any cylinder. Technician B believes that it is good policy to always reinstall an injector into the same cylinder. Does it matter? If no, why not? If yes, give your reasons.

30. Technician A says that most intake and exhaust valves are machined with a 30° angle on their faces. Not so says technician B; a 45° angle is much more common. Who is correct?

31. True or False: If a cylinder head is being removed with the injectors in place, the head should not be placed on a bench; it should be supported on wooden blocks or a head support bracket.

32. Technician A says that cylinder head bolts should be loosened off in the reverse order that they were torqued in, which is from the outside of the head toward the center. Technician B disagrees, saying that you should always start by loosening the head bolts from the center and working outward. Which technician is correct?

33. Technician A says that when remachining the fire deck of the cylinder head, you are limited to how much metal can be taken off. Therefore, refer to the engine manufacturer's specs for the minimum head thickness. Technician B says that it doesn't matter how much metal you remove; you can always use a thicker cylinder head gasket. Which technician knows the overhaul procedure best?

34. True or False: Heavy coolant scale buildup can result in cylinder head cracking due to overheating.

35. List the four methods that can be used to check a cylinder head for signs of cracks at engine overhaul.

36. Cleaning and polishing of the cylinder head fire deck can be performed using emery cloth with a grit rating of between
    a. 120 and 180
    b. 240 and 400
    c. 400 and 600
    d. 600 and 800

37. True or False: Cylinder head flatness can be checked by visually looking at the surface condition.

38. Technician A says that valve guide wear can be determined without removing the cylinder head by following a set procedure, which includes using a dial indicator. Technician B says that the only way to determine valve guide wear is to remove and disassemble the cylinder head assembly. Which technician is correct?

39. True or False: Some engine manufacturers supply valves with oversize valve stems to avoid having to replace the valve guides.

40. To check valve face-to-seat contact, the best method to use is to lightly coat the face with
    a. blue layout ink
    b. Prussian Blue paste
    c. Never-sieze
    d. line pencil marks

41. Technician A says that the best way to remove valve seat inserts is to use a small, sharp chisel and a hammer to split them. Technician B says that you should employ a special puller assembly. Which technician is correct?

42. Technician A says that when installing new valve seat inserts, you can heat the head in a temperature-controlled oven and chill the insert for best results, or use a guided installer and press or tap (hammer) the insert into place. Technician B says that you can simply drive the insert into the head with a hammer by working around the outer circumference of the insert. Who is correct?

43. If the cylinder head fire deck has to be remachined, technician A says that you should consider using thinner valve seat inserts. Technician B says that you can simply machine the hardened inserts during the head resurfacing procedure. Which technician is correct?

44. Technician A says that valve face seat contact width and placement are very important when regrinding valves and seats. Technician B says that it doesn't matter where the seat contact is as long as a good, wide seat exists to help to dissipate valve head heat. Which technician has a better understanding of the valve and seat grinding procedure?

45. True or False: The terms *overcutting* and *undercutting* refer to the procedure used when it is necessary to use a grinding stone or cutter with a larger or smaller angle.

46. The term *three-angle grinding* is often used by high-performance cylinder head rebuild shops. Describe what this term means.

47. What kinds of problems would exist if a valve had too much head protrusion?

48. What kinds of problems would exist if a valve had too much intrusion?

49. Too wide a valve seat face contact surface usually results in what types of problems?

50. Too narrow a valve seat face contact area usually results in what kinds of problems?

51. Technician A says that if a cylinder head has worn valve guides, these should be replaced before attempting to regrind the valve seat inserts. Technician B says that replacement will have no bearing on the finished valve seat grind quality, because either a grinding stone or cutter will be used. Which technician understands the factors behind a good valve seat reconditioning procedure?

52. Technician A believes that using a grinding stone produces a better valve seat insert finish than using a valve seat cutter with blades. What do you think? Give your reasons.

53. How would you check a valve to determine if it is bent when you cannot see that it is bent?

54. After regrinding a valve face, you discover that the head margin is too thin. What types of problems would occur if you reused the valve?

55. What is an interference angle between a valve and its seat insert? Does this feature provide any advantages?

56. Technician A says that when employing an interference angle the valve face is always ground at a smaller angle than the seat. Technician B says that it is the seat insert that has the smaller angle. Which technician knows theory of operation best?

57. Technician A says that an interference angle of the valve face to seat cannot be used when employing positive valve rotators. Technician B says it can be used. Which technician is correct and why?

58. Technician A says that all valves should be lapped into their seats after grinding to produce a smooth finish. Technician B says that lapping should only be used, and very lightly, if a sealing test indicates poor seat-to-face contact. Which technician is correct?

59. Technician A says that to check for tight valve face-to-seat sealing, you can employ a vacuum pump and suction cup over the valve head, or you can turn the cylinder head on its side and fill the intake and exhaust ports with diesel fuel and check for signs of fluid leakage. Technician B says that you should seal off both the intake and exhaust ports on the cylinder head with bolted plates drilled to take a compressed air fitting to check for effective valve seat sealing. Which technician knows the correct procedure?

60. List the checks required on all valve springs when performing a cylinder head rebuild.

61. Technician A says that all new cylinder head gaskets have to be coated with a suitable sealer prior to installation. Technician B says that most new gaskets are already coated and do not require additional sealant. Who is correct?

62. Technician A says that cylinder head gaskets are designed to be installed one way only. Technician B says that they can be installed in any direction since there is no top or bottom. Which technician is correct?

63. Technician A says that cylinder heads should be retorqued from the ends of the heads working toward the center. Technician B says that you should start the torquing sequence from the center of the head and work outwards in a CW direction. Which technician knows the procedure best?

64. Technician A says that all cylinder heads should be retorqued after a rebuilt engine has been run on a dynamometer or has accumulated a given number of hours or miles (kilometers). Technician B says that this is not necessary, unless specified by the engine manufacturer. Which technician is correct?

65. Technician A says that if you are installing a cylinder head and locating dowels are used on the cylinder block fire deck, it isn't necessary to use guide studs. Technician B says that you should always employ two guide studs to facilitate installation. Which technician knows good work practices?

66. Technician A says that cylinder head retaining bolts should be lightly coated with clean engine oil or International Compound No. 2 or equivalant on the threads, as well as underneath the hex head to provide for a more uniform torque loading of the bolt. Technician B says that you should flood the cylinder block oil hole with clean engine oil to ensure that proper torque is achieved. Which technician is correct and why?

67. Overtorquing of a cylinder head can result in
    a. bolt breakage
    b. head distortion
    c. head cracking
    d. coolant leakage into the cylinder
    e. all of the above

68. Undertorquing of a cylinder head can result in
    a. head gasket leakage
    b. head cracking
    c. valve breakage
    d. injector siezure

69. Torquing of very large engine cylinder head nuts is usually achieved by using a
    a. socket and long bar extension on the torque wrench
    b. gear-driven torque multiplier
    c. hydraulic tensioner
    d. portable hydraulic jack on the end of the torque wrench

70. Technician A says that cylinder head nuts and bolts should be taken to their final value in one step after snugging up. Technician B says that you should torque these up in incremental values using two to three steps because this procedure will provide a more even torque. Which technician is correct?

71. Technician A says that overtightening a unit injector type hold-down clamp bolt on a mechanical rack model can result in a sticking or binding rack condition. Technician B says that it will result in coolant leakage from the injector tube into the cylinder. Who is correct?

15 Pistons and Piston Rings

OVERVIEW

The pistons convert the chemical energy released from the fuel into mechanical energy to drive the connecting rod down the cylinder, which in turn rotates the engine crankshaft. The piston rings must seal the high-pressure gases of combustion from escaping from the cylinder. In this chapter, we discuss the various types of pistons and rings in use in today's high-speed, high-output electronically controlled diesel engines. The chapter also describes how to remove and install the pistons either alone or as a cylinder pack that includes the cylinder liner and connecting rod. Inspection, cleaning, measurement, and reassembly of all components are described.

TOPICS

- Piston function and nomenclature
- Basic piston designs
- Two-piece piston designs
- Piston crown shapes
- Piston operating temperatures
- Piston pins
- Piston skirt shape
- Piston Removal
- Piston disassembly inspection and reassembly
- Using a new piston
- Purpose and characteristics of piston rings
- Piston ring materials
- Types and designs of piston rings
- Piston ring wear and failure
- Piston ring installation
- Piston assembly installation
- Self-test questions

PISTON FUNCTION AND NOMENCLATURE

A piston, which is circular in shape, is one of the most important components of any internal combustion engine. The piston is designed to operate within the cylinder of the engine block; in so doing, it must retain the high-pressure gases of combustion created within the combustion chamber. This is achieved by employing a number of piston compression rings located in a ring belt on the upper half of the piston as shown in Figure 15–1. The burning of the liquid diesel or alternative fuel within the combustion chamber converts the chemical energy of the fuel into heat energy in the form of very-high-pressure gases acting on the top of the piston, which is commonly called the crown. This heat energy is transferred into mechanical energy by its downward thrust on the crown.

Depending on the design of the engine, the pressure of the expanding gases within the combustion chamber can drive the piston down the cylinder (vertically) or outward (horizontally). The piston pin, which is attached to both the piston and a connecting rod at its top end, is also bolted to the engine crankshaft at its bottom end. Therefore, the reciprocating (back and forward) motion of the piston and connecting rod causes the engine crankshaft to rotate.

Figure 15–2 illustrates the parts of a piston and the common terminology used to identify each.

BASIC PISTON DESIGNS

Pistons used in diesel engines are of two main designs: the one-piece *trunk-type model* shown in Figure 15–2 and, in high-output engines, the now more widely

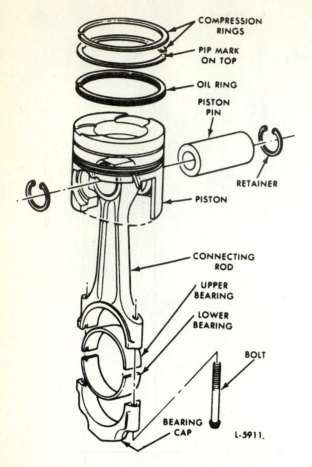

FIGURE 15–1   Piston details and relative location of component parts. (Courtesy of Detroit Diesel Corporation.)

used two-piece design referred to as *crosshead type* or an *articulated type* illustrated in Figure 15–3.

For many years, the majority of heavy-duty high-speed diesel engine manufacturers employed one piece trunk-type pistons made from either ductile cast iron or aluminum-silicon alloy. Now, however, internal engine design changes have been required because of exhaust emissions concerns of the U.S. EPA. One of these changes was the design and type of piston. Use of aluminum hypereutectic alloy pistons in marine and automotive two-stroke-cycle gasoline engines, showed that these materials could stand up to the arduous operating cycles. Consequently in the U.S. auto industry, these piston materials were used in the mid-1980s to avoid pound-out, microwelding, and durability problems that were being experienced by some major manufacturers of passenger cars. Piston ring wear has been virtually eliminated by the introduction of hypereutectic pistons. These pistons are compatible with both cylinder block cast iron and cylinder liners, and by dispersing primary silicon throughout the aluminum matrix, this hard silicon presents a durable and compatible bearing surface against which rings can seal. In addition, a higher fatigue strength is available from these types of pistons. Some of this same technology is now being applied to smaller-bore high-speed diesel engines, which require low-mass pistons.

Many trunk-type aluminum alloy pistons are produced from die castings that have been suitably heat-treated to bring out the optimum physical properties

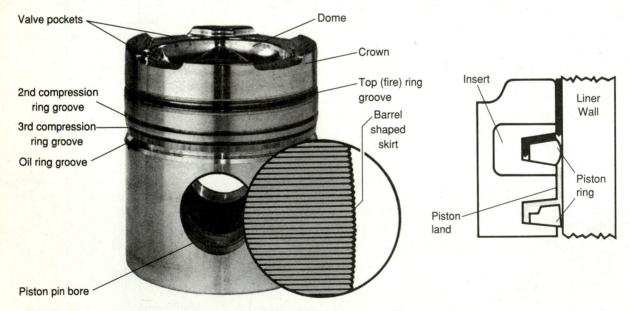

FIGURE 15–2   (a) One-piece trunk-type aluminum alloy piston and (b) nomenclature of specific areas. Note Ni-resist top ring piston insert and piston land. (Courtesy of Cummins Engine Company, Inc.)

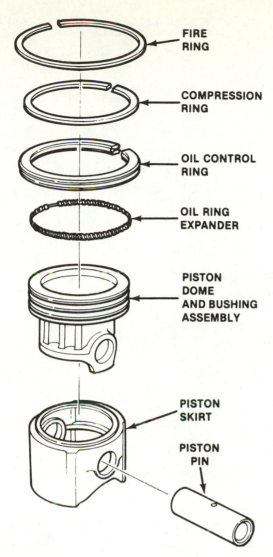

FIGURE 15–3 Two-piece crosshead, or articulated piston. The top of the piston (crown), which carries the rings, is entirely separate from the skirt; thus, each part can react independently to normal stresses developed during engine operation. In this three-ring arrangement, the top (fire) ring is only 3.8 mm (0.150 in.) from the piston crown. (Courtesy of Detroit Diesel Corporation.)

FIRE RING

COMPRESSION RING

OIL CONTROL RING

OIL RING EXPANDER

PISTON DOME AND BUSHING ASSEMBLY

PISTON SKIRT

PISTON PIN

of the material. Heavier sections are cast into both the crown and piston pin boss areas for added strength and to improve the heat flow through the piston. The co-efficient of expansion, or the increase in size per degree of temperature increase, of aluminum is approximately twice that of cast iron and steel. Also, the heat conductivity, or rate of heat flow, of aluminum is approximately three times that of cast iron—a condition that results in less variation in temperature from the top to the bottom of the piston. In addition, the weight of aluminum is 0.097 lb/cu in. and that of cast iron is 0.284 lb/cu in., or about three times that of alu-

minum. However, this does not mean that an aluminum piston weighs one-third that of a cast iron model, because strength and heat transfer problems dictate that the metal sections throughout the aluminum casting be made proportionately thicker. Aluminum melts at approximately 1220°F (660°C), compared to about 2800°F (1538°C) for cast iron. So to help strengthen the top of the aluminum piston, as well as improve the wear rate of the top piston ring grooves, a Ni-resist (nickel-chrome) band insert is metallurgically bonded into the piston top ring land area at the time of manufacture. (This can be seen in Figure 15–2 and Figure 15–4). The band insert may be in one or two top piston ring grooves depending on the demands, since the Ni-resist band creates structural integrity in the piston crown area. The addition of a Ni-resist insert further reduces the weight advantage of aluminum. The strength of aluminum also tends to decrease faster than that of cast iron or steel alloy when cylinder pressures and temperatures are increased. Similarly, the wear rate for an aluminum piston is usually greater when extremely heavy-load and high-speed applications are encountered.

Advanced casting techniques now allow a cooling oil gallery to be incorporated in SCFR (squeeze-cast fiber-reinforced) pistons. This offers the combined benefits of lower piston operating temperatures and greatly improved material strength. Squeeze casting is a die-casting technique that allows the high pressure applied during solidification to eliminate the microporosity inherent in all aluminum castings, thereby improving fatigue strength and permitting the incorporation of local fiber reinforcement. The adoption of gallery oil cooling increases piston bowl edge life by about a factor of one, and fiber reinforcement increases piston life by an order of magnitude of two. The combination of the two improves the life of the aluminum alloy piston by three orders of magnitude. Therefore, aluminum-silicon alloy trunk-type squeeze-formed pistons are emerging as a possible cost-effective solution to meet the performance and emissions requirements of diesel engines for both on- and off-highway applications. These pistons may very well challenge the more expensive two-piece piston design.

Figure 15–4 illustrates a SCFR trunk-type aluminum-silicon alloy piston from a Cummins C series engine used in 1994 on-highway truck applications of 250 bhp (186 kW) and above, with high peak torque above 700 lb-ft (949 N·m). A major production advantage of squeeze casting is that the piston can subsequently be machined using conventional tooling. The ceramic alumina fiber mesh reinforcement increases piston strength, reliability, and durability. The ceramic fibers have a polycrystalline structure consisting of

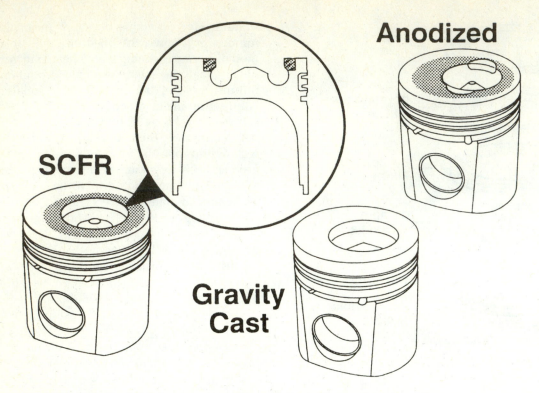

FIGURE 15–4 SCFR (squeeze-cast fiber-reinforced) one-piece trunk-type aluminum alloy pistons with an anodized crown for use in the C model engine. (Courtesy of Cummins Engine Company, Inc.)

alumina, zirconia, carbon, boron nitride, boron carbide, and silicon carbide. The aluminum fiber material is subjected, while still in a viscous (liquid) condition and prior to final solidification, to a process equivalent to that used in the forging process.

Ceramic-fiber-reinforced aluminum alloy, or CFA, pistons are now being used in both indirect- and direct-injection diesel engines. Figure 15–5 illustrates that the CFA material extends from the top of the piston down to below the top compression ring, as well as extending inward some distance toward the center of the crown. Tests indicate that the wear and siezure resistance of CFA pistons has been vastly improved compared to aluminum pistons and is equal to or superior to the Ni-resist insert that is still widely used in the top and/or second compression ring lands of many aluminum alloy pistons. In addition, the thermal (heat) conductivity of the CFA piston is better than an aluminum alloy piston using a Ni-resist insert; therefore, the overall operating temperatures of the CFA piston tend to run slightly cooler.

Industrial and automotive/truck applications for the same Cummins engines rated below 250 bhp (186 kW) and 700 lb-ft (949 N·m) have gravity cast pistons with an anodized coating on the piston crown. In addition, to minimize white smoke—particularly on cold

Thermal Comparison of CFA Piston and Niresist Insert Piston

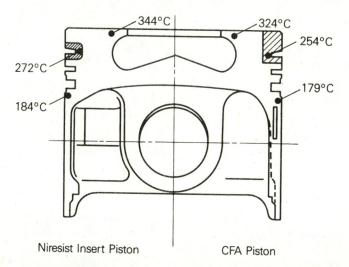

Niresist Insert Piston   CFA Piston

FIGURE 15–5 Thermal comparison of CFA (ceramic-fiber-reinforced aluminum alloy) piston versus a Ni-resist inset piston illustrates how the operating temperature throughout the piston varies during engine operation. (Courtesy of Cummins Engine Company, Inc.)

start up—and to optimize the piston height in each cylinder, all pistons have been graded into three sizes. In Cummins B series 1994 engines (used in the Dodge pickup truck application and others) the automotive ratings of below 190 bhp (142 kW) have the top piston ring location 8 mm (0.320 in.) down from the top of the piston. Automotive ratings at 190 bhp (142 kW) and higher continue to have the top ring location 14 mm (0.560 in.) down from the top of the piston.

In summary, CFA aluminum alloy pistons have the following advantages over a comparable cast iron model:

- Lighter weight therefore lower inertia forces
- Faster heat dissipation
- Good bearing surface (frictional) as well as running fairly quietly

TWO-PIECE PISTON DESIGNS

As U.S. EPA exhaust emissions standards became increasingly more stringent throughout the 1980s, heavy-duty high-speed diesel engine manufacturers such as Caterpillar, Cummins, Detroit Diesel, and Mack realized they had to make changes to meet on-highway truck emissions standards of the 1990s. They would have to redesign not only the fuel injection systems (higher injection pressures and electronic controls) but also the pistons within the cylinders. Aluminum alloys were reaching the limits of their capability to withstand the increased temperatures, pressures, and stresses created within the combustion chamber and cylinder during the power stroke. Two-piece pistons began to emerge in all of the high-speed heavy-duty on-highway truck engines; Detroit Diesel and Mack had already employed this concept for more than 20 years in a number of their engine models.

Research indicated that aluminum alloy pistons with top ring land heights of less than 4% of the piston diameter using single or double Ni-resist (Alfin process) ring carriers could withstand the higher pressures, temperatures, and stresses experienced in high-speed heavy-duty diesel engines. Consequently, both ferrous metal and aluminum alloy pistons in these heavier-duty applications have their compression ring and fire ring very close to the top of the piston crown to reduce the dead-air-space volume above the top piston ring. Another major change in pistons as a result of tighter exhaust emissions regulations is the redesign of the piston bowl geometry and size to provide optimum combustion conditions through increased air motion. The purpose of this change is to take advantage of better fuel atomization from the higher injection pressure injectors now in use, particularly on electronically controlled engines.

Major engine manufacturers at this time tend to employ one-piece trunk-type aluminum-silicon alloy pistons in their lower horsepower engines. Higher power models, such as those found in heavy-duty Class 8 truck applications employing electronically controlled fuel injection systems, use the stronger and superior performance two-piece unit. For example, Caterpillar uses a one-piece aluminum piston for the lower horsepower ratings in both its 3116 and 3406E engines; in its higher rated 3116 and 3406E (435 hp, 325 kW, and higher) engines, as well as its 3176B model truck engines, it employs a two-piece articulated piston that has a forged steel crown and aluminum alloy skirt. The Cat 3176B engine articulated piston is illustrated in Figures 15–6a and 15–6b; the 3406E employs a similar design arrangement. Cummins also employs an articulated piston in its higher power L10 engine, and the newer M11 and N14 Celect models have the two-piece piston assembly. Figure 15–7a illustrates a crosshead piston design used by Detroit Diesel in its 71, 92, and 149 series two-stroke engine models; Figure 15–3 illustrates the design used with its four-stroke-cycle Series 50 and 60 engine models.

Advantages of Two-Piece Pistons

The two-piece piston design has been in use for many years in large-bore, slow-speed two-stroke-cycle marine engines such as those of Sulzer, B&W, GMT, and Mitsubishi. Detroit Diesel was the first high-speed diesel engine manufacturer to employ the crosshead piston design in its engines. In the early 1970s Detroit Diesel used the design in its 92 series two-stroke cycle engines; then the company expanded use into its other series of two-stroke-cycle (53, 71, and 149 series) and four-stroke-cycle designs (Series 50 and Series 60 engines). The DDC two-piece piston has an all steel crown and skirt in the two-piece crosshead design. The malleable iron dome has greater strength than aluminum at operating temperatures and provides ring groove surfaces with very low wear rates, which are the result not only of material differences but of reduced dome motion inherent in the crosshead design. The iron piston skirt is tin plated to provide lower siezure susceptibility than a conventionally fitted aluminum piston while using a smaller skirt-to-liner clearance. This reduced clearance results in less noise due to piston slap and less liner excitation for reduced susceptibility to wet liner cavitation damage (pitting of the external liner surface).

Use of surface treatments has increased, for example, hard anodizing of the piston crown to resist thermal cracking and graphite coating of the aluminum skirt to achieve better resistance to scuffing. The Caterpillar 3176 model EUI engine two-piece articulated piston consists of a forged steel crown with pressed in bore bushings and a forged aluminum skirt. As with DDC

A

B

FIGURE 15–6 (a) Assembled view of a 1994 3176B engine articulated piston, which is 6% shorter than the 1991 model; (b) cutaway view of 3176B piston features an oil gallery closure plate inserted into the crown to permit pressurized lube oil to enter and be distributed evenly, to cool the piston dome; the outlet leads the oil toward the piston skirt where it drains back to the crankcase. (Courtesy of Caterpillar Inc.)

crosshead pistons, the steel crown has excellent high temperature strength and the ability to withstand much higher cylinder pressure and thermal loads than can an aluminum piston. Consider that the 3176 and 3406E engines have peak cylinder firing pressures of 2200 psi (15.2 mPa) plus, compared with 1700 to 1800 psi (11,722 to 12,411 kPa) capability of typical aluminum pistons that were used in the Caterpillar 3306 and 3406 B and C model engines.

In 1991, Cummins and Mack adopted two-piece crosshead pistons similar to those used by DDC and Caterpillar, although Mack had used a two-piece all-aluminum crosshead design for a number of years during the 1970s. Some of the major piston manufacturers now supply two-piece articulated pistons designed to cover bores of from 100 mm (4 in.) to 170 mm (6.6 in.) for high-speed diesel engines. Articulated pistons consisting of a steel crown and an aluminum skirt seem to be one of the most suitable designs to withstand the engine performance requirements of the 1990s.

The two-piece pistons are strictly for high-output performance engines and are constructed to separate piston guiding and sealing functions within the cylinder so that both parts, the crown (dome) and the skirt, are connected via the piston pin as shown in Figure 15–3. The current trend is to move away from an all-aluminum one-piece or two-piece piston to a two-piece iron-aluminum alloy design. This takes the form of a cast or forged steel crown and a cast or forged aluminum skirt. Forged pistons can withstand more severe operating conditions in heavy-duty diesel engines. The piston crown uses a variety of high-strength materials, including nodular cast iron, steel cast, or forged steel to transmit combustion gas pressure via the pin and connecting rod. This concept is necessary due to the higher cylinder temperatures and pressures now found in the combustion chambers of electronically controlled diesel engines that employ higher injection pressures and higher BMEPs (brake mean effective pressures) to comply with the strict EPA exhaust emissions standards. Peak cylinder temperatures of as high as 4000°F (2204°C), and peak pressures of 1800 to 2300 psi (12,411 to 15,858 kPa), require the piston head (crown) to be mechanically stronger and more heat resistant than it was in the past.

Construction of Two-Piece Pistons

The crosshead piston shown in Figure 15–7a illustrates the various parts of this type of piston. Note that a metal oil seal ring is used between the crown and skirt to prevent any excess oil used for under-piston cooling from flooding the cylinder above the oil control ring area. The actual crown and skirt are held together by the piston pin, which passes through the holes in the skirt and the mating holes in the extension struts of the crown. Because of the design characteristics of the crosshead piston, some models do not use the conventional eye- or hole-type connecting rod; instead, a con-rod such as that illustrated in Figure 15–7a is employed. The con-rod is bolted directly to the piston pin which also has a lube oil tube passing through it to deliver pressurized lube oil from the rifle drilled con-rod to the underside of the piston crown for cooling purposes.

The piston dome and skirt, can each react independently to normal stresses developed during engine operation. When the engine is running, the forces of the combustion chamber gases acting on top of the piston are absorbed directly by the piston pin after passing through the crown and struts and the large surface area of the slipper bearing (bushing). Because the skirt is separate from the crown, it is free from vertical load distortion and it receives less heat transfer from the crown, thereby allowing less thermal distortion. As the piston is forced down the cylinder, the con-rod swings off to the side as it rotates the engine crankshaft. During this action, the biggest part of the sidewise or thrust load is taken by the piston skirt; the crown area, which is separate or independent from the skirt, takes only a small portion of these side loads. The minimal side thrust on the crown ensures that the piston ring life will be extended, because as the piston if forced downward, the crown is not pushed sideways under the compression rings at the same time as they are pushed down hard against the bottom of their grooves during the actual power stroke.

Both crosshead and articulated pistons have the following major advantages over a one-piece trunk-type piston assembly:

- Piston-liner clearances are more tightly controlled due to the isolation of the skirt from the crown.
- The piston skirt maintains its designed shape better, thereby minimizing piston slap and lower engine noise.
- Piston ring and groove wear is reduced as a result of less piston crown motion.
- Increased lubrication and cooling of the piston crown occur due to the "cocktail shaker" action of the lube oil.
- Improved pin and bearing life occurs due to the increased slipper bearing area and less bending stress on the piston pin. This advantage can be clearly seen in Figure 15–7b, which illustrates the bending stresses imposed on the piston pin in a conventional trunk-type piston and shows how the crosshead and articulated piston design eliminates this bending stress.
- The two-piece piston is able to direct the force directly down to the connecting rod through the

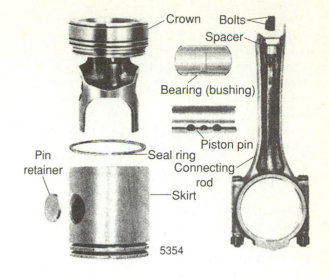

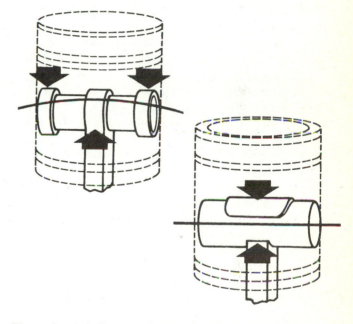

These sketches illustrate the bending stresses imposed on the piston pin in a conventional trunk-type piston—and shows how the cross-head piston eliminates this bending stress.

The cross-head piston is able to direct the force directly down to the connecting rod through the pin. Since both up and down forces are centered at the same point, the tendency of the pin to bend is eliminated.

FIGURE 15–7 (a) Component parts of a two-stroke-cycle DDC crosshead piston assembly; (b) comparison of the bending stresses imposed on the piston pin between a single-piece trunk-type piston and a two-piece crosshead or articulated piston assembly. (Courtesy of Detroit Diesel Corporation.)

pin. Since both up and down forces are centered at the same point, the tendency of the pin to bend is eliminated.

Even though the articulated and crosshead two-piece pistons have major advantages over the one-piece model, they are more expensive to manufacture, generally and are heavier, thereby creating higher inertia forces. Because of their backward and forward (reciprocating) motion, all pistons generate inertia loads (the tendency of a body, in this case the piston assembly, to want to keep moving in the same direction when it reaches the bottom of its stroke).

PISTON CROWN SHAPES

Piston crown shape is a critical factor in the reduction of diesel exhaust emissions. Major reductions in diesel emissions are possible by incorporating into the piston combustion bowl a feature commonly referred to as a *re-entrant chamber*, where the sides of the bowl slant inward toward the central axis of the piston as illustrated in Figure 15–8. This piston bowl design improves mixing and turbulence of the air and fuel in the combustion space, which leads to a cleaner exhaust stream from all emissions. Tests have shown, however, that there is a progressive and significant deterioration in piston life as the bowl shape becomes more re-entrant (the outer angle of the bowl becomes more severe). This flank angle should not exceed 15° to the vertical unless the piston is cooled by an oil gallery or reinforced.

Experience has proven that piston bowl shape, piston cooling, and piston material are major influences on crown life. Direct-injection heavy-duty truck diesel engines use a variety of piston crown shapes. Some employ high-air-swirl deep-bowl systems (Figure 15–4) with moderate injection pressures, while others favor quiescent shallow-bowl systems with much higher injection pressures (see Figure 15–3).

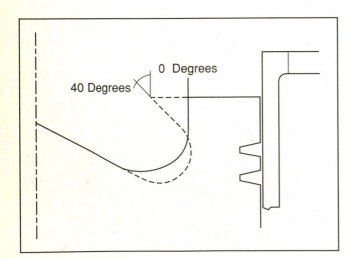

FIGURE 15–8 *Design concept of a re-entrant bowl piston crown.*

Research and development indicate that at this time both U.S. and European exhaust emissions regulations can be met using the quiescent combustion system with an optimized electronic unit injector. The actual shape of the piston crown determines to a great extent the amount of swirl imparted to the trapped cylinder air during the compression stroke.

Some engine manufacturers have adopted a bowl-in-crown design similar to that illustrated in Figure 15–5; this design is more commonly used on lower-horsepower engine models with one-piece trunk-type aluminum alloy pistons. Figure 15–10 illustrates one design of high-speed heavy-duty diesel engine piston crown used by a number of major engine manufacturers, including Caterpillar, Cummins, Detroit Diesel, and Mack, in their heavy-duty on-highway truck engines. Known as a concave design, it is also referred to as a *Mexican hat* shape because it resembles a sombrero. This piston offers the following major advantages:

- It reduces the risk of burning the center of the piston crown by direct flame impingement of fuel from the injector.
- It permits diffusion of the fuel spray further into the air mass for quicker and better mixing of injected fuel.
- It allows better relief from internal stresses in the metal due to expansion caused by heat.
- It allows considerably more squish effect of the injected fuel into the combustion chamber because of the high degree of swirl imparted to the air during the compression stroke.

PISTON OPERATING TEMPERATURES

Temperatures within the combustion chamber depend on a number of factors, but they can range between 2500°F and over 3500°F (1371 to 1927°C). Some of the newer high-speed electronically controlled engines can approach peak cylinder temperatures of 4000°F (2204°C). These high temperatures last for a very short time; the heat generated is dissipated to the surrounding cylinder head fire deck and valves as well as to the cylinder liner. The piston is forced down the cylinder by the expansion of the high-pressure gases on the power stroke; therefore, the piston metal and crown operating temperatures vary in different makes of engines depending on the speed and horsepower they produce. An uncooled cast iron piston can absorb as much as 15% to 18% of the heat created by the burning gases, leading to temperatures in the center of the crown in excess of 1000°F (538°C). In an uncooled aluminum piston, temperatures can run between 550° and 700°F (288 to 371°C).

As the thermal load of an engine increases, the material strength of the pistons decreases, carbon deposits on the piston increase, and scuffing of the piston and liner surfaces or cracks on the piston may appear. These types of problems are countered by designing a cooling cavity, by casting a cooling coil into the underside of the piston crown, or by bolting a forged aluminum skirt to a heat-resistant steel crown and leaving a cavity in between for oil flow. Because of the high pressures and temperatures now encountered in electronically controlled high-speed direct-injection heavy-duty diesel engines, some form of under-piston cooling is required. Pressurized engine lube oil sprays are the most popular. Figure 15–9 illustrates the results of a three-dimensional finite element analysis (FEA) of a Caterpillar 3176 engine piston which was conducted to evaluate the stresses created in the oil gallery of the piston undercrown area, the pinbore, and the pinbore strut from the thermal and peak firing pressure conditions. Maximum principle stresses were determined and the piston was designed to exceed the structural design goals for long life.

Control of higher piston crown temperatures is achieved by proper under-piston cooling via a lube oil cooling jet spray illustrated in Figure 15–10. This system is used in a number of Caterpillar and Mack engines. Some Cummins models employ strategically placed oil spray nozzles (Figure 15–11), which are inserted and retained externally into the side of the engine block so that they intersect with the main engine oil gallery to direct the pressurized cooling oil to the underside of the piston crown through a specifically located orifice. Another common lube oil cooling system is to rifle drill the con-rod and place a spray nozzle at its top end, which is fed through a drilled hole in the piston pin, to continuously spray pressurized lube oil to the underside of the piston crown—a system long used by Detroit Diesel and now by Cummins in its later model N14 engines. Some two-piece pistons employ a series of hollow undercrown support struts filled with spray nozzle supplied oil. This is referred to as a "cocktail shaker" system, since the up and down movement of the piston constantly throws the lube oil around to extract the heat. The hot

FIGURE 15–9 *Computer-generated finite element analysis profile used to show the maximum principal stresses imposed on a heavy-duty high-speed diesel engine piston during a typical thermal and pressure loading cycle. (Courtesy of Caterpillar Inc.)*

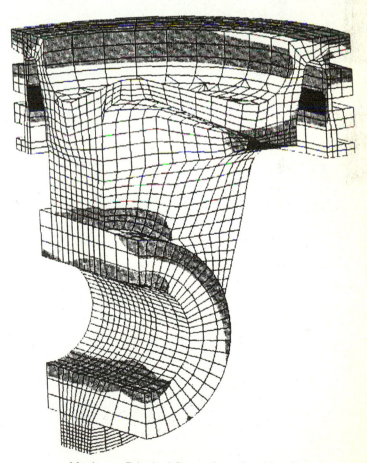

Maximum Principal Stress for a Combined
Loading of Thermal and Pressure

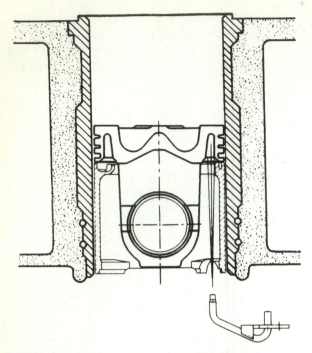

FIGURE 15–10 Example of the location of a piston cooling spray nozzle jet to direct pressurized engine lube oil to the underside of the piston crown for cooling purposes. (Courtesy of Mack Trucks, Inc.)

FIGURE 15–11 Location of piston cooling jet lube spray nozzles alongside the engine block of a Cummins 14L (855 cu in.) engine. (Courtesy of Cummins Engine Company, Inc.)

oil then exits through oil drain holes in the piston to the engine crankcase; the hot oil is constantly replenished by pressurized cooler oil from the spray nozzle. Due to the lower heat conductivity of the steel crown alloys (in comparison to aluminum alloys), the oil supply required to cool the piston has to be higher to prevent oil aging.

Figure 15–12a illustrates a drilled passage in the articulated Caterpillar 3176 engine piston skirt to allow a pressurized cooling jet of engine lube oil to reach the underside of the piston crown. In the cross section of the same piston in Figure 15–12b, the oil cooling gallery for the ring belt area is clearly shown. This gallery is formed by the channel forged into the crown that is behind the piston ring grooves. The oil returns to the engine crankcase or sump via the clearance gap that exists between the crown and the skirt. Additional piston cooling is provided by a second oil jet that is directed at the piston undercrown area. The relatively short heat path from the ring grooves to the cooling oil keeps the ring temperatures within safe operating conditions. Some larger-bore slower-speed engines use an external oil line running up the side of the connecting rod to deliver this oil to the piston pin and crown areas. As a general guide, in oil-cooled pistons approximately 3% to 5% of the heat released from the burning fuel is absorbed by the piston in quiescent combustion chamber engines above 6 in. (150 mm) in bore size. Between 6% and 8% of the released heat is absorbed by the piston in swirl-type chambers found in smaller high-speed engines. Typical piston crown apex temperatures on oil-cooled articulated pistons usually range between 300° and 325°C (572° to 617°F) at 100% oil flow and at rated power and speed. A slight temperature increase occurs at the peak torque rpm to around 350°C (662°F). Figure 15–13 illustrates one example of piston operating temperature distribution for a direct-injection heavy-duty electronically controlled engine. Although these temperatures may seem high, tests have indicated that no piston damage occurs on pistons manufactured from steel that meets SAE standard 4140 for temperatures up to 550°C (1022°F). The combination of lower thermal (heat) conductivity from the two-piece piston design, along with the more effective cooling of the cocktail shaker system, results in lower piston ring belt temperatures and 10% lower piston heat rejection than a typical one-piece trunk-type piston. In addition, the temperature at the high top piston ring groove is about the same as that found in the lower position of a typical aluminum piston, with the second compression ring groove temperature being significantly lower.

Aluminum piston manufacturers now use a mixture of composite and fiber-reinforced materials for added strength while maintaining the demands for a quieter running engine. Ceramic coatings are already in use in some specialized piston crown applications to improve heat rejection, and they are expected to gain in popularity as more stringent standards for exhaust emissions are enforced. In addition, ceramics also have better wear properties than steel or aluminum.

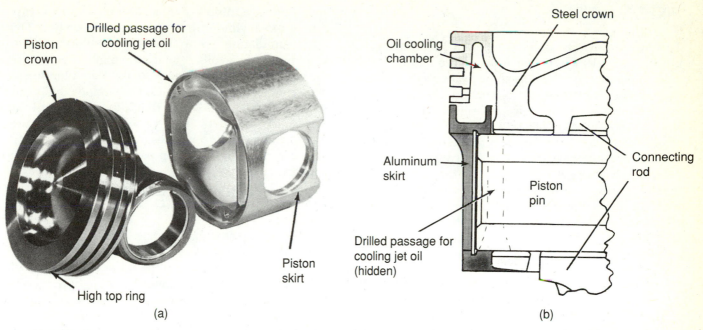

FIGURE 15–12 (a) Section through a Cat 3176 engine model articulated two-piece piston showing the piston skirt oil supply cooling passage to the crown; (b) cross section of the same piston assembly highlighting the oil flow up into the crown area. (Courtesy of Caterpillar Inc.)

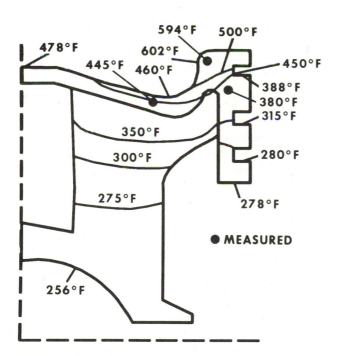

FIGURE 15–13 Typical operating temperatures encountered in the piston crown of a two-piece crosshead piston for a DDC Series 60 four-stroke-cycle engine. (Courtesy of Detroit Diesel Corporation.)

SAE paper 910460 (The Effects of Ceramic Coatings on Diesel Engine Performance and Exhaust Emissions, 1991, by Assanis, Wiese, Schwarz, and Bryzik) reports a variety of tests using plasma-sprayed zirconia-coated and insulated pistons with thicknesses of 0.5 and 1.0 mm (0.020 and 0.040 in.). The thinner ceramic coating generally resulted in improved performance over a noncoated piston due to the reduced heat loss. Fuel efficiency gains with the thinner-coated test pistons produced 10% higher thermal efficiency and 9% higher BMEP and torque than an uncoated piston with the engine running at 1000 rpm. The thicker 1 mm (0.040 in.) coated piston exhibited inferior performance to the noncoated piston. In addition, the emissions characteristics of the insulated engines at full load showed a reduction in CO (carbon monoxide) levels of between 30% and 60%, unburned HC (hydrocarbons) levels that were 35% to 40% lower, and NO_X (nitric oxide) concentrations that were between 10% and 30% lower, due to the changed nature of the combustion in the insulated engines compared to a noninsulated model. However, volumetric efficiencies for the ceramic-coated piston engine were lower than those of a noncoated piston engine because of the hotter cylinder temperatures and residual gases that decrease the density of the inducted air.

PISTON PINS

The piston pin acts as the important link and load-transmitting element between the piston and the con-rod. Depending on the stresses it encounters, the pin may be hollow or solid in construction. The piston pin is sometimes referred to as a wrist-pin or gudgeon pin. Pins are manufactured with a low-alloy, low-carbon steel and are case hardened or nitrided and tempered. A hard and wear-resistant layer surrounds a softer core, which is necessary to cope with the elastic deformation imposed by the engine's operation. In special heavy-load application engines, other steel alloys can be used to manufacture the piston pin.

The pin can be retained to the piston and connecting rod eye (small end) by one of three methods:

1. In a fully floating design, the pin is free to float, that is, move backward and forward within the con-rod and piston pin bore area. To prevent the pin from striking the cylinder wall, a snap ring or solid, thin spring steel retainer can be used. See Figures 15–1 and 15–7a.

2. In a semifloating design, the pin is usually clamped to the con-rod by a bolt located in the upper end of the con-rod. Some designs have a threaded bolt passing through the piston boss area to hold the pin from rotating.

3. In the two-piece crosshead piston design employed by DDC in its two-cycle engines and illustrated in Figure 15–7a, there is no round eye on the upper end of the con-rod. Within the hollow piston pin is a captive special nut, so that the two bolts passing through the con-rod saddle area thread into position. This allows retention of the piston pin to the con-rod saddle, yet provides for independent rotation of the pin within the bore of both the piston skirt and crown areas.

Figure 15–7a shows the solid retainer employed by Detroit Diesel in its two-stroke cycle engines. Note that the four-stroke-cycle DDC Series 50 and Series 60 engines (Figure 15–3) do not use piston pin retainers. The reasons for this are that the connecting rod is bolted to the piston pin and that the oil control rings on the piston are above the pin. In the two-stroke models, the oil control rings are located below the piston pin. In this case it is necessary to employ a solid piston pin retainer, because the pressurized engine lube oil that travels up through the rifle-drilled con-rod would flood out onto the cylinder liner wall if a Circlip (circular clip) were used, allowing excess lube oil to seep past the compression rings and into the combustion chamber. In addition, excess lube oil would escape through the cylinder liner ports into the air box. This oil accumulation within the engine block air box would result in an oil-air mixture being blown through the cylinders on the scavenge stroke, with blue smoke occurring in the exhaust gases. The engine would consume large amounts of oil! In addition, leaking solid piston pin retainers in a two-stroke DDC engine would allow the air box pressure created by the blower and turbocharger to seep past them, creating high crankcase pressure.

PISTON SKIRT SHAPE

Although the piston may visually appear to be straight from the top to the bottom, it is actually designed with a gradual taper that starts at the bottom of the ring belt area and becomes greater toward the top of the piston to allow for greater expansion caused by the higher operating temperatures in the compression ring area. The degree of expansion of the piston assembly varies with the load and speed applied to the engine. The piston diameter in the fire ring (top compression) area is the smallest, since it is in the area subjected to the greatest heat; therefore, the rate of expansion will be greater here. The taper in the ring belt area can be substantial.

Consider the amount of taper in the new generation two-piece piston engines, for example, the four-stroke-cycle Detroit Diesel Series 50 and 60 high-speed heavy-duty electronically controlled engines. The diameter specified for the piston dome above the top (fire) ring is listed as being between 5.035 and 5.043 in. (127.9 to 128.1 mm); below the second compression ring it is 5.095 to 5.098 in. (129.43 to 129.50 mm). The new cylinder liner diameter is listed as being between 5.118 and 5.120 in. (130.00 to 130.05 mm). Therefore, the clearance of the piston dome to the cylinder liner at the top ring is between 0.077 and 0.083 in. (1.955 to 2.108 mm), and below the second compression ring it drops to between 0.022 and 0.023 in. (0.558 to 0.124 mm). The taper on the piston dome below the second ring to above the top ring is between 0.055 and 0.060 in. (1.397 to 1.524 mm). Now you can appreciate just how much taper is required in the ring-belt area of a piston to allow for expansion due to the heat of combustion.

In addition to being tapered, some aluminum alloy pistons are cam-ground in the skirt area as illustrated in Figure 15–14. The cam-grinding process allows the piston to be fitted closely to the cylinder when cold. Excessive clearance would not only allow combustion gases to leak by, but would create a noise known as *piston slap* as the piston is driven down the cylinder on its power stroke. Piston slap is caused by the side thrust transmitted to the piston as it rocks at

TDC by the con-rod action to change its direction. Continued operation with excessive clearance can cause piston skirt and ring damage. On the other hand, what would happen if we fit the piston too tightly when cold? When the piston expands through heat, the lube oil on the cylinder wall would be sheared away, causing scuffing of the metal skirt-to-cylinder liner. This scuffing would allow metal to tear, and as metal accumulated between the skirt and cylinder wall, severe scoring followed by siezure would result.

Closer inspection of Figure 15–14 shows that a cam-ground aluminum piston is ground in an elliptical, or off-circle shape. Thus the diameter of the piston is less at the wrist pin bosses when the piston is cold. Because the expansion of the skirt is restricted by the cylinder wall, the piston is forced to expand in a crosswise direction toward the piston pin area as the temperature of the cylinder components increases. Because a greater mass or thickness of metal is required in the piston pin boss area for support and strength, greater expansion will occur here. Proper cam-grinding action is very important because it allows the skirt contact surfaces to retain their fit against the cylinder wall at all temperatures and to stabilize the piston and rings in the cylinder.

Although cam-ground pistons are more common in smaller-bore engines, the Caterpillar 3500 model engines with a bore and stroke of 6.7 × 7.5 in. (170 × 190 mm) employ a lightweight aluminum alloy piston, which is not only tapered but is ground elliptically (cam-ground) to precisely fit the cylinder at normal operating temperature and pressure and to provide longer ring life. This same piston has two oil cooling jets. One jet forces oil into a passageway within the piston to cool the ring area, while the second jet spray cools the piston undercrown area and lubricates the piston pin bearing.

Two-piece pistons do not encounter the same problems as does a one-piece trunk-type design. The independent operation of the piston crown and skirt in the two-piece piston tends to alleviate the excessive side thrusts to the skirt and crown during the power stroke.

In some aluminum alloy pistons, a vertical or angled slot may run from the base of the ring belt to the bottom of the skirt. This slot allows a tight fit of the piston to the cylinder when cold, to minimize piston slap. In other aluminum alloy pistons, you may notice a horizontal slot cut directly below the ring belt. Its main function is to act as a heat barrier or dam to minimize the transfer of heat to the lower portion of the skirt.

PISTON REMOVAL

Removal of the pistons and connecting rods is a major procedure. It can be done as an in-frame repair, with the engine remaining in place within the equipment. Alternatively, the engine can be removed for a complete overhaul. Regardless of the method chosen, the procedure is basically the same. If the cylinder is cast as part of the block (parent bore) or if it is designed to have a separate cylinder liner, the piston can be removed as a unit along with its connecting rod. In many cases, however, it is easier to remove the *cylinder pack*. This consists

The following diagram shows the comparison of a round piston compared to a cam-ground piston when cold and hot

Diagram of round piston in cylinder before heat causes it to expand. Note that piston has clearance all the way around.

Diagram of cam-ground piston in cold engine — "full-cam" position. Note that piston has cylinder-wall contact in the direction of thrust, and clearance along the axis of the pin bosses.

Diagram of cam-ground piston at engine operating temperature— "expanded cam" position. The piston has expanded till it is now practically round in the cylinder. Note that pin bosses are now further apart than when the piston was cold.

FIGURE 15–14   *Concept of operation for an aluminum alloy one-piece cam-ground piston assembly.*

of removing the piston, con-rod, and cylinder liner as a unit—a method commonly suggested by a number of major high-speed diesel engine manufacturers.

Remove Pistons and Connecting Rod Assemblies Alone

Steam clean or high-pressure wash the engine before you remove any components. Ensure that all intake and exhaust openings are taped shut and that fuel and lube lines are capped off during the cleaning procedure to avoid any possibility of dirt or cleaning liquid getting into these areas. Now follow these steps.

1. Begin by draining the oil from the engine. If an engine failure has occurred, save at least a liter of oil so that it can be analyzed for metal and contaminants in a test lab.

2. Using an air-impact socket and gun, remove the oil pan bolts. Leave at least one bolt tight at diagonally opposite ends of the pan finger to ensure that the oil pan does not drop under its own weight. Once you have arranged to support the pan, remove the remaining bolts.

3. Drain the engine coolant. Then remove the cylinder head(s) as described in Chapter 14.

4. On some four-stroke-cycle engines that have an underslung oil pump or a balancer shaft arrangement, remove these components to access the con-rod bolts.

5. On engines that employ internally mounted under-piston cooling nozzles (such as those used by Caterpillar and Mack), remove the nozzle tube retaining bolt and the piston oil cooling tube.

6. If the engine is equipped with externally mounted piston oil cooling nozzles (such as those found on some Cummins and Mack engines and illustrated in Figure 15–11), remove the retaining bolts, then the nozzles.

SERVICE TIP: Check the condition at the top inside bore of the cylinder or the cylinder liner for signs of a carbon ridge or for signs of an edge due to wear. See Figure 16–19. Failure to remove either one of these can result in a damaged piston during removal, since the piston rings will not slide freely past this ridge. By forcing the piston out by hammering from the underside, the rings and piston lands can be broken.

7. Remove the carbon ring or minor worn step edge at the top of the liner. Choose one of the following methods:
- Using a drill motor small rotary wire brush, or alternatively using an aluminum blade, carefully scrape the carbon away. Wear safety glasses when using the wire brush. Use lint-free paper to clean any loose carbon from the cylinders when finished.

- Use emery cloth to remove carbon. Some engine manufacturers are opposed to using 240 grit emery cloth to remove the carbon ridge because small particles of abrasive paper might be left in the engine. Some suggest soaking the emery cloth in a cleaning solvent to prevent the cloth from becoming saturated with carbon deposit material. If an in-frame repair is being performed, this precaution is valid. If you use emery cloth, exercise extreme care to ensure that all abrasives are thoroughly removed. If the repair involves a complete out-of-frame overhaul, the engine block is completely stripped and cleaned; therefore, this method of removing carbon is not a problem.

- If the top inside of the cylinder bore or liner has a distinct worn edge, use a ridge reamer (shown in Figure 16–20 and illustrated in place in the cylinder bore of Figure 15–15) to cut the ridge to allow free passage of the piston and rings. Exercise caution when using the ridge reamer; you do not want to make a deep cut into the bore. Remove only enough metal to allow passage of the piston and rings.

8. Manually rotate the crankshaft to place the cylinder piston at BDC (bottom dead center) to gain easy access to the con-rod bolts.

9. Loosen off the con-rod cap nuts or capscrews. Loosen off but do not attempt to remove the con-rod nuts or capscrews at this time. Use a rubber hammer to strike the underside of the rod cap to effectively loosen the cap from the rod. This is required, particularly on caps that are aligned to the rod by a dowel pin.

10. Remove the capscrews or nuts and pull the cap and lower bearing from the rod.

SERVICE TIP: On con-rods that employ retaining nuts, the bolts are a tight fit in the rod. Before pushing

FIGURE 15–15 Ridge reamer installed in the cylinder bore to remove the worn ridge that develops after many hours or miles (kilometers) of engine operation. (Courtesy of Cummins Engine Company, Inc.)

the piston and con-rod up and out from the bore, install short, snug pieces of rubber hose over the ends of the bolts to protect the crankshaft journal and cylinder from possible scoring during removal. Once you have started to push the con-rod free from the crankshaft journal, remove the upper con-rod bearing; otherwise, it will tend to fall out when you start pushing or tapping on the bottom of the rod to push the piston up and out of the cylinder bore.

11.   On con-rods that employ capscrews, once these have been removed, install con-rod guide pins. Then use a pusher T-handle as illustrated in Figure 15–16 to push the rod upward in the cylinder until the piston rings are free of the bore. You can then remove the piston and rod from the cylinder liners as shown in Figure 15–17; or, have an assistant grab the assembly as it leaves the top of the bore.

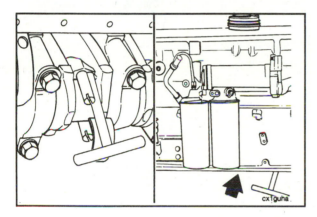

FIGURE 15–16 Using con-rod guide pins and a T-shaped pusher handle to push the con-rod upward through the cylinder until the piston rings are free of the bore. (Courtesy of Cummins Engine Company, Inc.)

FIGURE 15–17 Grasping a 3406 engine piston assembly (2) securely to remove it from the top of the cylinder bore. (Courtesy of Caterpillar Inc.)

12.   In the absence of a T-handle, use a hammer handle to push the piston and con-rod through the cylinder bore.

13.   Inspect the piston crown to determine if it is marked. If it is not, carefully mark the cylinder number on the top of each piston on the same side as the numbers on the con-rods. Many pistons will be stamped with the word *front* on the crown of the piston and a number or a directional arrow.

14.   Carefully place all of the removed pistons and con-rods in a suitable holding jig. If this is unavailable, turn them upside down and place them on a soft cover on a bench. Unless you are going to inspect the con-rod bearings immediately, install the caps on their mating rods along with their respective upper and lower bearings and hand-tighten the capscrews or nuts.

Remove Cylinder Pack

In some engines it is possible to remove the piston, con-rod, and cylinder liner as a complete assembly from the cylinder block bore. This is usually referred to as removing the *cylinder pack* or *cylinder kit*. Considerable time is saved during an in-frame overhaul when all of these components are replaced as a preassembled set. This procedure is also used when the liner is a dry-type slip-fit design in the block bore or a wet liner retained by O-ring seals, because in many cases when removing the piston and con-rod without using cylinder liner hold-down clamps, the liner will pop out of the block bore. You might want to remove the cylinder pack from engines such as the 3176 Cat, the 3406 Cat, the Cummins NT-855 (14L), and Detroit Diesel two-stroke-cycle models. Follow the same steps described earlier for piston and con-rod removal up to and including step 10. Then proceed as follows:

1.   Match-mark the cylinder liner to the engine block, so that if the liner is to be reused it will be reinstalled in the same position in the same cylinder. Also take note of the piston for any numbers or distinguishing marks that indicate "front" and so forth on the crown.

2.   Manually rotate the engine crankshaft to place the con-rod for the cylinder to be removed at the BDC position. This will facilitate removal of the con-rod cap.

3.   Use special tooling (Figure 15–18) to pull both the piston and liner as a unit from various engine models such as Cat, Cummins, and Detroit Diesel. The tool set includes a large expandable rubber plug sandwiched between two steel end plates. The large threaded rod that is securely attached to the lower round steel plate extends up to three large nuts, which are threaded onto the assembly. The first nut above the top plate of the rubber plug is used to expand the plug until it is

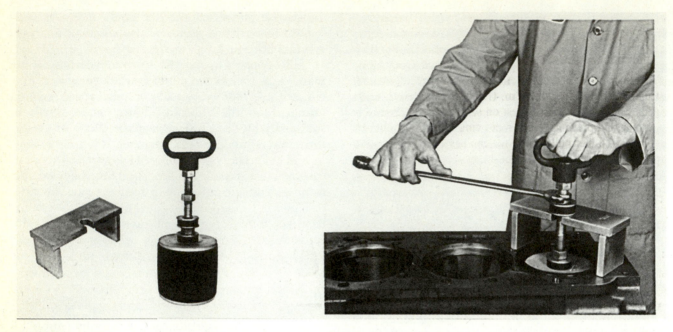

FIGURE 15–18 *Installing an expandable plug-type puller into a wet-type Cummins N14 cylinder liner and pulling (withdrawing) the piston and liner as a complete assembly. (Courtesy of Kent-Moore Division, SPX Corporation.)*

tight in the liner bore. The second nut up is the puller unit that, when tightened as shown in the diagram, will withdraw the cylinder kit from the block bore. The top nut is used to lock the handle in place so that you can hold onto the assembly while rotating the puller nut. The handle can then be used to lift the cylinder kit from the engine. Alternatively, you can loosen off the center nut first, withdraw the steel crab, then pull the cylinder kit. During initial installation of the large expandable rubber plug into the cylinder liner bore, the piston would be positioned at BDC. Some models of cylinder pack pullers can have the puller nut rotated clockwise by the aid of a deep socket and air-impact wrench to quickly and effectively pull the liner, piston, and connecting rod from the block bore as an assembly. Take care during this process, however, that the con-rod does not come into contact with the crankshaft journal and score it as it moves upward. (For details on how to remove the press-fit cylinder liner on its own, see Chapter 16.)

PISTON DISASSEMBLY, INSPECTION, AND REASSEMBLY

Once the piston and/or the cylinder pack has been removed from the engine block, take care not to damage any of the components. If a failure has occurred or the engine is still under warranty, you don't want to destroy any evidence that would help you or the fac-

FIGURE 15–19 *Example of fuel injector spray pattern commonly visible on top of a piston crown of an engine that has operated for some time.*

tory service representative analyze possible reasons for the failure.

SERVICE TIP: Prior to disassembling the pistons from the connecting rod or attempting to clean the tops of the pistons, carefully inspect the injector fuel spray pattern on the top of the piston crown (Figure 15–19). These patterns appear as visible lines within the bowl of the piston crown and generally are equally spaced. However, some nozzles have unequally spaced orifice holes. If there are six holes in the nozzle tip, a pattern indicating anything less means that one or more nozzle orifice holes are plugged with carbon. In addition, if any of the tracer lines across the piston crown bowl extend to the outside circumference of the piston, fuel has been over-

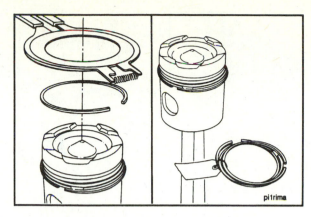

FIGURE 15–20 *Using a special piston ring expander tool to remove or install individual piston rings; tie removed rings together and identify the piston from which they were removed. (Courtesy of Cummins Engine Company, Inc.)*

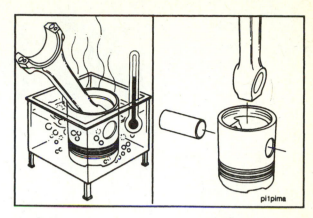

FIGURE 15–21 *Immersing an aluminum alloy piston into a container of boiling water to allow it to expand sufficiently so the piston pin can be thumb pressed from its bore. (Courtesy of Cummins Engine Company, Inc.)*

spraying. Overspraying occurs because of erosion of the orifice holes, which can be caused by using a wire brush instead of a brass-bristle brush when cleaning the injector spray tips to remove carbon accumulations. Enlargement of the orifice holes can also be caused by dirty fuel. In both cases, the larger orifice holes cause the spray-in angle of the fuel to flatten out. This results in overheating of the outer diameter periphery of the piston, which can usually be confirmed by signs of metal discoloration and possible piston breakup or cracking. Another problem associated with fuel overspray is cylinder wall wash, which breaks down the lube oil between the piston and liner surfaces, leading to eventual scuffing, scoring, and piston-to-liner siezure.

Disassembly

Disassembly should be performed with care. You don't want to scratch or score components that might be reusable. Piston components should be match-marked during disassembly to ensure that they are reassembled in the same position. Some service personnel prefer to remove the piston pin from the con-rod before removing the piston rings, but this procedure can make it harder to hold on to the piston during disassembly. It is advisable, therefore, to follow these steps.

1.   Install the piston and con-rod assembly vertically into a soft-jaw vise to facilitate easier removal of the piston rings. Lightly tighten the vise to secure the con-rod with the piston facing up and the bottom of the skirt resting lightly on the top of the vise jaws to prevent skirt rocking.

2.   Select a suitable piston ring expander—similar to that shown in Figure 15–20. Systematically remove each ring by applying pressure on the expander tool

handles to spread the rings only enough to remove them from the top of the piston.

3.   Once piston rings have been removed, always replace them with new ones. If the engine has experienced a failure, place a tag on each ring to record the cylinder number and the ring location on the piston for future reference; then wire them together as shown in Figure 15–20.

4.   Use internal snap-ring pliers to remove the piston retaining rings from a one-piece trunk-type piston. On aluminum alloy pistons, it is usually necessary to place the piston and con-rod assembly into a container of hot water for up to 15 minutes as illustrated in Figure 15–21. This procedure allows expansion of the piston material, so that the steel piston pin can be thumb pressed or lightly tapped from both the piston and con-rod eye.

5.   In an articulated piston used in the 3176 Cat engine, remove the snap rings on early models, or the solid plug on later models. Then remove the piston pin and separate the piston crown from the skirt; remove the con-rod.

6.   On Detroit Diesel Series 50 and 60 model engines refer to Figure 15–22 and place the crosshead piston into the special fixture plate. Slide the movable portion of the fixture until it contacts the piston pin and tighten the handle. Loosen the bolts that secure the con-rod to the piston and remove the two bolts and spacers. Remove the con-rod, followed by the piston, pin, and skirt, from the holding fixture. Withdraw the piston pin and separate the piston skirt from the piston dome.

7.   When disassembling a Detroit Diesel 53, 71, 92, or 149 crosshead piston (shown earlier in Figure 15–7a), punch a hole through the center of the solid

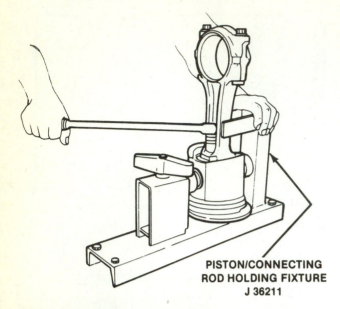

PISTON/CONNECTING
ROD HOLDING FIXTURE
J 36211

FIGURE 15–22 Using a special Kent-Moore piston and connecting rod fixture to remove the piston pin con-rod bolts and to disassemble the crosshead piston assembly. (Courtesy of Detroit Diesel Corporation.)

piston pin retainers with a narrow chisel or center punch. Then pry the retainer from the piston pin bore, being careful not to damage the piston or bushing during this procedure. To separate the piston dome from the skirt, it is necessary to compress the internal seal ring that exists between the two major components as shown in Figure 15–7a. A special tool may be used; or, the piston can be grasped by the skirt and the pin area of the dome brought down with enough force to separate the dome from the skirt. Take care during this procedure to keep your fingers out of the piston hole.

Cleaning Pistons and Components
On lightly carboned pistons, attempt to clean the components with diesel fuel oil. If the fuel oil doesn't remove the carbon deposits, use an approved chemical solvent that will not harm the tin plate on ferrous metal pistons. However, avoid using a chemical solvent on the bushing area of the piston pin bore. On aluminum alloy pistons, select a cleaning solvent that is approved for use with this material and that can be used either hot or cold. Figure 15–23 illustrates six trunk-type aluminum alloy pistons soaking in a hot soapy solution for up to 30 minutes before using a *nonmetallic brush* to remove carbon deposits. If a cold cleaner solution is being used, soaking the pistons overnight usually loosens any carbon deposits.

SERVICE TIP: Never use a metal-wire brush to clean aluminim alloy pistons; this type of brush will scratch and score the skirt as well as the piston ring grooves.

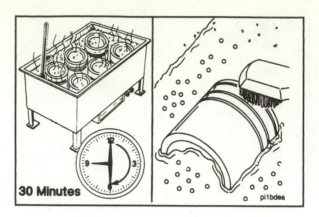

30 Minutes

pi1bdea

FIGURE 15–23 Soaking pistons in a hot soapy solution for up to 30 minutes before using a nonmetallic brush to remove carbon deposits. (Courtesy of Cummins Engine Company, Inc.)

Similarly, do not attempt to clean aluminum alloy piston ring grooves or the piston pin bores with glass beads or walnut shells, because this action can damage the pin bore surface finish or prevent the rings from seating correctly in the ring grooves. If the piston is fitted with Ni-resist ring groove inserts, then blasting with walnut shells may be done safely if the machine pressure is raised only enough to remove the carbon. Take care also not to concentrate the spray in one area (including the piston crown) for an extended period of time.

On ferrous metal piston domes, a wire brush can be used safely on both the piston dome and compression ring grooves to remove carbon; however, never use a wire brush on the piston skirt, particularly on Detroit Diesel pistons since they are tin coated (this applies to both the one-piece trunk-type and two-piece crosshead pistons). Removing this protective layer can result in scuffing, then scoring, of the skirt when it is operating in the cylinder liner.

If recommended in the service manual for the engine, clean the ring grooves of carbon deposits with a commercially available special ring groove tool. Many engine manufacturers recommend, however, using a piece of an old compression ring that has been lightly ground to a bevel edge, since the used ring is of the correct width for this purpose. Take care not to scratch or groove the ring sealing surface in the piston groove; this can cause carbon to form as well as possibly create a sticking ring. Any carbon left in the ring grooves will reduce piston ring clearance and prevent new rings from making good seals.

Detroit Diesel approves glass beading of the piston crown dome using Mico Bead Glass Shot MS-M, 0.0029 to 0.0058 in. (0.073 to 0.147 mm), using air pressure of 552 to 689 kPa (80 to 100 psi). Make certain that

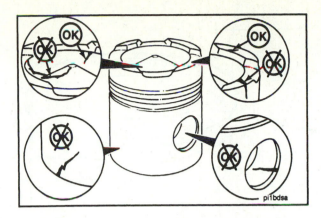

FIGURE 15–24 *Typical areas of a piston that should be inspected closely for signs of damage and cracks. (Courtesy of Cummins Engine Company, Inc.)*

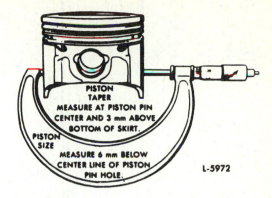

FIGURE 15–25 *Using an outside micrometer to gauge the piston for wear and suitability for reuse. (Courtesy of Detroit Diesel Corporation.)*

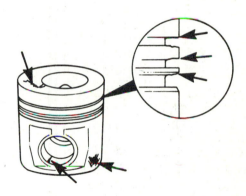

FIGURE 15–26 *Closely inspect the piston ring grooves for signs of wear and damage as well as for cracks in other highly stressed areas. (Courtesy of Cummins Engine Company, Inc.)*

no glass beads remain in the piston dome after cleaning! In addition, do not allow the glass beading to contact any area of the piston pin bushing. Avoid refinishing or polishing the piston pin.

After any cleaning solution has been used, whether on ferrous metal or aluminum alloy pistons, wear safety glasses and wash the pistons in a strong solution of laundry detergent in hot water. Some engine manufacturers allow steam cleaning of their aluminum alloy pistons. In both cases, dry off all components by using compressed air while wearing safety goggles. Make sure that all oil drain holes in the piston grooves are open and clean, as well as the oil supply cooling holes in the skirt and crown.

Inspection of Piston Components

Carefully inspect the piston ring grooves, lands, piston skirt, combustion bowl, and pin bore for wear, scuffing, cracks, or signs of blow-by. In addition, note any signs of overheating or burned spots. These could indicate an obstruction in the oil supply passage in the connecting rod, piston pin, or skirt that carries pressurized lube oil to the underside of the piston crown or to fuel injector overspray.

Inspect Piston for Cracks

Figure 15–24 illustrates the areas of the piston that should be inspected closely for signs of cracking. If a hairline crack appears, or if you suspect a crack that is not visible to the naked eye, use a dye penetrant and powder on aluminum alloy pistons in a manner similar to that described in Chapter 9 and Chapter 14 dealing with cylinder block and cylinder head checks. On ferrous metal piston domes, a magnetic particle or flourescent dye penetrant and a black light can be used.

Some Cummins, Caterpillar, and Mack models have pistons similar to that shown in Figure 15–24

where pockets are cast within the top of the piston to allow for clearance between the intake and exhaust valves. Carefully inspect these areas of the piston to ensure that there are no indentations, which would indicate contact between the piston and valves during engine operation. Also check the diameter of the piston skirt on the major axis of the piston skirt at 90° to the piston pin. This is illustrated in Figure 15–25 where measurements are taken using an outside micrometer at several positions starting from the bottom of the piston. In addition, measure at least two other areas of the skirt, one below and one above the piston pin bore area. These measurements are particularly important if you suspect that scuffing or highly polished spots are outside of the worn limits as stated in the service manual.

Inspect Piston Ring Grooves

When inspecting piston ring grooves, make sure they do not have a wear step as shown in Figure 15–26. Since most high-speed heavy-duty diesel engines now

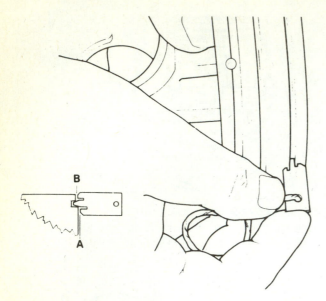

FIGURE 15–27 *Checking a piston fire (top) ring groove for wear with the aid of special keystone gauges. If gauge shoulder contacts piston at position A or B, replace piston. (Courtesy of Detroit Diesel Corporation.)*

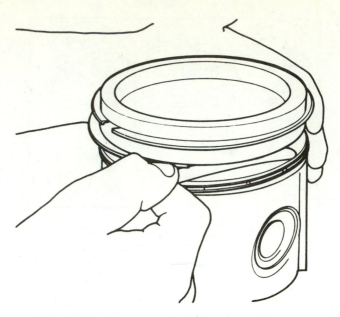

FIGURE 15–28 *Using a feeler gauge to measure and check piston ring side clearance. (Courtesy of Detroit Diesel Corporation.)*

employ *keystone* tapered rings, a special set of ring groove wear gauges is used to determine if there is excessive wear. Figure 15–27 illustrates the use of a typical keystone groove gauge used to check the top fire (compression) ring piston groove for wear at four places parallel to and at 90° to the wrist pin. The center tang of the gauge is inserted squarely into the ring groove as far as it will go. If the gauge shoulder makes contact with the piston at either position A or B, the ring groove is worn beyond usable limits and the piston should be discarded. In two-piece pistons, only the dome need be discarded if the skirt is serviceable.

Generally, if the top ring groove is OK, the lower ring grooves will be acceptable. In the absence of a ring groove gauge, you can check all grooves for wear by following this procedure: Install a new ring and hold it flush with the outside diameter of the piston. Then insert a feeler gauge of the recommended thickness as stated in the engine service manual between the upper land and the ring as illustrated in Figure 15–28. If the feeler gauge enters the groove without resistance, there is too much wear and the piston should be replaced.

Inspect Pin and Bore Wear

Aluminum alloy pistons generally do not have a bushing within the piston bore, since the pin rides directly on the aluminum. In ferrous metal pistons, however, a replaceable bushing is used in each side of the piston boss area. In both cases, the diameter of the bore and the pin must be checked. The inside diameter of the

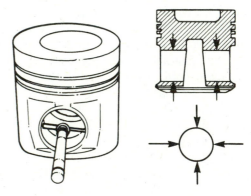

FIGURE 15–29 *Using a telescoping gauge to measure the piston pin bore at two locations 90° apart. (Courtesy of Cummins Engine Company, Inc.)*

piston pin bore can be checked using a telescoping gauge as shown in Figure 15–29 at 90° intervals. The diameter of the piston pin should be checked with an outside micrometer along its length at three places 90° apart. All readings should be compared to the specifications in the service manual.

Reassembly

Piston reassembly is basically the reverse of the disassembly procedure. More steps are involved in reassembling a two-piece crosshead or articulated piston, however, than in reassembling a one-piece type.

One-Piece Aluminum Piston

Follow these five steps to reassemble a one-piece piston:

1. On aluminum alloy trunk-type pistons, pre-heat the piston in boiling water (Figure 15–21) for 15 minutes or in a temperature-controlled oven set to 212°F (100°C) for 30 minutes. This step is required so that the steel piston pin can be safely installed with thumb pressure.

2. Use clean 15W-40 oil and lubricate both the con-rod piston pin bore and the piston pin.

3. While wearing insulated gloves, remove the piston from the hot water or oven. Make certain that the number or the word *front* stamped on top of the piston is facing toward the correct side of the con-rod (see Figure 15–60). Align the pin bore of the rod with that for the piston pin and slide the pin into position.

4. Install new snap rings into the piston pin bore groove.

5. Install the piston rings.

Reassembling a Two-Piece Crosshead Piston

The procedure for reassembling a crosshead or an articulated two-piece piston is similar but a bit more complicated. When reassembling a two-stroke-cycle crosshead piston, Detroit Diesel recommends that you lubricate all components with a mixture of eight parts of engine oil, and one part STP or equivalent. This lubricant adheres to parts longer than plain engine oil, thereby helping to avoid scuffing of parts after initial engine start-up. Refer to Figure 15–30 and turn the dome upside down. Then follow these steps:

1. Slide the piston pin slipper bearing (bushing) into the crown.

2. Lubricate the fluoroelastomer seal ring liberally with the STP-oil mix and install the ring.

3. Refer to Figure 15–22 and lower the piston skirt down over the dome and seal ring with care until the ring is compressed by the skirt coming into contact with the underside of the piston crown.

4. Carefully check that the skirt spins freely on the crown. (If it sticks, pull the skirt and check for high spots or nicks in the groove with a small, flat file. If this action does not relieve sticking, replace the piston crown.)

5. Lubricate the piston pin, and using the alignment tool shown in Figure 15–31, install the pin.

6. Lubricate the con-rod bolts with International Compound No. 2 or equivalent and install them finger-tight through the rod and into the captive piston pin bolt.

FIGURE 15–30 Installing the seal ring between the piston crown and skirt area for a two-piece crosshead piston assembly. (Courtesy of Detroit Diesel Corporation.)

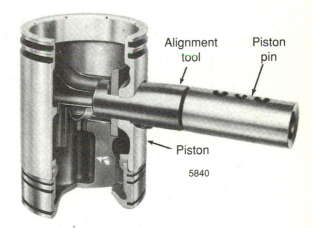

FIGURE 15–31 Installing a piston pin into a crosshead piston assembly using an alignment tool. (Courtesy of Detroit Diesel Corporation.)

7. With the con-rod and piston held securely in a soft-jaw vise, torque the bolts to 55 to 60 lb-ft. (75 to 81 N·m)

8. Refer to Figure 15–7a, which illustrates the solid piston pin retainers. With the piston

5362

A

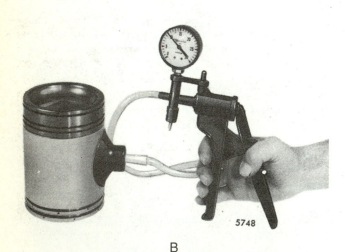

5748

B

FIGURE 15–32 (a) Installing a solid piston pin retainer into a two-stroke-cycle DDC engine piston; (b) using a hand-operated vacuum pump and gauge to check that the solid piston pin retainer is properly seated and will not leak. (Courtesy of Detroit Diesel Corporation.)

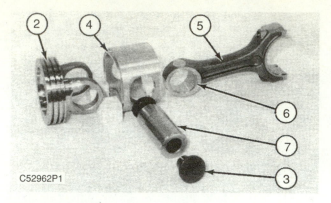

C52962P1

FIGURE 15–33 Components of a 3176B Cat articulated piston: 2 = piston crown; 3 = piston retaining plug; 4 = articulated piston skirt, 5 = connecting rod; 6 = bearing; 7 = piston pin. (Courtesy of Caterpillar Inc.)

assembly laying in the special fixture illustrated in Figure 15–32a, place the retainer into the piston pin bore area and lightly tap the retainer with special Kent-Moore tool (J23762-A) and a hammer. Strike the tool just hard enough to deflect the retainer and seat it evenly in the piston skirt groove. Do the same for the other pin retainer.

9. Refer to Figure 15–32 and check the retainers for possible leakage. Since the oil control rings on the two-stroke-cycle DDC engines are located below the piston pin bore, any leakage of pressurized engine oil that flows up through the rifle-drilled con-rod and past the solid retainers will leak onto the cylinder wall and up into the combustion chamber. Check for leakage using a vacuum pistol actuated to pull 10 in. on the gauge. A drop of the gauge needle indicates that the retainer is leaking. Try gently tapping the retainer once again with the installer tool. If the retainer still fails the vacuum test, remove it; inspect the piston skirt pin bore area for nicks, burrs, or damage. Clean the bore and retry a new retainer.

10. Note that the Caterpillar 3176B engine model also employs a solid type of piston pin retainer with its two-piece articulated piston design. This piston, you may recall from Figure 15–12, has a lube passage to carry oil to the crown. To control the amount of oil on the cylinder wall, a solid piston pin retainer plug is used. When reassembling the piston, *always* install a new piston pin plug (item 3 in Figure 15–33). Do not attempt to use an old plug!

USING A NEW PISTON

If cleaning and inspection reveal that a piston is not suitable for reuse, new pistons may be installed individually, or new cylinder kits may be installed. A new cylinder kit generally consists of the piston, pin, pin bushings, rings, pin retainers, and a new cylinder liner. Prior to installing a new cylinder kit, it is important to check the condition of all new components as well as clearance specifications. This check should include the checks already mentioned in this section regarding the piston and pin, as well as checks of piston ring end gaps and side clearance.

Finally, always check the piston-to-cylinder liner clearance in accord with the engine service manual specs. Figure 15–34 illustrates one method to check a new piston-to-liner clearance. The piston, minus its rings, is inserted upside down within the new liner using a selected feeler gauge and is checked in four places 90° apart. In this example, which shows the check for a Detroit Diesel two-stroke-cycle 92 series engine, a long feeler gauge attached to a spring scale is used to measure the force in pounds (kilograms) required to withdraw the feeler gauge. The specification for this piston-to-liner clearance with new parts ranges between 0.0051 and 0.0097 in. (0.129 to 0.246 mm). Since we require a minimum clearance of 0.005 in (0.129 mm), select a 0.004 in. (0.101 mm) feeler gauge and install it as shown in the diagram. If the spring scale requires a 6 lb (2.72 kg) pull to withdraw the feeler gauge, the piston to liner clearance will be 0.005 in. (0.129 mm). A 6 lb pull required to remove any feeler gauge indicates that the clearance will be 0.001 in. (0.0254 mm) greater than the gauge thickness.

In the absence of a spring scale, carefully measure the piston skirt diameter at room temperature (70°F, 21°C) lengthwise and crosswise of the piston pin bore and note the readings. Then measure the inside diameter of the new cylinder liner. Subtract the piston diameter readings from those of the liner to obtain the piston-to-liner clearance and compare these to the service manual specifications.

PURPOSE AND CHARACTERISTICS OF PISTON RINGS

It is impossible to fit the piston closely enough to the cylinder bore to maintain compression and firing pressures at varying loads and speed within the cylinder throughout the operating range of the engine. We need, therefore, to employ a number of expandable piston rings to effectively seal the combustion chamber gases.

Although deceptively simple in appearance, the compression rings used on a piston are designed to seal the high-pressure air created on the upward-mov-

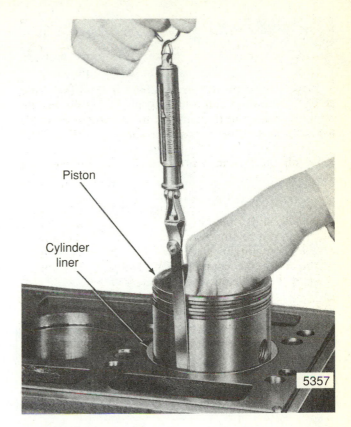

Piston

Cylinder liner

5357

FIGURE 15–34 *Measuring piston-to-liner clearance with a spring-loaded feeler gauge. (Courtesy of Detroit Diesel Corporation.)*

ing compression stroke of the piston, and to prevent the even higher pressure combustion gas from escaping into the engine crankcase during the power stroke. The ring face contact with the cylinder wall allows the heat absorbed by the piston to dissipate through the liner or block to the surrounding coolant passage. In addition, the oil control rings(s) are designed to distribute a controlled amount of engine lube oil on the cylinder wall during the upstroke—to provide piston skirt-to-liner lubrication—then to scrape it off on the downstroke.

Each compression ring is forced to operate within the high-pressure and high-stress areas of the engine. They seal the gases of combustion within the cylinder so that the expanding heat energy can be applied to the piston crown, where it can be converted into mechanical energy at the engine crankshaft and flywheel. Failure of the piston rings to effectively seal the high-pressure gases created within the cylinder leads to excessive blow-by into the engine crankcase, which causes sulfuric acid, sludging of the oil, and con-rod and main bearing pitting. It also creates burning oil within the combustion chamber, blue smoke in the exhaust, high exhaust emissions, a smoking exhaust from low compression, hard starting, lack of power, excessive fuel consumption, carbon buildup within the combustion chamber, carbon accumulation on the injector tips and valves, eventual engine failure from sticking rings, dilution of the crankcase oil from raw diesel fuel, scuffing and scoring of the piston to liner area, and engine failure either from siezure or from an accumulation of the problems listed.

For piston rings to effectively seal the gases of combustion, they must have a *free diameter* greater than the bore of the cylinder in which they operate. When these rings are inserted into the cylinder, they exert an outward pressure commonly known as *ring radial force*. This is desirable, of course, to ensure that the rings remain in fairly tight contact with the cylinder walls during engine operation so that neither compression air nor power

stroke gases escape. In addition, ring contact with the cylinder wall is important because it is the main avenue of heat dissipation from the piston. Figure 15–35 illustrates a piston ring in its confined state, as well as the terminology used to identify the areas of the ring. To allow for ring expansion within the cylinder as a result of heat, a ring gap must be provided as well as side clearance to prevent the ring from siezing in the piston ring groove.

When a piston ring operates within the cylinder as illustrated in Figure 15–36, the high-pressure gases of combustion force the ring downward against the lower part of the piston groove (land). Due to the ring side clearance, gas pressure also forces the ring outward hard against the cylinder wall to create effective sealing. These combined gas pressures, along with the irregular contact between the ring face and cylinder

FIGURE 15–35

Nomenclature of a piston ring assembly.

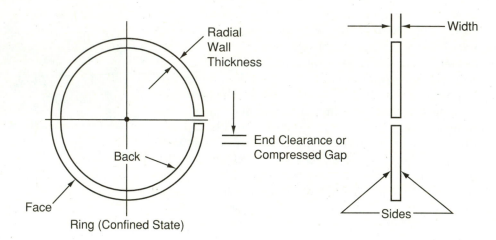

FIGURE 15–36   Identification of a piston and ring, and concept of how the combustion gas pressure within the cylinder acts to seal the piston ring against the cylinder wall.

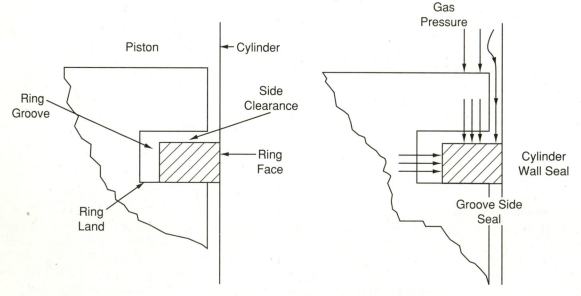

and the ring-to-piston groove clearances, can cause the ring to twist within the piston groove. This continuous cycling action as the piston moves up and down heavily stresses the ring. To avoid ring breakage, the ring must have high tensile strength, yet be flexible, somewhat like a heavy rubber band.

Flexibility of a piston ring is important to its ability to continually conform to the cylinder wall surface. The higher its modulus of elasticity, the more flexible the ring is; so it can be twisted and bent without losing its conformability—an important characteristic of any ring, but particularly a compression type. The combustion gas pressure exerted against the top compression, or fire, ring will always be greater than that on the lower compression rings; therefore, the sealing pressure on the second ring will only be what leaks past the first ring, and so on down through the remaining rings. Although a general rule of thumb assumes that the pressure at each succeeding ring location diminishes by half, current tests indicate that this is not necessarily so. The type of compression ring used, the contour of the ring face and cylinder wall surfaces, ring and cylinder wear, ring gap, and side clearance all have an influence on these succeeding pressures. (For more details on inter-ring gas pressures, refer to SAE technical paper 930792, 1993, by Dursunkaya and Keribar of Ricardo North America and Richardson of Cummins Engine Company, Inc.)

PISTON RING MATERIALS

To meet strength, scuff, and wear resistance requirements created within the combustion chamber and cylinders of high-speed heavy-duty electronically controlled engines yet remain cost-effective, piston rings are available in a wide variety of materials. Rings are generally manufactured from spun-cast sleeves or single-cast blanks. These include, spun-cast alloyed and heat-treated pearlitic nodular graphite cast iron, ductile cast irons, spun-cast carbidic malleable and flake graphite irons, carbon and high-alloyed steels, and heat-resistant nickel and cobalt alloys. Coatings to improve ring face wear from abrasives and scuffing include conventional electroplated nickel-chromium and plasma-sprayed complex chromium irons and molybdenum carbide for extreme operating conditions. Thermochemically treated chromium is generally used in top compression (fire) ring applications that require marginal lubrication. These materials also provide rapid seat-in and good oil control. With U.S. EPA exhaust emissions standards becoming increasingly more stringent, engine manufacturers have turned to tighter radial piston ring pressures top ring shapes, and coatings to reduce regular oil consumption within the combustion chamber—creating the term *dry engine*.

The heavy-duty trucking industry has come to expect engines that are capable of running for 500,000 to 1,000,000 miles (805,000 to 1,609,300 km), or the equivalent of 16,500 to 33,000 hours between engine overhauls. This capability requires that proper maintenance be scheduled regularly and demands piston ring materials that can operate for long periods. Spheroidal graphite material is highly resistant to fracture and is used for high-speed heavy-duty engine piston rings that experience severe dynamic conditions and for conditions that require high resistance to ring breakage.

To provide longer ring life, most high-speed heavy-duty engines now use *prestressed* piston rings. Figure 15–37 illustrates the basic difference between a conventional ring and a prestressed ring. Note the difference in stress distribution from the inside to the outside diameter of the steel ring. A manufacturing process significantly reduces the working stress as well as increases the fatigue life of the ring when it is installed and working in the cylinder. In this process the base metal is shot peened while the rings are held precisely to the actual bore size prior to chrome plating or coating. This process puts the outer surface of the steel ring into initial compression. When the ring is closed to bore size, the interface of the steel ring with the chrome plate approaches zero stress instead of approaching appreciable tension. Prestressing is said to increase ring life by a margin of ten to one.

TYPES AND DESIGNS OF PISTON RINGS

Basically, piston rings fall into one of two categories: compression ring or oil control ring. Although there are many different versions of both types of rings, the trend today in most high-speed heavy-duty diesel engines is toward a standardized ring package consisting of three rings on the piston (some manufacturers still employ four in some engine applications). The diagrams in this section illustrate a number of piston

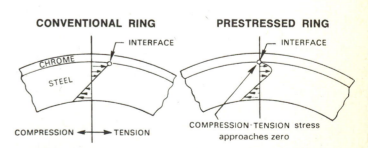

FIGURE 15–37 Comparison of a conventional piston ring and a prestressed ring. (Courtesy of Detroit Diesel Corporation.)

rings that are representative of typical designs found in diesel engines being manufactured by Caterpillar, Cummins, Detroit Diesel, Mack, Volvo, Navistar, MAN, DAF Trucks, Mercedes-Benz, and others.

The three-ring pack has been brought about in no small measure by the strict EPA exhaust emissions regulations in both North America and Europe. Figure 15–38 illustrates the three-ring pack arrangement used by Detroit Diesel in both its Series 50 and Series 60 four-stroke-cycle electronically controlled heavy-duty engine models. The top (fire) ring and the compression ring (second groove) are prestressed. Note that the top (fire) ring is a *keystone design*, that is, a ring with a taper on the upper and lower sides. This angle is usually between 12° and 15°, but it can range between 6° and 15° on other makes of engines. Due to the keystone shape, the piston ring lands are longer than a nontapered groove and consequently are stronger. In addition, the keystone shape causes relative motion between the ring and piston groove to effectively break up the formation of carbon, thereby preventing ring sticking. Also, the ring-to-piston groove side clearance increases slightly as face wear occurs, compensating for varnish, lacquer, or carbon formation that would tend to create ring sticking. The fire ring is also barrel faced and chrome plated to ensure quick seating of new rings and good resistance to corrosion and abrasion, thereby preventing scuffing. Good control of oil film is achieved using the keystone design; the ring is only 3.8 mm (0.150 in.) from the top of the piston crown to minimize any dead air space above the piston and ring. This design prevents tiny amounts of fuel from loitering unburned, then being pulled into the exhaust stream to become smoke, particulates, or other odorous gases.

In other makes of engines the barrel-face shape on the fire ring is contoured to assist in the development of a hydrodynamic oil film; the oil film has neutral oil control behavior since it has no upward or downward scraping action. However, some barrel-face rings have a nonsymmetrical shape to optimize generations of oil film and to provide more positive oil control, particularly in newer engines because of emissions standards.

The second groove in this piston ring (Figure 15–38) employs a rectangular compression ring, which is also chrome plated on the face. Note that the face has a small taper on it of 1° to 2° to allow its initial contact with the cylinder liner to form a line. Thus, unit pressures are fairly high, which allows the ring to seat more rapidly than a standard ring. The inner edge of this ring has an inside bevel that allows the ring to take a slight twist or dish shape when compressed to fit the cylinder. This causes the bottom edge of the ring to contact the cylinder with high unit pressures and results in very fast seating of a new ring.

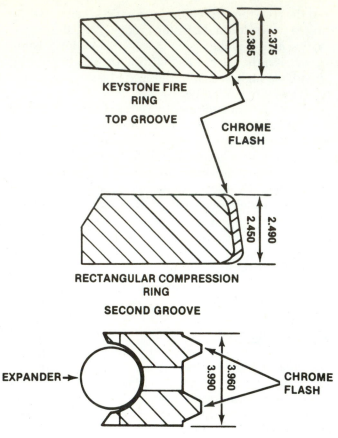

FIGURE 15–38 *Typical example of the arrangement of a three-ring piston assembly used on a Series 60 heavy-duty engine. Note different design concepts of the prestressed rings. (Courtesy of Detroit Diesel Corporation.)*

The one-piece oil control ring has an expansion spring (Figure 15–38) exerting radial pressure against the liner to effectively control oil distribution on the liner wall during the piston's upward stroke. Note also that the double-rail oil ring faces are chrome plated and have a channel between them to allow oil scraped from the cylinder wall on the pistons downward stroke to drain through the slot in the ring center and piston oil ring groove back to the crankcase. This type of a chrome-plated oil ring with a captive spring behind it is often referred to as a *conformable design*, because it exhibits good conformability to any bore distortion and provides long life in high-speed heavy-duty engines; ring wall pressures are possible up to 250 to 350 lb-ft/in.^{2} (1.72 to 2.41 MN/m^2). All three rings on this piston are identified by a small indentation dot mark on the top side, which indicates the side that faces the top of the piston when installed.

Illustrated in Figure 15–39 is a typical three-ring pack found on Cummins L10, M11, and N14 engine models (some other Cummins engine models employ a similar arrangement). The top piston ring on the new

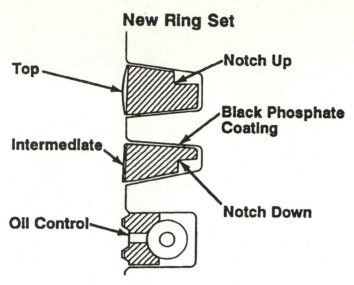

FIGURE 15–39 *Example of the three-ring arrangement used on Cummins L10, M11, and N14 engine models. (Courtesy of Cummins Engine Company, Inc.)*

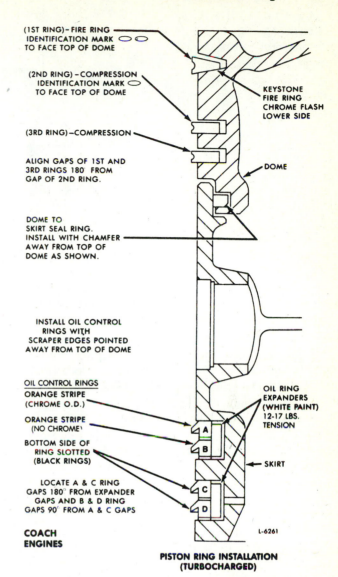

FIGURE 15–40 *Example of piston ring stack-up used by DDC on its V92 series of two-stroke-cycle transit bus engines. (Courtesy of Detroit Diesel Corporation.)*

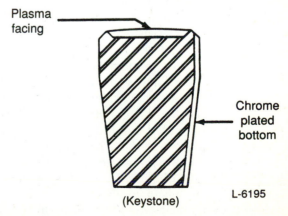

FIGURE 15–41 *Plasma-coated facing and chrome-plated bottom of a keystone piston ring. (Courtesy of Detroit Diesel Corporation.)*

ring set is a keystone design with a positive twist and a cutback notch on the top inside of the ring. This ring has a barrel-shaped face in contact with the cylinder liner, and the top of the ring has a bright metal appearance. The intermediate ring is a negative twist design with a cutback notch on the bottom side of the ring and a 2° taper face.

The intermediate ring has a black phosphate coating, which helps to distinguish it from the top ring. The oil ring is a conformable one with a coil expander somewhat similar to the type being used by other major engine manufacturers.

Figure 15–40 illustrates the piston ring arrangement in two-stroke DDC engines. The fire ring is a keystone design with a black oxide finish on its upper side and chrome flashing on its lower side as well as on its face. Some models now have a chrome-plated bottom and a plasma facing as shown in Figure 15–41. All of the rings are prestressed. Figure 15–42 illustrates that the second and third compression rings are rectangular in shape with a barrel-shaped and chrome-plated face. Some compression rings used on the two-cycle DDC engines also have a groove running around the center of the face as shown in Figure 15–42. This groove retains some lube oil, and it also allows inspection of the condition of the rings through the cylinder block air-box inspection covers for signs of wear or sticking rings.

Note carefully in Figure 15–40 the location of the oil control rings relative to their placement in a four-stroke-cycle engine design. The oil rings are located *below* the piston pin on two-stroke-cycle engines for these reasons: When the piston is at TDC, blower and turbocharger air

FIGURE 15–42
Comparison of a prestressed top groove keystone piston ring and a second groove rectangular ring. (Courtesy of Detroit Diesel Corporation.)

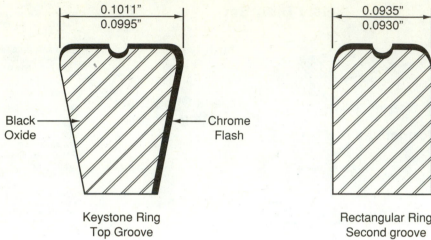

0.1011"
0.0995"

Black Oxide — → ← Chrome Flash

Keystone Ring
Top Groove

0.0935"
0.0930"

Rectangular Ring
Second groove

box pressure within the engine block would leak through the liner ports and past the piston into the crankcase creating high crankcase pressure. In addition, with oil rings located above the piston pin, engine oil would accumulate in the air box under light loads and at idle speeds. The oil ring expanders used with the two-cycle DDC engine provide ring tension against the cylinder wall ranging from 9 to 15 lb (4 to 7 kg) to as high as 16.5 to 22.5 lb (7.5 to 10.2 kg) in applications that require more strict control over oil distribution and retention (for example, city buses that spend considerable time idling). These models tend to employ higher-tension oil control rings, but these rings should not be used in intercity bus or truck engines since inadequate oil film on the cylinders and shortened cylinder kit life will result.

The oil ring expander used with many of these engines is known as a *peripheral abutment* type. When installed into the piston ring groove, the ends of the expander should face up as illustrated in Figure 15–43. Note also in Figure 15–40 that there are two oil scraping rings installed in each piston groove with their scraping edges facing downward so that they can effectively scrape oil from the cylinder wall on the downward stroke while distributing oil across the cylinder wall on the upstroke.

The three-ring pack arrangement is also being used on lighter-duty diesel engines as well as midrange truck applications. Figure 15–44 illustrates a 1995 Navistar T444E engine gravity cast M132 aluminum alloy piston with a cast-in Ni-resist insert for improved top ring groove wear. This engine is in the 140 to 160 kW (190 to 215 hp) range with a 17.5:1 compression ratio V8. The ring package for this engine follows the balanced-pressure design concept; the top ring is located approximately 9 mm (0.350 in.) below the piston crown. The top ring is a keystone, barrel-face design made of gravity cast ductile iron with a molyb-

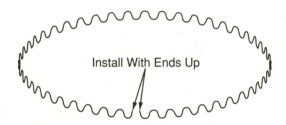

Install With Ends Up

FIGURE 15–43   Peripheral abutement type of oil ring expander used on two-stroke-cycle engine models. (Courtesy of Detroit Diesel Corporation.)

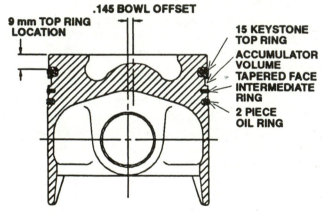

.145 BOWL OFFSET

9 mm TOP RING LOCATION

15 KEYSTONE TOP RING
ACCUMULATOR VOLUME
TAPERED FACE INTERMEDIATE RING
2 PIECE OIL RING

FIGURE 15–44   Piston cross section showing the combustion chamber bowl offset and the piston ring arrangement used in the Navistar T444E (7.3L) V8 diesel engine. (Reprinted with permission from SAE. Paper SP-961, copyright 1993, Society of Automotive Engineers, Inc.)

denum-plasma facing material. The second ring is a gray iron, negative twist, taper face rectangular ring. The oil ring is a 3.35 mm (0.132 in.) wide, gray iron, one-piece conformable ring with an expander spring.

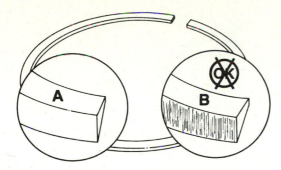

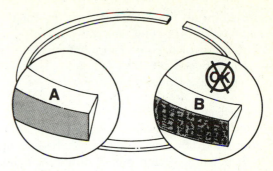

FIGURE 15–45 Compare the ring face condition of a new piston ring (A) with the face condition after an engine has ingested abrasive material due to poor air filter maintenance (B). (Courtesy of Cummins Engine Company, Inc.)

FIGURE 15–46 Part A illustrates a new piston ring face condition; part B indicates heavy metal scratches, metal discoloration, and void from scuffing and scoring. (Courtesy of Cummins Engine Company, Inc.)

From the three-ring piston pack arrangements just described, you can see that the basic shape of the piston rings used in high-speed heavy-duty engines is fairly standardized.

PISTON RING WEAR AND FAILURE

Typical causes of early piston ring failure can be attributed to engine overheating, dirty lube oil, dust-out (poor intake system maintenance), loss of under-piston cooling from plugged oil supply, cylinder glazing (wrong oil, excessive idling, light-load operations), incorrect ring end gap or side clearance, and insufficient piston-to-liner clearance. Other causes of piston ring wear and failure are discussed next.

Abrasive Wear

In Figure 15–45, first look at the surface finish condition of a new piston ring (A). Then consider the condition of the ring face (B) after the engine has ingested abrasive material (1) as a result of poor air filter maintenance, (2) from unfiltered air entering the engine from a leak in the air inlet piping between the air filter and the engine cylinders, (3) due to poor cleaning habits when the engine was repaired, or (4) from particles embedded in the cylinder liner surface.

Scuffing and Scoring

The term *scuffing* applies to the condition that occurs when miniaturized local welding between sliding surfaces takes place. Some very minor scuffing always takes place between new piston rings and the finished surface of the cylinder liner wall until they have conformed to one another's shape. With proper piston ring gaps, ring side clearance, piston-to-liner clearance, and adequate lubrication on the cylinder wall, this condition will not create any problems. However,

when abrasives are allowed to enter the air intake or lubrication system, or when insufficient clearances exist between running components within the cylinder, the tearing metal will create scuffing followed by *scoring* as the metal accumulates. Complete piston-to-liner siezure can result. Figure 15–46 illustrates the ring face condition when new (A) and the heavy metal scratches, metal discoloration, and voids from a scuffing and scoring condition (B). The damage at B can usually be traced to insufficient ring-to-liner wall clearance where the lube oil film was sheared away causing metal-to-metal contact. Common causes of scuffing can be traced to the following items:

- Engine coolant temperature (too hot) created by a lack of coolant flow, aerated coolant, faulty thermostats, scale buildup in the coolant passages
- Engine oil temperature (too hot), low oil level, wrong grade of oil, too much oil (foaming and aeration), plugged oil cooler, stuck-open bypass valve, faulty oil pump
- Incorrect grade of lubricant, oil dilution
- Cylinder liner surface finish (this is very important if the engine has been rebuilt and the liner or cylinder bore crosshatch is too shallow; see Chapter 16)
- Piston ring pack design (type of ring material in comparison to that in the bore or liner)
- Cylinder pressures and temperatures created
- Piston and ring clearance within the cylinder
- Incorrect combustion (carbon and ash buildup)
- Injector overspray creating cylinder wall wash
- High-sulfur diesel fuel

Chipping

Chrome-plated rings can be chipped as a result of careless handling, particularly when installing new rings onto the pistons. Always use the correct piston ring expander, and do not expand the rings more than necessary to install them onto the piston. Rings can also be chipped during engine operation if they stick or through incomplete combustion, which allows carbon to jam between the ring face and the cylinder wall. *Never* reuse a chipped ring.

Oil Ring Plugging

Figure 15–47 illustrates a new oil ring (A) and a plugging condition (B) that restricts oil drain back from the cylinder wall as the piston moves down the cylinder. This condition causes excessive amounts of oil to be retained on the cylinder wall; during the upward stroke of the piston, this oil saturates the compression rings as well as enters the combustion chamber. Burning oil will be visible as blue smoke in the exhaust gases and will increase the concentration of exhaust particulates. Burning oil, particularly around the compression ring grooves, can lead to varnish buildup and ring sticking, which slowly makes the condition worse. Causes of oil ring plugging can be attributed to low engine operating temperatures due to excessive idling, sustained light-load operating conditions, or an overcooling condition through a system malfunction. Ring groove deposits can also be caused by using the wrong grade or poor quality lube oil, plus too long a period between oil changes.

Ring Sticking

Many service personnel misunderstand cold-stuck, hot-stuck, and heat-set piston rings. Each of these three conditions is described next.

Cold-stuck rings means the ring is stuck in the piston ring groove. Usually this is caused by carbon deposits while the engine is *not* running. After engine start-up, the ring becomes free and functions normally. The entire face of a cold-stuck ring will have a normal shiny appearance, which indicates that the ring is sealing correctly. Consequently, cold-stuck rings should have no adverse effects on engine performance or life. It is not necessary to repair or replace cylinder kits because of cold-stuck rings.

Hot-stuck rings means the ring is actually stuck in the piston ring groove during engine operation. The ring face will exhibit a black face from compression blowby, and it will be scuffed as well as scored from improper lubrication. Any compression ring that is hot stuck will evolve into a major engine failure.

The heat-set ring (collapsed or broken ring) has lost all of its outward tension and is completely collapsed in its ring groove. The face of the ring appears black as it did in a hot-stuck condition, and it will be scuffed and scored from improper lubrication. Unlike a hot- or cold-stuck ring, however, when the heat-set ring is removed from the piston ring groove, it will have no

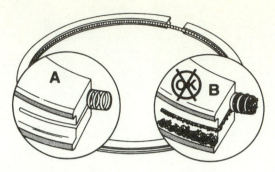

FIGURE 15–47   *Part A illustrates a new oil ring and part B shows a plugging condition which restricts oil drain back from the cylinder wall. (Courtesy of Cummins Engine Company, Inc.)*

outboard tension or free gap. Any ring that is heat set will evolve into a major engine failure.

Ring Breakage

One of the major causes of ring breakage is incorrect installation. Perhaps the ring was overexpanded during installation or maybe the wrong expander was used. These conditions can fracture a ring or overstress it, causing it to break into pieces during engine operation. Excessive ring-to-piston land side clearance causes the ring to flutter similar to a bird's wings, but at high speed. This will pound out the piston ring groove and lead not only to ring breakage but to possible breakup of the piston ring land area. Uneven piston ring groove land areas, or carbon jammed in the groove, can also cause ring breakage. Overloading of the engine can be another reason for ring breakage and piston damage.

External Piston Ring Inspection

One of the unique features of two-stroke-cycle engines is that the cylinder components can be inspected easily without disassembling the engine. If you suspect that the rings and cylinder surface are glazed, scuffed, scored, or damaged, remove the air box inspection covers from alongside the engine block. Use this procedure on small-displacement high-speed diesel engines (for example, any of the Detroit Diesel 53, 71, 92, and 149 engines) as well as on the very large deep-sea ship propulsion engines of up to 55,000 bhp (41,030 kW). Typical large ship engines of the two-stroke-cycle design include GMT, MAN, Mitsubishi, and Sulzer.

For inline Detroit Diesel 71 series engine models, a single, long bolt retains the air box cover to the engine block. Once the cover has been removed, the rings can be inspected as shown in Figure 15–48 to determine their condition (stuck, broken, glazed,

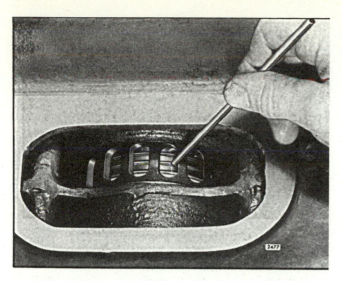

FIGURE 15-48 *Inspecting the condition of the piston rings after removal of the air box inspection cover from the side of the engine block on a DDC two-stroke-cycle engine. Use a blunt instrument to check the rings for loss of tension and sticking. (Courtesy of Detroit Diesel Corporation.)*

scuffed, scored, or badly worn). Use a blunt tool and gently push against the ring surface through the cylinder liner ports. A broken or stuck ring will have no compression or spring-back action. You can also manually rotate the engine over to inspect the piston, the piston crown, and the skirt, and by shining a small penlight or trouble light into the port area, you can determine the condition of the cylinder liner surface. You can also closely inspect the liners in the port belt area to determine if any cracks exist.

SERVICE TIP: When reinstalling the cover and bolt on inline engines, *do not* overtighten the bolt since it threads directly into the blcok casting alongside the cylinder liners. Overtightening can cause block bore distortion. Tighten the $3/8 \times 16$ in. bolt to 10 to 15 lb-ft. (14 to 20 N·m) torque value. The vee-type engine models have smaller air box covers on both sides of the engine block that are retained by several $5/16 \times 18$ in. bolts that should be retorqued to between 8 and 12 lb-ft. (11 to 16 N·m).

PISTON RING INSTALLATION

Cleaning and inspection of the piston assembly were discussed in the section on piston removal. Once the piston assembly has been checked and is considered serviceable, the piston rings must be checked for end-gap-clearance within the block bore or cylinder liner, and piston groove-to-ring side clearance.

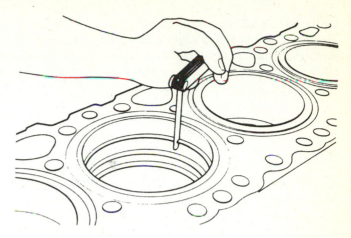

FIGURE 15-49 *Measuring piston ring gap with a feeler gauge after installing the rings into the cylinder and squaring them up with a piston inserted upside down. (Courtesy of Detroit Diesel Corporation.)*

End-Gap Clearance

Figure 15-49 illustrates how to correctly check end gap. Install the ring into the cylinder or liner in which it will be used. Then using a piston turned upside down (no rings on the piston), square the ring up in the bore and push it into the area where it will normally operate. Use a feeler gauge to measure the end gap and compare the figure to service manual specifications.

SERVICE NOTE: Piston ring end-gap clearances vary in engines based on the cylinder or liner bore size. In addition, the gap varies based on whether an aluminum piston or iron or steel crown is used. As a general rule of thumb, minimum acceptable end gaps with a new piston and liner would be between 0.003 and 0.004 in. (0.076 to 0.10 mm) for each inch of bore size on jacket water cooled engines. For air-cooled engines, this figure would be slightly greater: 0.004 to 0.005 in. (0.01 to 0.127 mm) per inch of cylinder bore size.

SERVICE TIP: If new piston ring gaps are found to be on the low side of the specification, they can be increased by filing or stoning the ends of the ring. Act with care to avoid chipping or peeling the chrome plate on the ring. *Make sure* that you file or stone both ends of the ring so that the cutting action is *always* from the outer diameter to the inner diameter (surface). Take extra care to ensure that the ends of the ring remain square and that the chamfer on the outer edge is maintained at approximately 0.015 in. (0.381 mm).

Side Clearance

A separate side clearance check is generally not required on keystone-type rings being installed in used pistons, since the piston groove wear check conducted with the special gauge shown in Figure 15–27 indicates the condition of the groove. However, when new pistons and rings are to be installed, it is wise to check side clearance. To effectively check the keystone piston ring-to-groove side clearance, refer to Figure 15–28. Use a selective feeler gauge inserted between the ring and groove to check the side clearance at four spots at 90° intervals. Acceptable side clearances vary in different makes of engines; some manufacturers quote as little as 0.001 to 0.005 in. (0.0254 to 0.127 mm) for the top compression (fire) ring. As a rule of thumb for top (fire) rings, side clearance is usually between 0.0025 and 0.0045 in. (0.064 to 0.114 mm) for cylinder bore sizes ranging between 3 and 7 in. (76 to 178 mm); this clearance is progressively greater as the bore size increases. Second and third rings usually have side clearances slightly larger than the top ring.

SERVICE TIP: On rectangular-shaped piston rings, side clearance can be checked before ring installation by taking a new ring and rolling it around and through the groove while you use a feeler gauge similar to that shown in Figure 15–50.

Ring Installation

To safely install the piston rings without damaging, stretching, or breaking them, always use a set of piston ring expanders similar to those shown in Figure 15–20. Check each ring carefully for an indentation or etched marking on each side, which will indicate the way the ring should face when installed on the piston. Usually this will be signified by the word *top*, *UP*, a ring supplier mark, a part number, a dot, or a dimple. In many cases, however, the piston ring shipping package identifies the location on each ring by part number. In the absence of any marking that signifies the top of the ring, carefully inspect both sides of the ring to see if one side has a black oxide or chrome flashing on it similar to that shown in Figure 15–51.

Since the oil control ring is generally less stressed than the compression rings, some manufacturers suggest that you refrain from using a ring expander to install it. Instead, they recommend manually stretching the ring just enough to spread it over the piston and into its groove.

Ring Gap Positioning

Once the rings have been correctly installed onto the piston, it is extremely important that they be properly positioned, or staggered, to ensure that during initial engine run-in the end gaps will not be subjected to the forces exerted on the thrust side of the piston. The ring gap should *not* be aligned with the piston pin or with any other ring. Rings with end gaps aligned would allow the high-pressure gases of combustion to leak through to the crankcase.

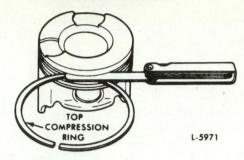

INSERT FEELER GAGE AT TOP OF RING GROOVE TO MEASURE RING SIDE CLEARANCE

TOP COMPRESSION RING

L-5971

FIGURE 15–50 *Using a feeler gauge to check piston ring side clearance. (Courtesy of Detroit Diesel Corporation.)*

Ring end-gap position and the number of degrees between each ring gap depend upon how many rings are in the ring pack. On a one-piece aluminum three-ring piston, the ring gaps should be 120° apart. Figure 15–51 illustrates the ring end-gap placement for a crosshead piston in the Detroit Diesel electronically controlled Series 50 and Series 60 four-stroke-cycle engines. Stagger the piston ring end gaps on a four-ring piston arrangement similar to that shown in Figure 15–51, where the ring gaps are positioned by the location of the inlet and exhaust valve pocket recesses cast into the aluminum alloy piston crown. Place the ring end gaps below the center of each valve pocket with position A representing the top (fire) ring, B the second ring, C the third ring, and D the oil control ring. The ring end gaps for positions A and D (rings one and four) would coincide with the front of the engine. If an oil control ring uses an individual expander similar to a peripheral abutment type, install the expander ring gap 180° from the gap of the oil ring.

Ring Compressors

With all of the rings installed and correctly staggered on the piston assembly, the rings must now be compressed to allow installation of the piston-ring assembly into either the engine block or the cylinder liner. Various types of piston ring compressors are available from major tool suppliers, and each engine manufacturer recommends a specific type for its engine models. On smaller-diameter bore pistons, the flexible steel band type of ring compressor shown in Figure 15–52 can be employed. The adjustable ring compressor must be tightened once it has been installed over the piston by use of a square metal Allen wrench.

Special ring compressors usually require no tightening of the compressor to facilitate piston installation into the cylinder or liner. Figure 15–53 illustrates a common *clamp-type ring compressor* used on some models of

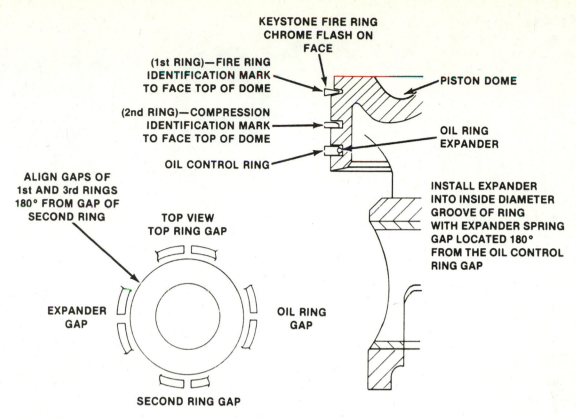

KEYSTONE FIRE RING
CHROME FLASH ON
FACE

(1st RING)—FIRE RING
IDENTIFICATION MARK
TO FACE TOP OF DOME

PISTON DOME

(2nd RING)—COMPRESSION
IDENTIFICATION MARK
TO FACE TOP OF DOME

OIL RING
EXPANDER

OIL CONTROL RING

ALIGN GAPS OF
1st AND 3rd RINGS
180° FROM GAP OF
SECOND RING

INSTALL EXPANDER
INTO INSIDE DIAMETER
GROOVE OF RING
WITH EXPANDER SPRING
GAP LOCATED 180°
FROM THE OIL CONTROL
RING GAP

TOP VIEW
TOP RING GAP

EXPANDER
GAP

OIL RING
GAP

SECOND RING GAP

FIGURE 15–51 *Piston ring identification markings and individual location of the piston ring gaps during installation for a Series 50 or 60 engine. (Courtesy of Detroit Diesel Corporation.)*

FIGURE 15–52 *An adjustable steel band clamp-type piston ring compressor for bore sizes in the range of 2.125 in. (54 mm) through 5 in. (127 mm). (Courtesy of Kent-Moore Division, SPX Corporation.)*

Caterpillar, Cummins, Detroit Diesel, Mack, and Navistar diesel engines. The two handles are opened by removing a pin, the compressor is installed over the piston and piston rings, the handles are pulled closed to compress the rings, and the retaining pin inserted. If the pin lock cannot be inserted, it indicates that the rings are *not* compressed; recheck for problems.

Figure 15–54 illustrates what is probably the best type of ring compressor available. Known as a *tapered-sleeve*, this ring compressor is manufactured with a large, gradual taper on its inside diameter to facilitate gradual compression of the rings during installation of the piston into the cylinder.

PISTON ASSEMBLY INSTALLATION

There are two methods for installing the piston assembly: (1) direct installation into the block bore or into the cylinder liner and (2) installation into the cylinder liner outside of the block followed by inserting the cylinder pack into the block as a complete assembly.

Note, however, that if the liner is press fit into the block bore, or if a wet cylinder liner is employed, many engine manufacturers recommend liner installation first, followed by piston assembly. Also, if it is not necessary to remove the liner but only the piston during a repair, then only the piston and piston rings require installation.

The following section describes how to install the piston and piston rings into the cylinder block bore or liner. The next section then describes how to install the piston and piston rings into the liner outside of the

FIGURE 15–53 Heavy-duty clamp-type piston ring compressor. (Courtesy of Kent-Moore Division, SPX Corporation.)

FIGURE 15–54 Tapered-sleeve ring compressor. (Courtesy of Kent-Moore Division, SPX Corporation.)

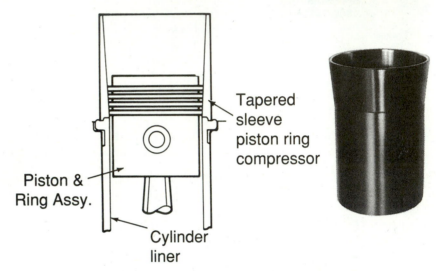

Tapered sleeve piston ring compressor

Piston & Ring Assy.

Cylinder liner

block, and how to install the cylinder pack as a unit into the bore of the engine block.

Piston-To-Block Bore Installation

Use the following procedure to correctly install the piston assembly into the cylinder block bore or preinstalled liner.

1. Refer to Figure 15–55 and carefully install the piston assembly into a container of clean 15W-40 engine oil. Remove the piston assembly from the container and let the excess oil drain from the piston.

2. If using the clamp-type ring compressor, lubricate it. Then install it around the piston as shown in Figure 15–53 to carefully compress the rings.

3. If using a tapered-sleeve-type ring compressor, install the piston dome down into a container of 15W-40 engine oil, with the piston rings staggered into their correct positions.

4. Coat the inside diameter of the ring compressor with liberal amounts of engine oil and place it over the bottom end of the piston and con-rod assembly as illustrated in Figure 15–56.

5. Slowly and carefully slide the tapered ring compressor down over the ring belt area. Then apply-

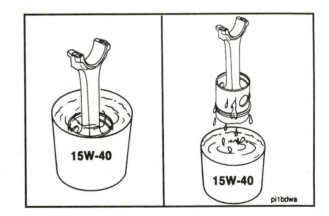

FIGURE 15–55 Submerging assembled piston, rings, and con-rod into a clean container of 15W-40 engine oil prior to using the piston ring compressor assembly. (Courtesy of Cummins Engine Company, Inc.)

ing gradual hand pressure evenly around the ring compressor to compress the rings, push down until the sleeve makes contact with the drain pan.

6. Manually rotate the engine crankshaft to place the con-rod journal for the cylinder you are working on at BDC.

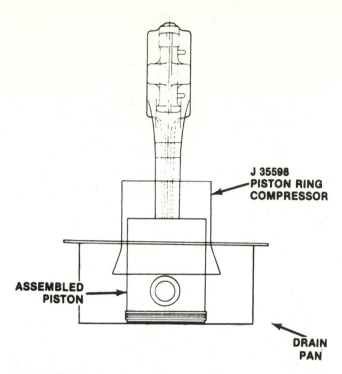

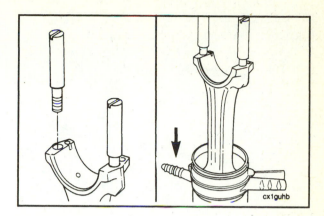

FIGURE 15–57 *Installing con-rod guide pins into the rod to avoid crankshaft journal damage during piston (rod) installation into the cylinder. (Courtesy of Cummins Engine Company, Inc.)*

FIGURE 15–56 *Installing the piston with its rings and con-rod assembly into a tapered-type piston ring compressor while inside a drain pan to prevent lube oil from spilling on the floor. (Courtesy of Detroit Diesel Corporation.)*

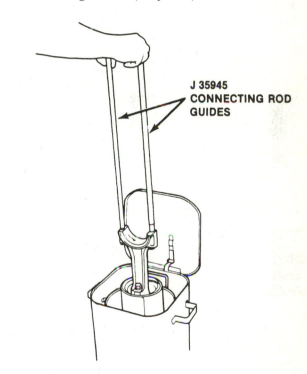

FIGURE 15–58 *Using long con-rod guides threaded over the existing con-rod bolts prior to piston (rod) assembly installation into a Series 50 or 60 cylinder. (Courtesy of Detroit Diesel Corporation.)*

7. Apply a heavy coat of 15W-40 engine oil around the cylinder bore or the liner with an oil squirt can.

8. Install the upper con-rod bearing into its saddle so that the bearing retaining tang aligns with the slot in the saddle. Avoid touching the bearing surface. Lubricate the bearing shell with 15W-40 engine oil.

9. Refer to Figure 15–57 and install con-rod guide pins into the rod if the cap is retained by threaded bolts. If, however, the con-rod employs pressed-in bolts and retaining nuts, refer to Figure 15–58 and thread the con-rod guides over the ends of the con-rod bolts to prevent damaging the crankshaft journals or the machined joint face of the rod. These guide studs (rods) also prevent the con-rod from contacting and damaging the cylinder liner surface. If no guide studs are available to you, place small-bore rubber hose over the end of each rod bolt to prevent the bolts damaging the liner or scratching the crankshaft rod journal.

10. Securely lift the piston and ring compressor assembly into position over the cylinder bore as illustrated in Figure 15–59. Make sure that the numbered side of the con-rod is facing the camshaft side of the engine on inline type engines or toward the outside of the block on vee engines. On some pistons check to see

that the word *front* or an arrow is toward the front of the engine. On Caterpillar 3406 and 3116 engine models, a color code at the base of the piston skirt, as illustrated in Figure 15–60, helps to correctly install the piston and con-rod assembly.

11. Carefully lower the piston and con-rod assembly into the cylinder bore, avoiding contact with the liner surface, until the ring compressor is resting

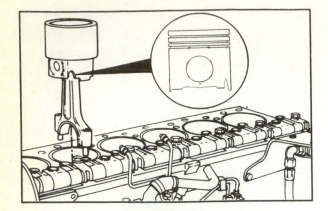

FIGURE 15–59 *Preparing to install the piston and installed ring compressor into the engine cylinder liner bore. Make sure that the numbered side of the con-rod is facing the correct side of the engine block. (Courtesy of Cummins Engine Company, Inc.)*

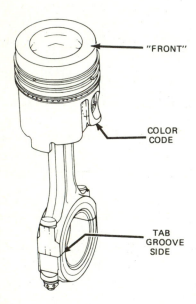

"FRONT"

COLOR CODE

TAB GROOVE SIDE

FIGURE 15–60 *Example of how some pistons are identified with the word front stamped or etched into the crown. Others employ a color code on the base of the skirt. (Courtesy of Caterpillar Inc.)*

flush and square with the top of the cylinder block deck surface.

12. Manually push the piston and connecting rod assembly down into the liner bore with your hand until the piston is free of the compressor. You can also use a soft-rag-covered wooden hammer handle or plug to *push* the piston into position. See Figure 15–61.

CAUTION: *Do not* attempt to drive the piston into the liner with the aid of a hammer or other metal object. Ring breakage can result as well as piston crown damage.

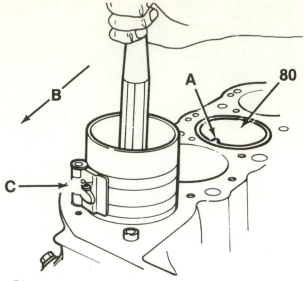

80. Piston
A. "Front" Mark
B. Front of Engine
C. Piston Ring Compressor Tool   W-00508

FIGURE 15–61 *Using a hammer handle to carefully but firmly push the piston assembly down into the cylinder bore and free of the piston ring compressor band. (Courtesy of GMC Trucks.)*

13. Remove the ring compressor. Then continue to push the piston all the way into the liner; or from the underside, pull on the guide studs until the upper con-rod bearing shell rests securely on the crankshaft journal. Remove the guide studs.

SERVICE TIP: Once the con-rod has been pulled into position over the crankshaft journal, make sure that the rod bolts have not been unseated or turned in their bores. Most rod bolts have a machined flat that *must* align with a mating flat on the rod shoulder to prevent its rotation when the retaining nut is tightened and torqued.

14. Refer to Figure 15–62 and install the bearing cap into position in its saddle. Make certain that the tang (2) is engaged with the cap slot (1). Make sure that the cap is match-numbered to the correct con-rod. Use clean 15W-40 engine oil to lubricate the bearing, although some engine manufacturers recommend that you lubricate the bearing shells with Lubriplate 105 or its equivalent.

15. Lubricate the rod retaining bolts, or the bolt threads, with clean 15W-40 engine oil. Some manufacturers specify 140W oil for this purpose or a special type of lubricant. Install the cap into position against the con-rod. Follow the engine manufacturers nut and

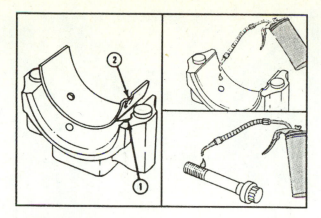

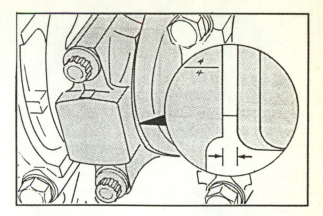

FIGURE 15–62 This illustration shows the precision shell bearing being installed into the con-rod cap so that its locating tang (2) engages with its mating slot (1). It also shows that the bearing shell should be well lubricated with clean engine oil and that the con-rod bolt threads should be cleaned and then lightly lubricated with clean engine oil. (Courtesy of Cummins Engine Company, Inc.)

FIGURE 15–63 Use a feeler gauge inserted between the con-rod and the crankshaft journal to check for adequate side clearance. (Courtesy of Cummins Engine Company, Inc.)

bolt tightening procedure. Usually this involves tightening the rod bolts and nuts alternately to a specified torque value. In some cases you have to perform a three-step procedure to gradually final torque the bolts and nuts. The bolts and nuts are then loosened off, and the process is repeated.

16. Using a feeler gauge, check for side clearance between the con-rod and the crankshaft journal as illustrated in Figure 15–63 by moving the rod from crank cheek to crank cheek.

NOTE: The connecting rod must move freely from side to side on the crankshaft journal to allow for heat expansion. If the rod does not move freely or has insufficient side clearance, remove the rod cap and make sure that the bearing shells are the correct size. Then check for dirt or damage on the crankshaft and bearing shells, misalignment of the cap to saddle, and signs of nicks, burrs, and so forth on the machined side faces of the rod and cap.

Cylinder Pack Installation

When it is desirable to install the piston assembly and cylinder liner as a cylinder pack (cylinder kit), the piston and rings are inserted into the liner outside of the engine block. Then the complete assembly is installed in the engine cylinder block bore area. Refer to Chapter 16 which describes the checks required for the liner and cylinder block before installation of the cylinder pack.

The procedure to install the cylinder pack involves using a piston ring compressor to compress the rings on the piston (see Figure 15–56) so that the piston and con-

rod can be inserted as an assembly into the cylinder liner outside of the engine block. We will discuss the installation of the cylinder pack for a 3176 Caterpillar engine as well as for a Detroit Diesel two-stroke-cycle engine.

Procedure for a Two-Cycle DDC Engine

1. Thoroughly lubricate the piston and rings as shown in Figure 15–55 using an 8:1 mixture of clean engine oil and STP or equivalent. On two-stroke DDC engines, the recommended engine oil is a straight 40 weight rather than the 15W-40 used in the four-stroke-cycle models.

2. Closely inspect the tapered ring compressor for signs of nicks, burrs, or deep scratches that could cause piston ring breakage during assembly.

3. Liberally coat the inside diameter of the ring compressor with the same oil mix used in step 1.

4. With the piston rings correctly staggered and the piston match-marked to the liner, carefully push the piston and con-rod assembly down into the tapered ring compressor as illustrated in Figure 15–64 (operation 1) until the piston crown contacts the wooden block.

5. Carefully lift and place the piston and rod assembly and ring compressor on the bottom of the cylinder liner as shown in operation 2 of Figure 15–64.

SERVICE TIP: Always load the piston into the cylinder liner from the bottom side, which contains a short machined taper to facilitate installation. This will also ensure that the oil scraping rings do not scratch or score the inside diameter of the liner, as they enter from the bottom rather than from the top side. In Figure 15–40 you can see that the oil rings have their scraping edges facing down so that they can effectively remove oil from the cylinder wall on the downward stroke of the piston.

OPERATION 1   OPERATION 2

5752

FIGURE 15–64 *Installing the piston and con-rod assembly into the cylinder liner of a two-stroke-cycle DDC engine using a special tapered-type ring compressor. (Courtesy of Detroit Diesel Corporation.)*

6. The stamped numbers on the rod and cap should be aligned with the match-mark that you placed on the liner flange-to-block surface previously.

7. Push the piston and con-rod assembly all the way down into the cylinder liner (see operation 2 in Figure 15–64) until the piston is free of the ring compressor. The peripheral abutment-type oil ring expanders used with these pistons (see Figure 15–43) exert considerable force on the two-piece oil scraping rings; therefore, don't unduly force the piston into the liner if it becomes stuck, otherwise ring breakage can result. Remove the piston assembly from the liner and check the ring condition. You may have to remove the piston from the ring compressor also to recheck ring condition.

8. Make sure that the liner seal ring grooves in the cylinder block are clean. Then install a new seal ring in each groove.

9. Use the same engine oil mix used in step 1 to lubricate the liner-to-block O-ring seals to help facili-

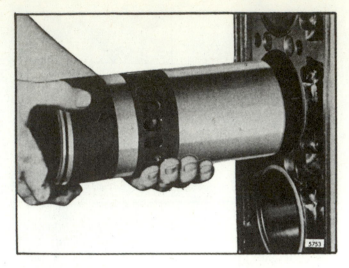

5753

FIGURE 15–65 *Installing the cylinder pack (piston, rod and liner) as a unit into the engine block as a complete assembly. (Courtesy of Detroit Diesel Corporation.)*

tate cylinder pack installation. *Do not* use hydrogenated vegetable oil or shortening on the O-ring seals.

10. Rotate the crankshaft to place the con-rod journal at BDC, and lubricate the journal with clean engine oil.

11. Install the con-rod upper bearing shell (one without the continuous oil groove) and lubricate it with clean engine oil.

SERVICE TIP: On vee-type engines, the crankshaft end of the con-rod is manufactured with an uneven width. Viewed from the side, it is wider on one side than the other. This allows proper alignment of the two con-rods when they are installed on the same crankshaft journal. Be sure that the narrow side of the con-rod is positioned so that when you install the cylinder pack the narrow side of the rod faces toward the center of the crankshaft journal and not away from it; otherwise, you will not be able to install the other cylinder pack that has its con-rod sharing the same journal.

12. Refer to Figure 15–65 and with the cylinder liner match-marks and cylinder stamped numbers on the con-rod facing the outside of the engine block on vee engines, carefully guide and direct the con-rod through the block bore. Use long-extension con-rod guide bolts or small-diameter rubber hose over the ends of the bolts to help protect the crankshaft journal if necessary.

13. Slide the cylinder liner straight into the block bore while supporting the cylinder pack to avoid dislodging the upper rod bearing. This action also allows you to feel the liner as it passes each one of the block-

FIGURE 15–66 *Cylinder liners held in place by special hold-down clamps to allow checking of the liner flange depth below the top face of the engine block on a two-stroke-cycle DDC 92 series engine. (Courtesy of Detroit Diesel Corporation.)*

FIGURE 15–67 *Installation of the liner seal (6) lubricated with clean engine oil into the cylinder block to facilitate ease of liner installation on a 3176 Cat engine model. (Courtesy of Caterpillar Inc.)*

to-liner O-seal rings until the liner flange rests within the block counterbore.

14. Push or pull the piston and rod into the liner until the upper bearing shell is firmly seated on the crankshaft journal.

15. Follow steps 14, 15, and 16 described under the subheading "Piston-to-Block-Bore Installation."

16. Once you have installed one cylinder pack use a set of cylinder liner hold-down clamps as illustrated in Figure 15–66 to prevent liner upward movement as you rotate the crankshaft over to install the other cylinder pack assemblies. In addition, the hold-down clamps ensure that the liner is bottomed in its counterbore. You must then use a gauge to determine if the liner flange is within the specifications for distance below the block surface. This is an important dimensional check because it ensures that the individual liner compression gaskets will seal effectively once the cylinder head is installed. On some four-stroke-cycle engines, the liner sits above the block surface.

Procedure for a 3176 Caterpillar Engine

1. Use a ring compressor to install the piston and piston rings into the cylinder liner similar to those shown in Figure 15–53 and Figure 15–54.

2. Thoroughly clean the cylinder liner mid-flange seat area, the top surface of the cylinder block, and the top of the block bore with Cat 8T9011 solvent cleaner.

SPECIAL NOTE: If you are installing a cylinder liner into the block of an earlier model 3176 engine, follow steps 3, 4, 5, and 6. Later 3176/B truck engine models employ a new cylinder liner with two seals where the liner has an additional seal groove. This new liner is a direct replacement for the earlier design with one seal. The manufacturer recommends that the two-seal liner be installed dry. If installation is difficult, however, a light application of engine oil on the new oil seal (6I3549) can be used; an antifreeze-water mixture can be used on the 4P9388 cylinder seal.

3. Install a new cylinder liner seal located at the base of the spacer block in the engine; lubricate it with clean engine oil to facilitate ease of liner installation. Figure 15–67 illustrates the location of this seal.

4. Paint a thin coat of Caterpillar 9U5839 liquid gasket material to the midstop location of the cylinder liner flange seat radius on the single-seal cylinder liner as illustrated in Figure 15–68 and allow it to dry to the touch. The liquid gasket material helps prevent oil leaks between the cast iron cylinder block and the aluminum spacer deck block.

5. Lubricate the lower portion of the liner with engine oil and rotate the crankshaft to place the con-rod journal for the cylinder at BDC.

6. Using the Caterpillar special tools illustrated in Figure 15–69, position the cylinder pack (5) and guide rod (A) into place.

7. Refer to Figure 15–70 and using tooling (B), press the cylinder pack into place in the block spacer plate until the liner is securely seated.

8. Repeat steps 14, 15, and 16 described under the subheading for the "Piston-to-Block Bore Installation"; then install the piston oil cooling jets below the cylinder liners.

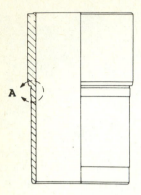

DETAIL A

FIGURE 15–68   Location of where to apply a bead of Cat 9U5839 liquid gasket material to the midstop cylinder liner flange seat radius on a 3176 model engine. (Courtesy of Caterpillar Inc.)

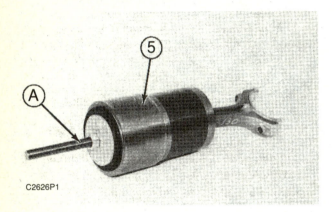

C2626P1

FIGURE 15–69   Using a liner-located rubber plug expander tool and guide rod (A) tightened into position securely to allow the cylinder pack (5) to be inserted as a unit into the block bore of a 3176 model engine. (Courtesy of Caterpillar Inc.)

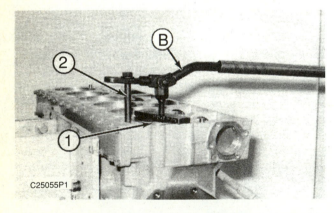

C25055P1

FIGURE 15–70   Using Cat special tooling (B), part number 2P8260, to correctly pull the installed cylinder pack into position in the block bore of a 3176 engine model. 2 = guide stud; 1 = cylinder liner installer plate. (Courtesy of Caterpillar Inc.)

SELF-TEST QUESTIONS

1. Describe the major purpose of a piston.
2. A trunk-type piston is a
   a. one-piece assembly
   b. two-piece assembly
3. Many heavy-duty high-speed engines in use today employ two-piece pistons. What are they called?
4. Technician A says that a trunk-type piston exerts less side thrust on the piston rings and cylinder wall than does a two-piece piston design. Technician B says that the two-piece piston design accomplishes this much better. Which technician understands piston design best?
5. List the advantages of a two-piece piston design over a single-piece design?
6. Technician A says that some aluminum alloy pistons are ground in an elliptical or barrel shape to provide a better piston-to-liner fit. Technician B says that this would lead to excessive ring blowby and piston slap when the engine was at normal operating temperature. Which technician understands the concept best?
7. The top of the piston is usually referred to as the
   a. crown
   b. skirt
   c. slipper bearing
   d. boss area
8. Aluminum alloy pistons normally employ a Ni-resist insert at the top and sometimes the second ring belt area. Describe this material and state the reason for its use.
9. Technician A states that when two-piece piston assemblies are used the crown is manufactured from a forged aluminum alloy to allow for greater expansion and better sealing, while the skirt is made from forged steel. Technician B says the reverse: the crown is steel and the skirt is aluminum alloy. Which technician is correct?
10. True or False: Since aluminum weighs approximately one-third that of cast iron and steel, an aluminum piston would be one-third of the weight of an equivalent steel model.
11. High-speed heavy-duty direct injection diesel engines normally employ pressurized under-piston lube oil cooling, according to technician A. Technician B says that this would result in unacceptable lube oil temperatures; therefore, an air intake system aftercooler is used instead. Which technician knows basic engine design theory best?
12. The letters SCFR mean that a piston, in addition to being manufactured from aluminum alloy, is
   a. special chrome ferrous-reinforced
   b. squeeze-cast fiber-reinforced
13. The advantage of using SCFR in the manufacture of a piston is to
   a. improve fatigue strength
   b. provide better piston-to-liner clearance
   c. provide longer piston ring life
   d. improve piston scuffing characteristics

14. One of the coatings that is sometimes used on pearlitic malleable iron piston skirts to improve scuff resistance is
    a. tin
    b. solder
    c. chrome
    d. copper

15. One of the coatings sometimes used on aluminum alloy piston skirts to improve scuff resistance is
    a. graphite
    b. tin
    c. solder
    d. powdered cast iron

16. True or False: Two-piece pistons generally have a piston pin bearing that is referred to as a slipper bearing.

17. Current high-speed heavy-duty diesel engines tend to employ a piston crown that is shaped similar to a
    a. saucer
    b. Mexican hat (concave)
    c. bowl-in-crown

18. List the advantages of using the piston design selected in your answer for Question number 17.

19. Some heavy-duty high-speed diesel engines use a piston crown shape that is known as a *re-entrant chamber*. What are the advantages of this design?

20. Technician A says that a piston crown with a quiescent combustion chamber shape does not impart a suitable swirling action to the air for use in high-speed engines. Technician B says that the quiescent design is most often used in slower running engines which operate with a large quantity of excess air. Are both technicians correct in their statements?

21. Technician A says that the average operating temperature in the center of the piston crown of a heavy-duty high-speed diesel engine is in the range of 475° to 600°F (246 to 315°C). Technician B says that the temperature has to be higher than this and suggests it is closer to 1000° to 1200°F (538 to 649°C). Which technician is closer to reality?

22. True or False: The thermal (heat) conductivity of steel is slower than that of aluminum; consequently, a higher cooling oil flow is required to prevent oil aging when a steel crown is used.

23. True or False: Some very-high-output horsepower high-speed diesel engines employ ceramic-coated piston crown assemblies.

24. The most widely used design of piston pin in high-speed heavy-duty diesel engines is
    a. semifloating
    b. fixed
    c. fully floating

25. True or False: A hollow piston pin is more widely used than a solid pin.

26. Piston pin retainers are generally of what type?

27. Technician A says that two-stroke-cycle DDC engines employ solid piston pin retainers because the oil control rings are located toward the base of the piston skirt. Technician B says the solid retainers are strictly to prevent the fully-floating piston pin from striking the ports in the cylinder liner. Which technician knows theory best?

28. Technician A says that piston crowns tend to be manufactured with a taper that increases toward the top of the piston. Technician B disagrees, saying that only the piston skirt is tapered to allow for expansion. Which technician is correct?

29. True or False: Prior to removing a piston from the cylinder, you may have to use a ridge reamer.

30. Failure to perform the task in question 29 can lead to damage of the piston, particularly in what area?

31. True or False: Pistons should always be identified as to cylinder number to ensure they will be replaced in the same position.

32. Technician A says that the best way to clean a piston of carbon at overhaul is to glass bead the complete assembly. Technician B disagrees, saying that this procedure would remove any protective coating from the piston skirt and should be avoided. Technician B says crushed walnut shells in a glass-bead-type machine are better for cleaning carbon from the piston ring belt area. Which technician is correct?

33. Technician A says that careful inspection of the injector spray pattern on the crown of the piston can indicate plugged nozzle orifices or injector overspray. Technician B says that you have to remove and test the injector to confirm any nozzle wear. Which technician is correct?

34. Aluminum alloy pistons employing fully-floating piston pins should be preheated to facilitate piston pin hand insertion or removal, according to technician A. Technician B disagrees, saying that the pin should be pressed or hammered in or out. Which technician is correct?

35. True or False: The term *fire ring* in relation to a piston ring means that it is the top ring on the piston.

36. True or False: The purpose of placing the top ring very close to the piston crown on high-speed heavy-duty engines is to reduce the dead air space that exists with lower-positioned rings. This results in more effective combustion.

37. True or False: Piston rings should always be removed using a special piston ring expander.

38. Most high-speed heavy-duty diesel engines now employ rings shaped in a
    a. keystone design
    b. rectangular design
    c. square design
    d. bevel-faced design

39. The advantage of using the ring in your answer to Question 38 is that it tends to minimize
    a. combustion gas blowby
    b. ring sticking
    c. pumping oil
    d. ring scuffing

40. The ring in your answer to Question 38 generally has sides that are

a. flat
b. oval
c. tapered
d. convex

41. True or False: Aluminum alloy pistons can be checked for cracks by using a magnetic particle detection procedure.

42. True or False: Forged steel piston crowns can be checked for cracks only by using a dye penetrant method.

43. Technician A says that all piston rings have a free diameter that is greater than the cylinder bore. Technician B says that this is not true; the rings would not fit into the cylinder when assembled onto the piston. Which technician is correct?

44. Name the two main piston ring clearances.

45. Piston ring wear groove gauges are generally used to check the following design of piston ring:
a. Square
b. Rectangular
c. Bevel faced
d. Keystone

46. An insufficient piston ring gap can result in
a. ring breakage
b. combustion blowby
c. piston land damage
d. scoring of the liner
e. all of the above

47. True or False: Insufficient piston ring side clearance can result in ring sticking.

48. True or False: A prestressed piston ring results in lower overall ring stress and a more rugged piston ring.

49. To offer scuff and corrosion resistance, top piston rings are generally coated with
a. molybdenum
b. chrome
c. graphite
d. nickel

50. Technician A says that during piston ring installation, you must look for a dot, part number, the word *top*, or a black phosphate coating to determine how to install the ring. Technician B says that the ring can be installed in any direction without any problems. Which technician is correct?

51. Technician A says that to inspect for piston ring damage on a two-cycle engine, you can remove the block air box inspection covers. Technician B says that you need to pull out the piston assembly to determine this. Who is correct?

52. True or False: Cylinder combustion gas pressures are the same on all piston rings during engine operation.

53. A *high modulus of elasticity* is a desired feature on a piston ring. What does this term mean?

54. Technician A says that the purpose of an oil control ring is to prevent oil from being burned in the combustion chamber. Technician B says that it is designed to distribute oil across the face of the cylinder wall on the upstroke and to scrape it off on the downstroke. Which technician is correct?

55. Name two commonly used types of oil ring expanders.

56. What condition is most likely to cause very early ring failure after a rebuild resulting in low compression, hard starting, and burning of oil?
a. Dust-out through unfiltered air
b. Use of the wrong grade of oil
c. Insufficient ring gap
d. Too much ring gap

57. Using the wrong grade of oil and light-load operation after new piston rings have been installed will usually result in
a. cylinder liner glazing
b. stuck rings
c. broken rings
d. siezed pistons and liners

58. List the causes that might lead to surface scuffing of the piston ring and cylinder liner.

59. When checking piston rings to determine the difference between a cold-stuck and hot-stuck condition, what features should you look for?

60. Technician A says that piston rings must be staggered around the piston so that their gaps are not aligned. Technician B says that since the rings rotate during engine operation, it doesn't matter where you place the individual ring gaps. Which technician is better trained?

61. Technician A says that on some pistons the design of the crown makes it necessary that the piston be installed facing in only one direction. Technician B says that pistons can be installed in any position. Which technician is correct?

62. Technician A says that the cylinder liner must be installed into the block bore before the piston and rings can be installed. Technician B says that on many engines the piston and liner can be installed as a complete assembly. Which technician is correct?

16 Cylinder Liners

OVERVIEW

The cylinder liner acts as a replacement surface against which the piston and rings run. The liner can be a dry press-fit or slip-fit design, or it can have engine coolant in direct contact with part or all of its outside diameter. In this chapter we discuss the various types of cylinder liners in use and how to remove, clean, inspect, measure, and install them.

TOPICS

- Function
- Types of liners
- Liner materials
- Liner removal and inspection
- Liner surface finish and engine break-in
- Liner glazing
- Cylinder hones
- Cylinder liner measurement
- Installing a dry press-fit liner
- Wet liner installation
- Installation of a dry slip-fit liner
- Self-test questions

FUNCTION

Although there are a number of current four-stroke-cycle diesel engines that do not use separate cylinder liners, such as the 3116 Caterpillar, the Cummins B series, the Navistar T 444E, and Ford's own truck diesels, most heavy-duty high-speed diesel engines now in use employ replaceable cylinder liners. Engines manufactured by Caterpillar, Cummins, Detroit Diesel, Mack, Volvo, DAF Trucks, Scania, Navistar, Mercedes-Benz, Hino, Izusu, MAN, Deere, and Perkins have replaceable cylinder liners. Cylinder liners are readily available in bore sizes ranging from 50 to 1000 mm (2 to 39.4 in.) and in lengths from 100 to 3600 mm (3.9 to 142 in.).

The function of the cylinder liner is to provide a running surface for the piston and rings. When worn, the cylinder liner can be replaced so that the actual cylinder block metal does not have to be rebored. In conjunction with the piston and rings and the cylinder head and gasket, the cylinder liner (more commonly referred to as a *liner*) retains the high-pressure gases of combustion within its bore. In a *wet-type liner,* the liner transfers the high heat of combustion through its base metal to the surrounding coolant. In a *dry-type liner* heat is transferred through the liner's base metal, which is in close contact with the engine block bore, then into the engine coolant passages.

TYPES OF LINERS

Despite many design differences between the various liners used in specific engine makes and models, liners basically fall into three distinct categories: dry type, wet type, and integral. The characteristics of each model are discussed next.

Dry Type
Dry-type liners can be either slip fit (hand push) or interference fit (press) in the engine block bore; usually they require use of a hydraulic press or mechanical puller to install and remove them. Dry liners are

generally more common to engines with bore sizes under 152.4 mm (6 in.). Since no engine coolant is in contact with the outside diameter of the liner, the liner dissipates its heat through contact between the outside diameter of the liner and the engine block metal. Coolant passages cast within the block allow coolant to circulate around the block casting to carry away liner heat. Therefore, dry liners must have good, even contact throughout their length and diameter. Press-fit models have wall thicknesses in heavy-duty high-speed truck engines of approximately 2.54 mm (0.100 in.). Liner thicknesses of as little as 1 to 1.5 mm (0.040 to 0.060 in.) are not uncommon, however, in smaller-bore engines, because the high pressures generated from combustion can be absorbed by the liner which is securely pressed into the engine block bore. Figure 16–1 illustrates a dry-type press-fit liner from a four-stroke-cycle Mack engine.

Dry-type slip-fit liners used by Detroit Diesel in its two-stroke cycle Series 71 engines have wall thicknesses of 4.76 mm (0.1877 in.) and are designed to have a slip fit or hand push of between 0.0127 and 0.0635 mm (0.0005 to 0.0025 in.) when installed in the cylinder block bore. Shims are often required under the cylinder liner flange (see Figure 16–1) to ensure that the correct protrusion (liner height) of the liner can be maintained above or below the engine block (intrusion) for effective sealing of the cylinder liner gasket or cylinder head gasket.

Wet Type

Wet-type liners, which are widely used by many major engine manufacturers of both two-stroke and four-stroke-cycle heavy-duty high-speed engines, always contain a flange at their top end to support the liner in the engine block counterbore (Figure 16–2a). The wet-type liner can have engine coolant in direct contact with its outside diameter (OD) from the top to the bottom of the liner. Some may have contact with the engine coolant in only over half their length, normally the upper half which is the hottest running part of the cylinder. Since coolant is in contact with the liner, several O-ring seals (Figure 16–2b) must be located either on the OD of the liner in machined grooves or in machined grooves within the cylinder block bore and in direct contact with the liner on its machined OD. Figure 16–2a illustrates a four-stroke-cycle engine liner that has coolant in direct contact with its OD throughout its length. Note the location of the seal rings necessary to prevent coolant from entering the engine oil pan. This type of a liner arrangement is commonly employed by Detroit Diesel, Cummins, and Caterpillar in their four-stroke-cycle engines. The crevice seal shown in the diagram is recessed in a groove in the liner and helps to stabilize the liner in the cylinder block

FIGURE 16–1 A dry-type press-fit cylinder liner showing the liner flange shim used to obtain the correct flange protrusion. (Courtesy of Mack Trucks, Inc.)

bore as well as acts as a seal between the cooling system and the lube oil areas within the block, including the crankcase. The two Teflon-coated, D-shaped seal rings recessed in grooves in the liner are used specifically to prevent water leakage between the liner and block bore.

Figure 16–3 illustrates a four-cycle engine liner with coolant in contact with only one-half of the liner. Commonly known as a *mid-stop design*, this arrangement is currently used by Caterpillar in its 10.3L (629 cu in.) 3176 model engine as well as by Cummins in its 8.3L (505 cu in.) C series engines and by Mack in its six-cylinder E7 model shown in Figure 16–4.

The Cat 3176 mid-stop liner is manufactured from a statically cast gray iron with an induction-hardened bore. The liner guides in the engine block crankcase directly below the midsupported liner seat as well as at the bottom of the liner. The 3176 liner has the cooling water jacket extended to nearly the top of the liner. This feature results in low liner bore temperatures at the top of the liner, which provides excellent ring-to-liner durability with the ring located near the top of the piston. Liner O-ring grooves were avoided in the 3176 engine because FEA (finite element analysis) indicated that the O-rings would cause unacceptable distortion of the liner.

Wet-type flanged liners are generally a press fit between the liner and block at its upper end to provide coolant sealing at the top of the liner while an O-ring seal is used at the mid-stop portion of other liners for sealing purposes. Should the seal rings leak on a wet-type liner, coolant can enter the crankcase and contaminate the engine lube oil. Although commonly found on larger slow-speed marine and industrial engines, Detroit Diesel employs a similar arrangement in its four-stroke-cycle Series 50 and 60 engines as illustrated in Figure 16–5. A weep hole for each cylinder is drilled

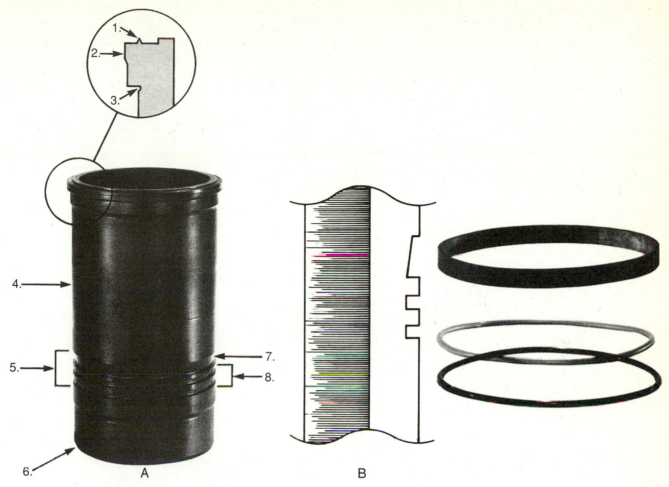

FIGURE 16–2 Features of a typical wet-type cylinder liner assembly and the seal rings required to retain the engine coolant within the engine block passages and around the outside diameter of the liner. 1, Bead; 2, Press fit; 3, Relief; 4, Wall; 5, Sealing area; 6, Chamfer; 7, Crevice seal groove; 8, Packing ring grooves. (Courtesy of Cummins Engine Company, Inc.)

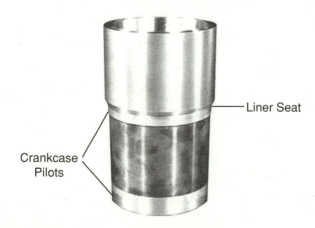

FIGURE 16–3 Mid-stop design cylinder liner employed by Cat in its 3176 engine model. (Courtesy of Caterpillar Inc.)

through the cylinder block exterior into the cylinder bore area. This weep hole is located between the two D-shaped seal rings and is used to determine if engine coolant is leaking past the upper liner seal ring. Small push-in rubber plugs are inserted into the weep holes during normal engine operation to prevent the entrance of any dirt or contaminants into the seal ring cavity.

Figure 16–6 illustrates a wet-type liner used in Detroit Diesel's two-stroke-cycle 53, 92, and 149 series engines with coolant in direct contact only with the upper half of the liner assembly. The flange at the top of the liner rests on a counterbore in the block and sits on a replaceable cast iron insert that permits accurate alignment of the liner. Two Teflon-coated seal rings installed in machined grooves of the cylinder block bore are used to prevent water leakage between the liner and block. The lower half of the liner is cooled by water inside the cylinder block water jacket that surrounds the liner. The

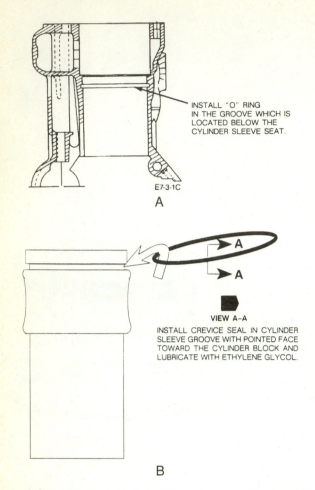

INSTALL "O" RING
IN THE GROOVE WHICH IS
LOCATED BELOW THE
CYLINDER SLEEVE SEAT.

E7-3-1C

A

VIEW A-A

INSTALL CREVICE SEAL IN CYLINDER
SLEEVE GROOVE WITH POINTED FACE
TOWARD THE CYLINDER BLOCK AND
LUBRICATE WITH ETHYLENE GLYCOL.

B

FIGURE 16–4   (a) Mack E-7 engine wet/dry liner O-ring groove; (b) Mack E-7 liner crevice seal groove. (Courtesy of Mack Trucks Inc.)

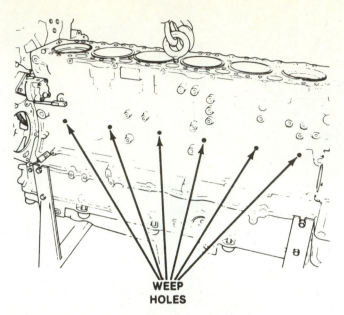

WEEP HOLES

FIGURE 16–5   Example of cylinder-block-located weep holes which indicate when engine coolant leaks past the upper liner seal ring of a Series 60 four-stroke-cycle electronically controlled engine. (Courtesy of Detroit Diesel Corporation.)

large air volume at the air inlet ports supplied from the gear-driven blower and turbocharger also cools the liner in this area.

A number of 1994 electronically controlled diesel engines have a groove cut in the top of the liner to circulate coolant around the hottest part of the liner just below the flange area as illustrated in Figure 16–7. This concept is used by Deere in its 6101 engines (replacing the 6619 models) and is referred to by Deere as *directed cooling*. Detroit Diesel uses this same design feature in its Series 50 and 60 engines. Cylinder head gasket temperatures are reduced by as much as 100°F (38°C), and the liner temperature in this area is reduced by as much as 130°F (54°C). Longer piston ring life is also achieved.

Integral Type
Very-large-displacement slow-speed engines, such as those in deep-sea marine and stationary power-gener-

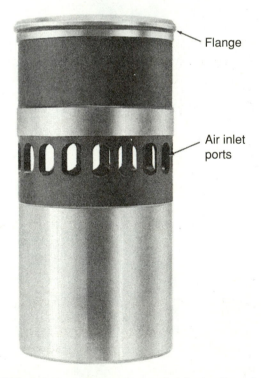

Flange

Air inlet ports

FIGURE 16–6   Wet-type ported cylinder liner for a two-stroke-cycle DDC 92 series engine model. (Courtesy of Detroit Diesel Corporation.)

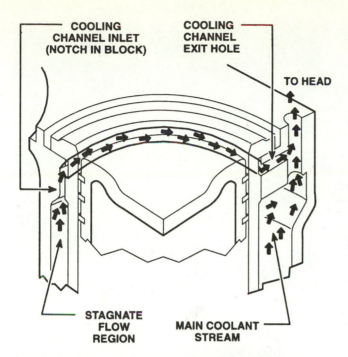

COOLING CHANNEL INLET (NOTCH IN BLOCK)

COOLING CHANNEL EXIT HOLE

TO HEAD

STAGNATE FLOW REGION

MAIN COOLANT STREAM

FIGURE 16–7 *Design concept of the top liner cooling principle employed by Detroit Diesel in its latest Series 50 and 60 engine models. Longer top ring life results from a cooler running top liner band area. (Courtesy of Detroit Diesel Corporation.)*

ation applications, can be of either a four-stroke or two-stroke-cycle design. The liner is generally water cooled. Coolant may be in direct contact with the outside diameter of the liner or a design known as an *integral liner* may be used. This type of design employs a thick-walled hollow liner that has been cast and machined to allow coolant to be directed through a series of hollow struts, particularly when a ported two-cycle liner is used. In other variations, a series of internal or external cast loops with a sleeve surrounding a liner permit the coolant to enter the bottom of the liner and centrifuge itself around the liner, thereby achieving improved coolant flow. Warm coolant then leaves the top area of the liner and passes into the cylinder head area.

Figure 16–8 illustrates a series of very-large-displacement two- and four-stroke cycle marine engine cylinder liners. To gain an appreciation of the actual dimension of these liners, note the size of the technician on the left-hand side of the illustration. The liners at the front are four-cycle designs. In some cases, large worn liners are rebuilt by power honing and glass beading; then they are rechromed. The checks and tests that must be done on these liners follow the same routine as those for smaller high-speed engine models.

LINER MATERIALS

Liner materials are available in up to 21 material specifications. In addition, a broad variety of bore and surface finish treatments are available depending on the demands under which the engine is to operate. Electric arc melting furnaces provide highly accurate quality control during material production, and centrifugal casting produces clean, sound castings with fine grain structures and excellent physical and mechanical properties. Machining is carried out with numerically controlled computers and robotic material-handling equipment for maximum efficiency.

Special high-alloyed cast irons are commonly used for liner construction. Basic grade cast iron consists of uniformly distributed flake graphite in a pearlite matrix (the embedding or enclosing mass surrounding the metal) and is used for applications that require high-wear resistance and normal mechanical properties. For more severe applications, the cast iron base material consists of an improved flake graphite alloyed to provide very high wear resistance by the addition of hard steadite (an extremely hard complex carbide) uniformly distributed in a pearlite matrix. To provide antiscuffing properties, very fine carbides of niobium uniformly distributed in the pearlitic matrix are added to specially alloyed cast iron. Other alloys used in liner construction include ductile iron with well-dispersed spheroidal graphites in a pearlitic matrix. When increased durability and piston ring life, along with reduced oil consumption and longer overhaul periods are desired, porous chrome-plated liner bores are used. The porosity percentage, liner plateau finish size, and the depth of cavities can be controlled to suit a variety of engine specifications.

The term *plateau honing* is often used in reference to the finished inside diameter of liners. This process provides superior performance in easy engine break-in, resistance to wear, and lower oil consumption. The process also controls liner surface crosshatch angle, plateau area and length, and surface depth to meet specific requirements for the types of pistons and rings being used. Liners can be as thin as 1 mm (0.040 in.) to as thick as 38 mm (1.5 in.), and the inside diameter can be chromium plated or silicon carbide impregnated for high resistance to scuffing and abrasion. For the prevention of cavitation erosion which occurs on the outside of wet-type cylinder liners, various metallic coatings are often used. Chrome is one of these. In smaller engines such as the air-cooled engines in motorcycles and snowmobiles, a process that bonds aluminum casting alloy with a cast iron liner is now widely used.

FIGURE 16–8 Example of the physical size of a large slow-speed diesel engine integral (wet) type of cylinder liner assembly. Note size of technician inspecting the liners. (Courtesy of Hyundai Engine & Machinery Co., Ltd., Seoul, Korea.)

LINER REMOVAL AND INSPECTION

NOTE: Cylinder liners can be removed from the engine block on their own, but on a number of engine makes there is another option. You can remove the liner and assembled piston, rings, and con-rods as a complete assembly. This is commonly referred to as removing the *cylinder kit* or *cylinder pack* and involves special tooling. See Chapter 15, Figure 15–18 dealing with piston removal. To effectively install a cylinder pack, refer to Figures 15–65 and 15–69.

Remove Cylinder Liner

The difficulty in removing a cylinder liner is relative to whether it is a slip-fit or interference (press-fit) design. To successfully remove and install a cylinder liner from an engine block, a variety of special pullers and installers are readily available from tool suppliers. Even though the liner may be slip fit in the block bore, after many hours or miles of engine operation and the heating and cooling that takes place, the liner can become tight. Therefore, a puller may be required to withdraw it from its bore.

Some wet-type liners are constructed so that the liner flange is press fit in the cylinder block counterbore; consequently, a puller is generally needed to remove or install it. Figure 16–9 illustrates a universal liner puller that can be employed with all wet liners from 4 to 6.25 in. (101.6 to 158.75 mm) bore diameter and up to 16 in. (406.4 mm) in length. An extension arm allows sleeve removal up to 18 in. (457.2 mm) in length. With spring-loaded feet, the tool automatically adjusts to fit the liner diameter. Care should be taken that the puller does not contact the block casting; otherwise, cylinder block damage can result. The liner

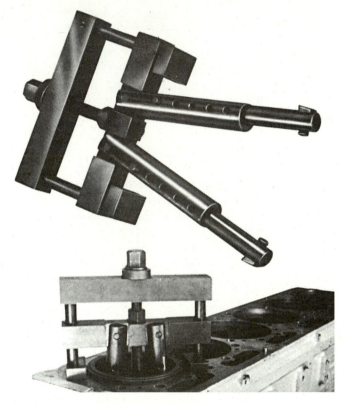

FIGURE 16–9 Example of a typical universal cylinder liner puller. (Courtesy of Kent-Moore Division, SPX Corporation.)

puller should be placed across the block at right angles to the centerline of the crankshaft.

SERVICE TIP: All liners should be match-marked to the engine block, so that if they are to be reused they will be replaced in the same position in their counterbore. Once the liner has been removed, write the cylinder number on its outer surface with a liquid metal market or Dykem, and tag any shims from below the liner flange to ensure that they will be used with the same liner. This will allow you to retain the same cylinder liner protrusion or intrusion, depending on the type of liner used. Should the liner be removed due to failure, use match-marks and numbers so that upon closer inspection, the technician or factory service representative can determine the cause of failure.

By using an air-impact wrench to rotate the hex nut on top of the tool, quick liner removal is assured. A tool such as this allows the technician to pull six stubborn wet liners in less than 4 minutes. By means of adapters, this same tool can be made to fit a wide variety of diesel engine cylinder liners.

A simpler liner puller with a variety of pivoting liner shoe adapter plates of different diameters is illustrated in Figure 16–10. Some models simply employ a slide hammer to dislodge the liner from the cylinder block bore. There are also liner puller tools that use an air-over hydraulic pump; these tools have up to a 20 ton capacity to pull even the most stubborn dry-type liners, particularly those in larger-bore size cylinders.

Inspect Cylinder Liner

When a wet cylinder liner has been removed at major overhaul or because of leaking liner seal rings, consider whether the liner might be used again. If so, it must be thoroughly cleaned and then inspected. After removing the liner seal rings, wash the liner in detergent soap and warm water and clean the inside diameter with a stiff nonmetallic brush to remove dirt and impurities. Use a high-quality steel wire brush to clean the liner flange seating area. If the outside diameter of the liner is scaled from coolant, check to see how thick the scale buildup is. Use a wire brush on the liner to remove the scale, since using a strong caustic solution could leave stains on the machined inside diameter of the liner. Then use a steam cleaner or solvent in a tank to clean the liner. Dry the liner with compressed air and lightly lubricate the machined surfaces to prevent any possibility of rusting. This also allows the oil to work its way into the surface finish.

SERVICE TIP: If the liners are not going to be inspected or used right away, always store them in an upright position until ready for use. Experience has shown that liners left on their sides for any length of time can become egg shaped and distorted, thereby making reinstallation in the block bores very difficult—sometimes even impossible.

Once a liner has been cleaned thoroughly, closely inspect it to determine if it has the following characteristics:

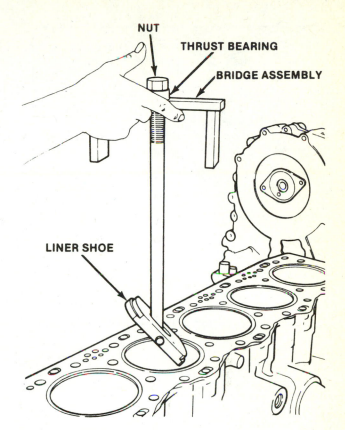

FIGURE 16–10   *A pivoting shoe-type of cylinder liner puller with its bridge assembly and puller screw— Kent-Moore part number J35791. (Courtesy of Detroit Diesel Corporation.)*

1. Surface finish and/or crosshatch irregularities. Refer to Figure 16–11 (left-hand side) and check for a moderate polish. A moderate polish means a bright mirror finish exists only in areas that are worn and some traces of the original hone marks, or an indication of an etch pattern, are still visible. The right-hand side of the diagram illustrates a near mirror-like finish in the worn area with no traces of the original hone marks or an etch pattern. Replace the liner if a heavy polish is visible over 20% of the piston ring travel area or if 30% of the ring travel area has both a moderate and a heavy polish while the other half shows a heavy polish.

2. Scuffing, scoring, gouging, or low spots on the inside diameter. If your fingernail catches in a scratch, the liner should be replaced.

3. Taper, wear, and ovality on the inside diameter, determined by using a dial bore gauge.

4. Signs of cracking, particularly at the flange, and around the port belt area of two-stroke-cycle engines. (It may be necessary to

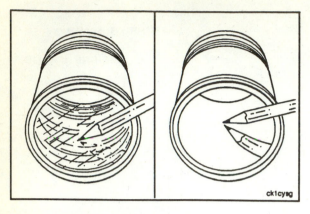

FIGURE 16–11 *Used cylinder liner. Left-hand side shows signs of a moderate polish yet still exhibits some traces of the original hone marks and an indication of the etch pattern. Right-hand side exhibits a near mirror-like finish on the surface of the liner with no traces of the original hone or etch marks. (Courtesy of Cummins Engine Company, Inc.)*

employ a nondestructive magnetic particle, flourescent magnetic particle, and a black light, or a flourescent penetrant method similar to that described for checking an engine block or crankshaft, if cracks cannot be seen clearly with the naked eye.)

5. Additional flange irregularities. Check for smoothness and flatness on the top and bottom surfaces.

6. A smooth and flat hardened liner insert, if used below the flange. Replace the insert if it shows signs of indentations.

7. Cavitation erosion, severe corrosion, or pitting on the outside surface of wet-type liners. Reject the liner if deep pits are visible or if the corrosion cannot be removed with a fine emery cloth.

8. Dark spots, stains, or low-pressure areas on the outside diameter of dry-type liners. This indicates poor liner-to-block contact.

9. Shiny areas on the outside diameter or flange area. These usually indicate liner movement (wet or dry type).

10. Fretting on the outside diameter of the liner, particularly below the ports on two-cycle engines, which is the result of slight movement of the liner during engine operation causing block metal to adhere to the liner. These metal particles can be removed from the surface of the liner with a coarse, flat stone.

LINER SURFACE FINISH AND ENGINE BREAK-IN

Manufacturing techniques today have produced outstanding metallurgical component parts as well as extremely close tolerances between moving parts. Surface finishes, such as plateau honing on cylinder liners, plus prefinished piston rings have drastically reduced the time required on both new and used engines for mating adjustment between the cylinder liner surface and piston rings during the run-in or break-in period. Nevertheless, it is important to follow the engine manufacturer's run-in procedure, particularly when an engine has undergone a major overhaul.

For years, oil consumption has been used as a measurement to determine when the piston rings have seated to the liner surface, although oil may be lost or consumed in other ways. As a result of tighter ring clearances and different ring designs, many newer engines, particularly those with electronic controls, consume far less oil than older mechanical models. Because correct sealing efficiency is not attained until new rings have seated and conformed to the liner surface, a "green" (new or rebuilt) engine has more blow-by and is more easily damaged by excessive loading than a broken-in engine. Major engine manufacturers such as Detroit Diesel, Caterpillar, and Cummins test their new engines with a dynamometer before they leave the factory, so the rings have seated, or are very close to being seated, to the liner surface.

To fully understand the conditions that exist within the engine cylinder during the break-in period of either a new or a rebuilt engine, let's review some of the major factors that come into play. Two major factors are the piston ring and the cylinder liner, since their respective surface finishes are always in contact. Consider that in an engine with a 6 in. (152.4 mm) stroke running at 2100 rpm, the piston will travel at 2100 ft/min (640 m/min) which is equivalent to 24 mph (39 km/h). If the average rpm of the engine throughout its working life is 1500 rpm, then the average piston speed is 1500 ft/min (457 m/min), or 17 mph (27 km/h). Should the engine accumulate 15,000 hours, or the equivalent of 450,000 miles (724,185 km) in an on-highway truck between overhauls, the piston rings will "slide" the equivalent of 255,000 miles (402,325 km).

The U.S. EPA exhaust smoke emissions standards have caused engine designers to tighten-up on the amount of oil that is retained on the cylinder wall, since even a small amount of lube oil entering the combustion chamber can contribute to the particulate content in the exhaust stream. Tests have shown that up to one-third of exhaust particulates can originate from lube oil that has been allowed to enter the combustion chamber. Therefore, today's high-speed engines have been engineered to run almost as a dry engine, with less lube oil being allowed to escape into the combustion chamber. Piston rings, particularly the fire ring (top), are subjected to higher pressures and temperatures.

All of the various functions of the piston rings must be performed continuously under the following range of conditions in a diesel engine.

1. On the intake stroke of a non-turbocharged engine (naturally aspirated) the air pressure in the cylinder is a partial vacuum, since it is less than atmospheric pressure (see the discussion of volumetric efficiency in Chapter 1). In a gear-driven blower (two-stroke Detroit Diesel) or any turbocharged engine, cylinder pressure is higher than atmospheric pressure. The intake airflow creates some internal cooling of cylinder components as well as of the valves. During this process, some oil can tend to flow upward, particularly if there is uneven piston ring-to-cylinder contact.

2. During the compression stroke, cylinder temperatures and pressures rise substantially. On high-speed turbocharged and air-to-air aftercooled engines, the air entering the cylinder can be in the region of 100° to 110°F (38° to 43°C), with temperatures at the end of compression ranging between 1000° and 1200°F (538° to 649°C) and 450 to 550 psi (3103 to 3792 kPa). As pressure increases, oil that was spread across the cylinder wall by the rings is blown downward.

3. On the power stroke, peak firing pressures in high-speed electronically controlled diesel engines can range between 1800 and 2300 psi (12,411 to 15,856 kPa); peak temperatures, which last for only a very short time can be between 3000° and 4000°F (1649 to 2204 C). Any oil that has seeped into the combustion chamber will burn and increase the particulate matter in the exhaust gases. Any oil on the hot cylinder wall will tend to burn and be blown downward.

4. When the exhaust valves open, the decreasing cylinder firing pressures and temperatures drop off as the blower or turbocharger scavenging airflow enters the cylinder. Very little to no oil is left on the cylinder walls at this time.

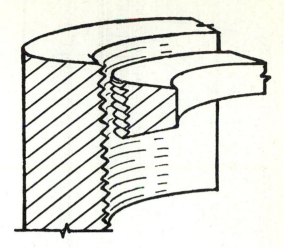

FIGURE 16–12 *Magnified view of a new piston ring and cylinder liner face surface. Note coarse-like thread pattern. (Courtesy of Cummins Engine Company, Inc.)*

In a typical engine running at 2100 rpm, this complete range of pressures, temperatures, and forces occurs 16 times every second. Thus, it is easy to appreciate why the surface finish of piston rings to the cylinder liner is extremely important and deserves maximum consideration during any repair or overhaul procedure.

Magnification of new piston ring faces will reveal that they usually have a coarse thread-like pattern, even though they may feel relatively smooth to the touch. This pattern forms the break-in surface of the ring. Figure 16–12 illustrates a magnified view of a cross section of a new cylinder wall and piston ring surfaces. The peaks on both the ring and cylinder represent the initial contact area. During the initial start-up and engine running procedure, pressure per unit of area is very high and tends to produce a high wear rate as a result of the localized high heat from the frictional contact. Recall from our discussion on how rings seal (see Figure 15–36) that the ring contact pressure is created by combustion gas pressure behind the ring. This gas pressure is proportional to the amount of fuel being burned in the combustion chamber (related to engine load and horsepower developed). It is necessary, therefore, to start with light loads and gradually increase speed and load to allow gradual seating of the rings as the wear-in period progresses and friction between the liner and ring surfaces is lowered. Figure 16–13 illustrates the same piston ring and liner surface shown in Figure 16–12 after a short period of gradual break-in. Notice that the sharp peaks shown in Figure 16–12 have been lapped away, leaving flat-topped ridges with open valleys between them. The unit of

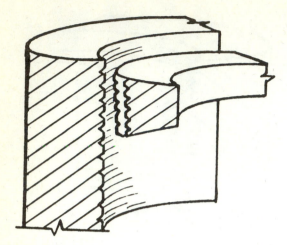

FIGURE 16–13   Magnified view of the piston ring and liner surfaces after initial break-in of rebuilt engine. (Courtesy of Cummins Engine Company, Inc.)

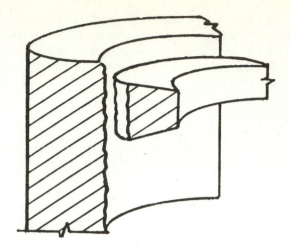

FIGURE 16–14   Magnified view of a closed wall cylinder liner surface where hot combustion gases soften the factory-produced hone pattern causing metal smearing. (Courtesy of Cummins Engine Company, Inc.)

area loading has now dropped to a smaller value as a result of the increase in ring-to-liner surface contact. Engine oil usage and any trace of blue exhaust smoke should have all but disappeared at this point.

Refer to the designs of piston rings illustrated in Figures 15–39 and 15–40. The top ring must seal against the highest temperature zone with the least amount of lubrication; this is why either a plasma or chromium coating is required on the top (fire) compression ring and often on the second one also. The top ring must not only withstand the high pressures and temperatures of combustion, but it must also be resistant to airborne dust or dirt and soot and carbon from the combustion process. The second compression ring is designed to distribute and control oil as well as seal against combustion pressures. These rings are generally designed to twist slightly under heat and pressure, so that the lower edge of the face contacts the cylinder wall surface more firmly than the top edge to permit the ring to form a line contact with the cylinder, thereby providing high sealing contact pressures. In addition, this design enables the ring to spread oil on the upstroke, and the lower edge acts to scrape the oil off the cylinder wall during the downstroke.

The oil ring is an oil metering device used to spread engine lube oil on the upstroke and scrape it off on the downstroke, thereby efficiently regulating the quantity of oil on the cylinder wall at any given time. The design of typical oil rings (Figure 15–39 and Figure 15–40) can consist of a wide two-rail ring design that contacts the cylinder wall. A channel between the oil ring rails allows oil to escape through the piston ring groove oil drain holes to allow oil scraped from the cylinder walls to return (drain) to the

engine crankcase. A two-piece oil scraper ring may also be used. All piston rings are subjected to carbons, soot, varnish, and gums that are formed during the combustion process. The degree of these accumulated contaminants depends on many factors, such as the mechanical state of the engine (amount of wear), the degree of load, and type of fuel and lube oil used. Oil rings in three-ring pistons receive some pressure from the combustion gases, although this tends to be very low. The compression rings are held against the cylinder wall by gas pressure, whereas the oil ring is held in a sealing position by its designed-in tension or by the use of an expander.

LINER GLAZING

Liners that have been subjected to periods of operation that are too long can develop a glass-like (glaze) surface on their inside diameter as a result of the rubbing action of the piston rings. In some cases, cylinder glazing occurs in new or rebuilt engines due to the use of the improper grade of lube oil; this is usually indicated by continuous oil consumption with low mileage on the engine. Scores and scuffing between the piston rings and cylinder liner surface, as well as other damage, will cause oil consumption to increase on any engine. A worn but undamaged cylinder wall surface tends to present a smooth, shiny appearance. The following two conditions are causes of glazing.

The first condition, shown in Figure 16–14, creates a *closed wall* where hot combustion gases soften the factory- or overhaul-produced hone pattern, causing metal smearing to obliterate the crosshatch pattern on the liner surface. This condition usually reflects itself in the form of irregularly shaped spots which are so hard that a hone may not cut through them. If the hone cannot cut through the spots, high blowby conditions will occur leading to possible scuffing of the piston, piston rings, and cylinder liner. The scuffing condition will tend to create a hot-spot condition within the cylinder, and this condition will lead to small metal particle buildup that eventually results in scoring and possible piston to liner siezure. This same scuffing condition can be caused by improper engine break-in conditions, such as applying a heavy load too early.

A second condition, shown in Figure 16–15, that can lead to glazing is referred to as a *filled wall*. The valleys created by the honing pattern are filled with carbon from burned oil, residue from incomplete fuel combustion, gum and varnish from unsuitable fuel and oil, coolant or antifreeze residues from internal leaks, or any combination of these. Excessive periods of idling or continual light-duty operation can also accelerate this condition. It becomes almost impossible for the piston ring to effectively seal, since the character of the liner surface is changing constantly as deposits are burned away and others are added. It is extremely hard for any lube oil to penetrate this type of a surface buildup; therefore, high friction can occur under load due to a lack of lubrication. Often when an engine with this condition is worked hard for some time, a reduction in oil consumption and blowby may result. If the operating conditions that initially created the problem are resumed, however, the engine once again will exhibit oil consumption and blowby.

Any glaze must be removed if liners are going to be reused. If it is not removed, the rings will take much longer to seat or may fail to seat at all. Glazing can be removed by the use of a hone, which is described next.

CYLINDER HONES

A power honing machine is described in Chapter 9 in reference to cylinder block reconditioning. Major tool and equipment suppliers offer hones in a variety of styles. Basically, however, there are three main types of hand-operated hones used to recondition cylinder block bores or liners:

1. The spring-loaded hone shown in Figure 16–16 can be adjusted to suit different bore sizes. This type of hone tends to follow the contours of a worn bore due to the spring pressure exerted on the stones; therefore, it is used to quickly deglaze a bore or a liner. Do not use

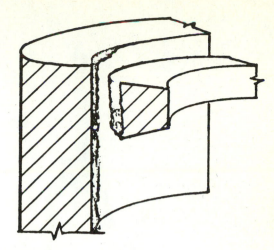

FIGURE 16–15 A filled-wall cylinder liner and ring condition that can lead to glazing. The valleys created by normal liner honing are filled with carbon from burned oil, incomplete combustion, and so forth. (Courtesy of Cummins Engine Company, Inc.)

this type of equipment when attempting to hone a just completed cylinder block bore to achieve the correct piston-to-liner clearance as well as the correct surface finish crosshatch pattern.

2. A ball-type hone, or flexi-hone, illustrated in Figure 16–17 is also used mainly to create effective cylinder wall deglazing or to clean a used liner by lightly roughening up the surface to facilitate new piston ring seating.

3. A fixed-type hone, illustrated in Figure 16–18, can be set to a specific diameter by rotating a knurled knob above the stones until the expanding mechanism (stones) make firm but light contact with the cylinder wall. This type is used to hone a cylinder or block bore after reboring to achieve the correct crosshatch pattern, and desired piston-to-liner clearance.

Reasons for Honing

It is *not* necessary to hone a new cylinder liner to modify its inside diameter surface finish. The liner has already undergone a machine-honing process at the factory, and any change to the crosshatch pattern will adversely affect the seating of the piston rings. When reusing liners, some engine manufacturers support honing and others are opposed to it. By way of background information, Detroit Diesel, Mack, and a number of major European and Japanese diesel engine manufacturers are in favor of honing used liners if they are to be reused. There are several reasons why

Range 2" to 7"

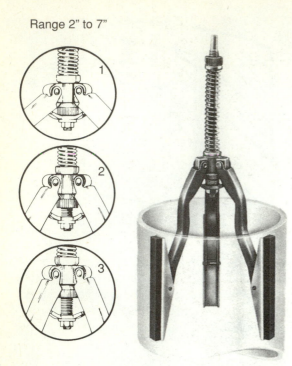

3-Stone Glaze Breaker Hone
ADJUSTABLE TENSION

Full range 2" to 7" diameter. Fully adjustable for both diameter and tension. Rugged construction. Flexible drive shaft. Equipped with three 220 grit stones recommended for ring seating.

Spreader Limiter permits easy insertion in the cylinder bore or when changing from cylinder to cylinder.
1. Spread Limiter adjustment nut shown in position to allow hone to open to full capacity.
2. Spread Limiter adjustment shown turned up on shaft to limit arm diameter to open to about half capacity of the hone.
3. Spread Limiter adjustment nut turned up on shaft to limit the arm's diameter to open for a smaller diameter job.

FIGURE 16–16 Example of a spring loaded adjustable cylinder liner hone that can be employed to lightly clean or to deglaze a liner. (Courtesy of Hastings Manufacturing Co.)

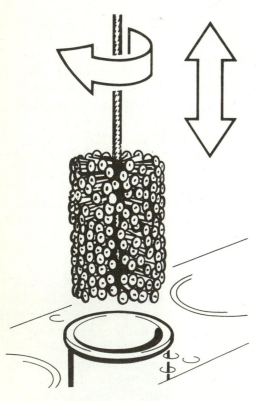

FIGURE 16–17 A ball-type hone, or flexi-hone, used mainly to deglaze cylinder liners, or to clean up a used liner to provide a seat for new piston rings. (Courtesy of DAF Trucks, Eindhoven, Netherlands.)

many engine manufacturers recommend honing a liner prior to reuse:

- To break any glaze and to obtain the correct surface roughness, so that the piston rings can seat against the cylinder wall as quickly as possible with minimum wear; otherwise, the piston ring seating time will be lengthened or piston rings may fail to seat correctly.
- To obtain a surface structure that allows optimum adhesion of the lube oil, so that a film of oil is maintained between the piston rings and the liner.
- To create a crosshatch pattern on the inside diameter of the liner. This will optimize the distribution and removal of oil from the cylinder wall when the piston moves down. Too steep a crosshatch pattern can lead to excessive oil consumption, whereas too narrow a pattern can lead to scuffing of the rings, inadequate lubrication, and damage to the cylinder kit.
- Any deep ridge at the top of the liner similar to that illustrated in Figure 16–19 would invariably render the liner unfit for further use. You may need to use a ridge reamer (see Figure 16–20) to remove this ridge before attempting to pull the piston and rings from the liner or block bore in a press-fit liner. A small ridge formed at the top of the liner by the piston rings can be removed with

A

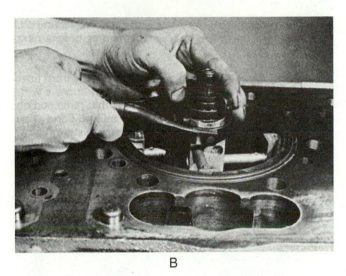

B

FIGURE 16–18 (a) Installing an adjustable hone set into the cylinder liner or block bore. (Courtesy of Sunnen Products Company). (b) Adjusting the hone to a fixed position within the cylinder liner to obtain a specific crosshatch finish on either the cylinder liner or block bore after machining. (Courtesy of Cummins Engine Company, Inc.)

a hone; if it is not removed, interference with the travel of the new rings may result in actual compression ring breakage.

Holding Fixture

You cannot effectively hone a liner when it is outside of the engine block without using a suitable holding fixture. Ideally, a scrap cylinder block makes the best fixture! If you choose to install the liner in a cylinder block that is to be reused, the block should be dismantled and then cleaned thoroughly after the liner honing process. The type of hone recommended and the stone grit required to successfully hone a liner depend on the liner material used. Cast iron liners, hardened cast iron, steel, and even aluminum cylinders dictate the honing stones and materials that should be used. Major manufacturers of hones and stones for all facets of the automotive and diesel industry, such as Sunnen Products Company, include with their products honing instructions for reconditioning cylinders and liners. Refer to these directions along with the engine manufacturer's service manual procedure prior to honing. For best results, thoroughly wash out all cylinders before honing.

Liner Surface Finish

Correct honing procedures produce a cylinder liner surface finish that exhibits a crosshatch pattern similar to that illustrated in Figure 16–21, which shows a 20° to 25° and a 40° to 50° example. This illustration is magnified many times for instructional purposes. Each engine manufacturer specifies in its service manual what angle of crosshatch pattern and what surface finish are desired. Surface finish is usually stated as being in the region of 20 to 35 RMS (root mean square), which is simply a mathematical term

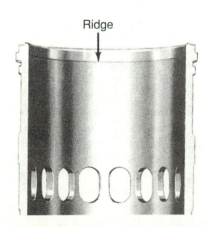

Ridge

FIGURE 16–19 Wear ridge on a used cylinder liner or block bore. (Courtesy of Detroit Diesel Corporation.)

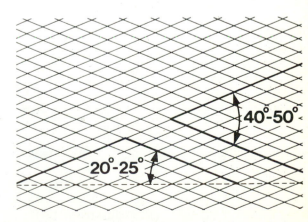

40°-50°

20°-25°

FIGURE 16–21 Example of how to identify a cylinder liner or block bore surface finish crosshatch pattern in degrees. (Courtesy of Cummins Engine Company, Inc.)

FIGURE 16–20 Clamshell-design ridge reamer tool that can be adjusted to cut the worn ridge within a cylinder liner or cylinder block bore. (Courtesy of Hastings Manufacturing Co.)

Ridge Reamers

QUICK-CUT—FEED UP

This extra-sturdy, extra-durable ridge reamer will handle all modern engines with bores including canted and most short stroke types. Tool sits solidly in the cylinder, with holding blades maintaining hook wall contact for smooth cut. Cutter head guide plate locks on both sides. Tungsten carbide Saf-T-Blade will not overcut, chatter or dig in. Smooth cutting action of this ridge reamer is attained by fine-thread feed-up. Accuracy maintained by heavy, heat-treated center bolt. Steel collar on center bolt protects threads from wrench damage. Three position setting of spring-loaded cutter head permits change from one cylinder to another without adjusting cutter head assembly.

Clamshell package

indicating the average irregularity in millionths of an inch (0.000001 in.). This angle of surface finish is usually referred to as a *microinch finish* because the actual surface finish on the liner inside diameter would appear to the naked eye similar to that shown in Figure 16–22.

The actual microinch surface finish is controlled by the proper selection of honing stone used—the grit. For example, both roughing and finishing stones are available with grits ranging from 70 to 600: the 70 grit stones are regarded as roughing types, 150 grit as finishing, 220 grit as a medium finishing set, 280 grit as a polishing set, 400 grit as a fine set, and 600 grit as an extra-fine finishing set. Keep in mind that the rougher the stone grit used, the larger will be the microinch surface finish. Consider the finish on a liner or sleeve surface from the following information:

FIGURE 16–22 Example of a properly finished crosshatch liner surface pattern. (Courtesy of Cummins Engine Company, Inc.)

STONE TYPE USED

	70 grit	150 grit	220 grit	280 grit	400 grit	600 grit
Liner material	Liner Microinch Surface Finish					
Cast iron	100	32	20	12	6	3
Hardened sleeve	25	20	. . .	12	5	1
Steel sleeve	. . .	35	. . .	20	7	2

Hone Driving Power and Adjustment

When using a hone, the drive motor (air or electric) must be set to rotate the assembly in a clockwise direction at speeds between 250 and 450 rpm. The size of

drive motor required depends on the diameter of stones being used. It is advisable to use a 1/2 in. (12.7 mm) capacity drill motor for bore sizes up to 3 in. (76.2 mm), a 5/8 in. (16 mm) motor for up to 4.75 in. (121 mm), and a 3/4 in. (19 mm) motor for bore sizes larger than 4.75 in. (121 mm).

A ball-type hone offers no adjustment, but it does come in a range of sizes to suit different diameter bores and liners. Some spring-loaded hones can be adjusted, and all fixed hones are equipped with an adjustment knob to allow expansion of the stones until they have a firm but light drag on the cylinder wall. Figure 16–18 illustrates placement of a fixed, adjustable Sunnen hone into the cylinder or liner. The pinion is raised about 1/4 in. (6 mm) then turned counterclockwise to set the stones to the approximate diameter of the cylinder and liner. Push the pinion down until it engages with the outside gear on the hone body. Expand the combination of two stones and two guides firmly against the cylinder-liner wall by turning the hone ring wrench clockwise (see Figure 16–18). While making this adjustment, the tops of the stones and guides should not extend more than 1/2 in. (12.7 mm) out of the top of the liner.

Honing Process

Honing stones can be used either dry or wet. When used dry, stones cut faster; when used wet, a honing oil must be employed. Metal removal can be achieved faster in a cast iron liner when dry honing is done; honing oil is recommended when a 280, 400, or 600 grit stone is used. Honing oil should always be used when honing steel or aluminum. Use a squirt can or brush to apply a continuous flow to the stones and cylinder. If a recommended honing oil is not readily available, smear vegetable shortening liberally on the cylinder and the stones.

SERVICE TIPS: Never attempt to employ previously wetted stones for dry honing, because the stones tend to load up with finely removed liner material and no longer cut. If a cylinder is scored, remove all built-up metal before honing or the stones may chip. New stones do not require truing; however, when employing *used stones*, always true in the stone set using a truing sleeve available from the hone manufacturer for the diameter range required. If you do not, the stones may not have time to become fully trued in before final size or surface finish is reached, particularly when simply honing a used liner for reuse. Mount the truing sleeve in a vise and hone it with a constant steady stroke, allowing the stones to pass through the sleeve about 25.4 mm (1 in.) at both ends of the stroke. With wet stones, apply liberal amounts of honing oil and continue honing through the truing sleeve until the entire surface of the stone contacts the sleeve. You are now ready to hone the cylinder. If no truing sleeve is available, and you are using either new or used adjustable stones, to allow the stones to seat to the cylinder radius, stroke the hone up and down the cylinder a few times; then expand the stones by the adjuster ring and repeat the process. Note that new stones will often appear to wear rapidly until their curvature is the same as the cylinders.

It is important to thoroughly inspect liners before honing to avoid wasting time on those that are damaged severely or are worn and in an out-of-round condition beyond acceptable service manual specifica-

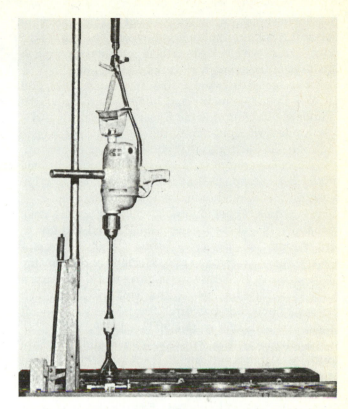

FIGURE 16–23 Special honing fixture to support a heavy-duty variable speed drill motor used to drive the honing stones when cleaning up a liner or block bore. (Courtesy of Cummins Engine Company, Inc.)

tions. The smaller the amount of material that can be removed from the used liner to lightly clean it up the better. However, avoid casual roughing up of the cylinders, since too coarse a crosshatch pattern will show deep scratches that will permit leakage between the rings and cylinder wall as well as wearing the new rings excessively. If wear limits published in the engine service manual are exceeded after honing, new rings will not have sufficient wall tension due to the size increase, and new liners will be required.

The purpose of honing a used cylinder liner is simply to deglaze the surface with minimal removal of metal. The intent is not to enlarge the bore size. Consequently, it takes very little effort and time to accomplish this procedure. Always exercise care when honing to avoid removing excess material from the cylinder or liner.

With the honing tool fixture (correct stone grit?) inserted into and adjusted to the cylinder or liner bore size, connect the top of the hone drive shaft to a drive motor. Using the chuck key, tighten the chuck securely.

SERVICE TIP: Support the drive motor on an overhead support bracket similar to the one illustrated in Figure 16–23. This tool allows you to adjust a stroking rod to prevent the hone from moving too far through the cylinder at the bottom; otherwise, the stones can strike the lower end of the block strengthening struts, resulting in breakage of the stones and damage to the hone.

The speed at which you manually push/pull (stroke) the drive motor and hone up and down the cylinder will determine the finished crosshatch angle. The stone grit determines the RMS surface finish. Figure 16–24 illustrates that you need to use short up-and-down overlapping strokes equal to about one stroke per second. Detroit Diesel recommends a 120 grit stone set when honing its four-stroke cycle Series 50 and Series 60 engine cylinder liners, while Mack recommends a stone set between 150 and 250 grit to "glaze bust" its dry-type liners. Cummins recommends a 280 grit stone set to deglaze and clean the cylinder bores of its B series engines that do not use a liner. Cummins further recommends that a fine grit ball-type hone and a mixture of equal parts of mineral spirits and SAE 30W engine oil be used.

Remember these two steps when honing. First, on used liners or bores always start stroking at the bottom or least worn section of the liner or bore using short strokes to concentrate honing in the smallest diameter of the cylinder. Gradually lengthen the stroke as metal is removed and the stones make contact higher up the cylinder. Allow the stones to extend about 1/2 in. (13 mm) from the cylinder at the top of its stroke.

Second, work the hone up and down the full length of the liner with the drive motor running at between 300 and 400 rpm. Do this a few times (about 15 seconds maximum) or after about 10 full strokes of the hone. The result should be a crisscross pattern that produces hone marks on an axis stated by the engine manufacturer in the respective engine service manual. For example, DDC states that the liner should be honed to produce between a 22° and 32° crisscross (crosshatch) pattern in its Series 50 and Series 60 cylinder liners, while Mack recommends that a diamond crisscross pattern of 20 to 35 microinch RMS finish be achieved. On Cummins B series engines that use no liner, the block bore finish should be honed to produce a correctly deglazed surface and crosshatched appearance with the lines at a 15° to 25° angle with the top of the cylinder block as shown in Figure 16–25 (or a 30° to 50° included angle). When bringing the drive motor to a stop *do not* allow the hone to come to a stop in the same position. Keep it moving so that no one area of the bore ends up with too narrow a crosshatch pattern. In addition, to avoid vertical scratches up and down the length of the cylinder, relieve the tension on the hone before removing it from the cylinder. Otherwise, these vertical scratches can form a path for combustion gases to blow by.

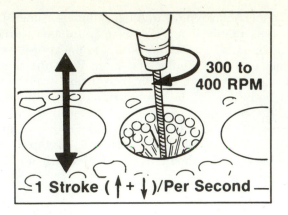

FIGURE 16–24   Honing drill speed and the number of strokes per second determines the correct liner or block bore crosshatch pattern. (Courtesy of Cummins Engine Company, Inc.)

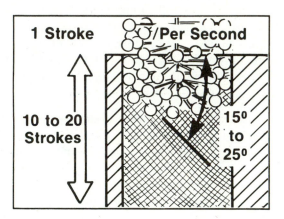

FIGURE 16–25   Vertical strokes of the hone must be smooth, continuous passes along the full length of the bore to obtain the desired crosshatch pattern. This example shows a Cummins B series engine block bore (no liner used) when using a hone. (Courtesy of Cummins Engine Company, Inc.)

SERVICE TIP: When the wrong crosshatch pattern appears, it can be traced back to several possible problems. Figure 16–26 illustrates a crosshatch angle of approximately 70° caused either by moving the hone too fast vertically up and down the cylinder or by employing a drive motor that rotates too slowly. Too steep a crosshatch pattern allows the piston rings to pump oil up the cylinder, leading to excessive oil consumption. On the other hand, if the crosshatch pattern appears too shallow as shown in Figure 16–27, the drill speed is either too fast or the vertical stroke of the hone is too slow. Too narrow a crosshatch pattern leads to tearing or scuffing of the piston ring-to-liner surface.

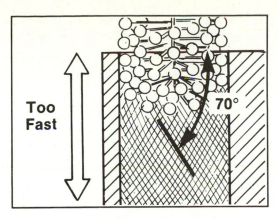

FIGURE 16–26   Too great a crosshatch angle caused by moving the hone too fast up and down the cylinder or by using a drive motor that rotates too slowly. (Courtesy of Cummins Engine Company, Inc.)

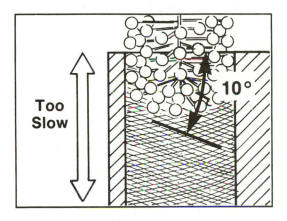

FIGURE 16–27   Too shallow a crosshatch pattern caused by too great a drill speed or a vertical stroke of the hone that is too slow. (Courtesy of Cummins Engine Company, Inc.)

In both cases, if you assemble the cylinder kits, you will invariably have to disassemble the engine again to correct the problems associated with an improper crosshatch angle. A reduction in drive motor speed during honing usually indicates a tight spot in the bore (smaller diameter). Therefore, localize the stroking procedure at these areas until the drill speed is constant over at least 75% of the cylinder length; then stroke the full length of the cylinder.

NOTE: Many cylinder liners now have a plateau finish, which was described earlier in this section. If a plateau finish is required on the liner surface, use 600 grit stones, with honing oil as an option; then hone for about 45 seconds per cylinder.

Cleaning the Liner or Block after Honing

The ideal liquid for washing or cleaning a liner or cylinder block may seem to be gasoline, diesel fuel, or solvent. Tests have shown, however, that on liner surfaces cleaned in this manner, too much grinding and honing dust is left in the crosshatch surface grooves. Subsequently this will cause damage to the liner and the piston rings. After honing, wash the inside surface of the liner with a solution of household laundry detergent and scrub with a stiff nonmetallic bristle brush to remove as much of the honing debris as possible. Rinse with hot water and blow-dry. After the bore is dry, coat it with clean engine oil and allow it to soak in for 10 minutes. Wipe the lube oil from the bore with a clean white cloth or white paper towel. If the cloth or towel shows evidence of gray or darker stains, honing debris is still present on the cylinder liner surface. Repeat the oil application and wiping procedure until no evidence of stain appears on the cloth or towel. Use a brass or steel wire brush to clean the top of the liner flange.

NOTE: If you are honing an engine block with no liner (that is, where the piston runs directly in the block bore), after the honing procedure is complete and before engine reassembly, thoroughly clean the cylinder block, oil galleries, and cylinder bores using a solution of strong detergent and water. Incomplete cleaning will lead to piston siezure or rapid wear of the cylinder bores or sleeves, pistons, and rings!

CYLINDER LINER MEASUREMENT

After a liner or cylinder block bore has been lightly honed, it must be checked closely for wear, taper, and out-of-round condition. Use a cylinder dial bore gauge similar to the one illustrated in Figure 9–10 dealing with engine block servicing.

Make sure that you check the liner inside diameter in a minimum of four places spaced 90° apart. This is commonly referred to as using an X and Z and a Y and W axis of measurement (see Figure 9–11). One axis represents the lengthwise, or longitudinal, axis of the engine; the other axis represents the crosswise, or transverse, axis of the engine. All measurements should be checked and compared with the service manual specifications for allowable taper, ovality, and maximum allowable wear dimensions. When checking a two-stroke engine ported-type cylinder liner, use a dial gauge and measure the inside diameter of the liner using the X - Z and Y - W method of measurement; measure 90° apart at seven points throughout the liner length. To determine the difference between taper, ovality, and wear, let's assume that the inside diameter of a new cylinder liner is quoted in the engine service manual as being 130 to 130.05 mm (5.118 to 5.120 in.). These dimensions are minimums and maximums for new parts. If we take four main measurement points from the top to the bottom of the liner and number these from the top as 1 through 4, and if we obtained the following measurements from a used liner, we would be able to effectively determine the taper and ovality limits.

	Dimension W-Y axis	Dimension X-Z axis
Position 1	5.1215 in. (130.08 mm)	5.122 in. (130.09 mm)
(top)		
Position 2	5.121 in. (130.07 mm)	5.1215 in. (130.08 mm)
Position 3	5.120 in. (130.05 mm)	5.121 in. (130.07 mm)
Position 4	5.119 in. (130.02 mm)	5.120 in. (130.05 mm)

Taper is the difference in measurement from the top to the bottom of the liner on either axis. In our example, our greatest taper occurs on the W-Y axis; the reading at position 1 minus that obtained at position 4 is equal to 0.0025 in. (0.0635 mm). There is also a taper on the X-Z axis, but it is only 0.002 in. (subtract the reading at position 4 from that at position 1). Therefore, the maximum taper is known to be 0.0025 in. (0.0635 mm). The engine service information states that the allowable taper for a liner is 0.001 in. (0.025 mm), so these liners are not acceptable for reuse.

Ovality is the difference in measurement at any two points at the same position (for example, position 1 on the W-Y versus position 1 on the X-Z axis). In our sample measurements, we have the following ovality readings:

Position 1	= 0.0005 in. (0.0127 mm)
Position 2	= Same
Position 3	= 0.001 in. (0.025 mm)
Position 4	= Same

Therefore, position 3 exhibits the greatest ovality—0.001 in. (0.0254 mm). Maximum allowable ovality is stated as being 0.001 in. (0.0254 mm), so we are at the maximum limit here. A close check of the engine service manual will normally reveal that the maximum allowable taper and ovality for a used liner is approximately 0.0005 to 0.001 in. (0.0127 to 0.0254 mm) greater than that for a new liner.

In addition to checking the liner inside diameter, some models of wet liners are press fit at their top flange area. Therefore, you also have to measure the outside diameter of the liner at the top to determine if the dimension is within specifications. The dimensional tolerance for this diameter is always stated in the respective service manual. For example, the Cummins L10 liner press-fit tolerance at the top flange allows a minimum reading of 5.7465 to 5.7495 in. (145.962 to

146.038 mm), or a tolerance of 0.003 in. (0.0762 mm). You also have to check the flange thickness for distortion and so on.

INSTALLING A DRY PRESS-FIT LINER

Dry liners that are press fit or interference fit into the cylinder block are between 0.0004 and 0.0008 in. (0.010 to 0.020 mm) larger on their outside diameter than the block bore. Follow these steps to achieve proper installation of the liner:

1. Select a hydraulic or mechanical press and suitable guide adapters that can be inserted across the liner at the top. Figure 16–28 is a mechanical puller arrangement. The left side of the figure shows removal of the liner; the right side shows the tooling required to press the liner back into place.

2. Refer to Figure 16–1 and make sure that any shims from under the liner flange that were removed when it was pulled from the block bore are reinstalled into the block counterbore prior to installation.

3. Position the liner squarely with the machined surface of the top of the engine block. Although this can be determined visually, if you use a small try square placed at 90° intervals around the liner outside diameter prior to installation, you can lightly hand bump the liner to square it up.

4. Apply a small amount of light lube oil to the top edge of the block bore if necessary. Be careful—excessive amounts can create heat transfer problems between the outside diameter of the block bore and the liner during normal operation.

5. Carefully press the liner into the block bore. Then check the liner flange protrusion height above the machined surface of the block as illustrated in Figure 16–29. Obtain this specification from the engine service manual. Then you can lay a small straightedge across the top of the liner and gauge the protrusion with a feeler gauge, although the use of a dial indicator mounted on a sled gauge as illustrated is preferable. Securely hold the liner in position during the protrusion check with two cylinder liner hold-down clamps, which are shown in Figure 16–29. Liner protrusion is needed to allow the cylinder head gasket to seal correctly. If the liner protrusion is not within published specs, you will have to pull it back out. By using different liner-to-block counterbore shims, proper protrusion can be achieved. However, you may have to clean or remachine the counterbore to square it up again (refer to Chapter 9).

NOTE: Press-fit dry-liner installation can be made easier by chilling the liner. Pack in dry ice for 35 to 45 minutes to allow it to cool before installation. If you

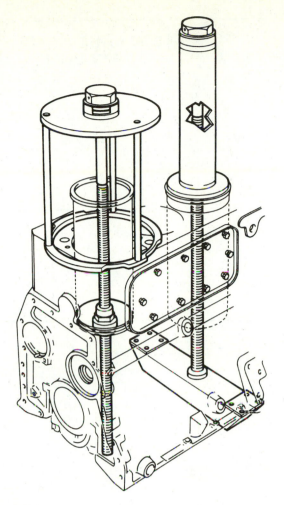

FIGURE 16–28 *Installation tooling used to install a cylinder liner assembly into the block bore when it is a press fit or interference fit. (Courtesy of DAF Trucks, Eindhoven Netherlands.)*

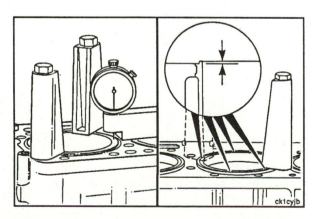

FIGURE 16–29 *Employing two cylinder liner hold-down clamps while using a sled-mounted dial gauge to check liner protrusion. (Courtesy of Cummins Engine Company, Inc.)*

choose this method, *be very careful* to avoid serious injury when handling dry ice or parts that have been chilled. Dry ice can cause skin burns and eye injury if not handled properly. Always wear safety gloves and goggles. Never seal dry ice in an airtight container because it may cause the container to explode or burst. Follow these two steps:

1. When removing the liner from the dry ice, *do not* wrap a shop cloth or towel around it, because it may stick to the liner surface.

2. Using safety gloves, quickly insert the liner into the block bore; make sure that it is square to the top of the block. Then pull the liner into position as shown in Figure 16–28 (right-hand side) or by using a hydraulic press.

INSTALLING A WET LINER

A wet liner can be installed on its own or as part of a cylinder pack that includes the assembled piston, piston rings, and con-rod. (The cylinder pack is described in detail in Chapter 15.)

If the measurements of the outside diameter and thickness of the liner flange area are outside of specifications, the liner will have to be replaced. If the cylinder block counterbore is damaged, refer to Chapter 9 and remachine it and/or install a sleeve. Many engine manufacturers supply liners of oversize flange diameter and thickness to allow reuse of an engine block. For example, in the Cummins NT-855 (14L) engine series, you can obtain liners with a 0.020 in. (0.51 mm) larger outside diameter flange and liners with a 0.010 in. (0.25 mm) thicker flange. You can install a wet liner into the cleaned block bore minus any of the seal rings, pull the liner into position and secure it in place with liner hold-down clamps, and check the flange protrusion. Then you can add or delete liner flange shims to obtain the correct specifications.

Follow this procedure to install a wet liner:

1. Engine manufacturers suggest that you lubricate the liner crevice and seal rings shown in Figure 16–2. These seals are installed into respective machined grooves on the liner; however, on Detroit Diesel's two-stroke wet-liner models, the liner seal rings are installed into the cylinder block bore machined grooves. Refer to Figure 9–11 in Chapter 9 for positioning of these seal rings. Check the service manual for your engine since the liner seal material will usually dictate the type of lubricant to use. Consider the following suggested lubricants:

- Cummins NT-855 (14L) engine liner: vegetable oil
- Cummins L10 engine liner: 15W-40 engine oil
- Detroit Diesel two-stroke 92 series: clean engine oil

- Detroit Diesel four-stroke-cycle Series 50 and 60 engine liners: clean petroleum jelly
- Caterpillar 3176 engine: clean engine oil
- Caterpillar 3406 engine liner: liquid soap on early O-ring seals; engine oil on the crevice seal and later O-rings

CAUTION: Many engine manufacturers oppose the use of hydrogenated vegetable shortening as a seal lubricant because of the adverse effects that it has on the seal ring material.

2.   Some engine manufacturers suggest that you apply a bead of RTV (room temperature vulcanizing) sealant on either the cylinder block counterbore or on the underside of the liner flange. The diameter of the bead should be between 3/64 in. (0.047 in., or 1.19 mm) and 1/16 in. (0.0625 in., or 1.58 mm). Figure 16–30 and Figure 15–68 illustrate where to apply this sealer bead. Note that the liner *must* be installed within 5 minutes, maximum, after bead installation; otherwise, the RTV sealer will have dried out and may not effectively seal.

3.   Manually insert the liner carefully into the block bore (align the previous match-marks to the block) and push it down squarely as far as you can.

4.   Using a properly sized cylinder liner diameter driver and handle, gently tap the liner all the way into the block counterbore. When the liner reaches bottom you will hear a dull thud. If you have a suitable liner installer similar to that illustrated in Figure 16–28, you can pull the liner squarely into position. This allows you to recheck the liner protrusion with a dial gauge (Figure 16–29), which clearly shows where cylinder liner protrusion is measured in relation to the top machined surface of the engine block. If a liner press is not available, once the liner has been driven home, you may have to install a cylindrical liner clamping plate bolted to the cylinder block upper deck to ensure that the liner is completely bottomed in the block counterbore. Recheck the liner protrusion with either a dial sled gauge, or a straight edge and feeler gauges, at four points 90° apart. If the protrusion is not within the service manual specifications, try reshimming; or, the liner may have to be repulled and both the liner flange and block counterbore rechecked for possible problems.

5.   Some engine manufacturers recommend that once protrusion has been checked, you should use a feeler gauge to measure the clearance between the liner and its lower bore to ensure that no distortion has occurred during installation. Figure 16–31 illustrates this particular check where one manufacturer's spec calls for a clearance of 0.002 to 0.006 in. (0.05 to 0.15 mm).

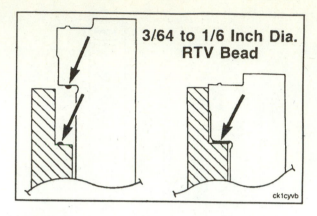

FIGURE 16–30   *Where to apply a bead of RTV (room temperature vulcanizing) sealant between the cylinder liner flange and engine block counterbore. (Courtesy of Cummins Engine Company, Inc.)*

FIGURE 16–31   *Using a feeler gauge around the bottom circumference of a wet-type cylinder liner after installation to check for any signs of liner distortion due to rolled or twisted seal rings. (Courtesy of Cummins Engine Company, Inc.)*

6.   Take a dial bore gauge and recheck the liner inside diameter for out-of-roundness at five points throughout the liner length. Then take another set of readings at a 90° axis to the first.

7.   If the liner protrusion, lower liner block check with the feeler gauge, or the liner bore out-of-round condition are not within specs, repull the liner and check for possible rolled or twisted seal rings, or clean the liner flange or cylinder block counterbore.

8.   On Detroit Diesel two-stroke-cycle engines, once the liner has been installed, use a liner hold-down clamp and check the distance (intrusion) of the liner below the cylinder block machined surface. Figure 16–32 illustrates that these engines employ a hardened steel insert in the block counterbore on which the liner flange sits and an individual cylindri-

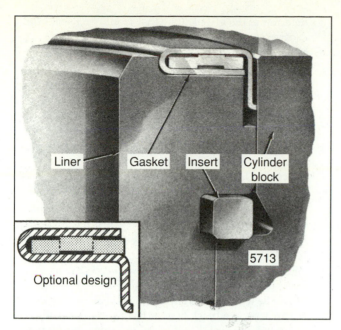

FIGURE 16–32 *Example of a hardened steel insert in the cylinder liner block counterbore and the placement of the individual sealing gasket employed by Detroit Diesel on its 71 series engine models that use a dry slip-fit liner. (Courtesy of Detroit Diesel Corporation.)*

cal sealing gasket that sits on the liner flange. When the cylinder head is torqued down, this gasket is compressed and acts as a seal between the combustion chamber, liner, head, and block.

INSTALLING A DRY SLIP-FIT LINER

Detroit Diesel's two-stroke 71 series engine model has a dry cylinder liner that is a slip-fit design in the engine block bore. The service manual specification calls for a liner-to-block bore clearance of between 0.0005 and 0.0025 in. (0.0127 to 0.0635 mm) on used parts. Before removing a liner from the block, match-mark it with a metal marker to ensure that when it is reinstalled it will be inserted into the same position. If the cylinder block has to be lightly honed at overhaul, Detroit Diesel supplies 0.001 in. (0.0254 mm) oversize outside diameter liners to allow a closer fit to the block bore. If however, the cylinder block has to be rebored oversize, oversize *outside diameter only* liners will be required. These liners are available in 0.001, 0.005, 0.010, 0.020, and 0.030 in. oversize (0.0254, 0.127, 0.254, 0.508, and 0.762 mm). Take careful note that the liners are *only* available in oversize outside diameter, and *no* oversize pistons are available! If a liner is replaced, it can be reused with a used or a new standard diameter piston assembly. Liner-to-block clearances after reboring should fall within 0.0005 to 0.0015 in. (0.013 to

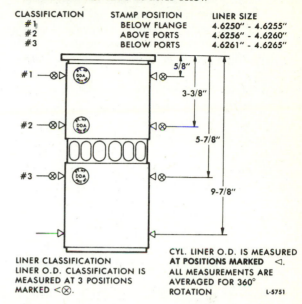

FIGURE 16–33 *Dry-type slip-fit cylinder liner classification used by Detroit Diesel to identify oversize outside diameter liners for its 71 series two-stroke cycle engine models. (Courtesy of Detroit Diesel Corporation.)*

0.038 mm). The oversize dimension of the liner is etched on its outside diameter; a new standard size outside diameter cylinder liner is classified as a #1, #2, or #3 as illustrated in Figure 16–33.

SELF-TEST QUESTIONS

1. List the three most commonly used types of cylinder liners.

2. True or False: All cylinder liners are press fit in the cylinder block bore.

3. A common material used to cast cylinder liners is
   a. chrome
   b. cast gray iron
   c. molybdenum
   d. aluminum alloy

4. Which current high-speed heavy-duty diesel engine manufacturer employs telltale weep holes along the side of its engine block to indicate that coolant is leaking past the first liner seal O-ring?

5. True or False: A number of cylinder liners are chrome plated on their inside diameter.

6. Technician A says that cylinder liners should not only be numbered but should be match-marked before removal to ensure that they are reinstalled in the same cylinder bore. Technician B says that numbering is

required, but it doesn't matter where you reinsert the liner. Which technician is correct and why?

7. Technician A says that liners should be stored horizontally before and after inspection. Technician B says that they should be stored vertically (standing up); otherwise, they can become egg shaped or distorted after a period of time. Which technician is correct?

8. What condition is indicated by a very high glass-like polish on the inside surface of a liner?

9. The condition existing in Question 8 is usually caused by what operating parameters?

10. Technician A says that to successfully repair the condition in Question 8, you need to rebore the block or liner. Technician B says that by using a fine-grit ball-type hone and a mixture of equal parts of mineral spirits and 30 weight engine oil you can correct this condition. Which technician is correct?

11. When inspecting a used cylinder liner bore, a bright mirror finish in certain areas is indicative of
    a. wear
    b. glazing
    c. scuffing
    d. scoring

12. Liners should always be checked with a dial bore gauge to determine what three conditions?

13. Cavitation corrosion on the outside surface of a wet-type liner is usually caused by what operating condition(s)?

14. Dark spots, stains, or low-pressure areas on the outside diameter of dry-type liners generally indicate what type of a condition?

15. Shiny spots or areas on the outside diameter or flange area of a cylinder liner are usually indicative of
    a. movement during engine operation
    b. overheating
    c. coolant leakage
    d. distortion

16. Cracking of a cylinder liner flange can usually be attributed to
    a. sloping counterbores in the block
    b. liner movement
    c. overheating
    d. light-load operation

17. True or False: A liner crosshatch pattern can be established to produce any surface angle finish.

18. Cylinder liner glaze must be broken using
    a. emery cloth
    b. glass beading
    c. reboring
    d. cylinder hone

19. List the three basic types of cylinder hones that are widely used.

20. Technician A says that any grade grit honing stone can be used to finish the desired crosshatch pattern on the inside diameter of a block bore or liner assembly. Not so says technician B; the type of block or liner material

determines the grit of stone that would be used. Who is correct?

21. True or False: Honing stones should always be used dry.

22. If a cylinder block bore requires that an oversize liner be used, technician A says that a boring machine must be employed. Technician B says that a power hone could also be used. Are both technicians correct in their statements?

23. True or False: In Question 22, if a boring machine is used, you still need to employ a fixed hone to produce the correct liner surface crosshatch pattern.

24. Technician A says that too steep a crosshatch pattern on a block bore or liner surface would result in scuffing and tearing of the new piston rings. Technician B believes that it would result in pumping oil. Which technician is correct?

25. Technician A says that too shallow a crosshatch pattern in a block bore or liner would result in pumping oil, while technician B says that too shallow a crosshatch angle in a block bore or liner surface would result in tearing and scuffing of the rings. Which technician is correct?

26. True or False: To achieve the desired crosshatch pattern in the block bore or liner, the speed at which you stroke the honing stones up and down is the key factor.

27. True or False: If a plateau finish is required on the block bore or cylinder liner surface, you should use a 200 grit honing stone and hone for about 20 seconds per cylinder.

28. True or False: Honing debris is best removed by submerging the liners in a tank with hot caustic solution.

29. Describe how you would best remove all traces of honing dust from a liner or block bore.

30. Technician A says that liners should always be clamped down prior to checking the liner flange protrusion limit. Technician B says that this isn't necessary since most liners are press fit at the flange area anyway. Which technician is correct?

31. Too much cylinder liner protrusion would result in (possibly more than one correct answer)
    a. liner movement
    b. cracking of the liner flange
    c. cracking of the cylinder head
    d. head gasket leakage

32. Insufficient cylinder liner protrusion would result in (possibly more than one correct answer)
    a. liner movement
    b. head gasket leakage
    c. liner distortion
    d. liner flange cracking

33. To correct for insufficient liner protrusion, what remedy would you use?

34. If too much liner protrusion existed, what remedy would you use?

35. True or False: Wet-type cylinder liner seals should usually be lubricated prior to liner installation in the

block. If your answer is true, what lubricant would
you use? If your answer is false, why so?

36. Some engine manufacturers suggest that you apply a
thin bead of RTV sealant to what two areas of the
cylinder liner during installation?

37. After you install a wet-type cylinder liner, the lower
inside bore of the liner indicates some distortion. What
condition do you think might cause this problem?

38. Technician A says that cylinder liners are available in
both oversize inside and outside diameter.
Technician B disagrees, stating that all cylinder liners
retain a standard inside bore diameter and are oversize only on their outside diameter. Which technician
is correct?

39. True or False: Most cylinder liners require removal
and installation by use of a special liner puller.

17 Connecting Rods

OVERVIEW

The connecting rod, or con-rod, extends between the piston at its upper end and the engine crankshaft at its lower end. It transfers the reciprocating (backward and forward motion) from the piston to rotate the crankshaft. In this chapter we discuss the various types of con-rods now in use and how to check for twists and bends, cracks, wear on piston pin bushings, and rod bore ovality.

TOPICS

- Function and design
- Materials
- Checking for twists and bends
- Checking for cracks
- Cleaning oil passages
- Checking piston pin bushing for wear
- Checking rod bore ovality
- Self-test questions

FUNCTION AND DESIGN

The connecting rod, or what is more commonly called the *con-rod*, connects the piston pin to the crankshaft. The force of the combustion chamber expanding gases that drive the piston down the cylinder (reciprocating or straight-line motion) is converted to rotary motion at the crankshaft by the transfer of power from the lower end of the con-rod, which is bolted to the crankshaft. Con-rods are subjected to tremendous loads and stresses as they move up and down the cylinder. They are constantly placed under compression and elongation (lengthening). Consider, for example, that a 300 mm (11.81 in.) long con-rod can stretch by as much as 0.15 mm (0.0059 in.) when running in a fully loaded engine.

Loads of up to 6 tons are commonly encountered by the con-rod during the engine power stroke. In two-stroke-cycle engines, the load on the rod is partly released during the operational cycle, but there is always a load on the rod due to the compression of the air on the upstroke and the pressure of the expanding gases on the down (power) stroke. In four-stroke-cycle engines, there is a reversal of loading on the rod from compression to tension on each cycle. On both the upstroke of compression and the downstroke of power, compression loads are absorbed, while during the last part of the exhaust stroke and the beginning of intake, the rod is placed under tension to absorb the inertia forces (tendency of a body to want to keep moving in the same direction), since there is no gas pressure in the cylinder.

The con-rod stress reversal in a four-stroke-cycle engine tends to be more severe than that experienced in the two-stroke-cycle engine. This is so because of the partially relieved compressive load experienced by the two-stroke-engine near bottom dead center (scavenge blow-through air). In addition, when the con-rod reaches BDC, it is pulled back in the opposite direction of rotation by the action of the spinning crankshaft. This tends to create an increasing whip effect the faster the engine rotates and induces a bending stress. The longer and heavier the rod, the greater will be the bending stress, which reaches its maximum when the crankshaft rod journal and the con-rod are at right angles to one another. Because of the operating strokes (one piston stroke up and one down) in a two-stroke-cycle engine, both the con-rod bolt and cap loads are very low.

Basically, there are two-types of con-rods used in high-speed diesel engines:

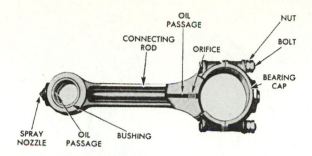 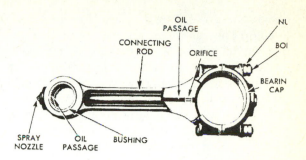

FIGURE 17–1 Typical closed hub style con-rod assembly with a rifle-drilled oil passage to carry oil to the underside of the piston crown via a spray nozzle. (Courtesy of Detroit Diesel Corporation.)

FIGURE 17–2 An open or saddle type design con-rod commonly employed with two-piece crosshead or articulated piston assemblies (Courtesy of Detroit Diesel Corporation.)

1. The *closed hub* style illustrated in Figure 17–1 normally contains a pressed-in bushing at the upper or small end of the rod (often called the eye). This bushing is generally a steel-backed bronze design. At the lower (big) end of the rod is a split bearing cap. Some con-rods used by Cummins, Caterpillar, and Mack employ rods with a taper machined at the piston pin end of the rod; usually this is in the region of 12°. This design feature reduces the unit load in the piston pin bearing created by the peak cylinder pressures by using the available space more efficiently than a straight rod eye.

2. The *open* or *saddle* style con-rod shown in Figure 17–2 is commonly used with two-piece crosshead or articulated type pistons. This type of a con-rod has two bolts at the upper end which are screwed into a captive bolt within the hollow piston pin. The pin in turn is housed within the bore of the piston dome and the independent skirt assembly.

Many con-rods used in current high-speed heavy-duty engines have a rifle-drilled oil passage throughout the length of the rod to allow pressurized lube oil flow to both the piston pin and bushing, as well as to the underside of the piston crown via a spray nozzle as shown in Figure 17–1. (For more information on piston lube oil cooling, refer to Chapter 15 on pistons.) Larger-bore, slow- to medium-speed engines, often employ an external lube oil pipe that runs up the length of the rod to carry needed lube oil to the piston pin and piston for lubrication purposes.

Due to the reciprocating mass of the con-rod and piston assembly, all rods are fully balanced so that their weight is the same within an acceptable tolerance. Consequently, the bearing cap at the lower (big) end is match-marked to a specific rod and should

never be intermixed with other con-rods. Some engine manufacturers employ a stamping mark, color-coded paint stripe, or colored paint dots on the con-rod to identify the different weight classes of various con-rods. For example, Mack stamps all of its con-rod bearing caps on the E7 engines with either an M1, M2, or M3 so that rods within a particular class *do not* vary more than 1/4 ounce in total weight to ensure a smooth vibration-less engine. An M1 weighs 5.098 kg (11.239 lb), an M2 weighs 5.265 kg (11.609 lb), and an M3 weighs 5.433 kg (11.979 lb). The installation of the same M number is preferred when installing a single replacement con-rod. For example, if an M2 weight class is not available, a M1 or M3 rod may be used. If M1 is used with M2, then M3 must not be used since the weight difference between M1 and M3 would be 0.0335 kg (0.074 lb or 1.184 oz). Mercedes-Benz truck diesel engines have two painted dots along the side of the con-rod body; they are yellow, red, blue, green, or white to indicate a specific con-rod weight. Mercedes-Benz indicates that the maximum permissible difference between con-rods of an engine should not be more than 40 grams (1.41 oz).

MATERIALS

Con-rods are generally made from medium-carbon forged steel, alloy steel forgings that can contain nickel, or in some cases manganese steel in the shape of an I-section. They are then heat-treated and are often shot peened to relieve stresses and add fatigue strength. Because of the extreme stress factors created in a con-rod, the rod is generally manufactured to exhibit a *safety factor* far in excess of the forces that it will be subjected to while in an engine. For example, steel used in bridge construction usually has a safety factor of 5 (five times stronger than what it will actually require), while a con-rod has a safety factor of 16.

Bolts used with con-rods are always Grade 8 material. Some rods employ bearing cap bolts that are pressed into place through the upper part of the rod and then secured with nuts, whereas others employ capscrews that pass through bearing cap holes and then thread into the rod shank. Bolts are generally made from nickel steel, high-carbon steel, or an alloy steel, and they are heat-treated to provide high strength with good fatigue-resistant properties. On very large slow-speed heavy-duty high-horsepower (kilowatt) engines, when cylinder packs are pulled out at a major overhaul, the con-rod bolts are removed and annealed to prevent fatigue breakdown. In typical high-speed heavy-duty truck-type engines, many manufacturers recommend that the con-rod bolt, or nut and bolt, be replaced at major overhaul. The minimum replacement should include new self-locking nuts.

A series of necessary checks must be performed to determine if a connecting rod is suitable for reuse. These include the items discussed in the following sub-headings.

CHECKING FOR TWISTS AND BENDS

Con-rods should always be checked for signs of twists or bends. A rod should be replaced if it is twisted or bent. Figure 17–3 clearly illustrates the difference between a *twisted* and a *bent* rod. When a con-rod is found to be twisted or bent, close inspection of the engine and its component parts will usually reveal the reason(s) behind the damage.

One of the most common causes of bent con-rods is a *hydrostatic lock* as a result of liquid in the cylinder. A general law of physics states that you cannot compress a liquid (although we can pressurize it such as in a fuel, lube, or cooling system), so any trapped liquid within the engine combustion chamber resists compression. When a liquid is trapped in a cylinder and its volume exceeds the clearance volume between the piston and the cylinder head, it will stop any upward movement of the piston. During the compression stroke, or even during cranking, the piston simply locks up due to the resistance of the liquid being compressed. Even though the piston has stopped moving, the crankshaft contin-

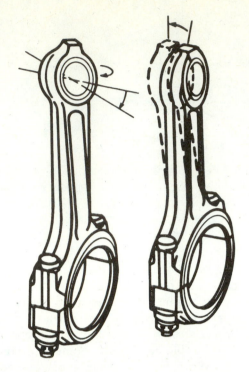

FIGURE 17–3 Example of twist on left side and bend on right side of a connecting rod. (Courtesy of Caterpillar Inc.)

ues to rotate; this action forces the crankshaft against the con-rod, resulting in a bent rod.

Figure 17–4 illustrates the effects of a hydrostatic lock in a two-stroke Detroit Diesel 92 series engine. First the rod bent, causing piston and liner damage; then it broke, causing both piston and cylinder liner failure. This kind of damage can also severely damage the engine block.

In addition to bending the con-rod, a hydrostatic lock can crack or lift the cylinder head as well as blow the head gasket, and in some engines it may even crack the cylinder bore.

Hydrostatic lock can occur as a result of coolant leakage from a leaking head gasket, distorted head, or incorrect cylinder liner intrusion or protrusion. Other causes of liquid entering the engine cylinder are also possible:

- On vehicles or equipment with vertical exhaust stacks (no rain cap or a partially stuck open rain cap), rain can enter the exhaust manifold and flow in through an open exhaust or intake valve.
- On marine installations that have been shut down, sea water can back up in the exhaust system and enter the cylinder through an open intake or exhaust valve.

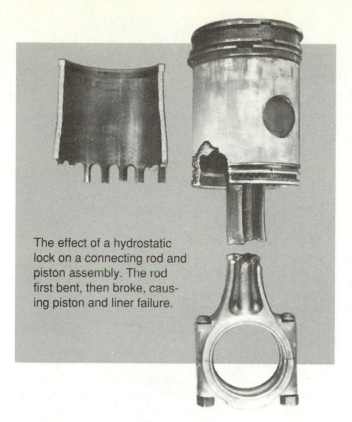

The effect of a hydrostatic lock on a connecting rod and piston assembly. The rod first bent, then broke, causing piston and liner failure.

FIGURE 17–4 *Example of how a hydrostatic lock (fluid trapped in cylinder) first bent a con-rod, then broke it, causing piston and liner failure. (Courtesy of Detroit Diesel Corporation.)*

- Coolant can seep in through a cracked cylinder head, a cracked cylinder liner, a cracked water cooled exhaust manifold, or a leaking injector tube.
- On engine installations with a gravity feed fuel tank (tank is higher than the engine), faulty injectors can allow fuel to dribble onto the piston crown recess and actually fill up the cylinder combustion space.

If you suspect that an engine may have water or fuel trapped in the cylinder, place the fuel control linkage in the STOP position on mechanically governed engines. Then manually bar over (rotate) the engine in its normal direction of rotation at least two complete revolutions to confirm that it is in fact free to rotate.

A variety of special tooling is available to correctly check a con-rod for twists or bends. If such special tooling is not available to you, check the con-rod by laying it flat on a machined surface table. Then insert two round mandrel pins that are of the same diameter as the large and small end of the con-rod and support them between two vee blocks (as shown in Figure 17–5. A surface gauge or a dial gauge mounted on a

machined sled can be used to determine if any difference in height exists between the sides of the mandrel pins. If no gauge is available, measure the vertical drop from each side of the pins to the machined surface table by the use of vernier calipers. Another easy way to check the con-rod, particularly on rods that have the same thickness at the small and big ends, is to lay the rod on a surface table, place light pressure on it, and run a feeler gauge around the machined surface of the rod that is resting on the table. Do this at both ends. If the con-rod has a tapered small end, lay the rod flat on the surface table and check the big end first by the feeler gauge method; then repeat the check at the small end by holding its machined surface against the table.

One type of dual dial gauge for checking con-rod twist and bend is shown in Figure 17–6a where the rod is being checked for a bend condition. With a mandrel pin inserted into the piston pin bore end, the mandrel expanding arbor is adjusted to hold the rod assembly snug at the crankpin end. Both dial gauges are placed against the piston pin (preloaded slightly) and set to zero. The rod is lifted out and turned 180° and set back into the fixture. The dial gauges are adjusted to divide any difference between the first and second readings to effectively calibrate the gauges. The measurements that are then read directly from the dial indicator show the comparative length and misalignment of the piston pin and crankpin bores of the rod.

To check for con-rod twist, refer to Figure 17–6b which illustrates that by using a selective feeler gauge between the piston pin and dial holding plate, you can effectively gauge how much twist exists. Compare all readings to specifications in the engine service literature.

The latest electronic con-rod gauges employ digital readouts similar to the one illustrated in Figure 17–7 to measure the degree to which the centerline of the wrist-pin bore is out of parallel with the centerline of the crankpin bore (bend or twist). This fixture checks center-to-center, bend, and twist—all at the same time. Various expanding mandrel blades allow checks to be made on crankpin diameters from 1 9/16 in. (39.7 mm) to 4 1/8 in. (104.8 mm). This gauge can handle con-rods up to a center-to-center distance of 22 in. (558 mm). It is calibrated to show total wrist pin displacement from parallel and register out-of-parallel to the nearest 0.001 in. (0.025 mm) for bend or twist on two separate indicators.

Checking for Cracks

Con-rods are generally checked for signs of cracks by the *magnetic particle method*. If this method is not readily available to you, refer to Chapter 14 on cylinder heads; the chapter describes four methods commonly used to check component parts of the engine for cracks.

FIGURE 17–5 A simplified method that can be used to determine if a con-rod is bent or twisted while the rod is mounted on a machined surface table.

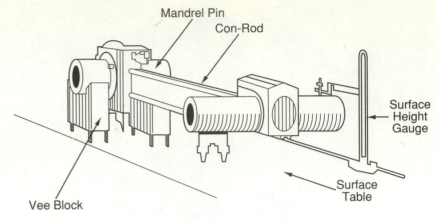

Checking alignment of pins.

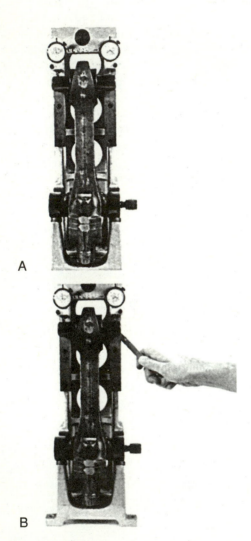

FIGURE 17–6 Using a special con-rod checker with two dial gauges to check for (a) bends and (b) twists in a con-rod. (Courtesy of Cummins Engine Company, Inc.)

The magnetic particle method involves magnetizing the con-rod and covering it with a fine magnetic powder or solution. Any flaw, such as a crack, forms a small local magnet, which causes the magnetic particles in the powder or solution to gather there. The technician then can visually determine where a crack is located. The con-rod *must* be demagnetized after this test. Figure 17–8 illustrates where fatigue cracks may appear on an I-beam con-rod, as well as areas of the rod that require special visual attention during any checking procedure. A deep dent or scratch on the side of the rod can cause a stress riser that eventually leads to rod breakage. These nicks or dents can be very carefully ground to produce proper blending of the area to form a smooth surface. Once again, some engine manufacturers suggest that you replace the con-rod if the I-beam is nicked or damaged. Check the service manual.

CLEANING OIL PASSAGES

Although compressed air can be blown through the rifle-drilled oil passage in the rod, it is preferable to use a stiff nylon-bristle brush to effectively remove any possible coagulated oil or dirt that has been trapped in the rod. Use solvent or steam clean the rod; then dry the rod with compressed air.

Checking Piston Pin Bushing for Wear

On closed-eye con-rods, use a telescoping gauge as illustrated in Figure 17–9 to check the dimension of the piston pin bushing. Compare your readings to the service manual specifications. If a new bushing is required, use a suitable mechanical or hydraulic press. Figure 17–10 shows that a pin slightly smaller in diameter than the bushing wall thickness can be used to drive it from the rod eye with a hammer and punch. Installation of a new bushing is the reverse of removal,

FIGURE 17–7 *Sunnen Model R1-9000 electronic gauge for checking con-rod twists and bends. (Courtesy of Sunnen Products Company, St. Louis, MO.)*

but use fine emery cloth to clean out the piston pin bore first and clean it completely. Prior to installing a new bushing, refer to Figure 17–10 and align an oil hole, if used. Some new bushings require that oil holes be drilled once they have been installed. If the bushing

is a split-type design, install it with the joint toward the top of the con-rod. Note that some engines may use two bushings (one pressed in from each side of the rod) to provide a space between them for pressurized engine lube oil that flows up the rifle-drilled con-rod

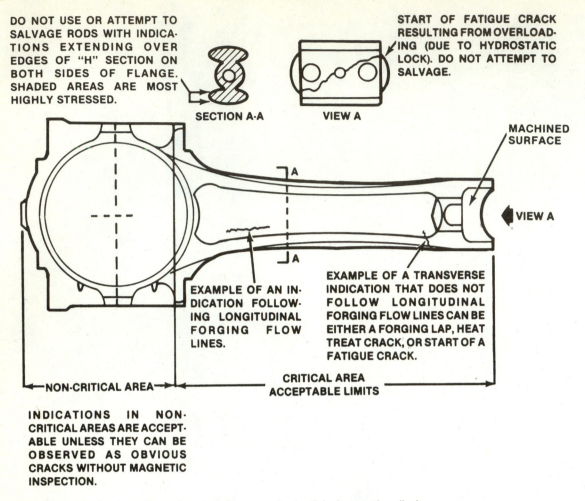

DO NOT USE OR ATTEMPT TO SALVAGE RODS WITH INDICATIONS EXTENDING OVER EDGES OF "H" SECTION ON BOTH SIDES OF FLANGE. SHADED AREAS ARE MOST HIGHLY STRESSED.

SECTION A-A

START OF FATIGUE CRACK RESULTING FROM OVERLOADING (DUE TO HYDROSTATIC LOCK). DO NOT ATTEMPT TO SALVAGE.

VIEW A

MACHINED SURFACE

VIEW A

EXAMPLE OF AN INDICATION FOLLOWING LONGITUDINAL FORGING FLOW LINES.

EXAMPLE OF A TRANSVERSE INDICATION THAT DOES NOT FOLLOW LONGITUDINAL FORGING FLOW LINES CAN BE EITHER A FORGING LAP, HEAT TREAT CRACK, OR START OF A FATIGUE CRACK.

NON-CRITICAL AREA

CRITICAL AREA ACCEPTABLE LIMITS

INDICATIONS IN NON-CRITICAL AREAS ARE ACCEPTABLE UNLESS THEY CAN BE OBSERVED AS OBVIOUS CRACKS WITHOUT MAGNETIC INSPECTION.

FIGURE 17–8 Location of con-rod magnetic particle inspection limits allowed by DDC. (Courtesy of Detroit Diesel Corporation.)

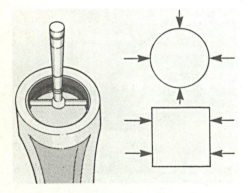

FIGURE 17–9 Using a telescoping gauge to measure the wear in a con-rod pin bushing. (Courtesy of Cummins Engine Company, Inc.)

to feed the oil spray nozzle at the top of the rod for piston cooling purposes. Once the new bushing has been installed, it can either be hand reamed or power honed to provide the correct piston pin-to-bushing clearance.

Some engine manufacturers provide oversize bushings and piston pins for use in repairing a con-rod at major overhaul. On two-piece crosshead-type pistons similar to that employed by Detroit Diesel in its two-stroke and four-stroke-cycle engines, a slipper bearing (half-moon shaped, shown in Figure 15–7a) must be checked for signs of scoring, overheating, or other damage. In addition, measure the thickness of the bushing along its center axis with a ball-type micrometer and compare your measurement to specs or to a new one. Use crocus cloth wet with fuel oil to remove any trace of fretting or corrosion on the con-rod slipper bearing saddle at the piston pin contact surface area before reassembly. Do not, however, attempt to use emery or crocus cloth to polish or refinish the piston pin.

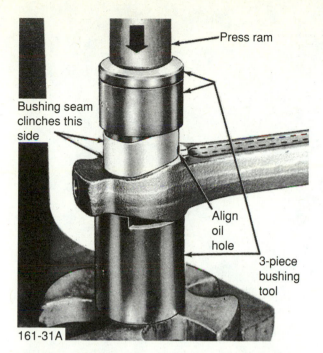

FIGURE 17–10 *Pressing a new bushing into a con-rod. (Courtesy of Mack Trucks, Inc.)*

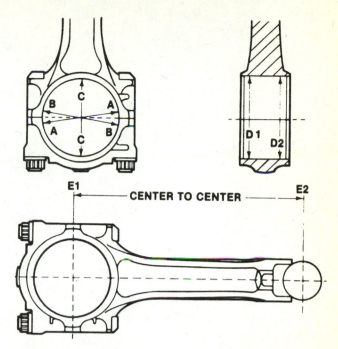

FIGURE 17–11 *Dimensions of a crosshead piston con-rod that should be checked with either a telescoping gauge (similar to Figure 17–9) or a dial bore gauge. (Courtesy of Detroit Diesel Corporation.)*

CHECKING ROD BORE OVALITY

Closely inspect the con-rod bearing cap and saddle area for any signs of dark spots, which usually indicate poor contact of the precision shell bearing contact. Also check for color discoloration throughout the rod; this could indicate overheating, which affects rod strength. Look for signs of bluing at either the top or bottom end of the rod, and replace the rod if it is severely discolored.

With the con-rod and cap assembled and torqued to specs, use a dial bore or telescoping gauge to measure the distortion and ovality of the rod bore as illustrated in Figure 17–11. After many hours, or miles (kilometers) of operation, the con-rod bolts can stretch, and ovality may be indicated when you check the crankpin end of the rod. Taper may also be indicated by comparing the readings obtained at positions D1 and D2 (see Figure 17–11); the center-to-center distance could indicate a bent rod. Closely inspect the rod and cap at the split parting line for any signs of fretting, which would signify bearing cap movement. Signs of movement or rod bore ovality may require that the rod be replaced. Check the engine manufacturer's service literature. The bearing cap and saddle can be parted (machined flat) on a cap and rod grinder similar to the one shown in Figure 17–12. Grinding the parting surface of either the

crankshaft main or con-rod bearing caps leaves all the main bearing and rod cap bores *undersize* when the caps are bolted back in place. Main bearing bores can be *line honed* as shown in Chapter 9 (Figure 9–31), while con-rods can be power honed back to a stock bore size on a machine similar to the one illustrated in Figure 17–13.

CAUTION: Some engine manufacturers are opposed to parting and remachining the con-rod since when metal is removed, the weight of the rod as well as the clearance height of the piston to cylinder head fire deck are changed. Thus the cylinder compression and injector spray distribution throughout the combustion chamber are altered. Always check the engine service manual closely to determine if remachining is an acceptable practice. Detroit Diesel is one major engine manufacturer that cautions against any such remachining of its connecting rods.

Most manufacturers suggest that rod bolts be replaced at each major overhaul, or at least that the self-locking nuts be replaced. Inspect the rod bolts for signs of fretting (movement), thread damage, or bolt stretch, and compare them to a new bolt. If new nuts are used, install them in the proper direction so that the hardened machined face bottoms against the rod cap.

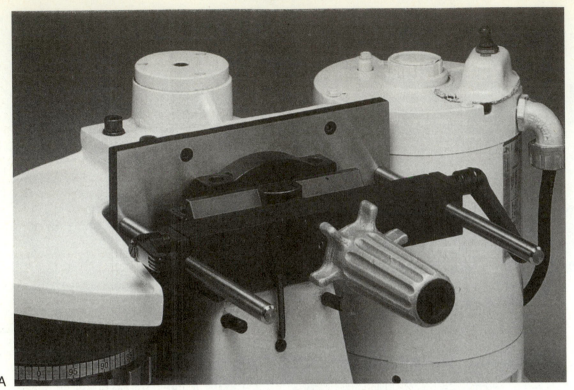

A

B

FIGURE 17–12 (a) Grinding of the parting line surface of the con-rod
bearing cap; (b) grinding of the con-rod parting line flat machined surface using
a cap and rod grinder. (Courtesy of Sunnen Products Company, St. Louis, MO.)

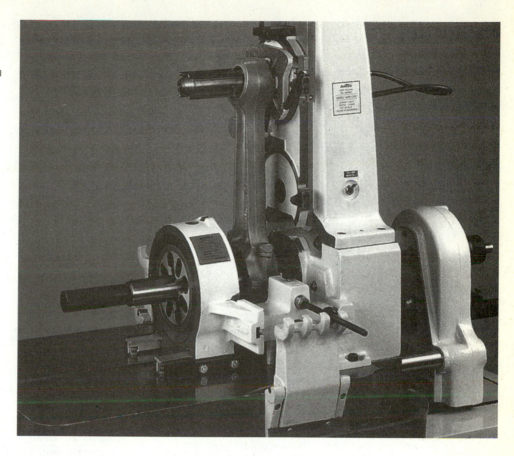

FIGURE 17–13 *Power honing the large end of a con-rod on a Model PM-300 machine. (Courtesy of Sunnen Products Company, St. Louis, MO.)*

SELF-TEST QUESTIONS

1. Tue or False: All connecting rods are designed to transmit the reciprocating or straight-line motion at the piston to rotary motion at the crankshaft.

2. True or False: On four-stroke-cycle engines during the compression and power strokes, the rod is placed under tension, while during the last part of the exhaust stroke and the beginning of the intake stroke, the rod is placed under the forces of compression.

3. True or False: On two-stroke-cycle engines, the con-rod is less highly stressed than in a four-cycle engine.

4. List the two types of con-rods that are widely used in high-speed diesel engines.

5. What is the purpose of rifle-drilling some connecting rods?

6. True or False: Technician A says that all con-rods are balanced, so you should never mix the caps and rods on an engine. Technician B says that since all rods are balanced, it wouldn't make any difference. Who is correct?

7. Con-rods are generally manufactured from a single forging. What metals are used in their construction?

8. What alphabetical letter would best describe the cross-sectional shape of a typical con-rod?
   a. I-beam
   b. H-beam
   c. O-section
   d. A-beam

9. Steel used in bridge construction usually has a built-in safety factor of 5. What is the safety factor in a con-rod?

10. Technician A says that bolts used with con-rods are normally a Grade 5 or Grade 6. Technician B says that Grade 8 or higher should always be used. Which technician is correct?

11. True or False: Rod bolts or nuts should be replaced automatically at each major overhaul.

12. Dark spots in the bearing cap or saddle area of a con-rod are usually indications of
    a. bearing movement
    b. poor bearing contact
    c. insufficient bearing-to-journal clearance
    d. too much bearing-to-journal clearance

13. Shiny areas at the parting line of the con-rod cap to rod are indicative of
    a. cap movement
    b. bearing movement
    c. insufficient bearing clearance
    d. too much bearing clearance

14. True or False: All con-rods are subjected to stretch during engine operation, therefore if the rod cap bore end is tapered or oval, the rod should be replaced.

15. Rehoning of a con-rod on a power honing machine at overhaul involves what specific steps to recondition it, particularly at the crankshaft journal end?

16. If a con-rod is honed at its crank journal end, does this have any effect on the compression ratio in that cylinder?

17. If con-rods are honed at overhaul, does this action have any effect on the weight of the finished product and therefore the balance of the other con-rods?

18. List the procedure(s) that can be used at the time of overhaul to determine if a con-rod is twisted or bent.

19. One of the more common conditions that leads to bending of a con-rod is
    a. a hydrostatic lock (water in the cylinder)
    b. overspeeding of the engine
    c. uneven cylinder balance
    d. trapped fuel or oil in the cylinder

20. What might cause the condition to the answer you chose in Question 19?

21. Con-rods can be checked for cracks at inspection or rebuilt by using what type of nondestructive testing procedure?

22. Technician A says that minor nicks or burrs on the con-rod can be relieved by grinding to produce proper blending of the ground area to form a smooth surface. Technician B says that the con-rod should be discarded if any such irregularities are discovered. Which technician is correct?

23. Most diesel engines use bushings in the piston pin bore area of the con-rod that are replaceable. If no bushing is used, are oversize pins available?

24. Technician A says that the top and bottom bearing of the con-rod are identical. Not so says technician B and if the wrong bearing is used, the oil hole through the rifle-drilled con-rod can be blocked. Is there any validity in technician B's statement of concern?

25. True or False: Con-rod bearings can be identified in regard to size and position by etched or stamped numbers on the backside.

26. What gauge should you use to check con-rod bearing clearances?

27. True or False: When installing con-rods and pistons into an engine cylinder, the numbered sides of the rod and cap should always face one another.

28. Technician A says that once a con-rod has been installed over the crankshaft journal and its bolts have been torqued to spec, you should always check the rod side clearance with a feeler gauge. Technician B says that as long as the engine crankshaft can be rotated manually, this check is not necessary. Which technician is correct?

29. In vee-type engines where two con-rods are located on one journal, a lack of side clearance between the rods could be caused by
    a. bent rods
    b. twisted rods
    c. one rod installed backwards on the journal

30. Technician A says that the numbers on the con-rod of an inline engine are usually designed to face a specific side of the engine block, such as the camshaft or oil cooler side. Technician B says the way the numbers face makes no difference. Which technician is correct and why?

31. In engines using two-piece crosshead or articulated pistons, the con-rod has an open saddle at the piston pin end. How are the piston and pin attached to the rod?

32. True or False: Main bearing wear results in oil starvation of the con-rod bearings.

33. Technician A says that if the crankshaft con-rod journals are in need of regrinding to a smaller diameter, the main bearing journals also have to be reground to the same size. Not so says technician B; only the rod journals need to be reground. Which technician is correct?

34. True or False: A properly fitted and operating con-rod shell bearing usually appears dull gray in color after a reasonable period of service.

35. Technician A says that a con-rod bearing noise is generally more noticeable when the engine is unloaded; technician B says the noise is more noticeable when the engine is loaded. Who is correct?

18

Lubrication Systems

OVERVIEW

The engine lubrication system is extremely important to the longevity of all the operating components. In this chapter we discuss the various types and grades of lube oils commonly recommended by the OEM. We also trace lube oil system flows and discuss the components that form the operational lube system, for example, the oil pump, filters, and oil cooler assemblies.

TOPICS

CRUDE OIL REFINING AND ADDITIVES

Engine oils, which come primarily from petroleum, consist of mixtures of hydrocarbons—chemical compounds composed solely of carbon and hydrogen—and carefully chosen chemicals that are called additives. Not all of the elements in crude oil are desirable in an engine, so the base crude oil must be refined at an oil refinery through a process called *fractional distillation*. This process divides the crude oil into portions according to their boiling point ranges. Products that are normally obtained from a supply of crude oil consist of gasoline, jet fuel, diesel fuel, and lube oil itself, which is one of the heavier fractions.

After this first separation, another distillation procedure separates the oils into fractions ranging from thin to thick. Each fraction is then processed to remove small amounts of undesirable components. One of these known as *wax* is part of the paraffin base of crude oil. Perhaps you experienced hard starting of a diesel engine in cold weather and found that the fuel filters were plugged with a greasy wax-like formation. Portions of the crude oil started to gel (solidification of wax crystals) at low ambient temperatures. This problem is referred to as the *cloud point of the fuel* (see Chapter 3). Too much wax would cause the engine lube oil to become solid at a given ambient temperature; therefore, most of the wax is removed during the lube oil refining procedure.

Once the crude oil has gone through the first stages of refining, we are left with what is commonly known as *base stocks*. These base stock oils are unsuitable, however, for the high pressures and temperatures in today's engines. Lube oil additives must be chemically mixed

471

FIGURE 18-1   Typical lube oil additives and reasons for use. Reprinted with permission by Chevron Research and Technology Company, a division of Chevron, U.S.A. Inc.; copyright Chevron Research Company (1995).

Type	Reason for Use	Typical Compounds
Dispersants, detergents	Keep sludge, carbon and other deposit precursors suspended in the oil	Succinimides, neutral metallic sulfonates, phenates, polymeric detergents, amine compounds
Basic metal compounds	Neutralize acids, prevent corrosion from acid attack	Overbased metallic sulfonates and phenates
Oxidation inhibitors	Prevent or control oxidation of oil, formation of varnish, sludge, and corrosive compounds; limit viscosity increase	Zinc dialkyldithiophosphates; aromatic amines, sulfurized products, hindered phenols
Extreme pressure (EP) antiwear additives	Form protective film on engine parts, reduce wear, prevent scuffing and seizing	Zinc dialkyldithiophosphates; tricresylphosphates, organic phosphates, chlorine and sulfur compounds
Friction modifiers	Reduce or modify friction, improve fuel economy	Long-chain polar compounds, (amides, phosphates phosphites, acids, etc.)
Rust inhibitors	Prevent the formation of rust on metal surfaces by formation of surface film or neutralization of acids	High base additives, sulfonates, phosphates, organic acids or esters, amines
Viscosity index improvers	Reduce the rate of viscosity change with temperature; reduce fuel consumption; maintain low oil consumption; allow easy cold starting	Polyisobutylene, mathacrylate, acrylate polymers, olefin copolymers; may incorporate dispersant groups
Metal deactivators	Form surface films so that metal surfaces do not catalyze oil oxidation	Zinc dialkyldithiophosphates, metal phenates, organic nitrogen compounds
Pour point dispersants	Lower "freezing" point of oils, assuring free flow at low temperatures	Low molecular weight methacrylate polymers
Antifoamants	Reduce foam in crankcase	Silicone polymers

with the base stock to achieve desired operating characteristics. Additives are chemicals that, when added to an oil, affect or enhance desirable functional properties. Basically, they improve lubrication and protect engines and equipment from deposits, wear, rust and corrosion, oxidation, and friction. Figure 18–1 lists some of the more widely used additives and the reasons for their use.

Two of the most common additive packages are the *dispersants* and *detergents*. The dispersants are chemical additive packages that disperse sludge, carbon, and other deposits in the oil, and the detergents displace gum deposits from within the engine interior. Other additives—the oxidation inhibitors—prevent oxidation of the oil when the engine is running continually at elevated operating temperatures. Oxidation of the lube oil leads to viscosity increases and deposits

and corrosion. The oxidation inhibitors also prevent formation of varnish and sludge. Antiwear and extreme pressure additives are used to form a protective film on metal surfaces. Viscosity improvers and wear inhibitors prevent foaming of the oil by the use of silicone compounds and also act as friction modifiers.

Additive packages are used in dosages such as these:

- Industrial lubricants = 0.5% to 2% by weight
- Tractor hydraulic fluid gear oils = 4% to 7% by weight
- Automotive/truck engine oils = 3% to 16% by weight
- Zinc-free railroad diesel engine oils = 7% to 20% by weight
- Marine engine oils = 10% to 30% by weight

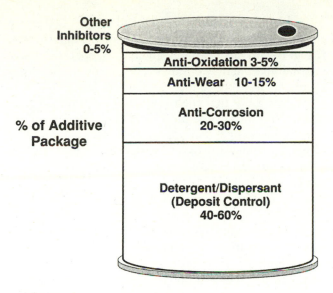

FIGURE 18-2 Additives in a typical can of lube oil. Reprinted with permission by Chevron Research and Technology Company, a division of Chevron, U.S.A. Inc.; copyright Chevron Research Company (1995).

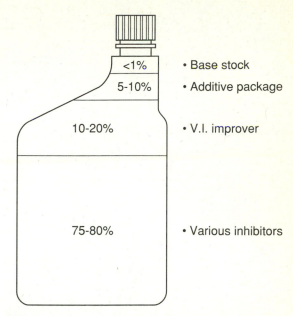

FIGURE 18-3 Contents of a fully formulated lube oil. V.I. = viscosity index. Reprinted with permission by Chevron Research and Technology Company, a division of Chevron, U.S.A. Inc.; copyright Chevron Research Company (1995).

Figure 18-2 illustrates a typical additive package for heavy-duty high-speed diesel engine oils. Figure 18-3 illustrates the contents of a fully formulated quart (liter) of oil. Note that the base stock crude oil accounts for less than 1%, the additive package for 5% to 10%, the V.I. (viscosity index improver) for 10% to 20%, and the various inhibitors for 75% to 80%.

Hundreds of commercially available engine oils are produced worldwide, and labeling terminology and grading differ among suppliers. Some marketers of engine lube oils may claim that their lubricant is suitable for all makes of diesel engines. Such claims should be checked with the recommendations of a specific engine's manufacturer. Engines manufactured in North America require a lube oil that is selected based on SAE (Society of Automotive Engineers) viscosity grade and API (American Petroleum Institute) service designations, although OEM and U.S. military specifications are also often quoted. In Europe, military specifications and the CCMC (The Comite des Constructeurs du Marche Commun) represent the requirements of European lube oil manufacturers for engine oil quality. In North America both the SAE and API standards are displayed, and only oils meeting these recommended properties should be considered as suitable for a given engine. Figure 18-4 illustrates a typical oil can symbol that indicates the lube oil meets an enhanced level of lubricant performance of the API CF-4 category.

NOTE: In January 1995, the API began voluntarily licensing of API CG-4 lubricating oils for use in on-highway truck engines. To conform with this change, it is now recommended that heavy-duty electronically controlled diesel engines operating on low-sulfur fuel (0.05%) use API CG-4 designated lube oils. The phase in of API CG-4 oils was not immediate; therefore, API CF-4 oils may continue to be used until CG-4 products become available.

The use of CG-4 lube oils is recommended by Detroit Diesel in both its Series 50 and Series 60 four-cycle engine models; other engine OEMs are scheduled to follow this same recommendation. The recommended lube oil viscosity grade continues to be 15W-40 for heavy-duty high-speed on-highway truck engines manufactured by all of the major OEMs. The use of a CG-4 lubricant does not permit extension of normal oil drain intervals. CG-4 lube oil does have several advantages:

- Better control of engine deposits and prevention of corrosive wear
- Reduced oil consumption and improved oil viscosity control
- Control of combustion soot dispersancy, oxidation, and lube oil shear

VISCOSITY OF OILS

Oils are classified by a numbering system to indicate basic viscosity grading. For example, in Figure 18-4

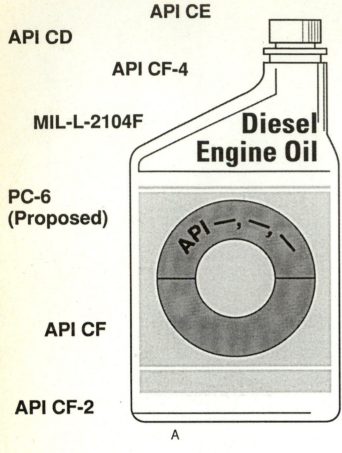

API CE

API CD

API CF-4

MIL-L-2104F

PC-6
(Proposed)

API CF

API CF-2

Diesel Engine Oil

A

API Symbol:

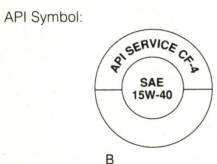

B

FIGURE 18–4 *API and SAE symbols on a typical lube oil container. Reprinted with permission by Chevron Research and Technology Company, a division of Chevron, U.S.A. Inc.; copyright Chevron Research Company (1995).*

note that the oil is a 15W-40 grade, which is a multi-viscosity lubricant. The 15W indicates that the oil has a viscosity of 15 when cold (W = winter). The 40 indicates that when the oil is hot, its additives allow it to thicken to an equivalent viscosity of 40 weight oil. Some oils may be labeled as a single-weight lubricant such as 30, 40 or 50. Various alphabetical letters have appeared on oil containers for years; these letters have

changed as lubricating oils have improved. Letters on an oil can such as, SA, SB, SC, SD, SE, SF, or SG signify that the oil has been designed for S (spark ignition) internal combustion engines. Diesel engine lubricant containers have the letters CA, CB, CC, CD, CD-11, CE, or CF to signify that the oil is intended for a C (compression ignition) type diesel engine.

Engine oil viscosity was first defined by Isaac Newton as a measure of the resistance offered when one layer of the fluid moves relative to an adjacent layer similar to that illustrated in Figure 18–5, where the letters AW indicate an *adhesive wear* additive. The higher the viscosity or thickness of the fluid film, the greater is the internal resistance to motion. Newton discovered that the viscosity of a fluid or lube oil will remain constant if both the temperature and pressure are held constant. Within an engine subjected to changing operating conditions, however, these two "constants" are regularly subjected to change. Most single-grade lube oils such as a 30, 40, or 50 are sometimes referred to as being Newtonian, whereas multigrade oils are non-Newtonian because they don't obey the basic law as we shall see. Several factors affect lube oil viscosity:

- Composition of the refined oil with its additives
- Operating temperature of the oil
- Pressure (loads) between two lubricated parts

The ASTM (American Society for Testing and Materials) created a method to provide a number called the VI (viscosity index). The VI is related to the amount of change for a given oil compared to two reference oils over a range of 40° to 100°C (104° to 212°F). On the ASTM scale, most engine oils have a VI of 90 or more, although it is not uncommon for light, multigrade oils to have a VI approaching 200 due to the additive packages used with them. Single-weight oils are more successful in some engine designs than others, but they have the disadvantage of having a much higher drag when cranking the engine over in cold-weather operation. Non-W-grades of lube oil are based only on their viscosities at 100°C (212°F). Multiviscosity oils are formulated to meet the W-grade criterion of a relatively thin oil at a particular low temperature, yet meet the standards for a thicker, non-W-grade oil at a higher temperature (usually 100°C, 212°F).

Therefore, the base stocks used with multigrade oils are of lower viscosity than a single-weight oil, but the multiviscosity oil is thickened with additives called viscosity index improvers. These are giant molecules made by chemically linking together a large number of smaller ones in a process called *polymerization*. The polymers may have molecular weights 1000 times or more greater than the base crude oil stock used. This is

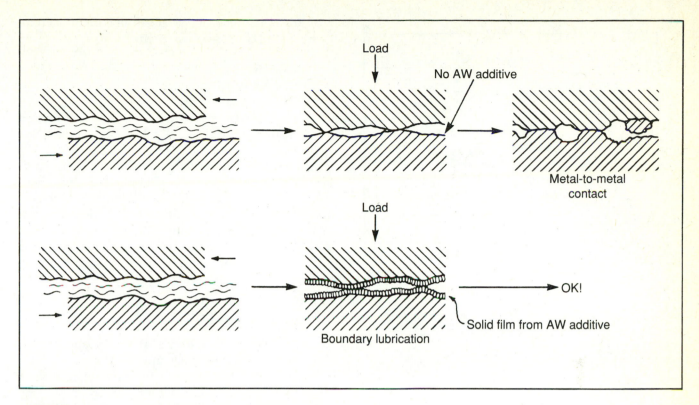

FIGURE 18–5 Example of the resistance between two moving pieces of metal. The letters AW indicate an adhesive wear additive. Reprinted with permission by Chevron Research and Technology Company, a division of Chevron, U.S.A. Inc.; copyright Chevron Research Company (1995).

important to understand because the viscosity of the resulting lube oil blend increases, but to a much greater degree at higher temperatures than at lower temperatures. So the reduced effect of engine oil temperature on viscosity means a higher VI for that oil. Consequently, these polymers are classified as being VI improvers.

One of the drawbacks of using a multigrade lube oil is that under high-shear stress conditions within an operating engine, these polymers are either squeezed to a more compact form or align themselves in the direction of motion that results in a reduction of the oil film resistance. This causes the lube oil viscosity to drop to that of the base stock oil, which lowers the fluid friction. In certain locations within the engine this can be advantageous. For example, the shear rate in the engine ring belt area is fairly low, allowing the multigrade oil to maintain a good oil film in a critical wear location in addition to controlling oil consumption. The graphs in Figure 18–6 and Figure 18–7 illustrate the viscosity changes to a single-weight and a multigrade lube oil. Note in Figure 18–6 that the SAE 30 oil has a higher kinematic viscosity, cSt (centistokes), at a lower ambient temperature than does the multiviscosity oil. Figure 18–7 illustrates the condi-

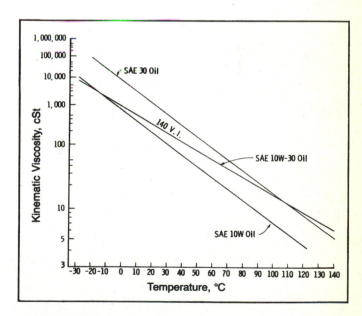

FIGURE 18–6 Graph showing the viscosity characteristics of a single-grade and multigrade oil. Reprinted with permission by Chevron Research and Technology Company, a division of Chevron, U.S.A. Inc.; copyright Chevron Research Company (1995).

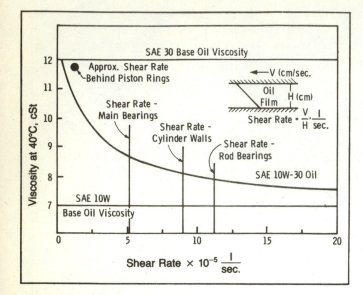

FIGURE 18-7 *Graph showing the effect of shear rate on oils of differing viscosities. Reprinted with permission by Chevron Research and Technology Company, a division of Chevron, U.S.A. Inc.; copyright Chevron Research Company (1995).*

tions of the two oils (a single SAE 30 base oil and a 10W-30 multiviscosity blend) under shear stresses within an operating engine. Note how the shear rate affects both oils at different locations throughout the engine. There is always some permanent viscosity loss in multiviscosity oils as the polymer molecules are broken down into smaller ones. Good multiviscosity oils are generally designed to take this shear condition into account, so that the oil remains within its designed grade limits throughout its period of engine use prior to normal oil-change intervals. Almost all heavy-duty high-speed diesel engines, such as Caterpillar, Cummins, Detroit Diesel, Volvo, Navistar, and Mack, recommend use of 15W-40 multiviscosity oils in their four-stroke-cycle engines.

Regardless of whether the engine is a two-stroke or a four-stroke-cycle model, if the oil is too viscous engine drag is increased, particularly during cranking in cold ambient temperatures. Too viscous an oil can cause these problems:

- Hard starting (engine will not crank over fast enough)
- Lower power output and reduced engine lube oil cooling
- Higher fuel consumption
- Higher wear rate during initial engine start-up, particularly in cold weather
- Higher overall engine operating temperatures

If, on the other hand, the selected lube oil is too thin, the following conditions can occur:

- Higher than normal oil consumption
- Increased oil leakage
- Noisier engine operation
- Metal-to-metal contact creating increased friction and a higher wear rate of lubricated components

Lubricants that meet engine manufacturers' specifications already contain a balanced additive treatment. The use of supplemental additives such as break-in oils, top oils, graphitizers, and friction-reducing compounds is generally not necessary and can even be harmful. Engine damage resulting from the use of nonrecommended additives could result in voidance of the engine warranty!

TWO-CYCLE ENGINE OILS

Two-stroke-cycle engines are always loaded, since every time the piston moves upward it is under compression, and every time it moves downward it is on the power stroke. Unlike a four-stroke-cycle engine which has a separate intake and exhaust stroke, the two-cycle-engine completes both its intake and exhaust strokes when the ports in the liner are opened for about 120 crankshaft degrees (although the exhaust valves do open at about 95° to 100° ATDC).

In a two-cycle diesel multiviscosity oils tend to break down faster than a single-weight engine oil due to mechanical and thermal stresses that result in a loss of viscosity and premature engine wear. Detroit Diesel two-cycle engines have been shown to achieve significantly longer time between overhaul on 40 or 50 single-grade lube oil than on any other available lubricant. This oil is more effective in reducing wear on critical engine parts. On DDC 149 series two-cycle engine models, 50-grade oil is recommended for engines operating in continuous high-temperature conditions (over 94°C, 200°F, coolant out) and for applications where ambient temperatures are above 35°C (95°F). This oil has given superior performance under these conditions. *Do not*, however, use 50-grade oil at temperatures below 10°C (50°F).

Although multiviscosity oils exhibit lower drag and easier engine cranking in cold ambient temperatures, DDC recommends that auxiliary starting aids be used to provide reliable starting without sacrificing engine life. Synthetic oils may be used if suitable viscosity ranges are available. In cases where consistent operation in cold ambient temperatures is unavoidable, you can use a lighter-weight lube oil; however, expect less than optimum engine life. DDC also cautions against the use of an SAE 30-grade oil in any two-stroke marine engines or Series 149 engines under any circumstances.

SYNTHETIC LUBE OILS

The history of synthetic oils dates back to World War II when they were developed to meet the critically high standards of the aviation industry. Synthetic oils have been used in various forms for diesel truck applications since the early to mid-1960s, particularly for differentials and transmissions. Because of their superior cooling quality and service life much longer than that of mineral oils, they have found favor in severe-duty service off-road operations for diesel engines. Although more expensive than mineral oils, synthetic lubricants can be the ideal choice under heavy loads and steep operating grades. Synthetic oil is a far more refined, purer product than mineral oil, which is one reason it costs more. In addition, synthetic oil tends to be stickier than mineral oil and provides a better oil wedge between gear teeth on differentials and transmissions. As stricter emissions standards become a fact of life, synthetic engine oils are on the horizon for heavy-duty diesel engines as well as for gasoline-powered passenger cars.

EXHAUST EMISSIONS AND LUBE OIL

Electronically controlled diesel engines now operate in an era dominated by low-emissions fuels. Engine lube oil plays an important role in meeting stringent exhaust limits. Engine oils are being formulated to handle the side effects of EPA mandates.

Low-sulphur fuel (0.05%), which was introduced in October 1993, does allow the engine to burn cleaner, but it also affects key engine parts. To meet the strict standards for diesel particulate emissions, engine manufacturers have changed their piston designs by moving the rings closer to the top of the piston crown; thus, the crevice volume (area above the top ring and piston crown) is reduced but the rings are subjected to hotter temperatures. To protect the engines, lubricants have to control deposits at elevated temperatures. Since the top piston rings now operate in a much hotter environment, top ring groove deposits may increase, as well as oil viscosity. Improved additive packages help to minimize these new deposit configurations, thereby reducing wear and oil consumption. Improved oxidation inhibitors keep the oil viscosity within its designed grade level for longer periods.

To reduce nitrogen oxide emissions, many new engines use retarded injection timing, a feature that

can substantially increase soot loading in the oil film on the cylinder walls. Advanced dispersancy additives help to keep this extra load of soot suspended instead of attaching internally to key engine parts. When the oil is drained, the soot is removed with the used oil. Dispersed soot is what makes the engine oil "black," and it can also cause the oil to thicken in time. Dispersancy-type oil additives provide reduced abrasive wear, fewer plugged filters, cleaner engines, and excellent pumpability during cold-weather start-up. Much of the particulate exhaust emissions in the newer diesel engines consist of unburned oil escaping through the exhaust gases.

The new characteristics of the widely used 15W-40 oils in high-speed heavy-duty engines also offer fleets the possibility of extending oil drain intervals without suffering any loss of performance. An oil drain interval of 30,000 miles (48,279 km) is not uncommon in many of today's newer engines. Accumulated mileages of between 800,000 and 1 million miles (1,287,440 to 1,609,300 km) are becoming standard practice between overhauls. The 15W-40 multiviscosity oil is also designed to be compatible with oil oxidation catalysts that will be required on many smaller, high-speed diesel engines throughout the 1990s (see Chapter 20).

The main elements of these new engine oils is that there is only 1% ash content, which is held in check by ashless dispersants, and that the TBN (total base number) is 9. TBN is an indication of the depletion rate of the oil's additive package. Low ash in lube oils is key to reducing deposits in the piston top ring groove area; any such deposits can cause ring sticking, blowby, and high oil consumption.

OIL RECOMMENDATIONS

Engine manufacturers recommend engine oils based on their experience with oil viscosities. Manufacturers do not specifically state that a certain *brand name* lube oil be used. Rather, the key is that the oil brand selected meet the minimum specs stated in the engine manufacturer's technical data.

Although some OEMs offer engine oils under their own name, any brand name engine oil can be used as long as it meets the standards and specifications specified by the engine manufacturer regarding sulfated ash and so on. Always refer to the engine service manual, operator manual, or lube oil spec sheets to ensure that the oil you choose for a certain engine make and model does in fact comply with the specs of the OEM. Failure to do so could have a detrimental effect on engine oil consumption and engine life and MAY void the existing warranty for the engine.

Some typical lube oil recommendations as specified by engine manufacturers follow:

- Caterpillar: Cat diesel engine oil CF-4, CE/SG (15W-40, 10W-30), CD11 (15W-40), CD/SD (10W, 30, 40). For Cat natural gas engine operation use NGEO (natural gas engine oil) SAE 30 or 40.

- Cummins: Cummins Premium Blue SAE 15W-40, CE, CF-4, SF, Cummins NTC-400, and Cummins NTC-444. Cummins Premium Blue 2000 SAE 15W-40 meeting Cummins Engineering Standard 20066 may be used where CF-4 oils are required.

- Mack: Bulldog Premium EO-L (engine oil lube) meeting the T-8 engine test.

- Detroit Diesel: DDC manufactures two-stroke and four-stroke-cycle engines; therefore its recommended lube oil viscosities are that a single-weight lube oil be used in its two-cycle models. SAE 40 is typically used in Series 71 and 92 engines; for 149 series and high-output 71 and 92 engines, SAE 50 is recommended. For Series 50 and 60 engines, 15W-40 oil is the base oil, and current engines have a decal on the rocker cover recommending the use of a 15W-40 Mobil Delvac 1300 Super product. In all DDC engines, any engine oil that meets the company's specifications for CG-4 lubricants can be used.

To avoid possible engine damage, do not use single-grade (monograde) lubricants in Detroit Diesel four-cycle Series 50 and Series 60 engines, regardless of API classification.

OIL CHANGE INTERVALS

During use, engine lubricating oil undergoes deterioration from combustion by-products and contamination by the engine. Certain components in a lubricant additive package are designed to deplete with use. For this reason, regardless of the oil formulation, regular oil drain intervals are necessary. These intervals may vary in length, depending on engine operation, fuel quality, and lubricant quality. Generally, shorter oil drain intervals extend engine life through prompt replenishment of the protection qualities in the lubricant.

The oil drain intervals listed in Figure 18-8 should be considered **maximum** and should not, under any circumstances, be exceeded. Always install new engine oil filters when the oil is changed.

Proper drain intervals for engine oil require that the oil be drained before the contaminant load becomes so great that the oil's lubricating function is impaired or heavy deposits of suspended contaminants occur. Oil and filter change intervals are usually recommended by each engine manufacturer for various operating conditions. This information is usually contained in service manual literature as well as operator manuals (engine,

vehicle, equipment) and is provided simply as a general guide. Engine operating environments, speeds, loads, idling time, ambient air temperature, grades encountered with mobile equipment, and airborne dust all affect the lube oil life cycle. Some truck fleets base their engine oil change interval on average vehicle fuel consumption in mpg (L/100 km) as well as the average oil consumption rate of the engine. This is known as using the *chart method.* To convert miles to kilometers, multiply the miles by 1.609. For example, 1000 miles = 1609 km.

New electronic engines have made key improvements in engine oil consumption. In fact, many new engines use such little oil that they are referred to as *dry engines.* For example, consider that the 1991 model Cummins L10 managed about 2000 miles (3219 km) per U.S. quart (0.946 L) of oil. The new M11 model, which has superseded the L10, and the N14 Celect engines are up to approximately 3200 miles (5150 km) per U.S. quart, with some customers claiming up to 6000 miles (9656 km).

Assume that a line-haul truck operation was changing oil on its trucks at 10,000 miles (16,093 km) or 6 months. This interval may be ideal for one fleet operation, but totally inadequate for another based on the abovementioned operating conditions. For example, Cummins Premium Blue 2000 engine oil, which is recommended for use in NT/N14 or L10/M11 line-haul applications, is formulated to extend maintenance intervals by up to 50% to 15,000 miles (24,140 km) or 6 months without the risk of decreased engine life or increased reliability problems that result in downtime. Depending on the actual fuel consumption of a particular engine coupled with the workload, however, Cummins indicates that using a premium engine oil may extend maintenance schedules as far as 22,000 miles (35,404 km) for L10 engines and 27,000 miles (43,451 km) for NT/N14 models.

Regardless of the type of oil used, it is always wise to have a schedule for oil sampling in a fleet operation to determine the best mileage (hours, time) at which to change the engine lube oil and filter(s). Another method for determining the oil and filter change interval if no service literature is available is to use kilometers (miles) hours, or months—whichever comes first. On industrial and marine engine applications, oil change intervals are normally based on accumulated engine hours; the type of application, loads, and speeds play a large part in determining the recommended oil drain period. The type of diesel fuel used and the sulfur content also are relevant. Because of the many factors involved, the change interval can range from as low as 50 hours to 500 hours or 6 months maximum.

Figure 18–8 illustrates normal oil change intervals based on engine application and engine series recommended by Detroit Diesel. On larger diesel engines,

FIGURE 18-8 *Recommended maximum allowable oil drain intervals under normal operation for various models and applications of DDC engines. (Courtesy of Detroit Diesel Corporation.)*

Service application	Engine series	Oil drain interval
Highway truck and motor coach	40, 50, 60, 71, 92	15,000 miles (24,000 km)
City transit coaches	50, 53, 71, 92	6000 miles (9600 km) or 3 months*
Pickup and delivery, Stop and go, short trip	53, 71, 92	12,000 miles (19,000 km)
	40, 50	6000 miles (9600 km)
Industrial, agricultural, and marine	149	300 hours of 1 year*
	53, 60, 71, 92	150 hours
Stationary units, continuous	53, 71, 92, 149	300 hours or 3 months*
Stationary units, standby	53, 71, 92, 149	150 hours or 1 year*

*Whichever comes first.

total fuel consumed is often used as a measure of when to change both the engine lube oil and filters. For a specific make, model, and engine application always refer to the engine service manual.

LUBE OIL DILUTION

During normal daily checks of the engine lube oil by the operator or service technician, unusual oil color is an indication of an internal problem with the engine. The color of diluted engine oil depends on whether the oil is being contaminated by diesel fuel or engine coolant. In Figure 18–9 note that thin black oil is an indication of diesel fuel in the oil. Such contamination can originate at injector O-ring seals or from fuel lines or fuel studs located underneath the valve rocker cover areas. In extreme cases a cracked cylinder head may be the culprit. Don't confuse dark-colored lube oil with thin oil diluted by fuel. Normal engine lube oils turn dark when they are doing their job properly; the contaminants from unburned fuel (carbon particles) cause this change. The detergent or dispersant additives within the oil are designed to handle this contamination. A quick method to check for fuel contamination is to pull the dipstick and feel the oil viscosity between your fingers. In addition, smell the oil between your fingers; if it is diluted with diesel fuel, you can normally smell it.

When the oil appears milky white or grey in color, usually there is coolant in the lube oil. Coolant can originate from a leaking cylinder head gasket, engine oil cooler, air aftercooler, wet cylinder liner seals, cracked wet-type liner, cracked cylinder head or block, or leaking core plugs in the cylinder head

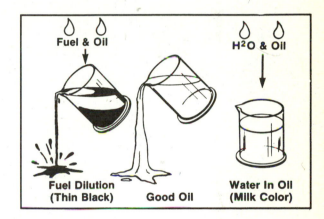

FIGURE 18–9 *Visual lube oil color when diluted with either diesel fuel or engine coolant. (Courtesy of Cummins Engine Company, Inc.)*

assembly. Keep in mind that during engine operation, the lube oil pressure is higher than the coolant pressure. A leak in the oil cooler will show as oil in the coolant; however, after engine shutdown, as the engine cools, the residual pressure in the cooling system will cause coolant to seep through the leak path and into the lube oil system.

WASTE OIL DISPOSAL

Over 1 billion gallons of waste oil is generated annually in the United States alone. Waste oil has now been legislated as a hazardous waste material and must be disposed of according to the local, state, provincial, and federal laws. Collection and recycling companies pick up used oil and try to recycle it to a rerefining manufacturer. Many major engine manufacturers are now permitting the use of rerefined oils in their engines, provided that the rerefined oils meet the SAE viscosity and API specifications for new oils.

OIL ANALYSIS

An oil analysis program involves saving at least a liter of drained oil in a clean sealed container with the engine serial number, number of hours or miles (kilometers), and the make and weight of oil clearly identified on the container. Many equipment companies, marine organizations, and heavy-duty truck fleets use an oil analysis program to monitor the condition of the crankcase oil. Engine lube oil analysis is conducted primarily to determine the overall condition of the lube oil, but it also reveals the state of the internal components of the engine. Oil analysis can be relied on to assist effective engine maintenance only if proper sampling is conducted over a relatively long period of time. In this way, varying engine operating conditions and applications allow a fleet to determine a practical oil drain interval.

The oil sample can detect undesirable contaminants such as diesel fuel, combustion soot, coolant, salt, airborne sand, dirt or dust, and trace wear metals from internal components. Contaminant identification allows maintenance personnel to take corrective action to eliminate their causes or to determine when component repair or engine overhaul is required. To determine a baseline value, or average mathematical change point for the oil, the first three or four samples taken from the engine (drained at the same hours, miles, kilometers, or time interval) should be monitored closely.

Drawing an Oil Sample

Any drained oil sample must be secured in the proper manner to avoid the entrance of outside contaminants that would affect analysis. Most oil sampling labs provide a container and often the required equipment for drawing an oil sample. Oil samples should always be taken from an engine which is at normal operating temperature, since this will ensure that any contaminants and trace wear metals are still in suspension within the oil and have not had time to deposit themselves internally within the engine block. It is also important to thoroughly clean the area around which the oil sample will be drawn.

Ideally, oil samples can be taken from the engine crankcase or oil pan. This can be done by removing the drain plug in most engines; however, on applications such as marine units, oil can be sucked from the dipstick tube using a suitable pump system. Exercise caution here to allow at least a liter of oil to drain from the engine before you collect the sample; this usually minimizes the possibility of picking up debris from the bottom of the oil pan or from the dipstick tube. Whatever type of container is being used for the oil sample must be clean; otherwise, any contaminants added to the oil will create false interpretations of the lab results. Make sure that you seal the container and label it with the engine serial number; total hours or miles (kilometers) of accumulated engine operating time; the number of hours, miles (kilometers), or time interval since the last oil change; and the sample date.

Interpreting Oil Analysis Results

Oil sampling is generally performed by a local lab that produces a computer printout of the trace wear metals and other contaminants. Baseline oil values can be used to determine an average trend for the maximum allowable warning limits of wear metal and other contaminants. These limits are determined by adding the warning values obtained to those for the baseline values. Figure 18–10a illustrates in table form the types of conditions that can be measured for two- and four-cycle engine models. The numbers listed for the two- and four-stroke cycle engines refer to ppm (parts per million).

One of the most important warning values of a used lube oil is the TBN (total base number), which is a measure of the reserve alkalinity of the oil. One function of a lube oil is to neutralize acids that occur from water vapor and combustion blowby. Engine damage can occur when sulfur oxides react with water vapor to form sulfur and sulfuric acids. As these vapors condense in the valve guides and piston ring area, the acids can chemically attack the metal surfaces and cause corrosive wear. The alkaline compound additives in the lube oil act to neutralize these acids. Protective TBN comes from oil-soluble bases derived from calcium, magnesium, sodium, and barium. When oil is in service, the TBN value gradually decreases, because the materials that provide the TBN consistency are depleted. New oil TBN does not reveal much about an oil's ability to provide corrosive wear protection, although the recent shift in North America to low-sulfur diesel fuel (0.05% sulfur) will certainly help in reducing the total acidic value created in running engines. The ASTM-D2896 TBN test allows used oil to be tested so that a correlation with engine wear protection can be determined.

Soot levels in Detroit Diesel two-stroke cycle 71 and 92 series transit coach engines should not exceed 0.8% according to the TGA (thermogravimetric analysis) method. Since soot contributes to engine wear, oil change intervals should be planned at 6000 miles (9600 km) or 3 months, whichever comes first, to ensure that soot levels do not exceed this maximum acceptable level.

FIGURE 18-10A (a) Oil wear warning limits for two-stroke and four-stroke cycle DDC engine models; (b) used lube oil wear metal elements and warning limits in parts per million found in a typical heavy-duty high-speed diesel engine. (Courtesy of Detroit Diesel Corporation.)

	ASTM designation	Condition measured	Two cycle		Four cycle 40, 50, 60
			53, 71, 92	149	
Pentane insolubles % Max.	D893	Engine combust.	1.0	1.0	1.0
Carbon (soot) content, TGA mass % max.	E-1131	Engine combust.	0.8	0.8	1.5
Viscosity at 40°C cS	D445 & D2161	Engine and oil			
% Max. increase			40.0	40.0	40.0
% Max. decrease			15.0	15.0	15.0
Total base number (TBN)					
Min.	D664 or D4739	Oil	1.0	1.0	1.0
Min.	D2896		2.0	2.0	2.0
Water content (dilution) Vol. % max.	D95	Engine	0.30	0.30	0.30
Flash point °C reduction max.	D92	Engine fuel dil.	20.0	20.0	20.0
Fuel dilution vol. % max.	*	Engine	2.5	2.5	2.5
Glycol dilution ppm max.	D 2982	Engine	1000	1000	1000
Iron content ppm Fe max.	**	Engine wear	150	35	150
Copper content ppm Cu max.	**	Engine wear	25	25	30
Sodium content ppm NA Over baseline max.	**	Engine coolant	50	50	50
Boron content ppm B Over baseline max.	**	Engine coolant	20	20	20

* Various methods
** Elemental analyses are conducted using either emission or atomic absorption spectroscopy. Neither method has an ASTM designation.

FIGURE 18-10B

Wear metals elements	Warning limits above recommended values (parts per million)
Iron	250
Lead	25
Chromium	5
Aluminum	5
Tin	50
Silicon	5
Copper	25
Sodium	50
Boron	20

Wear Limits

Typical wear metals found in the oil analysis can indicate areas in the engine that may be wearing prematurely. Figure 18–10b lists typical wear metal elements, both ferrous and nonferrous, that might show up in an oil sample along with the established warning limits above the recommended values in parts per million. Values in excess of the limits are most likely indicative of internal engine problems requiring immediate attention. Such values also suggest that much closer monitoring of the engine condition should be initiated and that corrective action should be taken to identify possible sources of lube oil contamination.

Sources of Wear

Most heavy-duty high-speed engines employ similar base metals in their construction; however, specific makes and models may have different metals in their components. Once the make of engine has been identified, a suitable listing of possible wear metals can be compiled. Figure 18–11 is a chart than can be helpful in locating the source of a particular wear metal from an engine. The types of metals listed are specific to certain engine makes and models, but a similar chart can be constructed for any make of engine. In this example, a simultaneous increase toward the warning values in iron, tin, chromium, and silicon would indicate that the wear metals are most likely due to cylinder kit wear (piston, liner, and piston rings) and that the cause of the wear may very well be linked to airborne dirt bypassing the air cleaner element(s). The finest lapping compound available for a running engine consists of very fine dirt or dust particles mixed with cylinder wall lube oil. The constant up and down rubbing action between the piston rings and cylinder liner provides the ideal lapping surface condition. If oil analysis showed only trace iron increases since the previous oil sample was taken, the cylinder kits are probably not the problem. Careful inspection and analysis of other engine areas would be required to determine what is causing the iron increase.

Electronic Diesels and Reduced Engine Wear

Some transit bus fleets take oil samples approximately every 9500 miles (15,288 km) when the oil is changed. In industry studies of 361 samples of oil from two- and four-stroke cycle engines, both mechanically and electronically controlled, there was a dramatic reduction in wear for engines equipped with electronic controls.

Basically, a tenfold reduction in metallic iron wear occurred in the electronically equipped engines. This finding can be attributed to much better fuel injection control with less washing away of the lubricating oil from the cylinder walls; subsequently, less cylinder wear occurs.

ENGINE LUBE OIL FLOW

All internal combustion engines, gasoline and diesel powered, are equipped with gear-driven oil pumps. The pumps provide pressurized lube oil flow throughout the engine to those parts that require continuous lubrication between their surfaces. The diesel engine has eight basic components of the lube system:

1. Gear-driven oil pump assembly
2. One of more full-flow oil filters
3. Optional bypass lube oil filter(s)
4. Lube oil cooler assembly
5. Pressure regulating system consisting of both a system control pressure valve and an oil pump bypass (safety) valve to dump oil back to the crankcase (oil pan)
6. Oil reservoir generally in the form of an oil pan
7. Dipstick to check the oil level
8. Ventilation system.

The specific plumbing (pipes and hoses) as well as the design of oil pump and distribution of the oil vary slightly in different makes and models of engines. Nevertheless, we can consider the oil flow system to be fairly common in most high-speed heavy-duty diesel engines in use today. Figure 18–12 illustrates pressurized oil flow through a Detroit Diesel electron-

FIGURE 18-11 *Sources of wear metal and lube oil analysis elements. (Courtesy of Detroit Diesel Corporation.)*

Element	Source of element part metallurgy
Aluminum (AL)	Blower (aluminum alloy), camshaft intermediate bearings, turbo bearings and crankshaft thrust bearings
Boron (B)	Supplementary coolant inhibitor additive, lube oil additive
Chromium (Cr)	Piston ring face ("chrome")
Copper (Cu)	Slipper (wrist pin) bushing, connecting rod and crankshaft main bearing matrices, cam follower roller bushings, rocker arm clevis bushings, connecting rod bushings, camshaft thrust washers. Also used in some latter oil additive packages for anti-wear characteristic.
Iron (Fe)	Gray iron cylinder liners, malleable iron pistons, hardened steel camshafts crankshafts, gears. Cast iron induction-hardened rocker arms, valve bridges, alloyed steel cam follower rollers, etc.
Lead (Pb)	Babbitt overlay and alloy matrix of connecting rod and crankshaft main bearings
Silicon (Si)	Print-O-Seal silicon gasket, silicon anti-foam additive in lube oil, silicon dioxide from ingested airborn sand or dust.
Sodium (Na)	Supplementary coolant inhibitor additive, lube oil additive or salt
Tin (Sn)	Piston plate coating (tin), babbitt overlay of connecting rod and crankshaft main bearings.

ically controlled unit injector Series 60 model diesel engine. Although this system has a spin-on bypass filter, this filter was not considered necessary for later model Series 60 engines. The oil flow through this engine system is as follows:

The engine crankshaft-driven gear pump circulates oil through the full-flow filters to an oil cooler and then into the main oil gallery within the cylinder block. From there, oil is distributed to the crankshaft main bearings, the connecting-rod bearings, and the overhead camshaft bearings. Pressurized lube oil passes up through each rifle-drilled con-rod where it lubricates the piston pin and sprays oil to the underside of the piston crown for cooling purposes. If a bypass filter is used, a portion of the pressurized oil is continually bled off and fed through this filter; the oil is then returned to the engine oil pan. Excessive oil pump pressure is controlled by a spring-loaded relief valve within the oil pump body, which directs oil back to the pan when the pressure exceeds approximately 105 psi (725 kPa). Main oil gallery pressure is controlled by a spring-loaded regulator valve that is set to open and dump oil back to the oil pan when pressure exceeds 50 psi (345 kPa). This oil pressure would be normal with an oil temperature of 230°F (110°C), which is typical of an engine operating in service.

Oil also flows to the adjustable idler and bull gear within the front housing of the engine. Oil from the camshaft bearings is then directed to the rocker arm shafts. Each rocker is drilled to supply oil to the valve adjuster screw, valve button, retainer clip, intake and exhaust valve stems, and the fuel injector follower. Oil then drains through passages in the cylinder head and block and back to the oil pan. If the oil cooler becomes plugged, the oil flows from the pump through a restricted passage directly into the main oil gallery. A bypass valve in the filter adaptor opens at aproximately 18 to 21 psi (124 to 145 kPa) to bypass the oil filters if they become clogged or plugged. Pressurized lube oil is also fed to both the engine gear-driven air compressor as well as to the exhaust-gas-driven turbocharger. Oil supplied to the compressor exits through a hole in the housing and into the front gear case where it lubricates the compressor accessory drive gear. A flexible oil line from the oil filter adaptor housing carries pressurized oil to the turbocharger bearings and shaft and is returned to the oil pan through another external line.

Another example of a pressurized lube oil system is shown in Figure 18–13 for a 3176B Caterpillar electronically controlled unit injector engine. Normal oil pressure for this engine at 230°F (110°C) oil temperature is 40 psi (276 kPa). The oil pump on this engine is similar in design to that used by Cummins on its L10/M11 and N14 models: it is an externally mounted

gear-type pump located below the water pump on the front gear train. Pressurized lube oil flow to the major engine components is somewhat similar to that described for the DDC Series 60. In the 3176B, however, a thermostatically controlled valve bypasses the oil cooler when the oil temperature is below 212°F (100°C) to reduce the oil pump load (parasitic losses). This results in an improvement in fuel consumption during warm-up and in cold weather. The oil filtration system gives the user a choice of two optional engine-mounted bypass oil filters: a spin-on paper element or a centrifuge filter with a disposable cartridge. The integral centrifuge bypass filter shown in Figure 18–14 mounts directly to the filter base next to the full-flow filter, thereby eliminating the need for additional lines and mounting hardware. Undercrown piston cooling on the 3176B is similar to that used by Cummins, Mack, and several others; that is, small piston cooling jets are bolted to the block where oil from the main oil gallery is fed to them. A small orifice in the cooling jet pipe is positioned to spray pressurized lube oil to the underside of the piston.

The lubrication system on Caterpillar's larger on-highway truck model, the 3406E electronically controlled unit injector engine, has many of the features of the 3406C PEEC (programmable electronic engine controls). The oil flow channels remain the same in the block and bottom end of the engine. Oil sump capacities, oil change intervals, and recommended oil viscosity are the same as those for the 3406C engine.

OIL PUMPS

The location and design of the oil pump depends on the make and model of the engine. Some typical locations include these:

- Base of the engine block and contained within the oil pan. Manufacturers that locate the oil pump here are Detroit Diesel, Mack, Volvo, Mercedes-Benz, DAF Trucks, Perkins, Rolls-Royce, MAN, Mitsubishi, and Isuzu.
- Externally mounted and gear driven from the backside of the engine gear train front cover: Cummins N14 and Cat 3176B.
- Gear driven from behind the engine gear train front cover: Cummins B, C, and L10 models.

Figure 18–15 illustrates the location of the oil pump pickup screen, inlet pipe, and discharge pipe for a Series 60 DDC model with the engine oil pan removed. The DDC Series 50 oil pump is similar, since it is a four-cylinder version of a 12.7L Series 60. The oil pump is mounted to the underside of the cylinder block and is gear driven from the front end of the

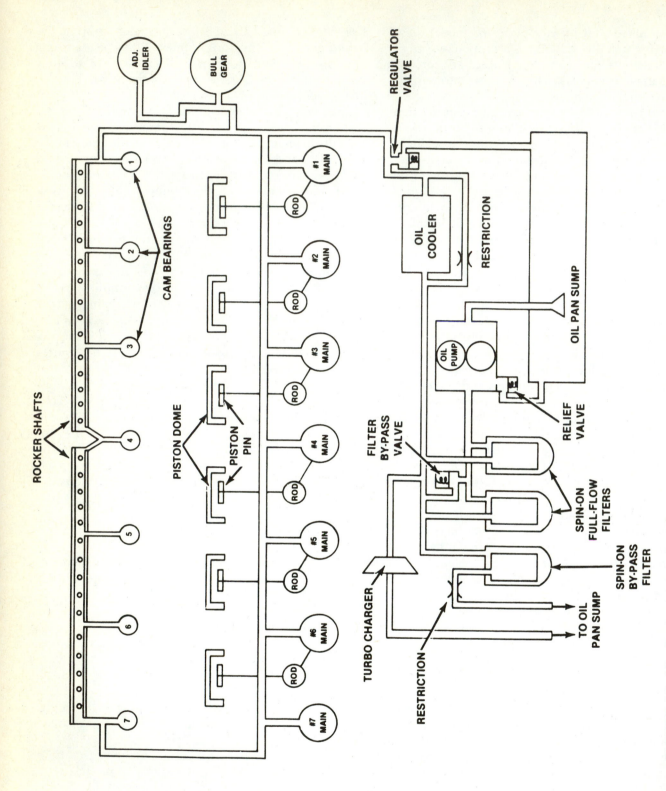

FIGURE 18-12 Engine lube oil flow schematic for a Series 60 four-stroke-cycle DDC electronically controlled diesel engine. (Courtesy of Detroit Diesel Corporation.)

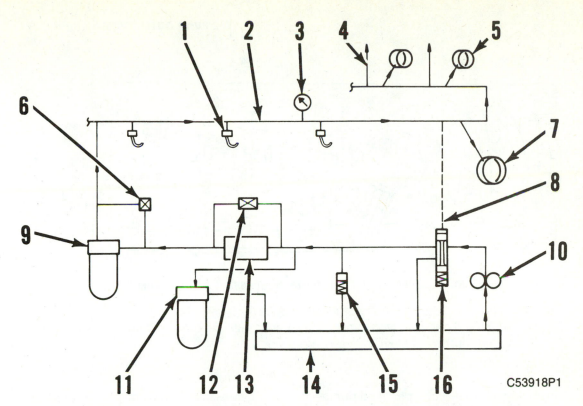

FIGURE 18–13 Engine lube oil flow schematic for a Caterpillar 3176B EUI-controlled engine. 1 = piston cooling jets; 2 = main oil gallery (in cylinder block); 3 = engine oil pressure sensor; 4 = oil flow to valve mechanism; 5 = camshaft journals; 6 = oil filter bypass valve; 7 = main bearings; 8 = signal line; 9 = oil filter (full flow); 10 = oil pump; 11 = bypass oil filter; 12 = oil cooler bypass valve; 13 = oil cooler; 14 = oil pan (sump); 15 = high-pressure relief valve; 16 = oil pump bypass valve. (Courtesy of Caterpillar Inc.)

FIGURE 18–14 Optional centrifuge bypass oil filter assembly available on certain models of Cat engines. (Courtesy of Caterpillar Inc.)

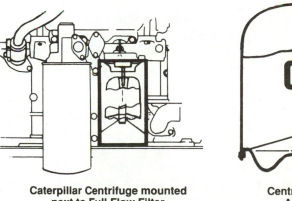

Caterpillar Centrifuge mounted next to Full Flow Filter

Centrifuge Rotor Assembly

crankshaft. An exploded view of the pump, which contains helical gears rotating within a housing, is illustrated in Figure 18–16 along with the relative location and names of the parts. Basically, both the drive and driven gears are pressed onto their respective shafts which are in turn supported inside the pump housing

on two bushings. A plunger-type bypass relief valve (items 12 through 17) is used to bypass oil into the oil pan when the pump pressure exceeds 725 kPa (105 psi).

The oil pump inlet screen shown in Figure 18–15 should be cleaned each time the oil pan is removed for any reason and during major engine overhaul. When

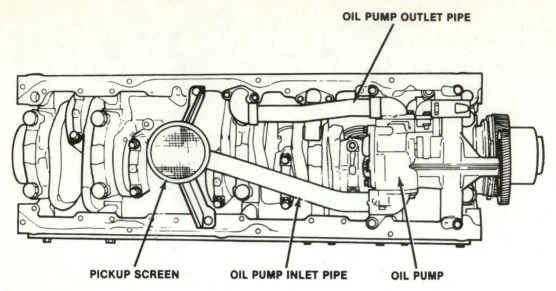

FIGURE 18–15 *View of the underside of a Series 60 four-stroke-cycle engine with the oil pan removed. Note the inlet and outlet pipes to and from the oil pump. (Courtesy of Detroit Diesel Corporation.)*

removing or installing these in-pan types of oil pumps, remember that the gear backlash between the oil-pump-driven gear and the engine crankshaft gear is maintained by shims inserted between the oil pump mounting flange and the engine machined pad. Therefore, when removing the oil pan always note where the shims came from and how many there are. A good practice is to tie or wire these together for reinstallation of the pump at a later time. Overhaul of the oil pump requires complete disassembly, close inspection, and measurement of parts.

Before disassembling the oil pump, always match-mark the housing and covers with a small scribe or center punch to ensure that all reused parts will be reassembled in the same position. Wash all oil pump parts in clean diesel fuel or solvent and dry them with compressed air. Remove all gaskets and seal rings if used. Inspect the shaft support bushings for severe scoring, overheating, and damage. Measure the bushing inside diameter and compare your figure to service manual specs. If the gear teeth contact areas show severe polish or are scored, or the gear backlash exceeds the spec, replace the gears. Gears are generally press fit on the shaft and therefore require a hydraulic press to remove and install them. Worn gears result in low oil pressure which can cause both the main and con-rod bearings to fail. In addition, low oil pressure to the underside of the piston crown from the cooling jets or spray nozzle can cause overheating of the piston crown and eventual failure of the fire ring, piston crown, and/or piston to liner seizure.

Disassemble and inspect the oil pump relief valve for freedom of movement, a weak or broken spring, and a scored or damaged piston; check the bore of the relief valve piston housing for scoring or wear. When a pump is reassembled, always use new gaskets and seals where applicable. Lubricate the drive shaft bushings and associated gears with clean engine oil. You can also coat the bore of the drive gear with a light film of Lubriplate extra heavy gear shield or equivalent. Once the pump has been reassembled and the cover or housing bolts have been installed hand tight, ensure that the pump rotates freely by hand. Any sign of a binding condition would necessitate pump disassembly again to determine the cause. If the pump rotates freely, tighten and torque the cover (housing) bolts to the service manual specs. Then recheck that the pump does in fact still rotate freely by hand.

To install the pump onto the engine, most pumps have locating dowels that serve as guides. Be sure to install any shims that were removed earlier between the mounting feet (flanges) and the engine block; then torque the retaining bolts to spec. Refer to Figure 18–17 and with a dial indicator in position as shown against the tooth of the oil pump drive gear, grasp and rotate the pump backward and forward while noting the reading on the face of the dial gauge. Compare this reading to the service manual specs. Adding selective shims between the pump mounting surface and block increases the gear backlash, while removing some decreases the backlash condition.

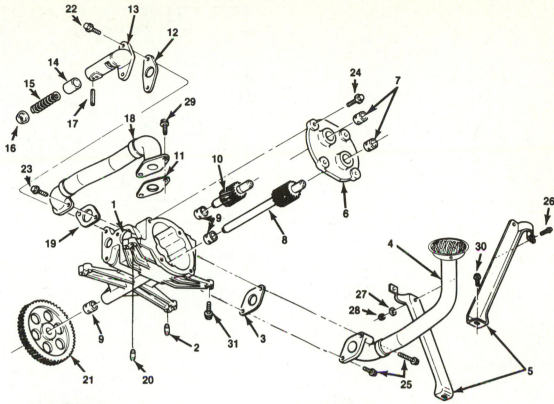

1. **Body, Oil Pump**
2. **Dowel, Oil Pump Locating (Round)**
3. **Gasket, Inlet Pipe-to-Pump**
4. **Pipe and Screen Assembly, Inlet**
5. **Bracket, Inlet Pipe (2)**
6. **Cover, Oil Pump Housing**
7. **Bushing, Oil Pump Cover (2)**
8. **Drive Shaft and Gear Assembly**
9. **Bushing, Oil Pump Housing (3)**
10. **Driven Shaft and Gear Assembly**
11. **Gasket, Outlet Pipe-to-Cylinder Block**
12. **Gasket, Relief Valve-to-Oil Pump**
13. **Body, Relief Valve**
14. **Valve, Relief**
15. **Spring, Relief Valve**
16. **Spring Seat**
17. **Pin, Retaining**
18. **Pipe, Outlet**
19. **Gasket, Outlet Pipe-to-Oil Pump**
20. **Dowel, Oil Pump Locating (Diamond)**
21. **Gear, Oil Pump Drive**
22. **Bolt, Oil Pressure Relief Valve-to-Oil Pump Housing (2)**
23. **Bolt, Outlet Pipe-to-Oil Pump Housing (2)**
24. **Bolt, Oil Pump Cover (4)**
25. **Bolt, Inlet Pipe-to-Pump Body (2)**
26. **Bolt, Screen Bracket-to-Inlet Pipe (2)**
27. **Washer, Screen Bracket-to-Inlet Pipe (2)**
28. **Nut, Screen Bracket-to-Inlet Pipe (2)**
29. **Bolt, Outlet Pipe-to-Cylinder Block (2)**
30. **Bolt, Inlet Pipe Bracket-to-Cylinder Block (2)**
31. **Bolt Pump Body to Block**

FIGURE 18–16 Exploded view of the oil pump components for a Series 60 engine model. (Courtesy of Detroit Diesel Corporation.)

CAUTION: It is important that the shims underneath each mounting foot (flange) contain the same stack-up; otherwise, the pump will not sit square (level) on the engine block.

Too much backlash can result in noisy pump operation and eventual gear damage, not only between the engine crank and oil pump drive gear but also within the oil pump body. Drive gear tooth breakage can eventually result with this condition. Insufficient gear backlash usually results in a whine during operation and can result in overheating of the crank to pump gear,

which leads to gear tooth failure. Make certain that any inlet and outlet pipes and the pump pickup screen have been cleaned thoroughly before they are installed. After engine overhaul and prior to start-up, refer to Figure 18–42 and prelube the oil system as described.

Figure 18–18 illustrates another type of oil pump assembly that is accessed by removing the front timing cover of the engine gear train. This is common to the design used by Cummins on its B and C series engines and is known as a *gerotor*-type pump. The word is derived from a combination of the words *gear* and

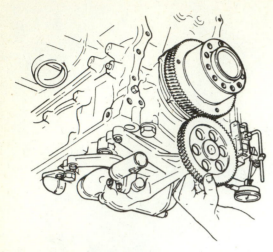

FIGURE 18–17 *Using a dial indicator to check the gear backlash between the engine crankshaft gear and the oil pump drive gear for a Series 60 engine. (Courtesy of Detroit Diesel Corporation.)*

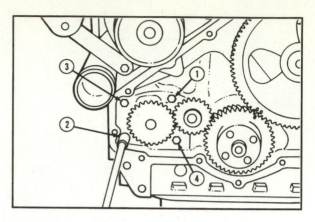

FIGURE 18–18 *Engine front timing cover removed to show the location of the retaining bolts to access the gerotor-type lube oil pump for Cummins model B and C series engines. (Courtesy of Cummins Engine Company, Inc.)*

rotor. Checks on this pump include inspecting the housing and gerotor drive for scoring, damage, and wear. As shown in Figure 18–19, you should also measure the clearance of the gerotor planetary (star-shaped inner components) to the body bore with a feeler gauge. In addition, lay a straightedge across the top of the housing as shown in Figure 18–20 and check the clearance of the gerotor drive/gerotor planetary to port plate for wear. Refer to the service manual specs for these clearances.

Figure 18–21 shows an externally mounted oil pump commonly used by Cummins on its N14 (855 cu in.) inline six-cylinder heavy-duty models. The pump is located on the backside of the engine front cover, which would be on your right-hand side when facing the engine from the front. Figure 18–21 shows the pump location and its drive gear, which is gear train driven, as well as the main oil pressure regulator valve. A lube oil suction tube extends from the underside of the oil pump and is bolted to the oil pan as shown in Figure 18–22. This diagram also illustrates a DFC (demand flow cooling) line, a system employed by Cummins to regulate oil flow and oil cooling only on demand rather than continuously at maximum capacity. Advantages of this system are better control of oil pressure and temperature. It also reduces the parasitic power losses of the oil pump to improve fuel economy. The DFC signal line shown in Figure 18–22 is connected between the main oil rifle (gallery) and the internal oil pump pressure regulator. When the main oil rifle pressure exceeds 40 psi (276 kPa) the pump regulator valve is opened and dumps oil back to the oil pan to relieve the pump workload.

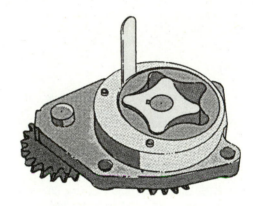

FIGURE 18–19 *Checking the clearance between the gerotor planetary and the body with a feeler gauge. (Courtesy of Cummins Engine Company, Inc.)*

FIGURE 18–20 *Using a small steel straightedge and feeler gauge to check the clearance of the gerotor drive/gerotor planetary and port plate end play. (Courtesy of Cummins Engine Company, Inc.)*

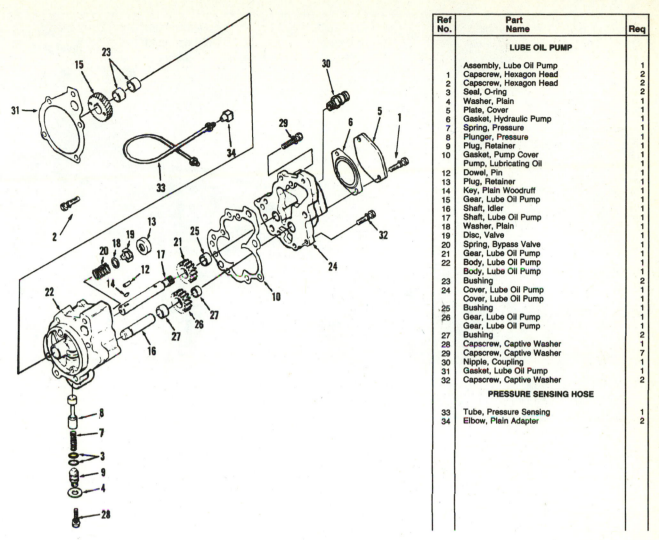

Ref No.	Part Name	Req
	LUBE OIL PUMP	
	Assembly, Lube Oil Pump	1
1	Capscrew, Hexagon Head	2
2	Capscrew, Hexagon Head	2
3	Seal, O-ring	2
4	Washer, Plain	1
5	Plate, Cover	1
6	Gasket, Hydraulic Pump	1
7	Spring, Pressure	1
8	Plunger, Pressure	1
9	Plug, Retainer	1
10	Gasket, Pump Cover	1
	Pump, Lubricating Oil	1
12	Dowel, Pin	1
13	Plug, Retainer	1
14	Key, Plain Woodruff	1
15	Gear, Lube Oil Pump	1
16	Shaft, Idler	1
17	Shaft, Lube Oil Pump	1
18	Washer, Plain	1
19	Disc, Valve	1
20	Spring, Bypass Valve	1
21	Gear, Lube Oil Pump	1
22	Body, Lube Oil Pump	1
	Body, Lube Oil Pump	1
23	Bushing	2
24	Cover, Lube Oil Pump	1
	Cover, Lube Oil Pump	1
25	Bushing	1
26	Gear, Lube Oil Pump	1
	Gear, Lube Oil Pump	1
27	Bushing	2
28	Capscrew, Captive Washer	1
29	Capscrew, Captive Washer	7
30	Nipple, Coupling	1
31	Gasket, Lube Oil Pump	1
32	Capscrew, Captive Washer	2
	PRESSURE SENSING HOSE	
33	Tube, Pressure Sensing	1
34	Elbow, Plain Adapter	2

FIGURE 18–21 Oil pump details for a Cummins N14 engine model. (Courtesy of Cummins Engine Company, Inc.)

Scavenge Oil Pumps

In engine applications that are subjected to steep oil pan operating angles, such as in off-highway equipment or certain marine models, it is necessary to employ a double oil pump arrangement to ensure that the engine oil pump pickup screen is never starved temporarily for oil. Figure 18–23 illustrates the oil pump inlet screen and the scavenging pump inlet screen located on the underside of the engine with the oil pan(s) removed. The scavenging pump shown in Figure 18–23 is mounted in tandem with the regular engine oil pump and is used in conjunction with a deep-style oil pan that has a shallow reservoir at one end. Oil that flows to the shallow end of the pan during inclined engine operation is picked up and transferred to the deep end by the action of the scavenge pump gears. The regular engine oil pump then picks

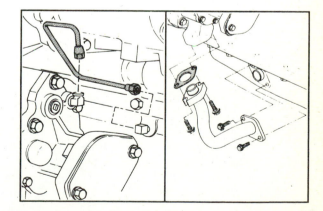

FIGURE 18–22 Location of an N14 engine lube oil pump suction tube and a DFC (demand flow cooling) line. (Courtesy of Cummins Engine Company, Inc.)

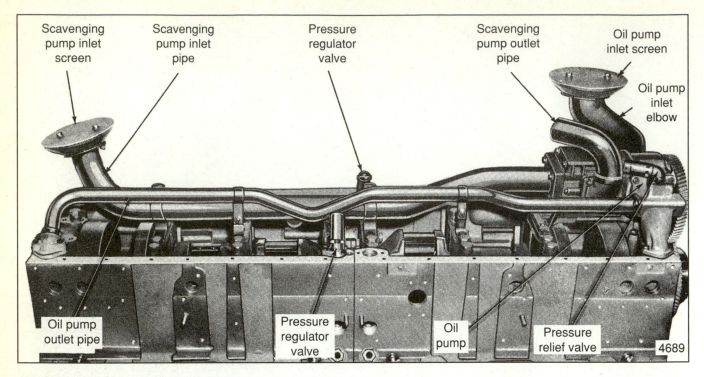

FIGURE 18–23   *Typical oil pump and scavenge pump mounting and associated piping for a 149 series DDC engine. (Courtesy of Detroit Diesel Corporation.)*

up this oil and distributes it throughout the engine. Figure 18–24 illustrates the details of a combination scavenge and engine lube oil pump assembly. The oil pump drive gear is driven from the crankshaft-mounted gear. Inspection of this type of a pump follows the same as that for a single oil pump. This system is used by Detroit Diesel on its 149 series engines which are available in V8, V12, V16, and V20 models. Both the V12 and V16 models employ a minimum of four oil filters and two oil coolers since the V12 models consist of two V6s bolted together, while the V16 uses two V8s bolted together. The latest V20 model consists of two V6s and a V8 in the middle bolted together.

OIL FILTERS

Oil filters are a very important part of any lube oil system because good filtration increases engine service life. All diesel engines today employ one or more full-flow filters, and all of the circulated oil from the oil pump is directed through the filter(s). Some engines also use a *bypass* type of lube oil filter. This filter is designed to provide finer filtration of the oil than does a full-flow type. It receives its oil through a restricted fitting so that only about 10% of the oil passes through at a given time.

Filter performance is based on the optimum combination of filter micron ratings, filter capacity, and the integrity of the filter element used. Depending on the type of filter used and the make, most full-flow lube filters have ratings between 30 and 45 microns; bypass models are designed to filter out dirt products down to approximately 10 microns. Remember a *micron* is 1/1,000,000th of a meter or 0.00003937 in. On engines that use full-flow filters and no bypass filter assembly, a 25 to 28 micron rating is often quoted. Other engines demand a micron rating of as low as 12 at a 98% single oil pass efficiency.

Although all oil filters appear alike, they differ in construction, type of material used, and micron ratings. Some engine manufacturers caution against using certain types of filters. For example, DDC warns against using filters such as the AC-PF911L or equivalent model in its four-cycle series 50 or 60 models because the filter is made from a fiberglass medium, which is unsuitable for these electronically controlled diesel engines.

Figure 18–25 illustrates a typical full-flow oil filter of the *spin-on* type, although some engines still use the more robust *shell and element* style shown in Figure 18–26. Oil under pressure flows into the top of the filter housing and totally surrounds the filter. The filtering medium can be a treated and pleated paper material similar in design to both a fuel filter and an air filter. The actual material used for filter construction can

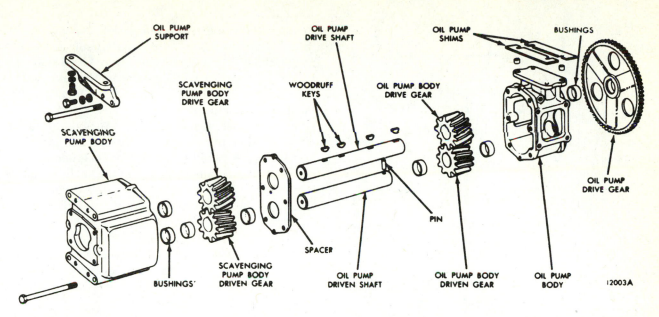

FIGURE 18–24 *Details of a combination lube oil pump and scavenge pump assembly for a 149 Series two-stroke-cycle engine. (Courtesy of Detroit Diesel Corporation.)*

vary. An organic (cellulose) filtering medium is commonly used, but a synthetic fiberglass material is also used in some filters. As the pressurized oil forces its way through the filtering medium, the small dirt particles are trapped in the element. The clean oil enters the central passage within the filter assembly and flows out of the filter adaptor and onto the oil cooler assembly. Item 1 in Figure 18–25 is a nonreturn valve, item 2 is the paper element, and item 3 is the pressure relief valve to allow oil to bypass the filter when it is clogged or plugged. Unfiltered oil would then pass onto the engine oil cooler assembly. In some engine makes the oil flow from the pump is directed first to the *oil cooler* before it is routed to the filter(s).

Many large engines that run 24 hours a day are equipped with tandem lube and fuel filter arrangements, which consist of any number of filters connected together. These are generally referred to as *duplex* filter systems. These types of filtration systems are arranged so that a main control valve lever can be rotated to direct lube oil through one set of oil filters while the other ones are being changed and the engine is still running. At the completion of the filter change, the control valve lever can be moved to the opposite position and the second set of filters can be changed while the engine is running.

Oil Filter Maintenance

With spin-on filters, it is a fairly straightforward job to use either a strap wrench or a 12-point socket on the base of some models to remove the filter. Figure 18–27

illustrates a heavy-duty high-speed engine filter pack assembly mounted to and bolted on the side of the engine block. Inspect used filters to determine if heavy sludge deposits are evident. This is easier to do on a shell and element type than on a spin-on model. If in doubt, simply use a cutting tool to open up the spin-on type, or use a hacksaw to cut the spin-on filter open. Sludge is an indication that the oil detergency has been exhausted; therefore, a shorter lube and filter change period is required.

Always clean the filter adaptor with a clean, lint-free cloth. Fill the spin-on filter two-thirds full with clean engine oil before installing it. This ensures that oil will reach the bearing surfaces of the engine quickly. Also, if you don't do this on electronically controlled diesel engines, a faulty low oil pressure code may be logged into the ECM memory. Lightly coat the new spin-on oil filter seal with clean engine oil and thread it onto the housing. All spin-on filters have a label that indicates the degree of tightness required once the seal touches the adaptor head. Follow these directions, which are normally somewhere between one-half and two-thirds of a turn. Avoid overtightening a spin-on filter since this can buckle the housing or crack the filter adaptor and/or make it extremely hard to remove at the next service interval.

If the oil filter is of the shell and element type as illustrated in Figure 18–26, remove the drain plug from the base of the shell to drain the oil into a container. Loosen off the center stud bolt to withdraw the shell and element. Discard the dirty filter element.

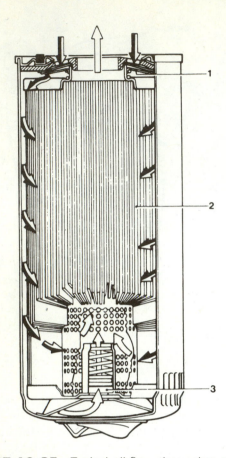

FIGURE 18–25 Typical oil flow through a spin-on type of full-flow lube oil filter assembly. 1 = nonreturn valve; 2 = treated and pleated paper element filter; 3 = pressure relief valve which opens when the filter is plugged allowing oil to bypass the filter and enter the lube system unfiltered. (Courtesy of DAF Trucks, Eindhoven, Netherlands.)

Remove the center stud and gasket. Save the gasket unless it appears to require replacement. Remove the nut on the full-flow filter center stud. Use a sharp pick to remove the large O-ring seal from the filter adaptor. Install the new seal which comes in the filter box (bag). Wash the filter shell in clean solvent and clean the adaptor or base. Reassemble the parts that you have removed; then install a new filter over the center stud and within the shell. Note that overtightening of the center stud can cause damage to the shell or adaptor; refer to the service manual for the recommended torque on the stud. Install the drain plug back into the shell and tighten it accordingly. On filter models that allow access to the filter bypass valve, as shown in both Figure 18–26 and in Figure 18–27, remove the plug and gasket and withdraw the spring and bypass valve. Wash all of the parts and dry them with compressed air. Worn parts should be replaced.

With either a spin-on or shell and element filter, start and run the engine at low rpm for a short time while checking for any signs of oil leaks from the filter area. After at least a 5 to 10 minute drain back period, remove the oil pan dipstick and recheck the oil level.

Tattle Tale Filter

One of the problems that many fleets and equipment operators face under the environmental laws now in place is the disposal of used engine oils and equipment fluids as well as used filter assemblies. To avoid the problem of having to dispose of used filters, the Racor Division of the Parker Hannifin Corporation offer a filter-less method of trapping dirt and contaminants through the *Tattle Tale filter* assembly, which is capable of being used for lube oil, hydraulic fluid, transmission oil, power steering, and coolant systems.

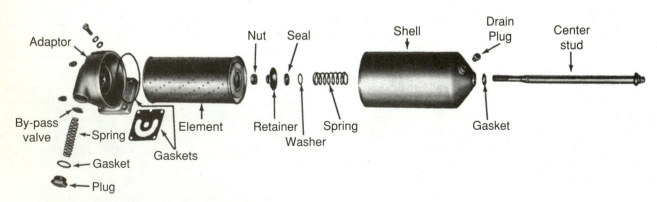

FIGURE 18–26 Details of a full-flow oil filter of the shell and element type with a replaceable filter. Shell must be cleaned in solvent and dried at filter replacement. (Courtesy of Detroit Diesel Corporation.)

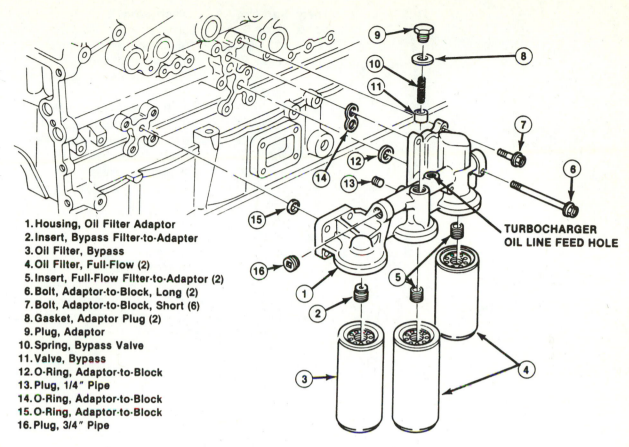

1. Housing, Oil Filter Adaptor
2. Insert, Bypass Filter-to-Adapter
3. Oil Filter, Bypass
4. Oil Filter, Full-Flow (2)
5. Insert, Full-Flow Filter-to-Adaptor (2)
6. Bolt, Adaptor-to-Block, Long (2)
7. Bolt, Adaptor-to-Block, Short (6)
8. Gasket, Adaptor Plug (2)
9. Plug, Adaptor
10. Spring, Bypass Valve
11. Valve, Bypass
12. O-Ring, Adaptor-to-Block
13. Plug, 1/4" Pipe
14. O-Ring, Adaptor-to-Block
15. O-Ring, Adaptor-to-Block
16. Plug, 3/4" Pipe

TURBOCHARGER OIL LINE FEED HOLE

FIGURE 18–27 *Series 60 engine DDEC I and early DDEC II lube oil filter adaptor, bypass valve, and related parts. Later DDEC II and all DDEC III models use only two oil filters as shown in Figure 1–1a. (Courtesy of Detroit Diesel Corporation.)*

Figure 18–28 illustrates the construction and arrangement of the Tattle Tale device. The unit consists of an adapter that can be installed onto the current engine or equipment filter mounting area. The Tattle Tale is available in varying flow rate sizes of 6 gpm (23 L), 16 gpm (61 L), 20 gpm (76 L), and 45 gpm (170 L) as well as in differing micron filtration ratings: 28 micron (0.0011 in.), 40 micron (0.0016 in.), 60 micron (0.0024 in.), and 115 micron (0.0045 in.).

The Tattle Tale system has full-flow units that contain a reusable, stainless steel wire cloth filter between die-cast aluminum housings. The filter is designed to trap damaging solids and is available in four micron ratings. The draining, crushing, accounting, and related liabilities associated with disposal of used filters are eliminated with this permanent filter design. The wire cloth filter is also effective as a visual diagnostic tool to monitor potential engine wear. Cleanup of the wire cloth filter is easy. The filter can be soft brushed in solvent or cleaned in a parts washer, then reinserted between the permanent housings. The standard oil filter is replaced by an adapter that spins onto the filter header. Adapters are available to fit any engine. Some housings feature two inlets and outlets for flexible installation and SAE O-ring ports. When the wire cloth filter reaches its restriction capacity, the system goes into a bypass mode and the Tattle Tale light signals the operator there is a need for service. Frequency of filter cleaning is determined by the contamination levels present in the fluid. (The cleaning interval may be more frequent when first installed.) The units are rated by the flow rate of the fluid.

Service of the Tattle Tale is a simple procedure as illustrated in Figure 18–29, which also shows the assembled unit and plumbing.

OIL TEMPERATURE

The two major functions of engine lube oil are to cool and lubricate, so the operating temperature of the oil

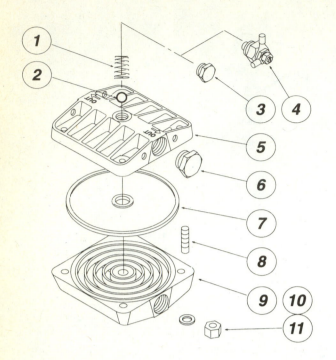

Item	Part No.	Description	Qty.
1	46020	Spring, 9" series	1
2	LFS RK90BB	Check Ball, 1 1/16" diameter	1
3	46021	Plug/Gasket, 9" series	1
4	LFS RK9LS	Light Sensor Switch/Gasket*	1
5	46025	Housing, Outlet	1
6	46030	Port Plug, #16/Bracket Bolt Kit	2
7	9028WCF	28 Micron Stainless Steel Filter	1
	9040WCF	40 Micron Stainless Steel Filter	1
	9060WCF	60 Micron Stainless Steel Filter	1
	90115WCF	115 Micron Stainless Steel Filter	1
8	LFS RK90SK	Stud, 5/8"–18 X 2 1/8"	4
9	46024	Housing, Inlet	1
11	46028	Washer	4
12	46029	Nut, 5/8"–18	4
13	46026	Mounting Bracket (not shown)	1
14	LFS 90MFK	9" Optional Multi–filter Kit (See Accessories for illustration)	1

*Do not use when filtering gasoline or volatile fluids.
Refer to the Accessories Section for fittings, hose information, adapters and optional accessories.

FIGURE 18–28 Construction and arrangement of a Tattle Tale filter unit. (Courtesy of Parker Hannifin Corporation, Racor Division.)

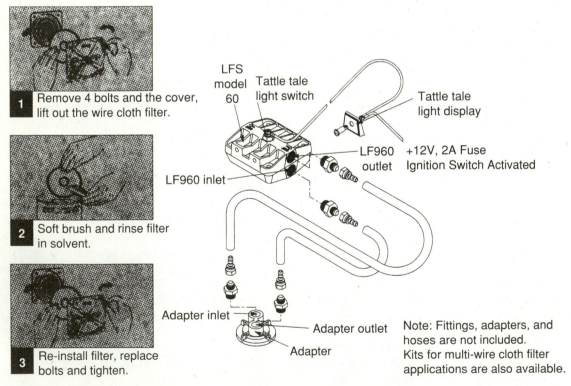

1 Remove 4 bolts and the cover, lift out the wire cloth filter.

2 Soft brush and rinse filter in solvent.

3 Re-install filter, replace bolts and tighten.

LFS model 60 Tattle tale light switch

Tattle tale light display

LF960 outlet

+12V, 2A Fuse Ignition Switch Activated

LF960 inlet

Adapter inlet

Adapter outlet

Adapter

Note: Fittings, adapters, and hoses are not included. Kits for multi-wire cloth filter applications are also available.

FIGURE 18–29 Installation hookup for a Tattle Tale filter assembly. (Courtesy of Parker Hannifin Corporation, Racor Division.)

must be kept within prescribed limits. If the oil is too cold, it will not flow freely. If the oil is too hot, it cannot support the bearing loads, it cannot dissipate and carry away the heat generated between moving parts, and it may result in too great an oil flow. Consequently, oil pressure may drop below acceptable limits, oil consumption may become excessive, and crankshaft and con-rod bearing damage may result. In addition, the cooling oil fed to the underside of the piston crown may be unable to adequately cool this area, so the piston overheats. This can cause rings to stick in their grooves and possibly break up, score the liner, and lead to eventual siezure. The piston crown may also overheat and suffer damage.

On electronically controlled diesel engines such as those used by DDC, Caterpillar, Cummins, Volvo, and Mack, an oil temperature sensor sends a signal to the engine ECM when an oil overtemperature condition occurs. A trouble code is logged in computer memory for retrieval by the service technician at a later date. More importantly, a yellow warning light on the instrument panel is illuminated or a digital readout monitor, on engines so equipped, indicates to the operator that a hot-oil condition had been detected. Thus, the operator can cut back on speed and load to reduce the overtemperature condition. Since the ECM engine protective system is usually programmed to monitor out-of-parameter conditions, an automatic engine *power-down feature* may be activated based on the engine being used and the degree of oil overtemperature condition. If the oil temperature reaches a preprogrammed maximum level, the ECM illuminates a *red* warning light on the instrument panel and/or a buzzer, and the engine automatically shuts off within a 30 second time period to prevent serious damage. This engine shutoff temperature varies in different makes and models of engines, but generally it is somewhere between 251° and 260°F (122° to 127°C).

Most heavy equipment and on- and off-highway trucks contain an oil temperature gauge set within the instrument cluster. The normal full-load operating temperature on an engine depends on the make and model; usually the range is 30° to 40°F (10° to 15°C) higher than the engine coolant-out temperature at the thermostat. Therefore, an engine with a steady engine coolant operating temperature of 195° to 200°F (90.5° to 93°C) should have an oil temperature within the range of approximately 225° to 235°F (107° to 113°C). The difference in temperature between the coolant and oil is referred to as the *water-to-oil differential*. The maximum allowable safe operating temperature for engine oil is generally 250°F (121°C); however, each engine manufacturer lists the allowable limits for its particular make and model of engines. Keep in mind that the lower the engine speed and load, the lower will be the engine oil temperature.

LUBE OIL COOLERS

Engine lube oil coolers vary in physical size and location in different engines. Figure 18–30 shows a typical location of an oil cooler in a heavy-duty high-speed electronically controlled diesel engine. Note the tube and hose connection from the base of the water pump to direct pressurized coolant flow to and through the oil cooler and into the engine block area.

Oil Cooler Types
In oil coolers in heavy-duty diesel engines, generally engine coolant surrounds the cooler assembly to extract the dissipated heat from the hotter running oil. However, in air-cooled diesel engines (such as many of the Deutz-KHD models) an airflow-cooled type of oil cooler is employed. Usually it is located within the cover (housing) area that is used to direct the engine cooling fan airflow to and around the individual cylinder barrels, which are finned similar to a motorcycle engine cylinder barrel. Two types of oil coolers are common in heavy-duty diesel engines:

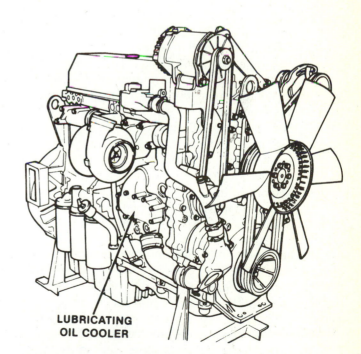

LUBRICATING OIL COOLER

FIGURE 18–30 *Location of the engine lube oil cooler for a Series 60 DDC engine model. Later model DDEC II and all DDEC III units employ an oil cooler mounted at an angle as shown in Figure 1–1a. (Courtesy of Detroit Diesel Corporation.)*

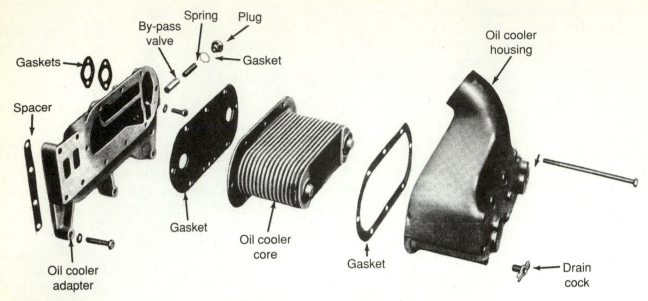

FIGURE 18–31   Details of a plate-type oil cooler assembly. (Courtesy of Detroit Diesel Corporation.)

1. The plate type, which is sometimes referred to as a cellular type, is illustrated in Figure 18–31. This oil cooler can be used for an engine or hydraulic marine gear cooler. Chapter 19 describes a marine gear oil cooler located within or at the base of the cooling system expansion tank.

2. The tube type, which usually requires more space, is illustrated in Figure 18–32. Note in this diagram that both an engine oil cooler and a powershift transmission cooler are cooled by engine coolant flow. On some applications, you may find only an engine oil cooler. On some lighter-duty automotive and truck applications, an automatic transmission oil cooler is assembled into the bottom tank of the radiator with steel lines carrying the fluid into and out of the cooler from the transmission case.

On marine applications, either of these two types of oil coolers can be used. Both the hydraulic marine gear and the engine oil can be cooled by fresh engine coolant circulating through the respective coolers. On some larger marine applications, raw sea water can be employed to cool the various operating equipment fluids.

The plate-type oil cooler shown in Figure 18–31 consists of a series of plates constructed with a space between the plates to allow engine coolant to circulate. The oil flows internally within each plate, which is constructed somewhat like corrugated cardboard. This allows the oil to spread over a greater cross-sectional

surface area for improved cooling efficiency. The number of plates depends on the size of engine and its horsepower rating; the number must be adequate to handle the generated heat load of the oil. Inlet and outlet oil passages are provided in the cooler. Some models are marked I/L and O/L to identify the passages. Identification is important because if the oil cooler is reassembled backwards, the cooler will be reverse flushed and contaminated dirt particles can enter the engine. Always match-mark a cooler core before removing it so it will be reinstalled in the same flow direction! In both types of oil coolers, if the cooler becomes clogged a bypass relief valve (which is assembled into the cooler housing) is designed to open so that engine oil under pressure can still flow to the engine main bearings, and so forth.

The tube-type oil cooler is constructed of a nest of tubes mounted into two end support plates, and the core assembly is mounted inside a housing. Figure 18–33 illustrates that the coolant water enters one end of the oil cooler, flows through the nest of tubes, and exits at the opposite end. The engine oil enters at the top of the cooler housing and is forced to spiral its way around the outside of the tubes by the insertion of baffles within the housing. This causes the hot oil to dissipate its heat more efficiently to the cooler tubes. Note also that to increase cooler efficiency, water enters at the end opposite that for the oil. If the oil were directed into the same end as the water, they would both flow in the same direction and less heat would be extracted from the oil.

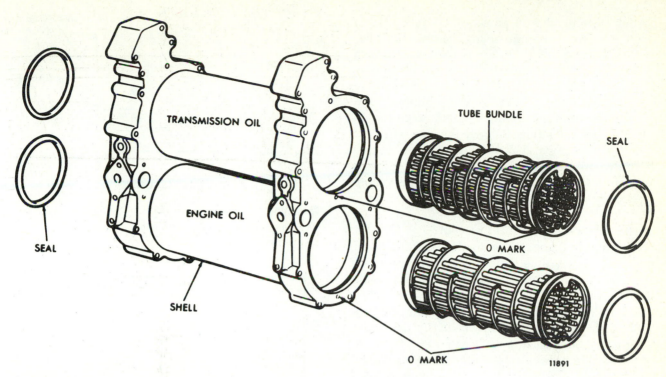

FIGURE 18–32 Tandem-mounted tube-type lube oil coolers (removable bundles) for an engine and powershift transmission arrangement. (Courtesy of Detroit Diesel Corporation.)

Cleaning Oil Cooler Cores

Clean oil cooler cores only if the engine has *not* experienced a main or con-rod bearing failure. *Do not* reuse an oil cooler core after an engine bearing failure, because there is no practical method to clean such a core. Metal particles that may have circulated through the lube system may remain in the cooler core and cause engine damage.

Do not allow dirt or gasket material to enter the oil passageways when cleaning the oil cooler and the cylinder block surface. Work in an open or well-ventilated area and use safety breathing equipment.

Clean the oil passages in the core of a plate-type cooler by circulating a solution of 1, 1, 1-trichloroethane through the passages with a force pump. If sludge has hardened, or if the oil passages are badly clogged, circulate an alkaline cleaning solution through the core and flush it with clean, hot water. To effectively clean the core of a tube-type oil cooler, use a set of long, narrow cleaning brushes to ream out each tube. Alternatively, remove and replace the bypass valve assembly with a long tube connected between the front and rear end castings of the cooler. Seal both the oil inlet and outlet to the filter with fabricated steel covers and gaskets. Attach a steel plate with a compressed air fitting to the oil outlet in the cooler front cover. Stand the

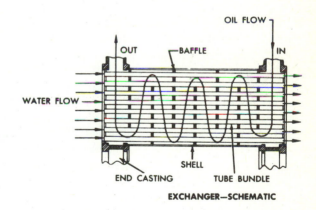

FIGURE 18–33 Typical lube oil flow through a tube-type oil cooler. (Courtesy of Detroit Diesel Corporation.)

oil cooler on its end so that the internal baffles inside the shell are in a horizontal position. Suspend the oil cooler in a barrel so that as the sludge is expelled it is trapped in the barrel rather than blowing all over. Fill the oil cooler with a cleaning solvent and apply air pressure as recommended by the engine manufacturer (this can vary between 60 and 100 psi, 414 to 690 kPa). Repeat the same procedure by reversing the cleaning solvent flow several times until it appears that the system is clean.

After cleaning the oil passages, clean the water side of the oil cooler by immersing the core in a solution of one-half pound (0.226 kg) of oxalic acid to each 2.5 U.S. gallons (9.5 L) of a solution composed of one-third muriatic acid and two-thirds water. The cleaning action takes between 30 and 60 seconds. Bubbling and foaming will occur as soon as you submerge the oil cooler core in the solution. Remove the core when the bubbling action stops and flush the oil cooler core thoroughly with clean, hot water. After cleaning the oil cooler core and blowing it dry with compressed air, dip the cooler core in light oil.

Pressure Checking the Oil Cooler

The oil cooler should be checked for leaks during major overhaul, or at any time that lube oil appears in the engine coolant and the oil cooler core is suspected as the culprit. Figure 18–34 illustrates the method to use when checking a plate-type oil cooler core for leakage. Use a suitable steel test plate as shown bolted to the cooler core with a rubber gasket in between for effective sealing. Attach an air hose to the plate and submerge the oil cooler assembly into a suitably large container filled with hot water—approximately 180° to 200°F (82° to 93°C). Refer to the engine service manual for the recommended air pressure to use; normally, it is about 75 to 100 psi (517 to 690 kPa) for plate-type oil coolers. Any leaks will be indicated by air bubbles emanating from the core. Replace a leaking oil cooler core.

Figure 18–35 illustrates the method for pressure checking a tube-type oil cooler core. Visually inspect the cooler core housing and bypass filter head for any signs of cracks or damage. If an oil cooler test kit bracket unit is available from the engine manufacturer, mount and bolt it to the end of the oil cooler core as shown in the diagram. As an alternative, use a rubber gasket and suitable steel plate bolted to the head end of the cooler core and drilled and tapped to take a compressed air fitting. The test water should be preheated to between 180° and 200°F (82° to 93°C) to allow expansion of the cooler core similar to what might exist in a running engine. Apply approximately 414 kPa (60 psi) to the test plate adaptor. If any leaks are indicated by the presence of air bubbles, replace the oil cooler core.

REGULATING AND RELIEF VALVES

All lube oil systems are equipped with a number of oil pressure valves. A bypass relief valve is normally found in the lube oil filter, the oil cooler, and the oil pump assemblies. The relief valve in the oil filter and the cooler is designed to open when a predetermined restriction to oil flow occurs. This permits engine oil to

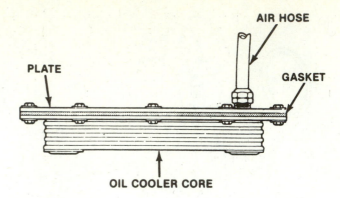

FIGURE 18–34 Preparing a plate-type oil cooler for pressure checking. (Courtesy of Detroit Diesel Corporation.)

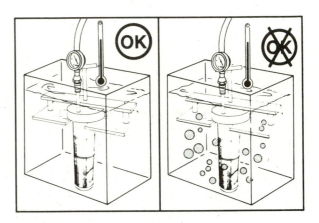

FIGURE 18–35 Submerging a tubular-type oil cooler core into a container of heated water to check for signs of air bubbles from the compressed air supply. (Courtesy of Cummins Engine Company, Inc.)

bypass the plugged system and direct either unfiltered or uncooled oil through to the main oil gallery (rifle). In addition to these valves, a main oil pressure regulating valve and high-pressure relief valve are required. These are generally located on the underside of the engine block and within the oil pan area.

The various regulating and relief valves provide stabilized lube oil pressure in the engine at all speeds, regardless of the oil temperature. The regulating valve controls the designed operating pressure within the main oil gallery, or rifle, of the engine. For example, this pressure may be set to 50 psi (345 kPa), while the relief valve is set to a much higher pressure, usually in the region of 100 psi (690 kPa), and is used to bypass excess oil pressure to the oil pan. The relief valve usually operates in conditions of cold engine start-up in low-ambient-temperature conditions when the oil tends to be thicker and higher initial pressures are created. In addition, if the regulator valve becomes stuck

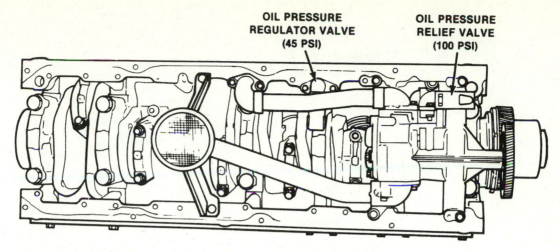

FIGURE 18–36 *Location of the lube oil pressure regulator and oil pressure relief valves on a Series 60 engine model. (Courtesy of Detroit Diesel Corporation.)*

closed, the relief valve limits the maximum oil pressure developed within the lube system.

Figures 18–12 and 18–13, which illustrated oil flow through two typical engine lube systems, show the location of the various control valves within the system. Figures 18–16 and 18–21 illustrate the location of the oil pump pressure relief valve for their respective systems, and Figure 18–23 shows the location of the main pressure regulator valve for a 12V-149 DDC engine model. The built-in bypass valve for both an oil filter and a lube oil cooler can be seen, respectively, in Figures 18–26 and 18–31. The location of the oil pressure regulating and relief valves for a DDC Series 60 electronically controlled diesel engine can be seen in Figure 18–36. Note that the relief valve on 1991 and later models is located beside the outlet flow from the oil pump tube at the No. 4 main bearing cap. The regulating valve is situated at the end of a vertically drilled passage in the cylinder block, opposite the No. 3 main bearing cap located on the oil cooler side that connects with the main cylinder block oil gallery.

In many engines, both the oil pressure regulating valve and relief valves use the same casting and component parts. They differ only in the location of the retaining pin as illustrated in Figure 18–37, although there may also be a slightly different bypass opening machined into the side of the housing. With the retaining pin inserted into hole A, the length of the compressed spring holding the valve closed is longer than it would be if the pin were inserted into hole B. The spring is shorter and stronger with the pin in hole B and requires a higher oil pressure acting on the piston valve to cause it to open. In this example for DDC Series 50 and 60 engines, with the pin in hole A the valve would open at approximately 45 psi

(310 kPa), whereas with the pin in hole B the valve would open at approximately 100 psi (690 kPa).

Service of the oil pressure regulating and relief valves is normally not required until major engine overhaul. Service may also be necessary, however, if the lube system is being inspected and repaired during the service life of the engine due to conditions of low oil pressure, which could be caused by one or both of these valves being stuck open.

Valve Inspection

Once the oil has been drained from the system, remove the oil pan to access the regulator and relief valves. On externally mounted oil pumps such as the one shown in Figure 18–21 for a Cummins 14L engine model, the regulator valve can be removed without taking the oil pump off. However, the oil pump does require removal and disassembly to access the internal relief valve.

During inspection of these valves clean all of the components in fuel oil and dry them with compressed air. Carefully inspect the spring for both its *free* and *compressed* length as you would inspect a valve spring. Refer to the service manual for specifications. Replace the spring if it is weak or shows signs of fretting (high polish marks on the coils) or if the coils are off square when you stand the spring on its end (vertically). Also, replace a spring that shows severe pitting or if any of the coils are broken. Closely inspect the valve bore for signs of scoring or damage; this condition can usually be remedied with fine emery cloth. Check the valve body itself for signs of scoring, wear, or damage. The valve must slide freely within its bore to function correctly. A badly scored or damaged valve or bore requires installation of a new regulator or relief valve.

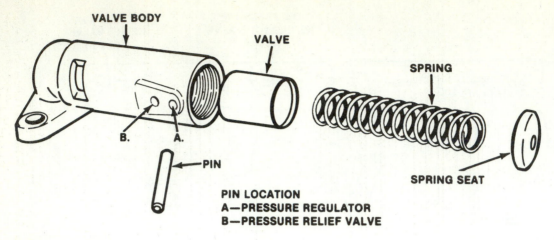

VALVE BODY

VALVE

SPRING

B.   **A.**

PIN

SPRING SEAT

PIN LOCATION
A—PRESSURE REGULATOR
B—PRESSURE RELIEF VALVE

FIGURE 18–37 *Details and relative location of parts of oil pressure regulator and relief valves. (Courtesy of Detroit Diesel Corporation.)*

ENGINE OIL PANS

Automotive, light and heavy-duty trucks, and high-speed industrial and marine engines employ an oil reservoir contained within what is commonly called a sump or *oil pan.* The type of oil pan and its reservoir capacity depend on the make and model of engine. Oil pans are manufactured from stamped steel, cast iron, or cast aluminum, although a number of newer high-speed engines have an oil pan made from FRP (fiberglass-reinforced plastic) or vinyl ester (plastic) such as the one illustrated in Figure 18–38. In this example only 10 bolts physically clamp the oil pan to the underside of the engine block; in contrast, two to three times that amount are necessary on most cast or pressed steel pans. The diagram shows that a one-piece reusable isolator seal is employed rather than a gasket. Rubber isolators are also used between the flat washer and the oil pan rail at each oil pan attaching bolt to distribute the clamping pressure evenly. A metal sleeve spacer is inserted through the isolator to limit the distance that the oil pan bolts can be run in. This prevents possible overtightening and damage to the FRP oil pan assembly.

On most high-speed engines it is possible to remove the oil pan from the engine without removing the engine from its application. If the engine is being removed for a major overhaul, however, leave the oil pan in place until the engine has been removed from its equipment. In either case, before removing the oil pan, always drain the oil first by removing the oil drain plug. On cast iron, large aluminum, or pressed steel pans, it is advisable to use a small air-impact wrench and socket to loosen and remove all of the oil pan bolts, other than one or two at each end which should be left in place to support the oil pan. This is a safety measure for heavy oil pans. You should also position a hydraulic

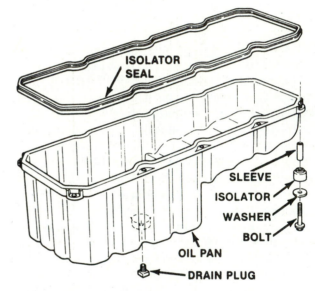

ISOLATOR SEAL

SLEEVE

ISOLATOR

WASHER

BOLT

OIL PAN

DRAIN PLUG

FIGURE 18–38 *Example of a lube oil pan assembly manufactured from FRP (fiberglass-reinforced plastic) and used on some models of the Series 60 engine. The oil pan is retained in place by a minimum number of bolts and rubber isolators. (Courtesy of Detroit Diesel Corporation.)*

jack with suitable wooden blocking, or use a transmission-style cradle, to take the weight of the oil pan as you remove the remaining bolts. If the oil pan gasket has been cemented in place, you may have to use a rubber mallet to strike the pan to break it loose. Carefully lower the oil pan to ensure that it does not damage the oil pump pickup or scavenge pump screens.

On pressed and stamped steel oil pans, carefully inspect the pan rail area for signs of distortion or damage. Lay the pan upside down on a flat surface and see if there are signs of irregular contact. You may have to use a rubber or plastic mallet to strike the oil pan rail area to bring it back to a true flat surface. Failure to do this can result in continuous oil leakage from the pan area when it is bolted to the engine. Also check and remove any dents within the oil pan surface of pressed steel pans, particularly in the area of the oil pump pick-up screen. Inspect the oil drain plug threads for damage. Threaded inserts can be installed to repair these. Oil pans should always be thoroughly cleaned prior to reinstallation. On heavy-duty cast iron or aluminum pans, any visible oil pan cracks should be repaired by welding. Severe damage requires the installation of a new oil pan assembly. When reinstalling large, heavy oil pans, it is helpful to employ several slotted and threaded guide studs in opposite holes of the block oil pan rail. This facilitates retention of the oil pan gasket and allows you to carefully guide the pan into position while you insert the various retaining bolts without disturbing or damaging the gasket.

Dipstick and Oil Filler Tube

All engines must be equipped with some means of checking the level of the lube oil in the engine base reservoir or oil pan. The common method is a steel ribbon-type dipstick, although round, cold-rolled steel types may be found on some engine models. The dipstick is usually located in a tube that is attached to a threaded adaptor on the side of the engine block casting as illustrated in Figure 18–39.

Use of the correct dipstick is critical to the proper functioning of the lube system, since using the wrong dipstick can cause either too much or too little oil to be added to the crankcase. Sometimes dipsticks are inadvertently switched by service personnel between the same make and model of engine. Not all engines are equipped with the same type of oil pan. The physical size and shape of the oil pan, and the operating angle, may be different. Therefore, before switching a dipstick from one engine to another, be certain that engines do in fact use the same oil pan assembly. Too much oil can result in frothing or foaming and aeration of the oil as the crankshaft rotates. This condition can cause low oil pressure as well as increase the operating temperature of the oil. The condition can also be accompanied by an increase in crankcase pressure that results in seal leakage and oil consumption in the engine. Too little oil increases the operating temperature of the oil and causes the pump to suck air. This condition can also create low oil pressure. Anything that increases the engine lube oil temperature can result in crankshaft, camshaft, bearing, and piston crown damage (cooling jet oil too hot). A reduction in oil pressure can also occur because of thinning of the oil. In electronically controlled engines, an automatic reduction in engine speed and

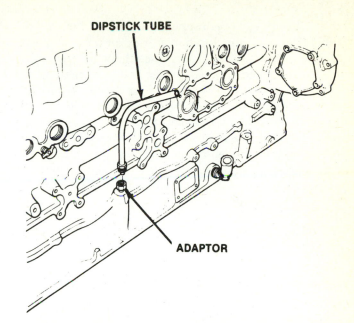

FIGURE 18–39 *Example of a typical engine oil dipstick tube mounting alongside the engine block. (Courtesy of Detroit Diesel Corporation.)*

power occurs when the oil temperature sensor indicates to the ECM that the oil is outside of a normal operating parameter, and a dash-mounted yellow warning light is illuminated. When the oil temperature reaches a maximum operating value, a red warning light and/or buzzer are activated followed shortly thereafter by automatic engine shutdown.

The oil level should always be checked when the equipment or vehicle is on a level surface both longitudinally and transversely. The dipstick is marked with a high and low oil level on the steel ribbon or rod; some may be marked *add* also. Usually it is advantageous at the time of an oil and filter change to fill the oil to just below the *full* mark. This allows the oil to be circulated to all filters, oil cooler cores, and so on and be distributed throughout the system. Start and run the engine for a minimum of 5 minutes. Allow at least 10 minutes of drain-back time once the engine has been shut off so all of the oil can drain back to the crankcase or oil pan before pulling the dipstick to check the correct level. Keep in mind that oil expands when hot. If the oil added when the engine is cold is already at the full mark, you may find that the level is too high on the dipstick during normal engine operating temperature.

NOTE: Some industrial and marine engines are equipped with a dipstick that is calibrated and marked to allow the operator to actually check the oil level when the engine is running. These dipsticks are marked with a *running* and *stopped* oil level condition on them.

All engines are equipped with an oil filler cap, or tube. The common location is the rocker cover, the engine front cover, or the flywheel housing area, or it may be attached to a side cover bolted to the engine block. A rubber plug within the cap can be expanded within its tube by rotating the cap handle until tight. In some engines the oil filler cap also serves as a ventilation system to the atmosphere, although due to environmental concerns many engines now route all crankcase gases and fumes back into the engine, or alternatively, trap them in a container that requires regular preventive maintenance.

CRANKCASE VENTILATION SYSTEMS

Harmful crankcase vapors formed during engine operation are usually removed by a continuous pressurized ventilating system. Normally some *slight* leakage past the piston rings occurs in all internal combustion engines, and this creates a small amount of crankcase pressure. In addition, the downward moving pistons tend to pressurize the air within the crankcase during engine operation. In some engines a small pump extractor system is designed to constantly draw these fumes from the engine crankcase area. In addition, on Detroit Diesel two-stroke-cycle engine models, the air box pressure from the blower and turbocharger is designed to let a small degree of air seep past the piston oil control rings and escape into the crankcase through the oil drain holes in the piston ring land area, when the piston is at the top of its stroke. This provides a *positive crankcase* ventilation system that allows all gases within the crankcase to be swept up through the engine and pass through the crankcase breather located on the valve rocker cover or other suitable location.

Some engines have a wire mesh element within the breather cap or oil filler cap that can be removed for cleaning at regular service intervals; some have a spring wire clip to hold the element in place. The wire mesh element can be cleaned in diesel fuel and dried with compressed air. If high crankcase pressure is suspected at any time, the element can be checked using a *water manometer* (described in detail in Chapter 20). In high-speed, heavy-duty, high-performance, marine diesel engine pleasure craft applications, the engine uses a closed crankcase emissions system similar to the one shown in Figure 18–40, which is incorporated within the air cleaner unit. The system is designed to eliminate crankcase vapors in the engine room by separating the oil from the dry gases, returning the oil to the oil pan, and directing the gases to the intake air. When the engine is running, intake air passes through the air cleaner to the turbocharger and a slight vacuum is created within the separator housing. Crankcase fumes are drawn out of the engine breather through a hose connected to this low-pressure area within the separator housing, where the oil vapor is removed from the gases and returned to the oil pan through a drain line. In this oil drain line, a one-way check valve prevents oil from being drawn into the separator. Normally an 8 in. (203 mm) drain line between the separator housing and the check valve is required to provide the proper amount of head pressure to cause oil to flow past the check valve to the sump. This arrangement allows crankcase pressure to be maintained at 2 in. (50.8 mm) of water by the vacuum limiter. (Service of this system is described in Chapter 20.)

CRANKCASE EXPLOSIONS

In large-displacement high- and low-speed diesel engines such as those found in mining trucks, locomotives, and industrial and marine applications, too much crankcase pressure accompanied by a hot engine running condition can result in a crankcase explosion. These explosions can create serious damage to the engine as well as personal injury. Because of the size of many of the large-displacement slow-speed engines, bolted crankcase inspection covers are large enough to allow a service technician or marine engineer to physically enter the base of the engine. Attached to these inspection covers are explosion relief valves similar to the one in Figure 18–41.

The cause of crankcase explosions, particularly in large-bore slow-speed engines of up to 60,000 horsepower (44760 kW), is a gathering of a combustible mixture of air/fuel and lube oil mist in the base of the engine. Spontaneous combustion can occur at a temperature of 270°C (518°F) with a mixture having an oil content of approximately 13% by weight. An explosive mixture can be created by overheating of mechanical parts within the engine or a *hot spot* that leads to auto-ignition of the fuel and oil mixture. In large slow-speed engines, the crankcase normally contains a mixture of mechanically generated spray and a small amount of condensed mist from lube oil vaporization as a result of the operating temperature of the components within the base of the engine. This mist is not a problem in an engine that is running correctly. When a hot spot occurs, however, it leads to accelerated vaporization of the oil mist and an auto-ignition temperature condition. Research has proven that if stable conditions in the crankcase persist, the presence of a hot spot may not necessarily lead to a crankcase explosion. Only when cracking of the oil and subsequent oxidation of the oil forms gases and vapors, will the hot spot possibly create an explosion.

FIGURE 18–40 *Closed crankcase emissions system and a vacuum limiter for a high-output 3408/3412 Cat marine engine application. (Courtesy of Caterpillar Inc.)*

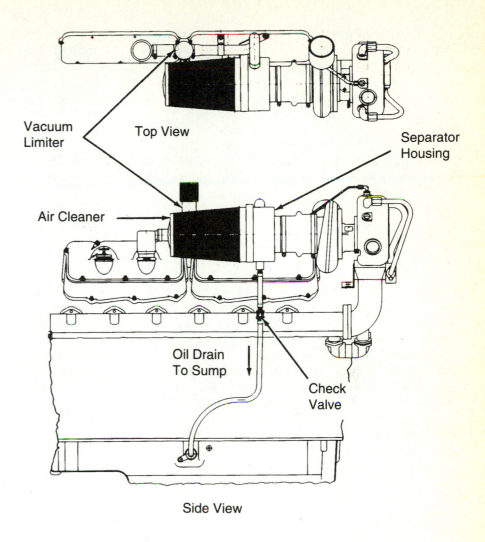

Vacuum Limiter

Top View

Separator Housing

Air Cleaner

Oil Drain To Sump

Check Valve

Side View

FIGURE 18–41 *Sectional arrangement of a typical crankcase explosion relief valve.*

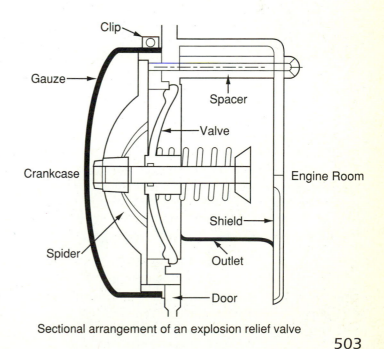

Clip

Gauze

Spacer

Valve

Crankcase

Engine Room

Shield

Spider

Outlet

Door

Sectional arrangement of an explosion relief valve

When an explosion within the engine crankcase occurs, it can range from a fairly mild puff of white smoke from the relief valve assembly shown in Figure 18–41 to a serious explosion with generated pressures depending on the composition and quantity of the explosive mist, the speed of flame propagation, and the pressure rise within the crankcase. The primary explosion can be followed by a secondary explosion if air is permitted to enter the crankcase, since this action allows further mixing of the oil and air. Although in extreme cases loss of engine room personnel and/or serious personal injury have been documented, modern well-maintained large-displacement slow-speed engines seldom experience catastrophic failures of this nature. Crankcase breather pipes fitted with flame arrestors and piped to a safe place on deck are used today on a number of these types of engines.

The crankcase explosion relief valve illustrated in Figure 18–41 is usually located on the side of the engine and fitted to one of the inspection doors. The relief valve is normally fitted with a flame trap to prevent emission of flame. A number of regulations cover the size, number, and location of these relief valves on specific displacement engines. Some sensing systems for detecting the possibility of excessive oil mist within the crankcase on larger engines involve the use of a light beam directed toward a photocell. The opacity, or denseness, of the oil mist passes through an optical-electrical measuring system where the reduction in the intensity of the light falling on the photo-diode is decreased, which leads to actuation of an alarm.

On larger-displacement high-speed diesel engines such as the Caterpillar 3500 and 3600 models, Cummins K V12 and V16 models, Detroit Diesel 149 series models, GM-EMD 567, 645, and 710 models, and most of the well-known large slow-speed marine engines (such as GMT, MAK, MAN, Sulzer, Mitsubishi), crankcase pressure relief valves, pressure sensors, or combination explosion doors with relief valves are fitted to the side of the engine inspection cover areas. On the Detroit Diesel 149 series engine models equipped with the DDEC system, the ECM can be programmed to either warn the operator or shut the engine down after a pre-programmed time period when a high crankcase pressure condition occurs. Maritime regulations prevent automatic stopping of the engine in many instances because of the possible ramifications when a vessel is docking or maneuvering.

ENGINE PRELUBRICATION

When an engine is completely disassembled, all parts are cleaned, dried, and inspected. When the engine is reassembled with used or new parts, the engine oil galleries must be filled with oil, and all lubricated components such as crankshaft bearings and thrust washers, camshafts, roller followers, rocker arms, pushrods, and oil pumps must be liberally coated with engine oil to ensure that a dry-start condition does not occur. Tests of various engines that have not been prelubed indicate that it can take from 30 to 60 seconds for the pressurized lube oil to reach all areas of an engine after initial start-up of a new engine and longer if the engine has been stopped or stored for long periods in cold ambient conditions.

During the reassembly process that follows replacement of major parts or engine overhaul, certain load-bearing components require prelubrication. This is to ensure that they receive adequate lubrication between initial engine start-up and the complete pressurizing of the lube system by the lube oil pump. In any engine assembly operation, the primary prelubricant is clean engine oil of the correct grade as recommended by the engine manufacturer. Usually, this is 15W-40 multigrade for many heavy-duty four-stroke-cycle engines and straight 40 oil on two-stroke Detroit Diesel engines. Some engine manufacturers recommend liberal use of special lubricants, such as Lubriplate or equivalent, during component assembly.

Failure to prelubricate parts while rebuilding the engine or prior to initial start-up can result in severe wear and damage to the components and engine downtime. Many major tool and equipment suppliers offer engine *prelubers,* which consist of an air- or electric-motor-driven pump and oil reservoir tank that can be filled with clean engine oil.

Figure 18–42 illustrates a prelubricating electric-motor-driven pump sitting on top of an oil barrel with its suction hose extending down into the reservoir. A flexible hydraulic hose can be connected between the pump outlet side and the engine main oil gallery or suitable tap point, so that when the unit is switched on pressurized lube oil can be sent through all oil passages to actively fill and prelubricate all component parts within the engine.

The prelube procedure has several steps:

1. Remove the valve rocker cover(s).
2. Remove a main oil gallery plug from the engine block; if no plug is accessible, remove the oil pressure gauge sensing unit or the sensor on an electronically controlled engine.
3. Refer to Figure 18–42 and connect the hydraulic hose and connector from the preluber to the engine block main oil gallery or oil filter head. On Cummins 14L engines, you can prime the lube system by removing the pipe plug from the external oil pump

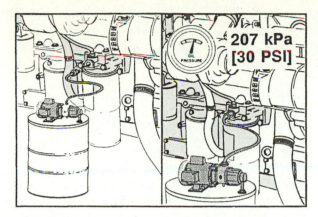

FIGURE 18–42 *Using an electric-motor-driven pump to prelubricate the engine after an overhaul and prior to initial start-up. (Courtesy of Cummins Engine Company, Inc.)*

cover. On some engines it may be easier to remove the 1/2 in. (12.7 mm) pipe plug from the oil filter head above the full-flow oil filter such as that illustrated in Figure 18–42.

4. Fill the preluber reservoir with the recommended grade of lubricant for the engine. Refer to the service manual.

5. With the prelube pump regulated to 25 to 35 psi (172 to 241 kPa), allow oil to flow into the engine. Generally, the preluber is equipped with a bypass regulating valve to control the maximum delivery pressure.

6. When oil is visibly flowing from the rocker arms, the engine oil galleries are primed. Manually rotate the engine over one-half turn to ensure that the oil penetrates all areas. In addition, if the oil pressure gauge is connected, once the gauge registers pressure, you know that the system is primed.

7. On turbocharged engines, disconnect the oil supply line at the turbo center bearing housing and fill the housing cavity with approximately a 1/2 L (pint) of the same grade of engine lube oil. Be sure to manually rotate the turbo wheel during this procedure to coat all internal surfaces with oil; then reinstall the supply line, but leave it between one-half to one-full turn loose.

8. Allow the prelube oil to drain to the crankcase for at least 5 minutes; then add the remaining quantity of engine oil to bring the level to the full mark on the dipstick. Pour this oil slowly over the rocker arms, followers, and camshaft pocket areas to ensure that all of the component parts are adequately lubricated.

9. Disconnect the preluber and plug the main oil gallery.

10. Crank the engine with the governor control in the no-fuel position on mechanical engines until oil pressure starts to register on the gauge.

11. Prior to starting the engine, make sure that the fuel system has been bled of air and that the engine can be *shut down* for any reason. It is sometimes wise to have a suitable blanking plate that can be placed over the air inlet system to kill (stop) the engine should it not shut off in the normal manner.

12. Once the engine cranks, or as soon as it starts, be prepared to tighten up the turbocharger oil supply line, which was left loose in step 7, as soon as oil flow is visible. If no oil flow is apparent to the turbocharger within 20 to 30 seconds, shut the engine off and determine the cause.

SELF-TEST QUESTIONS

1. Refined crude oil is commonly referred to as a
   a. base stock
   b. mineral oil
   c. vegetable oil
   d. additive package

2. List some of the more commonly used oil additives and the reasons for their use.

3. Technician A says that oxidation of engine lube oil can lead to viscosity increases, engine deposits, and corrosion. Technician B says that the oxidation would decrease the oil viscosity, reduce engine oil pressure, and increase the oil temperature. Which technician is correct?

4. Technician A says that viscosity improvers and wear inhibitors prevent thinning of the oil and therefore wear of bearings. Technician B says that they prevent foaming of the oil as well as act as friction modifiers. Which technician knows the purpose of these two additives?

5. A typical dosage of an additive package in a typical heavy-duty diesel engine lube oil used in automotive or truck applications consists of
   a. 0.5% to 2% by weight
   b. 3% to 5% by weight
   c. 3% to 16% by weight
   d. 10% to 30% by weight

6. What percentage of the following items constitute a typical lube oil package?
   a. Base stock crude
   b. Additive package
   c. Viscosity index improver
   d. Various inhibitors

7. Lube oils in North America are manufactured to various standards set down by these organizations. What do the letters represent?
   a. SAE
   b. API
   c. ASTM

8. Technician A says that letters appearing on any oil container that begin with S indicate a diesel engine lubricant. Technician B says that the letter C indicates a diesel engine lubricant, since the letter S is used for gasoline spark-ignited engines. Which technician is correct?

9. True or False: Oil viscosity rating is a measure of the oil's resistance when one layer of the fluid moves relative to an adjacent layer.

10. True or False: An oil referred to as Newtonian (Issac Newton) is a multiviscosity weight (grade) lube oil.

11. True or False: An oil referred to as non-Newtonian is a straight weight (grade) lube oil.

12. True or False: An oil with a higher viscosity number means the thickness of the fluid film is greater.

13. Multiviscosity oils are identified by an alphabetical letter following the first number. This letter is
    a. C
    b. F
    c. S
    d. W

14. True or False: The viscosity of multigrade oils is based on their ability to meet an ASTM W-grade standard of a relatively thin oil at a particular low temperature, while also meeting the standards for a thicker, non-W-grade oil at a higher temperature (usually 100°C/212°F).

15. True or False: Base stocks used to formulate multigrade oils are of low viscosity and are thickened with additive packages called VI (viscosity index) improvers.

16. True or False: The term *polymerization* refers to the chemical linking together of giant molecules to a large number of smaller ones.

17. The most frequently recommended oil grade for use in heavy-duty high-speed four-stroke-cycle engines such as those of Caterpillar, Cummins, Detroit Diesel, Volvo, Mack, and Navistar is
    a. 5W-20
    b. 10W-30
    c. 10W-40
    d. 15W-40

18. Why does the two-cycle DDC engine require a different oil grade than that for the DDC four-cycle models?

19. The engine oil recommended for two-stroke-cycle Detroit Diesel engines is
    a. 10W-30
    b. 15W-40
    c. 30
    d. 40 or 50

20. List the problems that will occur if a lube oil with too thick a viscosity grade is used.

21. List the problems that will occur if a lube oil with too thin a viscosity grade is used.

22. Technician A says that synthetic lube oils are far more refined and therefore a purer product than mineral oils. Technician B says that synthetic oil tends to be stickier than mineral oil and that is why synthetic oils are more expensive. Is one of the technicians correct, or are both statements valid?

23. Technician A says that the reason diesel engine oil tends to appear much blacker than the oil used in gasoline engines over the same hours (miles, kilometers) is they are subjected to much greater pressures and stresses. Technician B disagrees, saying that the dispersed soot from the combustion phase is the cause. Which technician is correct?

24. Technician A says that the newer electronic engines use retarded injection timing to meet the more stringent EPA exhaust emissions regulations and to reduce NO_x emissions. Technician B says that injection timing has been advanced to reduce NO_x. Who is right?

25. Based on your answer to Question 24, does this feature increase or decrease soot loading on the cylinder walls?

26. True or False: The letters TBN stand for total base number.

27. Technician A says that TBN means the oil has started to thicken and it should be changed more frequently. Technician B says that TBN is an indication of the depletion rate of the oil's additive package. Which technician is correct?

28. True or False: An oil with a high ash content helps to reduce deposits in the piston top ring groove area, which can cause ring sticking, blowby, and high oil consumption.

29. List three methods that could be used to determine the best point at which to change the engine lube oil and filter.

30. Describe how a lube oil analysis program can help determine when internal engine components are wearing prematurely or are close to a failure level.

31. Why has the use of electronic fuel injection been able to reduce metallic iron wear in engines compared to that normally found in mechanically governed and controlled engines?

32. Technician A says that the typical oil temperature in a high-speed heavy-duty diesel engine is normally 230°F (110°C). Technician B says that oil temperature should be closer to 195°F (91°C). Who is correct?

33. Maximum engine lube oil temperatures should not exceed
    a. 200°F (93°C)
    b. 215°F (102°C)
    c. 235°F (113°C)
    d. 250°F (121°C)

34. Name the two spring-loaded valves within the lube oil system that control normal and maximum operating pressures.

35. What prevents starvation of lube oil to the engine if and when the full-flow oil filter(s) becomes plugged?

36. If the engine oil cooler becomes plugged, what device would still allow oil to flow to the engine components?

37. True or False: Most oil pumps are gear driven from the crankshaft.

38. The word *gerotor* describes an oil pump that is a combination of
    a. gear and rotor
    b. piston and gear
    c. piston and rotor
    d. dual gears

39. Technician A says that a scavenge pump is used to supply lube oil to the opposite end of the oil pan in engine applications that operate at steep angles. Technician B says that this pump is used on large engines to supply half of the oil flow throughout the engine. Which technician is correct?

40. High-speed diesel engine full-flow oil filters are generally rated for a micron filtration size of approximately
    a. 30
    b. 25
    c. 20
    d. 10

41. Bypass oil filters that filter approximately 10% of the total oil flow are micron rated in the range of
    a. 20 to 30
    b. 20 to 25
    c. 15 to 20
    d. 10 to 15

42. Technician A says that when a duplex filtration system is used one or more filters can be changed while the engine is running. Technician B says that the engine must be stopped to change an oil filter. Who is correct?

43. True or False: The appearance of sludge is an indication that the oil and filter should be changed more frequently.

44. True or False: Thin black oil is an indication of fuel in the oil.

45. True or False: Milky discoloration of the oil is an indication of coolant in the oil.

46. Overtightening of a spin-on lube oil filter can result in what type of a problem?

47. Shell and element lube oil filters should be drained and washed in clean solvent and dried with compressed air. What other service items need to be replaced with this type of a filter assembly?

48. Describe the basic theory of operation of a Tattle Tale filter used on heavy-duty engines.

49. True or False: The difference in temperature between the engine cooling system and the oil is generally within a range of 30° to 40°F (17° to 23°C).

50. Name the two types of engine oil coolers that are used on heavy-duty diesel engines.

51. Technician A says that a leaking oil cooler core during engine operation will result in water in the oil. Not so says Technician B, who believes that lube oil would enter the cooling system instead. Who is correct and state your reasons why?

52. Describe what method you would use to clean an oil cooler core.

53. Describe how you would perform a pressure check on an oil cooler core.

54. The crankcase ventilation system ensures that harmful crankcase vapors can be recirculated through the engine. How would you determine if high crankcase pressure existed, and how would you check it?

55. Describe what conditions can lead to a crankcase explosion on a large-displacement diesel engine. What component is employed to prevent this condition from happening?

56. Describe how you would prelubricate an engine.

Cooling Systems

OVERVIEW

This chapter begins with a description of how the cooling system functions and the heat loads it must handle. Next we discuss coolant flow determination and treatment; the relationship of coolant to cylinder liner pitting; the effects of antifreeze; coolant testing; and scale buildup. Specific features of the coolant system are then highlighted, for example, filters, radiators, jacket water aftercoolers, thermostats, and fans.

TOPICS

- Basic function
- Engine heat loads
- Coolant flow determination and treatment
- Cylinder liner pitting
- Antifreeze
- Testing the coolant
- Scale buildup
- Coolant filters
- Flushing the system
- Pressure caps
- Pressure checking the coolant system
- Radiators
- Jacket water aftercoolers
- Thermostats
- Radiator shutters
- Fans
- Expansion tanks and heat exchangers
- Raw water pumps
- Keel cooling systems
- Self-test questions

BASIC FUNCTION

All internal combustion engines require water within a radiator system, heat exchanger, keel cooler, or cooling tower to prevent the engine from overheating and boiling over. Documented studies have shown that more than 40% of all engine problems are directly or indirectly related to improper maintenance of the cooling system.

The basic function of a cooling system is to dissipate a portion of the heat created within the engine combustion chamber. Heat absorbed by the pistons, rings, liners, cylinder heads, and cylinder block during engine operation that is not directly converted into useful power at the flywheel, must be handled by the cooling system. A properly designed cooling system must maintain the coolant operating temperature within a fairly narrow band to ensure proper combustion, minimize blowby, and allow the engine lube oil to function correctly. Tests have proven that wear on cylinder walls can be up to eight times greater with a coolant temperature of 100°F (38°C) compared to one of 180°F (82°C). Normal engine operating temperatures are generally controlled by one or more temperature regulators or thermostats. Typical coolant temperatures under loaded engine conditions fall within 180° to 200°F (82° to 93°C).

ENGINE HEAT LOADS

Heat dissipated to the coolant at rated power and peak torque engine speeds is used to define the heat load that must be dissipated by the cooling system, either to a radiator or heat exchanger system such as that found in industrial and marine applications. The energy distribution from combustion of the injected fuel can be split into four categories:

508

1. Useful work or power available after frictional losses

2. Exhaust gases (which recapture some heat energy to drive a turbocharger)

3. Cooling system (which recaptures some energy, for example, as an in-cab heater and defroster)

4. Heat radiation from the engine

Exact heat loads vary in specific makes of engines. In modern electronically controlled engines, TE (thermal efficiency), or the heat efficiency and useful work from the engine, approaches 40% to 42%. Typical heat rejection values for today's engines can range from as high as 14,000 Btu per minute (10,440 kW) in high-output electronically controlled engines to as little as 4000 Btu per minute (2,983 kW) in low-horsepower engines. Average heat rejection to the cooling system is usually in the range of 30 to 35 Btu/hp/min for a basic engine. The addition of accessories to the coolant system, such as transmission and marine gear oil coolers, can increase the cooling system heat load to between 40 and 50 Btu/min.

Assume that an engine is rated at 450 bhp (335.6 kW) with a heat load of 14,000 Btu/min (10,440 kW). If we divide the heat load by 450 bhp (335.6 kW), then the cooling system would have to absorb 31 Btu/hp/min. In a smaller engine rated at only 150 bhp (112 kW) with a heat load of 4000 Btu/min, the cooling system has to absorb 27 Btu/hp/min (0.471 kW/min). As you can see, there isn't too much of a difference between the cooling system heat absorption requirements of the smaller and larger rated engines. For example, the 3176B Caterpillar inline six-cylinder four-stroke-cycle engine which has electronically controlled unit injectors is a 10.3L (629 cu in.) displacement engine. Although initially designed for heavy-duty truck applications, it is now used in a variety of applications. Total heat rejection on this engine is 27 Btu/hp/min, with 17 Btu from the engine cooling jacket and 10 Btu from the ATAAC (air-to-air aftercooler) charge air system.

Thermal efficiency (or heat efficiency) simply means that if the engine has a 42% TE, for every $1 of fuel injected into the combustion chamber, there is a 42 cent return at the flywheel as usable power. This means that approximately 58% of the heat developed from combustion is wasted and dissipated to the cooling, exhaust, friction, and radiation areas. If we assume that our example engine is rated at 450 bhp (335.6 kW) and the cooling system handles 14,000 Btu/min (10,440 kW), then in 1 hour the cooling system has to handle 60 × 14,000 = 840,000 Btu. If we divide this figure by 450 bhp (335.6 kW), the cooling system load is 1866.66 Btu/hp/hr.

From the discussion in Chapter 1 we know that a perfect engine incurring no heat losses would require enough injected fuel to release 2545 Btu of heat within the cylinder to produce 1 hp (0.746 kW) over a 1 hr period. If this 2545 Btu/hp/hr represents usable power with a 42% TE value, we can factor out the remaining Btu heat losses. If the engine has a fuel consumption of 0.310 lb/bhp/hr (188.5 g/kW-h), then at a rating of 450 bhp (335.6 kW) in 1 hr the engine consumes 450 × 0.310 = 139.5 lb (63.27 kg) of fuel. If the fuel has an API rating of 38, it weighs 6.95 lb/U.S. gallon (3.15 kg/3.78 L). The engine consumes, therefore, 20.07 U.S. gallons/hr (75.97 L/h). A 38 API fuel contains 137,000 Btu HHV (high heat value) per U.S. gallon, so in 1 hour the total heat released into the engine cylinders is 137,000 × 20.07 = 2,749,590 Btu. If we divide this total heat released by the power rating of 450 bhp (335.6 kW), the engine requires 6110.2 Btu to produce 1 horsepower over a 1 hr period. We know that only 2545 Btu of this heat was actually useful power; therefore, 6110.2 − 2545 = 3565.2 Btu was lost to the cooling system, exhaust, friction, and radiation. The 1866.66 Btu/hp/hr is equal to 30.54% of the total heat used (6110.2 Btu). Added to the 42% TE, we have now accounted for 42 + 30.54 = 72.54% of the fuel heat released into the combustion chamber. This means that the remaining 27.46% of dissipated heat losses was accounted for by the exhaust and friction and radiation area, which represents 1698.54 Btu.

COOLANT FLOW DETERMINATION AND TREATMENT

Although the service technician is seldom required to determine the water flow through an engine, it is helpful to appreciate what the coolant flow demands are on various diesel engines. A reduction in coolant flow from a faulty water pump, a restricted radiator caused by scale buildup or plugging, collapsed top and bottom hoses, and faulty thermostats can all affect the flow rate through the engine water jackets.

Let's say we were asked to consider the rate of water flow in gpm (gallons per minute) or lpm (liters per minute) required to cool an engine rated at 450 bhp with a heat rejection rate to the cooling water of 1500 Btu/bhp/hr (25 Btu/bhp/min) with a water inlet temperature to the engine of 170°F (76.6°C), and a thermostat outlet temperature of 195°F (90.5°C). We need to apply a known formula to determine the cooling flow rate solution:

$$\text{gpm} = \frac{\text{bhp (Btu per bhp per hour)}}{(t1 - t2)\ 500}$$

where $t1$ is the outlet temperature and $t2$ is the coolant inlet temperature.

$$\text{gpm} = \frac{450\,(1500)}{(195 - 170)\,500} = \frac{450\,(1500)}{(25)\,500} = \frac{675,000}{12,500}$$
$$= 54 \text{ U.S. gpm (204.5 L)}$$

Using the same formula, if the same engine rated at 450 bhp had a heat rejection rate of 2000 Btu/bhp/hr (33.3 Btu/bhp/min) and the same water inlet and outlet temperatures, the water flow requirements through the engine would be 72 U.S. gpm (272.5 L). On a 3000 bhp engine with a heat rejection rate of 1800 Btu/bhp/hr (30 Btu/bhp/min) and the same water inlet and outlet temperatures, the required coolant flow rate through this engine would be 432 U.S. gpm (1635 L).

Water tends to be the major constituent in all engine cooling systems. Any water, whether of drinking quality or not, produces a corrosive environment within the cooling system. If the mineral content of the water is over 300 ppm hardness or the corrosive chemicals are over 100 ppm chloride or sulfate, the water is unfit for use in the cooling system and will invariably allow deposits of scale to form on all of the internal cooling surfaces. Therefore, all water used in a cooling system must be chemically treated and tested on a regular basis to ensure that it is suitable for continued use. Generally, most engine manufacturers state that coolant solutions must meet the following requirements:

- Provide for adequate heat transfer
- Provide a corrosion-resistant environment in the cooling system
- Prevent formation of scale or sludge deposits in the cooling system
- Be compatible with cooling system hose and seal materials
- Provide adequate freeze protection during cold-weather operation and boil-over protection in hot weather

SCAs (supplemental coolant additives) have been used in coolant systems since the mid-1950s. Although the first types were chromate based, these were phased out in the mid-1970s because of concerns about toxicity. Coolants used in current systems consist of antifreeze, water, and SCAs; these three ingredients combine to protect the engine and cooling system components. SCAs are formulated to provide protection against deposits, corrosion, and pitting that is not provided by the chemicals in the antifreeze. SCAs extend the life of antifreeze by adding to and replenishing the chemicals that tend to deplete after about 3 to 6 months or 30,000 miles (48,279 km) of normal operation. Keep in mind, however, that SCAs *do not* extend the freeze protection of the antifreeze.

The type of SCAs now being used in heavy-duty diesel engine coolants employ water-soluble polymers and detergents that often are not included in automotive antifreezes. All antifreezes create a percentage of salts (inhibitors) that can increase the percentage of electrolytes. The process is similar to that in batteries, in that the salts cause an increase in electrical activity that leads to greater corrosion potential between the dissimilar metals used in engines and radiators. To reduce corrosion that occurs as a result of the difference in electrical potential between two parts, many heavy-duty trucks and equipment with aluminum radiators have a ground strap or wire that runs from the radiator to the vehicle frame.

CYLINDER LINER PITTING

One of the most serious problems that can occur in a wet-type cylinder liner is *liner pitting* (see Figure 19–1). The liner metal is actually eaten away.

The definition of liner pitting is *cavitation-accelerated corrosion*. Pitting is caused by high-pressure combustion gases that tend to cause a rocking motion on the piston skirt when it is driven down the cylinder. This is usually referred to as *piston slap* (not to be confused with the slap noise that occurs in a worn cylinder) and is more pronounced on a one-piece design than on a two-piece crosshead or articulated design. Piston slap subjects the liner to intense vibration at a high frequency, which results in cavitation (vapor bubble formation and collapse) of the coolant surrounding the outer wall of the liner. The high-frequency vibration causes the pressure in the layer of coolant next to

FIGURE 19–1   *A liner with an acceptable degree of pitting and a severely pitted, nonreusable liner. (Courtesy of Cummins Engine Company, Inc.)*

the liner to change drastically. Although the liner wall movement is very small, when it moves away from the coolant the pressure decreases, and bubbles that consist of both coolant vapor and air form. As the liner moves back toward the coolant, surface pressure again increases and the bubbles formed under low pressure now collapse, or implode, exerting forces as high as 60,000 psi (413,700 kPa) on the liner surface. These tremendous shock waves from bubble collapse hammer the liner and result in a highly stressed surface that is susceptible to corrosion. When an engine is not running, the static conditions create corrosion of the cast iron liner through heavy rust deposits, which eventually slow the corrosion process. In a running engine however, the rust and corrosion products are literally blasted away from the liner surface.

A wet liner can be perforated in less than 80,465 km (50,000 miles) if the coolant chemistry is not maintained properly. Coolant can then enter the engine crankcase or the cylinder area and cause destruction of the engine. Wet-liner corrosion can be prevented by using a GM-6038-M permanent-type antifreeze and a mixture of SCAs that contain nitrites or a mixture of nitrite, molybdate, and chromate. These prevent liner pitting by promoting a thin, tough, protective oxide layer on the liner surface. As the coolant film is broken by the collapse of a cavitation bubble, the protective film is rapidly reformed. This isolates the liner from the water, oxygen, and coolant impurities that cause the corrosion.

ANTIFREEZE

The AF (antifreeze) used in diesel engines can be of the EG (ethylene-glycol) type or the aqueous PG (propylene-glycol) type. PG is essentially EG with a methyl group attached to one end, and its chemistry is similar to that of EG. PG is propylene oxide combined with water to form the glycol.

One of the major advantages of PG is that the U.S. Food and Drug Administration has classified it as GRAS (generally regarded as safe). EG, however, is frequently responsible for poisoning cats and dogs who are drawn to its sweet taste. Consider also that 32 fluid ounces (950 milliliters) of ingested PG can be fatal to a 150 lb (68 kg) person, while less than 4 fluid ounces (100 milliliters) of EG is fatal. In the United States, the Clean Air Act considers EG a hazardous air pollutant. In addition, the U.S. Occupational Safety and Health Administration (OSHA), which regulates workplace safety, has placed an 8 hour average exposure standard for EG at 50 ppm. On the other hand, PG has not been considered dangerous enough to require safety legislation standards. In the face of increasing environmental concerns regarding EG, the adoption of PG-based antifreezes can be expected in heavy-duty diesel trucks and equipment.

All AFs must be disposed of in a safe manner. Most local regulations consider used AF a hazardous waste due to the heavy metals that accumulate. Because of their high biochemical oxygen demands, neither EG or PG can be disposed of in sewer systems. Check with local, state, provincial, or federal agencies for the proper disposal guidelines. Take careful note that both EG and PG antifreeze can now be cleaned and recycled, and both are biodegradable. A variety of portable AF recycling machines are available from most major equipment and tool suppliers.

Tests have shown that PG used with the same SCA package that is used with EG provides extra cavitation corrosion protection equivalent to at least 20% to 40%. Thus, it offers significant advantages to users of heavy-duty diesel engines.

Antifreeze is used for boil-over protection, freeze protection, and some corrosion protection. AF solutions should be used year-round to provide a stable environment for seals and hoses. The freeze protection value depends on the concentration of AF used. A 40% AF-to-water mix offers freeze protection to about $-10°F$ ($-23°C$), while a 60% AF-to-water mix offers protection to about $-65°F$ ($-55°C$). Never use more than a 67% maximum AF-water solution; more than that can adversely affect coolant freezing and boiling temperatures, increase silicate levels, and reduce heat transfer. A 50% glycol mix is considered optimal. Table 19–1 illustrates various cooling system capacities in U.S. gallons and the freeze protection offered when using EG-type AF based on the volume of AF that is added to the system. The cooling system capacity is generally listed in the engine or vehicle service literature. When adding or topping off coolant, never use a 100% AF solution as makeup coolant or straight water; always mix AF with water to provide the same concentration as the initial fill. Otherwise, dilution or possible overconcentration of the system coolant can occur.

Heavy-duty diesel engine antifreeze consists of a number of chemicals and is formulated with a balance of nitrite, nitrate, borate, small amounts of sodium silicate, and azoles to protect soft metals. These additives provide a very effective corrosion inhibitor, particularly for aluminum components. As sodium silicate depletes over time, it can "drop out" of the coolant solution through a process called catalytic polymerization. In this process, individual silicate molecules unite in the presence of engine heat and form larger particles that precipitate in the form of gel, which can plug coolant passages.

TABLE 19–1 SELECTION GUIDE FOR COOLING SYSTEM FREEZE PROTECTION[a]

7[c]	2[b]	3	4	5	6	7	8	9	10	11	12	13	14	15	16	17	18
7[c]	6°[d]	−17°	−54°														
8	10°	−7°	−34°	−62°													
9	14°	0°	−21°	−50°													
10	16°	4°	−12°	−34°	−62°												
11	18°	8°	−6°	−23°	−47°	−62°											
12	19°	10°	0°	−15°	−34°	−57°											
13	21°	13°	3°	−9°	−25°	−45°	−62°										
14		15°	6°	−5°	−18°	−34°	−54°										
15		16°	8°	0°	−12°	−26°	−43°	−62°									
16		17°	10°	2°	−8°	−19°	−34°	−52°	−62°								
17		18°	12°	5°	−4°	−14°	−27°	−42°	−58°								
18		19°	14°	7°	0°	−10°	−21°	−34°	−50°	−62°							
19		20°	15°	9°	2°	−7°	−16°	−28°	−42°	−56°							
20			16°	10°	4°	−3°	−12°	−22°	−34°	−48°	−62°						
21			17°	12°	6°	0°	−9°	−17°	−28°	−41°	−54°	−62°					
22			18°	13°	8°	2°	−6°	−14°	−23°	−34°	−47°	−59°					
23			19°	14°	9°	4°	−3°	−10°	−19°	−29°	−40°	−52°	−62°				
24			19°	15°	10°	5°	0°	−8°	−15°	−24°	−34°	−46°	−58°				
25			20°	16°	12°	7°	1°	−5°	−12°	−20°	−29°	−40°	−52°	−62°			
26			21°	17°	13°	8°	3°	−3°	−9°	−16°	−25°	−34°	−45°	−57°			
27				17°	14°	9°	4°	0°	−6°	−13°	−22°	−30°	−38°	−50°	−62°		
28				18°	15°	10°	6°	1°	−5°	−11°	−18°	−27°	−34°	−44°	−55°	−62°	
29				18°	15°	11°	7°	3°	−2°	−8°	−15°	−23°	−30°	−38°	−48°	−58°	
30				19°	16°	12°	8°	4°	0°	−6°	−12°	−19°	−26°	−34°	−43°	−53°	−62°

Source: Courtesy of Peterbilt Motors Company, Division of PACCAR.

[a]Ethylene-glycol

base antifreeze	25%	33%	40%	50%	60%
Protects to	10°	0°	−12°	−34°	−62°

Note: 60% ethylene-glycol base antifreeze and 40% water by volume gives maximum protection. *Never* use concentrated ethylene-glycol base antifreeze as it will freeze at approximately 0° F.

[b]Gallons of ethylene-glycol base antifreeze required

[c]Cooling system capacity in gallons

[d]Degrees of temperature in Fahrenheit.

Gel is sometimes referred to as green slime, goo, or hydrogel. Always use a low silicate AF containing not less than 0.10% silicate (measured as Na_2SiO_3), for example, any AF that meets General Motors Engineering standard GM-6038-M (this number is usually listed on the AF container). This AF limits the maximum amount of silicate to 0.15%. When new heavy-duty trucks leave the factory, they are generally filled with this type of antifreeze. The use of AFs with sealer additives may cause plugging throughout the cooling system and is *not* recommended. Dowtherm 209 full-fill coolant should not be mixed with AF because it is not compatible with AF solutions and inhibitors.

The increased use of aluminum parts, for example, in radiators, was a key factor that led antifreeze manufacturers to reformulate their products to include increased amounts of silicates to protect these parts from corrosion. If an AF solution is overconcentrated or too much of a corrosion inhibitor supplement is used, the excess silicate drops out of the coolant and silica gel builds up in the coolant and low-flow areas of the engine, particularly the radiator, the oil cooler core, heater core, and the turbocharger engine-mounted JWAC (jacket water aftercooler). The reduced coolant flow that results from silica gel buildup can lead to engine overheating and serious engine dam-

age. In the wet state, the silica gel takes on the color of the AF or inhibitor supplements used in the system. Although silica gel is nonabrasive, it can pick up solid particles in the coolant and become a gritty, abrasive deposit that can cause excessive wear of water pump seals and other components of the cooling system. When the silicate is allowed to dry as shown in Figure 19-2, it appears as a white powdery substance.

Other conditions can contribute to silicate dropout:

- Air trapped in the coolant
- A reduced flow condition
- High engine operating temperatures
- Poor system maintenance
- Low coolant level
- Faulty pressure cap or the wrong rating
- Use of hard water in coolant solutions

If an engine overheating problem and coolant passage plugging can be traced to silicate dropout, use a commercially available nonacidic cleaner to remove the silica gel from the system. This can be done without disassembling the engine. Typical no-acid cleaners are Fleet Restore (Fleetguard, Inc.), Nalprep or Nalclean (Power Fleet Division, The

FIGURE 19—2 Example of hardened coolant gel in a plugged radiator passage. (Courtesy of Power Fleet Division, The Penray Companies, Inc., Elk Grove, Il.)

Penray Companies, Inc.), and Peak Professional Cooling System Cleaner (Northern Petrochemical Company). Follow the manufacturer's directions for use, which normally appear on the container. If this treatment does not remove the silicate deposits (engine continues to overheat), you will have to disassemble the affected engine components from the engine. The engine will have to be submerged in an agitated caustic solution, and the radiator will have to be stripped and cleaned ultrasonically (the preferred method). If this cannot be done, clean and rod out the rad core (you cannot rod out turbulated or Z-wire tubes).

Engine coolant water, antifreeze, and SCAs should generally be changed and the system cleaned and flushed every 2 years due to additive depletion. Use of SCAs and Need Release filters can extend this to as much as 600,000 miles (965,580 km), 10,000 hours, or 5 years. When it is desirable to check the freeze protection of an AF, check EG by means of a hydrometer (not accurate for PG) or a refractometer. A hydrometer is not accurate for testing PG because the specific gravity of water with a rating of 1.0 weighs 10 lb per Imperial gallon, or the equivalent of 4.546 L, while the PG AF weighs 1.04. To test the PG AF, use a test strip (can also be used to measure the total amount of mixed EG or PG in a coolant) or a refractometer that is scaled for PG, not EG. Make sure that the measuring window is clean. A sample of coolant is drawn off by the small tube attached to the refractometer and a drop of coolant is placed on the measuring window. Close the cover plate and point the tester toward a light source as you look into the eyepiece. The internal scale will indicate the degree of AF protection (see Figure 23–14).

Several problems are caused by poor AF concentration control:

- Below 30% concentration: head/block cracking in cold ambient temperatures, coolant freezeup, increased liner pitting
- Above 75% concentration: water pump leakage, slushing of coolant, additive precipitation, poor heat transfer and overheating

TESTING THE COOLANT

Fleet service technicians are charged with the responsibility of maintaining the cooling system. Typical coolant should be maintained with a 50% to 67% antifreeze precharged with 3% Nalcool; then a Need Release filter should be installed to safeguard the system. This coolant mix will establish a recommended inhibitor level for cost-effective protection. Two tech-

nologies are dominant in heavy-duty diesel engine cooling systems today:

1. Nalcool 3000, distributed through the Power Fleet Division, The Penray Companies, Inc., is the primary SCA used by Caterpillar and Detroit Diesel.
2. DCA-4 (diesel coolant additive, fourth generation) is the primary SCA used by Cummins, which owns Fleetguard.

SPECIAL NOTE: Since most heavy-duty diesel engines employ either the Penray Nalcool or Fleetguard SCA products, a conversion factor of recommended SCA levels from Nalcool to Fleetguard DCA units and vice versa is required. One DCA unit is equivalent to 2.0 volume percent Nalcool measured as 800 ppm (parts per million) nitrite.

The SCAs must be checked closely and analyzed to ensure that the coolant mix is within levels recommended by engine manufacturers. Control of the SCAs is one of the major reasons for field and lab analysis of heavy-duty diesel engine coolants; therefore, it is very important that the diesel technician understand this test procedure.

Most SCAs are formulated for use with both EG and PG antifreeze. Nevertheless, if you are using PG check with the SCA supplier to make sure that its package will work with PG. Remember, using an SCA package that is not suitable for PG will result in coolant dropout.

Overconcentration of SCAs causes a high level of solids to gather in the cooling system. Chemical deposits at the water pump seal weep hole are usually an indication of overconcentration. Underconcentration of SCAs can result in pitting of liner surfaces. Checking for overconcentration of SCAs can be done by testing reserve alkalinity and conductivity, but usually checking requires special kits or a coolant sample taken to a lab for analysis. Overconcentration of SCAs can lead to these conditions:

- Deposits on heat-transfer surfaces and fouling of the cooling system with precipitated additives
- Water pump seal leaks
- Plugging of coolant passages from solder bloom/corrosion or silicate gelation

To effectively test the condition of the coolant for glycol and nitrite as well as TDS (total dissolved solids), a number of coolant test kits are available commercially. These kits allow the technician to test the coolant for proper SCA concentration as well as TDS and pH level, which is a measure of the degree of alkalinity or acidity of the coolant. The optimum pH is generally within the range of 7.5 to 11.0. A reading below 7.5 pH indicates acidity, while one above 11.0 pH indicates an alkaline concentration. Consider the following cooling pH scale:

0	7.5	11	14
Acidic corrosion of iron, steel, copper, brass	Optimum coolant pH range	Alkaline corrosion of aluminum and solder	

Acids can form when glycol degrades or gases bleed past gaskets into the coolant. The Nalcool/Penray two-way test strip kit includes directions on the strip container to guide the technician on how to interpret and compare the nitrite and glycol content, as well as the acidity or alkaline level of the coolant. After dipping a test strip into the coolant and removing it, the color change on the test strip is compared with the colored blocks on the container to determine coolant SCA condition. Another test kit is used to check for MBT (mercaptobenzothiazole) and nitrite in a coolant sample. Directions in this container describe how to draw a small sample of coolant and how to mix the solutions in the various plastic bottles until a specific color change to the coolant is noted. Record the number of drops of solution required to cause a coolant color change; then refer to the directions to determine if additional SCAs need to be added. If you are using a Cummins Fleetguard test kit, (Figure 19–3), note that this same procedure will indicate how many DCA-4s are required. Too much SCA can lead to silcate dropout, while too little SCA can create corrosion and cavitation. A TDS (total dissolved solids) tester can quickly indicate the solid particle percentage in the coolant when dipped into the radiator top tank by measuring the conductivity between two probes of the tester. The level of dissolved solids in the coolant water should generally not exceed 340 ppm (20 grams per gallon). The higher a coolant's TDS, the greater the amount of corrosion and scale buildup that will occur.

SCALE BUILDUP

All engines radiate a great deal of heat, which is normally removed by the coolant as it flows through the engine. Scale or rust developed in the coolant passages acts as an insulator and blocks heat transfer. Scale occurs when magnesium and calcium (always present in tap water) are deposited on the heated metal surfaces inside the cooling system. Normally scale occurs where temperatures are highest, such as at the cylinder head and the outside of wet-type lin-

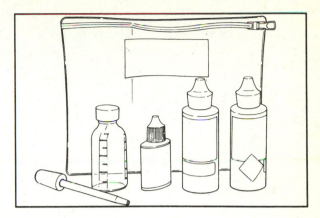

FIGURE 19–3   Coolant test kit to check DCA-4 concentration. (Courtesy of Cummins Engine Company, Inc.)

ers, as well as in heat exchanger cores or radiator cores. Depending on the water used (hardness, alkalinity, acidity, and so on), scale tends to form a hard white crust. Scale deposits on the outside of a wet-type liner can cause it to expand unevenly, and the liner metal can actually bulge inward in the areas of hot spots. As the pistons and rings move up and down within the liners, irregular ring and liner wear occur. This causes metal scuffing to take place between the rings, pistons, and the liner surface. Eventually, metal scoring occurs, which is an advanced stage of scuffing. The tearing metal creates stuck or broken rings, piston damage, and possible piston-to-liner siezure. Cylinder head cracking is another inevitable result.

For example, a 1/16 in. (1.58 mm) thick coating of scale on a 1 in. (25.4 mm) thick section of cast iron reduces the heat transfer ability of the iron to that of approximately 4.25 in. (114.3 mm) of cast iron as illustrated in Figure 19–4. Scale buildup does not happen overnight but gradually over weeks or months. Use a good-quality cooling system corrosion inhibitor and coolant stabilizer, such as Nalcool 3000 containing Stabil-Aid, a patented scale suppressant that helps prevent scale deposits (but never add it to a cooling system until the system has been cleaned and flushed with a cleaner such as Nalprep 2001). Another serious problem when scale buildup occurs is that it prevents coolant temperature sensors from sensing the engine block cooling temperature. This can prevent heavy-duty fan clutches from turning on, which will cause boil over of the coolant from the radiator. In electronic engines, both the coolant level and coolant temperature sensors can be affected by scale buildup. Another item affected is the engine coolant block heater assembly.

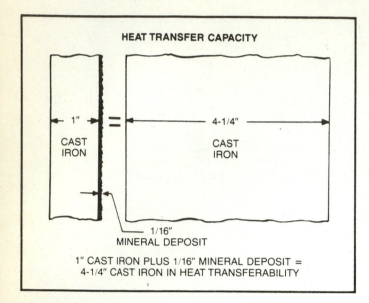

FIGURE 19–4 How scale buildup insulates and retards heat transferability. (Courtesy of Detroit Diesel Corporation.)

COOLANT FILTERS

Many heavy-duty engines employ coolant filter conditioners that have two basic functions: to provide the most effective way of controlling the addition of SCAs and to provide the benefits of mechanical filtration. These filters, which are the bypass type, are plumbed into the system so that coolant under pressure from the engine block enters the inlet side of the filter assembly and returns to a low-pressure side of the coolant system (back toward the suction side of the water pump). Two shutoff valves allow the technician to prevent any coolant loss from the block when changing the coolant filter.

Some coolant filters are the spin-on throw-away type, but many larger engines employ an actual filter housing with a filter element. Larger engines may also have more than one filter assembly attached to a coolant header or manifold assembly. Certain models of filter assemblies may contain a sacrificial zinc corrosion resistor plate/electrode, which tends to be eaten away by any electrolysis that occurs in the engine. Electrolysis takes place because the engine coolant is basically like a battery electrolyte; that is, the galvanic action that occurs due to dissimilar metals in contact through the engine block and coolant (electrolyte) tends to eat away the weakest link in the system. Within the water filter, the sacrificial element is eaten away (corrodes) during engine operation. Each time that the filter is changed, a new corrosive element is installed automatically. On very large diesel engines,

such as deep-sea marine applications, a small generator is sometimes used. This generator is designed to cause a predetermined small electrical current to flow between an engine-mounted cathode and anode to counteract the effects of electrolysis. Also, the water filter contains a powder that is absorbed by the coolant. This powder contains additives that prevent rust and corrosion by forming a protective film on all metal surfaces. The powder also maintains the coolant PH level (acidic versus alkalinity) and softens the water to minimize scale deposits.

Figure 19–5 illustrates a typical coolant filter for a heavy-duty high-speed engine. This particular Need Release filter assembly, which is manufactured by Penray/Nalcool, is designed to release the correct amount of SCAs into the coolant during engine operation to provide complete cooling system protection for up to 1 year or 120,000 miles (193,116 km). As the chemically balanced SCAs (inhibitors) within the coolant deplete, the metal alloy membranes within the filter cartridge detect the need for additional corrosion protection. Before the system reaches a corrosive condition, the *Need Release membranes* release the exact amount of treatment necessary to adjust the system to the proper level of corrosion protection.

FLUSHING THE SYSTEM

The cooling system should be flushed at a recommended time interval as stated by the engine manufacturer in the service literature. Suggested mileage or time was discussed in the "Antifreeze" section of this chapter. After draining and flushing the system, follow the manufacturer's recommendation for precharging the cooling system.

If the coolant system has developed *soft gel* formations, these can be removed by using a commercial cleaner such as Nalprep 2001. If the gel has dried, however, the radiator will have to undergo ultrasonic cleaning at a rad shop. Coolant gel is gelatinous polymerized silica in its wet form and a light-colored powder or scale in its dry form. It traps antifreeze phosphates, hard water salts, and coolant additive ingredients, as well as corrosion products, to form a gritty material that is abrasive to cooling system components. Figure 19–2 illustrates radiator tubes that have been plugged with coolant gel in as little as 18,000 miles (28,967 km). You cannot flush hardened gel from a radiator core. Acid-based cleaners tend to be ineffective in cleaning gel. If the system is totally plugged, similar to the conditions shown in Figure 19–2, take the radiator to a rad shop and have it boiled out and rodded, although the latest and most effective method now used is ultrasonic cleaning.

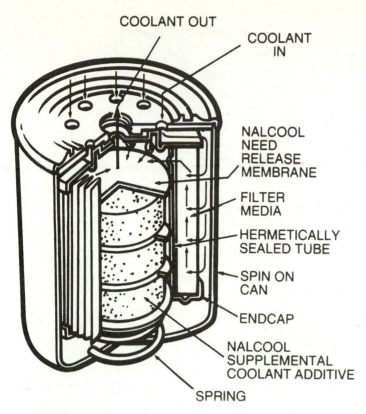

COOLANT OUT
COOLANT IN

NALCOOL NEED RELEASE MEMBRANE
FILTER MEDIA
HERMETICALLY SEALED TUBE
SPIN ON CAN
ENDCAP
NALCOOL SUPPLEMENTAL COOLANT ADDITIVE
SPRING

FIGURE 19–5 Cutaway view of a typical coolant system filter assembly. (Courtesy of Power Fleet Division, The Penray Companies, Inc., Elk Grove Village, IL.)

CAUTION: Service personnel often back, or reverse, flush the cooling system. In this procedure a pressurized water hose is connected to the bottom rad hose or heat exchanger to force liquid out of the top hose outlet. This reverse flushing procedure should only be considered a salvage operation. Back flushing can loosen scale formations that cause the cooling system to clog at a later date during the operation.

Each time that the antifreeze is changed, the coolant system should be cleaned (flushed) with Nalprep 2001, Fleetguard Restore, or an equivalent to ensure that the system is thoroughly clean before adding Nalcool 3000 or equivalent, followed by a water-antifreeze mix. Follow these steps when flushing the system:

1. Thoroughly power flush the complete cooling system using a flushing kit. Limit the air pressure to 138 kPa (20 psi) because excess pressure applied to the water can damage the radiator, thermostat, and water pump seals. Back, or reverse, flushing the cooling system can be considered a salvage operation, if after using a commercially available chemical cleaner the radiator core is still partially dirty. Figure 19–6 illustrates how to reverse flush the radiator core using hot water forced through the system in the opposite direction to normal coolant flow.

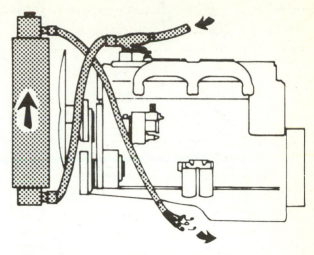

FIGURE 19–6 Hookup procedure used to reverse, or back flush a radiator. (Courtesy of Cummins Engine Company.)

CAUTION: Reverse flushing can cause small loosened scale particles to damage internal seals within the water pump and thermostat areas. It is better to remove the radiator and have it repaired at a rad shop.

2. Add 2 L of Nalprep 2001 or equivalent for every 30 L of water. If using Fleetguard Restore, add 1 U.S. gallon (3.8 L) for each 10 to 15 U.S. gallons (38 to 57 L) of water.

3. Start and run the engine for 1.5 to 2 hours. This can be done in the shop or yard area, or the vehicle can be road tested to ensure circulation of the cleaner from all cooling system surfaces and passages.

4. Allow the engine to cool, then drain the cooling system and flush it with fresh water, or fill the system with clean fresh water and run the engine for 5 minutes at high idle with the coolant temperature above 185°F (85°C).

NOTE: If the cooling system has already started to overheat due to severe gelling problems, a longer cleaning period may be required. Proceed to step 5 if this is the case.

5. Perform steps 1 and 2. Then leave the cleaner, such as Nalprep 2001 or equivalent, in the cooling system for 250 hours, 30 days, or 16 to 20,000 km (9942 to 12,428 miles), whichever comes first. Nalprep 2001 will not harm cooling system metals, seals, or hoses. It will not cause deterioration of cooling system sealants as some high PH cleaners will.

6. Completely drain the coolant from the engine and flush with fresh water as in step 4. Add Nalcool

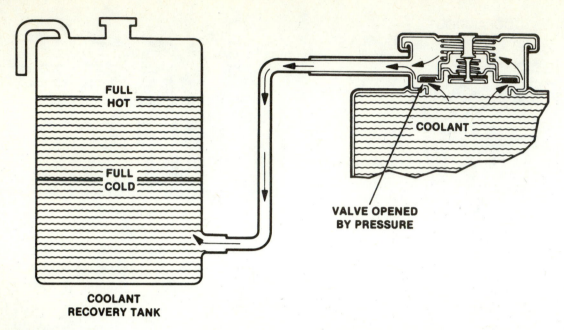

FIGURE 19–7 *Process of radiator pressure cap opening and directing expanded coolant to a recovery tank. (Courtesy of Detroit Diesel Corporation.)*

3000 (with Stabil-Aid) or equivalent; then add a mixture of antifreeze and water to the cooling system. On a Cummins engine, install a new *initial charge* coolant filter and a 50-50 mix of antifreeze to ensure the correct DCA-4 concentration.

PRESSURE CAPS

There are two descriptive terms that you may come across when dealing with cooling systems regardless of whether a radiator or heat exchanger system is being used. The first term is *A/W* (air-to-water differential) and is the difference between engine *coolant out*, or the top tank temperature, and the ambient air temperature. For example, with a stabilized top tank temperature of 185°F (85°C), and with air entering the radiator at 100°F (38°C), the differential is 85°F (29°C). The second term is *ATB* (air-to-boil) and represents the ambient air temperature at which top tank boiling occurs. The boiling point should always be considered as 212°F (100 °C). For example, consider the same engine operating at 185°F (85°C) with air at 100°F (38°C): 212°F (100°C) − 185°F (85°C) = 27°F (15°C) + 100°F (38°C) ambient = 127°F (53°C) air-to-boil.

All cooling systems are able to handle a specific heat load from a given engine and are designed to prevent engine overheating at sea level without the use of a pressure cap. A pressure cap, illustrated in Figure 19–7, is used to protect against boiling at above baseline elevations. System pressure is required to maintain water pump performance at elevated coolant tempera-

ture, to prevent loss of coolant at low-boiling-point altitudes, and to reduce coolant loss due to after boil at engine shutdown. Each pound of pressure applied to the cooling system raises the boiling point of the coolant by approximately 3°F (1.7°C); therefore, a 7 lb (48 kPa) pressure cap on a cooling system will raise the boiling point of the coolant from 212°F (100°C) at sea level to 232.5°F (111°C). For each 1000 ft (305 m) in altitude, the boiling point decreases by approximately 1.25°F (0.5°C). The opening pressure for all pressure caps is stamped or inscribed on the top of the cap in psi (kPa). For example, a number 12 indicates a 12 psi (83 kPa) cap.

Figure 19–7 illustrates a typical pressure cap for a cooling system. When the coolant pressure acting on the underside of the pressure cap seal against the spring becomes high enough, the valve unseats and hot coolant is normally routed to a surge tank to prevent any loss of coolant. When the spring pressure is greater than that developed in the cooling system, the valve closes. When an engine is shut down and the coolant starts to lose its temperature, it contracts, thereby reducing the pressure within the radiator, surge tank, or bottle and cooling system. To prevent collapse of hoses and other nonsupported components, a second and smaller valve within the pressure cap assembly opens as this vacuum is created. Figure 19–8 illustrates the action of this small valve, which usually opens at approximately ⅝ of a pound (4.3 kPa). The vacuum created as the fluid cools, sucks fluid from the radiator overflow line, which is normally connected to a separate surge tank or plastic bottle, and replenishes the radiator coolant volume.

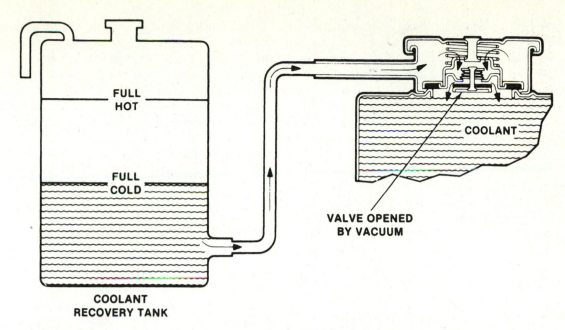

FIGURE 19–8 Opening of radiator cap vacuum valve as the engine cools to allow coolant to be recovered from the expansion tank, thereby preventing collapse of radiator hoses. (Courtesy of Detroit Diesel Corporation.)

To check the operating condition of the pressure cap, refer to Figure 19–9 which shows a hand tester installed on the cap. Pump up the pressure to the value stamped on the cap and note the rate of decrease on the gauge. If the pressure doesn't hold for approximately 10 seconds, replace the cap.

PRESSURE CHECKING THE COOLING SYSTEM

When coolant loss or overheating is a problem, the cooling system can be pressurized to help determine the location of the leak and to determine the causes of overheating under various operating conditions. Check the following areas:

Components that leak	Reasons for overheating
Hoses and clamps	Thermostat problem
Radiator cap	Aeration
Head and gasket	Shutter control thermostat
Water pump	Thermatic (thermally
Cylinder liner O-rings	activated) fan thermostat
or counterbore	Clogged Rad fins
Radiator, oil cooler,	Plugged radiator tubes
aftercooler and heater	Faulty water pump
cores	(slipping belt, broken
	impeller, or spinning of the
	impeller on its shaft)

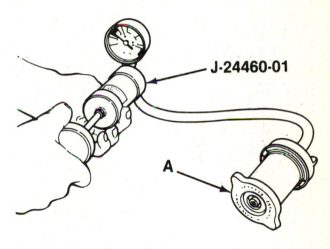

A. Radiator Cap

F-01021

FIGURE 19–9 Using a pressure pump to establish the opening pressure of the radiator cap. (Courtesy of GMC Trucks.)

A pressure check of the system can be performed in the following situations:

- During an engine rebuild when wet liners are replaced and before the oil pan is installed to check that the liner O-rings are not leaking
- During engine service when coolant is found in the engine oil and the liner O-rings may be the cause

- Suspected leak of a cylinder head water seal ring or gasket
- Suspected leak of an injector sleeve
- Suspected leak of fluid by the external engine cooling system components
- Checking the radiator or heat exchanger pressure cap for its opening pressure as well as the vacuum portion of the cap when the engine is shut down.

Figure 19–9 illustrates a standard cooling system pressure tester kit, which consists of a special graduated pressure gauge mounted to a hand-operated pump, a rad filler neck adaptor, a pressure cap adaptor, a rubber filler neck plug, and a hose assembly. Some models of cooling system analyzer kits come with a temperature probe to allow the technician to check the exact temperature of the cooling system while under pressure. The kit also allows troubleshooting of thermostat openings, thermatic fan operating range, and electronic temperature sensors, and it monitors new and rebuilt engines through warm-up cycles. The cooling system is easily checked for pressure by hooking up the shop-regulated air supply to a pressure probe and dialing in the desired test pressure. Unlike a hand operated pump test system, by using shop air the cooling system can be left pressurized for an extended period of time to find difficult and intermittent leaks. In addition, with the kit pressure probe, the cylinder head can be diagnosed for cracks, blown head gaskets, and leaking piston sleeves.

Attach the hand pump shown in Figure 19–9 to the radiator expansion/surge tank cap neck to check the cooling system for suspected leaks. Build up the system pressure by viewing the gauge until it registers the release pressure stamped on the rad cap. The system should hold pressure for about 2 minutes; if it doesn't, check for signs of external or internal leaks.

RADIATORS

A radiator is a form of heat exchanger that is designed to allow hot coolant from the engine to flow through a series of tubes or cores to dissipate its heat. The heat is dissipated by air being drawn through the radiator fins when the vehicle is stationary by an engine-driven suction fan; when the vehicle is moving, ambient ram (forced or pushed) air passes through the radiator. When a radiator is used on a stationary piece of equipment such as a portable air compressor, a *blower fan* pulls ambient air from below the unit and forces it through the radiator core in the opposite direction to what occurs on a car, truck, or piece of mobile equipment capable of being driven at a reasonable speed. There are three main types of radiators in use:

1. In a *downflow* design, the coolant flows from the top to the bottom of the radiator core. The effect of gravity in this type of system generally minimizes the restriction to the suction side of the water pump. Figure 19–10 illustrates a downflow system. Typical

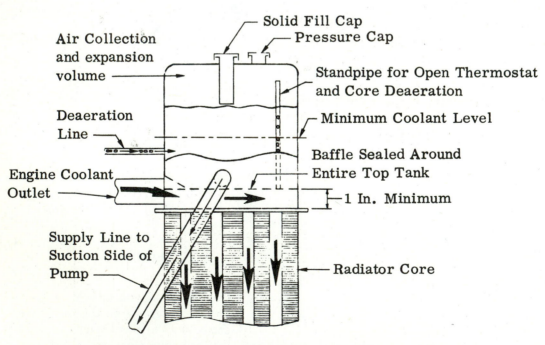

FIGURE 19–10 *Typical design of a heavy-duty downflow tube and fin radiator highlighting the baffled top tank. (Courtesy of Detroit Diesel Corporation.)*

heavy-duty Class 8 diesel trucks employ radiators with a frontal area ranging from 1000 to 1700 sq in. (6451 to 10,967 cm sq) depending on the engine power rating and the required heat loads.

2. In another design the hot coolant from the thermostat housing enters either the top or bottom of the radiator first and circulates through a series of tubes and liquid-tight baffles in a crossflow, downward, or upward loop. The number of passes of the coolant through these types of radiators depends on the heat transfer level required. Figure 19–11 illustrates a two-

pass crossflow radiator, and Figure 19–12 illustrates a two-pass counterflow design. A greater number of coolant passes increases the velocity of the coolant. In recent years, a two-pass design commonly referred to as LFC (low-flow-cooling) has been used by Cummins on a number of its truck engines. Figure 19–13 illustrates the basic flow from the engine to and through this system for a 14L engine. The main difference between an LFC system and a traditional system is that the LFC design has a reduced coolant flow rate through the radiator and usually operates with a higher pressure

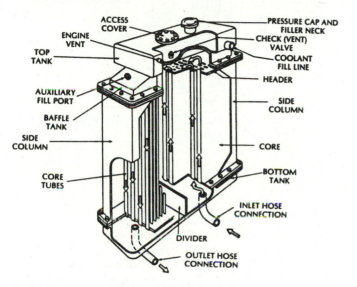

FIGURE 19–11 Coolant flow through a two-pass crossflow heavy-duty truck radiator. (Courtesy of Cummins Engine Company, Inc.)

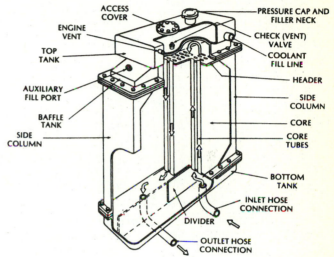

FIGURE 19–12 Coolant flow through a heavy-duty truck two-pass counterflow radiator. (Courtesy of Cummins Engine Company, Inc.)

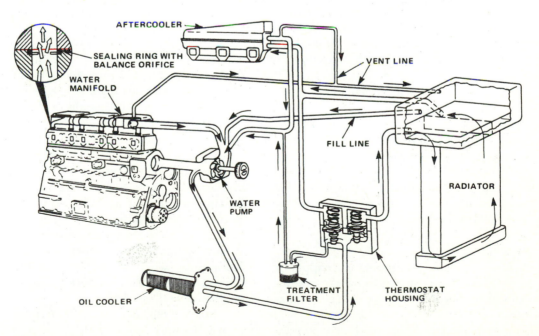

Figure 19–13 Coolant flow paths through a Cummins NTC (14L) engine low-flow cooling system. (Courtesy of Cummins Engine Company, Inc.)

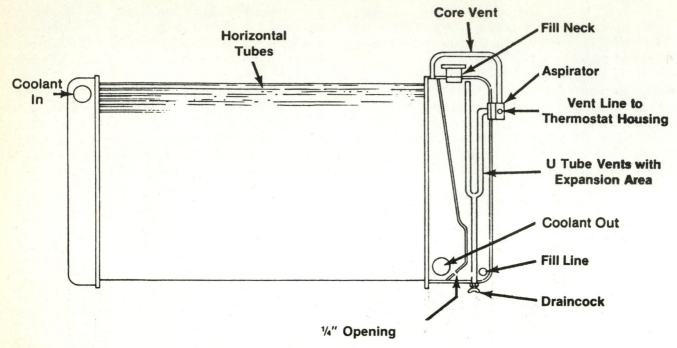

FIGURE 19–14 *Identification of components of a crossflow radiator system. (Courtesy of Cummins Engine Company, Inc.)*

cap, since system pressures can exceed 40 psi (276 kPa). The two-pass LFC radiator directs the engine coolant down one side of the core and up the other to increase tube velocity and keep the coolant in the radiator as long as possible. This results in a lower-temperature coolant to the water-cooled engine aftercooler, which lowers the charge temperature of the pressurized air flowing from the turbocharger to the engine. This in turn provides a denser air charge to the cylinders, resulting in improved fuel economy and lower exhaust emissions. The LFC system is generally not required on engines employing AAACs (air-to-air aftercoolers).

3. In a *crossflow* design the coolant enters the radiator along one of the side headers and flows horizontally through the core to the opposite side. Figure 19–14 illustrates a typical crossflow rad design for an inline engine. In vee-type engines two thermostat housings would be connected together, or alternatively, have two outlets to the radiator. The crossflow design allows a lower overall hood height, which is often necessary with aerodynamic truck styling.

Construction

Many heavy-duty trucks and equipment use copper or brass radiators, although the use of aluminum radiators is well underway. With the move in recent years to more aerodynamic heavy trucks, the nose of vehicles has become smaller. This has created a frontal downsizing that has forced radiator manufacturers to

handle increased cooling system loads in a smaller space for the higher-horsepower electronically controlled diesel engines. Throughout the 1970s, the common radiator consisted of four-and five-tube plate- and fin-type cores that were heavy and reliable. Coolant leaving the engine thermostat(s) is directed through the top rad hose to the top tank of the radiator where the hot coolant spreads across the tops of a series of vertical tubes and flows downward to the bottom tank as shown in Figure 19–15. The design of these tubes can vary. Figure 19–16 illustrates a smooth tube and a turbulated tube, and some tubes may incorporate a Z-wire arrangement assembled inside the tube. These tubes are usually a thin-wall brass construction but aluminum is a possibility. The number of tubes across the radiator and the number of rows employed (one behind the other) determine the heat load capability of the radiator. To increase the efficiency of the radiator, a series of *fins* are assembled around the tubes to provide an extended heat-transfer surface through which the air flows. Figure 19–17 illustrates two common types of fins, which are usually made from very-light-gauge copper, although some may use aluminum. When these fins become plugged with debris, the airflow is reduced substantially and the engine coolant overheats.

In the 1980s manufacturers started to develop less expensive and lighter-weight radiators that contain many aluminum components. Although the inside

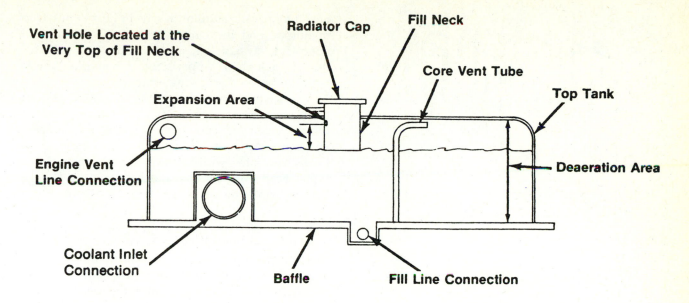

Vent Hole Located at the
Very Top of Fill Neck

Radiator Cap

Fill Neck

Core Vent Tube

Top Tank

Expansion Area

Engine Vent
Line Connection

Deaeration Area

Coolant Inlet
Connection

Baffle

Fill Line Connection

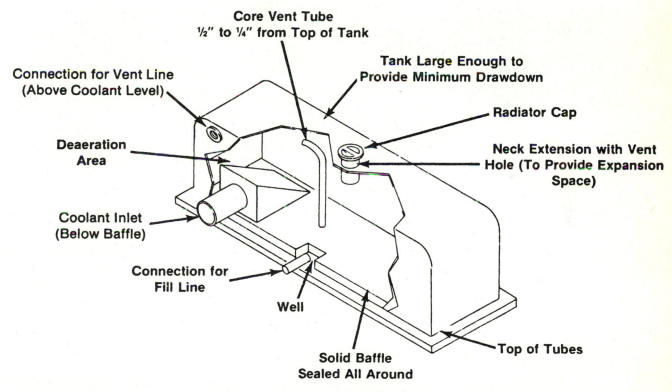

Core Vent Tube
½" to ¼" from Top of Tank

Tank Large Enough to
Provide Minimum Drawdown

Connection for Vent Line
(Above Coolant Level)

Radiator Cap

Deaeration
Area

Neck Extension with Vent
Hole (To Provide Expansion
Space)

Coolant Inlet
(Below Baffle)

Connection for
Fill Line

Well

Top of Tubes

Solid Baffle
Sealed All Around

FIGURE 19–15   *Design details of the deaerating type of radiator top tank of a heavy-duty truck. (Courtesy of Cummins Engine Company, Inc.)*

diameter of the tubes increased, the number of rows tended to decrease, and the durability of heavy-duty radiators suffered. In addition, the substitution of plastic crimped-on tanks for the traditional steel, bolt-on type of rad tank affected durability. Radiators account for 25% to 40% of cooling system costs and are the

third costliest maintenance item in heavy-truck fleets (daily fuel and tires are more costly).

Aluminum radiators are used in approximately 90% of the passenger cars in Europe, and usage in the United States is expected to increase from a level of about 57% to 72% within the next few years. Over the

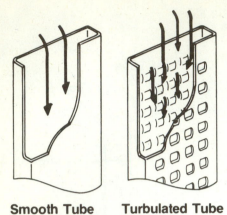

Smooth Tube   Turbulated Tube

FIGURE 19–16 *Two types of radiator tubes: smooth tube and turbulated tube. (Reprinted with permission from SAE Paper SP-824, copyright 1990, Society of Automotive Engineers, Inc.)*

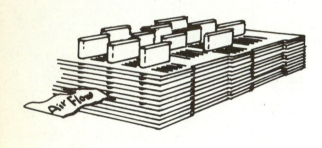

Plate Fin

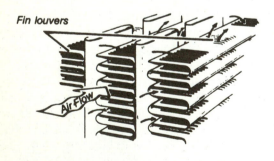

Serpentine Fin

FIGURE 19–17 *Types of radiator fins: plate fin and serpentine fin. (Reprinted with permission from SAE paper SP-824, copyright 1990, Society of Automotive Engineers, Inc.)*

next 3 to 5 years, aluminum rads in heavy-duty trucks in Europe and the United States will increase from approximately 62% to 75%. Aluminum rads seem to be durable enough in comparison to copper rads, but they tend to be less forgiving of poor coolant quality. Experience has shown that aluminum rads with round tubes are more susceptible to tube-end corrosion and disintegration when poor water quality and low coolant levels are encountered. The many epoxies, rods, and fluxes associated with the sealing and repair of these types of radiators tend to make these rads less forgiving than the earlier model copper or brass systems.

Maintenance

The life expectancy of a typical heavy-duty radiator has much to do with the coolant treatment and service, the application and operating conditions, abuse, and cleaning all dirt and grit regularly from the fins. In one of its recommended practices, the Maintenance Council of the American Trucking Associations states that the following average life (in mileage or years) should be expected from Class 6, 7, and 8 truck radiators:

Class and GVW (gross vehicle weight)	Engine size in liters	Life in miles/years
6: 19,501 to 26,000 lb (8846-11,794 kg)	Less than 10 L	250,000/5 (402,325 km)
7: 26,001 to 33,000 lb (11,794 to 14, 969 kg)	All engines	700,000/5 (1,126,510 km)
8: 33,000 lb (14,969 kg)	10 L and over	700,000/5 (1,126,510 km)

Causes of radiator failure can usually be traced to cracked radiator end tanks, fin rotting caused by sulfur oxide, leaks at surge tank seams, and vibration-induced tube breaks at the area where the tubes join with header tanks. In multiple-pass coolant flow rads, baffle leakage and failed RTV seals can cause the engine to run hotter. Failure of the radiator to maintain the coolant temperature prescribed by the engine manufacturer can create serious engine problems. A radiator that allows the coolant temperature to rise by 20° to 30°F (11° to 17°C) will substantially increase the engine lube oil temperature to the point where it may exceed the allowable maximum of 250°F (121°C), and oil degradation can quickly occur.

The state-of-the-art procedure for cleaning radiator cores is to employ *ultrasound* rather than to submerge the rad in a chemical bath and solvent flush, which was used for many years.

System Flow

Even though a number of different radiator systems are in use on heavy-duty trucks and equipment, the flow through the systems is similar. Figure 19–13 illustrates the basic flow through the engine and radiator when the engine thermostat(s) is closed (cold engine), and when the thermostat(s) is open when the engine has obtained normal operating temperature. Many heavy-duty trucks employ a *rapid warm-up* cooling system to allow the engine to reach its normal operating temperature as soon as possible. These systems require a radiator with a horizontal baffle in the top tank as shown in Figure 19–15. The baffle should completely seal the top tank from the radiator core and contain a J-tube that allows for deaeration lines with a continuous upward slope between the thermostat housing and/or the bypass tubes in vee-type engines and the top tank of the radiator.

The radiator top tank can be soldered or brazed to the core, crimped with seal rings, or bolted using seal strips. In Figure 19–15 the supply line to the suction side of the pump allows coolant that has not passed through the radiator to be used by the pump as needed. This uncooled liquid provides a faster engine warm-up. Note that the engine block deaeration lines are connected to the top tank, or surge tank, to vent all entrapped air from the engine and to prevent the possibility of air being taken from the top tank when the thermostats are open, at which time the deaeration line may sense pump suction. Deaeration lines are generally designed to limit the flow rate to a maximum of 5% system capacity.

To correctly fill these types of systems, the top tank should contain a minimum 1 in. (25.4 mm) fill line, which must slope downward toward the water pump inlet and not have any horizontal travel. The reason is that during initial filling of the cooling system, any air in the horizontal areas of the fill line can be trapped. The cooling system can become airbound causing overheating or water pump damage. Always idle the engine for several minutes, recheck the coolant level, and add coolant as needed. Figure 19–7 illustrates a typical radiator cooling system with a coolant recovery, or surge tank, system and the various plumbing requirements.

Servicing

When it becomes necessary to service a radiator, generally the technician has to drain it and remove it from the equipment. In most cases, the radiator is sent to a rad shop for inspection, descaling, rodding out of the tubes, and replacement of necessary components. If the core needs service, the technician may have to disassemble the radiator. Sometimes the service technician must inspect and replace components or seals, such as in the heavy-duty bolted-type radiator in Figure 19–11.

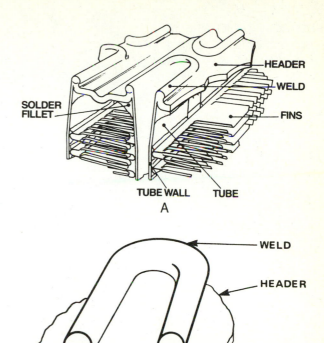

FIGURE 19–18 Construction features of (a) a heavy-duty radiator tube and fin system and a (b) soldered header and tube assembly. (Reprinted with permission from SAE Paper SP-824, copyright 1990, Society of Automotive Engineers, Inc.)

Regular service of the radiator on the vehicle or equipment requires that any coolant spilled onto the core fins be removed, because spilled antifreeze can form a sticky residue that quickly attracts dust and dirt and plugs the fins. High accumulations of dirt, dust, or bugs may require air pressure, steam, or water to dislodge them. Avoid *high pressure washers* since they can damage the rad fins. You may need to gently brush off the fins using a soft-bristle brush. Always direct steam or air pressure through the radiator core from the back to the front side; otherwise, dirt or bugs can become trapped as you drive them further into the core.

On radiators that have welded tube and header joints, such as the two examples shown in Figure 19–18, there is no solder on the water side of the header. Repair the header joint by reflowing solder on the air side. A leak in the tube can be repaired by a low-melting-point 50-50 solder. If a welded tube leaks and is not accessible for repair, it can be soldered shut on both ends to stop the leak. Very thin cracks on the

FIGURE 19–19 *System check for baffle leakage in a heavy-duty radiator. (Courtesy of Cummins Engine Company, Inc.)*

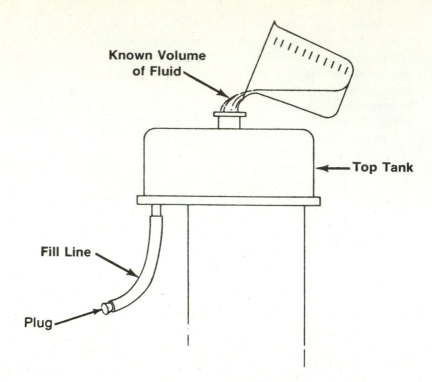

radiator header tank may be repaired temporarily using silver solder and flux.

In heavy-duty truck radiators that have a divided upper header tank, a baffle separates the header tank from the deaeration chamber as illustrated in Figure 19–15. After steel wool or a brush is used to clean and remove the old sealant, the baffle *must* be resealed using a new extruded seal and silicone sealant. Then wash with a low-residue solvent. It is very important to run the bead of new sealant in the V-clip as well as at the corners. With this type of sealant, it is advisable to store the radiator overnight in a warm area to allow the sealant to cure properly before attempting to add coolant to the system. If this seal leaks during engine operation, the engine can overheat as coolant leaks past the baffle seal, which will prevent it from passing through the radiator core. Although the coolant can return to the inlet side of the water pump, it will do so by flowing through the small-bore makeup line only.

If a top tank baffle is suspected of leaking, there are several methods to check the system. Begin by draining the coolant.

Procedure 1

1. Also drain the coolant from the deaeration area through the fill line as shown in Figure 19–19.
2. Plug off the fill line with a watertight plug.
3. Obtain a measured container that will allow you to determine how much coolant will be added to the top tank.

4. Fill the radiator top tank to the bottom of the fill neck with a measured amount of coolant. Do not attempt to add water beyond this level.
5. Allow the water added to the top tank to sit for at least 10 minutes.
6. Obtain a container that will hold the amount of coolant that was added to the top tank.
7. Remove the small fill-line plug and carefully measure the drained coolant.

Coolant retrieved that is less than that added initially to the top tank, confirms a leak in the baffle, radiator core vent tube, or the radiator inlet connection. Leaks in any of these areas allow coolant to flow through the radiator core with a fully blocking-type thermostat in the closed position.

Procedure 2

1. If the radiator is left in the vehicle, refer to Figure 19–20 and with the truck parked on a level surface, drain the coolant. Then connect the test hoses and equipment as shown.
2. If possible, use a regulated air supply of 1 psi (6.895 kPa) to pressurize the system. Alternatively, attach a 1 in. (25.4 mm) inside diameter clear plastic line about 12 ft (3.7 m) long to the inlet connection.
3. Fill the radiator with coolant through the funnel until the rad is full. Apply low air pressure until the water level on the inlet side is just above the bottom header by about ½ in. (12.7 mm).

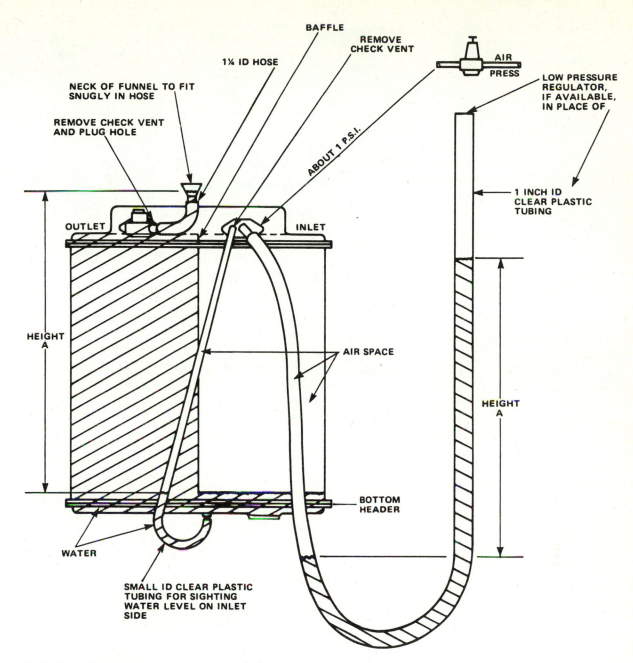

FIGURE 19–20 Hookup requirements for conducting a baffle seal leak test of a heavy-duty radiator with the radiator in the vehicle. (Courtesy of Peterbilt Motors Company, Division of PACCAR).

4. By monitoring the small ID plastic tubing, do not allow the water level to drop below the header during the filling stage.

5. Allow the system to sit for 3 to 5 minutes. If bubbles appear in the outlet hose there is a baffle leak.

If a pressure regulator system is not available, fill the rad slowly through the outlet hose until you can see water through the clear tubing reach a level of about 3 in. (76 mm) above the bottom header. Move to the larger 1 in. (25.4 m) clear plastic tubing and continue to add water until there is at least 3.5 ft (1.1 m) of air space between the water in this tube and the inlet to the rad top header tank. Go back to the top header outlet connection and slowly add water while raising the 1 in. (25.4 mm) clear tubing on the inlet side to balance the pressure. A large baffle leak will cause the water level to continue rising in this clear 1 in. (25.4 mm) tube as you pour water into the outlet side. If this does not occur, continue filling through the outlet fitting until full. Slowly raise the clear inlet hose until the water is about 1 in. above the bottom rad header. Allow the system to sit for 3 to 5 minutes. If air bubbles appear, there is a baffle leak.

Procedure 3

1. Drain the cooling system.
2. Remove the radiator from the vehicle. Class 8 trucks employ large and heavy radiators, so safely sling the rad to support it during removal.
3. Once removed, turn it upside down.
4. Pour coolant into the radiator with the fill hose attached to the side of the rad.
5. After 15 minutes, check the radiator. If the coolant level has dropped, the internal baffle seal is leaking.

Aeration Check

Air trapped in a cooling system can cause overheating as well as cause the water pump to become *air bound.* Air may be trapped in the cooling system when the system has been refilled after draining or flushing the system. When refilling a system, always open the vent cocks, particularly around the thermostat housing(s). Run the engine at an idle speed until a steady stream of coolant flows from the vent cocks, then close them. Air can also enter the cooling system because of a low coolant level in the radiator or expansion tank, through a suction leak on the inlet side of the water pump or loose hose connections, or by combustion gases escaping into the coolant.

To check a system for aerated coolant, remove the system pressure cap and replace it with a nonpressurized cap. You can use an old rad cap that has had the spring and the pressure relief valve removed to allow free flow of engine coolant from the rad or expansion tank connection. Figure 19–21 illustrates a solid rad cap in place with an overflow hose connected and submerged in a clear container of water. Proceed as follows:

1. Run the engine until it attains normal operating temperature.
2. Ideally, connect the engine to a dynamometer. If the engine is in a truck, place the engine on a chassis dynamometer. This is necessary so that the engine can be fully loaded to check if air bubbles might be caused by a leaking cylinder head gasket, and so on.
3. Refer to Figure 19–21 and check for signs of air bubbles in the clear container.

At rated speed and load, continuous air bubbles in the container indicate aeration is being induced through one

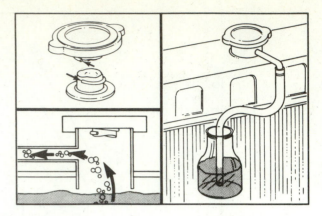

FIGURE 19–21 Hookup to determine if aerated coolant is present. (Courtesy of Cummins Engine Company, Inc.)

of the following causes: leaking cylinder head gasket, jacket water aftercooler core leakage, air compressor head or head gasket leakage, (since most heavy-duty units are cooled by coolant from the engine), defective fan or shutter air control valves (compressed air leakage), cracked cylinder head, cracked cylinder liner, or incorrect cylinder liner protrusion after overhaul.

Air leaks suspected to be induced by the cooling system can usually be traced by installing short pieces of thick, heavy-duty, round, clear plastic sections into the system supply and discharge lines and checking for air bubbles.

Winterfronts

A *winterfront,* illustrated in Figure 19–22, is an insulated covering located in front of the radiator. Usually it is manufactured from a plasticized fabric that is fastened with zippers, snaps, or a combination of the two. Designed to keep the engine coolant within normal temperature ranges when operating in severe cold weather, the winterfront also helps to further insulate the vehicle cab from severe wind-chill factors. Although used for many years on diesel-powered trucks and in engines equipped with jacket water aftercooling systems, it is not recommended for vehicles with AAAC (air-to-air aftercooled) engines. Blocking off airflow can cause reduced engine life, (pistons and valves), loss of power, and poor fuel economy. Refer to Chapter 20 for specific details related to winterfronts and AAAC systems.

In cases where a heavy truck operates in extremely cold ambient temperatures and a winterfront is used, it should *never* be closed completely. When used with a viscous fan assembly, there should be at least a 203 mm (8 in.) diamond area that is open permanently. This opening should be centered on the radiator—not at the top, bottom, or other off-center position. If more than

FIGURE 19–22 Typical location of a winterfront snapped to a heavy-duty truck radiator. (Courtesy of Detroit Diesel Corporation.)

one opening is used, these openings should be the same size at the top and bottom, or on the left- and right-hand sides, to produce a balanced airflow across the fan blades. Never install a winterfront directly in front of the radiator grill; leave at least 51 mm (2 in.) of air space between it and the radiator to ensure sufficient bypass cooling in the event that a winterfront is not opened in warming temperatures. When open, winterfronts should provide an airflow passage equal to or greater than 40% of the radiator core area. When outside temperatures are continually above 4.5°C (40°F), winterfronts should be removed.

JACKET WATER AFTERCOOLERS

Although most heavy-duty trucks are now equipped with AAACs (air-to-air aftercoolers—see Chapter 20), many stationary and marine engines employ JWAC (jacket water aftercoolers). In these systems the engine coolant is piped through the aftercooler core, as illustrated in Figure 19–23, to reduce the temperature of the pressurized turbocharger air flowing into the engine cylinders. The coolant that has passed through the engine is routed through the JWAC core and back toward the thermostat housing, where the warm coolant is circulated through the radiator and back to the water pump. Figure 19–24 illustrates an aftercooler contained within the intake manifold housing assembly. This location is common in a wide variety of four-stroke-cycle engines such as some Cummins and

Caterpillar models. Detroit Diesel two-stroke-cycle engines using JWACs have the cooler core located in the vee of the engine block air box, below the gear-driven roots blower assembly.

A JWAC system lowers the air temperature from the outlet side of the turbocharger under full load from about 300°F (149°C) to about 200°F (93°C). Some engines are equipped with an aftercooler system that plumbs the cool water from the base of the radiator through the aftercooler core first. This system, known as ALCC (advanced liquid charge cooling), can lower the full-load turbocharger air temperature from about 300°F (149°C) to approximately 160°F (71°C).

Marine Charge Air Cooling

A number of marine applications employ both a turbocharger IC (intercooler) and a fresh water engine-cooled aftercooler. This option is usually available on very-high-output engines only, for example, a V92 Detroit Diesel two-stroke-cycle engine equipped with two turbo-chargers (Figure 19–25). The turbocharger intercooler is placed between the air discharge side of the turbochargers and the air inlet side of the engine gear-driven blower. The intercooler has raw sea water pumped through it from an engine-driven raw water pump. The raw water usually makes about six passes through the intercooler core and is then discharged overboard. The turbocharger air enters the finned side of the intercooler opposite the water inlet and moves in a counterflow direction to that of the core water.

1. **Water Pump Outlet**
2. **Oil Cooler**
3. **Bypass Thermostat**
4. **Radiator Thermostat**
5. **Engine Water Outlet**
6. **Engine Water Inlet**
7. **Aftercooler Inlet**
8. **Aftercooler Outlet**
9. **Water Pump Inlet**

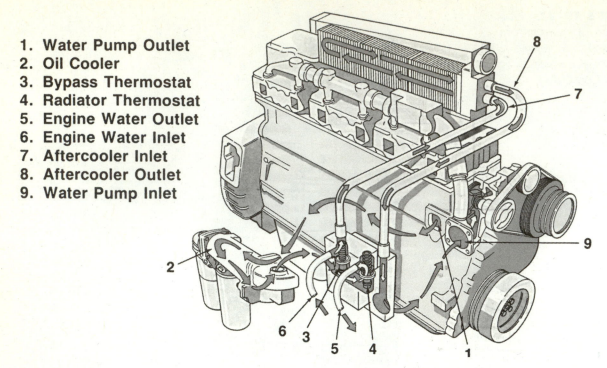

FIGURE 19–23 Coolant flow through a Cummins 14L Big Cam IV engine. Note the jacket water aftercooler. (Courtesy of Cummins Engine Company, Inc.)

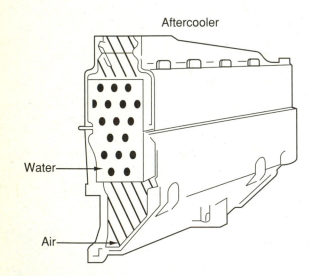

FIGURE 19–24 Sectionalized view of an aftercooler core. (Courtesy of Cummins Engine Company, Inc.)

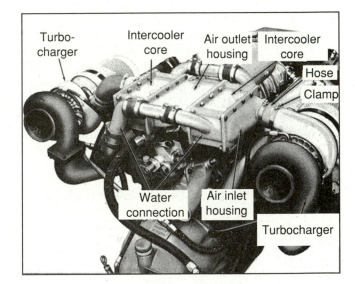

FIGURE 19–25 Turbocharger intercooler mounting and component identification for a very-high-output V92 DDC engine in a marine application using charge air cooling. (Courtesy of Detroit Diesel Corporation.)

JWAC and turbocharger intercoolers can be cleaned and descaled by using an ultrasound procedure similar to that for a radiator core or by immersing the core in a chemical solution. To clean the intercooler shown in Figure 19–25, use a solvent consisting of 0.22 kg (½ pound) of oxalic acid to each 9.5 L (2.5 U.S. gallons) of a solution consisting of one-third muriatic acid and two-thirds water. Note that this cleaning process requires only about 30 to 60 seconds, and when the core is immersed in the solution a brisk bubbling and foaming action results. The core should be flushed thoroughly with clean, hot water under pressure at the completion of the descaling proce-

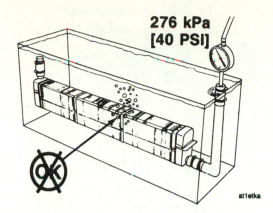

276 kPa [40 PSI]

at1etka

FIGURE 19–26 *Method used to pressure test an aftercooler core. (Courtesy of Cummins Engine Company, Inc.)*

dure. To clean the jacket water aftercooler core illustrated in Figure 19–24, immerse the core in a tank filled with a solution of clean-parts dip such as Soak-NS or equivalent for approximately 12 hours; then rinse thoroughly with a steam cleaner or high-pressure water unit.

Both a JWAC and a turbocharger intercooler core can be pressure checked to ensure there are no leaks. Figure 19–26 illustrates a JWAC core from a Cummins 14L engine with the coolant outlet hose sealed off and an adapter for a pressurized air fitting attached to the inlet side. The JWAC core is submerged in a test tank with the surrounding water heated to approximately 180°F (82°C). A turbocharger intercooler core can be tested in the same way. Cummins recommends that 276 kPa (40 psi) be applied to the core. DDC recommends only 138 kPa (20 psi) be applied to the turbocharger intercooler core. Any sign of air bubbles at the core during the test indicates a cracked or damaged core, which should be repaired or replaced.

THERMOSTATS

Purpose and Function

Although the radiator or heat exchanger system absorbs and dissipates the rejected heat to the cooling system, to maintain a steady coolant temperature under all operating conditions, all internal combustion engines employ temperature controlled thermostats (stats) or regulators. The thermostat(s) is normally located within a bolted housing at the top front of the engine block as illustrated in Figure 19–27. To perform effectively, a stat must operate as follows:

- Start to open at a specified temperature.
- Be fully open at a specified number of degrees above the *start-to-open* temperature.
- Allow a specified amount of coolant under pressure to flow when the stat is fully open.
- Block all coolant flow to the radiator when in the closed position.

As you can see in Figure 19–27b, all engine coolant flows through a bypass pipe (hose) back to the suction side of the water pump at temperatures below the opening point of the stat. Additional coolant requirements of the pump during this period are supplied through a makeup or fill line. When the engine coolant reaches the stat opening temperature, engine coolant flows through the open stat to the top rad hose as shown in Figure 19–28 to the baffle area of the radiator top tank. This hot coolant then passes through the radiator tubes where it gives up its heat to the airflow moving through the rad fins.

Types

Depending on the cooling system design three basic types of thermostats can be used in diesel engines: full blocking, nonblocking, and partial blocking. Let's look more closely at each one of these types.

Figure 19–29 illustrates the full-blocking type of stat. Figure 19–28 depicts the actual flow of coolant through the stat to the radiator HE (heat exchanger) as well as the bypass circuit. During engine warm-up, all engine coolant flows through the bypass circuit, thereby preventing any coolant from being exposed to heat loss by flowing through the rad or HE. This provides for a faster warm-up period. As the thermostat begins to open, increasing amounts of engine coolant flow to the rad or HE, and bypass flow is correspondingly reduced. At approximately 15° to 20°F (8° to 11°C) above the opening temperature of the stat, the bypass opening is fully blocked and the total flow of coolant is directed into the radiator or HE.

The partial blocking type of stat shown in Figure 19-30 directs coolant to a bypass passage connected to the water pump when cold (closed), but directs all coolant flow to the radiator or HE when hot (open). Figure 19-31 illustrates a partial blocking, or shielded stat assembly as it would actually appear.

Figure 19-32 illustrates a non-blocking (choke or poppet-type) thermostat which will always bypass some coolant down the bypass line to the water pump while the stat is open or closed.

Construction and Operation

Engine coolant is corrosive even when properly maintained and treated with antifreeze and SCAs. Stats, therefore, are normally made from brass or

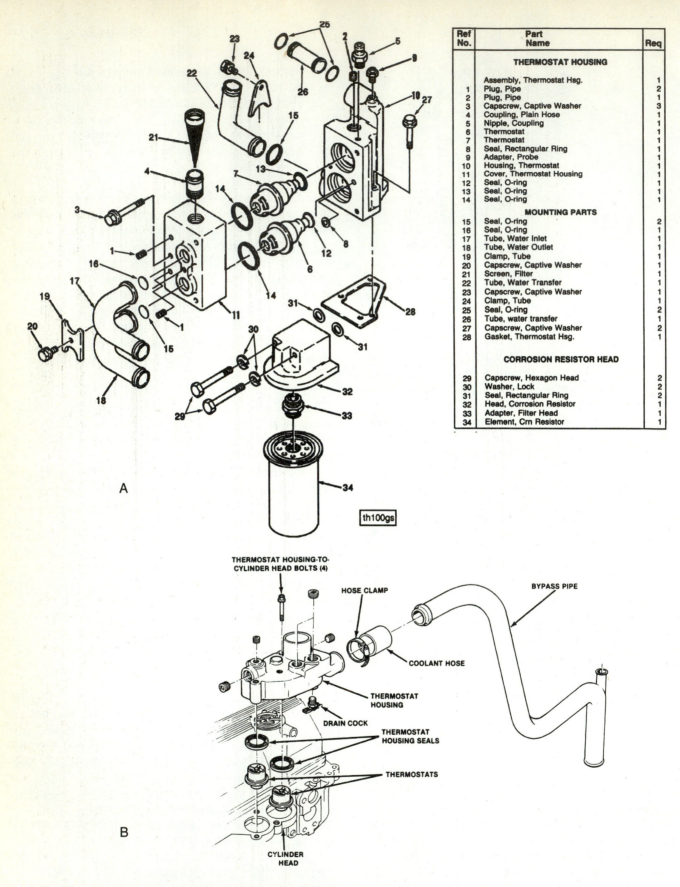

Ref No.	Part Name	Req
	THERMOSTAT HOUSING	
	Assembly, Thermostat Hsg.	1
1	Plug, Pipe	2
2	Plug, Pipe	1
3	Capscrew, Captive Washer	3
4	Coupling, Plain Hose	1
5	Nipple, Coupling	1
6	Thermostat	1
7	Thermostat	1
8	Seal, Rectangular Ring	1
9	Adapter, Probe	1
10	Housing, Thermostat	1
11	Cover, Thermostat Housing	1
12	Seal, O-ring	1
13	Seal, O-ring	1
14	Seal, O-ring	1
	MOUNTING PARTS	
15	Seal, O-ring	2
16	Seal, O-ring	1
17	Tube, Water Inlet	1
18	Tube, Water Outlet	1
19	Clamp, Tube	1
20	Capscrew, Captive Washer	1
21	Screen, Filter	1
22	Tube, Water Transfer	1
23	Capscrew, Captive Washer	1
24	Clamp, Tube	1
25	Seal, O-ring	2
26	Tube, water transfer	1
27	Capscrew, Captive Washer	2
28	Gasket, Thermostat Hsg.	1
	CORROSION RESISTOR HEAD	
29	Capscrew, Hexagon Head	2
30	Washer, Lock	2
31	Seal, Rectangular Ring	2
32	Head, Corrosion Resistor	1
33	Adapter, Filter Head	1
34	Element, Crn Resistor	1

FIGURE 19–27 (a) Exploded view of the component parts of the thermostat housing used on N14 model engines. (Courtesy of Cummins Engine Company, Inc.) (b) Thermostats and related parts for a Series 60 DDC engine model. (Courtesy of Detroit Diesel Corporation.)

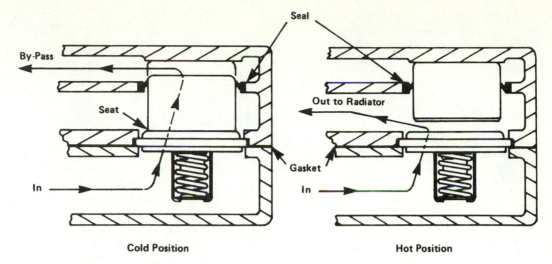

FIGURE 19–28 Coolant flow to the bypass pipe and to the radiator in the cold and hot positions when using a fully blocking type of thermostat. (Courtesy of Cummins Engine Company, Inc.)

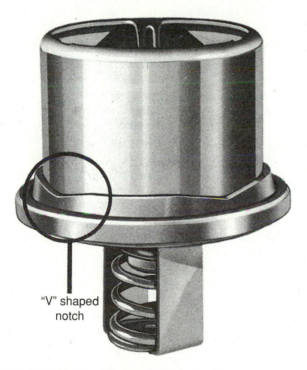

FIGURE 19–29 Weir-type fully blocking thermostat design. (Courtesy of Detroit Deisel Corporation.)

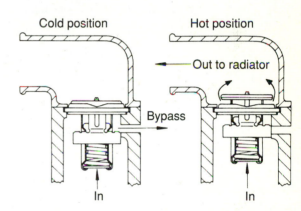

FIGURE 19–30 Coolant flow through a partial blocking thermostat. (Courtesy of Detroit Diesel Corporation.)

brass-coated materials. The stat consists of a brass cup filled with a heat-expansive, wax-like material (sometimes referred to as beeswax) retained within the cup by an elastomeric seal. The stat valve is connected to a piston which is held on the elastomer by a spring. Figure 19–33 illustrates the basic construction and operation of a thermostat.

A stat can be vented or nonvented. The *vent* refers to the deaeration capability of the cooling system. The design of the cooling system determines whether the stat is vented, or not. In a vented system, venting is accomplished by drilling a small hole in the stat valve or notching the valve at its seat (see the design shown in Figure 19–29). Nonvented stats should only be installed in cooling systems of the positive deaeration type. This is usually the case if one or more deaeration lines (hoses) extend from the stat housing area to the rad or HE top tank.

Designs

Engine manufacturers employ various types of stats and locate one or more within a housing similar to

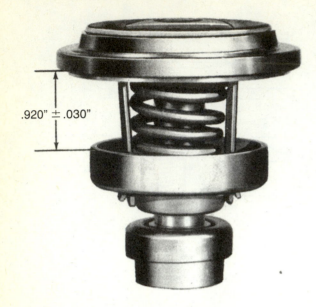

.920" ± .030"

Current

FIGURE 19–31 *Partial, or semi-blocking (shielded) thermostat. (Courtesy of Detroit Diesel Corporation.)*

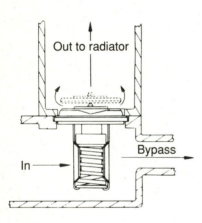

Out to radiator

In →

Bypass

FIGURE 19–32 *Coolant flow through a nonblocking (choke or poppet) thermostat. (Courtesy of Detroit Diesel Corporation.)*

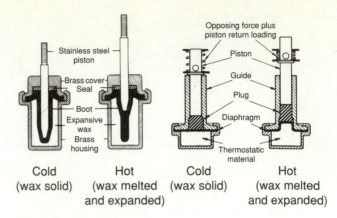

FIGURE 19–33 *Construction and operation of a typical thermostat assembly. (Courtesy of Detroit Diesel Corporation.)*

that shown in Figure 19–27. For example, in the Cummins optimized JWAC and LFC radiator cooling system, two stats are used within a common housing; one stat is a bypass type while the other is a radiator type. At engine start-up, the bypass stat is wide open and the radiator stat is closed. Coolant flows through the stat housing to the JWAC aftercooler inlet to allow the gradually warming coolant to heat the intake air for more efficient combustion. When the coolant temperature reaches 160°F (71°C), flow to the aftercooler decreases as the bypass stat begins to close. At coolant temperatures below 175°F (79°C), there is no coolant flow through the radiator core; all of the coolant flows through the bypass stat to the aftercooler. Take careful note that at 175°F (79°C) the rad stat begins to open and some coolant begins to flow to the radiator; therefore between 175° and 185°F (79° to 85°C), the two stats operate together to control the flow and temperature of coolant flow to the aftercooler and the radiator.

At engine coolant temperatures above 185°F (85°C), the bypass stat to the JWAC is fully closed. The radiator stat continues to open until it is fully open at 195°F (91°C) or higher and all engine coolant flows to and through the radiator as illustrated in Figure 19–13. The maximum allowable coolant temperature in these engines is 212°F (100°C). Depending on the Cummins engine model in use, 10 to 20 U.S. gpm (38 to 76 L) of coolant flows through the radiator stat to the low-flow rad.

Removal and Inspection

In cases of engine or coolant overheating, many service personnel remove the thermostats. This should only be done, however, as a temporary measure to allow possible relocating of the vehicle or equipment when all else fails. Stat removal normally should *not* be done. Operating an engine without a stat is not recommended because the engine will run too cool, thereby causing condensation of water and incomplete combustion, which results in corrosive acids and sludge forming in the lube oil. This can restrict lube oil flow and accelerate engine wear. In addition, poor combustion causes rough idling and increased amounts of exhaust pollutants and white smoke (water vapor). When using full- or partial-blocking type stats that fail to open fully (or stick closed), the bypass system will remain open and prevent a suffi-

FIGURE 19–34 *Temporary installation of a section of hose in a thermostat leakage test. (Courtesy of Cummins Engine Company, Inc.)*

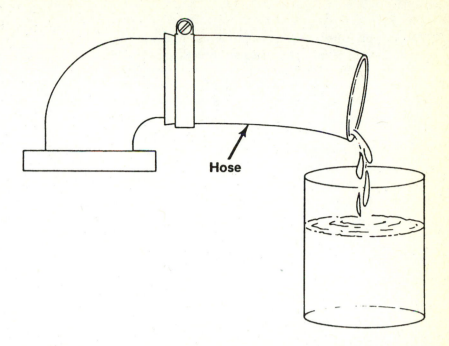

Hose

cient flow of coolant to the radiator or HE. As a result, the engine coolant temperature may rise even higher.

The actual stat location and housing shape vary in different makes and models of engines. We can assume, however, that most diesel engines place their stat close to the top end of the engine in a manner similar to that shown in Figure 19–27b for a DDC Series 60 four-stroke-cycle engine. Some engines employ a single stat while others may employ two or more based on flow rate requirements to the rad or HE when open. Sufficient coolant must be drained from the system to prevent loss of coolant when removing the stat housing.

Figure 19–27a identifies the major components of the stat assembly and seals used with a full-blocking type of arrangement. Even if the stat is functioning correctly, leaking seals will allow coolant to continue to flow to the bypass passage when the engine is warm and the stat is open. Leaking seals also allow some coolant to leak to the rad or HE when the engine is cold. Review Figure 19–28, which illustrates coolant flow in closed and open stat conditions. To check for leaking stat seals, perform these steps:

1. Make sure the engine is *cold* to ensure that the stat is closed.
2. Remove the upper rad hose from the stat housing.
3. Temporarily install a section of hose as shown in Figure 19–34 to direct coolant discharged from the housing.
4. Start the engine and note if any coolant pours from the hose.

5. Slowly accelerate the engine to wide open throttle for 1 minute.
6. Measure the accumulated coolant. It should not exceed 100 cc/min (3.3 fluid ounces/min), which is less than one-half cup. If leakage exceeds this rate, either the stat or seal is leaking.
7. Remove the stat and check it visually for any signs of scoring or damage. Both stat and seal damage can be due to dirty coolant or silica dropout. Although silica gel from overconcentrated antifreeze or SCAs is nonabrasive, it can pick up solid particles in the coolant and become a gritty abrasive deposit that can cause excessive wear of water pump and other seals.
8. Check the stat housing for correct alignment between the two halves, and check that the gasket has been properly positioned and aligned.

Opening Temperature and Distance

Each stat is designed and constructed to start to open at a specific temperature, which is stamped on the stem or housing area. The stat control section moves through a set distance to its fully open position. For example, Figure 19–31 shows that this stat should move through a distance of 23.36 mm ± 0.76 mm (0.920 in. ± 0.030 in.). Failure of the stat to open fully will restrict the engine coolant from reaching the rad or HE. For example, a 180°F (82°C) stat would have a start-to-open temperature in the range of 177° to 183°F (81° to 83°C) and should be fully open at approximately 197°F (92°C).

Operational Check

Never apply direct flame heat to a stat to cause it to open. Do not allow the stat to sit directly against the bottom of a metal container filled with water during the test. Ideally, the stat should be suspended in a container of clean water as shown in Figure 19–35 along with a suspended thermometer. Some stat test kits include a small drive motor that spins a propeller to constantly agitate the water. If this is not available, stir the water during the heating process.

Follow these steps as part of your operational check of a thermostat:

1. Note the temperature stamped on the stat.
2. Carefully record the temperature at which the stat starts to open. It may take 10 minutes for some stats to reach their full open condition.
3. Carefully watch the thermometer; the stat should be *fully open* at approximately 15° to 20°F (8° to 11°C) above the stamped value on the stat.
4. Using vernier calipers, carefully measure the distance that the stat has moved from closed to open. Figure 19–31 shows one example of a stat opening distance. Refer to the engine service literature for the spec relative to your engine make and model.
5. Replace a stat that fails to open at the correct temperature or fails to open fully.

Stats can become damaged from an overheated engine condition, which may be due to restriction to coolant flow through the rad or HE (scale, hardened gel), collapsed or weak hoses, slipping fan belts, coolant leaks, or aerated coolant. Stats that are stuck open prevent the engine from reaching its normal operating temperature. A stat that does not open, or only opens partially, can cause engine overheating. Prior to replacing stats, make sure that the stat housing seating/seal and gasket areas are cleaned of rust and scale buildup. When installing a new seal (see Figure 19–27), make certain that the seal is installed in the proper direction and use a seal driver so that the seal is not kinked or installed off square when driven into the housing(s). Apply a small amount of clean engine oil to lubricate the seal lips before pushing the stats into position. Some engines employ horizontally installed stats and seals, whereas others have vertically installed stats and seals. When installing the stat housing gasket, be careful not to apply excessive amounts of gasket cement. Cement can damage the seal lip or accumulate on the stat. If a stat housing drain cock or vent cock is used, apply a coating of Loctite Pipe Sealer with Teflon or equivalent to the threads.

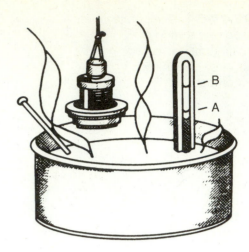

A – Starts to open
B – Fully open

FIGURE 19–35 Test equipment needed to perform a thermostat operational check. (Courtesy of Detroit Diesel Corporation.)

RADIATOR SHUTTERS

Some heavy-duty trucks and tractors have a venetian-blind type of mechanism mounted directly in front of the radiator core. This device is known as a *shutter assembly*, and it is designed to control cooling air flow across the radiator. Certain truck models may install the radiator shutters behind the radiator core. Figure 19–36 illustrates both types of systems. Both shutter assemblies have horizontal vanes, but some crossflow radiator designs employ vertical vanes. The shutter assembly is designed to maintain and control the operating temperature of the engine coolant within a given range. It is commonly used on trucks operating in cold ambient conditions.

CAUTION: Shutters are commonly used on trucks that employ JWAC systems. Shutters should not be used on engines equipped with AAAC systems unless the installation provides for mounting the shutter between the AAAC core and the radiator core. Mounting a shutter assembly in front of the AAAC core will result in hot air from the turbocharger compressor entering the engine. This can cause short valve and piston life as well as poor fuel economy and a reduction in engine power.

Shutters are only used in conjunction with a clutch fan. With the shutters in the closed position, a fan would be highly stressed in attempting to pull air through a closed rad core. To prevent this condition from occurring, a thermally operated fan clutch is used, which can be disengaged until the radiator shutters are opened.

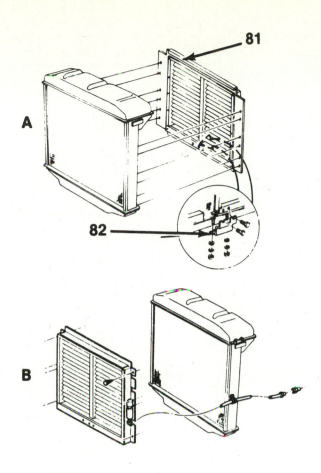

81. **Shutter Assembly**
82. **Bracket**
A. **Rear Installation**
B. **Front Installation**

F-03883

FIGURE 19–36 *Heavy-duty radiator shutter arrangement showing (a) the shutter assembly located behind the radiator core and (b) the shutter located in front of the radiator core. (Courtesy of GMC Trucks.)*

The actual engine coolant temperature at which the shutters and thermatic fan engage depends on the opening temperature of the engine coolant thermostat. The basic sequence of events for a heavy-duty Class 8 truck equipped with 82°C (180°F) coolant thermostats, shutters, and a thermatic clutch fan is presented in Figure 19–37. The vanes, or individual blinds, of the shutter assembly are connected by mechanical rod-type linkage so that they can be opened or closed to suit engine operating temperature conditions.

The power unit that rotates the vanes is an air cylinder which operates on compressed air from the vehicle air brake reservoir. The shutters are either fully open or fully closed. To prevent overheating of the engine in the event of a system malfunction, the shut-

ters are normally held open by spring pressure and closed by air pressure. Figure 19–38 illustrates one example of a shutter system used in conjunction with a compressed-air disengaged fan clutch. Some shutters are open upon initial engine start-up, and between 275 and 380 kPa (40 to 55 psi) is required to close them. They remain closed until the engine coolant temperature is hot enough to trigger the shutter *thermostat*, which is located close to the engine thermostat(s). In addition to maintaining engine coolant temperature, the shutters can function on *Freon* pressure to meet air-conditioning demands.

Figure 19–39 illustrates a typical shutter thermostat, which is generally referred to as a *shutterstat*. This stat is the ON/OFF switch for the shutter system. The stat is installed in the engine water manifold close to the coolant outlet to respond to the hottest coolant temperature. When the engine is cold, the shutterstat allows vehicle compressed air to enter one side of it and exit on the other. This compressed air is directed to a radiator shutter air cylinder, illustrated in Figure 19–38, where the bushing connected to the shutter vane linkage causes the vanes to close, thereby preventing any cooling air from moving through the radiator core. If we assume that the shutterstat is set to begin opening at 85°C (185°F), when this temperature is reached the shutterstat shuts off air supply to the air cylinder while simultaneously exhausting air from the cylinder. With no compressed air to hold the vanes closed, a heavy-duty spring connected to the shutter linkage pulls them open to allow cooling air to the radiator core.

Shutter Operational Checks

Failure of the shutters to open at the desired setting temperature results in the engine running hot. On the other hand, failure of the shutters to close can cause a cold-running engine. The operational check consists of five main tasks:

1. Check the shutter thermostat.
2. Check the air-operated shutter controls.
3. Check for air leaks.
4. Check the operating linkage for binding.
5. Check the vanes for bends or twists.

If the shutter system is not functioning correctly, proceed as follows.

1. If the engine is running cold, start and run the engine at between 900 and 1000 rpm. With the engine running and the shutters closed, hold a large sheet of paper across the front of the vanes. The sheet of paper should not remain in position when you release it. If it does, this usually indicates there is air passing through the vanes and radiator (suction). This

Figure 19–37 Heavy-duty truck cooling system operating temperatures for various components when using a 180°F opening thermostat(s).

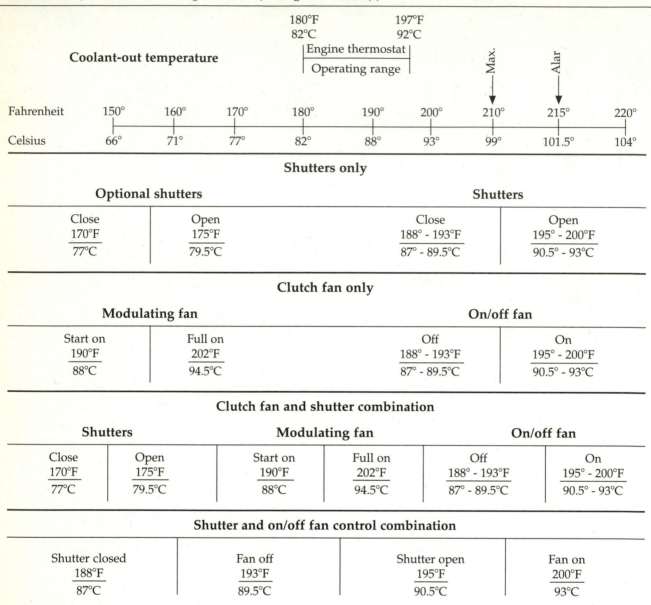

	Shutters only		
Optional shutters		**Shutters**	
Close 170°F ―――― 77°C	Open 175°F ―――― 79.5°C	Close 188° - 193°F ―――――――― 87° - 89.5°C	Open 195° - 200°F ―――――――― 90.5° - 93°C

	Clutch fan only		
Modulating fan		**On/off fan**	
Start on 190°F ―――― 88°C	Full on 202°F ―――― 94.5°C	Off 188° - 193°F ―――――――― 87° - 89.5°C	On 195° - 200°F ―――――――― 90.5° - 93°C

		Clutch fan and shutter combination			
Shutters		**Modulating fan**		**On/off fan**	
Close 170°F ―――― 77°C	Open 175°F ―――― 79.5°C	Start on 190°F ―――― 88°C	Full on 202°F ―――― 94.5°C	Off 188° - 193°F ―――――――― 87° - 89.5°C	On 195° - 200°F ―――――――― 90.5° - 93°C

	Shutter and on/off fan control combination		
Shutter closed 188°F ―――― 87°C	Fan off 193°F ―――― 89.5°C	Shutter open 195°F ―――― 90.5°C	Fan on 200°F ―――― 93°C

can cause the engine to run cold. Check the individual vanes and the operating linkage for sticking or bending. Open the shutters at the air cylinder to check the condition of the vane seals and replace these if worn. If the seals are in good condition, check their sealing status by closing the shutters and inserting a 0.38 mm (0.015 in.) feeler gauge between the vanes. If there is a drag when removing the gauge, vane adjustment is OK. If not, adjust the shutter linkage by applying air to the air cylinder (see Figure 19–38) and loosen the jam nut located under the rocker arm; then tighten the jam nut on top of the rocker arm to close the vanes. If adjustment fails to repair the problem, closely check the linkage for wear and replace necessary components.

2. When an engine overheating problem exists and the shutters are suspected as being the cause, proceed as follows. Install either a master temperature gauge or a thermocouple in the engine at the upper front water manifold. Restrict the radiator airflow if necessary to block all airflow. Operate the engine at high idle or on a chassis dynamometer until it reaches the temperature stamped on the shutter thermostat assembly (see Figure 19–39). Refer to the thermocouple or master temperature gauge and see if the shutters open fully at this point. Allow the engine to return to idle and remove the rad restriction cover. As the engine cools off, carefully note when the shutters close; normally this occurs at

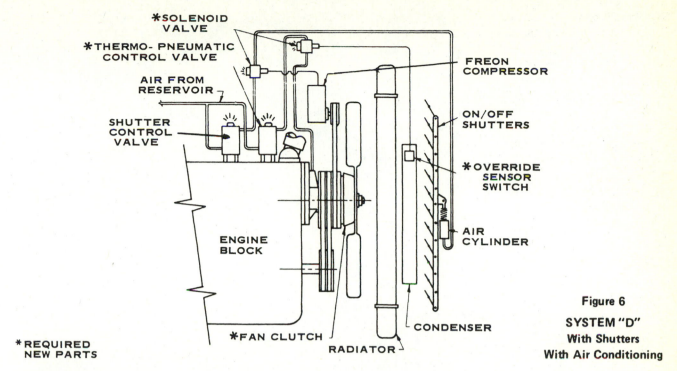

FIGURE 19–38 *Component arrangement of heavy-duty truck cooling system showing the shutter, fan clutch, and air-conditioning condenser control system. (Courtesy of Allied Signal Truck Brake Systems Company).*

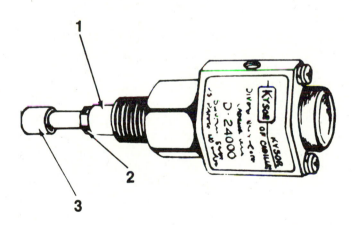

1. Shutterstat Base
2. Jam Nut
3. Power Element

B-02736

FIGURE 19–39 *Features of a typical radiator shutter thermostatic control unit. (Courtesy of GMC Trucks.)*

approximately 6°C (10°F) below the temperature stamped on the shutterstat.

3. The shutterstat can be removed and tested in the same way the engine thermostat assembly was tested (as described earlier in this chapter). During this test, compressed air can be plumbed to the *inlet* port of the shutterstat with a small pressure gauge connected

to the outlet port. The gauge should register air pressure when the stat is submerged in water below its trigger temperature. When the heated water reaches the temperature stamped on the shutterstat, the gauge pressure should drop to zero. If the shutterstat fails to operate within a 5°F (3°C) range of that stamped on the housing, replace the shutterstat.

4. Refer to Figure 19–38, which includes the shutter air cylinder. Disconnect the vehicle air supply line from this cylinder and hook an air supply line directly to it that is teed into a good pressure gauge. Refer to the service literature and apply the recommended pressure to the cylinder to determine if it operates as specified. Also check for air leaks from the cylinder assembly.

5. Most trucks are equipped with a shutter protection valve that can be located at the air reservoir, cowl junction block, instrument package manifold valve, or other accessory air port. The valve is designed to cut off air supply to the shutter system if pressure in the air tanks drops below a given level; approximately 450 kPa (65 psi) is a normal value. This protection valve can be checked by exhausting air from the system and connecting a pressure gauge to the supply side of the valve between the tank and valve. Allow the pressure to build up to the valve trigger pressure. If we assume that this is 450 kPa (65 psi) as indicated on the gauge, this pressure should cause the valve to open and result

FIGURE 19-40

Determining the characteristics of a heavy-duty truck fan assembly. A = swept diameter; B = hub pilot hole diameter; C = bolt circle diameter; D = fan blade pitch width; E = front-to-back distance. To the right are fan-to-shroud and bade-tip-to-shroud clearances. (Courtesy of Kysor/Cadillac, Division of Kysor Industrial Corporation, Cadillac, MI).

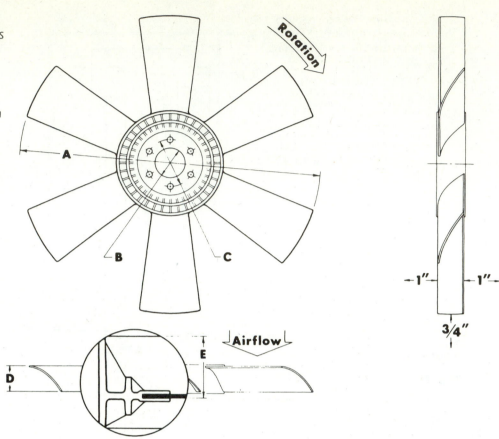

in a delivery pressure of 345 kPa (50 psi). If the pressures do not meet specifications, replace the valve.

6. Shutterstat fluid or penetrating oil can be used to lubricate the shutter control linkage. This would include the vane pins, bearings, and surfaces, including the control bar. Manually operate the vanes until they move freely; then remove excess fluid with rags and a suitable solvent.

FANS

The engine-driven fan assembly is designed to provide cooling airflow through the radiator core as well as to circulate air across the engine block and components. The effectiveness of the radiator depends on the cooling air that moves through its core. Although flow of coolant through the radiator is extremely important, the flow of air through the radiator is more critical.

The quantity of air moved through a radiator depends on fan diameter, number of blades and pitch, speed, fan-to-rad position, shroud design, and overall system air pressure. A guideline to determine adequate air flow is based on the temperature rise of the air (40° to 50°F) as it passes through the rad core and picks up heat from the coolant flowing through the rad cores. This can be estimated as follows: total Btu input

to coolant × 1.25 = cfm (cu ft/min) for a 450 bhp (336 kW) engine with a 33 Btu/hp/min heat rejection to the cooling system, 450 × 33 × 1.25 = 18,563 cfm at 500 ft (152 m) above sea level.

Fan manufacturers can supply a listing of their various fans and the airflow movement at a given speed. The construction of the radiator (rows of tubes, fins per inch, fin design, and so forth) affects the airflow and the system working pressure. In general, the denser the rad core and the higher the airflow of the fan assembly, the higher will be the operating pressure.

Figure 19-40 illustrates the method used to determine the characteristics of a given fan assembly. Refer to the figure and follow this explanation:

1. Dimension A is the swept diameter of the fan.
2. Dimension B is the hub pilot hole diameter.
3. Dimension C is the bolt circle diameter.
4. Dimension D is the fan blade pitch width, which can be determined by laying the fan on a flat surface and measuring the distance from the lowest to the highest point of the fan blade.
5. Dimension E, known as the front-to-back distance, is determined by laying the fan on a flat surface with the side that faces the radiator

core up. Measure the vertical distance from this surface to the highest point of the fan. Then measure the vertical distance from the surface to the bottom edge of the pilot hole, and subtract this distance from the first one. The purpose of obtaining this dimension is to establish that sufficient clearance will be available when the fan is installed.

6. The maximum fan speed can be calculated by measuring the diameter of the driving and driven pulleys according to this formula:

$$\text{fan rpm} = \text{engine rated rpm} \times \frac{\text{driving pulley diameter}}{\text{driven pulley diameter}}$$

7. The right side of the fan diagram illustrates suggested fan-to-shroud clearances of 1 in. (25.4 mm) and blade-tip-to-shroud clearance of ¾ in. (19 mm).

Most radiator fans are driven by *multiple belts*; of vee- or polyvee-design belts on heavy-duty trucks and equipment. The fan is mounted and supported on a hub, which consists of a shaft and support bearings similar to that illustrated in Figure 19–41. Tests over many years have proven that the fan assembly is only required for a short time during engine operation on mobile equipment such as heavy-duty trucks due to the ram airflow through the radiator core at vehicle speed. An average requirement for fan usage is between 5% and 10% throughout the life of an engine. The number of blades, their angle and width, fan diameter, and driven speed have an influence on the power required to drive a fan, with some fans drawing as much as 37 kW (50 hp). Other factors influencing fan performance are air temperature, atmospheric pressure, and humidity. Proper fan selection is necessary to ensure maximum efficiency.

On constantly driven fans or thermatic-type fans, the power required to drive them at maximum speed should be kept to approximately 6% of basic engine horsepower. The most efficient installation is usually a fan with the largest possible diameter rotating at the lowest speed to deliver the desired amount of air. Because of the move to smaller radiators in many heavy-duty trucks, however, radiators must be made thicker with more fins and/or tubes forming a denser core. Therefore, fans have to be driven faster or their blade angle must be increased to produce a greater static pressure capacity. Tests indicate that at fan blade angles beyond 35°, only an increase in fan speed will produce additional airflow. Although many fan blades are manufactured from pressed steel, one-piece thermoset polyester (fiberglass) fans that are stronger than

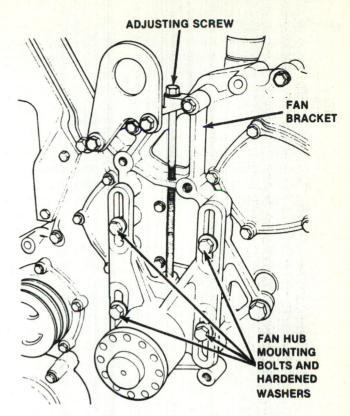

FIGURE 19–41 Typical fan hub mounting arrangement for a heavy-duty truck diesel engine (Series 60). To adjust the fan belts, the fan hub mounting bolts are loosened off; the long adjusting screw is rotated CCW to remove the belts and tightened CW to adjust the belts. (Courtesy of Detroit Diesel Corporation.)

steel are now widely used on heavy-duty Class 8 trucks and equipment. Their lighter weight moves air with less horsepower (kW) and increases fan hub or fan clutch life. Fans are significant contributors to vehicle noise when they are operating.

Blower Versus Suction Fans

If you have ever stood in front of a stationary piece of equipment, such as a portable air compressor when the engine is running, you probably felt a blast of air coming out of the radiator core. If the compressor side covers are left open, this is contrary to the operating direction labels attached to the covers and the engine can overheat. On a stationary piece of equipment, the fan cannot move the desired quantity of air when the side covers are left open. A blower fan blows air through the rad core from the inside rather than sucking it through the front as a suction fan does. The blower fan is designed to pull air at ambient temperature from underneath the machine up and over the engine.

This air is cooler than the air that is pulled through the rad core by a suction fan. So operating the equipment with the side covers left open severely reduces the ability of the blower fan to move sufficient air across the engine and through the radiator core. A blower fan receives air at a lower temperature than a suction fan, which receives the warm air that has passed through the rad core. Therefore, for the power expended to drive the fan, a blower fan is more efficient in terms of mass airflow than a suction fan. Blower fans, however, require more attention to shroud configuration to realize this inherent higher efficiency.

Fans and Shrouds

Fan position in relation to the radiator depends on the fan diameter and the radiator frontal area. When the fan diameter is approximately equal to the radiator swept area, the fan should be located between 51 and 101 mm (2 to 4 in.) from the rad core. When the fan diameter is less than the size of the radiator swept area, the fan should be moved back from the core to allow the airflow to spread over the full surface of the core. This will not occur if the fan is placed too close to the back side of the rad core. In addition to fan placement, a well-fitted *shroud* can ensure that the fan air will not be dispersed around the rad core and recirculated.

Basically three types of fan shrouds are in use, and these are illustrated in Figure 19–42: the well-rounded-entrance Venturi type, the ring type, and the box type. In all cases, maximum fan air delivery is obtained by using a tight-fitting shroud to prevent air recirculation around the rad core. Rad guards, grills, and other obstructions to air flow may cause air to recirculate. Of the three shrouds listed, the most efficient type is the close-fitting Venturi model. Regardless of the type of fan shroud, the closer the fan blade tips are positioned to the shroud diameter, the more efficient the fan airflow will be. To allow for fan belt adjustment, however, many diesel engines require that the fan hub actually be raised or lowered, which limits the clearance of fan blade tip to the shroud. One way around this is to employ a separate fan belt idler pulley instead of moving the actual fan and hub assembly. Ideally, fan blade-tip-to-shroud clearance should be kept to a minimum of 13 mm (½ in.) or less. In some trucks, the fan shroud can be adjusted to maintain this spec.

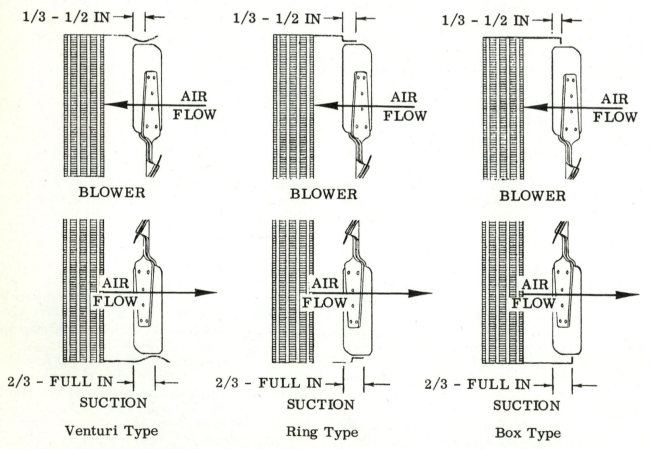

FIGURE 19–42 *Identification and features of three commonly used types of fan shrouds. (Courtesy of Detroit Diesel Corporation.)*

The diesel technician must ensure that broken or damaged fan shrouds are repaired as soon as possible, because engine overheating may result under certain operating conditions of heavy load and peak torque. Another important point for the technician to remember is that fan placement into or out of the shroud also affects the efficiency of the fan. Figure 19–42 indicates the relative position of the fan blades in the shroud assembly.

NOTE: The 1/3 – 1/2 IN (in Figure 19–42) does *not* refer to inches; it refers to the actual fan blade width in relation to its position in or out of the shroud assembly.

Fan Clutches

Since fans are only required for between 5% and 10% of the operational time of the engine, there are a number of automatic engagement and disengagement types on the market for trucks and equipment. Thermatically controlled fan clutches can save up to 10% fuel consumption and up to 10% horsepower. These fan clutches are designed to operate based on air, springs, or engine oil controlled from an engine coolant temperature sensor. Note that some thermatic fans rely on radiator air temperature directed against the heat-sensing center hub of the fan. Figure 19–43 illustrates that regardless of clutch type, the actual fan hub pulley is driven by a multiple-belt arrangement from the engine

crankshaft front pulley. Although the fan hub rotates, the power required to drive it is marginal when the fan clutch is not engaged. During this disengaged position, the fan blades do not rotate. When the fan clutch is engaged, the fan blades rotate as their belt-driven hub engages with the fan clutch portion of the assembly. Fan drives without a clutch require maintenance of only shaft bearings. Fan drives with a clutch engagement mechanism require bearing, clutch facing, seal, and air or electrical supply maintenance. Some of the more popular fan clutches on the market are manufactured by Bendix, Rockford, Horton, Facet, Kysor/Cadillac, Eaton, Evans, and Schwitzer.

Fan Clutch Operation

Engine fan clutch engagement, other than in the thermomodulated models, is automatically controlled in all cases by a coolant temperature sensing valve (thermopneumatic) illustrated in Figure 19–38. Schwitzer models gradually increase the fan speed rotation as the air temperature flowing through the radiator acts on a fan-hub-mounted sensor which causes internal and external drive and driven clutch plates to move closer together, thereby shearing a silicone fluid to transfer power. The Rockford wet clutch is controlled by a thermal air valve located in the cooling system. On this clutch, the degree of engagement and fan speed are controlled by the distance that the valve is

FIGURE 19–43 Features of a spring-engaged, air-pressure-disengaged fan clutch assembly. (Courtesy of Allied Signal Truck Brake Systems Company).

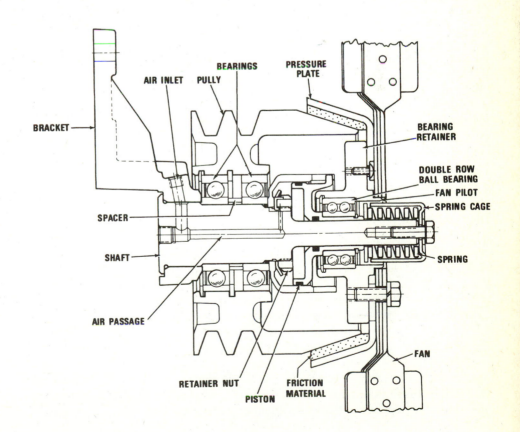

opened based on engine coolant temperature. This valve functions similarly to the radiator shutterstat (see Figure 19–39), whereby the expansion of the wax within the thermal portion of the assembly controls the degree of valve opening.

Figure 19–43 illustrates a spring-engaged and air-pressure-disengaged fan clutch model, which is the concept used by Bendix and Kysor/Cadillac. In this design, when a cold engine is first cranked and started, the control valve that senses engine coolant temperature is open and allows air pressure of 70 to 75 psi (483 to 517 kPa) to gradually disengage the fan rotation as it overcomes the clutch hub spring force. This is accomplished by the fact that the air pressure fills the clutch hub piston cavity, which pushes the piston, lining assembly, and fan forward to the disengaged position. Under this condition, there is no fan load on the drive belts or the engine; however, some fan clutches will freewheel at about 300 rpm due to internal drag. When the engine coolant temperature reaches the control valve setting, air pressure is exhausted from the clutch through the control valve. The internal spring forces the piston, lining assembly, and fan into the engaged position. When the engine coolant temperature has dropped sufficiently, the control valve opens and allows the air pressure to once again disengage the fan clutch mechanism.

On fan clutches similar to the Horton models, the fan clutch is air pressure engaged and spring disengaged; therefore, the operation is basically the reverse of that described for the Bendix model shown in Figure 19–43. The Horton models feature a fan clutch that employs a set of drive and driven discs as shown in Figure 19–44. Another common fan clutch design is that of Facet, which is illustrated in Figure 19–45. In this system, when the engine coolant reaches a preset temperature, the fan clutch temperature sensor completes the electrical circuit, and electrical current is allowed to flow through the coil within the magnet body to magnetically attract the armature to the inner body, somewhat similarly to the operation of an air-conditioning pump. This action brings the fan into engagement. As the engine cools off, the coil is demagnetized and internal springs pull the armature away from the inner body, allowing the fan to coast down to an idle or off condition.

In Class 8 heavy-duty trucks such as those manufactured by PAACAR (Kenworth and Peterbilt), when an air-conditioning condensor is mounted in front of the radiator, the thermal switch is overridden by the firewall-mounted *trinary switch* (Freon pressure switch). The same solenoid valve supplies air to the fan clutch. In addition, a fan clutch override switch on the vehicle instrument panel turns the fan on when all other switches are off. In this case, the fan clutch oper-

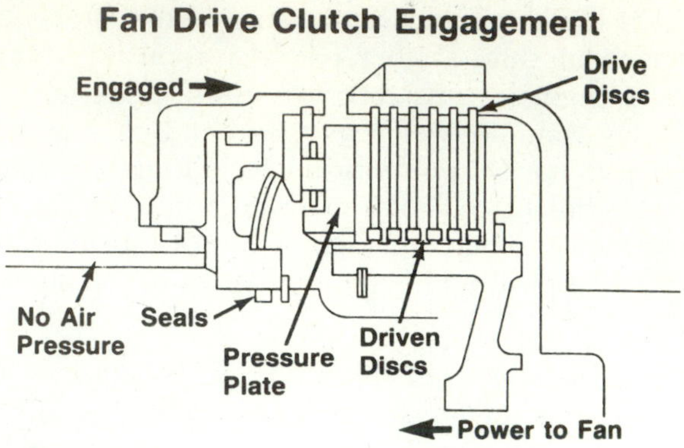

FIGURE 19–44 *Features of an air-pressure-engaged, spring-disengaged fan clutch assembly. (Courtesy of Cummins Engine Company. Inc.)*

ates just like an ON/OFF model with no modulation (change to fan speed). Air pressure is required to disengage this particular fan clutch.

The electrical circuit used with a fan clutch system can be either a NC (normally closed) or NO (normally open) type of switch (see Figure 19–46). Two optional control systems are available:

1. Combination of basic control and an optional air-conditioning control system
2. Combination of basic control system and a manual bypass system with a dash-mounted indicator light and optional air-conditioning control. The dash indicator light indicates to the driver when the fan is engaged.

Figure 19–37 illustrates the fan clutch engagement temperatures for an engine using an 82°C (180°F) coolant thermostat. Generally there are three temperature settings for the fan clutch sensing switch, 85°, 88°, and 91°C (185°, 190°, 195°F) with a 6° to 8°F variation between the clutch engaging and disengaging points.

Emergency Clutch Engagement
Horton fan clutches can be engaged in the event of a fan clutch or control malfunction as shown in Figure 19–46 by using the following procedure:

1. Disconnect and plug the air line to the fan clutch.
2. Align two holes in the piston (friction) disc with two holes in the sheave as shown in the diagram.
3. Install two 5⁄16 in. − 18 NC × 1 in. Grade 8 socket head screws, or the equivalent metric bolts, and tighten to 25 lb-ft (34 N·m) torque. Note that when the bolts are tightened they force the internal clutch plates together. This

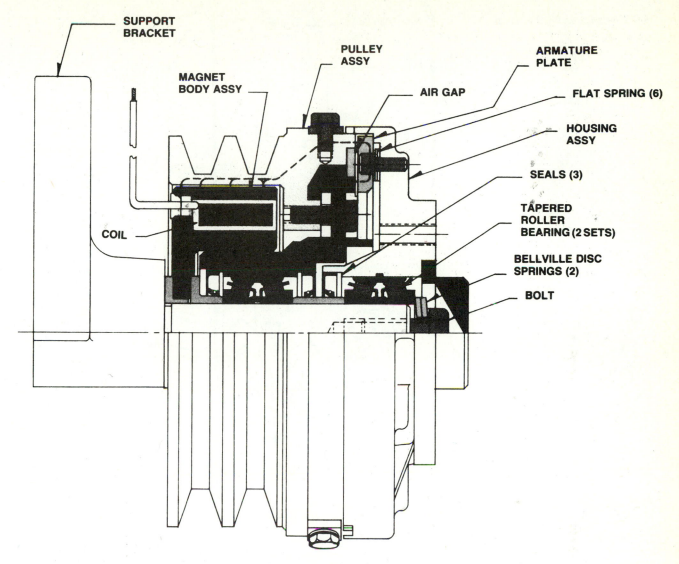

FIGURE 19–45 Features of an electromagnetically applied fan clutch assembly. (Courtesy of Cummins Engine Company. Inc.)

procedure should only be used as a temporary solution until the fan clutch can be repaired. Air leaks from fan clutches require complete overhaul of the assembly.

Oil-Pressure-Operated Fans

Some engine manufacturers use a fan clutch assembly that operates on engine oil that is continually delivered to the drive hub assembly. This fan clutch design is used by GMC in trucks and buses. Operation of the drive assembly is controlled by a combination-type valve installed in the engine water jacket. As engine oil is delivered to the drive assembly, it lubricates the clutch assembly seals and bearings, where the oil is bled off to the engine crankcase from the port on the

front of the housing. When the engine is cold, the engine oil pressure is maintained at between 28 and 48 kPa (4 to 7 psi); oil simply drains from the drive assembly and the fan is disengaged. Note, however, that the fan tends to turn slowly at this time. When the engine coolant temperature reaches 88° to 89°C (190° to 192°F), a fan combination valve shown in Figure 19–47 closes. This action allows engine oil under pressure to collect within the fan clutch hub and fill it. With the housing filled with pressurized engine oil, the fan shaft rotates according to the fluid coupling principle. The fan blade assembly is connected to the drive shaft. Within the combination valve is a pressure relief valve that opens at between 159 and 186 kPa (23 to 27 psi), thereby allowing some oil to drain to the engine

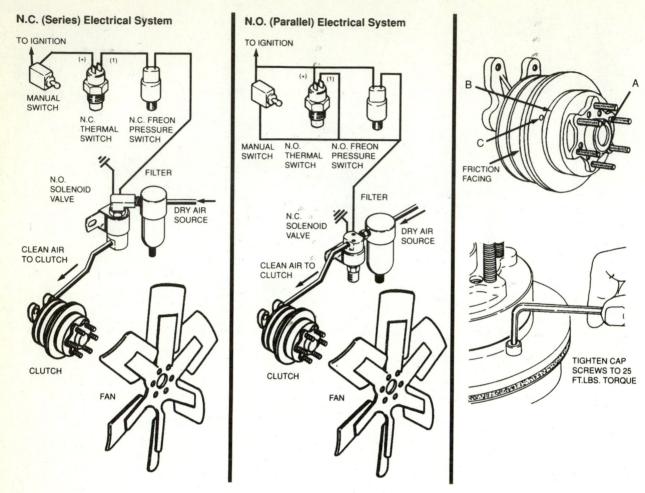

FIGURE 19–46 *Features of a Horton fan clutch assembly. Note location of the two access holes (c) to allow the insertion of two 5/16 − 18 NC × 1 in. long Grade 8 socket head screws to engage the fan clutch in an emergency caused by fan clutch or control system malfunction. (Courtesy of Horton Manufacturing Co., Inc.)*

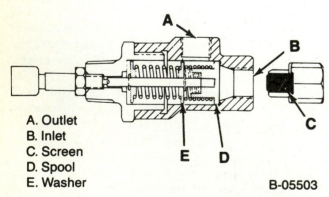

A. Outlet
B. Inlet
C. Screen
D. Spool
E. Washer

B-05503

FIGURE 19–47 *Oil-pressure-operated fan clutch with combination valve. (Courtesy of GMC Trucks.)*

crankcase. When the coolant temperature is equal to or greater than 88°C (190°F), the oil pressure is between 28 and 186 kPa (4 to 27 psi); no oil flows to the sump and the fan rotates at full speed. This type of fan has a screen located in a brass fitting threaded into the control valve (item C in Figure 19–47). This screen should be cleaned every 40,000 km (24,000 miles).

Thermomodulated Fans
A heavy-duty high-speed thermomodulated viscous fan drive assembly for a diesel engine regulates the speed of the fan based on the temperature of the air that flows through the radiator core. Within the fan hub are a series of drive and driven plates that are similar to the concept shown in Figure 19–44. The clutch plates are separated by a silicone fluid film. The thermostatic control element, which is located at the front center of the unit, reacts to changes in air temperature and varies the fluid

film thickness between the plates to change the fan speed. The fan hub that supports the fan blades is mounted to and driven by multiple belts from the engine crankshaft pulley. The internal drive plates of the fan rotate with the belt-driven fan hub. The only connection between the drive and driven plates is through the fluid film. The air temperature acting on the fan temperature control assembly changes and shears the fluid film thickness to obtain the change in fan speed.

On light- and medium-duty truck applications a similar type of thermomodulated fan drive assembly is also used. This type of fan clutch employs a bimetallic coil connected to the fan hub arm shaft. The temperature at which the fan clutch engages and disengages is controlled by the setting of the coil. When the engine is started in cold ambient conditions or during high-speed heavy-load driving conditions, silicone fluid contained within the fan clutch reservoir allows the fan to spin in the "engaged mode." Greatest fan speed occurs when the silicone fluid completely fills the grooves between the clutch body and the clutch plate. The speed of the fan decreases when the air temperature acting on the bimetallic spring drops.

Fan Drive Belts

Fan hubs are generally driven by a set of multiple belts or by a wide multiple-groove polyvee-type belt (see Figure 19–48). When more than one belt is necessary, the belts are sold in matched sets to ensure they are the same length. This is essential to divide the drive loads equally between the belts. When a multiple-belt set experiences a failure of one or more of the belts, always replace *all* belts. If you fail to do so, the used belts will have experienced a degree of stretch greater than the new belt(s). Consequently, the fan drive hub load will be concentrated on the newer, less stretched belt.

NOTE: Any drive belt is considered to be used if it has been in operation for 10 minutes or longer, since this time period allows the belt assembly to be stretched.

Belt Adjustment

Fan belts are generally driven from the crankshaft pulley. The speed ratio is related to the fan size, desired speed, and airflow movement requirements. Some drive belts employ an idler pulley with an adjustable bracket, whereas others require you to actually raise or lower the fan hub bracket assembly to adjust the tension of the fan belts. Attempting to adjust a fan belt set by the degree of slack between the pulleys by feel invariably results in either overtension or undertension. Figure 19–49 illustrates three examples of where the belt tension reading should be measured. Overtightening multiple-belt drives can create severe bending stresses on the front crankshaft main bearing assembly. Failure analysis studies

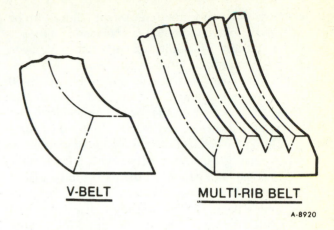

FIGURE 19–48 *V-belts or multirib belts drive a fan hub. (Courtesy of GMC Trucks.)*

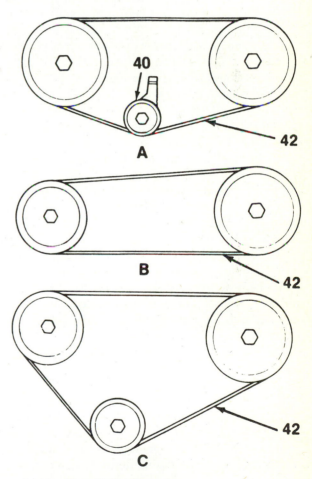

A. Use Two Pulley Tension
B. Use Two Pulley Tension
C. Use Three Pulley Tension
40. Idler Pulley
42. Belt   M-01210

FIGURE 19–49 *Three examples of where fan belt tension should be checked. (Courtesy of GMC Trucks.)*

have shown that many front crankshaft failures can be traced directly to overtightened fan belt assemblies.

To avoid any possibility of belts that have been adjusted too loosely or too tightly, always use a commercially available *belt tensioner gauge*. Figure 19–50 illustrates an example of a widely used Vee-belt tensioner which is scaled on the face to indicate the belt tension in pounds or newton-meters. To use the gauge, while holding the black knob in the palm of your hand, simultaneously grasp the crossbar with your fingers. This allows the hooked end of the gauge to be placed over the belt where it is sandwiched between the hooks and a plunger flat at the base of the circular gauge. The spring-loaded gauge will record the opposing tension of the belt by rotating the round colored faceplate to a position that allows you to read how much tension the belt exhibits. Note that on multiple-belt drives, each belt in the set should be checked individually for tension (see Figure 19–51).

The amount of belt tension depends on the physical size of the belt. The tension is measured in the center span of the pulleys as shown in Figure 19–49. Fan belt tension can be seen on the dial face of the gauge. If the belt(s) requires adjustment, and an idler pulley is used, loosen off the idler pulley retaining bolt and rotate the pulley to alter the belt tension. Some idler pulleys are equipped with an eccentric (off center) adjusting bolt to facilitate ease of adjustment; others may require you to use a bar to force the pulley to move within its adjustment bracket slot. Always tighten the retaining bolt(s) after any adjustment and recheck the belt tension with the gauge. On many heavy-duty trucks, the belts are adjusted by loosening off a locknut first, followed by rotation of an adjustment bolt. Figure 19–41 illustrates this arrangement whereby the adjustment bolt actually causes the fan pulley bracket to be raised or lowered. Always recheck the fan belt tension after locking the retaining bolt(s).

In the absence of a recommended belt tensioner similar to the one shown in Figure 19–50, refer to Figure 19–52 which illustrates how best to check the belt for free play or slack. This procedure should only be used in emergencies where no belt tensioner is readily available. Push down on the belt with your finger and gauge how much deflection is apparent. A general rule of thumb is to allow the following deflection distances:

Belt width	Deflection per foot (or per 31 cm of span)
½ in. (12.7 mm)	¹³⁄₃₂ in. (10.3 mm)
¹¹⁄₁₆ in. (17.5 mm)	¹³⁄₃₂ in. (10.3 mm)
¾ in. (19 mm)	⁷⁄₁₆ in. (11 mm)
⅞ in. (22.2 mm)	½ in. (12.7 mm)
1 in. (25.4 mm)	9.16 in. (14.3 mm)

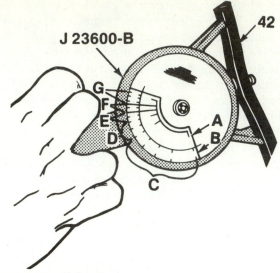

A. "Newtons" Scale
B. "Lbs." (Pounds) Scale
C. "Too Low" Range
D. "Used Belt" Range
E. Overlap Area
F. "New" Range
G. "Too High" Range
42. Belt   M-01209

FIGURE 19–50 *Using a belt tension gauge.* (Courtesy of GMC Trucks.)

Belts should not be allowed to bottom on the pulley groove or rub against adjacent parts. The top belt edge should not protrude more than ¹⁄₁₆ in. (1.6 mm) above the top edge of the pulley groove.

Belt Cleaning and Storage

Occasionally, drive belts may be exposed to leaking antifreeze mixtures, diesel fuel, or engine oil, and this causes them to slip in the pulley grooves. Sometimes the belts may be reusable after cleaning; however, heavily oil-soaked belts generally require replacement. *Never* attempt to clean drive belts while the engine is running, since cleaning equipment can be caught in the rotating assembly and cause serious personal injury. *Do not* use flammable cleaning solvent. Remove all grease and oil from the drive belts by means of a clean cloth. Use a nonflammable cleaner or solvent to remove grease; alternatively, use water and detergent soap.

Always store new belts in a clean, cool, dry place. Storing belts in a damp environment or near excessive heat sources can shrink or deteriorate the belts. Keep the belts away from direct sunlight and heat, and do not stack belts in bins for long time periods as this can distort the belts. Avoid hanging heavy belts or belt sets on pegs or nails, because this action can also weaken

BELT TENSION CHART										
BELT SIZE	WIDTH BELT TOP		WIDTH TOP OF PULLEY GROOVE		BELT TENSION "INITIAL"* GAUGE READING		BELT TENSION "USED"** GAUGE READING		BORROUGHS GAUGE NUMBERS	
	mm	in.	mm	in.	N	lb	N	lb	OLD GAUGE NO.	NEW GAUGE NO.
3/8	10.72	.422	9.65	.380	445 ± 22	100 ± 5	400 ± 22	90 ± 5	BT-33-95	BT-33-97
1/2	13.89	.547	12.70	.500	534 ± 22	120 ± 5	400 ± 44	90 ± 10	BT-33-95	BT-33-97
5V	15.88	.625	15.24	.600	534 ± 22	120 ± 5	400 ± 44	90 ± 10	BT-33-72-4-15	BT-33-72C
11/16	17.48	.688	15.88	.625	534 ± 22	120 ± 5	400 ± 44	90 ± 10	BT-33-72-4-15	BT-33-72C
3/4	19.05	.750	17.53	.690	534 ± 22	120 ± 5	400 ± 44	90 ± 10	BT-33-72-4-15	BT-33-72C
15/16	23.83	.983	22.30	.878	534 ± 22	120 ± 5	400 ± 44	90 ± 10	BT-33-72-4-15	BT-33-72C
8K	27.92	1.099			800 ± 22	180 ± 5	489 ± 44	110 ± 10		BT-33-109
MEASURE TENSION OF BELT FARTHEST FROM THE ENGINE										

*"INITIAL" BELT TENSION is for a new belt.
**"USED" BELT TENSION is for a belt which has more than 30 minutes of operation at rated speed of engine.   A10232-4P1

FIGURE 19–51   Belt tension chart. (Courtesy of Caterpillar Inc.)

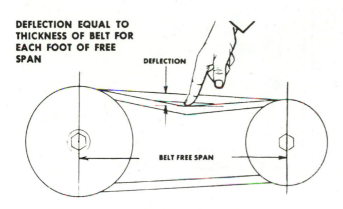

DEFLECTION EQUAL TO THICKNESS OF BELT FOR EACH FOOT OF FREE SPAN

DEFLECTION

BELT FREE SPAN

FIGURE 19–52   Example of how to check belt tension in the absence of a belt tensioner gauge.

or distort the belts. If the engine is to be stored for any length of time, the belt tension should be released.

EXPANSION TANKS AND HEAT EXCHANGERS

In stationary gen-set or marine engine applications, the radiator and fan cooling system is replaced by an ET (expansion tank) and HE (heat exchanger) core.

The ET is a large cast-iron receptacle that acts as a header tank; it is similar to the top tank and/or ET used in a radiator and fan system. See Figure 19–53. Note that the expansion tank on high-performance marine engines illustrated in Figure 19–53, is used in conjunction with deaerators on 3408/3412 Caterpillar engines. The deaerators shown in Figure 19–54 are designed to remove tiny air bubbles from the coolant. Excessive air bubbles can lead to water pump cavitation and reduced coolant flow; therefore, proper deaer-

ation is mandatory. This is achieved by means of two swirl chamber air separator housings on Vee-model engines from each cylinder bank. These deaerators allow a much smaller expansion tank to be used, and they are designed to operate on the principle of a centrifuge. As the hot coolant enters the chamber, it begins to swirl and forces the coolant to the outside and onto the heat exchanger. The air bubbles move to the center of the deaerator and exit through a short hose to the expansion tank as can be seen in Figure 19–54.

Directly below the ET is a tubular-type heat exchanger assembly with an engine-driven raw water pump connection (see Figure 19–53). The coolant pump flow through the 3606 engine is quoted as being 228 U.S. gallons per minute (880 L) at 1000 rpm engine speed; for the 3616 model, it is 546 U.S. gallons per minute (2100 L) at 1000 engine rpm. The ET has a filler cap that may or may not contain a spring-loaded pressure cap. An overflow tube is generally plumbed into the ET; the tube can be routed to a receptacle, or it may vent directly into the bilge on a marine installation. The ET provides a means of filling the engine cooling system as well as providing space for fluid expansion of the coolant as its temperature rises.

In the HE system, the engine is filled with a fresh water coolant mixture similar to that used in a radiator system. To cool the hot, fresh engine coolant, raw sea water, city water, or lake water can be pumped through the HE core in a direction opposite to the flow of the fresh water. The raw water is circulated by the action of a gear-driven or belt-driven raw water pump (described later in this chapter). The sealed HE ensures that both the engine coolant and raw water flows never mix, since they are plumbed through separate tubing or cores. This can be seen in Figure 19–55 where the hot

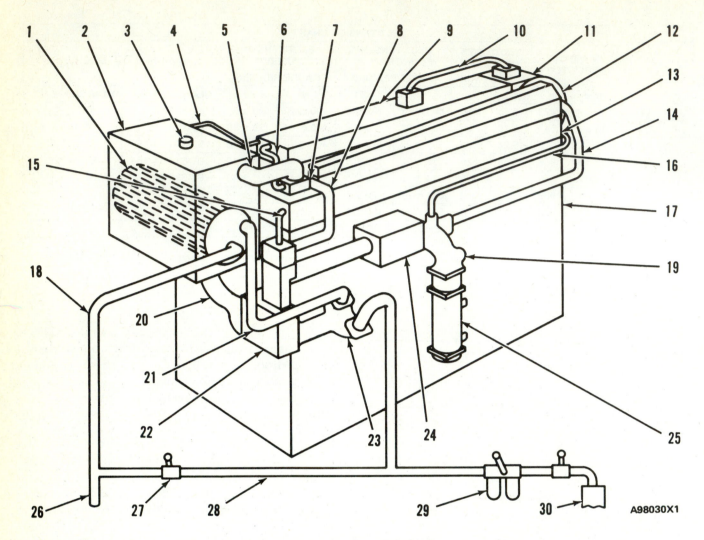

COOLING SYSTEM SCHEMATIC

1. Heat exchanger. 2. Expansion tank. 3. Pressure cap. 4. Vent line. 5. Outlet line. 6. Outlet line. 7. Regulator housing. 8. Aftercooler inlet line. 9. Water cooled manifold. 10. Outlet line. 11. Water cooled turbocharger. 12. Aftercooler housing. 13. Cylinder head. 14. Aftercooler outlet line. 15. Internal bypass (shunt) line. 16. Turbocharger inlet line. 17. Cylinder block. 18. Outlet line. 19. Bonnet. 20. Inlet line. 21. Inlet line. 22. Water pump. 23. Sea water pump. 24. Engine oil cooler. 25. Auxiliary oil cooler. 26. Outlet for sea water circuit. 27. Bypass valve. 28. Bypass line. 29. Duplex strainer. 30. Inlet for sea water circuit.

FIGURE 19–53 Flow path through a marine engine heat exchanger cooling system with a JWAC feature to reduce the temperature of the turbocharger boost air. (Courtesy of Caterpillar Inc.)

engine coolant flows from the cylinder head water manifold through the thermostat(s) to the ET. The coolant then flows vertically through the cells of the HE core. The raw water flowing horizontally between the cells of the HE core lowers the temperature of the engine coolant as it passes through the cells. This engine coolant can then flow over a marine gear oil cooler and the engine oil cooler to lower the operating temperature of these two lubricants. The coolant is then directed into the suction side of the engine fresh water pump and is circulated through the engine block and cylinder head.

Smaller-horsepower (kW) high-speed marine installations have a cellular-type HE assembly that is usually contained within the expansion tank. Some larger applications may employ a tubular type of HE that is bracket mounted alongside the engine. To ensure proper filling of the HE cooling system, an air-bleed hose must be installed between the top of each thermostat housing and the top of the expansion tank.

Two raw water pumps on large vee engines supply the raw water flow to and through the HEs. The warm raw water is then plumbed overboard on a

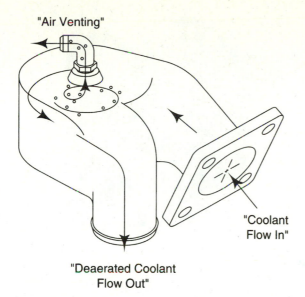

FIGURE 19–54 *Swirl chamber design of coolant deaerator housing used with a heat exchanger type of cooing system. (Courtesy of Caterpillar Inc.)*

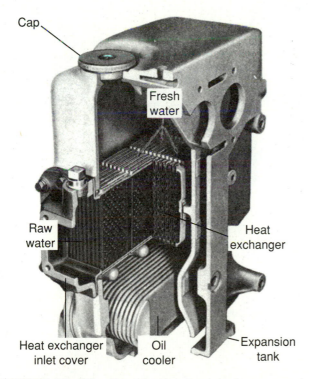

FIGURE 19–55 *Combination heat exchanger and expansion tank arrangement also showing the engine oil cooler. (Courtesy of Detroit Diesel Corporation.)*

marine application. In some industrial HE applications, a raw water cooling tank is used to recirculate the raw city water to and through the HE system to minimize water usage.

Zinc Electrodes

To counteract electrolysis or galvanic action within the cooling system, zinc electrodes are normally screwed into and located in the HE inlet cover and the raw water pump(s) inlet elbow. Most electrodes can be identified by their square brass head which allows removal with a wrench. These electrodes act as sacrificial elements within the cooling system; that is, the electrolysis tends to corrode them rather than the other metal components within the cooling system.

Electrodes should be removed at given service intervals and inspected after cleaning with a wire brush. If an electrode is worn excessively, it should be replaced. To determine the condition of a used electrode, strike it sharply against a hard metal surface; a weakened electrode will break.

Clean Heat Exchanger Core

As with a radiator cooling system, after many hours of operation, scale deposits can accumulate within the core of the heat exchanger, thereby reducing its efficiency. Soft water plus a good grade of antifreeze should be used as an engine coolant. At major engine overhaul, or if the heat exchanger fails to maintain the fresh engine coolant within its designed range, the HE may require cleaning. Follow these steps:

1. Drain the cooling system.
2. Remove the heat exchanger housing and/or core.

NOTE: To prevent drying and hardening of accumulated foreign substances, the HE core must be cleaned as soon as possible after removing it from service. The core can be cleaned at a commercial facility that has an ultrasound cleaning system, or use step 3 as follows.

3. Immerse the HE core in a scale solvent consisting of one-third muriatic acid and two-thirds water to which ½ lb (0.226 kg) of oxalic acid has been added to each 2 ½ U.S. gallons (9.5 L) of solution.
4. Remove the core when foaming and bubbling stops, which normally is about 30 to 60 seconds.
5. Flush the core thoroughly with clean hot water under pressure.

RAW WATER PUMPS

When a heat exchanger cooling system is used on an industrial or marine installation, a water pump(s) is required to circulate cooling raw water through the HE core. Most RWP (raw water pumps) are gear driven on diesel engines, but it is possible for these units to be belt driven. The RWP drive location varies in different makes and models of engines. Figure 19–56, a view across the center of the RWP, shows the normal flow of raw water. Note that both the inlet and outlet passages are located on the top of the pump housing. Because these pumps are widely used in marine applications with salt water, the pump housing is usually manufactured from a bronze or brass material, and the impeller is manufactured from a rubber or neoprene material. In applications where the vessel may be running in frigid waters, a special impeller material must be used to avoid cracking of the impeller blades.

Figure 19–57 is a cutaway view of a typical RWP manufactured by Jabsco. The pump drive shaft (213) is supported by a prelubricated, shielded, double-row ball bearing (222). An oil seal (247 and 249) prevents oil leakage from the bearing compartment and a rotary seal (256) prevents water leakage along the shaft. A rubber/neoprene-type impeller (220) is splined to the end of the drive shaft (213) and is self-lubricated by the pumped water. Never run the pump any longer than required for the pump to prime itself; otherwise, impeller damage can occur. A wear plate (255) in the impeller compartment prevents wear of the pump housing and can be reversed if wear on the plate becomes excessive. A slot machined in the outer periphery of the wear plate registers with a dowel in the pump housing, thereby preventing the plate from rotating with the shaft assembly.

The flexible impeller allows these pumps to be operated in either a clockwise or counterclockwise direction. The pump end cover is marked with an arrow and the letters RH or LH to show the outlet port for either of these rotations. Once the pump has been operated in one direction, attempting to reverse its rotation will result in the impeller cracking at the base of the individual blades (vanes). Within the pump housing is an offset cam (250) designed to direct the flow within the housing. This cam causes the impeller to take up a set curvature during pump operation. Any time you attempt to manually rotate the engine over, keep this caution in mind: Turning the engine opposite its normal rotation more than about one-eighth of a turn can result in impeller damage. If you have to rotate the engine in a direction opposite to its normal rotation beyond this limit, disconnect the RWP from the engine.

The seal parts of a RWP may be replaced without removing the pump from the engine as follows:

1. Remove the pump cover screws and take off the cover and gasket.
2. Using two pliers, grasp an impeller blade at each side and pull the impeller from the shaft. The spline plug will come out with the impeller.

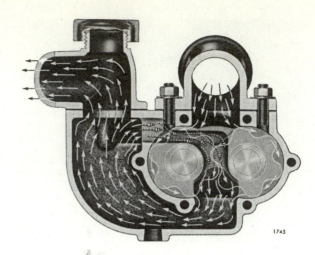

FIGURE 19–56 View across the center of a Jabsco raw water pump illustrating the normal flow of water and recirculation of priming water through the channel at the rear of the pump housing. (Courtesy of Detroit Diesel Corporation.)

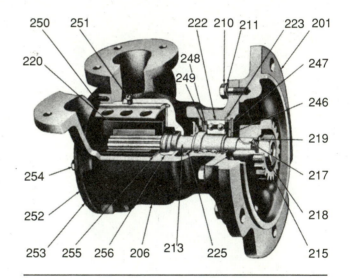

201. Adaptor – pump	225. Oil slinger – shaft
206. Housing – pump	246. Washer – felt
210. Bolt – housing to adaptor	247. Seal – bearing
211. Lock washer	248. Washer – felt
213. Shaft – drive	249. Seal – bearing
215. Gear – drive	250. Cam – offset
217. Key – woodruff	251. Bolt – cam
218. Nut – gear retaining	252. Cover
219. Lock washer	253. Gasket – cover
220. Impeller	254. Bolt – cover
222. Ball bearing	255. Wear plate
223. Retainer – bearing	256. Seal assy.

FIGURE 19–57 Identification of components of a Jabsco raw water pump. (Courtesy of Detroit Diesel Corporation.)

3. Insert two wires with a hook fashioned into each end and insert between the pump housing and the seal with the hooks over the edge of the carbon seal. Pull the seal assembly from the shaft.

4. Remove the seal and gasket in the same manner if they require replacement.

5. Assemble the carbon seal, seal ring, and washer in the correct relative positions and slide them over the shaft and against the seal seat. Make sure the seal ring is contained snugly within the ferrule.

6. Install the Marcel washer (deformed one) next to the flat washer.

7. Compress the impeller blades to clear the offset cam and press the impeller onto the splined shaft; then install the spline plug.

8. Manually rotate the impeller several turns in the direction that it will normally run to position the blades correctly.

9. Install a new gasket between the pump housing and cover.

KEEL COOLING SYSTEMS

In many marine applications where dirty raw water makes the use of a heat exchanger system impractical, a keel cooling system such as that illustrated in Figure 19–58 can be used. This cooling system is similar to the HE system just described: however, the heat transfer of the engine fresh water coolant occurs in a nest of tubes that are mounted to the hull of the ship below the waterline rather than in the HE core mounted in the engine ET. The ET used can be the same as that for an HE system.

In this example, when the thermostat(s) is open, the engine coolant flows to the keel cooling tubes or coils where it transfers its heat to the surrounding seawater. The return coolant is drawn through the vertical pipes and the ET by the engine water pump. When the thermostat(s) is closed, coolant entering the stat housing is bypassed directly to the engine water pump inlet where it remixes with the coolant from the water-cooled exhaust manifold jacket. The coolant is then circulated through the engine cylinder block and head. A percentage of the coolant leaving the head is routed through pipes or hoses to the hollow core exhaust manifold to minimize heat radiation into the engine room. This hot coolant leaving the exhaust manifold is then routed to the expansion tank. Since no engine coolant passes to the keel cooler with closed thermostats, a fairly rapid warm-up of the engine is assured.

SELF-TEST QUESTIONS

1. Technician A says that typical coolant system temperatures should be between 140° and 165°F (60° to 74°C). Technician B disagrees, stating that normal coolant temperature should be between 185° and 200°F (85° to 93°C). Which technician do you believe?

2. True or False: Wear on cylinder walls can be up to eight times greater with a coolant temperature of 100°F (38°C) than one of 180°F (82°C).

3. Describe by approximate percentage the heat losses from an engine from the injected fuel used to produce power.

4. Technician A says that in a perfect engine with no heat losses 3300 Btu (966 W) is needed to produce 1 hp (0.746 kW) per hour. Technician B states that a perfect engine requires 2545 Btu/hp/hr (746 W). Which technician knows heat engine theory best?

5. The average heat rejection to the cooling system in current high-speed high-output engines is approximately
   a. 30 to 35 Btu/hp/min (9 to 10 W/kW/min)
   b. 40 to 50 Btu/hp/min (12 to 15 W/kW/min)
   c. 50 to 60 Btu/hp/min (15 to 18 W/kW/min)
   d. 60 to 70 Btu/hp/min (18 to 20 W/kW/min)

6. True or False: Electronically controlled diesel engines are more thermally efficient than mechanically controlled models.

7. Calculate the heat load in Btu (W) that a Caterpillar 3176B EUI engine cooling system would have to absorb and dissipate from the following information: Engine is rated at 350 bhp (261 kW); fuel used has a LHV of 18,390 Btu/lb (42,780 kJ/kg) and weighs 7.001 lb/U.S. gal (839g/l). Fuel consumption is 0.319 lb/hp/hr (194 g/kW-h). The engine has a TE of 43.38%; the cooling system absorbs 27.61% of the total heat load. Determine the total heat that this engine would produce in 1 hour; then calculate how many Btu/hp/min (W/kW/min) the cooling system would handle.

8. From your answer to question 7, and using information in Chapter 19, determine the coolant flow rate that would be required through this Cat engine with a water inlet temperature to the engine of 170°F (77°C) and a thermostat outlet temperature of 195°F (90.5°C).

9. From the information in Chapter 19, how many ppm (parts per million) hardness content, or corrosive chemicals of chloride or sulfate, would make water unfit for cooling system usage?

10. What does the chemical symbol PH represent in relation to coolant? Allowable PH is generally within the range of
    a. 3.5 to 5
    b. 5 to 7
    c. 7.5 to 11
    d. 12 to 16.5

11. What is the purpose of using SCAs in a cooling system?

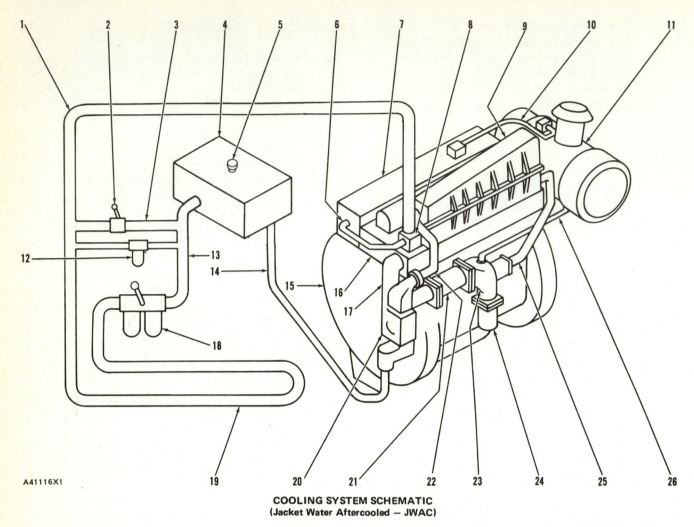

COOLING SYSTEM SCHEMATIC
(Jacket Water Aftercooled — JWAC)

1. Outlet line. 2. Bypass valve. 3. Bypass line. 4. Expansion tank. 5. Pressure cap. 6. Outlet line. 7. Water cooled manifold. 8. Regulator housing. 9. Aftercooler housing. 10. Outlet line. 11. Water cooled turbocharger. 12. Bypass filter. 13. Inlet line. 14. Inlet line. 15. Cylinder block. 16. Cylinder head. 17. Internal bypass (shunt) line. 18. Duplex strainer. 19. Keel cooler tubes. 20. Water pump. 21. Engine oil cooler. 22. Aftercooler inlet line. 23. Bonnet. 24. Auxiliary oil cooler. 25. Aftercooler outlet line. 26. Turbocharger inlet line.

FIGURE 19–58 *Schematic of a marine keel cooling system featuring JWAC to reduce the temperature of the turbocharger boost air supply. (Courtesy of Caterpillar Inc.)*

12. Describe what actually causes wet-type cylinder liner pitting. What can be done to minimize this condition?

13. Name the two common types of permanent antifreeze used in modern engines.

14. Which one of the two antifreezes listed in your answer for Question 13 is considered by the U.S. EPA to be a hazardous air pollutant?

15. True or False: Antifreeze is considered to be a nonhazardous waste.

16. Technician A says that used antifreeze must be disposed of once it is drained from an engine. Technician B says that all types of antifreeze can be cleaned and recycled. Which technician is aware of current technology?

17. Which one of the two types of antifreeze listed in your answer to Question 13 offers improved protection against cavitation corrosion, particularly in wet-liner engines?

18. Technician A says that too great a concentration of antifreeze can result in gelling of the coolant. Technician B believes that in very low ambient operating conditions, the greater the percentage of antifreeze used the better. Which technician is correct?

19. The maximum recommended concentration of antifreeze should never exceed
    a. 50%
    b. 57%
    c. 63%
    d. 67%

20. What additive in antifreeze acts as a corrosion inhibitor?

21. When maintenance personnel talk about silicate *dropout* in a coolant, what actually transpires and what problems occur from this action?

22. A widely used antifreeze spec is the General Motors standard GM-6038-M, which is listed on the antifreeze container. What does this standard limit, and to what percentage?

23. What antifreeze additive actually causes plugging of internal cooling passages and when allowed to dry appears as a white powdery substance?

24. Technician A says that if an engine overheating problem and coolant passage plugging can be traced to a silicate dropout condition, you would have to disassemble the radiator and engine to effectively clean the system. Technician B believes that you can use a commercially available nonacidic cleaner to remove the silica gel from the system without disassembling the engine. Which technician knows cooling system maintenance best?

25. If the procedure used in Question 24 doesn't work successfully, what would you do next? Describe the method(s) that would have to be employed.

26. True or False: Antifreeze protection level can be checked quickly by using a hydrometer or a refractometer similar to that for a battery.

27. List the problems that would occur to engine components if an antifreeze concentration was below 30%.

28. List the problems associated with using an antifreeze concentration above the maximum recommended level.

29. True or False: Chemical deposits at the water pump seal weep hole are usually an indication of possible overconcentration of SCAs.

30. True or False: SCA concentration must be checked regularly with a kit to determine the condition of the coolant.

31. When checking SCA concentration, what two additives relate directly to cylinder liner pitting concentration?

32. Scale buildup within a cooling system insulates and blocks heat transfer. What chemicals in tap water promote scale buildup?

33. Technician A says that 0.0625 in. (1.58 mm) of mineral scale deposit on a cylinder liner is equivalent to 1 in. of additional cast iron in insulating quantity. Technician B suggests that this amount of scale on the liner walls would be equivalent to approximately 4.25 in. (108 mm) of additional cast iron in insulating quality. Which technician is correct?

34. Name one cooling system corrosion inhibitor and stabilizer product that contains a patented scale suppressant to help prevent scale deposits.

35. One of the most effective ways to control coolant system SCAs is
   a. using a coolant filter
   b. flushing the system regularly
   c. changing the antifreeze mixture twice a year
   d. using a thermostat with a high opening temperature

36. List the various functions of a coolant filter assembly.

37. When radiators become plugged and have to be cleaned, the most popular method in use today is
   a. boiling the rad in a caustic solution
   b. cleaning by ultrasonic methods
   c. using solvent and rod cleaning brushes
   d. pressure steam cleaning or using high-pressure hot water

38. Describe what the term *reverse flushing* means.

39. What is the main reason for using a radiator pressure cap (other than to prevent a loss of coolant)?

40. Technician A says that the term *ATB* represents the difference between engine coolant out, or the top tank temperature, and the ambient air temperature. Technician B says that it is the ambient temperature at which radiator top tank boiling occurs. Who is correct?

41. True or False: Each radiator or cooling system pressure cap has the opening pressure stamped on the cap.

42. What prevents the radiator or cooling system hoses from collapsing when the engine is stopped and the coolant begins to cool, thereby creating a partial vacuum?

43. How can a rad pressure cap be checked to determine if it is operating correctly?

44. True or False: All radiators in use today are of the downflow type.

45. What major engine manufacturer employs LFC (low-flow cooling) systems on some of its engines?

46. True or False: All radiators employ one-pass coolant flow?

47. What feature of radiator design determines its rated cooling capacity?

48. What two materials are most widely used in the construction of heavy-duty truck radiators?

49. When radiator fins become soft or rotted, what is the usual cause?

50. True or False: Technician A says that the top tank of heavy-duty truck radiators contains two tanks within one, separated by a baffle arrangement.

51. Technician A says that cleaning radiator fins should never be done by employing high-pressure washers because this will damage the fins. Technician B says that high-pressure washer cleaning is required to dislodge bugs and so forth from the fins and is a recommended practice. Which technician is correct?

52. What types of problems does aerated coolant cause?

53. Describe how you would check a cooling system to determine if coolant is being aerated.

54. Technician A says that in cold-weather operation, all heavy-duty trucks should employ winterfronts that can be completely closed to keep the engine coolant operating temperature within specs. Technician B says that closing the winterfront completely could cause serious problems with the air-to-air aftercooler system. Which technician understands the theory of operation best?

55. A JWAC usually lowers the turbocharger boost air temperature under full-load conditions from approximately 300°F (149°C) to about
    a. 250°F (121°C)
    b. 200°F (93°C)
    c. 160°F (71°C)
    d. 110°F (43°C)

56. ALCC (advanced liquid charge cooling) is capable of lowering turbocharger boost temperatures down to which one of the answers in Question 55?

57. What is the difference between JWAC and ALCC?

58. Describe how you would clean or service either a JWAC or an ALCC system.

59. What are the three common types of thermostats used in diesel engines?

60. Describe how a thermostat actually opens and closes.

61. Operating an engine without a thermostat is not recommended. Give the reasons why.

62. What is the purpose of using thermostat seals, and what problems exist if they leak?

63. Describe how you would check a thermostat for effective operation. List the specific checks to confirm whether a thermostat is good or bad.

64. Why would a truck or stationary engine application use shutterstats?

65. Describe briefly how a shutterstat system operates.

66. List the operational checks that you would follow to check a shutterstat for correct operation on an engine.

67. Provide an example of the opening temperatures for a heavy-duty truck engine that employs a thermostat, a shutterstat, and a thermatic fan.

68. What would be the approximate fan airflow requirements for an engine rated at 470 hp (351 kW) with a 35 Btu/hp/min (10.25 W) heat rejection to the cooling system?

69. Technician A says that radiator fans on highway trucks are normally required for only between 5% and 10% of engine operating time. Technician B says that the fan must operate most of the time to keep the engine coolant within the designed operating temperature. Which technician knows cooling theory best?

70. The horsepower required to drive a truck fan should not exceed which of the following percentages of the engine's developed horsepower?
    a. 2%
    b. 4%
    c. 6%
    d. 9%

71. True or False: A suction fan is designed to blow air through the radiator core.

72. True or False: A blower fan is designed to pull air through the radiator core.

73. For the amount of power expended to drive a fan, technician A says that the suction fan is more effective. Technician B believes that the blower fan is more effective. Give the reasons why you believe Technician A or B is correct.

74. On a portable application such as a trailer or skid-mounted unit with a large diesel-driven air compressor, would the engine-driven fan be of the suction or blower type? Why?

75. Describe the three commonly used designs of fan shrouds.

76. Why is a fan shroud a widely used item? Describe the main reason for employing one.

77. Technician A says that a fan should always be mounted as close as possible to the radiator core. Do you agree or disagree with this statement? Give your reasons for your answer.

78. True or False: All thermatically operated fans use air pressure to function.

79. Technician A says that thermatic fans must have their hub belt driven from the engine crankshaft. Technician B says that no belt drive is necessary. Which technician is correct?

80. Technician A says that a Bendix and Kysor/Cadillac thermatic fan hub assembly is applied by spring pressure; technician B says the assembly is applied by air pressure. Who is correct?

81. True or False: A thermomodulated fan hub assembly relies on coolant temperature within the engine block to activate it.

82. True or False: Fan belts should always be adjusted using a fan belt tensioner gauge.

83. Technician A says that when multiple belts are used to drive a fan hub assembly, if one belt requires replacing, all of the belts should be changed since they are a matched set. Not so says technician B; you only need to change the damaged, worn, or broken belt. Who is correct?

84. True or False: Marine engine applications use raw seawater routed through the engine cooling system and plumb fresh water through the heat exchanger to cool the hot, raw seawater.

85. True or False: Raw water pumps usually employ a special rubber or neoprene type of impeller.

86. The purpose of zinc electrodes in marine engine cooling systems is to
    a. counteract electrolysis
    b. prevent scale buildup
    c. maintain the correct PH control level
    d. prevent silica dropout in the antifreeze

87. How would you clean a marine engine heat exchanger core?

88. Describe briefly how a marine engine keel cooling system operates.

20 Air Inlet and Exhaust Systems

OVERVIEW

In this chapter the air inlet and exhaust system is explained in terms of its importance to the combustion system. In addition to operational aspects of the system, we discuss the major components that contribute to air and exhaust flow into and from the engine cylinders.

TOPICS

- The air supply
- Air temperatures
- Intake and exhaust system flow
- Airflow requirements
- Dust ingestion
- Air cleaners
- Air ducting inspection
- Use of starting fluids
- Aftercoolers
- Engine compression check
- Turbochargers
- Exhaust mufflers and particulate traps
- Gear-driven blowers
- Marine engine applications
- Troubleshooting using manometers
- Exhaust brake devices
- Self-test questions

THE AIR SUPPLY

All internal combustion engines need an adequate supply of air that is clean, dry, filtered, fresh, and cool. Damp air contains less oxygen than dry air, thus it reduces engine power. The power loss is usually negligible unless conditions of very high humidity are encountered in warm countries. On naturally aspirated (non-turbocharged) and particularly on turbocharged engines, air is as necessary to successful operation as is the quality of the fuel used. Lack of sufficient airflow to an engine can result in these conditions:

- High air inlet restriction
- Low turbocharger or blower boost pressure
- Higher exhaust temperatures
- Incomplete combustion
- Lower fuel economy
- Lack of power
- Smoke at the exhaust stack
- Increased exhaust emissions
- Shorter valve and piston life
- Noisier operation
- Increased lube oil usage

Heavy-duty diesel engines with electronically controlled unit injectors are designed to provide minimum exhaust emissions, superior fuel economy, and high power outputs. Most of these engines are equipped with a variety of engine sensors. The air inlet system is equipped with one or more of the following sensors: ambient air pressure sensor for altitude compensation, intake manifold temperature sensor, and turbocharger boost pressure sensor. These three sensors can quickly determine a problem and cause the engine ECM to reduce speed and power. The sensors are normally mounted on the intake manifold similar to that shown in Figure 5–46 for the DDC Series 50 and 60 and Figure 5–57 and 5–58 for the Caterpillar 3176B and 3406E; and Figure 5–69 illustrates the location of these sensors on a Cummins N14 engine.

Black exhaust smoke pouring from any engine, particularly from a mechanically governed one, is a direct indication of either air starvation or engine over-fueling. Unburned fuel doesn't all flow from the exhaust stack! Some of it actually washes down the cylinder wall and causes lube oil dilution. Some changes to carbon, which can stick to pistons, rings, and valves as well as plug the orifice holes in the injector tip.

Unfiltered air can rapidly wear out an engine—a condition often referred to as *dusting out* an engine. This condition is particularly noticeable when an engine has been overhauled but after a short period of time loses compression and power and emits heavy smoke at the exhaust stack. Tests by major diesel engine manufacturers have shown that as little as two tablespoons of dirt can dust out an engine within a very short time. All air contains small particles of dirt and abrasive material that are not always visible to the naked eye. Dirty intake air is the main cause today for wear on pistons, rings, liners, valves, and other internal engine components.

AIR TEMPERATURES

The temperature of the ambient air delivered to a naturally aspirated engine, or the pressurized airflow from the turbocharger, can drastically affect the combustion process within the engine cylinders. Diesel engines perform best at nominal air inlet temperatures of 49°C (120°F). Control of these air supply and combustion chamber temperatures depends on several factors:

- Ambient air temperature
- Use of glow plugs
- Turbulence of the inlet air
- Use of aftercoolers or intercoolers
- Underhood air versus external air supply
- Engine compression ratio
- Piston crown design
- Precombustion versus direct-injection design

Air Too Cold

Air that is too cold or too warm can adversely affect the combustion process. Air that is too cold results in a longer ignition delay once fuel is injected. This occurs because the air temperature is much lower toward the end of the compression stroke. The piston crown shape and the turbulence created within the cylinder during the compression stroke has a bearing on this final air temperature. A drop in ambient air inlet temperature from +27°C (80°F) in the summer to −29°C (−20°F) in the winter can result in the air temperature toward the end of compression being between 110° and 149°C

(230° to 300°F) lower. Therefore, the ability of the injected and atomized fuel to change from a liquid state to a vaporized state is severely affected. Even a drop in intake air temperature of 15.5°C (60°F) can result in a compression temperature loss of approximately 71°C (160°F). The lower the air temperature, the longer the ignition delay (time required for the injected atomized liquid fuel to change to a vapor). Consequently, the degree of combustion knock noise that you here after engine start-up in cold weather is directly related to the air temperature and the quality of the fuel that is being used.

Low compression temperatures have the following four effects on engine operation:

1. The time required for the injected fuel to vaporize and mix with the oxygen molecules is lengthened, thereby delaying fuel ignition.

2. Ignition delay increases the quantity of fuel that is injected before it starts to burn. Therefore, peak cylinder pressures are higher, combustion knock is louder, and white smoke in the exhaust is much more visible.

3. The engine runs rougher, particularly at idle speed, due to the irregular combustion process.

4. Excessively long ignition delay periods can result in a failure of the fuel to ignite at all. This causes lube oil dilution problems from cylinder wall wash and severe wear within the cylinder pack assembly.

Current electronically controlled diesel engines are capable of starting unaided (no starting fluid or ether) at lower ambient temperatures than mechanically governed engines. In extremely cold ambient temperatures, however, starting aids such as measured-shot starting fluids may be necessary. In precombustion chamber engines, and in some of the newer direct-injection electronic engines (such as the Navistar-Ford 444 HEUI engine), a glow plug is used to facilitate faster engine start-up. In heavy-duty engine applications, particularly in off-highway equipment, many equipment manufacturers and operators have recognized the advantages of controlling the inlet air temperature during operations in extremely cold weather by employing an air cleaner system with a *flip valve* (See Figure 20–1). This valve in the duct work has to be manually rotated, or flipped, to either the outside air or underhood air position. In turbocharged and aftercooled engines, a study must be performed to ensure that the air entering the cylinders will not be too warm when using this system; otherwise, engine power loss and short valve life could result.

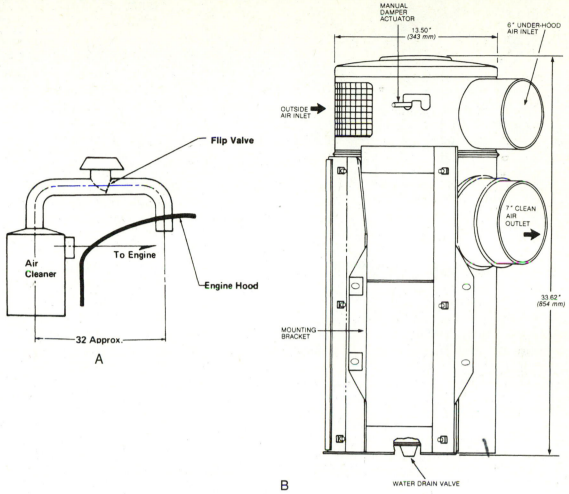

FIGURE 20–1 (a) Exterior-mounted truck air cleaner with a flip valve for summer and winter operation; (b) close-up of a heavy-duty air cleaner with a manually operated damper inside the cap to control the inlet air source—from the outside or from under the hood. (Courtesy of Farr Company, Los Angeles, CA.)

Air Too Hot

Air entering the engine cylinders when it is too warm results in a loss of air density (weight). This causes an approximate 1.5% engine power loss and other problems for each 38°C (100°F) that the air inlet temperature is above the nominal temperature. More details on the use of warm air are provided in this chapter in the section on aftercoolers. An increase in altitude can also affect the denseness of the air charge. A general rule of thumb is that in non-turbocharged engines, a 1% power loss occurs for every 100 m (328 ft) in altitude.

INTAKE AND EXHAUST SYSTEM FLOW

Four-Cycle Engines

Figure 20–2 illustrates the flow of the air in a turbocharged engine. The pressurized air flows into the cylinders through the open intake valve. The exhaust gases flow from the cylinder through the open exhaust valve(s) through the manifold and piping to the muffler assembly. This same airflow pattern is typical of turbocharged *intercooled* high-output heavy-duty engine models.

The intake charge is routed through a cast intake manifold bolted to the cylinder head. The manifold is designed and contoured to provide a minimum restriction to the airflow. In addition, most high-performance diesel engines employ four valve heads (two intake and two exhaust) in what is known as a crossflow head design. See Figure 14–3, which shows that the air enters one side of the cylinder head and exits on the opposite side. This configuration provides for very short, unobstructed intake and exhaust ports for efficient airflow, low pumping losses, and reduced heat transfer, so the engine breathes more freely and runs cooler.

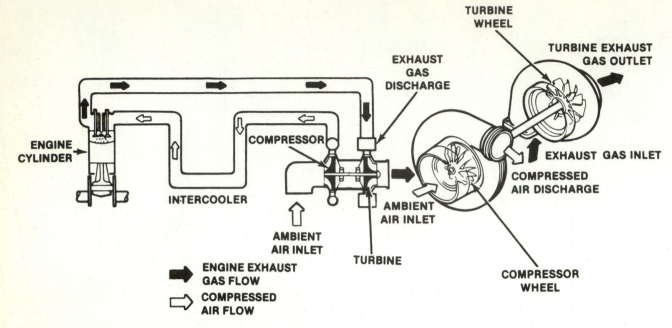

FIGURE 20–2 *Schematic of the air and exhaust flow for a heavy-duty high-speed turbocharged and intercooled diesel engine. (Courtesy of Detroit Diesel Corporation.)*

The valve operating mechanism used with current high-output direct-injection electronically controlled diesel engines is moving toward the overhead camshaft design. Refer to Figure 13–3 in Chapter 13. In addition, Chapter 13 has illustrations showing the design arrangement of the in-block camshaft and pushrod-operated valve mechanism.

Two-Cycle Engines

The largest engine manufacturer of two-cycle heavy-duty engines is Detroit Diesel. The two-stroke-cycle engine differs from the four-cycle model in that it does not use intake valves. All poppet-type valves contained in the cylinder head are *exhaust only;* usually there are four valves per cylinder on high-speed heavy-duty models.

Basic airflow through a vee-design DDC engine is illustrated in Figure 1–8. Note that a gear-driven blower is used to force the pressurized air into an *airbox* which completely surrounds each cylinder. The cylinder liner contains a row of helically shaped ports to create high air turbulence as air flows into the cylinder. These ports serve as the intake system. The conventional intake and exhaust strokes of four-stroke-cycle engines are eliminated in the two-stroke engine. Every piston upstroke is compression, and every downstroke is power; however to provide for the flow of the exhaust gases from the cylinder, the power stroke is shorter than on a four-cycle engine. The exhaust valve is typically opened at approximately 90° to 95° ATDC,

while the liner ports are opened at about 120° ATDC and remain open to approximately 60° ABDC for a duration of about 120 crankshaft degrees. During this time period, the blower and/or combination blower and turbocharger scavenges the cylinder of burnt gases, cools the internal cylinder components and valves, and supplies fresh air for combustion purposes.

AIRFLOW REQUIREMENTS

Different engine makes and models require specific airflows. The airflow requirements of a given engine are calculated by an engineer during the initial design stage of the engine. Nevertheless, the technician must be familiar with the basic airflow demands for the engine. The technician may be involved in switching air cleaners between engines or selecting a replacement air cleaner assembly for a damaged unit. Placing the air cleaner from a similarly power-rated four-stroke engine on a two-stroke model can result in severe air starvation, black smoke, and a lack of power. These conditions occur because the two-cycle engine needs greater airflow for scavenging purposes.

The cubic inch, or cubic centimeter, displacement of an engine and its power setting determine how much airflow will be required. Higher horsepower (kW) ratings require a greater airflow supply. The VE (volumetric efficiency) of an engine indicates how efficiently the engine inhales and retains its air charge. The higher the VE, the more fuel that can be injected to sustain a given power-development cycle. Consequently, the use of an exhaust-driven turbocharger is one common method for increasing the air delivery rate to an engine. The airflow requirements also vary between four-stroke-cycle and two-stroke-cycle engines, and they depend on whether the engine is naturally aspirated, turbocharged, and/or turbocharged and aftercooled. The VE varies with engine design, but for instructional purposes, we can assume VE to be between 85% and 90% for naturally aspirated four-stroke-cycle diesel engines and in excess of 100% for turbocharged models. With atmospheric air pressure at sea level being approximately 101.4 kPa (14.7 psi), a VE of 0.85 means that the air charge within the cylinder will hover around 85% of atmospheric pressure, or 86 kPa (12.5 psi).

Typical average VE for two-cycle and four-stroke cycle diesel engines is usually as follows:

- Four-cycle diesel supercharged: 1.3 VE
- Four-cycle valve-in-head naturally aspirated diesel engine: 0.90 VE
- Four-cycle valve-in-head turbocharged diesel: 1.35 VE
- Two-cycle diesel blower scavenged: 1.3 VE
- Two-cycle diesel blower and turbocharged: 1.7 VE

In two-stroke-cycle engines, since there is no actual piston intake and exhaust stroke, the airflow requirements are higher than those needed for an equivalent four-stroke engine. The volume requirement for two-cycle diesel engines is usually considered to be between 1.4 and 1.6 (140% to 160%) of the cylinder displacement to allow for scavenging air. Therefore, the average airflow requirements of an engine in cubic meters (cubic feet) per minute per horsepower (kW) at 15.5°C (60°F) and a barometric pressure of 760 mm Hg (29.92 in. mercury) atmospheric pressure can be considered from the following average values:

- Naturally aspirated four-cycle engine: 0.062 to 0.077 cm/min/0.746 kW (2.2 to 2.75 cfm/bhp)
- Turbocharged four-cycle engine: 0.084 to 0.099 cm/min/0.746 kW (3.0 to 3.5 cfm/bhp)
- Two-cycle engine with Roots blower: 0.084 to 0.141 cm/min/0.746 kW (3.0 to 5.0 cfm/bhp)

The average airflow volume requirement should generally be increased by 1% for every 2.8°C (5°F) above 15.5°C (60°F) and 3% for each inch (25.4 mm) of mercury (in. Hg) pressure below 29.92 in.Hg (760 mm Hg).

NOTE: The airflow requirements when a turbocharger is added to the gear-driven blower on the two-cycle

engine increase the airflow demands substantially. The following airflows, which are for rough comparison only, allow you to compare the differences between a non-turbocharged DDC two-cycle 8V-92 engine (not released commercially) and its turbocharged sibling. Keep in mind that the size of the unit fuel injector used (mechanical or electronic) determines the engine power output; therefore, a turbocharger with different A/R ratio (area over radius of the turbine housing) may be required.

Naturally aspirated 8V-92 **Turbocharged 8V-92**
1800 rpm: 28 cm/m 1800 rpm: 37 cm/m
  (980 cfm) (1300 cfm)
2100 rpm: 32.6 cm/m 2100 rpm: 45.3 cm/m
  (1150 cfm) (1600 cfm)

To determine the average airflow requirements of a given four-stroke-cycle engine, use the following formula:

$$\frac{\text{cubic inch displacement} \times \text{rpm}}{3456} \times \text{volumetric efficiency} = \text{cfm}$$

For example, according to this formula, a 14L (855 cu in.) naturally aspirated engine running at a full-load rated speed of 2100 rpm would require an average airflow of

$$\frac{855 \times 2100}{3456} \times 0.90 = 467.5 \text{ cfm (13.23 cubic meters)}$$

Of course, engines in use today use turbochargers and aftercoolers so you could expect a similar 14L (855 cu in.) displacement engine to require twice as much airflow, or between 24 and 27 cm/m (850 to 950 cfm) while producing twice as much power.

The formula remains the same for two-stroke-cycle engines except that the constant figure of 3456 is cut in half due to twice as many compression/power strokes (one power stroke every 360°) as the 720° engine crankshaft rotation for the four-cycle engine. The formula is

$$\frac{\text{cubic inch displacement} \times \text{rpm}}{1728} \times \text{volumetric efficiency} = \text{cfm}$$

For example, a 6V-92 DDC model with a 8.95L (546 cu in) displacement, running at 2100 rpm rated speed, and with a VE of 1.3 would require

$$\frac{546 \times 2100 \times 1.3}{1728} = 862.6 \text{ cfm (24.42 cubic meters)}$$

This same two-cycle engine running at the same speed, but with a turbocharger added to the system, would require approximately 1200 cfm (34 cubic meters)—approximately a 28% higher airflow rate through the engine, or 1.4 times more airflow.

As these examples demonstrate, the airflow requirements change substantially for different engines, and a higher airflow rate is required when a turbocharger is added to the system. You can readily obtain charts of engine airflow requirements from either the engine manufacturer or one of the major OEMs of air cleaners.

DUST INGESTION

As just described, a high-speed diesel engine requires a substantial amount of air to operate successfully. Although the air that we breathe may seem to be reasonably clean, even in fairly clean areas, the air carries approximately 0.2 grains of dust per 28.3 cm (1000 cu ft). With 7000 grains being equal to 0.453 kg (1 lb), it doesn't take long for a high-speed diesel engine to inhale substantial amounts of dust or dirt.

How much dust would enter the cylinder of a diesel engine that operated without an air cleaner? Let's assume that a heavy-duty on-highway truck engine was operated for 6 days a week for 10 hours a day on a long-haul application and that the engine was rated at 298 kW (400 bhp). Let's also assume that the average dust content of the air throughout its trips was 1.2 grains per 28.3 cm (1000 cu ft). The amount of air entering the engine depends on whether the engine is a four-stroke-cycle non-turbocharger or turbocharger model, or a two-stroke-cycle turbocharged (blower) model. If we accept that this engine inhales 0.107 cm (3.8 cu ft) per minute per 0.746 kW or for each horsepower, the volume of air taken into the engine per hour can be computed as follows:

$$400 \text{ bhp} \times 3.8 \text{ cu ft/minute} \times 60 \text{ min/hr} =$$
$$91{,}200 \text{ cu ft/hr (2583 cm/h)}$$

From this answer, we can further determine that the dust entering the engine per hour is equal to 1.2 grains × 91,200/1000 cu ft (1.2 grains × 2583/28.3 cm) = 109.44 grains. Therefore, the dust entering the engine intake system in 1 year can be computed as 109.44 × 10 hr/day × 312 days/year = 341,453 grains.

Since 7000 grains equals 1 lb (0.453 kg), the dust entering the air intake system in 1 year equals 341,453 divided by 7000: 48.8 lb (22 kg). Since it takes approximately two tablespoons of dust to wear out an engine, you can readily appreciate the need for an air cleaner and filter system as well as the need for regular filter service!

AIR CLEANERS

A large number of different air cleaner (filter) models are in use. We can categorize them into three general types: oil bath (seldom used), single-stage dry element, and two-stage dry element.

The oil bath air cleaner is seldom used now because it is less efficient at lower engine speeds when the airflow entering the engine is lower. This lower airflow reduces the agitation of the oil within the air cleaner sump and, therefore, does not trap airborne dust or dirt as well. In addition, overfilling an oil bath air cleaner can result in engine oil pullover, which causes engine overspeed. In cold weather, the oil can freeze; the result is high air inlet restriction and/or poor dust/dirt trapping ability. Operating a piece of equipment at steep angles can result in air restriction problems and possible oil pullover. An oil bath air cleaner must be serviced more frequently than a dry type, and the process is more time consuming. In addition, the oil bath air cleaner offers a higher initial restriction to airflow.

Dry-Type Air Cleaners

The major advantage of a dry-type air filter is that it allows much longer periods between service intervals. Up to 160,930 km (100,000 miles) is not uncommon on heavy-duty on-highway trucks. The dry filter is capable of trapping dust or dirt with equal efficiency throughout the speed range. The filter element is made from treated paper that has been pleated and assembled into a continuous vee-form throughout its circumference. In some filter models, this pleated paper element can be opened to a full length of 12 to 18 m (40 to 60 ft). The dry filter element increases in efficiency as the dirt load builds up a cake or bed in the valley of the vee pleats—upward from a minimum efficiency of 99.5% to as high as 99.99%—and remains constant throughout the engine speed range.

The paper element is surrounded and protected by a perforated steel mesh screen (shell). Dry filters are available in either a cylindrical or square/rectangular panel shape. Figure 20–3 illustrates a Donaldson dual-filter element—composite, dry and horizontally mounted—which has primary and secondary units. In composite filters, dirty air enters through the inlet opening where it travels through a plastic ring of vanes (called a precleaner) around the outside of the element. These vanes are designed to create a *cyclonic twist* to the air to throw the heavier dust and dirt particles outward by centrifugal force and downward into the dust cup area. The dust cup is held in place by a large heavy-duty clamp. On the composite heavy-duty, vertical-tube type shown in Figure 20–4, dirty air passes through the inlet and flows onto a series of

FIGURE 20–3 (a) Dual-filter air cleaner, which is a composite, dry, and horizontally mounted unit featuring a vacuator valve to expel 90%+ of the inlet laden dust or dirt by a centrifuge design; (b) same air filter assembly but in exploded view. (Courtesy of Donaldson Co., Inc.)

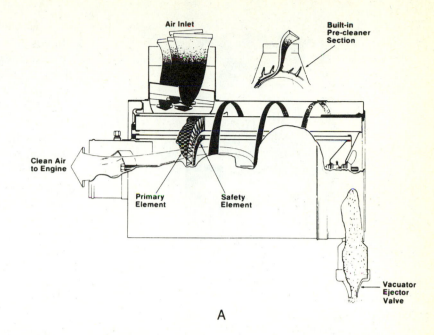

A

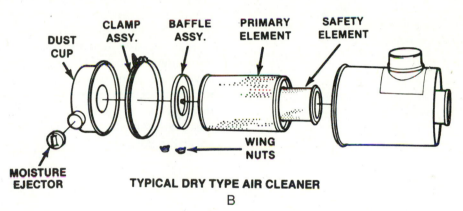

TYPICAL DRY TYPE AIR CLEANER

B

tubes that are vertically mounted inside the air cleaner. The hard plastic tubes contain vanes, which create a cyclonic twist similar to that described for the single and dual elements. Centrifugal action throws the heavier dust or dirt particles to the outside of the tube where they drop downward to the removable dust cup. The clean air then passes upward through the center of the tubes and into the air filter where minute dust and dirt particles can be removed.

An optional dust removal design is shown in Figure 20–3. In addition to the cyclonic action described, the dust that has been spun outward along the wall of the cleaner is directed toward a *Vacuator* dust ejector. This filter design can be mounted horizontally, as shown, or vertically with the Vacuator located at the base of the dust cup.

Precleaners and Screens

In heavy dust conditions, for example in situations involving off-highway trucks and equipment, pre-

cleaners such as those shown in Figure 20–5 are often used. These precleaners reduce the frequency of service by spinning the dust-laden air outward as shown in Figure 20–5. This dust is trapped and stored in a heavy-duty, hard, clear plastic bowl and cover assembly. When the dirt reaches the level indicated by a painted arrow on the bowl, remove the cover by loosening off the wing nut, lift off the plastic body, and empty the dust.

Many engines and equipment operate in areas where coarse or fuzzy material such as chaff, lint, or leaves is continually airborne. To prevent any of this material from entering the engine, a snap-on pre-screener can be used (Figure 20–5). Equipment applications using dry-type filters that fight forest fires or operate in municipal garbage dumps where sparks from burning debris are often airborne, a fine prefilter screen is necessary. This screen prevents sparks from being pulled into the air cleaner and damaging the plastic cylconic tubes.

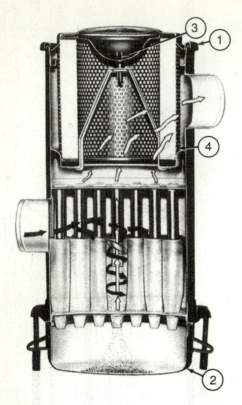

FIGURE 20–4 Vertically mounted, composite, cyclonic type of heavy-duty air cleaner. 1-top cover; 2-dust cup; 3-wing bolt; 4-filter element. (Courtesy of Donaldson Co., Inc.)

Many heavy-duty Class 8 on-highway trucks have air cleaner assemblies mounted on the engine intake manifold (see Figure 20–6).

Another very popular air cleaner for on-highway as well as stationary industrial engine applications is the ECO series manufactured by the Farr Company. Figure 20–7 illustrates this model, which is a spin-on disposable unit. The air filter has a tapered offset cone design and can be mounted either horizontally or vertically. This design feature ensures that airflow distribution and dirt loading are uniform throughout the core, resulting in lower overall restriction, between three to five times longer filter life, and better fuel economy. The air inlet shown at the top can also be at the side if desired.

Cartridge Panel Air Cleaners

In the cartridge panel air cleaner shown in Figure 20–8 the filter element is square or rectangular in shape rather than round. These types of filters are more commonly used on larger equipment such as mining trucks, graders, and bottom-dump scrapers, where extremely heavy dust and dirt conditions are regularly encountered. Most of these designs employ an exhaust gas aspirator assembly, which is also illustrated in Figure 20–8. This system directs exhaust gas flow through the piping to the aspirator funnel which creates a constant suction to the base of the dustbin located at the bottom of the centrifugal air cleaner panel.

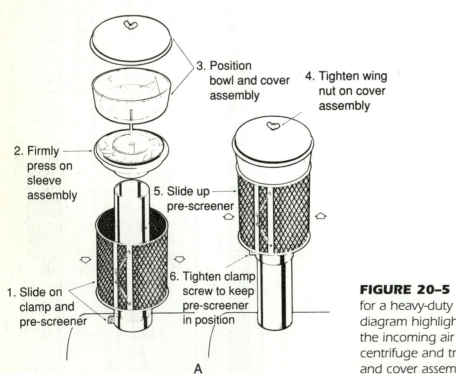

3. Position bowl and cover assembly

4. Tighten wing nut on cover assembly

2. Firmly press on sleeve assembly

5. Slide up pre-screener

1. Slide on clamp and pre-screener

6. Tighten clamp screw to keep pre-screener in position

A

Pre-cleaned air   Contaminated air

B

FIGURE 20–5 a) Features of a snap-on prescreener for a heavy-duty air cleaner assembly; (b) airflow diagram highlighting the spinning action imparted to the incoming air in the precleaner assembly to centrifuge and trap dust or dirt in the clear plastic bowl and cover assembly. (Courtesy of Donaldson Co., Inc.)

FIGURE 20–6 Features of a heavy-duty on-highway truck DynaCell air cleaner assembly. (Courtesy of Farr Company, Los Angeles, CA.)

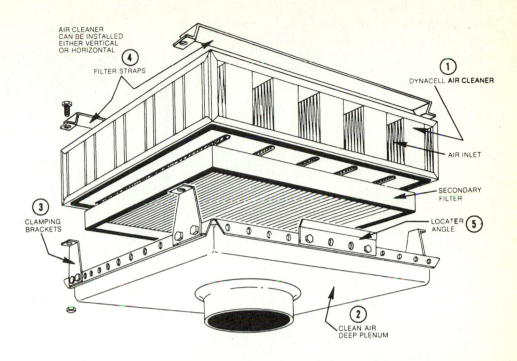

TAPERED OFFSET CONE DESIGN assures uniform air distribution...it minimizes air restriction and maximizes element service life. Illustration shows intake airflow at end, but can also be from the side.

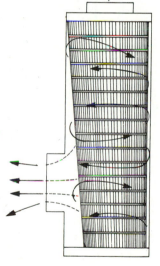

FIGURE 20–7 Design of an Ecolite air cleaner with a tapered offset cone filter assembly. (Courtesy of Farr Company, Los Angeles, CA.)

Heavily laden dusty air is spun outward as shown in Figure 20–9 by the shape of the deflector vanes at the inlet tubes, and 90% of the dirt is drawn off through the dustbin which is constantly subjected to the exhaust aspirator suction. Protecting the exhaust system from rain, fog, and other moisture is important to prevent corrosion of the exhaust piping. Either a balanced rain cap or smooth elbow-design raincap should be used on the end of the aspirator as illustrated in Figure 20–9. An optional dust ejector system shown in Figure 20–10

uses a supply of vehicle compressed air to bleed airflow through a nozzle in the Rotopamic or ultra-heavy-duty model precleaner panel.

In applications where moisture is a continuing problem (for example, on marine applications or in coastal logging equipment), a moisture eliminator pre-screen can be used. The moisture eliminator is fitted in front of the filter cartridge to attract moisture and dust. The coils of the eliminator cause the moisture-laden air to be trapped and drain by gravity to the base of the precleaner eliminator, which has a series of horizontal slots to allow the accumulated water to drain.

In heavy-duty off-highway equipment applications such as 170 and 200 ton mining vehicles, multiple air cleaners are required to handle the large airflow requirements of engines rated at 1600 to 2300 hp (1194 to 1716 kW). Figure 20–11 illustrates four UHD (ultra-heavy-duty) Farr air cleaners mounted on the forward bulkhead of a typical mining truck. These particular air cleaner models offer three stages of filtration for large trucks, drill rigs, shovels, and so on. The first stage of UHD filtration occurs through the *superclone* precleaner. This precleaner operates similarly to the one shown in Figure 20–9 where up to 93% of the dirt and 90% of any water entering the system are removed. The UHD air cleaner uses a small amount of vehicle compressed air to provide bleed airflow for self-cleaning action in the precleaner section, which is located in the swing-away heavy-gauge forward metal grid that protects the precleaner section (see Figure 20–10). The compressed air source can be supplied from the air compressor, the pressure side of the

FIGURE 20–8 Component parts of a two-stage dry-type air cleaner featuring an exhaust gas aspirator to withdraw and expel 90%+ of the dust-laden intake air. (Courtesy of Farr Company, Los Angeles, CA.)

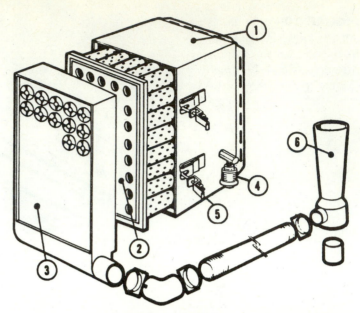

Mounting flanges are an integral part of all Series-D housings.

BASIC TWO-STAGE KIT INCLUDES

1. Air Cleaner Housing
2. Pamic Filter
3. Pre-Cleaner
4. Service Indicator
5. Fasteners
6. Aspirator Kit

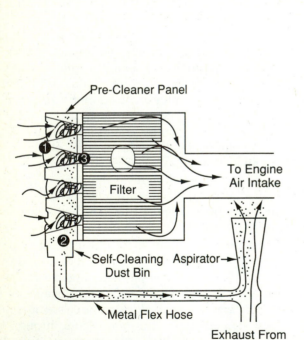

❶ Air enters pre-cleaner panel and is spun to remove 90% of dust particles.

❷ The separated dust falls into dust bin and is drawn out through aspirator.

❸ Pre-cleaned air now enters Pamic after-cleaner for second-stage cleaning.

A

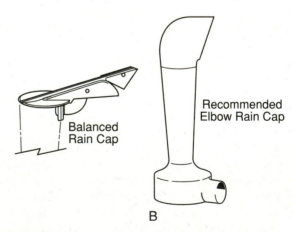

B

FIGURE 20–9 (a) Operational schematic of the two-stage Rotopamic heavy-duty air cleaner equipped with an exhaust gas aspirator; (b) outlet options for the Rotopamic heavy-duty air cleaner exhaust aspirator.

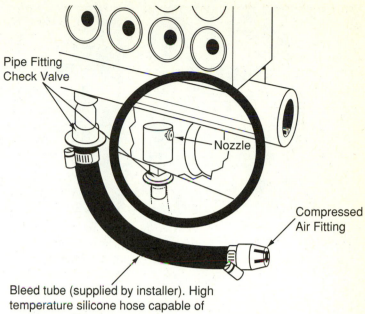

FIGURE 20–10 Features of a compressed air aspirator bleed-tube option used with a heavy-duty Rotopamic air cleaner. (Courtesy of Farr Company, Los Angeles, CA.)

Pipe Fitting
Check Valve

Nozzle

Compressed
Air Fitting

Bleed tube (supplied by installer). High temperature silicone hose capable of handling positive pressure is recommended.

FIGURE 20–11 Location of four ultra-heavy-duty dry-type air cleaner assemblies on the front of a large mining truck. (Courtesy of Farr Company, Los Angeles, CA.)

turbocharger, or the air box of naturally aspirated two-cycle engines. The second stage employs a primary filter to remove 99.9% of the dirt that gets through the precleaner (see Figure 20–9a). The third stage safety filter is designed to trap the small amount of dirt or dust that may get past the primary filter, so that the total system efficiency of 99.99% will be maintained.

Servicing the UHD air cleaner simply involves loosening the three latches on the side of the air cleaners to open the swing-away protective grate door. The primary element is held in place by two vertical straps. After loosening off the bolt at the top and bottom of each strap, swing the strap away. Insert the fingers of

both hands into the access holes of the air cleaner element and pull it straight out. Thoroughly wipe out the housing with a clean cloth. If the safety element requires changing (normally only at engine overhaul), note that it is held in place by a bolt and tab at each corner. Each bolt has a safety wire through its head to discourage unnecessary tampering. Cut the safety wires and remove the bolts. Grasp the element and pull it straight out of the housing.

In applications that operate in conditions of severe dust, it is extremely important to ensure that all ducting and piping to the air cleaner and engine are dust tight. Leaky connections, holes in piping, or other system faults must be avoided. Since only a couple of tablespoons of dust wear an engine out, several air cleaner manufacturers offer *dust detector kits* that are installed in the actual air cleaner to engine duct work.

Restriction Indicators

The most effective methods of determining when to service a dry-type filter element are by measuring the AIR (air inlet restriction) with a water manometer or by employing an air cleaner service indicator. Both gauges operate when there is a vacuum condition, that is, when the pressure within the air cleaner and ducting on the suction side of the turbocharger is less than atmospheric pressure. Consequently, a vacuum gauge can also be used to monitor AIR.

The restriction indicator gauge can be attached to the air cleaner housing or remotely mounted on the dash area of a heavy-duty truck or piece of equipment.

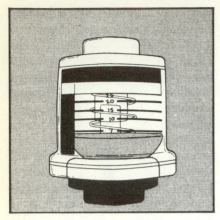

5" to 10"
Normal clean filter. (Initial restriction varies with each system design.)

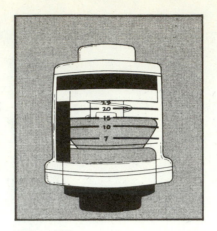

15" to 18"
The filter element is loading up with contaminants, but still has much useful life left. Fuel consumption is probably increasing.

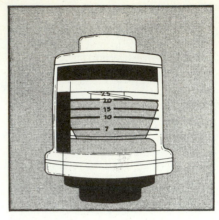

20" to 25"
The filter element should be replaced. The engine is probably using more fuel with slight loss of power. This upper limit will vary depending on whether equipment is diesel or gasoline fueled, and your fuel consumption experience.

FIGURE 20–12 Graduated Filter Minder air restriction indicator which reads in inches of water to indicate to the operator or service technician the degree of air filter plugging. (Courtesy of Farr Company, Los Angeles, CA.)

A small-bore plastic tube connects the indicator with a fitting on the ducting at the engine. Figure 20–12 illustrates a common type of restriction indicator (Filter Minder). This model contains a clear plastic window so that when the air filter becomes plugged, the restriction (vacuum) pulls a small float gauge into view within the small inspection window. Once the system has been serviced, the gauge can be reset by pushing a small release button on the bottom of the gauge. The restriction gauge shown actually allows the operator or technician to visually determine the degree of AIR based on the graduated scale on the *Filter Minder* gauge. Restriction gauges are calibrated in inches of water and are available for different maximum settings.

Servicing Air Cleaners

Nothing will wear out an engine faster than unfiltered air entering the system. The finest lapping compound in the world is a combination of fine dust mixed with oil on the cylinder walls. Think also of the continuous rubbing action of the piston rings against the liner surface and you can readily appreciate the rapid wear condition that is present.

Although oil bath air cleaners are *seldom* found on modern diesel engines, you may be faced with servicing one of these older assemblies. The oil sump must be removed and the dirty oil disposed of safely. The oil sump can be washed in solvent, and the internal wire-mesh filter assembly can be washed in solvent and blown dry with an air hose. Using a steam cleaner tends to pack dirt tighter into the wire-mesh screen. Check all gaskets and seals for an air- and oil-tight fit. Refill the oil reservoir with the same grade of oil that is used in the engine. *Do not* overfill the air cleaner sump; check the sump for the oil level *full* mark. Overfilling an oil bath air cleaner can cause oil pullover and engine overspeed.

On dry-type filters, check the manufacturer's specifications and service recommendations closely prior to service, since *not all* dry filter elements can be washed. A filter restriction indicator lets you know when the filter and system require servicing. When restriction readings indicate that the filter element is plugged, perform the following procedure:

1. Clean off the access cover before removing any clamps or bolts.

2. Remove the necessary clamps, bolts, or wing nuts to gain access to the air cleaner filter. Dust cups should be dumped when they are two-thirds full by removing the large clamp at the base of the filter housing. Precleaners can be dumped when the dust reaches the level indicated on the clear heavy-duty plastic bowl (see Figure 20–5). On cleaners equipped with the Donaldson Vacuator valve (see Figure 20–3), make sure the valve is not damaged or plugged. Is the cup joint sealing?

3. On heavy-duty air cleaners that have cyclonic tubes, light dust plugging can be removed as illustrated in Figure 20–13 by using a stiff-fiber brush. If heavy plugging with fibrous material is evident, remove the lower body section for cleaning with compressed air and warm water at a temperature not exceeding 71°C (160°F). Avoid steam cleaning cyclonic tubes because the heat can melt the plastic.

4. Remove the filter by loosening off the large wing nut that retains it. On square and rectangular models, there are usually four or more large external wing nuts. On cartridge-type filters, carefully insert several fingers into the tube holes and work the element free from the housing as shown in Figure 20–14.

5. On reusable dry filter elements, take care not to pound, tap, or rap the dust out of them as severe damage can result. Dust and loose dirt can be removed by directing compressed air through the element in the opposite direction to normal airflow.

CAUTION: Do not allow the air nozzle to touch the element paper directly since this can rupture it. Keep the nozzle at least 51 mm (2 in.) away from the filter element. Reduced air pressure should be used, in the range of 345 to 414 kPa (50 to 60 psi), although some manufacturers allow up to 690 kPa (100 psi).

6. Thoroughly clean the filter with warm water. Many filter manufacturers offer a sudsy cleaning solution that can be mixed with warm water for cleaning purposes. The filter element should be soaked for at least 15 minutes in a large receptacle of the cleaning solution. Rinse it in clean warm water; then use a pressure air hose with a maximum of 276 kPa (40 psi) to remove excess water. Refer to Figure 20–15.

7. Once a filter element has been cleaned, dry it using warm flowing air at a maximum temperature of 71°C (160°F). This can be accomplished by setting the filter on a drying rack or placing it in a temperature-controlled oven.

8. Once the filter has been dried, inspect it for rips or tears. This is a *very important* step. The best method to use is to place the filter over a vertically mounted lightbulb and rotate it slowly. You can also use a Trouble-light, as illustrated in Figure 20–16, to look for signs of damage.

9. Check all air cleaner system seals and gaskets and replace if damaged. Look for dust trails, which indicate leaky gaskets. Many heavy-duty round air filters have a soft rubber compressible seal glued to one or both ends. This seal can permanently compress (set) so that it flattens out; the result is that when the air cleaner cover is installed, it does not produce a dust-tight seal. Compare the height of this seal with that of a new filter element. If the seal is badly set,

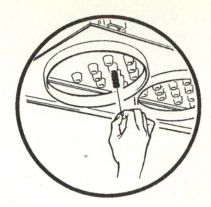

FIGURE 20–13 *Using a stiff-bristle brush to clean out the cyclonic tubes of a heavy-duty air cleaner assembly. (Courtesy of Donaldson Co., Inc.)*

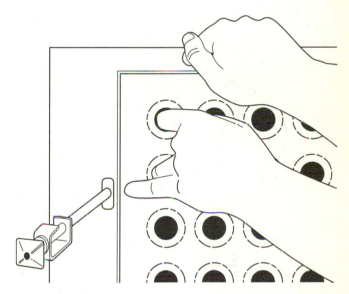

FIGURE 20–14 *Removal of the molded air filter element from a heavy-duty cartridge-type air cleaner assembly. (Courtesy of Farr Company, Los Angeles, CA.)*

replace the filter element. If starting aid fittings are used, inspect them to make sure they are tight and free of leaks.

10. On square or rectangular cartridge-type air filters, the filter elements are encased in a heavy molded rubber or neoprene casing. When the filter is changed, therefore, a new seal is automatically assured. Prior to installing the new filter, always clean out the air cleaner housing using a damp cloth to pick up any dirt or dust. Do not blow pressurized air into the housing unless a safety element is in position; otherwise, dirt may enter the turbocharger and/or engine intake manifold. Figure 20–14 illustrates the replacement of a rectangular cartridge-type filter element.

FIGURE 20–15 Using a pressurized air nozzle to remove excess warm fresh water that was used to rinse the dry-type air filter element after cleaning in a sudsy solution. Never use more than 276 kPa (40 psi) of air pressure, and never place the air nozzle directly against the filter to avoid tearing (rupturing) the element. (Courtesy of Donaldson Co., Inc.)

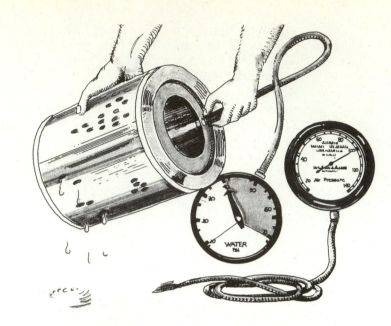

FIGURE 20–16 Using a Trouble-light inserted inside the air filter element to check for signs of paper damage, tears, or ruptures. (Courtesy of Donaldson Co., Inc.)

11. On air cleaner systems employing exhaust gas aspirators, ensure that the aspirator tube (piping) is not plugged. Plugging of these tubes can cause exhaust gas recirculation to melt the cyclonic tubes in the filter assembly. If components are melted, it is also possible that the assembly is located too close to an exhaust pipe. In addition, engine exhaust can rapidly plug dry filter elements, so make sure that exhaust gases are directed above and away from the air inlet system.

Remember that using a badly restricted (plugged) filter element results in excessive fuel consumption, loss of power, increased engine operating temperature, and shortened cylinder kit life. Using a damaged filter element results in rapid piston, ring, and cylinder wear and severe damage to the engine.

AIR DUCTING INSPECTION

The air induction piping functions with the air cleaner to carry clean air into the turbocharger and engine. In addition to servicing the air cleaner filter assembly, it is extremely important to check the piping hoses, elbows, and clamps for looseness, tears, or ruptures. Ignoring these components can lead to unfiltered air entering the system and destroying the engine in a very short time. Every time you service the air filter, inspect the intake ducting (piping) and elbows. Typical piping and connecting hose are illustrated in Figure 20–17a. Molded heavy-duty rubber elbows, which are approximately 6.25 mm (1/4 in.) thick with ribbed reinforcement, are widely used and secured by

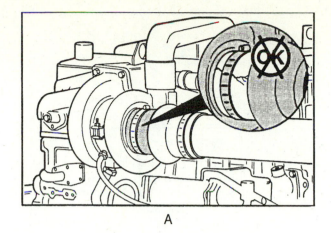

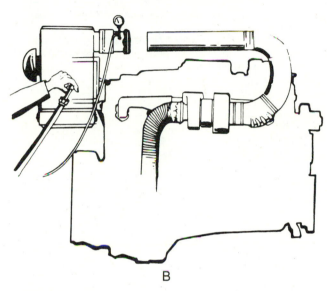

FIGURE 20–17 *(a) Inspection of air inlet ducting heavy-duty elbows for signs of cracking, looseness, or damage; (b) sealed air inlet ducting being pressurized to check for signs of air leaks. (Courtesy of Cummins Engine Company, Inc.)*

T-bolt hose clamps. Metal tubing should be spaced at least 19 mm (3/4 in.) apart from the hose clamps.

To check heavy-duty elbows and hoses, depress the hose where it is secured by the clamp and visually inspect it for signs of cutting or cracking as shown in Figure 20–17a. If you suspect that the tubing is not air-tight, disconnect it at both the air cleaner outlet and the turbocharger inlet. Install heavy plastic shipping caps or light metal blanking plugs at each end and clamp them into position. Drill and tap one sealing plate, or use the air inlet restriction pipe plug, to adapt an air pressure fitting. Connect a hand pump or use a low-pressure regulator at a wall valve to limit the pressure to 14 kPa (2 psi). Apply liquid spray soap or use a brush and apply sudsy soap solution to each joint. Air bubbles indicate a leak.

If you suspect that the air cleaner assembly is pulling in unfiltered air, remove the dry filter element and install a dummy one, or install a prewrapped one for the test. Refer to Figure 20–17b. Clamp a rubber sheet tightly over the air cleaner inlet and outlet connections. Prepare an air fitting connection on the air cleaner, or clamp a used tire tube with its Schraeder valve over the inlet or outlet connection. Use liquid spray soap on the inlet and outlet connections as well as at the dust cup of the cleaner. Apply 14 kPa (2 psi) maximum and look for signs of air bubbles, which would indicate a leak. Clean the inside of piping and flexible connectors before replacing them on the engine.

USE OF STARTING FLUIDS

In very cold ambient operating conditions, particularly when an engine has been cold-soaked overnight or for several days, the temperature at the end of the compression stroke is often too low to allow vaporization of the injected and atomized diesel fuel. For example, when the ambient temperature drops from 80°F (27°C), to −20°F (−29°C), the air temperature at the end of the compression stroke can be lowered by between 200° to 300°F (93° to 149°C). Engine compression ratio, cranking speed, and combustion chamber design all affect the temperature drop at the end of the compression stroke. Typical vaporization points for diesel fuel are listed in Table 3–2 dealing with diesel fuels. In cold weather, a combination of reduced cylinder compression temperatures and low cranking speeds severely affect the vaporization point of the diesel fuel.

For example, a typical no. 2 diesel fuel grade has an end boiling, or 100% vaporization point, of approximately 675°F (357°C). Obtaining this temperature would be hard under the operating conditions just discussed. Ethyl ether, or starting fluid, has an auto-ignition temperature of approximately 356°F (180°C); therefore when injected into the intake manifold of a diesel engine, it will initiate the cylinder combustion process within a reasonable time period after engine cranking. Although ethyl ether can facilitate starting in cold weather, excess amounts inhaled into the engine cylinders by an overzealous operator or service technician using a can of aerosol spray can wreak havoc with internal engine components. Using starting fluids in an uncontrolled manner can dispense as much as 12 cc of ether per second and cause severe damage. Ether used in this way can blow a cylinder head gasket, crack a piston or cylinder head, bend connecting rods, break cylinder head bolts, and damage cylinder liners. Uncontrolled amounts of ether also tend to act as a drying agent to the upper cylinder lubricant, resulting in lockup, or cause flaming in the cylinder area. In two-stroke-cycle diesel engines, loading of the cylinder

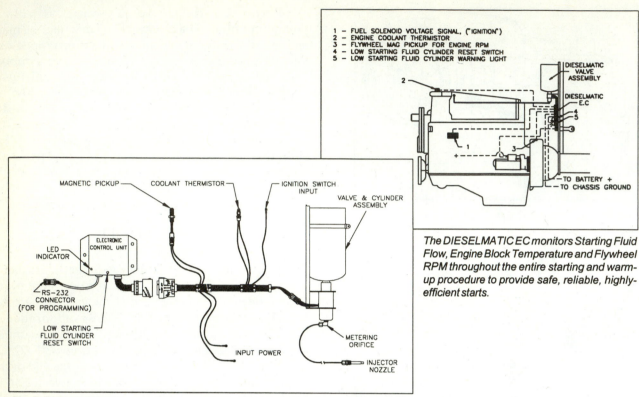

1 – FUEL SOLENOID VOLTAGE SIGNAL, ("IGNITION")
2 – ENGINE COOLANT THERMISTOR
3 – FLYWHEEL MAG PICKUP FOR ENGINE RPM
4 – LOW STARTING FLUID CYLINDER RESET SWITCH
5 – LOW STARTING FLUID CYLINDER WARNING LIGHT

The DIESELMATIC EC monitors Starting Fluid Flow, Engine Block Temperature and Flywheel RPM throughout the entire starting and warm-up procedure to provide safe, reliable, highly-efficient starts.

The DIESELMATIC EC insures that starting fluid will be injected into the engine in only the proper amount and only at the proper time.

FIGURE 20–18   KBI Dieselmatic electronically controlled starting fluid system with electrical accessories and hookup kit for use on heavy-duty on-highway, off-road industrial, construction, and agricultural equipment (Courtesy of Kold Ban International Ltd., Lake In The Hills, IL.)

block air box during ether injection, along with the rapid combustion that occurs, can blow the air box cover gaskets along the side of the engine block as the cylinder liner ports open and vent this combustible mixture into the air box.

To avoid the dangerous conditions caused by uncontrolled use of an ether aerosol spray can, a number of diesel starting fluid systems are designed to automatically control a measured (metered) shot of starting fluid that can enter the engine air intake manifold at any one time. Two manufacturers are Phillips & Temro Industries (Zerostart cold-weather starting products) and KBI (Kold Ban International, Ltd.). Generally, about 6 cc of starting fluid is needed in the air intake stream, metered over 3 to 5 seconds, to start a typical 800 cu in. (13.1L) high-speed heavy-duty diesel engine. Compare this amount to the uncontrolled introduction of ether by an operator from an aerosol spray—12 cc per second over a 3 second time period. This results in 36 cc of ether in the engine, or approximately six times the amount required to start the engine in low-temperature conditions. High-pres-

sure starting fluid systems have an excellent safety record and have been endorsed, specified, and recommended by virtually all of the leading diesel engine manufacturers worldwide.

In electronically controlled heavy-duty high-speed diesel engines, the ECM can be employed to safely start diesel engines in cold ambient operating conditions. Figure 20–18 is a schematic of the electronically controlled engine starting fluid injection system offered by KBI. In a paper published in the 1993 issue of *Truck Technology International,* James O. Burke, Vice President of marketing for KBI, described the research and development for adopting the KBI ethyl ether starting system to electronic engines. Basically, this system taps into the power of the engine microprocessor and various sensors. (The function and operation of an engine ECM is described in Chapter 5.) By monitoring input signals from the engine or vehicle ignition switch, the engine speed sensor magnetic pickup, the coolant system thermistor (temperature and resistance), and an optional exhaust gas temperature sensor, the ECM activates the Dieselmatic pressurized starting cylinder to open the metering orifice. The starting fluid within the cylinder is approximately 148 psi (1020 kPa) at 20°C (68°F), and when exposed to atmospheric pressure, the propellants contained in the fluid begin to boil off and force the liquid starting fluid and vapors through a 1/8 in. (3.175 mm) nylon tube line to an injector nozzle located on the pressure side of the turbocharger, which is most often the intake manifold. A precisely controlled amount of vaporized starting fluid permits an optimal engine start condition and smooth warm-up, while eliminating white smoke and other detrimental effects otherwise associated with cold-start conditions. Major advantages of using the KBI cold-start electronically controlled system, include these:

- Decreases engine starter motor cranking time
- Eliminates additional cranking cycles on cold-soaked engines
- Reduces engine vibration caused by uneven combustion chamber firing through ECM sensor monitoring during the warm-up period, and provides precise, metered quantities of starting fluid until the engine is running smoothly
- Minimizes lube oil dilution that normally occurs due to nonvaporized diesel fuel by reducing the time period that combustion chamber misfire exists
- Substantially reduces (along with the ECM controls) white exhaust smoke caused by partially burned fuel droplets from misfiring cylinders
- Indicates when the starting fluid cylinder is low by activating a low cylinder dash-mounted warning light.
- Eliminates operator abuse through fully automatic controls that cannot be overridden
- Offers a replacement and recyclable spin-on high-pressure cylinder.

AFTERCOOLERS

As the U.S. EPA exhaust emissions standards have become stringent, an area of engine design that has received more attention involves the temperature of the air that leaves the turbocharger and enters the engine intake manifold. One of the most important components in use today on electronically controlled high-speed heavy-duty diesel engines is the turbocharger-pressurized-air *aftercooler*.

Ideal air temperature for operating engines is usually in the region of 35° to 38°C (95° to 100°F). An engine rated at 187 kW (250 hp) would lose approximately 7.5 kW (10 hp) if the intake air temperature were allowed to rise to 54°C (130°F). The higher the ambient air temperature, the greater the expansion of the air; therefore, a loss of engine power always

results. Depending on the rise in ambient air temperature and the engine design features, an engine can lose between 0.15% and 0.7% horsepower per cylinder for every 6°C (10°F) rise beyond 32°C (90°F), or approximately 1% power loss for each 6°C (10°F) of intake temperature rise above 32°C (90°F).

There are four basic types of aftercoolers:

1. Intercooler-aftercooler combination often used on high-output marine engines. This system uses raw sea or lake water to cool the intercooler, while the aftercooler is cooled by fresh engine coolant (refer to Chapter 19).
2. JWAC (jacket water aftercooler—see Chapter 19).
3. ALCC (advanced liquid charge cooling) see Chapter 19.
4. AAAC (air-to-air aftercooler)

The terms *intercooler* and *aftercooler* are interchangeable descriptions used by engine manufacturers. The word *inter* means in between the turbocharger and engine intake manifold; the word *after* means that a cooler is located after the pressurized air leaves the cold end of the turbocharger. Both words indicate that the pressurized turbocharger air is cooled by directing it through a cooler system, which can be either air or water cooled. Figure 20–2 shows the general location of an intercooler, while Figure 20–19 shows a charge air cooler system mounted in front of the radiator. Pressurized turbocharger air that is directed through the charge air cooler core is cooled by forced air as a vehicle moves along the highway. Most heavy-duty highway trucks powered by Caterpillar, Cummins, Detroit Diesel, Mack, and Volvo engines now use a system similar to that shown in Figure 20–19, where the charge air cooler is mounted in front of the radiator assembly. Some very-high-output marine engine applications employ both an intercooler and an aftercooler. In Figure 19–25 the pressurized turbocharger air is intercooled before it enters the gear-driven blower. Once it passes through the blower, it is directed through an aftercooler and into the air box of this two-stroke-cycle engine.

Water Aftercooling

Water-type inlet air aftercoolers are discussed in detail in Chapter 19. Briefly, a JWAC engine employs fresh engine coolant routed through its water jacket to reduce the temperature of the pressurized air flowing through it from the turbocharger. A JWAC is capable of lowering the full-load engine turbocharger boost air from a temperature of about 149°C (300°F) down to approximately 93°C (200°F). The ALCC system is capable of lowering the turbo boost air temperature down to approximately 74°C (165°F).

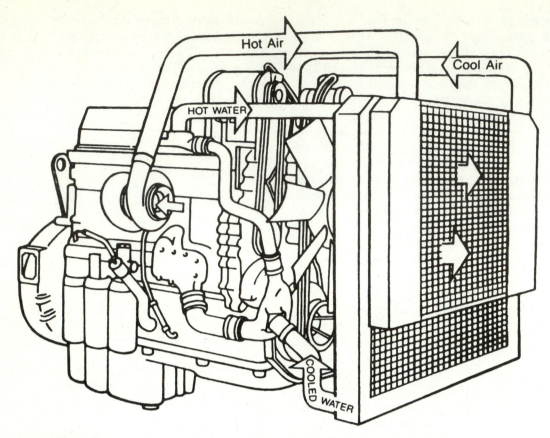

FIGURE 20–19 *Design of a heavy-duty highway truck engine ATAAC (air-to-air aftercooler) which is mounted in front of the radiator. (Courtesy of Detroit Diesel Corporation.)*

Air-to-Air Aftercooling

The most efficient and widely used turbocharger boost air aftercooler on heavy-duty trucks and buses is the AAAC, or ATAAC as some engine manufacturers refer to it. The engine turbocharger is driven by hot pressurized exhaust gases flowing from the exhaust manifold into the turbine side. These gases drive the turbine wheel at speeds in excess of 100,000 rpm, where they then leave the system at the exhaust piping and flow through the muffler system. Inlet air is pulled through the air cleaner, compressed, and heated by the compressor wheel (cold side); then it is pushed through the AAAC core and it then moves to the engine intake manifold.

Cooling of the pressurized intake air increases combustion efficiency, which in turn lowers fuel consumption, increases horsepower, and helps to minimize exhaust emissions. The AAAC system increases the engine fuel economy by approximately 4% over a JWAC engine. Today, high BMEPs, high torque rise, and maximum engine power are being developed at mid-range engine speeds, particularly on heavy-duty truck engines. Without the AAAC, the pressurized air

leaving the turbocharger under full-load operation, at temperatures as high as 149°C (300°F), and entering the cylinder would result in short valve and piston crown life, since there would be insufficient cooling airflow. In addition, the reduction in air density would lower the mass air charge for the combustion process resulting in a loss of power. This problem would be more severe on a two-stroke-cycle engine model where approximately 30% of the engine cooling is performed by the mass airflow rate.

Figure 20–19 illustrates a typical AAAC located in front of the radiator. Ambient air is moved across the aftercooler core and then the radiator core by means of the engine fan and also by the ram-air effect created when a truck is moving along the highway at vehicle speed. Consequently the use of radiator shutters and/or winterfronts should be avoided. Any airflow restriction to the aftercooler core can cause higher exhaust temperatures, power loss, excessive fan usage, and a reduction in fuel economy. Figure 19–22 illustrates a typical winterfront located in front of the radiator. In cases where heavy-duty trucks operate in extremely cold weather conditions and a winterfront

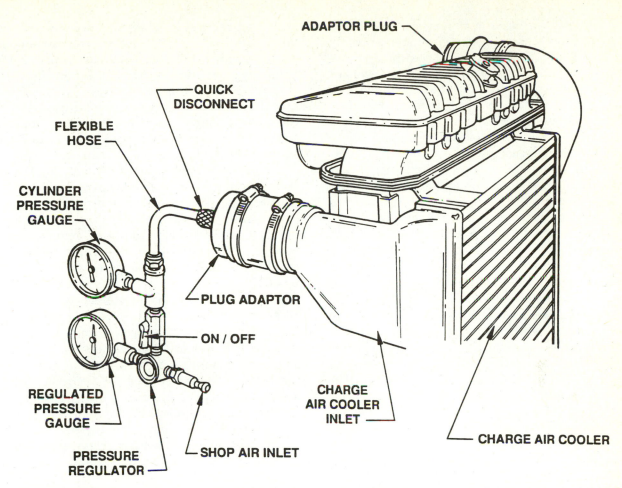

FIGURE 20–20 *Charge air cooler pressure, test hookup. (Courtesy of Detroit Diesel Corporation.)*

must be used, it should *never* be closed completely. Generally, a minimum of 20% airflow to the AAAC core must remain. When used with a viscous fan assembly, there should be at least a 203 mm (8 in.) diamond permanently open in the winterfront. This opening should be centered on the radiator, not at the top, bottom, or other off-center position. If more than one opening is used in the winterfront, these should be the same size at the top and bottom, or on the left and right sides, to produce a balanced airflow across the AAAC core as well as the fan blades. Winterfronts should always be completely removed when operating in ambient air temperatures above 4.5°C (40°F). Also, never install a winterfront directly against the AAAC core or radiator core or shutter. Install it in front of the truck grill with at least 51 mm (2 in.) of air space between the winterfront and the AAAC or rad core to ensure sufficient bypass cooling in the event that the winterfront is not fully opened in warming temperatures. When winterfronts are fully open, the airflow passage should be equal to or greater than 40% of the radiator core area.

Pressurized turbocharger air flowing through the AAAC core assembly dissipates its heat to the cooler ram air entering the grill at the front of the vehicle. This design of aftercooler reduces the turbocharger air temperature from 149°C (300°F) to between 38° and 43°C (100° to 110°F) before it flows into the intake manifold. Note that the AAAC has no water or coolant running through it. The aftercooler core consists of a series of tubes surrounded by metal fins somewhat similar to a radiator. The fins disperse the cooling air much more effectively around the tubes through which the turbocharger boost air flows. On a heavy-duty truck, flexible rubber elbows, couplings, and hose clamps are used to secure the duct work to the turbocharger, aftercooler inlet and outlet, and also at the intake manifold.

Heavy-duty electronically controlled diesel engines employ a number of sensors to accurately control the exhaust emissions levels, fuel consumption, and engine power. A number of sensors are used for the air system. An ambient air pressure (barometric pressure) sensor, an intake manifold air temperature sensor, and a turbocharger boost sensor are commonly used to monitor the airflow system. These three sensors are usually mounted directly on the intake manifold or mounted on brackets close to the intake manifold.

Checking AAAC Types

The AAAC does not have coolant flowing through it, so it can be checked using the test equipment illustrated in Figure 20–20. The core of the aftercooler should be kept free of bugs, dust, dirt, and antifreeze spilled from the radiator cooling system. Antifreeze forms a sticky substance that can attract dust and dirt. When cleaning the aftercooler core, always blow air through the core from the back side, since blowing it from the front will push it further into the aftercooler core and the radiator core when mounted on the vehicle. Regulate the air supply to 172 to 207 kPa (25 to 30 psi) when cleaning the core. Examine the core fins for external damage, debris, and corrosion from road salt.

To check the AAAC core for leaks, refer to Figure 20–20. Fabricate air inlet adaptor plugs to fit into the charge air cooler inlet and outlet connections. Fit a 0 to 414 kPa (0 to 60 psi) gauge and open/close air valve, preferably with an adjustable air-inlet control knob to regulate the air pressure to 172 kPa (25 psi). With the test equipment in position, apply 172 kPa (25 psi) to the cooler core. Apply a water-soap spray solution to each hose connection across the face of the charge air cooler and also at the intake manifold-head mating area. Closely check all welds on the charge air cooler and the tube header areas for stress cracks and signs of air bubbles, which would indicate a leak in the system. If the cooler core can hold 172 kPa (25 psi) with less than a 35 kPa (5 psi) loss in 15 seconds after the air supply hand valve is turned off, the core should be considered acceptable for use.

On heavy-duty trucks that employ air brakes, the engine-driven air compressor often draws its air supply from the engine intake manifold. The system *air dryer* can also be checked for correct operation while pressure checking the aftercooler core as just described. Use shop air to recharge the truck air brake reservoirs to 827 kPa (120 psi) so that you can force the air compressor governor to the unloaded position. This will allow charge air pressure to be directed to the air dryer through the air compressor. If the air dryer is leaking, it should be repaired as soon as possible.

ENGINE COMPRESSION CHECK

The inlet air system flow is critical to the efficient combustion and cooling of the engine cylinder components. High AIR (air inlet restriction) will result in low

turbocharger boost pressures and incomplete combustion accompanied by an increase in exhaust emissions. Similarly, high EBP (exhaust back pressure) will adversely affect turbocharger operation. If both the AIR and EBP have been confirmed as being within specifications after a water and mercury manometer check, the engine cylinders may have low compression caused by leaking valves, worn rings, scored liners, leaking cylinder head gasket, and so on.

When an engine is suspected of having low compression in one or more cylinders, a compression check can be performed. Depending on the make of engine, this compression check can be performed in one of three ways. First, however, remove the unit injector (mechanical or electronically controlled), the nozzle on an inline multiple-pump-type fuel system, or the glow plug on a precombustion-chamber-type engine. Some engine manufacturers recommend that all nozzles or glow plugs be removed, particularly if the procedure calls for a cranking motor engine rotation test. If, however, the engine manufacturer calls for a running compression check, a *dummy injector* and fuel bypass line must be used. On electronic engines, a dummy injector can be used, but the injector wiring harness must be disconnected at the ECM to prevent any system damage. *Always* run the engine until normal operating temperature is reached before performing the compression test; this will provide a more accurate reading.

Follow the steps outlined for the principal methods of performing a compression test.

Inline or Distributor Pump Fuel System.

1. If the engine is a precombustion chamber design, remove the glow plug from the cylinder to be checked; if checking all cylinders, remove all glow plugs (some manufacturers suggest that all glow plugs be removed to allow faster engine rotation during the cranking test).

2. If the engine is a direct-injection model, remove the nozzle from the cylinder head after disconnecting the high pressure fuel supply and/or return line.

3. Install a threaded adapter into the glow plug or nozzle hole and tighten to specs.

4. Place and secure the fuel pump control lever into the stop position.

5. Attach a pressure gauge to the threaded adapter which has been tightened into the glow plug hole (see Figure 20–21).

6. Crank the engine over on the starter motor for between 6 and 10 full revolutions or until the gauge stops moving.

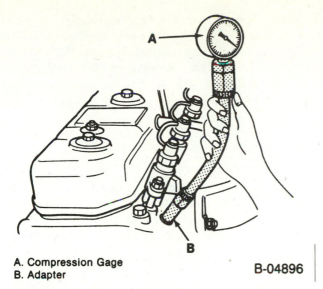

A. Compression Gage
B. Adapter

B-04896

FIGURE 20–21 *Example of a cylinder compression check on a precombustion chamber engine showing the gauge adaptor installed into the access hole of the cylinder head glow plug. The injectors can be removed to adapt the compression gauge on direct-injected engines. (Courtesy of GMC Trucks.)*

7. Record the compression reading and compare to the service literature specs.

Mechanical Unit Injector System (for example, DDC two-stroke-cycle models).

1. Remove the fuel lines from the injector assembly.
2. Remove the rocker arm hold-down studs on the cylinder to be checked.
3. Tip back the rocker arms.
4. Remove the injector hold-down stud and clamp.
5. Install a dummy injector and torque the retaining clamp to specs.
6. Reinstall the rocker arm assemblies into position and torque their hold-down bolts to specs.
7. Employ a fuel jumper line between the inlet and return cylinder head fuel studs to bypass fuel from the inlet directly to the return.
8. Connect a quick-connector coupler to the dummy injector adapter to support the pressure gauge.
9. Start and run the engine (DDC recommends that you run its two-stroke-cycle engines at 600 rpm).

10. When the gauge needle stops moving, stop the engine and record the pressure; compare to specs.
11. Depress the gauge line quick-pressure release button to vent all compressed air from the line.
12. Make sure compression pressure between cylinders does not vary more than 25 psi (172 kPa) on DDC two-stroke-cycle engines (for other engines, refer to the service manual).

Electronic Unit Injector Systems. Before beginning the test procedure, clean and then remove the rocker cover assembly. Disconnect the fuel supply line of the secondary fuel filter to cylinder head and be prepared to catch spilling fuel from the line into a container. Using regulated low-pressure shop air (30 psi, 207 kPa) direct the air into and through the cylinder head fuel inlet fitting for 20 to 30 seconds or until all fuel has been blown from the cylinder head fuel galleries.

CAUTION: Failure to remove fuel from the head passages can result in raw fuel draining onto the top of the piston crown. This can result in a hydrostatic lock and/or cause cylinder wall wash-down during engine start-up.

Individual cylinders can be checked or multiple cylinders can be checked at the same time. This depends on the particular make of engine. Most electronically controlled unit injector engines have a series of drivers to control a given number of injectors; these are wired from the ECM to specific injector assemblies. Let's consider a compression test on a Series 60 inline six-cylinder DDC four-stroke-cycle engine model where we can check compression of three cylinders at once.

1. Remove the three rocker shaft mounting bolts and nuts from the three forward cylinders. A special lifting bracket can be used to lift the assembly up and off of the head.
2. Carefully loosen the injector wire terminal screws. *Do not* attempt to completely remove these screws or you may break them; these are captive screws and should only be loosened off two full turns to accomodate pushing the wire terminal forward and up (off) of the screw.
3. Loosen off and remove the injector hold-down crabs.
4. Remove the three injectors from cylinders 1, 2, and 3.
5. Refer to Figure 20–22 and install three dummy injector compression test adaptors (Kent-Moore J38768-1A) into the injector tube holes.

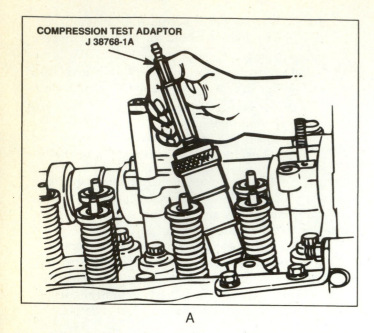

COMPRESSION TEST ADAPTOR
J 38768-1A

A

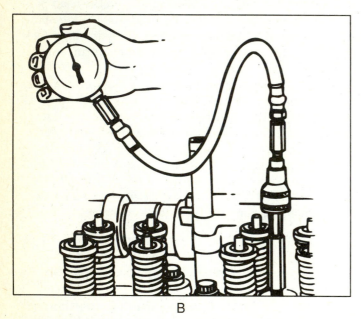

B

FIGURE 20–22   *(a) Installing a special compression test adaptor (dummy injector) into the cylinder head injector sleeve of a DDC Series 50 or 60 engine; (b) attaching a compression gauge to the dummy injector. (Courtesy of Detroit Diesel Corporation.)*

6. Torque the injector hold-down crabs to 58 to 66 N·m (43 to 49 lb-ft).

7. Remove the shaft from the rocker arm assembly and place it on a bench.

8. Remove the three INJECTOR rocker arms and replace them with oil control sleeves (Kent-Moore N J 38768-5).

9. Using clean 15W-40 engine oil, lube each shaft. With the sleeves in position, install the shaft through each rocker arm shaft, making sure that the cup plug end faces inboard.

10. Install the modified rocker arm shaft assembly onto the cylinder head; if Jake brakes are employed, use non-Jake rocker arm shaft bolts (J8929129) and torque the three bolts to 102 to 108 N·m (75 to 80 lb-ft).

11. Reconnect and prime the fuel system.

12. Carefully disconnect the gray connector from the ECM for the A-bank injectors (this isolates the driver signal).

13. Since the engine will be running during the compression test, and to avoid excessive oil throw-off, install the bottom half of the rocker cover and gasket and snug down with a few bolts (some dealers fabricate an old damaged rocker cover assembly for this specific purpose).

14. Prior to engine start-up, check that no equipment or tools are within the vicinity of rotating engine components.

15. Start and run the engine until a minimum coolant-out temperature of 38°C (100°F) is obtained.

16. Attach a cylinder compression gauge with a quick-connect coupler to one cylinder compression test adapter as shown in Figure 20–22.

17. Carefully note the gauge pressure reading, and while the engine is running (wear safety gloves), depress the gauge pressure relief valve several times so that the highest reading is obtained. Typical values should be between 3102 and 3793 kPa (450 to 550 psi). Cylinder compression values should *not* vary more than 276 kpa (40 psi).

18. At the completion of the compression test for cylinders 1, 2, and 3, remove the test equipment. Install the three injectors and wiring and repeat all of these steps for cylinders 4, 5, and 6.

Cylinder Leak-Down Test

Loss of compression pressure in an engine could be caused by a number of faults: worn or broken piston rings, worn cylinder walls, scored or cracked cylinder liners, damaged pistons (cracked or holed), cracked cylinder head, damaged or leaking cylinder head gasket, and burned, pitted, or worn valves and seats. Although a compression check such as that just described can determine that the pressure within a given cylinder is low, another method is often recommended by engine manufacturers to determine the *reason* for a loss of compression pressure. This method is commonly referred to as a *cylinder leak-down test*, or CLDT. The procedure is similar to that described for the compression test in that the individual injectors are removed and a dummy injector is installed and clamped into position.

For the sake of continuity, let's consider performing a CLDT on a four-stroke-cycle electronically controlled DDC Series 50 or 60 engine model. Follow these steps:

1. Bring the engine to normal operating temperature.

2. Remove the ducting (piping) to the intake manifold assembly.

CAUTION: Wear a pair of insulated gloves to protect yourself during removal of hot components.

3. Remove the exhaust piping from the turbocharger outlet.

4. Drain the cylinder head of diesel fuel (see the compression check procedure for electronic unit injector systems).

5. Refer to Figure 20–23 and install a Kent-Moore injector adaptor and whistle assembly into the cylinder head injector hole.

6. Torque down the adaptor with the injector hold-down crab and washer to a value of 58 to 66 N·m (43 to 49 lb-ft).

7. The CLDT must be performed with the piston at TDC compression. This can be determined by manually barring the engine over clockwise from the front using a 19 mm (3/4 in.) short extension on a heavy-duty bar inserted into the square hole in the crankshaft pulley. As the piston slowly moves up the cylinder on its power stroke, air will escape from the whistle causing an audible sound. TDC is indicated just as the sound from the whistle fades.

8. Disconnect and remove the whistle, but leave the adaptor in position in the head.

9. Refer to Figure 20–24 which illustrates the various special test tools required to perform the CLDT.

10. With the gauge set in position attached to a dummy injector, connect a hose from a regulated shop air supply to the gauge set air inlet. This air pressure usually runs between 690 and 862 kPa (100 to 125 psi).

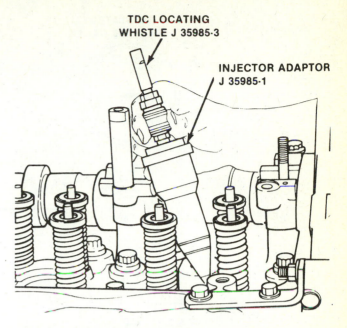

FIGURE 20–23   Installation of a TDC locating whistle into the injector bore of the cylinder head on a Series 50 or 60 engine to perform a cylinder leak-down test. (Courtesy of Detroit Diesel Corporation.)

11. Adjust the regulator pressure gauge by use of the knurled knob until the air pressure registers 552 kPa (80 psi). On an engine that is not running, normal internal clearances will prevent the cylinder from retaining more than this pressure.

CAUTION: If when the air is relayed to the cylinder, the engine starts to rotate, you will have to repeat step 7 to ensure that the piston is in fact at true TDC.

12. Allow the 552 kPa (80 psi) air pressure to stabilize in the cylinder for up to 1 minute. The air pressure on the cylinder pressure gauge will always read less than the reading from the air supply due to normal leakage.

13. Carefully listen for signs of air loss at the intake manifold, the turbocharger exhaust outlet, the crankcase oil filler tube, and the adjacent injector tubes on either side of the cylinder being tested.

If the cylinder pressure gauge maintains a value of 386 kPa (56 psi) or greater, then this cylinder is OK. No cylinder should register lower than 330 kpa (48 psi); if it does, leakage is not acceptable. Further investigation would be required to pinpoint the cause of the low pressure condition. If a cylinder shows low pressure, manually rotate the engine over two complete turns (720°) and repeat the CLDT.

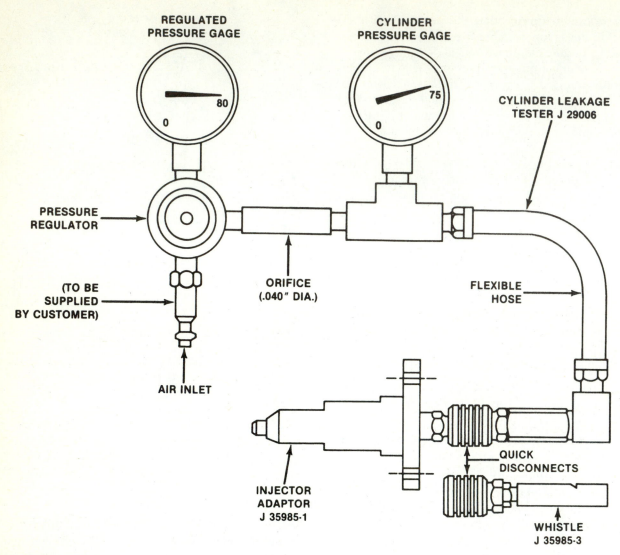

FIGURE 20–24 Test tools required to perform a cylinder leak down test. (Courtesy of Detroit Diesel Corporation.)

Possible causes for low air pressure retention can usually be traced to one of the following conditions:

Air leaks from	Probable cause
Air intake manifold	Intake valve face-to-seat leakage
Oil fill tube	Piston rings worn, hole in piston, worn cylinder liner
Adjacent injector holes	Leaking or damaged head gasket
Turbo exhaust outlet	Burned or pitted exhaust valves
Bubbles in radiator	Damaged head gasket, cracked liner or cylinder head

Experience has indicated that air leakage from the oil fill tube is normaly caused by a cylinder leak past the piston and piston rings or piston and piston liner assembly. To confirm where the leakage might be, follow these steps:

1. Carefully determine if the air is leaking from the intake or exhaust valves. Solidly rap the top of each valve with a rubber or plastic mallet and listen for air leakage.

2. Very slowly rotate the engine over manually (CW) in 10° increments. Note the cylinder pressure gauge value. If the gauge needle increases and the air leakage tends to fade, this confirms that the liner bore is tapered or less worn in the cooler areas of the cylinder. A consistent cylinder gauge reading accompanied by a steady air loss as you slowly rotate the engine over confirms that the piston rings are worn.

TURBOCHARGERS

Basic Information

The key factor to increasing the power output of a given displacement engine model is to trap a greater air mass and density of charge air in the cylinders. The main advantage of using a TC (turbocharger) assembly is that it allows more air to be packed into the engine cylinders, thereby increasing the VE (volumetric efficiency). The higher the VE, the greater is the quantity of fuel that can be injected and burned to completion. This results in a more thermally efficient engine, and one that can produce substantial increases in both engine power and torque characteristics over its naturally aspirated or non-turbocharged sibling.

There are several methods by which the mass of trapped air within the engine cylinders can be increased. One method is to use an engine gear-driven assembly similar to the *Roots blower*, which is widely used by Detroit Diesel and the General Motors Electro-Motive Division on their two-stroke-cycle engine models. The power requirements needed to drive the blower are not required, however, when an exhaust-gas-driven turbocharger is used. Virtually all of the exhaust energy leaving the cylinders is available to drive the TC turbine wheel shown in Figure 20–2. Only about 5% is lost to heat transfer of the surrounding components, and even less is lost when water-cooled exhaust manifolds are employed as in marine engine applications. The blower does have the advantage of producing a positive airflow at lower speeds and light loads, when the pressure and flow rate of the engine exhaust gases are lower than at rated full-load speed. The response time of the TC is generally slower than a gear-driven blower due to the small time lag involved when additional fuel must be injected until the higher pressure and flow of exhaust gases are available to drive the turbine.

Either one of these systems delivers boost air to the engine cylinders that is in excess of atmospheric pressure. The greater the air charge that can be retained within the engine cylinders at the start of the compression stroke, then the larger is the fuel volume that can be injected to produce a higher horsepower (kW). The pressure of the trapped air within the cylinders is controlled by the TC airflow capacity and, most importantly, by the intake and exhaust valve timing. The basic term for an engine that uses any device to increase the cylinder air charge is *supercharged*. A supercharged engine is an engine that takes air under pressure into the cylinders during the intake stroke and then compresses it. The degree of supercharging depends on the valve timing, since this controls when the intake valves close as the piston moves up the cylinder from BDC. Generally, gear-driven blowers are

referred to as superchargers, while the exhaust-driven TC is simply called by the descriptive term *turbocharger*. Keep is mind, however, that both devices are capable of supplying air pressure to the engine cylinders that is higher than atmospheric pressure.

Each TC model is designed for a given displacement engine. The performance of a TC is defined by the pressure ratio, mass airflow rate, and the efficiency characteristics of both the compressor and turbine, as well as the mechanical efficiency of the bearing support assembly of the rotating components. The TC identification tag riveted on the center housing usually indicates the name of the manufacturer, the model and part number, and an A/R ratio—the area over radius of the turbine housing. The letter A is the area of the exhaust gas inlet to the turbine wheel, and the letter R is the radius of the spiral of the turbine housing. This A/R number is very important because each number indicates a slightly different housing is determined by turbocharger efficiency, airflow through the engine, engine application and speed range, and engine load (the unit injector size, or on inline injection pumps, the rack setting dimension).

Typical TC pressure ratios for high-speed diesel engines usually fall within the range of 2 to 2.5:1. The engine TC maximum boost pressures are determined by using a mercury (Hg) manometer connected to the inlet manifold (described later in this chapter). This is usually stated in inches of Hg at full-load rated speed in the engine service manual.

Turbocharger Types

The two main types of turbocharging are the CPTC (*constant pressure turbocharging*) model and the PTC (*pulse turbocharging*) model. In the CPTC system, the exhaust ports from all cylinders are connected to a single exhaust manifold whose volume is large enough to provide a near constant pressure feed to the TC turbine housing inlet. This system has the advantage of providing a near constant gas flow rate; therefore, the TC can be matched to operate at optimum efficiency at specified engine operating conditions, particularly on applications that run at fairly constant loads and speeds. The disadvantage is that the energy entering the turbine is low because the pulsing energy of the gases leaving each cylinder in firing order sequence is damped out through the single exhaust manifold assembly. This represents a loss of potential energy to the turbine.

The majority of high-speed heavy-duty diesel engines in use today, particularly the electronically controlled unit injector models of Caterpillar, Cummins, and Detroit Diesel, favor the pulse turbocharging design. In addition they employ specially designed exhaust manifolds to increase the efficiency of the exhaust gases flowing into the TC turbine housing.

FIGURE 20–25
Turbocharger with a ceramic turbine wheel and pulse recovery exhaust manifold used with the Series 50 8.5L four-cylinder electronically controlled engine model. (Courtesy of Detroit Diesel Corporation.)

Figure 20–25 illustrates the DDC Series 50 and 60 pulse recovery exhaust manifold, which improves TC efficiency at low engine speeds.

Pressure waves are generated in the manifold by the exhaust gases rushing past the valves as they begin to open. The length of these passages is tuned to create a response within the manifold that directs the pressure waves to the hot turbine wheel where some of the kinetic energy is recovered. Tuned TCs also improve white smoke cleanup by producing higher engine intake air boost pressure at lower engine speeds, as well as improved TC bearing temperature control. In addition, turbocharger designs are usually of the type described as a single-stage radial flow compressor, and a radial flow turbine with both components mounted to the same shaft.

Figure 20–2 illustrates a typical TC system and the air and exhaust flow passages to and from the engine cylinders. Basically, the TC consists of a housing, illustrated in Figure 20–26, that is a bolted unit with both a turbine and a compressor housing. The turbine end of the TC is often referred to as the *hot* side since the exhaust gases enter here. The compressor end is often referred to as the *cold* end, because this is where the intake air from the air cleaner system enters the housing.

In the center housing of the TC is a one-piece support shaft that has a vaned turbine and compressor wheel pressed onto each end. The compressor wheel is usually retained by a self-locking nut, while the turbine wheel is often part of the support shaft assembly. The rotating components are supported within the TC housing by bearings (bushings) that are pressure lubri-

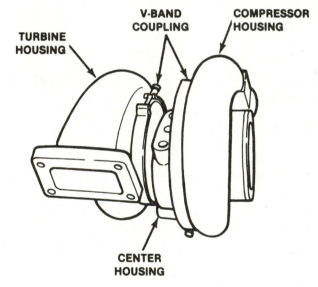

FIGURE 20–26 Major components of a typical turbocharger assembly. (Courtesy of Detroit Diesel Corporation.)

cated by engine oil directed to the center housing by a hydraulic or steel-braided hose. This allows a constant reservoir of oil to be maintained in the center housing. The pressurized oil supply actually results in the rotating shaft and components being supported on an oil film during high-speed engine operation. Therefore, the term *floating bearings* is often used to describe this type of system. Figure 20–27 illustrates these floating bearings on the support shaft. The bearings also act as thrust surfaces to absorb the thrust loads as the rotat-

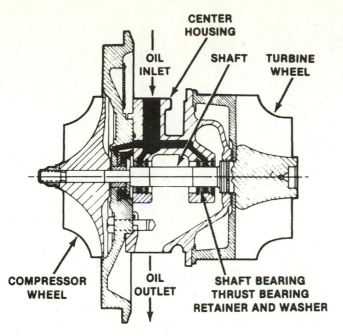

FIGURE 20–27 *Sectional view of a turbocharger identifying the major components and showing the pressurized inlet oil flow and the low-pressure drain line. (Courtesy of Detroit Diesel Corporation.)*

ing assembly changes position during engine operation. Figure 20–28 illustrates the TC lubrication supply and drain lines, while Figure 20–27 shows the actual pressurized oil flow within the TC center housing. The large drain line allows hot oil to return to the engine crankcase. On some TC models, oil drains directly through a passageway in the engine block or through the blower end plate on some DDC two-stroke-cycle engines where the TC is mounted directly to the gear-driven blower.

The easiest way to understand TC operation is to view it as a large air pump. The hot pressurized exhaust gases leaving the exhaust manifold are directed into the turbine area. As these gases expand through the housing to the atmosphere, they cause rotation of the turbine wheel and shaft. The compressor wheel mounted on the opposite end of the support shaft is driven at the same speed. This speed of rotation averages about 100,000 rpm; speeds may be higher or lower depending on the design characteristics of the TC assembly. The compressor wheel draws air in through the air cleaner system, compresses it, and delivers it to the engine intake manifold on four-stroke-cycle models. On two-stroke-cycle DDC engines, the TC delivers its airflow to the gear-driven engine Roots-type blower. The TC responds to engine airflow demands by reacting to the flow of exhaust gases. As the power demands of the engine increase and the operator depresses the throttle, the exhaust gas flow increases causing an

increase in the speed of the rotating components. Since the TC relies on exhaust gas flow, there is always a small time lag between the additional injected fuel and the actual TC response. This time has been reduced to almost an unnoticeable point on new TCs by use of smaller and lighter rotating components that are often made of ceramics rather than aluminum alloy metals. Many diesel TCs employ engine coolant passages cast within the center housing to assist in maintaining the lube oil below the *coking* temperature. Otherwise, hot oil (particularly after engine shutdown) can actually boil and create carbon buildup within the lube oil passages and eventual plugging of the lube oil supply to the TC support bearings.

When air is pressurized, its temperature increases and its mass (density) decreases accordingly. Either JWAC or AAAC systems are widely employed on modern engines to reduce the temperature of the pressurized air entering the engine intake manifold or the two-stroke-cycle air box.

Engine Exhaust Gas Temperatures

The temperature of the engine exhaust gases is controlled by the speed and load applied to the engine. All four-stroke-cycle diesel engines experience higher exhaust temperatures than two-stroke-cycle models. This is so because the two-cycle engine has a higher airflow rate, particularly when a gear-driven blower and turbocharger are used together in series such as two-stroke DDC models. The two-cycle engine also has a much shorter power stroke than its equivalent-power-rated four-stroke model. Since the two-cycle engine has no actual intake and exhaust stroke as does the four-cycle engine, the actual scavenging of exhaust gases, cooling of cylinders and components, and fresh air for combustion occurs in approximately 120° of crankshaft rotation. Approximately 30% of the cooling in a two-stroke-cycle DDC engine model is achieved by airflow. Therefore, a 10% reduction in flow of cooling air will more adversely affect the operating temperature of the engine than a similar reduction in flow of coolant water.

Actual exhaust temperatures for different makes and models of engines vary based on power ratings and whether they are two-stroke or four-stroke-cycle models. Generally, the average full-load rated speed exhaust temperatures are as follows for a high-speed heavy-duty electronically controlled unit injector engine rated between 298 and 373 kW (400 to 500 hp) at 2100 rpm on an on-highway Class 8 truck:

	Two-stroke cycle	Four-stroke cycle
Full load	357° to 371°C (675° to 700°F)	413° to 440°C (775° to 825°F)
Peak torque	399° to 427°C (750° to 800°F)	482° to 510°C (900° to 950°F)

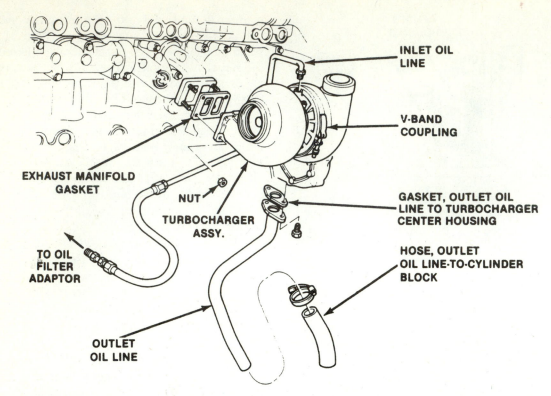

FIGURE 20–28 *Location of the turbocharger oil supply and drain lines for a heavy-duty high-speed engine. (Courtesy of Detroit Diesel Corporation.)*

The exhaust temperatures on some four-stroke-cycle engines can exceed 538°C (1000°F), while some high-output two-cycle models can approach 454°C (850°F). Engine manufacturers list exhaust temperatures in their service literature.

Wastegate Turbochargers

Many current high-speed on-highway truck diesel engines have wastegate turbochargers. Examples are the 5.9L Cummins engine used in the Dodge Ram pickup truck, the 7.3L Navistar engine used in Ford and Navistar trucks, and the 6.5L GMC V8 diesel. Heavier-duty engines using this TC include the Cat 3116 and the Cat 3406E—ratings of 435 bhp (325 kw) and higher. Engines rated below 435 bhp use a fixed, nonceramic wheel that spins 6% faster than the 3406C engine model T/C. A wastegate TC is designed to improve engine low-end performance and transient response, limit peak cylinder pressures, lower heat rejection and turbo speed, and reduce exhaust emissions. In addition, use of a wastegate allows very close matching to either an overdrive or manual transmission used in vehicles. The wastegate system can be adjusted to limit the maximum amount of boost depending on specific application needs, and the system provides improved throttle response at both the low-end and midrange loads.

An example of the location of a turbocharger wastegate can be seen in Figure 20–29 on a Cat 3406E series engine. A hose is connected to the body of the wastegate from the cold end of the outlet of the turbo assembly. Pressurized air (turbo boost) is routed into the wastegate control housing where it works against a spring-loaded diaphragm and linkage connected to the housing at the hot side (exhaust gas outlet) of the turbocharger. When the air pressure exceeds the spring setting in the control housing, the wastegate linkage shifts a small butterfly-type valve within the exhaust manifold porting area. This routes the exhaust gas flow around the turbine wheel, thereby bypassing, or *wasting*, the heat energy around the turbine housing and back into the upstream side of the exhaust manifold piping. When the boost pressure within the intake manifold of the engine is reduced, the spring within the turbo wastegate control housing automatically reopens the wastegate valve to redirect the hot exhaust gases back into the turbine wheel area of the turbo, allowing boost to once again be delivered to the engine. There is usually an adjustable pushrod, as shown in Figure 20–29, that must be set to ensure that the butterfly valve within the wastegate remains in either the fully open or fully closed position.

A

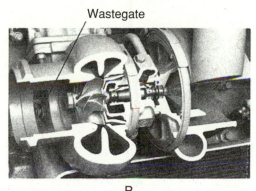

Wastegate

B

FIGURE 20–29   (a) Design features of the high-tech turbocharger used by Caterpillar on its 3406E engine models. Note linkage connection to the wastegate to bypass exhaust gases around the turbine in order to limit the turboboost pressure supply; (b) cutaway view of wastegate turbocharger which improves transient response, limits peak cylinder pressure, and lowers heat rejection and turbo speed. (Courtesy of Caterpillar Inc.)

Turbocharger Back Pressure Device

Another unique design feature in use on some turbochargers in high-speed diesel engines is the exhaust gas back pressure device. It is being used on the Navistar 7.3L T 444E V8 engine that employs hydraulically actuated electronic unit injectors. Since this is a direct-injection design engine, less heat is rejected to the coolant than in an indirect-injection engine. To provide rapid warm-up in cold ambient conditions, an exhaust gas back pressure device is employed within the turbocharger (Figure 20–30). This device consists of a butterfly valve controlled and actuated by a sole-

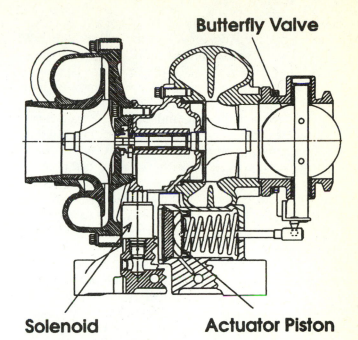

Butterfly Valve

Solenoid   **Actuator Piston**

FIGURE 20–30   Concept of an exhaust gas back pressure device used on the Navistar 7.3L T 444E V8 hydraulically actuated electronic unit injector engine model. (Reprinted with permission from SAE publication SP-930629, copyright 1994, Society of Automotive Engineers, Inc. Warrendale, PA.)

noid and actuator piston. The butterfly valve is powered hydraulically with engine oil supplied to the turbocharger bearings. The valve is only operational at idle and light load, when engine temperature and ambient temperature are low; therefore, once the engine is warmed up, the device is turned off. At temperatures below approximately 3°C, the device is activated by the electronic control unit on the vehicle, which is a variant of Ford Motor Company's EEC-1V control module. A signal from the control module opens an oil passage to charge the actuator cylinder, which in turn moves the actuator piston and closes the butterfly valve located in the exhaust outlet area of the turbocharger to restrict the exhaust flow. This action increases the exhaust back pressure and consequently the pumping effort required by the engine. This back pressure is monitored by a pressure sensor in the exhaust manifold. Thus, an electronic closed-loop strategy ensures that the exhaust back pressure is held at levels that will not affect drivability under varying speed, load, and acceleration conditions over a limited range of engine temperature.

Turbocharger Maintenance

Properly maintained TCs should provide trouble-free service between engine overhauls. The three key maintenance items that affect the life of a turbocharger are excessive AIR (air inlet restriction), high EBP (exhaust back pressure), and lubrication of bearings. Unfiltered air entering the TC can cause fine lapping of the rotating components, and high AIR can cause lube oil to be drawn past the seals. On mechanically governed engines, high AIR and high EBP can create incomplete combustion which leads to carbon buildup on the rotating turbine wheel. This, in turn, can create an imbalance condition of the rotating components and the turbine blading may actually come into contact with the housing. On electronically controlled diesel engines, the various intake system sensors prevent the engines from being overfueled as a result of a high AIR condition.

Leaks at the TC exhaust gaskets can prevent the rotating components from reaching the proper speed under load. This, in turn, reduces the boost pressure to the engine cylinders. Leaking gaskets or intake manifold seal rings on the outlet side of the TC compressor wheel can create a high-pitched whistle, particularly under load as the boost pressure forces its way past these areas.

TC inspection is best performed with the engine stopped and the intake ducting removed. Check for dirt and dust buildup on the compressor wheel impeller and in the housing. Excessive signs of dirt suggest that the air inlet ducting is not airtight, so perform the checks discussed earlier in this chapter and shown in Figure 20–17. You can also disconnect the exhaust piping to inspect the hot end of the turbo. Pay particular attention to the condition of the carbon buildup on the turbine vanes. Light carbon usually is indicative of light-load operation and/or excessive periods of idling. Do not attempt to remove carbon buildup from the vanes without removing the TC from the engine and disassembling it. Any signs of physical damage to either the compressor or turbine wheels are sufficient reason for immediate removal and replacement of these rotating assemblies. If damaged TC blading disintegrated during engine operation and the parts were inhaled into the engine cylinders, complete engine failure might be the result.

With the engine stopped, rotate the turbine wheel by hand to check for smooth and free operation. Any tight spots or signs of turbine or compressor wheel contact with their respective housings require TC removal and disassembly. Also examine the TC compressor intake area for signs of oil leaks. If oil is found, both the *axial* and *radial* clearances of the rotating assembly should be checked. These checks can be performed by means of a dial indicator gauge assembly

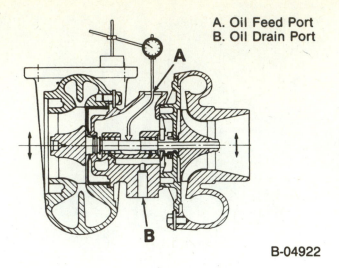

A. Oil Feed Port
B. Oil Drain Port

B-04922

FIGURE 20–31 *Using a dial indicator gauge to check the turbocharger bearing radial clearance. (Courtesy of GMC Trucks.)*

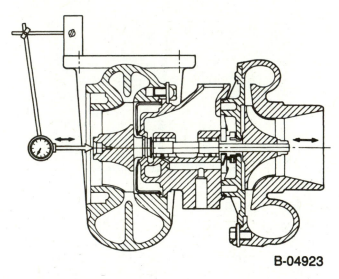

B-04923

FIGURE 20–32 *Dial indicator mounting required to check the turbocharger rotating assembly axial (end) play. (Courtesy of GMC Trucks.)*

mounted over the TC as illustrated in Figures 20–31 and 20–32. When checking the TC radial clearance with a dial gauge, use an offset gauge plunger as shown so that it comes into contact with the shaft through the oil inlet hole. Grasp the TC main shaft and slowly move it up and down while reading the dial gauge. To check the axial clearance (end to end), install and preload the dial gauge so that its pointer rests against the end of the shaft as shown in Figure 20–32. Push and pull the shaft backward and forward to record the end play.

Compare the radial and axial readings obtained to the specifications listed in the TC or engine service manual literature. Both of these clearances are fairly small on high-speed engine TCs. Radial clearances are usually in the range of 0.15 to 0.53 mm (0.006 to 0.021 in.); axial clearances usually run between 0.025 and 0.35 mm (0.001 to 0.014 in.), although specific models may allow greater clearances than these. If a dial indicator is not readily available, radial clearance can be checked by using a wire-type feeler gauge between the vanes and housing. Hold the TC shaft towards the feeler gauge to check this dimension.

When a suspected oil leak at the TC seal from the hot end (turbine) cannot be confirmed on a stopped engine, a commercially available fluorescent tracer liquid additive can be mixed with the engine lube oil. Normally, add one unit of the tracer to each 38 L (10 U.S. gallons) of engine lube oil. Refer to the packaging for specific directions.

CAUTION: Under certain engine and turbocharger running test conditions, it may be necessary to remove the inlet ducting. If this is the case, refer to Figure 20–33 and *always* install a TC inlet shield to prevent the possibility of foreign objects or loose clothing being pulled into the rotating components. *Never* run a TC engine with this shield removed since serious personal injury can result.

To test a TC seal for leakage, follow these steps:

1. Start and run the engine until normal operating temperature is reached.
2. Stop the engine and add the recommended amount of fluorescent tracer to the engine oil.
3. Start and operate the engine at low idle for 10 minutes.
4. Stop the engine.
5. Allow the turbocharger to cool and remove the exhaust pipe from the hot end (turbine) of the housing.
6. Use a high-intensity *black light* to inspect the turbine outlet for oil.
7. A dark-blue glow usually indicates a raw fuel leak, while a yellow glow is indicative of a lube oil leak.
8. Remove the TC oil drain line and check it carefully. Lube oil leaks may be traced back to restrictions within this drain line. Clean any restrictions and/or replace a damaged or collapsed drain line or hose.
9. Check for restrictions in the engine breather or tube, because high crankcase pressure can also cause the TC seals to leak.

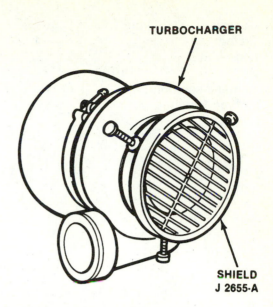

FIGURE 20–33 *Installation of a turbocharger safety shield when running the engine with the air inlet piping disconnected. (Courtesy of Detroit Diesel Corporation.)*

Turbocharger Removal and Disassembly

Removal of the TC from the engine is a fairly straightforward process. Refer to Figure 20–28 and note that the TC hot-end housing flange is bolted to a mating flange on the engine exhaust manifold. A gasket is located between the mating surfaces. The cold end of the TC is usually connected to the air inlet piping or ducting by use of a heavy-duty thick-wall rubber hose and clamp arrangement. In addition, the various lube oil supply and drain lines must be disconnected. Carefully sling the TC with a suitable lifting tackle prior to removing the retaining bolts that hold it to the exhaust manifold.

If it is necessary to disassemble the TC assembly, always match-mark the hot and cold ends of the housing to the center housing assembly to allow reinstallation of the components in the same position. Figure 20–34 illustrates the three main TC components split apart after either loosening off the special band clamps or removing the bolts on some models. Most service facilities simply replace a damaged TC with a new or rebuilt one, since special equipment is required to overhaul and rebalance the rotating components. If however, the TC is to be disassembled, the self-locking retaining nut on the compressor wheel end of the assembly must be removed and the back side of the compressor wheel must be supported on a hydraulic press: Use an old nut over the threads while applying pressure to it so the shaft and turbine wheel assembly pop from the compressor wheel.

64. Compressor Housing
65. Clamp
66. Lock Plate
67. Bolt
68. Center Assembly
69. Turbine Housing

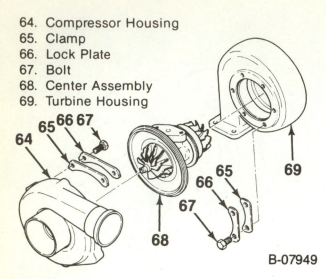

B-07949

FIGURE 20–34 *Three main components of a typical turbocharger assembly. (Courtesy of GMC Trucks.)*

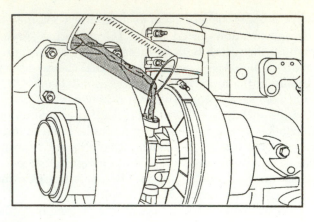

FIGURE 20–35 *Priming the turbocharger oil reservoir with clean engine oil prior to engine start-up after installation of a new or rebuilt unit. (Courtesy of Cummins Engine Company, Inc.)*

Special pliers are usually required to remove the snap rings to reach the seals and bearings (bushings). In some cases a series of small bolts at the center housing must also be removed to access these components.

Carefully inspect all disassembled components. Compare all dimensions of the parts with those in the service manual. Replace all worn or damaged components. When reassembling the TC, make sure to align the match-marks that were applied during the disassembly procedure.

Reinstall the TC assembly onto the engine using the reverse procedure of removal. Always use new self-locking nuts to retain the TC to the exhaust manifold. Remember that a new or rebuilt TC must be prelubricated before engine start-up. Refer to Figure 20–35 and pour clean engine oil into the bearing housing cavity while turning the rotating assembly by hand to lubricate all of the internal components. With the turbo guard shown in Figure 20–33 in position, start the engine and run at an idle speed; do not use a WOT (wide open throttle) condition. It is also usually good practice to leave the oil supply line slightly loose on initial engine start-up, until you can confirm that a steady flow of lube oil is reaching the TC center housing. If no lube oil is evident within 30 seconds maximum, shut the engine down and determine the cause.

Once the engine has warmed up, carefully listen for any unusual metallic rattles or scraping sounds. After the engine has been stopped, the TC should coast freely and smoothly to a stop. Any signs of a jerky or sudden stop should be investigated and corrected.

Troubleshooting Turbochargers

Generally, when a turbocharged engine lacks power, emits black smoke, or shows signs of oil (blue smoke) at the exhaust stack, the turbocharger may not be at fault. Often the cause is TC related, but other factors can cause or contribute to these symptoms. Spend a few minutes first in checking possible causes before you start to remove the TC from the engine.

One of the easiest and most useful methods is to *listen, look, and feel* as described next.

Listen. Since the turbocharger is a standard item on most heavy-duty diesel engines manufactured today, most of us know what a normal-running turbocharger sounds like. Unusual TC operating sounds that you should be aware of include these:

- A high-pitched whine, particularly under load, can be created by an exhaust gas leak or by a leak in the air induction piping between the TC and the engine intake manifold.
- A sharp high-pitched scream is generally indicative of worn bearings or possibly that the turbine or compressor wheel is rubbing on its housing.
- A cycling up and down in sound pitch can indicate air starvation or blockage in the air inlet duct system, a restricted air cleaner, or a buildup in dirt on the compressor wheel or diffuser vanes within the TC housing.

Look. One of the most important tools for troubleshooting is sight. Disconnect the exhaust and inlet piping from the TC housing assembly. Then make the following visual determinations:

- Use either a flashlight or Trouble-light and carefully look into the turbine and compressor end of the TC. Are there any signs of rubbing marks (polishing) on either the wheels or the housing?
- Are any of the blades (vanes) on the turbine or compressor wheels bent or damaged?
- Is there heavy dirt buildup on the compressor wheel? This would indicate unfiltered air, possibly coming from a leak in the air ducting, or poor filter maintenance intervals.
- Check for signs of heavy carbon or soot buildup on the vanes of the turbine wheel. This is indicative of incomplete combustion or burning oil (possibly from TC seals).
- If heavy oil accumulations are noticeable, check for the possible source. Oil may be from TC seals, although oil in the compressor inlet may not necessarily be coming from the TC seals. Also check that the engine air compressor is not pumping oil.
- Oil at the turbine end usually indicates an engine fault rather than a TC problem. Check the exhaust manifold for signs of engine oil accumulations, which may be from worn or broken rings on the pistons or worn valve guides. On two-stroke-cycle DDC models, leaking blower seals could contribute to the oil accumulations as well as leaking solid piston pin retainers or operation of the engine for long idle periods or under light-load conditions.
- Turbochargers generally use metal piston-type seal rings rather than lip-type seals that are used on crankshafts. Therefore, the oil sealing on the TC is known as *dynamic sealing*. Oil slingers keep the oil away from the seal ring areas. Check these common causes of leaking TC seals: excessive engine idling, plugged crankcase breather system (high crankcase pressure), sludge buildup or accumulations within the center housing of the TC, high air inlet restriction conditions, plugged or kinked TC oil drain line, damage to the TC bearings or wheels, and worn piston rings in the engine (blowby).

Heavy carbon buildup on the turbine wheel can be cleaned once the end housing has been removed to allow access. Use a noncorrosive cleaning solvent and a soft-bristle brush. Avoid the use of a wire brush, screwdriver, or gasket scraper which could scratch, damage, or nick the blades. It is important that carbon be thoroughly removed; if not, an imbalance condition could lead to the wheel striking the housing once the engine is started. If the TC has to be completely disassembled to clean the carbon, a glass-beading machine can be used. Make sure you use only the recommended material for cleaning, for example, walnut shells.

Feel.   To avoid personal injury, make sure the engine is stopped and the TC has been allowed to cool off. Then perform the following checks:

- Slowly rotate the turbo wheels by hand. They should turn easily and smoothly.
- Push inward against each wheel one at a time as you rotate it by hand. Once again, it should rotate smoothly and freely.
- Determine if there are any signs of rubbing or scraping; these indicate a major problem.
- Determine if the TC rotates smoothly and freely; if it does not, a major problem is indicated.
- After replacing a new or rebuilt TC, always prelube the turbo as shown in Figure 20–35. Check the intake and exhaust system ducting (piping) for any signs of foreign objects. Check the TC oil supply and return line and the air filter ducting to ensure that all connections are airtight. Do the same on the exhaust system.

Figure 20–36 lists typical operational conditions that you may experience when dealing with turbochargers along with possible causes and suggested corrections.

EXHAUST MUFFLERS AND PARTICULATE TRAPS

Mufflers used on diesel engines can vary tremendously in physical size and design. Their purpose, however, is the same: to allow the escaping exhaust gases, which are under pressure, to expand within the muffler, thereby reducing the noise emitted as they exit into the atmosphere. Exhaust noise is caused by sound pressure waves that cause small changes in atmospheric pressure. The frequency, or pitch, of sound pressure waves is measured in cycles per second. Typical noise levels from a heavy-duty highway truck or trailer are usually within the range of 80 to 86 decibels (dB).

Two typical muffler designs are illustrated in Figure 20–37. In the straight-through design, baffles located between the inlet and outlet cause the pressurized exhaust gases to follow a given path through connecting tubes. In the reverse-flow muffler design, the gases flow through connecting tubes. The muffler can be mounted either horizontally or vertically, as is the case on many heavy-duty on- and off-highway trucks and equipment.

Sometimes a small, round *spark arrestor* is added to the pipe exiting from the muffler assembly. This spark arrestor traps most incendiary sparks, thereby reducing any fire hazard, which is important in logging

Engine lacks power	Black exhaust smoke	Excessive engine oil consumption	Blue exhaust smoke	Turbocharger noisy	Cyclic sound from turbocharger	Oil leak from compressor seal	Oil leak from turbine seal	CAUSE	CORRECTION
•	•		•	•		•		Clogged air filter element	Replace element according to engine service manual recommendations
	•	•	•	•	•	•		Obstructed air intake duct to turbo compressor	Remove obstruction or replace damaged parts as required
•	•		•					Obstructed air outlet duct from compressor to intake/manifold	Remove obstruction or replace damaged parts as required
•	•		•					Obstructed intake/manifold	Refer to engine service manual & remove obstruction
			•					Air leak in duct from air cleaner to compressor	Correct leak by replacing seals or tightening fasteners as required
•	•	•	•	•				Air leak in duct from compressor to intake/manifold	Correct leak by replacing seals or tightening fasteners as required
•	•	•	•	•				Air leak at intake/manifold engine inlet	Refer to engine service manual & replace gaskets or tighten fasteners as required
•	•	•	•	•		•		Obstruction in exhaust manifold	Refer to engine service manual & remove obstruction
•	•					•		Obstruction in muffler or exhaust stack	Remove obstruction or replace faulty components as required
•	•		•			•		Gas leak in exhaust manifold to engine connection	Refer to engine service manual & replace gaskets or tighten fasteners as required
•	•		•			•		Gas leak in turbine inlet to exhaust manifold connection	Replace gasket or tighten fasteners as required
			•					Gas leak in ducting after the turbine outlet	Refer to engine service manual & repair leak
		•	•			•	•	Obstructed turbocharger oil drain line	Remove obstruction or replace line as required
		•	•			•	•	Obstructed engine crankcase vent	Refer to engine service manual, clean obstruction
		•	•			•	•	Turbocharger center housing sludged or coked	Change engine oil & filter, overhaul or replace turbo as required
•	•							Fuel injectors incorrect output	Refer to engine service manual — replace or adjust faulty component(s) as required
•	•							Engine camshaft timing incorrect	Refer to engine service manual & replace worn parts
•	•	•	•			•	•	Worn engine piston rings or liners (blowby)	Refer to engine service manual & repair engine as required
•	•	•	•			•	•	Internal engine problem (valves, pistons)	Refer to engine service manual & repair engine as required
•	•	•	•	•	•	•	•	Dirt caked on compressor wheel and/or diffuser vanes	Clean using a *Non-Caustic* cleaner & *Soft Brush*. Find & correct source of unfiltered air & change engine oil & oil filter
•	•	•	•	•		•	•	Damaged turbocharger	Analyze failed turbocharger, find & correct cause of failure, overhaul or replace turbocharger as required

FIGURE 20–36 Turbocharger troubleshooting chart. (Courtesy of Detroit Diesel Corporation.)

Slight wear or scratches	Moderate to heavy gooving on O.D. only	Moderate to heavy grooving on O.D. & I.D.	Extruded, or pounded. (May be stuck in ctr. hsg.)	Smooth undersized O.D.	Cracked or broken	Deep groove around center of O.D.	Oil holes fully or partially closed	Oil holes plugged with carbon	I.D. Polished looking O.D.	Melted (aluminum bearing)	CONDITION	PROBABLE CAUSE
•											Normal Use	Acceptable operating & maintenance procedures
	•										Contaminated oil (dirt in oil)	Engine oil & oil filter(s) not changed frequently enough, unfiltered air entering engine intake, malfunction of oil filter bypass valve
		•		•							Severely contaminated (dirty oil)	
			•	•	•						Pounded by eccentric shaft motion	Foreign object damage, coked or loose housing, excessive bearing clearance due to lube problem
		•					•				Center housing bearing bores, rough finish	Incorrect cleaning of center housing during overhaul of turbo. (Wrong chemicals, bores sand or bead blasted)
					•						Metal or large particle oil contamination	Severe engine wear. i.e., Bearing damage, camshaft or lifter wear, broken piston
						•				•	Lack of lube, oil lag, insufficient lube	Low oil level, high speed shutdowns, lube system failure, turbo plugged with hose fitting sealants
							•				Coking	Hot shutdowns, engine overfueled, restricted or leaking air intake/inlet
			•					•	•		Fine particles in oil (contaminated oil)	See contaminated oil
									•		Rough bearing journals on shaft	Bearing journals not protected from sand or bead blast cleaning during overhaul

GLOSSARY OF TERMS

ALIGNMENT — Proper position of parts.

BURR — Sharp metal.

COLD END — Compressor end of turbocharger.

CONTAINER — A box used to hold material.

DISCOLORATION — Change in color.

DISSIPATED — Dispersing or dispelling of heat.

DO NOT REUSE — Excessive damage - part requires replacement or possible remanufacturing.

EROSION — Gradual wear of material.

EXCESSIVE — Too much.

GLASS BEADING — Procedure used to clean parts where air under pressure is used to force small glass particles at a high rate of speed against the surface of the part.

HOT SHUTDOWN — Shutdown at high rpm will cause the turbocharger to continue spinning after the lubricant supply from the oil pump has stopped. Bearings will not be adequately lubricated or cooled.

HOT SIDE — Turbine side of turbocharger.

NICK — Small notch.

PITTING — Wear that causes holes in the material.

POLISH — To clean and smooth the surface.

REUSE — Parts that require inspection and reconditioning according to published specifications.

ROTATING UNIT — Compressor wheel-shaft-turbine assembly.

RUBBING — Contact between two parts.

SEVERELY — To a large degree.

SLIGHTLY — To a small degree.

STRAIGHTEN — Make straight.

WARP — To twist or bend out of shape.

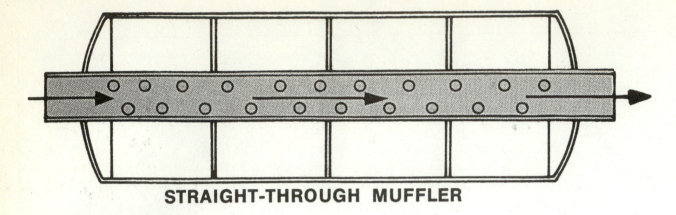

STRAIGHT-THROUGH MUFFLER

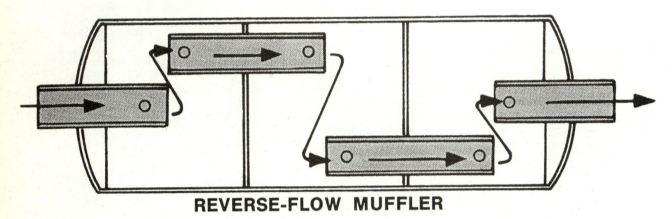

REVERSE-FLOW MUFFLER

FIGURE 20–37 *Exhaust gas flow through two typical muffler assemblies.*

equipment, for example. The venting of glowing carbon particles blown out with the exhaust gases can retain sufficient heat to ignite surrounding materials. Stainless steel vanes inside the inlet tube spin exhaust gases and solid particles. Centrifugal force throws particles to the periphery of the tube where they move in an ascending spiral. When the particles pass the end of the inlet tube, they are thrown out of the gas stream into the outer chamber of the spark arrestor where they fall through a baffle and are collected in the carbon trap where they remain until the unit is serviced. The trap can be serviced by removing a clean-out plug located on the underside of the body. Any crust that has been formed over the hole can be broken with a screwdriver. Start the engine and run it at high idle to blow collected particles out of the clean-out hole. Replace the plug when finished.

A fairly widely used exhaust silencer is the *COWL* spiral silencer manufactured by Phillips & Temro (Figure 20–38). The exhaust gases are routed through an aluminum-coated 14 or 16 gauge cold-rolled steel housing. This type of a silencer is much more compact than the conventional exhaust muffler system and offers superior noise reduction. The COWL silencer consists of a spiral passage of constant cross-sectional area. The spiral is partially lined with noise absorbing stainless steel wool. The exhaust gases can pass from one spiral passage to another through bleed holes within the spiral body. Since sound waves travel in straight lines at a speed much higher than the speed of the exhaust gases passing through the silencer, they are continually bounced off the smooth wall of the spiral. Some of these sound waves are reflected into the wool-covered wall where they are diffused. Other sound waves pass through the bleed holes, progressively attenuating the sound by wave cancellation as the gases pass through the multiple turns of the spiral. Any contaminants flowing into the silencer are centrifugally forced to the smooth outer surface and pass through the silencer, thus ensuring that no buildup of deposits occur.

FIGURE 20–38 Features of a COWL spiral exhaust silencer. (Courtesy of Temro Division, Budd Canada Inc.)

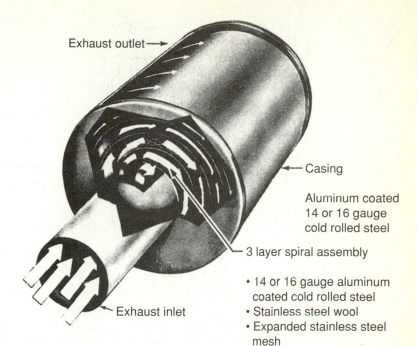

Exhaust outlet →

← Casing

Aluminum coated 14 or 16 gauge cold rolled steel

3 layer spiral assembly

- 14 or 16 gauge aluminum coated cold rolled steel
- Stainless steel wool
- Expanded stainless steel mesh

← Exhaust inlet

Calculation of Exhaust Gas Flows

As with air cleaners, the size of a muffler or silencer required depends on the exhaust gas flow that it needs to handle while maintaining a minimum exhaust back pressure. A rule of thumb for calculating exhaust gas flows for high-speed heavy-duty diesel engines operating between 1800 and 2100 rpm is to allow 7 cfm (0.198 cu m) per horsepower (0.746 kW) for two-stroke-cycle DDC type engines and 6 cfm (0.168 cu m) for four-cycle engines. You can specifically calculate the exhaust gas flow requirements by the following methods:

- Two cycle engines

$$\text{cfm} = \frac{\text{CID}}{1728} \times \text{rpm} \times \frac{T + 460}{Ta + 460} \times 1.4 \text{ (if turbocharged)}$$
$$\times 1.3 \text{ (if intercooled/aftercooled)}$$

- Four-cycle engines

$$\text{cfm} = \frac{\text{CID}}{1728} \times \frac{\text{rpm}}{2} \times \frac{T + 460}{Ta + 460} \times 1.4 \text{ (if turbocharged)}$$
$$\times 1.3 \text{ (if intercooled/aftercooled)}$$

where T = exhaust gas temperature in degrees F. Ta = ambient temperature in degrees F, and cid = cubic inch displacement.

Exhaust Catalyst After-Treatment Devices

The U.S. EPA as well as other government bodies in various countries are charged with setting standards to control the exhaust emissions of internal combustion engine vehicles. At the time of this writing, a number of lighter- and mid-duty diesel engines have been unable to meet the stringent 1994 EPA on-highway vehicle exhaust emissions particulate standards without resorting to the use of an exhaust after-treatment device. Most engine manufacturers have adopted electronic controls on their inline and distributor-type fuel injection pumps or are using electronic unit fuel injectors on their heavy-duty engine models to allow them to comply with the emissions standards. However, some of the lighter, mid- and heavy-duty diesel models have had to use an exhaust catalyst design similar to those of gasoline engines. Figure 20–39 illustrates a diesel exhaust soot filter that is designed to remove up to 90% or more of visible smoke and soot. Manufactured by Englehard Corporation, the soot filter is a ceramic flow-through design retrofittable in a stainless steel canister. It is designed to catalytically burn trapped particles. When exhaust temperatures exceed 375°C (707°F), the system reliably self-generates and burns collected soot. The self-cleaning process revolves around a proprietary precious metal catalyst coating that lowers the temperature at which trapped particles vaporize.

Most catalysts are contained within a coating on a ceramic substrate in the exhaust system in a remote location from the engine. These types of catalysts are capable of reducing exhaust particulates by approximately 30%.

FIGURE 20–39 Features of a diesel exhaust soot filter designed to remove up to 90% or more of visible smoke and soot. (Courtesy of Engelhard Corporation.)

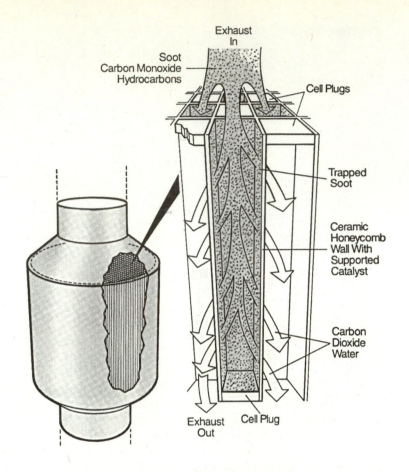

The particulate composition is split between the soot portion and the SOF (soluble organic fraction or VOF (volatile organic fraction). The catalytic converter particulate reduction mechanism absorbs the VOF during lower exhaust temperature ranges, below 150°C (302°F), and oxidizes it during higher temperature operation. Exhaust temperatures play an important part in the selection of what metals to use in the converter. For example, platinum is more active and better for lower engine exhaust temperatures, whereas palladium is less active (and less expensive) and is better for higher temperature applications. On its 6.5L V8 HD turbo model, GMC determined that average exhaust temperature during the emissions test cycle was about 250°C (482°F); on the LD engine, for both the turbo and naturally aspirated models, the exhaust temperatures averaged only 150°C (302°F) during the emissions test cycle. These temperatures are acceptable when using a catalytic converter on diesel engines, because if the exhaust temperature at the converter inlet exceeds 400°C (752°F), the sulfur in the exhaust from the diesel fuel can oxidize. This can form sulfates on the surface of the material used within the converter, thereby rending its function inoperable. This problem has been reduced substantially with the use of the newer classified 0.05% sulfur fuels.

Both GMC and Navistar employ a ceramic substrate flow-through monolith catalytic converter to further reduce the soluble organic fractions of the particulate emissions from their 6.5L (GMC) and Navistar T 444E (7.3L) direct-injection turbocharged and electronically controlled V8 diesel engine. This engine is widely used in various Ford pickup truck and van models, as well as by Ford and International in school buses and medium-sized truck applications. Figure 20–40 illustrates a typical Corning catalytic converter used by Cummins to comply with 1994 U.S. EPA emissions regulations. Engines affected include the 5.9L B series, which are widely used in Dodge Ram pickup trucks, as well as midrange vocational truck applications. These Cummins-developed catalysts are available to muffler manufacturers who package the catalysts in one of two ways: as a separate catalyst in a dedicated housing, similar to that in a passenger car; or in an integrated catalyst muffler where the catalyst is housed inside the muffler, which may be the same size or somewhat larger than current mufflers. The catalyst cores used with the B series engines are packaged in an 8 in. (203 mm) shell; however, the catalyst core and shell are then packaged in a larger round or oval shell, which forms the body of the muffler-catalyst assembly.

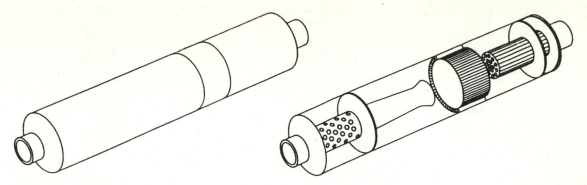

FIGURE 20–40 *Basic design of a diesel catalytic converter. (Courtesy of Cummins Engine Company, Inc.)*

A major manufacturer in North America of catalytic converter substrates for diesel trucks is Corning Incorporated, which also has companies in Hong Kong, Japan, Germany, Korea, Singapore, and Taiwan. The company has stated that total worldwide demand for truck exhaust treatment substrates is expected to grow from 80,000 in 1993 to more than 375,000 in 1994 and to 730,000 by 1998. This growth is being fueled by the 1990 U.S. Clean Air Act Amendments which call for significant reductions in diesel particulate emissions; these amendments became effective in the 1994 model year.

Currently, most heavy-duty engine manufacturers can meet existing regulations without catalytic converters by using improved combustion technology or by banking and trading exhaust emissions credits. The North American exhaust emissions standards are far stricter at this time than those in Europe and Japan; however, the standards of Europe and Japan are expected to match those of North America as time goes by. The Corning diesel substrates are coated with precious-metal catalysts which reduce diesel-particulate emissions by as much as 50%.

Diesel Exhaust Filter Operation

Many long-haul trucks using low-sulfur diesel fuel and electronic unit injectors can meet current exhaust particulate emission standards. Some, however, have to use a catalyst substrate to comply with the more stringent 1996 emissions levels mandated by U.S. EPA and other government regulatory bodies. The Corning catalyst converts noxious carbon monoxide and hydrocarbon gases in the exhaust stream into carbon dioxide and water vapor. Figure 20–41 illustrates a typical example of the operation of the exhaust gas filtering system. It oxidizes the exhaust SOF (soluble organic fraction), which would otherwise condense to form solid particulates. The Corning exhaust filters exploit the inherent porosity of *cordierite* ceramics to trap the soot produced by buses and other diesel vehi-

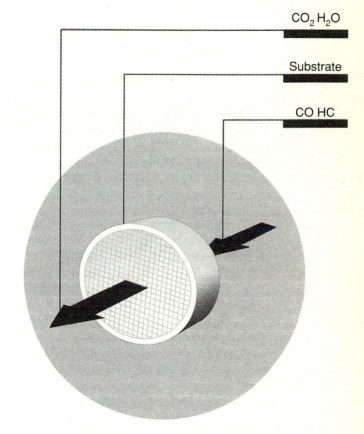

FIGURE 20–41 *Example of how the porous cordierite ceramic material in a diesel exhaust filter oxidizes the SOF (soluble organic fractions) to prevent solid particulates from being expelled into the atmosphere. (Courtesy of Corning, Inc.)*

cles. The channels of the filter are open at one end but plugged at the other as illustrated in Figure 20–39. The exhaust gases are able to escape through the pores in the cell wall and exit the filter through the neighboring channel. Solid exhaust particulates are too large to escape and are trapped on the wall of the channel. The exhaust soot is then oxidized when the filter reaches its load limit, thus regenerating the filter.

The typical truck substrate has 400 cells per square inch (6.45 sq cm), is 260 mm (10.25 in.) in diameter, and is 180 mm (7.0 in.) long. When coated with a catalyst, however, the substrate provides the surface area of two football fields. Substrates can also be used with alternative-fueled engines. Cordierite ceramics have a very low (near zero) thermal expansion coefficient; thus they can tolerate extreme thermal cycling. In addition, they offer high-temperature resistance and high-temperature mechanical strength, and their yield strength actually increases as they are heated to as high as 1200°C (2192°F).

GEAR-DRIVEN BLOWERS

A blower is a mechanical air pump used to force low-pressure air into engine cylinders. The blower, or what is often referred to as a supercharger, is usually gear driven from the engine, although belt drives are also common. Blowers are used on both gasoline and diesel engines, most widely on Detroit Diesel two-stroke-cycle engine models (the 53, 71, 92, and 149 series engines). These two-cycle engines also employ exhaust-gas-driven turbochargers and aftercoolers.

In the four-stroke-cycle line, Volvo Penta uses a crankshaft belt-driven mechanical compressor, which is referred to as a supercharger on its 42 series marine pleasure craft diesel engines. This supercharger provides the performance of a gasoline engine with diesel engine economy and durability. Figure 20–42 illustrates the Volvo system; both a belt-driven supercharger engaged through an electromagnetic clutch, similar to an air-conditioning pump drive, and an exhaust-gas-driven turbocharger are employed. Low-end engine torque is increased by the use of the mechanical supercharger. During accleration, the throttle is set to maximum and a kick-down function engages the supercharger, which uses two rotors alternating in four compression positions per revolution to provide pressurized air to the turbocharger. This has the affect of immediately improving low-end engine torque and eliminating turbo lag.

Once the turbocharger boost starts to increase, at an engine speed of approximately 3100 rpm, a valve in the air system is actuated, causing the air stream to bypass the mechanical supercharger. An electronic circuit breaker turns off the supercharger and the engine then operates as a conventional turbocharged diesel engine. The supercharger is designed to function automatically when cruising between 1700 rpm and 2500 rpm, which makes the engine less sensitive to load. Acceleration is improved by up to 40% over a non-supercharged model with a substantial increase in horsepower. Both the engine and turbocharger are cooled by fresh water.

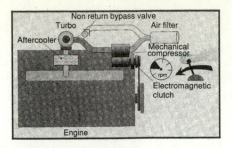

FIGURE 20–42   Example of a mechanical compressor, or supercharger, operation used on four-cycle Volvo Penta engines. (Courtesy of *Diesel Progress, Engines and Drives,* Business Journals Inc.)

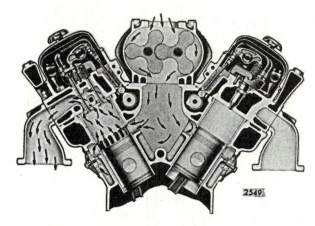

FIGURE 20–43   Airflow into and through the gear-driven blower, the engine block air box, ported liners, cylinder, and exhaust system for a two-stroke cycle vee-configuration engine. (Courtesy of Detroit Diesel Corporation.)

Figure 20–43 illustrates airflow through the engine of a vee-model DDC engine. On larger models, two blowers are used, and on the DDC 20V-149 engine model three blower assemblies are needed since this engine consists of a V6–V8–V6 arrangement bolted together. The major function of the blower in two-stroke engines is to supply air at pressures between 4 and 7 psi (27 to 48 kPa) to the engine *air box* area, which acts as a reservoir for a header of charged air. Remember, in a two-cycle engine the intake and exhaust strokes are physically eliminated, so pressurized air is needed and is used for several purposes:

- Supply fresh air for combustion
- Cool the cylinder liner, piston crown, and exhaust valves
- Scavenge waste exhaust gases from the cylinder
- Allow a controlled amount of air leakage past the piston oil control rings when at TDC to provide for positive crankcase ventilation

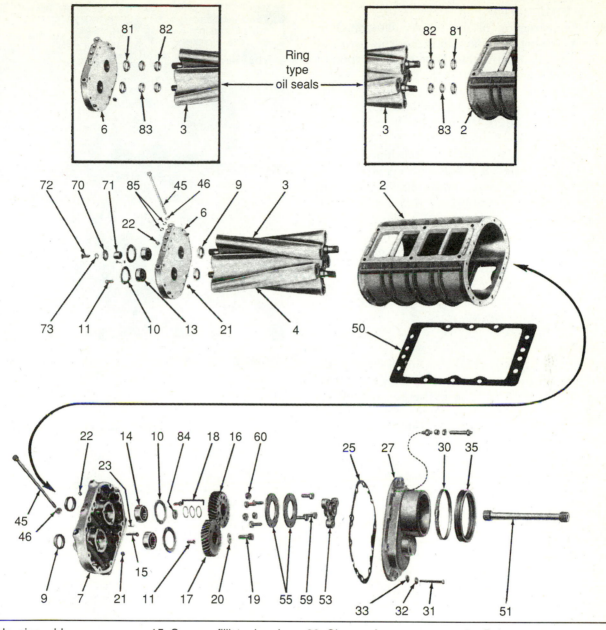

FIGURE 20–44 *Exploded view illustrating the component parts of a gear-driven blower assembly for a DDC two-stroke-cycle engine. (Courtesy of Detroit Diesel Corporation.)*

2. Housing – blower
3. Rotor Assy. – R.H. helix
4. Rotor Assy. – L.H. helix
6. Plate – blower front end
7. Plate – blower rear end
9. Seal – oil
10. Retainer – blower bearing
11. Retainer – lock screw
13. Bearing – blower rotor front (roller)
14. Bearing – blower rotor rear (ball)
15. Screw – fillister head
16. Gear – R.H. helix rotor
17. Gear – L.H. helix rotor
18. Shim – blower gear
19. Bolt – blower gear
20. Washer
21. Strainer – end plate oil passage
22. Plug – oil passage
23. Orifice – oil passage
25. Gasket – cover
27. Cover – rear end plate
30. Clamp – hose
31. Bolt – cover
32. Lock washer
33. Washer – special flat
35. Hose – blower drive cover
45. Bolt – blower mounting
46. Lock washer
50. Gasket
51. Shaft – blower drive
53. Hub – drive
55. Plate – flexible
59. Bolt
60. Spacer
70. Disc – fuel pump drive
71. Spacer – fuel pump drive disc
72. Bolt – drive disc
73. Lock washer
81. Collar – blower end plate
82. Carrier – seal ring
83. Ring – seal (piston type)
84. Spacer
85. Seal ring

Basic Construction

The basic construction of the blower illustrated in Figure 20–44 consists of an aluminum housing, two end plates, and two aluminum three-lobe rotors supported on ball and roller bearings within the end plates. As the blower rotates, air is trapped between the lobes and the housing to produce a positive air displacement into the engine air box. Figure 20–44 illustrates the major parts of a typical blower assembly used on a DDC V92 series engine. The blower is mounted on a machined pad on top of the engine block between both cylinder heads and is bolted in position. A splined shaft driven from the rear of the engine (gear train end) is also splined into a blower drive gear at the rear end of the right-hand rotor. On mechanically governed engines, the front end plate of the blower supports and drives the fuel transfer pump as well as the governor assembly. On DDEC engine models, the blower front end plate simply supports the fuel pump, since all engine governing is controlled from the engine ECM.

Operation

The airflow rates of blowers depend on their physical size and speed of rotation. Typical airflow rates were discussed earlier in this chapter. The power required to rotate a gear- or belt-driven blower can be substantial; for example, average power is between 25 and 30 horsepower on many high-speed automotive truck-type engines when running at maximum rated speed. To reduce this parasitic power loss, Detroit Diesel uses a bypass-type blower arrangement on its two-stroke-cycle engine models, which are also equipped with a turbocharger assembly. Recall that a turbocharger only provides pressurized airflow once the engine is running and under load. It is necessary, therefore, on two-cycle engines to employ a gear-driven blower so that a positive air displacement can be supplied to the engine for starting purposes and light-load operation. Once the engine is placed under load, the hot pressurized exhaust gases allow the turbocharger to supply all of the necessary air requirements for the engine, and the gear-driven blower becomes unnecessary.

The principle employed by DDC to disengage the blower is a *bypass valve*. This bypass valve and its location are shown in Figure 20–45, and the concept of operation is illustrated in Figure 20–46. The spring-loaded bypass relief valve contained within the rear end plate of the blower is held closed during initial engine start-up and also during low rpm and light-load conditions. When the engine speed is increased and load is applied, the turbocharger boost air pressure increases to raise the air pressure within the engine air box area. On 6V and 8V-92 model DDC engines, when this air box pressure reaches approxi-

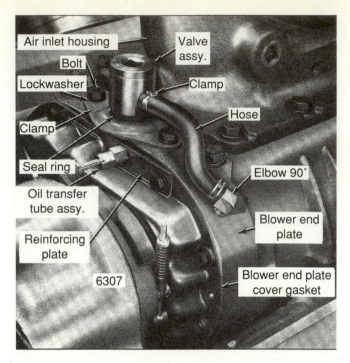

FIGURE 20–45 Location of the gear-driven blower bypass valve assembly used on DDC two-stroke-cycle engine models. (Courtesy of Detroit Diesel Corporation.)

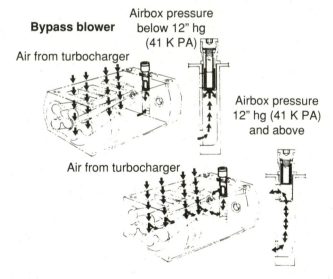

FIGURE 20–46 Schematic illustrating the airflow through a mini-bypass gear-driven blower assembly. (Courtesy of Detroit Diesel Corporation.)

mately 6 psi (12 in. Hg/305 mm manometer fluid displacement) or 41 kPa, the spring-loaded bypass valve opens. Under this valve-open condition, turbocharger boost air is free to bypass the blower rotors and enter the engine air box. The blower is gear driven so it will continue to rotate, but since the bypass valve is wide open, all of the required air pressure is being supplied from the turbocharger assembly and the pressure rise across the blower (inlet to outlet) is greatly reduced. During this bypass mode of operation (reduced pumping losses) the blower requires very little power to drive it; therefore, a substantial improvement occurs in brake specific fuel consumption.

Blower Removal

The blower must be removed if a major overhaul of the engine is to be performed or if the blower assembly requires major servicing. The blower assembly has either lip-type oil seals (item 9) or hook-type piston seal rings (item 83, Figure 20–44) in both the front and rear end plates. These seals are required to prevent pressurized lube oil on vee engines, or drain oil on inline models, which lubricate the rotor support bearings from entering the blower rotor housing. In addition, they prevent blower air pressure from entering the engine crankcase and creating high crankcase pressure. If the seals are suspected of leaking, check them as follows:

1. Make sure engine is stopped.
2. Remove the air inlet housing from the blower.
3. Remove the blower safety screen if used.
4. Start and run the engine at idle. Exercise extreme care to prevent any loose clothing or foreign objects from entering the blower.
5. If the seals are leaking, use a Trouble-light or flashlight and look into the housing; you will see oil spiral along the length of the rotors.

In addition to the seal check, note if there are signs of rotor-to-rotor contact throughout their length. Contact is an indication that the bearings (items 13 and 14 in Figure 20–44) are worn and/or that excessive gear backlash might exist in the drive and driven gears. Perform one more check before removing the blower. With the engine stopped, grasp one blower rotor and push the other one downward, then let it go; it should spring back slightly. This indicates that the blower drive hub and flex coupling are operating correctly. Any looseness detected in the rotors during this check indicates damage to the blower drive hub assembly.

When removing a DDC blower assembly, remember that minor variations will exist between a mechanically governed engine and an electronically controlled one, since there are no injector control tubes or fuel rods in the DDEC system. Nevertheless, the basic removal procedure can be considered common for most engines.

SPECIAL NOTE: In the following description the letter *M* indicates that a step is relevant *only* to a *mechanically governed* engine and not a DDEC-equipped model.

To remove the blower from the engine, proceed as follows:

1. Loosen the oil pressure supply line from the flywheel housing blower drive area to the blower rear plate.
2. Loosen the hose clamp on the blower drive support to blower seal.
3. If a mechanical tachometer drive is used, remove the cable from the adaptor at the rear of the blower.
4. Remove the flywheel housing accessory drive cover to gain access to the blower drive shaft.
5. Remove the snap ring of the blower drive shaft.
6. Pull the blower drive shaft from the blower.
7. Remove the fuel inlet/outlet lines from the fuel pump.
8M. Remove the mechanical governor top cover and remove the left and right bank pins from the inside of the governor linkage that are connected to the fuel rods.
9M. Remove the rocker covers and pull the split cotter pins from the fuel control tube to fuel rod pins.
10M. Remove the fuel rod pins and remove the fuel rods.
11M. Loosen off the small hose clamps on the fuel rod cover tube hoses at each cylinder bank at the front; slide each hose and clamp up on the tube in the governor housing.
12. Remove or disconnect the breather pipe at the top of the cylinder block.
13. On some engines you may choose to drain the cooling system and slide the hoses back on the bypass tube between the thermostat housings. Then remove the bypass tube.
14. You may also have to remove the engine front lifter bracket on some models.
15. Remove the two bolts and hardened washers through the top of each blower end plate, which are threaded into the engine block.
16. Remove the blower-to-block bolts and special clamp washers from along each side of the blower.
17M. On 12V and 16V engines, depending on the actual engine model, you may have to disconnect the governor linkage and/or remove the mechanical governor. Either

blower may be removed without disturbing the other blower.

18. Thread eyebolts into diagonally opposite tapped holes in the top of the blower housing. Then use an overhead chain hoist to lift the blower up slightly. Move the blower forward to disconnect the large blower drive seal hose at the rear; then lift the blower up and clear from the engine.

Blower Overhaul

The blower must be disassembled in a systematic way using some special tools. Figure 20–44 is an exploded view of all of the component parts of a typical DDC V-92 engine blower. Always match-mark each end plate to the blower housing to ensure that they are replaced in the same position.

NOTE: Refer to the exploded view in Figure 20–44 for the individual items listed in the following disassembly procedure.

1. Once the blower accessories and front and rear cover plates (item 27) have been removed, refer to Figure 20–47 and jam a soft folded rag between the rotors (items 3 and 4). This will allow you to loosen and remove the gear retaining bolts that are threaded into each rotor. The blower drive and driven gears shown in Figure 20–47 *must* be removed using the two special Kent-Moore pullers which have been bolted to the rear of each gear.

2. Leave the folded rag between the rotors as you tighten the puller center bolts; otherwise, the rotors would continue to spin during this tightening process. Alternately tighten each puller bolt so that the helical cut gears do not bind into one another.

3. Once the gears have been removed, take careful note of the hardened spacers and shims (item 18) behind each gear. Tie or wire these together so that they can be reinstalled in the same position upon reassembly.

4. Remove the three bearing retainer screws from each retainer at the front and rear of the blower. Remove the retainers (item 10).

5. Using the same pullers that were employed in Figure 20–47, attach the pullers to the blower end plate with bolts threaded into the bearing retainer holes.

6. Remove the two fillister heads (large slotted screws, item 15) that are located diagonally opposite one another in the end plate.

FIGURE 20–47 Using two Kent-Moore gear pullers to remove the drive and driven gears from the rear of a two-stroke-cycle engine blower assembly. (Courtesy of Detroit Diesel Corporation.)

7. Jam the rotors with a soft folded rag and tighten the puller center bolts alternately to remove the end plate with its bearings from the blower housing.

8. At the front end plate on mechanically governed engines, remove the fuel pump drive bolt (item 72), washer, and spacer, as well as the two fillister head end plate retaining screws.

9. Using the same pullers that were employed in Figure 20–47, repeat the same procedure to remove the front end plate (item 6) and bearings (item 13) from the housing.

NOTE: The rotors can be pulled with the end plate and then pressed from the bearings, or they can be separated by leaving the fillister head screws in position and pushed out of the bearings.

10. Remove the end plate bearings and seals from the front and rear plates by supporting the plate on wooden blocks or an arbor press and using suitable pressing stub shafts. Take note that the front end plate bearings (item 13) are of a roller design, while the rear end plate (gear end) has double-row radial and thrust ball bearings (item 14).

11. On turbocharged engines, the blower rotors employ seal ring carriers (item 82) that support piston type seal rings (item 83). Remove these seals using a pair of suitable snap-ring pliers.

12. If the seal ring carrier is damaged, remove it using a Kent-Moore puller similar to those shown in Figure 20–47.

Blower Inspection

After washing all parts in clean fuel oil, dry them with compressed air and lint-free rags. Carefully inspect the blower parts for any signs of severe scoring on the rotors, the end plates, the blower end plate mounting surface, and inside the blower housing. Minor imperfections can be removed using fine emery cloth in all areas. Note, however, that each blower end plate is bolted directly to the blower housing without a gasket, although a nonhardening sealer can be used. Any scoring, nicks, or burrs at either the end plate or housing can lead to leakage of air from the end plate to housing. Severely scored or damaged end plates should be replaced.

If the rotor support shaft serrations are worn or damaged, they can be replaced. The shafts are short-stub shafts that are pressed into and pinned to the hollow rotor lobes. Carefully inspect the end plate bearings for signs of pitting, flaking, or corrosion. *Never* spin a ball or roller bearing using air pressure because bearing damage can occur. Lubricate each bearing lightly with clean engine oil, and while holding the inner race from rotation, manually rotate the outer race slowly by hand to determine if any rough spots exist. The gear end plate double-row ball bearings are preloaded and so have no end play. A new bearing thus will have a certain amount of resistance to motion when rotated by hand. Check the oil seal rings, carriers, and collars for wear or scoring and replace them if worn excessively. When lip-type oil seals are used, oversize oil seals and spacers can be employed on worn or grooved rotor shafts. Carefully examine the inside serrations on each blower gear for signs of wear or damage. If the gears are worn so that gear backlash is in excess of 0.004 in. (0.1 mm), both gears must be replaced as a set.

Blower Assembly

Each hollow aluminum alloy rotor is supported by bearings in each end plate. The rotors are designed to turn freely on these bearings so that at no time do the rotors actually come into contact with one another, the end plates, or the blower housing. When the blower is being reassembled, use the reverse procedure that was used for disassembly. Important points to remember during reassembly are listed next.

1. Note that the rotors are machined so that one is a right-hand helix, and the other is a left-hand helix.

2. The right-hand helix rotor is marked *gear end;* the left-hand rotor is the end with the serrated shaft. When viewing the blower from the drive end, the right-hand helix rotor is on the right and the left-hand helix rotor is on your left.

3. The rotors must be timed to one another. This is achieved by placing the rotors in mesh with the omitted serrations (Figure 20–48) on the rotor stub shaft in a horizontal position and facing to the left as viewed from the gear end. Failure to time the rotors correctly will result in binding of the assembly when you attempt to turn it.

4. Support the front-end plate on two wooden blocks, similar to Figure 20–49) that are high enough to prevent the rotor shafts from contacting the bench top. Always install the rotors into the front end plate first. Use seal protectors (lip-type seals), or take care when compressing the piston-type seal rings (lightly lubricated with oil) on the rotors as you push them into the end plate.

5. Apply a light coating of permatex Form-A-Gasket No. 2 or an equivalent sealant to the mating surfaces of the end plate and the blower housing (no gasket is used here).

6. Lower the blower housing over the top of the two rotors which are supported in the front end plate horizontally.

7. Install the rear end plate, and insert and tighten the fillister head screws to retain each end plate to the blower housing.

8. Install the front and rear end plate bearings (roller type in the front plate; double row in the rear). Lubricate the bearings with engine oil, and with the numbered side facing up toward you, use a suitable bearing driver and hammer to tap them into the housing bore over the rotor shafts.

9. Install the bearing retainers and tighten their screws.

10 Take the previously tied (wired) together shims that were removed earlier and install them behind the correct gear along with the hardened spacer.

11. Place both of the rotor-omitted spline serrations in a horizontal position to the left. Align the omitted serrated spline on each gear hub with the one on each rotor shaft. A center punch mark in the end of each rotor shaft at the omitted serration will assist you in aligning the gears on the shafts. Gently push and tap each gear onto the shaft. Use a rubber mallet to drive each gear on by alternating between them.

12. Jam a soft folded rag between the rotors and tighten the gear retaining bolts to the recommended torque for your blower model. Torque on these bolts for DDC 92 engines is between 100 and 110 lb-ft. (136–150 N·m).

13. Refer to Figure 20–50 which illustrates the location of the various minimum clearances for the blower rotor to housing. These are identified as A, B, C, CC, D, and E, and they are checked by inserting a long feeler gauge into the various positions illustrated

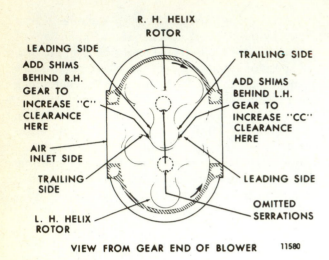

FIGURE 20–48 Diagram showing the areas of the blower that must be checked for correct clearances and the location of selective thickness shims required to correct rotor lobe clearances. (Courtesy of Detroit Diesel Corporation.)

in the clearance diagram. These dimensions are not the same for every model of engine blower. For example, they might be as follows:

A	0.007 in. (0.177 mm)
B	0.012 in. (0.304 mm)
C	0.010 in. (0.254 mm)
CC	0.006 in. (0.152 mm)
D	0.015 in. (0.381 mm)
E	0.005 in. (0.127 mm)

It is usually easier to use laminated shims stacked together when checking clearances in excess of 0.005 in. (0.127 mm). However, major tool suppliers can supply you with a specially designed feeler gauge set for this purpose.

14.   If the various clearances are outside of the stated limits, refer to Figure 20–48. The figure indicates the proper location of shims to alter a given dimension.

15.   When more or fewer shims are required behind a gear to alter the rotor clearances, both gears must be removed using the special pullers shown earlier in Figure 20–47. In addition, both gears must be installed together to prevent binding between the helical gear teeth.

16.   To alter the rotor clearance, place a 0.003 in. (0.076 mm) shim behind a rotor gear to revolve the rotor approximately 0.001 in. (0.025 mm). This is achieved because of the helical design of the rotor. Shims force one rotor ahead of and rotates it away from the opposite rotor to effect a change in the clearance.

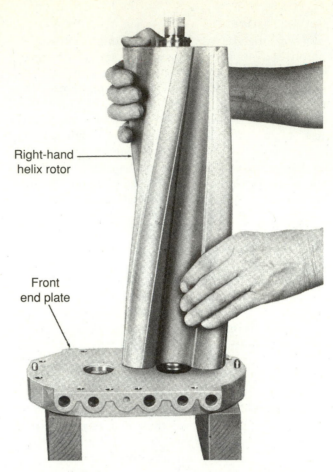

FIGURE 20–49 Installing the blower rotor in the front end plate. (Courtesy of Detroit Diesel Corporation.)

17.   Reinstall any accessory items, such as the fuel pump drive. Install new gaskets between the end plates and the end covers.

18.   Install a new blower-to-block basket.

19.   Use guide studs to align the blower to the block and to keep the gasket in position. Lower the blower into position. Install all of the items removed during blower removal, and tighten (torque) all bolts into position.

MARINE ENGINE APPLICATIONS

Air Silencers

Many marine applications, such as workboats, tugs, logging boom boats, are equipped with conventional types of air cleaners. In certain applications they may even employ a *moisture eliminator* described earlier in this chapter. Some pleasure craft may also employ some form of air filter/cleaner system; however, many such marine applications often use what is commonly called an *air silencer*. These may take the form of a rec-

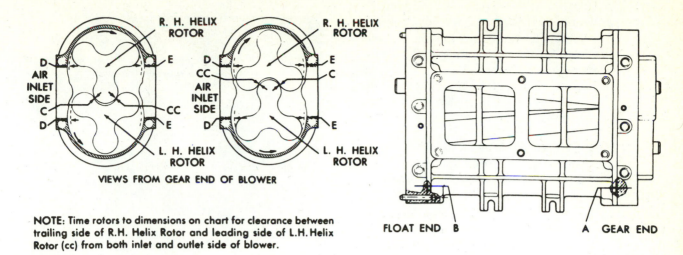

NOTE: Time rotors to dimensions on chart for clearance between trailing side of R.H. Helix Rotor and leading side of L.H. Helix Rotor (cc) from both inlet and outlet side of blower.

FIGURE 20–50 *Diagram illustrating where all of the blower clearances must be checked. (Courtesy of Detroit Diesel Corporation.)*

tangular shaped device, or be a system similar to that illustrated in Figure 20–51. Although no servicing is required on the air silencers shown, it has to be removed to perform other service operations. Some silencers contain a perforated steel partition welded into place parallel with the outside faces, thereby dividing the silencer into two sections. Between the outer wall and the perforated partition (internal), a sound absorbent, flame proof, felted cotton waste is used.

The air separator filter element (or closed crankcase vapor collector) illustrated in Figure 20–51 is now common in pleasure craft marine applications. To operate efficiently, air separator filters and vacuum limiters must be maintained properly. Generally, there are three recommended service intervals for these systems:

1. Every 250 hours of engine service, clean and reoil the air separator filter elements and vacuum limiters.

2. Every 500 hours of engine operation, or once a year, replace the filter elements. The vacuum limiter can be replaced every 2 years or every 1000 hours of engine operation.

3. Clean and reoil filter elements and vacuum limiters any time that the restriction gauge shows red, or if so equipped, any time that the restriction indicator gauge reaches its designed limit.

Servicing of these elements is similar to that for dry-type heavy-duty air filters. Once the precleaner element has been removed from the air separator, tap it gently to dislodge any large embedded dirt particles. Then gently clean the outside of the element with a soft-bristle brush. To clean the element, obtain and spray a commercially

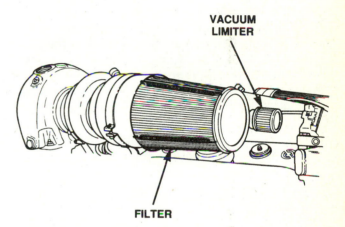

FIGURE 20–51 *Air silencer showing location of air separator and vacuum limiter. (Courtesy of Detroit Diesel Corporation.)*

available liquid such as Walker solution onto the element and allow it to soak in for at least 20 minutes. *Never* use gasoline, steam, high-pressure water, compressed air cleaners, caustic solutions, strong detergents, or cleaning solvents. If you do, filter damage is more than likely to occur! Rinse the element with clean, fresh water from the inside toward the outside. Shake off excess water after rinsing and allow the element to dry in ambient air. *Do not* use compressed shop air to dry the element since this may rupture it. Also, avoid using temperature-controlled ovens or heat dryers to dry the element because heat will shrink the cotton filter. Finally, reoil the element by squeezing Walker air filter oil out of the application bottle and into the valley of each filter pleat; make only one pass per pleat. Do not use a fluid such as engine oil, diesel fuel, WD-40, transmission fluid, or other lightweight oil because they can damage the filter element. Allow the oil to soak into the element for approximately 15 to 20 minutes; then reoil any dry (white) spots on the element. Reinstall it.

Clean the vacuum limiter after removing the complete assembly (do not detach the filter element). Use the same service procedure as that for the air filter element.

Water-Cooled Exhaust Manifolds

A water-cooled exhaust manifold(s) is necessary because of the high heat radiation from the engine of marine applications into the engine room. Basically, the manifold consists of an integral casting that contains a hollow jacket surrounding the regular exhaust manifold. This type of a manifold is, therefore, substantially larger in diameter than a conventional air-cooled design. Figure 20–52 illustrates one example of a water-cooled exhaust manifold for either an industrial or marine application. Note that both an inlet line and outlet line are connected at opposite ends of the manifold to allow constant coolant circulation through the integral water jacket that surrounds the manifold. The coolant flow is directed from the engine water jacket system under pressure, with a constant bypass into the exhaust manifold(s). The coolant leaves the forward end of the exhaust manifold and is discharged toward the thermostat housing area where the hot coolant can circulate through an expansion tank and heat exchanger or keel-cooled system. A drain plug is normally located below the exhaust manifold to allow water drainage when required; another drain plug allows moisture condensed from exhaust gases to be drained.

TROUBLESHOOTING USING MANOMETERS

All internal combustion engines require an adequate supply of clean filtered air to operate. Once combustion takes place, the exhaust gases exit the cylinders and normally expend their stored energy in driving a turbocharger. So both the *inlet* and the *exhaust* systems must be fairly free-flowing to avoid possible restrictions to either the air supply or the exhaust gases. Engine models operate at a given rpm where they are designed to produce a specific rated horsepower. If the airflow into the engine is affected in any way, not only will poor combustion result, but a number of other problem areas can surface: visible exhaust smoke, carbon deposits within the cylinders, high exhaust temperatures, a lack of power, and poor fuel economy.

The engine manufacturer usually places a limit on the amount of AIR (air inlet restriction) that the engine can handle without a loss in performance. This restriction within the air system occurs at maximum airflow

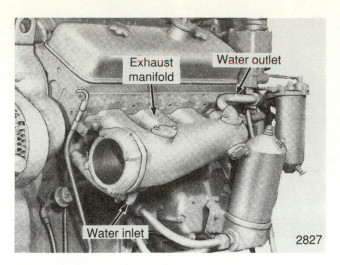

FIGURE 20–52 *Example of a water-cooled exhaust manifold. (Courtesy of Detroit Diesel Corporation.)*

requirement operating conditions of rated full load. On a naturally aspirated engine, the maximum airflow occurs at the maximum no-load or high-idle speed without regard to engine power. On turbocharged engines, the maximum airflow only occurs at the full-load (rated) engine speed, since the rotative speed of the turbocharger only produces maximum boost under this operating condition. Most engine manufacturers suggest a maximum restriction of between 510 and 635 mm (20 to 25 in.) of water for diesel engines; the allowable level is printed in the service manual or literature.

Generally, the maximum allowable AIR for naturally aspirated engines is 510 mm (20.0 in.) of water; for turbocharged engines, 635 mm (25 in.) is fairly standard. Excessive restriction affects the flow of air to the cylinders. On mechanically governed engine models, this will result in poor combustion and lack of power; the engine will tend to overheat; the exhaust, coolant and oil temperatures will climb; and fuel economy will increase. On electronically controlled engines, the turbo boost sensor will limit the unit injector PWM (pulse width modulated) signal, thereby limiting the amount of fuel delivered. This will result in a controlled loss of engine power and speed. If the engine oil temperature drifts outside of the preset parameters, a further reduction in engine power will occur. Excessively high oil temperatures will result in an automatic engine shutdown.

Manometer Use

When dealing with air inlet and exhaust systems, a number of air restriction (vacuum) and air pressure values can be determined by using both a water (H_2O) and mercury (Hg) *manometer* assembly. A manometer allows the service technician to quickly and accurately determine the following engine operating conditions:

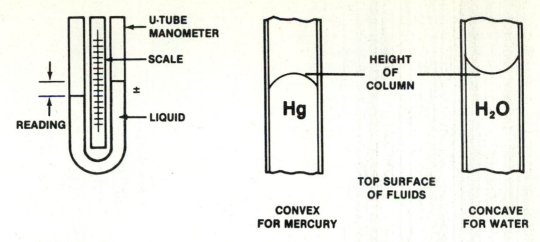

FIGURE 20–53 *Comparison of column height for both a mercury and a water manometer. (Courtesy of Detroit Diesel Corporation.)*

- AIR (air inlet restriction)—H$_2$O manometer
- Turbocharger boost pressure (two or four cycle)— Hg manometer
- ABP (air box pressure on a two cycle only)—Hg manometer
- EBP (exhaust back pressure)—Hg manometer
- Crankcase pressure—H$_2$O manometer

These manometers consist of a slack or solid tube formed into a U-shape as illustrated in Figure 20–53. A sliding scale allows the technician to calibrate the gauge to *zero* before use. At the top of each tube is a screw valve that allows the water or mercury within the tube to be retained when not in use and when transporting the manometers in service trucks or toolboxes. Before using a manometer, both valves at the top of the U-shaped tubes must be screwed open (one-half to one turn) to allow atmospheric air pressure to balance the fluid within each side of the tube.

Note in Figure 20–53 that the liquid within the two manometer tubes takes opposite shapes. Mercury, which is heavier than water, will not wet the inside of the tube and it forms what is commonly called a *convex miniscus*. Water, on the other hand, does wet the inside of the tube and forms a *concave miniscus*. Therefore, when zeroing-in the manometer prior to use, open both valves at the top of each tube and carefully move the sliding scale until the zero (0) on the ruler is opposite the fluid as shown. During a manometer test, read the water type by sighting horizontally between the bottom of the concave water surface and the scale. Read a mercury manometer by sighting horizontally between the top of the convex mercury surface and the scale. Both sides of the displaced fluid are added together when using a *full-scale* model where the distance on the scale is equal to that found on a ruler or tape measure.

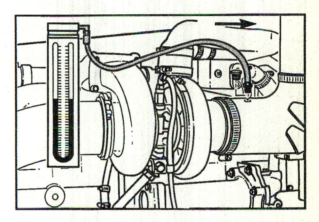

FIGURE 20–54 *Water manometer hookup to the air inlet ducting on the suction side of the turbocharger to check the air inlet restriction. (Courtesy of Cummins Engine Company, Inc.)*

On half-scale manometer models, read only one side of the displaced fluid scale.

If one column of fluid travels further than the other, disregard this occurrence. Minor variations within the inside diameter of the tube (particularly when heavy-duty clear plastic models are used) are the cause. The accuracy of the reading will not be impaired. Depending on the particular make and model of engine, the connection tap point for the manometer fitting will vary, but it is common for most engines. Check the AIR, EBP, ABP, and turbo boost at the following recommended positions:

1. Figure 20–54 illustrates where the AIR can be checked. AIR is checked using a water manometer at a point between 101 and 203 mm (4–8 in.) away from the turbocharger air inlet by removing a small pipe plug screwed into the inlet piping. Install a suitable brass fitting to which you can connect a small flexible rubber

hose; the opposite end should fit over one of the open manometer valves. Note that the manometer has been *zeroed* by opening both valves and moving the sliding scale. If possible, operate the engine on a chassis or engine dyno at WOT and full-rated horsepower. Refer to Figure 20–55, which illustrates the water displacement on both sides of the manometer. On full-scale manometers, add both sides together; on a half-scale manometer, read only one side. A loss of 6.895 kPa (1 psi) of suction air pressure due to restriction in a system would be equivalent to a displacement of 27.7 in. (704 mm) on the H_2O manometer. Therefore when the engine manufacturer's limit of say 25 in. (635 mm) H_2O of restriction is reached, this means that the air pressure within the air inlet ducting to the suction side of the turbocharger is 0.9 psi (6.2 kPa) lower than atmospheric pressure. Compare your reading with that listed in the service manual.

2. Check turbocharger boost pressure using a Hg manometer. Remove a small plug located in the intake manifold or at the outlet side of the turbocharger assembly. Install a suitable brass fitting with a small-bore rubber hose connected between the fitting and the manometer. Repeat the same procedure as described for the AIR check and compare your results to the service manual specs. Failure to fully load the engine during this test will result in a low turbocharger boost reading. On two-stroke cycle DDC engine models, ABP can be checked using a Hg manometer by connecting a tight-fitting rubber hose over one end of the engine block air box drain tube and the opposite end to the manometer valve. EBP is checked using a Hg manometer connected into a brass fitting installed in the exhaust piping approximately 152 mm (6 in.) from the exhaust outlet from the turbocharger. Always use a brass fitting, and make sure that the pipe plug that is installed into the hot exhaust at the completion of the test is *brass* not steel, since a steel plug will tend to freeze in position. Figure 20–56 illustrates a Hg manometer connected to the exhaust system to measure the EBP. Repeat the same procedure described for the AIR check and compare your results to specs.

3. Engine crankcase pressure can be checked using an H_2O manometer connected to one of several sources. You can place a small-bore tight-fitting hose over the oil level dipstick shroud; if the shroud extends below the oil level in the pan, however, you will not be able to record a reading. You can usually gain access to and remove a small pipe plug located in the side of the engine block above the pan rail. On some engine makes and models, the oil filler cap can be removed from a rocker cover, and an expandable rubber plug can be installed and tightened into position. A small connection on the adaptor plug can be

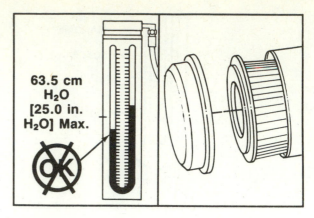

FIGURE 20–55 *Fluid displacement in a water manometer during a running engine test to check the air inlet restriction. In this example the maximum allowable restriction is quoted as being 25 in. H_2O (63.5 cm). Add both sides of the manometer together when using a full-scale model; read only one side when using a one-half scale model. (Courtesy of Cummins Engine Company, Inc.)*

used to connect a small-bore rubber hose to the H_2O manometer (see Figure 21–5). Once again, a more accurate reading can be obtained by running the engine or vehicle on a dynamometer.

Manometer Specifications

Each engine manufacturer lists the allowable specifications for its engine manometers in the service manuals. These values are normally listed for a given engine rpm and also in inches of water or mercury. For example, you might find the following engine operating conditions listed for a given turbocharged engine:

	1800 rpm	2100 rpm
Air inlet restriction kPa (in. water)		
Full-load maximum— dirty air cleaner	5 kPa (20 in.)	Same
Full-load maximum— Clean air cleaner	3 kPa (12 in.)	Same
Air inlet manifold pressure (in. Hg)		
Minimum at full load	159 kPa (47 in.)	152 kPa (45 in.)
Crankcase pressure	0.5 kPa (2 in.)	Same
Exhaust back pressure kPa (in. mercury)		
Maximum value, full load	10.1 kPa	(3 in. Hg)

Often it is necessary to convert the manometer reading into other units of measurement. Use the following pressure conversion values:

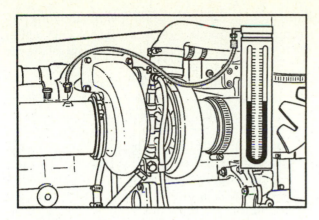

FIGURE 20–56 Connection between the exhaust manifold and an Hg (mercury) manometer required to measure the exhaust back pressure. (Courtesy of Cummins Engine Company, Inc.)

1 in. (25.4 mm) water	=	0.0735 in. Hg/1.86 mm Hg
1 in. (25.4 mm) water	=	0.0361 psi/0.248 kPa
1 in. (25.4 mm) mercury	=	13.60 in. H_2O/345.44 mm H_2O
1 in. (25.4 mm) mercury	=	0.491 psi/3.385 kPa
1 psi (6.895 kPa)	=	27.70 in. H_2O/703.6 mm H_2O
1 psi (6.895 kPa)	=	2.036 in. Hg/52 mm Hg
Note: 1 psi	=	6.895 kPa; 1 kPa
	=	0.145 psi.

Causes for High or Low Manometer Readings

After you perform an AIR check, a turbocharger boost check, an EBP check, or a crankcase pressure check, you may find that the manometer values you obtained are higher or lower than those listed in the engine service manual. The only value that could be both high or low is the turbocharger boost value. The typical causes for high manometer readings in the AIR, EBP, and crankcase pressure operating conditions are described next.

High Air Inlet Restriction

High AIR results in poor combustion, lack of power, poor fuel economy, and higher than normal exhaust temperatures, particularly on two-stroke-cycle DDC engine models where approximately 30% of the engine cooling is achieved by airflow through the ported cylinders. The following conditions are typical of those that might cause high AIR:

- Plugged or dirty air cleaner (precleaner or main element)
- Too small an air filter assembly (improperly sized to pass the required cfm of air)
- Intake piping diameter too small
- Intake piping too long
- Intake piping containing too many elbows or bends
- Crushed intake piping (hole free)
- Damaged air cleaner assembly
- Collapsed rubber hoses in intake piping
- Water-soaked paper filter element (employ a moisture eliminator assembly when operating in heavy rainfall and high humidity areas)
- Coal dust plugging in mine sites (short filter life; use two-stage filters and exhaust gas aspirators)

Low Turbocharger Boost Pressure

Many of the causes of low turbocharger boost pressure are similar for two-stroke and four-stroke-cycle engines. Some causes, however, are unique to the two-stroke cycle models because they employ a gear-driven blower assembly in addition to the exhaust-gas-driven turbocharger. Strategically placed small pipe plugs on the engine can be accessed to isolate the TC boost pressure from the air box pressure on two-cycle engines such as the DDC models. Reasons for low boost pressure can usually be traced to the following conditions:

- Anything that creates a high AIR condition
- High EBP condition
- Exhaust gas leaks feeding to turbo from engine
- Leaking fittings, connections, or intake manifold gasket from outlet side of turbo (usually accompanied by a high-pitched whistle under load due to pressurized air leaks)
- Plugged turbocharger safety screen if used on the inlet or outlet side
- Plugged or damaged air system aftercooler
- Possible turbocharger internal damage (visually check the condition of the turbine and compressor blading vanes, for damage with the engine stopped)
- Leaking gasket between direct-mounted TC and the blower housing on a DDC two-cycle engine
- Low air box pressure on a two-cycle DDC engine caused by any of the above conditions plus leaking hand-hole inspection covers on the block, leaking cylinder block-to-end-plate gaskets, a clogged blower inlet screen, or a partially stuck closed emergency air system shutdown valve
- Defective or damaged blower on a two-cycle DDC engine
- High air box pressure on a DDC two-cycle engine usually traced to high exhaust back pressure or partially plugged cylinder liner ports (normally related to carbon buildup)

High Exhaust Back Pressure

A slight pressure in the exhaust system is normal, but excessive EBP will seriously affect the operation of the engine. Some of the causes of high EBP are these:

- Stuck rain cap at the end of a vertical exhaust stack
- Crushed exhaust piping
- Crushed or damaged muffler
- Too small a muffler
- Exhaust piping diameter too small
- Exhaust piping too long
- Exhaust piping with too many elbows or bends
- Excessive carbon buildup in exhaust system
- Obstruction in exhaust system or piping

High Crankcase Pressure

Crankcase pressure indicates the amount of compression leakage and/or air box pressure leakage between the piston rings. All engines operate with a slight crankcase pressure, which is highly desirable since a low pressure prevents the entrance of dust as well as keeps any dust or dirt within suspension so that it can flow through the crankcase and be trapped in the engine breather system. Any signs of engine lube oil escaping from the engine breather tube, crankcase ventilator, dipstick tube hole, crankshaft oil seals, or air box drain tubes on two-cycle DDC engines may be a positive indicator of a high crankcase pressure condition. Causes of high crankcase pressure can usually be traced to the following conditions:

- Too much oil in crankcase (check level after adequate drain-back time after engine shutdown)
- Plugged crankcase breather or tube system
- High EBP
- Excessive cylinder blowby (worn rings, scored liner, cracked piston, or a hole)
- On two-stroke DDC engine models, loose piston pin retainers, worn or damaged blower oil seals, leaking cylinder block-to-end-plate gaskets or a defective blower

EXHAUST BRAKE DEVICES

An exhaust gas pressure engine retarding device is a widely used option found on many light- and mid-duty truck applications, both gasoline and diesel powered. The two common types currently in use are illustrated in Figure 20–57. The device shown in Figure 20–57a uses a sliding-gate type of valve, while the model in b employs a butterfly-type valve assembly. The exhaust brake, which is installed as shown in Figure 20–57, restricts engine exhaust flow when it is activated, thereby slowing the vehicle by increasing the pressure acting on the upward moving pistons during the regular exhaust stroke. This action tends to transform the engine into a low-pressure air compressor.

The brake is installed in the exhaust pipe downstream from the turbocharger and before the catalytic converter and muffler. The exhaust brake valve can be actuated by either a pneumatic cylinder with air from the onboard air system of the vehicle for trucks equipped with air brakes or by an auxiliary 12 V electric air system supply. Typical exhaust brake actuation and release time is approximately 2/10's of a second. ON/OFF controls are normally mounted on the dashboard and activated through a rocker switch. When the rocker switch is placed in the ON position, the accelerator pedal is in the idle position, the clutch pedal is up (clutch engaged), the exhaust brake circuit is activated, and compressed air flows to the actuating cylinder to move either the sliding-gate or butterfly valve to the closed position. If the accelerator pedal is depressed past the normal idle position, the brake will be released automatically by breaking the electrical circuit to the brake actuating controls. Some exhaust brake manufacturers offer either hand or foot controls where the normal service brake is synchronized with the use of the exhaust brake. In addition, exhaust brake actuation can be wired to illuminate the stoplights of the vehicle during operation.

Minimum supply pressure of the exhaust brake compressed air is generally 85 psi (586 kPa) to overcome the force of the valve return spring. Maximum supply pressure is usually set at the same value as that for the air compressor governor, thereby limiting excessive supply pressure. Material used in the construction of the exhaust brake is usually ductile iron; in the operating cylinder the common material is anodized aluminum.

The exhaust brake restriction created affects the degree of braking that occurs. On butterfly-type valves, a factory drilled orifice (size depends on engine make and model) is used to maintain exhaust back pressure within limits set by the OEM. For example, this is limited to below 60 psi (414 kPa) on Cummins six-cylinder B5.9 engines and to below 65 psi (448 kPa) on Cummins six-cylinder C8.3 engine models. The Caterpillar 3116 engine is limited to 55 psi (379 kPa); Detroit Diesel Series 60 is limited to 45 psi (310 kPa); and the Navistar DTA-466 is limited to 28 psi (193 kPa). The braking horsepower generated depends on several factors:

- Engine design and the allowable back pressure it can withstand
- Engine displacement
- Speed of the engine during exhaust brake activation

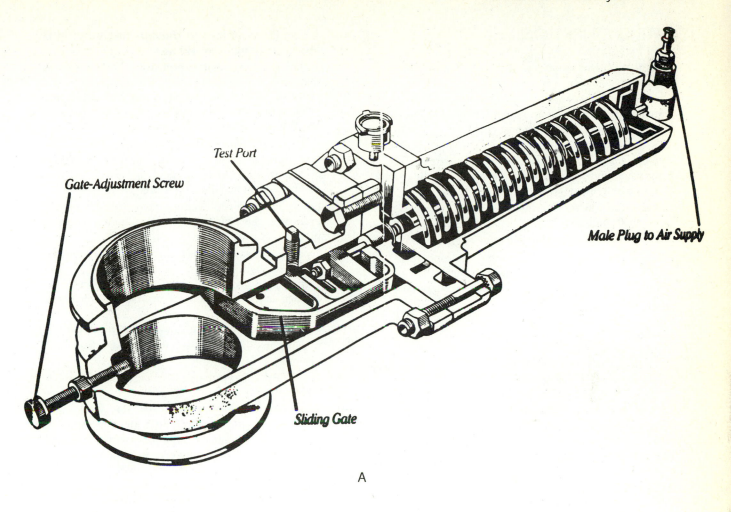

Gate-Adjustment Screw

Test Port

Male Plug to Air Supply

Sliding Gate

A

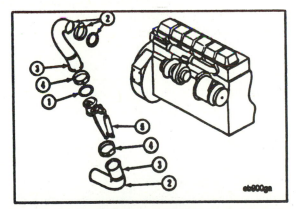

1. Gasket 2. Original Equipment 3. Exhaust Sleeve 4. V Clamp 5. EXTARDER Assembly

B

FIGURE 20–57 (a) Sliding-gate type of exhaust valve brake. (Courtesy of Williams Controls, Dana Corporation, Portland, OR.) b) Butterfly-type of exhaust valve brake. (Courtesy of Cummins Engine Company, Inc.)

- Transmission and axle gear ratios
- Placement and model of exhaust brake in use

To obtain maximum performance from the exhaust brake, the truck operator should select a gear that will cause the engine to operate at its normal governed rpm, consistent with the road conditions and engine rpm limits.

CAUTION: When driving on wet, slick, or icy roads, keep the exhaust brake control switch in the OFF position.

When an exhaust brake with an automatic transmission (such as an Allison model) is used, maximum braking will only occur if the transmission is equipped with a torque converter lockup clutch. The brake can still be used in an automatic transmission without a lockup clutch; however only 70% to 75% efficiency will be obtained due to the normal hydraulic slippage that occurs within the turbocharger.

SELF-TEST QUESTIONS

1. List the problems associated with lack of sufficient airflow to an engine.

2. On electronically controlled high-speed heavy-duty diesel engines, list the various sensors used to monitor air system operating conditions.

3. True of False: An equivalent reduction of airflow on a two-cycle Detroit Diesel engine will affect the engine operating temperature more adversely than will a similar reduction in coolant flow.

4. List the four functions of the airflow on a two-stroke-cycle DDC engine.

5. What does the term *dusting-out* of an engine mean?

6. Technician A says that as little as two tablespoons of unfiltered air can severely damage an engine. Technician B says that it would take several pounds. Which technician is correct?

7. Diesel engines perform best at air inlet temperatures between
   a. 40° and 60°F (4.5° to 15.5°C)
   b. 60° and 90°F (15.5° to 32°C)
   c. 90° and 115°F (32° to 46°C)
   d. 120° and 150°F (49° to 65°C)

8. Technician A says that an air inlet temperature that is too cold allows the engine to produce more power due to a more dense air charge. Technician B says that this would result in a longer ignition delay once the fuel is injected. Which technician knows thermodynamics theory best?

9. A reduction in ambient air inlet temperature from 80°F (27°C) in summer operation to −20°F (−29°C) in the winter will severely affect the air temperature at the end of the compression stroke. The amount of variation depends on the piston crown shape and the turbulence that is created. Usually the heat loss is approximately
   a. 100° to 130°F (38° to 54°C)
   b. 150° to 180°F (65° to 82°C)
   c. 190° to 220°F (88° to 104°C)
   d. 230° to 300°F (110° to 149°C)

10. Because of the problems associated with the answer to Question 9, diesel fuel characteristics must be altered when operating in winter conditions. Refer to Chapter 3 for information on how fuels vary between summer and winter. What characteristics would be altered?

11. Make a list of the visible and audible changes that result when the air inlet charge is too cold, such as during winter operation.

12. Technician A says that in cold-weather operation, engine air can be drawn from underhood or from within the engine compartment. Technician B says that this would result in air starvation. Which technician is correct?

13. True or False: Air inlet temperature that is too hot results in an engine power loss.

14. Technician A says that on non-turbocharged engines, there will be a power loss of approximately 1% for every 100 m (328 ft) in operating altitude. Technician B believes that the power loss will be greater—closer to 5%. Which technician is correct?

15. Describe the meaning of the term *volumetric efficiency*.

16. Determine the airflow requirements for a two-stroke cycle blower and turbocharged engine with a displacement of 736 cu in. (12.06 L) at 2100 rpm.

17. Determine the airflow requirements for a four-stroke cycle turbocharged and aftercooled engine with a displacement of 855 cu in. (14 L) at 2100 rpm.

18. Technician A says that oil bath air cleaners have been almost totally replaced by dry-type designs. Technician B says that there are more oil bath air cleaners in use than there are dry types. Which technician is up to date?

19. List and compare the advantages and disadvantages of using an oil bath versus a dry-type air cleaner assembly.

20. True or False: Dry-type air filters cannot be cleaned when service is required.

21. Technician A says that ultra-heavy-duty air cleaner systems used in mining and off-highway equipment employ a three-stage cleaning process. Technician B believes that it is only a two-stage cleaning process. Which technician is correct?

22. True of False: Some heavy-duty off-highway air cleaner systems offer a dust sight glass to determine if unfiltered air is entering the system.

23. The purpose of an air system restriction indicator is to warn the operator or service technician of
   a. high exhaust back pressure
   b. high turbo boost pressure
   c. high crankcase pressure
   d. high air inlet restriction

24. The maximum allowable air system flow restriction on high-speed heavy-duty diesel engines is normally within the range of
   a. 10 to 15 in. water
   b. 10 to 15 in. mercury
   c. 20 to 25 in. water
   d. 20 to 25 in. mercury

25. Technician A says that when servicing dry-type air filters or when drying a cleaned filter it is acceptable to use up to 120 psi (827 kPa) of air pressure. Technician B says that this much air pressure would rupture the paper element; instead, air pressures should normally be reduced to a level between 50 and 60 psi (345 to 414 kPa). Which technician is correct?

26. Describe the best method to inspect a dry-type air filter element for signs of holes or tears.

27. List the sequential steps that you would employ to fully service a heavy-duty dry-type filter assembly.

28. Technician A says that some models of two-and three-stage air filter assemblies employ either an exhaust gas aspirator or a pressurized air supply to help to remove up to 90% of the initial stage of air filtration. Technician B says that exhaust gases would burn the filter and that air pressure would rupture the element. Which technician is correct?

29. List the engine problems that would be associated by continuing to operate with a high air inlet restriction condition.

30. Describe how you would inspect and check the air inlet ducting for signs of unfiltered air.

31. List the problems that can occur to the engine through excessive use of starting fluid, particularly in cold-weather operation.

32. Technician A says that an intercooler and aftercooler are basically designed to cool the turbocharger boost air before it enters the intake manifold. Technician B says that an intercooler is designed to cool the air charge, while an aftercooler is used to cool the exhaust gases. Which technician understands the purpose and function of the coolers?

33. Describe the three basic types of aftercoolers/intercoolers and the features of each.

34. Name the most common type of aftercooler used on heavy-duty high-speed engines in on-highway vehicles.

35. Describe a situation in where both an intercooler and aftercooler might be employed on the same engine and discuss the function and purpose of each.

36a. True or False: In an AAAC system the sue of fully closed winterfronts should be avoided in cold-weather operation. Describe the reasons for your answer.

36b. Technician A says that approximately 10% of the cooling on a DDC two-stroke cycle engine is achieved by turbo blower air flow? Technician B says that it is closer to 30%. Which technician knows the product best?

37. True or False: If an AAAC system is employed, radiator shutterstats cannot be used.

38. Describe the method that you would use to check an AAAC core for possible leakage on a truck application.

39. List the three ways to perform an engine cylinder compression check on different types of diesel engines.

40. What conditions might cause low cylinder compression?

41. How does a cylinder leak-down check differ from an engine compression check?

42. Technician A says that most heavy-duty high-speed engine turbochargers are designed to rotate at speeds close to, and in some cases in excess of, 100,000 rpm. Impossible says technician B; at this elevated speed the turbocharger would disintegrate. Which technician is correct?

43. The turbocharger is
   a. exhaust gas driven
   b. gear driven
   c. belt driven
   d. chain driven

44. What does the term *supercharged* engine mean?

45. True or False: All DDC two-stroke cycle engines that employ a Roots blower are supercharged.

46. DDC engines that use Roots blowers are normally
   a. belt driven
   b. chain driven
   c. exhaust gas driven
   d. gear driven

47. True or False: Roots blowers can produce a more positive airflow at a lower speed than can a turbocharger.

48. Describe what the term *A/R ratio* means in relation to a turbocharger.

49. Describe what problems would exist on an engine fitted with the wrong model of A/R turbocharger.

50. What is the basic conceptual difference between a constant pressure type of TC and a pulse turbocharger?

51. Typical engine full-load turbocharger boost pressures on heavy-duty high-speed engines usually ranges between
   a. 10 and 12 psi (69 to 83 kPa)
   b. 17 and 22 psi (117 to 152 kPa)
   c. 28 and 30 psi (193 to 207 kPa)
   d. 36 and 42 psi (248 to 289 kPa)

52. True or False: Some newer heavy-duty high-speed diesel engines employ ceramic turbine wheels in the turbocharger.

53. Technician A says that tuned intake manifolds and TCs are designed to improve white smoke clean-up by producing higher intake manifold air boost pressures at lower engine speeds. Technician B says that this design feature is primarily used to reduce intake air restriction. Which technician is correct?

54. Technician A says that the turbocharger rotating components are supported on pressure lubricated ball bearings. Not so says technician B; they use pressure lubricated bushings. Which technician is correct?

55. True or False: Exhaust gas temperatures on a four-cycle engine are generally higher than those for a two-cycle engine.

56. Technician A says that a TC wastegate is employed to bypass exhaust gas flow around the turbine wheel to limit the maximum amount of boost pressure. Technician B believes that the wastegate is used to recirculate exhaust gases to lower combustion chamber temperatures and therefore improve exhaust gas emissions. Which technician is correct?

57. Can a TC wastegate be adjusted to control its opening pressure?

58. Describe how a TC wastegate differs from a TC back pressure device that is used on the Navistar 7.3L/444E V8 engine model.

59. List the three key maintenance items that affect the life of a turbocharger.

60. A TC with no physical signs of damage has a high-pitched whine noise while the engine is under load. This is probably due to
    a. lack of oil to the TC bearings
    b. leaking intake or exhaust piping (hoses) on the outlet side of the TC
    c. high exhaust gas back pressure
    d. high air inlet restriction

61. A sharp high-pitched scream from a TC is usually indicative of one or more of the following problems:
    a. Exhaust gas leakage
    b. Turbo boost air leakage
    c. Worn TC bearings
    d. Turbine or compressor wheel rubbing on the housing

62. A speed cycling sound from a TC could indicate which one or more of the following problems:
    a. High air inlet restriction
    b. High exhaust back pressure
    c. Dirt buildup on the compressor wheel

63. With the engine stopped and the intake and exhaust piping removed from the TC, how would you check to see if the TC bearings were worn?

64. You are using a fluorescent tracer liquid engine oil additive to inspect a TC at the hot exhaust outlet side along with a black light. A yellow glow would indicate a
    a. raw fuel leak
    b. engine oil leak
    c. coolant leak from a cracked cylinder head
    d. high-pressure air leak

65. Following the same procedure as in Question 64, a dark-blue glow usually indicates a
    a. raw fuel leak
    b. engine oil leak
    c. coolant leak
    d. high-pressure air leak

66. Describe in list form how you would disassemble a turbocharger assembly and the necessary precautions required.

67. When a new or rebuilt turbocharger is installed back onto the engine, what should be done before cranking and immediately after engine start-up?

68. Signs of oil at the TC inlet side could be caused by leaking oil seals according to technician A. Technician B says they may be caused by an air compressor pumping oil. Is only one of the technicians correct or are both correct?

69. True or False: Signs of engine oil at the turbine (hot end) of the TC usually indicate an engine fault rather than a TC seal problem.

70. List the most common causes of leaking TC seals.

71. Typical noise levels from a heavy-duty tractor or trailer moving along the highway at regulated speed levels are usually within the range of:

a. 54 to 64 dB
b. 65 to 70 dB
c. 74 to 79 dB
d. 80 to 86 dB

72. How would you calculate the exhaust gas flow for a four-stroke cycle turbocharged diesel engine running at 1800 rpm at an ambient air temperature of 75°F (24°C) and a full-load exhaust gas temperature of 925°F (496°C)?

73. Describe the basic concept of operation of a diesel exhaust catalyst muffler (silencer) system. Why is it required on some models of current diesel engines?

74. List some diesel engines that were forced into using exhaust gas after-treatment devices to comply with the 1994 EPA exhaust emissions limits.

75. The type of blower assembly used by DDC in its two-stroke cycle engines is known as a
    a. Roots type
    b. pulse type
    c. constant pressure type
    d. supercharger

76. True or False: Rotors used in DDC blowers never touch each other or the housing since they are supported on fully floating bearings.

77. True or False: Signs of oil flowing along the blower rotors when the engine is running are indicative of leaking blower oil seals.

78. The DDC blower assembly on current model engines employs a bypass blower design. Describe what this actually means and how it operates.

79. Average air delivery pressure available from the gear-driven blower on DDC two-cycle engines is in the range of
    a. 4 to 7 psi (27 to 48 kPa)
    b. 8 to 12 psi (55 to 83 kPa)
    c. 15 to 19 psi (103 to 131 kPa)
    d. 21 to 24 psi (145 to 165 kPa)

80. True or False: Signs of rotor-to-rotor lobe contact on a DDC blower usually indicate that the blower bearings are worn.

81. Technician A says that the DDC two-cycle engine blower is usually gear driven at the same speed as the engine crankshaft. Technician B believes that the blower is driven at approximately twice engine speed. Which technician is right?

82. True or False: The blower rotors on DDC engines must be timed to one another during reassembly.

83. True or False: DDC blower rotor clearances are obtained by using selective shims behind the drive or driven gear of the assembly.

84. Describe the service required on a marine engine air separator and vacuum limiter filter assemblies.

85. True or False: Most marine engines employ dry-type exhaust manifolds.

86. What are the two types of manometers that are widely used to troubleshoot diesel engines?

86. List what engine system checks you could perform with manometers and indicate the type of manometer you would use for each check.

87. True or False: Fluid displacement in an H_2O manometer is equal to 2.036 in. (52 mm) for every 1 psi (6.895 kPa) of air pressure applied to it.

88. True or False: Fluid displacement in an Hg manometer is equal to 27.7 in. (704 mm) for every 1 psi (6.895 kPa) of pressure applied to it.

89. List the causes of a high AIR condition.

90. List the causes of low TC boost pressure.

91. List the causes of low ABP on a DDC two-stroke-cycle engine.

92. List the causes of high EBP.

93. List the causes of high crankcase pressure.

21

Engine Run-in (Testing)

OVERVIEW

This chapter describes the proper steps and presents guidelines for preparing to start, run, and test a rebuilt engine with a dynamometer. Necessary adaptation hardware and safety checks and tests are also discussed.

TOPICS

- General Information
- Engine dynamometers
- Dyno run-in procedures
- Chassis dyno run-in procedures
- On-highway engine run-in procedures
- Off-highway equipment run-in procedures
- Marine engine run-in procedures
- Self-test questions

GENERAL INFORMATION

The durability and service life of an overhauled engine is directly related to its initial *run-in* (testing) after repair. Ideally, testing should be performed on an engine dynamometer. When a dynamometer is not readily available, the engine can be run-in correctly by following a procedure related to the type of equipment application in which the engine is used. On-highway trucks or mobile equipment can be run-in on a *chassis dynamometer*. The advantage of using a dynamometer is that the engine can be loaded gradually at different speeds. In addition, the technician can observe and record the engine coolant temperature, oil pressure and temperature, fuel pressure, turbocharger boost, and crankcase pressure conditions as well as note any leakage of fluid or air.

The actual run-in routine varies slightly depending on the rpm, rating, and displacement of the engine; for our purposes here, the process can be considered common for all engines. Each engine manufacturer describes and explains the recommended run-in procedure, speeds, loads, and time under load for their particular model of engine. This information can be found in most service manuals or in special publications readily available from a local engine dealer or distributor.

ENGINE DYNAMOMETERS

Ideally, an engine dynamometer (dyno for short) should be placed in a soundproof room to minimize noise radiation throughout the shop area. A dyno room should be equipped with all of the necessary coolant, lube, fuel, air, and exhaust connections. The engine must be securely bolted to a frame that is itself secured to the floor of the dyno room. Portable dyno models such as the one shown in Figure 21–1 bolt directly to the engine flywheel. A splined driveshaft extending from the center of the dyno is attached to a drive plate hub that has been bolted to the engine flywheel; the dyno housing is secured by bolts to the flywheel housing. Fixed or stationary dynamometers which are mounted to a frame and bolted to the shop floor, require that a heavy-duty short-length driveshaft similar to that used in Class 8 trucks be bolted to the dyno-driven member at one end while the opposite end is bolted to the engine flywheel. When using the driveshaft system, make sure that both ends of the flanges are parallel to one another and that a small angle exists along the length of the driveshaft. Mounting the driveshaft so that it is perfectly flat

FIGURE 21–1 *Portable engine dynamometer bolted to the engine flywheel. (Courtesy of SuperFlow Corporation.)*

will prevent the universal joints at each end from functioning. This will be noticeable by a vibration or rattling noise when the engine is running and can damage or shear the U-joints.

Although an engine can be dyno tested using its own radiator or heat exchanger system, it is preferable to employ the cooling tower system of the dyno manufacturer; (a large electric fan can be placed in front of the radiator and ATAAC core to keep the engine from overheating). This tower contains an inlet and outlet connection as well as deaeration lines from the engine to vent all air from the cooling system. In addition, the cooling tower can use city water, and a built-in temperature regulator can be adjusted to maintain the flow of water in and out of the cooling tower to ensure that a preset engine coolant temperature is maintained. If a pressurized cooling system is preferred, two cooling tower options are available that allow the use of glycol for cooling the engine in a closed-loop system. Another option is a separate engine tubular-type oil cooler for use in high-horsepower engines or when performing lengthy dyno or engine endurance testing. The oil cooler is cooled by city water plumbed through it.

The rate of water circulation through the engine should be sufficient to maintain the engine within the maximum recommended operating temperature under all loads and conditions during the test. Normally, the water outlet temperature from the thermostat housing should be maintained at no more than a 10°F (5.6°C) difference between the water inlet temperature back into the engine water pump. On some engines that are used in equipment with automatic

(powershift type) transmissions, where the transmission oil cooler dissipates its heat to the engine jacket water, a 15°F (9.4°C) coolant temperature difference is allowable.

Dynamometer loads on modern engines are usually electronically monitored with a panel that indicates digitally the engine rpm, horsepower, and torque. More expensive models can be programmed to perform a detailed engine dyno run-in procedure on its own from a PC controlled by a technician in a separate soundproof room. The test cell is equipped with a safety glass window through which the technician can visibly monitor the engine during the test routine. All diesel engines are dyno tested at the factory and cycled through a series of speed and load profiles to check them for performance. In addition, exhaust emissions are checked to ensure that the engine complies with the U.S. EPA heavy-duty transient cycle. Figure 21–2 is a graph showing an automatic dyno test sequence that an engine manufacturer might program into its test routine. This test will start the engine, warm it up, loop through a sequence of stages two times, cool the engine down, and shut it off. Throughout the test procedure, the technician can specify emergency actions such as aborting the test or shutting off power, or a warning can be flashed to the technician's screen. In addition, limits can be evaluated as a group and action taken only when certain combinations of limits are exceeded. During the test, engine sensor outputs are compared to programmed limits. These are checked and data are gathered and stored on a PC high-capacity fixed disk or on diskettes. The test information can be extracted to a printer or

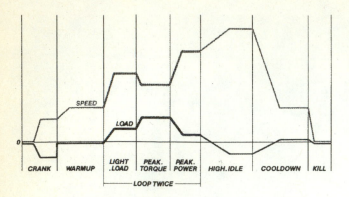

Speed, Load Profile of "TURBO. DIESEL. TEST."

FIGURE 21–2 *Sample automatic dyno test sequence showing the speed and load profile for a turbocharged diesel engine. (Courtesy of SuperFlow Corporation.)*

remote computer screens for the engine manufacturer's internal records and to satisfy government emissions agencies. Figure 21–3 lists the typical U.S. Federal Register specifications for a routine engine test sequence.

The power absorbed by the dyno is generally measured as a torque value (twisting and turning force). A calibrated scale then converts this value along with the known engine speed to an equivalent horsepower (kilo-watt) readout. This is accomplished by the following formula:

$$bhp = \frac{T \times RPM}{5250}$$

where bhp = brake horsepower
  T = torque in lb-ft (N·m)
  rpm = engine speed
  5250 = constant number to determine power

This formula is generally not required on current dynamometers since they are calibrated to read both torque and horsepower at the push of a selector button. The formula does apply if an older-model dyno is being used that requires the technician to add weights to the end of a brake arm. If the technician wants to check that the instrumentation on a newer dyno is calibrated correctly, he or she can insert the engine rpm into the formula along with the torque gauge readout value and determine what the horsepower should be. The torque meter can also be checked by using this formula:

$$torque = \frac{5252 \times bhp}{rpm}$$

Some dynamometers operate on water pressure and others use electricity (eddy currents) to provide the rotating resistance to the engine flywheel. The water-type dyno can be connected to a city water supply, or it may have its own water reservoir and pump system. Both water inlet and outlet control valves are connected to the dyno control panel. Within the load cell of the dyno is a vaned impeller, which is similar to that found on a water pump and not unlike the impeller found in the Allison and Voith transmission hydraulic retarders or the Caterpillar 3406 engine Brakesaver.

If the water outlet valve is closed and the inlet valve is opened, the dyno load cell is filled with water under pressure. By manipulation of the inlet and outlet valves, the technician can determine how much trapped water is allowed to remain in the dyno load cell. This controls the resistance to engine flywheel rotation as the dyno impeller is driven against the water within its housing. A hydraulic dyno uses fluid instead of water to apply the load. On electric dynamometers, a resistance control knob allows the technician to vary the current supplied to a series of electromagnets surrounding the dyno driveshaft. The stronger the magnetic force developed, the greater is the load applied to the engine flywheel.

Pre-Run-In Checks

Before you conduct a run-in, follow these preparatory steps:

1. Open the dyno coolant supply to fill and deaerate the system. If no deaeration lines are routed from the engine thermostat housings to the cooling tower, open up the petcock on the taps at the housings to completely vent the system of all entrapped air. Failure to properly deaerate the cooling system can lead to an air lock, and serious overheating may result.

2. Ensure that a fully charged battery (or batteries) is used. This is very important when testing electronically controlled diesel engines to be sure that the ECM will function properly.

3. Prelube the engine as described in Chapter 18 (see Figure 18–42).

4. Install all gauges required to monitor the following systems and conditions: lube oil pressure, lube oil temperature, coolant temperature, crankcase pressure (water manometer), turbocharger boost pressure (mercury manometer or pressure gauge), fuel temperature, fuel pressure, exhaust temperature (pyrometer), air inlet restriction (water manometer or vacuum gauge), air inlet temperature, exhaust back pressure, and fuel consumption check.

5. Install a fuel cooler if the fuel supply to the engine is from a fuel tank that allows the fuel temperature to exceed recommended maximums. Ideally, the fuel temperature should be maintained between 90°

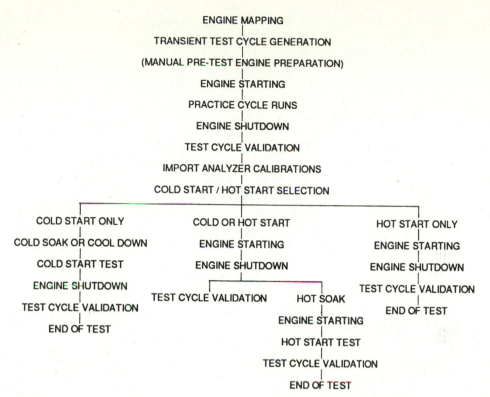

**FEDERAL REGISTER
SPECIFICATIONS
FOR
TEST SEQUENCE**

Note: This overview
illustrates the typical
sequence of steps followed
by the dynamometer
controller. The dyna-
mometer controller enters
and exits the major
functions independently
of the others. It is possible
to map the engine only,
generate test cycles only,
do practice cycles only, do
Cold Starts only, do Hot
Starts only, perform cycle
validation only, or any
combination.

FIGURE 21–3 Overview of a typical U.S. Federal Register specifications for a heavy-duty diesel engine dyno test. (Courtesy of SuperFlow Corporation.)

and 95°F (32° to 35°C) since a horsepower loss of approximately 1% will occur on non-turbo engines and of 1.5% on turbo engines for every 10° F (5.6°C) rise beyond this range. This occurs due to the expansion of the fuel—meaning that a less dense fuel charge is metered and injected. The maximum fuel temperature should never be allowed to exceed 150°F (66°C). Note also that on electronically controlled engines, fuel temperatures in excess of 140°F (60°C) can damage the electronics within the ECM.

6. Ensure that a regular supply of cool air is available to the engine intake system. Usually this means that the air inlet ducting must be pulled from outside the building. Warm air also causes a reduction in engine horsepower, and on heavy-duty truck electronic engines that are designed for use with AAACs (air-to-air aftercoolers), some means must be provided to ensure that the air inlet temperature is cool enough. Most AAACs are designed to reduce the pressurized air temperature from the turbocharger from 300°F (149°C) to between 100° and 110°F (38° to 43°C). Engine operating temperature and piston and valve cooling can be adversely affected by hot air entering the engine.

7. Plumb the exhaust system to the outside to minimize heat radiation within the dyno room. Some systems use water-cooled exhaust manifolds. Another

possibility is to heat wrap (insulate) the exhaust piping within the dyno room.

8. Make sure all engine adjustments such as valve and injector timing and initial governor controls (mechanical engines only) have been performed. Check that the *buffer screw* on DDC mechanical engine models has been backed out; otherwise, engine overspeed can occur.

DYNO RUN-IN PROCEDURES

Prior to actually starting the engine, obtain the recommended specs and operating conditions from the manufacturer. The recommended minimum idle speed, maximum no-load (high idle) and full-load (rated) speeds, as well as the engine horsepower, can be found on the engine decals attached to the rocker cover or engine block. The maximum peak torque value and engine speed are normally not listed on the engine decal, so obtain a sales brochure for your engine to review all of the specs.

Perform the following steps of the run-in procedure:

1. As soon as the engine is started at idle, check the oil pressure gauge. Continue to run the engine at an idle speed for at least 1 minute on all turbocharged engines to ensure that there is oil pressure to the turbo oil supply line.

2. With the engine running at 800 to 1000 rpm, inspect all systems for signs of leaks. Fix if necessary. If there are no leaks, allow the engine to run for a maximum of 5 to 8 minutes while you listen for any unusual rubbing noises, tapping or clacking (valves), hum, deep base noises, knocking, scraping, and so forth. Make sure there is no significant oil pressure drop on the gauge.

3. Slowly increase the engine rpm to WOT and using an accurate tachometer, note and record the speed. On mechanical engines, adjust the governor assembly to obtain the recommended maximum no-load (high idle) rpm. This can be found on either the engine decal or in the engine service manual or sales literature spec sheet. Note and record the engine oil pressure.

4. Allow the engine to return to its low idle speed and check that this rpm is correct. On mechanical engines, adjust the idle speed to specs. On some engines such as DDC two-stroke cycle models, you may also have to adjust the governor buffer screw to prevent engine surge (hunt). Engines using multiple-plunger inline pumps may also require adjustment to the low idle speed and the bumper spring to prevent engine roll.

5. With the engine and dyno both operating correctly, refer to the engine manufacturer's dyno run-in spec sheet. An example is given in Figure 21–4 for a Detroit Diesel Series 60 four-stroke-cycle heavy-duty electronically controlled engine.

6. Increase the engine rpm to half speed and apply the load shown in the spec sheet of Figure 21–4 (under warm-up) for 5 minutes or longer to allow the coolant temperature to stabilize at its normal operating level. During this time, repeat the same checks that you did in step 2. On this engine, normal coolant temperature is controlled by a 180°F (82°C) thermostat system. Under full-load conditions, coolant operating temperatures will be maintained within a range of 180° to 197°F (82° to 92°C). Under certain ambient temperatures, grades and loads, however, coolant temperatures may approach higher levels than this. Under no circumstances should the coolant temperature be allowed to exceed 210°F (99°C) because serious engine damage could result.

7. Refer to the run-in spec sheet and proceed through the individual steps while applying the recommended percentage of full load. Note that the run-in times are minimum values, so the engine can be run or loaded for longer periods of time if necessary. During all speeds and load levels, record all of the information relative to the systems shown and any others listed under the engine pre-run-in checks. In addition, closely monitor the engine for any speed changes, fluid or air leaks, and unusual noises.

8. Excessive blowby indicated by steady fumes emanating from the breather cap, or by the water manometer displacement, indicates possible valve stem, piston ring, liner, or turbocharger malfunction. Crankcase pressure can be checked as shown in Figure 21–5. A connection is made to the engine rocker cover breather, or a bottle-stopper type of plug can be inserted in place of the breather. A handle or knob can be tightened on the rubber stopper to expand it tightly. It also has a tap point for a rubber hose to connect to a water manometer. On some engines, crankcase pressure can be monitored through the dipstick tube or by removing an inspection plug alongside the engine block which sits above the oil pan rail. Check the service specs to determine the maximum allowable crankcase pressure. The engine may require slightly longer time under load to allow the piston rings to seat; however, failure of the blowby condition or engine crankcase pressure to stabilize might require engine component disassembly to correct the cause.

9. When the engine has been cycled through the run-in procedure, gradually reduce the load from the dyno and allow it to remain at these reduced load (speed) levels for several minutes each. This allows the various components such as the cylinder head, valves, pistons, and turbocharger to dissipate their heat gradually.

10. Once the engine has been reduced to an idle speed, let it run for at least 3 minutes to allow the turbocharger to cool off.

11. Shut the engine off!

NOTE: Some engine manufacturers recommend that the cylinder head bolts be retorqued after a dyno run-in. Be sure to check the service manual for your specific engine to determine if this is necessary.

12. Once the engine has cooled, if it is to be stored for any length of time, the fuel system should be rust-proofed, the cooling system filled with a rust inhibitor, and the crankcase filled with a lube oil preservative. All intake and exhaust openings should be plugged with plastic shipping caps and/or masked closed. The same procedure should be done for the coolant, fuel, and lube systems.

CHASSIS DYNO RUN-IN PROCEDURES

Although chassis dynamometers can be used to run-in an engine after a major overhaul, most truck service dealers employ this type of load device to troubleshoot complaints of low engine power and/or possible driveline problems and horsepower losses. The OEM or truck manufacturer may use a chassis dyno to monitor and test new truck designs. Current

SERIES 60 ENGINE TEST REPORT

Date: _____   Unit Number: _____
Repair Order Number: _____   Model Number: _____
PROM Part Number: _____   Engine Size: _____
Rated F/L RPM: _____   Max. N/L RPM: _____
Idle RPM: _____

A. PRESTART

1. PRIME LUBE OIL SYSTEM	2. PRIME FUEL OIL SYSTEM	3. FILL COOLING SYSTEM

B. START UP AND IDLE FOR 30 SECONDS.

START_____STOP_____OIL PRESSURE_____WATER TEMPERATURE_____

C. WARM UP—5 MINUTES   START_____ STOP_____

RPM MAX. SPEED	LOAD 50%	OIL PRESSURE	WATER TEMPERATURE
1. LUBE OIL LEAKS	2. FUEL OIL LEAKS	3. COOLANT LEAKS	4. LOOSE BOLTS

D. RUN IN—5 MINUTES   START_____ STOP_____

RPM MAX. SPEED	LOAD 75%	OIL PRESSURE	WATER TEMPERATURE

E. FINAL RUN IN—20 MINUTES   START_____ STOP_____

RPM MAX. SPEED	LOAD 100%	CRANKCASE PRESSURE AT F/L	EXHAUST BACK PRESSURE AT F/L
LUBE OIL PRESSURE AT F/L	LUBE OIL TEMPERATURE AT F/L	FUEL OIL TEMPERATURE AT F/L	FUEL OIL PRESSURE AT F/L
WATER TEMPERATURE AT F/L	TURBO BOOST PRESSURE AT F/L	LUBE OIL PRESSURE AT IDLE	IDLE RPM

REMARKS: _____
_____

OK_____Reject_____Dynamometer Operator_____Date_____

Figure 21–4 Sample of a dyno test report for a DDC Series 60 four-stroke-cycle electronically controlled diesel engine. (Courtesy of Detroit Diesel Corporation.)

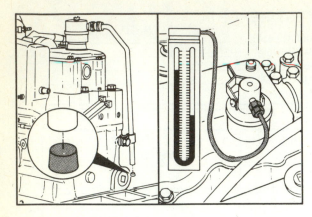

FIGURE 21–5 *Water manometer connections to monitor engine crankcase pressure. (Courtesy of Cummins Engine Company, Inc.)*

MEASURES AND CALCULATES:

1. Engine speed	26. Corrected BSFC
2. Vehicle power	27. Aftercooler temperature
3. Roll 1 speed	28. Air temperature
4. Roll 2 speed	29. Fuel temperature
5. Roll % difference	30. Exhaust temperature
6. Roll 1 power	31. Coolant out temperature
7. Roll 2 power	32. Coolant in temperature
8. Corrected Vehicle Speed	33. Oil out temperature
9. Corrected Vehicle Power	34. Oil in temperature
10. Caterpillar Balance Point	35. Extra temperature
11. Manifold pressure	36. Caterpillar rack switch %
12. Air inlet pressure	37. Current date and time
13. Fuel pressure	38. Test time
14. Exhaust back pressure	39. Voltage D.C.
15. Rail pressure	40. Engine blow-by*
16. Coolant pressure	41. Exhaust opacity*
17. Oil pressure	42. Engine dyno power*
18. Barometric pressure	43. Engine corrected power*
19. Extra pressure	44. Engine torque*
20. Fuel API	45. Current to 1000 amps*
21. Fuel mass flow	46. Airflow 1*
22. Fuel volume flow	47. Airflow 2*
23. Fuel economy	48. Air-fuel ratio*
24. Vehicle BSFC	49. Engine volumetric efficiency*
25. Engine BSFC	50. Coolant flow*

*Items 40-50 are extra cost options.
All items may be displayed and stored in English or Metric units.

FIGURE 21–6 *Example of items that can be measured and calculated on a typical microprocessor-controlled heavy-duty truck chassis dynamometer. (Courtesy of SuperFlow Corporation.)*

microprocessor-controlled chassis dynamometers typically measure and calculate the items listed in Figure 21–6.

Vehicle wheel horsepower (kW) output on a chassis dyno will always be lower than that specified for the engine itself due to driveline efficiency and engine-driven accessories. The wheel horsepower will usually be reduced by approximately 20% for a single-axle vehicle and 25% for tandem-axle vehicles. These percentages are used in relation to engine run-in only and are not to be considered absolute figures. *Always* refer to the vehicle service literature of the OEM to establish what these wheel horsepower (kW) figures should be for a given model of truck. Figure 21–7 illustrates a Class 8 heavy-duty tandem-axle truck sitting on a dual-roller system. The technician can sit in the vehicle cab during the dyno test to control the transmission gear selection. By using a handheld terminal, the technician can control the operation and load characteristics of the dyno assembly. A computer mounted inside or outside of the dyno test cell records all of the accumulated test data. Most computerized chassis and engine dynamometers today can maintain a selected roll speed to within ± 0.8 km/h (0.5 mph), engine speed to ± 5 rpm, and power to ± 1 hp (0.75 kW). At the end of the test period, printed copies can be extracted for the technician to study and for the customer to consult. In addition, the test data can be analyzed using a graphic plotting system to compare the test results to the engine or truck manufacturer's standards.

If the chassis dyno is being used to run-in an overhauled engine, chassis dyno manufacturers caution against employing recapped or snow-tread tires mounted on the vehicle. They also issue some cautions against using radial-ply tires. Low-profile radial tires are more sensitive to heat than bias-ply tires. Excessive operating time at full load can damage tires as a result of overheating. Tire manufacturers can advise on the maximum allowable chassis dyno operating time. Recap tires can experience tread separation, while snow tires may upset and reduce dyno readings due to their different grip characteristics on the dyno rollers. Never operate with tires that have been used less than 160 km (100 miles). Some dyno manufacturers suggest that a set of *slave tires* with a cross-ply tread design of minimum depth be used during the chassis dyno test. Check the information for the specific dyno that you are using. Also be aware that the vehicle chassis power reading can be affected by heavy truck bodies and tanks and excessively loaded vehicles.

Figure 21–8 illustrates a heavy-duty truck sitting on a chassis dyno with a single set of rollers. Either a large single-roller or double-roller type can be used. During testing, the vehicle transmission is shifted into gear to allow the rear axle(s) tires to drive the dyno rollers. The load applied to the rollers is similar to that described for an engine dynamometer. When using the chassis the vehicle frame *must* be securely tied down. This is usually done with safety chains connected to the rear of the vehicle, as shown in Figure 21–9, and anchored through shackles to hold-down eyes in the cement floor to prevent any possible truck breakaway under load testing. In addition, refer to Figure 21–9 and chock the front wheels; or, as shown in Figure 21–10, use chains to securely hold each front wheel to

FIGURE 21–7 *Example of a heavy-duty Class 8 highway tractor connected to a dual-roller chassis dynamometer. Also shown are the dyno controls and handheld terminal controls. (Courtesy of SuperFlow Corporation.)*

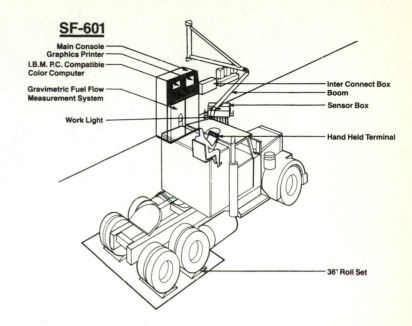

SF-601

Main Console
Graphics Printer
I.B.M. P.C. Compatible
Color Computer

Gravimetric Fuel Flow
Measurement System

Work Light

Inter Connect Box
Boom
Sensor Box

Hand Held Terminal

36" Roll Set

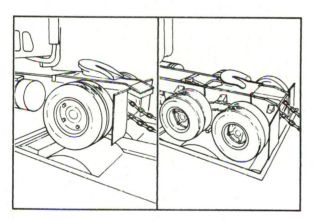

FIGURE 21–8 *Example of a heavy-duty truck mounted on a large single-roll chassis dynamometer. Notice the safety hold-down chains connected between the truck frame and the shop floor tie-downs. (Courtesy of Cummins Engine Company, Inc.)*

FIGURE 21–9 *Safety chain tie-downs and front wheel chocks to prevent vehicle movement during a chassis dyno test. Notice the overhead exhaust pipe connection. (Courtesy of Cummins Engine Company, Inc.)*

rails embedded in the concrete floor. Also connect the overhead exhaust stack(s) to the dyno ducting as indicated in Figure 21–9.

Most turbocharged trucks today employ AAACs mounted in front of the radiator core. The AAAC depends on forced air driven through its core when the vehicle is moving along the highway. Therefore, it is necessary to install a suitable electric-driven blower fan in front of the truck radiator to ensure adequate airflow through the AAAC as well as the radiator cores during chassis dyno testing.

All of the necessary engine checks and instrumentation discussed under the previous section on dyno run-in procedures can be applied to a chassis

dyno test. In addition, the instrumentation and gauges on the truck can be used to monitor various systems. Prior to testing, all tires should be checked for equal pressures and for matched size. Use a matching stick, square, or string wound around the circumference of each tire. Mismatched tires can cause interaxle fight and one side of an axle to rotate through more revolutions per mile (km) than the other. Tire size differences vary by tire manufacturer; however the widely used standard is that dual tires should not differ more than 1/4 in. (6.35 mm) in diameter or more than 3/4 in. (19 mm) in circumference when mounted on the same dual wheel. If differences are unavoidable, place the larger or less worn tire on

FIGURE 21–10 *Optional chaining down of front wheels to securely anchor the vehicle to the rails embedded in the concrete floor. (Courtesy of SuperFlow Corporation.)*

the outside. If the tires mounted on the forward-rear axle are larger than those on the rear-rear axle, a difference in speed between the two axles results. With the forward- and rear-rear axles connected, the rear-rear axle attempts to overrun the slower turning forward axle, and the forward axle attempts to slow down the rear axle; the result is wheel fight between the two axles. The propeller shaft tries to wind up, and the axle shafts try to do the same. The axle gear teeth are loaded to very high pressures, which causes overloading of the bearings and eventual failure of the bearings and possibly the axle gear teeth.

During testing, axle speed difference must not exceed 5 mph (8 km/h). With the engine at the speed to be tested and the dyno unloaded, the two load buttons for the dyno (*load* and *unload*) must be applied slowly and evenly while observing the road speed meters to be sure that the allowable axle speed difference is not exceeded. On vehicles equipped with an interaxle *power divider* lockout control, the lockout should be engaged during testing. All-wheel drive vehicles should have the front propellor shaft disconnected, and the transfer case lockup clutch should be engaged.

SAFETY TIPS: Check that all safety chains are secured to both the truck frame and floor hooks. The tie-down chains *must* have some slack in them to avoid damage to the chassis dyno rollers. Check that all stones have been removed from the tire treads because they can fly out with destructive force.

Although the vehicle is securely chained down, never stand in front or behind a truck or bus during a chassis dyno test run! Make sure that there are no other vehicles or shop components parked in front of the test truck.

Perform the following steps in the chassis dyno run-in:

1. With all checks and conditions performed as just described, start the engine with the transmission in neutral and allow the engine to warm up until the air compressor has cut out at its maximum value. You can warm up the engine by operating the truck on the dyno in a gear range with about 25% of rated engine load between 1200 and 1500 rpm for about 15 minutes or until the coolant gauge indicates that normal operating temperature has been reached (at least 160°F, 71°C).

2. Release the spring parking brakes.

3. Place the transmission in *direct gear*, not overdrive to produce a road speed of 90 to 95 km/h (55 to 60 mph).

NOTE: Depending on the engine model used, the actual time and loads applied to the vehicle will vary. The following steps refer to one example. The truck manufacturer's service manual and/or engine service manual will provide you with specific run-in details.

4. Select an engine speed and gear range that permits the engine to operate at or near the full-load governed speed for 15 to 30 minutes for run-in. Note and record all operating data in a manner similar to that for an engine dyno test described earlier.

5. Starting at a high engine rpm, conduct a power test at each decreasing 200 rpm. One test should be made 100 rpm below engine governed speed and continued down to the engine peak torque rpm. Hold full load for approximately 3 min-

utes with the transmission in direct drive in each speed range. Take careful note of all power levels and engine/vehicle operating conditions, particularly the axle oil temperatures.

ON-HIGHWAY ENGINE RUN-IN PROCEDURES

In an on-highway truck application in which either a new or rebuilt engine has been installed or an in-frame overhaul has been performed, the engine can be *on-road* dyno tested, in the absence of an engine or chassis dynamometer, to check for possible problem areas. Note that on electronically equipped diesel engines, a hand-held diagnostic data reader (see Figures 5–39, 5–40, 5–64, and 5–74) or a portable PC can be connected to the on-board computer (ECM) of the vehicle, and a snapshot of the accumulated data can be stored for retrieval after the road test. A review of the stored data, operating parameters, and sensor performance can indicate the condition of the engine. Follow this procedure:

1. Check that all engine fluid levels are correct and that the maximum no-load and idle speeds have been adjusted properly.
2. Perform a vehicle *pre-trip* inspection to ensure that all components are operating correctly.
3. Load the vehicle to its usual maximum GVW (gross vehicle weight—straight truck body) or GCVW (gross combination vehicle weight—semitrailer).
4. Use a progressive shift technique and operate the vehicle through all gear ranges for at least 30 minutes. Take care that the engine speed does not exceed approximately 1800 rpm. Regularly check all of the gauges on the instrument panel.
5. With the vehicle on a suitable road surface, continue to operate it at or near its maximum governed speed for between 30 and 60 minutes. Regularly check all the gauges on the instrument panel.
6. When back at home base, recheck the engine maximum no-load (high idle) speed as well as the idle rpm and reset if necessary.
7. Allow the engine to idle for 3 to 5 minutes after the run-in so the turbocharger can cool down.
8. Check all fluids and inspect the engine closely for any signs of leaks or unusual noises.

NOTE: If the engine manufacturer specifies a cylinder head bolt retorque, perform it now.

OFF-HIGHWAY EQUIPMENT RUN-IN PROCEDURES

Off-highway engines can be operated in the equipment for at least 3 hours after overhaul, but avoid running the engine higher than 75% of throttle while loaded. Do not operate the engine at rated speed and full-load for more than 5 minutes at any one time. Do not idle the engine for more than 5 minutes at any one time either. Take careful note of crankcase blowby or fumes, leaks, and any unusual noises during the run-in time.

MARINE ENGINE RUN-IN PROCEDURES

On many marine applications, overhaul of the engine must be performed inside the engine room, unless accessible deck plates can be removed to allow engine removal. In some situations (steel workboats and so on), the deck plates have to be cut out and rewelded into place after completion of the repairs.

After prelubrication of the engine as described and illustrated in Figure 18–42, start the engine(s). The governed speed of the engine will, of course, determine the specific test speeds to follow. Assume that we are preparing to run-in a high-speed high-output engine(s) and follow this typical procedure:

1. Allow the engine(s) to idle with the marine gear in *neutral* for approximately 10 minutes. Carefully check all fluid levels; look for signs of fluid leakage at the engine and marine gear, exhaust system, air intake ducting, and so forth.
2. With the marine gear still in neutral, increase the engine(s) speed to 1200 rpm and operate here for 20 minutes. Monitor and record all pressure and temperature gauges for both the engine and marine gear.
3. Engage the marine gear in *forward,* and with the vessel underway, run the engine(s) at the following time intervals: 800 rpm for 20 minutes, 1000 rpm for 20 minutes, 1600 rpm for 20 minutes, 1800 rpm for 30 minutes, 2000 rpm for 30 minutes, 2100 rpm for 30 minutes, and maximum full-load speed for 30 minutes.

SELF-TEST QUESTIONS

1. Describe the various types (not makes) of engine and vehicle dynamometers being used.
2. How does the water dynamometer effectively load or unload an engine?

3. Technician A says that the power absorbed by a dyno is a direct horsepower (kW) value. Technician B says that it is a torque value that is then calibrated to an hp reading. Which technician knows dyno theory best?

4. Describe how you would prelubricate an engine after overhaul and prior to dyno testing.

5. Ideally, during dyno testing the diesel fuel temperature should be maintained between
   a. 65° and 70°F (18° to 21°C)
   b. 75° and 80°F (24° to 27°C)
   c. 85° and 90°F (29° to 32°C)
   d. 90° and 95°F (32° to 35°C)

6. True or False: On initial engine start-up, run the engine at approximately 1500 rpm to quickly allow oil to circulate.

7. What check should be done on the turbocharger as soon as the engine starts?

8. What other checks should be performed as soon as the engine starts?

9. True or False: Oil pressures less than 30 psi at idle speed indicate a serious oil pressure condition.

10. Typical oil pressures on high-speed heavy-duty diesel engines at close to regulated speed usually range between
    a. 30 and 40 psi (207 to 276 kPa)
    b. 40 and 50 psi (276 to 345 kPa)
    c. 50 and 60 psi (345 to 414 kPa)
    d. 60 and 80 psi (414 to 552 kPa)

11. Under full-load engine operating conditions, what is a normal engine coolant temperature range?

12. What is the maximum allowable coolant temperature range for a typical high-speed heavy-duty engine under full load in a dyno test?

13. Describe the normal variation in engine oil temperature and engine coolant temperature for a high-speed heavy-duty diesel engine under load in a dyno test run.

14. Failure of an engine to show a reduction in crankcase pressure after several hours on a dyno would usually be indicative of
    a. failure of the piston rings to seat properly
    b. cracked piston
    c. cracked liner
    d. cracked cylinder head

15. The shortest run-in time on a dyno test should not be less than
    a. 15 minutes
    b. 30 minutes
    c. 60 minutes
    d. 2 hours

16. An engine in a dyno test should be capable of producing its rated power output within
    a. ± 5%
    b. ± 8%
    c. ± 10%
    d. ± 12%

17. Once an engine has been warmed up on a dyno, it should be loaded down to no more than what percentage of its rated output?
    a. 25%
    b. 35%
    c. 50%
    d. 60%

18. What systems and gauge readings should you monitor and record during an engine/vehicle dyno test? Make a list.

19. Technician A says that when running a truck or tractor on a chassis dyno, you should never use recap or snow-tread tires. Describe the reasoning behind this precaution.

20. What other checks must be done on truck or tractor tires prior to a chassis dyno test of the vehicle?

21. If testing a heavy-duty high-speed truck or tractor on a chassis dyno, or an engine on a dyno that is equipped with an ATAAC, what step must be employed to prevent damage to the engine valves, pistons, and cylinder head(s)?

22. To prevent a truck or tractor from moving on a chassis dyno test, what safety precautions should be employed?

23. List the engine speeds and times that you would employ to run-in a rebuilt engine on a marine application.

22 Engine Troubleshooting

OVERVIEW

This chapter stresses that both mechanical and electronically controlled diesel engines encounter problems that can be mechanical, electrical, or a combination of both. We discuss the diagnostic procedures to follow when tracing a problem. Several troubleshooting charts are presented to assist the technician in systematically analyzing potential fault areas.

TOPICS

- Getting started
- Troubleshooting tips
- Engine idling
- Sequential troubleshooting steps
- General procedure for checking engine and vehicle
- Exhaust smoke color
- Exhaust smoke detection
- Checking the fuel system
- Primary engine checks
- Troubleshooting charts
- Self-test questions

GETTING STARTED

The introduction of electronically controlled diesel fuel injection systems has made pinpointing a problem area in the fuel control and engine systems easier for the technician. Plug-in diagnostic equipment is now readily available and recommended by the engine manufacturer (See chapter 5 for details). With this diagnostic equipment hooked into the microprocessor, the system performs a self-diagnostic run through and issues trouble codes from those stored in computer memory. The technician can then zero in on a specific area, conduct a series of tests, and pinpoint the exact problem fairly easily. In some cases, a particularly tough problem may require the technician to follow closely a step-by-step service manual procedure to pinpoint one or more problems in the system. The use of electronic diagnostic tools does not mean that the technician can simply plug in the unit and sit back. On the contrary, often the electronic components are blamed for a particular problem. Fully 50% of supposedly faulty computers are found by the manufacturers to be completely operational when they are returned under warranty. The technician did not check closely enough to determine if the problem could have been a simple mechanical one. So don't condemn the onboard computer system before making a number of basic system checks, examples of which are given in this chapter.

Effective troubleshooting is an art that can only be developed over a period of time. How quickly you become proficient at it depends on a number of factors, one of which is how often you have the opportunity to pursue this process which requires an active and quick mind. The ability to be able to diagnose an engine problem quickly and effectively is related to the following basic conditions:

- A thorough understanding of the fundamentals of what actually goes on within an internal combustion engine
- The amount of experience of the technician involved

- How familiar the technician is with a particular make of engine; also, how up to date he or she is
- The ability to be analytical
- The ability to control one's temper when an irate customer or operator is pushing for an answer
- The ability of the technician not to second guess himself or herself (if in doubt, check it out)
- A willingness, if necessary, to refer to the manufacturer's specifications or troubleshooting charts in the appropriate engine service manual.

People often refer to someone as being a really good mechanic. How do you think that person achieved such respect? In many instances experience is gained through a series of mistakes in the apprenticeship stage. Nevertheless, one must have a genuine desire to succeed—to be the best in the field of diesel technology. Certainly, in this ever-changing technological era, especially with high labor costs and overhead, it is easy to become simply the "parts replacer" instead of a highly skilled and dedicated technician. In many instances, of course, a new part may be required. There are many, many instances, however, when a new component part is installed and within a short time, the same problem exists, leading you to scratch your head and ask why.

Unless a part shows particular excessive wear or damage, do not accept at face value that it is nonserviceable. Learn to accept, where possible, nothing less than the best; in every job think of the engine or equipment as your own. People will remember your abilities as a first-class technician only as long as you produce first-class work. Foul up once, and that is the job that stays in their minds, regardless of how many jobs you completed successfully for them at other times.

It is hard work to stay abreast of the many changes that occur constantly in the field of modern diesel technology. Accept the challenge as a person and as a skilled technician. Tackle a troubleshooting problem with an open and keen mind. Don't panic, take it easy, and eventually you will find that most problems are of a minor nature.

The problems that can relate to the fuel system of an engine are diversified in nature. The method chosen to pinpoint a particular problem will depend on how familiar you are with the make of engine. However, if you systematically collect all the information available regarding what led up to the problem, you should be able to analyze on a step-by-step basis the reason for the problem. Remember, satisfactory operation of the engine depends primarily on the following nine items:

1. Adequate supply of clean, relatively cool air, which once in the cylinder can be compressed to a high enough pressure to effect proper combustion

2. Injection of the correct amount of fuel at the proper time during the compression stroke

3. Use of the proper grade of fuel for the environment in which the engine operates

4. Ability to maintain the fuel oil, if possible, at an optimum temperature range of 90° to 95°F (32° to 36°C) for high-speed diesel operation (maximum allowable of 150°F (65°C).

5. Clean, sediment- and water-free filtered fuel.

6. Maintenance of the proper engine water temperature. Most high-speed diesel engines operate between 180° and 200°F (82° to 83°C). Satisfactory water treatment.

7. Maintenance of exhaust back pressure within specifications.

8. Use of the proper grade of oil with proper service intervals.

9. Proper selection and application of the engine for what it was intended.

When collecting information before analyzing a problem, keep an open mind. There will always be those who are ready to tell you what the problem is. Listen to their suggestions, but remember *you* are the trained and skilled technician. It is easy to become sidetracked into believing that what an operator says is in fact the cure for the problem. Maybe it is, but think before jumping to conclusions.

Suppose you find yourself in this situation: You are called to repair a heavy-duty truck. As you step out of the truck you see the contractor, loader operator, and a couple of truck drivers. The contractor has been "chewing out" the operator; the scene is tense. When you enter the area, the contractor starts in on you, much to the relief of the operator and the amusement of the truck drivers. You are drawn into the tension whether you like it or not. As the contractor vents frustration and anger, nothing constructive is learned. The regular toolbox isn't much use at this point, but the two tools of self-control and reason are!

What should you do with the customer's opinions? Use your reasoning ability. Sift the answers to questions as they come. Some will be factual and pertinent to the problem. Others will be incidental or entirely unrelated. Sort out the facts and list them. Do not discard any related facts, even though they may seem unimportant. When everything is examined together, one seemingly unimportant fact may be the key to the problem.

Through questioning and testing, you gather all the facts. You can now make some decision concerning the cause of the problem and the procedure to use in correcting it. In examining the facts, look beyond the individual parts. Visualize the whole system and how it functions. (Like a jigsaw puzzle, you cannot get the picture from the individual parts.) Relate the facts to the whole system and the possible causes for the failure will be more evident.

Through testing, questioning, and analyzing answers, the technician lays the groundwork for the repairwork that follows. All this scrutiny and study often takes place in an atmosphere of tension and pressure. Each job experience will be different, but this only points out more strongly the need for self-control and reason.

In these days of high labor costs, it is more profitable in the long run to spend 5 or 10 minutes on basic checks and collecting your thoughts so you are able to arrive at a solution to the problem rather than going off haphazardly. Given the high costs involved in purchasing equipment, most companies have a reasonably good maintenance program that in most instances is reflected in minimum engine failures and downtime. When a problem occurs, then, you will find that many times it is of a minor nature. Do not automatically suspect a major reason for failure. Consider the procedure illustrated in Figure 22–1 to systematically determine the reasons and causes for a suspected problem.

TROUBLESHOOTING TIPS

When faced with a troubleshooting problem, learn to complement your mechanical expertise and knowledge with four faculties that are always at your disposal. Figure 22–2 illustrates the most important tools available to you when troubleshooting a complaint—faculties that if used correctly might pinpoint one or more problems without your having to pull out any tools or special diagnostic equipment. They often will lead you to the system that may be causing the problem, although they may not spell out the exact cause of the problem.

Consider item 1, your eyesight, which allows you to quickly view the color of the exhaust smoke, signs of fuel oil, lube oil or coolant system leaks, and any signs of damage—collapsed intake piping; damaged air cleaner assembly; crushed exhaust piping, muffler, stack exhaust pipe, or rain cap; signs of overheated components; loose or corroded wiring, particularly on electronically equipped fuel-injected engines such as those of DDC; Caterpillar, Cummins, Mack, and Volvo. Take a few minutes to look for telltale signs before jumping to any conclusions.

Item 2, your hearing, allows you to listen for unusual noises such as air or exhaust leaks, particularly on turbocharged engines, or for sounds that are not usually associated with a mechanically sound engine. A misfiring cylinder or cylinders or rough-running engine can be heard immediately. Complement your hearing by using a stethoscope to pinpoint and pick up the intensity of noises at each injector, fuel pump plunger, valve train mechanism, bearing noise, and so on. If a stethoscope is unavailable, use a metal rod or pipe, screwdriver, or similar object to intensify the sounds to your ear.

Item 3, your sense of smell, allows you to pick up the aroma of burning lube oil, fuel oil, coolant, wire insulation, hoses, and so on. In addition, your sense of touch can lead you to a possible problem area, such as a small vibration, particularly on engines with externally mounted injectors and high-pressure fuel lines. An injector or pumping plunger in the injection pump which is at fault will exhibit a different feel when you lightly place your fingers over a high-pressure fuel line. Placing your hand along the cylinder block to determine possible variations in operating temperature, or lightly touching an exhaust manifold on a cold engine immediately after start-up, can let you feel if one cylinder is running cooler than another. A heat-indicating crayon can be used to make marks on the exhaust manifold opposite each cylinder; as the engine warms up, look to see if the crayon marks all melt together. If not, place a pyrometer on each manifold and check to ensure that each cylinder exhaust operating temperature is within 50°F (10°C) maximum of the others. Any spread greater than this indicates either lower compression in that cylinder or less fuel being delivered through that injector.

Item 4 involves gathering as much information as you can through dialogue with the equipment operator.

Another helpful tool that can be used to check an engine internally (such as the condition of valves and cylinders, crankcase state, overheated bearings) is the *borescope*, a tool used for many years by aircraft mechanics on gas turbine engines. This tool comes in varying lengths with a flexible body that can bend in and around curves and irregular shapes. Complete with a small light and magnifying window, it allows you to peer into components and areas without having to remove major engine components.

Exhaust smoke meters are manufactured by a variety of companies, two of which are Hartridge Equipment and Robert Bosch. Expensive though they are, smoke meters are necessary tools of engine manufacturers, distributors/dealers, federal and state truck licensing agencies and police traffic organizations, and large fleets that need to know and maintain engines within the legislated U.S. EPA exhaust emissions regulations. Many additional special tools are available, such as fuel injection test equipment, fuel consumption testers, and electronic diagnostic equipment, particularly for use with electronic fuel injection control systems.

The Diagnostic Process

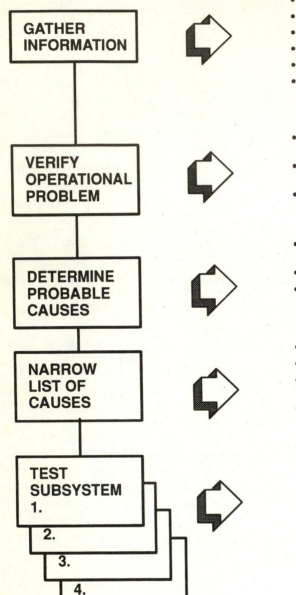

GATHER INFORMATION

- Talk to driver directly, if possible.
- What exactly are the symptoms?
- Under what conditions does the problem occur?
- When did the symptoms begin?
- Check repair history of vehicle.
- What happened, in what order (be specific)?

VERIFY OPERATIONAL PROBLEM

- Is complaint due to parameters or incorrect programming?
- Is engine performing as expected (see System Operation description)?
- When possible, repeat conditions to repeat problem.

DETERMINE PROBABLE CAUSES

- Repair any ACTIVE Diagnostic Codes immediately!
- What subsystem could cause the problem?
- What subsystem does the manual suggest?

NARROW LIST OF CAUSES

- Use driver information gathered above.
- Check LOGGED Diagnostic Codes.
- If more than one symptom, are there common causes?
- AVOID PRE–CONCEIVED IDEAS!

TEST SUBSYSTEM
1.
2.
3.
4.

- Test most likely cause first.
- Perform visual inspection.
- Use procedure in manual.
- Connector checks are **extremely** important, check **every** pin and wire.

FIGURE 22–1   *Sequential procedure to use when troubleshooting any system. (Courtesy of Caterpillar, Inc.)*

ENGINE IDLING

Sometime you may be considering a performance complaint on an engine that deals with a rough-idle situation or unusual exhaust smoke color at low speed. Keep in mind that excessive amounts of engine idling, particularly in cold-weather environments, will cause incomplete combustion, slobbering, or wet stacking at the exhaust stack (unburned raw fuel) and white smoke for up to 5 minutes or longer after initial engine start-up, particularly on nonelectronic controlled engines. Idling an engine for long periods results in a rapid loss of heat from the cooling system because the small amount of fuel required to keep the engine running at an idle speed does not generate enough heat rejection to the surrounding water jack-

FIGURE 22–2 *Before attempting to trace a problem, stop and use the four most important troubleshooting tools at your disposal: 1 = seeing; 2 = listening; 3 = smelling; 4 = questioning.*

ets. If an engine is to be idled for longer than 5 minutes, it should be shut off.

Tests on midrange and heavy-duty trucks that operate in a wide variety of applications in North America have shown that the average 1 year idling period for a typical over-the-road truck or tractor totals 800 hours, equivalent to 64,000 miles (103,000 km). Idling causes engine damage through rapid oil breakdown and increased combustion chamber deposits. Idling wastes fuel and tends to wash down the cylinder liner. The incomplete combustion can result in deposits forming not only in the combustion chamber, but also on exhaust valves and around piston rings. For this reason, current high-performance heavy-duty diesel truck engines equipped with electronic controls offer an optional 3 to 100 minute idle shutdown system. This system automatically stops the engine after this period should the operator leave the engine running unattended.

SEQUENTIAL TROUBLESHOOTING STEPS

It is not the intent of this chapter to include all the complaints you will come across when maintaining, servicing, or troubleshooting engines. The various troubleshooting charts within this chapter will provide you with a lengthy list of typical conditions that can result in a given symptom. Keep in mind, however, that problems associated with one make and type of engine (two-stroke versus four-stroke) may not occur exactly in the same way in another.

For example, particular features on one four-stroke-cycle engine may not appear on another because of the type of fuel system used and the optional features on that engine. Follow the basic troubleshooting steps listed next *prior to* rolling up your sleeves and trying to pinpoint a problem area:

1. Obtain as much information as possible concerning the complaint.
2. Analyze the problem in detail first, beginning with the smallest and simplest things.
3. Relate the problem symptoms to the basic engine systems and components.
4. Consider any recent maintenance or repair job that might relate to the problem.
5. Always double-check and think about the problem before disassembling anything.
6. Try to solve the problem by checking the easiest and simplest things first.
7. Refer to various troubleshooting charts in this chapter to assist you.
8. If possible, use the special tools and diagnostic equipment at your disposal to verify a complaint and pinpoint the general area.
9. Determine the cause(s) of the problem and carry out the repair.
10. Operate the engine and road test the vehicle to confirm that the problem has been corrected.

GENERAL PROCEDURE FOR CHECKING ENGINE AND VEHICLE

A general procedure is essential to effectively troubleshoot and isolate a cause for a lack of power complaint or an engine that runs rough under load. Follow these steps:

1. Determine from discussions with the operator if possible, just when the problem occurs. Possibly the operator's driving habits require modification and/or the horsepower setting for the engine is not suitable for the application.
2. On mobile equipment, always check to ensure that the brakes are not dragging, or that the axles are not misaligned (dog-legging), or that a problem does not exist in the driveline (bearings and so on).
3. Check the brakes by feeling all the brake drums. If the brakes of a wheel do not completely release, the brake drum for that wheel will be hotter than the brake drums for the other wheels. With the truck lifted with a jack, the wheels must have free rotation when turned by hand.
4. Check the color of the exhaust smoke at no load and full load. Perform an AIR check, turboboost check, EBP check, and crankcase pressure check with water and mercury manometers if unusual smoke is detected.
5. Air coming into the engine must be cool for the engine to have full horsepower. If the air inlet system is not of correct design or is not in good

mechanical condition, hot air can come into the engine, causing a loss of horsepower. To check the inlet air temperature, install a thermistor-thermometer into the engine air inlet pipe.

6. Check that full throttle is being obtained, with an accurate tachometer, particularly if there is no visible or unusual smoke at the exhaust stack. Is the engine obtaining maximum no-load rpm in accord with the option plate or rocker cover decal (label)? Check the governor linkage as well, through to the injection pump, or injector control tube and racks. Is there any binding—particularly if the rocker covers have been improperly installed or if they have been dented or crushed?

7. Ask the operator if any repairs were performed recently. If the vehicle is fairly new, check that any related engine parts have been correctly installed at the OEM. Components such as fuel filters and lines, as well as intake and exhaust system components, are often installed by the OEM and not by the engine manufacturer.

8. It is possible for a transmission or rear axle to use extra horsepower because of these conditions: being damaged, not being in correct adjustment, having the wrong type of fluid or not enough fluid, or having an inside mechanical problem. If a part of the drive train unit operates at a higher temperature than normal, it may be the problem. Check this part of the unit before working on any other part of the unit. Powershift or automatic transmissions can cause vehicle performance to be low if they are out of adjustment or not working correctly. See the transmission service manual for the correct adjustments.

9. The tire size, rear axle ratio, and transmission gear ratios must be correct to obtain maximum engine performance. If the transmission gear ratios are wrong, they can cause the engine rpm to go low enough during shifting that the engine does not have correct *acceleration* (increase in speed). A rear axle gear ratio that supplies too high a vehicle speed with the engine at a low rpm during normal vehicle operation will cause the engine to be *lugging* (when the truck is used in a gear too high for engine rpm to go up as the accelerator pedal is pushed farther down, or when the truck is used in a gear where engine rpm goes down with the accelerator pedal at maximum travel). Application personnel can give you the correct tire sizes and gear ratios for your operation.

10. Perform a fuel spill-back check as shown in Figure 22–3. This test is a quick way to determine if the fuel system is, in fact, receiving sufficient fuel during engine operation. If an engine lacks power and the exhaust smoke is not an unusual color, it is probably starving for fuel. This may be due to a plugged prima-

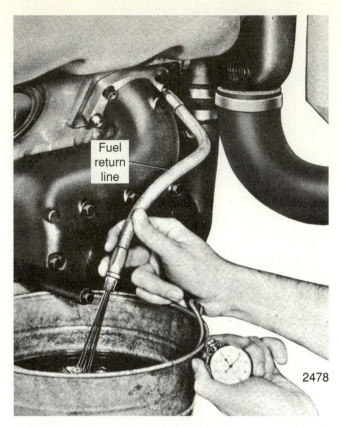

FIGURE 22–3 Performing a fuel spill-back test on a running engine for 1 minute to determine if system is receiving sufficient fuel flow and is free of air. (Courtesy of Detroit Diesel Corporation.)

ry fuel filter, a plugged secondary fuel filter, a fuel line restriction, or drawing air on the suction side of the fuel system. The spill-back test is a common procedure on all models of Detroit Diesel two- and four-stroke-cycle engines. It involves disconnecting the fuel return line between the engine and fuel tank, then running the engine at rated speed (usually 1800 or 2100 rpm) for 1 minute to measure the quantity of fuel returned, or spilled back. This quantity can be compared to the specification in the service manual. For example, if an 0.080 in. (2.03 mm) restricted fitting (Series 60 engine) is used in the fuel return line, the fuel spill back should be a minimum of 1.08 U.S. gallons per minute (4.1 L). While performing this test, the technician can also submerge the return line below the level of the spilling fuel within the container to look for signs of air bubbles, which would indicate that the fuel pump is drawing air on the suction side (between the fuel tank and the inlet side of the fuel pump). Signs of air would result in a low spill back. Check all of the fuel lines and fittings between the fuel tank and fuel pump inlet for leakage (drawing air).

11. Perform a fuel system restriction check by removing the small pipe plug located on the outlet side of the primary fuel filter assembly. Screw in a suitable small brass fitting at the filter that can have a small-bore rubber hose connected to it; connect the opposite end to a Hg (mercury) manometer or vacuum gauge. Start and run the engine at idle and slowly accelerate to a WOT position while carefully noting the fuel system restriction. Compare the reading to that in the engine service manual. A reading that exceeds the limits indicates either a plugged primary fuel filter or a restriction between the fuel tank and inlet side of the transfer pump, possibly caused by a kinked or collapsed fuel line. In addition, check to ensure that the fuel lines are of the correct size. For example, DDC recommends that this restriction should not exceed 6 in. (15.24 mm) of Hg when using a clean primary fuel filter and no more than 12 in. (30.48 mm) when a filter has been in service. Other engine manufacturers such as Cummins call for the following restrictions:

- 14L, L10, and M11 engine models: 4 in. (102 mm) Hg with a clean fuel filter; 8 in. (203 mm) Hg with a dirty filter. The fuel drain line maximum restriction without check valves is 2.5 in. (64 mm) Hg; with check valves, it is 6.5 in. Hg (165 mm).
- C and B model engines: fuel lift pump maximum inlet restriction not exceeding 3.75 in. (95 mm); fuel return line maximum restriction not exceeding 20.4 in. (518 mm)

12. Check the fuel system operating pressure by installing a gauge on the inlet and outlet side of the secondary fuel filter assembly. This is accomplished easily by removing the small square or Allen-head access pipe plug located on the filter cover. Now check the fuel transfer pump delivery pressure and the pressure drop through the filter itself. Generally, the allowable pressure drop through a secondary fuel filter should not exceed 5 psi (34.5 kPa). Normal fuel system pressures for various engines running at rated speed (usually 1800 or 2100 rpm) are as follows:

- Detroit Diesel two-cycle engines: 50 to 70 psi (345 to 483 kPa); DDC Series 50 and 60 four-stroke engines: 65 psi (450 kPa).
- Caterpillar 3176B and 3406E engines: 91 psi (630 kPa) at rated rpm
- Cummins Celect engines: 140 psi (965 kpa)

NOTE: Keep in mind that warm fuel allows the fuel to expand. On mechanically governed engines, this will result in a power loss due to less fuel (denseness) being metered. On electronically controlled engines, a fuel temperature sensor continually sends a signal to the ECM to advise it of any change in fuel system operating temperature. The ECM then alters the PWM (pulse width modulation) signal to the electronically controlled unit injectors or pump injectors to maintain a steady horsepower (kilowatt) output for a given throttle position.

13. Check the API gravity of the fuel being used. Engines are set at the factory to produce rated power with a fuel of a specific API number. Fuel with higher API gravities (number) will produce less horsepower. For more information on API numbers, refer to Chapter 3.

14. Check the customer engine and vehicle order specification and vehicle road speeds.

15. Check the mechanical throttle delay, fuel modulator, or AFC (air/fuel control) setting and operation.

16. Check all adjustments; the engine may need a tune-up.

17. If the engine is fitted with a Jake brake, check it for proper operation and adjustment.

18. Check for hard starting which might indicate low compression, which is usually accompanied by white smoke. Check the piston rings through the air box inspection covers on DDC two-stroke-cycle series engines (see Figure 15–48). If necessary, perform a compression check as shown in Figure 20–21 and 20-22. On four-cycle engines, you can also perform a cylinder leak-down test as shown in Figure 20–24.

19. Test the engine/truck with a dynamometer to confirm that the published horsepower is being obtained.

EXHAUST SMOKE COLOR

One of the easiest methods to use when troubleshooting an engine for a performance complaint is to visually monitor the color of the smoke emanating at the exhaust stack. This is particularly true when a low-power complaint is received, because the smoke color allows you to determine fairly quickly whether the engine is exhibiting an internal mechanical problem and leads you to the air intake, exhaust, or fuel system to find the reason for the complaint. Four basic colors may exit from the exhaust system at any time during engine operation—white, gray, black, or blue. Each is a clue to what the problem is and where the problem might be located.

In this section we discuss why one color of exhaust smoke may lead you to a specific problem area. To thoroughly understand the reasons behind exhaust smoke, refer to Chapter 2, where the theory and dynamics of the combustion phase in an internal combustion diesel engine are described.

White Smoke

White smoke is generally most noticeable at engine start-up, particularly during conditions of low ambient temperatures when the air drawn into the engine is cold. Although more dense than warmer air, this cold air will result in lower temperatures and pressures at the end of the piston's compression stroke. Consequently, all of the fuel will not burn to completion in the cylinder; when the exhaust valves open, these fuel droplets are exhausted into the atmosphere as unburned hydrocarbons which cool, condense, and appear as white smoke. Recollect from the discussion in Chapter 2 that hydrocarbons are basically soot produced from the carbon in the diesel fuel. Operating an engine at 20°F (-7°C) in the winter months versus 80°F (27°C) in the summer results in a reduction in the intake air temperature of 100°F (38°C). At the end of the compression stroke, the temperature of this pressurized air can be anywhere between 230° and 300°F (110° to 149°C) lower, depending on the compression ratio of the engine and the shape of the piston crown, which controls the degree of air swirl within the cylinder and combustion chamber. This colder air results in a longer ignition delay period, which can be offset slightly by use of a more volatile higher-cetane-number diesel fuel. As the combustion and cylinder temperatures increase during the first few minutes of engine operation, this white smoke generally starts to disappear in a mechanically sound engine.

If the white smoke takes longer than 3 to 5 minutes to start to disappear, the problem may be caused by low cylinder compression from worn rings, scored piston or liner, or valve seating problems, as well as from faulty injectors or the use of a low-cetane diesel fuel. The time for the white smoke to disappear depends on how cold the outside air is, the design of the engine, and how quickly it warms up. White smoke on start-up is much more predominant on high-horsepower fixed-injection timing engines because the fuel and combustion systems have been optimized for maximum performance, reliability, and durability under high-load operating conditions.

Excessive white smoke at idle speed, or some sign of white smoke once the engine is up to operating temperature, could be associated with any one of the conditions listed in the troubleshooting chart (see Figure 22–6) for excessive white smoke at idle. In addition to the conditions listed in the chart, keep in mind that white smoke at idle or when the engine is up to operating temperature can also be attributed to low cylinder compression or to coolant leakage into the combustion chamber from a leaking cylinder head gasket, injector copper tube, or cracked head or liner.

Black or Gray Smoke

Black or gray smoke should be checked with the engine at a minimum operating temperature of 160°F (71°C). Generally, either color of exhaust smoke is caused by the same conditions; the difference in color is due to the opacity or denseness of smoke. Less than 5% exhaust smoke opacity is hardly visible to the naked eye. Acceptable standards being set in North America by the U.S. EPA currently allow a maximum opacity of 20% during acceleration, 15% under engine lug, and 50% under peak-load operation. Each engine manufacturer must certify that its engines comply with the limits of maximum allowable exhaust smoke emissions under a variety of situations that include full-load acceleration, transient response under load, and lug-down conditions. Once an engine is certified to comply with legislated exhaust emissions, it becomes the maintenance technician's job to ensure that each engine continues to perform according to this certification. Heavy fines are levied by state and federal authorities on companies that allow their heavy-duty truck exhaust emissions to exceed regulated limits. In addition, abnormal amounts of exhaust smoke emission is an indication that the engine is not operating correctly, resulting in a lack of power as well as decreased fuel economy. Excessive black or gray exhaust smoke is generally caused by an improper grade of diesel fuel, air starvation, or high exhaust back pressure.

The grade of fuel must meet the engine manufacturer's specifications according to the service manual and special bulletin information. Anything that causes a high-AIR condition or aftercooler plugging, resulting in hot air entering the engine, is a typical reason for air starvation. In this chapter we describe how to check for high AIR. Similarly, a high-EBP condition can create problems in both the exhaust and air intake systems, particularly on two-stroke-cycle engines and turbocharged four-stroke-cycle models.

Other reasons for black or gray exhaust smoke include these:

- Incorrect fuel injection timing
- Incorrect fuel setting (delivery rate)
- Faulty nozzles or injectors
- Incorrect-thickness washer installed under the nozzle seat in the bore in the cylinder head, or two washers installed instead of one
- Incorrect valve adjustment clearances or valve seat leakage
- Faulty fuel injection pump
- Faulty automatic timing advance unit

Blue Smoke

Blue exhaust smoke is attributable to oil entering the combustion chamber and being burned or blown through the cylinder and burned in the exhaust manifold or turbocharger. Check the simplest things first, such as too much oil in the crankcase or a plugged crankcase ventilation system breather (or the items listed in Figure 22–12). More serious causes can be worn valve guides, piston rings, or cylinder walls; scored pistons or cylinder walls; broken rings; turbocharger seal ring leakage; glazed cylinder liner walls through use of the wrong type of oil; improper run-in procedures of a new or rebuilt engine; or excessive periods of idling and/or light-load conditions. A cylinder leak-down check can be used to confirm whether the problem is in the valves or rings (see Figure 20–24). If a cylinder leak-down kit is not available, perform a compression check on the engine. On two-stroke-cycle DDC engines, the condition of the pistons, rings, and liners can be checked visually, with the engine stopped, by removing an air box inspection cover on the side of the engine block and accessing the components through the cylinder liner ports (see Figure 15–48).

EXHAUST SMOKE DETECTION

Although smoke meters are readily available, not everyone has such a device. A Ringelmann-type smoke chart can be used to approximate the density of the exhaust smoke emanating from the stack (see Figure 22–4). A Ringelmann smoke scale enables you to observe conveniently the approximate density of the smoke coming out of the engine exhaust stack. The scale should be held at arm's length, at which distance the shaded areas on the chart can be compared to the shade or density of the smoke coming from the exhaust stack. Your line of observation should be at right angles to the direction of smoke travel and not be less than 100 ft (30.48 m) or more than a 1/4 mile (0.4 km) from the stack. The background directly beyond the top of the exhaust stack should be free of buildings or other dark objects and direct sunlight. By recording the changes in smoke density, the average *percentage of smoke density* for any period of time can be approximated.

Mechanical Engines—Causes of Exhaust Smoke

The causes for a particular color of exhaust smoke vary somewhat in mechanically governed engines and electronically controlled engines. In this section we discuss the causes for exhaust smoke in the mechanical engines. Reasons for unusual colored exhaust

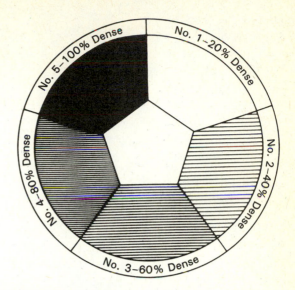

FIGURE 22–4 Example of a Ringelmann-type exhaust smoke chart which indicates the percentage opacity (denseness) and color of various degrees of incomplete combustion. (Courtesy of Detroit Diesel Corporation.)

smoke in electronic engines are given in the next section. Although many of the causes for a particular color of exhaust smoke can be the same for both types of engines, electronic sensors and circuits are added variables that we normally don't have to deal with on mechanical engines.

Black or Gray Smoke

The procedure to follow when black or gray smoke is detected is shown in Figure 22–5.

Possible Causes and Corrections

1. *Incompletely burned fuel.* High exhaust back pressure or a restricted air inlet causes insufficient air for combustion and results in incompletely burned fuel. Excessive exhaust back pressure may be caused by faulty exhaust piping or muffler obstruction and is measured at the exhaust manifold outlet from the turbocharger with a manometer or suitable gauge. Replace faulty parts. You can also check by removing the exhaust pipes from the exhaust manifolds. With the exhaust pipes removed, start and load the engine on a chassis dynamometer to see if the problem is corrected.

2. *Excessive fuel or irregular fuel distribution.* Check for the following conditions:
   a. *Misadjusted throttle delay mechanisms or fuel modulators.* This affects smoke at excessive acceleration but not smoke at constant speed.

Figure 22–5 Black or gray exhaust smoke analysis chart. (Courtesy of Detroit Diesel Corporation.)

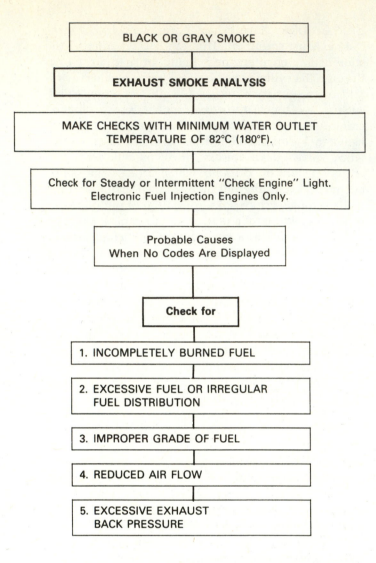

b. *Bad fuel nozzle(s).* Bad fuel nozzles normally cause the engine to misfire and run rough, but they can cause too much smoke with the engine still running smooth. Remove the fuel nozzles and test.

c. *Wrong seal washer installed under nozzle(s).* The use of incorrect washers changes the location of the fuel injection nozzles in the combustion chamber. This affects smoke.

d. *Fuel injection timing not correct.* Check and make the necessary adjustments. Check for improperly timed injectors and improperly positioned injector rack control levers. Time the fuel injectors and perform the appropriate governor tune-up. Replace faulty injectors if this condition persists after timing the injectors and performing the engine tune-up. Avoid lugging the engine, as this will cause incomplete combustion.

e. *Fuel setting not correct.* Check and make necessary adjustments as described in the service manual.

f. *Bad fuel injection pump.* An injection pump can have a good fuel flow coming from it but cause rough running because of slow timing caused by wear on the bottom end of the plunger. Fuel pumps that are severely scored from debris can cause rough running, but fuel dilution usually occurs before horsepower is affected. Low installation torque on the fuel pump retaining nut can cause misfire, rough running, and low power.

g. *Automatic timing advance not operating correctly.* A timing advance that does not operate correctly on engines equipped with an inline pump can cause delays on the engine acceleration at some rpm before high idle, or possibly cause the engine to run rough and have exhaust noise (backfire) during acceleration. This condition is difficult to find if engine acceleration is slow or at a constant engine rpm.

    h. *Air in the fuel system.* With air in the fuel system, the engine will normally be difficult to start, particularly on inline-pump-equipped engines, run rough, and release a large amount of white smoke. If the engine does not start, loosen a fuel injection line nut and crank the engine until fuel comes out. Tighten the fuel line nut. If the engine still does not run smooth or releases a large amount of white smoke, loosen the fuel line nuts one at a time until the fuel that comes out is free of air. Tighten the fuel line nuts. If the air cannot be removed this way, put 35 kPa (5 psi) of air pressure to the fuel tank. Check for leakage at the connections between the fuel tank and the fuel transfer pump. If leaks are found, tighten the connections or replace the lines. If there are no visual leaks, remove the fuel supply line from the tank and connect it to an outside fuel supply. If this corrects the problem, the suction line (standpipe) inside the fuel tank has a leak.

  3. *Low-quality fuel.* Check for use of an improper grade of fuel. The use of low-cetane fuel will cause exhaust smoke. Refer to the fuel specifications section of the engine service manual. See also Chapter 3 in this book.

  4. *Reduced airflow.* Reduced airflow to the engine cylinders is caused by a restricted intercooler or air cleaner, an air leak in the piping between the air cleaner and the intake manifold, or a faulty turbocharger. Check, clean, and/or repair these items as necessary. Restricted air inlet to two-stroke-cycle engine cylinders is caused by clogged cylinder liner ports, air cleaner, or blower air inlet screen. Clean these items. Check the emergency stop to make sure that it is completely open and readjust it if necessary.

    a. *Air inlet piping damage or restriction.* Make a visual inspection of the air inlet system and check for damage to piping, rags in the inlet piping, or damage to the rain cap or the cap pushed too far on the inlet pipe. If no damage is seen, check inlet restriction with a clean air cleaner element.

    b. *Dirty air cleaner.* Check if the air cleaner has a restriction indicator. See Figure 20–12. If there is no restriction indicator, restriction can be checked with a water

manometer or a vacuum gauge (which measures in inches of water). Make a connection to the piping between the air cleaner and the inlet of the turbocharger. Check with the engine running at full-load rpm. Maximum restriction is usually between 20 and 25 in. (500 to 635 mm) of water. If a gauge is not available, visually check the air cleaner element for dirt. If the element is dirty, clean the element or install a new element.

    c. *Valve adjustment not correct or valve leakage.* Check and make necessary adjustments. Valve leakage normally causes the engine to misfire and run rough.

  5. *High or excessive exhaust back pressure.* Refer to Figure 20–56.

White Smoke

The procedure to follow when white smoke is detected is shown in Figure 22–6a.

Possible Causes and Corrections

  1. Misfiring cylinders. To check for a misfiring cylinder, you can short out the mechanical unit injector by running the engine at an idle rpm. To do this, manually depress and hold down the injector follower using a large screwdriver or a hooked adaptor under the rocker arm assembly, and force and hold down the injector follower. If there is no significant change in the operational sound of the engine when you do this, then the injector is not functioning correctly. On engines equipped with an inline pump system, loosen off each individual nozzle fuel line nut one at a time as shown in Figure 22–7 to determine the same situation. Keep in mind, however, that low cylinder compression can cause a cylinder misfire condition as well as low cetane fuel.

CAUTION: On the Detroit Diesel four-stroke-cycle 8.2L V8 engine, which uses a unit injector, do *not* attempt to hold the injector follower down to short it out as you would do with the two-stroke-cycle model, since the injector pushrod on the four-stroke engine is not threaded into the rocker arm as it is on the two-stroke engine. Consequently, if you hold the injector follower down with a large screwdriver while the engine is running, the pushrod will either fly out of the engine or drop off to the side and be bent. To short out the unit injector on the 8.2L engine, individually push the injector fuel rack into its full-fuel position. This is known as flooding the cylinder. The engine should pick up speed when you do this to confirm that it is firing. If there is no change in speed, the injector is faulty.

EXHAUST SMOKE ANALYSIS

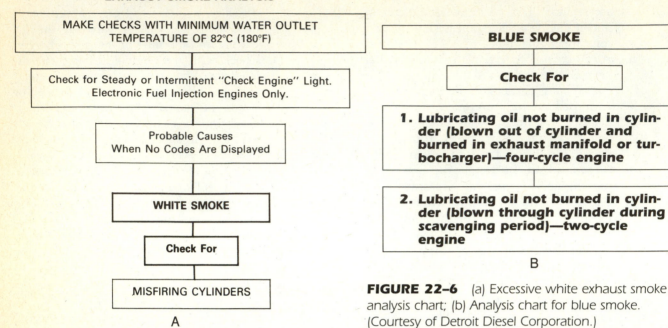

A

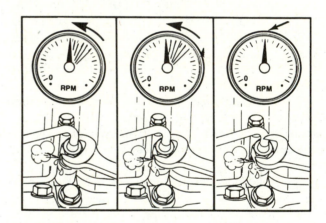

B

FIGURE 22–6 (a) Excessive white exhaust smoke analysis chart; (b) Analysis chart for blue smoke. (Courtesy of Detroit Diesel Corporation.)

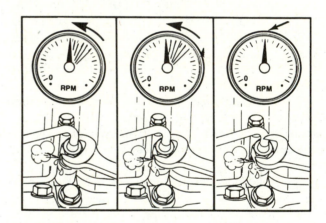

FIGURE 22–7 Loosening off a high-pressure fuel line at the injector nozzle to determine if the fuel injector is firing correctly. (Courtesy of Cummins Engine Company, Inc.)

2. *Miscellaneous causes*
   a. *Cold outside temperatures.* When the air outside is cold, the cylinder temperature is cooler. Not all the fuel will burn in the cylinders. The fuel that does not burn comes out the exhaust as white smoke. White smoke is normal in cold temperatures until the engine operates long enough to become warm. There will be less white smoke if No. 1 diesel fuel is used.
   b. *Long idle periods.* When an engine runs at idle speed for a long period of time, the cylinders cool and all of the fuel does not burn. Do not idle an engine for a long period of time. Stop an engine when it is not in use. If long idle periods are necessary, use No. 1 diesel fuel.
   c. *Engine operating temperature too low.* This can cause white smoke on start-up. If the smoke is slow to clear from the exhaust, check and make a replacement of the thermostat if needed.
   d. *Low-quality fuel.* Test the engine using fuel according to recommendations by the engine manufacturer.
   e. *Air in the fuel system.* If there is air in the fuel system, the engine will normally be difficult to start, run rough, and release a large amount of white smoke. If the engine does not start, loosen a fuel injection line nut and crank the engine until fuel comes out. Tighten the fuel-line nut.

Start the engine. If the engine still does not run smooth or releases a large amount of white smoke, loosen the fuel-line nuts one at a time until the fuel that comes out is free of air. Tighten the fuel-line nuts. If the air cannot be removed in this way, put 35 kPa (5 psi) of air pressure to the fuel tank. Check for leakage at the connections between the fuel tank and the fuel transfer pump. If leaks are found, tighten the connections or replace the lines. If there are no visual leaks, remove the fuel supply line from the tank and connect it to an outside fuel supply. If this corrects the problem, the suction line (standpipe) inside the fuel tank has a leak.

f. *Fuel injection timing not correct.* Check and make the necessary adjustments as described for Figures 13–49 and 13–50.

g. *Value adjustment not correct.* Check and make the necessary. adjustments as described in Chapter 13.

h. *Bad fuel nozzle(s).* Bad fuel nozzles normally cause the engine to *misfire* and run rough, but they can cause too much smoke with the engine still running smooth. Remove the fuel nozzles and test as described in testing and adjusting section of various chapters in this book.

i. *Coolant leakage into combustion chamber.* Coolant in the combustion chamber can cause white smoke. A cracked cylinder head or liner, or a bad cylinder head gasket, is a possible cause for this condition.

j. *Low compression.* Worn piston rings and cylinder liners lower compression pressures, which can cause white exhaust smoke.

Blue Smoke

Possible Causes and Corrections

1. *Fuel or oil leaks.*

   a. *Engine oil level too high.* Do not put too much oil in the crankcase. If the oil level in the crankcase goes up as the engine is used, check for fuel in the crankcase.

   b. *Oil leaks.* Check for internal lubricating oil leaks and refer to the high lubricating oil consumption chart (see Figure 22–11).

   c. *Worn valve guides.* Consult the specifications section of the service manual for the maximum permissible wear of the valve guides.

   d. *Worn piston rings and/or cylinder walls.* Worn piston rings and/or cylinder walls can be the cause of blue smoke and can cause a loss of compression. Make a visual inspection of the cylinder walls and piston rings. If necessary, measure the cylinder walls and piston rings. For the cylinder and piston ring specifications, see the specifications section of the service manual.

NOTE: High wear at low mileage is normally caused by dirt coming into the engine with the inlet air.

   e. *Wear or damage to pistons.* Check the piston ring grooves for wear. Most high-speed, heavy-duty engines have piston grooves

and rings of the keystone (taper) design. A piston ring groove gauge is available to check the top two ring grooves in the piston. Pistons that have worn grooves and pistons with damage or defects can cause blue smoke and too much oil consumption. Make sure that the oil return holes under the oil ring are open.

Electronic Engines—Causes of Exhaust Smoke Color

Causes for a particular color of exhaust smoke are similar regardless of whether the engine is mechanically or electronically controlled. When an *electronically controlled* engine has been operating normally, and a performance complaint is registered that deals with either white or black exhaust smoke include the following checks.

White Smoke

1. Remember some white smoke is normal when an engine is started and running, particularly during cold outside temperatures.

2. Check and recalibrate the engine speed or timing sensor (for example, Cat 3176 and 3406E engines).

3. Check the fuel system for either low- or high-pressure combustion gas or air in the fuel (perform a fuel spill-back test as shown in Figure 22–3). Check for poor fuel quality.

4. Check the intake manifold air temperature sensor signal. If ambient air is cool while the engine is idling, or after extended idling, monitor the intake manifold air temperature. If the reading is significantly higher than ambient air temperature at idle, it could be because of intake manifold heat soak: there is insufficient airflow for the sensor to accurately measure the air temperature, and the sensor is detecting conducted heat from the manifold. This could be normal operation after an extended idle period. Drive the vehicle to see if the airflow eliminates the problem.

5. Use a DDR or an ECAP (Cat) and check for atmospheric pressure sensor diagnostic codes. Monitor atmospheric pressure sensor status with a DDR or ECAP and compare with known atmospheric pressure for your area and elevation. If atmospheric pressure is 1 psi (6.895 kPa) higher than the known atmospheric pressure for your area, inspect the crankcase breather for restrictions. Remove a valve cover and recheck the DDR or ECAP pressure reading. If removing the valve cover

solves the problem, replace the breather assembly. If the breather is not restricted, check the operating condition of the atmospheric pressure sensor.

6. Using either a DDR or ECAP, check for any coolant temperature sensor diagnostic codes. Monitor the coolant temperature sensor status, and if a problem is detected, perform a coolant temperature sensor circuit test.

7. Check for security of the individual unit injector plug-in harness connections, and make sure they are free of corrosion. Inspect the ECM injector harness end connections. Perform a cylinder cut-out test using the DDR or ECAP to isolate a misfiring cylinder.

8. Use either a DDR or an ECAP and check to make sure that the EEPROM or Personality Module (Cat) is programmed correctly for the engine hardware.

9. Use either a DDR or ECAP and check for a positive 5 V sensor supply from the ECM. If this check is OK, perform a sensor supply circuit test.

Black Smoke

1. Check for high air inlet restriction
2. Check for restricted fuel supply
3. Check for poor fuel quality
4. Check for incorrect intake and exhaust valve adjustment
5. Check for defective unit injector. Perform a cylinder cut-out test using the DDR (see Figure 5–42).
6. Inspect the ECM connector for full connection and corrosion.
7. Check boost pressure or atmospheric pressure sensor signal. Check the ECM with the DDR to see if a logged trouble code has been stored in memory. You can also run the engine through a full-range speed test, and by using the DDR, program it to perform a boost pressure test; then compare the readings with test specs.
8. Connect a DDR or ECAP (Cat) and check to make sure the correct Personality Module is installed compared to the engine hardware.

CHECKING THE FUEL SYSTEM

If an engine is misfiring, running rough, and lacking power, refer to the appropriate troubleshooting charts in this chapter. They will guide you to the possible problem areas. Note whether the condition occurs only at an idle rpm, high idle (maximum no-load speed), or only under acceleration or at loaded conditions, since the troubleshooting charts will guide you through each general condition. A quick way to determine if the fuel system is the problem is to note whether there is an unusual smoke color at the exhaust stack and to compare this with the exhaust smoke analysis chart (see Figure 22–4). Generally speaking, if there is no unusual exhaust smoke color, but the engine lacks power, then the engine is not starving for airflow, does not have high EBP, and is mechanically sound. Suspect simple things such as plugged fuel filters or a restriction to fuel flow somewhere, since the engine can still run with a lack of fuel but will fail to accelerate properly, can run rough at idle, and will most likely have trouble reaching the maximum no-load rpm. If it does reach the no-load rpm, but dies when a load is applied to it, fuel starvation is more than likely the cause. Nevertheless consider all possible areas listed in the troubleshooting charts, start with the simplest possibilities first and move to the more complex. The first rule of effective troubleshooting is to walk before you run.

Fuel Temperature

On high-speed diesel engines, fuel temperature can adversely affect the horsepower output of the engine. The optimum fuel temperature should be kept between 90° and 95°F (32° to 35°C). With each 10°F temperature rise beyond these figures, there is approximately a 1% loss in horsepower due to expansion in the fuel on a conventional engine. On turbocharged-aftercooled engines, each 10°F fuel temperature rise beyond 95° to 100°F (32° to 38°C) results in approximately a 1½% horsepower loss. Therefore, if you were running at a fuel temperature of 135° to 140°F (57° to 60°C), theoretically your engine would be producing approximately 4% less horsepower on a conventional engine and closer to 6% less on a turbocharged and aftercooled engine. On a 350 hp engine, this would amount to about 14 hp (10.4 kW) on a conventional engine and closer to 21 hp on the turbocharged and aftercooled engine. Maximum temperature should *NEVER* be allowed to exceed 150°F (65°C). A reduction in engine horsepower can also result due to an increase in air temperature (ambient), since this causes the air to expand and therefore become less dense. On a turbocharged engine, this is offset by the increase in airflow and pressure increase and the use of an aftercooler or intercooler.

On most high-speed engines, a power decrease can be expected of between 0.15 and 0.5 hp (0.11 to 0.373 kW) per cylinder, depending on the delivery capability of the fuel injector or pump for each 10°F (5°C) air temperature rise above 90°F (32°C). Therefore, when investigating complaints of low horsepower, always check to ensure that these two temperatures are within specifications. If you don't, you could spend a lot of time trying to find the reason for the complaint, which is not directly related to the normal mechanical operation of the engine fuel or air inlet system.

If the engine fails to reach its maximum governed speed and generally seems to be starving for fuel, install a fuel pressure gauge into the secondary filter, run the engine, and check the fuel pressure with the engine manufacturer's specifications. On Detroit Diesel engines, perform a fuel spill-back check. Some engines have a small filter screen located just under the cover of the fuel transfer pump; check that this is not plugged.

If a fuel strainer or fuel water separator is used, check it for plugging and excessive amounts of water. Check that all fuel lines are free of sharp bends and kinks. Check the tightness of all fittings and connections from the suction side of the transfer pump back to the fuel tank. Install a clear test line connection into the suction line to check for air bubbles. You may have to undertake a restriction check to the fuel flow as discussed in Chapter 5.

Check the fuel transfer pump drive for security and proper engagement. Ensure that there are no external fuel leaks, especially at the pump or injectors. Also, if more than one fuel tank is employed, check to see that the balance-line valve is open between them; if a three-way valve is employed, check that it is in the correct position. In certain instances you may also find that there is a restriction to fuel flow from inside the fuel tank caused by sediment or some foreign object that has dropped into the tank either during filling or maintenance checks.

One complaint that you may occasionally come across is that the engine runs well in the early part of a shift, but stalls and lacks power as the day wears on. This could be caused by debris, such as a piece of wood or bark, especially around logging equipment. A restriction to fuel flow is created as the level in the fuel tank drops and the debris is drawn over the suction line.

If the engine has been overhauled recently or the injection pump or injectors serviced, double-check the injection pump timing, injector release pressure, or injector timing.

If the engine has a considerable amount of hours or miles on it, it very well may be in need of a tune-up; however, this alone may not be the cause of the problem. Too many people immediately assume that if an engine is lacking power the answer is to tune it up. Although many large companies have developed a sequence of checks to be carried out at certain intervals of time, a tune-up should be done only if other checks show that everything else is according to specifications.

When conducting a tune-up, do not back off all adjustments and start from scratch. Check each adjustment first and if necessary, readjust. One of the first checks that should be made is to disconnect the throttle linkage and manually hold the speed control lever on the governor to the full-fuel position and accurately record the maximum governed engine rpm. Reconnect the throttle linkage, place it in the full-fuel position, and compare the readings. If they are not the same, adjust the linkage to correctly obtain the maximum engine rpm. Similarly, the maximum governor no-load speed setting may require adjustment. Ensure that there is no binding anywhere in the fuel control linkage.

Fuel Flow

When an engine is suspected of using too much fuel, a close check of daily fuel usage versus miles (km) covered can be made. In addition, fuel flow measurement systems are available from some major truck manufacturers. On board computer monitoring devices are now being widely used by many truck fleets to keep an accurate check of vehicle fuel mileage.

A bad speedometer does not give the correct speed or the correct indication of fuel consumption. An indication of low speed can cause the operator to think there is a power problem.

PRIMARY ENGINE CHECKS

Engine Timing

Improper engine timing, improper valve adjustment clearances, or an out of adjustment sequence can lead to physical, or mechanical damage, such as valves hitting pistons.

If the injection pump timing or injector timing is off, problems of smoking exhaust, low power, high-fuel consumption, and internal engine damage can result. Always ensure that the engine is timed according to the manufacturer's specifications and that injection pump and injectors are timed for the particular application for which the engine is being employed. An engine timing indicator that operates off fuel pressure through a transducer pickup can be used on engines that employ a high-pressure fuel system.

Pyrometers

Exhaust temperature gauges, more commonly called *pyrometers*, are extremely helpful when checking an engine for a lack-of-power complaint. Most heavy-duty highway trucks with diesel engines are equipped with dash-mounted pyrometers, which can readily assist you in determining if both engine banks are running at the same temperature on vee-type engines. On inline engines, the pyrometer can establish whether the engine is operating within the range specified by the engine manufacturer.

The most common form of pyrometer uses a pick-up, or thermocouple, consisting of two wires of different metals welded together at their ends—a *hot junction.* The metals used in these wires are selected for their response to temperature and ability to withstand high heat. As the hot junction is exposed to a heat source, a small electric current is generated at the junction; it flows through the wires to the measuring instrument, which is a *millivoltmeter.* The amount of current flow is proportional to the heat created at the hot junction.

Many companies offer pyrometers that can be readily used by one person during troubleshooting. These are of the handheld type; they have a heat probe that registers temperature upon contact with the surface to be checked. The newer pyrometers that offer a digital readout are very helpful. Just point the infrared thermometer, pull the pistol trigger, and an instant reading is recorded on the face.

Engine exhaust temperatures vary in engine types based on fuel setting, horsepower, speed, and load conditions. Typical full-load exhaust temperatures can range as follows:

- Two-stroke-cycle diesel: 585° to 740°F (307° to 393°C)
- Four-stroke cycle diesel: 647° to 1030°F (342° to 554°C)

Peak torque exhaust temperatures, which occur at a lower engine speed, will consistently show higher temperatures of 200°F (93°C) plus over those encountered under full-load engine speed conditions at the rated governed engine rpm.

Two-stroke-cyle engines run cooler than four-stroke cycle engines due to the shorter power stroke in crankshaft degrees, plus the fact that almost twice the airflow is pumped through the two-cycle engine. Approximately 30% of the cooling on a two-stroke-cycle diesel engine is achieved by airflow alone.

Engine Overspeed

The maximum speed of diesel engines is controlled either by a mechanical or electronic governor assembly (see Chapter 6). Causes of possible engine overspeed can usually be traced to the following conditions:

1. Maximum governed rpm adjustment improperly set. Use an accurate digital tachometer to determine engine speeds.
2. Internal governor problem
3. Oil pullover from an oil bath air cleaner or other external fuel source such as blower or turbocharger seals
4. Running the engine with the governor linkage disconnected
5. Operator problem. This particular problem is not unusual on mobile equipment and highway truck operation. If an operator allows the engine rpm to climb beyond the maximum safe road speed for a particular gear, in effect, the vehicle's road wheels become the driving member. As there is a direct mechanical link from the road wheels to the differential and the driveline, this increased road wheel speed works through the transmission, causing the engine to be the driven member instead of the driving member. During this time, it matters not that the operator has his or her foot on the throttle, since the governor will react to pull the engine to a decreased fuel situation. Even if the operator has the throttle in the idle speed position, the road wheels as the driving member can spin the engine to a point that the valves strike the piston crown, leading to mechanical failure of the engine. Therefore, caution drivers and operators about excessive road speed when going down long inclines and steep hills.

Detonation

Do not confuse the normal combustion sound within the engine for this complaint. Some engines do run louder than others, and many of them have a peculiar sound common to that particular engine or application. Pressure pulsations within the engine cylinder create the condition often referred to as *diesel knock;* it is an inherent characteristic of all diesel engines.

Experience will tune your ear to pick up sounds other than the normal combustion pressure sounds. Often it is helpful, even to an experienced mechanic, to isolate any irregular noises with the use of an engine *stethoscope,* which amplifies sounds remarkably well. A piece of welding rod or even a lead pencil placed on the engine with the other end at your ear can magnify sounds reasonably well.

If detonation occurs, check for the following conditions:

- Lube oil picked up by the air intake stream to the engine; this also causes engine overspeed
- Low coolant temperature caused by excessive periods of idling and light-load operation or cold-weather operation without proper attention to maintaining coolant operating temperatures
- Faulty injectors: leaking fuel, fuel spray-in pressure low

High-Horsepower Complaint

Both mechanically governed and electronically controlled diesel engines are adjusted for a specific horsepower (kW) at a specific engine speed setting. If the mechanical governor settings are tampered with, or the ECM-EEPROM settings are reprogrammed, it is possible to increase the maximum rated power output of the engine for a given application. This can cause an increase in fuel consumption, higher noise levels, and shorter engine, clutch, transmission, and driveline life. If a complaint of this nature is made, carefully check the engine power setting by running the engine on a dyno, or if in a vehicle, on a chassis dyno, to confirm the settings. The ECM options and power settings on electronic engines can be checked by accessing the ECM programming with the aid of a DDR or an ECAP (see Figures 5–40 and 5–64).

Crankcase Oil Dilution

This complaint is sometimes referred to by mechanics as "the engine is making oil," meaning that the engine oil level continually rises above the full mark on the dipstick. This is generally due to fuel oil leakage from under a rocker cover fuel line connection or from leaking injector O-ring seals. Crankcase dilution of DDC two-stroke 71 and 92 series engines can be caused by overtightening of the fuel pipe retaining nuts on the injector body fuel stud. Additional fuel leakage on these engines can occur from the fuel stud that is screwed into the cylinder head. On DDC four-stroke engines, fuel leakage can occur at the injector upper seal rings (see Figure 5–36a). On Cummins 14L (855 cu in.) and L10 and MII engines, fuel leakage can occur from O-rings (see Figure 5–70). Caterpillar electronic unit injectors have several O-rings around the body (see Figure 5–32). On the Caterpillar 3116 engine mechanical injector assembly, there is an O-ring seal on the body. On Mack engines, check the injector nozzle holder O-ring seals for signs of leakage.

To check for fuel leaks under the rocker cover, start and run the engine with the cover off, if possible. If it is not possible to run the engine, simply seal off the fuel return line from the injection pump or engine return line and apply low pressure (not to exceed normal fuel system pressure) to the system with a small priming pump. Carefully check all fuel lines and the injectors for signs of fuel leakage and correct as necessary. In some cases it may be necessary to remove the injector or nozzle holder assembly and mount it in a pop-tester. The fuel pressure can then be raised to just below the nozzle/injector release pressure; then the pop-tester valve can be closed and an inspection made for signs of fuel leakage at the suspected areas.

Piston Scuffing, Scoring, and Possible Seizure

These problems are often caused by injectors either dribbling raw fuel into the combustion chamber, due to a faulty check valve, or by a combination of water and dirt entering the injector. On multihole fuel injectors, water can blow the tip off the end of the injector. With dirt passing through the small spray tip holes, they can become enlarged, leading to a flattening out of the fuel spray-in angle. This can create what is commonly called *wall wash,* since the fuel tends to penetrate the outer periphery of the piston crown, causing burning of the outer circumference of the piston and leading to increased piston temperatures and seizure or breakup of the fire ring. If the fuel sprays onto the cylinder wall, this creates wall wash and lube oil dilution, leading to eventual scuffing and scoring of the cylinder and piston.

Engine Vibration

Misfiring cylinders as a result of low compression or faulty injectors, improper timing of individual pumping units or injectors, valves set too tight, improperly balanced cylinder banks or individual injector racks, water in the fuel, or plugged fuel filters are some of the typical causes of engine vibration. However, vibration may be caused by accessory items on the engine; if so, conduct a more thorough analysis with a vibration meter.

Compression Checks

A compression check may be necessary to determine the condition of the valves and rings. On many engines this check is done with the use of a dummy injector and with the engine running (see Figure 20–22). Each make of engine will have some variation in the sequence of events required for the compression check. Check the engine manufacturer's service manual for the routine and specifications. A crankcase pressure check conducted using a water manometer can alert you to worn rings, as can an exhaust smoke analysis, hard starting, and low power.

Dynamometers

The quickest and most effective method of determining if an engine is producing its rated horsepower is through the use of a dynamometer. A variety of load-testing machines are available for any purpose and application. Basically, they are as follows:

- A truck or bus chassis dynamometer (see Figure 21–7). The rear driving wheels of the vehicle are forced to drive against either a single or double set of rollers connected to the dynamometer. This allows road wheel horsepower to be read directly from the dyno instrument cluster or a hard copy of test results to be printed out from a computerized interface system.
- A stationary dynamometer that can have an engine coupled to either end of it for convenience. Only one engine can be tested at a time.
- A portable, compact, relatively lightweight dynamometer that can be bolted to the engine flywheel housing and driven from the engine flywheel. This type can also be readily adapted to truck applications simply by disconnecting the driveline and coupling up the dynamometer unit.

Chassis dynamometers can be a great help in testing a vehicle for engine performance if they are in good condition and used correctly. When the dynamometer is not in good condition, or a bad operating procedure is used, the result will be incorrect readings. To achieve good comparison of horsepower readings from different vehicles, use the same dynamometer with the same operator.

Manometers

One of the most effective troubleshooting tools that you can use is a set of manometers, one a water type and the other a mercury type. These can be of a solid-tube fashion mounted on a stand or cabinet fixture, which is usually more common in a shop setup. Many mechanics prefer to use a *slack tube* manometer, which is a clear, heavy-plastic tube. It is less susceptible to breakage and can be easily packed in a toolbox or service truck. Both types perform the same function. Both are known as U-tube manometers because of their shape, and they are available in sizes from 12 to 48 in. (30.48 to 122 cm), with longer units available if required.

Manometers measure either a pressure or vacuum reading on the engine. This is done through a sliding scale connected to the manometer, as shown in Figure 20–53, which can be adjusted before use to a zero position. The scale is calibrated in either English or metric units or a combination of both. The scale reflects water or mercury displacement within the U-shaped tube in either inches or millimeters. Most engine manufacturers list relative specifications in their service manuals for the particular test that you wish to conduct. A typical pressure conversion chart is given in the last section of chapter 20 for converting from inches or millimeters to either pounds per square inch (kiloPascals) or back and forth between water and mercury.

Diesel Fuel Quality Tester

Often the cause of lack of power can be attributed directly to the quality of the fuel being used in the engine. Many hours can be spent in analyzing and troubleshooting performance complaints, only to find that there is nothing out of adjustment and that the engine is mechanically sound. Remember, the wrong grade of fuel can affect the horsepower developed by the engine. To determine if diesel fuel quality should be considered as a possible problem area when diagnosing a lack-of-power complaint in an engine, use a simple *diesel fuel quality tester*—basically a hydrometer (see Figure 3–5).

TROUBLESHOOTING CHARTS

The troubleshooting charts shown in Figures 22–8 through 22–15 deal with a variety of problems related to various diesel engines that do not necessarily use the same type of fuel injection system. Specific types of fuel injection systems will exhibit particular problems related to their design that may not necessarily be reflected in the same manner in another. Some commonality does exist, however, between engines and fuel systems regardless of whether the engine is a two-stroke or four-stroke-cycle model. When using these troubleshooting charts, keep in mind that a suggested cause may not apply directly to the type of fuel injection system or engine you are dealing with.

If the engine is equipped with an electronically controlled fuel injection system, the special diagnostic equipment that can be plugged into these systems will quickly direct you to a stored trouble code in computer memory, so you can go to the system or area in which the problem lies. Keep in mind, however, that although these engines may use electronic controls, the cause of a problem may be a simple mechanical condition that would also occur in a nonelectronically equipped engine. Accept the trouble code(s) output by the computer, but also use the faculties that were discussed earlier (see Figure 22–2), and you will solve the problem or problems. Good luck in your endeavors, and keep a high standard of excellence in all your efforts.

Hard Starting

Figure 22–8 is the troubleshooting chart for hard starting.

Possible Causes and Corrections

1. *Engine cannot be rotated.* Bar the engine over at least two complete revolutions. If the engine cannot be rotated, internal damage is indicated and the engine must be disassembled to ascertain the extent of damage and the cause.
   a. *Transmission or power takeoff (if so equipped) problem prevents crankshaft from turning.* If the crankshaft cannot be turned by hand, disconnect the transmission and power takeoff. If crankshaft now turns, find the cause of the problem in the transmission or power takeoff and make necessary corrections.
   b. *Inside problem prevents engine crankshaft from turning.* If the crankshaft cannot be turned after disconnecting the transmission and power takeoff, remove the fuel nozzles and check for fluid in the cylinders while turning the crankshaft. If fluid in the cylinders is not the problem, the engine must be disassembled to check for other inside problems. Some of these inside problems are bearing seizure, piston seizure, and valves making contact with pistons.

2. *Oil too thick for free crankshaft rotation.* Use the correct SAE grade oils for the temperatures in which the engine is operated (refer to chapter 18). At temperatures below 0°C (32°F), it may be necessary to warm the oil for free crankshaft rotation.
   a. *Cold outside temperatures.* It may be necessary to use starting aids or to heat engine oil or coolant at temperatures below −12°C (°F).

3. *Battery voltage is low or nonexistent.* Check battery voltage. If battery voltage is less than 8 volts for a 12 volt system, or 16 volts for a 24 volt system, put a charge to the batteries. Recharge the battery if a light-load test indicates low or no voltage. Replace the battery if it is damaged or will not hold a charge.

4. *Terminals are damaged or corroded.* Clean or replace terminals that are damaged or corroded.

5. *Cranking System has problems.*
   a. *Bad switch, bad wiring, or bad connection in switch circuit.* With ignition switch in the START position, check the voltage at the switch connection on the starter solenoid. If there is no voltage, or if the volt-

age is low at this connection, check the wiring, connections, ignition switch, and magnetic switch (if used).
   b. *Bad cable or connection—battery to starter.* With the ignition switch in the START position, check voltage at the connection of the battery cable to the starter. If there is no voltage, or if the voltage is low at this connection and there is good voltage at the battery, check for a bad cable or connection between the battery and the starter.
   c. *Bad starter solenoid.* Remove and repair a solenoid that does not work when voltage is correct at both the battery and ignition switch connections.
   d. *Bad starter motor.* If the solenoid works and the starter motor does not turn the crankshaft, the starter motor is bad. Before removing the starter motor, turn the crankshaft by hand to be sure that a mechanical failure inside the engine, transmission, or power takeoff is not preventing the crankshaft from turning. If the crankshaft turns freely by hand, engage the starter motor again. If the starter motor still will not work, remove the starter motor and repair it, or install a new starter motor.
   e. *Extra outside loads.* Damage to the power takeoff equipment (if so equipped) and/or transmission can put extra load on the engine. This prevents free rotation of the crankshaft. To check, disconnect the transmission and power takeoff, and start the engine.
   f. *Mechanical problem inside engine.* Take the engine apart and check all components for damage.

6. *Exhaust smoke cannot be seen while starting.*
   a. *No fuel in tank(s).* Check fuel level visually (do not use the fuel gauge only). Be sure that the dual tank selection valve is open to the tank with fuel in it. Be sure that the valve in the fuel line between the tanks is open and/or the check valve is correctly installed.

7. *Fuel separator (if equipped) may have water in the bowl.*
   a. *Low fuel pressure.* Change the primary and secondary fuel filters and check to make sure that the fuel lines are not plugged or damaged. If the filters or lines are not the cause, repair or replacement of the fuel transfer pump is needed.

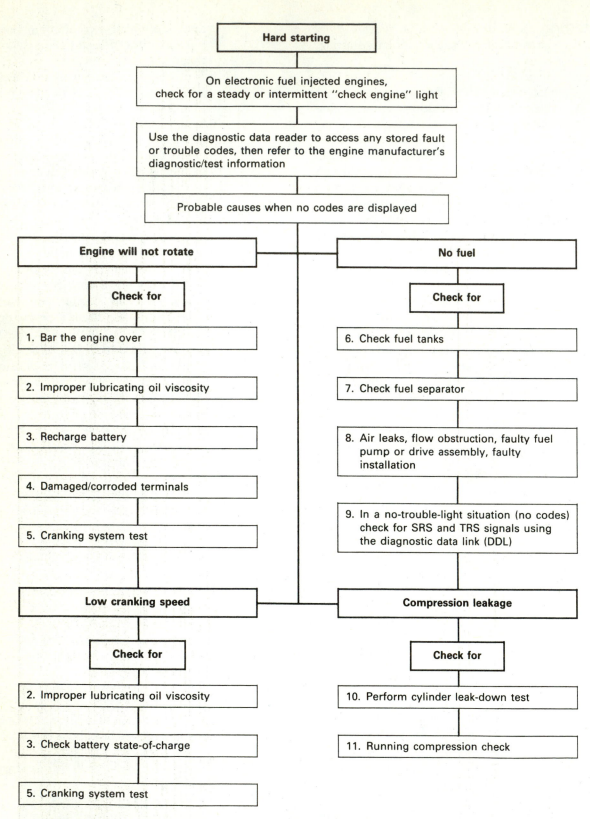

FIGURE 22–8 Troubleshooting chart for an engine hard-starting condition. (Courtesy of Detroit Diesel Corporation.)

8. *There may be air leaks, flow obstruction, faulty fuel pump, faulty fuel pump drive, or faulty installation.*

   a. *Air in the fuel system.* If there is air in the fuel system, the engine will normally be difficult to start, run rough, and release a large amount of white smoke. If the engine does not start, loosen a fuel-injection-line nut at the through-the-head adapter and crank the engine until fuel comes out. Tighten the fuel-line nut. Start the engine. If the engine still does not run smooth or releases a large amount of white smoke, loosen the fuel-line nuts one at a time at the through-the-head adapters until the fuel that comes out is free of air. Tighten the fuel-line nuts. If the air cannot be removed in this way, put 35 kPa (5 psi) of air pressure to the fuel tank.

NOTE: Do not use more than 55 kPa (8 psi) of air pressure in the fuel tank, or damage to the tank may result. Check for leakage at the connections between the fuel tank and the fuel transfer pump. If leaks are found, tighten the connections or replace the lines. If there are no visual leaks, remove the fuel supply line from the tank and connect it to an outside fuel supply. If this corrects the problem, the suction line (standpipe) inside the fuel tank has a leak.

   b. *Low-quality fuel.* Remove a small amount of fuel from the tank and check for water in the fuel. If there is water in the fuel, remove fuel from the tank until it is free of water and fill with a good-quality fuel. Change the fuel filter and *prime* (remove the air and/or low-quality fuel from the fuel system) the fuel system with the fuel priming pump. If there is no water in the fuel, prime and start the engine by using an outside source of fuel. If the engine starts correctly using different fuel, remove all fuel from the tank and fill with good-quality fuel. Prime the fuel system, if necessary.

   c. *No fuel from fuel injection pump.* Loosen a fuel-injection-line nut at the through-the-head adapter. With ignition switch in the ON position and accelerator in the FUEL ON position, turn the engine with the starter to be sure there is no fuel from the fuel injection pump. To find the cause for no fuel, perform the following steps—1 through 4—until the problem is corrected:

      (1) Use the priming pump to make sure the fuel lines and fuel injection pump housing are full of fuel

      (2) Check the shutoff solenoid. With the ignition switch on, the plunger should be fully retracted to allow full-rack travel. Also, remove the rack position indicator cover and check to see if the fuel rack has moved to the FUEL ON position (toward the rear of the engine). This can be an indication of possible governor problems. If rack travel is restricted, replace the solenoid or repair the governor.

      (3) If you are not using a good-quality fuel at temperatures below −12°C (10°F), it is possible that the fuel in the system can *wax* (not have correct flow characteristics) and cause a restriction in the fuel system. Install a new fuel filter. It may be necessary to drain the complete fuel system and replace with a No. 1 grade of fuel.

      (4) Check for fuel supply line restriction by removing the fuel supply line for the fuel filter base. Put 35 kPa (5 psi) of air pressure to the fuel tank. If there is no fuel, or only a weak flow of fuel from the fuel supply line, there is a restriction in the fuel supply line and/or the fuel tank.

   d. *Check the air inlet and exhaust systems for restrictions.*

9. *Check for SRS and TRS signals using the diagnostic data link reader on electronically equipped engines.*

10. *Perform a cylinder leak-down test* (as outlined in Chapter 20 (Figure 20–24) or *an engine compression check* (as shown in Figures 20–21 and 20–22).

Abnormal Engine Operation

The troubleshooting chart for abnormal engine operation is shown in Figure 22–9.

Misfiring and Running Rough

Possible Causes and Corrections

1. *Perform a cylinder cutout test.* Refer to the engine manufacturer's diagnostic troubleshooing guide or to the information in this chapter dealing with mechanical and electronic unit injectors as well as inline pump and nozzle systems.

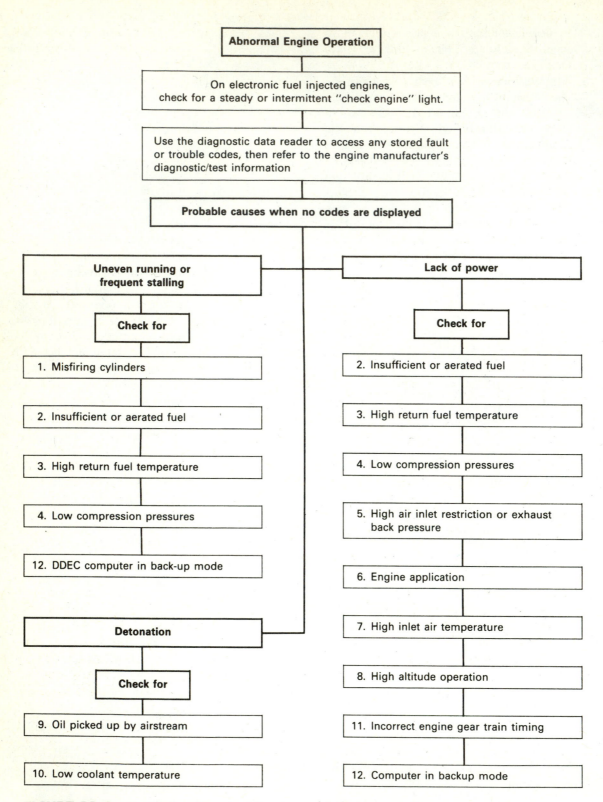

FIGURE 22–9 Troubleshooting chart for abnormal engine operation. (Courtesy of Detroit Diesel Corporation.)

a. *Air or water in fuel system.* If there is air in the fuel system, the engine will normally be difficult to start, run rough, and release a large amount of white smoke. If the engine does not start, loosen a fuel-injection-line nut at the through-the-head adapter and crank the engine until fuel comes out. Tighten the fuel-line nut. Start the engine. If the engine does not run smooth or releases a large amount of white smoke, loosen the fuel-line nuts one at a time at the through-the-head adaptors until the fuel that comes out is free of air. Tighten the fuel-line nuts. If the air cannot be removed in this way, put 35 kPa (5 psi) of air pressure to the fuel tank.

NOTE: Do not use more than 55 kPa (8 psi) of air pressure in the fuel tank, or damage to the tank may result.

Check for leaks at the connections between the fuel tank and the fuel transfer pump. If leaks are found, tighten the connections or replace the lines. If there are no visual leaks, remove the fuel supply line from the tank and connect it to an outside fuel supply. If this corrects the problem, the suction line (standpipe) inside the fuel tank has a leak. Water in the fuel can cause rough running and possible fuel system damage.

b. *Valve adjustment not correct.* Check and make necessary adjustments according to the engine service manual. Also check closely for a possible bent or broken pushrod.

c. *Bad fuel nozzle(s).* Find a bad nozzle by running the engine at the rpm where it runs rough. Loosen the high-pressure fuel-line nut at the cylinder head enough to stop fuel supply to that cylinder (see Figure 22–7). Each cylinder must be checked this way. If a cylinder is found where loosening of the nut makes no difference in the rough running, remove and test the nozzle for that cylinder.

d. *Fuel leakage from fuel-injection-line nut.* Tighten the nut to specs. Again check for leakage. Be sure to check the fuel injection lines inside the valve cover base.

e. *Bad fuel injection pump.* An injection pump can have good fuel flow coming from it but cause rough running because of slow timing that is caused by wear on the bottom end of the plunger. Fuel pumps that are severely scored from debris can cause rough running, but fuel dilution usually occurs before horsepower is affected. Low installation torque on the fuel pump retaining nut can cause misfire, rough running, and low power.

f. *Fuel with a high cloud point.* In cold-weather operation, this condition should be checked first. The fuel *cloud point* is the temperature at which wax begins to form in the fuel. If the atmospheric temperature is lower than the cloud point of the fuel, wax will form and plug the filter. Change the filter and drain the tank and the complete fuel system. The replacement fuel must be of a better grade with a lower cloud point.

g. *Fuel injection timing not correct.* Check and make necessary adjustments.

h. *Automatic timing advance not operating correctly.* Check with engine warm. Use the engine manufacturer's timing indicator group. If not available, make a rapid *acceleration* (increase in speed) from low idle to high idle. Engine must have smooth acceleration. A timing advance that does not operate correctly can cause delays of the engine acceleration at some rpm before high idle, or possibly cause the engine to run rough and have exhaust noise (backfire) during acceleration. This condition is difficult to find if engine acceleration is slow or at a constant engine rpm.

i. *Fuel return line has restriction.* This condition blocks or slows the fuel flow back to the fuel tank. The result is higher fuel temperatures in the fuel injection pump housing. Also, the removal of air from the fuel is prevented. Make a visual inspection of the fuel lines and fittings for damage and make repairs or replacements as needed.

j. *Valve leakage; wear or damage to pistons and/or piston rings; wear or damage to cylinder walls.* The cylinder head will have to be removed to make a visual inspection of these inside problems.

k. *Cylinder head gasket leakage.* Leakage at the gasket of the cylinder head can show as an outside leak or can cause loss of coolant through the radiator overflow. Remove the radiator filler cap and, with the engine running, check for air bubbles in coolant caused by combustion gases.

WARNING: Do *not* loosen the filler cap or pressure cap on a hot engine. Steam or hot coolant can cause severe burns.

1. *Check the throttle position sensor signal and circuit as well as the intake manifold air temperature sensor signal.*

2. *Perform a fuel flow test.* Determine if sufficient fuel quantity is being delivered. If less than the specified amount is returning, or if the fuel is aerated, check for a fuel system restriction using a mercury manometer connected to the primary fuel filter.

3. *Check the fuel spill-back temperature.* The relative fuel temperature should be less than 60°C (150°F) or a loss of horsepower may occur. Ideal fuel temperature should be between 90° and 95°F (32° to 35°C), since for every 10°F (6°C) rise in fuel temperature above this, horsepower losses can run between 1% and 1.5%. Note that 150°F (60°C) is the allowable maximum. Continuing to operate an engine with temperatures higher than this will result in injection component damage as well as possible ECM damage.

4. *Perform a cylinder leak-down test.* (as outlined in Figure 20–24), *or perform an engine compression test* (see Figure 20–21).

5. *Check that the air inlet restriction and exhaust back pressures are within prescribed limits.* Repair or replace defective parts as necessary. Use a water manometer to check the air inlet restriction and a mercury manometer to check the exhaust back pressure.

Low-Power Complaint

When a low-power complaint is received, determine after discussions with the operator whether the lack of power is consistent or if intermittent power cutouts are the main problem. Using electronic diagnostic equipment, check that the ECM operating parameters are set according to the desired horsepower setting. On electronically controlled engines, poor electrical connections could be the cause, so check the vehicle harness and connectors, the ECM power, and ground connections. Using a DDR or ECAP system, check for active or historical codes in ECM memory. For either a consistent or intermittent low-power complaint, check the valve and injector settings, engine brake, fuel temperature, turbocharger boost sensor, throttle position sensor, and vehicle speed sensor signal. Perform a cylinder cutout procedure, check the fuel supply system for restrictions and correct delivery pressure, check fuel quality, perform an air-to-air aftercooler leakage test, check air inlet or exhaust restrictions.

If the low-power complaint is ongoing, and you have made all of the primary engine checks, use an engine or chassis dynamometer to save a lot of diagnostic time.

Possible Causes and Corrections

1. *High inlet air temperature.* Air coming into the engine must be cool for the engine to have full horsepower. If the air inlet system is not of correct design or is not in good mechanical condition, hot air can come into the engine, causing a loss of horsepower. Check the air inlet temperature to the engine. The engine should not be operated with a winter shield (radiator cover) in front of the intercooler. The nominal air inlet temperature should be 49°C (120°F). An approximate 1.5% power loss will be noted for each 38°C (100°F) the inlet air temperature is above nominal. If high air inlet temperature is noted, check and clean the exterior intercooler and radiator cores. Check the fan, fan drive, and fan shroud to ensure maximum airflow is provided. To check the inlet air temperature, install a thermistor-thermometer into the engine air inlet pipe.

2. *High-altitude operation.* An engine loses horsepower with an increase in altitude. The percentage of power loss is governed by the altitude at which the engine is operated. On many current heavy-duty high-speed truck engines, there is no effect on the horsepower of the engine for the first 2280 m (7500 ft) above sea level of operation.

3. *Examine the air intake piping after the turbocharger for evidence of oil from a malfunctioning turbocharger.*

4. *Check the engine coolant temperature gauge for accuracy.* If the coolant temperature does not reach a minimum temperature of 180°F (82°C) while the engine is operating, consult the abnormal engine coolant temperature chart (see Figure 22–14).

5. *Check the engine gear train timing.* An improperly timed gear train results in a loss of power due to the valves and injectors being actuated at the wrong time in the engine operating cycle.

6. *Examine the check-engine light.* A steady check-engine light, with no codes, may indicate that the electronic control module is in the backup mode. Refer to the engine manufacturer's diagnostic troubleshooting guide.

No Fuel or Insufficient Fuel

The troubleshooting chart for no fuel or insufficient fuel is shown in Figure 22–10.

Possible Causes and Corrections

1. The fuel tank should be filled above the fuel suction (pickup) tube in the tank.

2. Perform a fuel flow test. If air is present, check all fuel lines and connections for cracks or damage. Tighten all connections. Check the fuel filters for cracks or damage, and be sure that they have been properly installed. Repair worn or broken components as necessary.

3. With all fuel lines, filters, and connections correctly installed and tightened, and air in the fuel system still present, check and/or replace questioned injectors. Faulty or incorrectly seated injectors are usually associated with a darkening of the fuel.

4. Check the restricted fitting on the fuel return line at the rear of the cylinder head for the correct size.

5. Check the primary and secondary fuel filters for plugging. Replace as necessary.

6. Check the fuel lines for pinching, damage, obstruction, or incorrect routing. Be sure that the fuel lines are of adequate size.

7. Check for correct installation and operation of the fuel check valve or shutoff valve (if so equipped).

8. Check for fuel temperature being less than 6°C (10°F) above the pour point of the fuel.

9. Bypass the electronic control module cold plate.

10. Check the fuel pump and relief valve. Check the fuel pump drive and coupling. Repair or replace worn or damaged components as necessary.

11. In the event of a no-fuel/no-start situation and no check-engine light displayed, check for voltage at the electronic injector terminals while cranking the engine. If no voltage is present, consult the engine manufacturer's diagnostic troubleshooting guide.

High Fuel Consumption

A measurement of fuel consumption is used to check fuel system performance. If fuel consumption of an engine is within OEM specifications, the fuel system is performing correctly and no additional time should be spent checking fuel delivery.

- *Fuel consumption.* If the specified amount of fuel is being injected into the engine, the fuel delivery specification is being met. Therefore, the basic fuel system (fuel pump and lines, transfer pump, filters, and primary fuel pressure) is within functional limits. Additional time spent troubleshooting these components is probably not justified.

- *Fuel system timing.* Fuel cannot be burned efficiently if it is not injected into the cylinder at the correct time. Because engines develop horsepower only when they are running, timing must be measured when they are running. The static pin timing of the engine is not adequate. Timing must be measured throughout the speed range (this also checks the timing advance operation).

- *Intake manifold pressure.* Manifold pressure is an indication of the overall health of the engine. Boost is affected by any one or all of the following: fuel consumption, compression (valve condition, piston ring condition), turbocharger performance, intake restriction (air filters), exhaust restriction (muffler), and timing.

Complaints about fuel consumption are related to engine owners' expectations. They may be related to the engine itself or causes other than the engine; in some cases, the fuel consumption may be normal for the application. Only a good discussion with the owner/operator, as described next, will guide you to a correct repair or prevent unnecessary repairs

The following questions should be asked before beginning any diagnosis or repair for an engine performance complaint. *There are no hard and fast answers for these questions.* Many factors can cause poor fuel mileage, or make users believe they are getting poor fuel mileage. Customer expectations are also a factor. The answers to these questions will give you a better understanding and perspective on the complaint and may identify characteristics that will help pinpoint the cause of the complaint quickly.

1. *Are miles measured accurately?* A most common problem in determining mpg is errors in recording the number of miles traveled.

   a. *Is this vehicle hub or cab odometer accurate?* The easiest way to check an odometer is to install a hub odometer known to be accurate and appropriate for the tire size on the truck. Run the truck over several hundred miles and compare the reading with the reading of the original odometer. Odometers may also be checked by comparing them to interstate mile posts or by

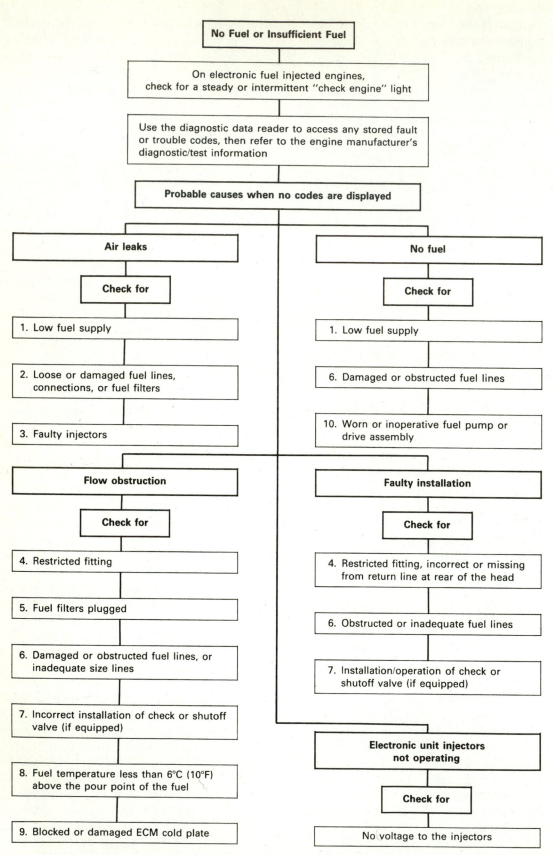

FIGURE 22–10 Troubleshooting chart for no fuel or insufficient fuel. (Courtesy of Detroit Diesel Corporation.)

running over a course of known length—50 miles is required to get a good check.

2. *Is fuel measurement accurate?* There are a number of ways in which fuel measurement can be the source of mpg problems.

   a. *Are fuel pumps calibrated?* If fuel tickets come from company-owned fuel pumps, there can be errors because nonrevenue fuel pumps do not have calibration requirements in many states.

   b. *Are road fuel tickets accurate?* The only way to verify fuel additions when road fuel tickets are used is a laborious ticket-by-ticket audit ensuring that the correct amount of fuel has been entered for the vehicles in question and that there are no indications of incorrect entries.

NOTE: Onboard vehicle computer recording devices are helpful in determining fuel consumption usage (see Figure 5–44).

3.

   a. *Is the wheel horsepower comparable?* When checking wheel horsepower, compare the horsepower ratings of competitive fleet engines; if one make of engine has more wheel horsepower or power at higher rpm, the competitive engine has an advantage.

   b. *Is the maximum vehicle speed comparable?* When you give the driver of the vehicle higher rpm and more power, it gives the vehicle the potential to go faster. The faster the truck goes, the more fuel it will burn.

   c. *Is wheel horsepower and vehicle speed higher than unit with better mpg?* If an engine is set to specifications and this does not equalize the wheel horsepower and vehicle speed, the use of an alternate lower-horsepower rating—when available for the same engine—should be considered.

4. *Are the tractor specifications comparable?* Often, a general discussion or questioning of a tractor's specifications will uncover a significant difference that leads to differences in mpg results.

   a. *Tires.* The difference in fuel efficiency between radial and bias-ply tires is well known. A vehicle or a fleet of vehicles that have bias-ply tires will have worse fuel consumption than those with radial tires. Also, tire size changes have the same effect as changes in rear end ratio.

   b. *Rear end ratio.* One objective in choosing a rear end (axle) ratio for optimum fuel consumption is to limit the engine rpm at the user's desired road speed. Normally, a higher ratio (lower number) will yield better fuel consumption at a given speed. In some situations, however, the higher ratio can give additional vehicle speed, which will hurt the fuel consumption if the higher potential vehicle speed is used.

   c. *Transmission ratios.* The transmission ratio difference that has the greatest effect is an overdrive transmission versus a direct transmission with the same rear end ratio. Obviously, the overdrive ratio allows the vehicle to go faster, which can hurt mpg; but overdrives can be used to reduce average engine rpm at a low vehicle speed, which helps mpg. Therefore, the same situation exists as with rear end ratios. What can be good in one application can be bad in another. The number of gears in the transmissions can also be significant. The effect of the number of gears depends on the skill and motivation of the driver. Again, general rules do not always apply, but less skillful drivers would probably get better mpg results with 7 or 9 speed transmissions than with a 13 speed transmission. A very skillful driver may be able to get better mpg with a 13 speed transmission.

   d. *Temperature-controlled fan.* A malfunctioning or poorly engineered temperature-controlled fan can be a very significant contributor to an mpg complaint. An appropriate question for all mpg complaints is, Does the temperature-controlled fan run often? If the answer to that question is "yes," normally there is something wrong with the way the temperature-controlled fan is installed or engineered, or there has been a system malfunction. Normally the fan will operate about 10% of the time!

   e. *Cab aerodynamics or cab style.* There can be significant differences in aerodynamics, and therefore, mpg between two cab designs. The effects are not always predictable. When cab designs of two vehicles are different, it is difficult to make comparisons or prove that engines are the source of mpg complaints.

   f. *Air deflector and air deflector setting.* Use of wind screens or air deflectors is common today. Obviously, different brands of air deflectors perform differently. Also, some deflectors may be adjusted to various settings that affect their performance.

g. *Gap between back of cab and trailer.* The performance of air deflectors and the fuel consumption of tractors without deflectors are greatly influenced by the distance between the back of the cab and the front of the trailer. The wheelbase of the tractor, and therefore, distance between the back of the cab and the front of the trailer, significantly affect mpg. The closer the trailer is to the tractor, the better the mpg will be.

5. *Is the operation the same for all units?* For dump trucks, mixers, garbage trucks, and so on, variations in the operation that can be very difficult to find may have significant effects on mpg.

a. *Assigned or slip-seat drivers.* With assigned drivers, the driver's driving habits are applied to the vehicle directly. The assigned driver can be the total problem. In a slip-seat operation where different drivers drive the truck every trip, the effect of the driver on fuel consumption is essentially eliminated.

b. *Routes.* If vehicles consistently run different routes, there is an effect on mpg.

c. *Equal loads.* If one vehicle is consistently at a significantly higher gross weight than another vehicle, it will have poorer fuel consumption than the lighter unit.

d. *Assigned trailers, trailer aerodynamics, and trailer tires.* If one tractor always pulls a vertical rib trailer and another tractor always pulls a smooth-sided trailer, the tractor pulling the smooth-sided trailer has an advantage as far as fuel consumption is concerned. The same is true if one trailer has radial tires and another trailer has bias-ply tires; if one trailer is properly aligned and another is not; or if one trailer is higher than another.

e. *Operational changes and weather changes.* Some mpg complaints can result from operational changes. Moving trucks from one location to another can have a dramatic effect on fuel consumption. Changes in the weather also change fuel mileage dramatically. An industry rule of thumb of 10% to 15% loss in fuel mileage from summer to winter is a close approximation of actual results for fleets that run throughout the country.

Possible Cause and Corrections

1. *Check records used to determine fuel consumption.* Make sure that the records are accurate. The minimum period for accurate fuel records is 1 month or 10,000 miles. Check the tires (air pressure and size), the gap between the tractor and trailer, air deflectors, trailer width, trailer type, engine cooling fan, and driver habits.

2. *Determine minor operating faults.* To help identify a problem before a more involved troubleshooting procedure is started, follow the procedure given in the section "Primary Engine and Vehicle Checks."

3. *Fix an air/fuel ratio control that is out of adjustment or bad.*

4. *Check engine performance.* Be sure to make a record of the temperatures for inlet air, fuel (at filter base), lubricating oil, and coolant. Also, check for excessive exhaust smoke. At this point, the governor fuel settings should be verified.

5. *Replace worn fuel nozzles.* Check the horsepower on a dynamometer. Make a replacement of the fuel injection nozzles and check the horsepower output again. If there is more than 10 hp difference, the old nozzles had eroded orifices and were causing high fuel rate.

Fuel in Crankcase Oil

Possible Causes and Corrections

1. *Loose inner fuel-injection-line nut(s).* A loose fuel-injection-line nut or a bad O-ring seal on the end of the adapter inside the cylinder head can cause fuel leakage into the crankcase. Check for a bad O-ring seal and tighten nuts to specifications. On DDC engines (two-stroke models), distorted or bent fuel jumper lines or damaged pipe flared-end conditions can cause severe crankcase oil dilution

2. *Fuel nozzle leaks.* A loose bleed screw (Cat 3406 model mechanical fuel systems) or leaking bleed screw washer will cause fuel dilution in the crankcase. Check for bad bleed screw washers or damaged bleed screw washer face. Make sure that the bleed screws are tightened to specifications.

3. On unit injectors, check for fuel leakage at the injector O-rings.

High Lubricating Oil Consumption

The troubleshooting chart for high lubricating oil consumption is shown in Figure 22–11.

NOTE: Lube oil consumption must be verified after each repair is made.

Possible Causes and Corrections

1. Check the oil dipstick, tube, and engine installation angle for proper oil level.

2. Check the air storage tanks for oil. If oil is found, check the air compressor or discharge line for oil. If oil is found, repair or replace as necesssary.

3. Steam clean the engine. Start the engine and bring it to operating temperature (82°C, or 180°F). Check for oil leaks at lines, connections, mating joints, seals, and gaskets. Correct the source of the leak.

4. Check crankcase pressure. Clean the breather and recheck the pressure.

5. Check for indications of oil at the turbocharger compressor outlet and the turbine inlet to determine turbocharger oil seal leakage.

6. Remove the exhaust manifold and inspect the exhaust ports and manifolds for wetness or oil discharge. Determine if the oil appears to originate from the cylinder or around the valve stem. If the oil appears to originate from the cylinder, perform a cylinder leak-down test (refer to Figure 20–24). If the oil appears to originate around the valve stem, check for worn or damaged valve stem seals or excessive clearance between the valve stem and valve guide.

7. Pressure test the cooling system. Inspect the coolant for lube oil contamination and the lubricating oil for coolant contamination. Pressure test the oil cooler core. If contamination is found, correct the source and clean the affected system.

8. Perform a cylinder leak-down test as outlined. If the cylinder pressure is below the recommended minimum, listen for air leakage at the oil filler tube, intake manifold, or turbocharger exhaust outlet. Also look for bubbles in the engine coolant. Excessive leakage heard at the oil filler tube indicates worn or damaged cylinder kit components. Removal of the cylinder head is necessary to determine and correct the cause.

9. If the cylinder kits are worn, check the engine air intake system for a possible source of contaminated air entrance.

Excessive Crankcase Pressure

The troubleshooting chart for excessive crankcase pressure is shown in Figure 22–12.

Possible Causes and Corrections

1. Clean and repair or replace breather assembly.

2. Perform a cylinder leak-down test (see Figure 20–24). If the cylinder pressure is below recommended minimum, listen for air leakage at the oil fill tube, intake manifold, or the turbocharger exhaust outlet. Also look for bubbles in the engine coolant at the radiator. Leakage heard at the oil fill tube indicates worn or damaged cylinder kit components. Removal of the cylinder head is necessary to verify. Bubbles in the radiator coolant indicate a leaking head gasket or damaged cylinder head. Valve leakage could be indicated by air leakage heard at the intake manifold or turbocharger exhaust outlet.

3. Check the exhaust back pressure. Repair or replace the muffler and/or piping if an obstruction is found or it is determined that the piping is too small, too long, or has too many bends.

Low Oil Pressure

The troubleshooting chart for low oil pressure is shown in Figure 22–13.

Possible Causes and Corrections

1. Check the engine oil level. Bring it to the proper level on the dipstick. Ensure the proper engine installation angle.

2. Be sure the correct lubricating oil is being used. Refer to the service manual for recommended grade and viscosity.

3. Pressurize the appropriate system (fuel or coolant) and closely examine components for leakage. After completing the checks, bar the engine over at least two revolutions (by hand) to ensure against possible hydrostatic lock.

4. A plugged oil cooler is indicated by excessively high lubricating oil temperature. Remove and clean the oil cooler core.

5. Remove the bypass valve from the oil filter adapter. Clean and inspect the valve, valve spring, and bore. Replace worn or damaged parts. Always replace the copper washer whenever the adapter plug is removed.

6. Remove the pressure regulator valve. Clean and inspect the valve, valve body, and spring. Replace any worn or damaged parts.

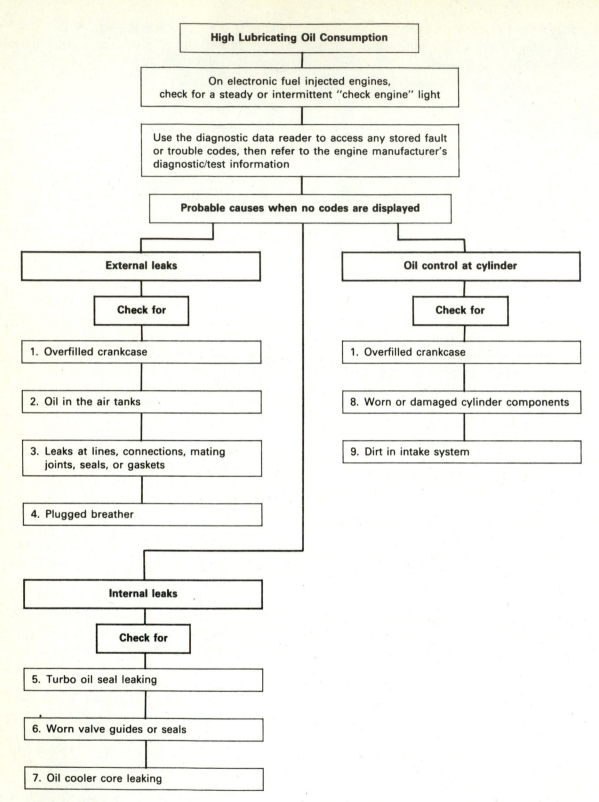

FIGURE 22–11 Troubleshooting chart for high lube oil consumption. (Courtesy of Detroit Diesel Corporation.)

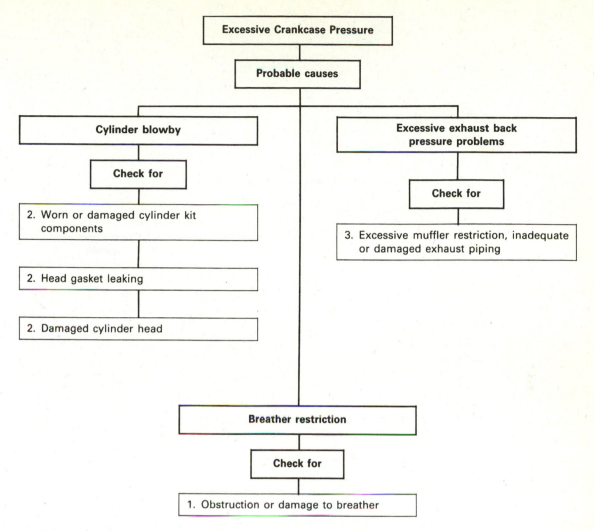

FIGURE 22–12 *Troubleshooting chart for excessive crankcase pressure. (Courtesy of Detroit Diesel Corporation.)*

7. Check for missing plugs at each end of the rocker shafts. Replace any missing plugs.

8. Remove, clean, and inspect the oil pickup tube and screen assembly. If cracked or damaged, repair or replace the assembly. Always use a new pickup tube flange-to-oil pump gasket upon reassembly.

9. Inspect the crankshaft main bearings for wear and/or correct clearance.

10. Check the oil pressure with a reliable gauge. Replace the oil pressure gauge if it is faulty.

11. Remove and clean the oil gauge line and gauge orifice.

12. Remove, clean, and inspect the pressure relief valve. Clean and inspect the valve, valve body, and spring. Replace any worn or damaged parts.

13. Remove the oil pump-to-cylinder block tube assembly. Clean and inspect the assembly for cracks or damage. Also inspect the flanges for flatness of the mating surface. Always use new gaskets upon reassembly.

14. Remove the oil pump assembly. Clean and inspect the pump for wear or damage. Replace all worn or damaged parts.

Cooling System

The troubleshooting chart for the cooling system is shown in Figure 22–14.

Overheating

Possible Causes and Corrections

1. *Low coolant level.* If the coolant level is too low, not enough coolant will go through the engine and radiator. This lack of coolant will not take

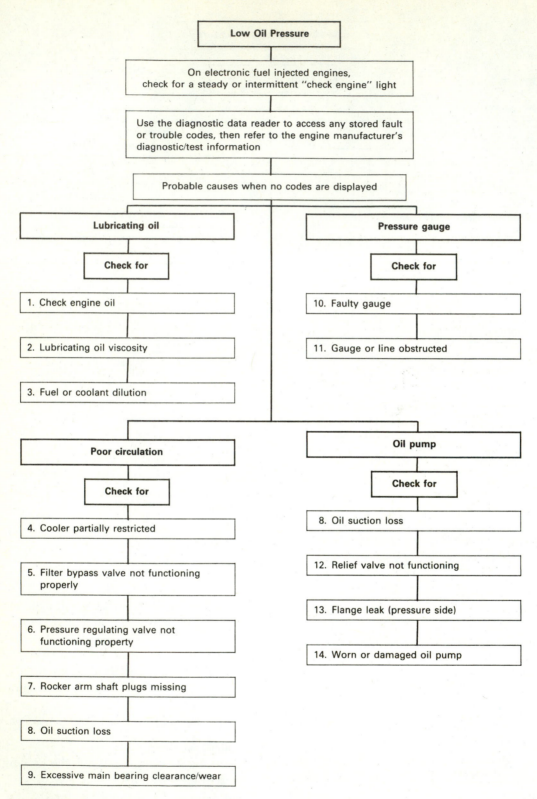

FIGURE 22–13 Troubleshooting chart for low oil pressure. (Courtesy of Detroit Diesel Corporation.)

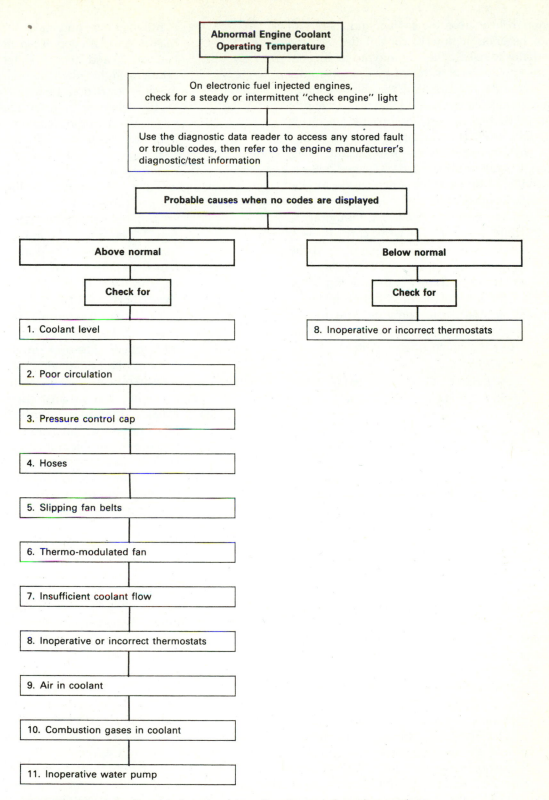

FIGURE 22–14 Troubleshooting chart for abnormal engine coolant operating temperature. (Courtesy of Detroit Diesel Corporation.)

enough heat from the engine, and there will not be enough flow of coolant through the radiator to release the heat into the cooling air. Low coolant level is caused by leaks or under filling of the radiator. With the engine cool, be sure that coolant can be seen at the low end of the fill neck on the radiator top tank. Check the coolant level. The coolant should be within 2 in. of the radiator filler neck (if coolant is low, and no fault or trouble code is logged, refer to the diagnostic troubleshooting guide for the particular make of engine).

   a. *Bad temperature gauge.* A temperature gauge that does not work correctly will not show the correct temperature. If the temperature gauge shows that the coolant temperature is too hot but other conditions are normal, either install a gauge that you know is functioning properly or check the cooling system with a thermistor-thermometer tool.

2. *Poor circulation*

   a. *Dirty radiator.* Check the radiator for debris between the fins of the radiator core, which prevents free airflow through the core. Check the radiator for debris, dirt, or deposits on the inside of the radiator core; this prevents free flow of coolant through the radiator. Clean the exterior of the radiator and intercooler to remove dirt and debris; this will permit complete airflow. If so equipped, remove the front winter shield (radiator cover). Some engines should not be operated with a winter shield in front of the intercooler. Check for damaged, incorrectly positioned, or inadequate shrouding. Check for an incorrectly sized radiator.

   b. *Shunt line restriction.* A restriction of the shunt line from the radiator top tank to the engine front cover, or a shunt line not installed correctly, will cause a reduction in water pump efficiency. The result will be low coolant flow and overheating.

   c. *Air inlet restriction.* Restriction of the air coming into the engine causes high cylinder temperatures and more than normal amount of heat to pass to the cooling system. Check for a restriction with a water manometer or a vacuum gauge (which measures in inches of water). Connect the gauge to the engine air inlet between the air cleaner and the inlet to the turbocharger. With the gauge installed, run the engine at full-load rpm and check the restriction. Maximum restriction of the air inlet varies between 20 and 30 in. of water. If the indication is higher than the maximum permissible restriction, remove the dirt from the filter element, or install a new filter element and check the restriction again. If the indication is still too high, there must be a restriction in the inlet piping.

   d. *Exhaust restriction.* Restriction in the exhaust system causes high cylinder temperatures and a higher than normal amount of heat to pass to the cooling system. To see if there is an exhaust restriction, make a visual inspection of the system. Check for damage to piping or for a bad muffler. If no damage is found, check the system for back pressure from the exhaust (pressure difference measurement between exhaust outlet and atmosphere). The back pressure must not be more than the engine manufacturer's specs. You can also check the system by removing the exhaust pipes from the exhaust manifolds. With the exhaust pipes removed, start and run the engine to see if the problem is corrected.

   e. *High outside temperature.* When outside temperatures are too high for the rating of the cooling system, there is not enough temperature difference between the outside air and coolant temperatures. To get better cooling, use the truck in a lower gear.

   f. *Operating at high altitude.* The cooling capacity of the cooling system goes down as the truck is used at higher altitudes. A system, under pressure, large enough to keep the coolant from boiling must be used.

   g. *Engine used in a lug condition. Lugging* (means the truck is used in a gear too high for engine rpm to go up as the accelerator pedal is pushed farther down, or the truck is used in a gear where engine rpm goes down with the accelerator pedal at maximum travel). Lugging the engine causes the engine rpm and fan rpm to be low. This low rpm causes a reduction in airflow through the radiator and a reduction in the flow of coolant through the system. This combination of less air and less coolant flow during high input of fuel causes above normal heating.

h. *Fuel injection timing not correct.* Check and make necessary adjustments as described in the testing and adjusting section of the appropriate service manual.

i. *Transmission problems.* Powershift or automatic transmissions that are cooled by the engine cooling system can cause above normal heating if they are out of adjustment or not working correctly. See the transmission service manual for the correct adjustments.

j. *Radiator too small.* A radiator that is too small does not have enough area to release the heat to the cooling air. This causes the engine to run at higher than normal temperatures. Make sure that the radiator size is in accord with the recommendations of the truck manufacturer.

3. *Pressure control cap.* Check for an inoperative or incorrect pressure control cap.

4. *Bad hose(s).* Inspect the cooling system for any soft, deteriorated, or collapsed hoses. Replace any suspected hoses. Bad hoses with leaks normally can be seen. Hoses that have no visual leaks can "collapse" (pull together) during operation and cause a restriction in the flow of coolant. Hoses become soft and/or get cracks after a period of time, and they must be changed after specific miles or time. The inside can become loose, and the loose particles of the hose can cause a restriction in the flow of coolant.

5. *Loose belt(s).* Loose fan or water pump belts will cause a reduction in air or water flow. Adjust the fan drive belts to the correct tension to prevent slippage. Replace any damaged, frayed, glazed, or worn belts.

a. *A wrong fan, fan or shroud not in correct position.* A wrong fan, or a fan or shroud in a wrong position, will cause a reduction or a loss of airflow through the radiator. The fan must be large enough to send air through most of the area of the radiator core. Make sure that the fan size, fan shroud, and position of fan and shroud are in accord with the recommendations of the truck manufacturer.

b. *Not enough airflow through radiator because of restriction in engine compartment.* The airflow through the radiator comes out of the engine compartment. Make sure that the filters, air conditioners, and similar items are not installed in a way that prevents free flow of air into and out of the engine compartment.

6. *Inoperative fan clutch.* Repair or replace an inoperative fan.

7. *Insufficient coolant flow.* Check the flow of coolant through the radiator. Clean the cooling system with a good cooling system cleaner and thoroughly flush the system to remove all scale deposits.

8. *Thermostats.* Remove, inspect, and test the thermostats for correct operation. Replace any thermostats that are not operating properly. Always replace the thermostat seals in the housing whenever the thermostats are removed.

a. *Bad water temperature regulators.* A regulator that does not open, or opens only part of the way, can cause above normal heating.

b. *Shutters not opening correctly.* Check the opening temperature of the shutters. The shutters must be completely closed at a temperature below the fully open temperature of the water temperature regulators. Also, verify that fan control switches on viscous fans are operating correctly.

9. *Air in the cooling system* Air can get into the cooling system in different ways. The most common causes are not filling the cooling system correctly and combustion gas leaking into the system. Combustion gas can get into the system through inside cracks or bad cylinder head gaskets. Air in the cooling system causes a reduction in coolant flow and bubbles in the coolant. Air bubbles hold coolant away from engine parts, preventing heat flow. Check for the presence of air in the cooling system. The presence of air or gases in the cooling system may be detected by connecting a rubber hose from the overflow pipe and submerging the other end in a container of water. Another method is inserting a section of clear, thick-wall Pyrex tube between the thermostat housing and the top radiator hose and observing for bubbles. If bubbles are present, check for leaks on the suction side of the water pump.

Air in the cooling system can also be found by the *bottle test*. The equipment needed to make this test is a pint bottle, a bucket of water, and a hose that fits the end of the overflow pipe of the radiator. Before testing, make sure that the cooling system is filled correctly. Use a wire to hold the relief valve in the radiator cap open. Install the radiator cap and tighten it. Put the hose over the end of the overflow pipe. Start the engine and oper-ate it at high idle rpm for a minimum of 5 minutes after the engine is at normal operat-ing temperature. Use a cover on the radiator core to keep the engine at operating tempera-ture. After 5 or more minutes at operating temperature, place the loose end of the hose in the bottle filled with water. Put the bottle in the bucket of water with the top down. If the water gets out of the bottle in less than 40 sec-onds, there is too much exhaust gas leakage into the cooling system. Find the cause of the air or gas getting into the cooling system and correct as necessary.

10. *Gases in coolant* If no leaks were detected in step 9, and bubbles remain present, perform a cylinder leak-down test.

11. *Bad water pump.* Check the water pump for a loose or damaged impeller. A water pump with a loose impeller does not pump enough coolant for correct engine cooling. A loose impeller can be found by removing the water pump and by pushing the shaft backward and pulling it forward. If the impeller has no damage, check the impeller clearance.

Overcooling

Possible Causes and Corrections

1. *Long idle periods.* When the engine is running with no load, only a small quantity of fuel is burned and engine heat is removed too quickly.

2. *Very light load.* Very light loads and a very slow speed or downhill travel can cause over-cooling because of the low heat input of the engine. The installation of shutters helps to correct this condition.

3. *Bad water temperature regulators.* A regulator that is stuck open (will not move to the closed position) will cause overcooling. A thermostat that is stuck between the open and closed positions, or opens only part of the way, can cause overcooling when the truck has a light load. Also, coolant leaks around the thermostat, such as vent lines, can cause overcooling.

Loss of Coolant

Outside Leaks

Possible Causes and Corrections

1. *Leaks in hoses or connections.* Check all hoses and connections for visual signs of leakage. If no leaks are seen, look for damage to hoses or loose clamps.

2. *Leaks in the radiator and/or expansion tank.* Put pressure to the radiator and/or expansion tank with the cooling system pressurizing pump and check for leaks.

3. *Leaks in the heater.* Put pressure to the cooling system with the cooling system pressurizing pump and check the heater for leaks.

4. *Leaks in the water pump.* Check the water pump for leaks before starting the engine; then start the engine and look for leaks. If there are leaks at the water pump, repair or install a new water pump.

5. *Cylinder head gasket leakage.* Look for leaks along the surface of the cylinder head gasket. If you see leaks, install a new head gasket.

Coolant Leaks at the Overflow Tube

Possible Causes and Corrections

1. *Bad pressure cap or relief valve.* Check the seal-ing surfaces of the pressure cap and the radi-ator to be sure that the cap is sealing correctly. Check the opening pressure and sealing abili-ty of the pressure cap or relief valve with the cooling system pressurizing pump.

2. *Engine runs too hot.* If coolant temperature is too high, pressure will be high enough to move the cap off of the sealing surface in the radiator and cause coolant loss through the overflow tube.

3. *Expansion tank too small or installed incorrectly.* The expansion tank can be a part of the radia-tor or it can be installed separately from the radiator. The expansion tank must be large enough to hold the expansion of the coolant as it gets warm or has sudden changes in pressure. Make sure that the expansion tank is installed correctly and that the size is in accord with the recommendations of the truck manufacturer.

4. *Cylinder head gasket leakage or crack(s) in cylin-der head or cylinder block.* Remove the radiator cap and, with the engine running, look for air bubbles in the coolant. Bubbles in the coolant are a sign of probable leakage at the head gas-ket. Remove the cylinder head from the engine. Check the cylinder head, cylinder walls, and head gasket surface of the cylinder block for cracks. When the head is installed, use a new head gasket, spacer plate gasket, water seals, and O-ring seals.

Inside Leakage

Possible Causes and Corrections

1. *Cylinder head gasket leakage.* If the cylinder head gasket leaks between a water passage and an opening into the crankcase, coolant will get into the crankcase.
2. *Crack(s) in the cylinder head.* Crack(s) in the upper surface of the cylinder head, or an area between a water passage and an opening into the crankcase, can allow coolant to get into the crankcase.
3. *Crack(s) in the cylinder block.* Crack(s) in the cylinder block between a water passage and the crankcase will let coolant get into the crankcase.

Inline Pumps

High-pressure inline multiple-plunger fuel injection pump systems can exhibit symptoms that are unique to their particular design characteristics. Much of the information contained in this chapter can be applied to general troubleshooting techniques for these types of pumps manufactured by companies such as Robert Bosch, Zexel USA, Nippondenso, Lucas, and licencees of these manufacturers. Many light-, medium-, and heavy-duty diesel engines today employ inline pumps. Table 22–1 lists typical problems, possible causes, and corrections to consider when you are troubleshooting.

SELF-TEST QUESTIONS

1. Technician A says that self-control and reason are two of the most important faculties to use when faced with an irate customer during a troubleshooting problem. Technician B says that your sense of vision, hearing, smell, and touch are the four most important faculties that you possess. Who is correct here?
2. Technician A says that a slobbering exhaust is usually caused by unburned raw fuel after initial engine start-up from cold and that it will usually clear up within a 5 minute time period. Technician B feels that a slobbering exhaust is indicative of worn piston or turbocharger seal rings, allowing oil to enter the exhaust stream. Who is correct here?
3. If an engine is to be idled for longer than 5 minutes, technician A feels that it should be shut off. Technician B says that as long as there is no slobbering at the exhaust, the engine can be left idling for any length of time with no problems. Who is correct?
4. True or False: Electronically equipped engines can be fitted with automatic 3 to 100 minute idle shutdown timers.
5. Technician A says that a lack of power complaint can best be diagnosed by monitoring the exhaust smoke color for possible clues. Technician B says that you

should first check the maximum no-load (high idle) engine speed setting. Who is right?
6. Technician A says that white smoke at the exhaust stack after starting a diesel truck engine, particularly in cold ambient conditions, may be due to a leaking cylinder head gasket, which as the engine warms up will expand and seal. Technician B says that this is a natural phenomenon caused by unburned fuel droplet hydrocarbons. Who is correct?
7. Technician A says that exhaust smoke cannot exceed 5% opacity under any operating condition, whereas technician B says that the U.S. EPA stipulates acceptable smoke limits under a variety of conditions that include full-load acceleration, transient response under load, and lug-down conditions. Who is right?
8. Technician A says that black exhaust smoke is an indication of using the improper grade of diesel fuel. Technician B says that it can only be caused by air starvation (plugged air filter element). Who is correct here?
9. Technician A says that blue exhaust smoke indicates that the piston rings or intake valve guides are worn. Technician B says that this could be caused by leaking turbocharger seals. Who is right?
10. Technician A says that the best way in which to determine if the piston rings are worn on a two-stroke-cycle DDC engine is to remove the air box inspection covers and check the condition of the rings. Technician B says that the type and design of the engine may require a leak-down check. Who is correct?
11. Technician A says that a compression check on all diesel engines should be performed with a dummy injector and the engine running at an idle speed. Technician B disagrees, saying that a compression check will differ between makes of engines. Who is correct?
12. Technician A feels that if an engine lacks power and there is no unusual color exhaust smoke, the problem is more than likely restriction of fuel flow. Technician B, on the other hand, believes that this condition could be due to misadjusted throttle linkage, which does not allow full-rack travel. Who might be right here?
13. Technician A says that when diesel fuel filter plugging occurs in cold weather, it is due to using a fuel with too low a pour point. Technician B disagrees, saying that the problem is caused by using fuel with not a low enough cloud point for the ambient temperature encountered. Who understands fuel theory?
14. Technician A says that an engine that reaches its maximum no-load (high idle) rpm but then dies when a load is applied to it is more than likely experiencing fuel starvation. Technician B says that this condition is due to a faulty governor. Who is correct?
15. An engine performs well until it has been working under load for some time; then starts to lose power, particularly in warm-weather operation. Technician A believes that this situation could be caused by the fuel becoming too hot. Technician B says that it is probably

TABLE 22–1 Diagnosis Chart For Troubleshooting An Inline High-Pressure Fuel Injection Pump System

Problem	Possible causes	Correction
Hard starting	1. Empty fuel tank 2. Blocked fuel vent 3. Air in the fuel system 4. Misadjusted stop cable 5. Plugged fuel filter 6. Broken or restricted injection lines 7. Incorrect injection timing 8. Low compression 9. Internal injection pump problem 10. Incorrect valve adjustment 11. Glow plugs not operating properly	1. Fill the tank and prime the fuel system. 2. Clean the fuel vent. 3. Bleed the fuel system. 4. Adjust the cable. 5. Replace the filter. 6. Replace injection lines. 7. Time the injection pump. 8. Do a compression test. 9. Remove the injection pump and have it serviced by an authorized dealer. 10. Adjust valves. 11. Check for current flow.
Surge at idle	1. Blocked fuel vent 2. Air in the system from loose connections 3. Idle speed misadjusted 4. Governor defective or misadjusted 5. Injection pump not operating properly 6. Cold engine oil affecting the governor	1. Clean the fuel vent. 2. Repair the loose fittings. Bleed the fuel system. 3. Adjust the idle speed. 4. Remove the injection pump and have it serviced by an authorized dealer. 5. Remove the injection pump and have it serviced by an authorized dealer. 6. Run the engine until the oil warms up.
Rough idle	1. Air in the fuel system 2. Injector nozzle not working 3. Wrong firing order or misrouted injection line 4. Low or uneven engine compression 5. Misadjusted fuel injection pump	1. Bleed the fuel system. 2. Replace the nozzle. 3. Correct to the right firing order. 4. Perform a compression test. 5. Remove the injection pump and have it serviced by an authorized dealer.
Incorrect idle speed or no-load high idle	1. Low idle not adjusted 2. No-load high idle not adjusted 3. Governor not working properly 4. Accelerator linkage out of adjustment	1. Adjust the low idle. 2. Adjust no-load high idle. 3. Remove the injection pump and have it serviced by an authorized dealer. 4. Adjust the accelerator linkage.
Engine misses under load	1. Blocked fuel vent 2. Air in the fuel system 3. Plugged fuel filter 4. Plugged injection line 5. Incorrect injection timing 6. Injection nozzle not working 7. Injection pump not operating properly	1. Clean the fuel vent. 2. Bleed the fuel system. 3. Replace the fuel filter. 4. Replace the injection line. 5. Time the injection pump. 6. Replace the nozzle. 7. Remove the injection pump and have it serviced by an authorized dealer.

TABLE 22–1, *continued*

Low power	1. Plugged fuel filter	1. Replace the fuel filter.	
	2. Leaking or restricted injection lines	2. Replace injection lines.	
	3. Incorrect injection timing	3. Time the injection pump.	
	4. Injection nozzle not working	4. Replace the nozzle.	
	5. Restricted air filter	5. Replace the air filter.	
	6. Incorrect firing order	6. Correct to the proper firing order.	
	7. Fuel pump timing assembly gear not working	7. Replace the timing assembly.	
	8. Incorrect valve adjustment	8. Adjust valves.	
	9. Injection pump not working properly	9. Remove the injection pump and have it serviced by an authorized dealer.	
	10. Accelerator linkage not adjusted properly	10. Adjust linkage.	
Excessive fuel consumption	1. Incorrect injection timing	1. Time the injection pump.	
	2. Leaking injection lines	2. Replace the injection line and test the nozzle.	
	3. Restricted air filter	3. Replace the air filter.	
	4. Low idle speed	4. Adjust the idle speed.	
	5. Fuel pump timing assembly gear not working	5. Replace the timing assembly.	
	6. Governor not working	6. Remove the injection pump and have it serviced by an authorized dealer.	
Black smoke	1. Air in the fuel system	1. Bleed the fuel system.	
	2. Leaking or restricted injection line	2. Replace the injection line.	
	3. Incorrect injection timing	3. Time the injection pump.	
	4. Leaking injection nozzle	4. Test and replace the nozzle if necessary.	
	5. Restricted air filter	5. Replace the air filter.	
	6. Incorrect firing order	6. Correct to the proper firing order.	
	7. Timing gear in full advance	7. Replace the time gear.	
	8. Low compression	8. Do a compression test.	
	9. Injection pump or governor adjusted improperly	9. Remove the injection pump and have it serviced by an authorized dealer.	
	10. Incorrect valve adjustment	10. Adjust valves.	
White or blue smoke	1. Air in the fuel system	1. Bleed the fuel system	
	2. Plugged fuel filter	2. Replace the fuel filter.	
	3. Leaking or restricted injection lines	3. Replace injection line.	
	4. Incorrect injection timing	4. Time the injection pump.	
	5. Incorrect firing order	5. Correct to the proper firing order.	
	6. Fuel pump timing gear assembled incorrectly	6. Replace the gear.	
	7. Injection pump or governor not adjusted properly	7. Remove the injection pump and have it serviced by an authorized dealer.	
	8. Incorrect valve adjustment	8. Adjust valves	

Source: GMC Trucks.

due to a sticking fuel rack when hot. Who do you think might be right here?

16. An engine performs well with a full tank of fuel, but it loses power toward the end of the daily shift as the fuel level drops in the tank. Technician A says that this could be caused by water vapor through condensation of the warm air in the tank. Technician B believes that it is more likely due to a piece of floating debris aligning itself with the fuel pickup tube as the fuel drops. Who do you think is correct?

17. Technician A says that failure of the engine to obtain its maximum no-load speed rpm is probably due to a fuel system restriction, whereas Technician B says that the throttle linkage may be in need of adjustment. Who is right?

18. Technician A says that if an engine fails to crank or cranks too slowly, the cause could be a low battery. Technician B says it could be a no-voltage condition at the starter solenoid. Who might be right here?

19. An engine cranks over satisfactorily on the starter motor but fails to start and there is no smoke from the exhaust stack. Technician A says that the problem is more than likely no fuel in the tank. Technician B feels that the problem is probably caused by a faulty electrical fuel solenoid assembly that does not allow the fuel to flow. Who is right?

20. The reason an engine is hard to start may be the intake and exhaust valves being adjusted incorrectly, according to Technician A's theory, since exhaust smoke is present at the stack. Technician B says this theory is wrong. Who is right?

21. Air in the fuel system could result in an engine starting but not continuing to run according to Technician A. Technician B says that the engine would not start at all if air was present in the fuel system. Who is correct?

22. Technician A says that a rough idle on a warm engine could be the result of one or more cylinders losing compression. Technician B says that this could not be the cause; otherwise, the engine would fail to start. Who is correct here?

23. An engine that surges at idle could be due to an incorrectly adjusted buffer screw or bumper spring according to Technician A. Not so says Technician B, who thinks that this condition is more likely caused by air in the fuel system. Who is correct?

24. A Cummins NTC engine has a slow throttle response and tends to die when motoring downhill on a closed throttle. Technician A believes this is due to the PT pump throttle leakage being too low. Technician B says that it is more than likely caused by air starvation. Who is correct here?

25. Engine misfire can be caused by low compression in one or more cylinders, according to Technician A. Technician B says that it would be due to incorrect valve adjustment. Who is right?

26. Technician A says failure of an engine to reach rated speed under load could be caused by the throttle link-

age being out of adjustment. Technician B says that this is not possible, since the governor will always ensure that full fuel is obtained. Who is correct?

27. Technician A says that a low-power complaint can be caused by an air leak between the turbocharger and exhaust manifold, whereas Technician B says that an air leak between the turbocharger and intake manifold would result in low boost and therefore low power. Who is right?

28. Technician A says that a high intake air temperature will cause a low-power complaint in warm weather. Technician B says that low power will occur only when intake air temperatures are low, such as when operating below 0°C (32°F). Who understands theory of combustion?

29. Technician A says that an engine should be derated at altitudes above 1000 m (3300 ft); Technician B says that this is necessary only at altitudes above 3600 m (12,000 ft). Who knows what they are talking about?

30. Confirmation of a damaged or cracked injector cup in a Cummins L10 or NTC 14L engine can be confirmed only by removing the injector from the engine according to Technician A. Technician B says that you can check this by holding the injector down at idle and observing the change in the smoke level at the exhaust stack. Who is right?

31. Technician A says that excessive white smoke at idle can be caused by poor fuel quality and you can check it by using a portable fuel quality tester similar to a hydrometer. Technician B says that you should verify this possibility by operating the engine from a temporary fuel tank that contains a known, good-quality fuel. Whose advice will you follow?

32. Technician A says that excessive exhaust smoke that occurs only under load could be due to a plugged air cleaner. Technician B says that if the air cleaner were plugged, smoke would occur under both a no-load and a full-load condition. Who is correct in this instance?

33. True or False: Excessive black smoke under load could be caused by a faulty turbocharger (air leak).

34. An engine that fails to shut off when the ignition key switch is turned OFF could be caused by a faulty electric fuel shutdown solenoid, according to Technician A. Technician B thinks that it could also be caused by an external source of fumes or oil pullover. Does Technician B's statement have any validity here?

35. Technician A says that a compression or fuel knock in the engine can be caused by air in the fuel system. Technician B does not believe that air in the fuel system could cause such a condition. Who is correct?

36. Excessive fuel consumption could be attributed to poor operator driving techniques according to technician A. Technician B thinks that it is more than likely due to a high intake air restriction or high exhaust back pressure. Who is right?

37. Technician A says that air in the fuel system usually reflects itself as a rough-running engine, a stumble at idle, failure to accelerate smoothly, and a lack of power under load. Technician B says that air in the system creates nothing more than a fuel knock. Who is right?

38. Technician A says that low fuel delivery can be caused by plugged fuel filters or an air leak on the suction side of the system. Technician B says that this condition could only be caused by a fuel leak on the pressure side of the system. Is technician B totally correct?

39. Technician A says that to quickly determine the condition of a low-power complaint on a DDC engine with no unusual exhaust smoke color, you should monitor the fuel pressure at the secondary fuel filter. Technician B believes that a fuel spill-back check would be more appropriate. Whose advice will you take?

40. Technician A says that to conduct a fuel system restriction check, you should connect a mercury manometer to the suction side of the fuel system as close as possible to the transfer pump. Technician B says that you should connect it to the secondary fuel filter. Who is right here?

41. Technician A believes that the use of low-cetane fuel will result in gray exhaust smoke, whereas technician B thinks that it will cause white smoke and a misfiring cylinder condition. Who is correct?

42. Technician A says that an engine that is out of time may result in higher exhaust temperatures. Technician B says that it is liable to cause possible preignition, uneven running, and a loss of power. Who is correct?

43. An engine hunting condition on a DDC two-stroke-cycle engine can be caused by a misadjusted buffer screw, according to technician A. Technician B says that mistimed injectors could case this. Who is right?

44. Technician A says that enlarged orifices in the injector spray tip will result in an increased flow rate and therefore greater than normal power output. Technician B says that such a condition will decrease the fuel atomization and reduce engine power. Who is right?

45. Technician A also believes that enlarged orifice holes in the spray tip can cause possible piston and cylinder wall damage. Technician B says that burned exhaust valves could result. Who has a good understanding of the combustion problems associated with this situation?

46. Technician A says that when operating an engine at altitudes in excess of 5000 ft (1524m), you should consider the use of the next-lighter grade of fuel. Technician B believes that a heavier grade of fuel should be used to offset the power loss due to the lower atmospheric pressure at altitude. Who understands this concept?

47. Technician A says that high exhaust back pressure can result in white exhaust smoke. Technician B says that it will cause a loss of engine power and a tendency for gray to black smoke. Who is right?

48. When setting the injector timing height on DDC engines, Technician A says that using a longer pin than necessary will result in retarded ignition timing. Technician B says that it will result in advanced ignition timing. Who is correct?

49. Technician A says that a rough-running engine under half load or more is probably the result of a faulty automatic timing advance unit. Technician B says that this condition is more likely to be caused by a plugged air filter assembly. Who is right?

50. Technician A says that a popping sound at the exhaust stack is most likely caused by a burned exhaust valve, whereas Technician B leans more toward a burned intake valve. Who is right here?

51. Technician A says that air inlet restriction can be monitored and measured with a water manometer. Technician B says that you should use a mercury manometer. Whose advice will you follow?

52. Technician A says that turbocharger boost pressure should be monitored and checked by using a mercury manometer, whereas Technician B says that you should use a water manometer. Who is right here?

53. Technician A says that you should always check exhaust back pressure by using a mercury manometer, but Technician B says that you should use a water manometer. Who is right?

54. Technician A says to check crankcase pressure by using a water manometer. Technician B says to use a mercury manometer. Which manometer will you use?

55. Engine detonation can be caused by oil picked up in the airstream, according to Technician A. Technician B says that it is more likely to be caused by retarded injection timing. Who is right?

Index